MW01015208

Election Law

Election Law

Cases and Materials

SEVENTH EDITION

Daniel Hays Lowenstein
Professor of Law Emeritus
UCLA School of Law

Richard L. Hasen
Chancellor's Professor of Law and Political Science
UC Irvine School of Law

Daniel P. Tokaji
Fred W. & Vi Miller Dean and Professor of Law
University of Wisconsin Law School

Nicholas O. Stephanopoulos
Kirkland & Ellis Professor of Law
Harvard Law School

Carolina Academic Press
Durham, North Carolina

ISBN 978-1-5310-2081-1
eISBN 978-1-5310-2082-8
LCCN 2021947132

Carolina Academic Press
700 Kent Street
Durham, NC 27701
(919) 489-7486
www.cap-press.com

Printed in the United States of America

For
Sharon
Aaron, Jessie, Asa, and Sadie
Nathan, Elham, and Adam
—D.H.L.

For
Lori
Deborah
Shana
Jared
—R.H.

For
Renuka
Aria
Mohan
—D.T.

For
Ruth
Iliana
—N.S.

To the memory of
our friend and colleague,
Gary Schwartz
—D.H.L. and R.H.

Summary of Contents

Contents

Introduction to the Seventh Edition

Readers of this book may well find nothing surprising about its existence. After all, Election Law is a course taught at many law schools and political science departments across the country. There are a growing number of competing casebooks, a quarterly journal dedicated to the field (*Election Law Journal*), and regular conferences and law review symposia dedicated to election law issues such as campaign finance, voting rights, redistricting, election administration, ballot measures and other topics.

But when the First Edition of this book first appeared in 1995, written solely by Daniel Hays Lowenstein, it was the first modern casebook on the subject. Things have changed much since Professor Lowenstein wrote in the First Edition's Introduction: "So election law has not been a subject in the university." Lowenstein was one of a handful of pioneers in the field, and his book helped define the range of topics which would come to fall under the "election law" category, the theoretical approaches which would be brought to bear on the subject matter, and the importance of empirical political science and political theory to a full examination of the questions raised in this book.*

The First Edition also spoke in Lowenstein's distinctive voice: a mixture of dry and self-deprecating humor, a healthy skepticism of courts and abstract legal theory, and unremitting grammatical correctness.

The Seventh Edition of this casebook appears twenty-seven years after the First Edition, and is written by Professor Rick Hasen of UC Irvine, Dean Dan Tokaji of the University of Wisconsin, and Professor Nicholas Stephanopoulos of Harvard; Lowenstein retired from the field over a decade ago and the book now bears less of Lowenstein's voice. But it kept the sensibility that Lowenstein articulated in the First Edition: "Although I have not attempted to conceal my own views on the subjects treated in this book, I have tried to assure that the book is not a brief for those or any other views. But I hope the book is animated by a respect for truth and a regard for the public good."

---

* A special "festschrift" issue of the *Election Law Journal* (Volume 9, Number 4, December 2010) considers Lowenstein's considerable contributions to the field. Lowenstein and Hasen served as founding co-editors of *ELJ* from 2001–2010. Tokaji served as co-editor from 2011-2013.

We have tried to emulate Lowenstein's ethos, something particularly important in this hyperpartisan era following the 2020 election when there is so much mistrust and misinformation about the voting and election process.

The goals of this Seventh Edition of the casebook are the same as Lowenstein's ambition with the First: to shed more light than heat on a disputed subject; to give students and their instructors a fair presentation of the cases and scholarship in the key areas of election law; to bring in political science evidence with which to evaluate legislative and judicial interventions into democratic processes; and to do all of this in clear language.

As always, we welcome your comments on how we can improve on this book. No doubt the book is already greatly improved thanks to the generosity of earlier readers.

Conventions Used in This Book

In the interest of saving the publisher's space and the reader's time, most of the materials reprinted in this book have been significantly edited. Insertions are indicated with brackets. Deletions are indicated with brackets or ellipses. However, footnotes have been deleted and citations have been deleted or altered without signalling. Sometimes, formatting of the original sources has been revised. For purposes of serious research, the reader should consult the original sources.

Footnotes that are signalled with a number are from the original work and retain the numbers that they have in the original. Footnotes signalled with a letter are those of the Editors.

Opinions differ on the extent to which law school casebooks should contain references to the scholarly literature. The interdisciplinary nature of this book has persuaded us that these annotations are appropriate. Very few readers of this book — whether instructors, students, or general readers — will have a strong background on all the subjects presented. The references are intended to facilitate further reading on matters of interest and to provide a head start on research projects. They are not intended to be intimidating, and we hope they will not have that effect.

Although the references are extensive, they are not remotely exhaustive. In most cases they should be sufficient to get you into the literature that interests you.

Acknowledgments

Before this Seventh Edition of the book, we republished in each edition the Introduction to the prior editions. We are no longer continuing this tradition to save ink and space, but the one thing lost from cutting those older Introductions are the names of all the people who helped make this book better through comments, research, proofreading, and overall assistance. Please refer to the Sixth Edition, pages xv-xxviii, for the earlier acknowledgments.

For this Seventh Edition of the Casebook, we thank Sara Sampson for her contribution of the updated Appendix on election law research. We also thank our research assistants: Hannah Bartlett, Alyx Bogus, Timothy Duong, Anna Setyaeva, Katy Shanahan, Timothy Duong and Xuechun Wang. We thank Stacy Tran for excellent administrative assistance and the team at Carolina Academic Press for wonderful production assistance.

RICK HASEN
Los Angeles, CA

DAN TOKAJI
Madison, WI

NICHOLAS STEPHANOPOULOS
Cambridge, MA

August 2021

Copyright Acknowledgments

We gratefully acknowledge the permission granted by authors, publishers, and organizations to reprint portions of the following copyrighted materials.

CQ Press, *Illustration:* North Carolina — Districts Established February 6, 1992; in Congressional Districts in the 1990s: A Portrait of America (1993). Reprinted by permission.

Ellis, R., Democratic Delusions: The Initiative Process in America 26–43 (2002). Copyright 2002 by the University Press of Kansas. All Rights Reserved. Reprinted with permission.

Foley, E., Equal-Dollars-Per-Voter: A Constitutional Principle of Campaign Finance, 94 Columbia Law Review 1204 (1994). Reprinted by permission.

Lowenstein, D., Associational Rights of Major Political Parties: A Skeptical Inquiry. Published originally in 71 Texas Law Review 1741 (1993). Copyright © 1993 by the Texas Law Review Association. Reprinted by permission.

Mayer, K., Werner, T., & Williams, A., *Do Public Funding Programs Enhance Electoral Competition?* in The Marketplace of Democracy 245–67 (Michael P. McDonald & John Samples eds. 2006). Copyright 2006 Brookings Institution Press. Reprinted with permission.

Rossiter, C. (ed.), The Federalist #10 (Madison), The Federalist Papers, NAL/Dutton (1961), pp. 77–84.

Election Law

Chapter 1

Introductory Readings

It has been said, "there is no democratic theory—there are only democratic theories."[a] Probably most such theories would include at least two fundamental concepts, however differently they may be defined and combined: first, that certain basic rights or liberties should be guaranteed to each individual, and second, that each individual should have an equal opportunity to participate in the making of public policy so that each individual's interests will be served.[b]

In this book, our primary concern will be with how the laws governing elections and politics further (or hinder) the attainment of these democratic goals. Our emphasis will be on statutes that have been enacted and legal doctrines that have been developed, primarily since the early 1960s, with the intention of reforming the political system in the direction of greater equality. Among the most important of these developments are the adoption of the one person, one vote rule by the Supreme Court; the adoption and amendment by Congress of the Voting Rights Act; the adoption by Congress and state legislatures of campaign finance regulations; and, more recently, various reforms in election administration.

Some of our attention will be on constitutional law, which may be an instrument of reform, as in the case of the one person, one vote rule, or may be an impediment to some proposed reforms, as in the case of campaign finance regulation. (The word "reform," as used throughout this book, is likely to be a source of controversy. Probably a good working definition of "reform" is a proposed or actual change that at least some people claim will be for the better.) The constitutional issues we will be considering often reflect the tensions long recognized between the twin goals of liberty and equality, or between either of these goals and the need for secure, workable, and efficient processes.

Most of the book deals with elections, the most fundamental mechanism for achieving equality in a democracy. The book also will consider some of the influences most likely to affect political equality that are brought to bear on public officials. Throughout the book we shall be alert to empirical findings of social scientists that cast light on the likely consequences of reforms that have been enacted or proposed.

---

a. Robert A. Dahl, A Preface to Democratic Theory 1 (1956). See also J. Roland Pennock, Democratic Theory xiii (1979).

b. See, *e.g.*, John Rawls, A Theory of Justice 60–65 (1971).

I. Factions and the Public Interest

We begin with a sampling of theoretical writings on the relationship between majorities and minorities, between public and private interests, and between citizens and representatives. It should be apparent that even if the entire book were devoted to these theoretical questions we could do little more than introduce them. Nevertheless, this chapter will help give us a broader framework against which to consider the legal and empirical materials that follow.

The first selection is an essay by James Madison that is possibly the most influential work of political theory ever written by an American. The Federalist Papers were a series of essays by Madison, John Jay, and Alexander Hamilton in which they attempted to persuade the citizens of New York that the new constitution, proposed by the convention that met in Philadelphia in 1787, should be ratified. In the tenth essay in the series, Madison addresses the dangers that are posed for a republic by the existence of "factions." If you substitute "special interest group" for Madison's word "faction," you may be surprised at how germane the issues raised by Madison are to contemporary debates over democracy.

James Madison, The Federalist Papers, No. 10

(Clinton Rossiter, ed., 1961)

Among the numerous advantages promised by a well-constructed Union, none deserves to be more accurately developed than its tendency to break and control the violence of faction. The friend of popular governments never finds himself so much alarmed for their character and fate, as when he contemplates their propensity to this dangerous vice. He will not fail, therefore, to set a due value on any plan which, without violating the principles to which he is attached, provides a proper cure for it. The instability, injustice, and confusion introduced into the public councils, have, in truth, been the mortal diseases under which popular governments have everywhere perished, as they continue to be the favorite and fruitful topics from which the adversaries to liberty derive their most specious declamations. The valuable improvements made by the American constitutions on the popular models, both ancient and modern, cannot certainly be too much admired; but it would be an unwarrantable partiality to contend that they have as effectually obviated the danger on this side, as was wished and expected. Complaints are everywhere heard from our most considerate and virtuous citizens, equally the friends of public and private faith and of public and personal liberty, that our governments are too unstable, that the public good is disregarded in the conflicts of rival parties, and that measures are too often decided, not according to the rules of justice and the rights of the minor party, but by the superior force of an interested and overbearing majority. However anxiously we may wish that these complaints had no foundation, the evidence of known facts will not permit us to deny that they are in some degree true. It will be found, indeed, on a candid review of our situation, that some of the distresses under which we labor have been erroneously charged on the operation of our governments; but it will be found, at the same time, that other causes will not alone account for many of our heaviest misfortunes; and, particularly, for that prevailing and increasing distrust of public engagements and alarm for private rights which are echoed from one end of the continent to the other. These must be chiefly, if not wholly, effects of the unsteadiness and injustice with which a factious spirit has tainted our public administration.

By a faction, I understand a number of citizens, whether amounting to a majority or minority of the whole, who are united and actuated by some common impulse of passion, or of interest, adverse to the rights of other citizens, or to the permanent and aggregate interests of the community.

There are two methods of curing the mischiefs of faction: the one, by removing its causes; the other, by controlling its effects.

There are again two methods of removing the causes of faction: the one, by destroying the liberty which is essential to its existence; the other, by giving to every citizen the same opinions, the same passions, and the same interests.

It could never be more truly said than of the first remedy that it was worse than the disease. Liberty is to faction what air is to fire, an aliment without which it instantly expires. But it could not be less folly to abolish liberty, which is essential to political life, because it nourishes faction than it would be to wish the annihilation of air, which is essential to animal life, because it imparts to fire its destructive agency.

The second expedient is as impracticable as the first would be unwise. As long as the reason of man continues fallible, and he is at liberty to exercise it, different opinions will be formed. As long as the connection subsists between his reason and his self-love, his opinions and his passions will have a reciprocal influence on each other; and the former will be objects to which the latter will attach themselves. The diversity in the faculties of men, from which the rights of property originate, is not less an insuperable obstacle to a uniformity of interests. The protection of these faculties is the first object of government. From the protection of different and unequal faculties of acquiring property, the possession of different degrees and kinds of property immediately results; and from the influence of these on the sentiments and views of the respective proprietors ensues a division of the society into different interests and parties.

The latent causes of faction are thus sown in the nature of man; and we see them everywhere brought into different degrees of activity, according to the different circumstances of civil society. A zeal for different opinions concerning religion, concerning government, and many other points, as well of speculation as of practice; an attachment to different leaders ambitiously contending for pre-eminence and power; or to persons of other descriptions whose fortunes have been interesting to the human passions, have, in turn, divided mankind into parties, inflamed them with mutual animosity, and rendered them much more disposed to vex and oppress each other than to co-operate for their common good. So strong is this propensity of mankind to fall into mutual animosities that where no substantial occasion presents itself the most frivolous and fanciful distinctions have been sufficient to kindle their unfriendly passions and excite their most violent conflicts. But the most common and durable source of factions has been the various and unequal distribution of property. Those who hold and those who are without property have ever formed distinct interests in society. Those who are creditors, and those who are debtors, fall under a like discrimination. A landed interest, a manufacturing interest, a mercantile interest, a moneyed interest, with many lesser interests, grow up of necessity in civilized nations, and divide them into different classes, actuated by different sentiments and views. The regulation of these various and interfering interests forms the principal task of modern legislation and involves the spirit of party and faction in the necessary and ordinary operations of the government.

No man is allowed to be a judge in his own cause, because his interest would certainly bias his judgment, and, not improbably, corrupt his integrity. With equal, nay with greater reason, a body of men are unfit to be both judges and parties at the same time; yet what are many of the most important acts of legislation but so many judicial determinations, not indeed concerning the rights of single persons, but concerning the rights of large bodies of citizens? And what are the different classes of legislators but advocates and parties to the causes which they determine? Is a law proposed concerning private debts? It is a question to which the creditors are parties on one side and the debtors on the other. Justice ought to hold the balance between them. Yet the parties are, and must be, themselves the judges; and the most numerous party, or in other words, the most powerful faction must be expected to prevail. Shall domestic manufacturers be encouraged, and in what degree, by restrictions on foreign manufacturers? are questions which would be differently decided by the landed and the manufacturing classes, and probably by neither with a sole regard to justice and the public good. The apportionment of taxes on the various descriptions of property is an act which seems to require the most exact impartiality; yet there is, perhaps, no legislative act in which greater opportunity and temptation are given to a predominant party to trample on the rules of justice. Every shilling with which they overburden the inferior number is a shilling saved to their own pockets.

It is in vain to say that enlightened statesmen will be able to adjust these clashing interests and render them all subservient to the public good. Enlightened statesmen will not always be at the helm. Nor, in many cases, can such an adjustment be made at all without taking into view indirect and remote considerations, which will rarely prevail over the immediate interest which one party may find in disregarding the rights of another or the good of the whole.

The inference to which we are brought is that the *causes* of faction cannot be removed and that relief is only to be sought in the means of controlling its *effects*.

If a faction consists of less than a majority, relief is supplied by the republican principle, which enables the majority to defeat its sinister views by regular vote. It may clog the administration, it may convulse the society; but it will be unable to execute and mask its violence under the forms of the Constitution. When a majority is included in a faction, the form of popular government, on the other hand, enables it to sacrifice to its ruling passion or interest both the public good and the rights of other citizens. To secure the public good and private rights against the danger of such a faction, and at the same time to preserve the spirit and the form of popular government, is then the great object to which our inquiries are directed. Let me add that it is the great desideratum by which this form of government can be rescued from the opprobrium under which it has so long labored and be recommended to the esteem and adoption of mankind.

By what means is this object attainable? Evidently by one of two only. Either the existence of the same passion or interest in a majority at the same time must be prevented, or the majority, having such coexistent passion or interest, must be rendered, by their number and local situation, unable to concert and carry into effect schemes of oppression. If the impulse and the opportunity be suffered to coincide, we well know that neither moral nor religious motives can be relied on as an adequate control. They are not found to be such on the injustice and violence of individuals, and lose their efficacy in proportion to the number combined together, that is, in proportion as their efficacy becomes needful.

From this view of the subject it may be concluded that a pure democracy, by which I mean a society consisting of a small number of citizens, who assemble and administer the government in person, can admit of no cure for the mischiefs of faction. A common passion or interest will, in almost every case, be felt by a majority of the whole; a communication and concert results from the form of government itself; and there is nothing to check the inducements to sacrifice the weaker party or an obnoxious individual. Hence it is that such democracies have ever been spectacles of turbulence and contention; have ever been found incompatible with personal security or the rights of property; and have in general been as short in their lives as they have been violent in their deaths. Theoretic politicians, who have patronized this species of government, have erroneously supposed that by reducing mankind to a perfect equality in their political rights, they would at the same time be perfectly equalized and assimilated in their possessions, their opinions, and their passions.

A republic, by which I mean a government in which the scheme of representation takes place, opens a different prospect and promises the cure for which we are seeking. Let us examine the points in which it varies from pure democracy, and we shall comprehend both the nature of the cure and the efficacy which it must derive from the Union.

The two great points of difference between a democracy and a republic are: first, the delegation of the government, in the latter, to a small number of citizens elected by the rest; secondly, the greater number of citizens and greater sphere of country over which the latter may be extended.

The effect of the first difference is, on the one hand, to refine and enlarge the public views by passing them through the medium of a chosen body of citizens, whose wisdom may best discern the true interest of their country and whose patriotism and love of justice will be least likely to sacrifice it to temporary or partial considerations. Under such a regulation it may well happen that the public voice, pronounced by the representatives of the people, will be more consonant to the public good than if pronounced by the people themselves, convened for the purpose. On the other hand, the effect may be inverted. Men of factious tempers, of local prejudices, or of sinister designs, may, by intrigue, by corruption, or by other means, first obtain the suffrages, and then betray the interests of the people. The question resulting is, whether small or extensive republics are most favorable to the election of proper guardians of the public weal; and it is clearly decided in favor of the latter by two obvious considerations:

In the first place it is to be remarked that however small the republic may be the representatives must be raised to a certain number in order to guard against the cabals of a few; and that however large it may be they must be limited to a certain number in order to guard against the confusion of a multitude. Hence, the number of representatives in the two cases not being in proportion to that of the constituents, and being proportionally greater in the small republic, it follows that if the proportion of fit characters be not less in the large than in the small republic, the former will present a greater option, and consequently a greater probability of a fit choice.

In the next place, as each representative will be chosen by a greater number of citizens in the large than in the small republic, it will be more difficult for unworthy candidates to practice with success the vicious arts by which elections are too often carried; and the suffrages of the people being more free, will be more likely to center on men who possess the most attractive merit and the most diffusive and established characters.

It must be confessed that in this, as in most other cases, there is a mean, on both sides of which inconveniencies will be found to lie. By enlarging too much the number of electors, you render the representative too little acquainted with all their local circumstances and lesser interests; as by reducing it too much, you render him unduly attached to these, and too little fit to comprehend and pursue great and national objects. The federal Constitution forms a happy combination in this respect; the great and aggregate interests being referred to the national, the local and particular to the State legislatures.

The other point of difference is the greater number of citizens and extent of territory which may be brought within the compass of republican than of democratic government; and it is this circumstance principally which renders factious combinations less to be dreaded in the former than in the latter. The smaller the society, the fewer probably will be the distinct parties and interests composing it; the fewer the distinct parties and interests, the more frequently will a majority be found of the same party; and the smaller the number of individuals composing a majority, and the smaller the compass within which they are placed, the more easily will they concert and execute their plans of oppression. Extend the sphere and you take in a greater variety of parties and interests; you make it less probable that a majority of the whole will have a common motive to invade the rights of other citizens; or if such a common motive exists, it will be more difficult for all who feel it to discover their own strength and to act in unison with each other. Besides other impediments, it may be remarked that, where there is a consciousness of unjust or dishonorable purposes, communication is always checked by distrust in proportion to the number whose concurrence is necessary.

Hence, it clearly appears that the same advantage which a republic has over a democracy in controlling the effects of faction is enjoyed by a large over a small republic—is enjoyed by the Union over the States composing it. Does this advantage consist in the substitution of representatives whose enlightened views and virtuous sentiments render them superior to local prejudices and schemes of injustice? It will not be denied that the representation of the Union will be most likely to possess these requisite endowments. Does it consist in the greater security afforded by a greater variety of parties, against the event of any one party being able to outnumber and oppress the rest? In an equal degree does the increased variety of parties comprised within the Union increase this security. Does it, in fine, consist in the greater obstacles opposed to the concert and accomplishment of the secret wishes of an unjust and interested majority? Here again the extent of the Union gives it the most palpable advantage.

The influence of factious leaders may kindle a flame within their particular States but will be unable to spread a general conflagration through the other States. A religious sect may degenerate into a political faction in a part of the Confederacy; but the variety of sects dispersed over the entire face of it must secure the national councils against any danger from that source. A rage for paper money, for an abolition of debts, for an equal division of property, or for any other improper or wicked project, will be less apt to pervade the whole body of the Union than a particular member of it, in the same proportion as such a malady is more likely to taint a particular county or district than an entire State.

In the extent and proper structure of the Union, therefore, we behold a republican remedy for the diseases most incident to republican government. And according to the degree of pleasure and pride we feel in being republicans ought to be our zeal in cherishing the spirit and supporting the character of federalists.

Notes and Questions

1. Consider carefully Madison's definition of the term "faction" in the second paragraph of *Federalist No. 10.* Does this definition enable you to identify those groups Madison would regard as factions and those he would not? Is it necessary, for Madison's purposes, to be able to identify particular groups as factions? Which terms in Madison's definition, if any, seem subject to differing interpretations? How would you interpret those terms? Do you think you can improve on Madison's definition?

2. Peter H. Schuck, *Against (And For) Madison: An Essay in Praise of Factions*, 15 Yale Law & Policy Review 553, 555–557 (1997), argues that to be useful in current times, Madison's definition of "faction" must be modified:

> Madison asserts the objectivity of the public interest ("the permanent and aggregate interest of the community")—a conception that stands above and apart from any special interest or from any combination of such interests—including those of a majority. Such a transcendent conception, of course was hardly Madison's invention. In one form or another, it had constituted a convention of most political philosophy stretching back through the writings of Rousseau, Aquinas, Aristotle, and Plato....
>
> [O]ne of the most significant innovations of liberal political theory, especially of the American variety, is its challenge to the Madisonian conception of the public interest. Much of modern liberalism has repudiated this conception in favor of one defined in terms of process values and political participation through group activity. This procedural notion of the public interest is the dominant one today, essentially accepted even by progressives and social democrats on the left and by market and libertarian conservatives on the right....
>
> To understand the role of special interest groups in the American polity today, then, we must define faction in a way that does not depend—as Madison's definition manifestly does—on a transcendent conception of the public interest that no longer elicits strong defense or justification, even from those who most vehemently condemn pluralism's processes and policies. All definitions of "special" interests can be criticized for being underinclusive, arbitrary, or subjective. To characterize any interest as "general," to assert that its goals correspond with those of the community at large, is not simply a presumptuous claim but also inevitably a form of approbation. To characterize an interest as "special," in contrast, is to ascribe to it a partial, parochial, or narrowly self-interested quality; in common parlance this label is almost always deprecatory.

If Schuck correctly describes the dominant view among contemporary theorists as rejecting substantive conceptions of the public interest in favor of procedural ones, are the theorists correct? Consider the proposition that economic prosperity consistent with environmental protection is in the public interest. Or that citizens should have the right to speak freely and exercise religion as (and if) they choose. Or that bribery in the conduct of government should be minimized. Is there any significant body of opinion that disagrees that such goals are in the public interest or that citizens ought to have such rights? Theorists might respond that such substantive conceptions of the public interest are too general, that as soon as we begin to address the tradeoffs—for example, between economic prosperity and environmental protection, or the limits to such rights as freedom of speech and freedom of religion, or the determination of what is a bribe—consensus will disappear. But is it any different with process issues? Everyone might favor a campaign finance system that assures electoral competition, minimizes corruption, and maximizes freedom to engage in political activity, but would there be more agreement on the tradeoffs between these goals than on the tradeoffs between economic growth and environmental protection? For a negative answer, see Daniel H. Lowenstein, *Political Reform Is Political*, in The U.S. House of Representatives: Reform or Rebuild 194, 195–200 (Joseph F. Zimmerman and Wilma Rule, eds., 2000).

3. Madison says it is the "diversity in the faculties of men, from which the rights of property originate. . . . The protection of these faculties is the first object of government." In making this statement, was Madison speaking for a faction? Whether or not he was, the approval of the federal constitutional system advocated by Madison was certain to benefit some groups and harm others. As Justice Felix Frankfurter observed,

> Hardly any distribution of political authority that could be assailed as rendering government non-republican would fail . . . to operate to the prejudice of some groups, and to the advantage of others, within the body politic. . . . No shift of power but works a corresponding shift in influence among the groups composing a society.

Baker v. Carr, 369 U.S. 186, 266, 299 (1962) (dissenting opinion).

Throughout this book, we shall see changes in the political system being proposed, opposed, adopted, or rejected in legislatures, courts, and administrative agencies. The reformers, their opponents, and the decision-makers normally justify their positions by reference to the public interest and democratic principles. In addition to these considerations, bear in mind which interest groups will gain and which will lose from the actual or proposed changes. Does the question of who will gain and who will lose affect what interests line up on each side and the eventual outcome? Should it? Suppose it is shown that a proposed law will benefit a particular group—incumbent legislators, for example, or labor unions, or law students. Would that be a legitimate argument against the proposal?

4. According to Madison, factions can consist of a majority or a minority of the population, but only a majority faction is likely to have its way under a republican constitution. Why? Many contemporary reformers, both conservative and liberal, believe minority interests too often can veto or bring about changes in a manner contrary to the public interest and opposed by the majority. Are these reformers wrong? Was Madison wrong? Have conditions changed in relevant ways since Madison's time? What conditions?

5. In *Federalist No. 10* Madison points to a sharp contrast between a democracy and a republic. The differences are "the delegation of the government, in the latter, to a small number of citizens elected by the rest; secondly, the greater number of citizens and greater sphere of country over which the latter may be extended." One conclusion that some have drawn is that the initiative process, which we examine in Chapter 7, is anti-republican because it bypasses the representative legislature. But that conclusion emphasizes Madison's first difference at the expense of the second.

Morton White, Philosophy, The Federalist, and the Constitution 137–38 (1987), summarizes his reading of Madison on this point as follows:

> [T]he small population of a pure democracy—its first fundamental feature—makes it very likely that a pure democracy will contain a small-numbered majority which has a factious *motive.* And the fact that the citizens of a pure democracy must assemble and administer the government in person—the second fundamental feature of a pure democracy—makes it likely that a factious majority in a pure democracy will have an *opportunity* to "concert and execute their plans of oppression." Finally, according to Madison, if a small-numbered majority has both a factious motive and an opportunity to act, it will in all likelihood invade the rights of others or act against the common good. . . .

On White's reading of Madison, is it correct to conclude that the initiative process is anti-republican?

6. Concern that majorities will tyrannize over minorities in a democracy has continued. John C. Calhoun, in *A Disquisition on Government* (published posthumously in 1853) claimed that Madison's solution to the problem of faction was insufficient to protect minorities. Calhoun proposed instead a requirement that the government act with the approval of a "concurrent majority," meaning that all major interests must concur. Beginning with a similar impulse, a more recent influential book argued that, in principle, unanimous consent should be required for government action, but that since the cost of obtaining unanimity on any specific proposal would be prohibitive, the unanimity requirement should be applied only to the adoption of a constitution, which would permit day-to-day decisions to be made with less than unanimous approval. James M. Buchanan & Gordon Tullock, The Calculus of Consent (1962). For a cogent criticism of the ethical desirability of a unanimity rule, see Douglas W. Rae, *The Limits of Consensual Decision*, 69 American Political Science Review 1270 (1975).

7. How persuasive do you find Madison's arguments for larger legislative districts? Do you think his views would be the same if he were writing under modern conditions?

II. Citizens and Representatives

The next selection is a speech by Edmund Burke, one of the great British statesmen of the late eighteenth century. Burke had just been elected to the House of Commons from Bristol, and was addressing his constituents in 1774. His speech followed the other person who had been elected from Bristol at the same time as Burke. The other candidate had expressed views favorable to "instructions," by which was meant the practice of constituents binding their representative to vote on legislative matters in accordance with the opinion of the constituents. Burke's response is the centerpiece for what has become one of the leading debates in democratic theory.

Edmund Burke, Speech to the Electors of Bristol

1 Burke's Works 442, 446–48 (1854)

GENTLEMEN, . . .

I am sorry I cannot conclude without saying a word on a topic touched upon by my worthy colleague. . . .

He tells you that "the topic of instructions has occasioned much altercation and uneasiness in this city;" and he expresses himself (if I understand him rightly) in favour of the coercive authority of such instructions.

Certainly, gentlemen, it ought to be the happiness and glory of a representative to live in the strictest union, the closest correspondence, and the most unreserved communication with his constituents. Their wishes ought to have great weight with him; their opinion, high respect; their business, unremitted attention. It is his duty to sacrifice his repose, his pleasures, his satisfactions, to theirs; and above all, ever, and in all cases, to prefer their interest to his own. But his unbiassed opinion, his mature judgment, his enlightened conscience, he ought not to sacrifice to you, to any man, or any set of men living. These he does not derive from your pleasure; no, nor from the law and the constitution. They are a trust from Providence, for the abuse of which he is deeply answerable. Your representative owes you, not his industry only, but his judgment; and he betrays, instead of serving you, if he sacrifices it to your opinion.

My worthy colleague says, his will ought to be subservient to yours. If that be all, the thing is innocent. If government were a matter of will upon any side, yours, without question, ought to be superior. But government and legislation are matters of reason and judgment, and not of inclination; and what sort of reason is that, in which the determination precedes the discussion; in which one set of men deliberate, and another decide; and where those who form the conclusion are perhaps three hundred miles distant from those who hear the arguments?

To deliver an opinion, is the right of all men; that of constituents is a weighty and respectable opinion, which a representative ought always to rejoice to hear; and which he ought always most seriously to consider. But *authoritative* instructions; *mandates* issued, which the member is bound blindly and implicitly to obey, to vote, and to argue for, though contrary to the clearest conviction of his judgment and conscience,—these are things utterly unknown to the laws of this land, and which arise from a fundamental mistake of the whole order and tenor of our constitution.

Parliament is not a *congress* of ambassadors from different and hostile interests; which interests each must maintain, as an agent and advocate, against other agents and advocates; but parliament is a *deliberative* assembly of *one* nation, with *one* interest, that of the whole; where, not local purposes, not local prejudices, ought to guide, but the general good, resulting from the general reason of the whole. You choose a member indeed; but when you have chosen him, he is not member of Bristol, but he is a member of *parliament*. If the local constituent should have an interest, or should form an hasty opinion, evidently opposite to the real good of the rest of the community, the member for that place ought to be as far, as any other, from any endeavour to give it effect. I beg pardon for saying so much on this subject. I have been unwillingly drawn into it; but I shall ever use a respectful frankness of communication with you. Your faithful friend, your devoted servant, I shall be to the end of my life: a flatterer you do not wish for. On this point of instructions, however, I think it scarcely possible we ever can have any sort of difference. Perhaps I may give you too much, rather than too little, trouble.

Notes and Questions

1. Would Madison have agreed with Burke?

2. Is Burke's argument undercut by modern communications, which make the debate on public issues accessible to each representative's constituents?

3. When Burke spoke, the British Parliament included so-called "pocket boroughs," districts with little or no population whose members could in effect be chosen by a wealthy landlord or nobleman. Some of these seats in Parliament were for sale, but others would be awarded to leaders of the parliamentary faction favored by the individual who controlled the district. Accordingly, Burke was assured of being returned to Parliament even if, as occurred in 1780, he failed to win reelection from Bristol.

Is Burke's view of the proper conduct of a legislative representative realistic under modern American conditions? Is it consistent with democratic principles? What changes—in our electoral system, in our attitudes toward elective office, or otherwise—would be necessary to induce modern legislators to act consistently with Burke's views?

4. A 19th-century Englishman, W.S. Gilbert, expressed a different view of the "M.P.'s" (i.e., Member of Parliament's, or legislator's) role:

When in that House M.P.'s divide,
If they've a brain and cerebellum, too,
They've got to leave that brain outside,
And vote just as their leaders tell 'em to.
But then the prospect of a lot
Of dull M.P.'s in close proximity,
All thinking for themselves, is what
No man can face with equanimity.

Gilbert & Sullivan, Iolanthe, Act II.

Notice that the system described by Gilbert and still prevailing in Britain and to varying degrees in many other democracies is different from either of the alternatives considered by Burke. Instead of following his or her own judgment or the views of his or her constituents, the representative is bound by the dictates of the party leadership. Would Burke approve? Would you?

5. Burke's speech provides the leading text for one of the longest-running debates in democratic theory. An excellent commentary may be found in Hanna Pitkin, The Concept of Representation (1967).

A great deal of empirical research in the United States has attempted to discern the influences that affect legislative behavior. One of the many leading works is David R. Mayhew, Congress: The Electoral Connection (2d ed. 2004). See also John W. Kingdon, Congressmen's Voting Decisions (3d ed. 1989); R. Douglas Arnold, *Can Inattentive Citizens Control Their Elected Representatives?* in Congress Reconsidered 401 (Lawrence C. Dodd & Bruce I. Oppenheimer, eds., 5th ed. 1993). There is also a substantial and growing literature on the problem of political polarization, discussed in Chapter 8, Part I.

6. Would you favor a system in which measures could be put on the ballot by petition to permit voters to inform their legislators how the voters think a public policy question should be resolved? If so, should the result be binding on legislators or only advisory? How broadly would you define the scope of public policy questions that could be put before the voters in this manner. For example, would the question whether individual human life begins at (a) conception; (b) viability; (c) birth; or (d) a different biological stage be permissible for the ballot? See *New England Christian Action Council v. Secretary of the Commonwealth*, 532 N.E.2d 40 (Mass. 1989).

7. In the late 1990s, proponents of term limits sponsored initiatives instructing members of Congress to vote for an amendment to the Constitution establishing congressional term limits. Those candidates who failed to sign a pledge supporting the particular term limit specified in the Amendment would have the words "DECLINED TO PLEDGE TO SUPPORT TERM LIMITS" printed next to their names on the ballot. Those Congressional incumbents who failed to support the measure in Congress were branded as having "DISREGARDED VOTERS' INSTRUCTION ON TERM LIMITS."

In *Cook v. Gralike*, 531 U.S. 510 (2001), the Supreme Court struck down a Missouri initiative along these lines. The Court first held that Missouri failed to demonstrate "that either the people or the States had a right to give legally binding, *i.e.*, nonadvisory, instructions to their representatives . . . , much less that such a right would apply to federal representatives." The Court further held that even assuming a state had such a power, it could not use ballots for congressional elections as a means of giving its instructions binding force.

What would be the harm of the Missouri initiative? The Court wrote that "it seems clear that the adverse labels handicap candidates at the most crucial stage in the election process—the instant before the vote is cast." If voters have a preference for term limits, and the initiative provides additional information about term limits, is the "handicap" unfair? See Elizabeth Garrett, *The Law and Economics of "Informed Voter" Ballot Notations*, 85 Virginia Law Review 1533 (1999). According to the Court in *Cook*, how competent are voters to make decisions about candidates at the time they cast their ballots? See James A. Gardner, *Neutralizing the Incompetent Voter: A Comment on* Cook v. Gralike, 1 Election Law Journal 49 (2002).

8. Burke's speech is most often recalled in connection with the question whether representatives should act on their own or their constituents' views, when the two conflict. A related and equally important question addressed in the speech that should not be overlooked is how the representative should balance the interests of his or her constituency with those of the nation as a whole. What values are served by a district orientation on the part of representatives? Is excessive parochialism inevitable in a district-based democratic system? Is a strong party system along the lines described by W.S. Gilbert likely to be beneficial in accomplishing a balance between local and nationwide interests? For the suggestion that strong presidential leadership may offset the parochialism of Congress, see Michael Fitts & Robert Inman, *Controlling Congress: Presidential Influence in Domestic Fiscal Policy*, 80 Georgetown Law Journal 1737 (1992).

III. Pluralism and Progressivism

A contemporary school of thought whose proponents claim to be the heirs of James Madison is known as "pluralism." The following essay describes the intellectual history of pluralism, several of its variants, and some of the criticisms that have been leveled at it.

Richard J. Ellis, Pluralism[c]

The concept of "pluralism" is usually associated with post-war American behavioral political science, but pluralism's roots extend back to the early twentieth century, and are as much European as American. The Englishman Harold Laski introduced the term "pluralism" into political science in a number of essays he published mostly while teaching at Harvard University between 1916 and 1920.

Laski and other English pluralists sought to vindicate the rights and autonomy of associations by challenging the modern doctrine of an unlimited and unitary state sovereignty. Sovereignty was a myth. The world, Neville Figgis explained, is "not, as a fact, composed of a few vast unities known as States, set over against crowds of isolated individuals." Rather each society "is a society of societies, each and all with rights, liberty and life of their own."[1] The history of societies, Laski agreed, showed repeatedly that organized groups, even unpopular ones like militant female suffragists, striking miners, or conscientious objectors, imposed limits on the allegedly sovereign state, forcing public officials to adopt policies to which they were opposed.[2]

---

c. We are grateful to Professor Ellis for preparing this essay for this volume.

1. Cited in David Nicholls, The Pluralist State 140 (1975).

2. Harold J. Laski, Studies in the Problem of Sovereignty 12 (1917).

Although pluralists frequently appealed to "the real facts of human society"[3] their challenge to what they termed "the monistic theory of the state" was more normative than empirical, though typically the "is" and the "ought" were woven seamlessly together. In arguing that "the state is only one among many forms of human association,"[4] for instance, Laski meant not only to highlight the empirical fact of the social and political importance of associations and groups, but also, and more importantly, to advance a radically anti-statist normative vision. For the young Laski, the state was owed no more loyalty than other groups; each group, including the state, deserved only the loyalty it earned "by virtue of its achievement."[5]

Not all pluralists shared Laski's anarchic and syndicalist sympathies. Others, like Figgis and Barker, allowed that the state had an important role to play in regulating conflict between associations and thus in creating the political conditions necessary for associations to pursue their own ends. But the main objective of the English pluralists was to help the groups they cared most deeply about, which for Figgis, for example, meant religious associations but for Laski and others meant labor and the trade unions. And herein lies an explanation for English pluralism's precipitous decline in the 1920s. For pluralists failed to persuade others, or even eventually themselves, that pluralism was the most effective means to help the groups they wanted to assist. Laski himself gradually abandoned or watered down his pluralist ideas, because along with the rest of the left he came to believe, particularly after the Great Crash of 1929, that labor had more to gain from an active, even paternal state than from a minimal, pluralist state.

Ironically, at the same time that English pluralism as a normative vision and intellectual force was in decline, the empirical study of organized groups was gaining ground in American universities. The American political scientists believed, with Arthur Bentley, that there was too much moralizing about the evils of special interest groups and too little objective empirical description and analysis of group behavior in the political process. By 1950, when David Truman's landmark book, *The Governmental Process*, was published, the discipline was relatively rich in empirical studies of interest group influence. Though the term "pluralism" was rarely if ever used, political scientists were beginning to speak of the "group basis of politics"[6] or the "group theory of politics." Truman and others had helped to revive interest in Bentley who, in his 1908 book, *The Process of Government*, had argued that groups, not laws, institutions or constitutions, were the essential "raw materials" of government. Truman followed Bentley in trying to understand the governmental process by treating groups, specifically interest groups, as "a primary unit of analysis."[7] Over

3. Nicholls, *supra*, at 141.
4. Laski, *supra*, at 65.
5. Harold J. Laski, The Foundations of Sovereignty and Other Essays 170 (1917).
6. Earl Latham, The Group Basis of Politics (1952).
7. David Truman, The Governmental Process: Political Interests and Public Opinion xix (2d ed. 1971 [1951]).

the next decade this increasingly influential mode of analysis would become known by advocates and even more frequently by detractors as "analytical pluralism" or simply "pluralism."

Critics were quick to charge pluralists with believing that groups were all that mattered, often pointing to Bentley's remark that "when the groups are adequately stated, everything is stated."[8] But most of those tagged as pluralists, including most especially Truman, never maintained anything so implausible. Pluralists looked to groups as "*a* major explanatory variable,"[9] but explicitly rejected the notion that government officials passively registered or mirrored the sum total of organized group preferences. The relative importance of groups and government officials in the shaping of policy, Truman emphasized, was an empirical question, not one to be settled by "preassigning weights and roles."[10] Analytic pluralists, to be sure, generally avoided using the term, "the state," but this was not because their explanations were "society-centered" or because they believed government officials lacked autonomy or importance vis-à-vis societal groups. Rather it was because they doubted, for epistemological as well as empirical reasons, that the myriad institutions and officials of government, particularly in the United States, were coherent enough to warrant a locution that treated the government as a unitary actor with a single will. The same doubts fed pluralists' skepticism of concepts like "the public interest" or "the will of the people," since society no less than the state was a complex mix of rival interests and objectives. In this respect, the modern American pluralists were kindred spirits of the early twentieth century English pluralists.

Another strain in criticism of American pluralism objected not to its focus on societal groups but to its portrayal of the distribution of power within the United States as dispersed. Pluralists, it was claimed, slighted the severe inequalities in resources and power in American society, and mistakenly believed that the system was self-correcting, that the mobilization of one group would necessarily lead to the mobilization of an equal and opposite countervailing pressure. Pluralists were also said to believe that all important or legitimate interests and opinions were represented within the political system, or even that all groups had substantially equal access to the policy-making process. As the ideological dust kicked up in the 1960s has slowly settled, scholars have begun to recognize that few if any of those scholars commonly described as pluralists harbored such naive views of the political process.[11] The important question, in any event, is not whether it is possible to find someone myopic enough to believe that all groups have equal or nearly equal power, but whether pluralists are logically committed to these propositions. How widely dispersed power is within any given policy domain or in any given place or time is

8. Arthur F. Bentley, The Process of Government 209 (1967 [1908]).

9. Truman, *supra*, at xxii (emphasis added).

10. *Id.* at xxv.

11. Martin J. Smith, *Pluralism, Reformed Pluralism and Neopluralism: The Role of Pressure Groups in Policy-making*, 38 Political Studies 302–22 (1990).

an empirical question that cannot be settled by methodological or theoretical fiat. Nor can it be satisfactorily answered without a comparative perspective: the same distribution of power may be reasonably characterized as either concentrated or dispersed depending on one's comparative referent or on one's normative benchmark. There is no inherent reason that an empirical commitment to the study of interest groups ala Truman need predispose the analyst to find any given distribution of political power. Nor need a normative commitment to pluralism, understood as wide dispersion of political influence and power, necessarily predispose one to find pluralism as a socio-political fact in any given setting.

The term "pluralist" is a particularly confusing label because it is often applied to those who conclude that power in a given locale is dispersed rather than concentrated. Pluralism can be a useful term to describe either an empirical reality—one in which there is, for example, widespread dispersal of power, and bargaining rather than hierarchical decision-making—or a normative commitment to such dispersed power, but it does not help to call those scholars who find dispersed power "pluralists." When Robert Dahl[12] finds a pattern of dispersed influence in contemporary New Haven politics that no more makes him a pluralist than his discovery of concentrated oligarchic power in early New Haven makes him an elitist.

Dahl remains the archetypal pluralist in the minds of many, even though he is not a group theorist on the model of Bentley and Truman. Whether or not Dahl counts as a pluralist, he is certainly among the keenest students of the dilemmas of pluralism. Dahl maintained that it was one thing to recognize (as Laski did) that government officials often could not "enforce decisions by unilateral, hierarchical means" but must often bargain with powerful and autonomous groups to negotiate "temporary armistices,"[13] but it was "quite another to turn this social fact into a prescription of the desirable, and to argue in effect that politicians should not even attempt to exercise 'the last say,' but should turn that power over to national organizations bargaining among themselves."[14] The fundamental dilemma of a pluralist democracy, in Dahl's view, is that autonomous associations, groups, or organizations are highly desirable and yet also capable of great harms if not controlled by a central authority.[15]

Why is pluralism desirable? Advocates of pluralism see autonomous organizations fulfilling a variety of beneficial purposes. Some emphasize pluralism's role in facilitating individual development and self-expression[16] while others emphasize the importance of groups in integrating the individual into society.[17] Associations

---

12. Robert A. Dahl, Who Governs? Democracy and Power in an American City (1961).

13. Robert A. Dahl & Charles Lindblom, Politics, Economics and Welfare 498 (1953).

14. *Id.* at 507.

15. Robert A. Dahl, Dilemmas of Pluralist Democracy: Autonomy vs. Control (1982)

16. Nancy L. Rosenblum, Membership and Morals: The Personal Uses of Pluralism in America (1998).

17. Robert A. Nisbet, The Twilight of Authority (1975).

are also seen as seedbeds of civic virtue, an enabling environment in which citizens learn the habits of self-government.[18] A different emphasis is evident among those who stress pluralism's defensive political function, as an organizational counterweight to the coercive powers of the central government.[19]

Pluralism may be essential to the functioning of large-scale democracies but that does not mean, as Dahl emphasizes, that pluralism is without disadvantages. To begin with, group leaders may dominate or oppress group members, particularly where the costs of exit from a group are high. Less ominously, the group's elites may fail to represent the opinions of its membership — the elites may be more conservative or more radical, more compromising or more confrontational, than the membership.

A second problem with organizational pluralism is that all groups are not created equal: organized interests, all other things being equal, have an advantage over unorganized interests, and some interests are easier to organize than other interests.[20] Autonomy for the lambs may well mean a quick dinner for the wolves. It is the weaker groups, as Schattschneider argued, who generally have the greatest interest in "enlarging the scope of conflict" by appealing to public authority and thereby modifying the imbalance in private power relations.[21] Recognition that group autonomy may serve the interests of the most powerful groups is a powerful argument against the radically anti-statist vision of the English pluralists, but not nearly so troubling to the pluralist vision of post-war American political scientists, most of whom were New Deal Democrats. The problems of group autonomy are real, but they need to be counterbalanced with an appreciation for the limits of central control. Absent the articulation of group preferences and mobilization of group interests, a central political authority would define who was a group and what were legitimate interests. Without group pressures, the state would find it difficult if not impossible to gauge the intensity with which preferences were held. If group autonomy without central control is bad for the lambs, central control without group autonomy is no better.

Other critics worry that even if all groups were equal, pluralism might, in Dahl's words, "deform civic consciousness" by fostering particularistic or short-run demands at the expense of a broader common good or long-run social needs.[22] Whether civic consciousness is higher or the common good is more closely attended to in those countries or policy domains where interest groups are less prevalent or less assertive is an empirical question, the answer to which is far from self-evident. A related concern is that private associations may be given essentially public functions,

---

18. Robert D. Putnam, Bowling Alone: The Collapse and Revival of American Community (2000).

19. Judith N. Shklar, *The Liberalism of Fear*, in Liberalism and the Moral Life (Nancy Rosenblum, ed., 1989).

20. Mancur Olson, Jr., The Logic of Collective Action (1965).

21. E.E. Schattschneider, The Semisovereign People (1960).

22. Dahl, Dilemmas, *supra*, at 43.

thereby removing or reducing democratic control over governmental decisions. One manifestation of this problem is European-style corporatism, in which bargains are worked out between peak associations representing labor, business and farmers. In the United States, the problem of alienating democratic control may take the form of powerful groups capitalizing on the fragmentation of the system by "capturing" governmental officials in a specialized policy domain.[23] Dispersed power is not inconsistent with groups monopolizing power in specialized segments of the political system. Again the extent to which this accurately describes policy-making in any given system or policy domain is an empirical question.

Among the most common criticisms of pluralism is that it was little more than an apologia for American or, alternatively, Western democracy. Whether or not those who were associated with pluralist ideas were satisfied with the state of democracy in America or Western Europe, pluralism as a normative vision is not inherently conservative. In much of the non-Western world, for example, even the most modest pluralist ideas pose a subversive challenge to entrenched state power and economic privilege. In 1968 Henry Kariel wrote an obituary for pluralism, which, he said, "as an ideology . . . only lingers quietly as a submerged, inarticulate ingredient of Western liberalism."[24] Over three decades later it would appear that reports of pluralism's decline let alone its death have been greatly exaggerated. Particularly as a normative vision, as an antidote to plebiscitary democracy and to centralized state control, political pluralism has shown renewed appeal and relevance across the globe.

Notes and Questions

1. Was James Madison a pluralist?

2. Robert Dahl, mentioned by Ellis, placed great emphasis on the concept of "intensity," the strength of an individual's or group's support or opposition to a government policy. Dahl maintained that the best protection for minority groups against tyranny by majorities lay not in constitutional safeguards but in the operation of the political system along pluralist lines. The idea was that groups whose freedoms or vital interests were threatened by a proposed policy would feel the most intensely about the issue. That intensity would be reflected in increased political activity. "All other things being equal," Dahl concluded, "the outcome of a policy decision will be determined by the relative intensity of preference among the members of a group."

Dahl also asserted that "intensity is almost a modern psychological version of natural rights." Would Madison agree? Do you? How, if at all, would Madison's definition of "faction" be affected if the term "intense preferences" were substituted for "rights"?

---

23. Grant McConnell, Private Power and American Democracy (1966); Theodore J. Lowi, The End of Liberalism (1969).

24. Henry S. Kariel, *Pluralism*, in International Encyclopedia of the Social Sciences 168 (David L. Sills, ed., 1968).

3. One influential criticism of pluralism mentioned briefly by Ellis is based on the problem of the "free rider." According to this line of thought, a government policy beneficial to a number of people is a "collective good" for that group. That is, either the policy will be adopted and benefit all members of the group, or it will not be adopted and none of the members will benefit. An obvious example is governmental protection of air quality. There is no way for individuals to obtain the benefit of cleaner air for themselves without obtaining it for everyone. If a lot of organizing activity and substantial resources are needed to obtain the benefit, the free rider analysis yields the paradoxical result that a small group may be better situated than a large group. Each member of the small group, perhaps a concentrated industry, will regard its own contribution to the collective effort as crucial, and therefore will be motivated to contribute. But members of a large group, such as consumers, individual taxpayers, or small businesspersons, may be motivated to take a free ride. That is, each such individual will reason that his or her own contribution is such a minute percentage of the whole that the overall success of the effort will not be affected. "Better to take a free ride," individuals might reason. "If others contribute, I will benefit from the favored policy and be even better off because I will have saved the time or money I declined to contribute. If others also opt for a free ride none of us will get the government policy we want, but at least I will save by not contributing to a losing effort."

The classic work on the free rider problem is Mancur Olson, The Logic of Collective Action (1965).

4. Although Ellis criticizes use of the word "pluralism" to refer to a descriptive theory of politics, nevertheless the term is commonly used for that purpose. On the other hand, critics have attacked pluralism less for its description of government policy as the outcome of the struggle of interest groups than for its normative conclusion that this outcome is satisfactory. Are the struggles over reform of the political system, with which much of this book deals, the practical counterpart of the theoretical debate over pluralism? For one view, see J. Skelly Wright, *Politics and the Constitution: Is Money Speech?*, 85 Yale Law Journal 1001 (1976).

5. During the 1950s pluralism was probably the dominant normative theory in American political science. Criticisms that were developed in the 1960s, including the free rider problem and the criticisms described by Ellis, have had their effect. Nevertheless, it is probably still true that the majority of political scientists and many journalists, judges, and people active in electoral politics are greatly influenced by the pluralist outlook and by related theories centered around political parties, described in Chapter 8. Pluralism also underlies the process-based theory of judicial review associated with *United States v. Carolene Products*, 304 U.S. 144, 152 n.4 (1938) (discussed in Chapter 3, Part I, in the notes following *Reynolds v. Sims* and *Lucas v. 44th General Assembly of Colorado*).

As Ellis mentions, many of the normative criticisms of pluralism are based on concerns about arguably unjust differences in the power and influence of various groups. One early version of this criticism was probably unfair to pluralism. During the 1950s, the most flagrant instance of inequality in the United States was the disfranchisement and subjugation of African-Americans in the South. Pluralism, however, assumes basic political rights for all such as freedom of speech, freedom of association, and the right to vote. Therefore, the subjugation of southern blacks was not a failure of pluralism but a failure to implement pluralism.

Pluralism could not evade responsibility so easily for other possible inequalities. The free rider problem and other theoretical issues—for example, the view that dispersed groups can be satisfied with symbolic gestures, while concentrated groups with lobbyists in Washington or the state capitol demand substantive benefits[d]—suggested that broadly based interests would face an unequal struggle against concentrated interests, especially economic interests. These criticisms of pluralism suggested that interests such as the natural environment, consumers, women's groups, small businesses, general taxpayers, and low income people would suffer and corporate interests as well as those of well-organized labor unions would have unfair advantages. The criticisms have undeniable force. Yet history, as she often does, played an ironic game with the critics of pluralism. Just as these criticisms were being forcefully articulated, American society saw the emergence of a potent "public interest" movement. Environmental organizations such as the Sierra Club, the Natural Resources Defense Council, and the Environmental Defense Fund, women's groups such as the National Organization for Women, political reform organizations such as Common Cause, and even more specialized groups such as Americans for Nonsmokers' Rights not only were able to enlist large numbers of members, but won major political successes. There is, however, recent empirical research suggesting that groups representing business interests have substantial influence on public policy, while less affluent citizens lack such influence. Martin Gilens, Affluence and Influence: Economic Inequality and Political Power in America (2012); Martin Gilens & Benjamin I. Page, *Testing Theories of American Politics: Elites, Interest Groups, and Average Citizens*, 12 Perspectives on Politics 564 (2014); Nicholas Stephanopoulos, *Political Powerlessness*, 90 New York University Law Review 1527 (2015).

6. As Ellis' essay suggests, much of the development and criticism of American pluralist thought occurred in the 1950s and 1960s. The story did not end there, as Andrew S. McFarland, Neopluralism (2004) demonstrates in a very useful review and interpretation of subsequent research. McFarland groups critics such as Mancur Olson, Jr., E.E. Schattschneider, and Grant McConnell as "multiple-elite theorists," because they claimed on various grounds that a pluralist system would be dominated by relatively few "elites," though they conceded that different individuals would have influence in different policy sectors. McFarland writes, at 9–10:

> But by 1980, the new multiple-elite theory was being overturned. Later researchers studying questions of power, policymaking, and interest groups

---

d. See Murray J. Edelman, The Symbolic Uses of Politics (1964).

usually found well-organized representation of interest groups on two or more sides of an issue, a finding repeated more than a dozen times. The frequency of such findings contradicted multiple-elite theory. The research finding of a number of well-organized groups wielding power in public policy areas might be termed *neopluralism*; it is different from the original pluralist theory, in that it recognizes that subgovernments sometimes exist and that Olson's logic of collective action has a major impact.

[Next came] research explaining why interest groups exist when we would not expect them to exist, according to Olson's theory. [Researchers pointed to] the existence of . . . "interest group sustainers." These included patrons, such as government, foundations, or wealthy persons who give resources to a group. Another interest group sustainer is a policy network, a communications network of persons concerned with policymaking in some area who have high personal stakes in a policy for occupational or other reasons and therefore participate in policymaking. A third interest group sustainer is social movements, which motivate persons to form groups in a way not explainable by Olson.

7. Although pluralism remains an important strain in popular political thought in America, the dominant strain probably is a conception most often associated with the Progressive movement of the early twentieth century but extending back to Thomas Jefferson and beyond. In what we shall call the *progressivist* view, the individual citizen is taken as the unit of analysis, in contrast to the pluralists' concentration on groups. Citizens are thought of as rational, reasonably well-informed, concerned about public issues, and desirous of resolving issues in accord with the common good. Their political beliefs are not entirely dominated by the particular interests of groups to which they belong. Candidates for office compete by debating the substance of issues in the manner befitting a rational, informed, public-spirited and actively involved audience. Once elected, representatives act pretty much like the voters who elected them. That is, they consider each issue of public policy individually, voting in accordance with their informed, rational sense of what is in the public interest.

Probably very few people past junior high school age believe that American democracy actually operates in this manner most of the time. Nevertheless, popular progressivist thinking holds up something like this as the ideal. Social prejudice and selfish pursuit of economic and political interests will constantly cause departures from the ideal, but the progressivist goal is to cultivate civic virtue in the individual and design institutions to minimize these departures.

8. This book focuses on pluralism, political party theories, and progressivism rather than on any of a number of other academic theories—such as feminism, critical race theory, or law and economics—because most courts and other political actors have tended to view the field through these lenses. However, students and instructors with an interest in other academic perspectives will find grist for their theoretical mills in the issues dealt with in this book. Two additional academic

theories, one related to pluralism and one related to progressivism, bear mentioning here because they have appeared in numerous scholarly articles (and occasional court cases) discussing election law:

Public Choice Theory. Public choice theory, which applies economic models of rational[e] decisionmaking to issues of political science, is closely related to the pluralist conception of politics. Public choice theory assumes that politicians rationally seek to maximize the chances of reelection and individuals rationally seek government action furthering self-interested goals. Like progressivism, it begins at the level of the individual, but like pluralism, it believes that much political action occurs when individuals organize for group action. If truth be known, we have already smuggled in a central concept of public choice theory, that of the free rider: In the struggle among interest groups, small, cohesive groups enjoy disproportionate influence over the political process.

Public choice theory also has a normative component that focuses on how to make the political process "efficient," that is, maximizing social wealth without regard to its distribution. In other words, public choice theorists care about the size of the pie, not how large a piece each person gets. But in the interest group struggle, inefficiency is a common problem:

> When interest groups use their political capital to secure goods from the state, they engage in "rent seeking." Rent seeking occurs when resources are used in order to capture a monopoly right instead of being put to a productive use. For example, when firms compete for the exclusive control of a local cable television franchise, they use their resources lobbying the local regulatory board, instead of investing those resources productively. Like these potential cable franchisees, organized interest groups expend their resources competing for political favors, such as tax breaks or subsidies, instead of putting them to some productive use. Rent seeking is . . . inefficient because it leads to an overall decline in social wealth. . . .

Richard L. Hasen, *Clipping Coupons for Democracy: An Egalitarian/Public Choice Defense of Campaign Finance Vouchers*, 84 California Law Review 1, 9–11 (1996). Thus, under the normative public choice vision, election laws should be written to make it more difficult for groups to engage in socially wasteful rent seeking. How does that differ from the normative vision of pluralists? Of progressives?

For an introduction to the use of public choice theory in law, see Daniel A. Farber and Philip P. Frickey, Law and Public Choice: A Critical Introduction (1991). The use of economic models to explain politics has become very popular in the political science literature as well, where it is commonly referred to as "rational choice

---

e. By "rational," public choice theorists do not mean "sensible." Rather, they mean that an individual makes choices in accord with a consistent set of preferences: thus, if one prefers liver to ice cream for dessert, one rationally chooses liver when offered the choice of liver or ice cream for dessert.

theory." For a book-length critique of rational choice theory, see Donald P. Green and Ian Shapiro, Pathologies of Rational Choice Theory: A Critique of Applications in Political Science (1994). For defenses by a number of rational choice theorists, see The Rational Choice Controversy: Economic Models of Politics Reconsidered (Jeffrey Friedman, ed., 1996).

Civic Republicanism. Civic republicanism does not necessarily reject pluralism as an accurate description of the current American political system. Like progressivism, however, civic republicanism argues for a politics aimed at promoting the common good. It rejects the normative notion that politics should be merely about structuring interest group competition. Where civic republicanism differs from progressivism is in civic republicanism's special emphasis on facilitating *deliberation* among legislators:

> Many republican conceptions treat politics as above all deliberative; and deliberation is to cover ends as well as means.... [T]he belief in political deliberation is a distinctly American contribution to republican thought. The function of politics, on this view, is not simply to implement existing private preferences. Political actors are not supposed to come to the process with pre-selected interests that operate as exogenous variables. The purpose of politics is not to aggregate private preferences, or to achieve an equilibrium among contending social forces. The republican belief in deliberation counsels political actors to achieve a measure of critical distance from prevailing desires and practices, subjecting these desires and practices to scrutiny and review.
>
> To say this is not to suggest that deliberation calls for some standard entirely external to private beliefs and values (as if such a thing could be imagined). The republican position is instead that existing desires should be revisable in light of collective discussion and debate, bringing to bear alternative perspectives and additional information. Thus, for example, republicans will attempt to design political institutions that promote discussion and debate among the citizenry; they will be hostile to systems that promote lawmaking as "deals" or bargains among self-interested private groups; they may well attempt to insulate political actors from private pressure; and they may also favor judicial review designed to promote political deliberation and perhaps to invalidate laws when deliberation has not occurred.
>
> ... The antonym of deliberation is the imposition of outcomes by self-interested and politically powerful private groups; republicans emphasize that deliberative processes are often undermined by intimidation, strategic and manipulative behavior, collective action problems, adaptive preferences, or—most generally—disparities in political influence. The requirement of deliberation is designed to ensure that political outcomes will be supported by reference to a consensus (or at least broad agreement) among political equals.

Cass R. Sunstein, *Beyond the Republican Revival*, 97 Yale Law Journal 1539, 1548–50 (1988). As Sunstein suggests, civic republicans place an emphasis on political equality: "Political equality, in republican terms, is understood as a requirement that all individuals and groups have access to the political process; large disparities in political influence are disfavored." *Id.* at 1552.

Assuming that "insulat[ing] political actors from private pressure" is indeed possible, is it desirable? How would a believer in strong political parties respond? Consider Michael A. Fitts, *Look Before You Leap: Some Cautionary Notes on Civic Republicanism*, 97 Yale Law Journal 1651, 1657 (1988):

> According to the political science literature, insulation of individual government actors and dispersion of government power is a serious *problem* in government, both as an impediment to effective and coordinated action and as a system that facilitates the influence and power of concentrated and wealthier special interest groups. Political parties, which seek to overcome those discrete sources of influence, are thus "the special form of political organization adapted to the mobilization of the majority."
>
> Not surprisingly, the political party literature views political dialogue and ideological politics, especially in the extreme, more skeptically. According to Sunstein, modern civic republicanism envisions rational dialogue as a "Rawlsian ideal"—by leading participants to "think from the point of view of everyone," a type of consensus is often achieved. Much of the political science literature suggests, however, that ideological debate—discussing public problems in terms of fundamental questions and beliefs—can sometimes create and exacerbate divisions and disputes in a public political context. Deep moral discussion can thus *undermine* the ability to reach consensus, and take action.

For an elaboration on these themes, see Michael A. Fitts, *The Vices of Virtue: A Political Party Perspective on Civic Virtue Reforms of the Legislative Process*, 136 University of Pennsylvania Law Review 1567 (1988).

9. Regardless of the perspectives employed to understand it, the field of election law has grown dramatically over the last few decades. No doubt some of that growth reflects the attention that the United States Supreme Court has paid to the topic. From the period 1901–1960, the Court decided an average of 10.3 election law cases per decade with a written opinion. From 1961–2000, that figure jumped to 60 per decade. The trend also appears when one considers the percentage of election law cases on the Supreme Court's docket. In the earlier period, election law cases made up 0.7% of the cases the Court decided by written opinion; in the latter period, that percentage increased seven and one-half times to an average 5.3% of cases. Richard L. Hasen, The Supreme Court and Election Law, Judging Equality from Baker v. Carr to Bush v. Gore 1–2 (2003). In the 2001–2010 decade, however, the number of election law cases in the Supreme Court fell dramatically, to 30 cases. For the most recent data on election litigation, see the notes following *Bush v. Gore* in Chapter 6.

Chapter 2

The Right to Vote

If the election mechanism is at the heart of any democracy, then the right to vote in elections is a central democratic right and the act of voting is the most elemental form of democratic participation. The simplest and most natural place to begin our study of election law is thus with the right to vote itself. Who is entitled to the franchise? And when should courts interfere with a state's decision to limit the franchise to particular groups? The remaining chapters in this book will consider the electoral system within which the right to vote is located.

For two centuries the history of the United States (and of much of the rest of the world) has usually been in the direction of allowing more people to vote in more elections that increasingly have controlled the most important aspects of government policymaking. The suffrage was limited in important ways when the United States Constitution was adopted. Property qualifications, denial of the vote to racial groups (African Americans and Native Americans), and restriction of the vote to men were the most important departures from universal suffrage. In the course of American history, each of these restrictions on the right to vote and numerous others have been eliminated. In Part I of this chapter, we shall provide a brief overview of this history.

Whether we are more impressed with the progress that these developments reflect or with the unfortunate fact that they were necessary in the first place, we should not assume that the direction of change has always been toward extension of the franchise. As we shall see, the late nineteenth and early twentieth centuries comprised a cruelly regressive period during which the hard-won right for African Americans to vote in the southern states was taken away for all practical purposes. That right was finally restored in the mid-twentieth century. Another group, resident aliens, was permitted to vote in many states during much of the nineteenth century. That extension of the franchise was revoked around the turn of the century and, with minor exceptions, has not been restored. The constitutionality of denying the vote to noncitizens is considered later in this Chapter.

In Part II of this Chapter, we consider the role of courts in policing legislative limits on the franchise. May a state limit voting to those who (1) pay a poll tax; (2) are literate; (3) are residents; (4) are non-felons; or (5) are citizens? In recent years, the courts have read the U.S. Constitution to prohibit some, but not all, of these limits on the franchise. Which voter qualifications, if any, should be a matter of legislative prerogative? We then turn to a related question: once a state grants the right to vote to a particular group in general elections, may it limit the franchise in particular *types* of elections, such as school board elections?

Whether people actually vote after they are granted the right to do so may seem more a question for political scientists and party activists than for students of the law. However, voting procedures that are either fixed by law or amenable to legal reform may affect turnout—and election outcomes—and the distinction between procedural barriers and the denial of the right to vote is not a sharp one. During the post-Reconstruction period, the Fifteenth Amendment precluded white southern Democrats from overtly denying the vote to African Americans. Instead, they relied on a variety of devices that made voting so difficult that the practical effect was almost as great as a denial of the right to vote. No such extreme restrictions are in effect today in the United States, but various requirements for voting, especially the requirement that individuals take the initiative to register if they wish to be eligible to vote, may be significant causes of low turnout in American elections, compared to those in other industrialized democracies. Chapter 6 looks at registration rules as well as other election administration issues.

Many people nowadays agree that the right to vote should be nearly universal, but that has not always been the case.[a] Opponents of extending the franchise have argued at various times that the masses would so misuse the vote that, far from being benefited, their lot would be worsened; that mass suffrage would be futile, for power would always remain in an elite class; and that even if extension of the right to vote furthered the goal of political equality, this would be more than offset by harmful effects on other values, such as liberty.

Although no one seriously proposes cutting back the right to vote in dramatic ways, past criticisms of universal suffrage cannot all be dismissed as insincere or lacking in substance. Similar arguments are heard today in opposition to proposals to make voting easier. Political columnist Jonah Goldberg argues: "[V]oting should be harder, not easier—for everybody. . . . If you are having an intelligent conversation with somebody, is it enriched if a mob of uninformed louts, never mind ex-cons and rapists, barges in? People who want to make voting easier are in effect saying that those who previously didn't care or know enough about the country to vote are exactly the kind of voters this country needs now." Jonah Goldberg, *The Cellblock Voting Bloc*, Los Angeles Times, Mar. 8, 2005, at B11. Lurking behind these and many of the legal and policy disputes reviewed in this book is the question whether democracy should be thought of as competition among interests or as a deliberative process seeking the common good. Measures that some have believed would

---

a. Albert O. Hirschman, The Rhetoric of Reaction (1991), provides a lively account of the history of conservative arguments against the extension of the franchise over a period of two centuries. He concludes that the arguments have tended to reflect dogmatic assumptions that could be and have been levied against virtually all proposed social, economic, and political reforms, but that these assumptions often have little empirical grounding. In a concluding chapter, Hirschman finds that liberal reformers tend to rely on a set of similarly dogmatic opposing assumptions.

improve the deliberative quality of democracy—restricting the vote to property-owners or to people who can read and write, or requiring would-be voters to take the time to register and thereby demonstrate a sense of the responsibilities of a citizen—have appeared to others as self-interested devices to enhance the political power of certain groups or parties. For example, is the 18-year-old age requirement for voting a desirable assurance of maturity in public decision-making, or is it a device for reinforcing adult society's strict control over younger teenagers?

I. A Brief History of the Right to Vote in the United States

A. The Extension of the Suffrage

1. The Attainment of White Male Suffrage

The American colonies inherited property qualifications for voting that had been established in England at least as early as the fifteenth century. In addition, British law excluded women, Catholics, Jews, aliens, and servants from the franchise. However, because of cheap land and lax administration, suffrage was far more widespread in practice in the colonies during the eighteenth century than in England.

Although estimates of the percentage of people who were eligible to vote during the colonial and revolutionary periods are uncertain, it appears that at least half the white adult males could vote before the Revolution in all states, and that in some states at least three-quarters and perhaps nearly 100 percent could vote. Because of cheap land and scarce labor, most white men who could not meet the property qualifications during their youth could do so by the time they had attained middle age.

The fact that the property qualifications were not extremely restrictive in practice was one reason that their imposition did not become a major point of contention during the period leading up to the Revolution. Another reason was that the restrictions sometimes were not enforced or were easily evaded, especially when political contests were highly competitive and individuals therefore had the greatest incentive to vote. In addition to these practical considerations, there was no ideological consensus during the eighteenth century in favor of universal white male suffrage. Before the Revolution, the prevailing political theory was influenced by Aristotle's idea of balanced government, which held that tyranny would result if either the monarchical, the aristocratic, or the democratic principle dominated the others. Finally, in the absence of a secret ballot, voting by tenants, employees, or paupers was regarded as likely to lead to corruption or coercion, with a consequent magnification of influence by the wealthy.

The Constitution of the United States did not purport to regulate the franchise. The only federal officials chosen by direct election under the original Constitution were the members of the House of Representatives, and Article I, § 2 of the Constitution said that "the Electors in each State shall have the Qualifications requisite for Electors of the most numerous Branch of the State Legislature."[b] What those qualifications were to be was entirely up to the states. Nor was there any impetus in the direction of universal suffrage from the federal government. The Northwest Ordinance and other laws governing territories imposed landowning requirements for voting. Difficulties with land titles and other practical problems quickly made property requirements a dead letter in much of the west, however.

With the arrival of the nineteenth century, the idea of universal white manhood suffrage became ascendant. The Aristotelian view was opposed by a Puritan belief that for purposes of secular politics, people should be treated as if they were equal and, increasingly, by natural rights theories of political equality.

Religious tests for voting and exclusion on the basis of status as a servant or employee (but not as a slave) were largely eliminated by the end of the revolutionary period. With one significant exception (Rhode Island, discussed below), property qualifications more or less petered out over the three-quarters of a century following the Revolution. In many places, the payment of a tax was permitted as an alternative to satisfying the property qualifications. Although the poll tax later became a prominent device for *denying* the vote to blacks and poor whites in the South, in the eighteenth century it was a liberalizing device that opened the franchise to persons whose wealth did not take the form of land. Similarly, service in the militia was increasingly accepted as an alternative to owning land or paying taxes, thereby extending the right to vote to a higher percentage of young men.

During the Jeffersonian period, several states adopted universal white male suffrage or regulations that came very close. The trend continued throughout the first half of the nineteenth century, though at a very uneven pace in different states. Often the movement toward extension of the franchise was pushed forward by party competition, as each party sought to benefit by extending the franchise to new groups of voters who would, it was hoped, reward the party with their votes. The movement also benefited from less savory considerations, such as the contention in Virginia and North Carolina that universal white male suffrage was needed to assure unity among whites in the event of a slave rebellion. Despite this argument, these two states were among the last to adopt universal white male suffrage, in the 1850s.

The only truly dramatic event in the early extension of suffrage occurred in Rhode Island. In that state during the Jeffersonian period, the property qualifications did not prevent most adult males from voting, so there was no strong pressure to eliminate them. After the War of 1812, as industry began to develop and cities to grow, it became apparent that the non-landowning working class would be composed of immigrants, largely Catholic. Resistance to suffrage reform became strong

---

b. The Seventeenth Amendment, providing for direct election of Senators, contains a virtually identical clause. Note also that the Guarantee Clause of Article IV, which states that "[t]he United States shall guarantee to every State in this Union a Republican Form of Government," could in theory have implications for voting if certain franchise restrictions were deemed unrepublican. But any such potential in the Guarantee Clause has remained almost entirely untapped.

in rural areas, where Protestant farmers had no desire to share political power with these newcomers. Pressure for a liberalized franchise grew, but was stoutly resisted by the rural interests who controlled the state government.

In 1841, a group called the Rhode Island Suffrage Association, under the leadership of Thomas Dorr, called for a constitutional convention, delegates to which would be elected by universal white male suffrage. Dorr's convention competed with a constitutional convention sponsored by the official state government. The official convention's Charter retained property qualifications, and for a time it appeared that popular support for Dorr might result in the overthrow of the Charter government. However, the national government under President John Tyler supported the Charter government, and the following year the constitution was liberalized to allow native-born citizens the right to qualify to vote with personal rather than real property. Dorr was forced to flee from Rhode Island, which for many years continued to discriminate between native-born and naturalized citizens, but whose new constitution was, in one important respect, more liberal than Dorr's, in that it permitted African Americans to vote.

By the time of the Civil War, adult white male suffrage was the rule in most of the states, with relatively minor exceptions. Although limited voting by women had been permitted in New Jersey until 1807, the almost universal rule restricted voting to men. For African Americans, there had actually been a regression since the colonial period, when a number of states, northern and southern, had permitted voting by free blacks. By 1860, most states restricted voting to whites, with most of the exceptions located in New England.[c]

2. The Fifteenth Amendment and Its Betrayal

As the Civil War ended, black suffrage not only was the exception rather than the rule in the North, but also was unpopular, as evidenced by its defeat in several (though not all) referendums that occurred in the 1860s. Accordingly, in 1865 and 1866, the Republicans, uncertain of their electoral prospects, did little to promote voting rights for African Americans. The Fourteenth Amendment, proposed in 1866 and ratified in 1868, made African Americans citizens and guaranteed "equal protection of the laws." It did not, however, expressly prohibit voting discrimination, though it did reduce the representation in Congress of states that denied voting rights to male inhabitants 21 and over. In 1866, the congressional Republicans won a landslide victory and thus felt safe in ordering black suffrage in areas where doing so would not arouse opposition in their northern constituencies. In 1867, blacks were given the franchise in the District of Columbia and in federal territories. The Reconstruction Act of 1867 required that blacks be allowed to vote in southern states as a condition of readmission.

c. There was also a regression in the first half of the nineteenth century in the number of states permitting noncitizens to vote. The history of voting by noncitizens is sketched briefly in Note 3 following *Skafte v. Rorex, infra.*

By 1868, the Democrats were resurgent and although Ulysses Grant, the Republican candidate, was elected in 1868, the margin was perilously close in many northern states. Republicans also began to fear that some black voters in the South were in danger of being won over by the Democrats. The Republicans responded to these concerns by rushing the Fifteenth Amendment through the lame duck session of Congress in January and February, 1869. This was accomplished with some difficulty, and the final version of the Fifteenth Amendment was something of a compromise, falling short of the hopes of some that the federal Constitution would impose universal adult male suffrage or bar literacy and property tests. As adopted, the Fifteenth Amendment reads as follows:

> Section 1. The right of citizens of the United States to vote shall not be denied or abridged by the United States or by any State on account of race, color, or previous condition of servitude.
>
> Section 2. The Congress shall have power to enforce this article by appropriate legislation.

Ratification by the requisite number of states was completed within thirteen months, but only after considerable uncertainty. Ratification was assisted by legislation requiring Georgia, Mississippi, Texas, and Virginia to ratify the Fifteenth Amendment as a condition of readmission to the Union.

One impetus for the Fifteenth Amendment was the principled view of many that it was wrong to deny the vote on grounds of race, especially to a group whose vulnerability as recently emancipated slaves made the protection accorded by the right to vote particularly important. Section 2 provided express authority for legislation to safeguard their voting rights, an opportunity of which Congress availed itself through several laws enacted in succeeding years. Perhaps an even greater impetus for the Fifteenth Amendment came from the desire of the Republican Party for electoral advantage. Black voters in many northern states, though few in number, could be expected to reinforce shaky Republican majorities, while the gratitude of African Americans in North and South would strengthen their voting loyalty to the GOP. The Fifteenth Amendment also benefitted northern Republicans by ending a potentially divisive debate. Once black voting was a fait accompli, Democrats could no longer exploit the *threat* of black voting as a way of appealing to white voters. It would thus be a mistake to assume that the Fifteenth Amendment was aimed primarily at the South. In the southern states, extension of the vote to blacks had been accomplished by military reconstruction and by the constitutions of the states that had already been readmitted.

The Fifteenth Amendment had the dual purpose of enfranchising African Americans in the northern states and reinforcing the right to vote in the South. The first purpose was successfully accomplished and, for a while, the second was accomplished too. African Americans did not only vote but were also elected to office in substantial numbers, with over 300 elected from southern states by 1872.

But despite the Fifteenth Amendment, a disastrous retrenchment was to occur in the South.

The year 1877, when Union soldiers were removed from the South as part of the settlement of the disputed presidential election of 1876, is often given as the end of Reconstruction. It is easy to imagine that from 1877 on, the Solid South system—an almost exclusively white electorate, ubiquitous control by the Democratic Party, and low voter turnout—was firmly entrenched. In reality, it took thirty years of concentrated effort to accomplish this result. The driving forces were racism, partisanship, and class politics.

Partisan political competition was a reality in the South until nearly the end of the nineteenth century. It is true that the Democrats carried every southern state in presidential elections from 1880 on, but the vote was not always lopsided, and state and local races were often more competitive. Republicans or the candidates of a variety of third parties occasionally won statewide elections and often mounted a serious threat. Although the number of southern black legislators began to decline in the 1870s, some continued to serve through the 1890s.

White support for disenfranchisement of African Americans came primarily from "black belt counties" (those with especially large African American populations) and from wealthier areas. Typical leaders in the disenfranchisement movement were wealthy, well-educated, and from established families. White opposition to disenfranchisement came mostly from poorer and predominantly white areas, and from members of the Republican and other opposition parties. Their opposition to disenfranchisement may have been motivated by principle, but it certainly was motivated by recognition that their partisan and class interests had no hope of success without the support of black voters. Blacks themselves actively resisted disenfranchisement in both judicial and political arenas, though ultimately without success.

Roughly speaking, in the 1870s and 1880s, southern Democrats often relied on violence and fraud to gain or consolidate control of state legislatures. Violence was often ineffective. The use of fraud was more successful, but it created the danger that it would trigger a new round of federal intervention. Accordingly, in the 1880s and 1890s, southern Democratic legislatures adopted laws making it more difficult for blacks (and often poor whites) to vote. Finally, in the 1890s and the 1900s, constitutional conventions were summoned. The discriminatory laws that had already been passed helped to assure that these conventions would be dominated overwhelmingly by Democrats. The new constitutions that emerged entrenched even stronger discrimination devices.

The following is a description of some of the leading devices that were adopted in the southern states during this period, together with a brief indication of their subsequent history:

Secret Ballots: Although ostensibly introduced as a good government device to reduce voter corruption and preserve the integrity of the ballot box, the secret ballot was also favored in the South (and perhaps in the North as well) as a device to prevent illiterates from voting. In the South, this had a detrimental effect on blacks, who had been denied education as slaves and subjected to inferior education after the Civil War. Furthermore, election officials could discriminatorily provide assistance to white voters who needed it, while denying assistance to black voters. In South Carolina and Florida, the "eight-box" device was used, to similar effect. Voters had to place separate ballots for different offices in separate ballot boxes, and ballots placed in the wrong box were not counted. Precinct officials gave no assistance to illiterate blacks, and the boxes could be moved around frequently during the day of the election, to confound any outside person who might seek to instruct black voters on which box was which.

Currently, most Americans are sufficiently literate that the secret ballot is not a major barrier to voting. Furthermore, the 1982 amendments to the Voting Rights Act mandate that any voter who needs assistance because of blindness, disability or illiteracy is entitled to receive it from a person of the voter's choice.[d]

The adoption of the secret ballot may have reduced turnout by as many as seven percentage points, but this effect was no greater in the South than in the rest of the country. See Jac C. Heckelman, *The Effect of the Secret Ballot on Voter Turnout Rates*, 82 Public Choice 107 (1995). Heckelman argues that the effect on turnout was not primarily caused by deterrence of voting by illiterates. He contends that party symbols that were usually placed on ballots made it possible for illiterates to vote when they were permitted to do so. Furthermore, literacy tests were a much more direct and potent way of preventing voting by illiterates. Rather, Heckelman contends that bribery of voters, a common practice in the nineteenth century, became impractical once a state adopted the secret ballot, because there was no way of assuring that the voter had voted as desired. The elimination of bribery also eliminated the incentive for some people to vote.

Poll Tax: Georgia adopted a poll tax in 1877. Other southern states did not follow suit until the 1890s, but by 1904 all the former states of the Confederacy had adopted a poll tax. The poll tax was justified by its proponents as a device to disenfranchise blacks, but it also had the effect, and probably the intent, of lowering white turnout. The poll tax was a particularly severe obstacle to voting in some states, which required an individual to pay not only the current year's tax but also unpaid taxes from previous years.

---

d. Voting Rights Act § 208, 52 U.S.C. § 10508.

The Twenty-Fourth Amendment, added to the Constitution in 1964, banned poll taxes in federal elections. Two years later, the Supreme Court in *Harper v. Virginia State Board of Elections*, 383 U.S. 663 (1966), ruled that the use of the poll tax in any election violated the Equal Protection Clause. We consider *Harper* in Part II of this Chapter.

Literacy Tests: Literacy tests were among the most important devices adopted at the disenfranchisement conventions in the decades before and after the turn of the century. They were often accompanied by escape provisions, the best known of which was the "grandfather clause," which waived the literacy test for persons who were eligible to vote or whose ancestors were eligible to vote on a date prior to the initial enfranchisement of African Americans. Grandfather clauses were declared unconstitutional in *Guinn v. United States*, 238 U.S. 347 (1915), but literacy tests could be and were administered in a discriminatory manner against blacks. By the 1950s and early 1960s, discriminatory literacy tests were the most important devices for restricting voting by African Americans in the South.

In *Lassiter v. Northampton County Board of Elections*, 360 U.S. 45 (1959), the Supreme Court held that a literacy test, fairly applied, did not violate the Equal Protection Clause:

> The ability to read and write likewise has some relation to standards designed to promote intelligent use of the ballot. Literacy and illiteracy are neutral on race, creed, color, and sex, as reports around the world show. Literacy and intelligence are obviously not synonymous. Illiterate people may be intelligent voters. Yet in our society where newspapers, periodicals, books, and other printed matter canvass and debate campaign issues, a State might conclude that only those who are literate should exercise the franchise. It was said last century in Massachusetts that a literacy test was designed to insure an "independent and intelligent" exercise of the right of suffrage. North Carolina agrees. We do not sit in judgment on the wisdom of that policy. We cannot say, however, that it is not an allowable one measured by constitutional standards.
>
> Of course a literacy test, fair on its face, may be employed to perpetuate that discrimination which the Fifteenth Amendment was designed to uproot. No such influence is charged here.... The present requirement, applicable to members of all races, is that the prospective voter "be able to read and write any section of the Constitution of North Carolina in the English language." That seems to us to be one fair way of determining whether a person is literate, not a calculated scheme to lay springes for the citizen. Certainly we cannot condemn it on its face as a device unrelated to the desire of North Carolina to raise the standards for people of all races who cast the ballot.

Id. at 51–54. Literacy tests in the South often were *not* fairly applied, but proving discrimination on a case-by-case basis was a laborious chore. The Voting Rights Act of 1965 banned literacy tests in most of the Deep South. In *South Carolina v. Katzenbach*, 383 U.S. 301 (1966), the Supreme Court held that the literacy test ban was a permissible exercise of Congress's power to enforce the Fifteenth Amendment, despite the fact that the literacy test itself was not unconstitutional. In the 1970 amendments to the Voting Rights Act, Congress extended the literacy test ban to the entire country, but only until 1975.[e] In 1975 the ban was made permanent. See 52 U.S.C. § 10303(e)(2).

e. The Supreme Court upheld the nationwide literacy test ban in *Oregon v. Mitchell*, 400 U.S. 112 (1970).

Louisiana Literacy Test from the 1960s

The State of Louisiana

Literacy Test (This test is to be given to anyone who cannot prove a fifth grade education.)

Do what you are told to do in each statement, nothing more, nothing less. Be careful as one wrong answer denotes failure of the test. You have 10 minutes to complete the test.

1. Draw a line around the number or letter of this sentence.

2. Draw a line under the last word in this line.

3. Cross out the longest word in this line.

4. Draw a line around the shortest word in this line.

5. Circle the first, first letter of the alphabet in this line.

6. In the space below draw three circles, one inside (engulfed by) the other.

7. Above the letter X make a small cross.

8. Draw a line through the letter below that comes earliest in the alphabet.

   Z V S B D M K I T P H C

9. Draw a line through the two letters below that come last in the alphabet.

   Z V B D M K T P H S Y C

10. In the first circle below write the last letter of the first word beginning with "L".

11. Cross out the number necessary, when making the number below one million.

    10000000000

12. Draw a line from circle 2 to circle 5 that will pass below circle 2 and above circle 4.

13. In the line below cross out each number that is more than 20 but less than 30.

    31 16 48 29 53 47 22 37 98 26 20 25

14. Draw a line under the first letter after "h" and draw a line through the second letter after "j".

abcde fghijklmnopq

15. In the space below, write the word "noise" backwards and place a dot over what would be its second letter should it have been written forward.

16. Draw a triangle with a blackened circle that overlaps only its left corner.

17. Look at the line of numbers below, and place on the blank, the number that should come next.

2 4 8 16 ____

18. Look at the line of numbers below, and place on the blank, the number that should come next.

3 6 9 ____ 15

19. Draw in the space below, a square with a triangle in it, and within that same triangle draw a circle with a black dot in it.

20. Spell backwards, forwards.

21. Print the word vote upside down, but in the correct order.

22. Place a cross over the tenth letter in this line, a line under the first space in this sentence, and circle around the last the in the second line of this sentence.

23. Draw a figure that is square in shape. Divide it in half by drawing a straight line from its northeast corner to its southwest corner, and then divide it once more by drawing a broken line from the middle of its western side to the middle of its eastern side.

24. Print a word that looks the same whether it is printed frontwards or backwards.

25. Write down on the line provided, what you read in the triangle below:

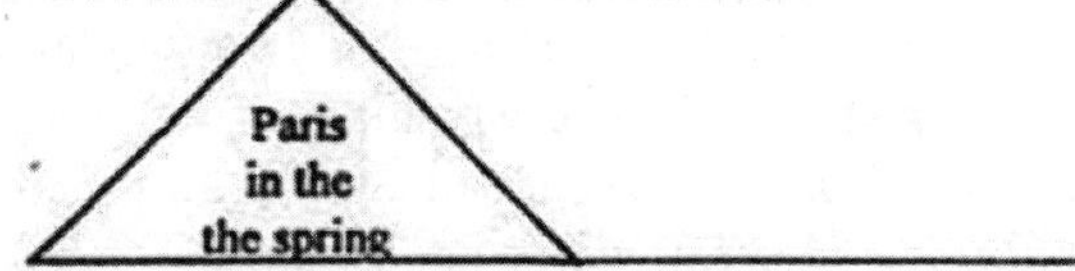

26. In the third square below, write the second letter of the fourth word.

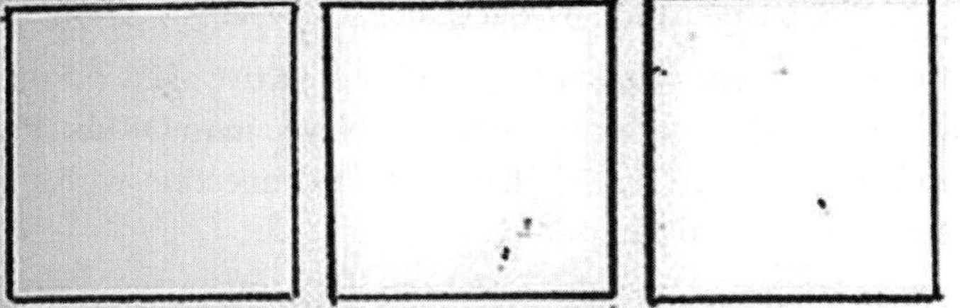

27. Write right from the left to the right as you see it spelled here.

28. Divide a vertical line in two equal parts by bisecting it with a curved horizontal line that is only straight at its spot bisection of the vertical.

29. Write every other word in this first line and print every third word in same line, (original type smaller and first line ended at comma) but capitalize the fifth word that you write.

30. Draw five circles that one common inter-locking part.

Source: Rebecca Onion, Take the Impossible "Literacy" Test Louisiana Gave Black Voters in the 1960s, Slate, June 28, 2013, https://perma.cc/FF4X-JFYV

White Primary: Democratic primaries were held in some local elections in the South beginning in the 1870s as a device to coopt opposition or to assure a unified party vote. Apparently the first statewide primary held anywhere in the country was held in Louisiana in 1892, to prevent an intra-party division over the state lottery from leading to a Republican or Populist victory. Black voting in Democratic primaries was sometimes permitted until around the turn of the century, and was not much of an issue. Until the 1930s, the overwhelming majority of African Americans wanted to vote *against* the Democrats in the South, not to vote in their primaries. However, once interparty opposition was essentially eliminated, the white primary helped preserve the Democratic monopoly and provided an extra barrier against effective participation by black voters.

The elimination of the white primary was a major objective of civil rights litigation from the 1920s until success was finally achieved in the 1940s. The *White Primary Cases* are described in Chapter 8, in connection with the constitutional status of political parties.

Intimidation and Violence: When the above devices failed to stop African Americans from trying to register and vote, southern whites frequently resorted to intimidation and violence. The Supreme Court had a chance to combat these practices in *Giles v. Harris*, 189 U.S. 475 (1903), in which 5,000 blacks in Montgomery, Alabama complained that they had been unconstitutionally prevented from registering to vote despite satisfying all applicable requirements. Writing for the Court, Justice Holmes rejected this challenge on the grounds that the Court did not wish to involve itself in Alabama's unlawful activity and that any remedy the Court ordered would be ineffective:

> The difficulties which we cannot overcome are two, and the first is this: The plaintiff alleges that the whole registration scheme of the Alabama Constitution is a fraud upon the Constitution of the United States, and asks us to declare it void. But, of course, he could not maintain a bill for a mere declaration in the air. He does not try to do so, but asks to be registered as a party qualified under the void instrument. If, then, we accept the conclusion which it is the chief purpose of the bill to maintain, how can we make the court a party to the unlawful scheme by accepting it and adding another voter to its fraudulent lists? ...
>
> The other difficulty is of a different sort, and strikingly reinforces the argument that equity cannot undertake now, any more than it has in the past, to enforce political rights.... [T]he court has [no] practical power to deal with the people of the state in a body. The bill imports that the great mass of the white population intends to keep the blacks from voting. To meet such an intent something more than ordering the plaintiff's name to be inscribed upon the lists of 1902 will be needed. If the conspiracy and the intent exist, a name on a piece of paper will not defeat them.

> Unless we are prepared to supervise the voting in that state by officers of the court, it seems to us that all that the plaintiff could get from equity would be an empty form. Apart from damages to the individual, relief from a great political wrong, if done, as alleged, by the people of a state and the state itself, must be given by them or by the legislative and political department of the government of the United States.

Id. at 486-88. *Giles* reflects Justice Holmes's view that the courts cannot be expected to achieve dramatic change in the face of popular opposition. See David Luban, *Justice Holmes and the Metaphysics of Judicial Restraint*, 44 Duke Law Journal 449, 515 (1994) (noting "his insistence on viewing electoral majorities as unanswerable military victors"). *Giles* also represents the nadir of the Court's efforts to protect African Americans from disenfranchisement and other forms of electoral discrimination. See Richard H. Pildes, *Democracy, Anti-Democracy, and the Canon*, 17 Constitutional Commentary 295 (2000) (arguing for this reason that *Giles* should be included in the "anti-canon" of the Court's most objectionable decisions).

3. *Votes for Women*

Enactment of the constitutional amendment guaranteeing the vote to racial minorities was accomplished relatively quickly, but the Fifteenth Amendment marked only the beginning of the long struggle to make suffrage for blacks a permanent reality. The struggle for the enfranchisement of women was similarly long, but the sequence was the opposite. The adoption of the Nineteenth Amendment took more than three-quarters of a century, but once it was accomplished, the struggle was over.

The beginning of the American women's rights movement is commonly dated from an 1848 meeting in Seneca Falls, New York, led by Elizabeth Cady Stanton and Lucretia Mott. The demand for the right to vote contained in the Declaration of Sentiments adopted at Seneca Falls was regarded as particularly radical. The founders of the women's movement were abolitionists, and their call for the right to vote was motivated in part by the desire to win the right to participate more effectively in the movement to end slavery. Leaders of the movement, including Lucy Stone and Susan B. Anthony, worked actively to support the Union cause during the Civil War. Many of them were disillusioned when, after the war, the Republican Party pushed for votes for blacks but not for women. Efforts to obtain judicial relief also failed when the Supreme Court ruled that the Fourteenth Amendment did not prevent denying women the right to vote. *Minor v. Happersett*, 88 U.S. 162 (1875).

The appellant's claim in *Minor* was that Missouri's grant of suffrage to men alone abridged the "privileges or immunities of citizens of the United States" protected by the Fourteenth Amendment. The Court agreed that women are American citizens (and, indeed, had been even before the Amendment's ratification). But the Court disagreed that the right to vote is one of the "privileges or immunities" guaranteed to American citizens. "It certainly is nowhere made so in express terms. The United States has no voters in the States of its own creation. The elective officers of the

United States are all elected directly or indirectly by State voters." *Id.* at 170. Moreover, "[u]pon an examination of those [state] constitutions [in effect at the Framing] we find that in no State were all citizens permitted to vote.... In this condition of the law in respect to suffrage in the several States it cannot for a moment be doubted that if it had been intended to make all citizens of the United States voters, the framers of the Constitution would not have left it to implication. So important a change in the condition of citizenship as it actually existed, if intended, would have been expressly declared." *Id.* at 172-73.

In 1890, two women's suffrage groups merged to form the National American Woman Suffrage Association ("NAWSA"). By this time several states allowed women to vote in school or municipal elections and, in 1890, Wyoming was admitted as the first state to allow full woman suffrage. Colorado, Utah, and Idaho followed suit by 1896, but it was not until 1910 that Washington became the next state to do so. After 1910, several more states joined the fold, and New York's doing so in 1917 became the turning point in the effort to obtain women's suffrage nationwide. By that time, enough representatives had voting female constituents to provide impetus to the approval by Congress of the Nineteenth Amendment in 1919. The amendment was ratified by the 36th state and became part of the Constitution in August, 1920.

In the 1890s, arguments for women's suffrage were cast largely in terms of equality and individual rights. However, around the turn of the century, the appeal of arguments based on the principle of universal suffrage diminished, as opposition to voting by immigrant groups in the North and blacks in the South mounted. One of the leading arguments made against suffrage for women was that it would give more influence to "the poor, the ignorant, and the immoral," groups who were often assumed to be identical by proponents of this viewpoint.

The leaders of the women's suffrage movement were mainly white, native-born, middle-class women who were by no means immune to the prejudices that characterized their period. Accordingly, arguments for women's suffrage shifted from arguments based on equality and the principle of universal suffrage to arguments based on reforms that women would favor and help to bring about, particularly prohibition of alcoholic beverages and a variety of reforms espoused by the Progressive movement.

In contrast to the highly partisan politics that led first to the granting of the franchise to blacks and then to the denial of it to blacks in the South, party played a much smaller role in the struggle for women's suffrage. The NAWSA was consistently nonpartisan. Indeed, many of its members shared the general anti-party views common among Progressive reformers. It is true that as a general rule, Republican legislators were more likely to support women's suffrage than Democrats, at least in part because women were expected to support prohibition, a cause supported by more Republicans than Democrats. A group known as the Women's Party, smaller and more militant than the NAWSA, in 1914 and 1916 urged women in states where they could vote to oppose Democrats because of President Wilson's lack of leadership in support of women's suffrage. However, there is little evidence that such campaigning was effective. As the inevitability of nationwide women's suffrage began to be clear, representatives of both parties joined the bandwagon so as not to provoke opposition from the new class of voters.

Contemporaries expected that voting by women would boost two political causes: peace and prohibition. Whether this would have occurred is hard to say, because World War I ended and the prohibition amendment (the Eighteenth) was enacted before women's suffrage was accomplished. As Aileen S. Kraditor, a historian of the women's suffrage movement, has written:

> The addition of women to the electorate has not significantly altered American voting patterns as the suffragists predicted it would.[f] But it would not be correct for that reason to deny that an enormous change took place with the enactment of the Nineteenth Amendment. Even those many suffragists who wanted the vote primarily to enact reforms became suffragists partly because of the intense shame they felt at being thought unfit to help govern their country. When they acquired that right they felt a new pride in American democracy and a new respect for themselves.[g]

4. The Reenfranchisement of African Americans in the South

In 1910, when racial segregation and disenfranchisement of blacks were firmly established in the South and when belief in racial equality was at a low point throughout the nation, blacks and whites who retained a commitment to civil rights formed the National Association for the Advancement of Colored People. Reenfranchisement was one of the NAACP's major goals, and litigation was one of its major weapons.

The NAACP's most important litigation campaign relating to voting rights was a sustained attack on the white primary. The key victory, in *Smith v. Allwright*, 321 U.S. 649 (1944), was largely responsible for an increase in black registration in the South from an estimated 250,000 in 1940, to as many as 775,000 in 1947.

A second disenfranchisement device, the poll tax, was vulnerable to political attack because it prevented some whites as well as blacks from voting and was sometimes associated with corrupt political machines, which would pay the poll tax for voters expected to be reliable machine supporters. The poll tax was repealed in North Carolina in 1920, and in five other states, Florida, Georgia, Louisiana, South Carolina, and Tennessee, between 1937 and the mid-1950s.

---

f. Kraditor was writing in 1965. Beginning in the 1980s political analysts have sometimes observed a "gender gap," consisting of somewhat greater support for Democrats by women and Republicans by men.

g. Aileen S. Kraditor, The Ideas of the Woman Suffrage Movement, 1890–1920, at 263–64 (1965). See also Adam Winkler, *A Revolution Too Soon: Woman Suffragists and the "Living Constitution,"* 76 New York University Law Review 1456 (2001).

In addition to attacks on legal impediments to registering, action to encourage registration of blacks began in earnest after World War II. In Mississippi, returning African American veterans led registration efforts, and although these did not achieve great numerical success, Mississippi's discriminatory practices received nationwide exposure during a Senate investigation into the Democratic senatorial primary of 1946. The NAACP and a variety of voter leagues and other civil rights organizations conducted intense registration drives.

These legal and political efforts were by no means without effect. By the mid-1950s, over a million African Americans were registered in the South, representing 20 to 25 percent of the voting age black population, as compared with about 5 percent before *Smith v. Allwright*. However, the gains were concentrated in the upper South and the largest cities of the deep South. In 24 deep South black belt counties, not a single African American was registered at the end of 1952. Literacy tests and often flagrantly discriminatory administration of the registration system, supplemented by violence and economic retaliation sometimes directed against African Americans who sought to register, blocked further progress. It became the consensus among voting rights supporters that federal action would be necessary.

Voting rights legislation was passed by Congress in 1957 and 1960, and there were relatively minor voting provisions in the Civil Rights Act of 1964. The general thrust of these laws was to enable the Justice Department and private citizens to bring actions in federal courts to enforce nondiscriminatory voting procedures. It would be an exaggeration to say that these reforms were a failure. By 1964, an estimated 38 percent of southern voting age blacks were registered, a significant increase from a decade before. The 1957 and 1960 civil rights laws contributed to this progress, which also was prompted by intensified registration drives conducted by the NAACP and newer organizations such as the Student Non-Violent Coordinating Committee, the Congress of Racial Equality, and the Southern Christian Leadership Conference. Still, the laws that had been passed were not sufficient to bring about equal access to the ballot box throughout the South. The key flaw was that the burden of initiating litigation was on the Justice Department or on voting rights proponents. Case-by-case litigation was slow and costly.[h]

Events in Selma, Alabama, in 1965, led the voting rights issue to a climax. Martin Luther King, who had recently been awarded the Nobel Peace Prize, led a series of voting rights demonstrations in Selma. Two thousand demonstrators, including King, were arrested. King later met with President Lyndon Johnson, who agreed to seek legislation prohibiting literacy tests and eliminating local officials' discretion

h. Nevertheless, litigation has continued to be a significant device for those seeking to protect or extend the franchise to minority group members. See Peyton McCrary, *Bringing Equality to Power: How the Federal Courts Transformed the Electoral Structure of Southern Politics, 1960–1990*, 5 University of Pennsylvania Journal of Constitutional Law 665 (2003).

by imposing federal registrars where necessary. On March 7, 1965, demonstrators marching from Selma to Montgomery were beaten by state troopers and county police. A week later, in a dramatic address to Congress, President Johnson employed the civil rights slogan, "We shall overcome," in demanding strong voting rights legislation. In August, he was able to sign the Voting Rights Act of 1965 into law.[i]

Sections 2 and 3 of the Act were permanent additions to law and generally applicable. Section 2 essentially restated the Fifteenth Amendment, barring states and localities from employing voting mechanisms that would deny or abridge on account of race or color the right of American citizens to vote. Section 3 further strengthened the remedies in suits brought by the Justice Department to enforce the Fifteenth Amendment. Although Section 2 was later to become, in an amended form, a key provision of the Act, in 1965 Sections 2 and 3 were regarded as relatively unimportant.

The provisions that were dramatically new and that would make the Fifteenth Amendment a reality were in Sections 4 through 9, which were to be in effect only for five years and were applicable only in states or localities that in 1964 used a literacy or other test as a condition for registering or voting and in which less than half the voting age population voted in the 1964 presidential election. As a practical matter, the areas "covered" by the Act were Alabama, Georgia, Louisiana, Mississippi, South Carolina, Virginia, and large parts of North Carolina.

Section 4 of the act prohibited the use of literacy tests and other tests or devices in covered areas. Sections 6 through 8 authorized the federal government, under specified circumstances but without the need for judicial proceedings, to appoint federal registrars and election observers, to assure nondiscriminatory election administration. To prevent states from devising new means of disenfranchisement, Section 5 required covered states and localities to submit changes in "any voting qualification or prerequisite to voting, or standard, practice or procedure with respect to voting" to either the Attorney General or to the U.S. District Court for the District of Columbia for "preclearance." No such change could be implemented without preclearance, but if preclearance were denied by the Attorney General, it could be sought judicially.

The Voting Rights Act proved to be one of the most successful civil rights measures in American history. In the words of one leading student of the Act:

> In Mississippi, that stronghold within a stronghold, black voter registration increased from 6.7 percent before the act to 59.8 in 1967. The act simply overwhelmed the major bulwarks of the disenfranchising system. In the seven states originally covered, black registration increased from 29.3 percent in

i. 52 U.S.C. § 10301 et seq. Provisions of the Voting Rights Act are commonly referred to by the Act's internal section numbers rather than by their codification in the United States Code, and that practice will be followed henceforth in this volume.

> March 1965 to 56.6 percent in 1971–72; the gap between black and white registration rates narrowed from 44.1 percentage points to 11.2.[j]

The great effect that the reenfranchisement of African Americans has had on southern politics is manifested in many ways. One is economic. Blacks living in areas covered by the Act experienced reductions in both poverty and black-white income inequality compared to blacks living in non-covered areas. This progress is presumably attributable to the political mobilization of African Americans that the Act enabled. See Abhay P. Aneja, *Voting for Welfare: The Voting Rights Act as Socioeconomic Empowerment*, 109 California Law Review (forthcoming 2021). Additionally, the Act likely contributed to the migration of most southern whites, over a period lasting several decades, from the Democratic to the Republican Party. Across almost the entire South, the vast majority of blacks are Democrats, and the vast majority of whites now affiliate with the Republican Party. This fact—a stark reversal of the once all-Democratic "Solid South"—means that Republicans now dominate southern state legislatures and congressional delegations, and that Democratic representation is largely (though not entirely) limited to majority-minority districts electing minority officeholders.

Notably, the fact that the major provisions of the Act were temporary has turned out to be an advantage to proponents of minority voting rights rather than a hindrance, for each time the Act has been scheduled to expire it has not only been renewed, but strengthening or broadening amendments have been added. For example, in 1970, the coverage formula was updated to refer to the 1968 rather than the 1964 presidential election, thereby considerably expanding the covered areas. In addition, the 1970 amendments made the ban on literacy tests nationwide for a five-year period.

The Act was again renewed and amended in 1975. The nationwide ban on literacy tests was made permanent, and plaintiffs were given new advantages in litigation brought under the Act, including the possibility of being awarded attorneys' fees. The most important of the 1975 amendments extended the protection of the Act beyond racial minorities to specified language minorities—Asian Americans, Native Americans, Alaskan natives, and persons of Spanish heritage. Concomitantly, coverage was extended to three new states, Alaska, Arizona, and Texas, and portions of many other states around the country. Congress renewed the Act once again in 1982, giving it considerably more teeth. Additionally, Congress expanded the coverage of one portion of the Act, requiring bilingual voting assistance in specified areas, in 1992.

The most recent extension and amendment of the Voting Rights Act occurred in 2006, with the language provisions set to expire in 2031 and Section 5 preclearance

j. Chandler Davidson, *The Voting Rights Act: A Brief History*, in Controversies in Minority Voting: The Voting Rights Act in Perspective 7, 21 (Bernard Grofman and Chandler Davidson, eds., 1992).

in 2032. The most significant change was to impose a higher standard for preclearance, one that focuses on racial minorities' opportunity to elect their preferred candidate of choice. The latest amendment did not change the formula for coverage, a drafting choice that led to litigation, ultimately successful, claiming the provision is unconstitutional as exceeding congressional power to enforce the Fourteenth and Fifteenth Amendments. In Chapter 5, we consider the 1982 and 2006 amendments, along with the doctrine of racial vote dilution, that is, efforts to reduce minority representation through means other than disenfranchisement. In Chapter 6, we consider the doctrine of racial vote *denial*, that is, measures that make it more difficult for minority members to vote or otherwise participate in elections.

5. Additional Extensions of the Franchise

The elimination of property qualifications and of racial and gender discrimination have been the most important extensions of the franchise in American history, but by no means the only ones. A few additional ones are worthy of brief consideration, some of which we will revisit in Chapter 6.

Age: Until 1970, most states set the minimum voting age at 21. The 1970 amendments to the Voting Rights Act prohibited states from setting a minimum voting age above 18. In *Oregon v. Mitchell*, 400 U.S. 112 (1970), four justices believed Congress had no power under the Constitution to set a voting age, but four justices believed Congress was acting within its power to enforce the Fourteenth Amendment. The remaining member of the Court, Justice Black, believed Congress had the power to set the voting age for federal elections but not state and local elections. An arguable problem with this interpretation is that it disregarded the Constitution's text. Article I, § 2 and the Seventeenth Amendment prescribe that the qualifications for congressional electors are to be the same as the qualifications for electors for the most numerous branch of the state legislature. Justice Black's view nevertheless prevailed, because there were five justices who believed Congress could set the voting age in federal elections and there were five who believed Congress could not set the voting age for state and local elections. The anomaly was eliminated in 1971 by adoption of the Twenty-Sixth Amendment, which prohibits a state from setting a voting age above 18.

Durational residency: Prior to 1972, states commonly denied the right to vote to persons who had recently moved into the state. Typically, a residency period of one year was required. Because of the high rate of transiency in the United States, lengthy durational residency requirements prevented significant numbers of people from voting. However, the Supreme Court struck down a Tennessee requirement of one year's residency in the state and three months' residency in the county, observing that "30 days appears to be an ample period of time for the State to complete whatever administrative tasks are necessary to prevent fraud." *Dunn v. Blumstein*, 405 U.S. 330, 348 (1972). Despite this statement, the next year the Court upheld Arizona's 50-day durational residence requirement, *Marston v. Lewis*, 410 U.S. 679

(1973), and Georgia's 50-day pre-election cut-off for registering to vote, *Burns v. Fortson*, 410 U.S. 686 (1973).

The registration cut-off is distinct from, though related to, the durational residence requirement. Long-time residents of the state who satisfy the durational residence requirement will be barred from voting if they miss the registration cut-off. The difference between a 50-day and a 30-day residency requirement is not particularly great, because it affects only people who move into the jurisdiction within a twenty-day period. The same 20-day difference in the registration cut-off may have a much more substantial effect on turnout, because the closer to the election, the more likely people are to have developed an interest in the campaign that generates an incentive to register. We explore the legal significance of this and other election administration rules affecting turnout in Chapter 6.

Marston and *Burns* notwithstanding, nearly all states have 30-day residency requirements and registration cut-offs or less. An important reason for this near-uniformity is that Section 202 of the Voting Rights Act, added in 1970, sets a maximum 30-day residence and registration period for voting in presidential elections. States that might otherwise prefer longer than a 30-day period no doubt would find it more trouble than it is worth to retain one deadline for presidential registration and another for all other elections. Section 202 also requires states to provide absentee ballots for presidential voting to voters who will be out of the state on election day, and it permits voters who move during the thirty days before a presidential election to vote for president in their old state of residence.

6. *New Battles*

In the current century, we have seen renewed battles over the ballot box, including over rules for providing voter identification at the polls, private voter registration efforts, the periods when early voting is available, the availability of absentee voting, and the decisions made by partisan election officials at the state and local levels. The uptick in litigation and public attention to these matters corresponded to a general increase in partisanship of the electorate and Congress, the contested 2000 presidential election, culminating in recounts in Florida and the United States Supreme Court's controversial decision in *Bush v. Gore*, and the unique 2020 presidential election, held in the throes of a pandemic and featuring an avalanche of spurious claims of fraud by the defeated candidate. The amount of election litigation has more than doubled during this period.[k]

In addition, scholars and election officials have paid new attention to the voting rights of people with disabilities, both to ensure that those with physical disabilities are able to use appropriate technology to cast a ballot, and that those with mental

k. We pay extensive attention to these developments in Chapter 6, on election administration.

disabilities are competent to vote and not being unduly influenced in their voting decisions.

Notes and Questions

1. *Bibliographical Note*: An excellent overview of the history of the franchise in America is provided in J. Morgan Kousser, *Suffrage*, in 3 Encyclopedia of American Political History 1236 (Jack P. Greene, ed., 1984). The above account has drawn primarily on Kousser's essay and on the following sources: Chandler Davidson, *The Voting Rights Act: A Brief History*, in Controversies in Minority Voting: The Voting Rights Act in Perspective 7–51 (Bernard Grofman & Chandler Davidson, eds., 1992); William Gillette, The Right to Vote: Politics and the Passage of the Fifteenth Amendment (1965); Alexander Keyssar, The Right to Vote: The Contested History of Democracy in the United States (revised ed. 2009); J. Morgan Kousser, The Shaping of Southern Politics: Suffrage Restriction and the Establishment of the One-Party South, 1880–1910 (1974); Aileen S. Kraditor, The Ideas of the Woman Suffrage Movement, 1890–1920 (1965); Steven F. Lawson, Black Ballots: Voting Rights in the South, 1944–1969 (1976); and Chilton Williamson, American Suffrage: From Property to Democracy, 1760–1860 (1960). See also Pamela S. Karlan, *Ballots and Bullets: The Exceptional History of the Right to Vote*, 71 University of Cincinnati Law Review 1345 (2003), and Richard L. Hasen, The Voting Wars: From Florida 2000 to the Next Election Meltdown (2012).

2. This section has dealt with the broadening of categories of people who are generally eligible to vote. It is worth noticing, in passing, that the scope of the right to vote also has expanded enormously. When the Constitution was adopted, only one chamber — the House of Representatives — of one of the three branches of government was subject to direct popular control. By 1800, the selection of electors for president and vice-president became, in reality, a process of popular election in most states. In 1913, the Seventeenth Amendment made the Senate subject to popular elections as well.

State governments may have been more democratically controlled from the start than the federal government, but the domain of popular elections has expanded even further at the state level. All state legislative chambers are chosen in direct elections, as are governors and, in most states, other executive officials such as attorneys general and treasurers. In many states, judges are elected. In 1818, Connecticut adopted a constitution providing that future constitutional amendments would be subject to popular approval. Today, every state but Delaware subjects constitutional amendments to an election, and most states submit bond measures or other types of special legislation to popular approval as well. Since early in the twentieth century, about half the states have employed the initiative and referendum devices to permit a vote of the people on particular legislative proposals.

3. Neither the original Constitution, nor any amendment to it, includes an *affirmative* right to vote. As noted above, the original Constitution's only explicit reference to the franchise is Article I, § 2's requirement that voters in elections for the

House of Representatives possess the same qualifications as voters in state house elections. The Fifteenth, Nineteenth, Twenty-Fourth, and Twenty-Sixth Amendments then all exhibit the same structure. They state that the right to vote shall not be denied or abridged on the basis of some forbidden factor (respectively, race, gender, failure to pay a poll tax, and age above eighteen). But the provisions' prohibitions are only *negative*; while they bar certain restrictions of the franchise, they do not actually give anyone the right to vote.

In contrast to the United States Constitution, almost every foreign democracy's constitution recognizes an affirmative right to vote. See Alexander Kirshner, *The International Status of the Right to Vote*, available at https://perma.cc/9JPV-JCZ5 (finding that 108 of 119 democracies' constitutions include this right, with almost all of the exceptions being former British colonies). Almost every American *state* constitution also contains direct language granting the franchise. See Joshua A. Douglas, *The Right to Vote Under State Constitutions*, 67 Vanderbilt Law Review 89 (2014) (finding that 49 of 50 state constitutions—all but Arizona—include this right). Why might the United States Constitution *not* bestow the right to vote? Is this omission simply a function of the document's age? Or might it be attributable to other factors, such as an embrace of a political theory resistant to popular participation or a desire to exclude certain groups from voting? If the American Constitution were being redrafted, could you imagine it continuing to lack an affirmative grant of the franchise?

4. What is the point of the right to vote? In a well-known article, Pamela S. Karlan, *The Rights to Vote: Some Pessimism About Formalism*, 71 Texas Law Review 1705 (1993), provides a taxonomy of the interests protected by the franchise. The first of these (and the focus of this chapter) is voters' interest in casting a ballot that is, in fact, counted. This is the interest that is threatened by outright disenfranchisement as well as measures that make it more difficult (if not impossible) to vote. A second conception of the franchise is "voting as aggregation." This conception is based on the reality that votes determine election outcomes only when they are aggregated. *How* exactly votes are aggregated—through which district maps and voting rules—is therefore vitally important. A third and final view of the franchise is "voting as governance." This view goes beyond the identities of the prevailing candidates to ask what policies are enacted and how closely they reflect voters' interests and preferences. How helpful do you find Karlan's taxonomy? To what extent are "voting as aggregation" and "voting as governance" the same as descriptive and substantive representation, respectively?

5. Aside from disenfranchising African Americans, how did the exclusionary devices of the Jim Crow South, in particular the poll tax and the literacy test, affect southern politics? Timothy Besley and Anne Case, *Political Institutions and Policy Choices: Evidence from the United States*, 41 Journal of Economic Literature 7 (2003), studied this question empirically using state-level data on turnout and legislative composition. They found that the poll tax reduced turnout by about 16 percentage points and increased the fraction of Democrats in the state legislature by roughly

3 percentage points. Similarly, the literacy test cut turnout by about 14 percentage points and raised the Democratic seat share by roughly 8 percentage points. Given these results, it seems likely that proponents of the poll tax and the literacy test were motivated by *both* animus against African Americans *and* a desire to maintain their hold on power—which full black participation threatened. See also Thomas A. Husted & Lawrence W. Kenny, *The Effect of the Expansion of the Voting Franchise on the Size of Government*, 105 Journal of Political Economy 54 (1997) (finding that the elimination of the poll tax and the literacy test led to higher turnout, a poorer median voter, and a sharp rise in welfare spending).

6. What about women's suffrage—what political consequences did it have? The conventional wisdom is that it had few salient effects because women's political preferences were not too different from men's. However, John R. Lott, Jr. and Lawrence W. Kenny, *Did Women's Suffrage Change the Size and Scope of Government?*, 107 Journal of Political Economy 1163 (1999) have challenged this account. Unsurprisingly, they found that enfranchising women dramatically increased the share of the adult population voting. More interestingly, they found that women's suffrage caused a leftward shift in the voting records of members of Congress as well as rises in governmental revenue and spending. Lott and Kenny therefore conclude that, long before the emergence of the "gender gap" between male and female voting patterns in the 1970s, women's suffrage significantly reshaped American politics.

7. The Nineteenth Amendment has prompted almost no litigation and played a very minor role in subsequent case law on discrimination against women. Reva B. Siegel, *She The People: The Nineteenth Amendment, Sex Equality, Federalism, and the Family*, 115 Harvard Law Review 947 (2002), explains that the Nineteenth Amendment's ratification amounted to a rejection of the traditional view that women were already represented electorally by their husbands, fathers, and brothers. Siegel also argues for a "synthetic" reading of the Fourteenth and Nineteenth Amendments, under which interpretations of the Equal Protection Clause would incorporate the Nineteenth Amendment's renunciation of women's subordination in the family. According to Siegel, this reading would disrupt the doctrine's current focus on gender classifications (rather than policies that perpetuate inequality between the sexes) and give Congress more power to enact federal laws that redress problematic state regulations of the family. To what extent, if any, should subsequent constitutional amendments be understood to revise earlier ones? Can the Nineteenth Amendment fairly be construed as extending beyond the franchise? For an argument that Congress can pass extensive voting rights legislation under its broad powers to enforce the Nineteenth Amendment, see Richard L. Hasen and Leah M. Litman, *Thin and Thick Conceptions of the Nineteenth Amendment and Congress's Power to Enforce It*, 108 Georgetown Law Journal 27 (19th Amend. edition 2020).

II. Court Review of State Limitations on the Franchise

Harper v. Virginia State Board of Elections

383 U.S. 663 (1966)

Mr. Justice DOUGLAS delivered the opinion of the Court.

These are suits by Virginia residents to have declared unconstitutional Virginia's poll tax.[1] The three-judge District Court, feeling bound by our decision in *Breedlove v. Suttles*, 302 U.S. 277 [1937], dismissed the complaint. The cases came here on appeal and we noted probable jurisdiction.

While the right to vote in federal elections is conferred by Art. I, § 2, of the Constitution (*United States v. Classic*, 313 U.S. 299, 314–315 [1941]), the right to vote in state elections is nowhere expressly mentioned. It is argued that the right to vote in state elections is implicit, particularly by reason of the First Amendment and that it may not constitutionally be conditioned upon the payment of a tax or fee. We do not stop to canvass the relation between voting and political expression. For it is enough to say that once the franchise is granted to the electorate, lines may not be drawn which are inconsistent with the Equal Protection Clause of the Fourteenth Amendment. That is to say, the right of suffrage "is subject to the imposition of state standards which are not discriminatory and which do not contravene any restriction that Congress, acting pursuant to its constitutional powers, has imposed." *Lassiter v. Northampton County Board of Elections*, 360 U.S. 45, 51 [1959]. We were speaking there of a state literacy test which we sustained, warning that the result would be different if a literacy test, fair on its face, were used to discriminate against a class.[3]

---

1. Section 173 of Virginia's Constitution directs the General Assembly to levy an annual poll tax not exceeding $1.50 on every resident of the State 21 years of age and over (with exceptions not relevant here). One dollar of the tax is to be used by state officials 'exclusively in aid of the public free schools' and the remainder is to be returned to the counties for general purposes. Section 18 of the Constitution includes payment of poll taxes as a precondition for voting. Section 20 provides that a person must 'personally' pay all state poll taxes for the three years preceding the year in which he applies for registration. By § 21 the poll tax must be paid at least six months prior to the election in which the voter seeks to vote. Since the time for election of state officials varies, the six months' deadline will vary, election from election. The poll tax is often assessed along with the personal property tax. Those who do not pay a personal property tax are not assessed for a poll tax, it being their responsibility to take the initiative and request to be assessed. Enforcement of poll taxes takes the form of disenfranchisement of those who do not pay, § 22 of the Virginia Constitution providing that collection of delinquent poll taxes for a particular year may not be enforced by legal proceedings until the tax for that year has become three years delinquent.

3. We recently held in *Louisiana v. United States*, 380 U.S. 145 [1965], that a literacy test which gave voting registrars "a virtually uncontrolled discretion as to who should vote and who should not" had been used to deter Negroes from voting and accordingly we struck it down. While the "Virginia poll tax was born of a desire to disenfranchise the Negro" (*Harman v. Forssenius*, 380 U.S. 528, 543 [1965]), we do not stop to determine whether on this record the Virginia tax in its modern setting serves the same end.

But the *Lassiter* case does not govern the result here, because, unlike a poll tax, the 'ability to read and write . . . has some relation to standards designed to promote intelligent use of the ballot.' *Lassiter.*

We conclude that a State violates the Equal Protection Clause of the Fourteenth Amendment whenever it makes the affluence of the voter or payment of any fee an electoral standard. Voter qualifications have no relation to wealth nor to paying or not paying this or any other tax.[4] Our cases demonstrate that the Equal Protection Clause of the Fourteenth Amendment restrains the States from fixing voter qualifications which invidiously discriminate. Thus without questioning the power of a State to impose reasonable residence restrictions on the availability of the ballot, we held in *Carrington v. Rash*, 380 U.S. 89 [1965], that a State may not deny the opportunity to vote to a bona fide resident merely because he is a member of the armed services. "By forbidding a soldier ever to controvert the presumption of non-residence, the Texas Constitution imposes an invidious discrimination in violation of the Fourteenth Amendment." Previously we had said that neither homesite nor occupation "affords a permissible basis for distinguishing between qualified voters within the State." *Gray v. Sanders*, 372 U.S. 368 [1963]. We think the same must be true of requirements of wealth or affluence or payment of a fee.

Long ago in *Yick Wo v. Hopkins*, 118 U.S. 356 [1886] the Court referred to "the political franchise of voting" as a "fundamental political right, because [it is] preservative of all rights." Recently in *Reynolds v. Sims* [377 U.S. 533 (1964), *infra* Chapter 3], we said, "Undoubtedly, the right of suffrage is a fundamental matter in a free and democratic society. Especially since the right to exercise the franchise in a free and unimpaired manner is preservative of other basic civil and political rights, any alleged infringement of the right of citizens to vote must be carefully and meticulously scrutinized." There we were considering charges that voters in one part of the State had greater representation per person in the State Legislature than voters in another part of the State. We concluded:

> A citizen, a qualified voter, is no more nor no less so because he lives in the city or on the farm. This is the clear and strong command of our Constitution's Equal Protection Clause. This is an essential part of the concept of a government of laws and not men. This is at the heart of Lincoln's vision of "government of the people, by the people, (and) for the people." The Equal Protection Clause demands no less than substantially equal state legislative representation for all citizens, of all places as well as of all races.

We say the same whether the citizen, otherwise qualified to vote, has $1.50 in his pocket or nothing at all, pays the fee or fails to pay it. The principle that denies the State the right to dilute a citizen's vote on account of his economic status or other such factors by analogy bars a system which excludes those unable to pay a fee to vote or who fail to pay.

---

4. Only a handful of States today condition the franchise on the payment of a poll tax. . . .

It is argued that a State may exact fees from citizens for many different kinds of licenses; that if it can demand from all an equal fee for a driver's license, it can demand from all an equal poll tax for voting. But we must remember that the interest of the State, when it comes to voting, is limited to the power to fix qualifications. Wealth, like race, creed, or color, is not germane to one's ability to participate intelligently in the electoral process. Lines drawn on the basis of wealth or property, like those of race are traditionally disfavored. To introduce wealth or payment of a fee as a measure of a voter's qualifications is to introduce a capricious or irrelevant factor. The degree of the discrimination is irrelevant. In this context—that is, as a condition of obtaining a ballot—the requirement of fee paying causes an "invidious" discrimination that runs afoul of the Equal Protection Clause. Levy "by the poll," as stated in *Breedlove* is an old familiar form of taxation; and we say nothing to impair its validity so long as it is not made a condition to the exercise of the franchise. *Breedlove* sanctioned its use as "a prerequisite of voting." To that extent the Breedlove case is overruled.

We agree, of course, with Mr. Justice Holmes that the Due Process Clause of the Fourteenth Amendment "does not enact Mr. Herbert Spencer's Social Statics" (*Lochner v. People of State of New York*, 198 U.S. 45 [1905]). Likewise, the Equal Protection Clause is not shackled to the political theory of a particular era. In determining what lines are unconstitutionally discriminatory, we have never been confined to historic notions of equality, any more than we have restricted due process to a fixed catalogue of what was at a given time deemed to be the limits of fundamental rights. Notions of what constitutes equal treatment for purposes of the Equal Protection Clause do change. This Court in 1896 held that laws providing for separate public facilities for white and Negro citizens did not deprive the latter of the equal protection and treatment that the Fourteenth Amendment commands. *Plessy v. Ferguson*, 163 U.S. 537 [1896]. Seven of the eight Justices then sitting subscribed to the Court's opinion, thus joining in expressions of what constituted unequal and discriminatory treatment that sound strange to a contemporary ear. When, in 1954—more than a half-century later—we repudiated the "separate-but-equal" doctrine of *Plessy* as respects public education we stated: "In approaching this problem, we cannot turn the clock back to 1868 when the Amendment was adopted, or even to 1896 when *Plessy v. Ferguson* was written." *Brown v. Board of Education*, 347 U.S. 483, 492 [1954].

In a recent searching re-examination of the Equal Protection Clause, we held, as already noted, that "the opportunity for equal participation by all voters in the election of state legislators" is required. *Reynolds*. We decline to qualify that principle by sustaining this poll tax. Our conclusion, like that in *Reynolds v. Sims*, is founded not on what we think governmental policy should be, but on what the Equal Protection Clause requires.

We have long been mindful that where fundamental rights and liberties are asserted under the Equal Protection Clause, classifications which might invade or restrain them must be closely scrutinized and carefully confined. Those principles apply here. For to repeat, wealth or fee paying has, in our view, no relation to voting qualifications; the right to vote is too precious, too fundamental to be so burdened or conditioned.

Reversed.

Mr. Justice BLACK, dissenting.

... It should be pointed out at once that the Court's decision is to no extent based on a finding that the Virginia law as written or as applied is being used as a device or mechanism to deny Negro citizens of Virginia the right to vote on account of their color. Apparently the Court agrees with the District Court below and with my Brothers HARLAN and STEWART that this record would not support any finding that the Virginia poll tax law the Court invalidates has any such effect. If the record could support a finding that the law as written or applied has such an effect, the law would of course be unconstitutional as a violation of the Fourteenth and Fifteenth Amendments and also [52 U.S.C. § 10301(a)].... What the Court does hold is that the Equal Protection Clause necessarily bars all States from making payment of a state tax, any tax, a prerequisite to voting.

[I] think the interpretation that this Court gave the Equal Protection Clause in *Breedlove* was correct. The mere fact that a law results in treating some groups differently from others does not, of course, automatically amount to a violation of the Equal Protection Clause. To bar a State from drawing any distinctions in the application of its laws would practically paralyze the regulatory power of legislative bodies. Consequently "The constitutional command for a state to afford 'equal protection of the laws' sets a goal not attainable by the invention and application of a precise formula." Voting laws are no exception to this principle. All voting laws treat some persons differently from others in some respects. Some bar a person from voting who is under 21 years of age; others bar those under 18. Some bar convicted felons or the insane, and some have attached a freehold or other property qualification for voting. The *Breedlove* case upheld a poll tax which was imposed on men but was not equally imposed on women and minors, and the Court today does not overrule that part of *Breedlove* which approved those discriminatory provisions. And in *Lassiter*, this Court held that State laws which disqualified the illiterate from voting did not violate the Equal Protection Clause. From these cases and all the others decided by this Court interpreting the Equal Protection Clause, it is clear that some discriminatory voting qualifications can be imposed without violating the Equal Protection Clause....

Mr. Justice HARLAN, whom Mr. Justice STEWART joins, dissenting.

The final demise of state poll taxes, already totally proscribed by the Twenty-Fourth Amendment with respect to federal elections and abolished by the States themselves in all but four States with respect to state elections, is perhaps in itself not of great moment. But that fact that the coup de grace has been administered by this Court instead of being left to the affected States or to the federal political process should be a matter of continuing concern to all interested in maintaining the proper role of this tribunal under our scheme of government....

Property qualifications and poll taxes have been a traditional part of our political structure. In the Colonies the franchise was generally a restricted one. Over the years, these and other restrictions were gradually lifted, primarily because popular theories of political representation had changed. Often restrictions were lifted only after wide public debate. The issue of woman suffrage, for example, raised question of family relationships, of participation in public affairs, of the very nature of the type of society in which Americans wished to live; eventually a consensus was reached, which culminated in the Nineteenth Amendment no more than 45 years ago.

Similarly with property qualifications, it is only by fiat that it can be said, especially in the context of American history, that there can be no rational debate as to their advisability. Most of the early Colonies had them; many of the States have had them during much of their histories; and, whether one agrees or not, arguments have been and still can be made in favor of them. For example, it is certainly a rational argument that payment of some minimal poll tax promotes civic responsibility, weeding out those who do not care enough about public affairs to pay $1.50 or thereabouts a year for the exercise of the franchise. It is also arguable, indeed it was probably accepted as sound political theory by a large percentage of Americans through most of our history, that people with some property have a deeper stake in community affairs, and are consequently more responsible, more educated, more knowledgeable, more worthy of confidence, than those without means, and that the community and Nation would be better managed if the franchise were restricted to such citizens. Nondiscriminatory and fairly applied literacy tests, upheld by this Court in *Lassiter*, find justification on very similar grounds.

These viewpoints, to be sure, ring hollow on most contemporary ears. Their lack of acceptance today is evidenced by the fact that nearly all of the States, left to their own devices, have eliminated property or poll-tax qualifications; by the cognate fact that Congress and three-quarters of the States quickly ratified the Twenty-Fourth Amendment; and by the fact that rules such as the "pauper exclusion" in Virginia law, have never been enforced.

Property and poll-tax qualifications, very simply, are not in accord with current egalitarian notions of how a modern democracy should be organized. It is of course entirely fitting that legislatures should modify the law to reflect such changes in popular attitudes. However, it is all wrong, in my view, for the Court to adopt the political doctrines popularly accepted at a particular moment of our history and to declare all others to be irrational and invidious, barring them from the range of choice by reasonably minded people acting through the political process. It was not too long ago that Mr. Justice Holmes felt impelled to remind the Court that the Due Process Clause of the Fourteenth Amendment does not enact the laissez-faire theory of society, *Lochner.* The times have changed, and perhaps it is appropriate to observe that neither does the Equal Protection Clause of that Amendment rigidly impose upon America an ideology of unrestrained egalitarianism. . . .

Notes and Questions

1. *The Equal Protection Clause.* In a number of the cases in this book, persons claim that an election regulation, such as the denial of the right to vote challenged in *Harper,* violates the Equal Protection Clause. That clause appears in Section 1 of the Fourteenth Amendment, which reads in part as follows:

> No State shall make or enforce any law which shall abridge the privileges or immunities of citizens of the United States; nor shall any state deprive any person of life, liberty, or property, without due process of law; *nor deny to any person within its jurisdiction the equal protection of the laws.* [Emphasis added.]

There is no occasion here to consider in depth the intricacies of equal protection doctrine, but the following very simplified summary should assist persons who have never studied constitutional law to understand the equal protection cases contained in this book.

Although the phrase "equal protection of the laws" might seem to suggest that the clause is more concerned with the enforcement of laws than with their content, the overwhelming majority of controversies under the Equal Protection Clause arise because of attacks on classifications that are explicitly or implicitly written into statutes. However, as the Supreme Court has often recognized, almost all legislation classifies people and thus treats them differently. Persons who engage in certain economic transactions are subjected to different forms of taxation and regulation than persons who engage in different types of transactions. Persons convicted of engaging in certain forms of conduct are punished by the criminal law while others who refrain from such conduct are not. And so on.

Because the Supreme Court has not wanted the Equal Protection Clause to be a means of voiding virtually all legislation, it has said that only "invidious" distinctions are prohibited. Since World War II, and especially as constitutional law developed in the 1960s with cases like *Harper,* the Court's determination of what distinctions are invidious has tended to depend on the nature of the classification and on the nature of the benefit or penalty that is contingent on the classification.

Certain types of classifications are regarded as "suspect." Classifications drawn according to race or national origin are examples. When a law draws a suspect classification, the Court will subject it to "strict scrutiny" under the Equal Protection Clause. It will be struck down unless the law is shown to be "narrowly tailored" to promote a "compelling state interest." (Strict scrutiny that requires narrow tailoring to a compelling state interest is not limited to equal protection cases. In this book, we shall see essentially the same concept applied in many cases arising under the First Amendment.)

Even if the classification drawn by a statute is not suspect, it will still be subject to strict scrutiny if the classification burdens or denies a "fundamental right" for some people while not burdening or denying the rights of others. As we shall see, one of the fundamental rights that triggers strict scrutiny under the Equal Protection Clause has been the right to vote. The *Harper* opinion does not use the term "strict scrutiny" in reaching its result, describing the Virginia poll tax as "irrational," although it does say that classifications burdening fundamental rights like voting "must be closely scrutinized and carefully confined." Later, the Supreme Court adopted strict scrutiny terminology in many of its right to vote cases, saying that laws infringing on the fundamental right to vote must be narrowly tailored to serve a compelling interest.

If the classification being challenged is not suspect and does not burden a fundamental right, then it will not be subjected to strict scrutiny. Instead, it will be upheld so long as it has a rational basis.[1] This is usually a standard that statutes can meet, since the Court will accept any legitimate interest the statute may be intended to further. The Court will not even require a showing that a statute actually accomplishes its purposes, so long as the legislature could have believed it would. Although there are exceptions, some of which we shall encounter in this book, statutes that are subjected to strict scrutiny usually are struck down, and those that are tested for a rational basis usually are upheld.

2. At issue in *Harper* is whether the Equal Protection Clause bars the use of a poll tax (which the Court assumes is not administered as a means to discriminate against African American voters). How should the Court decide whether the Equal Protection Clause bars the use of a poll tax? Should it defer to the practice of most states? What if such practices change over time, as was the case with the poll tax? By the time the Court decided *Harper*, all but four states had eliminated poll taxes for voting in state elections. Is that an argument for or against the Supreme Court's decision in this case to bar the practice in the four outlier states? See generally Justin Driver, *Constitutional Outliers*, 81 University of Chicago Law Review 929 (2014).

3. Both the majority and dissenters in *Harper* appear to agree that a fairly-applied literacy test would not violate the Equal Protection Clause under the authority of the 1959 *Lassiter* case. (Recall from Part I of this chapter that Congress has banned the use of literacy tests under the Voting Rights Act. But that is a statute that—in theory—Congress could repeal at any time.) If the constitutional question ever arose again, should *Lassiter* be overruled? Are *Lassiter* and *Harper* inconsistent? Compare Richard H. Pildes, *Why Rights Are Not Trumps: Social Meanings, Expressive Harms, and Constitutionalism*, 27 Journal of Legal Studies 725, 746 (1998) (no), with Richard L. Hasen, *Bad Legislative Intent*, 2006 Wisconsin Law Review 843, 878–879 (yes).

---

1. In some cases, the Court engages in "intermediate scrutiny," which is not as severe as "strict scrutiny" but not as lax as the "rational basis" test. For example, different statutory treatment of men and women receives intermediate scrutiny. See *Craig v. Boren*, 429 U.S. 190 (1976). By and large, the equal protection cases contained in this book do not raise questions of intermediate scrutiny. However, in *Anderson v. Celebrezze*, discussed in Chapter 9, in the notes following *Munro v. Socialist Workers Party*, the Supreme Court articulated a comparable, "flexible" standard to be used in some election law cases.

In *United States v. Carolene Products*, 304 U.S. 144, 152 n.4 (1938), the Supreme Court made a celebrated statement regarding its function of reviewing the constitutionality of state and federal laws, especially under broadly worded constitutional guarantees such as "due process of law" and "equal protection of the laws." The Court explained that ordinarily, legislatures would be given broad leeway to enact laws deemed to be in the public interest. Legislatures were more likely than courts to be aware of the varied consequences of legislative policies, and interest groups were presumably capable of defending themselves against unjustifiably harsh policies by exercising their political rights. In the famous footnote 4, however, the Court mentioned several possible exceptions to this generally deferential approach, one of which was "whether legislation which restricts those political processes which can ordinarily be expected to bring about repeal of undesirable legislation [might] be subjected to more exacting judicial scrutiny under the general prohibitions of the Fourteenth Amendment than are most other types of legislation." Surely the most basic process that might be used by a group seeking repeal of undesirable legislation is the right to vote. Does that fact justify the Court's decision in *Harper*? If so, what of the Court's decision in *Lassiter* upholding a literacy test?

4. *The Secret Drafting History of* Harper. Consider the following history gleaned from the files of deceased Supreme Court Justices and recounted in Richard L. Hasen, The Supreme Court and Election Law: Judging Equality from *Baker v. Carr* to *Bush v. Gore* 37–38 (2003):

> Although *Harper* . . . stated its principles as self-evident, the result in the 6–3 case reversing the lower court was hardly inevitable. The case began as a proposed a 6–3 *per curiam* summary affirmance (that is, without a written opinion) of the lower court decision upholding the poll tax. Justice Goldberg, joined by Chief Justice Warren and Justice Douglas, circulated a proposed dissent. Relying on *Reynolds*, *Gray*, and *Carrington*, along with the Virginia poll tax's legislative history evincing intent to discriminate against both African Americans and poor whites, Justice Goldberg would have held that "no reasonable state interest is served by barring from voting those citizens who desire to vote but who lack the requisite funds."
>
> Justice Goldberg sought to explain the limits of the equal protection principle that would bar the use of a poll tax in elections:
>
>> The application of these principles obviously does not mean that Government—State or Federal—must equalize all economic inequalities among citizens. Nor does it mean that the Government cannot impose burdens or exactions which by reason of economic circumstances fall more heavily upon some than others. Nor however desirable it may be as a matter of social and legislative policy, does it require the State affirmatively to provide relief for all the incidents of poverty. The Constitution does not command absolute equality in all areas. It does mean, however, that a State may not frustrate or burden the exercise of the basic and precious right to vote by imposing substantial obstacles upon that

> exercise by a class of citizens not justified by any legitimate state interest. In particular it means that with respect to the fundamental right to vote, a reverse means test cannot be applied. A classification based upon financial means embodied in a voting statute is inherently not "reasonable in light of . . . [the statute's] purpose."

Justice Goldberg further rejected the long American history of tolerance for property qualifications and poll taxes as irrelevant for contemporary application of constitutional principles. "[W]e must consider voting rights in light of their full development, their 'present place in American life throughout the nation,' cf. *Brown v. Board of Education*, and our present conception of the meaning and application of the Equal Protection Clause."

Only one day after Justice Goldberg's dissent circulated, Justice Black circulated a memorandum to the other Justices asking that the case be put for a full hearing. Justice Black perhaps expected from the initial 6–3 vote for summary affirmance that the case would lead to a similar 6–3 vote on an opinion affirming the validity of the poll tax and distinguishing the cases cited by Justice Goldberg. If so, his expectations were dashed, because Justices Brennan, Clark, and White changed positions. Justice Black ultimately issued a dissent arguing the question of poll taxes should be left to the states unless Congress wanted to use its enforcement powers to ban the practice.

What, if anything, does this history tell you about how the Supreme Court Justices create election law precedents? About how they *should* do so?

5. The Supreme Court was not the only body to attack the poll tax in the 1960s. The Twenty-Fourth Amendment, passed by Congress in 1962 and ratified by the states in 1964, prohibited the poll tax in federal elections. Similarly, the Voting Rights Act, enacted in 1965, included a provision harshly criticizing the poll tax and calling upon the Attorney General to challenge it under the Act wherever possible. "The Congress finds that the requirement of the payment of a poll tax as a precondition to voting (i) precludes persons of limited means from voting or imposes unreasonable financial hardship upon such persons as a precondition to their exercise of the franchise, (ii) does not bear a reasonable relationship to any legitimate State interest in the conduct of elections, and (iii) in some areas has the purpose or effect of denying persons the right to vote because of race or color." 52 U.S.C. § 10306(a). Why, then, did the Court strike down the poll tax as a violation of the *Fourteenth Amendment* (rather than the Twenty-Fourth Amendment or the Voting Rights Act) in *Harper*? For an argument that the Court should not have invoked the Fourteenth Amendment—and that *Harper* has improperly erased the memories of the other efforts to end the poll tax—see Bruce Ackerman and Jennifer Nou, *Canonizing the Civil Rights Revolution: The People and the Poll Tax*, 103 Northwestern University Law Review 63 (2009). Notably, Justice Goldberg's initial dissent in *Harper*, excerpted above, focused far more than Justice Douglas's eventual opinion for the Court on the Twenty-Fourth Amendment. What would have been the pros and cons of this alternative doctrinal approach?

6. If you were a *legislator* rather than a *judge*, would you support the imposition of literacy tests or poll taxes (assuming the Constitution did not bar such limits)? Why or why not? What about limiting the franchise on the basis of (1) citizenship; (2) residency; or (3) non-felon status? We consider some of these additional restrictions below.

Skafte v. Rorex

553 P.2d 830 (Colo. 1976),
appeal dismissed, 430 U.S. 961 (1977)

PRINGLE, Chief Justice.

[Appellant Skafte, a permanent resident alien, was denied the right to register to vote in school elections and then challenged the constitutionality of a Colorado statute permitting only United States citizens to vote. The District Court ruled that the statute was valid, and the Colorado Supreme Court affirmed on the grounds stated in this opinion.]

I

The appellant asserts that the statutes prohibiting permanent resident aliens from voting in school elections violate the Equal Protection Clause.

A

At the outset, the registrar contends that the Equal Protection Clause has no application to the issue in this case. For this proposition, she relies on section 2 of the Fourteenth Amendment. Section 2 provides, in part:

> [W]hen the right to vote at any election for the choice of electors for President and Vice President of the United States, Representatives in Congress, the Executive and Judicial officers of a State, or the members of the Legislature thereof, is denied to any of the male inhabitants of such state, being twenty-one years of age, *and citizens of the United States*, or in any way abridged, except for participation in rebellion or other crime, the basis of representation therein shall be reduced in the proportion which the number of such male citizens shall bear to the whole number of male citizens twenty-one years of age in such State. [Emphasis supplied.]

The registrar argues that section 2 makes the Equal Protection Clause of the Fourteenth Amendment inapplicable to this case, since the specific wording of the section shows that those adopting the Fourteenth Amendment considered citizenship a valid classification in legislation dealing with the franchise. We do not agree with this contention.

Local school elections are not contained in the types of elections expressly listed in section 2. Moreover, the implicit sanction of a citizenship requirement contained in section 2 for the elections there listed does not warrant a conclusion that the Equal Protection Clause is inapplicable in the instant case. Indeed, the United States Supreme Court has rejected the general proposition that section 2 was intended to supplant the Equal Protection Clause in the area of voting rights. *Richardson v. Ramirez*, 418 U.S. 24 (1974); *Reynolds v. Sims*, 377 U.S. 533 (1964).

Nevertheless, we do believe that section 2 is helpful in deciding the constitutional questions raised in this appeal. The section demonstrates, as an historical matter, that the requirement of citizenship to exercise the franchise was assumed to be a valid one at the time the Fourteenth Amendment was adopted. Hence, in deciding the constitutional issues in this case, we are mindful of the language of section 2.

B

The appellant asserts that the alienage classification created here requires strict judicial scrutiny. The United States Supreme Court has consistently used language suggesting that citizenship with respect to the franchise is not a suspect classification and that therefore the compelling interest test does not apply. See *Hill v. Stone*, 421 U.S. 289 (1975); *Sugarman v. Dougall*, 413 U.S. 634 (1973); *Kramer v. Union Free School District No. 15*, 395 U.S. 621 (1969) [*infra*].

C

We hold that the state's citizenship requirements for a school district election do not contravene the Equal Protection Clause of the Fourteenth Amendment. The state has a rational interest in limiting participation in government to those persons within the political community. Aliens are not a part of the political community.

The United States Supreme Court has recognized a state's valid interest in establishing a government and in limiting participation in that government to those within the concept of a political community. *Sugarman*, 413 U.S. at 642. The Supreme Court has noted that "alienage itself is a factor that reasonably could be employed in defining 'political community.'" *Sugarman, supra*, at 649. Indeed, the Court has further stated that "implicit in many of this Court's voting rights decisions is the notion that citizenship is a permissible criterion for limiting such rights." *Sugarman, supra*, at 649.

The appellant contends that this justification satisfies the Equal Protection requirement only as it pertains to voting in *general* elections. He contends, however, that a school election is a "special interest" election, and therefore the proposition that a citizenship requirement is valid for general elections does not apply.

We believe that a school election is an election which falls within the class of cases prohibiting aliens from voting contemplated by the Supreme Court in *Sugarman*. We point out that school districts are governmental entities.... Further, in *Kramer v. Union Free School District No. 15, supra*, the Supreme Court indicated that school elections are elections involving participation by the political community.

Moreover, voting in school elections involves participation in the decision making process of the polity, a factor which indicates the "general" nature of such elections. It is in fact a determination of participation or not in the government policymaking process which often has been crucial in deciding cases contesting alienage classifications. The Supreme Court in *In Re Griffiths*, 413 U.S. 717 (1973), held unconstitutional a requirement that bar examinees be citizens. The court noted that the acts of a lawyer "hardly involve matters of state policy" and that the status of holding a license to practice law does not "place one so close to the core of the political process as to make him a formulator of government policy." 413 U.S. at 729 (footnote omitted).

The administration of school districts, however, does involve . . . matters of "state policy" and entails the formulation of such policy. Therefore, voting in school elections constitutes participation in the government policy-making process.

[The court stated that the denial of suffrage to resident aliens "is properly tailored to the state's interest," citing an earlier decision upholding the exclusion of aliens from juries on the ground that aliens as a group did not owe allegiance to the United States. Although many aliens do in fact hold such allegiance, the court said there was no test short of citizenship that would distinguish those who did from those who did not.]

Thus, we conclude that the State has shown a reasonable basis justifying the classification here challenged. Consequently, the citizenship requirement in school elections does not deprive the appellant of equal protection of the laws.

[In Part II, the court rejected appellant's argument that the prohibition against voting by resident aliens created an unconstitutional "conclusive presumption." In Part III, it rejected the assertion that the prohibition was an interference with Congress' power to regulate immigration and naturalization.]

The judgment is affirmed.

Notes and Questions

1. *The Equal Protection Clause and Citizenship Status.* In cases such as *Sugarman*, cited in *Skafte*, the Supreme Court has treated most laws discriminating against noncitizens as "suspect," but has made an exception for laws restricting the ability of noncitizens to participate in government. It was because of this exception that the denial of suffrage to noncitizens was not regarded as a suspect classification in *Skafte*. But even assuming there was no suspect classification, should the court have applied strict scrutiny on the ground that the fundamental right to vote was granted to some (citizens) and denied to others (resident aliens)? For a strong argument to this effect, see Gerald M. Rosberg, *Aliens and Equal Protection: Why Not the Right to Vote?*, 75 Michigan Law Review 1092, 1106–09 (1977).

2. What state interests might justify the denial of the right to vote to noncitizens? Rosberg, *supra*, considers a number of possible state interests, including that noncitizens may have less of a stake in the outcome of elections than citizens; that noncitizens are likely to lack the information and understanding of politics needed to vote intelligently; and that noncitizens may have less of a commitment to the well-being of the United States and its states and localities than citizens. Rosberg argues that none of these alleged interests holds much water, though he acknowledges that some of them may be plausible enough to pass a rational basis test.

Rosberg's unstated assumption is that denial of suffrage to noncitizens must serve some instrumental purpose of the state. Unquestionably, the right to vote serves instrumental purposes for individuals and groups, namely protecting their interests that are affected by public policy decisions. If that is the primary reason for the importance of the right to vote, then the denial of the suffrage to noncitizens in the absence of a strong instrumental purpose served by that denial may be quite troubling. In *Skafte*, the court justifies the denial as a limitation of the vote to "persons within the political community." Is this an instrumental purpose? Is the right to vote important not only as a means of protecting the rights and interests of individuals and groups but as a means for a community as a whole to define and govern itself? If so, is it legitimate for the community to protect its own self-definition by determining which individuals will be deemed members of the community and therefore entitled to participate in its self-government? These general questions are discussed in Frank I. Michelman, *Conceptions of Democracy in American Constitutional Argument: Voting Rights*, 41 Florida Law Review 443 (1989).

Sanford Levinson, *Suffrage and Community: Who Should Vote?*, 41 Florida Law Review 545, 557 (1989), doubts whether denial of the vote to noncitizens can be justified under a conception of voting either as an instrumental means of protecting individual interests or as an expression of the "shared values" embodied in a community:

> If we asked persons only five yes-or-no questions to figure out their basic values, would citizenship be one of them? If the answer is "no," because a person's citizenship conveys too little relevant information, then we might ask why something as important as the vote is based on citizenship, even within a communalist perspective.
>
> [A] conception of citizenship as a surrogate for shared interests is a fatally underinclusive category because the universe of people whose interests are vitally affected by any given election is far larger than the universe of those who are allowed to participate . . . If we view citizenship as a surrogate for shared values, then it may be grossly overinclusive: the set of people sharing the (proper) values may be far smaller than the set of people designated as citizens. Noncitizens also may share what are thought to be the requisite values.

3. According to Rosberg, *supra*, 75 Michigan Law Review at 1094–1100, noncitizen voting was fairly widespread at the end of the eighteenth century, but in the first half of the nineteenth there was a trend toward making citizenship a requirement for voting. This trend was reversed after the Civil War, and by the end of the nineteenth century, about half the states had had some experience with noncitizen suffrage. Starting in the 1890s, a reaction set in, which received additional impetus from the assassination of President McKinley in 1901 by an immigrant and from World War I. The last state to repeal noncitizen suffrage was Arkansas in 1926. More recently, noncitizens have been permitted to vote in decentralized school elections in Chicago and New York City, and several towns in Maryland have permitted noncitizens to vote in municipal elections.

If, as *Skafte* holds, resident aliens do not have a constitutional right to vote, is it an unconstitutional abridgement of citizens' right to vote if noncitizens are given the suffrage? In Germany, where immigration has been a controversial political issue, the Federal Constitutional Court has so ruled. See Gerald L. Neuman, *"We Are the People": Alien Suffrage in German and American Perspective*, 13 Michigan Journal of International Law 259, 283–87 (1992). Neuman acknowledges that from a communitarian perspective a plausible case could be made that permitting noncitizens to vote is unconstitutional in the United States, but he concludes that American courts would be unlikely to intervene because

> Popular sovereignty in the United States has been a flexible notion, which has not restricted political power by a rigid definition of the 'People,' and certainly not by the legal category of national citizenship.

Id. at 324.

4. Jamin B. Raskin, *Legal Aliens, Local Citizens: The Historical, Constitutional and Theoretical Meanings of Alien Suffrage*, 141 University of Pennsylvania Law Review 1391, 1417–41 (1993), maintains that extending the franchise to resident aliens is neither prohibited nor required by the Constitution. Doctrinally, he bases his disagreement with Rosberg's view that the vote is constitutionally required on Section 2 of the 14th Amendment and *Richardson*. He adds an additional and broader point:

> [E]ven if we follow the doctrinal somersaults required to arrive at Rosberg's position, his argument is not wholly persuasive as a description, historical or normative, of how the franchise expands in the American polity. None of the principal excluded national groups who gained access to the ballot in American history did so by way of judicial action through the Equal Protection Clause. Rather, they fought their way in through political agitation. This history encloses an important democratic logic: it is the standing citizenry, after hearing and debating appeals from the voteless, that must extend rights of political membership to disenfranchised outsiders seeking entry and equality.

Id. at 1431–32.

5. The *Skafte* opinion refers to *Richardson v. Ramirez*, 418 U.S. 24, 41–56 (1974), in which the Supreme Court upheld provisions of the California Constitution denying the vote to persons who had been convicted of felonies, even after they had finished their sentences and paroles. The Court relied primarily on Section 2 of the Fourteenth Amendment:

> Representatives shall be apportioned among the several States according to their respective numbers, counting the whole number of persons in each State, excluding Indians not taxed. But when the right to vote at any election for the choice of electors for President and Vice President of the United States, Representatives in Congress, the Executive and Judicial officers of a State, or the members of the Legislature thereof, is denied to any of the male

> inhabitants of such State, being twenty-one years of age, *and citizens of the United States*, or in any way abridged, *except for participation in rebellion, or other crime*, the basis of representation therein shall be reduced in the proportion which the number of such male citizens shall bear to the whole number of male citizens twenty-one years of age in such State. [Emphasis added.]

Section 2 thus imposes a sanction consisting of reduced representation in the House of Representatives upon a state that denies suffrage to its inhabitants, but specifies a number of grounds upon which suffrage may be denied that are exempt from the sanction. One of these exempt grounds for denial of suffrage is participation in rebellion or other crime. In *Richardson*, Justice Rehnquist wrote for the majority that Section 1 of the Fourteenth Amendment, which contains the Equal Protection Clause, "in dealing with voting rights as it does, could not have been meant to bar outright a form of disenfranchisement which was expressly exempted from the less drastic sanction of reduced representation which § 2 imposed for other forms of disenfranchisement." 418 U.S. at 55. He added that "the exclusion of felons from the vote has an affirmative sanction . . . which was not present in the case of the other restrictions on the franchise which were invalidated in [earlier Supreme Court] cases." *Id.* Note that the penalty in Section 2 also is inapplicable when a state denies the franchise to noncitizens. Why did the *Skafte* court not regard *Richardson* as dispositive? Should it have? See Rosberg, *supra*, 75 Michigan Law Review at 1102–04.

Richardson has come in for severe criticism from some scholars. See Laurence H. Tribe, American Constitutional Law 1094 (2d ed. 1988); David L. Shapiro, *Mr. Justice Rehnquist: A Preliminary View*, 90 Harvard Law Review 293, 302–04 (1976). For an argument that the Fifteenth Amendment repealed Section 2 of the Fourteenth Amendment, and therefore that *Richardson* erred in concluding that felon disenfranchisement is constitutionally authorized, see Gabriel J. Chin, *Reconstruction, Felon Disenfranchisement, and the Right to Vote: Did the Fifteenth Amendment Repeal Section 2 of the Fourteenth Amendment?*, 92 Georgetown Law Journal 249 (2004).

More recently, Richard M. Re and Christopher M. Re, *Voting and Vice: Criminal Disenfranchisement and the Reconstruction Amendments*, 121 Yale Law Journal 1584 (2012), have defended *Richardson* and disagreed that the Fifteenth Amendment implicitly repealed Section 2 of the Fourteenth Amendment. Re and Re argue that a particular political philosophy underlay all of the Reconstruction Amendments: "the view that a legitimate political order distinguishes persons by their actions and not by their station," which entailed "the liberation and then enfranchisement of former slaves, but also . . . the disenfranchisement of criminals, rebels, and other wrongdoers." *Id.* at 1590. On this account, *Richardson* was correct to rely so heavily on the Fourteenth Amendment's "other crime" exception, since it represented "the textual expression of a deep political principle." *Id.* Likewise, the Fifteenth Amendment could not have abridged part of the Fourteenth Amendment since it was rooted in the very same principle—that disenfranchisement is appropriate for those who commit bad acts, but not for those of a particular race or color.

6. *Richardson* does *not* mean that all restrictions on the franchise for persons convicted of crimes are constitutional. In *Hunter v. Underwood*, 471 U.S. 222 (1985), the Supreme Court considered a provision of the Alabama Constitution that made conviction for "any crime . . . involving moral turpitude" a basis for lifetime disenfranchisement. The Court unanimously stated that, notwithstanding *Richardson*, "we are confident that § 2 [of the Fourteenth Amendment] was not designed to permit . . . purposeful racial discrimination." *Id.* at 233. The Court also concluded that the moral turpitude provision had both a racially discriminatory purpose and a disparate racial impact. It "was enacted with the intent of disenfranchising blacks" and "'establish[ing] white supremacy in this State,'" and blacks were "'at least 1.7 times as likely as whites to suffer disenfranchisement'" under it. *Id.* at 227, 229. The provision therefore violated the Equal Protection Clause.

In 1996, Alabama enacted a constitutional amendment virtually identical to the one struck down in *Hunter*: "No person convicted of a felony involving moral turpitude . . . shall be qualified to vote. . . ." Ala. Const. § 177(b). Is this provision necessarily unconstitutional under binding Supreme Court precedent, or does the answer depend on whether it can be shown to have been motivated by a racially discriminatory purpose? If the latter, what are the implications for the Court's current approach to equal protection? See *Thompson v. Merrill*, 505 F. Supp. 3d 1239 (M.D. Ala. 2020) (upholding the revised Alabama provision against a claim of intentional racial discrimination).

7. In recent years, courts around the world have grappled with the disenfranchisement of prisoners. In 2002, the Supreme Court of Canada, by a 5–4 decision, held that the disenfranchisement of prisoners serving terms longer than two years violated the Canadian Charter of Rights and Freedoms. The chief justice wrote:

> The government's novel theory that would permit elected representatives to disenfranchise a segment of the population finds no place in a democracy built upon principles of inclusiveness, equality, and citizen participation. That not all self-proclaimed democracies adhere to this conclusion says little about what the Canadian vision of democracy embodied in the Charter permits. Moreover, the argument that only those who respect the law should participate in the political process cannot be accepted. Denial of the right to vote on the basis of attributed moral unworthiness is inconsistent with the respect for the dignity of every person that lies at the heart of Canadian democracy and the Charter.

Sauvé v. Canada (Chief Electoral Officer), [2002] 3 S.C.R. 519, 522 (Can.). The high courts of Australia and South Africa have also struck down bans on voting by incarcerated persons. See *Roach v. Electoral Commissioner*, [2007] HCA 43 (Austl.) (requiring the franchise for prisoners serving terms shorter than three years); *Minister of Home Affairs v. National Institute for Crime Prevention and the Re-Integration of Offenders*, 2005 (3) SA 280 (CC) (S. Afr.) (requiring the franchise for all prisoners). However, when the European Court of Human Rights invalidated the United Kingdom's complete ban on prisoner voting, see *Hirst v. United Kingdom*, [2005] Eur. Ct. H.R. 681, the British government defied the court's ruling. Parliament voted not to comply and British prisoners remain disenfranchised while serving their terms. See also *Scoppola v. Italy*, [2012] Eur. Ct. H.R. 868 (upholding Italy's disenfranchisement of prisoners serving terms longer than three years).

For comparative discussions of judicial decisions on prisoner disenfranchisement, see Reuven Ziegler, *Legal Outlier Again? U.S. Felon Suffrage: Comparative and International Human Rights Perspectives*, 29 Boston University International Law Journal 197 (2011); Michael Plaxton & Heather Lardy, *Prisoner Disenfranchisement: Four Judicial Approaches*, 28 Berkeley Journal of International Law 101 (2010); and Graeme Orr & George Williams, *The People's Choice: The Prisoner Franchise and the Constitutional Protection of Voting Rights in Australia*, 8 Election Law Journal 123 (2009).

8. Denial of the franchise to currently incarcerated felons is almost universal in the United States.[m] Additionally, felons who have completed their punishments (including parole or probation) are denied the franchise in about a third of the states. Strenuous efforts to end the latter denial are underway. Litigation is one form of these efforts. *Richardson* seems to suggest that the denial is consistent with the Constitution. Nevertheless, litigation surrounding felon voting rights has continued, with none of the legal challenges succeeding so far.

In *Simmons v. Galvin*, 575 F.3d 24 (1st Cir. 2009), the First Circuit rejected a claim that Massachusetts's felon disenfranchisement law violated Section 2 of the Voting Rights Act. The First Circuit concluded that Congress did not intend to include felon disenfranchisement within the qualifications covered by that statute. In *Farrakhan v. Gregoire*, 590 F.3d 989 (9th Cir. 2010), a panel of the Ninth Circuit initially ruled that Washington's felon disenfranchisement law violated Section 2 of the Voting Rights Act. The majority relied on evidence of racial discrimination in Washington's criminal justice system, and the disparate impact that felon disenfranchisement has on minority voting power. Sitting en banc, however, the Ninth Circuit vacated the panel opinion and rejected the Section 2 claim, based on the lack of evidence of intentional racial discrimination. 623 F.3d 990 (9th Cir. 2010). See also *Hayden v. Pataki*, 449 F.3d 305 (2d Cir. 2006) (en banc) (rejecting a Voting Rights Act challenge to New York's felon disenfranchisement law); *Johnson v. Governor of Florida*, 405 F.3d 1214 (11th Cir. 2005) (en banc) (same with Florida's disenfranchisement law). We cover the application of the Voting Rights Act to measures that deny the franchise, or burden its exercise, in Chapter 6.

---

m. The exceptions are Maine and Vermont. See Rosanna M. Taormina, Comment, *Defying One-Person, One-Vote: Prisoners and the "Usual Residence" Principle*, 152 University of Pennsylvania Law Review 431, 460 (2003) (appendix).

There have also been some recent constitutional challenges to felon disenfranchisement laws — all of which have failed as well. In *Hayden v. Paterson*, 594 F.3d 150 (2d Cir. 2010), the Second Circuit rejected a constitutional challenge to New York's felon disenfranchisement law, finding plaintiffs' allegations of discriminatory intent implausible. In an opinion by retired Supreme Court Justice Sandra Day O'Connor, sitting by designation, the Ninth Circuit rejected a constitutional challenge to Arizona's felon disenfranchisement law. *Harvey v. Brewer*, 605 F.3d 1067 (9th Cir. 2010). And in *Johnson v. Bredesen*, 624 F.3d 742 (6th Cir. 2010), the Sixth Circuit rejected a constitutional challenge to Tennessee's law conditioning restoration of voting rights upon former felons' payment of restitution and child support. The court applied rational basis review to uphold this requirement against an equal protection challenge. The court also rejected plaintiffs' argument that the requirement imposed an impermissible poll tax in violation of the Twenty-Fourth Amendment. The court reasoned that the requirement did not abridge a right, but simply imposed conditions for restoration of one's voting rights. Is this a tenable distinction? Does the greater power to deny ex-felons their voting rights entirely include the lesser power to condition those rights on restitution and payment of child support?

9. In 2018, Florida voters approved a constitutional amendment restoring the voting rights of ex-felons "after they complete all terms of their sentence." The Florida Legislature subsequently passed a statute implementing the amendment and defining the completion of "all terms of their sentence" to include the payment of all outstanding fines and fees. Hundreds of thousands of Florida ex-felons owe legal financial obligations. Until these debts are repaid, under the implementing statute, these individuals will be unable to vote. In *Jones v. Governor of Florida*, 975 F. 3d 1016 (11th Cir. 2020) (en banc), the Eleventh Circuit upheld the implementing statute against claims that it violated the Equal Protection Clause, the Twenty-Fourth Amendment, and other provisions. On the equal protection issue, the court's key move was to portray the statute's classification as one "between felons who have completed all terms of their sentences, including financial terms, and those who have not." *Id.* at 1030. Because this is not a suspect classification, it triggered only rational basis review, which it easily survived. On the question of whether the statute amounted to a poll tax in violation of the Twenty-Fourth Amendment, the court reached two contestable conclusions. One is that "court costs and fees are not *taxes*" because they are penalties rather than revenue-generating mechanisms. *Id.* at 1037 (emphasis added). The other conclusion is that the Twenty-Fourth Amendment only "prohibits denials of the right to vote *motivated* by a person's failure to pay a tax." *Id.* at 1045 (emphasis added). How persuasive do you find the court's reasoning?

10. What are the electoral consequences of felon disenfranchisement? In a pair of papers, Jeff Manza and Christopher Uggen estimated the turnout and voting preferences that felons would have exhibited had they been allowed to vote from 1972 to the present. They then combined these estimates with actual election results to determine how many senatorial and presidential races would have had different outcomes had felons not been barred from participation. If all felons (including

prisoners) had been enfranchised, seven Senate races and the 2000 presidential election would have come out differently. If only ex-felons had been enfranchised, three Senate races and the 2000 presidential election would have had different winners. See Jeff Manza & Christopher Uggen, *Punishment and Democracy: Disenfranchisement of Nonincarcerated Felons in the United States*, 2 Perspectives in Politics 491 (2004); Christopher Uggen & Jeff Manza, *Democratic Contraction? Political Consequences of Felon Disenfranchisement in the United States*, 67 American Sociological Review 777 (2002). But see Thomas J. Miles, *Felon Disenfranchisement and Voter Turnout*, 33 Journal of Legal Studies 85 (2004) (finding that laws disenfranchising ex-felons do not reduce the state-level turnout of African American men); Michael Morse, *The Future of Felon Disenfranchisement Reform: Evidence from the Campaign to Restore Voting Rights in Florida*, 109 California Law Review 1143 (2021) (finding that Florida's re-enfranchisement of ex-felons would have minor partisan implications).

11. *Residency.* As we have seen, though voting is a fundamental right which often triggers strict scrutiny, strict scrutiny does not apply to discrimination in voting on the basis of citizenship or felon-status. The same is true of discrimination against non-residents. Though the Supreme Court has held it unconstitutional to discriminate against *residents* of a jurisdiction whose residence began after they had joined the military, see *Carrington v. Rash*, 380 U.S. 89 (1965), discrimination against non-residents is generally constitutionally permissible under rational basis review. In *Holt Civic Club v. City of Tuscaloosa*, 439 U.S. 60 (1978) plaintiffs lived within the "police jurisdiction" of Tuscaloosa, Alabama which consisted of the area outside but within three miles of the city limits. Under Alabama law, city criminal ordinances were applicable and the jurisdiction of the municipal courts extended to the police jurisdiction. In addition, businesses located within the police jurisdiction had to pay a license tax half the amount they would be required to pay if they were within the city. However, the city's power of zoning, eminent domain, and ad valorem taxation did not extend to the police jurisdiction. The Supreme Court majority rejected plaintiffs' claim they were denied equal protection because they were denied the vote in Tuscaloosa city elections:

> Appellants' argument that extraterritorial extension of municipal powers requires concomitant extraterritorial extension of the franchise proves too much. The imaginary line defining a city's corporate limits cannot corral the influence of municipal actions. A city's decisions inescapably affect individuals living immediately outside its borders. The granting of building permits for high rise apartments, industrial plants, and the like on the city's fringe unavoidably contributes to problems of traffic congestion, school districting, and law enforcement immediately outside the city. A rate change in the city's sales or ad valorem tax could well have a significant impact on retailers and property values in areas bordering the city. The condemnation of real property on the city's edge for construction of a municipal

> garbage dump or waste treatment plant would have obvious implications for neighboring nonresidents. Indeed, the indirect extraterritorial effects of many purely internal municipal actions could conceivably have a heavier impact on surrounding environs than the direct regulation contemplated by Alabama's police jurisdiction statutes. Yet no one would suggest that nonresidents likely to be affected by this sort of municipal action have a constitutional right to participate in the political processes bringing it about. And unless one adopts the idea that the Austinian notion of sovereignty, which is presumably embodied to some extent in the authority of a city over a police jurisdiction, distinguishes the direct effects of limited municipal powers over police jurisdiction residents from the indirect though equally dramatic extraterritorial effects of purely internal municipal actions, it makes little sense to say that one requires extension of the franchise while the other does not.

Id. at 69-70. The dissenters in *Holt* did not disagree with the majority that a jurisdiction could deny the vote to non-residents. Instead, Justice Brennan, writing for the dissenters, argued that the majority impermissibly allowed the jurisdiction to define "residency" too narrowly:

> The criterion of geographical residency is thus entirely arbitrary when applied to this case. It fails to explain why, consistently with the Equal Protection Clause, the "government unit" which may exclude from the franchise those who reside outside of its geographical boundaries should be composed of the city of Tuscaloosa rather than of the city together with its police jurisdiction. It irrationally distinguishes between two classes of citizens, each with equal claim to residency (insofar as that can be determined by domicile or intention or other similar criteria), and each governed by the city of Tuscaloosa in the place of their residency.
>
> The Court argues, however, that if the franchise were extended to residents of the city's police jurisdiction, the franchise must similarly be extended to all those indirectly affected by the city's actions. This is a simple non sequitur. There is a crystal-clear distinction between those who reside in Tuscaloosa's police jurisdiction, and who are therefore subject to that city's police and sanitary ordinances, licensing fees, and the jurisdiction of its municipal court, and those who reside in neither the city nor its police jurisdiction, and who are thus merely affected by the indirect impact of the city's decisions. This distinction is recognized in Alabama law, and is consistent with, if not mandated by, the very conception of a political community underlying constitutional recognition of bona fide residency requirements.

Id. at 87 (Brennan, J., dissenting). Should restrictions based on citizenship, residency, and non-felon status be subject to a more permissive constitutional standard than other restrictions? What about laws prohibiting minors from voting? Does the 26th Amendment's prohibition on denying voting rights to those *over* eighteen imply that voting discrimination against those *under* eighteen is permissible?

12. What would happen if everyone voted (say, due to the adoption of compulsory voting)? Turnout would clearly skyrocket, but would there be partisan consequences? For decades, political scientists' answer was no. Nonvoters were thought not to have materially different preferences from voters, meaning that universal turnout generally would not change election outcomes. See, *e.g.*, Raymond E. Wolfinger & Steven J. Rosenstone, Who Votes? (1980); Bernard Grofman et al., *Rethinking the Partisan Effects of Higher Turnout: So What's the Question*, 99 Public Choice 357 (1999). More recently, however, Jack Citrin, Eric Schickler, and John Sides have challenged this conventional wisdom. They estimated voters' and nonvoters' preferences in dozens of Senate races, and found that in the vast majority of cases, nonvoters leaned somewhat more Democratic than voters. Full turnout would therefore have benefited Democrats, albeit rarely enough to flip election outcomes. See Jack Citrin et al., *What if Everyone Voted? Simulating the Impact of Increased Turnout in Senate Elections*, 47 American Journal of Political Science 75 (2003).

13. Once a state grants the right to vote to adult, citizen, resident non-felons, may a state limit the franchise in *particular elections*, such as school board elections, to a subset of otherwise eligible voters? Consider the next case.

Kramer v. Union Free School District No. 15

395 U.S. 621 (1969)

Mr. Chief Justice WARREN delivered the opinion of the Court.

In this case we are called on to determine whether § 2012 of the New York Education Law is constitutional. The legislation provides that in certain New York school districts residents who are otherwise eligible to vote in state and federal elections may vote in the school district election only if they (1) own (or lease) taxable real property within the district, or (2) are parents (or have custody of) children enrolled in the local public schools. Appellant, a bachelor who neither owns nor leases taxable real property, filed suit in federal court claiming that § 2012 denied him equal protection of the laws in violation of the Fourteenth Amendment....

I

[In school] districts such as the one involved in this case, which are primarily rural and suburban, the school board is elected at an annual meeting of qualified school district voters ...

Appellant is a 31-year-old college-educated stockbroker who lives in his parents' home in the Union Free School District No. 15, a district to which § 2012 applies. He is a citizen of the United States and has voted in federal and state elections since 1959. However, since he has no children and neither owns nor leases taxable real property, appellant's attempts to register for and vote in the local school district elections have been unsuccessful....

II

At the outset, it is important to note what is *not* at issue in this case. The requirements of § 2012 that school district voters must (1) be citizens of the United States, (2) be bona fide residents of the school district, and (3) be at least 21 years of age are not challenged. . . . The sole issue in this case is whether the *additional* requirements of § 2012—requirements which prohibit some district residents who are otherwise qualified by age and citizenship from participating in district meetings and school board elections—violate the Fourteenth Amendment's command that no State shall deny persons equal protection of the laws.

"In determining whether or not a state law violates the Equal Protection Clause, we must consider the facts and circumstances behind the law, the interests which the State claims to be protecting, and the interests of those who are disadvantaged by the classification." *Williams v. Rhodes*, 393 U.S. 23, 30 (1968). And, in this case, we must give the statute a close and exacting examination. "[S]ince the right to exercise the franchise in a free and unimpaired manner is preservative of other basic civil and political rights, any alleged infringement of the right of citizens to vote must be carefully and meticulously scrutinized." *Reynolds v. Sims* [*infra* Chapter 3]. This careful examination is necessary because statutes distributing the franchise constitute the foundation of our representative society. Any unjustified discrimination in determining who may participate in political affairs or in the selection of public officials undermines the legitimacy of representative government.

Thus, state apportionment statutes, which may *dilute* the effectiveness of some citizens' votes, receive close scrutiny from this Court. *Reynolds*. No less rigid an examination is applicable to statutes *denying* the franchise to citizens who are otherwise qualified by residence and age. Statutes granting the franchise to residents on a selective basis always pose the danger of denying some citizens any effective voice in the governmental affairs which substantially affect their lives. Therefore, if a challenged state statute grants the right to vote to some bona fide residents of requisite age and citizenship and denies the franchise to others, the Court must determine whether the exclusions are necessary to promote a compelling state interest.

And, for these reasons, the deference usually given to the judgment of legislators does not extend to decisions concerning which resident citizens may participate in the election of legislators and other public officials. Those decisions must be carefully scrutinized by the Court to determine whether each resident citizen has, as far as is possible, an equal voice in the selections. Accordingly, when we are reviewing statutes which deny some residents the right to vote, the general presumption of constitutionality afforded state statutes and the traditional approval given state classifications if the Court can conceive of a "rational basis" for the distinctions made are not applicable. The presumption of constitutionality and the approval given "rational" classifications in other types of enactments are based on an assumption that the institutions of state government are structured so as to represent fairly all the people. However, when the challenge to the statute is in effect a challenge of this basic assumption, the assumption can no longer serve as the basis for presuming constitutionality. And, the assumption is no less under attack because the legislature which decides who may participate at the various levels of political choice is fairly elected. Legislation which delegates decision making to bodies elected by only a portion of those eligible to vote for the legislature can cause unfair representation. Such legislation can exclude a minority of voters from any voice in the decisions just as effectively as if the decisions were made by legislators the minority had no voice in selecting....

Nor is the need for close judicial examination affected because the district meetings and the school board do not have "general" legislative powers. Our exacting examination is not necessitated by the subject of the election; rather, it is required because some resident citizens are permitted to participate and some are not....

III

Besides appellant and others who similarly live in their parents' homes, the statute also disenfranchises the following persons (unless they are parents or guardians of children enrolled in the district public school): senior citizens and others living with children or relatives; clergy, military personnel, and others who live on tax-exempt property; boarders and lodgers; parents who neither own nor lease qualifying property and whose children are too young to attend school; parents who neither own nor lease qualifying property and whose children attend private schools.

Appellant asserts that excluding him from participation in the district elections denies him equal protection of the laws. He contends that he and others of his class are substantially interested in and significantly affected by the school meeting decisions. All members of the community have an interest in the quality and structure of public education, appellant says, and he urges that "the decisions taken by local boards ... may have grave consequences to the entire population." Appellant also argues that the level of property taxation affects him, even though he does not own property, as property tax levels affect the price of goods and services in the community.

We turn therefore to question whether the exclusion is necessary to promote a compelling state interest. First appellees argue that the State has a legitimate interest in limiting the franchise in school district elections to "members of the community of interest" — those "primarily interested in such elections." Second, appellees urge that the State may reasonably and permissibly conclude that "property taxpayers" (including lessees of taxable property who share the tax burden through rent payments) and parents of the children enrolled in the district's schools are those "primarily interested" in school affairs.

We do not understand appellees to argue that the State is attempting to limit the franchise to those "subjectively concerned" about school matters. Rather, they appear to argue that the State's legitimate interest is in restricting a voice in school matters to those "directly affected" by such decisions. The State apparently reasons that since the schools are financed in part by local property taxes, persons whose out-of-pocket expenses are "directly" affected by property tax changes should be allowed to vote. Similarly, parents of children in school are thought to have a "direct" stake in school affairs and are given a vote.

Appellees argue that it is necessary to limit the franchise to those "primarily interested" in school affairs because "the ever increasing complexity of the many interacting phases of the school system and structure make it extremely difficult for the electorate fully to understand the whys and wherefores of the detailed operations of the school system." Appellees say that many communications of school boards and school administrations are sent home to the parents through the district pupils and are "not broadcast to the general public"; thus, nonparents will be less informed than parents. Further, appellees argue, those who are assessed for local property taxes (either directly or indirectly through rent) will have enough of an interest "through the burden on their pocketbooks, to acquire such information as they may need."

We need express no opinion as to whether the State in some circumstances might limit the exercise of the franchise to those "primarily interested" or "primarily affected." Of course, we therefore do not reach the issue of whether these particular elections are of the type in which the franchise may be so limited. For, assuming, *arguendo*, that New York legitimately might limit the franchise in these school district elections to those "primarily interested in school affairs," close scrutiny of the § 2012 classifications demonstrates that they do not accomplish this purpose with sufficient precision to justify denying appellant the franchise.

Whether classifications allegedly limiting the franchise to those resident citizens "primarily interested" deny those excluded equal protection of the laws depends, *inter alia*, on whether all those excluded are in fact substantially less interested or affected than those the statute includes. In other words, the classifications must be tailored so that the exclusion of appellant and members of his class is necessary to achieve the articulated state goal. Section 2012 does not meet the exacting standard of precision we require of statutes which selectively distribute the franchise. The classifications in § 2012 permit inclusion of many persons who have, at best, a remote and indirect interest, in school affairs and, on the other hand, exclude others who have a distinct and direct interest in the school meeting decisions.[15]

Nor do appellees offer any justification for the exclusion of seemingly interested and informed residents — other than to argue that the § 2012 classifications include those "whom the State could understandably deem to be the most intimately interested in actions taken by the school board," and urge that "the task of . . . balancing the interest of the community in the maintenance of orderly school district elections against the interest of any individual in voting in such elections should clearly remain with the Legislature." But the issue is not whether the legislative

15. For example, appellant resides with his parents in the school district, pays state and federal taxes and is interested in and affected by school board decisions; however, he has no vote. On the other hand, an uninterested unemployed young man who pays no state or federal taxes, but who rents an apartment in the district, can participate in the election.

judgments are rational. A more exacting standard obtains. The issue is whether the § 2012 requirements do in fact sufficiently further a compelling state interest to justify denying the franchise to appellant and members of his class. The requirements of § 2012 are not sufficiently tailored to limiting the franchise to those "primarily interested" in school affairs to justify the denial of the franchise to appellant and members of his class.

Mr. Justice STEWART, with whom Mr. Justice BLACK, and Mr. Justice HARLAN join, dissenting.

In *Lassiter*, this Court upheld against constitutional attack a literacy requirement, applicable to voters in all state and federal elections, imposed by the State of North Carolina. Writing for a unanimous Court, Mr. Justice Douglas said:

> The States have long been held to have broad powers to determine the conditions under which the right of suffrage may be exercised, absent of course the discrimination which the Constitution condemns.

Believing that the appellant in this case is not the victim of any "discrimination which the Constitution condemns," I would affirm the judgment of the District Court....

Although at times variously phrased, the traditional test of a statute's validity under the Equal Protection Clause is a familiar one: a legislative classification is invalid only "if it rest[s] on grounds wholly irrelevant to achievement of the regulation's objectives." It was under just such a test that the literacy requirement involved in *Lassiter* was upheld. The premise of our decision in that case was that a State may constitutionally impose upon its citizens voting requirements reasonably "designed to promote intelligent use of the ballot." A similar premise underlies the proposition, consistently endorsed by this Court, that a State may exclude nonresidents from participation in its elections. Such residence requirements, designed to help ensure that voters have a substantial stake in the outcome of elections and an opportunity to become familiar with the candidates and issues voted upon, are entirely permissible exercises of state authority. Indeed, the appellant explicitly concedes, as he must, the validity of voting requirements relating to residence, literacy, and age. Yet he argues — and the Court accepts the argument — that the voting qualifications involved here somehow have a different constitutional status. I am unable to see the distinction.

Clearly a State may reasonably assume that its residents have a greater stake in the outcome of elections held within its boundaries than do other persons. Likewise, it is entirely rational for a state legislature to suppose that residents, being generally better informed regarding state affairs than are nonresidents, will be more likely than nonresidents to vote responsibly. And the same may be said of legislative assumptions regarding the electoral competence of adults and literate persons on the one hand, and of minors and illiterates on the other. It is clear, of course, that lines thus drawn can not infallibly perform their intended legislative function. Just as "[i]lliterate people may be intelligent voters," nonresidents or minors might also in some instances be interested, informed, and intelligent participants in the electoral process. Persons who commute across a state line to work may well have a great stake in the affairs of the State in which they are employed; some college students under 21 may be both better informed and more passionately interested in political affairs than many adults. But such discrepancies are the inevitable concomitant of the line drawing that is essential to law making. So long as the classification is rationally related to a permissible legislative end, therefore—as are residence, literacy, and age requirements imposed with respect to voting—there is no denial of equal protection.

Thus judged, the statutory classification involved here seems to me clearly to be valid. New York has made the judgment that local educational policy is best left to those persons who have certain direct and definable interests in that policy: those who are either immediately involved as parents of school children or who, as owners or lessees of taxable property, are burdened with the local cost of funding school district operations. True, persons outside those classes may be genuinely interested in the conduct of a school district's business—just as commuters from New Jersey may be genuinely interested in the outcome of a New York City election. But unless this Court is to claim a monopoly of wisdom regarding the sound operation of school systems in the 50 States, I see no way to justify the conclusion that the legislative classification involved here is not rationally related to a legitimate legislative purpose....

With good reason, the Court does not really argue the contrary. Instead, it strikes down New York's statute by asserting that the traditional equal protection standard is inapt in this case, and that a considerably stricter standard—under which classifications relating to "the franchise" are to be subjected to "exacting judicial scrutiny"—should be applied. But the asserted justification for applying such a standard cannot withstand analysis.

The Court is quite explicit in explaining why it believes this statute should be given "close scrutiny":

> The presumption of constitutionality and the approval given "rational" classifications in other types of enactments are based on an assumption that the institutions of state government are structured so as to represent fairly all the people. However, when the challenge to the statute is in effect a challenge of this basic assumption, the assumption can no longer serve as the basis for presuming constitutionality.

I am at a loss to understand how such reasoning is at all relevant to the present case. The voting qualifications at issue have been promulgated, not by Union Free School District No. 15, but by the New York State Legislature, and the appellant is of course fully able to participate in the election of representatives in that body. There is simply no claim whatever here that the state government is not "structured so as to represent fairly all the people," including the appellant.

In any event, it seems to me that under *any* equal protection standard, short of a doctrinaire insistence that universal suffrage is somehow mandated by the

Constitution, the appellant's claim must be rejected. First of all, it must be emphasized—despite the Court's undifferentiated references to what it terms "the franchise"—that we are dealing here, not with a general election, but with a limited, special-purpose election. The appellant is eligible to vote in all state, local, and federal elections in which general governmental policy is determined. He is fully able, therefore, to participate not only in the processes by which the requirements for school district voting may be changed, but also in those by which the levels of state and federal financial assistance to the District are determined. He clearly is not locked into any self-perpetuating status of exclusion from the electoral process....

Notes and Questions

1. The argument of the school district was that the franchise may be limited to those with an "interest" in decisions of the district, in the sense of being "directly affected" by the decisions as opposed to being "subjectively concerned." In which of these senses is the Court using the term in the next-to-last paragraph of the majority opinion?

2. In footnote 15, the Court describes a hypothetical individual with supposedly less of a stake in school district elections than Kramer, but who is eligible to vote because he is a tenant. Is the Court correct in assuming that a person who is a tenant is unaffected by fiscal decisions of the school district? Consider *City of Phoenix v. Kolodziejski*, 399 U.S. 204, 210 (1970), in which the Court wrote:

> Property taxes may be paid initially by property owners, but a significant part of the ultimate burden of each year's tax on rental property will very likely be borne by the tenant rather than the landlord since . . . the landlord will treat the property tax as a business expense and normally will be able to pass all or a large part of this cost on to the tenants in the form of higher rent.

3. (a) Suppose Paula is a 31-year-old who resides with her parents just outside the boundaries of District No. 15. She does most of her shopping in the district and has recently completed a doctoral dissertation on the operations of District No. 15. Will the Court order the District to let her vote in District elections? Would it make any difference if she owns commercial property in the District and runs a business there, and if her school-age children reside with her former husband within the District and attend the public schools? See *Hill v. Stone*, 421 U.S. 289, 302, 306 (1975) (Rehnquist, J., dissenting); *Reeder v. Bd. of Supervisors of Elections*, 305 A.2d 132 (Md. 1973). See also *Millis v. Bd. of Cy. Com'rs. of Larimer Cy.*, 626 P.2d 652 (Colo. 1981) (fact that in-state nonresidents of a district were allowed to vote did not preclude the district from denying the vote to out-of-staters).

(b) Would it make any difference if Paula is African American and proves that the District boundaries were drawn to exclude her neighborhood because most of the residents are African American? Cf. *Gomillion v. Lightfoot*, 364 U.S. 339 (1960). Because of a belief that voters in her neighborhood would tend to vote in a particular manner, *e.g.*, for higher (or lower) school budgets? Cf. *Carrington v. Rash*, 380 U.S. 89, 94 (1965).

(c) Suppose the New York statute were amended to permit non-residents who own property subject to property taxation in the District to vote in school board elections. Would the Court hold that the votes of residents had been diluted unconstitutionally? See *Spahos v. Mayor and Councilmen of Savannah Beach*, 207 F. Supp 688 (S.D. Ga. 1962), aff'd. per curiam 371 U.S. 206 (1962); *Brown v. Bd. of Com'rs. of Chattanooga*, 722 F. Supp. 380, 397–400 (M.D. Tenn. 1989).

Permitting nonresident landowners to vote in Town elections was upheld in *May v. Town of Mountain Village*, 132 F.3d 576 (10th Cir. 1997), cert. denied 524 U.S. 938 (1998). This is the majority position; courts typically reason that rational basis review applies to a jurisdiction's decision to allow nonresidents to vote, and that the decision is rational because the nonresidents permitted to vote have a substantial interest in the election. See, *e.g.*, *Duncan v. Coffee Cty.*, 69 F.3d 88 (6th Cir. 1995); *Collins v. Town of Goshen*, 635 F.2d 954 (2d Cir. 1980); *Cantwell v. Hudnut*, 566 F.2d 30 (7th Cir. 1977).

However, extraterritorial voting was struck down as an unconstitutional dilution of residents' votes in *Board of County Commissioners of Shelby County v. Burson*, 121 F.3d 244 (6th Cir. 1997), cert. denied *sub nom. Walkup v. Board of Commissioners of Shelby County*, 522 U.S. 1113 (1998). In that case, Shelby County was divided into two school districts, one consisting of the city of Memphis (Memphis City Schools) and the other consisting of the rest of the county (Shelby County School District). The school board members of the latter district were regarded as county officials, which meant that under the Tennessee constitution, all residents of the county, including residents of Memphis, were permitted to vote for them. The Sixth Circuit did not regard this extraterritorial voting as per se unconstitutional, but struck it down after considering a number of factors, including that Memphis made up about three-fourths of the county population. See also *Locklear v. North Carolina State Bd. of Elections*, 514 F.2d 1152 (4th Cir. 1975) (invalidating North Carolina laws that allowed residents of city school districts in Robeson County also to vote in elections for the county school board).

4. In *Wit v. Berman*, 306 F.3d 1256 (2d Cir. 2002), plaintiffs divided their time between living in New York City and living in houses in the Hamptons at the far end of Long Island. They voted in their Long Island communities. Had they not done so, they would have been eligible to vote in New York City. The Second Circuit rejected a claim that their being denied the vote in New York City violated the Equal Protection Clause. Judge Winter pointed out that residence for voting purposes is closely tied to the legal concept of domicile, which is premised on the idea that one may be domiciled at only one place at a given time. Judge Winter continued:

> At first blush, it may seem that domicile plays such a key role because it is a close proxy for determining the election district in which a voter has

the greatest stake in the outcome of elections. This is an oversimplification, however.

Particularly in modern times, domicile is very often a poor proxy for a voter's stake in electoral outcomes because many of an individual voter's varied interests are affected by outcomes in elections in which they do not vote. Some, or even many, voters may reasonably perceive that their primary political concerns are affected more by outcomes in elections in which they do not vote than by outcomes in elections in which they do vote. There are endless examples of the bad fit between domicile and a voter's interest in electoral outcomes. For example, a person who works in a factory, or owns one, located in a municipality other than where the person lives, has interests in that municipality's tax, traffic, law enforcement, and other policies. . . .

However, while one may mount ethereal arguments against the single-domicile-registration rule, the administrative problems that interests-based rules would cause for thousands of registrars of voters render those rules virtually unthinkable. Voter registration is generally a nondiscretionary function of local government carried out by low level officials. Absent meaningful guidance, some registrars (even in the same precinct) would use a "whatever-you-say" approach, others will adopt a "show-me-beyond-a-reasonable-doubt" stance, while yet others will resort to *ad hoc, ad hominem,* or whimsical standards.

Given the need for workable standards, determination of where one may vote based on interests in electoral outcomes is not a manageable rule. Honoring the desires of voters to vote in other districts based on their expression of subjective interests in the political decisions of those other districts would essentially lead to a "vote-in-however-many-districts-you-please" rule. Such a rule would be truly chaotic, save for the small measure of order that corruption would bring to it. An objective test of voter interests is equally unworkable. At the very least, it would involve an ever-changing analysis by registrars of the merits of political issues — e.g., does an employee of a firm in one city who lives in another have a sufficient interest in the traffic and tax policies of the former to vote there, or is there sufficiently harmful acid rain in Vermont as a result of loose environmental standards in Ohio to justify a Vermonter voting in Ohio — and would also be chaotic.

Domicile as a rule may have its philosophical defects, therefore, but it has enormous practical advantages over the alternatives. It almost always insures that a voter has *some* stake in the electoral outcome in the domiciliary district and almost always does not involve large numbers of disputes over where one may vote. The domicile rule informs would-be voters where they may vote, a vital function that encourages registration and voting. Moreover, it gives voters the notice required for the enforcement

> of criminal laws against individuals voting in places where they are not eligible....
>
> To be sure, domicile as a test entails administrative difficulties at the margins. The domicile of students is an example. So too is the registration of the homeless. However, these difficulties are slight compared to those that abandonment of the domicile rule and its one domicile/one electoral district restriction might entail.

Id. at 1261-62.

5. The majority in *Kramer* argues that the usual presumption of constitutionality is based on the belief that everyone is represented in the governmental process that leads to the policy in question. Therefore, the presumption of constitutionality should not apply in a case where the complainant is denied the right to vote. Justice Stewart rebuts this contention by pointing out that the voting restriction was enacted by the New York State Legislature, in which Kramer was fully represented. Are you persuaded by Justice Stewart's argument? Would Justice Stewart's position be undermined if it can be shown that as a practical matter, Kramer's chances of getting the legislature to change the rules regarding school district voting were nil? See Mark Tushnet, *Darkness on the Edge of Town: The Contributions of John Hart Ely to Constitutional Theory*, 89 Yale Law Journal 1037, 1048–51 (1980).

6. Recall that, in *Harper*, the Court struck down the poll tax on the ground that it was "not germane" to voting, had "no relation to voting qualifications," and represented "a capricious or irrelevant factor." This may sound like rational basis review, yet *Harper* also quoted *Reynolds v. Sims* (excerpted in Chapter 3) for the proposition that restrictions on voting must be "be carefully and meticulously scrutinized." In *Kramer*, the Court employs the classic terminology of strict scrutiny. It carries out "a close and exacting examination" of New York's limits on participation in school board elections, requiring them to be "necessary to promote a compelling state interest." *Kramer*'s approach represents current black-letter law for measures that completely bar certain persons from voting. But as we shall see in Chapter 6, a different sliding-scale approach applies to less severe burdens on voting. Why shouldn't strict scrutiny be applied to all electoral regulations? Or rational basis review?

7. In a 9–0 decision issued the same day as *Kramer*, the Court in *Cipriano v. City of Houma*, 395 U.S. 701 (1969), struck down a Louisiana statute that permitted only property owners to vote in elections to approve *revenue* bond issues for municipally-owned utilities. The next term a 5–3 majority reached the same conclusion in a case involving Arizona provisions which gave only property owners the right to vote in elections to approve *general obligation* bonds. *City of Phoenix v. Kolodziejski*, 399 U.S. 204 (1970).

When a government issues bonds, it borrows money from the purchasers of the bonds. In the case of revenue bonds, the loans will be repaid only from revenues of the project (for example, a municipal parking garage) for which the bonds are issued. General obligation bonds give the bondholders a right to be repaid from the jurisdiction's general revenues and are backed by the full faith and credit of the jurisdiction. Can you see why some justices concurred in *Cipriano* but dissented in *Kolodziejski*?

8. Despite the holding of *Kramer*, we shall see in the next chapter that the Supreme Court has permitted states to deny the franchise in certain "special purpose districts" such as water storage districts and to weight those votes unequally. Before turning to that material, we begin with the permissibility of unequally weighted votes in congressional, state, and local elections.

Chapter 3

Representation and Districting

In Chapter 2 we saw that the United States Constitution does not directly grant the right to vote to individuals but that numerous amendments to the Constitution prohibit denying the franchise on a variety of grounds and that the right to vote has been further extended by statutes and by court decisions. In this chapter and the two that follow, the right to vote is considered in its relationship to the system of representation of which it is a part, including the districts that are used to elect representatives.

Cases involving the equal *weighting* of votes have had both practical and theoretical significance. In *Reynolds v. Sims*, the Supreme Court imposed the "one-person, one-vote" standard on state legislative districts. This decision required the restructuring of at least one house of the state legislature in nearly every state. Although we shall limit ourselves to relatively brief excerpts from *Reynolds* and its companion cases, the reader should not draw the inference that it is an unimportant case. To the contrary, most observers would list it as one of the landmark decisions in Supreme Court history. The excerpts we shall consider show the conflicting theoretical perspectives from which different justices viewed the question of "malapportionment" (i.e., unequally populated legislative districts). The reason for not dwelling further on the many issues and sub-issues making up the original malapportionment debate is that *Reynolds* has been so successful that these topics, though still of intellectual interest, are no longer of great practical significance. However, the desire to extend *Reynolds* in different directions has generated many additional issues, and these will provide the focus of our study.

At present, the most contentious malapportionment matters in state and federal elections pertain to race, partisanship, and the meaning of equal population. After considering these issues, we proceed to extension of the one-person, one-vote rule to local government. When this was accomplished in *Avery v. Midland County*, the theoretical disputes began to resemble those in the *Kramer* line of cases, which we considered in Chapter 2. The two lines converged in *Salyer Land Co. v. Tulare Lake Basin Water Storage District* and *Ball v. James*. Voting schemes in which only property owners could vote and votes were weighted on a one dollar (or one acre), one vote basis were upheld by the Supreme Court in the case of local districts with specialized functions. Although these cases have had relatively small practical importance, they bring into question the nature of representation and its relation to interest group influence and political power. Among other issues, they raise the question of whether government must always represent an undifferentiated public interest or, alternatively, may it represent specialized constituencies without losing its "public" character.

At the end of this chapter, we consider criteria other than population equality that might be taken into consideration when drawing legislative districts. These include contiguity, compactness, respect for political subdivisions, and respect for communities of interest. Such factors lay the groundwork for the questions surrounding judicial intervention in the redistricting process, which we consider in Chapters 4 and 5.

I. The Right to an Equally Weighted Vote

It has long been recognized that severe population disparity between different districts that elect representatives to a legislative or other governmental assembly creates a serious theoretical and practical inequality between voters in the respective districts. See, *e.g.*, John Locke, Two Treatises on Government 390–91 (Peter Laslett, ed., 2d ed. 1964). Yet until the 1960s, the Supreme Court refused to rule on matters of legislative apportionment, regarding them as nonjusticiable political questions. The most famous statement of this position comes from Justice Frankfurter's plurality opinion in *Colegrove v. Green*, 328 U.S. 549, 552–56 (1946):

> This is not an action to recover for damage because of the discriminatory exclusion of a plaintiff from rights enjoyed by other citizens. The basis for the suit is not a private wrong, but a wrong suffered by Illinois as a polity. In effect this is an appeal to the federal courts to reconstruct the electoral process of Illinois in order that it may be adequately represented in the councils of the Nation. Because the Illinois legislature has failed to revise its Congressional Representative districts in order to reflect great changes, during more than a generation, in the distribution of its population, we are asked to do this, as it were, for Illinois.
>
> ... Nothing is clearer than that this controversy concerns matters that bring courts into immediate and active relations with party contests. From the determination of such issues this Court has traditionally held aloof. It is hostile to a democratic system to involve the judiciary in the politics of the people. And it is not less pernicious if such judicial intervention in an essentially political contest be dressed up in the abstract phrases of the law.
>
> The petitioners urge with great zeal that the conditions of which they complain are grave evils and offend public morality. The Constitution of the United States gives ample power to provide against these evils. But due regard for the Constitution as a viable system precludes judicial correction. Authority for dealing with such problems resides elsewhere. ... The short of it is that the Constitution has conferred upon Congress exclusive authority to secure fair representation by the States in the popular House and left to that House determination whether States have fulfilled their responsibility.

> If Congress failed in exercising its powers, whereby standards of fairness are offended, the remedy ultimately lies with the people. Whether Congress faithfully discharges its duty or not, the subject has been committed to the exclusive control of Congress....
>
> To sustain this action would cut very deep into the very being of Congress. Courts ought not to enter this political thicket. The remedy for unfairness in districting is to secure State legislatures that will apportion properly, or to invoke the ample powers of Congress....

Two milestone cases in the 1960s, however, dramatically changed the Court's disposition toward legislative apportionment, and revealed its new willingness to foray into the political thicket. The first, *Baker v. Carr*, 369 U.S. 186 (1962), held that challenges to malapportioned districts under the Equal Protection Clause *are* justiciable in federal courts, but did not decide when such districts are unconstitutional. The Court listed several circumstances that render disputes nonjusticiable: "a textually demonstrable constitutional commitment of the issue to a coordinate political department; or a lack of judicially discoverable and manageable standards for resolving it; or the impossibility of deciding without an initial policy determination of a kind clearly for nonjudicial discretion; or the impossibility of a court's undertaking independent resolution without expressing lack of the respect due coordinate branches of government." *Id.* at 217. The Court then explained that none of these situations applied to claims of malapportionment:

> ... The question here is the consistency of state action with the Federal Constitution. We have no question decided, or to be decided, by a political branch of government coequal with this Court. Nor do we risk embarrassment of our government abroad, or grave disturbance at home if we take issue with Tennessee as to the constitutionality of her action here challenged. Nor need the appellants, in order to succeed in this action, ask the Court to enter upon policy determinations for which judicially manageable standards are lacking. Judicial standards under the Equal Protection Clause are well developed and familiar, and it has been open to courts since the enactment of the Fourteenth Amendment to determine, if on the particular facts they must, that a discrimination reflects no policy, but simply arbitrary and capricious action.

Id. at 226.[a]

---

a. Baker v. Carr: *A Commemorative Symposium*, 80 North Carolina Law Review 1103 (2002) marked the 40th anniversary of the celebrated case, with contributions by Guy-Uriel E. Charles; Robert J. Pushaw, Jr.; Mark Tushnet; James A. Gardner; Sanford Levinson; Nathaniel A. Persily, Thad Kousser & Patrick Egan; Heather K. Gerken; Luis Fuentes-Rohwer; Richard L. Hasen; and Roy A. Schotland. *Baker*'s 50th anniversary was the subject of another symposium, Baker v. Carr *After 50 Years: Appraising the Reapportionment Revolution*, 62 Case Western Law Review 941 (2012), with contributions by Margo Anderson; Tom Brunell; Justin Buchler; John Griffin; Candice Hoke; Nelson Lund; Michael McDonald & Micah Altman; Michael Solimine; and Daniel Tokaji.

The second groundbreaking case, *Reynolds v. Sims*, 377 U.S. 533 (1964), was presaged by *Gray v. Sanders*, 372 U.S. 368 (1963), striking down the unequal weighting of votes within a single constituency, and by *Wesberry v. Sanders*, 376 U.S. 1 (1964), requiring that congressional districts be drawn on an equal population basis. *Gray* prevented states from using a system analogous to the Electoral College in electing statewide officials and did not involve the more common question of a multimember legislative body.[b] *Wesberry* was not decided under the Equal Protection Clause but rather under Article I, Section 2 of the Constitution, and was thus applicable only to the United States House of Representatives. The constitutional requirements that would be applicable to state legislatures and to elected local government bodies remained undecided—but not for long.

In *Reynolds*, Alabama voters challenged unequally populated state legislative districts as violative of the Equal Protection Clause. The Supreme Court struck down the Alabama districts and, in companion cases decided on the same day, invalidated state legislative districts in Colorado, Delaware, Maryland, New York, and Virginia. In these cases, the Court required that seats in both houses of a bicameral state legislature be apportioned on a substantially equal population basis—in short, "one-person, one-vote." Following are excerpts from *Reynolds* and the Colorado case, which raises the interesting question of whether underrepresented voters may *approve* malapportionment that seems to disadvantage them.

Reynolds v. Sims

377 U.S. 533 (1964)

MR. CHIEF JUSTICE WARREN delivered the opinion of the Court....

III

A predominant consideration in determining whether a State's legislative apportionment scheme constitutes an invidious discrimination violative of rights asserted under the Equal Protection Clause is that the rights allegedly impaired are individual and personal in nature. As stated by the Court in *United States v. Bathgate*, 246 U.S. 220, 227, "[t]he right to vote is personal...." While the result of a court decision in a state legislative apportionment controversy may be to require the restructuring of the geographical distribution of seats in a state legislature, the judicial focus must be concentrated upon ascertaining whether there has been any discrimination against certain of the State's citizens which constitutes an impermissible impairment of their constitutionally protected right to vote.... Undoubtedly, the right of suffrage is a fundamental matter in a free and democratic society. Especially since the right to exercise the franchise in a free and unimpaired manner is preservative of other basic civil and political rights, any alleged infringement of the right of citizens to vote must be carefully and meticulously scrutinized....

---

b. Is the Electoral College, which is used to elect the President of the United States, itself unconstitutional? Not according to *New v. Ashcroft*, 293 F. Supp. 2d 256 (E.D.N.Y. 2003).

Legislators represent people, not trees or acres. Legislators are elected by voters, not farms or cities or economic interests. As long as ours is a representative form of government, and our legislatures are those instruments of government elected directly by and directly representative of the people, the right to elect legislators in a free and unimpaired fashion is a bedrock of our political system. It could hardly be gainsaid that a constitutional claim had been asserted by an allegation that certain otherwise qualified voters had been entirely prohibited from voting for members of their state legislature. And, if a State should provide that the votes of citizens in one part of the State should be given two times, or five times, or 10 times the weight of votes of citizens in another part of the State, it could hardly be contended that the right to vote of those residing in the disfavored areas had not been effectively diluted. It would appear extraordinary to suggest that a State could be constitutionally permitted to enact a law providing that certain of the State's voters could vote two, five, or 10 times for their legislative representatives, while voters living elsewhere could vote only once. And it is inconceivable that a state law to the effect that, in counting votes for legislators, the votes of citizens in one part of the State would be multiplied by two, five, or 10, while the votes of persons in another area would be counted only at face value, could be constitutionally sustainable. Of course, the effect of state legislative districting schemes which give the same number of representatives to unequal numbers of constituents is identical. Overweighting and overvaluation of the votes of those living here has the certain effect of dilution and undervaluation of the votes of those living there. The resulting discrimination against those individual voters living in disfavored areas is easily demonstrable mathematically. Their right to vote is simply not the same right to vote as that of those living in a favored part of the State. Two, five, or 10 of them must vote before the effect of their voting is equivalent to that of their favored neighbor. Weighting the votes of citizens differently, by any method or means, merely because of where they happen to reside, hardly seems justifiable. One must be ever aware that the Constitution forbids "sophisticated as well as simpleminded modes of discrimination." . . .

State legislatures are, historically, the fountainhead of representative government in this country. . . . But representative government is in essence self-government through the medium of elected representatives of the people, and each and every citizen has an inalienable right to full and effective participation in the political processes of his State's legislative bodies. Most citizens can achieve this participation only as qualified voters through the election of legislators to represent them. Full and effective participation by all citizens in state government requires, therefore, that each citizen have an equally effective voice in the election of members of his state legislature. Modern and viable state government needs, and the Constitution demands, no less.

Logically, in a society ostensibly grounded on representative government, it would seem reasonable that a majority of the people of a State could elect a majority of that State's legislators. To conclude differently, and to sanction minority control of state legislative bodies, would appear to deny majority rights in a way that far surpasses any possible denial of minority rights that might otherwise be thought to result. Since legislatures are responsible for enacting laws by which all citizens are to be governed, they should be bodies which are collectively responsive to the popular will. And the concept of equal protection has been traditionally viewed as requiring the uniform treatment of persons standing in the same relation to the governmental action questioned or challenged. With respect to the allocation of legislative representation, all voters, as citizens of a State, stand in the same relation regardless of where they live. Any suggested criteria for the differentiation of citizens are insufficient to justify any discrimination, as to the weight of their votes, unless relevant to the permissible purposes of legislative apportionment. Since the achieving of fair and effective representation for all citizens is concededly the basic aim of legislative apportionment, we conclude that the Equal Protection Clause guarantees the opportunity for equal participation by all voters in the election of state legislators. Diluting the weight of votes because of place of residence impairs basic constitutional rights under the Fourteenth Amendment just as much as invidious discriminations based upon factors such as race or economic status. Our constitutional system amply provides for the protection of minorities by means other than giving them majority control of state legislatures. And the democratic ideals of equality and majority rule, which have served this Nation so well in the past, are hardly of any less significance for the present and the future.

We are told that the matter of apportioning representation in a state legislature is a complex and many-faceted one. We are advised that States can rationally consider factors other than population in apportioning legislative representation. We are admonished not to restrict the power of the States to impose differing views as to political philosophy on their citizens. We are cautioned about the dangers of entering into political thickets and mathematical quagmires. Our answer is this: a denial of constitutionally protected rights demands judicial protection; our oath and our office require no less of us. . . .

To the extent that a citizen's right to vote is debased, he is that much less a citizen. The fact that an individual lives here or there is not a legitimate reason for overweighting or diluting the efficacy of his vote. The complexions of societies and civilizations change, often with amazing rapidity. A nation once primarily rural in character becomes predominantly urban. Representation schemes once fair and equitable become archaic and outdated. But the basic principle of representative government remains, and must remain, unchanged — the weight of a citizen's vote cannot be made to depend on where he lives. Population is, of necessity, the starting point for consideration and the controlling criterion for judgment in legislative apportionment controversies. A citizen, a qualified voter, is no more nor no less so because he lives in the city or on the farm. This is the clear and strong command of our Constitution's Equal Protection Clause. This is an essential part of the concept of a government of laws and not men. This is at the heart of Lincoln's vision of "government of the people, by the people, [and] for the people." The Equal Protection

Clause demands no less than substantially equal state legislative representation for all citizens, of all places as well as of all races.

V

... [O]ne of the proposed plans ... at least superficially resembles the scheme of legislative representation followed in the Federal Congress. Under this plan, each of Alabama's 67 counties is allotted one senator, and no counties are given more than one Senate seat. Arguably, this is analogous to the allocation of two Senate seats, in the Federal Congress, to each of the 50 States, regardless of population....

We agree with the District Court, and find the federal analogy inapposite and irrelevant to state legislative districting schemes. Attempted reliance on the federal analogy appears often to be little more than an after-the-fact rationalization offered in defense of maladjusted state apportionment arrangements. The original constitutions of 36 of our States provided that representation in both houses of the state legislatures would be based completely, or predominantly, on population. And the Founding Fathers clearly had no intention of establishing a pattern or model for the apportionment of seats in state legislatures when the system of representation in the Federal Congress was adopted. Demonstrative of this is the fact that the Northwest Ordinance, adopted in the same year, 1787, as the Federal Constitution, provided for the apportionment of seats in territorial legislatures solely on the basis of population.

The system of representation in the two Houses of the Federal Congress is one ingrained in our Constitution, as part of the law of the land. It is one conceived out of compromise and concession indispensable to the establishment of our federal republic. Arising from unique historical circumstances, it is based on the consideration that in establishing our type of federalism a group of formerly independent States bound themselves together under one national government.... The developing history and growth of our republic cannot cloud the fact that, at the time of the inception of the system of representation in the Federal Congress, a compromise between the larger and smaller States on this matter averted a deadlock in the Constitutional Convention which had threatened to abort the birth of our Nation....

Political subdivisions of States—counties, cities, or whatever—never were and never have been considered as sovereign entities. Rather, they have been traditionally regarded as subordinate governmental instrumentalities created by the State to assist in the carrying out of state governmental functions....

[W]e necessarily hold that the Equal Protection Clause requires both houses of a state legislature to be apportioned on a population basis. The right of a citizen to equal representation and to have his vote weighted equally with those of all other citizens in the election of members of one house of a bicameral state legislature would amount to little if States could effectively submerge the equal-population principle in the apportionment of seats in the other house. If such a scheme were permissible, an individual citizen's ability to exercise an effective voice in the only instrument of state government directly representative of the people might be almost as effectively thwarted as if neither house were apportioned on a population basis. Deadlock between the two bodies might result in compromise and concession on some issues. But in all too many cases the more probable result would be frustration of the majority will through minority veto in the house not apportioned on a population basis, stemming directly from the failure to accord adequate overall legislative representation to all of the State's citizens on a nondiscriminatory basis.

VI

. . . In implementing the basic constitutional principle of representative government as enunciated by the Court in *Wesberry*—equality of population among districts—some distinctions may well be made between congressional and state legislative representation. Since, almost invariably, there is a significantly larger number of seats in state legislative bodies to be distributed within a State than congressional seats, it may be feasible to use political subdivision lines to a greater extent in establishing state legislative districts than in congressional districting while still affording adequate representation to all parts of the State. To do so would be constitutionally valid, so long as the resulting apportionment was one based substantially on population and the equal-population principle was not diluted in any significant way. Somewhat more flexibility may therefore be constitutionally permissible with respect to state legislative apportionment than in congressional districting. . . .

A State may legitimately desire to maintain the integrity of various political subdivisions, insofar as possible, and provide for compact districts of contiguous territory in designing a legislative apportionment scheme. Valid considerations may underlie such aims. Indiscriminate districting, without any regard for political subdivision or natural or historical boundary lines, may be little more than an open invitation to partisan gerrymandering. . . .

History indicates, however, that many States have deviated, to a greater or lesser degree, from the equal-population principle in the apportionment of seats in at least one house of their legislatures. So long as the divergences from a strict population standard are based on legitimate considerations incident to the effectuation of a rational state policy, some deviations from the equal-population principle are constitutionally permissible with respect to the apportionment of seats in either or both of the two houses of a bicameral state legislature. But neither history alone, nor economic or other sorts of group interests, are permissible factors in attempting to justify disparities from population-based representation. Citizens, not history or economic interests, cast votes. Considerations of area alone provide an insufficient justification for deviations from the equal-population principle. Again, people, not land or trees or pastures, vote. Modern developments and improvements in transportation and communications make rather hollow, in the mid-1960's, most claims that deviations from population-based representation can validly be based solely on geographical considerations. Arguments for allowing such deviations in order to insure effective representation for sparsely settled areas and to prevent legislative districts from becoming so large that the availability of access of citizens to their representatives is impaired are today, for the most part, unconvincing.

A consideration that appears to be of more substance in justifying some deviations from population-based representation in state legislatures is that of insuring some voice to political subdivisions, as political subdivisions. . . . Local governmental entities are frequently charged with various responsibilities incident to the operation of state government. In many States much of the legislature's activity involves the enactment of so-called local legislation, directed only to the concerns of particular political subdivisions. And a State may legitimately desire to construct districts along political subdivision lines to deter the possibilities of gerrymandering. However, permitting deviations from population-based representation does not mean that each local governmental unit or political subdivision can be given separate representation, regardless of population. Carried too far, a scheme of giving at least one seat in one house to each political subdivision (for example, to each county) could easily result, in many States, in a total subversion of the equal-population principle in that legislative body.

MR. JUSTICE HARLAN, dissenting. . . .

Today's holding is that the Equal Protection Clause of the Fourteenth Amendment requires every State to structure its legislature so that all the members of each house represent substantially the same number of people; other factors may be given play only to the extent that they do not significantly encroach on this basic 'population' principle. Whatever may be thought of this holding as a piece of political ideology—and even on that score the political history and practices of this country from its earliest beginnings leave wide room for debate—I think it demonstrable that the Fourteenth Amendment does not impose this political tenet on the States or authorize this Court to do so.

The Court's constitutional discussion . . . is remarkable . . . for its failure to address itself at all to the Fourteenth Amendment as a whole or to the legislative history of the Amendment pertinent to the matter at hand. Stripped of aphorisms, the Court's argument boils down to the assertion that appellees' right to vote has been invidiously 'debased' or 'diluted' by systems of apportionment which entitle them to vote for fewer legislators than other voters, an assertion which is tied to the Equal Protection Clause only by the constitutionally frail tautology that 'equal' means 'equal.'

Had the Court paused to probe more deeply into the matter, it would have found that the Equal Protection Clause was never intended to inhibit the States in choosing any democratic method they pleased for the apportionment of their legislatures. This is shown by the language of the Fourteenth Amendment taken as a whole, by the understanding of those who proposed and ratified it, and by the political practices of the States at the time the Amendment was adopted. It is confirmed by numerous state and congressional actions since the adoption of the Fourteenth Amendment, and by the common understanding of the Amendment as evidenced by subsequent constitutional amendments and decisions of this Court before *Baker v. Carr, supra*, made an abrupt break with the past in 1962.

The failure of the Court to consider any of these matters cannot be excused or explained by any concept of 'developing' constitutionalism. It is meaningless to speak of constitutional 'development' when both the language and history of the controlling provisions of the Constitution are wholly ignored. Since it can, I think, be shown beyond doubt that state legislative apportionments, as such, are wholly free of constitutional limitations, save such as may be imposed by the Republican Form of Government Clause, the Court's action now bringing them within the purview of the Fourteenth Amendment amounts to nothing less than an exercise of the amending power by this Court....

The Court's elaboration of its new 'constitutional' doctrine indicates how far—and how unwisely—it has strayed from the appropriate bounds of its authority. The consequence of today's decision is that in all but the handful of States which may already satisfy the new requirements the local District Court or, it may be, the state courts, are given blanket authority and the constitutional duty to supervise apportionment of the State Legislatures. It is difficult to imagine a more intolerable and inappropriate interference by the judiciary with the independent legislatures of the States....

Records such as these in the cases decided today are sure to be duplicated in most of the other States if they have not been already. They present a jarring picture of courts threatening to take action in an area which they have no business entering, inevitably on the basis of political judgments which they are incompetent to make. They show legislatures of the States meeting in haste and deliberating and deciding in haste to avoid the threat of judicial interference....

Generalities cannot obscure the cold truth that cases of this type are not amenable to the development of judicial standards. No set of standards can guide a court which has to decide how many legislative districts a State shall have, or what the shape of the districts shall be, or where to draw a particular district line. No judicially manageable standard can determine whether a State should have single-member districts or multimember districts or some combination of both. No such standard can control the balance between keeping up with population shifts and having stable districts. In all these respects, the courts will be called upon to make particular decisions with respect to which a principle of equally populated districts will be of no assistance whatsoever. Quite obviously, there are limitless possibilities for districting consistent with such a principle. Nor can these problems be avoided by judicial reliance on legislative judgments so far as possible. Reshaping or combining one or two districts, or modifying just a few district lines, is no less a matter of choosing among many possible solutions, with varying political consequences, than reapportionment broadside....

In one or another of today's opinions, the Court declares it unconstitutional for a State to give effective consideration to any of the following in establishing legislative districts: (1) history; (2) 'economic or other sorts of group interests'; (3) area; (4) geographical considerations; (5) a desire 'to insure effective representation for sparsely settled areas'; (6) 'availability of access of citizens to their representatives'; (7) theories of bicameralism (except those approved by the Court); (8) occupation; (9) 'an attempt to balance urban and rural power.' (10) the preference of a majority of voters in the State. I know of no principle of logic or practical or theoretical politics, still less any constitutional principle, which establishes all or any of these exclusions. Certain it is that the Court's opinion does not establish them.

Lucas v. 44th General Assembly of Colorado

377 U.S. 713 (1964)

MR. CHIEF JUSTICE WARREN delivered the opinion of the Court....

II

At the November 1962 general election, the Colorado electorate adopted proposed Amendment No. 7 by a vote of 305,700 to 172,725, and defeated proposed Amendment No. 8 by a vote of 311,749 to 149,822. Amendment No. 8, rejected by a majority of the voters, prescribed an apportionment plan pursuant to which seats in both houses of the Colorado Legislature would purportedly be apportioned on a population basis. Amendment No. 7, on the other hand, provided for the apportionment of the House of Representatives on the basis of population, but essentially maintained the existing apportionment in the Senate, which was based on a combination of population and various other factors....

III

Several aspects of this case serve to distinguish it from the other cases involving state legislative apportionment also decided this date.... [T]he Colorado scheme of legislative apportionment here attacked is one adopted by a majority vote of the Colorado electorate almost contemporaneously with the District Court's decision on the merits in this litigation. Thus, the plan at issue did not result from prolonged legislative inaction....

IV

... [W]e find no significance in the fact that a nonjudicial, political remedy may be available for the effectuation of asserted rights to equal representation in a state legislature. Courts sit to adjudicate controversies involving alleged denials of constitutional rights.... [I]ndividual constitutional rights cannot be deprived, or denied judicial effectuation, because of the existence of a nonjudicial remedy through which relief against the alleged malapportionment, which the individual voters seek, might be achieved. An individual's constitutionally protected right to cast an equally weighted vote cannot be denied even by a vote of a majority of a State's electorate, if the apportionment scheme adopted by the voters fails to measure up to the requirements of the Equal Protection Clause. Manifestly, the fact that an apportionment plan is adopted in a popular referendum is insufficient to sustain its constitutionality or to induce a court of equity to refuse to act. . . . A citizen's constitutional rights can hardly be infringed simply because a majority of the people choose that it be. We hold that the fact that a challenged legislative apportionment plan was approved by the electorate is without federal constitutional significance, if the scheme adopted fails to satisfy the basic requirements of the Equal Protection Clause, as delineated in our opinion in *Reynolds v. Sims*. . . .

MR. JUSTICE STEWART, whom MR. JUSTICE CLARK joins, dissenting.

It is important to make clear at the outset what these cases are not about. They have nothing to do with the denial or impairment of any person's right to vote. Nobody's right to vote has been denied. Nobody's right to vote has been restricted. Nobody has been deprived of the right to have his vote counted. The voting right cases which the Court cites are, therefore, completely wide of the mark. Secondly, these cases have nothing to do with the "weighting" or "diluting" of votes cast within any electoral unit. The rule of *Gray v. Sanders* is, therefore, completely without relevance here. . . .

The question involved here in these cases is quite a different one. Simply stated, the question is to what degree, if at all, the Equal Protection Clause of the Fourteenth Amendment limits each sovereign State's freedom to establish appropriate electoral constituencies from which representatives to the State's bicameral legislative assembly are to be chosen. The Court's answer is a blunt one, and, I think, woefully wrong. The Equal Protection Clause, says the Court, "requires that the seats in both houses of a bicameral state legislature must be apportioned on a population basis."

After searching carefully through the Court's opinions . . . , I have been able to find but two reasons offered in support of this rule. First, says the Court, it is "established that the fundamental principle of representative government in this country is one of equal representation for equal numbers of people. . . ." With all respect, I think that this is not correct, simply as a matter of fact. It has been unanswerably demonstrated before now that this "was not the colonial system, it was not the system chosen for the national government by the Constitution, it was not the system exclusively or even predominantly practiced by the States at the time of adoption of the Fourteenth Amendment, it is not predominantly practiced by the States today." Secondly, says the Court, unless legislative districts are equal in population, voters in the more populous districts will suffer a "debasement" amounting to a constitutional injury. As the Court explains it, "To the extent that a citizen's right to vote is debased, he is that much less a citizen." We are not told how or why the vote of a person in a more populated legislative district is "debased," or how or why he is less a citizen, nor is the proposition self-evident. I find it impossible to understand how or why a voter in California, for instance, either feels or is less a citizen than a voter in Nevada, simply because, despite their population disparities, each of those States is represented by two United States Senators.

To put the matter plainly, there is nothing in all the history of this Court's decisions which supports this constitutional rule. The Court's draconian pronouncement, which makes unconstitutional the legislatures of most of the 50 States, finds no support in the words of the Constitution, in any prior decision of this Court, or in the 175-year political history of our Federal Union. With all respect, I am convinced these decisions mark a long step backward into that unhappy era when a majority of the members of this Court were thought by many to have convinced themselves and each other that the demands of the Constitution were to be measured not by what it says, but by their own notions of wise political theory. The rule announced today is at odds with long-established principles of constitutional adjudication under the Equal Protection Clause, and it stifles values of local individuality and initiative vital to the character of the Federal Union which it was the genius of our Constitution to create.

I

What the Court has done is to convert a particular political philosophy into a constitutional rule, binding upon each of the 50 States, from Maine to Hawaii, from Alaska to Texas, without regard and without respect for the many individualized and differentiated characteristics of each State, characteristics stemming from each State's distinct history, distinct geography, distinct distribution of population, and distinct political heritage. My own understanding of the various theories of representative government is that no one theory has ever commanded unanimous assent among political scientists, historians, or others who have considered the problem. But even if it were thought that the rule announced today by the Court is, as a matter of political theory, the most desirable general rule which can be devised as a basis for the make-up of the representative assembly of a typical State, I could not join in the fabrication of a constitutional mandate which imports and forever freezes one theory of political thought into our Constitution, and forever denies to every State any opportunity for enlightened and progressive innovation in the design of its democratic institutions, so as to accommodate within a system of representative government the interests and aspiration of diverse groups of people, without subjecting any group or class to absolute domination by a geographically concentrated or highly organized majority.

Representative government is a process of accommodating group interests through democratic institutional arrangements. Its function is to channel the numerous opinions, interests, and abilities of the people of a State into the making of the State's public policy. Appropriate legislative apportionment, therefore, should ideally be designed to insure effective representation in the State's legislature, in cooperation with other organs of political power, of the various groups and interests making up the electorate. In practice, of course, this ideal is approximated in the particular apportionment system of any State by a realistic accommodation of the diverse and often conflicting political forces operating within the State.

I do not pretend to any specialized knowledge of the myriad of individual characteristics of the several States, beyond the records in the cases before us today. But I do know enough to be aware that a system of legislative apportionment which might be best for South Dakota, might be unwise for Hawaii with its many islands, or

Michigan with its Northern Peninsula. I do know enough to realize that Montana with its vast distances is not Rhode Island with its heavy concentrations of people. I do know enough to be aware of the great variations among the several States in their historic manner of distributing legislative power—of the Governors' Councils in New England, of the broad powers of initiative and referendum retained in some States by the people, of the legislative power which some States give to their Governors, by the right of veto or otherwise, of the widely autonomous home rule which many States give to their cities. The Court today declines to give any recognition to these considerations and countless others, tangible and intangible, in holding unconstitutional the particular systems of legislative apportionment which these States have chosen. Instead, the Court says that the requirements of the Equal Protection Clause can be met in any State only by the uncritical, simplistic, and heavy-handed application of sixth-grade arithmetic.

But legislators do not represent faceless numbers. They represent people, or, more accurately, a majority of the voters in their districts—people with identifiable needs and interests which require legislative representation, and which can often be related to the geographical areas in which these people live. The very fact of geographic districting, the constitutional validity of which the Court does not question, carries with it an acceptance of the idea of legislative representation of regional needs and interests. Yet if geographical residence is irrelevant, as the Court suggests, and the goal is solely that of equally "weighted" votes, I do not understand why the Court's constitutional rule does not require the abolition of districts and the holding of all elections at large.

The fact is, of course, that population factors must often to some degree be subordinated in devising a legislative apportionment plan which is to achieve the important goal of ensuring a fair, effective, and balanced representation of the regional, social, and economic interests within a State. And the further fact is that throughout our history the apportionments of State Legislatures have reflected the strongly felt American tradition that the public interest is composed of many diverse interests, and that in the long run it can better be expressed by a medley of component voices than by the majority's monolithic command. What constitutes a rational plan reasonably designed to achieve this objective will vary from State to State, since each State is unique, in terms of topography, geography, demography, history, heterogeneity and concentration of population, variety of social and economic interests, and in the operation and interrelation of its political institutions. But so long as a State's apportionment plan reasonably achieves, in the light of the State's own characteristics, effective and balanced representation of all substantial interests, without sacrificing the principle of effective majority rule, that plan cannot be considered irrational.

II

Moving from the general to the specific, I think that the Equal Protection Clause demands but two basic attributes of any plan of state legislative apportionment.

First, it demands that, in the light of the State's own characteristics and needs, the plan must be a rational one. Secondly, it demands that the plan must be such as not to permit the systematic frustration of the will of a majority of the electorate of the State. I think it is apparent that any plan of legislative apportionment which could be shown to reflect no policy, but simply arbitrary and capricious action or inaction, and that any plan which could be shown systematically to prevent ultimate effective majority rule, would be invalid under accepted Equal Protection Clause standards. But, beyond this, I think there is nothing in the Federal Constitution to prevent a State from choosing any electoral legislative structure it thinks best suited to the interests, temper, and customs of its people.

Notes and Questions

1. Not surprisingly, *Baker*, *Reynolds*, and the other redistricting cases prompted a flood of commentary. Among the better writings in the 1960s were Carl A. Auerbach, *The Reapportionment Cases: One Person, One Vote—One Vote, One Value*, 1964 Supreme Court Review 1 (1964), and Phil C. Neal, *Baker v. Carr: Politics in Search of Law*, 1962 Supreme Court Review 252 (1962). A prolific and highly regarded commentator on the redistricting cases was the late Robert G. Dixon, whose views in the 1960s were synthesized in his book, Democratic Representation: Reapportionment in Law and Politics (1968). Additional commentary may be found in two excellent anthologies, Reapportionment in the 1970's (Nelson W. Polsby, ed., 1971), and Representation and Redistricting Issues (Bernard Grofman et al., eds., 1982). For more recent accounts of the history and consequences of the reapportionment revolution, see Stephen Ansolabehere and James M. Snyder, Jr., The End of Inequality: One Person, One Vote and the Transformation of American Politics (2008), and J. Douglas Smith, On Democracy's Doorstep: The Inside Story of How the Supreme Court Brought "One Person, One Vote" to the United States (2015).

2. Whose position, as between Chief Justice Warren and Justice Stewart, would be preferred by James Madison? By a pluralist? In A Preface to Democratic Theory (1956), Robert A. Dahl emphasized that the minority should prevail over the majority when and only when its preference is more intense than the majority's. Other writers in the pluralist tradition have sharply criticized the one-person, one-vote rule. Bruce E. Cain, *Election Law as a Field: A Political Scientist's Perspective*, 32 Loyola of Los Angeles Law Review 1105, 1109 (1999), acknowledges that most political scientists probably support the one-person, one-vote rule, but regards *Reynolds* as a setback to Madisonian theory, whose

> basic premise was that the popular will was best checked by institutions that were insulated from public opinion, similar to courts, or by the competition between representatives from various types of constituencies. The *Reynolds* cases elevated majoritarian principles over the prudentially cautious design of the Founding Fathers. Skepticism about the public whim has given way to reverence for the majority will.

Another pluralist, John Moeller, *The Supreme Court's Quest for Fair Politics*, 1 Constitutional Commentary 203, 213 (1984), writes:

> The solution the courts have imposed ignores our Madisonian political tradition. Most Americans identify with one or more groups, and those groups, representing varying constituencies, compete with each other for advantage. One consequence of Madisonian politics is an inherent tension in the scheme of representation. It calls for majoritarian government, which requires that most of the time most of the people will rule. But it also calls for reflective representation, which means that the institutions will "reflect the people in all their diversity, so that all the people may feel that their particular interests and even prejudices . . . were brought to bear on the decision-making process."

See also Alexander M. Bickel, The Supreme Court and the Idea of Progress 108–13 (1978). But consider Daniel Hays Lowenstein, *The Supreme Court Has No Theory of Politics—And Be Thankful for Small Favors*, in The U.S. Supreme Court and the Electoral Process 245, 251 (David K. Ryden, ed., 2000):

> Some pluralist writers have been critical of the Supreme Court's ruling in *Reynolds*. Although this criticism may not be surprising in light of Chief Justice Warren's progressivist reasoning, it is misplaced. These writers have viewed the Court in *Reynolds* as detaching the Madisonian system of countervailing groups and factions from redistricting. Despite *Reynolds*' progressivist foundation, however, there was no good reason to suppose *a priori* that the "one-person, one-vote" rule's constraint on redistricting would fundamentally alter the pluralist process of negotiation and compromise that characterizes legislative redistricting.

3. In *United States v. Carolene Products*, 304 U.S. 144, 152 n.4 (1938), the Supreme Court famously suggested that "more exacting judicial scrutiny" is appropriate when "legislation . . . restricts those political processes which can ordinarily be expected to bring about repeal of undesirable legislation." Four decades later, John Hart Ely, Democracy and Distrust: A Theory of Judicial Review 103 (1980) based a prominent theory of judicial review on *Carolene Products*, arguing that courts should intervene when "the ins are choking off the channels of political change to ensure that they will stay in and the outs will stay out." The one-person, one-vote cases are commonly considered among the greatest triumphs of this approach, because they eliminated the malapportionment that had permitted rural minorities to maintain control of state legislatures (and congressional delegations) for generations. Do you agree with this perspective? Consider some possible objections: "Political process" theory finds little support in the Constitution's text or history. The meaning of democracy is hotly contested, so there is rarely consensus that any particular judicial action is pro- or anti-democratic. And while they eliminated malapportionment, the one-person, one-vote cases did *not* guarantee majority rule because they did nothing to combat gerrymandering (which is discussed in Chapter 4, *infra*).

4. *Baker*, *Reynolds*, and their progeny were decided under the Equal Protection Clause. Was this the most suitable provision for the cases to invoke? Michael W. McConnell, *The Redistricting Cases: Original Mistakes and Current Consequences*, 24 Harvard Journal of Law and Public Policy 103 (2000), argues that it would have been preferable for the cases to have relied on the Republican Guarantee Clause (Article IV, Section 4). According to McConnell, the logic of equal protection leads inexorably to a requirement of perfectly equal population, but overlooks the democratic soundness (or weakness) of the electoral system. In contrast, doctrine developed under the Republican Guarantee Clause would be less obsessed with minor population deviations and more attentive to the achievement (or frustration) of broader democratic values. This approach would also make it easier to fight gerrymandering, which "is designed to entrench a particular political faction against effective political challenge" and thus "is in obvious tension with the values of Republicanism." *Id.* at 116.

5. It is a "basic equal protection principle that the invidious quality of a law . . . must ultimately be traced to a . . . discriminatory purpose." *Washington v. Davis*, 426 U.S. 229, 240 (1976). Under conventional equal protection doctrine, governmental actions that do not employ suspect classifications such as race or sex also are subject to highly deferential rational basis review. Yet in the reapportionment context, discriminatory intent does *not* need to be shown. Nor would anyone characterize the operative test as highly deferential to governmental decision-makers. What accounts for these divergences from standard equal protection law? Could it be the relatively early dates of the reapportionment cases, prior to the development of modern equal protection doctrine in the 1970s and 1980s? Or could it be that the usual approach would not work for one-person, one-vote claims? After all, can an intent to malapportion be meaningfully distinguished from actual malapportionment, and if rational basis review applied, would any plan ever be invalid?

6. In the 1950s and 1960s, many people hoped or feared that if the Supreme Court imposed an equal population requirement on state legislative districts and, to a lesser extent, on congressional districts, the result would be a major shift in policy toward liberalism and a major partisan shift in favor of the Democrats. The reason was that the overrepresented rural areas tended to be more conservative and Republican than the underrepresented urban areas. No such massive shift took place. In retrospect the reason is clear. Had *Reynolds* been decided twenty or so years earlier, the shift might have occurred, but by 1964 the growth of suburbs, which at that time tended to be conservative and Republican, had about equalled the earlier growth of cities. Did *Reynolds* have any systematic and major policy consequences at all? Many people have found it difficult to believe that it did not, but social scientists generally have found weak effects. See, *e.g.*, Timothy G. O'Rourke, The Impact of Reapportionment 119–45 (1980). Most such studies looked for changes in policy direction caused by redistricting, such as an increase in overall state spending or spending in particular policy sectors. However, a more recent study focused on the

geographic distribution of spending and found substantial changes in favor of the counties that gained representation as a result of redistricting. See Stephen Ansolabehere, Alan Gerber & James M. Snyder, Jr., *Equal Votes, Equal Money: Court-Ordered Redistricting and the Distribution of Public Expenditures in the American States*, 96 American Political Science Review 767 (2002). Another study concluded that the one-person, one-vote cases eliminated the pro-Republican partisan bias that had characterized congressional elections prior to the mid-1960s. See Gary W. Cox & Jonathan N. Katz, Elbridge Gerry's Salamander: The Electoral Consequences of the Reapportionment Revolution (2002).

7. Whether or not districts are equal in population, they are likely to group together those interests that are geographically concentrated (e.g., farmers, poor people in cities, some racial and ethnic groups), but not groups that are dispersed (e.g., dentists, women, other racial and ethnic groups). Is a group better off politically if it is concentrated or dispersed? To what extent does the answer depend on the group's size and political cohesion? See generally James M. Buchanan & Gordon Tullock, The Calculus of Consent 217–20 (1962).

Andrew Rehfeld, The Concept of Constituency: Political Representation, Democratic Legitimacy, and Institutional Design (2005), argues against geographically defined districts precisely because he deems it arbitrary to represent spatially concentrated groups more effectively than spatially dispersed ones. Rehfeld also contends that, in the contemporary world, territorially defined communities have lost much of their historical salience. In place of geographically defined districts, Rehfeld advocates constituencies to which people would be assigned at birth and which would thus mirror the state demographically and politically. How theoretically attractive do you find Rehfeld's proposal? Practically, might it lead to a highly homogeneous legislature and large legislative swings from election to election?

8. At the time of *Reynolds*, many opponents of the Court's intervention invoked the so-called "federal analogy," arguing based on the United States Senate that states should be permitted to apportion one legislative chamber by providing equal representation to political subdivisions such as counties. The Court made short shrift of the federal analogy, pointing out that counties (unlike states) have never enjoyed sovereignty and that the Senate was the key to the compromise between large and small states that made the Constitution possible. Are you persuaded by the Court's response? Is it relevant that, in many states, counties *are* highly significant units with a good deal of policymaking authority? Even if the federal analogy is not historically accurate, why should states not be able to embrace a theory of democracy that requires equal county representation? Is this theory any less legitimate than the Court's vision of equal treatment of all individuals?

9. In *Lucas*, majorities in every county in Colorado voted *against* an amendment that would have required both legislative chambers to be reapportioned on the basis of population, and *for* a different proposal that authorized reapportionment based on population and factors such as geography, history, and economic activity. In the Court's view, the electorate's approval of malapportionment was irrelevant: "A

citizen's constitutional rights can hardly be infringed simply because a majority of the people choose that it be." Consider the following counterargument: Reapportionment requires tradeoffs between population equality on the one hand, and the representation of group interests on the other. When the very people who would reside in the overpopulated districts consent to their own numerical underrepresentation, there has been no injury. Those people have simply sacrificed a degree of population equality for a gain in other forms of representation. (But what about the rebuttal, hinted at by the Court, that not everybody in the overpopulated districts actually agreed to their underrepresentation?)

10. In *Reynolds*, the Court speaks interchangeably of districts with equal population and with equal numbers of voters. The number of actual voters changes enough from election to election that it would be difficult to draw district lines to equalize the number of votes, but the theoretical argument is sometimes made that a measure closer to actual voters than population should be used. See, *e.g.*, *Garza v. County of Los Angeles*, 918 F.2d 763, 778, 779–86 (9th Cir. 1990) (Kozinski, J., concurring and dissenting in part), cert. denied 498 U.S. 1028 (1991). Although the Supreme Court has upheld redistricting on a basis other than population, it has stated a preference for population, see *Burns v. Richardson*, 384 U.S. 73 (1966), and population is nearly the universal basis for districting in the United States. Scot A. Reader, *One Person, One Vote Revisited: Choosing a Population Basis to Form Political Districts*, 17 Harvard Journal of Law & Public Policy 521 (1994), argues that the logic of *Reynolds* and subsequent cases ought to require equal numbers of voters rather than equal population, but he is skeptical that the Constitution ought to be so interpreted. On the other hand, Joseph Fishkin, *Weightless Votes*, 121 Yale Law Journal 1888 (2012), argues that the one-person, one-vote rule is not really about the weight of individual votes at all, but instead about how much power different groups should have. If that is correct, and if the responsibility of government is to represent all of the people—including children and others who are not eligible to vote—then equal population (not equal voters) should presumably be the standard of measurement.

The Supreme Court recently weighed in on this debate in *Evenwel v. Abbott*, 136 S. Ct. 1120 (2016). The plaintiffs challenged the Texas state senate plan, whose districts had a total *population* deviation of 8 percent but a total *eligible voter* deviation above 40 percent. (This discrepancy arose primarily between heavily Latino districts with many ineligible voters and heavily white districts with few ineligible voters.) The Court unanimously upheld the plan, thus reaffirming that "it is plainly permissible for jurisdictions to measure equalization by the total population of state and local legislative districts." *Id.* at 1126-27. The Court pointed out that congressional districts are allocated *between* states based on population, so it would be odd for districts to be drawn *within* states on some other basis. The Court also observed that its precedents are equivocal on the appropriate metric for reapportionment. "For every sentence appellants quote from the Court's opinions, one could respond with a line casting the one-person, one-vote guarantee in terms of equality of representation, not voter equality." *Id.* at 1131. Lastly, and most importantly, the Court explained that there is a sound theoretical argument for population (rather than voter) equality:

> [R]epresentatives serve all residents, not just those eligible or registered to vote. Nonvoters have an important stake in many policy debates—children, their parents, even their grandparents, for example, have a stake in a strong public-education system—and in receiving constituent services, such as help navigating public-benefits bureaucracies. By ensuring that each representative is subject to requests and suggestions from the same number of constituents, total-population apportionment promotes equitable and effective representation.

Id. at 1132.

Justices Alito and Thomas concurred in the judgment in separate opinions. Justice Alito objected on historical grounds to the Court's argument regarding the allocation of congressional seats to states on the basis of population. "In light of the history of Article I, § 2, of the original Constitution and § 2 of the Fourteenth Amendment, it is clear that the apportionment of seats in the House of Representatives was based in substantial part on the distribution of political power among the States and not merely on some theory regarding the proper nature of representation. It is impossible to draw any clear constitutional command from this complex history." *Id.* at 1149 (Alito, J., concurring in the judgment). More fundamentally, Justice Thomas argued that there is no constitutional basis for choosing between voter equality and equality of representation:

> This inconsistency (if not opacity) is not merely a consequence of the Court's equivocal statements on one person, one vote. The problem is more fundamental. There is simply no way to make a principled choice between interpreting one person, one vote as protecting eligible voters or as protecting total inhabitants within a State. That is because, though those theories are noble, the Constitution does not make either of them the exclusive means of apportionment for state and local representatives. In guaranteeing to the States a "Republican Form of Government," the Constitution did not resolve whether the ultimate basis of representation is the right of citizens to cast an equal ballot or the right of all inhabitants to have equal representation. The Constitution instead reserves these matters to the people. The majority's attempt today to divine a single "'theory of the Constitution'"—apportionment based on representation—rests on a flawed reading of history and wrongly picks one side of a debate that the Framers did not resolve in the Constitution.

Id. at 1136 (Thomas, J., concurring in the judgment). Does the majority actually embrace a single theory of apportionment or, despite its favorable comments about equality of representation, does it leave the question open?

Assuming *Evenwel* allows (even if it does not require) jurisdictions to select a unit of apportionment other than total population, what would happen if states, in fact, made this choice? Jowei Chen and Nicholas O. Stephanopoulos, *Democracy's Denominator*, 109 California Law Review 1011 (2021), investigate this issue by simulating large numbers of district maps, one set using total population as the apportionment base, a second set using citizen voting-age population (CVAP). They find that switching from total population to CVAP would significantly reduce the numbers of districts in which minority voters are able to elect their preferred candidates, especially in racially diverse states. However, the *partisan* effects of changing the unit of apportionment would be muted: only about one percentage point more Republican seats in most states. Given these findings, how likely are jurisdictions to switch from total population to CVAP? With respect to jurisdictions that take this leap, could a racially discriminatory purpose be inferred from the large expected drop in minority representation paired with the small expected partisan impact?

11. One issue not addressed by *Reynolds* was precisely how equal the population of districts must be. In *Swann v. Adams*, 385 U.S. 440 (1967), the Court struck down Florida legislative maps where the largest deviation from the mean population for any one district was 18 percent and the ratios of the largest to the smallest district in each house were, respectively, 1.41 to 1 and 1.30 to 1. The Court said such discrepancies could not be upheld without a showing of some rational basis, which could not include "deference to area and economic or other group interests." *Id.* at 447. In subsequent cases, however, the Court was willing to find that adherence to municipal boundaries can justify moderate deviations from exact equality (up to about 17 percent) in state and local districting. See *Abate v. Mundt*, 403 U.S. 182 (1971); *Mahan v. Howell*, 410 U.S. 315 (1973); *Voinovich v. Quilter*, 507 U.S. 146, 161 (1993). Smaller deviations (up to 10 percent) at the state level were believed to require no justification at all. See *Gaffney v. Cummings*, 412 U.S. 735 (1973). In *Daly v. Hunt*, 93 F.3d 1212, 1220 (4th Cir. 1996), for example, the court stated that a plan under the ten percent threshold is presumed to be valid, but can be overturned if it is shown to be the result of "arbitrariness or discrimination" or was not the result of an "honest and good faith effort to construct districts . . . as nearly of equal population as is practicable" (quoting *Roman v. Sincock*, 377 U.S. 695 (1964) and *Reynolds*).

12. What if population deviations close to but not exceeding ten percent systematically favor one region of a state over another (and, not coincidentally, one party over the other)? Compare *Larios v. Cox*, 300 F. Supp. 2d 1320 (N.D. Ga. 2004) (striking down a Georgia legislative plan), with *Rodriguez v. Pataki*, 308 F. Supp. 2d 346 (S.D.N.Y. 2004) (upholding a New York state senate plan). The Supreme Court summarily affirmed the Georgia decision. See *Cox v. Larios*, 542 U.S. 947 (2004). While not endorsing the lower court's reasoning, the summary affirmance seemed to mean that a plan within the ten percent threshold can violate the one-person, one-vote rule. As Justice Stevens wrote in a brief concurrence, "The District Court correctly held that the drafters' desire to give an electoral advantage to certain regions of the State and to certain incumbents (but not incumbents as such) did not justify the conceded deviations from the principle of one person, one vote." *Id.* at 949 (Stevens, J., concurring).

The Supreme Court provided more clarity about small but (allegedly) improperly motivated population deviations in *Harris v. Arizona Independent Redistricting Commission*, 136 S. Ct. 1301 (2016). Arizona's legislative districts had a total population deviation of just 4 percent. However, nearly all of the underpopulated districts elected Democratic representatives and nearly all of the overpopulated ones elected Republicans. Most of the underpopulated districts were also heavily Latino and were arguably required by the Voting Rights Act. The Court held that "those attacking a state-approved plan must show that it is more probable than not that a deviation of less than 10% reflects the predominance of illegitimate reapportionment factors." *Id.* at 1307. Applying this standard, the Court upheld the map. Based on a detailed examination of the record, the Court concluded that "the population deviations were primarily a result of good-faith efforts to comply with the Voting Rights Act"—and not a desire to benefit Democrats or disadvantage Republicans. *Id.* at 1309.

13. In the case of congressional districting, which under *Wesberry v. Sanders* is governed by Article I, Section 2 and not by the Equal Protection Clause, the Court has come close to requiring *perfect* population equality. More precisely, the Court demands legitimate justifications even for de minimis population deviations far below the ten percent threshold that applies to state legislative elections. See, *e.g.*, *Kirkpatrick v. Preisler*, 394 U.S. 526 (1969); *White v. Weiser*, 412 U.S. 783 (1973).

Neither Article I, Section 2 nor the Equal Protection Clause contains an explicit requirement of "one-person, one-vote," much less an indication of how equal the districts must be. Accordingly, many commentators have been unimpressed by the Court's reliance on the two constitutional provisions as an explanation for the dramatically different population standards the Court has imposed. A different justification is proposed by Charles Black, *Representation in Law and Equity*, 10 Nomos: Representation 131 (1968). Black, a proponent of "structural interpretation" of the Constitution, argues that the federal government's greater interest in federal elections justifies a stricter standard of population equality for congressional elections than for state and local elections, in which the federal government has less interest. However, a political scientist finds it perverse to give state legislators greater leeway when they design their own districts than when they define those of the members of the House of Representatives. See James L. McDowell, *"One Person, One Vote" and the Decline of Community*, 23 Legal Studies Forum 131, 138 (1999).

In *Tennant v. Jefferson County Commission*, 567 U.S. 758 (2012), the Supreme Court may have relaxed somewhat its approach to population inequality in congressional plans. West Virginia's map had a total population deviation of 0.79 percent. The legislature selected this plan over an alternative featuring perfect population equality because it did not split any counties, shifted very few people into new districts, and did not pair any incumbents. The Court unanimously upheld the map against a one-person, one-vote challenge, reasoning that the legislature's goals were "valid, neutral state districting policies" and that "[n]one of the alternative plans came close to vindicating all three of the State's legitimate objectives while achieving a lower variance." *Id.* at 8. Does *Tennant* change or confirm the law applicable to congressional reapportionment?

14. In 1983, the Supreme Court handed down two 5–4 decisions on the same day. In *Karcher v. Daggett*, 462 U.S. 725 (1983), the Court struck down a New Jersey congressional districting plan where the population difference between the largest and smallest districts amounted to 0.6984 percent. Relying on *Kirkpatrick*, the Court refused to set any percentage below which population inequality in congressional districts would be regarded as de minimis. In *Brown v. Thomson*, 462 U.S. 835 (1983), a case whose unusual factual and procedural background may undermine its precedential value, the Court validated a Wyoming state legislative plan where the maximum population deviation amounted to 89 percent. Can *Karcher* and *Brown* be reconciled based on the facts that (1) the New Jersey plan, despite its very low population inequality, was an aggressive partisan gerrymander; and (2) the Wyoming plan, despite its very large population inequality, respected county boundaries "in a manner 'free from any taint of arbitrariness or discrimination'"? *Id.* at 843.

15. Though *Wesberry* and *Reynolds* were fiercely controversial when they were decided, the one-person, one-vote rule has become widely accepted in the United States. For that reason, and because legislative bodies do not wish to jeopardize their districting plans by straying too near the boundaries of the equal population standards that have been staked out by the Supreme Court, serious challenges to legislative districts on grounds of population have become relatively unusual.

When such cases are brought, the plaintiffs usually have concerns other than population inequality. *Larios*, in which Republicans opposed a plan adopted by Georgia Democrats, is one example. Another occurred in the 2000 cycle in Pennsylvania. As mentioned above, in *Karcher* the Court refused to set a level below which any population inequality in a congressional plan would be regarded as de minimis. Does that mean *any* inequality, no matter how trivial, constitutes a prima facie constitutional violation? Apparently so, according to *Vieth v. Pennsylvania*, 195 F. Supp. 2d 672 (M.D. Pa. 2002). In that case, Democrats successfully challenged a Republican-drawn congressional plan whose maximum population deviation consisted of nineteen people. The largest district had a population of 646,380 while the population of the smallest district was 646,361, and there was no legitimate explanation for this divergence. The laugh was on the Democrats, though, because the court permitted the legislature to make politically insignificant changes to correct the (so-called) population disparity. The Democrats also pressed a challenge to the plan as a partisan gerrymander, which was their real concern. As we shall see in Chapter 4, that claim was decided (against the Democrats) by a closely divided Supreme Court in 2004.

Even before the Pennsylvania decision striking down a plan because of an unjustified population deviation of nineteen people, many drafters of congressional districting plans were reducing the deviations in their plans to the absolute minimum. In addition, after the Supreme Court's summary affirmance in *Larios*, lower courts were unwilling to recognize a maximum deviation under ten percent as a safe harbor for state and local plans. Following the 2010 census, state and local as well as congressional redistricters often sought to reduce deviations to an absolute minimum. See *2010 Redistricting Deviation Table*, National Conference of State Legislatures (Jan. 23, 2012), https://perma.cc/T4LW-QEYK (showing that thirty current congressional plans have total population deviations of zero or one people, and that every state legislative chamber is currently below the ten percent threshold except the Delaware Senate, the Hawaii House and Senate, the Ohio House, and the Vermont House and Senate). Is any purpose served by such extreme legislative and judicial efforts to guarantee population equality?

16. How do foreign countries address population equality in district plans? Nicholas O. Stephanopoulos, *Our Electoral Exceptionalism*, 80 University of Chicago Law Review 769, 808–09 (2013), explains that the United States is an outlier in its rigid stance on the issue:

> Like the United States, all foreign jurisdictions that periodically redraw their districts abide by equal population requirements of one kind or another. However, these foreign requirements are never as strict as the American mandate for congressional districts, and in only a handful of cases—most notably, Australia, New Zealand, and, since 2011, the United Kingdom—are they even as rigorous as the American policy for state legislative districts. Permissible population ranges around the world are more commonly on the order of 20 percent (e.g., Belarus, the Ukraine), 30 percent (e.g., the Czech Republic, Germany), 40 percent (e.g., Papua New Guinea, Zimbabwe), or 50 percent (e.g., Canada, Lithuania)—where they are specified at all, which they often are not. Also notably, certain Australian states and Canadian provinces make exceptions to their regular rules for large and sparsely populated districts. For example, population ranges of up to 100 percent are allowed for northern districts in Alberta and Saskatchewan, while Queensland and Western Australia add "phantom" voters to the populations of districts in their vast and almost empty interiors.

17. Compliance with the equal protection requirement, however strict or lax the requirement may be, is based on the census, which is performed each decade in the year ending in zero. The census is used for many purposes, but its basis is Article I, Section 2 of the Constitution, which calls for an "actual enumeration" of the population of each state, "in such manner" as Congress may direct. The provision further calls for members of the House of Representatives as well as direct taxes to be apportioned on the basis of the census. For reasons unrelated to the subject matter of this book, the direct taxation provision has become a dead letter, meaning that reapportionment is the only constitutionally stated purpose for the census that has any practical importance. As Peter Skerry, Counting on the Census? Race, Group Identity, and the Evasion of Politics (2000), explains, the use of the census for apportionment created an incentive for states to seek to maximize their counted population, while the census's use for direct taxation gave the states an incentive to try to minimize their counted population. Consistent with the goal of James Madison and

many of the other framers to create offsetting political pressures within the federal system as a way of preventing abuses, states would be restrained in their efforts to influence the census, because whether they sought to increase or lower their own population counts, what they stood to gain in one area they would lose in the other. That balance has been upset by the practical elimination of the direct taxation function, so that states now have an undiluted incentive to increase their relative share of the nation's population as counted by the census. That incentive is supplemented by additional statutory inducements pointing in the same direction. The failure of the original constitutional plan to create offsetting pressures no doubt accounts in part for the contentiousness of politics surrounding the census.

Article I, Section 2 states that the *apportionment* of the House of Representatives—that is, the allocation of House seats among the states—will be based on the census. As a result of *Wesberry* and *Reynolds*, the census must also be used for *districting*—that is, establishing the boundaries of districts within which members of the House, state legislatures, and other governmental bodies are elected. In addition, the census is the basis for the distribution of grants and other benefits in numerous federal programs, as well as for an immense variety of publicly and privately sponsored research.

In recent decades, the question of whether statistical sampling can and should be used in the census has become a contentious partisan issue. It is generally conceded that the method that has been used in the recent past—a mail survey, followed by personal visits to households that do not respond—results in a significant undercount. Furthermore, the persons missed by the census are not a random sample of the public. In particular, the size of the undercount is considerably larger among certain racial and ethnic groups than among the population at large. Sampling, i.e., statistically based extrapolation from the people who are actually counted, would yield a more accurate total population figure than the methods that have been used in the past.

Without much controversy since at least the 1950s, the Census Bureau has used various forms of sampling to produce demographic, social, and economic data of various sorts. The proposal to extend the use of sampling has provoked considerable argument along two lines of cleavage. The first divides states and municipalities that stand to gain in relative population from sampling and those that stand to lose in relative population. Roughly, jurisdictions such as California and Texas with large immigrant populations are in the former category, and many midwestern and southern states are in the latter. Because allocations under many federal programs are based either on total population or population of ethnic, income, or other groups that are likely to be disproportionately undercounted, these jurisdictions stand to gain or lose substantial amounts in federal grants and subsidies. However, the dispute between states and municipalities has been overshadowed, politically, by the dispute between the parties. The most heavily undercounted groups tend to be disproportionately Democratic in their voting behavior. It is not surprising that with almost one voice Democrats have favored sampling and Republicans have opposed it. A five-member majority of the Supreme Court concluded that sampling *could not* be used for apportionment, under Section 195 of the Census Act. *Department of Commerce v. United States House of Representatives*, 525 U.S. 316 (1999). However, the Court did not reach the broader question of whether the constitutional phrase, "actual enumeration," might itself preclude sampling.

Although the political debate on the census issue is saturated with partisanship, there are strong policy considerations on both sides of the argument. As was mentioned above, the use of sampling would generate a more accurate population total and would reduce or eliminate inequity resulting from undercounts of varying margins among different population groups. On the other hand, when it comes to the methodological details, the use of statistical sampling techniques is as much an art as a science and may be subject to abusive manipulation when it occurs in such a politically charged context. Furthermore, though statistical techniques would generate more accurate results in the aggregate, the more local the analysis, the less accurate would be the techniques. Yet, for purposes of legislative districting and allocating some federal grants, local rather than aggregate numbers are most relevant. Skerry, *supra*, is highly skeptical of the use of sampling. Unfortunately, there is no similarly accessible and comprehensive statement of the opposing view. However, for one brief summary of arguments in favor of sampling, see Stephen E. Fienberg, *The New York City Census Adjustment Trial: Witness for the Plaintiffs*, 34 Jurimetrics 65 (1993). Many of Skerry's arguments are criticized by Nathaniel Persily, *The Right to Be Counted*, 53 Stanford Law Review 1077 (2001).

For a discussion of the controversies surrounding the census and its impact on the redistricting process, see Nathaniel Persily, *The Law of the Census: How to Count, What to Count, Whom to Count, and Where to Count Them*, 32 Cardozo Law Review 755 (2011). One of the most significant current issues surrounds the practice of counting prisoners where they are incarcerated, rather than where they are from or where they plan to go once released. This practice has a tendency to "pad" the population of rural communities in which prisons generally tend to be located. The effect can be dramatic, as Professor Persily notes, because in some legislative districts over 10 percent of the population resides in prison. To the extent that prisoners are disproportionately minorities, not allowed to vote (as is true in most states), and counted in predominantly white rural communities, the counting of prisoners where they are incarcerated raises questions of minority vote dilution, a topic addressed in Chapter 5. See Dale E. Ho, *Captive Constituents: Prison-Based Gerrymandering and the Current Redistricting Cycle*, 22 Stanford Law and Policy Review 355 (2011) (arguing that "prison-based gerrymandering" violates both the one-person, one-vote rule and the Voting Rights Act).

18. The Supreme Court recently addressed a different issue concerning the 2020 Census, one that has major implications for the apportionment of U.S. Representatives among the states as well as for the drawing of districts within states. In 2018, Secretary of Commerce Wilbur Ross announced that a question regarding

citizenship would be added to the census questionnaire. The Census Bureau has asked some people questions about citizenship in the past, but in recent decades, the question was asked as part of the American Community Survey (formerly known as the long-form questionnaire) that only a sampling of households receive, rather than the census questionnaire that all households receive. For background on the history of citizenship questions on the census, see Thomas P. Wolf and Brianna Cea, *A Critical History of the United States Census and Citizenship Questions*, 108 Georgetown Law Journal Online 1 (2019).

The Department of Commerce argued that the addition of the citizenship question was needed to facilitate enforcement of the Voting Rights Act (VRA). Claims of minority vote dilution under Section 2 of the VRA often rely on evidence of how many voting-age *citizens* of different races and ethnicities live in different regions (see Chapter 5). Opponents of the citizenship question argued that its addition would depress participation, especially among Latino households and those that include noncitizens, ultimately resulting in a less accurate count. They sued on multiple grounds, alleging that addition of the citizenship question would violate the Enumeration Clause of the U.S. Constitution, the Census Act, and the Administrative Procedures Act (APA).

A federal district court in New York ruled that the Department of Commerce's decision to add the citizenship question was "arbitrary and capricious." In an opinion by Chief Justice Roberts, the Supreme Court reversed in part and affirmed in part. *Department of Commerce v. New York*, 139 S. Ct. 2551 (2019). Different groups of justices joined different portions of the Chief Justice's majority opinion. In a section joined by the other conservative justices, the Court upheld the Department of Commerce's authority to ask about citizenship under the Enumeration Clause. That Clause, according to the majority, gives Congress—and by implication, the Department of Commerce—broad authority to decide what questions to add as part of the Census. The same group of justices found that the stated reason for adding the question, that it was needed to enforce the VRA, was "reasonable and reasonably explained." *Id.* at 2571. They also rejected the argument that the addition of the citizenship question violated the Census Act.

The Court nevertheless concluded that the Department of Commerce's decision-making process violated the APA. A different group of justices formed the majority for this part of the opinion, with four liberal justices joining the Chief Justice. The Court held that the Secretary's decision "rested on a pretextual basis," *id.* at 2573, therefore justifying remand to the Department of Commerce. The Court relied on evidence showing that improved enforcement of the VRA was not the real reason for adding the citizenship question to the 2020 census:

> [V]iewing the evidence as a whole, we share the District Court's conviction that the decision to reinstate a citizenship question cannot be adequately explained in terms of DOJ's request for improved citizenship data to better enforce the VRA. Several points, considered together, reveal

> a significant mismatch between the decision the Secretary made and the rationale he provided. . . .
>
> Altogether, the evidence tells a story that does not match the explanation the Secretary gave for his decision. In the Secretary's telling, Commerce was simply acting on a routine data request from another agency. Yet the materials before us indicate that Commerce went to great lengths to elicit the request from DOJ (or any other willing agency). And unlike a typical case in which an agency may have both stated and unstated reasons for a decision, here the VRA enforcement rationale—the sole stated reason—seems to have been contrived.
>
> We are presented, in other words, with an explanation for agency action that is incongruent with what the record reveals about the agency's priorities and decisionmaking process. It is rare to review a record as extensive as the one before us when evaluating informal agency action—and it should be. But having done so for the sufficient reasons we have explained, we cannot ignore the disconnect between the decision made and the explanation given. Our review is deferential, but we are "not required to exhibit a naiveté from which ordinary citizens are free." *United States v. Stanchich*, 550 F.2d 1294, 1300 (2nd Cir. 1977) (Friendly, J.). The reasoned explanation requirement of administrative law, after all, is meant to ensure that agencies offer genuine justifications for important decisions, reasons that can be scrutinized by courts and the interested public. Accepting contrived reasons would defeat the purpose of the enterprise. If judicial review is to be more than an empty ritual, it must demand something better than the explanation offered for the action taken in this case.

Id. at 2575-76. If enforcement of the VRA was not the Department of Commerce's real reason for adding the citizenship question, what then was the true explanation? The Court professed agnosticism on this question, saying that the reasons were "unknown." But documents that emerged shortly before the Court's decision shed some light on the answer. The documents came from the electronic files of the late Thomas B. Hofeller, a Republican political operative who has been referred to as the "Michelangelo of gerrymandering" for his role in designing redistricting plans favorable to the party. After his death in 2018, his estranged daughter turned over information from Hofeller's hard drives to Common Cause, an advocacy group involved in cases challenging partisan gerrymandering. See Michael Wines, *Deceased G.O.P. Strategist's Hard Drives Reveal New Details on the Census Citizenship Question*, N.Y. Times, May 30, 2019.

The information from Hofeller's hard drives included a 2015 analysis of how political representation would be affected if only voting-age citizens—rather than the entire population—were counted in drawing legislative districts. At the time, the plaintiffs in *Evenwel v. Abbott* (see *supra* note 10) were challenging Texas's use of total population to divide the state into legislative districts. Hofeller's analysis of Texas found that using only adult citizens (rather than total population) to draw districts "would be advantageous to Republicans and non-Hispanic whites." The problem was that the detailed citizenship data needed to draw districts in this way was lacking. As Hofeller put it, "the use of citizen voting age population is functionally unworkable" without a citizenship question on the 2020 Census. *Id.*

This evidence suggests that the real reason—at least the main one—for adding the citizenship question to the 2020 Census was to allow Republican-dominated legislatures to equalize the voting-age citizen population instead of the total population when drawing districts. Drawing districts in this way would presumably advantage Republicans, while disadvantaging Democrats and Latino voters. Even before the Hofeller documents became public, some speculated that this was the real reason for the Department of Commerce wanting to add the citizenship question. See Justin Levitt, *Citizenship and the Census*, 119 Columbia Law Review 1355 (2019).

Notwithstanding his administration's defeat in *Department of Commerce*, President Trump issued a memorandum in July 2020 announcing a policy of excluding undocumented noncitizens from the apportionment count that is used to allocate U.S. House members among states. Under this policy, the Secretary of Commerce would use administrative records and other information to identify these noncitizens and omit them from the apportionment count. In *Trump v. New York*, 141 S. Ct. 530 (2020), the Supreme Court ruled that a challenge to the policy was premature. "[T]he policy may not prove feasible to implement in any manner whatsoever," the Court observed, rendering overly speculative any evaluation of how the policy might affect apportionment or funding flows. *Id.* at 535. In the event, the Trump administration was unable to complete the project of excluding undocumented noncitizens from the apportionment count before its term expired, and the incoming Biden administration quickly reversed the policy. See Exec. Order No. 13,986, 86 Fed. Reg. 7015, 7016 (Jan. 20, 2021).

19. In reporting data for redistricting to the states, the Census Bureau announced that, for the 2020 Census, it will employ a procedure known as "differential privacy." This is a statistical algorithm that randomly varies the population counts of small geographic units in order to prevent Census respondents' identities from being identifiable. Alabama filed a suit objecting to the use of differential privacy on the grounds that it violates the Census Act, the Administrative Procedure Act, and various constitutional provisions. See *Alabama v. Department of Commerce*, No. 3:21-cv-211-RAH-ECM-KCN, 2021 WL 2668810 (M.D. Ala. June 29, 2021) (rejecting most of Alabama's claims). Scholars have published reports on differential privacy reaching divergent conclusions on whether it would materially affect district plans' partisan and racial characteristics. Compare Aloni Cohen et al., *Census TopDown: The Impacts of Differential Privacy on Redistricting* (Apr. 14, 2021, https://perma.cc/UBM6-9U3N) (no significant impact), with Christopher T. Kenney et al., *The Impact of the U.S. Census Disclosure Avoidance System on Redistricting and Voting Rights Analysis* (May 28, 2021, https://perma.cc/DH7G-9YTW) (significant impact).

20. One of the big questions left open by *Reynolds v. Sims* was whether and to what extent its doctrine was applicable to local government. Consider the following

cases, and observe the degree to which the argument over extending *Reynolds* parallels the arguments in the *Kramer* line of cases, reviewed in Chapter 2. In the cases in Part II of this chapter, the *Kramer* and *Reynolds* lines will converge.

Avery v. Midland County

390 U.S. 474 (1968)

Mr. Justice WHITE delivered the opinion of the Court.

[Petitioner challenged electoral districts of drastically unequal population, asserting that the one-person, one-vote rule should be applied to the Midland County, Texas, Commissioners Court, the governing body of the county.]

Midland County has a population of about 70,000. The Commissioners Court is composed of five members. One, the County Judge, is elected at large from the entire county, and in practice casts a vote only to break a tie. The other four are Commissioners chosen from districts. The population of those districts, according to the 1963 estimates that were relied upon when this case was tried, was respectively 67,906; 852; 414; and 828. This vast imbalance resulted from placing in a single district virtually the entire city of Midland, Midland County's only urban center, in which 95% of the county's population resides.

The Commissioners Court is assigned by the Texas Constitution and by various statutory enactments with a variety of functions. According to the commentary to Vernon's Texas Statutes, the court:

> is the general governing body of the county. It establishes a courthouse and jail, appoints numerous minor officials such as the county health officer, fills vacancies in the county offices, lets contracts in the name of the county, builds roads and bridges, administers the county's public welfare services, performs numerous duties in regard to elections, sets the county tax rate, issues bonds, adopts the county budget, and serves as a board of equalization for tax assessments.

The court is also authorized, among other responsibilities, to build and run a hospital, an airport, and libraries. It fixes boundaries of school districts within the county, may establish a regional public housing authority, and determines the districts for election of its own members. . . .

In *Reynolds v. Sims*, the Equal Protection Clause was applied to the apportionment of state legislatures. Every qualified resident, *Reynolds* determined, has the right to a ballot for election of state legislators of equal weight to the vote of every other resident, and that right is infringed when legislators are elected from districts of substantially unequal population. The question now before us is whether the Fourteenth Amendment likewise forbids the election of local government officials from districts of disparate population. As has almost every court which has addressed itself to this question, we hold that it does.

When the State apportions its legislature, it must have due regard for the Equal Protection Clause. Similarly, when the State delegates lawmaking power to local government and provides for the election of local officials from districts specified by statute, ordinance, or local charter, it must insure that those qualified to vote have the right to an equally effective voice in the election process. If voters residing in oversize districts are denied their constitutional right to participate in the election of state legislators, precisely the same kind of deprivation occurs when the members of a city council, school board, or county governing board are elected from districts of substantially unequal population. If the five senators representing a city in the state legislature may not be elected from districts ranging in size from 50,000 to 500,000, neither is it permissible to elect the members of the city council from those same districts. In either case, the votes of some residents have greater weight than those of others; in both cases the equal protection of the laws has been denied.

That the state legislature may itself be properly apportioned does not exempt subdivisions from the Fourteenth Amendment. While state legislatures exercise extensive power over their constituents and over the various units of local government, the States universally leave much policy and decisionmaking to their governmental subdivisions. Legislators enact many laws but do not attempt to reach those countless matters of local concern necessarily left wholly or partly to those who govern at the local level. What is more, in providing for the governments of their cities, counties, towns, and districts, the States characteristically provide for representative government — for decisionmaking at the local level by representatives elected by the people. And, not infrequently, the delegation of power to local units is contained in constitutional provisions for local home rule which are immune from legislative interference. In a word, institutions of local government have always been a major aspect of our system, and their responsible and responsive operation is today of increasing importance to the quality of life of more and more of our citizens. We therefore see little difference, in terms of the application of the Equal Protection Clause and of the principles of *Reynolds v. Sims*, between the exercise of state power through legislatures and its exercise by elected officials in the cities, towns, and counties.[6]

We are urged to permit unequal districts for the Midland County Commissioners Court on the ground that the court's functions are not sufficiently "legislative." The parties have devoted much effort to urging that alternative labels — "administrative" versus "legislative" — be applied to the Commissioners Court. As the brief

---

6. Inequitable apportionment of local governing bodies offends the Constitution even if adopted by a properly apportioned legislature representing the majority of the State's citizens. The majority of a State — by constitutional provision, by referendum, or through accurately apportioned representatives — can no more place a minority in oversize districts without depriving that minority of equal protection of the laws than they can deprive the minority of the ballot altogether, or impose upon them a tax rate in excess of that to be paid by equally situated members of the majority. . . .

description of the court's functions above amply demonstrates, this unit of local government cannot easily be classified in the neat categories favored by civics texts. The Texas commissioners courts are assigned some tasks which would normally be thought of as "legislative," others typically assigned to "executive" or "administrative" departments, and still others which are "judicial." In this regard Midland County's Commissioners Court is representative of most of the general governing bodies of American cities, counties, towns, and villages. One knowledgeable commentator has written of "the states' varied, pragmatic approach in establishing government." That approach has produced a staggering number of governmental units—the preliminary calculation by the Bureau of the Census for 1967 is that there are 81,304 "units of government" in the United States—and an even more staggering diversity. Nonetheless, while special-purpose organizations abound and in many States the allocation of functions among units results in instances of overlap and vacuum, virtually every American lives within what he and his neighbors regard as a unit of local government with general responsibility and power for local affairs. In many cases citizens reside within and are subject to two such governments, a city and a county.

The Midland County Commissioners Court is such a unit. While the Texas Supreme Court found that the Commissioners Court's legislative functions are "negligible," the court does have power to make a large number of decisions having a broad range of impacts on all the citizens of the county. It sets a tax rate, equalizes assessments, and issues bonds. It then prepares and adopts a budget for allocating the county's funds, and is given by statute a wide range of discretion in choosing the subjects on which to spend. In adopting the budget the court makes both long-term judgments about the way Midland County should develop—whether industry should be solicited, roads improved, recreation facilities built, and land set aside for schools—and immediate choices among competing needs.

The Texas Supreme Court concluded that the work actually done by the Commissioners Court "disproportionately concern[s] the rural areas." Were the Commissioners Court a special-purpose unit of government assigned the performance of functions affecting definable groups of constituents more than other constituents, we would have to confront the question whether such a body may be apportioned in ways which give greater influence to the citizens most affected by the organization's functions. That question, however, is not presented by this case, for while Midland County authorities may concentrate their attention on rural roads, the relevant fact is that the powers of the Commissioners Court include the authority to make a substantial number of decisions that affect all citizens, whether they reside inside or outside the city limits of Midland. The Commissioners maintain buildings, administer welfare services, and determine school districts both inside and outside the city. The taxes imposed by the court fall equally on all property in the county. Indeed, it may not be mere coincidence that a body apportioned with three of its four voting members chosen by residents of the rural area surrounding the city devotes most of its attention to the problems of that area, while paying for its expenditures with a tax imposed equally on city residents and those who live outside the city. And we might point out that a decision not to exercise a function within the court's power—a decision, for example, not to build an airport or a library, or not to participate in the federal food stamp program—is just as much a decision affecting all citizens of the county as an affirmative decision....

This Court is aware of the immense pressures facing units of local government, and of the greatly varying problems with which they must deal. The Constitution does not require that a uniform straitjacket bind citizens in devising mechanisms of local government suitable for local needs and efficient in solving local problems. Last Term, for example, the Court upheld a procedure for choosing a school board that placed the selection with school boards of component districts even though the component boards had equal votes and served unequal populations. *Sailors v. Board of Education of Kent County*, 387 U.S. 105 (1967). The Court rested on the administrative nature of the area school board's functions and the essentially appointive form of the scheme employed. In *Dusch v. Davis*, 387 U.S. 112 (1967), the Court permitted Virginia Beach to choose its legislative body by a scheme that included at-large voting for candidates, some of whom had to be residents of particular districts, even though the residence districts varied widely in population....

Mr. Justice HARLAN, dissenting.

... The argument most generally heard for justifying the entry of the federal courts into the field of state legislative apportionment is that since state legislatures had widely failed to correct serious malapportionments in their own structure, and since no other means of redress had proved available through the political process, this Court was entitled to step into the picture. While I continue to reject that thesis as furnishing an excuse for the federal judiciary's straying outside its proper constitutional role, and while I continue to believe that it bodes ill for the country and the entire federal judicial system if this Court does not firmly set its face against this loose and short-sighted point of view, the important thing for present purposes is that no such justification can be brought to bear in this instance.

No claim is made in this case that avenues of political redress are not open to correct any malapportionment in elective local governmental units, and it is difficult to envisage how such a situation could arise. Local governments are creatures of the States, and they may be reformed either by the state legislatures, which are now required to be apportioned according to *Reynolds*, or by amendment of state constitutions. In these circumstances, the argument of practical necessity has no force. The Court, then, should withhold its hand until such a supposed necessity does arise, before intruding itself into the business of restructuring local governments across the country....

The present case affords one example of why the "one man, one vote" rule is especially inappropriate for local governmental units. The Texas Supreme Court held as a matter of Texas law:

> Theoretically, the commissioners court is the governing body of the county and the commissioners represent all the residents, both urban and rural, of the county. But developments during the years have greatly narrowed the scope of the functions of the commissioners court and limited its major responsibilities to the nonurban areas of the county. It has come to pass that the city government . . . is the major concern of the city dwellers and the administration of the affairs of the county is the major concern of the rural dwellers.

Despite the specialized role of the commissioners court, the majority has undertaken to bring it within the ambit of *Reynolds* simply by classifying it as "a unit of local government with general responsibility and power for local affairs." Although this approach is intended to afford "equal protection" to all voters in Midland County, it would seem that it in fact discriminates against the county's rural inhabitants. The commissioners court, as found by the Texas Supreme Court, performs more functions in the area of the county outside Midland City than it does within the city limits. Therefore, each rural resident has a greater interest in its activities than each city dweller. Yet under the majority's formula the urban residents are to have a dominant voice in the county government, precisely proportional to their numbers, and little or no allowance may be made for the greater stake of the rural inhabitants in the county government.

This problem is not a trivial one and is not confined to Midland County. It stems from the fact that local governments, unlike state governments, are often specialized in function. Application of the *Reynolds* rule to such local governments prevents the adoption of apportionments which take into account the effect of this specialization, and therefore may result in a denial of equal treatment to those upon whom the exercise of the special powers has unequal impact. Under today's decision, the only apparent alternative is to classify the governmental unit as other than "general" in power and responsibility, thereby, presumably, avoiding application of the *Reynolds* rule. . . .

A common pattern of development in the Nation's urban areas has been for the less affluent citizens to migrate to or remain within the central city, while the more wealthy move to the suburbs and come into the city only to work. The result has been to impose a relatively heavier tax burden upon city taxpayers and to fragmentize governmental services in the metropolitan area. An oft-proposed solution to these problems has been the institution of an integrated government encompassing the entire metropolitan area. In many instances, the suburbs may be included in such a metropolitan unit only by majority vote of the voters in each suburb. As a practical matter the suburbanites often will be reluctant to join the metropolitan government unless they receive a share in the government proportional to the benefits they bring with them and not merely to their numbers. The city dwellers may be ready to concede this much, in return for the ability to tax the suburbs. Under the majority's pronouncements, however, this rational compromise would be forbidden: the metropolitan government must be apportioned solely on the basis of population if it is a "general" government. . . .

Mr. Justice FORTAS, dissenting.

I submit that the problem presented by many, perhaps most, county governments (and by Midland County in particular) is precisely the same as those arising from special-purpose units. The functions of many county governing boards, no less than the governing bodies of special-purpose units, have only slight impact on some of their constituents and a vast and direct impact on others. They affect different citizens residing within their geographical jurisdictions in drastically different ways.

Study of county government leaves one with two clear impressions: that the variations from unit to unit are great; and that the role and structure of county government are currently in a state of flux. County governments differ in every significant way: number of constituents, area governed, number of competing or overlapping government units within the county, form, and means of selection of the governing board, services provided, the number and functions of independent county officials, and sources of revenue.

Some generalizations can be made about county governments. First, most counties today perform certain basic functions delegated by the State: assessment of property, collection of property taxes, recording of deeds and other documents, maintenance of rural roads, poor relief, law enforcement, and the administration of electoral and judicial functions. Some counties have begun to do more, especially by the assumption of municipal and policy-making functions. But most counties still act largely as administrative instrumentalities of the State.

Second, "[t]he absence of a single chief executive and diffusion of responsibility among numerous independently elected officials are general characteristics of county government in the United States." Those who have written on the subject have invariably pointed to the extensive powers exercised within the geographical region of the county by officials elected on a countywide basis and by special districts organized to perform specific tasks. Often these independent officials and organs perform crucial functions of great importance to all the people within the county.

These generalizations apply with particular force in this case. The population of Midland County is chiefly in a single urban area. That urban area has its own municipal government which, because of home rule, has relative autonomy and authority to deal with urban problems. In contrast, the Midland County government, like county governments generally, acts primarily as an administrative arm of the State. It provides a convenient agency for the State to collect taxes, hold elections, administer judicial and peace-keeping functions, improve roads, and perform other functions which are the ordinary duties of the State. The powers of the Commissioners Court, which is the governing body of Midland County, are strictly limited by statute and constitutional provision. Although a mere listing of these authorizing statutes and constitutional provisions would seem to indicate that the Commissioners Court has significant and general power, this impression is somewhat illusory because very often the provisions which grant the power also circumscribe its exercise with detailed limitations.

For example, the petitioner cites [provisions] granting the Commissioners Court authority to levy taxes. Yet, at the time this suit was tried, . . . no county could levy a tax in excess of 80 cents on $100 property valuation. And . . . that 80 cents [was allocated] among the four "constitutional purposes" . . . (not more than 25 cents for general county purposes, not more than 15 cents for the jury fund, not more than 15 cents for roads and bridges, and not more than 25 cents for permanent improvements).

Another example is the authority to issue bonds. It is true, as the majority notes, that the Commissioners Court does have this authority. Yet . . . a detailed code [regulates] how and for what purposes bonds may be issued. Significantly, . . . county bonds "shall never be issued for any purpose" unless the bond issue has been submitted to the qualified property-taxpaying voters of the county.

More important than the statutory and constitutional limitations, the limited power and function of the Commissioners Court are reflected in what it actually does. The record and briefs do not give a complete picture of the workings of the Commissioners Court. But it is apparent that the Commissioners are primarily concerned with rural affairs, and more particularly with rural roads. . . .

Substance, not shibboleth, should govern in this admittedly complex and subtle area; and the substance is that the geographical extent of the Commissioners Court is of very limited meaning. Midland County's Commissioners Court has its primary focus in nonurban areas and upon the nonurban people. True, the county's revenues come largely from the City of Midland. But the Commissioners Court fixes the tax rate subject to the specific limitations provided by the legislature. It must spend tax revenues in the categories and percentages which the legislature fixes. Taxes are assessed and collected, not by it, but by an official elected on a countywide basis. It is quite likely that if the city dwellers were given control of the Commissioners Court, they would reduce the load because it is spent primarily in the rural area. This is a state matter. If the State Legislature, in which presumably the city dwellers are fairly represented (*Reynolds v. Sims*), wishes to reduce the load, it may do so. But unless we are ready to adopt the position that the Federal Constitution forbids a State from taxing city dwellers to aid their rural neighbors, the fact that city dwellers pay most taxes should not determine the composition of the county governing body. We should not use tax impact as the sole or controlling basis for vote distribution. It is merely one in a number of factors, including the functional impact of the county government, which should be taken into account in determining whether a particular voting arrangement results in reasonable recognition of the rights and interests of citizens. Certainly, neither tax impact nor the relatively few services rendered within the City of Midland should compel the State to vest practically all voting power in the city residents to the virtual denial of a voice to those who are dependent on the county government for roads, welfare, and other essential services.

Texas should have a chance to devise a scheme which, within wide tolerance, eliminates the gross underrepresentation of the city, but at the same time provides an adequate, effective voice for the nonurban, as well as the urban, areas and peoples.

[Justice STEWART also dissented.]

Notes and Questions

1. In *Board of Estimate v. Morris*, 489 U.S. 688 (1989), the Court struck down the system for selecting the membership of the New York City Board of Estimate, which had significant budgetary and other fiscal authority. Three members of the Board, who cast two votes each, were the mayor and two other officials who were elected citywide. The remaining members were the five borough presidents, each of whom was elected within his or her respective borough. The populations of the boroughs were unequal by a big margin. How can *Morris* be distinguished from *Sailors v. Board of Education*, described in the majority opinion in *Avery*?

Should the fact that the members who were elected citywide could control the Board on most issues have led the *Morris* Court to uphold the Board's structure? Justice White, writing for the Court, responded as follows:

> The city . . . erroneously implies that the board's composition survives constitutional challenge because the citywide members cast a 6-to-5 majority of board votes and hence are in position to control the outcome of board actions. The at-large members, however, as the courts below observed, often do not vote together; and when they do not, the outcome is determined by the votes of the borough presidents, each having one vote. Two citywide members, with the help of the presidents of the two least populous boroughs, the Bronx and Staten Island, will prevail over a disagreeing coalition of the third citywide member and the presidents of the three boroughs that contain a large majority of the city's population. Furthermore, because the mayor has no vote on budget issues, the citywide members alone cannot control board budgetary decisions.

Id. at 696. If the Mayor were permitted to vote on budgetary issues and if evidence showed that the citywide members of the Board usually voted as a bloc, would the result in *Morris* be different?

In some states, especially in the South, all state legislators elected from a county are formally or informally constituted as the "delegation" from that county. As a practical matter, these delegations are often given virtually complete control over legislation affecting that county. Because of the need to comply with the one-person, one-vote rule, the delegation may consist of a mixture of representatives whose districts are entirely or only partially within the county. See generally Binny Miller, *Who Shall Rule and Govern? Local Legislative Delegations, Racial Politics, and the Voting Rights Act*, 102 Yale Law Journal 105 (1992). Suppose a county contains two legislative districts entirely within the county and one-tenth of an additional district. Could residents of the fully contained districts challenge the make-up of the county's delegation on the ground that in-county residents of the fractional district have ten times more voting power on the delegation than members of the fully contained districts? See *Vander Linden v. Hodges*, 193 F.3d 268 (4th Cir. 1999).

2. Do you agree with the *Sailors* exception to the one-person, one-vote rule for "appointed" bodies? How would you determine if a body is "appointive" or "elective"?

Consider *Cunningham v. Municipality of Metropolitan Seattle*, 751 F. Supp. 885 (W.D. Wash. 1990). The Municipality of Metropolitan Seattle ("Metro") was created to control water pollution in King County, Washington. The 42 members of its governing council were chosen by various methods. Twenty-four were county or city elected officials who automatically became members of the Metro Council. Most of the rest were also elected local officials who did not automatically become members upon election but were chosen by the bodies on which they sat. For example, in a number of cities the mayor and city council selected a representative to the Metro Council from their own number. The *Cunningham* court was willing to assume that those who did not become members of the council automatically on election to their local office could be considered "appointive" rather than "elective." Nevertheless, the court found that the council as a whole was an elective body, because a majority of its members were elective. Since the one-person, one-vote rule was not satisfied, the Metro Council structure was declared unconstitutional.

The *Cunningham* approach could lead to some odd results. In *Cunningham*, all the members of the Seattle city council were members of the Metro Council, and therefore were regarded as elective rather than appointive members. This fact was decisive, because if the Seattle delegation had been appointive, so would a majority of the Metro Council, so that the council would have been treated as appointive under the *Cunningham* approach. The legislature could have avoided the constitutional violation by reducing the Seattle delegation, thus requiring appointment of some percentage of the Seattle city council members, in which case a majority of the Metro Council would have been appointive. Suppose Seattle voters had been underrepresented on the council, despite the entire city council sitting as Metro Council members.[c] In that hypothetical situation, the *Cunningham* court's approach apparently would have permitted the legislature to remedy the problem by aggravating Seattle's underrepresentation!

Does *Cunningham* lend credence to Justice Harlan's concern, expressed in his *Avery* dissent, that application of the one-person, one-vote rule to local government would discourage the formation of metropolitan government entities like Metro? The *Cunningham* court stated, without citing evidentiary support, that "[t]here is

---

c. In the actual *Cunningham* case, Seattle was overrepresented.

no reason to believe that the vigorous governments and citizens of this region will fail to make Metro a continuing success if a change in the method of selecting its council is required to meet constitutional standards." *Id.* at 889.

3. In *Hadley v. Junior College District*, 397 U.S. 50 (1970), the Court imposed the one-person, one-vote doctrine on a consolidated junior college district. The Court said constitutional distinctions could not "be drawn on the basis of the purpose of the election.... While there are differences in the powers of different officials, the crucial consideration is the right of each qualified voter to participate on an equal footing in the election process." *Id.* at 54–55. The Court went on to say that if the purpose of the election were determinative courts would have to distinguish between various types of elections. The Court could not "readily perceive judicially manageable standards to aid in such a task." However, the Court also said:

> It is of course possible that there might be some case in which a State elects certain functionaries whose duties are so far removed from normal governmental activities and so disproportionately affect different groups that a popular election in compliance with *Reynolds*, ... might not be required.

Id. at 56. Is this last quotation from *Hadley* consistent with the earlier two?

Even if *Hadley*'s pronouncements might seem internally inconsistent, did "judicially manageable standards" for distinguishing elections that are subject to the one-person, one-vote requirement from those that are not emerge in the *Salyer Land* and *Ball* cases, reprinted below?

4. Does a local jurisdiction's use of instant runoff voting (IRV) violate the one-person, one-vote rule? No, according to multiple lower court decisions: for example, *Minnesota Voters Alliance v. City of Minneapolis*, 766 N.W.2d 683 (Minn. 2009), and *Dudum v. Arntz*, 640 F.3d 1098 (9th Cir. 2011).

Sometimes known as ranked-choice voting, IRV is an election method under which voters rank their choices for a particular office in order of preference. The counting process then operates as a series of runoff elections, narrowing the field until candidates reach a designated threshold of votes—usually a majority for single-seat elections. Minneapolis voters approved a referendum in 2006 that adopted IRV for city offices. The plaintiffs in *Minnesota Voters Alliance* challenged the city's IRV system, on the ground that it violated the one-person, one-vote rule. Their reasoning was that some voters would have their votes counted multiple times, because those whose first-choice candidate is eliminated would have their votes for a second- or third-choice candidate counted in subsequent rounds. The court rejected this argument, finding that there was no unequal weighting of votes. In *Dudum*, the Ninth Circuit similarly rejected a constitutional challenge to San Francisco's IRV system, finding that it did not impose a severe burden on anyone's right to vote. For a range of materials about IRV, arguing that it can thwart gerrymandering, produce competitive elections, and assure minority representation, see FairVote, http://www.fairvote.org.

II. Voting, Representation, and "Special-Purpose" Elections

Salyer Land Co. v. Tulare Lake Basin Water Storage District

410 U.S. 719 (1973)

Mr. Justice REHNQUIST delivered the opinion of the Court.

... We are here presented with the issue expressly reserved in *Avery*:

> Were the [county's governing body] a special-purpose unit of government assigned the performance of functions affecting definable groups of constituents more than other constituents, we would have to confront the question whether such a body may be apportioned in ways which give greater influence to the citizens most affected by the organization's functions.

The particular type of local government unit whose organization is challenged on constitutional grounds in this case is a water storage district, organized pursuant to the California Water Storage District Act....

Appellee district consists of 193,000 acres of intensively cultivated, highly fertile farm land located in the Tulare Lake Basin. Its population consists of 77 persons, including 18 children, most of whom are employees of one or another of the four corporations that farm 85% of the land in the district.

Such districts are authorized to plan projects and execute approved projects "for the acquisition, appropriation, diversion, storage, conservation, and distribution of water...." Incidental to this general power, districts may "acquire, improve, and operate" any necessary works for the storage and distribution of water as well as any drainage or reclamation works connected therewith, and the generation and distribution of hydroelectric power may be provided for. They may fix tolls and charges for the use of water and collect them from all persons receiving the benefit of the water or other services in proportion to the services rendered. The costs of the projects are assessed against district land in accordance with the benefits accruing to each tract held in separate ownership. And land that is not benefited may be withdrawn from the district on petition.

Governance of the districts is undertaken by a board of directors. Each director is elected from one of the divisions within the district, and each must take an official oath and execute a bond....

It is the voter qualification for such elections that appellants claim invidiously discriminates against them and persons similarly situated. Appellants are landowners, a landowner-lessee, and residents within the area included in the appellee's water storage district.... They allege that [the procedures for electing board members] unconstitutionally deny to them the equal protection of the laws guaranteed by the Fourteenth Amendment, in that only landowners are permitted to vote in water storage district general elections, and votes in those elections are apportioned according to the assessed valuation of the land. . . .

I

It is first argued that [California Water Code] § 41000, limiting the vote to district landowners, is unconstitutional since nonlandowning residents have as much interest in the operations of a district as landowners who may or may not be residents. Particularly, it is pointed out that the homes of residents may be damaged by floods within the district's boundaries, and that floods may, as with appellant Ellison, cause them to lose their jobs. Support for this position is said to come from the recent decisions of this Court striking down various state laws that limited voting to landowners, *Kolodziejski*, *Cipriano*, and *Kramer*. . . .

Cipriano and *Phoenix* involved application of the "one-person, one-vote" principle to residents of units of local governments exercising general governmental power, as that term was defined in *Avery*. *Kramer* and *Hadley* extended the "one-person, one-vote" principle to school districts exercising powers which,

> while not fully as broad as those of the Midland County Commissioners, certainly show that the trustees perform important governmental functions within the districts, and we think these powers are general enough and have sufficient impact throughout the district to justify the conclusion that the principle which we applied in *Avery* should also be applied here. [*Hadley*.]

But the Court was also careful to state that:

> It is of course possible that there might be some case in which a State elects certain functionaries whose duties are so far removed from normal governmental activities and so disproportionately affect different groups that a popular election in compliance with *Reynolds* might not be required, but certainly we see nothing in the present case that indicates that the activities of these trustees fit in that category. Education has traditionally been a vital governmental function and these trustees, whose election the State has opened to all qualified voters, are governmental officials in every relevant sense of that term.

We conclude that the appellee water storage district, by reason of its special limited purpose and of the disproportionate effect of its activities on landowners as a group, is the sort of exception to the rule laid down in *Reynolds* which the quoted language from *Hadley* and the decision in *Avery* contemplated.

The appellee district in this case, although vested with some typical governmental powers,[7] has relatively limited authority. Its primary purpose, indeed the reason for its existence, is to provide for the acquisition, storage, and distribution of water

7. The board has the power to employ and discharge persons on a regular staff and to contract for the construction of district projects. It can condemn private property for use in such projects

for farming in the Tulare Lake Basin. It provides no other general public services such as schools, housing, transportation, utilities, roads, or anything else of the type ordinarily financed by a municipal body. There are no towns, shops, hospitals, or other facilities designed to improve the quality of life within the district boundaries, and it does not have a fire department, police, buses, or trains.

Not only does the district not exercise what might be thought of as "normal governmental" authority, but its actions disproportionately affect landowners. All of the costs of district projects are assessed against land by assessors in proportion to the benefits received. Likewise, charges for services rendered are collectible from persons receiving their benefit in proportion to the services. When such persons are delinquent in payment, just as in the case of delinquency in payments of assessments, such charges become a lien on the land. In short, there is no way that the economic burdens of district operations can fall on residents *qua* residents, and the operations of the districts primarily affect the land within their boundaries.

Under these circumstances, it is quite understandable that the statutory framework for election of directors of the appellee focuses on the land benefited, rather than on people as such. California has not opened the franchise to all residents, as Missouri had in *Hadley*, nor to all residents with some exceptions, as New York had in *Kramer*. The franchise is extended to landowners, whether they reside in the district or out of it, and indeed whether or not they are natural persons who would be entitled to vote in a more traditional political election. Appellants do not challenge the enfranchisement of nonresident landowners or of corporate landowners for purposes of election of the directors of appellee. Thus, to sustain their contention that all residents of the district must be accorded a vote would not result merely in the striking down of an exclusion from what was otherwise a delineated class, but would instead engraft onto the statutory scheme a wholly new class of voters in addition to those enfranchised by the statute.

We hold, therefore, that the popular election requirements enunciated by *Reynolds* and succeeding cases are inapplicable to elections such as the general election of appellee Water Storage District.

II

Even though appellants derive no benefit from the *Reynolds* and *Kramer* lines of cases, they are, of course, entitled to have their equal protection claim assessed to determine whether the State's decision to deny the franchise to residents of the district while granting it to landowners was "wholly irrelevant to achievement of the regulation's objectives." No doubt residents within the district may be affected by its activities. But this argument proves too much. Since assessments imposed by the district become a cost of doing business for those who farm within it, and that cost must ultimately be passed along to the consumers of the produce, food shoppers in

---

and may cooperate (including contract) with other agencies, state and federal. Both general obligation bonds and interest-bearing warrants may be authorized.

far away metropolitan areas are to some extent likewise "affected" by the activities of the district. Constitutional adjudication cannot rest on any such "house that Jack built" foundation, however. The California Legislature could quite reasonably have concluded that the number of landowners and owners of sufficient amounts of acreage whose consent was necessary to organize the district would not have subjected their land to the lien of its possibly very substantial assessments unless they had a dominant voice in its control. Since the subjection of the owners' lands to such liens was the basis by which the district was to obtain financing, the proposed district had as a practical matter to attract landowner support. Nor, since assessments against landowners were to be the sole means by which the expenses of the district were to be paid, could it be said to be unfair or inequitable to repose the franchise in landowners but not residents. Landowners as a class were to bear the entire burden of the district's costs, and the State could rationally conclude that they, to the exclusion of residents, should be charged with responsibility for its operation. We conclude, therefore, that nothing in the Equal Protection Clause precluded California from limiting the voting for directors of appellee district by totally excluding those who merely reside within the district. . . .

IV

The last claim by appellants is that § 41001, which weights the vote according to assessed valuation of the land, is unconstitutional. They point to the fact that several of the smaller landowners have only one vote per person whereas the J. G. Boswell Company has 37,825 votes, and they place reliance on the various decisions of this Court holding that wealth has no relation to resident-voter qualifications and that equality of voting power may not be evaded. See, *e.g.*, *Gray*; *Harper.*

Appellants' argument ignores the realities of water storage district operation. Since its formation in 1926, appellee district has put into operation four multimillion-dollar projects. The last project involved the construction of two laterals from the Basin to the California State Aqueduct at a capital cost of about $2,500,000. Three small landowners having land aggregating somewhat under four acres with an assessed valuation of under $100 were given one vote each in the special election held for the approval of the project. The J. G. Boswell Company, which owns 61,665.54 acres with an assessed valuation of $3,782,220 was entitled to cast 37,825 votes in the election. By the same token, however, the assessment commissioners determined that the benefits of the project would be uniform as to all of the acres affected, and assessed the project equally as to all acreage. Each acre has to bear $13.26 of cost and the three small landowners, therefore, must pay a total of $46, whereas the company must pay $817,685 for its part.[10] Thus, as the District

10. [S]mall landowners are protected from crippling assessments resulting from district projects by the dual vote which must be taken in order to approve a project. Not only must a majority of the votes be cast for approval, but also a majority of the voters must approve. In this case, about 189 landowners constitute a majority and 189 of the smallest landowners in the district have only 2.34% of the land.

Court found, "the benefits and burdens to each landowner . . . are in proportion to the assessed value of the land." We cannot say that the California legislative decision to permit voting in the same proportion is not rationally based.

Accordingly, we . . . hold that the voter qualification statutes for California water storage district elections are rationally based, and therefore do not violate the Equal Protection Clause.

Mr. Justice DOUGLAS, with whom Mr. Justice BRENNAN and Mr. Justice MARSHALL concur, dissenting.

The vices of this case are fourfold.

First. Lessees of farmlands, though residents of the district, are not given the franchise.

Second. Residents who own no agricultural lands but live in the district and face all the perils of flood which the district is supposed to control are disfranchised.

Third. Only agricultural landowners are entitled to vote and their vote is weighted, one vote for each one hundred dollars of assessed valuation. . . .

Fourth. The corporate voter is put in the saddle.

There are 189 landowners who own up to 80 acres each. These 189 represent 2.34% of the agricultural acreage of the district. There are 193,000 acres in the district. Petitioner Salyer Land Co. is one large operator, West Lake Farms and South Lake Farms are also large operators. The largest is J. G. Boswell Co. These four farm almost 85% of all the land in the district. Of these, J. G. Boswell Co. commands the greatest number of votes, 37,825, which are enough to give it a majority of the board of directors. As a result, it is permanently in the saddle. Almost all of the 77 residents of the district are disfranchised. The hold of J. G. Boswell Co. is so strong that there has been no election since 1947, making little point of the provision in § 41300 of the California Water Code for an election every other year.

The result has been calamitous to some who, though landless, have even more to fear from floods than the ephemeral corporation.

I

. . . Assuming, *arguendo*, that a State may, in some circumstances, limit the franchise to that portion of the electorate "primarily affected" by the outcome of an election, *Kramer*, the limitation may only be upheld if it is demonstrated that "all those excluded are in fact substantially less interested or affected than those the [franchise] includes." *Ibid.* The majority concludes that "there is no way that the economic burdens of district operations can fall on residents *qua* residents, and the operations of the districts primarily affect the land within their boundaries."

But, with all respect, that is a great distortion. In these arid areas of our Nation a water district seeks water in time of drought and fights it in time of flood. One of the functions of water districts in California is to manage flood control. That is general

California statutory policy. It is expressly stated in the Water Code that governs water districts. The California Supreme Court ruled some years back that flood control and irrigation are different but complementary aspects of one problem.

From its inception in 1926, this district has had repeated flood control problems. Four rivers, Kings, Kern, Tule, and Kaweah, enter Tulare Lake Basin. South of Tulare Lake Basin is Buena Vista Lake. In the past, Buena Vista has been used to protect Tulare Lake Basin by storing Kern River water in the former. That is how Tulare Lake Basin was protected from menacing floods in 1952. But that was not done in the great 1969 flood, the result being that 88,000 of the 193,000 acres in respondent district were flooded. The board of the respondent district—dominated by the big landowner J. G. Boswell Co.—voted 6–4 to table the motion that would put into operation the machinery to divert the flood waters to the Buena Vista Lake. The reason is that J. G. Boswell Co. had a long-term agricultural lease in the Buena Vista Lake Basin and flooding it would have interfered with the planting, growing, and harvesting of crops the next season.

The result was that water in the Tulare Lake Basin rose to 192.5 USGS datum. Ellison, one of the appellants who lives in the district, is not an agricultural landowner. But his residence was 15 1/2 feet below the water level of the crest of the flood in 1969.

The appellee district has large levees; and if they are broken, damage to houses and loss of life are imminent.

Landowners—large or small, resident or nonresident, lessees or landlords, sharecroppers or owners—all should have a say. But irrigation, water storage, the building of levees, and flood control, implicate the entire community. All residents of the district must be granted the franchise.

This case, as I will discuss below, involves the performance of vital and important governmental functions by water districts clothed with much of the paraphernalia of government. The weighting of votes according to one's wealth is hostile to our system of government. As a nonlandowning bachelor was held to be entitled to vote on matters affecting education, *Kramer*, so all the prospective victims of mismanaged flood control projects should be entitled to vote in water district elections, whether they be resident nonlandowners, resident or nonresident lessees, and whether they own 10 acres or 10,000 acres. Moreover, their votes should be equal regardless of the value of their holdings, for when it comes to performance of governmental functions all enter the polls on an equal basis.

The majority, however, would distinguish the water storage district from "units of local government having general governmental powers over the entire geographic area served by the body," *Avery*, and fit this case within the exception contemplated for "a special-purpose unit of government assigned the performance of functions affecting definable groups of constituents more than other constituents." *Id.* The Avery test was significantly liberalized in *Hadley*. . . . We said,

> [S]ince the [junior college] trustees can levy and collect taxes, issue bonds with certain restrictions, hire and fire teachers, make contracts, collect fees, supervise and discipline students, pass on petitions to annex school districts, acquire property by condemnation, and in general manage the operations of the junior college, their powers are equivalent, for apportionment purposes, to those exercised by the county commissioners in *Avery*.... [T]hese powers, while not fully as broad as those of the Midland County Commissioners, certainly show that the trustees *perform important governmental functions* ... and have *sufficient impact throughout the district* to justify the conclusion that the principle which we applied in *Avery* should also be applied here. (Emphasis added.)

Measured by the *Hadley* test, the Tulare Lake Basin Water Storage District surely performs "important governmental functions" which "have sufficient impact throughout the district" to justify the application of the *Avery* principle.

Water storage districts in California are classified as irrigation, reclamation, or drainage districts. Such state agencies "are considered exclusively governmental," and their property is "held only for governmental purpose," not in the "proprietary sense." They are a "public entity," just as "any other political subdivision." That is made explicit in various ways. The Water Code of California states that "[a]ll waters and water rights" of the State "within the district are given, dedicated, and set apart for the uses and purposes of the district." Directors of the district are "public officers of the state." The district possesses the power of eminent domain. Its works may not be taxed. It carries a governmental immunity against suit. A district has powers that relate to irrigation, storage of water, drainage, flood control, and generation of hydroelectric energy.

Whatever may be the parameters of the exception alluded to in *Avery* and *Hadley*, I cannot conclude that this water storage district escapes the constitutional restraints relative to a franchise within a governmental unit.

II

When we decided *Reynolds* and discussed the problems of malapportionment we thought and talked about people—of population, of the constitutional right of "qualified citizens to vote," of "the right of suffrage," of the comparison of "one man's vote" to that of another man's vote....

It is indeed grotesque to think of corporations voting within the framework of political representation of people. Corporations were held to be "persons" for purposes both of the Due Process Clause of the Fourteenth Amendment and of the Equal Protection Clause. Yet, it is unthinkable in terms of the American tradition that corporations should be admitted to the franchise. Could a State allot voting rights to its corporations, weighting each vote according to the wealth of the corporation? Or could it follow the rule of one corporation, one vote?

It would be a radical and revolutionary step to take, as it would change our whole concept of the franchise. California takes part of that step here by allowing corporations to vote in these water district matters that entail performance of vital governmental functions. One corporation can outvote 77 individuals in this district. Four corporations can exercise these governmental powers as they choose, leaving every individual inhabitant with a weak, ineffective voice. The result is a corporate political kingdom undreamed of by those who wrote our Constitution.

Notes and Questions

1. The majority notes that voting by corporations and non-resident landowners was not challenged. Why do you think this was the case? Would appellants have strengthened or weakened their chances of winning if they had urged that only residents should be permitted to vote?

2. Is *Salyer* consistent with the Court's earlier decisions? Consider Richard Briffault, *Who Rules at Home? One Person/One Vote and Local Governments*, 60 University of Chicago Law Review 339, 361–62 (1993):

> The Court in *Salyer* was markedly more deferential to state determinations concerning local arrangements and much less protective of the interest of local residents in voting in local elections than it had been previously. The Court predicated the exception from the model of local democratic government on the "special limited purpose" of the water storage district and the "disproportionate effect of its activities on landowners." But neither "special limited purpose," nor "disproportionate effect" was adequately defined.
>
> From the perspective of residents dependent on the district's water, it is not obvious that water storage is a more limited function than a junior college. Indeed, comparing governmental functions is just the sort of standardless exercise that *Hadley* had warned against in refusing to hinge the standard of review on the "importance" of an office. Furthermore, although the California water storage district legislation established a fairly tight nexus linking receipt of water, assessment for water project costs, and the local vote, the Court did not explain how the water district arrangement differed from the service-payment-franchise relationship in *Kramer*. Much as nonparents and nontaxpayers may be affected by the operations of a local school board, water storage district residents as well as landowners may be affected by district actions.

3. Would it be unconstitutional if only owners of land in the district were eligible for election to the board? In Missouri, the state constitution provided for appointment of a board to recommend to the voters a plan of local government reorganization for the St. Louis area. Membership on this board was limited to landowners. In *Quinn v. Millsap*, 491 U.S. 95 (1989), the Court struck down this requirement as a denial of equal protection to non-landowners who were denied the right to serve. *Salyer Land* and *Ball v. James*, *infra*, were distinguished on the ground that the St. Louis government reorganization plan was not as directly connected to landownership as the water operations of the districts in *Salyer* and *Ball*.

Suppose that landownership within the Tulare Lake Basin Water Storage District were a qualification for service on the board of directors and that this qualification were challenged by Boswell on the ground that none of the persons it wished to "elect" to the board owned land in the district. What result?

4. In *Ball* v. *James*, 451 U.S. 355 (1981), the Court rejected a challenge to the one acre, one vote system used to elect the board of the Salt River Project Agricultural Improvement and Power District, which stored and delivered water to landowners in a large part of central Arizona. The district had begun as a private association of farmers in the late 19th century, though it had received federal assistance since 1903. In 1906, it began supporting its water operations by generating and selling hydroelectric power. It converted into a public district under Arizona law to obtain relief from financial difficulties during the Depression. By converting, the District's bonds became exempt from federal taxation. However, the conversion was not accomplished until the Arizona statutes were amended to permit the acreage-based voting system.

By the time of this lawsuit, the district included almost half Arizona's population and provided electric power to a large part of Phoenix and other cities. Furthermore, although the landowner-voters who received subsidized water were theoretically subject to assessments on their land to support the district, since 1951 no assessments had been needed because of the revenues from the sale of electricity. Excerpts from Justice Stewart's opinion for the Court follow:

> First, the District simply does not exercise the sort of governmental powers that invoke the strict demands of *Reynolds*. The District cannot impose ad valorem property taxes or sales taxes. It cannot enact any laws governing the conduct of citizens, nor does it administer such normal functions of government as the maintenance of streets, the operation of schools, or sanitation, health, or welfare services.
>
> Second . . . , the District's water functions, which constitute the primary and originating purpose of the District, are relatively narrow. The District and Association do not own, sell, or buy water, nor do they control the use of any water they have delivered. The District simply stores water behind its dams, conserves it from loss, and delivers it through project canals. . . . [A]ll water delivered by the Salt River District, like the water delivered by the Tulare Lake Basin Water Storage District, is distributed according to land ownership, and the District does not and cannot control the use to which the landowners who are entitled to the water choose to put it. As repeatedly recognized by the Arizona courts, though the state legislature has allowed water districts to become nominal public entities in order to obtain inexpensive bond financing, the districts remain essentially business enterprises, created by and chiefly benefiting a specific group of landowners. As in *Salyer*, the nominal public character of such an entity cannot transform it into the type of governmental body for which the Fourteenth Amendment demands a one-person, one-vote system of election.

Finally, neither the existence nor size of the District's power business affects the legality of its property-based voting scheme. [T]he provision of electricity is not a traditional element of governmental sovereignty, and so is not in itself the sort of general or important governmental function that would make the government provider subject to the doctrine of the *Reynolds* case. In any event, since the electric power functions were stipulated to be incidental to the water functions which are the District's primary purpose, they cannot change the character of that enterprise. The Arizona Legislature permitted the District to generate and sell electricity to subsidize the water operations which were the beneficiaries intended by the statute. A key part of the *Salyer* decision was that the voting scheme for a public entity like a water district may constitutionally reflect the narrow primary purpose for which the district is created. In this case, the parties have stipulated that the primary legislative purpose of the District is to store, conserve, and deliver water for use by District landowners, that the sole legislative reason for making water projects public entities was to enable them to raise revenue through interest-free bonds, and that the development and sale of electric power was undertaken not for the primary purpose of providing electricity to the public, but 'to support the primary irrigation functions by supplying power for reclamation uses and by providing revenues which could be applied to increase the amount and reduce the cost of water to Association subscribed lands.'

... [N]o matter how great the number of nonvoting residents buying electricity from the District, the relationship between them and the District's power operations is essentially that between consumers and a business enterprise from which they buy. Nothing in the *Avery*, *Hadley*, or *Salyer* cases suggests that the volume of business or the breadth of economic effect of a venture undertaken by a government entity as an incident of its narrow and primary governmental public function can, of its own weight, subject the entity to the one-person, one-vote requirements of the *Reynolds* case.

The functions of the Salt River District are therefore of the narrow, special sort which justifies a departure from the popular-election requirement of the *Reynolds* case. And as in *Salyer*, an aspect of that limited purpose is the disproportionate relationship the District's functions bear to the specific class of people whom the system makes eligible to vote. The voting landowners are the only residents of the District whose lands are subject to liens to secure District bonds. Only these landowners are subject to the acreage-based taxing power of the District, and voting landowners are the only residents who have ever committed capital to the District through stock assessments charged by the Association. The *Salyer* opinion did not say that the selected class of voters for a special public entity must be the only parties at all affected by the operations of the entity, or that their entire economic well-being must depend on that entity. Rather, the question was

> whether the effect of the entity's operations on them was disproportionately greater than the effect on those seeking the vote.
>
> As in the *Salyer* case, we conclude that the voting scheme for the District is constitutional because it bears a reasonable relationship to its statutory objectives. Here, according to the stipulation of the parties, the subscriptions of land which made the Association and then the District possible might well have never occurred had not the subscribing landowners been assured a special voice in the conduct of the District's business. Therefore, as in *Salyer*, the State could rationally limit the vote to landowners. Moreover, Arizona could rationally make the weight of their vote dependent upon the number of acres they own, since that number reasonably reflects the relative risks they incurred as landowners and the distribution of the benefits and the burdens of the District's water operations.

Id. at 366-71. Justice Powell, who joined in the majority opinion, wrote a separate concurrence emphasizing that the district's electoral system was controlled by the state legislature, which of course was elected on a one-person, one-vote basis. Justice White wrote a dissenting opinion, joined by Brennan, Marshall, and Blackmun.

(a) Is mosquito abatement a "normal" function of government or a "traditional element of government sovereignty"? Running a library? Operation of day care centers? How would you decide? Would the "normality" of such government activities be relevant to deciding whether single purpose districts to carry them out are subject to the one-person, one-vote rule? Should it be?

(b) Suppose the Salt River District began to operate a garbage disposal service, at a profit, to help finance its water distribution services. The majority lists sanitation services as a "normal" government function, but in many places this function has been handed over to private enterprise. Would the result in *Ball v. James* be affected?

Consider Briffault, *supra*, 60 University of Chicago Law Review at 374–75:

> [It is not] obvious why "sanitation, health, or welfare services" are more normal functions of government than the storage and distribution of water. There are more than 3,000 local governments specially created to address water management functions. How can a governmental activity so widespread not be a normal function of government? It may be that the existence of private providers of water undercuts the appreciation of the extent of public water storage and distribution activity, but surely the determination of whether a public service is a normal function of government cannot turn on the absence of private sector alternatives, lest the role of private security forces, private carting services, and private schools undermine the "governmentalness" of the traditional governmental functions concerning public safety, sanitation, and primary education.

(c) A big city school district sets up a local school council for each of the more than 500 schools in the district. The main functions served by each council are to select the principal for the school and approve a plan for spending money appropriated to the school by the citywide board of education. Each council consists of the principal, two teachers, six parents of children in the school and two residents of the area served by the school. The latter eight members are elected by the residents. Are these elections subject to the one-person, one-vote rule? Judge Posner gave the following reasons for answering this question in the negative in *Pittman v. Chicago Board of Education*, 64 F.3d 1098 (7th Cir. 1995), cert. denied 517 U.S. 1243 (1996):

> The line between a general-purpose governmental body and a special-purpose . . . one is wavering and indistinct. We are not even certain that it is the correct line. [Judge Posner concedes that the Chicago local school councils involved the same governmental function, education, as was involved in *Kramer* and *Hadley*.] But there is an important distinction between *Kramer* and *Hadley* on the one hand and our case on the other hand. The school board in *Kramer* and the board of trustees of the junior college district in *Hadley* had the power to tax. The local school councils in our case do not. Taxation without representation is abhorrent to Americans, but these local school councils have no power to tax directly and they also have no power to tax indirectly, for they do not have the power to raise revenues through the sale of bonds or to increase the total spending on the schools. [T]he writ of each [council] runs no farther than a single school. Basically they select a principal and determine school expenditures but within budgetary limits set by the board of education. They have less power than the board of trustees of a private school.
>
> We are mindful that in neither *Kramer* nor *Hadley* did the Supreme Court single out the power to tax as critical to the decision; and when it came to distinguish these cases in the later irrigation-district decisions the basis for distinction that the Court offered was that nowadays education unlike irrigation is regarded as a vital government function—a point that had been stressed in *Hadley* itself. But the point has to be considered in context. The boards involved in *Kramer* and *Hadley* were the governing bodies of the schools and colleges, respectively, in the districts. . . . The governing body of the public schools of Chicago is the Board of Education of the City of Chicago, not these local councils. Vital public education may be, but these councils, unlike the boards in *Kramer* and *Hadley*, do not control it. The interest of the public at large in the councils is therefore attenuated.

5. Another line of cases has been compared with the *Avery-Salyer-Ball* line. In *Carrington v. Rash*, 380 U.S. 89 (1965), the Court struck down a Texas prohibition on voting by members of the Armed Services whose Texas residence began after they had joined the military. Likewise, in *Evans v. Cornman*, 398 U.S. 419 (1970), the Court struck down Maryland's denial of the vote to persons who resided on the grounds of the National Institutes of Health, a federal enclave located within Maryland.

Conversely, in *Holt Civic Club v. City of Tuscaloosa*, 439 U.S. 60 (1978), discussed in Chapter 2, plaintiffs lived within the "police jurisdiction" of Tuscaloosa, Alabama, which consisted of the area outside but within three miles of the city limits. Under Alabama law, city criminal ordinances were applicable and the jurisdiction of the municipal courts extended to the police jurisdiction. In addition, businesses located within the police jurisdiction had to pay a license tax half the amount they would be required to pay if they were within the city. However, the city's powers of zoning, eminent domain, and ad valorem taxation did not extend to the police jurisdiction. The Supreme Court majority rejected plaintiffs' claim that they were denied equal protection because they were denied the vote in Tuscaloosa city elections.

Can these cases really be understood in terms of the *interests* of those excluded from voting? James A. Gardner, *Liberty, Community and the Constitutional Structure of Political Influence: A Reconsideration of the Right to Vote*, 145 University of Pennsylvania Law Review 893 (1997), argues that they are better understood in terms of membership in the political community. While acknowledging that much of the rhetoric in Supreme Court decisions concerns the ability to defend one's interests, Gardner contends that the results over a broad range of cases are more consistent with a right to vote grounded in full membership in the political community:

> Compared to the plaintiffs in *Holt*, the plaintiff in *Kramer* had a far less plausible claim that his inability to vote impaired in any significant way his ability to protect his rights and liberties from government infringement....
>
> What really bothered [Kramer], it seems, was the *fact* of his exclusion, not the *result* of it. "All members of the community," he flatly asserted, "have an interest in the quality and structure of public education." Nor was there any evidence that the plaintiff or any other excluded individuals had ever actually been harmed by a decision of a school board. Under the circumstances, the interest claimed by the plaintiff seems to arise less in virtue of any impact on actual individuals like him than in virtue of community membership itself; the interest, in other words, is definitional—it defines who is and who is not a member of the community....
>
> The contrast with *Holt* is instructive. Both Kramer and the Holt residents were represented only virtually on the pertinent municipal councils because they could not vote. Moreover, the school board had much less power to harm Kramer than Tuscaloosa had to harm the citizens of Holt. The Holt residents, however, by living in the suburbs, had voluntarily excluded themselves from the municipal political community and thus were confined to basing their voting-rights claim on the need to protect their interests from infringement by a government in which they were unrepresented.

Suppose you are counsel representing plaintiffs before the Supreme Court in a case challenging an alleged denial or infringement of the right to vote, in which you could plausibly argue either that your clients are being excluded symbolically from the political community or that their ability to use the vote to defend their political interests is being impaired. If Gardner is correct that the Court's language in voting cases tends to emphasize interest-protection but that it is exclusion from the political community that drives results, which theory would you emphasize the most in your briefs and in your oral argument?

6. Can the *Salyer-Ball* exception be used to limit the right to vote to a group defined by race? The Supreme Court answered that question in the negative in *Rice v. Cayetano*, 528 U.S. 495 (2000). In that case, a Hawaiian agency called the Office of Hawaiian Affairs (OHA) administered programs intended to benefit "native Hawaiians," defined as individuals at least half descended from the original Hawaiians who lived there prior to 1778 when Europeans first visited the islands, and "Hawaiians," defined as those who were at all descended from the original pre-1778 Hawaiians. The plaintiff did not challenge the limitation of the benefits of the programs to native Hawaiians and Hawaiians. Rather, he challenged a provision of the state constitution permitting only native Hawaiians and Hawaiians to vote for members of the OHA.

The Court held in a 7–2 decision that the restriction violated the Fifteenth Amendment. Justice Kennedy, writing for five members of the Court, rejected the state's contention that the voting restriction could be upheld under the *Salyer-Ball* exception because of the limited purposes of the OHA: "The question before us is not the one-person, one-vote requirement of the Fourteenth Amendment, but the race neutrality command of the Fifteenth Amendment. Our special purpose district cases have not suggested that compliance with the one-person, one-vote rule of the Fourteenth Amendment somehow excuses compliance with the Fifteenth Amendment. We reject that argument here." *Id.* at 522.

In response to the state's claim that the voting restriction was justified because the OHA members could be likened to fiduciaries of a trust and the eligible voters to beneficiaries, Justice Kennedy made these broader comments regarding the Fifteenth Amendment:

> There is no room under the Amendment for the concept that the right to vote in a particular election can be allocated based on race. Race cannot qualify some and disqualify others from full participation in our democracy. All citizens, regardless of race, have an interest in selecting officials who make policies on their behalf, even if those policies will affect some groups more than others. Under the Fifteenth Amendment voters are treated not as members of a distinct race but as members of the whole citizenry. Hawaii may not assume, based on race, that petitioner or any other of its citizens will not cast a principled vote. To accept the position advanced by the State would give rise to the same indignities, and the same resulting tensions and animosities, the Amendment was designed to eliminate.

Id. at 523-24. For commentary on the case, see Ellen D. Katz, *Race and the Right to Vote after* Rice v. Cayetano, 99 Michigan Law Review 491 (2000).

III. Districting Criteria

The one-person, one-vote cases established that state and local districts must be approximately equal in population, while congressional districts must be almost exactly equal in population. Consistent with this constraint, there remain an almost infinite number of ways in which district lines can be drawn, and the differences between them may have enormous political consequences.[d] In this section, we consider redistricting criteria that some have proposed as desirable.

To illustrate the dramatically different political consequences that different criteria can have, consider a simplified hypothetical jurisdiction with 300 residents, all voters, and with three legislative districts. 160 residents always vote Democratic, and 140 always vote Republican. Consider the makeup of the legislature under each of the following plans, each of which complies perfectly with the one-person, one-vote rule.

Plan 1:

	Democrats	Republicans
District 1	90	10
District 2	35	65
District 3	35	65

Plan 2:

	Democrats	Republicans
District 1	60	40
District 2	60	40
District 3	40	60

Under Plan 1 the Republicans will control the legislature, whereas under Plan 2 the Democrats will prevail. It is not obvious, even in principle, what is the most just or most democratic basis on which to draw district lines. For example, in our hypothetical case it might be assumed that Plan 2 is preferable because it assures that the Democrats, who are in the majority, will control the legislature. But suppose District 1 in Plan 1 (which votes 90–10 Democratic) consists of a predominantly African-American, low-income central city area, and Districts 2 and 3 in that plan consist of predominantly white, middle-class suburbs with a modest Republican majority distributed fairly evenly throughout the two districts. Plan 1 might then be preferred by some, since it assures effective representation to the central city residents, who comprise a substantial minority with distinctive political needs. It also creates districts containing "communities of interest," favored by some.

Perhaps a third possibility exists. District 1 of Plan 1 might be preserved to assure a district in which African-American voters can select a candidate of their choice,

d. For a thoughtful discussion of the political consequences of redistricting and the political environment within which redistricting plans are enacted, see Bruce E. Cain, The Reapportionment Puzzle (1984).

but the other two districts might be rearranged so that the Democrats, with a majority of the total vote, would be assured a majority of the seats.

Plan 3:

	Democrats	Republicans
District 1	90	10
District 2	10	90
District 3	60	40

Suppose that in order to create the outcome in Plan 3, it is necessary that Districts 2 and 3 consist of fantastic shapes that divide numerous suburban cities between the two districts. Which of the three plans do you think is best? Which is worst? Of course, any real-life redistricting situation involves a vastly more complicated set of choices between large numbers of political and interest group concerns.

Many states have constitutional provisions setting forth redistricting criteria. The prescribed criteria vary widely from state to state. They include: (1) compactness, (2) contiguity, (3) keeping communities of interest together, (4) adhering to county, municipal, ward, and precinct boundaries, (5) following census tracts, (6) nesting state house districts in state senate districts, (7) avoiding favoritism for incumbents, (8) avoiding favoritism for any party, (9) encouraging competition, and (10) allowing racial, ethnic, or language minorities to elect their candidates of choice. For a summary of the criteria used in the states, see Brennan Center for Justice, A 50 State Guide to Redistricting (2011), https://perma.cc/5QDW-SYSV. For a sampling of the extensive literature advocating various districting criteria, see Daniel D. Polsby and Robert D. Popper, *The Third Criterion: Compactness as a Procedural Safeguard Against Partisan Gerrymandering*, 9 Yale Law & Policy Review 301 (1991) (endorsing compactness); Nicholas O. Stephanopoulos, *Redistricting and the Territorial Community*, 160 University of Pennsylvania Law Review 1379 (2012) (endorsing respect for geographic communities of interest); Samuel Issacharoff, *Gerrymandering and Political Cartels*, 116 Harvard Law Review 593 (2002) (endorsing competitiveness).

It is common for states to specify multiple criteria that should be followed—and sometimes, ones that should be avoided—when drawing congressional or state legislative lines. An example is the State of Florida. In 2010, a majority of Florida voters adopted initiatives amending the state constitution to prescribe criteria for state legislative and congressional redistricting. Amendment 6 prescribes the following standards for congressional district boundaries:

> (a) No apportionment plan or individual district shall be drawn with the intent to favor or disfavor a political party or an incumbent; and districts shall not be drawn with the intent or result of denying or abridging the equal opportunity of racial or language minorities to participate in the political process or to diminish their ability to elect representatives of their choice; and districts shall consist of contiguous territory.

> (b) Unless compliance with the standards in this subsection conflicts with the standards in subsection (a) or with federal law, districts shall be as nearly equal in population as is practicable; districts shall be compact; and districts shall, where feasible, utilize existing political and geographical boundaries.
>
> (c) The order in which the standards within subsections (a) and (b) of this section are set forth shall not be read to establish any priority of one standard over the other within that subsection.

Fla. Const. art. III, § 20. Amendment 5 prescribes the same criteria for state legislative districts.

The amendment governing congressional districts was challenged on the ground that it violated Article I, Section 4 of the U.S. Constitution, which provides that "[t]he Times, Places and Manner of holding Elections for Senators and Representatives, shall be prescribed in each State *by the Legislature* thereof," while giving Congress the power to make or alter those regulations. The plaintiffs in *Brown v. Secretary of State of Florida*, 668 F.3d 1271 (11th Cir. 2012), argued that Article I, Section 4 vests authority for prescribing districting criteria in the state legislature, thus precluding such criteria from being adopted through other means, including a ballot initiative. The Eleventh Circuit disagreed, concluding that the phrase "by the legislature" refers to the entire lawmaking process, and not merely to the state legislature. *Id.* at 1276–77. In a later case arising from a different state, the U.S. Supreme Court agreed. *Arizona State Legislature v. Arizona Independent Redistricting Commission*, 576 U.S. 787 (2015) (discussed *infra*, Chapter 7, Part III.D).

The Florida Supreme Court subsequently considered challenges to the state legislative and congressional plans. *In re Senate Joint Resolution of Legislative Apportionment 1176*, 83 So. 3d 597 (Fla. 2012); *League of Women Voters v. Detzner*, 172 So. 3d 363 (Fla. 2015). The court concluded that the state house plan complied with the new constitutional amendment, but that the state senate plan and the congressional plan did not. Specifically, the court found that some state senate and congressional districts were not compact, failed to follow political and geographical boundaries, deviated too much from population equality, or were intended to benefit incumbents and a political party. Is this sort of aggressive judicial enforcement of redistricting criteria advisable?

Another well-known set of criteria was authoritatively adopted in California in 1973, after a lengthy struggle between a Democratic legislature and Republican Governor Ronald Reagan resulted in a failure to adopt a redistricting plan. The Special Masters' report in *Legislature* v. *Reinecke*, 516 P.2d 6 (1973), recommended that certain criteria be used, and the California Supreme Court adopted those districts with minor changes. Here are the Special Masters' recommended criteria:[e]

---

e. Following the 1990 census, California again had a Democratic legislature and a Republican governor (Pete Wilson), with the result, again, that the California Supreme Court had to design

1. As required by the federal Constitution, the districts in each plan should be numerically equal in population as nearly as practicable, with strict equality in the case of congressional districts and reasonable equality in the case of state legislative districts. The population of senate and assembly districts should be within 1% of the ideal except in unusual circumstances, and in no event should a deviation greater than 2% be permitted....

2. The territory included within a district should be contiguous and compact, taking into account the availability and facility of transportation and communication between the people in a proposed district, between the people and candidates in the district, and between the people and their elected representatives.

3. Counties and cities within a proposed district should be maintained intact, insofar as practicable.

4. The integrity of California's basic geographical regions (coastal, mountain, desert, central valley and intermediate valley regions) should be preserved insofar as practicable.

5. The social and economic interests common to the population of an area which are probable subjects of legislative action, generally termed a "community of interests" should be considered in determining whether the area should be included within or excluded from a proposed district in order that all of the citizens of the district might be represented reasonably, fairly and effectively. Examples of such interests, among others, are those common to an urban area, a rural area, an industrial area or an agricultural area, and those common to areas in which the people share similar living standards, use the same transportation facilities, have similar work opportunities, or have access to the same media of communication relevant to the election process....

6. State senatorial districts should be formed by combining adjacent assembly districts, and, to the degree practicable, assembly district boundaries should be used as congressional district boundaries....

7.... In counties for which the U.S. Census Bureau has established census tracts, such tracts should be used as the basic unit for district formation, with division of such tracts being made only when necessary for population equality or to improve substantially compliance with other recommended criteria.

---

redistricting plans. The court instructed its masters to use the same criteria that were described by the masters in 1973. See *Wilson v. Eu*, 823 P.2d 545 (1992). Similarly, when California voters passed initiatives establishing state legislative and congressional redistricting commissions in 2008 and 2010, respectively, the measures prescribed criteria very similar to those used in *Reinecke* and *Eu*. See Cal. Const. art. 21, § 2(d).

> Census tracts are the basic unit used by the Census Bureau for measuring the characteristics of the population. Tracts average approximately 4,000 persons in size, and an effort has been made by the Census Bureau to make them homogeneous as to social characteristics and to use prominent natural or manmade geographical features as boundaries. Thus, following, rather than disregarding, census tracts will aid in establishing natural, well defined legislative districts and will aid in obtaining valid pertinent socio-economic data about such districts.

Id. at 411–13 (internal citations omitted throughout).

Do you agree with the Special Masters' choice of criteria to guide a court that is forced to create a districting plan? Do you think any or all of these criteria should be constitutionally mandatory for legislatures that adopt districting plans? Whether or not they are required constitutionally, do you believe these criteria embody the public interest and that a legislature that fails to follow them may justly be criticized? Would you want to add additional criteria that were not considered by the Special Masters, such as partisan fairness, competitiveness, or minority representation?

Most of the criteria in the Special Masters' report are of the type known as "formal" criteria. These are criteria that look to the characteristics of individual districts, such as their shapes (compactness and contiguity) and the areas and populations that they enclose (conformity to political subdivisions and communities of interest). Of the formal criteria, the one most often pointed to, especially in popular debate, is *compactness*. For most people, the surest sign of a gerrymander is an oddly-shaped district. However, it is not easy to articulate persuasive reasons why a compact district is superior to a noncompact district. Skepticism of compactness as a criterion is cogently expressed in *Shaw v. Hunt*, 861 F. Supp. 408, 472 n.60 (E.D.N.C. 1994):

> [Districts'] perceived "ugliness" — their extreme irregularity of shape — is entirely a function of an artificial perspective unrelated to the common goings and comings of the citizen-voter. From the mapmaker's wholly imaginary vertical perspective at 1:25,000 or so range, a citizen may well find his district's one-dimensional, featureless shape aesthetically "bizarre," "grotesque," or "ugly." But back down at ground or eye-level, viewing things from his normal closely-bounded horizontal perspective, the irregularity of outline or exact volume of the district in which he resides is not a matter of any great practical consequence to his conduct as citizen-voter. In the earth-bound, horizontal workaday world of his political and other lives, it surely never occurs to him — until aroused to dislike something else about his district or his representative — that the lines that include him with others in a particular electoral district wander irregularly rather than evenly to enclose them. What happens is that after every re-drawing of the lines of any of the various overlapping electoral districts in which he resides, he learns quickly enough (if interested enough), either by official notice or unofficially, that

> he is now in the same or a new district that is identified by a number. He has no idea where exactly on the earth's surface the lines of the district—mostly invisible from this live perspective—run throughout their course. Nor does he need to know in order to conduct his political affairs effectively as a citizen of the district. In due course he learns that candidates A and B are contending for his vote, learns what he wants to about them, re-learns where his present voting location is, casts his vote, and thereafter has whatever contact he wants with his representative, completely unaffected either by where exactly his district boundaries lie, his lack of exact knowledge of their location, or by any "ugliness" that may from the mapmaker's perspective result from their irregular shape.

See also *Parrott v. Lamone*, 2016 WL 4445319 (D. Md. Aug. 24, 2016), appeal dismissed, 2017 WL 69143 (U.S. Jan. 9, 2017) (rejecting a partisan gerrymandering challenge to certain Maryland congressional districts based on their extreme noncompactness); Stephen Ansolabehere & Nathaniel Persily, *Testing* Shaw v. Reno*: Do Majority-Minority Districts Cause Expressive Harms?*, 90 New York University Law Review. 1041 (2015) (finding that voters' racial attitudes do not vary between compact and noncompact majority-minority districts).

One response from defenders of the criterion is that compactness should be required, not because a compact district is necessarily inherently superior, but because compactness is a relatively objective criterion whose requirement, like that of equal population, will restrict the ability of line-drawers to gerrymander. For a forceful statement of this viewpoint, see Polsby and Popper, *supra*. For a generalization of the argument to all formal criteria, see Jonathan Winburn, The Realities of Redistricting: Following the Rules and Limiting Gerrymandering in State Legislative Redistricting (2008) (finding that gerrymandering is reduced in states where formal criteria are enforced more stringently). However, compactness as an inherently desirable attribute has had some defenders. Consider, for example, the following statement from *Prosser v. Elections Board*, 793 F. Supp. 859, 863 (W.D. Wis. 1992) (three-judge court, per curiam):

> The objections to bizarre-looking reapportionment maps are not aesthetic (except for those who prefer Mondrian to Pollock). They are based on a recognition that representative democracy cannot be achieved merely by assuring population equality across districts. To be an effective representative, a legislator must represent a district that has a reasonable homogeneity of needs and interests; otherwise the policies he supports will not represent the preferences of most of his constituents. There is some although of course not a complete correlation between geographical propinquity and community of interests, and therefore compactness and contiguity are desirable features in a redistricting plan. Compactness and contiguity also reduce travel time and costs, and therefore make it easier for candidates for the legislature to campaign for office and once elected to maintain close and continuing contact with the people they represent. Viewing legislators as agents

> and the electorate as their principal, we can see that compactness and contiguity reduce the "agency costs" of representative democracy. But only up to a point, for the achievement of perfect contiguity and compactness would imply ruthless disregard for other elements of homogeneity; would require breaking up counties, towns, villages, wards, even neighborhoods. If compactness and contiguity are proxies for homogeneity of political interests, so is making district boundaries follow (so far as possible) rather than cross the boundaries of the other political subdivisions in the state.

Prosser differed from *Hunt* in that in *Prosser*, the legislature had failed to adopt a districting plan and it was necessary for the court to design one. In *Hunt* (which, by the way, was reversed by the Supreme Court in 1996, as described in Chapter 5), the court was considering a challenge to a legislatively enacted plan. Could this difference help explain the greater regard for compactness expressed in *Prosser*?

Another formal criterion that is usually much less controversial than compactness is *contiguity*. Although some state constitutions call for compact districts, more call for contiguity, which is ordinarily understood to be a requirement whether or not it is specified. "Contiguous" is usually understood to mean, in the words of one dictionary definition, "touching or connected throughout in an unbroken sequence." Questions about contiguity, so understood, typically arise when those drawing a plan choose or are required to cross a body of water. Crossing water is required in the case of an island. It will be accepted without question in many situations, such as crossing a river, which may be necessary, for example, to avoid dividing a city. But what about a district that crosses a bay or lake without including the land in between? For example, would a district be contiguous if it included parts of San Francisco and Oakland but excluded the land around the northern and southern ends of San Francisco Bay?

A different conception of contiguity was suggested in *Wilkins v. West*, 571 S.E.2d 100 (Va. 2002). The lower court had invalidated a plan, not simply because the district crossed water, but because there was no publicly available transportation between the parts of the district without going through another district. The Supreme Court of Virginia reversed, explaining its position as follows:

> While ease of travel within a district is a factor to consider when resolving issues of compactness and contiguity, resting the constitutional test of contiguity solely on physical access within the district imposes an artificial requirement which reflects neither the actual need of the residents of the district nor the panoply of factors which must be considered by the General Assembly in the design of a district. Short of an intervening land mass totally severing two sections of an electoral district, there is no *per se* test for the constitutional requirement of contiguity. Each district must be examined separately.

Id. at 109. How would you advise the legislative leadership of Virginia regarding the requirement of contiguity in the state constitution?

Many reformers have favored a different kind of criteria, sometimes referred to as "result-oriented," instead of or in addition to formal criteria. Result-oriented criteria take into account the expected political consequences of the districts. Examples are that the districts should encourage partisan competition, that they should avoid favoritism for incumbents or any party, and that they should yield proportional results. Arizona, Colorado, and Washington are among the few states that currently endorse competitiveness. For a study finding that Arizona's provision has not actually yielded closer elections, despite protracted litigation on precisely this issue, see Barbara Norrander and Jay Wendland, *Redistricting in Arizona, in* Reapportionment and Redistricting in the West 177 (Gary F. Moncrief, ed., 2011). Partisan fairness criteria have been adopted by a number of jurisdictions. For a study finding that they too have enjoyed only limited success, see Nicholas O. Stephanopoulos, *The Consequences of Consequentialist Criteria*, 3 U.C. Irvine Law Review 669 (2013). Why might these requirements have been largely ineffective to date? How might they be made more potent?

When a districting plan is adopted legislatively, state courts sometimes apply state criteria in a permissive manner. For example, in *Kilbury v. Franklin County Board of Commissioners*, 90 P.3d 1071 (Wash. 2004) (en banc), the court applied a state requirement that districts be "as compact as possible" by asking whether the plan was adopted arbitrarily or capriciously. In Idaho, similarly, a plan adopted by a redistricting commission was attacked for a district unnecessarily made up of portions of two counties. The state constitution required that districts not be so formed if "ideal district size may be achieved by internal division of the county." The Idaho Supreme Court upheld the plan, saying "[w]e simply cannot micromanage all the difficult steps the Commission must take in performing the high-wire act that is legislative district drawing. Rather, we must constrain our focus to determining whether the split was done to effectuate an improper purpose or whether it dilutes the right to vote." *Bonneville County v. Ysursa*, 129 P.3d 1213 (Idaho 2005). In *Ysursa*, the only way to have avoided the split in question may well have been to split one or more other districts among counties. But if the commission split a district in a manner that was not dilutive and not improperly motivated but that nevertheless was not needed to attain equal population, what justification would there be under the Idaho constitution to uphold the split?

A similar question can be posed regarding a provision in the Rhode Island constitution requiring that districts be "as compact in territory as possible." In *Parella v. Montalbano*, 899 A.2d 1226 (R.I. 2006), the Rhode Island Supreme Court upheld a plan against a compactness challenge, reaffirming an earlier statement that the state constitution is "clearly intended to leave the [L]egislature with a wide discretion as to the territorial structuring of the electoral districts." Is that a correct reading of the compactness clause? It is perhaps worth noting that the legislature was undoubtedly under political stress when it adopted the plan in question, as it was the first redistricting following a constitutional amendment cutting the membership of the legislature by a fourth.

Not all courts have been so deferential. As noted above, the Florida Supreme Court rejected state senate and congressional plans adopted after a 2010 constitutional amendment prescribing new districting criteria. In so doing, the court rebuffed the state legislature's argument that those challenging the plan should be required to prove their case beyond a reasonable doubt. The Pennsylvania Supreme Court also struck down a plan drawn in 2011, although that plan was drawn by a commission rather than the legislature. *Holt v. 2011 Legislative Reapportionment Commission*, 38 A.3d 711 (Pa. 2012) (per curiam). Pennsylvania's reapportionment commission consisted of two commissioners chosen by each major party's legislative leadership and a fifth member selected by the Pennsylvania Supreme Court. Article 2, Section 16 of the Pennsylvania Constitution requires that districts "be composed of compact and contiguous territory" and prohibits counties and municipalities from being divided unless "absolutely necessary." The court found that the commission's plan split far more counties and municipalities than available alternatives, and also expressed "concerns" about compactness. It remanded for the commission to draw new state legislative districts. More generally, Professor Stephanopoulos summarizes the extensive litigation that has unfolded under provisions requiring districts to adhere where possible to communities of interest:

> [C]ourts in ten states (Alaska, Arizona, Colorado, Idaho, Kansas, Montana, North Carolina, Oregon, Rhode Island, and Vermont) have invalidated districts that did not correspond to geographic communities and upheld districts that did. These decisions . . . all were handed down between 1974 and 2006, with their frequency increasing in recent years. In Alaska, Arizona, Colorado, North Carolina, and Rhode Island, the decisions were based on state constitutional requirements that districts and communities coincide, while the Idaho, Kansas, Montana, Oregon, and Vermont cases relied on analogous statutory and guideline provisions. In sum, courts have assessed more than fifty districts based on their adherence to community boundaries, of which a solid majority have been upheld.

Stephanopoulos, *Redistricting and the Territorial Community*, *supra*, 160 University of Pennsylvania Law Review at 1426-27. For detailed data on court action on district plans in the 2000, 2010, and 2020 cycles, see *National Summary*, All About Redistricting, https://perma.cc/ZRB7-VP2P.

The Supreme Court has instructed lower federal courts to defer to state political determinations on redistricting, including districting criteria, so long as these are consistent with federal constitutional and statutory requirements. Should federal courts also defer to state *judicial* determinations? Yes, according to the Supreme Court. In *Scott v. Germano*, 381 U.S. 407 (1965), the Supreme Court stated that federal courts should defer to state courts when parallel redistricting cases were pending in both. In the years that followed, this instruction may often have been overlooked or honored in the breach. However, *Germano* was strongly reaffirmed by a unanimous Court in *Growe v. Emison*, 507 U.S. 25, 32–37 (1993). The Court characterized as "mistaken" the lower federal court's view that it need only defer to the state legislature, and not the state judiciary. Absent evidence that the state — including its judicial branch — would fail to perform its duty of drawing district lines each decade, "a federal court must neither affirmatively obstruct state reapportionment nor permit federal litigation to be used to impede it."

Especially when the legislative process has broken down, a court has considerable discretion to shape a redistricting plan as it sees fit. Many litigants in redistricting controversies believe that the exercise of this discretion tends to be influenced by foreseeable partisan or other political predilections on the part of judges. Does *Growe* encourage recourse to the state judiciary by litigants who believe they have a sympathetic majority on the state supreme court? If so, is this a good thing? Keep in mind that many state supreme court judges run as nominees of their party, as discussed in Chapter 10, Part III, *infra*. For a detailed discussion of the law and practice of judicially designed plans, see Nathaniel Persily, *When Judges Carve Democracies: A Primer on Court-Drawn Redistricting Plans*, 73 George Washington Law Review 1131 (2005).

Chapter 4

Partisan Gerrymandering and Political Competition

Concern in the United States over parties' use or abuse of redistricting for their own purposes is almost as old as the parties themselves. The chief concern is that those in power will draw districts to serve their own interests, thereby entrenching the party in power or incumbents generally. Part I of this chapter examines partisan gerrymandering as a conceptual phenomenon. Part II considers efforts—mostly unsuccessful—to enlist the aid of the federal courts to combat gerrymanders. Part III addresses the debate over whether courts should intervene to stop putatively anticompetitive election practices, including certain kinds of gerrymandering.

I. Defining and Identifying Gerrymanders

Gerrymandering has received various definitions, which tend to fall into one of three categories. The first type of definition refers to plans drafted with an improper intent. The second denotes plans that have unfair effects. And the third emphasizes the noncompliance of districts with traditional districting criteria such as compactness. Consider the following:

> Those who favor judicial policing of gerrymandering are fond of quoting Chief Justice Warren's statement in *Reynolds v. Sims*, that "fair and effective representation for all citizens is concededly the basic aim of legislative apportionment." For such writers the "gerrymander" is the antithesis of "fair and effective representation," and their definitions of "gerrymander" tend to be just as broad and vague as Chief Justice Warren's phrase with which they are so enamored. Thus, they define "gerrymandering" as "dilut[ing] the voting strength" of groups of voters, as "excessive manipulation" of the shapes of districts, as creation of an "unjustifiable advantage" for one party over others, as "discriminat[ion] against" one group compared to others, or in more down-to-earth language, as "the dishing of one political party by another."
>
> Now, it is hard to defend dilution of voting strength, manipulation (especially *excessive* manipulation), unjustifiable advantages, discrimination, and dishing of political parties. On the other hand, voting strength cannot be characterized as diluted unless it can be compared to a level of strength

> that is agreed to be normal; the drawing of lines cannot be characterized as manipulative (in a pejorative sense) unless there is a method of drawing lines that is agreed to be nonmanipulative; an advantage cannot be characterized as unjustifiable unless there is an agreed-upon standard of justification and, equally importantly, a state of affairs cannot be characterized as an "advantage" unless there is an agreed-upon state of affairs regarded as neutral; a state of affairs agreed to be nondiscriminatory is necessary before we can say a group is discriminated against; and one person's dishing may be another's self-defense.
>
> In short, definitions of "gerrymandering" of the sort just canvassed raise questions but do not answer them. The questions are: What, if anything, constitutes a "neutral" districting plan, and how can we recognize a neutral plan when we see one? To find concrete meanings for the various writers' conceptions of gerrymandering we must consider the specific criteria they have proposed for legislative districting. If those criteria cannot be demonstrated to be neutral and cannot be employed to distinguish neutral from nonneutral plans, they have no legitimate claim to the public interest label and they should not serve in court or elsewhere to identify gerrymanders.

Daniel H. Lowenstein & Jonathan Steinberg, *The Quest for Legislative Districting in the Public Interest: Elusive or Illusory?* 33 UCLA Law Review 1, 9–11 (1985).

Now consider the following rejoinder:

> The fundamental premise on which Lowenstein and Steinberg build is that something cannot be constitutionally unfair, unequal, and wrong unless there is a standard or measure of what is fair, equal, and right. They believe, therefore, that once they have shown that there is no single, objective, neutral set of electoral district boundaries for a given state with a given geography and demography, they will have shown that courts should not concern themselves with the constitutionality of district boundaries.
>
> The fundamental premise is not, however, jurisprudentially sound nor does it reflect the actual, historical behavior of the Supreme Court....
>
> [J]udges, and indeed all those called upon to make ethical decisions, are often in a position to identify *a* wrong without being able to define *the* right. Finding themselves in this position, they are ethically entitled to, and in fact do, intervene against the wrong....
>
> Since the very beginnings of American constitutional law, the Supreme Court has made this stance a central feature of major areas of its constitutional jurisprudence.

Martin Shapiro, *Gerrymandering, Unfairness, and the Supreme Court*, 33 UCLA Law Review 227, 227–28 (1985).

Notes and Questions

1. *Proportionality and Symmetry.* The United States inherited from Britain the so-called Westminster system of elections, in which legislators are elected, usually one apiece, from geographically defined districts, with the candidate receiving the most votes declared the winner. This system may have been inevitable in the Colonial and Revolutionary periods, when neither full-fledged political parties nor modern devices of transportation and communication existed. Since a separate winner-take-all election occurs in each district, when the elections are run along party lines there is no assurance that the statewide vote for a given party will be proportionate to the number of legislative seats it wins. For example, a minority party that is outvoted by a small margin in a large number of districts might win 45% of the vote and only win 30% of the seats. Very few democratic countries in the world other than those inheriting their political institutions from Great Britain use the Westminster system. To varying degrees, most systems used in other countries are more likely than the Westminster system to yield proportional results. For commentary on a variety of systems, see Choosing an Electoral System: Issues and Alternatives (Arend Lijphart & Bernard Grofman, eds., 1984).

Just as the one person, one vote rule provided a relatively simple and far-reaching solution to the complex difficulties that seemed to be created by *Baker v. Carr*'s decision that malapportionment questions are justiciable, some have urged that the constitutional solution to the gerrymandering problem should be a requirement of *proportionality*. See Ronald Rogowski, *Representation in Political Theory and in Law*, 91 Ethics 395 (1981); John R. Low-Beer, Comment, *The Constitutional Imperative of Proportional Representation*, 94 Yale Law Journal 163 (1984). Others have seen the prospect that there is no stopping point short of proportional representation as a good reason for the courts to avoid the question of gerrymandering. See Shapiro, *supra*, 33 UCLA Law Review at 252–56; Peter H. Schuck, *The Thickest Thicket: Partisan Gerrymandering and Judicial Regulation of Politics*, 87 Columbia Law Review 1325 (1987). The question of proportional representation is placed in a theoretical and historical framework in Sanford Levinson, *Gerrymandering and the Brooding Omnipresence of Proportional Representation: Why Won't It Go Away?* 33 UCLA Law Review 257 (1985).

Most reformers, recognizing that it is difficult to assure proportional results so long as the Westminster system is in use, have sought anti-gerrymandering criteria that do not require proportionality. One such proposal is that *partisan symmetry* be required rather than proportionality. Symmetry may be satisfied even if one party receives a disproportionately large number of seats, so long as any other party receiving the same percentage of the vote would have received the same disproportionately large number of seats. For example, if Republicans win 60% of the seats with only 52% of the statewide vote, the results would be symmetrical so long as the Democrats would also be likely to win 60% of the seats if they won 52% of the votes. See, *e.g.*, Andrew Gelman & Gary King, *Enhancing Democracy Through Legislative Redistricting*, 88

American Political Science Review 541 (1994); Anthony J. McGann et al., Gerrymandering in America: The House of Representatives, the Supreme Court, and the Future of Popular Sovereignty (2016). For criticism of symmetry as a criterion, see Lowenstein & Steinberg, *supra*, 33 UCLA Law Review at 55–60. And for a claim by two prominent political scientists that advanced statistical methods can solve some of symmetry's problems, see Bernard Grofman and Gary King, *The Future of Partisan Symmetry as a Judicial Test for Partisan Gerrymandering after* LULAC v. Perry, 6 Election Law Journal 2 (2007). As we shall see in the next section, the Supreme Court has not accepted proportionality, symmetry, or for that matter, any other test as the standard for partisan gerrymandering claims under the U.S. Constitution.

The most significant flaw of the traditional measure of symmetry, known as *partisan bias*, is that it requires consideration of a hypothetical election in which the parties' statewide vote shares flipped. This counterfactual election is quite implausible when states are uncompetitive, and it necessitates strong assumptions such as a uniform swing across all districts. In recent years, scholars such as Eric McGhee and Nicholas Stephanopoulos have popularized a new symmetry measure called the *efficiency gap* that seeks to remedy the shortcomings of partisan bias. See Eric McGhee, *Measuring Partisan Bias in Single-Member District Electoral Systems*, 99 Legislative Studies Quarterly 55 (2014); Nicholas O. Stephanopoulos & Eric M. McGhee, *Partisan Gerrymandering and the Efficiency Gap*, 82 University of Chicago Law Review 831 (2015). The efficiency gap is based on the fact that all partisan gerrymandering takes place either by *cracking* the opposing party's voters among a large number of districts in which their preferred candidates lose by relatively narrow margins, or by *packing* these voters in a few districts in which their preferred candidates win overwhelming majorities. Both cracking and packing produce *wasted votes* that fail to contribute to a candidate's victory: all votes cast for a losing candidate in the case of cracking, and all votes above the 50%-plus-one threshold needed for victory in the case of packing. The efficiency gap is simply one party's wasted votes in an election, minus the other party's wasted votes, divided by the total number of votes cast.

Stephanopoulos and McGhee show that the efficiency gap is much more reliable than partisan bias in uncompetitive states, and that the metrics converge in competitive states. They also calculate the efficiency gap for congressional and state legislative elections over a forty-year period. They find that both of these distributions are approximately normal and centered on zero, indicating that neither party has enjoyed a systematic advantage in the modern redistricting era. They further find that while the *direction* of the efficiency gap has shifted in a Republican direction since the 1990s, its *magnitude* remained roughly constant until the 2010 cycle—when it surged to the highest level in modern history. Stephanopoulos and McGhee argue as well that the efficiency gap could be incorporated into a judicial test for partisan gerrymandering. As discussed in Part II, *infra*, several lower courts were receptive to this proposal, but the Supreme Court ultimately rejected it.

Since it was introduced, the efficiency gap has been the subject of significant academic commentary. For criticisms, see Benjamin Plener Cover, *Quantifying*

Partisan Gerrymandering: An Evaluation of the Efficiency Gap Proposal, 70 Stanford Law Review 1131 (2018) (arguing that the efficiency gap is in tension with democratic values like competition, participation, and proportional representation), and Jonathan S. Krasno et al., *Can Gerrymanders Be Detected? An Examination of Wisconsin's State Assembly*, 47 American Politics Research 1162 (2019) (alleging that the efficiency gap is overly volatile). For responses to these and other points, see Nicholas O. Stephanopoulos and Eric M. McGhee, *The Measure of a Metric: The Debate over Quantifying Partisan Gerrymandering*, 70 Stanford Law Review 1503 (2018).

2. *The Seats/Votes Ratio.* A party's "seats/votes" ratio is often used in discussions of districting, whether to test a plan against criteria such as proportionality or symmetry, or simply to see how well a party seems to be treated by a particular districting plan. Indeed, the ratio is commonly used as a rhetorical device in political debate, as a plan is shown to be a partisan gerrymander because a given party received only *x* percent of the seats when it received *x* plus *y* percent of the votes. The seats/votes ratio is certainly relevant to the evaluation of a districting plan, but it must be examined with caution, for a number of reasons. One is that American legislative elections are only partly conducted on a party basis. American voters are sometimes inclined to vote for the candidates they prefer, regardless of party. Thus, normally Republican voters might vote for Democratic state legislators because of the personalities and issues at stake between the candidates in particular districts. Mechanical application of a seats/votes ratio would imply that those voters wanted a Democratically controlled state legislature, which might not reflect their intent at all.

A second reason for caution in interpreting a seats/votes ratio is more technical. In *Reynolds v. Sims*, the Court spoke interchangeably about equal numbers of *people* in districts and equal numbers of *voters*. As we saw in Chapter 3, the Court prefers, and almost all jurisdictions use, population rather than number of voters. Although it might seem at first that there would be little difference between the two, in fact they can vary enormously. Some areas have much higher percentages of people not eligible to vote, especially because they are too young or are not citizens. Furthermore, as we shall see in Chapter 6, Part III, people of lower socioeconomic status are less likely to register and vote than those who are wealthier and, especially, better educated. By and large, lower income areas with a large immigrant population and with large families — the areas likely to have the lowest ratio of voters to population — are likely to be the most Democratic areas, while wealthier areas with few immigrants are more likely to be Republican.

A seats/votes ratio that does not take these circumstances into account may be misleading. For example, suppose a state is divided into three equally populated congressional districts, one with 200,000 voters, all of whom vote for the Republican candidate, and two with 100,000 voters, in each of which the Democratic candidate receives all of the votes. A naive seats/votes approach would find that the Republicans received only a third of the seats despite winning half of the votes. But the disparity results from the population-based districting rule, not from gerrymandering.

This distortion can easily be avoided, though the necessary adjustment is rarely made when seats/votes ratios are deployed in public discussion of redistricting. The usual method of computing a party's vote percentage is simply to add up the votes for the party's candidates in all the districts, and divide that total by the statewide total of votes cast for the major party candidates. The adjusted method is to calculate the party's vote percentage *within* each district, and then take the average of the party's district percentages. In the above example, Republicans received a third of the adjusted total (the average of 100%, 0%, and 0%), exactly the same as their percentage of the seats. See generally Graham Gudgin & P.J. Taylor, Seats, Votes, and the Spatial Organization of Elections 56–57 (1979).

3. *Compactness and Spatial Diversity.* As discussed *supra*, in Chapter 3, Part III, some commentators have argued that requiring compact districts would limit partisan gerrymanders. See, *e.g.*, Daniel D. Polsby & Robert D. Popper, *The Third Criterion: Compactness as a Procedural Safeguard Against Partisan Gerrymandering*, 9 Yale Law & Policy Review 301 (1991). A different approach is suggested in Nicholas O. Stephanopoulos, *Spatial Diversity,* 125 Harvard Law Review 1903 (2012). Stephanopoulos defines "spatial diversity" (or spatial heterogeneity) as the "variation of a given factor over geographic space." He uses the following example to illustrate the concept:

> Consider an electoral district that is fifty percent white and fifty percent black (and that is located in a region with an identical racial makeup). This district typically would be deemed highly diverse, in terms of race, since it contains large (and proportionate) shares of both white and black voters. But this same district could be very spatially diverse or very spatially non-diverse depending on its geographic composition. The district would be highly spatially heterogeneous if most white voters lived in one area and most black voters lived in another. On the other hand, the district would be highly spatially homogeneous if both white and black voters were dispersed evenly throughout its territory.

Id. at 1906. Stephanopoulos then uses Census data to quantify the spatial diversity of U.S. House districts, with respect to variables including race, ethnicity, age, income, education, profession, marital status, and housing. Highly spatially diverse districts typically combine disparate geographic groups; conversely, highly spatially uniform districts usually coincide with a single geographic community. Stephanopoulos further examines how spatial diversity is related to district plans' partisan bias and responsiveness to shifts in the electorate's preferences. In general, plans whose districts are more spatially diverse tend to exhibit higher levels of bias and to be less responsive to changing voter preferences. More spatially homogeneous districts therefore seem to be desirable — due to both their greater congruence with underlying communities and the superior electoral performance they produce.

4. *Commissions and Other Procedural Reforms.* In Chapter 3, we discussed the various criteria that might be taken into consideration in drawing districts. One way of trying to curb partisan gerrymanders is to require that legislative bodies

consider prescribed criteria, as Florida voters did in 2010, adopting a state constitutional amendment requiring compactness, contiguity, adherence to geographic boundaries, and protection of racial and ethnic minorities, while prohibiting districts "drawn with the intent to favor or disfavor a political party or an incumbent." See Fla. Const. art. III, § 20.

Another possibility, favored by some supporters of reform, is to modify the procedures by which redistricting is done instead of or in addition to imposing substantive criteria. See Bruce E. Cain, *Redistricting Commissions: A Better Political Buffer?*, 121 Yale Law Journal 1808 (2012). Some reform procedures are internal to state legislatures, such as requirements for public hearings, the provision of adequate staff and data to the minority party, or supermajority thresholds for passing districting bills. The latter proposal would tend to give each of the major parties an effective veto in states with closely divided legislatures, thus potentially thwarting *partisan* but promoting *bipartisan* gerrymandering.

Alternatively, the districting power may be taken away from the legislature, usually in favor of a commission. The method of choosing members has varied in different proposals and, in some states, commissions actually created. A sharp distinction is sometimes drawn between "bipartisan" commissions, on which the assent of both major parties is needed for adoption of a plan, and "nonpartisan" commissions, which are directed to adopt a plan either without regard to political consequences or that will be "neutral" politically. For a summary of the structures, selection procedures, and line-drawing criteria of American redistricting commissions, see Campaign Legal Center, Designing Independent Redistricting Commissions (2018).

Through an initiative constitutional amendment passed in 2008, California voters took state legislative redistricting out of the hands of the legislature and gave it to a group of "citizen redistricters." Proposition 11 amended Article XXI, Section 2 of the California Constitution to require the creation of the California Citizens Redistricting Commission. The fourteen-member commission must consist of five Democrats, five Republicans, and four members of neither major party. Registered voters are permitted to apply to be a member of the commission, so long as they voted in two of the last three general elections and have not been candidates, lobbyists, or contributors of $2000 or more in the previous decade. California Common Cause and Republican Governor Arnold Schwarzenegger prominently supported Proposition 11, while the California Democratic Party—which controlled both houses of the legislature—opposed it. The measure narrowly passed, with 50.9 percent of the vote. In 2010, California voters approved Proposition 20, which gave the same citizen commission power over *congressional* redistricting too. See Cal. Const. art. XXI, § 1.

In August 2011, the California Citizens Redistricting Commission approved the final congressional and state legislative maps, by a 12–2 and 13–1 vote respectively. State and federal lawsuits challenging the commission's plans were rejected, but a referendum on the state senate plan qualified for the November 2012 ballot. The commission's plans are generally considered to have created more competitive, compact, and fair districts, although some Republicans have complained that they favor Democrats. See Vladimir Kogan & Eric McGhee, *Redistricting California: An Evaluation of the Citizens Commission Final Plans*, 4 California Journal of Politics and Policy 1 (2012) (finding improvements in minority representation, political subdivision splits, geographic compactness, electoral competitiveness, and partisan bias); Nicholas O. Stephanopoulos, *Communities and the California Commission*, 23 Stanford Law and Policy Review 281 (2012) (finding an improvement in spatial diversity).

Since California adopted redistricting commissions through direct democracy, several more states have followed suit. In 2018, voters approved measures creating redistricting commissions in Colorado, Michigan, and Ohio. In 2020, Virginia voters did the same. Thanks to these developments, significantly more congressional and state legislative districts will be designed by commissions in the 2020 cycle than ever before. See *Creation of Redistricting Commissions*, National Conference of State Legislatures (June 14, 2021), https://perma.cc/B2ZM-7QRX; see also For the People Act of 2021, H.R. 1, 117th Cong. (2021) (a bill passed by the U.S. House of Representatives that would mandate the use of commissions modeled on California's for the redrawing of congressional districts).

Should reapportionment be taken away from legislators and given to citizens without political connections or experience in drawing districts? What are the pros and cons of this new system? One of the arguments for divesting legislators from responsibility over redistricting is that doing so will increase the partisan fairness and competitiveness of elections. Empirical studies supporting this claim include Jamie L. Carson and Michael H. Crespin, *The Effects of State Redistricting Methods on Electoral Competition in United States House of Representatives Races*, 4 State Politics and Policy Quarterly 455 (2004), and Nicholas O. Stephanopoulos, *Arizona and Anti-Reform*, 2015 University of Chicago Legal Forum 477 (2015). On the other hand, Nathaniel Persily, *In Defense of Foxes Guarding Henhouses: The Case for Judicial Acquiescence to Incumbent-Protecting Gerrymanders*, 116 Harvard Law Review 649 (2002), argues that redistricting commissions are flawed both in practice and in theory. In practice, it is almost impossible to insulate commissions from political pressures, and in theory, perfectly disinterested commissions are undesirable because redistricting is an inherently political activity.

Unsurprisingly, sitting legislators are very reluctant to transfer redistricting authority to commissions. Redistricting vitally affects legislators' livelihoods, so they would prefer to draw the lines themselves (at least if they belong to the majority party) than to accept boundaries set by another institution. For this reason, many reform efforts have proceeded through voter initiatives, which do not require the elected branches' approval, rather than through conventional legislation. However, a significant majority (roughly two-thirds) of these initiatives have failed. The usual problem has been that the majority party in the state uniformly opposes the proposal, and successfully turns the vote into a purely partisan issue on which it (being the majority party) commands more popular support. Successful initiatives have tended to be ones in which reformers managed to *divide* the majority party, for example by pitting executive branch officials and retired politicians against sitting legislators. See Nicholas O. Stephanopoulos, *Reforming Redistricting: Why Popular Initiatives to Establish Redistricting Commissions Succeed or Fail,* 23 Journal of Law & Politics 331 (2007).

The United States is one of numerous countries, most with a history of British rule, that employs first-past-the-post voting in single-member districts. But America is virtually alone in allowing the elected branches to design these districts. Just about every other country with a similar electoral system — including Australia, Britain, Canada, India, New Zealand, and Pakistan — entrusts redistricting to an independent commission composed of nonpartisan government officials, judges, or academics. Interestingly, most of these nations *used* to redistrict in the same fashion as the United States. Eventually, though, resistance to this politicization grew and culminated in sweeping electoral reform. The limited comparative evidence also suggests that foreign redistricting commissions perform much better than American mapmakers in terms of partisan fairness and competitiveness. See Nicholas O. Stephanopoulos, *Our Electoral Exceptionalism*, 80 University of Chicago Law Review 769 (2013).

5. *Computers and Redistricting.* A different kind of "procedural" change that is espoused by some is to entrust redistricting to the automatic processes of a computer. One possibility would be to program the computer to create equally populated districts in a random manner. A variation on this idea is to test the partisan consequences of a plan adopted by the legislature or some other institution by considering the probability of these consequences resulting from a randomly devised plan. See Richard L. Engstrom, *The Supreme Court and Equipopulous Gerrymandering: A Remaining Obstacle in the Quest for Fair and Effective Representation*, 1976 Arizona State Law Journal 277, 314–18. Randomly generated plans would be subject to the objection that they would preclude proponents of formal criteria (like compactness or adherence to county boundaries) from seeking assurance that their favored criteria would be reflected in the plan. Randomness as a method for creating districts or as a test against which a districting plan should be measured is subject to the further objection that there is no assurance that the results most likely to be generated in a random process are the fairest. See Lowenstein & Steinberg, *supra*, 33 UCLA Law Review at 61–64.

However, recent work by Jowei Chen, Jonathan Rodden, and other scholars may satisfy these objections. Chen and Rodden employ an algorithm that randomly creates districts that are not just equally populated, but also compact, respectful of political subdivisions, and compliant with the Voting Rights Act. Additionally, while the *typical* randomly simulated plan may have no particular normative significance, the *range* of simulated maps may help to show what kinds of electoral consequences are possible while still complying with traditional districting criteria. See Jowei Chen & Jonathan Rodden, *Unintentional Gerrymandering: Political Geography and Electoral Bias in Legislatures*, 8 Quarterly Journal of Political Science 239 (2013); Jowei Chen & Jonathan Rodden, *Cutting Through the Thicket: Redistricting*

Simulations and the Detection of Partisan Gerrymanders, 14 Election Law Journal 331 (2015); Jowei Chen & Nicholas O. Stephanopoulos, *The Race-Blind Future of Voting Rights*, 130 Yale Law Journal 862 (2021).

A different critique of randomness as a methodology or test for redistricting is that it would take the politics out of a decision that many people believe involves the kinds of competing interests and values that should be resolved politically. One proposal that attempts to address this critique is to require that districts be drawn automatically by a computer but to allow the legislature to decide on any number of general criteria that should be built into the program that guides the computer:

> What is intriguing about computer technology is its ability to force decisionmakers into the position of fully obligating themselves before the fact to a verifiable program explicitly stating the aims and objectives of redistricting.
>
> If the technology indeed existed to run multiattribute problems so as to achieve globally optimal solutions to the reapportionment puzzle, then the material basis for forcing legislators into an externally constrained precommitment strategy would be at hand. The courts could obligate states to reduce their reapportionment objectives to a computer program before the final census data became available and to live with the consequences of the computer-automated redistricting. The controlling computer algorithm would make explicit and obvious the policy choices of the states in ways that would allow courts to review reasonably and intelligently the relevant choices for unconstitutional attributes. Reapportionment decisions could then be challenged on the basis of the constitutional legitimacy of the considerations taken into account in the program, rather than the claimed unfairness of the electoral outcomes.

Samuel Issacharoff, *Judging Politics: The Elusive Quest for Judicial Review of Political Fairness*, 71 Texas Law Review 1643, 1699 (1993). One difficulty, which Issacharoff acknowledges, is that current and immediately foreseeable technology may not permit such an automated process that would take into account more than a small number of criteria. But the obstacles may be more formidable than Issacharoff admits.

> Proponents of automation assume that despite current shortcomings, finding the optimal redistricting plan simply requires the development of faster computers. [T]his assumption is false—in general, redistricting is a far more difficult mathematical problem than has been recognized. In fact, the redistricting problem is so computationally complex that it is unlikely that any mere increase in the speed of computers will solve it.

Micah Altman, *The Computational Complexity of Automated Redistricting: Is Automation the Answer?* 23 Rutgers Computer & Technology Law Journal 81, 82 (1997). Altman adds:

> Practical computer methods capable of guaranteeing optimal districts do not exist, and probably never will. In the real world, automated redistricting proceeds through educated guesses at solutions and crude attempts to describe representational goals with mathematical formulas. As a consequence, automation may not eliminate the opportunity to manipulate politically, but instead shift that opportunity toward those groups that have access to the most extensive computing facilities and expertise. At the same time, automation shrouds the manipulation in the illusion of neutrality and behind a cloud of technical details. Even if computing resources are equal, districts can be politically influenced by the choice of how to characterize values and how to arrive at specific plans.

Id. at 136. But see Chen & Stephanopoulos, *Race-Blind Future*, *supra* (using a redistricting algorithm that employs multiple criteria, including all legally binding requirements, and produces plans that are representative of the universe of maps that satisfy these parameters). Aside from Altman's objections, not everyone would agree with Issacharoff that the "politics" of districting consists of the adoption of general criteria that can be implemented mechanically. Instead, some would argue, the political process consists of accommodating different interests and values through a mixed process of electoral competition and negotiation. Such a process could be expected to reflect, to varying degrees, the different criteria that are espoused within the jurisdiction, but neither the process nor the outcome would be bound by any consistent ordering of such criteria.

Another way in which computers might be harnessed to make the redistricting process fairer is by allowing interested members of the public to draw their own plans. Those plans can then be compared to the real ones proposed or adopted by legislative bodies, to judge their fairness. For more on this possibility, see Micah Altman & Michael McDonald, *The Promise and Perils of Computers in Redistricting*, 5 Duke Journal of Constitutional Law & Public Policy 69 (2010). In 2011, citizen groups in Ohio sponsored an open competition through which people could draw district maps that were then evaluated against prescribed criteria. District maps were scored based on four parameters: compactness, adherence to county and municipal boundaries, competitiveness, and representational fairness. All 53 of the congressional maps submitted to the competition earned a higher score than the plan approved by the state legislature.

You can try drawing your own district maps in a hypothetical jurisdiction by playing the Redistricting Game: https://www.redistrictinggame.org/.

6. *Consequences of Gerrymandering.* That redistricting can have a dramatic and sometimes decisive effect on the electoral prospects of individual incumbents and other aspirants for legislative office is beyond question. Nor does anyone doubt that a party has at least the opportunity to enhance its prospects if it controls the redistricting process. However, the magnitude and durability of this partisan advantage are matters of controversy and uncertainty. Some studies have found surprisingly

few partisan effects of districting, while others have found at least moderate gains in some but not all of the states in which gerrymanders are said to have occurred. For two studies that contain references to earlier research, see Peverill Squire, *The Partisan Consequences of Congressional Redistricting*, 23 American Politics Quarterly 229 (1995); and Harry Basehart and John Comer, *Redistricting and Incumbent Reelection Success in Five State Legislatures*, 23 American Politics Quarterly 241 (1995). For more recent studies finding larger effects, see Devin Caughey et al., *Partisan Gerrymandering and the Political Process: Effects on Roll-Call Voting and State Policies*, 16 Election Law Journal 453 (2017); and Nicholas O. Stephanopoulos, *The Causes and Consequences of Gerrymandering*, 59 William & Mary Law Review 2115 (2018).

II. Gerrymandering and the Constitution

While the Supreme Court did not squarely confront the constitutionality of partisan gerrymandering until 1986, the issue emerged tangentially in several earlier cases. In *Fortson v. Dorsey*, 379 U.S. 433 (1965), the Court upheld a Georgia senate plan that included several multimember districts. The Court warned, however, that a map might be invalid if it "operate[d] to minimize or cancel out the voting strength of racial *or political* elements of the voting population." *Id.* at 438 (emphasis added). In *Gaffney v. Cummings*, 412 U.S. 735, 752 (1973), the Court validated Connecticut plans that were the opposite of partisan gerrymanders because they sought to "achieve a rough approximation of the statewide political strengths of the Democratic and Republican Parties." In the Court's view, "judicial interest should be at its lowest ebb when a State purports fairly to allocate political power to the parties in accordance with their voting strength and, within quite tolerable limits, succeeds in doing so." *Id.* at 754.

And as noted in Chapter 3, in *Karcher v. Daggett*, 462 U.S. 725 (1983), the Court skirted the partisan gerrymandering question by holding that a blatantly discriminatory New Jersey congressional plan violated the one-person, one-vote rule. In a concurring opinion, Justice Stevens engaged with the partisan gerrymandering merits, examining "whether the plan has a significant adverse impact on an identifiable political group, whether the plan has objective indicia of irregularity, and then, whether the State is able to produce convincing evidence that the plan nevertheless serves neutral, legitimate interests of the community as a whole." *Id.* at 751 (Stevens, J., concurring). In Justice Stevens's view, the New Jersey map was highly problematic because of its extremely noncompact districts and the rushed and partisan manner in which it was enacted. Justice Stevens could not conclude that the plan was actually unconstitutional, though, since the state had not had the chance to present any justifications for its districting choices. *Id.* at 761-65.

After all this buildup, the Court finally tackled partisan gerrymandering head-on in *Davis v. Bandemer*, 478 U.S. 109 (1986). *Bandemer* was an appeal by Democrats who objected to a Republican-passed plan to redistrict the Indiana state legislature. In the background were controversies over congressional redistricting, especially in California, where Republicans objected strenuously to a plan enacted by Democrats. National Republicans filed amicus briefs in *Bandemer* supporting the Indiana Democrats while California Democrats weighed in to support the Republican-adopted Indiana plan. Who says parties don't take a disinterested view of constitutional questions?

The Supreme Court divided into three groups in *Bandemer*. The largest group consisted of Justice White, who wrote the plurality opinion, and Justices Blackmun, Brennan, and Marshall. The first question was whether a claim that a partisan gerrymander violates the Equal Protection Clause is justiciable. Justice White answered that question in the affirmative, and on that issue he wrote for the Court, because he was joined by Justices Powell and Stevens. Justice O'Connor wrote an opinion, joined by Chief Justice Burger and Justice Rehnquist, that the question was nonjusticiable.

On the merits, White and the plurality found the Indiana plan constitutional. Stevens wrote a dissenting opinion, joined by Powell. The four members of the plurality and the three justices who thought the issue was nonjusticiable made up a majority to uphold the Indiana plan. Outside of Indiana, the question that drew most attention was the constitutional standard for adjudicating partisan gerrymandering cases. Everyone agreed that in effect, White's opinion governed, but the proper interpretation of that opinion proved controversial. Here are excerpts:

> [T]he appellees' claim, as we understand it, is that Democratic voters over the State as a whole, not Democratic voters in particular districts, have been subjected to unconstitutional discrimination. Although the statewide discrimination asserted here was allegedly accomplished through the manipulation of individual district lines, the focus of the equal protection inquiry is necessarily somewhat different from that involved in the review of individual districts.
>
> [I]n order to succeed the Bandemer plaintiffs were required to prove both intentional discrimination against an identifiable political group and an actual discriminatory effect on that group. See, *e.g.*, *Mobile v. Bolden*, 446 U.S. 55 (1980) [discussed in Chapter 5]. Further, we are confident that if the law challenged here had discriminatory effects on Democrats, this record would support a finding that the discrimination was intentional....
>
> Indeed, quite aside from the anecdotal evidence, the shape of the House and Senate Districts, and the alleged disregard for political boundaries, we think it most likely that whenever a legislature redistricts, those responsible for the legislation will know the likely political composition of the new districts and will have a prediction as to whether a particular district is a safe one for a Democratic or Republican candidate or is a competitive district that either candidate might win....

As long as redistricting is done by a legislature, it should not be very difficult to prove that the likely political consequences of the reapportionment were intended.... The District Court held that because any apportionment scheme that purposely prevents proportional representation is unconstitutional, Democratic voters need only show that their proportionate voting influence has been adversely affected. Our cases, however, clearly foreclose any claim that the Constitution requires proportional representation or that legislatures in reapportioning must draw district lines to come as near as possible to allocating seats to the contending parties in proportion to what their anticipated statewide vote will be.

[T]he mere fact that a particular apportionment scheme makes it more difficult for a particular group in a particular district to elect the representatives of its choice does not render that scheme constitutionally infirm. [T]he power to influence the political process is not limited to winning elections. An individual or a group of individuals who votes for a losing candidate is usually deemed to be adequately represented by the winning candidate and to have as much opportunity to influence that candidate as other voters in the district. We cannot presume in such a situation, without actual proof to the contrary, that the candidate elected will entirely ignore the interests of those voters. This is true even in a safe district where the losing group loses election after election. Thus, a group's electoral power is not unconstitutionally diminished by the simple fact of an apportionment scheme that makes winning elections more difficult, and a failure of proportional representation alone does not constitute impermissible discrimination under the Equal Protection Clause.

As with individual districts, where unconstitutional vote dilution is alleged in the form of statewide political gerrymandering, the mere lack of proportional representation will not be sufficient to prove unconstitutional discrimination. Again, without specific supporting evidence, a court cannot presume in such a case that those who are elected will disregard the disproportionately underrepresented group. Rather, unconstitutional discrimination occurs only when the electoral system is arranged in a manner that will consistently degrade a voter's or a group of voters' influence on the political process as a whole.

Although this is a somewhat different formulation than we have previously used in describing unconstitutional vote dilution in an individual district, the focus of both of these inquiries is essentially the same. [In a footnote, Justice White made it clear he was referring to and relying on racial vote dilution cases discussed in Chapter 5.] In both contexts, the question is whether a particular group has been unconstitutionally denied its chance to effectively influence the political process. In a challenge to an individual district, this inquiry focuses on the opportunity of members of

> the group to participate in party deliberations in the slating and nomination of candidates, their opportunity to register and vote, and hence their chance to directly influence the election returns and to secure the attention of the winning candidate. Statewide, however, the inquiry centers on the voters' direct or indirect influence on the elections of the state legislature as a whole. And, as in individual district cases, an equal protection violation may be found only where the electoral system substantially disadvantages certain voters in their opportunity to influence the political process effectively. In this context, such a finding of unconstitutionality must be supported by evidence of continued frustration of the will of a majority of the voters or effective denial to a minority of voters of a fair chance to influence the political process.
>
> Based on these views, we would reject the District Court's apparent holding that *any* interference with an opportunity to elect a representative of one's choice would be sufficient to allege or make out an equal protection violation, unless justified by some acceptable state interest that the State would be required to demonstrate. In addition to being contrary to the above-described conception of an unconstitutional political gerrymander, such a low threshold for legal action would invite attack on all or almost all reapportionment statutes. District-based elections hardly ever produce a perfect fit between votes and representation.

Id. at 127-33. Justice White went on to enumerate several of the deficiencies in the evidence presented by the Democratic plaintiffs, given the standards he had set forth:

> Relying on a single election to prove unconstitutional discrimination is unsatisfactory. The District Court observed, and the parties do not disagree, that Indiana is a swing State. Voters sometimes prefer Democratic candidates, and sometimes Republican. The District Court did not find that because of the 1981 Act the Democrats could not in one of the next few elections secure a sufficient vote to take control of the assembly. Indeed, the District Court declined to hold that the 1982 election results were the predictable consequences of the 1981 Act and expressly refused to hold that those results were a reliable prediction of future ones. The District Court did not ask by what percentage the statewide Democratic vote would have had to increase to control either the House or the Senate. The appellants argue here, without a persuasive response from the appellees, that had the Democratic candidates received an additional few percentage points of the votes cast statewide, they would have obtained a majority of the seats in both houses. Nor was there any finding that the 1981 reapportionment would consign the Democrats to a minority status in the Assembly throughout the 1980's or that the Democrats would have no hope of doing any better in the reapportionment that would occur after the 1990 census. Without

> findings of this nature, the District Court erred in concluding that the 1981 Act violated the Equal Protection Clause.

Id. at 135–36.

In her opinion concluding that partisan gerrymandering is nonjusticiable, Justice O'Connor made two notable arguments. First, she contended that judicial intervention is unnecessary in this context because partisan gerrymandering is inherently self-limiting; a party that gerrymanders too aggressively will expose itself to large seat losses if voter sentiment shifts even modestly. Second, she asserted that the plurality's approach would inevitably collapse into a requirement of proportional representation.

> Indeed, there is good reason to think that political gerrymandering is a self-limiting enterprise. See B. Cain, The Reapportionment Puzzle 151–159 (1984). In order to gerrymander, the legislative majority must weaken some of its safe seats, thus exposing its own incumbents to greater risks of defeat-risks they may refuse to accept past a certain point. Similarly, an overambitious gerrymander can lead to disaster for the legislative majority: because it has created more seats in which it hopes to win relatively narrow victories, the same swing in overall voting strength will tend to cost the legislative majority more and more seats as the gerrymander becomes more ambitious. . . .
>
> Moreover, any such intervention is likely to move in the direction of proportional representation for political parties. This is clear by analogy to the problem that arises in racial gerrymandering cases: "in order to decide whether an electoral system has made it harder for minority voters to elect the candidates they prefer, a court must have an idea in mind of how hard it 'should' be for minority voters to elect their preferred candidates under an acceptable system." Any such norm must make some reference, even if only a loose one, to the relation between the racial minority group's share of the electorate and its share of the elected representatives. In order to implement the plurality's standard, it will thus be necessary for courts to adopt an analogous norm, in order to assess whether the voting strength of a political party has been "degraded" by an apportionment, either on a statewide basis or in particular districts. Absent any such norm, the inquiry the plurality proposes would be so standardless as to make the adjudication of political gerrymandering claims impossible.
>
> Implicit in the plurality's opinion today is at least some use of simple proportionality as the standard for measuring the normal representational entitlements of a political party. That is why the plurality can say that "a history (actual or projected) of disproportionate results," together with proof of "the denial of fair representation" and of "lack of political power," will constitute an equal protection violation. To be sure, the plurality has qualified its use of a *standard* of proportional representation in a variety of ways

> so as to avoid a *requirement* of proportional representation. The question is whether these qualifications are likely to be enduring in the face of the tremendous political pressures that courts will confront when called on to decide political gerrymandering claims. Because the most easily measured indicia of political power relate solely to winning and losing elections, there is a grave risk that the plurality's various attempts to qualify and condition the group right the Court has created will gradually pale in importance. What is likely to remain is a loose form of proportionality, under which *some* deviations from proportionality are permissible, but any significant, persistent deviations from proportionality are suspect. Courts will be forced to look for some form of "undue" disproportionality with respect to electoral success if political gerrymandering claims are justiciable, because otherwise they will find their decisions turning on imponderables such as whether the legislators of one party have fairly represented the voters of the other.

Id. at 152, 156-57 (O'Connor, J., concurring in the judgment).

Notes and Questions

1. What is the nature of the inequality or discrimination that Justice White holds could violate the Equal Protection Clause? What does it mean for a district plan to "consistently degrade" voters' "influence on the political process as a whole"? Can district boundaries ever affect voters' overall access to the political system?

2. Justice White's opinion prompted divergent interpretations. Perhaps the most common was that the opinion contained inadequate standards and thus provided little or no guidance to lower courts.

> Neither Justice White's nor Justice Powell's approach to the question of partisan apportionment gives any real guidance to lower courts forced to adjudicate this issue; thus, Justice O'Connor's apprehension that courts will resort to a standard of rough proportional representation appears well-founded.... Of course, the results that *Bandemer* will spawn remain uncertain, but the Court may well come to regret involving the judiciary so deeply in this delicate political sphere.

Laurence H. Tribe, American Constitutional Law 1083–84 (2d ed. 1988).

Another interpretation maintained that the standard for partisan gerrymandering established in *Bandemer* was one of degree.

> [T]here *is* a clear and manageable standard in *Davis v. Bandemer*—one offered in the plurality opinion. Under it, for partisan gerrymandering to be unlawful, it must be (1) intentional, (2) severe, and (3) predictably non-transient in its effects.
>
> ... The Supreme Court plurality in *Bandemer* was walking a tightrope. It wanted to set standards high enough to strongly discourage frivolous suits

> but low enough so that the most egregious partisan gerrymanders could be overturned by the courts. In my view the Supreme Court has succeeded admirably in that balancing act.

Bernard Grofman, *Toward a Coherent Theory of Gerrymandering: Bandemer and Thornburg*, in Political Gerrymandering and the Courts 29, 30–31 (Bernard Grofman, ed., 1990).

Yet another proposed interpretation maintained that the gerrymandering claim recognized in *Bandemer* would rarely be available to the major political parties, because it is not gerrymandering per se that is prohibited, but gerrymandering aimed at groups that need particular protection under the Fourteenth Amendment.

> A gerrymandering claim brought by a group not constituted by race or by some other classification that has been recognized as "suspect" for equal protection purposes must demonstrate that the group is the victim of pervasive discrimination in the political process to such a degree that it is reasonable to suppose a districting plan contrary to their interests is the result of prejudice and an animus well beyond the usual bounds of political opposition in our system.
>
> There is one other possibility. If a case should arise in which a partisan gerrymander between established political parties should be so effective as to virtually guarantee a minority group permanent dominance over state government, comparable to the situation that existed in *Baker v. Carr* and some of the other malapportionment cases, that might be unconstitutional as well. It [was] not necessary [in *Bandemer*] to determine whether gerrymandering really is a powerful enough tool to produce such a result, nor to decide exactly what the theory supporting judicial intervention in such a case would be.

Daniel Lowenstein, Bandemer's *Gap: Gerrymandering and Equal Protection*, in Political Gerrymandering and the Courts 64, 89–90 (Bernard Grofman, ed., 1990). Dean Alfange, *Gerrymandering and the Constitution: Into the Thorns of the Thicket at Last*, 1986 Supreme Court Review 175, reaches a somewhat similar conclusion, but is highly critical of the *Bandemer* decision thus interpreted.

3. Justice O'Connor claimed in her opinion concurring in the result that Justice White called for "at least some use of simple proportionality as the standard for measuring the normal representational entitlement of a political party." Do you agree? Is there a difference between objecting to extreme and persistent disproportionality and affirmatively requiring proportionality? Some commentators agreed that a *de facto* requirement of proportional representation would be the likely outcome of the *Bandemer* decision. See Schuck, *supra*. This did not in fact occur, as we shall see.

Justice O'Connor also argued that partisan gerrymandering is necessarily self-limiting. Suppose that a would-be Democratic gerrymanderer designs seven districts in which Democrats have a 57%-43% advantage and three districts in which

Republicans have a 80%-20% advantage. This is an extreme gerrymander; Democrats win 70% of the seats with just 46% of the vote. But is it also a fragile gerrymander, as O'Connor would expect? All seven Democratic districts would continue to elect Democrats unless they swung by more than *seven points* in a Republican direction—historically, a relatively large and improbable swing.

4. Was the standard of *Davis v. Bandemer* applicable when a court was not reviewing the constitutionality of a plan but instead was required to create a plan of its own, or choose among plans tendered to it, because the legislature had failed to adopt a plan? Consider the following, from *Prosser v. Elections Board*, 793 F. Supp. 859, 867 (W.D. Wis. 1992) (three-judge court, per curiam):

> [I]f we were reviewing an enacted plan we would pay little heed to cries of gerrymandering, because every reapportionment plan has some political effect, and so could be denounced as "gerrymandering" committed by the party that had pressed for its enactment. But we are not reviewing an enacted plan. An enacted plan would have the virtue of political legitimacy. We are comparing submitted plans with a view to picking the one (or devising our own) most consistent with judicial neutrality. Judges should not select a plan that seeks partisan advantage—that seeks to change the ground rules so that one party can do better than it would do under a plan drawn up by persons having no political agenda—even if they would not be entitled to invalidate an enacted plan that did so.

Consistent with this passage from *Prosser*, numerous courts have voluntarily sought to ensure partisan fairness when designing their own maps. See, *e.g.*, *Avalos v. Davidson*, 2002 WL 1895406, at *8 (D. Colo. Jan. 25, 2002); *Balderas v. Texas*, 2001 WL 36403750, at *3 (E.D. Tex. Nov. 14, 2001); *Diaz v. Silver*, 978 F. Supp. 96, 102-04 (E.D.N.Y. 1997); *Good v. Austin*, 800 F. Supp. 557, 566 (E.D & W.D. Mich. 1992); *Hastert v. State Bd. of Elections*, 777 F. Supp. 634, 659 (N.D. Ill. 1991). These efforts, however, have not been especially fruitful; after including relevant controls, plans drawn with partisan fairness as a criterion have not been significantly more symmetric than other plans. See Nicholas O. Stephanopoulos, *The Consequences of Consequentialist Criteria*, 3 U.C. Irvine Law Review 669 (2013).

5. Challenges based on *Bandemer* met with little success. See, *e.g.*, *Fund for Accurate & Informed Representation v. Weprin*, 796 F. Supp. 662, 668–69 (N.D.N.Y. 1992), aff'd mem. 506 U.S. 1017 (1992); *Illinois Legislative Redistricting Commission v. LaPaille*, 782 F. Supp. 1272, 1275–76 (N.D. Ill. 1991); *Republican Party of Virginia v. Wilder*, 774 F. Supp. 400, 403–6 (W.D. Va. 1991). Justice Scalia's plurality opinion in *Vieth v. Jubelirer* lists many more examples in his footnote 6. The trouble for claimants was twofold. First, *Bandemer*'s requirement that a plan "*consistently* degrade" voters' influence meant that challenges brought prior to the first election under a plan, or even after one or two elections, universally failed. Courts simply could not be sure that a party's electoral disadvantage would be durable rather than transient. Second, *Bandemer*'s reference to voters' influence "on the political process *as a whole*" convinced many courts that electoral disadvantage alone was not enough to call a

plan into question. Losses at the polls had to be combined with efforts to prevent a party's supporters from registering or voting—efforts that typically did not occur in this era.

The Long Partisan Gerrymandering Interregnum

After holding in *Bandemer* that partisan gerrymandering may violate the Constitution and is justiciable, too, the Court did not consider another case of this kind until *Vieth v. Jubelirer*, 541 U.S. 267 (2004). The plaintiffs in *Vieth* were Democratic voters in Pennsylvania who objected to the state's congressional plan, under which Republicans won a supermajority of the seats even though the state's voters were nearly evenly split between the parties. The plaintiffs also proposed a new test to replace the one adopted by the *Bandemer* plurality, which, as noted above, had proved impossible for litigants to satisfy. Under this test's intent prong, the predominant purpose for a district map had to be the pursuit of partisan advantage. See *id.* at 284 (plurality opinion). Under the test's effect prong, the cracking and packing of the targeted party's voters had to thwart their ability to translate a majority of votes into a majority of seats. See *id.* at 286-87.

A majority of the *Vieth* Court rejected as unworkable the plaintiffs' proposal, criticizing both its intent and its effect prongs as follows:

> "Predominant intent" to disadvantage the plaintiff's political group refers to the relative importance of that goal as compared with all the other goals that the map seeks to pursue—contiguity of districts, compactness of districts, observance of the lines of political subdivision, protection of incumbents of all parties, cohesion of natural racial and ethnic neighborhoods, compliance with requirements of the Voting Rights Act of 1965 regarding racial distribution, etc. Appellants contend that their intent test *must* be discernible and manageable because it has been borrowed from our racial gerrymandering cases. To begin with, in a very important respect that is not so. In the racial gerrymandering context, the predominant intent test has been applied to the challenged district in which the plaintiffs voted. Here, however, appellants do not assert that an apportionment fails their intent test if any single district does so.... [A]ppellants propose a test that is satisfied only when "partisan advantage was the predominant motivation *behind the entire statewide plan.*" Vague as the "predominant motivation" test might be when used to evaluate single districts, it all but evaporates when applied statewide. Does it mean, for instance, that partisan intent must outweigh all other goals—contiguity, compactness, preservation of neighborhoods, etc.—*statewide?* And how is the statewide "outweighing" to be determined? If three-fifths of the map's districts forgo the pursuit of partisan ends in favor of strictly observing political-subdivision lines, and only two-fifths ignore those lines to disadvantage the plaintiffs, is the observance of political subdivisions the "predominant" goal between those two? We are sure appellants do not think so....

The effects prong of appellants' proposal replaces the *Bandemer* plurality's vague test of "denied its chance to effectively influence the political process" with criteria that are seemingly more specific. . . . But a person's politics is rarely as readily discernible — and *never* as permanently discernible — as a person's race. Political affiliation is not an immutable characteristic, but may shift from one election to the next; and even within a given election, not all voters follow the party line. We dare say (and hope) that the political party which puts forward an utterly incompetent candidate will lose even in its registration stronghold. These facts make it impossible to assess the effects of partisan gerrymandering, to fashion a standard for evaluating a violation, and finally to craft a remedy.

Assuming, however, that the effects of partisan gerrymandering can be determined, appellants' test would invalidate the districting only when it prevents a majority of the electorate from electing a majority of representatives. Before considering whether this particular standard is judicially manageable we question whether it is judicially discernible in the sense of being relevant to some constitutional violation. Deny it as appellants may (and do), this standard rests upon the principle that groups (or at least political-action groups) have a right to proportional representation. But the Constitution contains no such principle. It guarantees equal protection of the law to persons, not equal representation in government to equivalently sized groups. It nowhere says that farmers or urban dwellers, Christian fundamentalists or Jews, Republicans or Democrats, must be accorded political strength proportionate to their numbers.

Even if the standard were relevant, however, it is not judicially manageable. To begin with, how is a party's majority status to be established? Appellants propose using the results of statewide races as the benchmark of party support. But as their own complaint describes, in the 2000 Pennsylvania statewide elections some Republicans won and some Democrats won. Moreover, to think that majority status in statewide races establishes majority status for district contests, one would have to believe that the only factor determining voting behavior at all levels is political affiliation. That is assuredly not true. . . .

But if we could identify a majority party, we would find it impossible to ensure that that party wins a majority of seats — unless we radically revise the States' traditional structure for elections. In any winner-take-all district system, there can be no guarantee, no matter how the district lines are drawn, that a majority of party votes statewide will produce a majority of seats for that party. . . . Whether by reason of partisan districting or not, party constituents may always wind up "packed" in some districts and "cracked" throughout others. Consider, for example, a legislature that draws district lines with no objectives in mind except compactness and respect for the lines of political subdivisions. Under that system, political groups that

> tend to cluster (as is the case with Democratic voters in cities) would be systematically affected by what might be called a "natural" packing effect.
>
> Our one-person, one-vote cases have no bearing upon this question, neither in principle nor in practicality. Not in principle, because to say that each individual must have an equal say in the selection of representatives, and hence that a majority of individuals must have a majority say, is not at all to say that each discernible group, whether farmers or urban dwellers or political parties, must have representation equivalent to its numbers. And not in practicality, because the easily administrable standard of population equality adopted by *Wesberry* and *Reynolds* [discussed in Chapter 3, Section 1] enables judges to decide whether a violation has occurred (and to remedy it) essentially on the basis of three readily determined factors—where the plaintiff lives, how many voters are in his district, and how many voters are in other districts; whereas requiring judges to decide whether a districting system will produce a statewide majority for a majority party casts them forth upon a sea of imponderables, and asks them to make determinations that not even election experts can agree upon.

Id. at 284-90. Do you agree that courts are incapable of determining whether partisan advantage was the predominant purpose of a district plan? Recall from the previous chapter that, under *Harris v. Arizona Independent Redistricting Commission*, 136 S. Ct. 1301 (2016), courts must strike down plans on one-person, one-vote grounds if their population deviations "reflect[] the *predominance* of illegitimate reapportionment factors," such as partisan gain. *Id.* at 1307 (emphasis added). With respect to the mutability of voter behavior, is empirical evidence relevant? While it was once common for voters to change their party allegiance from election to election, and to split their tickets even in a single election, these acts are now increasingly rare. And is the value of majoritarianism advocated by the *Vieth* plaintiffs really equivalent to proportional representation, as claimed by the *Vieth* majority? Is it not possible to think of many examples where majoritarianism is satisfied but proportionality is not, e.g., if a small statewide majority in votes translates into a large statewide majority in seats?

The *Vieth* majority also rejected several other suggested standards for partisan gerrymandering claims: (1) that adopted by the *Bandemer* plurality; (2) a district-specific predominant-partisan-intent requirement, offered by Justice Stevens; (3) a five-part approach modeled on the Court's racial vote dilution precedents and focusing on compliance with traditional districting criteria, offered by Justice Souter; and (4) a statewide test asking if a partisan minority has unjustifiably entrenched itself in power, offered by Justice Breyer. *See id.* at 277-301. A plurality of four Justices would have reversed *Bandemer* outright and held that all partisan gerrymandering claims are nonjusticiable. We bracket the arguments for and against justiciability until our discussion of *Rucho v. Common Cause*, which largely echoed the debate in *Vieth*. The reason the *Vieth* plurality's nonjusticiability conclusion commanded the support of only four Justices was that Justice Kennedy declined to embrace that position.

In his concurrence in the judgment, Justice Kennedy floated a First Amendment theory of partisan gerrymandering. As we shall see, this theory enjoyed some traction until it was ultimately rejected in *Rucho:*

> I note that the complaint in this case also alleged a violation of First Amendment rights. The First Amendment may be the more relevant constitutional provision in future cases that allege unconstitutional partisan gerrymandering. After all, these allegations involve the First Amendment interest of not burdening or penalizing citizens because of their participation in the electoral process, their voting history, their association with a political party, or their expression of political views. Under general First Amendment principles those burdens in other contexts are unconstitutional absent a compelling government interest.... As these precedents show, First Amendment concerns arise where a State enacts a law that has the purpose and effect of subjecting a group of voters or their party to disfavored treatment by reason of their views. In the context of partisan gerrymandering, that means that First Amendment concerns arise where an apportionment has the purpose and effect of burdening a group of voters' representational rights.
>
> The plurality suggests there is no place for the First Amendment in this area. The implication is that under the First Amendment any and all consideration of political interests in an apportionment would be invalid. That misrepresents the First Amendment analysis. The inquiry is not whether political classifications were used. The inquiry instead is whether political classifications were used to burden a group's representational rights. If a court were to find that a State did impose burdens and restrictions on groups or persons by reason of their views, there would likely be a First Amendment violation, unless the State shows some compelling interest....
>
> Where it is alleged that a gerrymander had the purpose and effect of imposing burdens on a disfavored party and its voters, the First Amendment may offer a sounder and more prudential basis for intervention than does the Equal Protection Clause. The equal protection analysis puts its emphasis on the permissibility of an enactment's classifications. This works where race is involved since classifying by race is almost never permissible. It presents a more complicated question when the inquiry is whether a generally permissible classification has been used for an impermissible purpose. That question can only be answered in the affirmative by the subsidiary showing that the classification as applied imposes unlawful burdens. The First Amendment analysis concentrates on whether the legislation burdens the representational rights of the complaining party's voters for reasons of ideology, beliefs, or political association. The analysis allows a pragmatic or functional assessment that accords some latitude to the States.

Id. at 314-15 (Kennedy, J., concurring in the judgment) (internal citations omitted). If the crux of a First Amendment challenge is the mapmaker's partisan intent—"burdening or penalizing citizens because of ... their association with a political party"—then would such a suit succeed whenever a single party has full control of the redistricting process and so is able to disadvantage its opponent? Alternatively, if a First Amendment claim requires both partisan intent and a "burden [on] a group's representational rights," then how is it different from an equal protection claim, which also includes intent and effect prongs?

Around the time of *Vieth*, the issue of *re*-redistricting—enacting a second district map in a decade, even though the initial map was lawful—arose in several states. In Colorado, the legislature changed a court-drawn congressional plan following a Republican victory in the 2002 election. The Colorado Supreme Court struck down the plan on state law grounds, ruling that the Colorado Constitution prohibited a second redistricting plan during the decade. *People ex rel. Salazar v. Davidson*, 79 P.3d 1221 (Colo. 2003) (en banc), cert. denied, *Colorado General Assembly v. Salazar*, 541 U.S. 1093 (2004). In New Hampshire, the legislature was unable to update its own districts after the 2000 election, so a court-drawn plan was used in 2002. The New Hampshire Supreme Court upheld under state law a plan that the new legislature adopted in 2004. *In re Below*, 855 A.2d 459 (N.H. 2004). The court held that the legislature had authority under the state constitution to adopt only a single plan each decade, but that its authority was not obviated by the occurrence of an election under a court-drawn plan.

The fiercest controversy was in Texas. As in Colorado and New Hampshire, a divided legislature and governor had failed to produce a congressional plan after the 2000 census. Republicans claimed that a court-drawn plan simply carried forward a Democratic gerrymander enacted in 1991. Republicans won control of the state government in the 2002 elections and decided to turn the tables. The nation was entertained by the spectacle of Democratic legislators fleeing to Oklahoma and New Mexico to prevent Republicans from obtaining a quorum. Eventually Republicans succeeded in passing their plan, and Democrats challenged it on a number of grounds. We shall discuss one of these claims, under Section 2 of the Voting Rights Act, in Chapter 5, Part II. More relevant here, Democrats argued that whatever the difficulty of finding constitutional standards in the case of ordinary redistricting addressed by *Vieth*, a mid-decade re-redistricting should be treated differently. Once a plan has been adopted that satisfies one-person, one-vote, no new plan is necessary. Therefore, a new plan adopted by a legislature controlled by one party should be treated as presumptively void.

The Supreme Court rejected this argument in *League of Unified Latin American Citizens v. Perry*, 548 U.S. 399 (2006) (*LULAC*). As in *Vieth*, Justice Kennedy wrote the pivotal opinion. In one paragraph joined by the four *Vieth* dissenters and therefore speaking for the Court, he stated that he would not revisit the holding of *Bandemer* that partisan gerrymandering claims are justiciable. Proceeding for himself only, Justice Kennedy disagreed with the plaintiffs that partisan gain is necessarily the "sole" motivation for re-redistricting. "Evaluating the legality of acts arising out of mixed motives can be complex, and affixing a single label to those acts can be hazardous." *Id.* at 418 (opinion of Kennedy, J.). More fundamentally, Justice Kennedy objected to striking down maps because of their subjective purposes alone. "[A] successful claim attempting to identify unconstitutional acts of partisan gerrymandering must do what appellants' sole-motivation theory explicitly disavows: show a burden, as measured by a reliable standard, on the complainants' representational rights." *Id.*

Justice Kennedy further commented on a "symmetry standard," proposed by a group of distinguished political scientist amici, "that would measure partisan bias by 'compar[ing] how both parties would fare hypothetically if they each (in turn) had received a given percentage of the vote.'" *Id.* at 419. "Under that standard the measure of a map's bias is the extent to which a majority party would fare better than the minority party, should their respective shares of the vote reverse." *Id.* at 420. Justice Kennedy observed that "[t]he existence or degree of asymmetry may in large part depend on conjecture about where possible vote-switchers will reside." *Id.* He added that he was "wary of adopting a constitutional standard that invalidates a map based on unfair results that would occur in a hypothetical state of affairs." *Id.* Moreover, "the counterfactual plaintiff would face the same problem as the present, actual appellants: providing a standard for deciding how much partisan dominance is too much." *Id.* Accordingly, "[w]ithout altogether discounting its utility in redistricting planning and litigation," Justice Kennedy "conclude[d] asymmetry alone is not a reliable measure of unconstitutional partisanship." *Id.*

Noticing that this passage did not definitively dismiss the relevance of partisan asymmetry, a group of plaintiffs challenged Wisconsin's state house plan in the 2010 cycle based in part on its extreme asymmetry. In particular, the plaintiffs showed that the plan exhibited some of the most pro-Republican efficiency gaps and partisan biases in modern history in the 2012 and 2014 elections. [See Part I, Note 1, *supra*, defining the efficiency gap and partisan bias.] For the first time since *Bandemer*, the three-judge district court invalidated the plan on partisan gerrymandering grounds. Specifically, the court adopted a three-part test, under which a plan (1) must be "intended to place a severe impediment on the effectiveness of the votes of individual citizens on the basis of their political affiliation"; (2) must "achieve[] the intended effect" by "burden[ing] the representational rights of [voters] by impeding their ability to translate their votes into legislative seats, not simply for one election but throughout the life of [the plan]"; and (3) must be incapable of being "justified by the legitimate state concerns and neutral factors that traditionally bear on the reapportionment process." *Whitford v. Gill*, 218 F. Supp. 3d 837 (W.D. Wis. 2016), *vacated*, 138 S. Ct. 1916 (2018).

Wisconsin appealed the district court's decision to the Supreme Court. In *Gill v. Whitford*, 138 S. Ct. 1916 (2018), the Court unanimously vacated the decision below on the ground that the plaintiffs had not yet proven (but might still show) their standing to sue. Standing in a partisan gerrymandering suit brought on a vote dilution theory, according to the Court, does *not* extend to all supporters of the victimized party. Rather, only voters who *themselves* were placed in cracked or packed districts — and who could have been placed in uncracked or unpacked districts by some other, fairer map — have standing:

> To the extent the plaintiffs' alleged harm is the dilution of their votes, that injury is district specific. An individual voter in Wisconsin is placed in a single district. He votes for a single representative. The boundaries of the district, and the composition of its voters, determine whether and to what extent a particular voter is packed or cracked. This "disadvantage to [the voter] as [an] individual[]" therefore results from the boundaries of the particular district in which he resides. And a plaintiff's remedy must be "limited to the inadequacy that produced [his] injury in fact." In this case the remedy that is proper and sufficient lies in the revision of the boundaries of the individual's own district....
>
> Here, the plaintiffs' partisan gerrymandering claims turn on allegations that their votes have been diluted. That harm arises from the particular composition of the voter's own district, which causes his vote — having been packed or cracked — to carry less weight than it would carry in another, hypothetical district. Remedying the individual voter's harm, therefore, does not necessarily require restructuring all of the State's legislative districts. It requires revising only such districts as are necessary to reshape the voter's district — so that the voter may be unpacked or uncracked, as the case may be....
>
> The plaintiffs argue that their legal injury is not limited to the injury that they have suffered as individual voters, but extends also to the statewide harm to their interest "in their collective representation in the legislature," and in influencing the legislature's overall "composition and policymaking." But our cases to date have not found that this presents an individual and personal injury of the kind required for Article III standing. On the facts of this case, the plaintiffs may not rely on "the kind of undifferentiated, generalized grievance about the conduct of government that we have refused to countenance in the past." A citizen's interest in the overall composition of the legislature is embodied in his right to vote for his representative. And the citizen's abstract interest in policies adopted by the legislature on the facts here is a nonjusticiable "general interest common to all members of the public."

Id. at 1930–31 (internal citations omitted). Is the Court's holding that standing in partisan gerrymandering cases is district-specific in tension with the theory of vote dilution? Vote dilution is typically understood as an aggregate concept: a particular group is underrepresented in the legislature because its members' votes have been diluted by district lines that crack and pack these voters. If this is what vote dilution means, does it make sense for partisan vote dilution standing to be district-specific?

On remand from the Court, the *Whitford* litigants added numerous new plaintiffs in state house districts across Wisconsin. They also compiled expert evidence that the plaintiffs lived in districts that (1) were cracked or packed; and (2) could be uncracked or unpacked by a different map. Does this prove that the plaintiffs had standing to allege partisan vote dilution? More importantly, after *Whitford*, three-judge district courts ruled in favor of partisan gerrymandering plaintiffs in cases from Maryland, Michigan, North Carolina, and Ohio. *See Ohio A. Philip Randolph Inst. v. Householder*, 373 F. Supp. 3d 978 (S.D. Ohio 2019), *vacated*, 140 S. Ct. 102 (2019); *League of Women Voters of Mich. v. Benson*, 373 F. Supp. 3d 867 (E.D. Mich. 2019), *vacated*, 140 S. Ct. 429 (2019); *Benisek v. Lamone*, 348 F. Supp. 3d 493 (D. Md. 2018), *vacated*, 139 S. Ct. 2484 (2019); *Common Cause v. Rucho*, 318 F. Supp. 3d 777 (M.D.N.C. 2018), *vacated*, 139 S. Ct. 2484 (2019).

Three of these cases (all but the Maryland litigation) involved partisan vote dilution claims like the one in *Whitford*. The plaintiffs showed that particular districts were intentionally cracked or packed, and could have been uncracked or unpacked by other maps. The plaintiffs also showed that each plan was extremely asymmetric by historical standards, based on metrics like the efficiency gap and partisan bias. The plaintiffs further showed that each plan was more asymmetric than thousands of maps generated randomly by a computer algorithm using nonpartisan districting criteria. In addition, all four cases included First Amendment claims along the lines described by Justice Kennedy in *Vieth* (as well as by Justice Kagan in *Whitford*). These claims were plan-wide in Michigan, North Carolina, and Ohio, and limited to a single district in Maryland. Regardless of their scope, the claims succeeded in the district courts because of evidence that the mapmakers intended to disadvantage certain voters due to their political beliefs and, in fact, imposed burdens on these voters' rights of free speech and association.

Two of the major post-*Whitford* cases, *Rucho* involving North Carolina's congressional plan and *Benisek* involving a single Maryland congressional district, were appealed to the Supreme Court and decided in June 2019. In these cases, there were five votes for the position that commanded only plurality support in *Vieth*: namely, that all partisan gerrymandering claims are nonjusticiable political questions.

Rucho v. Common Cause

139 S. Ct. 2484 (2019)

Chief Justice ROBERTS delivered the opinion of the Court....

These cases require us to consider once again whether claims of excessive partisanship in districting are "justiciable"—that is, properly suited for resolution by the federal courts. This Court has not previously struck down a districting plan as an unconstitutional partisan gerrymander, and has struggled without success over the past several decades to discern judicially manageable standards for deciding such claims. The districting plans at issue here are highly partisan, by any measure. The question is whether the courts below appropriately exercised judicial power when they found them unconstitutional as well.

I

A

The first case involves a challenge to the congressional redistricting plan enacted by the Republican-controlled North Carolina General Assembly in 2016. *Rucho v. Common Cause*. The Republican legislators leading the redistricting effort instructed their mapmaker to use political data to draw a map that would produce a congressional delegation of ten Republicans and three Democrats. As one of the two Republicans chairing the redistricting committee stated, "I think electing Republicans is better than electing Democrats. So I drew this map to help foster what I think is better for the country." He further explained that the map was drawn with the aim of electing ten Republicans and three Democrats because he did "not believe it [would be] possible to draw a map with 11 Republicans and 2 Democrats." One Democratic state senator objected that entrenching the 10–3 advantage for Republicans was not "fair, reasonable, [or] balanced" because, as recently as 2012, "Democratic congressional candidates had received more votes on a statewide basis than Republican candidates." The General Assembly was not swayed by that objection and approved the 2016 Plan by a party-line vote.

In November 2016, North Carolina conducted congressional elections using the 2016 Plan, and Republican candidates won 10 of the 13 congressional districts. In the 2018 elections, Republican candidates won nine congressional districts, while Democratic candidates won three. The Republican candidate narrowly prevailed in the remaining district, but the State Board of Elections called a new election after allegations of fraud. . . .

B

The second case before us is *Lamone v. Benisek*. In 2011, the Maryland Legislature — dominated by Democrats — undertook to redraw the lines of that State's eight congressional districts. The Governor at the time, Democrat Martin O'Malley, led the process. He appointed a redistricting committee to help redraw the map, and asked Congressman Steny Hoyer, who has described himself as a "serial gerrymanderer," to advise the committee. The Governor later testified that his aim was to "use the redistricting process to change the overall composition of Maryland's congressional delegation to 7 Democrats and 1 Republican by flipping" one district. "[A] decision was made to go for the Sixth," which had been held by a Republican for nearly two decades. To achieve the required equal population among districts, only about 10,000 residents needed to be removed from that district. The 2011 Plan accomplished that by moving roughly 360,000 voters out of the Sixth District and moving 350,000 new voters in. Overall, the Plan reduced the number of registered Republicans in the Sixth District by about 66,000 and increased the number of registered Democrats by about 24,000. The map was adopted by a party-line vote. It was used in the 2012 election and succeeded in flipping the Sixth District. A Democrat has held the seat ever since. . . .

II

A

Article III of the Constitution limits federal courts to deciding "Cases" and "Controversies." We have understood that limitation to mean that federal courts can address only questions "historically viewed as capable of resolution through the judicial process." *Flast v. Cohen*, 392 U.S. 83, 95 (1968). In these cases we are asked to decide an important question of constitutional law. "But before we do so, we must find that the question is presented in a 'case' or 'controversy' that is, in James Madison's words, 'of a Judiciary Nature.'" *DaimlerChrysler Corp. v. Cuno*, 547 U.S. 332, 342 (2006).

Chief Justice Marshall famously wrote that it is "the province and duty of the judicial department to say what the law is." *Marbury v. Madison*. Sometimes, however, "the law is that the judicial department has no business entertaining the claim of unlawfulness—because the question is entrusted to one of the political branches or involves no judicially enforceable rights." *Vieth*. In such a case the claim is said to present a "political question" and to be nonjusticiable—outside the courts' competence and therefore beyond the courts' jurisdiction. *Baker*. Among the political question cases the Court has identified are those that lack "judicially discoverable and manageable standards for resolving [them]." *Id*.

Last Term in *Gill v. Whitford*, we reviewed our partisan gerrymandering cases and concluded that those cases "leave unresolved whether such claims may be brought." This Court's authority to act, as we said in *Gill*, is "grounded in and limited by the necessity of resolving, according to legal principles, a plaintiff's particular claim of legal right." The question here is whether there is an "appropriate role for the Federal Judiciary" in remedying the problem of partisan gerrymandering—whether such claims are claims of legal right, resolvable according to legal principles, or political questions that must find their resolution elsewhere.

B

Partisan gerrymandering is nothing new. Nor is frustration with it. The practice was known in the Colonies prior to Independence, and the Framers were familiar with it at the time of the drafting and ratification of the Constitution. During the very first congressional elections, George Washington and his Federalist allies accused Patrick Henry of trying to gerrymander Virginia's districts against their candidates—in particular James Madison, who ultimately prevailed over fellow future President James Monroe.

In 1812, Governor of Massachusetts and future Vice President Elbridge Gerry notoriously approved congressional districts that the legislature had drawn to aid the Democratic-Republican Party. The moniker "gerrymander" was born when an outraged Federalist newspaper observed that one of the misshapen districts resembled a salamander. "By 1840, the gerrymander was a recognized force in party politics and was generally attempted in all legislation enacted for the formation of election districts. It was generally conceded that each party would attempt to gain power which was not proportionate to its numerical strength."

The Framers addressed the election of Representatives to Congress in the Elections Clause. That provision assigns to state legislatures the power to prescribe the "Times, Places and Manner of holding Elections" for Members of Congress, while giving Congress the power to "make or alter" any such regulations. Whether to give that supervisory authority to the National Government was debated at the Constitutional Convention. When those opposed to such congressional oversight moved to strike the relevant language, Madison came to its defense:

> "[T]he State Legislatures will sometimes fail or refuse to consult the common interest at the expense of their local coveniency or prejudices.... Whenever the State Legislatures had a favorite measure to carry, they would take care so to mould their regulations as to favor the candidates they wished to succeed."

During the subsequent fight for ratification, the provision remained a subject of debate. Antifederalists predicted that Congress's power under the Elections Clause would allow Congress to make itself "omnipotent," setting the "time" of elections as never or the "place" in difficult to reach corners of the State. Federalists responded that, among other justifications, the revisionary power was necessary to counter state legislatures set on undermining fair representation, including through malapportionment. The Federalists were, for example, concerned that newly developing population centers would be deprived of their proper electoral weight, as some cities had been in Great Britain.

Congress has regularly exercised its Elections Clause power, including to address partisan gerrymandering. The Apportionment Act of 1842, which required single-member districts for the first time, specified that those districts be "composed of contiguous territory" in "an attempt to forbid the practice of the gerrymander." Later statutes added requirements of compactness and equality of population. (Only the single member district requirement remains in place today.) Congress also used its Elections Clause power in 1870, enacting the first comprehensive federal statute dealing with elections as a way to enforce the Fifteenth Amendment. Force Act of 1870. Starting in the 1950s, Congress enacted a series of laws to protect the right to vote through measures such as the suspension of literacy tests and the prohibition of English-only elections.

Appellants suggest that, through the Elections Clause, the Framers set aside electoral issues such as the one before us as questions that only Congress can resolve. We do not agree. In two areas — one-person, one-vote and racial gerrymandering — our cases have held that there is a role for the courts with respect to at least some issues that could arise from a State's drawing of congressional districts.

But the history is not irrelevant. The Framers were aware of electoral districting problems and considered what to do about them. They settled on a characteristic approach, assigning the issue to the state legislatures, expressly checked and balanced by the Federal Congress. As Alexander Hamilton explained, "it will ... not be denied that a discretionary power over elections ought to exist somewhere. It will, I presume, be as readily conceded that there were only three ways in which this power could have been reasonably modified and disposed: that it must either have been lodged wholly in the national legislature, or wholly in the State legislatures, or primarily in the latter, and ultimately in the former." At no point was there a suggestion that the federal courts had a role to play. Nor was there any indication that the Framers had ever heard of courts doing such a thing.

C

Courts have nevertheless been called upon to resolve a variety of questions surrounding districting. [The Court then summarizes its one-person, one-vote and racial gerrymandering precedents. See Chapter 3, Part I and Chapter 5, Part III of the Casebook.] . . .

Partisan gerrymandering claims have proved far more difficult to adjudicate. The basic reason is that, while it is illegal for a jurisdiction to depart from the one-person, one-vote rule, or to engage in racial discrimination in districting, "a jurisdiction may engage in constitutional political gerrymandering." *Hunt v. Cromartie* [*infra* Chapter 5].

To hold that legislators cannot take partisan interests into account when drawing district lines would essentially countermand the Framers' decision to entrust districting to political entities. The "central problem" is not determining whether a jurisdiction has engaged in partisan gerrymandering. It is "determining when political gerrymandering has gone too far." *Vieth*. See *LULAC* (opinion of Kennedy, J.) (difficulty is "providing a standard for deciding how much partisan dominance is too much"). . . .

III

A

In considering whether partisan gerrymandering claims are justiciable, we are mindful of Justice Kennedy's counsel in *Vieth*: Any standard for resolving such claims must be grounded in a "limited and precise rationale" and be "clear, manageable, and politically neutral." An important reason for those careful constraints is that, as a Justice with extensive experience in state and local politics put it, "[t]he opportunity to control the drawing of electoral boundaries through the legislative process of apportionment is a critical and traditional part of politics in the United States." *Bandemer* (opinion of O'Connor, J.). An expansive standard requiring "the correction of all election district lines drawn for partisan reasons would commit federal and state courts to unprecedented intervention in the American political process." *Vieth* (opinion of Kennedy, J.).

As noted, the question is one of degree: How to "provid[e] a standard for deciding how much partisan dominance is too much." *LULAC* (opinion of Kennedy, J.). And it is vital in such circumstances that the Court act only in accord with especially clear standards: "With uncertain limits, intervening courts — even when proceeding with best intentions — would risk assuming political, not legal, responsibility for a process that often produces ill will and distrust." *Vieth* (opinion of Kennedy, J.).

If federal courts are to "inject [themselves] into the most heated partisan issues" by adjudicating partisan gerrymandering claims, *Bandemer* (opinion of O'Connor, J.), they must be armed with a standard that can reliably differentiate unconstitutional from "constitutional political gerrymandering."

B

Partisan gerrymandering claims rest on an instinct that groups with a certain level of political support should enjoy a commensurate level of political power and influence. Explicitly or implicitly, a districting map is alleged to be unconstitutional because it makes it too difficult for one party to translate statewide support into seats in the legislature. But such a claim is based on a "norm that does not exist" in our electoral system — "statewide elections for representatives along party lines." *Bandemer* (opinion of O'Connor, J.).

Partisan gerrymandering claims invariably sound in a desire for proportional representation. As Justice O'Connor put it, such claims are based on "a conviction that the greater the departure from proportionality, the more suspect an apportionment plan becomes." *Id.* "Our cases, however, clearly foreclose any claim that the Constitution requires proportional representation or that legislatures in reapportioning must draw district lines to come as near as possible to allocating seats to the contending parties in proportion to what their anticipated statewide vote will be." *Id.* (plurality opinion).

The Founders certainly did not think proportional representation was required. For more than 50 years after ratification of the Constitution, many States elected their congressional representatives through at-large or "general ticket" elections. Such States typically sent single-party delegations to Congress. That meant that a party could garner nearly half of the vote statewide and wind up without any seats in the congressional delegation. The Whigs in Alabama suffered that fate in 1840: "their party garnered 43 percent of the statewide vote, yet did not receive a single seat." When Congress required single-member districts in the Apportionment Act of 1842, it was not out of a general sense of fairness, but instead a (mis)calculation by the Whigs that such a change would improve their electoral prospects.

Unable to claim that the Constitution requires proportional representation outright, plaintiffs inevitably ask the courts to make their own political judgment about how much representation particular political parties *deserve* — based on the votes of their supporters — and to rearrange the challenged districts to achieve that end. But federal courts are not equipped to apportion political power as a matter of fairness, nor is there any basis for concluding that they were authorized to do so. As Justice Scalia put it for the plurality in *Vieth*:

> "'Fairness' does not seem to us a judicially manageable standard. . . . Some criterion more solid and more demonstrably met than that seems to us necessary to enable the state legislatures to discern the limits of their districting discretion, to meaningfully constrain the discretion of the courts, and

to win public acceptance for the courts' intrusion into a process that is the very foundation of democratic decisionmaking."

The initial difficulty in settling on a "clear, manageable and politically neutral" test for fairness is that it is not even clear what fairness looks like in this context. There is a large measure of "unfairness" in any winner-take-all system. Fairness may mean a greater number of competitive districts. Such a claim seeks to undo packing and cracking so that supporters of the disadvantaged party have a better shot at electing their preferred candidates. But making as many districts as possible more competitive could be a recipe for disaster for the disadvantaged party. As Justice White has pointed out, "[i]f all or most of the districts are competitive . . . even a narrow statewide preference for either party would produce an overwhelming majority for the winning party in the state legislature." *Bandemer* (plurality opinion).

On the other hand, perhaps the ultimate objective of a "fairer" share of seats in the congressional delegation is most readily achieved by yielding to the gravitational pull of proportionality and engaging in cracking and packing, to ensure each party its "appropriate" share of "safe" seats. Such an approach, however, comes at the expense of competitive districts and of individuals in districts allocated to the opposing party.

Or perhaps fairness should be measured by adherence to "traditional" districting criteria, such as maintaining political subdivisions, keeping communities of interest together, and protecting incumbents. But protecting incumbents, for example, enshrines a particular partisan distribution. And the "natural political geography" of a State—such as the fact that urban electoral districts are often dominated by one political party—can itself lead to inherently packed districts. As Justice Kennedy has explained, traditional criteria such as compactness and contiguity "cannot promise political neutrality when used as the basis for relief. Instead, it seems, a decision under these standards would unavoidably have significant political effect, whether intended or not." *Vieth* (opinion of Kennedy, J.).

Deciding among just these different visions of fairness (you can imagine many others) poses basic questions that are political, not legal. There are no legal standards discernible in the Constitution for making such judgments, let alone limited and precise standards that are clear, manageable, and politically neutral. Any judicial decision on what is "fair" in this context would be an "unmoored determination" of the sort characteristic of a political question beyond the competence of the federal courts. *Zivotofsky v. Clinton*, 566 U.S. 189, 196 (2012).

And it is only after determining how to define fairness that you can even begin to answer the determinative question: "How much is too much?" At what point does permissible partisanship become unconstitutional? If compliance with traditional districting criteria is the fairness touchstone, for example, how much deviation from those criteria is constitutionally acceptable and how should mapdrawers prioritize competing criteria? Should a court "reverse gerrymander" other parts of a State to counteract "natural" gerrymandering caused, for example, by the urban concentration of one party? If a districting plan protected half of the incumbents but redistricted the rest into head to head races, would that be constitutional? A court would have to rank the relative importance of those traditional criteria and weigh how much deviation from each to allow.

If a court instead focused on the respective number of seats in the legislature, it would have to decide the ideal number of seats for each party and determine at what point deviation from that balance went too far. If a 5–3 allocation corresponds most closely to statewide vote totals, is a 6–2 allocation permissible, given that legislatures have the authority to engage in a certain degree of partisan gerrymandering? Which seats should be packed and which cracked? Or if the goal is as many competitive districts as possible, how close does the split need to be for the district to be considered competitive? Presumably not all districts could qualify, so how to choose? Even assuming the court knew which version of fairness to be looking for, there are no discernible and manageable standards for deciding whether there has been a violation. The questions are "unguided and ill suited to the development of judicial standards," *Vieth* (plurality opinion), and "results from one gerrymandering case to the next would likely be disparate and inconsistent," *Vieth* (opinion of Kennedy, J.).

Appellees contend that if we can adjudicate one-person, one-vote claims, we can also assess partisan gerrymandering claims. But the one-person, one-vote rule is relatively easy to administer as a matter of math. The same cannot be said of partisan gerrymandering claims, because the Constitution supplies no objective measure for assessing whether a districting map treats a political party fairly. It hardly follows from the principle that each person must have an equal say in the election of representatives that a person is entitled to have his political party achieve representation in some way commensurate to its share of statewide support.

More fundamentally, "vote dilution" in the one-person, one-vote cases refers to the idea that each vote must carry equal weight. In other words, each representative must be accountable to (approximately) the same number of constituents. That requirement does not extend to political parties. It does not mean that each party must be influential in proportion to its number of supporters. As we stated unanimously in *Gill*, "this Court is not responsible for vindicating generalized partisan preferences. The Court's constitutionally prescribed role is to vindicate the individual rights of the people appearing before it."

Nor do our racial gerrymandering cases provide an appropriate standard for assessing partisan gerrymandering. "[N]othing in our case law compels the conclusion that racial and political gerrymanders are subject to precisely the same constitutional scrutiny. In fact, our country's long and persistent history of racial discrimination in voting—as well as our Fourteenth Amendment jurisprudence, which always has reserved the strictest scrutiny for discrimination on the basis of race—would seem to compel the opposite conclusion." *Shaw v. Reno* [*infra* Chapter 5]. Unlike partisan gerrymandering claims, a racial gerrymandering claim does not ask for a fair share of political power and influence, with all the justiciability conundrums that entails. It asks instead for the elimination of a racial classification. A partisan gerrymandering claim cannot ask for the elimination of partisanship.

IV

Appellees and the dissent propose a number of "tests" for evaluating partisan gerrymandering claims, but none meets the need for a limited and precise standard that is judicially discernible and manageable. And none provides a solid grounding for judges to take the extraordinary step of reallocating power and influence between political parties.

A

The *Common Cause* District Court concluded that all but one of the districts in North Carolina's 2016 Plan violated the Equal Protection Clause by intentionally diluting the voting strength of Democrats. In reaching that result the court first required the plaintiffs to prove "that a legislative mapdrawer's predominant purpose in drawing the lines of a particular district was to 'subordinate adherents of one political party and entrench a rival party in power.'" The District Court next required a showing "that the dilution of the votes of supporters of a disfavored party in a particular district—by virtue of cracking or packing—is likely to persist in subsequent elections such that an elected representative from the favored party in the district will not feel a need to be responsive to constituents who support the disfavored party." Finally, after a prima facie showing of partisan vote dilution, the District Court shifted the burden to the defendants to prove that the discriminatory effects are "attributable to a legitimate state interest or other neutral explanation."

The District Court's "predominant intent" prong is borrowed from the racial gerrymandering context. In racial gerrymandering cases, we rely on a "predominant intent" inquiry to determine whether race was, in fact, the reason particular district boundaries were drawn the way they were. If district lines were drawn for the purpose of separating racial groups, then they are subject to strict scrutiny because "race-based decisionmaking is inherently suspect." *Miller v. Johnson* [*infra* Chapter 5]. But determining that lines were drawn on the basis of partisanship does not indicate that the districting was improper. A permissible intent—securing partisan advantage—does not become constitutionally impermissible, like racial discrimination, when that permissible intent "predominates."

The District Court tried to limit the reach of its test by requiring plaintiffs to show, in addition to predominant partisan intent, that vote dilution "is likely to persist" to such a degree that the elected representative will feel free to ignore the concerns of the supporters of the minority party. But "[t]o allow district courts to strike down apportionment plans on the basis of their prognostications as to the outcome of future elections . . . invites 'findings' on matters as to which neither judges nor anyone else can have any confidence." *Bandemer* (opinion of O'Connor, J.). And the test adopted by the Common Cause court requires a far more nuanced prediction than simply who would prevail in future political contests. Judges must forecast with unspecified certainty whether a prospective winner will have a margin of victory sufficient to permit him to ignore the supporters of his defeated opponent (whoever that may turn out to be). Judges not only have to pick the winner—they have to beat the point spread.

The appellees assure us that "the persistence of a party's advantage may be shown through sensitivity testing: probing how a plan would perform under other plausible electoral conditions." Experience proves that accurately predicting electoral outcomes is not so simple, either because the plans are based on flawed assumptions about voter preferences and behavior or because demographics and priorities change over time. In our two leading partisan gerrymandering cases themselves, the predictions of durability proved to be dramatically wrong. In 1981, Republicans controlled both houses of the Indiana Legislature as well as the governorship. Democrats challenged the state legislature districting map enacted by the Republicans. This Court in *Bandemer* rejected that challenge, and just months later the Democrats increased their share of House seats in the 1986 elections. Two years later the House was split 50–50 between Democrats and Republicans, and the Democrats took control of the chamber in 1990. Democrats also challenged the Pennsylvania congressional districting plan at issue in *Vieth*. Two years after that challenge failed, they gained four seats in the delegation, going from a 12–7 minority to an 11–8 majority. At the next election, they flipped another Republican seat.

Even the most sophisticated districting maps cannot reliably account for some of the reasons voters prefer one candidate over another, or why their preferences may change. Voters elect individual candidates in individual districts, and their selections depend on the issues that matter to them, the quality of the candidates, the tone of the candidates' campaigns, the performance of an incumbent, national events or local issues that drive voter turnout, and other considerations. Many voters split their tickets. Others never register with a political party, and vote for candidates from both major parties at different points during their lifetimes. For all of those reasons, asking judges to predict how a particular districting map will perform in future elections risks basing constitutional holdings on unstable ground outside judicial expertise.

It is hard to see what the District Court's third prong—providing the defendant an opportunity to show that the discriminatory effects were due to a "legitimate redistricting objective"—adds to the inquiry. The first prong already requires the plaintiff to prove that partisan advantage predominates. Asking whether a legitimate purpose other than partisanship was the motivation for a particular districting map just restates the question.

B

The District Courts also found partisan gerrymandering claims justiciable under the First Amendment, coalescing around a basic three-part test: proof of intent to burden individuals based on their voting history or party affiliation; an actual burden on political speech or associational rights; and a causal link between the invidious intent and actual burden. Both District Courts concluded that the districting plans at issue violated the plaintiffs' First Amendment right to association. The District Court in North Carolina relied on testimony that, after the 2016 Plan was put in place, the plaintiffs faced "difficulty raising money, attracting candidates, and mobilizing voters to support the political causes and issues such Plaintiffs sought to advance." Similarly, the District Court in Maryland examined testimony that "revealed a lack of enthusiasm, indifference to voting, a sense of disenfranchisement, a sense of disconnection, and confusion," and concluded that Republicans in the Sixth District "were burdened in fundraising, attracting volunteers, campaigning, and generating interest in voting."

To begin, there are no restrictions on speech, association, or any other First Amendment activities in the districting plans at issue. The plaintiffs are free to engage in those activities no matter what the effect of a plan may be on their district.

The plaintiffs' argument is that partisanship in districting should be regarded as simple discrimination against supporters of the opposing party on the basis of political viewpoint. Under that theory, any level of partisanship in districting would constitute an infringement of their First Amendment rights. But as the Court has explained, "[i]t would be idle ... to contend that any political consideration taken into account in fashioning a reapportionment plan is sufficient to invalidate it." *Gaffney v. Cummings*. The First Amendment test simply describes the act of districting for partisan advantage. It provides no standard for determining when partisan activity goes too far.

As for actual burden, the slight anecdotal evidence found sufficient by the District Courts in these cases shows that this too is not a serious standard for separating constitutional from unconstitutional partisan gerrymandering. The District Courts relied on testimony about difficulty drumming up volunteers and enthusiasm. How much of a decline in voter engagement is enough to constitute a First Amendment burden? How many door knocks must go unanswered? How many petitions unsigned? How many calls for volunteers unheeded? The *Common Cause* District Court held that a partisan gerrymander places an unconstitutional burden on speech if it has more than a "*de minimis*" "chilling effect or adverse impact" on any First Amendment activity. The court went on to rule that there would be an adverse effect "even if the speech of [the plaintiffs] was not *in fact* chilled"; it was enough that the districting plan "makes it easier for supporters of Republican candidates to translate their votes into seats," thereby "enhanc[ing] the[ir] relative voice."

These cases involve blatant examples of partisanship driving districting decisions. But the First Amendment analysis below offers no "clear" and "manageable" way of distinguishing permissible from impermissible partisan motivation. The *Common Cause* court embraced that conclusion, observing that "a judicially manageable framework for evaluating partisan gerrymandering claims need not distinguish an 'acceptable' level of partisan gerrymandering from 'excessive' partisan gerrymandering" because "the Constitution does not authorize state redistricting bodies to engage in such partisan gerrymandering." The decisions below prove the prediction of the *Vieth* plurality that "a First Amendment claim, if it were sustained, would render unlawful *all* consideration of political affiliation in districting," contrary to our established precedent.

C

The dissent proposes using a State's own districting criteria as a neutral baseline from which to measure how extreme a partisan gerrymander is. The dissent would have us line up all the possible maps drawn using those criteria according to the partisan distribution they would produce. Distance from the "median" map would indicate whether a particular districting plan harms supporters of one party to an unconstitutional extent.

As an initial matter, it does not make sense to use criteria that will vary from State to State and year to year as the baseline for determining whether a gerrymander violates the Federal Constitution. The degree of partisan advantage that the Constitution tolerates should not turn on criteria offered by the gerrymanderers themselves. It is easy to imagine how different criteria could move the median map toward different partisan distributions. As a result, the same map could be constitutional or not depending solely on what the mapmakers said they set out to do. That possibility illustrates that the dissent's proposed constitutional test is indeterminate and arbitrary.

Even if we were to accept the dissent's proposed baseline, it would return us to "the original unanswerable question (How much political motivation and effect is too much?)." *Vieth* (plurality opinion). Would twenty percent away from the median map be okay? Forty percent? Sixty percent? Why or why not? (We appreciate that the dissent finds all the unanswerable questions annoying, but it seems a useful way to make the point.) The dissent's answer says it all: "This much is too much." That is not even trying to articulate a standard or rule.

The dissent argues that there are other instances in law where matters of degree are left to the courts. True enough. But those instances typically involve constitutional or statutory provisions or common law confining and guiding the exercise of judicial discretion. For example, the dissent cites the need to determine "substantial anticompetitive effect[s]" in antitrust law. That language, however, grew out of the Sherman Act, understood from the beginning to have its "origin in the common law" and to be "familiar in the law of this country prior to and at the time of the adoption of the [A]ct." *Standard Oil Co. v. United States*, 221 U.S. 1, 51 (1911). Judges began with a significant body of law about what constituted a legal violation. In other cases, the pertinent statutory terms draw meaning from related provisions or statutory context. Here, on the other hand, the Constitution provides no basis whatever to guide the exercise of judicial discretion. Common experience gives content to terms such as "substantial risk" or "substantial harm," but the same cannot be said of substantial deviation from a median map. There is no way to tell whether the prohibited deviation from that map should kick in at 25 percent or 75 percent or some other point. The only provision in the Constitution that specifically addresses the matter assigns it to the political branches. See [the Elections Clause]. . . .

V

Excessive partisanship in districting leads to results that reasonably seem unjust. But the fact that such gerrymandering is "incompatible with democratic principles" does not mean that the solution lies with the federal judiciary. *Arizona State Legislature v. Arizona Independent Redistricting Commission* [*infra* Chapter 7]. We conclude that partisan gerrymandering claims present political questions beyond the reach of the federal courts. Federal judges have no license to reallocate political power between the two major political parties, with no plausible grant of authority in the Constitution, and no legal standards to limit and direct their decisions. "[J]udicial action must be governed by *standard*, by *rule*," and must be "principled, rational, and based upon reasoned distinctions" found in the Constitution or laws. *Vieth* (plurality opinion). Judicial review of partisan gerrymandering does not meet those basic requirements.

Today the dissent essentially embraces the argument that the Court unanimously rejected in *Gill*: "this Court *can* address the problem of partisan gerrymandering because it *must*." That is not the test of our authority under the Constitution; that document instead "confines the federal courts to a properly judicial role."

What the appellees and dissent seek is an unprecedented expansion of judicial power. We have never struck down a partisan gerrymander as unconstitutional—despite various requests over the past 45 years. The expansion of judicial authority would not be into just any area of controversy, but into one of the most intensely partisan aspects of American political life. That intervention would be unlimited in scope and duration—it would recur over and over again around the country with each new round of districting, for state as well as federal representatives. Consideration of the impact of today's ruling on democratic principles cannot ignore the effect of the unelected and politically unaccountable branch of the Federal Government assuming such an extraordinary and unprecedented role.

Our conclusion does not condone excessive partisan gerrymandering. Nor does our conclusion condemn complaints about districting to echo into a void. The States, for example, are actively addressing the issue on a number of fronts. In 2015, the Supreme Court of Florida struck down that State's congressional districting plan as a violation of the Fair Districts Amendment to the Florida Constitution. The dissent wonders why we can't do the same. The answer is that there is no "Fair Districts Amendment" to the Federal Constitution. Provisions in state statutes and state constitutions can provide standards and guidance for state courts to apply. (We do not understand how the dissent can maintain that a provision saying that no districting plan "shall be drawn with the intent to favor or disfavor a political party" provides little guidance on the question.) Indeed, numerous other States are restricting partisan considerations in districting through legislation. One way they are doing so is by placing power to draw electoral districts in the hands of independent commissions. For example, in November 2018, voters in Colorado and Michigan approved constitutional amendments creating multimember commissions that will be responsible in whole or in part for creating and approving district maps for congressional and state legislative districts. Missouri is trying a different tack. Voters there overwhelmingly approved the creation of a new position — state demographer — to draw state legislative district lines.

Other States have mandated at least some of the traditional districting criteria for their mapmakers. Some have outright prohibited partisan favoritism in redistricting. See Fla. Const., Art. III, § 20(a) ("No apportionment plan or individual district shall be drawn with the intent to favor or disfavor a political party or an incumbent."); Mo. Const., Art. III, § 3 ("Districts shall be designed in a manner that achieves both partisan fairness and, secondarily, competitiveness. 'Partisan fairness' means that parties shall be able to translate their popular support into legislative representation with approximately equal efficiency."). . . .

As noted, the Framers gave Congress the power to do something about partisan gerrymandering in the Elections Clause. The first bill introduced in the 116th Congress would require States to create 15-member independent commissions to draw congressional districts and would establish certain redistricting criteria, including protection for communities of interest, and ban partisan gerrymandering.

Dozens of other bills have been introduced to limit reliance on political considerations in redistricting. In 2010, H.R. 6250 would have required States to follow standards of compactness, contiguity, and respect for political subdivisions in redistricting. It also would have prohibited the establishment of congressional districts "with the major purpose of diluting the voting strength of any person, or group, including any political party," except when necessary to comply with the Voting Rights Act of 1965.

Another example is the Fairness and Independence in Redistricting Act, which was introduced in 2005 and has been reintroduced in every Congress since. That bill would require every State to establish an independent commission to adopt redistricting plans. The bill also set forth criteria for the independent commissions to use, such as compactness, contiguity, and population equality. It would prohibit consideration of voting history, political party affiliation, or incumbent Representative's residence.

We express no view on any of these pending proposals. We simply note that the avenue for reform established by the Framers, and used by Congress in the past, remains open.

* * *

No one can accuse this Court of having a crabbed view of the reach of its competence. But we have no commission to allocate political power and influence in the absence of a constitutional directive or legal standards to guide us in the exercise of such authority. "It is emphatically the province and duty of the judicial department to say what the law is." In this rare circumstance, that means our duty is to say "this is not law."

The judgments of the United States District Court for the Middle District of North Carolina and the United States District Court for the District of Maryland are vacated, and the cases are remanded with instructions to dismiss for lack of jurisdiction.

It is so ordered.

Justice KAGAN, with whom Justice GINSBURG, Justice BREYER, and Justice SOTOMAYOR join, dissenting.

For the first time ever, this Court refuses to remedy a constitutional violation because it thinks the task beyond judicial capabilities.

And not just any constitutional violation. The partisan gerrymanders in these cases deprived citizens of the most fundamental of their constitutional rights: the rights to participate equally in the political process, to join with others to advance political beliefs, and to choose their political representatives. In so doing, the partisan gerrymanders here debased and dishonored our democracy, turning upside-down the core American idea that all governmental power derives from the people. These gerrymanders enabled politicians to entrench themselves in office as against voters' preferences. They promoted partisanship above respect for the popular will. They encouraged a politics of polarization and dysfunction. If left unchecked, gerrymanders like the ones here may irreparably damage our system of government.

And checking them is not beyond the courts. The majority's abdication comes just when courts across the country, including those below, have coalesced around manageable judicial standards to resolve partisan gerrymandering claims. Those standards satisfy the majority's own benchmarks. They do not require—indeed, they do not permit—courts to rely on their own ideas of electoral fairness, whether proportional representation or any other. And they limit courts to correcting only egregious gerrymanders, so judges do not become omnipresent players in the political process. But yes, the standards used here do allow—as well they should—judicial intervention in the worst-of-the-worst cases of democratic subversion, causing blatant constitutional harms. In other words, they allow courts to undo partisan gerrymanders of the kind we face today from North Carolina and Maryland. In giving such gerrymanders a pass from judicial review, the majority goes tragically wrong.

I

Maybe the majority errs in these cases because it pays so little attention to the constitutional harms at their core. After dutifully reciting each case's facts, the majority leaves them forever behind, instead immersing itself in everything that could conceivably go amiss if courts became involved. So it is necessary to fill in the gaps. To recount exactly what politicians in North Carolina and Maryland did to entrench their parties in political office, whatever the electorate might think. And to elaborate on the constitutional injury those politicians wreaked, to our democratic system and to individuals' rights. All that will help in considering whether courts confronting partisan gerrymandering claims are really so hamstrung—so unable to carry out their constitutional duties—as the majority thinks.

A

[Justice Kagan extensively discusses the facts in *Rucho* and *Lamone*, focusing on the raw partisan motives underlying the North Carolina and Maryland maps as well as the drafters' success, in subsequent elections, in accomplishing their objectives.]

B

Now back to the question I asked before: Is that how American democracy is supposed to work? I have yet to meet the person who thinks so.

"Governments," the Declaration of Independence states, "deriv[e] their just Powers from the Consent of the Governed." The Constitution begins: "We the People of the United States." The Gettysburg Address (almost) ends: "[G]overnment of the people, by the people, for the people." If there is a single idea that made our Nation (and that our Nation commended to the world), it is this one: The people are sovereign. The "power," James Madison wrote, "is in the people over the Government, and not in the Government over the people."

Free and fair and periodic elections are the key to that vision. The people get to choose their representatives. And then they get to decide, at regular intervals, whether to keep them. Madison again: "[R]epublican liberty" demands "not only, that all power should be derived from the people; but that those entrusted with it should be kept in dependence on the people." Members of the House of Representatives, in particular, are supposed to "recollect[] [that] dependence" every day. To retain an "intimate sympathy with the people," they must be "compelled to anticipate the moment" when their "exercise of [power] is to be reviewed." Election day—next year, and two years later, and two years after that—is what links the people to their representatives, and gives the people their sovereign power. That day is the foundation of democratic governance.

And partisan gerrymandering can make it meaningless. At its most extreme—as in North Carolina and Maryland—the practice amounts to "rigging elections." By drawing districts to maximize the power of some voters and minimize the power of others, a party in office at the right time can entrench itself there for a decade or more, no matter what the voters would prefer. Just ask the people of North Carolina and Maryland. The "core principle of republican government," this Court has recognized, is "that the voters should choose their representatives, not the other way around." *Arizona State Legislature*. Partisan gerrymandering turns it the other way around. By that mechanism, politicians can cherry-pick voters to ensure their reelection. And the power becomes, as Madison put it, "in the Government over the people."

The majority disputes none of this. I think it important to underscore that fact: The majority disputes none of what I have said (or will say) about how gerrymanders undermine democracy. Indeed, the majority concedes (really, how could it not?) that gerrymandering is "incompatible with democratic principles." *Id.* And therefore what? That recognition would seem to demand a response. The majority offers two ideas that might qualify as such. One is that the political process can deal with the problem—a proposition so dubious on its face that I feel secure in delaying my answer for some time. The other is that political gerrymanders have always been with us. To its credit, the majority does not frame that point as an originalist constitutional argument. After all (as the majority rightly notes), racial and residential gerrymanders were also once with us, but the Court has done something about that fact. The majority's idea instead seems to be that if we have lived with partisan gerrymanders so long, we will survive.

That complacency has no cause. Yes, partisan gerrymandering goes back to the Republic's earliest days. (As does vociferous opposition to it.) But big data and modern technology—of just the kind that the mapmakers in North Carolina and Maryland used—make today's gerrymandering altogether different from the crude linedrawing of the past. Old-time efforts, based on little more than guesses, sometimes led to so-called dummymanders—gerrymanders that went spectacularly wrong. Not likely in today's world. Mapmakers now have access to more granular data about party preference and voting behavior than ever before. County-level voting data has given way to precinct-level or city-block-level data; and increasingly, mapmakers avail themselves of data sets providing wide-ranging information about even individual voters. Just as important, advancements in computing technology have enabled mapmakers to put that information to use with unprecedented efficiency and precision. While bygone mapmakers may have drafted three or four alternative districting plans, today's mapmakers can generate thousands of possibilities at the touch of a key—and then choose the one giving their party maximum advantage (usually while still meeting traditional districting requirements). The effect is to make gerrymanders far more effective and durable than before, insulating politicians against all but the most titanic shifts in the political tides. These are not your grandfather's—let alone the Framers'—gerrymanders.

The proof is in the 2010 pudding. That redistricting cycle produced some of the most extreme partisan gerrymanders in this country's history. I've already recounted the results from North Carolina and Maryland, and you'll hear even more about those. But the voters in those States were not the only ones to fall prey to such districting perversions. Take Pennsylvania. In the three congressional elections occurring under the State's original districting plan (before the State Supreme Court struck it down), Democrats received between 45% and 51% of the statewide vote, but won only 5 of 18 House seats. Or go next door to Ohio. There, in four congressional elections, Democrats tallied between 39% and 47% of the statewide vote, but never won more than 4 of 16 House seats. (Nor is there any reason to think that the results in those States stemmed from political geography or non-partisan districting criteria, rather than from partisan manipulation.) And gerrymanders will only get worse (or depending on your perspective, better) as time goes on—as data becomes ever more fine-grained and data analysis techniques continue to improve. What was possible with paper and pen—or even with Windows 95—doesn't hold a candle (or an LED bulb?) to what will become possible with developments like machine learning. And someplace along this road, "we the people" become sovereign no longer.

C

Partisan gerrymandering of the kind before us not only subverts democracy (as if that weren't bad enough). It violates individuals' constitutional rights as well. That statement is not the lonesome cry of a dissenting Justice. This Court has recognized extreme partisan gerrymandering as such a violation for many years.

Partisan gerrymandering operates through vote dilution — the devaluation of one citizen's vote as compared to others. A mapmaker draws district lines to "pack" and "crack" voters likely to support the disfavored party. He packs supermajorities of those voters into a relatively few districts, in numbers far greater than needed for their preferred candidates to prevail. Then he cracks the rest across many more districts, spreading them so thin that their candidates will not be able to win. Whether the person is packed or cracked, his vote carries less weight — has less consequence — than it would under a neutrally drawn (non-partisan) map. In short, the mapmaker has made some votes count for less, because they are likely to go for the other party.

That practice implicates the Fourteenth Amendment's Equal Protection Clause. The Fourteenth Amendment, we long ago recognized, "guarantees the opportunity for equal participation by all voters in the election" of legislators. *Reynolds.* And that opportunity "can be denied by a debasement or dilution of the weight of a citizen's vote just as effectively as by wholly prohibiting the free exercise of the franchise." *Id.* Based on that principle, this Court in its one-person-one-vote decisions prohibited creating districts with significantly different populations. A State could not, we explained, thus "dilut[e] the weight of votes because of place of residence." *Id.* The constitutional injury in a partisan gerrymandering case is much the same, except that the dilution is based on party affiliation. In such a case, too, the districters have set out to reduce the weight of certain citizens' votes, and thereby deprive them of their capacity to "full[y] and effective[ly] participat[e] in the political process[]." *Id.* . . .

And partisan gerrymandering implicates the First Amendment too. That Amendment gives its greatest protection to political beliefs, speech, and association. Yet partisan gerrymanders subject certain voters to "disfavored treatment" — again, counting their votes for less — precisely because of "their voting history [and] their expression of political views." *Vieth* (opinion of Kennedy, J.). And added to that strictly personal harm is an associational one. Representative democracy is "unimaginable without the ability of citizens to band together in [support of] candidates who espouse their political views." *California Democratic Party v. Jones* [*infra* Chapter 8]. By diluting the votes of certain citizens, the State frustrates their efforts to translate those affiliations into political effectiveness. In both those ways, partisan gerrymanders of the kind we confront here undermine the protections of "democracy embodied in the First Amendment." *Elrod v. Burns* [*infra* Chapter 8].

Though different Justices have described the constitutional harm in diverse ways, nearly all have agreed on this much: Extreme partisan gerrymandering (as happened in North Carolina and Maryland) violates the Constitution. See, *e.g., Vieth* (plurality opinion) ("[A]n excessive injection of politics [in districting] is unlawful" (emphasis deleted)). . . . Once again, the majority never disagrees; it appears to accept the "principle that each person must have an equal say in the election of representatives." And indeed, without this settled and shared understanding that cases like these inflict constitutional injury, the question of whether there are judicially manageable standards for resolving them would never come up.

II

So the only way to understand the majority's opinion is as follows: In the face of grievous harm to democratic governance and flagrant infringements on individuals' rights—in the face of escalating partisan manipulation whose compatibility with this Nation's values and law no one defends—the majority declines to provide any remedy. For the first time in this Nation's history, the majority declares that it can do nothing about an acknowledged constitutional violation because it has searched high and low and cannot find a workable legal standard to apply.

The majority gives two reasons for thinking that the adjudication of partisan gerrymandering claims is beyond judicial capabilities. First and foremost, the majority says, it cannot find a neutral baseline—one not based on contestable notions of political fairness—from which to measure injury. . . . And second, the majority argues that even after establishing a baseline, a court would have no way to answer "the determinative question: 'How much is too much?'" . . .

I'll give the majority this one—and important—thing: It identifies some dangers everyone should want to avoid. Judges should not be apportioning political power based on their own vision of electoral fairness, whether proportional representation or any other. And judges should not be striking down maps left, right, and center, on the view that every smidgen of politics is a smidgen too much. Respect for state legislative processes—and restraint in the exercise of judicial authority—counsels intervention in only egregious cases.

But in throwing up its hands, the majority misses something under its nose: What it says can't be done has been done. Over the past several years, federal courts across the country—including, but not exclusively, in the decisions below—have largely converged on a standard for adjudicating partisan gerrymandering claims (striking down both Democratic and Republican districting plans in the process). And that standard does what the majority says is impossible. The standard does not use any judge-made conception of electoral fairness—either proportional representation or any other; instead, it takes as its baseline a State's own criteria of fairness, apart from partisan gain. And by requiring plaintiffs to make difficult showings relating to both purpose and effects, the standard invalidates the most extreme, but only the most extreme, partisan gerrymanders.

Below, I first explain the framework courts have developed, and describe its application in these two cases. Doing so reveals in even starker detail than before how much these partisan gerrymanders deviated from democratic norms. As I lay out the lower courts' analyses, I consider two specific criticisms the majority levels — each of which reveals a saddening nonchalance about the threat such districting poses to self-governance. All of that lays the groundwork for then assessing the majority's more general view, described above, that judicial policing in this area cannot be either neutral or restrained. The lower courts' reasoning, as I'll show, proves the opposite.

A

Start with the standard the lower courts used. The majority disaggregates the opinions below, distinguishing the one from the other and then chopping up each into "a number of 'tests.'" But in doing so, it fails to convey the decisions' most significant — and common — features. Both courts focused on the harm of vote dilution, though the North Carolina court mostly grounded its analysis in the Fourteenth Amendment and the Maryland court in the First. And both courts (like others around the country) used basically the same three-part test to decide whether the plaintiffs had made out a vote dilution claim. As many legal standards do, that test has three parts: (1) intent; (2) effects; and (3) causation. First, the plaintiffs challenging a districting plan must prove that state officials' "predominant purpose" in drawing a district's lines was to "entrench [their party] in power" by diluting the votes of citizens favoring its rival. Second, the plaintiffs must establish that the lines drawn in fact have the intended effect by "substantially" diluting their votes. And third, if the plaintiffs make those showings, the State must come up with a legitimate, non-partisan justification to save its map. If you are a lawyer, you know that this test looks utterly ordinary. It is the sort of thing courts work with every day.

Turn now to the test's application. First, did the North Carolina and Maryland districters have the predominant purpose of entrenching their own party in power? Here, the two District Courts catalogued the overwhelming direct evidence that they did. To remind you of some highlights: North Carolina's redistricting committee used "Partisan Advantage" as an official criterion for drawing district lines. And from the first to the last, that committee's chair (along with his mapmaker) acted to ensure a 10–3 partisan split, whatever the statewide vote, because he thought that "electing Republicans is better than electing Democrats." For their part, Maryland's Democrats — the Governor, senior Congressman, and State Senate President alike — openly admitted to a single driving purpose: flip the Sixth District from Republican to Democratic. They did not blanch from moving some 700,000 voters into new districts (when one-person-one-vote rules required relocating just 10,000) for that reason and that reason alone.

The majority's response to the District Courts' purpose analysis is discomfiting. The majority does not contest the lower courts' findings; how could it? Instead, the majority says that state officials' intent to entrench their party in power is perfectly "permissible," even when it is the predominant factor in drawing district lines. But that is wrong. True enough, that the intent to inject "political considerations" into districting may not raise any constitutional concerns. In *Gaffney*, for example, we thought it non-problematic when state officials used political data to ensure rough proportional representation between the two parties. And true enough that even the naked purpose to gain partisan advantage may not rise to the level of constitutional notice when it is not the driving force in mapmaking or when the intended gain is slight. But when political actors have a specific and predominant intent to entrench themselves in power by manipulating district lines, that goes too far. Consider again Justice Kennedy's hypothetical of mapmakers who set out to maximally burden (i.e., make count for as little as possible) the votes going to a rival party. Does the majority really think that goal is permissible? But why even bother with hypotheticals? Just consider the purposes here. It cannot be permissible and thus irrelevant, as the majority claims, that state officials have as their purpose the kind of grotesquely gerrymandered map that, according to all this Court has ever said, violates the Constitution.

On to the second step of the analysis, where the plaintiffs must prove that the districting plan substantially dilutes their votes. The majority fails to discuss most of the evidence the District Courts relied on to find that the plaintiffs had done so. But that evidence — particularly from North Carolina — is the key to understanding both the problem these cases present and the solution to it they offer. The evidence reveals just how bad the two gerrymanders were (in case you had any doubts). And it shows how the same technologies and data that today facilitate extreme partisan gerrymanders also enable courts to discover them, by exposing just how much they dilute votes.

Consider the sort of evidence used in North Carolina first. There, the plaintiffs demonstrated the districting plan's effects mostly by relying on what might be called the "extreme outlier approach." (Here's a spoiler: the State's plan was one.) The approach — which also has recently been used in Michigan and Ohio litigation — begins by using advanced computing technology to randomly generate a large collection of districting plans that incorporate the State's physical and political geography and meet its declared districting criteria, except for partisan gain. For each of those maps, the method then uses actual precinct-level votes from past elections to determine a partisan outcome (i.e., the number of Democratic and Republican seats that map produces). Suppose we now have 1,000 maps, each with a partisan outcome attached to it. We can line up those maps on a continuum — the most favorable to Republicans on one end, the most favorable to Democrats on the other. We can then find the median outcome — that is, the outcome smack dab in the center — in a world with no partisan manipulation. And we can see where the State's actual plan falls on the spectrum — at or near the median or way out on one of the tails? The further out on the tail, the more extreme the partisan distortion and the more significant the vote dilution.

Using that approach, the North Carolina plaintiffs offered a boatload of alternative districting plans — all showing that the State's map was an out-out-out-outlier. One expert produced 3,000 maps, adhering in the way described above to the districting criteria that the North Carolina redistricting committee had used, other than partisan advantage. To calculate the partisan outcome of those maps, the expert also used the same election data (a composite of seven elections) that

Hofeller had employed when devising the North Carolina plan in the first instance. The results were, shall we say, striking. Every single one of the 3,000 maps would have produced at least one more Democratic House Member than the State's actual map, and 77% would have elected three or four more. A second expert obtained essentially the same results with maps conforming to more generic districting criteria (e.g., compactness and contiguity of districts). Over 99% of that expert's 24,518 simulations would have led to the election of at least one more Democrat, and over 70% would have led to two or three more. Based on those and other findings, the District Court determined that the North Carolina plan substantially dilutes the plaintiffs' votes.[4] . . .

The majority claims all these findings are mere "prognostications" about the future, in which no one "can have any confidence." But the courts below did not gaze into crystal balls, as the majority tries to suggest. Their findings about these gerrymanders' effects on voters — both in the past and predictably in the future — were evidence-based, data-based, statistics-based. Knowledge-based, one might say. The courts did what anyone would want a decisionmaker to do when so much hangs in the balance. They looked hard at the facts, and they went where the facts led them. They availed themselves of all the information that mapmakers (like Hofeller and Hawkins) and politicians (like Lewis and O'Malley) work so hard to amass and then use to make every districting decision. They refused to content themselves with unsupported and out-of-date musings about the unpredictability of the American voter. They did not bet America's future — as today the majority does — on the idea that maps constructed with so much expertise and care to make electoral outcomes impervious to voting would somehow or other come apart. They looked at the evidence — at the facts about how these districts operated — and they could reach only one conclusion. By substantially diluting the votes of citizens favoring their rivals, the politicians of one party had succeeded in entrenching themselves in office. They had beat democracy.

B

The majority's broadest claim, as I've noted, is that this is a price we must pay because judicial oversight of partisan gerrymandering cannot be "politically neutral" or "manageable." . . . But [the majority] never tries to analyze the serious question presented here — whether the kind of standard developed below falls prey to those objections, or instead allows for neutral and manageable oversight. The

4. The District Court also relied on actual election results (under both the new plan and the similar one preceding it) and on mathematical measurements of the new plan's "partisan asymmetry." Those calculations assess whether supporters of the two parties can translate their votes into representation with equal ease. See Stephanopoulos & McGhee, *The Measure of a Metric*, 70 Stan. L. Rev. 1503, 1505–07 (2018). The court found that the new North Carolina plan led to extreme asymmetry, compared both to plans used in the rest of the country and to plans previously used in the State.

answer, as you've already heard enough to know, is the latter. That kind of oversight is not only possible; it's been done.

Consider neutrality first. Contrary to the majority's suggestion, the District Courts did not have to — and in fact did not — choose among competing visions of electoral fairness. That is because they did not try to compare the State's actual map to an "ideally fair" one (whether based on proportional representation or some other criterion). Instead, they looked at the difference between what the State did and what the State would have done if politicians hadn't been intent on partisan gain. Or put differently, the comparator (or baseline or touchstone) is the result not of a judge's philosophizing but of the State's own characteristics and judgments. The effects evidence in these cases accepted as a given the State's physical geography (e.g., where does the Chesapeake run?) and political geography (e.g., where do the Democrats live on top of each other?). So the courts did not, in the majority's words, try to "counteract 'natural' gerrymandering caused, for example, by the urban concentration of one party." Still more, the courts' analyses used the State's own criteria for electoral fairness — except for naked partisan gain. Under their approach, in other words, the State selected its own fairness baseline in the form of its other districting criteria. All the courts did was determine how far the State had gone off that track because of its politicians' effort to entrench themselves in office.

The North Carolina litigation well illustrates the point. The thousands of randomly generated maps I've mentioned formed the core of the plaintiffs' case that the North Carolina plan was an "extreme[] outlier." Those maps took the State's political landscape as a given. In North Carolina, for example, Democratic voters are highly concentrated in cities. That fact was built into all the maps; it became part of the baseline. On top of that, the maps took the State's legal landscape as a given. They incorporated the State's districting priorities, excluding partisanship. So in North Carolina, for example, all the maps adhered to the traditional criteria of contiguity and compactness. But the comparator maps in another State would have incorporated different objectives — say, the emphasis Arizona places on competitive districts or the requirement Iowa imposes that counties remain whole. The point is that the assemblage of maps, reflecting the characteristics and judgments of the State itself, creates a neutral baseline from which to assess whether partisanship has run amok. Extreme outlier as to what? As to the other maps the State could have produced given its unique political geography and its chosen districting criteria. Not as to the maps a judge, with his own view of electoral fairness, could have dreamed up.

The Maryland court lacked North Carolina's fancy evidence, but analyzed the gerrymander's effects in much the same way — not as against an ideal goal, but as against an ex ante baseline. To see the difference, shift gears for a moment and compare Maryland and Massachusetts — both of which (aside from Maryland's partisan gerrymander) use traditional districting criteria. In those two States alike, Republicans receive about 35% of the vote in statewide elections. But the political geography of the States differs. In Massachusetts, the Republican vote is spread evenly across the State; because that is so, districting plans (using traditional criteria of contiguity and compactness) consistently lead to an all-Democratic congressional delegation. By contrast, in Maryland, Republicans are clumped—into the Eastern Shore (the First District) and the Northwest Corner (the old Sixth). Claims of partisan gerrymandering in those two States could come out the same way if judges, à la the majority, used their own visions of fairness to police districting plans; a judge in each State could then insist, in line with proportional representation, that 35% of the vote share entitles citizens to around that much of the delegation. But those suits would not come out the same if courts instead asked: What would have happened, given the State's natural political geography and chosen districting criteria, had officials not indulged in partisan manipulation? And that is what the District Court in Maryland inquired into. The court did not strike down the new Sixth District because a judicial ideal of proportional representation commanded another Republican seat. It invalidated that district because the quest for partisan gain made the State override its own political geography and districting criteria. So much, then, for the impossibility of neutrality.

The majority's sole response misses the point. According to the majority, "it does not make sense to use" a State's own (non-partisan) districting criteria as the baseline from which to measure partisan gerrymandering because those criteria "will vary from State to State and year to year." But that is a virtue, not a vice—a feature, not a bug. Using the criteria the State itself has chosen at the relevant time prevents any judicial predilections from affecting the analysis—exactly what the majority claims it wants. At the same time, using those criteria enables a court to measure just what it should: the extent to which the pursuit of partisan advantage—by these legislators at this moment—has distorted the State's districting decisions. Sure, different non-partisan criteria could result, as the majority notes, in different partisan distributions to serve as the baseline. But that in itself raises no issue: Everyone agrees that state officials using non-partisan criteria (e.g., must counties be kept together? should districts be compact?) have wide latitude in districting. The problem arises only when legislators or mapmakers substantially deviate from the baseline distribution by manipulating district lines for partisan gain. So once again, the majority's analysis falters because it equates the demand to eliminate partisan gerrymandering with a demand for a single partisan distribution—the one reflecting proportional representation. But those two demands are different, and only the former is at issue here.

The majority's "how much is too much" critique fares no better than its neutrality argument. How about the following for a first-cut answer: This much is too much. By any measure, a map that produces a greater partisan skew than any of 3,000 randomly generated maps (all with the State's political geography and districting criteria built in) reflects "too much" partisanship. Think about what I just said: The absolute worst of 3,001 possible maps. The only one that could produce a 10–3 partisan split even as Republicans got a bare majority of the statewide vote. And again: How much is too much? This much is too much: A map that without any evident non-partisan districting reason (to the contrary) shifted the composition of a district from 47% Republicans and 36% Democrats to 33% Republicans and 42% Democrats. A map that in 2011 was responsible for the largest partisan swing of a congressional district in the country. Even the majority acknowledges that "[t]hese cases involve blatant examples of partisanship driving districting decisions." If the majority had done nothing else, it could have set the line here. How much is too much? At the least, any gerrymanders as bad as these.

And if the majority thought that approach too case-specific, it could have used the lower courts' general standard—focusing on "predominant" purpose and "substantial" effects—without fear of indeterminacy. I do not take even the majority to claim that courts are incapable of investigating whether legislators mainly intended to seek partisan advantage. That is for good reason. Although purpose inquiries carry certain hazards (which courts must attend to), they are a common form of analysis in constitutional cases. Those inquiries would be no harder here than in other contexts.

Nor is there any reason to doubt, as the majority does, the competence of courts to determine whether a district map "substantially" dilutes the votes of a rival party's supporters from the everything-but-partisanship baseline described above. (Most of the majority's difficulties here really come from its idea that ideal visions set the baseline. But that is double-counting—and, as already shown, wrong to boot.) As this Court recently noted, "the law is full of instances" where a judge's decision rests on "estimating rightly . . . some matter of degree"—including the "substantial[ity]" of risk or harm. *Johnson v. United States*, 135 S. Ct. 2551, 2561 (2015). The majority is wrong to think that these laws typically (let alone uniformly) further "confine[] and guide[]" judicial decisionmaking. They do not, either in themselves or through "statutory context." To the extent additional guidance has developed over the years (as under the Sherman Act), courts themselves have been its author—as they could be in this context too. And contrary to the majority's suggestion, courts all the time make judgments about the substantiality of harm without reducing them to particular percentages. If courts are no longer competent to do so, they will have to relinquish, well, substantial portions of their docket.

And the combined inquiry used in these cases set the bar high, so that courts could intervene in the worst partisan gerrymanders, but no others. Or to say the same thing, so that courts could intervene in the kind of extreme gerrymanders that nearly every Justice for decades has thought to violate the Constitution. Illicit purpose was simple to show here only because politicians and mapmakers thought their actions could not be attacked in court. They therefore felt free to openly proclaim their intent to entrench their party in office. But if the Court today had declared that behavior justiciable, such smoking guns would all but disappear. Even assuming some officials continued to try implementing extreme partisan gerrymanders, they would not brag about their efforts. So plaintiffs would have to prove the intent to entrench through circumstantial evidence—essentially showing that no other explanation (no geographic feature or non-partisan districting objective) could explain the districting plan's vote dilutive effects. And that would be impossible unless those effects were even more than substantial—unless mapmakers had packed and cracked with abandon in unprecedented ways. As again, they did here. That the two courts below found constitutional violations does not mean their tests were unrigorous; it means that the conduct they confronted was constitutionally appalling—by even the strictest measure, inordinately partisan.

The majority, in the end, fails to understand both the plaintiffs' claims and the decisions below. Everything in today's opinion assumes that these cases grew out of a "desire for proportional representation" or, more generally phrased, a "fair share of political power." And everything in it assumes that the courts below had to (and did) decide what that fair share would be. But that is not so. The plaintiffs objected to one specific practice—the extreme manipulation of district lines for partisan gain. Elimination of that practice could have led to proportional representation. Or it could have led to nothing close. What was left after the practice's removal could have been fair, or could have been unfair, by any number of measures. That was not the crux of this suit. The plaintiffs asked only that the courts bar politicians from entrenching themselves in power by diluting the votes of their rivals' supporters. And the courts, using neutral and manageable—and eminently legal—standards, provided that (and only that) relief. This Court should have cheered, not overturned, that restoration of the people's power to vote.

III

This Court has long understood that it has a special responsibility to remedy violations of constitutional rights resulting from politicians' districting decisions. Over 50 years ago, we committed to providing judicial review in that sphere, recognizing as we established the one-person-one-vote rule that "our oath and our office require no less." *Reynolds*. Of course, our oath and our office require us to vindicate all constitutional rights. But the need for judicial review is at its most urgent in cases like these. "For here, politicians' incentives conflict with voters' interests, leaving citizens without any political remedy for their constitutional harms." *Gill* (Kagan, J., concurring). Those harms arise because politicians want to stay in office. No one can look to them for effective relief.

The majority disagrees, concluding its opinion with a paean to congressional bills limiting partisan gerrymanders. "Dozens of [those] bills have been introduced," the majority says. One was "introduced in 2005 and has been reintroduced in every Congress since." And might be reintroduced until the end of time. Because what all these bills have in common is that they are not laws. The politicians who benefit from partisan gerrymandering are unlikely to change partisan gerrymandering. And because those politicians maintain themselves in office through partisan gerrymandering, the chances for legislative reform are slight.

No worries, the majority says; it has another idea. The majority notes that voters themselves have recently approved ballot initiatives to put power over districting in the hands of independent commissions or other non-partisan actors. Some Members of the majority, of course, once thought such initiatives unconstitutional. But put that aside. Fewer than half the States offer voters an opportunity to put initiatives to direct vote; in all the rest (including North Carolina and Maryland), voters are dependent on legislators to make electoral changes (which for all the reasons already given, they are unlikely to do). And even when voters have a mechanism they can work themselves, legislators often fight their efforts tooth and nail. Look at Missouri. There, the majority touts a voter-approved proposal to turn districting over to a state demographer. But before the demographer had drawn a single line, Members of the state legislature had introduced a bill to start undoing the change. I'd put better odds on that bill's passage than on all the congressional proposals the majority cites.

The majority's most perplexing "solution" is to look to state courts. "[O]ur conclusion," the majority states, does not "condemn complaints about districting to echo into a void": Just a few years back, "the Supreme Court of Florida struck down that State's congressional districting plan as a violation" of the State Constitution. And indeed, the majority might have added, the Supreme Court of Pennsylvania last year did the same thing. But what do those courts know that this Court does not? If they can develop and apply neutral and manageable standards to identify unconstitutional gerrymanders, why couldn't we?

We could have, and we should have. The gerrymanders here — and they are typical of many — violated the constitutional rights of many hundreds of thousands of American citizens. Those voters (Republicans in the one case, Democrats in the other) did not have an equal opportunity to participate in the political process. Their votes counted for far less than they should have because of their partisan affiliation. When faced with such constitutional wrongs, courts must intervene: "It is emphatically the province and duty of the judicial department to say what the law is." *Marbury*. That is what the courts below did. Their decisions are worth a read. They (and others that have recently remedied similar violations) are detailed, thorough, painstaking. They evaluated with immense care the factual evidence and legal arguments the parties presented. They used neutral and manageable and strict standards. They had not a shred of politics about them. Contra the majority, this was law.

That is not to deny, of course, that these cases have great political consequence. They do. Among the amicus briefs here is one from a bipartisan group of current and former Members of the House of Representatives. They describe all the ways partisan gerrymandering harms our political system — what they call "a cascade of negative results." These artificially drawn districts shift influence from swing voters to party-base voters who participate in primaries; make bipartisanship and pragmatic compromise politically difficult or impossible; and drive voters away from an ever more dysfunctional political process. Last year, we heard much the same from current and former state legislators. In their view, partisan gerrymandering has "sounded the death-knell of bipartisanship," creating a legislative environment that is "toxic" and "tribal." Gerrymandering, in short, helps create the polarized political system so many Americans loathe.

And gerrymandering is, as so many Justices have emphasized before, anti-democratic in the most profound sense. In our government, "all political power flows from the people." *Arizona State Legislature.* And that means, as Alexander Hamilton once said, "that the people should choose whom they please to govern them." But in Maryland and North Carolina they cannot do so. In Maryland, election in and election out, there are 7 Democrats and 1 Republican in the congressional delegation. In North Carolina, however the political winds blow, there are 10 Republicans and 3 Democrats. Is it conceivable that someday voters will be able to break out of that prefabricated box? Sure. But everything possible has been done to make that hard. To create a world in which power does not flow from the people because they do not choose their governors.

Of all times to abandon the Court's duty to declare the law, this was not the one. The practices challenged in these cases imperil our system of government. Part of the Court's role in that system is to defend its foundations. None is more important than free and fair elections. With respect but deep sadness, I dissent.

Notes and Questions

1. At first glance, *Rucho* is a puzzling decision. It holds that partisan gerrymandering claims are nonjusticiable even though majorities of the Justices had repeatedly concluded to the contrary—including as recently as the year before, in *Gill v. Whitford*. *Rucho* also ignores various passages in *Whitford* that seemed to be giving clues to future partisan gerrymandering litigants: for example, the Court's statement that evidence of partisan intent "may well be pertinent with respect to any ultimate determination whether the plaintiffs may prevail in their claims." *Whitford*, 138 S. Ct. at 1932. What explains these oddities? Could it be the Court's changed composition? Note that Justice Kennedy was on the Court (and its median voter on this issue) in *Vieth*, *LULAC*, and *Whitford*, but that, by the time *Rucho* was decided, he had been replaced by Justice Kavanaugh. Is there any reason to think that Justice Kennedy would have joined the *Rucho* majority? See Nicholas O. Stephanopoulos, *The Denouement of Kennedy's Retirement*, Election Law Blog (July 1, 2019), https://perma.cc/2XL4-JC5P.

2. Most of *Rucho* discusses one reason why a legal theory may be a nonjusticiable political question: that there exists "a lack of judicially discoverable and manageable standards for resolving it." *Baker v. Carr*, 369 U.S. 186, 217 (1962). However, the appellants argued that partisan gerrymandering claims are political questions for a second reason: because the Elections Clause assigns responsibility for regulating federal elections to state legislatures and to Congress—but not to courts. See *id.* (observing that nonjusticiability also follows when there is "a textually demonstrable constitutional commitment of the issue to a coordinate political department"). In what may have been the plaintiffs' only victory in *Rucho*, the majority rejected this argument. The majority did "not agree" that "through the Elections Clause, the Framers set aside electoral issues ... as questions that only Congress can resolve" because "[i]n two areas—one-person, one-vote and racial gerrymandering—our

cases have held that there is a role for the courts with respect to at least some issues that could arise from a State's drawing of congressional districts." *Rucho*, 139 S. Ct. at 2495-96.

Why did the majority dismiss the appellants' Elections Clause theory, even though it would have given the majority a second reason to hold partisan gerrymandering claims nonjusticiable? As the majority notes, the appellants' Elections Clause theory would seemingly have extended to one-person, one-vote and racial gerrymandering claims, since they too involve judicial intervention in the area of congressional redistricting. Would the theory have extended even further, to *all* judicial intervention with respect to congressional elections? Under the text or history of the Elections Clause, is there any way to distinguish redistricting from other aspects of electoral regulation? Note as well that, on its face, the Elections Clause is simply a power-conferring provision, bestowing certain authorities to state legislatures and to Congress. What implications would follow from the position that all power-conferring provisions are nonjusticiable unless they explicitly mention a role for the courts?

3. The *Rucho* majority mentions two other kinds of redistricting claims—one-person, one-vote and racial gerrymandering challenges—but pointedly makes no reference to a third category: racial *vote dilution* claims. As we shall see in Chapter 5, Part II, such claims have been recognized under the Fourteenth Amendment since the early 1970s. They typically attack an electoral arrangement, such as an at-large electoral system or a single-member-district map, on the ground that it intentionally dilutes the electoral influence of a racial minority group. Why might the *Rucho* majority have declined to discuss racial vote dilution claims? (It's not because the plaintiffs didn't bring them up; they featured heavily in the plaintiffs' briefs.) How similar are racial and partisan vote dilution? Racial vote dilution requires discriminatory intent as well as the effect of a minority group's reduced electoral influence, often achieved through district lines that crack or pack the group's members. And what would be the fate of Section 2 of the Voting Rights Act, which bans racial vote dilution as a statutory matter, if constitutional racial vote dilution is no longer a cognizable claim? See Nicholas O. Stephanopoulos, *The Erasure of Racial Vote Dilution Doctrine*, Election Law Blog (June 28, 2019), https://perma.cc/45VM-67E6.

4. One of the *Rucho* majority's key analytical moves takes the following form: (1) *Some* partisan motivation in redistricting is permissible. (2) The Constitution only prohibits *excessive* partisanship. (3) There is no way to distinguish reliably between some and too much partisanship. (4) Therefore, no judicially manageable partisan gerrymandering standard exists. One response to this reasoning is to attack its premise: that some partisan motivation in redistricting is constitutionally unobjectionable. True, the *Vieth* plurality said the same thing, but that view only gained the support of four Justices. As Justice Stevens remarked in dissent in *Vieth*, until the plurality's opinion in that case, "there ha[d] not been the slightest intimation in any opinion written by any Member of this Court that a naked purpose to disadvantage

a political minority would provide a rational basis for drawing a district line." *Vieth*, 541 U.S. at 337 (Stevens, J., dissenting). See also Michael S. Kang, *Gerrymandering and the Constitutional Norm Against Government Partisanship*, 116 Michigan Law Review 351 (2017) (arguing that any partisan motivation in redistricting is impermissible); Justin Levitt, *Intent Is Enough: Invidious Partisanship in Redistricting*, 59 William & Mary Law Review 1993 (2018) (same).

A different response is to argue that a *predominant*-partisan-intent requirement successfully navigates between acceptable and unacceptable levels of partisanship in redistricting. This is the tack taken by Justice Kagan in her dissent in *Rucho*. "[W]hen political actors have a specific and predominant intent to entrench themselves in power by manipulating district lines, that goes too far." *Rucho*, 139 S. Ct. at 2517 (Kagan, J., dissenting). But note that both the *Vieth* appellants and Justice Stevens in dissent in *Vieth* proposed predominant-partisan-intent criteria (plan-wide in the appellants' case, district-specific in Justice Stevens's), and that five Justices in *Vieth* rejected both formulations. How, then, can Justice Kagan maintain that this approach is still doctrinally available?

5. The *Rucho* majority insists that "[p]artisan gerrymandering claims invariably sound in a desire for proportional representation." *Rucho*, 139 S. Ct. at 2499. What does the majority mean here by proportional representation? In political science, proportional representation has a clear definition: a share of legislative seats for a party that is *equal* to its share of the vote. Under this definition, neither the plaintiffs nor the lower courts sought to impose proportional representation. In particular, the quantitative metrics on which the plaintiffs and the lower courts relied, such as the efficiency gap and partisan bias, capture a plan's deviation from *partisan symmetry*, not proportionality. [See the discussion in Part I, Note 1, *supra*.] But perhaps the *Rucho* majority means something broader by proportional representation, more like any argument that even looks to how a party's legislative representation compares to its popular support. In that case, it might be fair to label the efficiency gap and partisan bias as measures of disproportionality. But how tenable is this view? In a democracy, is it really possible, normatively, to divorce a party's legislative representation from its popular support?

6. The *Rucho* majority observes that there are multiple desiderata in redistricting. Some want "a greater number of competitive districts." Others prefer "to ensure each party its 'appropriate' share of 'safe' seats." Still others advocate "adherence to 'traditional' districting criteria, such as maintaining political subdivisions, keeping communities of interest together, and protecting incumbents." *Rucho*, 139 S. Ct. at 2500. What do these redistricting objectives have to do with claims of *partisan* gerrymandering? Would anyone call it a partisan gerrymandering challenge if a plaintiff wanted lines to be drawn to yield greater electoral competitiveness? Or if a plaintiff sought districts that better corresponded to political subdivisions or communities of interest? To put the point another way, would courts actually have to "decid[e] among . . . these different visions of fairness" to adjudicate partisan gerrymandering claims, *id.*, or could courts simply stay agnostic between them?

7. Prior to *Rucho*, the last time the Supreme Court held that a redistricting cause of action was nonjusticiable was in *Colegrove v. Green*, 328 U.S. 549 (1946). In that case, as we discuss in Chapter 3, Part I, a plurality of the Court deemed one-person, one-vote claims to be political questions. The *Colegrove* plurality, and the dissenters in the 1960s reapportionment cases (which reversed *Colegrove*), made a number of arguments reminiscent of the *Rucho* majority's reasoning. Among other things, they contended that (1) conventional modes of constitutional interpretation do not support the justiciability of one-person, one-vote claims; (2) no normative consensus exists as to what a fairly apportioned map is; (3) judges lack the empirical skills to tackle the quantitative issues associated with malapportionment; (4) it would be unseemly for the federal courts to involve themselves in redistricting; and (5) other actors, like legislatures and state courts, could solve the problem of malapportionment instead. See Nicholas O. Stephanopoulos, *The Anti-*Carolene *Court*, 2019 Supreme Court Review 111, 128-35 (tracing the parallels between the *Rucho* majority and the opponents of one-person, one-vote in the mid-twentieth century).

8. Perhaps the most powerful evidence relied on by the plaintiffs, the lower courts, and Justice Kagan are computer simulations of alternative district maps. The logic of these simulations is as follows: First, identify all redistricting criteria used by a jurisdiction *other* than partisan advantage. (These may include compactness, respect for political subdivisions, compliance with the Voting Rights Act, and any other nonpartisan goal.) Second, deploy a computer algorithm to generate randomly thousands of district maps based on these criteria. Third, use election results to estimate the likely partisan consequences of both the enacted plan and all of the computer-generated maps. And fourth, compare the enacted plan's partisan performance to that of the computer-generated maps. If the enacted plan is similar to the computer-generated maps, then it is unproblematic. But if the enacted plan is more biased than the computer-generated maps—yielding more seats for the line-drawing party—then one may infer partisan intent, partisan effect, and a lack of any legitimate justification for this impact.

The *Rucho* majority objects that "it does not make sense to use criteria that will vary from State to State and year to year as the baseline." *Id.* at 2505. But why isn't this fluctuating benchmark "a virtue, not a vice—a feature, not a bug," as Justice Kagan argues in her dissent? *Id.* at 2521 (Kagan, J., dissenting). After all, the Court has always given mapmakers a great deal of discretion in selecting parameters for redistricting. The fluctuating benchmark is simply a product of this discretion. The *Rucho* majority also complains that it is unclear *how* different from the computer-generated maps the enacted plan must be to be condemned. "Would twenty percent away from the median map be okay? Forty percent? Sixty percent?" *Id.* at 2505. The dissent does not propose a quantitative standard, like more than two standard deviations away from the median, or more biased than 95 percent of computer-generated maps. Should it have?

A different critique of the computer simulations is that they may not be a representative sample of the universe of district maps that satisfy the specified criteria. In that case, it is arguably irrelevant how near to, or far from, the median of the distribution of computer-generated maps the enacted plan happens to be. If this median is unrepresentative of the appropriate universe, then it may carry little or no normative weight. For scholars making this point, see Micah Altman et al., *Revealing Preferences: Why Gerrymanders Are Hard to Prove, and What to Do About It* (Mar. 23, 2015), and Benjamin Fifield et al., *A New Automated Redistricting Simulator Using Markov Chain Monte Carlo*, 29 Journal of Computational and Graphical Statistics 715 (2020). For an argument that certain computer simulation methods do, in fact, yield representative samples, see Daryl DeFord et al., *Recombination: A Family of Markov Chains for Redistricting*, 3 Harvard Data Science Review (2021).

9. The *Rucho* majority asserts that voters' partisan preferences may change from race to race and year to year. As a result, district plans alleged to be gerrymanders for one party (like the Indiana state house map at issue in *Bandemer* and the Pennsylvania congressional map at issue in *Vieth*) may produce majorities for the opposing party in subsequent elections. In her dissent, Justice Kagan calls these claims "unsupported and out-of-date musings about the unpredictability of the American voter." *Rucho*, 139 S. Ct. at 2519 (Kagan, J., dissenting). The political science literature backs her up. Modern American voters rarely split their tickets or switch their partisan preferences from one election to the next. See, for example, Donald P. Green et al., Partisan Hearts and Minds: Political Parties and the Social Identities of Voters (2002) and Corwin D. Smidt, *Polarization and the Decline of the American Floating Voter*, 61 American Journal of Political Science 365 (2017). But even if the *Rucho* majority is wrong empirically, could there be sound jurisprudential reasons to assume that voters do not necessarily follow the party line but, rather, make choices based on issues, candidates, and campaigns? For an exploration of this possibility, see Michael Morley, Rucho, *Legal Fictions, and the Judicial Models of Voters*, Election Law Blog (July 4, 2019), https://perma.cc/2AZ8-N5E8.

10. The *Rucho* majority makes short work of the argument that partisan gerrymandering is justiciable under the First Amendment. First, the *Rucho* majority claims that district plans impose "no restrictions on speech, association, or any other First Amendment activities" because "plaintiffs are free to engage in those activities no matter what the effect of a plan may be on their district." *Rucho*, 139 S. Ct. at 2504. But even if gerrymanders do not *directly* burden First Amendment rights, why don't they do so *indirectly*, through their chilling effects on targeted voters who realize that their speech and association have been rendered meaningless in gerrymandered districts? The Court has often recognized First Amendment claims of this kind. See, for example, *Buckley v. Valeo*, 424 U.S. 1, 65 (1976) (applying "exacting scrutiny" to disclosure requirements even though their associational burden "arises, not through direct government action, but indirectly as an unintended but inevitable result of the government's conduct"), and *NAACP v. Alabama*, 357 U.S. 449, 463 (1958) (striking down an order that the NAACP reveal its membership list because the order "may induce [NAACP] members to withdraw from the Association and dissuade others from joining it"). See also Nicholas O. Stephanopoulos &

Christopher Warshaw, *The Impact of Partisan Gerrymandering on Political Parties*, 45 Legislative Studies Quarterly 609 (2020) (finding empirically that when parties are disadvantaged by gerrymandering, associational functions such as running for office and donating money are impeded).

Second, the *Rucho* majority asserts that, under the First Amendment, "any level of partisanship in districting would constitute an infringement." *Rucho*, 139 S. Ct. at 2504. The First Amendment thus "provides no standard for determining when partisan activity goes too far." *Id.* Perhaps it is true that a theory of viewpoint discrimination would find a violation whenever district lines are drawn to benefit certain voters, and disadvantage other voters, because of their political beliefs. But is this also the case for an associational theory that focuses on the ways in which gerrymanders prevent likeminded voters from collaborating politically? As we discuss in Chapter 6, Part C and Chapter 9, associational claims typically trigger sliding-scale scrutiny, under which the stringency of judicial review varies based on the severity of the burden imposed on associational rights. Why wouldn't this approach prevent the outcome feared by the Court, namely, the invalidation of all districts drawn for partisan reasons? See Daniel P. Tokaji, *Gerrymandering and Association*, 59 William & Mary Law Review 2159 (2018).

11. In the final section of its opinion, the *Rucho* majority observes that state courts, unlike federal courts, may fight gerrymandering on the basis of state constitutional provisions that are more specific than any clause in the federal Constitution. "[T]here is no 'Fair Districts Amendment' to the Federal Constitution," as there is to the Florida Constitution. *Rucho*, 139 S. Ct. at 2507. But notice that the Pennsylvania Supreme Court recently struck down the state's congressional plan based on a provision stating only that "elections shall be free and equal." *League of Women Voters v. Commonwealth*, 178 A.3d 737 (Pa. 2018). Is this language any more determinate than the First Amendment or the Equal Protection Clause? Also note that, shortly after *Rucho*, a North Carolina trial court invalidated the state's legislative and congressional maps based on (among other theories) North Carolina's analogues to the First and Fourteenth Amendments. This court explicitly disagreed with the Supreme Court that these provisions are nonjusticiable in this context. See *Common Cause v. Lewis*, 2019 WL 4569584 (N.C. Super. Sept. 3, 2019). And observe (as Justice Kagan does in her dissent) that, prior to *Rucho*, district courts in Michigan, North Carolina, Ohio, and Wisconsin arrived at essentially the same three-part test for adjudicating claims of partisan vote dilution. Does this lower court consensus suggest that, even if the federal Constitution is highly abstract, its dictates can be made more concrete through conventional judicial interpretation? See Nicholas O. Stephanopoulos, *The Emerging Consensus of the Lower Courts*, Election Law Blog (Apr. 27, 2019), https://perma.cc/G92L-DVDC.

The *Rucho* majority further points out that gerrymandering may be combatted by voter initiatives that "mandate[] at least some of the traditional districting criteria" or "plac[e] power to draw electoral districts in the hands of independent commissions." *Rucho*, 139 S. Ct. at 2507. But how helpful is direct democracy in this context? Most attempts to reform redistricting through voter initiatives fail due to the ferocious opposition of sitting legislators. See Stephanopoulos, *Reforming Redistricting, supra.* Voter initiatives are also available in only about half the states; they are *not* available, for example, in Maryland, North Carolina, and Wisconsin—the states that gave rise to *Lamone*, *Rucho*, and *Whitford*, respectively. And the constitutionality of independent redistricting commissions remains hazy. Their validity was affirmed in *Arizona State Legislature v. Arizona Independent Redistricting Commission*, 576 U.S. 787 (2015), which we discuss in Chapter 7, Part III.D. But Chief Justice Roberts, joined by three other Justices, dissented on the ground that when a commission is responsible for redistricting, the Elections Clause is violated because the "Legislature" does not get to draw the lines. Now that Justice Kennedy is no longer on the Court, this position may well command five votes.

Much the same points apply to the *Rucho* majority's final option for thwarting gerrymandering: congressional legislation. How likely is it that, for the first time in American history, members of Congress, many of whom are elected from gerrymandered districts, will pass laws seriously restricting the practice? One might think, not very likely, except that the House of Representatives recently approved a bill that would mandate the use of redistricting commissions for congressional district plans. See For the People Act, H.R. 1, 117th Cong. §§ 2401-2415 (2021). However, it is highly uncertain as of this writing whether the Senate will take any action on this bill. In addition, is it obvious that congressional action in this area would be constitutionally permissible? Congress has near-plenary authority over congressional elections under the Elections Clause. But what if, in exercising this power, Congress orders states to take certain steps (like creating redistricting commissions)? Would such directives violate the anti-commandeering doctrine? And even if Congress can fight congressional gerrymandering, can it curb state and local gerrymandering? To do so, Congress would presumably have to invoke its Fourteenth Amendment enforcement authority. Any such invocation would require the Court to determine how "congruent and proportional" the legislation is to underlying constitutional offenses.

12. What will mapmakers do now that there is no possibility of federal courts checking partisan gerrymandering? More aggressive gerrymandering of the kind seen in the 2010 cycle, relying on the cracking and packing of the opposing party's voters, is a near-certainty. But consider the following additional steps that mapmakers could take: (1) using computer algorithms to maximize the size and durability of a party's redistricting advantage; (2) redrawing districts more frequently (as often as every two years) to keep fine-tuning a party's electoral position; and (3) creating noncontiguous districts that combine clusters of voters in different parts of a state. How plausible are these options? How much value do they add to traditional gerrymandering? And is it definitely the case that federal courts would stay on the sidelines if these tactics were tried? See Aaron Goldzimer & Nicholas O. Stephanopoulos, *Democrats Can't Be Afraid to Gerrymander Now*, Slate (July 3, 2019).

III. Competition and Election Law

Related to the partisan gerrymandering debate is a larger question about whether courts should exercise their power of judicial review to prevent incumbents from adopting electoral rules that stifle competition. In the past three decades, a number of election law scholars have called for heightened judicial oversight of rules and procedures that they believe "entrench" incumbents or parties or, using language from antitrust, "lock up" the "marketplace" of the electoral system. Two early statements of this view were Michael J. Klarman, *Majoritarian Judicial Review: The Entrenchment Problem*, 85 Georgetown Law Journal 491 (1997), and Samuel Issacharoff and Richard H. Pildes, *Politics as Markets: Partisan Lockups of the Democratic Process*, 50 Stanford Law Review 643 (1998). Issacharoff and Pildes went so far as to suggest that in judicial review of election law, the nurturing of competitiveness should displace the principles of rights and equality based on the text of the Constitution:

> In cases involving the regulation of politics, we argue that courts should shift from the conventional first-order focus on rights and equality to a second-order focus on the background markets in partisan control. Rather than seeking to control politics directly through the centralized enforcement of individual rights, we suggest courts would do better to examine the background structure of partisan competition. Where there is an appropriately robust market in partisan competition, there is less justification for judicial intervention. Where courts can discern that existing partisan forces have manipulated these background rules, courts should strike down those manipulations to ensure an appropriately competitive political environment.

Id. at 648. How does one know when a political market is "appropriately" robust or competitive? Richard L. Hasen, *The "Political Market" Metaphor and Election Law: A Comment on Issacharoff and Pildes*, 50 Stanford Law Review 719, 725–28 (1998) argues that Issacharoff and Pildes do not adequately define the meaning of these terms.

Issacharoff and Pildes criticize a number of Supreme Court cases including *Timmons v. Twin Cities Area New Party*, 520 U.S. 351 (1997), upholding a ban on fusion candidacies, and *Burdick v. Takushi*, 504 U.S. 428 (1992), upholding Hawaii's ban on write-in votes.[a] After declaring that a "political process case more wrongly decided than *Burdick* is difficult to imagine," the authors argue that the ban on write-in votes worked with other election laws to insure Democratic party dominance over Hawaii politics:

> The critical issue for the Court should not have been Burdick's individual interest in using the ballot for mere "expressive purposes," nor should it

a. *Burdick* is discussed and *Timmons* appears *infra* in Chapter 9, Part I.

> have been the purported abstract state interests. Instead, when interpreting the various constitutional provisions that protect self-government, such as the First Amendment, the Court should construe those provisions against a background conception of democracy that recognizes the importance of competitive political markets to ensuring appropriately responsive representation. As part of that inquiry, the Court ought to focus on whether the process remains sufficiently open to challenge and reform, or whether the costs of mobilizing effective challenge have been raised so high as to leave the system insufficiently responsive. In the one-party state of Hawaii . . . the state-enacted barriers to competition were ingeniously effective at stifling potential competition.[b] The state's ability to recite abstract state interests in political stability, avoidance of factionalism, or prevention of party raiding, should hardly obstruct more penetrating judicial analysis of the actual anti-competitiveness effects. Indeed, given the context [of the case], the very interests that could be asserted in the names of the states are no more than thinly veiled formulas for disguising self-serving arguments of incumbent powers. Far from justifying these state practices, such interests should be the very reason the Court strikes those practices down.

Id. at 673-74. The anti-entrenchment rationale is criticized in Daniel H. Lowenstein, *The Supreme Court Has No Theory of Politics—And Be Thankful for Small Favors*, in The U.S. Supreme Court and the Electoral Process 245, 263 (David K. Ryden, ed., 2000). Lowenstein faults Issacharoff and Pildes for focusing on election laws like Hawaii's ban on write-in votes rather than on the more significant legal structures favoring the two-party system like single-member districts and the direct primary:

> Issacharoff and Pildes do not expect the Supreme Court to eliminate single-member districts, presidential elections, or direct primaries. It is not clear, therefore, what difference it would make if the Court were to subscribe to their theory of partisan lockups as the key to election law adjudication. If the Court accepted the theory and were truly sophisticated regarding the causes of Democratic and Republican predominance in American politics, they would simply deconstitutionalize election law and have done with it.

Pildes and Issacharoff have separately responded to criticisms of their "political markets" approach in ways that suggest the two authors have diverged on how far their approach goes. In Richard H. Pildes, *The Theory of Political Competition*, 85 Virginia Law Review 1605 (1999), Pildes responds to an argument by Bruce Cain, *Garrett's Temptation*, 85 Virginia Law Review 1589, 1600 (1999), to the effect that the logical implication of the approach is court-mandated proportional representation. Pildes lists a number of "countervailing values [that] could be marshaled against

b. Linda Lingle, the former governor of the "one-party" Democratic state of Hawaii, first elected in 2002 and reelected in 2006, is a Republican.—Eds.

judicial imposition of [proportional representation]" including original intent, history, and the importance of public acceptability of judicial decisions. *Id.* at 1616. In Samuel Issacharoff, *Gerrymandering and Political Cartels*, 116 Harvard Law Review 593 (2002), Issacharoff calls upon the courts to strike down virtually all legislative districting conducted by partisan officials as unconstitutional, leading to districting conducted solely by nonpartisan commissions or by computer. To Issacharoff, the risk of gerrymandering is that it "constrict[s] the competitive processes by which voters can express choice." *Id.* at 600.

Nathaniel Persily disagrees with Issacharoff on the question of whether gerrymandering stifles political competition. See Persily, *supra.* Launching a broader attack on the political markets approach is Richard L. Hasen, The Supreme Court and Election Law: Judging Equality from *Baker v. Carr* to *Bush v. Gore* 138–56 (2003). Hasen sees connections between the Supreme Court's "structural equal protection" jurisprudence in *Shaw v. Reno* and *Bush v. Gore* and the "political markets approach," finding both "symptomatic of a belief in unlimited judicial wisdom." For more arguments against judicial intervention in gerrymandering, see Luis Fuentes-Rohwer, *Doing Our Politics in Court: Gerrymandering, "Fair Representation" and an Exegesis Into the Judicial Role*, 78 Notre Dame Law Review 527 (2002), and Franita Tolson, *Partisan Gerrymandering as a Safeguard of Federalism*, 2010 Utah Law Review 859 (2010).

Some political scientists also have become increasingly concerned by lack of competitiveness in some elections. A vigorous statement of this viewpoint is contained in Michael McDonald and John Samples, *The Marketplace of Democracy: Normative and Empirical Issues*, which is the introduction to their edited volume, The Marketplace of Democracy: Electoral Competition and American Politics (2006). McDonald and Samples begin with the idea that the best chance for a political system to avoid tyranny is the accountability imposed on public officials by competitive elections. They survey a number of respects in which they believe American elections are deficient in competitiveness. "Competition in the United States," they say, "bears a troubling resemblance to that in nations where candidates run unopposed or with token opposition, nations that American leaders condemn as lacking truly democratic or legitimate elections."

The contributors to *The Marketplace of Democracy*, including some of the best contemporary political science writers on American politics, provide a wealth of ideas and analysis on aspects of competitiveness in elections, though they vary widely in their agreement with the editors on the degree of the problem. Lowenstein concluded a review of the volume by observing:

> I, for one, marvel at those who find this the moment to bewail a supposed lack of competitiveness. We are living through a period featuring the most intense partisan competitiveness between the most evenly divided parties in my now lengthy lifetime (and a considerable period before that). Incumbent legislators may show lack of vision or lack of wisdom or lack of

> courage, but the one thing they do not show is a lack of concern for their districts, which presumably is what is meant by lack of accountability.

Daniel H. Lowenstein, *Competition and Competitiveness in American Elections*, 6 Election Law Journal 278, 293 (2007).

Not all political scientists agree that more competition is a good thing, however. Thomas Brunell has argued strongly that safe districts actually produce better representation. Thomas L. Brunell, Redistricting and Representation: Why Competitive Elections Are Bad for America (2008). As he puts it, "the more homogeneous a district, the better able the elected official is to accurately reflect the views of his constituents." Is Brunell right that competitive elections are something that should be avoided rather than pursued? If the only goal is to maximize the percentage of voters whose views line up with their elected representatives, then competitive districts may well be undesirable. On the other hand, if there are other values that a system of representation seeks to pursue, then some mix of competitive and uncompetitive districts might best serve them. Is the federal judiciary best positioned to assess the democratic values that our system of representation should promote and to determine what means will best promote them?

Supporters of the idea that the courts should police entrenchment took heart from the lead opinion in a campaign finance decision, *Randall v. Sorrell*, 548 U.S. 230 (2006), in which Justice Breyer spoke for himself, Chief Justice Roberts, and Justice Alito. *Randall*, which appears in Chapter 14, struck down a limit on campaign contributions that the Court regarded as too low. One reason for the decision, according to Justice Breyer, was that "contribution limits that are too low can ... harm the electoral process by preventing challengers from mounting effective campaigns against incumbent officeholders, thereby reducing democratic accountability." *Id.* at 232. On the other hand, in *New York State Board of Elections v. López Torres*, 552 U.S. 196 (2008), the Supreme Court rejected a First Amendment challenge to a state's system for selecting judges through a convention that was alleged to impede competition by giving too much power to party bosses. Justice Scalia's opinion for the majority reasoned:

> None of our cases establishes an individual's constitutional right to have a "fair shot" at winning the party's nomination. And with good reason. What constitutes a "fair shot" is a reasonable enough question for legislative judgment, which we will accept so long as it does not too much infringe upon the party's associational rights. But it is hardly a manageable constitutional question for judges — especially for judges in our legal system, where traditional electoral practice gives no hint of even the existence, much less the content, of a constitutional requirement for a "fair shot" at party nomination. Party conventions, with their attendant "smoke-filled rooms" and domination by party leaders, have long been an accepted manner of selecting party candidates. "National party conventions prior to 1972 were generally under the control of state party leaders" who determined the votes of state delegates. American Presidential Elections: Process, Policy, and

> Political Change 14 (H. Schantz ed.1996). Selection by convention has never been thought unconstitutional, even when the delegates were not selected by primary but by party caucuses. . . .
>
> Respondents put forward, as a special factor which gives them a First Amendment right to revision of party processes in the present case, the assertion that party loyalty in New York's judicial districts renders the general-election ballot "uncompetitive." They argue that the existence of entrenched "one-party rule" demands that the First Amendment be used to impose additional competition in the nominee-selection process of the parties. . . . This is a novel and implausible reading of the First Amendment. . . .
>
> The reason one-party rule is entrenched may be (and usually is) that voters approve of the positions and candidates that the party regularly puts forward. It is no function of the First Amendment to require revision of those positions or candidates. The States can, within limits (that is, short of violating the parties' freedom of association), discourage party monopoly—for example, by refusing to show party endorsement on the election ballot. But the Constitution provides no authority for federal courts to prescribe such a course. The First Amendment creates an open marketplace where ideas, most especially political ideas, may compete without government interference. See *Abrams v. United States*, 250 U.S. 616, 630 (1919) (Holmes, J., dissenting). It does not call on the federal courts to manage the market by preventing too many buyers from settling upon a single product.
>
> Limiting respondents' court-mandated "fair shot at party endorsement" to situations of one-party entrenchment merely multiplies the impracticable lines courts would be called upon to draw. It would add to those alluded to earlier the line at which mere party popularity turns into "one-party dominance." In the case of New York's election system for Supreme Court Justices, that line would have to be drawn separately for each of the 12 judicial districts—and in those districts that are "competitive" the current system would presumably remain valid. But why limit the remedy to *one*-party dominance? Does not the dominance of two parties similarly stifle competing opinions? Once again, we decline to enter the morass.

Id. at 205-09. For criticism of the Court's failure to inquire into the barriers to competition faced by Judge López Torres, see Ellen D. Katz, *Barack Obama, Margarita Lopez Torres, and the Path to Nomination*, 8 Election Law Journal 369 (2009).

Occasionally, lower court judges—like those in the Second Circuit decision reversed in *López Torres*—have shown some sympathy for the argument that the Constitution should be interpreted with an eye toward preventing anti-competitive election rules. Following is an excerpt from an opinion by federal appellate judge J. Harvie Wilkinson III, dissenting from denial of an en banc hearing to review a panel decision striking down an unusual nominating procedure in Virginia. The general statutory rule in Virginia was that party organizations could select from a number of different nominating procedures, including an open primary. An exception allowed an incumbent state legislator who was seeking reelection to choose a procedure, even if it was not the procedure favored by the party organization. Stephen Miller, an incumbent legislator, opted for an open primary. The party preferred a semi-closed primary, which was not a form recognized by Virginia law. Two constitutional issues were raised in the case. First, did the party have the right to a semi-closed primary in the face of Virginia law providing for an open primary? Second, was it constitutional to allow incumbents individually to select the procedure under which they would seek reelection?

Judge Wilkinson objected to the narrow grounds on which the panel ruled in favor of the party. The panel declared the Virginia statute unconstitutional, "but only 'as applied' to the situation in which an incumbent elects to hold an open primary against his party's wishes." In other words, the panel did not decide whether the party had the general right to opt for a semi-closed primary, nor did it decide whether it was generally unconstitutional to allow the incumbent to select the nomination method. Judge Wilkinson dissented from the denial of en banc review because he believed each of these questions ought to have been decided. In the course of his opinion he made these comments on the significance of incumbency in election law jurisprudence:

Miller v. Cunningham

512 F.3d 98 (4th Cir. 2007)

. . .

WILKINSON, Circuit Judge, dissenting from the denial of the petition for rehearing en banc:

. . . The first important issue not addressed by the panel opinion is the constitutionality of Virginia's incumbent selection provision, Va. Code Ann. § 24.2-509(B) (2006). To me, the unconstitutionality of this provision is clear. I fully recognize that governance is an immensely complicated business and that the ability of parties to re-nominate and electorates to re-elect incumbent officeholders is essential to the fund of experience and expertise that enables a large Commonwealth such as Virginia to be well-run. Notwithstanding the benefits that length of service confers upon the public welfare, the incumbent selection provision at issue here facially discriminates in favor of incumbents, shutting down the political process and violating the most essential requirements of equal protection. . . .

I believe that the constitutionality of § 24.2-509(B) is properly presented in this case: the parties are treating it as such, and the panel necessarily considered the provision in reaching its holding. However, failure to address the constitutionality of this provision can only mean more litigation down the road. I see no reason to refrain from striking down a provision that plainly runs afoul of our most fundamental constitutional rights.

A

I start my analysis of Virginia's incumbent selection provision with a very simple proposition: if there is going to be election law, it will be written and enacted by incumbents. Both the United States and Virginia Constitutions explicitly grant the legislative branch the authority to regulate elections. . . .

Given this, there is certainly nothing unconstitutional *per se* about incumbents shaping the electoral process to their advantage. This is merely a feature of American politics. The Framers were surely aware of the desire of those who hold elective office to retain elective office, yet they were clearly comfortable giving incumbents the authority to write election law. Judicial intervention into the electoral process, merely for the purpose of rooting out self-interested political behavior, would therefore be a "substantial" incursion into textually and traditionally legislative prerogatives. *See Vieth* (Kennedy, J., concurring in the judgment). Furthermore, elections are "pervasively regulated," Richard H. Pildes, *The Supreme Court, 2003 Term-Foreword: The Constitutionalization of Democratic Politics,* 118 Harv. L. Rev. 28, 51 (2004), and aggressive review of legislative motivation in this area would leave the federal judiciary time to do little else but analyze election laws. The Supreme Court has therefore been appropriately reluctant to police enactments in the election law context, even while explicitly recognizing that self-interest may be a partial driver of legislative action in this area. *See Vieth* (plurality opinion) (holding political gerrymandering to be non-justiciable for lack of a judicially manageable standard despite the fact that redistricting is always conducted with an intent to gain "political advantage").

Nonetheless, there are limits to this deference. As the Supreme Court suggested in the famous fourth footnote of *United States v. Carolene Products Co.,* 304 U.S. 144 (1938), the judiciary has a basic obligation to keep the political process open and well-functioning. "The first instinct of power is the retention of power," and those who hold public office can be expected to attempt to insulate themselves from meaningful electoral review. *McConnell v. FEC,* 540 U.S. 93, 263 (2003) (Scalia, J., concurring in part and dissenting in part). It is therefore necessary for an independent and co-equal branch of government—the judiciary—to ensure that incumbents are unable to create a system where the "ins . . . will stay in and the outs will stay out." John Hart Ely, *Democracy and Distrust* 103 (1980); *see also* Klarman, *supra.*

This is because any political system that lacks accountability, "democracy's essential minimal condition," Pildes, *supra,* at 44, does not conform with even the barest requirements of equal protection, which demand, at a minimum, that the majority is not systematically frustrated in enacting its policies into law.

At the very least, therefore, the need to "clear the channels of political change," *see* Ely, *supra,* at 105–34, requires the judiciary to presume that election laws that *facially* discriminate in *favor* of incumbents are unconstitutional.[c] Two reasons

c. Laws may, of course, facially benefit incumbents without posing constitutional problems. For example, laws that enable state legislators to provide constituent services—e.g., hire staff or

support this conclusion. First, election laws that facially discriminate in favor of existing officeholders simply go "too far": if incumbents are allowed to pass laws explicitly and exclusively for their own benefit, there would be no end to the advantages they could provide themselves. Incumbents could therefore diminish the possibility for change and competition in American politics to a degree never envisioned by the Constitution. Second, the problems presented by judicial intervention into the political process are not nearly as pronounced when the courts are faced with laws that facially favor incumbents. Facially neutral laws, like legislative redistricting schemes, may produce a *de facto* advantage for incumbents, but uncovering whether that advantage reaches unconstitutional limits requires an intrusive—and potentially error-prone—inquiry into legislative motive. The biases of facially discriminatory laws, on the other hand, are readily apparent.

Given the foregoing, Virginia's incumbent selection statute is plainly unconstitutional, at least when state legislators are passing laws dealing with their own re-election prospects. The statute facially discriminates in favor of existing officeholders, by compelling political parties to "nominate [their] candidate[s] for election . . . by the method[s] designated" by incumbents. In doing so, the law leaves no doubt as to who its purported beneficiaries are—the incumbents in Virginia's General Assembly. These incumbent legislators already possess numerous structural advantages over their electoral competition: money, name-recognition, staff, etc. To this pre-existing array of *de facto* advantages, Virginia's incumbent selection provision now adds the *de jure* advantage that the incumbent can dictate his or her recommended preference as to renomination procedures over a party's express wishes. Such an explicit advantage given to existing officeholders surely threatens to entrench Virginia's incumbents to an unconstitutional extent. . . .

Notes and Questions

1. If the state permits the word "incumbent" to appear on the ballot to identify incumbents seeking reelection, does the state "facially favor" incumbents so as to make the practice presumptively unconstitutional, under Judge Wilkinson's opinion?

2. In the book review referred to previously, Lowenstein distinguishes two distinct concepts signified by the word "competition," and designates one of them by the word "competition" and the other by "competitiveness":

> There are two senses in which the word "competitiveness" is used. For example, we say that baseball is a competitive sport. But suppose you go to a game in which the score is 12–1 in the second inning. Nothing much happens after that and the final score is 16–3. You might say that the game was

---

pay office expenses—are clearly constitutional, despite the fact that these statutes may provide resources that produce a *de facto* advantage for legislators in campaigning for reelection. But these laws are clearly passed for a legitimate purpose, unlike election laws passed solely to entrench incumbents in office.

not competitive. Yet, you would not mean by that to deny that baseball is a competitive sport or that the 16–3 game was a fair competition.

A few weeks later you go to another game. In the bottom of the ninth with the score 3–2, two out and runners on second and third, the batter hits a sinking line drive. The outfielder charges and reaches down to attempt a shoestring catch. A matter of an inch separates his making the catch and the ball skipping off the web of his mitt. On that inch the outcome of the game depends. This, you will say, was a highly competitive game. As spectator entertainment, it was also no doubt a much better game than the previous one. But there is a sense in which the purpose of the competition is that the team that plays the best should win. If the question is which game was better from this standpoint, surely the answer is the 16–3 game, even though the 3–2 game (or 4–3, depending on whether the ball stayed in the mitt) was by far the more "competitive."

... Unfortunately, the two conceptions of electoral competition—a system whose features make it freely open to contestation as opposed to closely contested races in particular elections—are easy to confuse. The conceptions are related to each other and our language uses the same terms—"competition" and "competitive"—to apply to each. To help keep the conceptions distinct, I shall use the noun "competition" (sometimes "free competition" for emphasis) to refer to the electoral system that freely allows for contestation, and "competitiveness" to refer to races that are actually closely contested. As there is only one adjective, I shall say "freely competitive" to describe the free system or elections within the free system, and simply "competitive" to describe the elections that are actually closely contested.

Lowenstein, *Competition and Competitiveness, supra*, 6 Election Law Journal at 280-81. Using this terminology, when Judge Wilkinson makes it presumptively unconstitutional to "facially favor" incumbents in a statute, is he protecting competition or competitiveness?

3. The simplest and most drastic way of eliminating the incumbency advantage is to prohibit incumbents from running for reelection. The principle of "rotation in office" was popular at the time of the American Revolution, and many state constitutions that were adopted in the mid-1770s restricted the ability of incumbents to run for reelection. The popularity of rotation diminished over the next decade. Although mandatory rotation for members of Congress was proposed at the constitutional convention in 1787, it was rejected.

Term limits for executive officials—governor and mayor, primarily—became fairly common in the United States in the twentieth century, and an executive term limit was added to the federal government system in 1951, with the approval of the Twenty-Second Amendment, which limits presidents to two terms. Legislative term limits were rare, however, until 1990, when initiatives were passed in Colorado, limiting terms of congressional representatives and state legislators, and in California and Oklahoma, limiting state legislative terms. By the end of 1994, 22 states had adopted congressional term limits (all but one, Utah, had done so by the initiative process), and a similar number had adopted state legislative term limits. A number of local governments, including the cities of New York and Los Angeles, also adopted term limits in the 1990s.[d]

The election returns suggest that the movement for term limits strongly resonated with popular sentiment in the early 1990s. Probably an equally strong majority of students of government have been opposed to term limits. The debate has been vigorous. In part it has been a partisan debate, but history has a way of confounding those who seek or oppose structural changes for short term partisan reasons. The Twenty-Second Amendment, for example, was advocated by Republicans who reacted to Franklin Roosevelt having been elected four times as a Democrat. Yet, three of the five presidents to date who have been affected by the Twenty-Second Amendment, Dwight Eisenhower, Ronald Reagan, and George W. Bush, were Republicans. Similarly, part of the drive for congressional term limits was supplied by Republicans hoping to break the long-term Democratic control of the House of Representatives. In 1994 the Republicans won control of Congress without the help of term limits, and many of them faced the prospect of their own careers being cut short. However, as discussed below, the Supreme Court gave them a reprieve by declaring congressional term limits unconstitutional.

Are term limits constitutional? Challenges to state and local term limits based on the First and Fourteenth Amendments have generally been rejected by both state courts, see, *e.g.*, *Legislature v. Eu*, 816 P.2d 1309 (Cal. 1991), cert. denied 503 U.S. 919 (1992); *U.S. Term Limits v. Hill*, 872 S.W.2d 349 (Ark. 1994), aff'd on other grounds 514 U.S. 779 (1995), and federal courts, see, *e.g.*, *Citizens for Legislative Choice v. Miller*, 144 F.3d 916 (6th Cir. 1998); *Bates v. Jones*, 131 F.3d 843 (9th Cir. 1997) (en banc), cert. denied 523 U.S. 1021. The constitutionality of *congressional* term limits was vigorously debated. The debate centered on the fact that the Constitution itself sets forth qualifications for Congress, primarily minimum age, citizenship and residency requirements. In 1995, the Supreme Court held that the "Qualifications Clauses" prohibit the states from imposing term limits or any other qualifications on candidates for Congress. *U.S. Term Limits v. Thornton*, 514 U.S. 779 (1995). Justice Thomas wrote a dissenting opinion joined by Chief Justice Rehnquist and Justices O'Connor and Scalia.

4. Nicholas O. Stephanopoulos, *Elections and Alignment*, 114 Columbia Law Review 283 (2014), challenges scholars' (and some judges') fixation on competition on another basis. He agrees that election law should focus on structural values—but contends that competition is not the most important of these considerations. More

---

d. For a description and evaluation of the New York City term limits, see Eric Lane, *The Impact of Term Limits on Lawmaking in the City of New York*, 3 Election Law Journal 670 (2004).

fundamental to democracy than competition, according to Stephanopoulos, is the *alignment* of voters' preferences with key governmental outputs. Stephanopoulos argues for alignment at the levels of both the individual district and the jurisdiction as a whole, and with respect to representatives' partisan affiliations, representatives' policy preferences, and, ultimately, enacted policies. He also identifies two ways in which alignment could be invoked doctrinally. Jurisdictions could cite it as a justification for policies alleged to violate some individual right. Or, more ambitiously, plaintiffs could allege *misalignment* as a reason for invalidating a certain practice.

Do you agree that alignment is a distinct value from electoral competition? If so, it is also separate from the goals of accountability and responsiveness that competition is meant to achieve? Stephanopoulos says yes: "[R]esponsiveness differs from alignment in that it refers to the *rate* at which these outputs change given some shift in public opinion. Alignment, in contrast, denotes whether or not the outputs are *congruent* with the public's preferences." *Id.* at 301. Similarly, "[w]ith respect to accountability, [alignment] provides a valuable benchmark by which the performance of elected officials can be assessed. Officials can be ousted from office when their records are incongruent with the preferences of their constituents and reelected when their records are congruent." *Id.* at 322.

Recall the critique, noted above, that the competition theory is flawed because it does not specify the optimal level of competition. (We would not want to *maximize* competition because then we would sacrifice other important values, such as political stability.) Does this attack also apply to the alignment approach? Stephanopoulos claims it does not because maximizing alignment, unlike maximizing competition, is desirable; doing so simply means that no disjunction arises between voters' preferences and key governmental outputs. In subsequent work, Stephanopoulos and his coauthors also show that alignment can be quantified using data on voters' and representatives' preferences, and that whether different policies are aligning or misaligning can be rigorously analyzed as well. See Nicholas O. Stephanopoulos et al., *The Realities of Electoral Reform*, 68 Vanderbilt Law Review 761 (2015). Is it realistic to expect litigants to present (or courts to evaluate) these sorts of empirical findings?

Chapter 5

Race and Redistricting

Equal treatment of racial, ethnic, and language minorities is a criterion for redistricting that has loomed so large that we must devote our longest chapter to it. Other representational arrangements besides districting—especially the selection of officials in at-large elections or from multi-member districts—have also been challenged as discriminating against minority groups. In this chapter we shall consider such practices as well. However, we shall *not* discuss here measures that make it more difficult for minority members to vote; we defer this topic to Chapter 6, *infra*.

As we shall see, most of the litigation on race and redistricting has occurred under the Voting Rights Act, first enacted in 1965 and later amended on several occasions. Our attention will be concentrated mainly on two sections of the Voting Rights Act, Sections 2 and 5. We shall also take notice of a series of constitutional decisions beginning in the 1990s, in which the Supreme Court placed some limits on the use of race in redistricting.

I. Section 5 of the Voting Rights Act

In Chapter 2, we saw that the Voting Rights Act of 1965 had the dramatic effect of breaking down the barriers that prevented African Americans from voting in the deep South. In the original "covered" states of Alabama, Georgia, Louisiana, Mississippi, South Carolina, Virginia, and much of North Carolina, the most important provisions that accomplished this result were the temporary ban on literacy tests (later made permanent and extended to the entire country), the appointment of federal registrars where necessary, and the "preclearance" requirement of Section 5.

Section 5, now codified at 52 U.S.C. §10304, states that whenever any covered jurisdiction "shall enact or seek to administer any voting qualification or prerequisite to voting, or standard, practice, or procedure with respect to voting," that jurisdiction must either "institute an action in the United States District Court for the District of Columbia for a declaratory judgment that such qualification, prerequisite, standard, practice, or procedure neither has the purpose nor will have the effect of denying or abridging the right to vote on account of race or color," or submit the new policy to the Attorney General. If "the Attorney General has not interposed an objection within sixty days after such submission," then the policy may be implemented. In other words, no covered jurisdiction may adopt any new electoral practice without the consent of either the Washington, D.C. district court or the Attorney General. Such consent, in turn, is provided only if the practice has neither the purpose nor the effect of denying or abridging the right to vote on racial grounds.

Which jurisdictions are covered by this requirement, and so must obtain preclearance before changing their electoral regulations? None at present, thanks to the Supreme Court's decision in *Shelby County v. Holder*, 570 U.S. 529 (2013), which we address at length below. Prior to 2013, though, Section 4 of the Voting Rights Act (as amended in 1970 and 1975) extended coverage to jurisdictions that (1) used a "test or device" such as a literacy test or a good moral character test in the 1964, 1968, or 1972 elections; and (2) had voter registration or voter turnout rates below 50 percent in those elections. 52 U.S.C. §10303(b), (c). These criteria originally applied to the jurisdictions in the deep South named above. However, the 1970 and 1975 amendments to Section 4 also encompassed Alaska, Arizona, and Texas, and portions of California, Florida, Michigan, New Hampshire, New York, and South Dakota. We note that while these jurisdictions are no longer bound by the preclearance requirement, they (or other jurisdictions) could again be affected were Congress to enact a new preclearance formula. Section 5 therefore remains relevant even though it currently lies dormant.

What kinds of electoral policies must be precleared before they can be put into effect? No one doubts that measures that disenfranchise minority voters or significantly burden their exercise of the franchise require preclearance; thwarting such laws was the point of Section 5's enactment. But what about practices that *dilute* the electoral influence of minority voters without making it more onerous for them to vote? The Court grappled with Section 5's applicability to vote dilution in the following case.

Allen v. State Board of Elections

393 U.S. 544 (1969)

MR. CHIEF JUSTICE WARREN delivered the opinion of the Court....

In these four cases, the States have passed new laws or issued new regulations. The central issue is whether these provisions fall within the prohibition of §5 that prevents the enforcement of [changes in voting qualifications and procedures] unless the State first complies with one of the section's approval procedures.

[In the first and most important of the cases, Mississippi amended its statutes to permit county boards of supervisors to change election procedures so that board members would be elected at-large (i.e., each member would be elected by the entire county) rather than from districts. In the second case, a Mississippi statute changed the office of county superintendent of education in eleven specified counties from elective to appointive. In the third case, Mississippi changed the requirements for independent candidates in general elections. In the fourth case, Virginia changed procedures for assisting illiterate voters who sought to vote for write-in candidates.]

[W]e turn to a consideration of whether these state enactments are subject to the approval requirements of § 5. These requirements apply to "any voting qualification or prerequisite to voting, or standard, practice, or procedure with respect to voting...." The Act further provides that the term "voting" "shall include all action necessary to make a vote effective in any primary, special, or general election, including, but not limited to, registration, listing ... or other action required by law prerequisite to voting, casting a ballot, and having such ballot counted properly and included in the appropriate totals of votes cast with respect to candidates for public or party office and propositions for which votes are received in an election." § 14(c)(1). Appellees in the Mississippi cases maintain that § 5 covers only those state enactments which prescribe who may register to vote. While accepting that the Act is broad enough to insure that the votes of all citizens should be cast, appellees urge that § 5 does not cover state rules relating to the qualification of candidates or to state decisions as to which offices shall be elective....

We must reject a narrow construction that appellees would give to § 5. The Voting Rights Act was aimed at the subtle, as well as the obvious, state regulations which have the effect of denying citizens their right to vote because of their race. Moreover, compatible with the decisions of this Court, the Act gives a broad interpretation to the right to vote, recognizing that voting includes "all action necessary to make a vote effective." We are convinced that in passing the Voting Rights Act, Congress intended that state enactments such as those involved in the instant cases be subject to the § 5 approval requirements....

The weight of the legislative history and an analysis of the basic purposes of the Act indicate that the enactment in each of these cases constitutes a "voting qualification or prerequisite to voting, or standard, practice, or procedure with respect to voting" within the meaning of § 5.

[The first of the four cases] involves a change from district to at-large voting for county supervisors. The right to vote can be affected by a dilution of voting power as well as by an absolute prohibition on casting a ballot. See *Reynolds*. Voters who are members of a racial minority might well be in the majority in one district, but in a decided minority in the county as a whole. This type of change could therefore nullify their ability to elect the candidate of their choice just as would prohibiting some of them from voting.

In [the second case] an important county officer in certain counties was made appointive instead of elective. The power of a citizen's vote is affected by this amendment; after the change, he is prohibited from electing an officer formerly subject to the approval of the voters. Such a change could be made either with or without a discriminatory purpose or effect; however, the purpose of § 5 was to submit such changes to scrutiny.

The changes in [the third case] appear aimed at increasing the difficulty for an independent candidate to gain a position on the general election ballot. These changes might also undermine the effectiveness of voters who wish to elect independent candidates....

The [last case involves] new procedures for casting write-in votes. As in all these cases, we do not consider whether this change has a discriminatory purpose or effect. It is clear, however, that the new procedure with respect to voting is different from the procedure in effect when the State became subject to the Act; therefore, the enactment must meet the approval requirements of § 5 in order to be enforceable....

All four cases are remanded to the District Courts with instructions to issue injunctions restraining the further enforcement of the enactments until such time as the States adequately demonstrate compliance with § 5....

MR. JUSTICE HARLAN, concurring in part and dissenting in part.

[T]he Court's construction ignores the structure of the complex regulatory scheme created by the Voting Rights Act. The Court's opinion assumes that § 5 may be considered apart from the rest of the Act. In fact, however, the provision is clearly designed to march in lock-step with § 4—the two sections cannot be understood apart from one another. Section 4 is one of the Act's central provisions, suspending the operation of all literacy tests and similar "devices" for at least five years in States whose low voter turnout indicated that these "tests" and "devices" had been used to exclude Negroes from the suffrage in the past. Section 5, moreover, reveals that it was not designed to implement new substantive policies but that it was structured to assure the effectiveness of the dramatic step that Congress had taken in § 4. The federal approval procedure found in § 5 only applies to those States whose literacy tests or similar "devices" have been suspended by § 4. As soon as the State regains the right to apply a literacy test or similar "device" under § 4, it also escapes the commands of § 5....

As soon as it is recognized that § 5 was designed solely to implement the policies of § 4, it becomes apparent that the Court's decision today permits the tail to wag the dog. For the Court has now construed § 5 to require a revolutionary innovation in American government that goes far beyond that which was accomplished by § 4. The fourth section of the Act had the profoundly important purpose of permitting the Negro people to gain access to the voting booths of the South once and for all. But the action taken by Congress in § 4 proceeded on the premise that once Negroes had gained free access to the ballot box, state governments would then be suitably responsive to their voice, and federal intervention would not be justified. In moving against "tests and devices" in § 4, Congress moved only against those techniques that prevented Negroes from voting at all. Congress did not attempt to restructure state governments. The Court now reads § 5, however, as vastly increasing the sphere of federal intervention beyond that contemplated by § 4, despite the fact that the two provisions were designed simply to interlock. The District Court for the District of Columbia is no longer limited to examining any new state statute that may tend to deny Negroes their right to vote, as the "tests and devices" suspended by § 4 had done. The decision today also requires the special District Court to determine whether various systems of representation favor or disfavor the Negro voter—an area well beyond the scope of § 4. . . . Moreover, it is not clear to me how a court would go about deciding whether an at-large system is to be preferred over a district system. Under one system, Negroes have *some* influence in the election of *all* officers; under the other, minority groups have *more* influence in the selection of *fewer* officers. If courts cannot intelligently compare such alternatives, it should not be readily inferred that Congress has required them to undertake the task.

Notes and Questions

1. Whether Congress contemplated in 1965 that Section 5 would extend to structural aspects of elections beyond the right to vote itself remains a controversial issue. However, its primary interest is historical. Most people would agree that Congress's extensions and amendments of the Voting Rights Act in 1970, 1975, 1982, and 2006, without inserting language seeking to overrule *Allen*, constitute a ratification of that decision. That view is not held universally, however, and was challenged by Justice Thomas in his concurring opinion in *Holder v. Hall*, portions of which are reprinted in Part II of this chapter.

2. The logic of *Allen* extends to aspects of the electoral system beyond those considered in the decision. In *Perkins v. Matthews*, 400 U.S. 379 (1971), for example, the Court held that annexations of new areas into cities are subject to preclearance, because the new voters added to the city could affect the voting power of prior residents, including protected minority groups. In *Georgia v. United States*, 411 U.S. 526 (1973), similarly, the Court concluded that legislative districting plans are subject to preclearance.

Allen and its progeny had a big practical impact, causing many more policies to require preclearance before being implemented. See, *e.g.*, Chandler Davidson, *The Voting Rights Act: A Brief History*, in Controversies in Minority Voting: The Voting Rights Act in Perspective 7, 28–29 (Bernard Grofman and Chandler Davidson eds., 1992):

> Until *Allen*, section 5 had been little used. The Justice Department, in the three and one-half years between passage of the act and the *Allen* decision, had objected to only six proposed changes in election procedure in covered jurisdictions, and none of these concerned vote dilution. In the three and one-half years following *Allen*, there were 118 objections, of which 88 involved dilution schemes. These included attempts to replace single-member district systems with multimember ones, to replace plurality rules by majority-vote requirements, to create numbered-place systems and staggered terms, and to annex disproportionately white suburbs. A tally at the end of 1989 revealed that 2,335 proposed changes had been objected to under section 5. The great majority of objections involved proposals that would have diluted the votes of racial groups or language minorities. Had it not been for section 5 and the *Allen* decision, almost all the proposals would have become law. Moreover, white officials in the South would surely have

implemented a much larger number of dilutionary changes had there been no section 5 to deter them.

This pattern of dilutive practices accounting for the bulk of preclearance objections continued until *Shelby County*. Between the 1982 and 2006 reauthorizations of Section 5, annexations and boundary changes constituted 45 percent of objections, changes to methods of election constituted 24 percent, and new districting plans constituted 16 percent. In contrast, measures making it more difficult to vote (such as polling place changes, the treatment of absentee ballots, and voter registration policies) represented only 5 percent of objections. U.S. Commission on Civil Rights, Voting Rights Enforcement and Reauthorization 33 (2006). Objections of all types, however, were quite rare and became less frequent over time. 5.5 percent of submitted changes were blocked from 1965 to 1974, 1.2 percent from 1975 to 1982, and 0.6 percent from 1982 to 2004. *Id.* at 27.

Geographically, just two states, Texas and Georgia, submitted more than half of all policy changes from 1982 to 2004. The pattern of preclearance objections was somewhat different, though. Georgia, Louisiana, Mississippi, South Carolina, and Texas each accounted for 10 to 20 percent of all objections in this period. *Id.* at 75.

3. *Allen* and the subsequent reauthorizations of the Voting Rights Act firmly established the principle that the Act extends to electoral mechanisms that affect the ability of minority voters as a group to make their votes count. However, the establishment of this principle did not, by itself, provide answers to questions raised by Justice Harlan in his *Allen* dissent regarding how the Justice Department and the courts should decide which electoral procedures impermissibly discriminate against minority groups.

The Supreme Court addressed these issues in 1976 in *Beer v. United States*, reprinted below. In that case, the Court established "nonretrogression" as the standard for applying Section 5. The Justice Department later took the view that under certain circumstances, preclearance could be denied even in the absence of retrogression. As we shall see, the Supreme Court has generally rejected that view. But the meaning of retrogression has continued to be a controversial issue, most recently addressed in the 2006 amendments to the Voting Rights Act.

Beer v. United States

425 U.S. 130 (1976)

Mr. Justice STEWART delivered the opinion of the Court....

The city of New Orleans brought this suit under § 5 seeking a judgment declaring that a reapportionment of New Orleans' councilmanic districts did not have the purpose or effect of denying or abridging the right to vote on account of race or color. The District Court entered a judgment of dismissal, holding that the new reapportionment plan would have the effect of abridging the voting rights of New Orleans' Negro citizens....

I

New Orleans is a city of almost 600,000 people. Some 55% of that population is white and the remaining 45% is Negro. Some 65% of the registered voters are white, and the remaining 35% are Negro. In 1954, New Orleans adopted a mayor-council form of government. Since that time the municipal charter has provided that the city council is to consist of seven members, one to be elected from each of five councilmanic districts, and two to be elected by the voters of the city at large. The 1954 charter also requires an adjustment of the boundaries of the five single-member councilmanic districts following each decennial census to reflect population shifts among the districts.

In 1961, the city council redistricted the city based on the 1960 census figures. That reapportionment plan established four districts that stretched from the edge of Lake Pontchartrain on the north side of the city to the Mississippi River on the city's south side. The fifth district was wedge shaped and encompassed the city's downtown area. In one of these councilmanic districts, Negroes constituted a majority of the population, but only about half of the registered voters. In the other four districts white voters clearly outnumbered Negro voters. No Negro was elected to the New Orleans City Council during the decade from 1960 to 1970.

After receipt of the 1970 census figures the city council adopted a reapportionment plan (Plan I) that continued the basic north-to-south pattern of councilmanic districts combined with a wedge-shaped, downtown district. Under Plan I Negroes constituted a majority of the population in two districts, but they did not make up a majority of registered voters in any district. The largest percentage of Negro voters in a single district under Plan I was 45.2%. When the city submitted Plan I to the Attorney General pursuant to § 5, he objected to it, stating that it appeared to "dilute black voting strength by combining a number of black voters with a larger number of white voters in each of the five districts." He also expressed the view that "the district lines (were not) drawn as they (were) because of any compelling governmental need" and that the district lines did "not reflect numeric population configurations or considerations of district compactness or regularity of shape."

Even before the Attorney General objected to Plan I, the city authorities had commenced work on a second plan—Plan II. That plan followed the general north-to-south districting pattern common to the 1961 apportionment and Plan I. It produced Negro population majorities in two districts and a Negro voter majority (52.6%) in one district. When Plan II was submitted to the Attorney General, he posed the same objections to it that he had raised to Plan I. In addition, he noted that "the predominantly black neighborhoods in the city are located generally in an east to west progression," and pointed out that the use of north-to-south districts in such a situation almost inevitably would have the effect of diluting the maximum potential impact of the Negro vote. Following the rejection by the Attorney General of Plan II, the city brought this declaratory judgment action in the United States District Court for the District of Columbia. . . .

II

. . . .

B

The principal argument made by the appellants in this Court is that the District Court erred in concluding that the makeup of the five geographic councilmanic districts under Plan II would have the effect of abridging voting rights on account of race or color. In evaluating this claim it is important to note at the outset that the question is not one of constitutional law, but of statutory construction. A determination of when a legislative reapportionment has "the effect of denying or abridging the right to vote on account of race or color," must depend, therefore, upon the intent of Congress in enacting the Voting Rights Act and specifically § 5.

The legislative history reveals that the basic purpose of Congress in enacting the Voting Rights Act was "to rid the country of racial discrimination in voting." *South Carolina v. Katzenbach*. Section 5 was intended to play an important role in achieving that goal:

> Section 5 was a response to a common practice in some jurisdictions of staying one step ahead of the federal courts by passing new discriminatory voting laws as soon as the old ones had been struck down. That practice had been possible because each new law remained in effect until the Justice Department or private plaintiffs were able to sustain the burden of proving that the new law, too, was discriminatory. . . . Congress therefore decided, as the Supreme Court held it could, "to shift the advantage of time and inertia from the perpetrators of the evil to its victim," by "freezing election procedures in the covered areas unless the changes can be shown to be nondiscriminatory." H.R. Rep. No. 94-196, pp. 57–58.

By prohibiting the enforcement of a voting-procedure change until it has been demonstrated to the United States Department of Justice or to a three-judge federal court that the change does not have a discriminatory effect, Congress desired to prevent States from "undo(ing) or defeat(ing) the rights recently won" by Negroes. H.R. Rep. No. 91-397, p. 8. Section 5 was intended "to insure that (the gains thus far achieved in minority political participation) shall not be destroyed through new (discriminatory) procedures and techniques." S. Rep. No. 94-295, p. 19.

When it adopted a 7-year extension of the Voting Rights Act in 1975, Congress explicitly stated that "the standard (under § 5) can only be fully satisfied by determining on the basis of the facts found by the Attorney General (or the District Court) to be true whether the ability of minority groups to participate in the political process and to elect their choices to office is *augmented, diminished, or not affected* by the change affecting voting. . . ." H.R. Rep. No.94-196, p. 60 (emphasis added). In other words the purpose of § 5 has always been to insure that no voting-procedure changes would be made that would lead to a retrogression in the position of racial minorities with respect to their effective exercise of the electoral franchise.

It is thus apparent that a legislative reapportionment that enhances the position of racial minorities with respect to their effective exercise of the electoral franchise can hardly have the "effect" of diluting or abridging the right to vote on account of race within the meaning of § 5. We conclude, therefore, that such an ameliorative new legislative apportionment cannot violate § 5 unless the new apportionment itself so discriminates on the basis of race or color as to violate the Constitution.

The application of this standard to the facts of the present case is straightforward. Under the apportionment of 1961 none of the five councilmanic districts had a clear Negro majority of registered voters, and no Negro has been elected to the New Orleans City Council while that apportionment system has been in effect. Under Plan II, by contrast, Negroes will constitute a majority of the population in two of the five districts and a clear majority of the registered voters in one of them. Thus, there is every reason to predict, upon the District Court's hypothesis of bloc voting, that at least one and perhaps two Negroes may well be elected to the council under Plan II. It was therefore error for the District Court to conclude that Plan II "will . . . have the effect of denying or abridging the right to vote on account of race or color" within the meaning of § 5 of the Voting Rights Act.

It is possible that a legislative reapportionment could be a substantial improvement over its predecessor in terms of lessening racial discrimination, and yet nonetheless continue so to discriminate on the basis of race or color as to be unconstitutional. The United States has made no claim that Plan II suffers from any such disability, nor could it rationally do so. . . .

Accordingly, the judgment of the District Court is vacated, and the case is remanded to that court for further proceedings consistent with this opinion.

Notes and Questions

1. Many voting rights activists were dissatisfied with the nonretrogression rule, because they believed it provided no relief to protected groups if they had been treated unfairly all along. In most jurisdictions as of the 1970s there were few and often no congressional, state or local districts in which African Americans predominated. During the redistricting of the 1980s and, especially, the 1990s, those in charge of redistricting often felt legal and sometimes political pressure to create additional "majority-minority districts." As a result, *reducing* the number of majority-minority districts often was not even possible and almost never was likely as a practical matter. Whatever could be said for or against *Beer* as a matter of statutory construction, for practical purposes the decision seemed to make Section 5 marginal at best to the redistricting process. As we shall see in Part III of this Chapter, the Justice Department found reason to believe that it was not limited by the *Beer* nonretrogression rule in the post-1990 redistricting cycle. But through the 1980s, most proceedings under the Voting Rights Act relating to redistricting arose under Section 2, which we shall consider in Part II.

2. Justice Stewart gives various reasons for his conclusion that only retrogressive changes justify denial of preclearance under Section 5, but his opinion contains almost no discussion of what is meant by retrogression. Preclearance of the New Orleans redistricting plan had been denied on the ground that it should have contained more districts in which blacks were a majority of registered voters. Once having interpreted Section 5 as embodying the nonretrogression rule, in a single conclusory paragraph Justice Stewart reached the "straightforward" conclusion that New Orleans, which increased the number of such districts from none to one, was entitled to preclearance.

Justice Stewart's "straightforward" conclusion glossed over difficult questions about what should be regarded as retrogression. Concentrating blacks into two districts so that they made up the majority of the population in both and the majority of registered voters in one meant that the percentage of blacks in the remaining three districts was much lower than it could have been if the black population had been more evenly divided among the five districts. Was there a reason why *that* did not constitute retrogression, other than the fact that all the participants in the controversy—the Justice Department, voting rights activists, and the city itself—proceeded on the opposite theory? The Court's failure to address this fundamental theoretical question—is a minority group better off controlling the highest possible number of districts or having a substantial presence in all or most districts?—has not itself been a great practical problem, because the same answer that was assumed in *Beer* continued to be assumed throughout the subsequent history of the Voting Rights Act, at least until *Georgia v. Ashcroft*, discussed below.

3. Through the 1990s round of redistricting, it was widely believed that even in the absence of actual or intended retrogression, preclearance could be denied if a plan was intentionally discriminatory against a protected minority group. The Supreme Court decided otherwise in *Reno v. Bossier Parish School Board*, 528 U.S. 320 (2000) (*Bossier Parish II*).[a] According to the Court, "the 'purpose' prong of § 5 covers only retrogressive dilution"—and thus does *not* cover discriminatory but non-retrogressive intent. *Id.* at 328. Would this holding effectively nullify the purpose prong? No, in the Court's view, because thanks to the prong, "the Government need only refute the covered jurisdiction's prima facie showing that a proposed voting change does not have a retrogressive purpose in order for preclearance to be denied." "This advantage, plus the ability to reach malevolent incompetence, may not represent a massive addition to the effect prong, but it is enough to justify the separate existence of the purpose prong in this statute. . . ." *Id.* at 332.

Bossier Parish II may seem like a highly technical decision resolving a minor issue of statutory interpretation, but it actually had a dramatic impact. In the 1990s, 43 percent of preclearance objections were made exclusively on discriminatory

a. We shall encounter *Bossier Parish I* in Part II, Note 9 following *Thornburgh v. Gingles*.

intent grounds, and another 31 percent were made partially on intent grounds. In the 2000s, however, the Justice Department "interposed only forty-one objections, compared with 250 during a comparable period a decade earlier," and "[v]irtually all objections after *Bossier II* were based on a finding of retrogressive effect; at most two of the forty-one objections were based on the elusive concept of retrogressive intent." For this reason, Peyton McCrary and his coauthors labeled *Bossier Parish II* "the most transformative decision regarding section 5" since *Beer.* Peyton McCrary et al., *The Law of Preclearance: Enforcing Section 5*, in The Future of the Voting Rights Act 20, 26–27, 29 (David Epstein et al., eds., 2006).

The 2006 reauthorization of the Voting Rights Act added a new paragraph to Section 5 overturning *Bossier Parish II* by stating that "[t]he term 'purpose' in subsections (a) and (b) of this section shall include any discriminatory purpose." 52 U.S.C. § 10304(c). See J. Morgan Kousser, *The Strange, Ironic Career of Section 5 of the Voting Rights Act, 1965–2007*, 86 Texas Law Review 667, 754 (2008) (referring to this amendment as the "most important part" of the 2006 renewal). Under this new language, what should the Justice Department and courts consider in assessing whether a plan has a discriminatory purpose? For a detailed discussion, see Michael J. Pitts, *Redistricting and Discriminatory Purpose*, 59 American University Law Review 1575 (2010). In 2011, the Justice Department promulgated regulations setting forth its Section 5 procedures. These regulations state that the analysis of discriminatory purpose will be "guided by the analysis in *Village of Arlington Heights v. Metropolitan Housing Development Corp.*, 429 U.S. 252 (1977)," 28 C.F.R. § 51.54(a), and list the following factors from that decision:

> (1) Whether the impact of the official action bears more heavily on one race than another;
>
> (2) The historical background of the decision;
>
> (3) The specific sequence of events leading up to the decision;
>
> (4) Whether there are departures from the normal procedural sequence;
>
> (5) Whether there are substantive departures from the normal factors considered; and
>
> (6) The legislative or administrative history, including contemporaneous statements made by the decision makers.

28 C.F.R. § 51.57(e). In *Village of Arlington Heights*, the Court set forth this nonexclusive list of factors relevant to the determination of discriminatory purpose under the Equal Protection Clause. Are these factors helpful in determining whether a districting plan violates the purpose prong of Section 5?

4. Although the focus of this chapter is on *vote dilution*, Section 5 also applies to changes that are alleged to burden or suppress minority voting, sometimes referred to as "vote denial." See Daniel P. Tokaji, *The New Vote Denial: Where Election Reform Meets the Voting Rights Act*, 57 South Carolina Law Review 689 (2006).

That category would include strict voter identification laws like those enacted prior to *Shelby County* in covered states South Carolina and Texas. It would also include other measures that arguably make it more difficult for minority members to vote, such as the cutback to early voting passed by Florida in 2011. Courts denied preclearance to (or insisted on the relaxation of) these measures, reasoning that they disproportionately harmed minority voters and thus reduced their electoral influence. See *South Carolina v. United States*, 898 F. Supp. 2d 30 (D.D.C. 2012); *Texas v. Holder*, 888 F. Supp. 2d 113 (D.D.C. 2012); *Florida v. United States*, 885 F. Supp. 2d 299 (D.D.C. 2012). For further discussion of the Voting Rights Act's application to vote denial, see *infra* Chapter 6, Part II.

5. In *Georgia v. Ashcroft*, 195 F. Supp. 2d 25 (D.D.C. 2002), a three-judge district court refused to grant preclearance to a state senate plan adopted by the Georgia legislature, even though most blacks in the state legislature had voted for the plan. The court was spared the possible problem of competing minority groups, because the only large minority group in question was African Americans. However, the court was *not* spared the equally vexing issue of how to assess minority electoral influence, as the plan "unpacked" certain black-majority districts and increased the proportions of blacks (and Democrats) in other districts.

In a contentious 5–4 decision, the Supreme Court overruled the district court on the merits. Writing for the Court, Justice O'Connor first described the old and new state senate plans:

> [Under the old plan,] 13 districts had a black population of at least 50%, with the black voting age population exceeding 50% in 12 of those districts.... The [new] plan as designed by Senator Brown's committee kept true to the dual goals of maintaining at least as many majority-minority districts while also attempting to increase Democratic strength in the Senate. Part of the Democrats' strategy was not only to maintain the number of majority-minority districts, but to increase the number of so-called "influence" districts, where black voters would be able to exert a significant—if not decisive—force in the election process.... According to the 2000 census, as compared to the benchmark plan, the new plan reduced by five the number of districts with a black voting age population in excess of 60%. Yet it increased the number of majority-black voting age population districts by one, and it increased the number of districts with a black voting age population of between 25% and 50% by four.

Georgia v. Ashcroft, 539 U.S. 461, 469–70 (2003). Justice O'Connor then argued that the retrogression inquiry should not overemphasize minority voters' ability to elect their preferred candidates. Rather, it should also take into account their ability to influence (but not determine) the outcome in certain districts, the quality of their representation, and other related factors:

> While we have never determined the meaning of "effective exercise of the electoral franchise," this case requires us to do so in some detail. First...

the inquiry must encompass the entire statewide plan as a whole. Thus, while the diminution of a minority group's effective exercise of the electoral franchise in one or two districts may be sufficient to show a violation of § 5, it is only sufficient if the covered jurisdiction cannot show that the gains in the plan as a whole offset the loss in a particular district.

Second, any assessment of the retrogression of a minority group's effective exercise of the electoral franchise depends on an examination of all the relevant circumstances, such as the ability of minority voters to elect their candidate of choice, the extent of the minority group's opportunity to participate in the political process, and the feasibility of creating a nonretrogressive plan. . . .

In assessing the totality of the circumstances, a court should not focus solely on the comparative ability of a minority group to elect a candidate of its choice. While this factor is an important one in the § 5 retrogression inquiry, it cannot be dispositive or exclusive. The standard in § 5 is simple — whether the new plan "would lead to a retrogression in the position of racial minorities with respect to their effective exercise of the electoral franchise." *Beer.*

The ability of minority voters to elect a candidate of their choice is important but often complex in practice to determine. In order to maximize the electoral success of a minority group, a State may choose to create a certain number of "safe" districts, in which it is highly likely that minority voters will be able to elect the candidate of their choice. Alternatively, a State may choose to create a greater number of districts in which it is likely — although perhaps not quite as likely as under the benchmark plan — that minority voters will be able to elect candidates of their choice.

Section 5 does not dictate that a State must pick one of these methods of redistricting over another. Either option "will present the minority group with its own array of electoral risks and benefits," and presents "hard choices about what would truly 'maximize' minority electoral success." *Thornburg* (O'CONNOR, J., concurring in judgment). On one hand, a smaller number of safe majority-minority districts may virtually guarantee the election of a minority group's preferred candidate in those districts. Yet even if this concentration of minority voters in a few districts does not constitute the unlawful packing of minority voters, such a plan risks isolating minority voters from the rest of the state, and risks narrowing political influence to only a fraction of political districts. And while such districts may result in more "descriptive representation" because the representatives of choice are more likely to mirror the race of the majority of voters in that district, the representation may be limited to fewer areas.

On the other hand, spreading out minority voters over a greater number of districts creates more districts in which minority voters may have the opportunity to elect a candidate of their choice. Such a strategy has the potential to increase "substantive representation" in more districts, by creating coalitions of voters who together will help to achieve the electoral aspirations of the minority group. It also, however, creates the risk that the minority group's preferred candidate may lose.... Section 5 gives States the flexibility to choose one theory of effective representation over the other.

In addition to the comparative ability of a minority group to elect a candidate of its choice, the other highly relevant factor in a retrogression inquiry is the extent to which a new plan changes the minority group's opportunity to participate in the political process....

Thus, a court must examine whether a new plan adds or subtracts "influence districts"—where minority voters may not be able to elect a candidate of choice but can play a substantial, if not decisive, role in the electoral process. In assessing the comparative weight of these influence districts, it is important to consider "the likelihood that candidates elected without decisive minority support would be willing to take the minority's interests into account." *Thornburg* (O'CONNOR, J., concurring in judgment). In fact, various studies have suggested that the most effective way to maximize minority voting strength may be to create more influence or coalitional districts.

Section 5 leaves room for States to use these types of influence and coalitional districts. Indeed, the State's choice ultimately may rest on a political choice of whether substantive or descriptive representation is preferable. The State may choose, consistent with § 5, that it is better to risk having fewer minority representatives in order to achieve greater overall representation of a minority group by increasing the number of representatives sympathetic to the interests of minority voters.

In addition to influence districts, one other method of assessing the minority group's opportunity to participate in the political process is to examine the comparative position of legislative leadership, influence, and power for representatives of the benchmark majority-minority districts. A legislator, no less than a voter, is "not immune from the obligation to pull, haul, and trade to find common political ground." *De Grandy*. Indeed, in a representative democracy, the very purpose of voting is to delegate to chosen representatives the power to make and pass laws. The ability to exert more control over that process is at the core of exercising political power. A lawmaker with more legislative influence has more potential to set the agenda, to participate in closed-door meetings, to negotiate from a stronger position, and to shake hands on a deal. Maintaining or increasing legislative positions of power for minority voters' representatives of choice, while not dispositive by itself, can show the lack of retrogressive effect under § 5.

> And it is also significant, though not dispositive, whether the representatives elected from the very districts created and protected by the Voting Rights Act support the new districting plan.... The representatives of districts created to ensure continued minority participation in the political process have some knowledge about how "voters will probably act" and whether the proposed change will decrease minority voters' effective exercise of the electoral franchise.

Id. at 479-84. Applying this approach to retrogression, Justice O'Connor concluded that the district court had misanalysed the issue. It had problematically focused on a handful of districts whose black populations had decreased, while overlooking other districts that might have offset this decline. Justice Souter dissented, joined by Justices Breyer, Ginsburg, and Stevens. He lamented that under the majority's standard, "The power to elect a candidate of choice has been forgotten; voting power has been forgotten. It is very hard to see anything left of the standard of nonretrogression." *Id.* at 495 (Souter, J., dissented).

6. For a study of the interaction of legal and political science issues raised in *Georgia v. Ashcroft*, see Richard H. Pildes, *Is Voting-Rights Law Now at War with Itself? Social Science and Voting Rights in the 2000s*, 80 North Carolina Law Review 1517 (2002). As Pildes discusses, there are several kinds of districts that are commonly implicated in Section 5 disputes: (1) *majority-minority districts*, where minority voters make up a clear majority of the population and so are able to elect their preferred candidates; (2) *crossover districts*, where minority voters make up a large minority of the population and again are able to elect their candidates of choice with the aid of white voters who "cross over"; (3) *coalition districts*, where different groups of minority voters (e.g., African Americans and Latinos) make up a combined majority of the population and work together to elect their mutually preferred candidates; and (4) *influence districts*, where minority voters are not numerous enough to elect their candidates of choice (typically minority Democrats), but *are* numerous enough to help elect their second-choice candidates (often white Democrats). The majority in *Georgia* seems to permit two kinds of tradeoffs among these district types. First, jurisdictions may substitute fewer packed majority-minority districts, crossover districts, and coalition districts for more packed majority-minority districts. Second, and more provocatively, jurisdictions may substitute (a larger number of) influence districts for (a smaller number of) districts where minority members are able to elect their preferred candidates.

7. The tension between descriptive and substantive representation that is at the heart of *Georgia v. Ashcroft* has been the subject of extensive empirical analysis. Scholars have found that the additional majority-minority districts that were drawn in the South in the 1990s cost the Democrats about ten congressional seats and anywhere from two to sixteen seats in each of ten southern state houses. See David T. Canon, Race, Redistricting, and Representation: The Unintended Consequences of Black Majority Districts (1999); David Lublin, The Paradox of Representation: Racial Gerrymandering and Minority Interests in Congress (1997); David Lublin &

Stephen Voss, *Racial Redistricting and Realignment in Southern State Legislatures*, 44 American Journal of Political Science 792 (2000). Scholars have also found that the ideological midpoint of congressional delegations and state legislative chambers shifted to the right in response to the creation of the new majority-minority districts. See Charles Cameron et al., *Do Majority-Minority Districts Maximize Substantive Black Representation in Congress?*, 90 American Political Science Review 794 (1996); David Epstein & Sharyn O'Halloran, *Measuring the Electoral and Policy Impact of Majority-Minority Voting Districts*, 43 American Journal of Political Science 367 (1999).

Nicholas O. Stephanopoulos, *Race, Place, and Power*, 68 Stanford Law Review 1323 (2016), disputes the conventional wisdom that descriptive and substantive representation necessarily conflict. When Republicans are responsible for redistricting, "there is indeed a tradeoff between electing minority legislators and electing Democrats to state houses over the 1972–2014 period," because Republicans tend to overconcentrate minority (and Democratic) voters in a few districts. *Id.* at 1390. However, "[t]he tradeoff is alleviated by Democratic line-drawers," who, like the mapmakers in *Georgia*, try to unpack majority-minority districts and design additional influence districts. *Id.* Stephanopoulos reports similar results for the ideology of the median state house member; "[t]here is again a descriptive-substantive tradeoff, and it is again eased by unified Democratic control but aggravated by unified Republican control." *Id.* at 1391.

8. By the terms of the 1982 amendments, Section 5 and related provisions of the Voting Rights Act were set to expire in 2007. They were renewed a year ahead of schedule, in the Fannie Lou Hamer, Rosa Parks, and Coretta Scott King Voting Rights Act Reauthorization Act and Amendment Act of 2006, known for short as the Voting Rights Act Reauthorization Act, (VRARA), or simply as the 2006 amendments. For excellent accounts of the law's history, see Kousser, *Strange, Ironic Career, supra*; Nathaniel Persily, *The Promise and Pitfalls of the New Voting Rights Act*, 117 Yale Law Journal 174 (2007); and James Thomas Tucker, *The Politics of Persuasion: Passage of the Voting Rights Act Reauthorization Act of 2006*, 33 Journal of Legislation 205 (2007). The new legislation contained a few notable changes to the Voting Rights Act. The most important of these changes were intended to nullify the Supreme Court's rulings in *Georgia* and, as we have seen, *Bossier Parish II*.

9. The "*Georgia v. Ashcroft* fix" appears in a new paragraph added to Section 5, as follows:

> Any voting qualification or prerequisite to voting, or standard, practice, or procedure with respect to voting that has the purpose of or will have the effect of diminishing the ability of any citizens of the United States on account of race or color, or in contravention of the guarantees [protecting language minorities], to elect their preferred candidates of choice denies or abridges the right to vote within the meaning of subsection (a) of this section.

52 U.S.C. § 10304(b). An additional new paragraph specifies that "[t]he purpose of subsection (b) of this section is to protect the ability of such citizens to elect their preferred candidates of choice." *Id.* 10304(d).

The purpose of these amendments to Section 5 was to change the law to what Congress perceived it to have been before *Georgia*. The House Report accompanying the renewal legislation stated:

> [L]eaving the *Georgia* standard in place would encourage States to spread minority voters under the guise of "influence" and would effectively shut minority voters out of the political process. In essence, the Committee heard that Section 5, if left uncorrected, would now allow "States to turn black and other minority voters into second class voters who can influence elections of white candidates, but who cannot elect their preferred candidates, including candidates of their own race." This is *clearly not* the outcome that Congress intended the Voting Rights Act and Section 5 to have on minority voters.

H.R. Rep. No. 109-478, at 70 (2006). The House Report stated the legislation's intent as follows:

> This change is intended to restore Section 5 and the effect prong to the standard of analysis set forth by this Committee during its examination of Section 5 in 1975, such that a change should be denied preclearance under Section 5 if it diminishes the ability of minority groups to elect their candidates of choice. Such was the standard of analysis articulated by the Supreme Court in *Beer v. United States*, the retrogression standard of analysis on which the Court, the Department of Justice, and minority voters relied for 30 years, and the standard the Committee seeks to restore. Voting changes that leave a minority group less able to elect a preferred candidate of choice, either directly or when coalesced with other voters, cannot be precleared under Section 5. Furthermore, by adding the adjective "preferred" before "candidate," the Committee makes clear that the purpose of Section 5 is to protect the electoral power of minority groups to elect candidates that the minority community desires to be their elected representative.

Id. at 71. The Senate Committee Report accompanying the 2006 reauthorization—which was not filed until six days after the Senate voted on the bill—describes the new effect standard differently:

> It is important to emphasize that this language does not protect any district with a representative who gets elected with some minority votes. Rather, it protects only districts in which "such citizens"—minority citizens—are the ones selecting their "preferred candidate of choice" with their own voting power. These two phrases have a limited but important purpose: protecting naturally occurring majority-minority districts. By limiting non-retrogression requirements to districts in which "such [minority] citizens" are able with their own vote power to elect "preferred" candidates

> of choice—not just a candidate of choice settled for when forced to compromise with other groups—the bill limits section 5 to protecting those naturally occurring, compact majority—minority districts with which section 5 was originally concerned.

S. Rep. No. 109-295, at 21 (2006). Is the difference between the House and Senate characterizations of the *Georgia v. Ashcroft* fix significant? In what cases might this difference matter? For extensive commentary on the questions raised by the fix, see Persily, *Promises and Pitfalls, supra*, 117 Yale Law Journal at 216–51.

10. Persily argued that, as revised, "Section 5 should be read as preventing new districting plans that reduce the aggregated probability across districts that minorities will elect the candidates that they prefer and that whites generally disfavor." *Id.* at 219. In other words, under the benchmark plan, the probability that minority voters will be able to elect their candidate of choice should be determined in each district. The sum of these probabilities should then be calculated, and the exercise should be repeated for the new plan. If the new plan's total is lower than the benchmark plan's total, then the new plan should be denied preclearance.

Whatever the theoretical appeal of this probabilistic approach, it was not adopted by the lone court to consider a district plan under Section 5 between the 2006 amendments and *Shelby County*. Presented with Texas's congressional and state legislative plans, the court concluded that a *binary* inquiry was necessary, under which each district either would or would not be deemed an "ability" district in which minority voters are able to elect their preferred candidate. As the court put it, the revised Section 5 "requires identifying districts in which minority citizens enjoy an existing ability to elect and comparing the number of such districts in the benchmark to the number of such districts in a proposed plan to measure the proposed plan's effect on minority citizens' voting ability." *Texas v. United States*, 831 F. Supp. 2d 244, 262 (D.D.C. 2011); see also Guidance Concerning Redistricting Under Section 5 of the Voting Rights Act, 76 Fed. Reg. 7470, 7471 (Feb. 9, 2011) ("That ability to elect either exists or it does not in any particular circumstance."). Applying this standard, the court denied preclearance to Texas's state house plan because it reduced by four the number of ability districts. *Texas v. United States*, 887 F. Supp. 2d 133, 166-77 (D.D.C. 2012). More controversially, the court also denied preclearance to Texas's congressional plan because it failed to *increase* the number of ability districts (from ten) even though the State gained four seats thanks to the 2010 census. *Id.* at 158.

11. Among the interesting features of the politics of the 2006 amendments were the divisions of opinion among scholars who in the past had been staunch supporters of the Voting Rights Act. There were some in this group who had serious doubts about whether Section 5, especially in its more rigid form as represented by the lower court decision in *Georgia* and in VRARA by the *Georgia v. Ashcroft* fix, might be doing more harm than good. They worried that rigid application could impede the ability of black and white politicians in the covered jurisdictions to work together in coalitions. For one expression of this view, see Samuel Issacharoff, *Is Section 5 of*

the Voting Rights Act a Victim of Its Own Success?, 104 Columbia Law Review 1710 (2004). For an opposing view, asserting that Section 5 remains very important at the local level, see Michael J. Pitts, *Let's Not Call the Whole Thing Off Just Yet: A Response to Samuel Issacharoff's Suggestion to Scuttle Section 5 of the Voting Rights Act*, 84 Nebraska Law Review 605 (2005).

A related perspective is that dramatic changes in the environment in which the Voting Rights Act operates called for a serious reconsideration of what form of regulation is best suited to present circumstances. Richard H. Pildes, *Political Avoidance, Constitutional Theory, and the VRA*, 117 Yale Law Journal Pocket Part 148, 149–50 (2007), criticizes Congress for not engaging in such a reconsideration:

> [I]t is useful to begin with the context of the VRA today, then turn to the legislative process itself and the political economy that drove it. First, on context: when Congress last revisited the VRA in 1982, there were few black elected officials; virtually no Republican Party at the state and local levels in much of the South; voting was extremely polarized along racial lines; and the central institutional devices that occupied Congress's attention were multimember and at-large election structures that contributed to the virtual absence of black political representation. In the last twenty-five years, all of these elements have changed, some in ways easily visible, some in ways experts recognize. There is now robust two-party competition in the South; a significant cohort of black elected officials now exists at all levels and in most states with significant minority populations, with black elected state legislators making up thirty-one to forty-five percent of *all* Democratic state legislators in the Deep South states of Alabama, Florida, Georgia, Louisiana, Mississippi, and South Carolina; the VRA must be applied in today's multiethnic America, not the biracial context of the South of decades past; and racially polarized voting has declined somewhat....
>
> The effects these changes ought to have on the structure of the VRA are, of course, much debated, but the fact of change since 1982 is not. Yet the VRA that emerged from Congress in 2006 reflects not a single one of these changes in any way. Though there are as many judicial findings of VRA section 2 violations since 1990 in Pennsylvania as in South Carolina, for example, section 5 continues to cover the latter and not the former. The regionally specific areas of the country singled out for special coverage are neither expanded nor contracted from what they have been since 1982 (indeed, the structure of coverage goes back even earlier).

12. The other reason for some usual supporters of strong voting rights legislation having reservations was their fear that the renewed Section 5 might be declared unconstitutional. Congress may act only pursuant to a power granted to it by the Constitution. In *South Carolina v. Katzenbach*, 383 U.S. 301 (1966), the Supreme Court, over the dissent of Justice Black, upheld the original preclearance provisions of Section 5 as a valid exercise of congressional power to "enforce" the Fifteenth

Amendment. In doing so, the Court took a notably deferential stance and expressed considerable sympathy for Congress's reasons for enacting Section 5:

> The basic test to be applied in a case involving s 2 of the Fifteenth Amendment is the same as in all cases concerning the express powers of Congress with relation to the reserved powers of the States. Chief Justice Marshall laid down the classic formulation, 50 years before the Fifteenth Amendment was ratified: 'Let the end be legitimate, let it be within the scope of the constitution, and all means which are appropriate, which are plainly adapted to that end, which are not prohibited, but consist with the letter and spirit of the constitution, are constitutional.' *McCulloch v. Maryland*. . . .
>
> Congress exercised its authority under the Fifteenth Amendment in an inventive manner when it enacted the Voting Rights Act of 1965. First: The measure prescribes remedies for voting discrimination which go into effect without any need for prior adjudication. This was clearly a legitimate response to the problem, for which there is ample precedent under other constitutional provisions. Congress had found that case-by-case litigation was inadequate to combat widespread and persistent discrimination in voting, because of the inordinate amount of time and energy required to overcome the obstructionist tactics invariably encountered in these lawsuits. After enduring nearly a century of systematic resistance to the Fifteenth Amendment, Congress might well decide to shift the advantage of time and inertia from the perpetrators of the evil to its victims. . . .
>
> Second: The Act intentionally confines these remedies to a small number of States and political subdivisions which in most instances were familiar to Congress by name. This, too, was a permissible method of dealing with the problem. Congress had learned that substantial voting discrimination presently occurs in certain sections of the country, and it knew no way of accurately forecasting whether the evil might spread elsewhere in the future. In acceptable legislative fashion, Congress chose to limit its attention to the geographic areas where immediate action seemed necessary. The doctrine of the equality of States, invoked by South Carolina, does not bar this approach, for that doctrine applies only to the terms upon which States are admitted to the Union, and not to the remedies for local evils which have subsequently appeared.

Id. at 326-29. The Court subsequently upheld Section 5 after it was reauthorized in 1970, 1975, and 1982. See *Lopez v. Monterey County*, 525 U.S. 266 (1999); *City of Rome v. United States*, 446 U.S. 156 (1980); *Georgia v. United States*, 411 U.S. 526 (1973).

However, in subsequent years, the Supreme Court underwent a "federalism revolution," construing congressional power over the states much more narrowly than it had in cases such as *South Carolina*. In a line of cases beginning with *City of Boerne v. Flores*, 521 U.S. 507 (1997), the Court scrutinized with varying degrees of care congressional actions against the state ostensibly taken under its power to enforce the Fourteenth Amendment. In *Boerne*, the Court explained that Congress's power under Section 5 of the Fourteenth Amendment is limited: "Congress does not enforce a constitutional right by changing what the right is. It has been given the power 'to enforce,' not the power to determine what constitutes a constitutional violation." *Id.* at 519. The Court further explained that "[t]here must be a congruence and proportionality between the injury to be prevented or remedied and the means adopted to that end." *Id.* at 520.

Two other cases, *Nevada Department of Human Resources v. Hibbs*, 538 U.S. 721 (2003), and *Tennessee v. Lane* 541 U.S. 509 (2004), appeared to give Congress more leeway. Nevertheless, some scholars urged Congress to extend Section 5 for five or seven years instead of the twenty-five that Congress actually settled on, to ease the ability of covered jurisdictions to "bail out" of coverage, and to make other changes that might improve the chances of the renewed preclearance requirement being upheld as constitutional. Indeed, some thought the *Georgia v. Ashcroft* fix, by removing a degree of flexibility, would increase the likelihood that Section 5 would be struck down.

The constitutionality of preclearance was raised but not decided in *Northwest Austin Municipal Utility District, Number One v. Holder*, 557 U.S. 193 (2009). In an opinion joined by eight justices (all but Justice Thomas), the Court in dicta expressed the view that "the Act imposes current burdens and must be justified by current needs." *Id.* at 203. The Court also noted that the preclearance regime differentiated among states, "despite our historic tradition that all the States enjoy 'equal sovereignty.'" *Id.* But *Northwest Austin* avoided deciding the constitutional question, instead interpreting the statute to allow the plaintiff, a local utility district, to seek bail-out from coverage. For an analysis of the Court's use of constitutional avoidance in this case and its failure to use avoidance under similar circumstances in the campaign finance context, see Richard L. Hasen, *Constitutional Avoidance and Anti-Avoidance by the Roberts Court*, 2009 Supreme Court Review 181 (2010). Only Justice Thomas reached the constitutional question in *Northwest Austin*, concluding in his concurring opinion that Section 5 exceeded Congress' enforcement power under the Fifteenth Amendment.

Many observers thought the handwriting was on the wall after *Northwest Austin*, with a majority of the Court poised to declare the coverage formula or preclearance requirement unconstitutional. Yet there was no serious effort in Congress to amend the statute. Four years later, a 5-4 majority of the Supreme Court held that the coverage formula exceeds Congress' power under the Fourteenth and Fifteenth Amendments.

Shelby County v. Holder

570 U.S. 529 (2013)

Chief Justice ROBERTS delivered the opinion of the Court.

The Voting Rights Act of 1965 employed extraordinary measures to address an extraordinary problem. Section 5 of the Act required States to obtain federal permission before enacting any law related to voting—a drastic departure from basic principles of federalism. And § 4 of the Act applied that requirement only to some States—an equally dramatic departure from the principle that all States enjoy equal sovereignty. This was strong medicine, but Congress determined it was needed to address entrenched racial discrimination in voting, "an insidious and pervasive evil which had been perpetuated in certain parts of our country through unremitting and ingenious defiance of the Constitution." *South Carolina v. Katzenbach.* As we explained in upholding the law, "exceptional conditions can justify legislative measures not otherwise appropriate." Reflecting the unprecedented nature of these measures, they were scheduled to expire after five years.

Nearly 50 years later, they are still in effect; indeed, they have been made more stringent, and are now scheduled to last until 2031. There is no denying, however, that the conditions that originally justified these measures no longer characterize voting in the covered jurisdictions. By 2009, "the racial gap in voter registration and turnout [was] lower in the States originally covered by § 5 than it [was] nationwide." *Northwest Austin.* Since that time, Census Bureau data indicate that African-American voter turnout has come to exceed white voter turnout in five of the six States originally covered by § 5, with a gap in the sixth State of less than one half of one percent.

At the same time, voting discrimination still exists; no one doubts that. The question is whether the Act's extraordinary measures, including its disparate treatment of the States, continue to satisfy constitutional requirements. As we put it a short time ago, "the Act imposes current burdens and must be justified by current needs." *Northwest Austin.*

I

...

B

Shelby County is located in Alabama, a covered jurisdiction. It has not sought bailout, as the Attorney General has recently objected to voting changes proposed from within the county. Instead, in 2010, the county sued the Attorney General in Federal District Court in Washington, D.C., seeking a declaratory judgment that sections 4(b) and 5 of the Voting Rights Act are facially unconstitutional, as well as a permanent injunction against their enforcement. The District Court ruled against the county and upheld the Act. The court found that the evidence before Congress in 2006 was sufficient to justify reauthorizing § 5 and continuing the § 4(b) coverage formula.

The Court of Appeals for the D.C. Circuit affirmed....

We granted certiorari.

II

In *Northwest Austin*, we stated that "the Act imposes current burdens and must be justified by current needs." And we concluded that "a departure from the fundamental principle of equal sovereignty requires a showing that a statute's disparate geographic coverage is sufficiently related to the problem that it targets." These basic principles guide our review of the question before us.[1]

A

The Constitution and laws of the United States are "the supreme Law of the Land." U.S. Const., Art. VI, cl. 2. State legislation may not contravene federal law. The Federal Government does not, however, have a general right to review and veto state enactments before they go into effect. A proposal to grant such authority to "negative" state laws was considered at the Constitutional Convention, but rejected in favor of allowing state laws to take effect, subject to later challenge under the Supremacy Clause.

Outside the strictures of the Supremacy Clause, States retain broad autonomy in structuring their governments and pursuing legislative objectives. Indeed, the Constitution provides that all powers not specifically granted to the Federal Government are reserved to the States or citizens. Amdt. 10. This "allocation of powers in our federal system preserves the integrity, dignity, and residual sovereignty of the States." But the federal balance "is not just an end in itself: Rather, federalism secures to citizens the liberties that derive from the diffusion of sovereign power."

More specifically, "'the Framers of the Constitution intended the States to keep for themselves, as provided in the Tenth Amendment, the power to regulate elections.'" Of course, the Federal Government retains significant control over federal elections. For instance, the Constitution authorizes Congress to establish the time and manner for electing Senators and Representatives. Art. I, §4, cl. 1. But States have "broad powers to determine the conditions under which the right of suffrage may be exercised." And "[e]ach State has the power to prescribe the qualifications of its officers and the manner in which they shall be chosen." Drawing lines for congressional districts is likewise "primarily the duty and responsibility of the State."

Not only do States retain sovereignty under the Constitution, there is also a "fundamental principle of equal sovereignty" among the States. *Northwest Austin*. Over a hundred years ago, this Court explained that our Nation "was and is a union of States, equal in power, dignity and authority." *Coyle v. Smith*. Indeed, "the constitutional equality of the States is essential to the harmonious operation of the scheme upon which the Republic was organized." *Coyle* concerned the admission of new

1. Both the Fourteenth and Fifteenth Amendments were at issue in *Northwest Austin*, and accordingly *Northwest Austin* guides our review under both Amendments in this case.

States, and *Katzenbach* rejected the notion that the principle operated as a bar on differential treatment outside that context. At the same time, as we made clear in *Northwest Austin*, the fundamental principle of equal sovereignty remains highly pertinent in assessing subsequent disparate treatment of States.

The Voting Rights Act sharply departs from these basic principles. It suspends "*all* changes to state election law—however innocuous—until they have been precleared by federal authorities in Washington, D.C." States must beseech the Federal Government for permission to implement laws that they would otherwise have the right to enact and execute on their own, subject of course to any injunction in a § 2 action. The Attorney General has 60 days to object to a preclearance request, longer if he requests more information. If a State seeks preclearance from a three-judge court, the process can take years.

And despite the tradition of equal sovereignty, the Act applies to only nine States (and several additional counties). While one State waits months or years and expends funds to implement a validly enacted law, its neighbor can typically put the same law into effect immediately, through the normal legislative process. Even if a noncovered jurisdiction is sued, there are important differences between those proceedings and preclearance proceedings; the preclearance proceeding "not only switches the burden of proof to the supplicant jurisdiction, but also applies substantive standards quite different from those governing the rest of the nation."

All this explains why, when we first upheld the Act in 1966, we described it as "stringent" and "potent." *Katzenbach*. We recognized that it "may have been an uncommon exercise of congressional power," but concluded that "legislative measures not otherwise appropriate" could be justified by "exceptional conditions." *Id.* We have since noted that the Act "authorizes federal intrusion into sensitive areas of state and local policymaking," *Lopez*, and represents an "extraordinary departure from the traditional course of relations between the States and the Federal Government." As we reiterated in *Northwest Austin*, the Act constitutes "extraordinary legislation otherwise unfamiliar to our federal system."

B

In 1966, we found these departures from the basic features of our system of government justified. The "blight of racial discrimination in voting" had "infected the electoral process in parts of our country for nearly a century." *Katzenbach*. Several States had enacted a variety of requirements and tests "specifically designed to prevent" African-Americans from voting. *Id.* Case-by-case litigation had proved inadequate to prevent such racial discrimination in voting, in part because States "merely switched to discriminatory devices not covered by the federal decrees," "enacted difficult new tests," or simply "defied and evaded court orders." *Id.* Shortly before enactment of the Voting Rights Act, only 19.4 percent of African-Americans of voting age were registered to vote in Alabama, only 31.8 percent in Louisiana, and only 6.4 percent in Mississippi. Those figures were roughly 50 percentage points or more below the figures for whites.

In short, we concluded that "[u]nder the compulsion of these unique circumstances, Congress responded in a permissibly decisive manner." *Id.* We also noted then and have emphasized since that this extraordinary legislation was intended to be temporary, set to expire after five years. *Id.*; *Northwest Austin.*

At the time, the coverage formula—the means of linking the exercise of the unprecedented authority with the problem that warranted it—made sense. We found that "Congress chose to limit its attention to the geographic areas where immediate action seemed necessary." *Katzenbach.* . . . We therefore concluded that "the coverage formula [was] rational in both practice and theory." *Id.* It accurately reflected those jurisdictions uniquely characterized by voting discrimination "on a pervasive scale," linking coverage to the devices used to effectuate discrimination and to the resulting disenfranchisement. *Id.* The formula ensured that the "stringent remedies [were] aimed at areas where voting discrimination ha[d] been most flagrant." *Id.*

C

Nearly 50 years later, things have changed dramatically. Shelby County contends that the preclearance requirement, even without regard to its disparate coverage, is now unconstitutional. Its arguments have a good deal of force. In the covered jurisdictions, "[v]oter turnout and registration rates now approach parity. Blatantly discriminatory evasions of federal decrees are rare. And minority candidates hold office at unprecedented levels." *Northwest Austin.* The tests and devices that blocked access to the ballot have been forbidden nationwide for over 40 years.

Those conclusions are not ours alone. Congress said the same when it reauthorized the Act in 2006, writing that "[s]ignificant progress has been made in eliminating first generation barriers experienced by minority voters, including increased numbers of registered minority voters, minority voter turnout, and minority representation in Congress, State legislatures, and local elected offices." The House Report elaborated that "the number of African-Americans who are registered and who turn out to cast ballots has increased significantly over the last 40 years, particularly since 1982," and noted that "[i]n some circumstances, minorities register to vote and cast ballots at levels that surpass those of white voters." H.R. Rep. 109–478 (2006). That Report also explained that there have been "significant increases in the number of African-Americans serving in elected offices"; more specifically, there has been approximately a 1,000 percent increase since 1965 in the number of African-American elected officials in the six States originally covered by the Voting Rights Act. . . .

The preclearance statistics are also illuminating. In the first decade after enactment of §5, the Attorney General objected to 14.2 percent of proposed voting changes. In the last decade before reenactment, the Attorney General objected to a mere 0.16 percent.

There is no doubt that these improvements are in large part *because* of the Voting Rights Act. The Act has proved immensely successful at redressing racial discrimination and integrating the voting process.... [T]here is no denying that, due to the Voting Rights Act, our Nation has made great strides.

Yet the Act has not eased the restrictions in § 5 or narrowed the scope of the coverage formula in § 4(b) along the way. Those extraordinary and unprecedented features were reauthorized—as if nothing had changed. In fact, the Act's unusual remedies have grown even stronger. When Congress reauthorized the Act in 2006, it did so for another 25 years on top of the previous 40—a far cry from the initial five-year period. Congress also expanded the prohibitions in § 5. We had previously interpreted § 5 to prohibit only those redistricting plans that would have the purpose or effect of worsening the position of minority groups. See *Bossier Parish II*. In 2006, Congress amended § 5 to prohibit laws that could have favored such groups but did not do so because of a discriminatory purpose, even though we had stated that such broadening of § 5 coverage would "exacerbate the substantial federalism costs that the preclearance procedure already exacts, perhaps to the extent of raising concerns about § 5's constitutionality," *Bossier Parish II*. In addition, Congress expanded § 5 to prohibit any voting law "that has the purpose of or will have the effect of diminishing the ability of any citizens of the United States," on account of race, color, or language minority status, "to elect their preferred candidates of choice." In light of those two amendments, the bar that covered jurisdictions must clear has been raised even as the conditions justifying that requirement have dramatically improved.

We have also previously highlighted the concern that "the preclearance requirements in one State [might] be unconstitutional in another." *Northwest Austin*. Nothing has happened since to alleviate this troubling concern about the current application of § 5.

Respondents do not deny that there have been improvements on the ground, but argue that much of this can be attributed to the deterrent effect of § 5, which dissuades covered jurisdictions from engaging in discrimination that they would resume should § 5 be struck down. Under this theory, however, § 5 would be effectively immune from scrutiny; no matter how "clean" the record of covered jurisdictions, the argument could always be made that it was deterrence that accounted for the good behavior.

The provisions of § 5 apply only to those jurisdictions singled out by § 4. We now consider whether that coverage formula is constitutional in light of current conditions.

III

A

When upholding the constitutionality of the coverage formula in 1966, we concluded that it was "rational in both practice and theory." *Katzenbach*. The formula looked to cause (discriminatory tests) and effect (low voter registration and turnout), and tailored the remedy (preclearance) to those jurisdictions exhibiting both.

By 2009, however, we concluded that the "coverage formula raise[d] serious constitutional questions." *Northwest Austin.* As we explained, a statute's "current burdens" must be justified by "current needs," and any "disparate geographic coverage" must be "sufficiently related to the problem that it targets." *Id.* The coverage formula met that test in 1965, but no longer does so.

Coverage today is based on decades-old data and eradicated practices. The formula captures States by reference to literacy tests and low voter registration and turnout in the 1960s and early 1970s. But such tests have been banned nationwide for over 40 years. And voter registration and turnout numbers in the covered States have risen dramatically in the years since. Racial disparity in those numbers was compelling evidence justifying the preclearance remedy and the coverage formula. See, *e.g., Katzenbach.* There is no longer such a disparity.

In 1965, the States could be divided into two groups: those with a recent history of voting tests and low voter registration and turnout, and those without those characteristics. Congress based its coverage formula on that distinction. Today the Nation is no longer divided along those lines, yet the Voting Rights Act continues to treat it as if it were.

B

The Government's defense of the formula is limited. First, the Government contends that the formula is "reverse-engineered": Congress identified the jurisdictions to be covered and *then* came up with criteria to describe them. Under that reasoning, there need not be any logical relationship between the criteria in the formula and the reason for coverage; all that is necessary is that the formula happen to capture the jurisdictions Congress wanted to single out.

The Government suggests that *Katzenbach* sanctioned such an approach, but the analysis in *Katzenbach* was quite different. *Katzenbach* reasoned that the coverage formula was rational because the "formula . . . was relevant to the problem": "Tests and devices are relevant to voting discrimination because of their long history as a tool for perpetrating the evil; a low voting rate is pertinent for the obvious reason that widespread disenfranchisement must inevitably affect the number of actual voters."

Here, by contrast, the Government's reverse-engineering argument does not even attempt to demonstrate the continued relevance of the formula to the problem it targets. And in the context of a decision as significant as this one—subjecting a disfavored subset of States to "extraordinary legislation otherwise unfamiliar to our federal system," *Northwest Austin*—that failure to establish even relevance is fatal.

The Government falls back to the argument that because the formula was relevant in 1965, its continued use is permissible so long as any discrimination remains in the States Congress identified back then—regardless of how that discrimination compares to discrimination in States unburdened by coverage. This argument does not look to "current political conditions," *Northwest Austin*, but instead relies on a comparison between the States in 1965. That comparison reflected the different histories of the North and South. It was in the South that slavery was upheld by law until uprooted by the Civil War, that the reign of Jim Crow denied African-Americans the most basic freedoms, and that state and local governments worked tirelessly to disenfranchise citizens on the basis of race. The Court invoked that history—rightly so—in sustaining the disparate coverage of the Voting Rights Act in 1966. See *Katzenbach* ("The constitutional propriety of the Voting Rights Act of 1965 must be judged with reference to the historical experience which it reflects.").

But history did not end in 1965. By the time the Act was reauthorized in 2006, there had been 40 more years of it. In assessing the "current need[]" for a preclearance system that treats States differently from one another today, that history cannot be ignored. During that time, largely because of the Voting Rights Act, voting tests were abolished, disparities in voter registration and turnout due to race were erased, and African-Americans attained political office in record numbers. And yet the coverage formula that Congress reauthorized in 2006 ignores these developments, keeping the focus on decades-old data relevant to decades-old problems, rather than current data reflecting current needs.

The Fifteenth Amendment commands that the right to vote shall not be denied or abridged on account of race or color, and it gives Congress the power to enforce that command. The Amendment is not designed to punish for the past; its purpose is to ensure a better future. To serve that purpose, Congress—if it is to divide the States—must identify those jurisdictions to be singled out on a basis that makes sense in light of current conditions. It cannot rely simply on the past. We made that clear in *Northwest Austin*, and we make it clear again today.

C

In defending the coverage formula, the Government, the intervenors, and the dissent also rely heavily on data from the record that they claim justify disparate coverage. Congress compiled thousands of pages of evidence before reauthorizing the Voting Rights Act. The court below and the parties have debated what that record shows—they have gone back and forth about whether to compare covered to noncovered jurisdictions as blocks, how to disaggregate the data State by State, how to weigh § 2 cases as evidence of ongoing discrimination, and whether to consider evidence not before Congress, among other issues. Regardless of how to look at the record, however, no one can fairly say that it shows anything approaching the "pervasive," "flagrant," "widespread," and "rampant" discrimination that faced Congress in 1965, and that clearly distinguished the covered jurisdictions from the rest of the Nation at that time. *Katzenbach*; *Northwest Austin.*

But a more fundamental problem remains: Congress did not use the record it compiled to shape a coverage formula grounded in current conditions. It instead reenacted a formula based on 40-year-old facts having no logical relation to the present day. The dissent relies on "second-generation barriers," which are not impediments to the casting of ballots, but rather electoral arrangements that affect the weight of minority votes. That does not cure the problem. Viewing the preclearance requirements as targeting such efforts simply highlights the irrationality of continued reliance on the § 4 coverage formula, which is based on voting tests and access to the ballot, not vote dilution. We cannot pretend that we are reviewing an updated statute, or try our hand at updating the statute ourselves, based on the new record compiled by Congress. Contrary to the dissent's contention, we are not ignoring the record; we are simply recognizing that it played no role in shaping the statutory formula before us today.

The dissent also turns to the record to argue that, in light of voting discrimination in Shelby County, the county cannot complain about the provisions that subject it to preclearance. But that is like saying that a driver pulled over pursuant to a policy of stopping all redheads cannot complain about that policy, if it turns out his license has expired. Shelby County's claim is that the coverage formula here is unconstitutional in all its applications, because of how it selects the jurisdictions subjected to preclearance. The county was selected based on that formula, and may challenge it in court.

D

The dissent proceeds from a flawed premise. It quotes the famous sentence from *McCulloch v. Maryland*, with the following emphasis: "Let the end be legitimate, let it be within the scope of the constitution, and *all means which are appropriate, which are plainly adapted to that end*, which are not prohibited, but consist with the letter and spirit of the constitution, are constitutional." (emphasis in dissent). But this case is about a part of the sentence that the dissent does not emphasize—the part that asks whether a legislative means is "consist[ent] with the letter and spirit of the constitution." The dissent states that "[i]t cannot tenably be maintained" that this is an issue with regard to the Voting Rights Act, but four years ago, in an opinion joined by two of today's dissenters, the Court expressly stated that "[t]he Act's preclearance requirement and its coverage formula raise serious constitutional questions." *Northwest Austin*. The dissent does not explain how those "serious constitutional questions" became untenable in four short years....

In other ways as well, the dissent analyzes the question presented as if our decision in *Northwest Austin* never happened. For example, the dissent refuses to consider the principle of equal sovereignty, despite *Northwest Austin*'s emphasis on its significance. *Northwest Austin* also emphasized the "dramatic" progress since 1965, but the dissent describes current levels of discrimination as "flagrant," "widespread," and "pervasive." Despite the fact that *Northwest Austin* requires an Act's "disparate geographic coverage" to be "sufficiently related" to its targeted problems, the dissent maintains that an Act's limited coverage actually eases Congress's burdens, and suggests that a fortuitous relationship should suffice. Although *Northwest Austin* stated definitively that "current burdens" must be justified by "current needs," the dissent argues that the coverage formula can be justified by history, and that the required showing can be weaker on reenactment than when the law was first passed.

There is no valid reason to insulate the coverage formula from review merely because it was previously enacted 40 years ago. If Congress had started from scratch in 2006, it plainly could not have enacted the present coverage formula. It would have been irrational for Congress to distinguish between States in such a fundamental way based on 40-year-old data, when today's statistics tell an entirely different story. And it would have been irrational to base coverage on the use of voting tests 40 years ago, when such tests have been illegal since that time. But that is exactly what Congress has done.

* * *

Striking down an Act of Congress "is the gravest and most delicate duty that this Court is called on to perform." We do not do so lightly. That is why, in 2009, we took care to avoid ruling on the constitutionality of the Voting Rights Act when asked to do so, and instead resolved the case then before us on statutory grounds. But in issuing that decision, we expressed our broader concerns about the constitutionality of the Act. Congress could have updated the coverage formula at that time, but did not do so. Its failure to act leaves us today with no choice but to declare § 4(b) unconstitutional. The formula in that section can no longer be used as a basis for subjecting jurisdictions to preclearance.

Our decision in no way affects the permanent, nationwide ban on racial discrimination in voting found in § 2. We issue no holding on § 5 itself, only on the coverage formula. Congress may draft another formula based on current conditions. Such a formula is an initial prerequisite to a determination that exceptional conditions still exist justifying such an "extraordinary departure from the traditional course of relations between the States and the Federal Government." Our country has changed, and while any racial discrimination in voting is too much, Congress must ensure that the legislation it passes to remedy that problem speaks to current conditions.

The judgment of the Court of Appeals is reversed.

It is so ordered.

[Justice THOMAS's concurring opinion is omitted. Justice Thomas joined the majority opinion in full, while expressing the view that Section 5 is also unconstitutional. According to Justice Thomas: "By leaving the inevitable conclusion unstated, the Court needlessly prolongs the demise of that provision."]

Justice GINSBURG, with whom Justice BREYER, Justice SOTOMAYOR, and Justice KAGAN join, dissenting.

In the Court's view, the very success of § 5 of the Voting Rights Act demands its dormancy. Congress was of another mind. Recognizing that large progress has been made, Congress determined, based on a voluminous record, that the scourge of discrimination was not yet extirpated. The question this case presents is who decides whether, as currently operative, § 5 remains justifiable, this Court, or a Congress charged with the obligation to enforce the post-Civil War Amendments "by appropriate legislation." With overwhelming support in both Houses, Congress concluded that, for two prime reasons, § 5 should continue in force, unabated. First, continuance would facilitate completion of the impressive gains thus far made; and second, continuance would guard against backsliding. Those assessments were well within Congress' province to make and should elicit this Court's unstinting approbation.

I

. . . Although the VRA wrought dramatic changes in the realization of minority voting rights, the Act, to date, surely has not eliminated all vestiges of discrimination against the exercise of the franchise by minority citizens. Jurisdictions covered by the preclearance requirement continued to submit, in large numbers, proposed changes to voting laws that the Attorney General declined to approve, auguring that barriers to minority voting would quickly resurface were the preclearance remedy eliminated. *City of Rome*. Congress also found that as "registration and voting of minority citizens increas[ed], other measures may be resorted to which would dilute increasing minority voting strength." *Id.* Efforts to reduce the impact of minority votes, in contrast to direct attempts to block access to the ballot, are aptly described as "second-generation barriers" to minority voting.

Second-generation barriers come in various forms. One of the blockages is racial gerrymandering, the redrawing of legislative districts in an "effort to segregate the races for purposes of voting." *Shaw v. Reno*. Another is adoption of a system of at-large voting in lieu of district-by-district voting in a city with a sizable black minority. By switching to at-large voting, the overall majority could control the election of each city council member, effectively eliminating the potency of the minority's votes. . . . Whatever the device employed, this Court has long recognized that vote dilution, when adopted with a discriminatory purpose, cuts down the right to vote as certainly as denial of access to the ballot.

In response to evidence of these substituted barriers, Congress reauthorized the VRA for five years in 1970, for seven years in 1975, and for 25 years in 1982. Each time, this Court upheld the reauthorization as a valid exercise of congressional power. As the 1982 reauthorization approached its 2007 expiration date, Congress again considered whether the VRA's preclearance mechanism remained an appropriate response to the problem of voting discrimination in covered jurisdictions.

Congress did not take this task lightly. Quite the opposite. The 109th Congress that took responsibility for the renewal started early and conscientiously. . . .

In the long course of the legislative process, Congress "amassed a sizable record." *Northwest Austin*. The House and Senate Judiciary Committees held 21 hearings, heard from scores of witnesses, received a number of investigative reports and other written documentation of continuing discrimination in covered jurisdictions. In all, the legislative record Congress compiled filled more than 15,000 pages. The compilation presents countless "examples of flagrant racial discrimination" since the last reauthorization; Congress also brought to light systematic evidence that "intentional racial discrimination in voting remains so serious and widespread in covered jurisdictions that section 5 preclearance is still needed."

After considering the full legislative record, Congress made the following findings: The VRA has directly caused significant progress in eliminating first-generation barriers to ballot access, leading to a marked increase in minority voter registration and turnout and the number of minority elected officials. But despite this progress, "second generation barriers constructed to prevent minority voters from fully participating in the electoral process" continued to exist, as well as racially polarized voting in the covered jurisdictions, which increased the political vulnerability of racial and language minorities in those jurisdictions.... The overall record demonstrated to the federal lawmakers that, "without the continuation of the Voting Rights Act of 1965 protections, racial and language minority citizens will be deprived of the opportunity to exercise their right to vote, or will have their votes diluted, undermining the significant gains made by minorities in the last 40 years."

Based on these findings, Congress reauthorized preclearance for another 25 years, while also undertaking to reconsider the extension after 15 years to ensure that the provision was still necessary and effective. The question before the Court is whether Congress had the authority under the Constitution to act as it did.

II

In answering this question, the Court does not write on a clean slate. It is well established that Congress' judgment regarding exercise of its power to enforce the Fourteenth and Fifteenth Amendments warrants substantial deference. The VRA addresses the combination of race discrimination and the right to vote, which is "preservative of all rights." When confronting the most constitutionally invidious form of discrimination, and the most fundamental right in our democratic system, Congress' power to act is at its height.

The basis for this deference is firmly rooted in both constitutional text and precedent. The Fifteenth Amendment, which targets precisely and only racial discrimination in voting rights, states that, in this domain, "Congress shall have power to enforce this article by appropriate legislation." In choosing this language, the Amendment's framers invoked Chief Justice Marshall's formulation of the scope of Congress' powers under the Necessary and Proper Clause:

> "Let the end be legitimate, let it be within the scope of the constitution, and *all means which are appropriate, which are plainly adapted to that end*, which are not prohibited, but consist with the letter and spirit of the constitution, are constitutional." *McCulloch v. Maryland* (emphasis added).

It cannot tenably be maintained that the VRA, an Act of Congress adopted to shield the right to vote from racial discrimination, is inconsistent with the letter or spirit of the Fifteenth Amendment, or any provision of the Constitution read in light of the Civil War Amendments. Nowhere in today's opinion, or in *Northwest*

Austin,[3] is there clear recognition of the transformative effect the Fifteenth Amendment aimed to achieve. . . .

The stated purpose of the Civil War Amendments was to arm Congress with the power and authority to protect all persons within the Nation from violations of their rights by the States. In exercising that power, then, Congress may use "all means which are appropriate, which are plainly adapted" to the constitutional ends declared by these Amendments. *McCulloch*. So when Congress acts to enforce the right to vote free from racial discrimination, we ask not whether Congress has chosen the means most wise, but whether Congress has rationally selected means appropriate to a legitimate end. "It is not for us to review the congressional resolution of [the need for its chosen remedy]. It is enough that we be able to perceive a basis upon which the Congress might resolve the conflict as it did."

Until today, in considering the constitutionality of the VRA, the Court has accorded Congress the full measure of respect its judgments in this domain should garner. *South Carolina v. Katzenbach* supplies the standard of review: "As against the reserved powers of the States, Congress may use any rational means to effectuate the constitutional prohibition of racial discrimination in voting." Faced with subsequent reauthorizations of the VRA, the Court has reaffirmed this standard. Today's Court does not purport to alter settled precedent establishing that the dispositive question is whether Congress has employed "rational means."

For three reasons, legislation reauthorizing an existing statute is especially likely to satisfy the minimal requirements of the rational-basis test. First, when reauthorization is at issue, Congress has already assembled a legislative record justifying the initial legislation. Congress is entitled to consider that preexisting record as well as the record before it at the time of the vote on reauthorization. This is especially true where, as here, the Court has repeatedly affirmed the statute's constitutionality and Congress has adhered to the very model the Court has upheld.

Second, the very fact that reauthorization is necessary arises because Congress has built a temporal limitation into the Act. It has pledged to review, after a span of years (first 15, then 25) and in light of contemporary evidence, the continued need for the VRA.

Third, a reviewing court should expect the record supporting reauthorization to be less stark than the record originally made. Demand for a record of violations equivalent to the one earlier made would expose Congress to a catch-22. If the statute was working, there would be less evidence of discrimination, so opponents might argue that Congress should not be allowed to renew the statute. In contrast, if the statute was not working, there would be plenty of evidence of discrimination, but scant reason to renew a failed regulatory regime.

3. Acknowledging the existence of "serious constitutional questions" does not suggest how those questions should be answered.

This is not to suggest that congressional power in this area is limitless. It is this Court's responsibility to ensure that Congress has used appropriate means. The question meet for judicial review is whether the chosen means are "adapted to carry out the objects the amendments have in view." The Court's role, then, is not to substitute its judgment for that of Congress, but to determine whether the legislative record sufficed to show that "Congress could rationally have determined that [its chosen] provisions were appropriate methods." *City of Rome*.

In summary, the Constitution vests broad power in Congress to protect the right to vote, and in particular to combat racial discrimination in voting. This Court has repeatedly reaffirmed Congress' prerogative to use any rational means in exercise of its power in this area. And both precedent and logic dictate that the rational-means test should be easier to satisfy, and the burden on the statute's challenger should be higher, when what is at issue is the reauthorization of a remedy that the Court has previously affirmed, and that Congress found, from contemporary evidence, to be working to advance the legislature's legitimate objective.

III

The 2006 reauthorization of the Voting Rights Act fully satisfies the standard stated in *McCulloch*: Congress may choose any means "appropriate" and "plainly adapted to" a legitimate constitutional end. As we shall see, it is implausible to suggest otherwise.

A

I begin with the evidence on which Congress based its decision to continue the preclearance remedy. The surest way to evaluate whether that remedy remains in order is to see if preclearance is still effectively preventing discriminatory changes to voting laws. On that score, the record before Congress was huge. In fact, Congress found there were *more* DOJ objections between 1982 and 2004 (626) than there were between 1965 and the 1982 reauthorization (490).

All told, between 1982 and 2006, DOJ objections blocked over 700 voting changes based on a determination that the changes were discriminatory. Congress found that the majority of DOJ objections included findings of discriminatory intent, and that the changes blocked by preclearance were "calculated decisions to keep minority voters from fully participating in the political process." H.R. Rep. 109–478 (2006). On top of that, over the same time period the DOJ and private plaintiffs succeeded in more than 100 actions to enforce the § 5 preclearance requirements.

In addition to blocking proposed voting changes through preclearance, DOJ may request more information from a jurisdiction proposing a change. In turn, the jurisdiction may modify or withdraw the proposed change. The number of such modifications or withdrawals provides an indication of how many discriminatory proposals are deterred without need for formal objection. Congress received evidence that more than 800 proposed changes were altered or withdrawn since the last reauthorization in 1982. Congress also received empirical studies finding that DOJ's requests for more information had a significant effect on the degree to which covered jurisdictions "compl[ied] with their obligatio[n]" to protect minority voting rights.

Congress also received evidence that litigation under § 2 of the VRA was an inadequate substitute for preclearance in the covered jurisdictions. Litigation occurs only after the fact, when the illegal voting scheme has already been put in place and individuals have been elected pursuant to it, thereby gaining the advantages of incumbency. An illegal scheme might be in place for several election cycles before a § 2 plaintiff can gather sufficient evidence to challenge it. And litigation places a heavy financial burden on minority voters. Congress also received evidence that preclearance lessened the litigation burden on covered jurisdictions themselves, because the preclearance process is far less costly than defending against a § 2 claim, and clearance by DOJ substantially reduces the likelihood that a § 2 claim will be mounted.

The number of discriminatory changes blocked or deterred by the preclearance requirement suggests that the state of voting rights in the covered jurisdictions would have been significantly different absent this remedy. Surveying the type of changes stopped by the preclearance procedure conveys a sense of the extent to which § 5 continues to protect minority voting rights. [Justice Ginsburg described some examples of changes blocked in the years preceding the 2006 reauthorization.]

True, conditions in the South have impressively improved since passage of the Voting Rights Act. Congress noted this improvement and found that the VRA was the driving force behind it. But Congress also found that voting discrimination had evolved into subtler second-generation barriers, and that eliminating preclearance would risk loss of the gains that had been made. Concerns of this order, the Court previously found, gave Congress adequate cause to reauthorize the VRA. Facing such evidence then, the Court expressly rejected the argument that disparities in voter turnout and number of elected officials were the only metrics capable of justifying reauthorization of the VRA.

B

I turn next to the evidence on which Congress based its decision to reauthorize the coverage formula in § 4(b). Because Congress did not alter the coverage formula, the same jurisdictions previously subject to preclearance continue to be covered by this remedy. The evidence just described, of preclearance's continuing efficacy in blocking constitutional violations in the covered jurisdictions, itself grounded Congress' conclusion that the remedy should be retained for those jurisdictions.

There is no question, moreover, that the covered jurisdictions have a unique history of problems with racial discrimination in voting. Consideration of this long history, still in living memory, was altogether appropriate. The Court criticizes Congress for failing to recognize that "history did not end in 1965." But the Court ignores that "what's past is prologue." W. Shakespeare, The Tempest, act 2, sc. 1. And "[t]hose who cannot remember the past are condemned to repeat it." 1 G. Santayana, The Life of Reason (1905). Congress was especially mindful of the need to reinforce the gains already made and to prevent backsliding.

Of particular importance, even after 40 years and thousands of discriminatory changes blocked by preclearance, conditions in the covered jurisdictions demonstrated that the formula was still justified by "current needs." *Northwest Austin.*

Congress learned of these conditions through a report, known as the Katz study, that looked at § 2 suits between 1982 and 2004. Because the private right of action authorized by § 2 of the VRA applies nationwide, a comparison of § 2 lawsuits in covered and noncovered jurisdictions provides an appropriate yardstick for measuring differences between covered and noncovered jurisdictions. If differences in the risk of voting discrimination between covered and noncovered jurisdictions had disappeared, one would expect that the rate of successful § 2 lawsuits would be roughly the same in both areas. The study's findings, however, indicated that racial discrimination in voting remains "concentrated in the jurisdictions singled out for preclearance." *Northwest Austin.*

Although covered jurisdictions account for less than 25 percent of the country's population, the Katz study revealed that they accounted for 56 percent of successful § 2 litigation since 1982. Controlling for population, there were nearly four times as many successful § 2 cases in covered jurisdictions as there were in noncovered jurisdictions. The Katz study further found that § 2 lawsuits are more likely to succeed when they are filed in covered jurisdictions than in noncovered jurisdictions. From these findings—ignored by the Court—Congress reasonably concluded that the coverage formula continues to identify the jurisdictions of greatest concern.

The evidence before Congress, furthermore, indicated that voting in the covered jurisdictions was more racially polarized than elsewhere in the country. While racially polarized voting alone does not signal a constitutional violation, it is a factor that increases the vulnerability of racial minorities to discriminatory changes in voting law....

The case for retaining a coverage formula that met needs on the ground was therefore solid. Congress might have been charged with rigidity had it afforded covered jurisdictions no way out or ignored jurisdictions that needed superintendence. Congress, however, responded to this concern. Critical components of the congressional design are the statutory provisions allowing jurisdictions to "bail out" of preclearance, and for court-ordered "bail ins." The VRA permits a jurisdiction to bail out by showing that it has complied with the Act for ten years, and has engaged in efforts to eliminate intimidation and harassment of voters. It also authorizes a court to subject a noncovered jurisdiction to federal preclearance upon finding that violations of the Fourteenth and Fifteenth Amendments have occurred there.

Congress was satisfied that the VRA's bailout mechanism provided an effective means of adjusting the VRA's coverage over time. Nearly 200 jurisdictions have successfully bailed out of the preclearance requirement, and DOJ has consented to every bailout application filed by an eligible jurisdiction since the current bailout procedure became effective in 1984. The bail-in mechanism has also worked. Several jurisdictions have been subject to federal preclearance by court orders, including the States of New Mexico and Arkansas.

This experience exposes the inaccuracy of the Court's portrayal of the Act as static, unchanged since 1965. Congress designed the VRA to be a dynamic statute, capable of adjusting to changing conditions. True, many covered jurisdictions have not been able to bail out due to recent acts of noncompliance with the VRA, but that truth reinforces the congressional judgment that these jurisdictions were rightfully subject to preclearance, and ought to remain under that regime.

IV

Congress approached the 2006 reauthorization of the VRA with great care and seriousness. The same cannot be said of the Court's opinion today. The Court makes no genuine attempt to engage with the massive legislative record that Congress assembled. Instead, it relies on increases in voter registration and turnout as if that were the whole story.... One would expect more from an opinion striking at the heart of the Nation's signal piece of civil-rights legislation.

I note the most disturbing lapses. First, by what right, given its usual restraint, does the Court even address Shelby County's facial challenge to the VRA? Second, the Court veers away from controlling precedent regarding the "equal sovereignty" doctrine without even acknowledging that it is doing so. Third, hardly showing the respect ordinarily paid when Congress acts to implement the Civil War Amendments, and as just stressed, the Court does not even deign to grapple with the legislative record.

A

Shelby County launched a purely facial challenge to the VRA's 2006 reauthorization. "A facial challenge to a legislative Act," the Court has other times said, "is, of course, the most difficult challenge to mount successfully, since the challenger must establish that no set of circumstances exists under which the Act would be valid."

... [T]he Court's opinion in this case contains not a word explaining why Congress lacks the power to subject to preclearance the particular plaintiff that initiated this lawsuit—Shelby County, Alabama. The reason for the Court's silence is apparent, for as applied to Shelby County, the VRA's preclearance requirement is hardly contestable.

Alabama is home to Selma, site of the "Bloody Sunday" beatings of civil-rights demonstrators that served as the catalyst for the VRA's enactment. Following those events, Martin Luther King, Jr., led a march from Selma to Montgomery, Alabama's capital, where he called for passage of the VRA. If the Act passed, he foresaw, progress could be made even in Alabama, but there had to be a steadfast national commitment to see the task through to completion. In King's words, "the arc of the moral universe is long, but it bends toward justice."

History has proved King right. Although circumstances in Alabama have changed, serious concerns remain. Between 1982 and 2005, Alabama had one of the highest rates of successful § 2 suits, second only to its VRA-covered neighbor Mississippi. In other words, even while subject to the restraining effect of § 5, Alabama was found to have "deni[ed] or abridge[d]" voting rights "on account of race or color" more frequently than nearly all other States in the Union.... Alabama's sorry history of § 2 violations alone provides sufficient justification for Congress' determination in 2006 that the State should remain subject to § 5's preclearance requirement. [Justice Ginsburg provided examples of recent voting discrimination in Alabama.]

These recent episodes forcefully demonstrate that § 5's preclearance requirement is constitutional as applied to Alabama and its political subdivisions.[8] And under our case law, that conclusion should suffice to resolve this case.

This Court has consistently rejected constitutional challenges to legislation enacted pursuant to Congress' enforcement powers under the Civil War Amendments upon finding that the legislation was constitutional as applied to the particular set of circumstances before the Court. A similar approach is warranted here.[9] . . .

B

The Court stops any application of § 5 by holding that § 4(b)'s coverage formula is un-constitutional. It pins this result, in large measure, to "the fundamental principle of equal sovereignty." In *Katzenbach*, however, the Court held, in no uncertain terms, that the principle "*applies only to the terms upon which States are admitted to the Union*, and not to the remedies for local evils which have subsequently appeared." . . .

Today's unprecedented extension of the equal sovereignty principle outside its proper domain—the admission of new States—is capable of much mischief. Federal statutes that treat States disparately are hardly novelties. Do such provisions remain safe given the Court's expansion of equal sovereignty's sway?

Of gravest concern, Congress relied on our pathmarking *Katzenbach* decision in each reauthorization of the VRA. It had every reason to believe that the Act's limited geographical scope would weigh in favor of, not against, the Act's constitutionality. Congress could hardly have foreseen that the VRA's limited geographic reach would render the Act constitutionally suspect.

In the Court's conception, it appears, defenders of the VRA could not prevail upon showing what the record overwhelmingly bears out, *i.e.*, that there is a need for continuing the preclearance regime in covered States. In addition, the defenders

---

8. Congress continued preclearance over Alabama, including Shelby County, *after* considering evidence of current barriers there to minority voting clout. Shelby County, thus, is no "redhead" caught up in an arbitrary scheme.

9. The Court does not contest that Alabama's history of racial discrimination provides a sufficient basis for Congress to require Alabama and its political subdivisions to preclear electoral changes. Nevertheless, the Court asserts that Shelby County may prevail on its facial challenge to § 4's coverage formula because it is subject to § 5's preclearance requirement by virtue of that formula. This misses the reality that Congress decided to subject Alabama to preclearance based on evidence of continuing constitutional violations in that State.

would have to disprove the existence of a comparable need elsewhere. I am aware of no precedent for imposing such a double burden on defenders of legislation.

C

The Court has time and again declined to upset legislation of this genre unless there was no or almost no evidence of unconstitutional action by States. No such claim can be made about the congressional record for the 2006 VRA reauthorization. Given a record replete with examples of denial or abridgment of a paramount federal right, the Court should have left the matter where it belongs: in Congress' bailiwick.

Instead, the Court strikes § 4(b)'s coverage provision because, in its view, the provision is not based on "current conditions." It discounts, however, that one such condition was the preclearance remedy in place in the covered jurisdictions, a remedy Congress designed both to catch discrimination before it causes harm, and to guard against return to old ways. Volumes of evidence supported Congress' determination that the prospect of retrogression was real. Throwing out preclearance when it has worked and is continuing to work to stop discriminatory changes is like throwing away your umbrella in a rainstorm because you are not getting wet.

But, the Court insists, the coverage formula is no good; it is based on "decades-old data and eradicated practices." Even if the legislative record shows, as engaging with it would reveal, that the formula accurately identifies the jurisdictions with the worst conditions of voting discrimination, that is of no moment, as the Court sees it. Congress, the Court decrees, must "star[t] from scratch." I do not see why that should be so.

... By [2006], the formula had been in effect for many years, and *all* of the jurisdictions covered by it were "familiar to Congress by name." The question before Congress: Was there still a sufficient basis to support continued application of the preclearance remedy in each of those already-identified places? There was at that point no chance that the formula might inadvertently sweep in new areas that were not the subject of congressional findings. And Congress could determine from the record whether the jurisdictions captured by the coverage formula still belonged under the preclearance regime. If they did, there was no need to alter the formula. That is why the Court, in addressing prior reauthorizations of the VRA, did not question the continuing "relevance" of the formula.

Consider once again the components of the record before Congress in 2006. The coverage provision identified a known list of places with an undisputed history of serious problems with racial discrimination in voting. Recent evidence relating to Alabama and its counties was there for all to see. Multiple Supreme Court decisions had upheld the coverage provision, most recently in 1999. There was extensive evidence that, due to the preclearance mechanism, conditions in the covered jurisdictions had notably improved. And there was evidence that preclearance was still having a substantial real-world effect, having stopped hundreds of discriminatory voting changes in the covered jurisdictions since the last reauthorization. In addition, there was evidence that racial polarization in voting was higher in covered jurisdictions than elsewhere, increasing the vulnerability of minority citizens in those jurisdictions. And countless witnesses, reports, and case studies documented continuing problems with voting discrimination in those jurisdictions. In light of this record, Congress had more than a reasonable basis to conclude that the existing coverage formula was not out of sync with conditions on the ground in covered areas. And certainly Shelby County was no candidate for release through the mechanism Congress provided.

The Court holds § 4(b) invalid on the ground that it is "irrational to base coverage on the use of voting tests 40 years ago, when such tests have been illegal since that time." But the Court disregards what Congress set about to do in enacting the VRA. That extraordinary legislation scarcely stopped at the particular tests and devices that happened to exist in 1965. The grand aim of the Act is to secure to all in our polity equal citizenship stature, a voice in our democracy undiluted by race. As the record for the 2006 reauthorization makes abundantly clear, second-generation barriers to minority voting rights have emerged in the covered jurisdictions as attempted *substitutes* for the first-generation barriers that originally triggered preclearance in those jurisdictions.

The sad irony of today's decision lies in its utter failure to grasp why the VRA has proven effective. The Court appears to believe that the VRA's success in eliminating the specific devices extant in 1965 means that preclearance is no longer needed. With that belief, and the argument derived from it, history repeats itself. The same assumption — that the problem could be solved when particular methods of voting discrimination are identified and eliminated — was indulged and proved wrong repeatedly prior to the VRA's enactment. Unlike prior statutes, which singled out particular tests or devices, the VRA is grounded in Congress' recognition of the "variety and persistence" of measures designed to impair minority voting rights. *Katzenbach*. In truth, the evolution of voting discrimination into more subtle second-generation barriers is powerful evidence that a remedy as effective as preclearance remains vital to protect minority voting rights and prevent backsliding.

Beyond question, the VRA is no ordinary legislation. It is extraordinary because Congress embarked on a mission long delayed and of extraordinary importance: to realize the purpose and promise of the Fifteenth Amendment. For a half century, a concerted effort has been made to end racial discrimination in voting. Thanks to the Voting Rights Act, progress once the subject of a dream has been achieved and continues to be made.

The record supporting the 2006 reauthorization of the VRA is also extraordinary. . . . After exhaustive evidence-gathering and deliberative process, Congress reauthorized the VRA, including the coverage provision, with overwhelming bipartisan support. It was the judgment of Congress that "40 years has not been a sufficient amount of time to eliminate the vestiges of discrimination following nearly 100 years of disregard for the dictates of the 15th amendment and to ensure that the right of all citizens to vote is protected as guaranteed by the Constitution." That determination of the body empowered to enforce the Civil War Amendments "by appropriate legislation" merits this Court's utmost respect. In my judgment, the Court errs egregiously by overriding Congress' decision.

Notes and Questions

1. The *Shelby County* majority concludes that the coverage formula used for Section 5 preclearance violates the "fundamental principle of equal sovereignty" among the states. The Court relies in part on *Coyle v. Smith*, which concerned the admission of new states to the Union, while acknowledging that *South Carolina v. Katzenbach* rejected the notion that this principle forbids differential treatment of states outside this context. What does the equal sovereignty principle entail? Why does the Court conclude that the principle applies to Congress' decision to subject certain jurisdictions to special requirements? For an argument that equal sovereignty, as developed in the state admission cases, means only that Congress may not impose an admission condition that violates *other* constitutional rules, see Leah M. Litman, *Inventing Equal Sovereignty*, 114 Michigan Law Review 1207 (2016). For a qualified defense of equal sovereignty, based on constitutional structure rather than case law, see Thomas B. Colby, *In Defense of the Equal Sovereignty Principle*, 65 Duke Law Journal 1087 (2016).

2. What is the constitutional standard for determining whether Congress acts within its power to enforce the Fourteenth and Fifteenth Amendments, when it accords differential treatment to states? In *Northwest Austin*, the Court wrote of a dispute among the parties over the appropriate standard:

> The parties do not agree on the standard to apply in deciding whether, in light of the foregoing concerns, Congress exceeded its Fifteenth Amendment enforcement power in extending the preclearance requirements. The district argues that "[t]here must be a congruence and proportionality between the injury to be prevented or remedied and the means adopted to that end," Brief for Appellant, quoting *Boerne*; the Federal Government asserts that it is enough that the legislation be a "'rational means to effectuate the constitutional prohibition,'" Brief for Federal Appellee, quoting *Katzenbach*. That question has been extensively briefed in this case, but we need not resolve it. The Act's preclearance requirements and its coverage formula raise serious constitutional questions under either test.

557 U.S. at 204. In *Shelby County*, the majority does not expressly address the disagreement over the level of scrutiny. In fact, the majority does not even cite *Boerne*, leading Justice Ginsburg in dissent to write: "Without even identifying a standard of review, the Court dismissively brushes off arguments based on 'data from the record,' and declines to enter the 'debat[e about] what [the] record shows.'" 570 U.S. at 580 (Ginsburg, J., dissenting). Why did the majority sidestep this issue?

Perhaps the majority opinion is best understood as assuming without deciding that the more deferential standard set forth in *Katzenbach* applies. *Katzenbach* concluded that the original Section 5's coverage formula was "rational in both practice and theory." That opinion in turn relied on Chief Justice Marshall's famous articulation of the scope of congressional power in *McCulloch v. Maryland*, stating that Congress may adopt "all means which are appropriate" and "plainly adapted" to permissible ends which are not prohibited. In similar language, the *Shelby County* majority asserted the "irrationality of continued reliance on the § 4 coverage formula," and claimed that it is "irrational for Congress to distinguish between States in such a fundamental way based on 40-year-old data." *Id.* at 554, 556. If these statements indicate that the majority applied *Katzenbach*-style rational basis review, was this form of review properly applied? In other words, did the coverage formula really lack any rational foundation?

3. Although Congress amassed a lengthy evidentiary record when it reauthorized the coverage formula and preclearance in 2006, most of that record highlighted continuing problems with vote denial and vote dilution in covered areas. Relatively little of the record explicitly *compared* conditions in covered and non-covered areas. However, a study by Ellen Katz, cited by the dissent, did find that verdicts for plaintiffs in published decisions under Section 2 of the Voting Rights Act were more likely in covered than in non-covered areas. A similar study by Peyton McCrary, considering published *and* unpublished Section 2 decisions, concluded that that "[o]f the eight states with the highest number of successful . . . section 2 cases per million residents — Alabama, Mississippi, Arkansas, Texas, South Carolina, Georgia, and the covered portions of South Dakota and North Carolina — all but one are covered." *Shelby County v. Holder*, 679 F.3d 848, 875 (D.C. Cir. 2012).

Adam Cox and Thomas Miles have criticized these studies on the ground that plaintiffs' success rates shed little light on the prevalence of underlying discriminatory conduct. "The central methodological difficulty with [the studies'] claims is that they draw inferences about the extent of discrimination and the efficacy of section 5 from a sample of cases that is almost surely not representative of the entire class of voting rights claims. . . . In asserting that plaintiff win rates are accurate measures of discrimination, [the studies] overlook this fundamental obstacle in drawing inferences from judicial decisions." Adam B. Cox & Thomas J. Miles, *Documenting Discrimination?*, 108 Columbia Law Review Sidebar 31, 35 (2008). Does the dissent offer any response to this critique? How compelling is the rejoinder that even if litigated Section 2 claims are not representative of all voting rights violations, there is no reason why they would be any *more* or *less* representative in covered or non-covered areas?

4. *Shelby County* strikes down the coverage formula, but arguably leaves the door open for Congress to adopt a new one. (Only arguably because the majority opinion states that the argument that "the preclearance requirement, even without regard to its disparate coverage, is now unconstitutional . . . ha[s] a good deal of force." 570 U.S. at 547.) The case thus stops Section 5 preclearance for now, while perhaps allowing for the possibility of its being revived down the road. Do you think it is likely

that a future Congress will agree on a new coverage formula? If you were counseling Congress, what kind of evidence would you advise that it develop to support a new coverage formula? One possibility is to base coverage on documented disparities in racial stereotyping, which vary among states and localities. See Christopher S. Elmendorf & Douglas M. Spencer, *The Geography of Racial Stereotyping: Evidence and Implications for VRA Preclearance After Shelby County*, 102 California Law Review 1123 (2014). Another option, noted by the dissent, is to base coverage on rates of racial polarization in voting—that is, the extent to which minority voters and white voters differ in their electoral choices. Polarization, however, is not typically considered a voting rights violation in and of itself; rather, it is usually viewed as a condition that makes such violations more likely.

Major bills responding to *Shelby County* were introduced in 2014, 2015, 2019, and 2021. The most recent (and ambitious) of these, the John Lewis Voting Rights Advancement Act of 2021 (JLVRAA), is pending in Congress as of this casebook's writing. Among other things, the JLVRAA would:

- *Expand "bail-in."* Section 3(c) would be amended to allow courts to subject state and local jurisdictions to preclearance for violations of the Voting Rights Act and other federal antidiscrimination laws, not just violations of the Fourteenth and Fifteenth Amendments.
- *Prescribe a new coverage formula.* A state would be covered if there have been fifteen or more voting right violations in the state within the previous twenty-five years, at least one of which was committed by the state itself (as opposed to a local subdivision). Under this new formula, Alabama, Florida, Georgia, Louisiana, Mississippi, North Carolina, South Carolina, and Texas would initially be subject to preclearance. Local jurisdictions would be subject to preclearance for three or more voting rights violations within the previous twenty-five years.
- *Impose practice-based preclearance.* In sufficiently diverse states and local jurisdictions, preclearance would be required for switches to at-large elections, changes to jurisdictional boundaries, enactments of new district plans, changes to polling places, and changes to voter roll maintenance policies. In all states and local jurisdictions, preclearance would be required for identification requirements for voting and registering to vote and for changes to multilingual voting materials.
- *Enact disclosure requirements.* All states and local jurisdictions would be required to make available on the Internet new voting rules adopted close to a federal election, polling place information, and changes to voting districts. No person could be prevented from voting on the basis of a rule that was not timely and properly disclosed.
- *Change the preliminary injunction standard* in voting rights lawsuits, allowing relief to be granted if the hardship on the defendant if relief is granted is less than the hardship on the plaintiffs if relief is denied.

- *Section 2 retrogression.* Create a new cause of action under Section 2 for retrogressive practices. The anti-retrogression requirement would thus apply nationwide, not just to jurisdictions subject to preclearance.

The JLVRAA would also take many steps not directly related to *Shelby County*, including amending Section 2 to recognize coalition claims (see note 7 after *Bartlett v. Strickland*), overriding *Brnovich v. Democratic National Committee* with respect to racial vote denial claims (see Chapter 6, Part II), and overriding the so-called *Purcell* principle that allows courts to deny relief due to the proximity of an election (see Chapter 6, Part IV). Is the JLVRAA an appropriate and constitutional response to *Shelby County*? For a generally positive analysis, see Travis Crum, *Revising Sections 2 and 5 in the John Lewis Voting Rights Advancement Act of 2021*, Election Law Blog (Aug. 18, 2021), https://perma.cc/HJ5P-THQX.

Other discussion since *Shelby County* has addressed measures Congress could take beyond enacting a new coverage formula. Some commentators have suggested a transparency requirement, under which state and local jurisdictions would be required to file a public statement indicating the rationales for and the likely effects of new voting changes. See Gilda R. Daniels, *Unfinished Business: Protecting Voting Rights in the Twenty-First Century*, 81 George Washington Law Review 1928 (2013). Another possibility — one focused on barriers to participation — is to enact uniform registration and identification rules for federal elections that would trump stricter state rules. See Daniel P. Tokaji, *Responding to* Shelby County*: A Grand Election Bargain*, 8 Harvard Law & Policy Review 71 (2014). A further option is to amend Section 2 of the Voting Rights Act so as to provide some of the procedural and substantive advantages previously conferred by Section 5: for instance, by instituting a burden-shifting framework under which the onus would switch to the jurisdiction after a plaintiff made a preliminary showing of harm, and by imposing liability whenever districts in which minority voters are able to elect their preferred candidates are dismantled. See Nicholas O. Stephanopoulos, *The South After* Shelby County, 2013 Supreme Court Review 55.

5. *Shelby County* declares Section 4(b)'s coverage formula unconstitutional, but it does not completely eliminate preclearance. Under Section 3(b) of the Voting Rights Act, state and local jurisdictions may be subjected to preclearance (or "bailed in") if a court concludes that they have violated the Fourteenth or Fifteenth Amendment. A handful of state and local jurisdictions have been "bailed in" under Section 3, including Arkansas, New Mexico, Los Angeles County, and the City of Chattanooga (Tennessee). See Travis Crum, *The Voting Rights Act's Secret Weapon: Pocket Trigger Litigation and Dynamic Preclearance*, 119 Yale Law Journal 1992 (2010). The week after the *Shelby County* decision, voting rights advocates moved to have the State of Texas bailed in to preclearance under Section 3, citing constitutional violations arising from its redistricting and voter identification laws. Can Section 3 be an effective tool for the enforcement of voting rights after *Shelby County*? See *Patino v. City of Pasadena*, 230 F. Supp. 3d 667 (S.D. Tex. 2017) (imposing preclearance for six years on Pasadena, Texas after the city was found to have intentionally diluted Latino

votes when changing its city council electoral system). But see *N.C. State Conf. of NAACP v. McCrory*, 831 F.3d 204 (4th Cir. 2016) (denying to impose preclearance on North Carolina even after finding that the state passed voting restrictions with racially discriminatory intent).

6. What will the consequences of *Shelby County* be, given that Section 2 of the Voting Rights Act continues to apply in the formerly covered areas? Stephanopoulos, *The South After* Shelby County, *supra*, argues that they will be significant, especially in the context of vote dilution. Stephanopoulos notes that Section 5 protects *all* districts in which minority voters are able to elect their candidates of choice. In contrast, thanks to a series of Supreme Court decisions (which are discussed in the next section), Section 2 shields such districts only if they are geographically compact, their minority populations are not overly heterogeneous, and their minority populations exceed 50 percent. Quite a few southern districts may fall into this "gap" between Section 2 and Section 5: 22 districts arguably are too noncompact to qualify for Section 2 protection, 146 districts potentially include overly heterogeneous minority populations, and 17 districts have minority populations below 50 percent. All of these districts could find themselves on thin ice in the next redistricting cycle—newly subject to elimination without violating the VRA.

II. Section 2 of the Voting Rights Act

Already a vitally important provision, Section 2 of the Voting Rights Act has become even more significant in the wake of *Shelby County*. It is now without a doubt the VRA's most potent operative requirement, barring both racial vote denial and racial vote dilution throughout the country. As we will see in the discussion that follows, Section 2 resembles Section 5 in certain respects but diverges from it in others. Above all, Section 2 is a legal *sword* that enables minority voters to *improve* their electoral position, while Section 5 is a *shield* that prevents minority voters' position from *worsening*.

To understand Section 2, it is necessary to begin with a series of constitutional cases brought under the Equal Protection Clause in the 1970s and early 1980s. The backdrop to these cases was minority voters' dissatisfaction with at-large elections and multi-member districts—both common electoral practices in this period. At-large elections occur, usually at the local level, when each office is voted upon throughout the jurisdiction, rather than the jurisdiction being divided into districts. Elections of officers such as governors and mayors who do not sit in collegial bodies are almost inevitably at-large. The controversy arises when members of a collegial body, such as a city council, are elected at-large. In the United States, at-large elections usually are run according to one of two methods. In the first, there is a separate jurisdiction-wide election for each seat. In the second, all candidates for office run against each other, each voter may cast a number of votes equal to the number of offices to be filled, and the top vote-getters are elected. For example, in an election to fill three seats on a city council, all voters in the city could vote for up to three candidates, and the top three candidates would be elected. In multi-member districts, which often occur in state legislative elections as well as some local elections,[b] more than one member but fewer than all of the members of a collegial body are elected from the same district.

The criticism of at-large elections and multi-member districts stems from the fact that they often prevent the election of representatives of minority groups that might be able to elect some legislators using single-member districts. Under polarized voting conditions, such groups are persistently outvoted even though, if districts were drawn around them, the groups would comprise local majorities. At-large elections are sometimes defended on the ground that the representatives are more likely to serve the community as a whole rather than the parochial interests of a particular locality. A similar defense of multi-member districts can be made, but is more attenuated.

Minority plaintiffs began challenging at-large elections and multi-member districts almost immediately after the reapportionment revolution of the 1960s. As early as 1965, the Supreme Court suggested that these arrangements could be unconstitutional under certain circumstances. "It might well be that, designedly or otherwise, a multi-member constituency apportionment scheme . . . would operate to minimize or cancel out the voting strength of racial or political elements of the voting population." *Fortson v. Dorsey*, 379 U.S. 433, 438 (1965). However, only one of these initial cases squarely presented the issue of racial vote dilution. See *Whitcomb v. Chavis*, 403 U.S. 124, 149 (1971) (rejecting a claim by African Americans in Indianapolis, largely due to a lack of evidence that "Negroes were not allowed to register or vote, to choose the political party they desired to support, [or] to participate in its affairs"). The Court's other preliminary forays in this area were decided on one-person, one-vote grounds. See, *e.g.*, *Burns v. Richardson*, 384 U.S. 73 (1966).

Texas's state house plan in the 1970s allowed the Court, for the first time, to rule in favor of minority plaintiffs alleging vote dilution. The Court upheld the plan as a whole against a one-person, one-vote challenge, in the process establishing the 10 percent population deviation threshold below which maps are presumptively constitutional. But the Court was less receptive to multimember districts in Dallas and Bexar Counties—areas with large African American and Latino populations, respectively.

---

b. In the past, elections for the House of Representatives occasionally were conducted in multi-member districts. Currently, federal law requires single-member districts. 2 U.S.C. § 2c.

White v. Regester

412 U.S. 755 (1973)

Mr. Justice WHITE delivered the opinion of the Court.

This case raises two questions concerning the validity of the reapportionment plan for the Texas House of Representatives adopted in 1970 by the State Legislative Redistricting Board: First, whether there were unconstitutionally large variations in population among the districts defined by the plan; second, whether the multimember districts provided for Bexar and Dallas Counties were properly found to have been invidiously discriminatory against cognizable racial or ethnic groups in those counties....

II

[The Court held that the plan's total population deviation of 9.9% was constitutional.] ...

III

We affirm the District Court's judgment, however, insofar as it invalidated the multimember districts in Dallas and Bexar Counties and ordered those districts to be redrawn into single-member districts. Plainly, under our cases, multimember districts are not per se unconstitutional, nor are they necessarily unconstitutional when used in combination with single-member districts in other parts of the State. But we have entertained claims that multimember districts are being used invidiously to cancel out or minimize the voting strength of racial groups. See *Whitcomb*; *Burns*; *Fortson*. To sustain such claims, it is not enough that the racial group allegedly discriminated against has not had legislative seats in proportion to its voting potential. The plaintiffs' burden is to produce evidence to support findings that the political processes leading to nomination and election were not equally open to participation by the group in question—that its members had less opportunity than did other residents in the district to participate in the political processes and to elect legislators of their choice. *Whitcomb*.

With due regard for these standards, the District Court first referred to the history of official racial discrimination in Texas, which at times touched the right of Negroes to register and vote and to participate in the democratic processes. It referred also to the Texas rule requiring a majority vote as a prerequisite to nomination in a primary election and to the so-called 'place' rule limiting candidacy for legislative office from a multimember district to a specified 'place' on the ticket, with the result being the election of representatives from the Dallas multimember district reduced to a head-to-head contest for each position. These characteristics of the Texas electoral system, neither in themselves improper nor invidious, enhanced the opportunity for racial discrimination, the District Court thought. More fundamentally, it found that since Reconstruction days, there have been only two Negroes in the Dallas County delegation to the Texas House of Representatives and that these two were the only two Negroes ever slated by the Dallas Committee for Responsible Government (DCRG), a white-dominated organization that is in effective control of Democratic Party candidate slating in Dallas County. That organization, the District Court found, did not need the support of the Negro community to win elections in the county, and it did not therefore exhibit good-faith concern for the political and other needs and aspirations of the Negro community. The court found that as recently as 1970 the DCRG was relying upon 'racial campaign tactics in white precincts to defeat candidates who had the overwhelming support of the black community.' Based on the evidence before it, the District Court concluded that 'the black community has been effectively excluded from participation in the Democratic primary selection process,' and was therefore generally not permitted to enter into the political process in a reliable and meaningful manner. These findings and conclusions are sufficient to sustain the District Court's judgment with respect to the Dallas multimember district and, on this record, we have no reason to disturb them.

IV

The same is true of the order requiring disestablishment of the multimember district in Bexar County. Consistently with *Hernandez v. Texas*, the District Court considered the Mexican-Americans in Bexar County to be an identifiable class for Fourteenth Amendment purposes and proceeded to inquire whether the impact of the multimember district on this group constituted invidious discrimination. Surveying the historic and present condition of the Bexar County Mexican-American community, which is concentrated for the most part on the west side of the city of San Antonio, the court observed, based upon prior cases and the record before it, that the Bexar community, along with other Mexican-Americans in Texas, had long 'suffered from, and continues to suffer from, the results and effects of invidious discrimination and treatment in the fields of education, employment, economics, health, politics and others.' The bulk of the Mexican-American community in Bexar County occupied the Barrio, an area consisting of about 28 contiguous census tracts in the city of San Antonio. Over 78% of Barrio residents were Mexican-Americans, making up 29% of the county's total population. The Barrio is an area of poor housing; its residents have low income and a high rate of unemployment. The typical Mexican-American suffers a cultural and language barrier that makes his participation in community processes extremely difficult, particularly, the court thought, with respect to the political life of Bexar County. '(A) cultural incompatibility ... conjoined with the poll tax and the most restrictive voter registration procedures in the nation have operated to effectively deny Mexican-Americans access to the political processes in Texas even longer than the Blacks were formally denied access by the white primary.' The residual impact of this history reflected itself in the fact that Mexican-American voting registration remained very poor in the county and that, only five Mexican-Americans since 1880 have served in the Texas Legislature from Bexar County. Of these, only two were from the Barrio area. The District Court also concluded from the evidence that the Bexar County legislative delegation in the House was insufficiently responsive to Mexican-American interests.

Based on the totality of the circumstances, the District Court evolved its ultimate assessment of the multimember district, overlaid, as it was, on the cultural and economic realities of the Mexican-American community in Bexar County and its relationship with the rest of the county. Its judgment was that Bexar County Mexican-Americans 'are effectively removed from the political processes of Bexar (County) in violation of all the *Whitcomb* standards, whatever their absolute numbers may total in that County.' Single-member districts were thought required to remedy 'the effects of past and present discrimination against Mexican-Americans,' and to bring the community into the full stream of political life of the county and State by encouraging their further registration, voting, and other political activities.

The District Court apparently paid due heed to *Whitcomb v. Chavis*, did not hold that every racial or political group has a constitutional right to be represented in the state legislature, but did, from its own special vantage point, conclude that the multimember district, as designed and operated in Bexar County, invidiously excluded Mexican-Americans from effective participation in political life, specifically in the election of representatives to the Texas House of Representatives. On the record before us, we are not inclined to overturn these findings, representing as they do a blend of history and an intensely local appraisal of the design and impact of the Bexar County multimember district in the light of past and present reality, political and otherwise.

Affirmed in part, reversed in part, and remanded.

Notes and Questions

1. The Court makes clear that disproportionately low representation for minority groups, standing alone, does not amount to a constitutional violation. There must also be "findings that the political processes leading to nomination and election were not equally open to participation by the group in question — that its members had less opportunity than did other residents in the district to participate in the political processes and to elect legislators of their choice." 412 U.S. at 766. How feasible is this additional inquiry? How much less opportunity must there be to participate politically or to elect preferred candidates?

2. In *Whitcomb*, the Court held at the outset that "there is no suggestion here that [the challenged multi-member district was] conceived or operated as [a] purposeful device[] to further racial or economic discrimination." 403 U.S. at 149. The Court nevertheless went on to consider at length the district's effects on African Americans in Indianapolis. In *White*, the Court repeatedly used the term "invidious" to describe the kind of discrimination that the plaintiffs had to prove in order to prevail on their claim. What, then, is the role of discriminatory intent in the constitutional

standard? Is it a prerequisite for liability? Something that can be inferred fairly easily even in the absence of direct evidence? A mere plus factor?

3. In *Whitcomb*, African American plaintiffs in Indianapolis lost even though they were socioeconomically disadvantaged, geographically concentrated, and underrepresented in the legislature. In *White*, conversely, black plaintiffs in Dallas County won even though they too were poor, segregated, and underrepresented. What accounts for the different outcome? Is it that Indiana does not share Texas's history of slavery, Jim Crow, and state-sanctioned racial discrimination?

Turning to the Mexican Americans in Bexar County, they were not faced with a racially discriminatory slating organization like the Dallas County Responsible Government, nor do there seem to have been many anti-Mexican racial appeals in Bexar County campaigns. So even if the African Americans in Dallas properly prevailed, why were the Mexican Americans entitled to victory? Nicholas O. Stephanopoulos, *Redistricting and the Territorial Community*, 160 University of Pennsylvania Law Review 1379 (2012), suggests an answer. In his view, the Supreme Court strongly favors vote dilution claims by minority groups that constitute distinct territorial communities. The typical remedy for such claims is a new single-member district corresponding to the community—a result of which the Court approves because it guarantees representation to a group the Court sees as deserving. The Court thus may have ruled for the Mexican American plaintiffs in *White* "in large part because it viewed [them] as a discrete and underprivileged geographic community." *Id.* at 1416.

4. Many vote dilution cases were brought between *White* and *City of Mobile v. Bolden*, 446 U.S. 55 (1980) (discussed below). The most notable of these was *Zimmer v. McKeithen*, 485 F.2d 1297 (5th Cir. 1973) (en banc), in which the Fifth Circuit struck down at-large elections for a Louisiana parish's police jury and school board. In its decision, the court listed a series of circumstances that support a finding of liability. These "*Zimmer* factors" were relied on by many other litigants and courts, and eventually made their way into the Senate report that accompanied the 1982 amendments to Section 2:

> [W]here a minority can demonstrate a lack of access to the process of slating candidates, the unresponsiveness of legislators to their particularized interests, a tenuous state policy underlying the preference for multi-member or at-large districting, or that the existence of past discrimination in general precludes the effective participation in the election system, a strong case is made. Such proof is enhanced by a showing of the existence of large districts, majority vote requirements, antisingle shot voting provisions and the lack of provision for at-large candidates running from particular geographical subdistricts. The fact of dilution is established upon proof of the existence of an aggregate of these factors.

Id. at 1305. Do the *Zimmer* factors accurately reflect the Supreme Court's analysis in *White*?

5. As noted above, *Whitcomb* and *White* were ambiguous as to whether discriminatory intent had to be established in a vote dilution claim. In *City of Mobile*, involving at-large elections for the City Commission of Mobile, Alabama, a four-justice plurality held that it indeed had to be shown:

> The Fifteenth Amendment does not entail the right to have Negro candidates elected.... That Amendment prohibits only purposefully discriminatory denial or abridgment by government of the freedom to vote "on account of race, color, or previous condition of servitude." Having found that Negroes in Mobile "register and vote without hindrance," the District Court and Court of Appeals were in error in believing that the appellants invaded the protection of that Amendment in the present case.
>
> ... Despite repeated constitutional attacks upon multimember legislative districts, the Court has consistently held that they are not unconstitutional per se. We have recognized, however, that such legislative apportionments could violate the Fourteenth Amendment if their purpose were invidiously to minimize or cancel out the voting potential of racial or ethnic minorities. To prove such a purpose it is not enough to show that the group allegedly discriminated against has not elected representatives in proportion to its numbers. A plaintiff must prove that the disputed plan was "conceived or operated as [a] purposeful devic[e] to further racial ... discrimination." *Whitcomb*.
>
> This burden of proof is simply one aspect of the basic principle that only if there is purposeful discrimination can there be a violation of the Equal Protection Clause of the Fourteenth Amendment. The Court explicitly indicated in *Washington v. Davis* that this principle applies to claims of racial discrimination affecting voting just as it does to other claims of racial discrimination.
>
> ... Although dicta may be drawn from a few of the Court's earlier opinions suggesting that disproportionate effects alone may establish a claim of unconstitutional racial voter dilution, the fact is that such a view is not supported by any decision of this Court. More importantly, such a view is not consistent with the meaning of the Equal Protection Clause as it has been understood in a variety of other contexts involving alleged racial discrimination.

446 U.S. at 65-67 (plurality opinion). However, Justice Stevens concurred only in the judgment, and explicitly criticized the plurality's reasoning:

> Today, the plurality rejects the *Zimmer* analysis, holding that the primary, if not the sole, focus of the inquiry must be on the intent of the political body responsible for making the districting decision. While I agree that the *Zimmer* analysis should be rejected, I do not believe that it is appropriate to focus on the subjective intent of the decisionmakers.

> In my view, the proper standard is suggested by three characteristics of the gerrymander condemned in *Gomillion [v. Lightfoot]*: (1) the 28-sided configuration was, in the Court's word, "uncouth," that is to say, it was manifestly not the product of a routine or a traditional political decision; (2) it had a significant adverse impact on a minority group; and (3) it was unsupported by any neutral justification and thus was either totally irrational or entirely motivated by a desire to curtail the political strength of the minority. These characteristics suggest that a proper test should focus on the objective effects of the political decision rather than the subjective motivation of the decisionmaker....
>
> Conversely, I am also persuaded that a political decision that affects group voting rights may be valid even if it can be proved that irrational or invidious factors have played some part in its enactment or retention.... The standard cannot, therefore, be so strict that any evidence of a purpose to disadvantage a bloc of voters will justify a finding of "invidious discrimination"; otherwise, the facts of political life would deny legislatures the right to perform the districting function. Accordingly, a political decision that is supported by valid and articulable justifications cannot be invalid simply because some participants in the decisionmaking process were motivated by a purpose to disadvantage a minority group.

Id. at 90-92 (Stevens, J., concurring in the judgment). Who has the better of this debate? What is the state of vote dilution law under the Fourteenth and Fifteenth Amendments given the Court's fragmentation in *City of Mobile*? This question is of more than academic interest, because Section 2, as amended in 1982, could be subject to constitutional challenges in the future. If the provision were ever invalidated, then the statutory cause of action would disappear but the theory would remain viable under the Fourteenth and Fifteenth Amendments.

6. The Supreme Court has decided only one constitutional vote dilution case since *City of Mobile*: *Rogers v. Lodge*, 458 U.S. 613 (1982). In *Rogers*, the Court upheld the invalidation of at-large elections for a Georgia county's board of commissioners even though the lower court had relied primarily on the *Zimmer* factors. According to the Court, an inference of discriminatory intent could be based on the "overwhelming evidence of bloc voting along racial lines," "the fact that [no African-American candidates] have ever been elected," "the impact of past discrimination on the ability of blacks to participate effectively in the political process," "[e]xtensive evidence ... that elected officials of Burke County have been unresponsive and insensitive to the needs of the black community," and "the depressed socio-economic status of Burke County blacks." *Id.* at 623-26. Were these facts any different than in *City of Mobile*? For a recent article praising *Rogers*'s seeming relaxation of the constitutional standard for liability, see Bertrall L. Ross, *The Representative Equality Principle: Disaggregating the Equal Protection Intent Standard*, 81 Fordham Law Review 175 (2012).

7. *City of Mobile* triggered an uproar in the civil rights community. The common view was that if discriminatory intent had to be proven—and if it had *not* been proven in a case as egregious as *City of Mobile*—then very few vote dilution claims would be able to succeed. This impression was confirmed by the facts that "after *Bolden* litigators virtually stopped filing new voting dilution cases" and that "the decision had a direct impact on voting dilution cases that were making their way through the federal judicial system." S. Rep. No. 97-417, at 26 (1982).

Fortuitously for voting rights advocates, Section 5 of the Voting Rights Act happened to be up for renewal in 1982, not long after *City of Mobile* was handed down. Critics of *City of Mobile* managed to convince Congress not only to reauthorize Section 5, but also to amend Section 2. This provision had previously parroted the words of the Fifteenth Amendment, and thus had produced "an effect no different from that of the Fifteenth Amendment itself." *City of Mobile*, 446 U.S. at 60 (plurality opinion). Now, though, Section 2 was revised to include a "results test":

> (a) No voting qualification or prerequisite to voting or standard, practice, or procedure shall be imposed or applied by any State or political subdivision *in a manner which results in a denial or abridgement* of the right of any citizen of the United States to vote on account of race or color....
>
> (b) A violation of subsection (a) is established if, based on the totality of circumstances, it is shown that the political processes leading to nomination or election in the State or political subdivision are not equally open to participation by members of a class of citizens protected by subsection (a) in that its members have less opportunity than other members of the electorate to participate in the political process and to elect representatives of their choice. The extent to which members of a protected class have been elected to office in the State or political subdivision is one circumstance which may be considered: Provided, That nothing in this section establishes a right to have members of a protected class elected in numbers equal to their proportion in the population.

52 U.S.C. § 10301 (emphasis added). Several features of Section 2's new language are notable. The first, of course, is the explicit inclusion of a results test, thus making clear that statutory liability may be established even in the absence of discriminatory intent. Second, subsection (b)'s reference to minority members having "less opportunity than other members of the electorate to participate in the political process and to elect representatives of their choice" self-consciously evokes the Court's decision in *White*. In the words of the Senate Report, "the subsection codifies the test for discriminatory result laid down by the Supreme Court in *White v. Regester*, and the language is taken directly from that decision." S. Rep. No. 97-417, at 67 (1982). There remains a strong link, then, between the pre-*City of Mobile* constitutional doctrine and the post-1982 case law on Section 2.

Third, the Senate Report lists numerous factors that courts may consider when evaluating "the totality of circumstances." These factors, too, are derived from *White* and *Zimmer*, and are emblematic of courts' reasoning in vote dilution cases between *White* and *City of Mobile*:

> 1. the extent of any history of official discrimination in the state or political subdivision that touched the right of the members of the minority group to register, to vote, or otherwise to participate in the democratic process;
>
> 2. the extent to which voting in the elections of the state or political subdivision is racially polarized;
>
> 3. the extent to which the state or political subdivision has used unusually large election districts, majority vote requirements, anti-single shot provisions, or other voting practices or procedures that may enhance the opportunity for discrimination against the minority group;
>
> 4. if there is a candidate slating process, whether the members of the minority group have been denied access to that process;
>
> 5. the extent to which members of the minority group in the state or political subdivision bear the effects of discrimination in such areas as education, employment and health, which hinder their ability to participate effectively in the political process;
>
> 6. whether political campaigns have been characterized by overt or subtle racial appeals;
>
> 7. the extent to which members of the minority group have been elected to public office in the jurisdiction.
>
> Additional factors that in some cases have had probative value as part of plaintiffs' evidence to establish a violation are:
>
> whether there is a significant lack of responsiveness on the part of elected officials to the particularized needs of the members of the minority group.
>
> whether the policy underlying the state or political subdivision's use of such voting qualification, prerequisite to voting, or standard, practice or procedure is tenuous.

Id. at 28-29.

Lastly, subsection (b)'s final proviso — that "nothing in this section establishes a right to have members of a protected class elected in numbers equal to their proportion in the population" was suggested by Senator Robert Dole as a way to reassure opponents that Section 2, as amended, would not mandate proportional representation for minority groups. Per the Senate Report: "This disclaimer [confirms] the absence of any right of proportional representation. It puts to rest any concerns that have been voiced about racial quotas." *Id.* at 31. See also Thomas M. Boyd & Stephen J. Markman, *The 1982 Amendments to the Voting Rights Act: A Legislative*

History, 40 Washington & Lee Law Review 1347 (1983) (discussing in depth the legislative history of the 1982 amendments).

8. The Supreme Court grappled with the revised Section 2 for the first time in the monumental 1986 case of *Thornburg v. Gingles*, involving North Carolina's allegedly dilutive state house and state senate plans. *Gingles* remains one of the most important election law cases in history, and is thus excerpted at length below.

Thornburg v. Gingles

478 U.S. 30 (1986)

Justice BRENNAN announced the judgment of the Court and delivered the opinion of the Court with respect to Parts I, II, III-A, III-B, IV-A, and V, and an opinion with respect to Part III-C, in which Justice MARSHALL, Justice BLACKMUN, and Justice STEVENS join, and an opinion with respect to Part IV-B, in which Justice WHITE joins.

This case requires that we construe for the first time § 2 of the Voting Rights Act of 1965, as amended June 29, 1982. The specific question to be decided is whether the three-judge District Court, convened in the Eastern District of North Carolina . . . correctly held that the use in a legislative redistricting plan of multimember districts in five North Carolina legislative districts violated § 2 by impairing the opportunity of black voters "to participate in the political process and to elect representatives of their choice." § 2(b).

I

Background

In April 1982, the North Carolina General Assembly enacted a legislative redistricting plan for the State's Senate and House of Representatives. Appellees, black citizens of North Carolina who are registered to vote, challenged seven districts, one single-member and six multimember districts, alleging that the redistricting scheme impaired black citizens' ability to elect representatives of their choice in violation of the Fourteenth and Fifteenth Amendments to the United States Constitution and of § 2 of the Voting Rights Act.

After appellees brought suit, but before trial, Congress amended § 2. The amendment was largely a response to this Court's plurality opinion in *Mobile v. Bolden*, which had declared that, in order to establish a violation either of § 2 or of the Fourteenth or Fifteenth Amendments, minority voters must prove that a contested electoral mechanism was intentionally adopted or maintained by state officials for a discriminatory purpose. Congress substantially revised § 2 to make clear that a violation could be proved by showing discriminatory effect alone and to establish as the relevant legal standard the "results test," applied by this Court in *White v. Regester*. . . .

The District Court applied the "totality of the circumstances" test set forth in § 2(b) to appellees' statutory claim, and, relying principally on the factors outlined in the Senate Report, held that the redistricting scheme violated § 2 because it resulted in the dilution of black citizens' votes in all seven disputed districts. In light of this conclusion, the court did not reach appellees' constitutional claims.

[At this point, Justice Brennan summarizes the findings of the District Court to the effect that most of the factors set forth in the Senate Report were present to a significant extent in the relevant North Carolina districts.]

Based on these findings, the court declared the contested portions of the 1982 redistricting plan violative of § 2 and enjoined appellants from conducting elections pursuant to those portions of the plan. Appellants, the Attorney General of North Carolina and others, took a direct appeal to this Court . . . with respect to five of the multimember districts — House Districts 21, 23, 36, and 39, and Senate District 22. . . . We . . . now affirm with respect to all of the districts except House District 23. With regard to District 23, the judgment of the District Court is reversed.

II

Section 2 and Vote Dilution Through Use of Multimember Districts

An understanding both of § 2 and of the way in which multimember districts can operate to impair blacks' ability to elect representatives of their choice is prerequisite to an evaluation of appellants' contentions. First, then, we review amended § 2 and its legislative history in some detail. Second, we explain the theoretical basis for appellees' claim of vote dilution.

A

Section 2 and its Legislative History

. . . The Senate Report which accompanied the 1982 amendments elaborates on the nature of § 2 violations and on the proof required to establish these violations. First and foremost, the . . . intent test was repudiated for three principal reasons — it is "unnecessarily divisive because it involves charges of racism on the part of individual officials or entire communities," it places an "inordinately difficult" burden of proof on plaintiffs, and it "asks the wrong question." The "right" question, as the Report emphasizes repeatedly, is whether "as a result of the challenged practice or structure plaintiffs do not have an equal opportunity to participate in the political processes and to elect candidates of their choice."

In order to answer this question, a court must assess the impact of the contested structure or practice on minority electoral opportunities "on the basis of objective factors." [Here, Justice Brennan summarizes the factors from the Senate Report, quoted above.] The Report stresses, however, that this list of typical factors is neither comprehensive nor exclusive. While the enumerated factors will often be pertinent to certain types of § 2 violations, particularly to vote dilution claims, other factors may also be relevant and may be considered. Furthermore, the Senate Committee observed that "there is no requirement that any particular number of factors be proved, or that a majority of them point one way or the other." Rather, the Committee determined that "the question whether the political processes are 'equally open' depends upon a searching practical evaluation of the 'past and present reality,'" and on a "functional" view of the political process.

Although the Senate Report espouses a flexible, fact-intensive test for § 2 violations, it limits the circumstances under which § 2 violations may be proved in three ways. First, electoral devices, such as at-large elections, may not be considered *per se* violative of § 2. Plaintiffs must demonstrate that, under the totality of the circumstances, the devices result in unequal access to the electoral process. Second, the conjunction of an allegedly dilutive electoral mechanism and the lack of proportional representation alone does not establish a violation. Third, the results test does not assume the existence of racial bloc voting; plaintiffs must prove it.

B

Vote Dilution Through the Use of Multimember Districts

Appellees contend that the legislative decision to employ multimember, rather than single-member, districts in the contested jurisdictions dilutes their votes by submerging them in a white majority,[11] thus impairing their ability to elect representatives of their choice.[12]

The essence of a § 2 claim is that a certain electoral law, practice, or structure interacts with social and historical conditions to cause an inequality in the opportunities enjoyed by black and white voters to elect their preferred representatives. This Court has long recognized that multimember districts and at-large voting schemes may "'operate to minimize or cancel out the voting strength of racial [minorities in] the voting population.'" *Burns v. Richardson* (quoting *Fortson v. Dorsey*). The theoretical basis for this type of impairment is that where minority and majority voters consistently prefer different candidates, the majority, by virtue of its numerical superiority, will regularly defeat the choices of minority voters.[14] Multimember

---

11. Dilution of racial minority group voting strength may be caused by the dispersal of blacks into districts in which they constitute an ineffective minority of voters or from the concentration of blacks into districts where they constitute an excessive majority.

12. The claim we address in this opinion is one in which the plaintiffs alleged and attempted to prove that their ability to elect the representatives of their choice was impaired by the selection of a multimember electoral structure. We have no occasion to consider whether § 2 permits, and if it does, what standards should pertain to, a claim brought by a minority group, that is not sufficiently large and compact to constitute a majority in a single-member district, alleging that the use of a multimember district impairs its ability to influence elections.

We note also that we have no occasion to consider whether the standards we apply to respondents' claim that multimember districts operate to dilute the vote of geographically cohesive minority groups, that are large enough to constitute majorities in single-member districts and that are contained within the boundaries of the challenged multimember districts, are fully pertinent to other sorts of vote dilution claims, such as a claim alleging that the splitting of a large and geographically cohesive minority between two or more multimember or single-member districts resulted in the dilution of the minority vote.

14. Not only does "[v]oting along racial lines" deprive minority voters of their preferred representative in these circumstances, it also "allows those elected to ignore [minority] interests without fear of political consequences," *Rogers v. Lodge*, leaving the minority effectively unrepresented.

districts and at-large election schemes, however, are not *per se* violative of minority voters' rights. Minority voters who contend that the multimember form of districting violates § 2 must prove that the use of a multimember electoral structure operates to minimize or cancel out their ability to elect their preferred candidates.

While many or all of the factors listed in the Senate Report may be relevant to a claim of vote dilution through submergence in multimember districts, unless there is a conjunction of the following circumstances, the use of multimember districts generally will not impede the ability of minority voters to elect representatives of their choice. Stated succinctly, a bloc voting majority must usually be able to defeat candidates supported by a politically cohesive, geographically insular minority group. These circumstances are necessary preconditions for multimember districts to operate to impair minority voters' ability to elect representatives of their choice for the following reasons. First, the minority group must be able to demonstrate that it is sufficiently large and geographically compact to constitute a majority in a single-member district.[16] If it is not, as would be the case in a substantially integrated district, the multi-member form of the district cannot be responsible for minority voters' inability to elect its candidates. Second, the minority group must be able to show that it is politically cohesive. If the minority group is not politically cohesive, it cannot be said that the selection of a multimember electoral structure thwarts distinctive minority group interests. Third, the minority must be able to demonstrate that the white majority votes sufficiently as a bloc to enable it—in the absence of special circumstances, such as the minority candidate running unopposed—usually to defeat the minority's preferred candidate. In establishing this last circumstance, the minority group demonstrates that submergence in a white multimember district impedes its ability to elect its chosen representatives.

Finally, we observe that the usual predictability of the majority's success distinguishes structural dilution from the mere loss of an occasional election. Cf. *Davis v. Bandemer.*

III

Racially Polarized Voting

Having stated the general legal principles relevant to claims that § 2 has been violated through the use of multimember districts, we turn to the arguments of appellants and of the United States as *amicus curiae* addressing racially polarized voting....

16. In this case appellees allege that within each contested multimember district there exists a minority group that is sufficiently large and compact to constitute a single-member district. In a different kind of case, for example a gerrymander case, plaintiffs might allege that the minority group that is sufficiently large and compact to constitute a single-member district has been split between two or more multimember or single-member districts, with the effect of diluting the potential strength of the minority vote.

A

The District Court's Treatment of Racially Polarized Voting

The investigation conducted by the District Court into the question of racial bloc voting ... relied principally on statistical evidence presented by appellees' expert witnesses, in particular that offered by Dr. Bernard Grofman ... Dr. Grofman subjected the data to two complementary methods of analysis — extreme case analysis and bivariate ecological regression analysis[20] — in order to determine whether blacks and whites in these districts differed in their voting behavior. These analytic techniques yielded data concerning the voting patterns of the two races, including estimates of the percentages of members of each race who voted for black candidates.

... The District Court found that blacks and whites generally preferred different candidates and, on that basis, found voting in the districts to be racially correlated ... Finally, adopting Dr. Grofman's terminology, the court found that in all but 2 of the 53 elections the degree of racial bloc voting was "so marked as to be substantively significant, in the sense that the results of the individual election would have been different depending upon whether it had been held among only the white voters or only the black voters." ...

B

The Degree of Bloc Voting that is Legally Significant Under § 2 ...

2

The Standard for Legally Significant Racial Bloc Voting ...

The purpose of inquiring into the existence of racially polarized voting is twofold: to ascertain whether minority group members constitute a politically cohesive unit and to determine whether whites vote sufficiently as a bloc usually to defeat the minority's preferred candidates. Thus, the question whether a given district experiences legally significant racially polarized voting requires discrete inquiries into minority and white voting practices. A showing that a significant number of minority group members usually vote for the same candidates is one way of proving the political cohesiveness necessary to a vote dilution claim and, consequently, establishes minority bloc voting within the context of § 2. And, in general, a white bloc vote that normally will defeat the combined strength of minority support plus white "crossover" votes rises to the level of legally significant white bloc voting. The amount of white bloc voting that can generally "minimize or cancel" black voters' ability to elect representatives of their choice, however, will vary from district to district according to a number of factors, including the nature of the allegedly dilutive electoral mechanism; the presence or absence of other potentially dilutive

20. The District Court found both methods standard in the literature for the analysis of racially polarized voting.

electoral devices, such as majority vote requirements, designated posts, and prohibitions against bullet voting; the percentage of registered voters in the district who are members of the minority group; the size of the district; and, in multimember districts, the number of seats open and the number of candidates in the field.

Because loss of political power through vote dilution is distinct from the mere inability to win a particular election, a pattern of racial bloc voting that extends over a period of time is more probative of a claim that a district experiences legally significant polarization than are the results of a single election. Also for this reason, in a district where elections are shown usually to be polarized, the fact that racially polarized voting is not present in one or a few individual elections does not necessarily negate the conclusion that the district experiences legally significant bloc voting. Furthermore, the success of a minority candidate in a particular election does not necessarily prove that the district did not experience polarized voting in that election; special circumstances, such as the absence of an opponent, incumbency, or the utilization of bullet voting, may explain minority electoral success in a polarized contest.

As must be apparent, the degree of racial bloc voting that is cognizable as an element of a § 2 vote dilution claim will vary according to a variety of factual circumstances. Consequently, there is no simple doctrinal test for the existence of legally significant racial bloc voting. However, the foregoing general principles should provide courts with substantial guidance in determining whether evidence that black and white voters generally prefer different candidates rises to the level of legal significance under § 2. . . .

C[c]

Evidence of Racially Polarized Voting

1

Appellants' Argument

North Carolina and the United States also contest the evidence upon which the District Court relied in finding that voting patterns in the challenged districts were racially polarized. They argue that the term "racially polarized voting" must, as a matter of law, refer to voting patterns for which the *principal cause* is race. They contend that the District Court utilized a legally incorrect definition of racially polarized voting by relying on bivariate statistical analyses which merely demonstrated a correlation between the race of the voter and the level of voter support for certain candidates, but which did not prove that race was the primary determinant of voters' choices. According to appellants and the United States, only multiple regression analysis, which can take account of other variables which might also explain voters'

c. Recall that this section is joined by only four justices: Brennan, Marshall, Blackmun, and Stevens. — Eds.

choices, such as "party affiliation, age, religion, income[,] incumbency, education, campaign expenditures," "media use measured by cost, . . . name, identification, or distance that a candidate lived from a particular precinct," can prove that race was the primary determinant of voter behavior.

[W]e disagree: For purposes of § 2, the legal concept of racially polarized voting incorporates neither causation nor intent. It means simply that the race of voters correlates with the selection of a certain candidate or candidates; that is, it refers to the situation where different races (or minority language groups) vote in blocs for different candidates. As we demonstrate below, appellants' theory of racially polarized voting would thwart the goals Congress sought to achieve when it amended § 2 and would prevent courts from performing the "functional" analysis of the political process and the "searching practical evaluation of the 'past and present reality'" mandated by the Senate Report.

2

Causation Irrelevant to Section 2 Inquiry

The first reason we reject appellants' argument that racially polarized voting refers to voting patterns that are in some way *caused by race*, rather than to voting patterns that are merely *correlated with the race of the voter*, is that the reasons black and white voters vote differently have no relevance to the central inquiry of § 2. By contrast, the correlation between race of voter and the selection of certain candidates is crucial to that inquiry.

Both § 2 itself and the Senate Report make clear that the critical question in a § 2 claim is whether the use of a contested electoral practice or structure results in members of a protected group having less opportunity than other members of the electorate to participate in the political process and to elect representatives of their choice. As we explained [above], multimember districts may impair the ability of blacks to elect representatives of their choice where blacks vote sufficiently as a bloc as to be able to elect their preferred candidates in a black majority, single-member district and where a white majority votes sufficiently as a bloc usually to defeat the candidates chosen by blacks. It is the *difference* between the choices made by blacks and whites — not the reasons for that difference — that results in blacks having less opportunity than whites to elect their preferred representatives. Consequently, we conclude that under the "results test" of § 2, only the correlation between race of voter and selection of certain candidates, not the causes of the correlation, matters.

The irrelevance to a § 2 inquiry of the reasons why black and white voters vote differently supports, by itself, our rejection of appellants' theory of racially polarized voting. However, their theory contains other equally serious flaws that merit further attention. As we demonstrate below, the addition of irrelevant variables distorts the equation and yields results that are indisputably incorrect under § 2 and the Senate Report.

3

Race of Voter as Primary Determinant of Voter Behavior

Appellants and the United States contend that the legal concept of "racially polarized voting" refers not to voting patterns that are merely *correlated with the voter's race*, but to voting patterns that are *determined primarily by the voter's race*, rather than by the voter's other socioeconomic characteristics.

The first problem with this argument is that it ignores the fact that members of geographically insular racial and ethnic groups frequently share socioeconomic characteristics, such as income level, employment status, amount of education, housing and other living conditions, religion, language, and so forth. Where such characteristics are shared, race or ethnic group not only denotes color or place of origin, it also functions as a shorthand notation for common social and economic characteristics. Appellants' definition of racially polarized voting is even more pernicious where shared characteristics are causally related to race or ethnicity. The opportunity to achieve high employment status and income, for example, is often influenced by the presence or absence of racial or ethnic discrimination. A definition of racially polarized voting which holds that black bloc voting does not exist when black voters' choice of certain candidates is most strongly influenced by the fact that the voters have low incomes and menial jobs—when the reason most of those voters have menial jobs and low incomes is attributable to past or present racial discrimination—runs counter to the Senate Report's instruction to conduct a searching and practical evaluation of past and present reality and interferes with the purpose of the Voting Rights Act to eliminate the negative effects of past discrimination on the electoral opportunities of minorities....

Second, appellants' interpretation of "racially polarized voting" creates an irreconcilable tension between their proposed treatment of socioeconomic characteristics in the bloc voting context and the Senate Report's statement that "the extent to which members of the minority group ... bear the effects of discrimination in such areas as education, employment and health" may be relevant to a § 2 claim. We can find no support in either logic or the legislative history for the anomalous conclusion to which appellants' position leads—that Congress intended, on the one hand, that proof that a minority group is predominately poor, uneducated, and unhealthy should be considered a factor tending to prove a § 2 violation; but that Congress intended, on the other hand, that proof that the same socioeconomic characteristics greatly influence black voters' choice of candidates should destroy these voters' ability to establish one of the most important elements of a vote dilution claim.

4

Race of Candidate as Primary Determinant of Voter Behavior

North Carolina's and the United States' suggestion that racially polarized voting means that voters select or reject candidates *principally* on the basis of the *candidate's race* is also misplaced.

First, both the language of § 2 and a functional understanding of the phenomenon of vote dilution mandate the conclusion that the race of the candidate *per se* is irrelevant to racial bloc voting analysis. Section 2(b) states that a violation is established if it can be shown that members of a protected minority group "have less opportunity than other members of the electorate to . . . elect representatives *of their choice*." (Emphasis added.) Because both minority and majority voters often select members of their own race as their preferred representatives, it will frequently be the case that a black candidate is the choice of blacks, while a white candidate is the choice of whites. Indeed, the facts of this case illustrate that tendency—blacks preferred black candidates, whites preferred white candidates. Thus, as a matter of convenience, we and the District Court may refer to the preferred representative of black voters as the "black candidate" and to the preferred representative of white voters as the "white candidate." Nonetheless, the fact that race of voter and race of candidate is often correlated is not directly pertinent to a § 2 inquiry. Under § 2, it is the status of the candidate as the chosen representative of a particular racial group, not the race of the candidate, that is important. . . .

5

Racial Animosity as Primary Determinant of Voter Behavior

Finally, we reject the suggestion that racially polarized voting refers only to white bloc voting which is caused by white voters' *racial hostility* toward black candidates. To accept this theory would frustrate the goals Congress sought to achieve by repudiating the intent test of *Mobile v. Bolden*, and would prevent minority voters who have clearly been denied an opportunity to elect representatives of their choice from establishing a critical element of a vote dilution claim. . . .

The grave threat to racial progress and harmony which Congress perceived from requiring proof that racism caused the adoption or maintenance of a challenged electoral mechanism is present to a much greater degree in the proposed requirement that plaintiffs demonstrate that racial animosity determined white voting patterns. Under the old intent test, plaintiffs might succeed by proving only that a limited number of elected officials were racist; under the new intent test plaintiffs would be required to prove that most of the white community is racist in order to obtain judicial relief. It is difficult to imagine a more racially divisive requirement.

A second reason Congress rejected the old intent test was that in most cases it placed an "inordinately difficult burden" on § 2 plaintiffs. The new intent test would be equally, if not more, burdensome. In order to prove that a *specific factor*—racial hostility—*determined* white voters' ballots, it would be necessary to demonstrate that other potentially relevant *causal factors*, such as socioeconomic characteristics and candidate expenditures, do not correlate better than racial animosity with white voting behavior. . . .

Focusing on the discriminatory intent of the voters, rather than the behavior of the voters, also asks the wrong question. All that matters under § 2 and under a functional theory of vote dilution is voter behavior, not its explanations. Moreover . . .

requiring proof that racial considerations actually *caused* voter behavior will result—contrary to congressional intent—in situations where a black minority that functionally has been totally excluded from the political process will be unable to establish a § 2 violation.

6

Summary

In sum, we would hold that the legal concept of racially polarized voting, as it relates to claims of vote dilution, refers only to the existence of a correlation between the race of voters and the selection of certain candidates. Plaintiffs need not prove causation or intent in order to prove a prima facie case of racial bloc voting and defendants may not rebut that case with evidence of causation or intent.

IV

The Legal Significance of Some Black Candidates' Success

A[d]

North Carolina and the United States maintain that the District Court failed to accord the proper weight to the success of some black candidates in the challenged districts. Black residents of these districts, they point out, achieved improved representation in the 1982 General Assembly election. They also note that blacks in House District 23 have enjoyed proportional representation consistently since 1973 and that blacks in the other districts have occasionally enjoyed nearly proportional representation. [A]ppellants and the United States contend that if a racial minority gains proportional or nearly proportional representation in a single election, that fact alone precludes, as a matter of law, finding a § 2 violation.

Section 2(b) provides that "[t]he extent to which members of a protected class have been elected to office . . . is one circumstance which may be considered." The Senate Committee Report also identifies the extent to which minority candidates have succeeded as a pertinent factor. However, the Senate Report expressly states that "the election of a few minority candidates does not 'necessarily foreclose the possibility of dilution of the black vote,'" noting that if it did, "the possibility exists that the majority citizens might evade [§ 2] by manipulating the election of a 'safe' minority candidate." . . . Thus, the language of § 2 and its legislative history plainly demonstrate that proof that some minority candidates have been elected does not foreclose a § 2 claim.

[T]he District Court could appropriately take account of the circumstances surrounding recent black electoral success in deciding its significance to appellees' claim. In particular . . . , the court could properly notice the fact that black electoral success increased markedly in the 1982 election—an election that occurred after the instant lawsuit had been filed—and could properly consider to what extent "the

d. In this section, Justice Brennan speaks for the Court.—Eds.

pendency of this very litigation [might have] worked a one-time advantage for black candidates in the form of unusual organized political support by white leaders concerned to forestall single-member districting."

Nothing in the statute or its legislative history prohibited the court from viewing with some caution black candidates' success in the 1982 election, and from deciding on the basis of all the relevant circumstances to accord greater weight to blacks' relative lack of success over the course of several recent elections. Consequently, we hold that the District Court did not err, as a matter of law, in refusing to treat the fact that some black candidates have succeeded as dispositive of appellees' § 2 claim. Where multimember districting generally works to dilute the minority vote, it cannot be defended on the ground that it sporadically and serendipitously benefits minority voters.

B[e]

The District Court did err, however, in ignoring the significance of the *sustained* success black voters have experienced in House District 23. In that district, the last six elections have resulted in proportional representation for black residents. This persistent proportional representation is inconsistent with appellees' allegation that the ability of black voters in District 23 to elect representatives of their choice is not equal to that enjoyed by the white majority.

In some situations, it may be possible for § 2 plaintiffs to demonstrate that such sustained success does not accurately reflect the minority group's ability to elect its preferred representatives, but appellees have not done so here. Appellees presented evidence relating to black electoral success in the last three elections; they failed utterly, though, to offer any explanation for the success of black candidates in the previous three elections. Consequently, we believe that the District Court erred, as a matter of law, in ignoring the sustained success black voters have enjoyed in House District 23, and would reverse with respect to that District.

V[f]

Ultimate Determination of Vote Dilution

Finally, appellants and the United States dispute the District Court's ultimate conclusion that the multimember districting scheme at issue in this case deprived black voters of an equal opportunity to participate in the political process and to elect representatives of their choice.

A

[The Court held that the District Court's findings of vote dilution should be affirmed if not clearly erroneous.]

---

e. This section is joined only by Justices Brennan and White. However, as may be seen below in Part IV of the O'Connor concurring opinion, four additional justices reached a similar conclusion. — Eds.

f. In Part V, Justice Brennan speaks for the Court. — Eds.

B

The District Court in this case carefully considered the totality of the circumstances and found that in each district racially polarized voting; the legacy of official discrimination in voting matters, education, housing, employment, and health services; and the persistence of campaign appeals to racial prejudice acted in concert with the multimember districting scheme to impair the ability of geographically insular and politically cohesive groups of black voters to participate equally in the political process and to elect candidates of their choice. It found that the success a few black candidates have enjoyed in these districts is too recent, too limited, and, with regard to the 1982 elections, perhaps too aberrational, to disprove its conclusion. Excepting House District 23, with respect to which the District Court committed legal error, we affirm the District Court's judgment....

The judgment of the District Court is

Affirmed in part and reversed in part.

Justice WHITE, concurring.

I join Parts I, II, III-A, III-B, IV-A, and V of the Court's opinion and agree with Justice BRENNAN's opinion as to Part IV-B. I disagree with Part III-C of Justice BRENNAN's opinion.

Justice BRENNAN states in Part III-C that the crucial factor in identifying polarized voting is the race of the voter and that the race of the candidate is irrelevant. Under this test, there is polarized voting if the majority of white voters vote for different candidates than the majority of the blacks, regardless of the race of the candidates. I do not agree. Suppose an eight-member multimember district that is 60% white and 40% black, the blacks being geographically located so that two safe black single-member districts could be drawn. Suppose further that there are six white and two black Democrats running against six white and two black Republicans. Under Justice BRENNAN's test, there would be polarized voting and a likely § 2 violation if all the Republicans, including the two blacks, are elected, and 80% of the blacks in the predominantly black areas vote Democratic. I take it that there would also be a violation in a single-member district that is 60% black, but enough of the blacks vote with the whites to elect a black candidate who is not the choice of the majority of black voters. This is interest-group politics rather than a rule hedging against racial discrimination. I doubt that this is what Congress had in mind in amending § 2 as it did, and it seems quite at odds with the discussion in *Whitcomb v. Chavis*....

Justice O'CONNOR, with whom THE CHIEF JUSTICE, Justice POWELL, and Justice REHNQUIST join, concurring in the judgment.

... In construing this compromise legislation, we must make every effort to be faithful to the balance Congress struck. This is not an easy task. We know that Congress intended to allow vote dilution claims to be brought under § 2, but we also know that Congress did not intend to create a right to proportional representation for minority voters. There is an inherent tension between what Congress wished to do and what it wished to avoid, because any theory of vote dilution must necessarily rely to some extent on a measure of minority voting strength that makes some reference to the proportion between the minority group and the electorate at large. In addition, several important aspects of the "results" test had received little attention in this Court's cases or in the decisions of the Courts of Appeals employing that test on which Congress also relied. Specifically, the legal meaning to be given to the concepts of "racial bloc voting" and "minority voting strength" had been left largely unaddressed by the courts when § 2 was amended.

The Court attempts to resolve all these difficulties today. First, the Court supplies definitions of racial bloc voting and minority voting strength that will apparently be applicable in all cases and that will dictate the structure of vote dilution litigation. Second, the Court adopts a test, based on the level of minority electoral success, for determining when an electoral scheme has sufficiently diminished minority voting strength to constitute vote dilution. Third, although the Court does not acknowledge it expressly, the combination of the Court's definition of minority voting strength and its test for vote dilution results in the creation of a right to a form of proportional representation in favor of all geographically and politically cohesive minority groups that are large enough to constitute majorities if concentrated within one or more single-member districts. In so doing, the Court has disregarded the balance struck by Congress in amending § 2 and has failed to apply the results test as described by this Court in *Whitcomb* and *White.*

I

... Although § 2 does not speak in terms of "vote dilution," I agree with the Court that proof of vote dilution can establish a violation of § 2 as amended. The phrase "vote dilution," in the legal sense, simply refers to the impermissible discriminatory effect that a multimember or other districting plan has when it operates "to cancel out or minimize the voting strength of racial groups." *White.* This definition, however, conceals some very formidable difficulties. Is the "voting strength" of a racial group to be assessed solely with reference to its prospects for electoral success, or should courts look at other avenues of political influence open to the racial group? Insofar as minority voting strength is assessed with reference to electoral success, how should undiluted minority voting strength be measured? How much of an impairment of minority voting strength is necessary to prove a violation of § 2? What constitutes racial bloc voting and how is it proved? What weight is to be given to evidence of actual electoral success by minority candidates in the face of evidence of racial bloc voting?

The Court resolves the first question summarily: minority voting strength is to be assessed solely in terms of the minority group's ability to elect candidates it prefers. Under this approach, the essence of a vote dilution claim is that the State has created single-member or multimember districts that unacceptably impair the minority group's ability to elect the candidates its members prefer.

In order to evaluate a claim that a particular multimember district or single-member district has diluted the minority group's voting strength to a degree that violates § 2, however, it is also necessary to construct a measure of "undiluted" minority voting strength.... Put simply, in order to decide whether an electoral system has made it harder for minority voters to elect the candidates they prefer, a court must have an idea in mind of how hard it "should" be for minority voters to elect their preferred candidates under an acceptable system.

Several possible measures of "undiluted" minority voting strength suggest themselves. First, a court could simply use proportionality as its guide.... Second, a court could posit some alternative districting plan as a "normal" or "fair" electoral scheme and attempt to calculate how many candidates preferred by the minority group would probably be elected under that scheme. There are ... a variety of ways in which even single-member districts could be drawn, and each will present the minority group with its own array of electoral risks and benefits; the court might, therefore, consider a range of acceptable plans in attempting to estimate "undiluted" minority voting strength by this method. Third, the court could attempt to arrive at a plan that would maximize feasible minority electoral success, and use this degree of predicted success as its measure of "undiluted" minority voting strength. If a court were to employ this third alternative, it would often face hard choices about what would truly "maximize" minority electoral success. An example is [a scenario] in which a minority group could be concentrated in one completely safe district or divided among two districts in each of which its members would constitute a somewhat precarious majority.

The Court today has adopted a variant of the third approach, to wit, undiluted minority voting strength means the maximum feasible minority voting strength....

The Court's definition of the elements of a vote dilution claim is simple and invariable: a court should calculate minority voting strength by assuming that the minority group is concentrated in a single-member district in which it constitutes a voting majority. Where the minority group is not large enough, geographically concentrated enough, or politically cohesive enough for this to be possible, the minority group's claim fails. Where the minority group meets these requirements, the representatives that it could elect in the hypothetical district or districts in which it constitutes a majority will serve as the measure of its undiluted voting strength. Whatever plan the State actually adopts must be assessed in terms of the effect it has on this undiluted voting strength. If this is indeed the single, universal standard for evaluating undiluted minority voting strength for vote dilution purposes, the standard is applicable whether what is challenged is a multimember district or a particular single-member districting scheme....

The Court's statement of the elements of a vote dilution claim also supplies an answer to another question posed above: *how much* of an impairment of undiluted minority voting strength is necessary to prove vote dilution. The Court requires the minority group that satisfies the threshold requirements of size and cohesiveness to prove that it will *usually* be unable to elect as many representatives of its choice under the challenged districting scheme as its undiluted voting strength would permit....

This measure of vote dilution, taken in conjunction with the Court's standard for measuring undiluted minority voting strength, creates what amounts to a right to *usual, roughly* proportional representation on the part of sizable, compact, cohesive minority groups....

As shaped by the Court today, then, the basic contours of a vote dilution claim require no reference to most of the "*Zimmer* factors" that were developed by the Fifth Circuit to implement *White*'s results test and which were highlighted in the Senate Report. If a minority group is politically and geographically cohesive and large enough to constitute a voting majority in one or more single-member districts, then unless white voters usually support the minority's preferred candidates in sufficient numbers to enable the minority group to elect as many of those candidates as it could elect in such hypothetical districts, it will routinely follow that a vote dilution claim can be made out, and the multimember district will be invalidated....

II

In my view, the Court's test for measuring minority voting strength and its test for vote dilution, operating in tandem, come closer to an absolute requirement of proportional representation than Congress intended when it codified the results test in § 2....

In my view, we should refrain from deciding in this case whether a court must invariably posit as its measure of "undiluted" minority voting strength single-member districts in which minority group members constitute a majority. There is substantial doubt that Congress intended "undiluted minority voting strength" to mean "maximum feasible minority voting strength." Even if that is the appropriate definition in some circumstances, there is no indication that Congress intended to mandate a single, universally applicable standard for measuring undiluted minority voting strength, regardless of local conditions and regardless of the extent of past discrimination against minority voters in a particular State or political subdivision. Since appellants have not raised the issue, I would assume that what the District Court did here was permissible under § 2, and leave open the broader question whether § 2 *requires* this approach.

[T]he District Court concluded that there was a severe diminution in the prospects for black electoral success in each of the challenged districts, as compared to single-member districts in which blacks could constitute a majority, and that this severe diminution was in large part attributable to the interaction of the multimember form of the district with persistent racial bloc voting on the part of the white majorities in those districts. But the District Court's extensive opinion clearly relies as well on a variety of the other *Zimmer* factors....

In enacting § 2, Congress codified the "results" test this Court had employed, as an interpretation of the Fourteenth Amendment, in *White* and *Whitcomb*.... In my view, therefore, it is to *Whitcomb* and *White* that we should look in the first instance in determining how great an impairment of minority voting strength is required to establish vote dilution in violation of § 2.

The "results" test as reflected in *Whitcomb* and *White* requires an inquiry into the extent of the minority group's opportunities to participate in the political processes. While electoral success is a central part of the vote dilution inquiry, *White* held that to prove vote dilution, "it is not enough that the racial group allegedly discriminated against has not had legislative seats in proportion to its voting potential," and *Whitcomb* flatly rejected the proposition that "any group with distinctive interests must be represented in legislative halls if it is numerous enough to command at least one seat and represents a majority living in an area sufficiently compact to constitute a single member district." To the contrary, the results test as described in *White* requires plaintiffs to establish "that the political processes leading to nomination and election were not equally open to participation by the group in question — that its members had less opportunity than did other residents in the district to participate in the political processes and to elect legislators of their choice." . . .

[A] court should consider all relevant factors bearing on whether the minority group has "less opportunity than other members of the electorate to participate in the political process and to elect representatives of their choice." The court should not focus solely on the minority group's ability to elect representatives of its choice. . . .

III

. . . Insofar as statistical evidence of divergent racial voting patterns is admitted solely to establish that the minority group is politically cohesive and to assess its prospects for electoral success, I agree [with the plurality in Part III-C of the Brennan opinion] that defendants cannot rebut this showing by offering evidence that the divergent racial voting patterns may be explained in part by causes other than race, such as an underlying divergence in the interests of minority and white voters. I do not agree, however, that such evidence can never affect the overall vote dilution inquiry. Evidence that a candidate preferred by the minority group in a particular election was rejected by white voters for reasons other than those which made that candidate the preferred choice of the minority group would seem clearly relevant in answering the question whether bloc voting by white voters will consistently defeat minority candidates. Such evidence would suggest that another candidate, equally preferred by the minority group, might be able to attract greater white support in future elections.

I believe Congress also intended that explanations of the reasons why white voters rejected minority candidates would be probative of the likelihood that candidates elected without decisive minority support would be willing to take the minority's interests into account. In a community that is polarized along racial lines, racial hostility may bar these and other indirect avenues of political influence to a much greater extent than in a community where racial animosity is absent although the interests of racial groups diverge. . . . Similarly, I agree with Justice WHITE that

Justice BRENNAN's conclusion that the race of the candidate is always irrelevant in identifying racially polarized voting conflicts with *Whitcomb* and is not necessary to the disposition of this case.

IV

[Though her specific analysis of some of the North Carolina multimember districts diverges in detail from Brennan's, Justice O'Connor agrees with Brennan and White that the history of black success in District 23 required reversal, but not in the other districts.]

V

... Compromise is essential to much if not most major federal legislation, and confidence that the federal courts will enforce such compromises is indispensable to their creation. I believe that the Court today strikes a different balance than Congress intended to when it codified the results test and disclaimed any right to proportional representation under § 2. For that reason, I join the Court's judgment but not its opinion.

Justice STEVENS, with whom Justice MARSHALL and Justice BLACKMUN join, concurring in part and dissenting in part.

In my opinion, the findings of the District Court ... adequately support the District Court's judgment concerning House District 23 as well as the balance of that judgment.

Notes and Questions

1. The Court identified three "necessary preconditions" that plaintiffs must establish to show that multimember districts violate Section 2:

> First, the minority group must be able to demonstrate that it is sufficiently large and geographically compact to constitute a majority in a single-member district.... Second, the minority group must be able to show that it is politically cohesive.... Third, the minority must be able to demonstrate that the white majority votes sufficiently as a bloc to enable it ... usually to defeat the minority's preferred candidate.

478 U.S. at 50-51. The three *Gingles* preconditions are sometimes referred to as "compactness," "political cohesiveness," and "majority bloc voting." The second and third *Gingles* prongs are often conflated and described jointly as "racial polarization." Note that liability does *not* follow automatically if the preconditions are satisfied; rather, the analysis then proceeds to the totality-of-circumstances stage, at which the Senate factors (and, as we shall see, other issues too) are considered.

Is *Gingles* sound as statutory interpretation? In particular, is it consistent with the proviso in Section 2 that proportional representation is not required? Justice O'Connor, concurring in *Gingles*, thought not. The same conclusion is reached by Daniel D. Polsby and Robert D. Popper, *Ugly: An Inquiry Into the Problem of Racial Gerrymandering Under the Voting Rights Act*, 92 Michigan Law Review 652 (1993).

Conversely, might the problem with *Gingles* be that it makes liability too *difficult* to establish, by requiring compactness and racial polarization to be proved in all cases even though these terms are nowhere to be found in the statutory text? For critiques along these lines, see Christopher S. Elmendorf et al., *Racially Polarized Voting*, 83 University of Chicago Law Review 587 (2016) (arguing that *Gingles*'s polarization prongs should be modified); and Nicholas O. Stephanopoulos, *Civil Rights in a Desegregating America*, 83 University of Chicago Law Review 1329 (2016) (arguing that *Gingles*'s compactness prong should be dropped).

2. What is the overarching theory of *Gingles*? Elmendorf et al., *Racially Polarized Voting, supra*, 83 University of Chicago Law Review at 630-36, lay out four alternatives:

> (a) *Proportional representation theory*. . . . On this view, voting power is defined in terms of the opportunity to elect ideally preferred representatives, and the fairness benchmark is proportionality: the ratio of the number of districts that provide the minority community with this opportunity to the total number of districts should roughly equal the ratio of the minority population to the total population. . . .
>
> (b) *Coalitional-breakdown theory*. . . . A political minority's vote is "diluted" if and only if it lacks the opportunities to participate in coalitional politics that political minorities normally enjoy. Racial vote dilution occurs when a racial minority that is also a political minority lacks such opportunities. . . .
>
> (c) *Voter-discrimination theory* . . . [This] theory emphasizes the reasons why minority-preferred candidates lost. The core issue is disparate treatment: whether white voters give less support to minority candidates than to otherwise-similar white candidates. . . .
>
> (d) *The LULAC*[g] *theory* . . . [This is] the proposition that § 2 protects all "naturally occurring" majority-minority districts — that is, those likely to be drawn by a politically neutral redistricter applying traditional criteria such as compactness, respect for communities of interest, and minimization of political subdivision splits.

Stephanopoulos, *Race, Place, and Power, supra*, 68 Stanford Law Review at 1337, responds that the first of these theories enjoys by far the most doctrinal support, but should be tweaked to take into account the ways in which compactness and polarization can limit a group's representation:

> [Under *Gingles*, a] minority group is entitled to descriptive representation (up to the ceiling of proportionality) to the extent that it is geographically compact and polarized in its voting patterns. In other words, if there is racial polarization, a group's spatial distribution determines the number of

g. This is a reference to *LULAC v. Perry*, 548 U.S. 399 (2005), which we discuss below.

> districts in which the group must be able to elect its preferred candidate. A group's descriptive representation is a function of its segregation and polarization. In brief, this is the "ultimate core value" that [Senator Orrin] Hatch demanded, that the drafters of the 1982 amendments could not name, and that *Gingles* finally provided.

3. *Scholarly Views on* Gingles. A vigorous theoretical and political debate rages around Section 2's application to minority vote dilution claims. We cannot hope to fully capture that debate here, but will consider three divergent responses.

(a) *The view that* Gingles *does not go far enough.* This view is most famously set forth in the writings of Lani Guinier. Guinier contends that the *Gingles* anti-dilution framework represents the "second generation" of the voting rights movement, the first generation having been the successful fight for the access to the vote in the 1960s.

> On the assumption that racial bloc voting by a white electoral majority will invariably result in the defeat of black representatives, second-generation voting rights litigants seek to integrate the legislature primarily through the subdivision of predominantly white electorates into single-member districts. The second-generation remedial agenda is premised on the notion that black representatives, elected from majority-black subdistricts and electorally accountable only to black voters, will represent those voters' concerns from their newly established legislative seats. Once integrated, legislative bodies will deliberate more effectively and will be "legitimated" as a result of their more inclusive character.

Lani Guinier, *No Two Seats: The Elusive Quest for Political Equality*, 77 Virginia Law Review 1413, 1415 (1991). Guinier does not doubt the value of the "authentic black representation" that second-generation claims have sought, but quarrels with the idea that districting should be the central mechanism for achieving equal representation. She instead argues for "proportionate interest representation," which would require basic changes to both electoral and legislative systems:

> Winner-take-all territorial districting imperfectly distributes representation based on group attributes and disproportionately rewards those who win the representational lottery. Territorial districting uses an aggregating rule that inevitably groups people by virtue of some set of externally observed characteristics such as geographic proximity or racial identity. In addition, the winner-take-all principle inevitably wastes some votes. The dominant group within the district gets all the power; the votes of supporters of nondominant groups or disaffected voters within the dominant group are wasted. Their votes lose significance because they are consistently cast for political losers....
>
> Given a system of winner-take-all territorial districts and working within the limitations of this particular election method, the courts have sought to achieve political fairness for racial minorities. As a result, there is some truth to the assertion that minority groups, unlike other voters, enjoy

> a special representational relationship under the Voting Rights Act's 1982 amendments to remedy their continued exclusion from effective political participation in some jurisdictions. But the proper response is not to deny minority voters that protection. The answer should be to extend that special relationship to *all* voters by endorsing *the equal opportunity to vote for a winning candidate* as a universal principle of political fairness.
>
> I use the term "one-vote, one-value" to describe the principle of political fairness that as many votes as possible should count in the election of representatives. One-vote, one-value is realized when everyone's vote counts for someone's election. The only system with the potential to realize this principle for *all* voters is one in which the unit of representation is political rather than regional, and the aggregating rule is proportionality rather than winner-take-all. Semiproportional systems, such as cumulative voting, can approximate the one-vote, one-value principle by minimizing the problem of wasted votes.

Lani Guinier, *Groups, Representation, and Race-Conscious Districting: A Case of the Emperor's Clothes*, 71 Texas Law Review 1589, 1592–94 (1993).

There is an extensive literature debating the pros and cons of the "semiproportional systems" that Guinier recommends. For a useful description of some of these systems by an articulate exponent of views similar to Guinier's, see Pamela S. Karlan, *Maps and Misreadings: The Role of Geographic Compactness in Racial Vote Dilution Litigation*, 24 Harvard Civil Rights-Civil Liberties Law Review 173 (1989). For a comparative examination of semiproportional systems used abroad, and a taxonomy of these systems in terms of the geographic distributions of the groups they benefit and the explicitness with which they allocate seats to racial minorities, see Nicholas O. Stephanopoulos, *Our Electoral Exceptionalism*, 80 University of Chicago Law Review 769 (2013). And for an empirical assessment of semiproportional systems used in the United States (mostly in small towns and counties), finding that they improve minority representation, electoral competition, and voter turnout, see Shaun Bowler et al., Electoral Reform and Minority Representation: Local Experiments with Alternative Elections (2003).

The debate over semiproportional systems is in turn part of a larger debate over the merits of proportional voting systems versus single-member districts. Support for proportional systems appears to be widespread among legal scholars who study election law and has received strong support from numerous political scientists. See, *e.g.*, Douglas J. Amy, Real Choices/New Voices: The Case for Proportional Representation Elections in the United States (1993); Richard L. Engstrom, *The Political Thicket, Electoral Reform, and Minority Voting Rights*, in Fair and Effective Representation? Debating Electoral Reform and Minority Rights 3 (Mark E. Rush & Richard L. Engstrom, eds., 2001).

Most courts have not been inclined to order semiproportional devices of the sort favored by Guinier as remedies for Section 2 violations. See, *e.g.*, *Cane v. Worcester*

County, 35 F.3d 921 (4th Cir. 1994) (holding that it was an abuse of discretion for a district court to impose cumulative voting as a remedy for a Section 2 violation without giving the county the opportunity to submit a single-member district plan). But there are exceptions. A district court in Ohio ordered a school board to implement "limited voting," under which each voter may vote for a single candidate for a multi-member board. *United States v. Euclid City School Board*, 632 F. Supp. 2d 740 (N.D. Ohio 2009). Another district court ordered cumulative voting as a remedy, rejecting the United States' proposal that single-member districts be drawn. *United States v. Village of Port Chester*, 704 F. Supp. 2d 411 (S.D.N.Y. 2010). Although the United States argued that cumulative voting had been consistently rejected, the court called this "a misstatement of the case law." Under the cumulative voting system adopted by Port Chester, each voter has six votes which may be cast any way he or she wishes—for example, one vote for six different candidates or all six for one candidate. In June 2010, after an extensive voter education program, a Latino was elected to Port Chester's board of trustees for the first time. See Kirk Semple, *First Latino Board Member Is Elected in Port Chester*, N.Y. Times, June 16, 2010.

(b) *The view that* Gingles *goes too far.* Soon after *Gingles* was issued, it received influential criticism in a book by Abigail M. Thernstrom, Whose Votes Count? (1987).[h] Thernstrom concluded that the Voting Rights Act's original, widely-supported goals of extending the right to vote and eliminating abusive practices in the South had been quietly transmuted into anticompetitive policies that enjoyed little public support.

> [O]ur sensitivity to the special significance of black officeholding in the South, where blacks were disfranchised before 1965, has shaded into a belief in the entitlement of black and Hispanic candidates everywhere to extraordinary protection from white competition.

Thernstrom updated her argument in Voting Rights—and Wrongs: The Elusive Quest For Racially Fair Elections (2009). Justice Thomas' concurring opinion in *Holder v. Hall*, reprinted at the end of this section, partly relies on the academic criticism of race-conscious districting by Thernstrom and others.

Some commentators who believe *Gingles* goes "too far" begin with the same recognition expressed by Lani Guinier: that in a country in which minority groups are, after all, minorities, only so much can be accomplished by providing such groups with the opportunity to elect their own representatives. Thus, Carol Swain writes:

> When African Americans question the common strategy of drawing legislative districts with large black majorities, they are sometimes viewed by other blacks with suspicion and regarded as "enemies of the group." Yet the

---

h. Thernstrom's book was controversial. For sharp criticism, see J. Morgan Kousser, *The Voting Rights Act and the Two Reconstructions*, in Controversies in Minority Voting 135, 166–76 (1992); Pamela S. Karlan & Peyton McCrary, *Without Fear and Without Research: Abigail Thernstrom on the Voting Rights Act*, 4 Journal of Law & Politics 751 (1988).

> electoral demography of the United States favors such a policy. The statistics on the distribution and concentration of blacks in the population reveal a need to look beyond the creation of majority-black political units as a way to increase political representation of African Americans. Blacks have already made the most of their opportunities to elect black politicians in congressional districts with black majorities.... Some experts suggest that African Americans and Hispanics might be able to find twelve to fifteen new districts for themselves after the 1990s redistricting. Beyond that, and in years to come, we can expect severe limitations on what can be achieved by relying on the creation of black districts to ensure the election of black politicians.

Carol M. Swain, Black Faces, Black Interests 200 (1993). Instead of calling for some sort of proportional representation, Swain believes minority groups should welcome districts in which they fall short of a majority but constitute a significant element. She argues that "multiracial coalitions" offer the best hope for minority groups, and dispersing minorities over more districts—rather than concentrating them in a few districts—"might encourage greater responsiveness from white elected officials." *Id.* at 210–11.

Even if one agrees that the compelled creation of majority-minority districts was necessary in the 1980s and 1990s, is it still necessary in the third decade of the 21st century? Even after the election of our first African American president?

(c) *The view that* Gingles *is about right.* Despite the criticism it has received, the *Gingles* regime also has numerous defenders. Among the more prominent are Bernard Grofman (who served as the plaintiffs' expert in *Gingles*), Lisa Handley, and Richard G. Niemi, the authors of Minority Representation. Responding to the view of some critics that *Gingles* reflects a group-based theory of politics that is contrary to the idea of a "color-blind" society, they write:

> We would emphasize, first, that the rights provided by the act are contingent, appropriate only when a significant liability threshold has been met. Only when African-Americans or Hispanics are made a "permanent minority" as a result of racial bloc voting by the majority or by various practices and procedures is there intervention under the Voting Rights Act. Intervention in such circumstances is, we believe, in accord with the Madisonian tradition ... which condemns factions, even majority factions, and seeks to design constitutional rules that serve as safeguards against the pernicious consequences of such factionalism.
>
> Because the rights are contingent, the applicability of Section 2 of the Voting Rights Act, like Section 5, is, in principle, "self-liquidating."... Moreover, the three conditions—residential segregation sufficient to allow the drawing of districts in which minority group members are a majority, racially polarized voting, and a "usual" lack of minority electoral success—are conditions that few people wish to see perpetuated. Thus, if minority

> assimilation proceeds in such a fashion that residential segregation becomes a thing of the past, minority groups will be unable to launch successful voting rights suits. Or if voting in a jurisdiction is no longer polarized along racial or linguistic/ethnic lines—or even if it is, but the level of white crossover voting permits significant and repeated minority access—the Voting Rights Act will become a dead letter in that jurisdiction.
>
> Second, though it is true that most other voting rights violations (e.g., of the one-person, one-vote standard) are customarily defined in terms of the violation of individual rights, clearly there are types of discrimination directed against individuals as a function of their status as members of a minority community. In such situations it seems foolish to think that liability and remedies cannot be race conscious. In the present context, because racially polarized voting is a prerequisite for a voting rights violation and residential segregation a prerequisite for submergence, it is not plausible to attempt only "color-blind" tests and solutions.
>
> Furthermore, to argue that policies in the voting rights area must be free of all considerations of race and ethnicity is like blaming the messenger for the message.

Minority Representation at 131–32.

Is *Gingles*, in the end, the best that can be done to ensure equal representation for racial minorities, at least in a country where districted elections are the near-universal norm?

4. Where did *Gingles*'s three famous preconditions come from? Interestingly, almost verbatim from a law review article written by two veteran voting rights litigators, which the majority cited more than a dozen times. See James U. Blacksher & Larry T. Menefee, *From* Reynolds v. Sims *to* City of Mobile v. Bolden: *Have the White Suburbs Commandeered the Fifteenth Amendment?*, 34 Hastings Law Journal 1 (1982). Even more interestingly, neither the preconditions nor Blacksher and Menefee's article appeared in the first draft of Justice Brennan's opinion. Apparently, he (or a clerk) found the piece while trying to respond to the first draft of Justice O'Connor's concurrence (and to keep Justice White's vote), thus changing the path of voting rights history. For more on *Gingles*'s drafting, see Daniel P. Tokaji, *Realizing the Right to Vote: The Story of* Thornburg v. Gingles, *in* Election Law Stories 127 (Joshua A. Douglas & Eugene D. Mazo, eds., 2016).

5. If Section 2 means what the Court says it does in *Gingles*, is it constitutional? The Supreme Court has never squarely addressed this question, though Justice O'Connor once noted that "lower courts have unanimously affirmed its constitutionality," adding that "[s]tatutes are presumed constitutional, and that presumption appears strong here in light of the weight of authority affirming the results test's constitutionality." *Bush v. Vera*, 517 U.S. 952, 991–92 (1996) (O'Connor, J., concurring). A challenge to Section 2 would presumably emphasize the disjunction between the constitutional standard for liability, which requires proof of discriminatory intent,

and the statutory standard, which explicitly abjures the need for such proof. The argument would be that, under *City of Boerne*, there is insufficient "congruence and proportionality" between Section 2's means and the underlying constitutional harms. For a thorough consideration of this argument, stressing the implications of the Court's loosening of the constitutional standard in *Rogers v. Lodge*, see Luke P. McLoughlin, *Section 2 of the Voting Rights Act and* City of Boerne: *The Continuity, Proximity, and Trajectory of Vote-Dilution Standards*, 31 Vermont Law Review 39 (2006).

6. Ellen Katz has conducted the most thorough study of how *Gingles* has been applied in the lower courts. To cite a few of her most important findings: Plaintiffs succeeded in roughly one-third of the lawsuits she identified. Plaintiffs' success rate has fallen steadily over time, from close to 50 percent in the 1980s, to near 40 percent in the 1990s, to only 15 percent since then. At-large elections were the practices most commonly challenged in the 1980s; since then, at-large elections and single-member district plans have been the most frequent targets of litigation. African Americans were the plaintiffs in about 80 percent of cases, Latinos in about 10 percent, and Native Americans and Asian Americans in the remainder. And plaintiffs that satisfied all three of *Gingles*'s preconditions ultimately prevailed more than 80 percent of the time. See Ellen Katz et al., *Documenting Discrimination in Voting: Judicial Findings Under Section 2 of the Voting Rights Act Since 1982*, 39 University of Michigan Journal of Law Reform 643 (2006).

Using Katz's dataset of Section 2 cases, Adam Cox and Thomas Miles carried out two additional studies. In one, they determined that black and Democratic-appointed judges are much more likely to rule in favor of Section 2 plaintiffs than white and Republican-appointed judges. Race and partisanship are also more powerful drivers of judicial decisions than the type of practice challenged, the location of the challenged practice, and the date of the lawsuit. See Adam B. Cox & Thomas J. Miles, *Judging the Voting Rights Act*, 108 Columbia Law Review 1 (2008). In the other, they found that Democratic and Republican appointees disagree at lower rates when evaluating *Gingles*'s rule-like preconditions than when assessing its standard-like totality of circumstances. The frequency with which Democratic appointees assigned liability after deeming the preconditions satisfied also fell over time, perhaps because these judges realized that victory for minority plaintiffs could spell trouble for Democratic candidates. See Adam B. Cox & Thomas J. Miles, *Judicial Ideology and the Transformation of Voting Rights Jurisprudence*, 75 University of Chicago Law Review 1493 (2008).

7. Did *Gingles* accomplish its primary goal of improving descriptive representation for minority groups? Stephanopoulos, *Race, Place, and Power*, *supra*, tries to answer this question using state house data from 1972 to 2014. He finds that, in the South, the share of seats held by African American legislators surged after *Gingles* from roughly 12 percent to 20 percent. On the other hand, in the non-South, this proportion only increased from 4 percent to 6 percent. And nationwide,

the share of seats held by Latino legislators only rose after *Gingles* from 2 percent to 5 percent.

More interestingly, was this improvement in descriptive representation accomplished through *Gingles*'s preconditions of compactness and racial polarization? For African Americans, the answer is yes. A black population of a given size, compactness, and polarization obtained significantly more state house representation after *Gingles* than before. For Latinos, though, the situation is more ambiguous. A Latino population of a given size, compactness, and polarization won about the same representation before and after *Gingles*. Stephanopoulos therefore concludes that his results are "at once heartening and sobering. Heartening in that blacks—the minority at issue in *Gingles* itself, and the group for whom the Voting Rights Act was enacted half a century ago—have indeed profited greatly from the decision, and in precisely the manner intended by the Court. But also sobering in that Hispanics, now America's largest minority, have not been aided to nearly the same extent." *Id.* at 1404.

8. *Section 2's Scope.* Does *Gingles* apply to claims that single-member district plans (as opposed to at-large elections or multi-member districts) dilute the votes of a protected minority? Footnote 12 of *Gingles* left this question open, but later cases clarify that it does. In *Voinovich v. Quilter*, 507 U.S. 146, 153–54 (1993), notably, the Supreme Court explained: "In the context of single-member districts, the usual device for diluting minority voting power is the manipulation of district lines.... Dividing the minority group among various districts so that it is a majority in none may prevent the group from electing its candidate of choice." So may "the concentration of minority voters within a district.... A minority group, for example, might have sufficient numbers to constitute a majority in three districts.... But if the group is packed into two districts in which it constitutes a super-majority, it will be assured only two candidates."

What about the election of judges—are they "representatives" covered by Section 2's assurance of equal opportunity for protected groups "to elect representatives of their choice"? The Court answered in the affirmative in *Chisom v. Roemer*, 501 U.S. 380, 399 (1991): "We think... that the better reading of the word 'representatives' describes the winners of representative, popular elections. If executive officers, such as prosecutors, sheriffs, state attorneys general, and state treasurers, can be considered 'representatives' simply because they are chosen by popular election, then the same reasoning should apply to elected judges." See also *Houston Lawyers' Association v. Attorney General of Texas*, 501 U.S. 419, 426 (1991) (holding that a state's interest in electing judges on a countywide, at-large basis "is a legitimate factor to be considered by courts among the 'totality of circumstances' in determining whether a § 2 violation has occurred").

Suppose in a municipality with a three-member elected governing body, there is a minority community that is too small to satisfy the first *Gingles* prong but would be large enough if the governing body were expanded to five members. Does the failure to expand violate Section 2? Similarly, does a municipality violate Section 2 by electing a single individual to carry out functions that could be carried out by an elected board on which minorities could expect representation? (We shall refer to such individuals as "sole officeholders." Though our locution is hardly mellifluous, the more common "single-member officers" is inaccurate. The officeholder is not a "member" of any body.)

A divided Supreme Court answered these questions in the negative in *Holder v. Hall*, 512 U.S. 874 (1994). Justice Kennedy, writing for himself, Chief Justice Rehnquist and Justice O'Connor, reasoned from the premise that any claim of vote dilution implies some non-dilutive benchmark against which the challenged system can be measured.

> [T]he search for a benchmark is quite problematic when a §2 dilution challenge is brought to the size of a government body. There is no principled reason why one size should be picked over another as the benchmark for comparison. Respondents here argue that we should compare Bleckley County's sole commissioner system to a hypothetical five-member commission in order to determine whether the current system is dilutive. [Several reasons had been advanced for selecting a five-member body for comparison, including that a Georgia statute authorized counties to replace single commissioners with five-member commissions and that Bleckley County itself had recently switched from a single superintendent of education to a five-member school board.]
>
> That Bleckley County was authorized by the State to expand its commission, and that it adopted a five-member school board, are ... irrelevant considerations in the dilution inquiry. At most, those facts indicate that Bleckley County could change the size of its commission with minimal disruption. But the county's failure to do so says nothing about the effects the sole commissioner system has on the voting power of Bleckley County's citizens. Surely a minority group's voting strength would be no more or less diluted had the State not authorized the county to alter the size of its commission, or had the county not enlarged its school board. One gets the sense that respondents and the United States have chosen a benchmark for the sake of having a benchmark. But it is one thing to say that a benchmark can be found, quite another to give a convincing reason for finding it in the first place.

Id. at 881-82 (plurality opinion). Justice Thomas, joined by Justice Scalia, concurred in the judgment but selected *Holder* for the statement of much broader views, as we shall see shortly. Four justices dissented.

9. The *Gingles* test for Section 2 vote dilution claims is quite different from the nonretrogression test for preclearance under Section 5. Did the 1982 amendments and their interpretation in *Gingles* affect Section 5? If Section 5 were governed solely by the nonretrogression principle, then many changes in electoral procedures

entitled to preclearance under Section 5 would still be vulnerable to attack under Section 2. To avoid this anomaly, the Justice Department adopted a regulation saying it would withhold preclearance if necessary "to prevent a clear violation of Section 2." In *Reno v. Bossier Parish School Board* (*Bossier Parish I*), 520 U.S. 471, 480 (1997), the Supreme Court ruled that the regulation was invalid:

> ... § 5, we have held, is designed to combat only those effects that are retrogressive. To adopt appellants' position, we would have to call into question more than 20 years of precedent interpreting § 5. This we decline to do. Section 5 already imposes upon a covered jurisdiction the difficult burden of proving the *absence* of discriminatory purpose and effect. To require a jurisdiction to litigate whether its proposed redistricting plan also has a dilutive "result" before it can implement that plan — even if the Attorney General bears the burden of proving that "result" — is to increase further the serious federalism costs already implicated by § 5.

10. Can white voters bring racial vote dilution claims under Section 2 of the Voting Rights Act? The statutory text, which refers to "a denial or abridgement of the right of *any citizen* ... to vote *on account of race or color*," suggests so. And that is indeed what most lower courts have held. However, even if they could satisfy the *Gingles* preconditions, white voters would presumably have a very difficult time establishing liability under the Senate factors, most of which involve the presence of historical and ongoing racial discrimination. For a recent case recognizing white voters' right to bring a racial vote dilution challenge, but ruling against them on the merits, see *Harding v. County of Dallas*, 948 F.3d 302 (5th Cir. 2020) (holding that plaintiffs failed to prove that a second Anglo opportunity county commissioner district could be drawn in Dallas County, Texas).

11. Gingles*'s First Prong.* Recall that, under *Gingles*'s first precondition, "the minority group must be able to demonstrate that it is sufficiently large and geographically compact to constitute a majority in a single-member district." This precondition raises two distinct questions: Is the minority group *numerically large* enough? And is the group *geographically compact* enough? As we shall see, the meaning of the first question — in particular, whether a minority group must constitute an outright majority of a potential single-member district — went unaddressed by the Supreme Court until *Bartlett v. Strickland*, 556 U.S. 1 (2009). On the other hand, both the lower courts and the Supreme Court commented extensively on the first precondition's compactness requirement.

In the lower courts, this requirement was interpreted quite flexibly in the first few years after *Gingles*. Representative of these early decisions was *Dillard v. Baldwin County Board of Education*, 686 F. Supp. 1459, 1465-66 (M.D. Ala. 1988), in which the district court reasoned as follows:

> By compactness, *Thornburg* does not mean that a proposed district must meet, or attempt to achieve, some aesthetic absolute, such as symmetry or attractiveness. An aesthetic norm, by itself, would be not only unrelated to

> the legal and social issues presented under § 2, it would be an unworkable concept, resulting in arbitrary and capricious results, because it offers no guidance as to when it is met....
>
> The court therefore believes, especially in light of § 2's strong national mandate, that a district is sufficiently geographically compact if it allows for effective representation. For example, a district would not be sufficiently compact if it was so spread out that there was no sense of community, that is, if its members and its representative could not effectively and efficiently stay in touch with each other; or if it was so convoluted that there was no sense of community, that is, if its members and its representative could not easily tell who actually lived within the district.... These are not, however, the only factors a court should consider in assessing a proposed district; because compactness is a functional concept, the number and kinds of factors a court should consider may vary with each case, depending on the local geographical, political, and socio-economic characteristics of the jurisdiction being sued.

The Supreme Court, however, took a harder line on compactness in a series of racial gerrymandering cases that it decided in the 1990s. (These cases are discussed in more detail in Part III.) In these cases, allegations were made that bizarre-looking majority-minority districts were unconstitutional racial gerrymanders. The districts were commonly defended on the ground that they were required to avoid liability under Section 2. In rejecting these defenses, the Court explained that highly noncompact districts could never be mandated by Section 2 because such districts would not satisfy *Gingles*'s first precondition. With respect to an elongated North Carolina congressional district that tracked highway I-85 through the state, for example, the Court held that it "could not remedy any potential § 2 violation." "No one looking at [the district] could reasonably suggest that the district contains a 'geographically compact' population of any race." *Shaw v. Hunt*, 517 U.S. 899, 916 (1996). Likewise, with respect to two highly irregular Texas congressional districts, the Court declared, "If, because of the dispersion of the minority population, a reasonably compact majority-minority district cannot be created, § 2 does not require a majority-minority district; if a reasonably compact district can be created, nothing in § 2 requires the race-based creation of a district that is far from compact." *Bush v. Vera*, 517 U.S. 952, 979 (1996).

In the wake of these cases, the content of *Gingles*'s compactness criterion seemed settled: Plaintiffs could not satisfy the criterion by proposing bizarrely-shaped districts, and such districts could not be defended on the basis of Section 2. In *LULAC v. Perry*, 548 U.S. 399 (2006), however, the Court introduced an additional complication. Compactness, the Court held, has a *cultural* as well as a *geographic* component.[i]

---

i. *LULAC* also raises interesting issues of partisan gerrymandering (which we discussed in Chapter 4) and racial gerrymandering (which we discuss below in Part III).

League of United Latin American Citizens v. Perry

548 U.S. 399 (2006)

Justice KENNEDY announced the judgment of the Court and delivered the opinion of the Court with respect to [Part III]....

III

Plan 1374C made changes to district lines in south and west Texas that appellants challenge as violations of § 2 of the Voting Rights Act and the Equal Protection Clause of the Fourteenth Amendment. The most significant changes occurred to District 23, which—both before and after the redistricting—covers a large land area in west Texas, and to District 25, which earlier included Houston but now includes a different area, a north-south strip from Austin to the Rio Grande Valley.

After the 2002 election, it became apparent that District 23 as then drawn had an increasingly powerful Latino population that threatened to oust the incumbent Republican, Henry Bonilla. Before the 2003 redistricting, the Latino share of the citizen voting-age population was 57.5%, and Bonilla's support among Latinos had dropped with each successive election since 1996. In 2002, Bonilla captured only 8% of the Latino vote and 51.5% of the overall vote. Faced with this loss of voter support, the legislature acted to protect Bonilla's incumbency by changing the lines—and hence the population mix—of the district. To begin with, the new plan divided Webb County and the city of Laredo, on the Mexican border, that formed the county's population base. Webb County, which is 94% Latino, had previously rested entirely within District 23; under the new plan, nearly 100,000 people were shifted into neighboring District 28. The rest of the county, approximately 93,000 people, remained in District 23. To replace the numbers District 23 lost, the State added voters in counties comprising a largely Anglo, Republican area in central Texas. In the newly drawn district, the Latino share of the citizen voting-age population dropped to 46%, though the Latino share of the total voting-age population remained just over 50%.

These changes required adjustments elsewhere, of course, so the State inserted a third district between the two districts to the east of District 23, and extended all three of them farther north. New District 25 is a long, narrow strip that winds its way from McAllen and the Mexican border towns in the south to Austin, in the center of the State and 300 miles away. In between it includes seven full counties, but 77% of its population resides in split counties at the northern and southern ends. Of this 77%, roughly half reside in Hidalgo County, which includes McAllen, and half are in Travis County, which includes parts of Austin. The Latinos in District 25, comprising 55% of the district's citizen voting-age population, are also mostly divided between the two distant areas, north and south. The Latino communities at the opposite ends of District 25 have divergent "needs and interests," owing to "differences in socio-economic status, education, employment, health, and other characteristics."

The District Court summed up the purposes underlying the redistricting in south and west Texas: "The change to Congressional District 23 served the dual goal of increasing Republican seats in general and protecting Bonilla's incumbency in particular, with the additional political nuance that Bonilla would be reelected in a district that had a majority of Latino voting age population—although clearly not a majority of citizen voting age population and certainly not an effective voting majority." The goal in creating District 25 was just as clear: "[t]o avoid retrogression under § 5" of the Voting Rights Act given the reduced Latino voting strength in District 23.

A

The question we address is whether Plan 1374C violates § 2 of the Voting Rights Act....

B

Appellants argue that the changes to District 23 diluted the voting rights of Latinos who remain in the district. Specifically, the redrawing of lines in District 23 caused the Latino share of the citizen voting-age population to drop from 57.5% to 46%. The District Court recognized that "Latino voting strength in Congressional District 23 is, unquestionably, weakened under Plan 1374C." The question is whether this weakening amounts to vote dilution.

To begin the *Gingles* analysis, it is evident that the second and third *Gingles* preconditions—cohesion among the minority group and bloc voting among the majority population—are present in District 23. The District Court found "racially polarized voting" in south and west Texas, and indeed "throughout the State."...

The first *Gingles* factor requires that a group be "sufficiently large and geographically compact to constitute a majority in a single-member district." Latinos in District 23 could have constituted a majority of the citizen voting-age population in the district, and in fact did so under Plan 1151C. Though it may be possible for a citizen voting-age majority to lack real electoral opportunity, the Latino majority in old District 23 did possess electoral opportunity protected by § 2.

While the District Court stated that District 23 had not been an effective opportunity district under Plan 1151C, it recognized the district was "moving in that direction." Indeed, by 2002 the Latino candidate of choice in District 23 won the majority of the district's votes in 13 out of 15 elections for statewide officeholders. And in the congressional race, Bonilla could not have prevailed without some Latino support, limited though it was. State legislators changed District 23 specifically because they worried that Latinos would vote Bonilla out of office.

Furthermore, to the extent the District Court suggested that District 23 was not a Latino opportunity district in 2002 simply because Bonilla prevailed, it was incorrect. The circumstance that a group does not win elections does not resolve the issue of vote dilution. We have said that "the ultimate right of § 2 is equality of opportunity, not a guarantee of electoral success for minority-preferred candidates of whatever race." In old District 23 the increase in Latino voter registration and overall population, the concomitant rise in Latino voting power in each successive election, the near-victory of the Latino candidate of choice in 2002, and the resulting threat to the Bonilla incumbency, were the very reasons that led the State to redraw the district lines. Since the redistricting prevented the immediate success of the emergent Latino majority in District 23, there was a denial of opportunity in the real sense of that term.

Plan 1374C's version of District 23, by contrast, "is unquestionably not a Latino opportunity district." Latinos, to be sure, are a bare majority of the voting-age population in new District 23, but only in a hollow sense, for the parties agree that the relevant numbers must include citizenship. This approach fits the language of § 2 because only eligible voters affect a group's opportunity to elect candidates. In sum, appellants have established that Latinos could have had an opportunity district in District 23 had its lines not been altered and that they do not have one now.

Considering the district in isolation, the three *Gingles* requirements are satisfied. The State argues, nonetheless, that it met its § 2 obligations by creating new District 25 as an offsetting opportunity district. It is true, of course, that "States retain broad discretion in drawing districts to comply with the mandate of § 2." This principle has limits, though. The Court has rejected the premise that a State can always make up for the less-than-equal opportunity of some individuals by providing greater opportunity to others. As set out below, these conflicting concerns are resolved by allowing the State to use one majority-minority district to compensate for the absence of another only when the racial group in each area had a § 2 right and both could not be accommodated.

As to the first *Gingles* requirement, it is not enough that appellants show the possibility of creating a majority-minority district that would include the Latinos in District 23. If the inclusion of the plaintiffs would necessitate the exclusion of others, then the State cannot be faulted for its choice. That is why, in the context of a challenge to the drawing of district lines, "the first *Gingles* condition requires the possibility of creating more than the existing number of reasonably compact districts with a sufficiently large minority population to elect candidates of its choice."

The District Court found that the current plan contains six Latino opportunity districts and that seven reasonably compact districts could not be drawn. Appellant GI Forum presented a plan with seven majority-Latino districts, but the District Court found these districts were not reasonably compact, in part because they took in "disparate and distant communities." While there was some evidence to the contrary, the court's resolution of the conflicting evidence was not clearly erroneous.

A problem remains, though, for the District Court failed to perform a comparable compactness inquiry for Plan 1374C as drawn. [*Johnson v. De Grandy*, reprinted later in this section] requires a comparison between a challenger's proposal and the "existing number of reasonably compact districts." To be sure, § 2 does not forbid the creation of a noncompact majority-minority district. The noncompact district cannot, however, remedy a violation elsewhere in the State. Simply put, the State's creation of an opportunity district for those without a § 2 right offers no excuse for its failure to provide an opportunity district for those with a § 2 right. And since there is no § 2 right to a district that is not reasonably compact, the creation of a noncompact district does not compensate for the dismantling of a compact opportunity district....

The District Court stated that Plan 1374C created "six *Gingles* Latino" districts, but it failed to decide whether District 25 was reasonably compact for § 2 purposes. It recognized there was a 300-mile gap between the Latino communities in District 25, and a similarly large gap between the needs and interests of the two groups. After making these observations, however, it did not make any finding about compactness. It ruled instead that, despite these concerns, District 25 would be an effective Latino opportunity district because the combined voting strength of both Latino groups would allow a Latino-preferred candidate to prevail in elections. The District Court's general finding of effectiveness cannot substitute for the lack of a finding on compactness, particularly because the District Court measured effectiveness simply by aggregating the voting strength of the two groups of Latinos. Under the District Court's approach, a district would satisfy § 2 no matter how noncompact it was, so long as all the members of a racial group, added together, could control election outcomes.

The District Court did evaluate compactness for the purpose of deciding whether race predominated in the drawing of district lines. The Latinos in the Rio Grande Valley and those in Central Texas, it found, are "disparate communities of interest," with "differences in socio-economic status, education, employment, health, and other characteristics." The court's conclusion that the relative smoothness of the district lines made the district compact, despite this combining of discrete communities of interest, is inapposite because the court analyzed the issue only for equal protection purposes. In the equal protection context, compactness focuses on the contours of district lines to determine whether race was the predominant factor in drawing those lines. Under § 2, by contrast, the injury is vote dilution, so the compactness inquiry embraces different considerations. "The first *Gingles* condition refers to the compactness of the minority population, not to the compactness of the contested district."

While no precise rule has emerged governing § 2 compactness, the "inquiry should take into account 'traditional districting principles such as maintaining communities of interest and traditional boundaries.'" The recognition of nonracial communities of interest reflects the principle that a State may not "assum[e] from a group of voters' race that they 'think alike, share the same political interests, and will prefer the same candidates at the polls.'" In the absence of this prohibited assumption, there is no basis to believe a district that combines two far-flung segments of a racial group with disparate interests provides the opportunity that § 2 requires or that the first *Gingles* condition contemplates. "The purpose of the Voting Rights Act is to prevent discrimination in the exercise of the electoral franchise and to foster our transformation to a society that is no longer fixated on race." We do a disservice to these important goals by failing to account for the differences between people of the same race.

While the District Court recognized the relevant differences, by not performing the compactness inquiry it failed to account for the significance of these differences under § 2. In these cases the District Court's findings regarding the different characteristics, needs, and interests of the Latino community near the Mexican border and the one in and around Austin are well supported and uncontested. Legitimate yet differing communities of interest should not be disregarded in the interest of race. The practical consequence of drawing a district to cover two distant, disparate communities is that one or both groups will be unable to achieve their political goals. Compactness is, therefore, about more than "style points," *post* (opinion of Roberts, C. J.); it is critical to advancing the ultimate purposes of § 2, ensuring minority groups equal "opportunity . . . to participate in the political process and to elect representatives of their choice." (And if it were just about style points, it is difficult to understand why a plaintiff would have to propose a compact district to make out a § 2 claim.) As witnesses who know the south and west Texas culture and politics testified, the districting in Plan 1374C "could make it more difficult for thinly financed Latino-preferred candidates to achieve electoral success and to provide adequate and responsive representation once elected." We do not question the District Court's finding that the groups' combined voting strength would enable them to elect a candidate each prefers to the Anglos' candidate of choice. We also accept that in some cases members of a racial group in different areas — for example, rural and urban communities — could share similar interests and therefore form a compact district if the areas are in reasonably close proximity. When, however, the only common index is race and the result will be to cause internal friction, the State cannot make this a remedy for a § 2 violation elsewhere. We emphasize it is the enormous geographical distance separating the Austin and Mexican-border communities, coupled with the disparate needs and interests of these populations — not either factor alone — that renders District 25 noncompact for § 2 purposes. The mathematical possibility of a racial bloc does not make a district compact.

Since District 25 is not reasonably compact, Plan 1374C contains only five reasonably compact Latino opportunity districts. Plan 1151C, by contrast, created six such districts. The District Court did not find, and the State does not contend, that any of the Latino opportunity districts in Plan 1151C are noncompact. Contrary to The Chief Justice's suggestion, moreover, the Latino population in old District 23 is, for the most part, in closer geographic proximity than is the Latino population in new District 25. More importantly, there has been no contention that different pockets of the Latino population in old District 23 have divergent needs and interests, and it is clear that, as set out below, the Latino population of District 23 was split apart particularly because it was becoming so cohesive. The Latinos in District 23 had found an efficacious political identity, while this would be an entirely new and difficult undertaking for the Latinos in District 25, given their geographic and other differences.

Appellants have thus satisfied all three *Gingles* requirements as to District 23, and the creation of new District 25 does not remedy the problem.

C

[The Court then proceeded to analyze the totality of circumstances. The Court's comments on how the proportionality of a minority group's representation should be calculated are discussed later in this section. The Court, though, added the following analysis of the changes to District 23.]

District 23's Latino voters were poised to elect their candidate of choice. They were becoming more politically active, with a marked and continuous rise in Spanish-surnamed voter registration. In successive elections Latinos were voting against Bonilla in greater numbers, and in 2002 they almost ousted him. Webb County in particular, with a 94% Latino population, spurred the incumbent's near defeat with dramatically increased turnout in 2002. In response to the growing participation that threatened Bonilla's incumbency, the State divided the cohesive Latino community in Webb County, moving about 100,000 Latinos to District 28, which was already a Latino opportunity district, and leaving the rest in a district where they now have little hope of electing their candidate of choice.

The changes to District 23 undermined the progress of a racial group that has been subject to significant voting-related discrimination and that was becoming increasingly politically active and cohesive. The District Court recognized "the long history of discrimination against Latinos and Blacks in Texas," and other courts have elaborated on this history with respect to electoral processes. . . . In addition, the "political, social, and economic legacy of past discrimination" for Latinos in Texas may well "hinder their ability to participate effectively in the political process," *Gingles* (citing Senate Report factors).

Against this background, the Latinos' diminishing electoral support for Bonilla indicates their belief he was "unresponsive to the particularized needs of the members of the minority group." *Ibid.* (same). In essence the State took away the Latinos' opportunity because Latinos were about to exercise it. This bears the mark of intentional discrimination that could give rise to an equal protection violation. Even if we accept the District Court's finding that the State's action was taken primarily for political, not racial, reasons, the redrawing of the district lines was damaging to the Latinos in District 23. The State not only made fruitless the Latinos' mobilization efforts but also acted against those Latinos who were becoming most politically active, dividing them with a district line through the middle of Laredo.

Furthermore, the reason for taking Latinos out of District 23, according to the District Court, was to protect Congressman Bonilla from a constituency that was increasingly voting against him. The Court has noted that incumbency protection can be a legitimate factor in districting, see *Karcher v. Daggett,* but experience teaches that incumbency protection can take various forms, not all of them in the interests of the constituents. If the justification for incumbency protection is to keep the constituency intact so the officeholder is accountable for promises made or broken, then the protection seems to accord with concern for the voters. If, on the other hand, incumbency protection means excluding some voters from the district simply because they are likely to vote against the officeholder, the change is to benefit the officeholder, not the voters. By purposely redrawing lines around those who opposed Bonilla, the state legislature took the latter course. This policy, whatever its validity in the realm of politics, cannot justify the effect on Latino voters. See *Gingles* (citing Senate Report factor of whether "the policy underlying" the State's action "is tenuous"). The policy becomes even more suspect when considered in light of evidence suggesting that the State intentionally drew District 23 to have a nominal Latino voting-age majority (without a citizen voting-age majority) for political reasons. This use of race to create the façade of a Latino district also weighs in favor of appellants' claim.

Contrary to The Chief Justice's suggestion that we are reducing the State's needed flexibility in complying with § 2, the problem here is entirely of the State's own making. The State chose to break apart a Latino opportunity district to protect the incumbent congressman from the growing dissatisfaction of the cohesive and politically active Latino community in the district. The State then purported to compensate for this harm by creating an entirely new district that combined two groups of Latinos, hundreds of miles apart, that represent different communities of interest. Under § 2, the State must be held accountable for the effect of these choices in denying equal opportunity to Latino voters. Notwithstanding these facts, The Chief Justice places great emphasis on the District Court's statement that "new District 25 is 'a more effective Latino opportunity district than Congressional District 23 had been.'" Even assuming this statement, expressed in the context of summarizing witnesses' testimony, qualifies as a finding of the District Court, two points make it of minimal relevance. First, as previously noted, the District Court measured the effectiveness of District 25 without accounting for the detrimental consequences of its compactness problems. Second, the District Court referred only to how effective District 23 "had been," not to how it would operate today, a significant distinction given the growing Latino political power in the district.

Based on the foregoing, the totality of the circumstances demonstrates a § 2 violation. Even assuming Plan 1374C provides something close to proportional representation for Latinos, its troubling blend of politics and race—and the resulting vote dilution of a group that was beginning to achieve § 2's goal of overcoming prior electoral discrimination—cannot be sustained. . . .

Notes and Questions

1. Under pre-*LULAC* case law, there is little doubt that the new District 25 would have been considered a valid replacement for the old District 23. The new District 25 had a clear Latino citizen voting-age majority, and its shape was not so strange as to render it an improper remedy. Nevertheless, the Court concluded that the new

District 25 did *not* count as a reasonably compact minority-opportunity district. The problem, according to the Court, was that the new District 25 merged Latino communities in Austin and along the Mexican border that had "divergent 'needs and interests,' owing to 'differences in socio-economic status, education, employment, health, and other characteristics.'" 548 U.S. at 424. "[T]here is no basis to believe a district that combines two far-flung segments of a racial group with disparate interests provides the opportunity that §2 requires or that the first *Gingles* condition contemplates." *Id.* at 433.

Scholars were quick to notice this development. Daniel R. Ortiz, *Cultural Compactness*, 105 Michigan Law Review First Impressions 48 (2006), dubbed as "cultural compactness" the Court's new emphasis on the socioeconomic similarities between minority members in a district. Richard H. Pildes, *The Decline of Legally Mandated Minority Representation*, 68 Ohio State Law Journal 1139, 1146 (2007), warned that if plaintiffs had to establish cultural as well as geographic compactness, "[s]tates might not then have VRA obligations to create districts that, for example, bring together urban and rural minorities, or suburban and city ones." And Stephanopoulos, *The South After* Shelby County, *supra*, quantified the socioeconomic heterogeneity of the Latinos in the new District 25, and compared it to that of minority residents in other minority-heavy districts in the South. He found that 146 such districts contained minority residents who were *more* socioeconomically heterogeneous than the new District 25's Latinos. May all of these districts now be dismantled without violating Section 2?

2. Weighing against the likelihood of such drastic change is the Court's statement that "it is the enormous geographical distance separating the Austin and Mexican-border communities, coupled with the disparate needs and interests of these populations — not either factor alone — that renders District 25 noncompact for §2 purposes." 548 U.S. at 435. This statement suggests that when culturally noncompact but geographically *proximate* communities are joined in a district, that district may constitute a perfectly valid Section 2 remedy. Also consistent with the idea that *LULAC* did not revolutionize Section 2 doctrine is the fact that relatively few lower courts have confronted *LULAC*-based arguments in the years since the decision. When such arguments *have* been raised, moreover, they have been resolved in narrow and fact-specific ways. See, *e.g.*, *Fletcher v. Lamone*, 831 F. Supp. 2d 887, 899 (D. Md. 2011) (rejecting a proposed district that combined distinct African American communities in the Baltimore and Washington, D.C. suburbs); *Benavidez v. City of Irving*, 638 F. Supp. 2d 709, 722 (N.D. Tex. 2009) (finding that although a district contained a Hispanic neighborhood that "may differ in some demographic characteristics from the core area," the neighborhood was "geographically close to that core" and thus the district was a valid Section 2 remedy).

3. The old District 23 — the constituency that Representative Bonilla was about to lose, and that was heavily revised to save him — was far from the only district redrawn by Texas's Republicans. To the contrary, the entire congressional plan was redone in a (highly successful) effort to elect more Republicans and fewer Democrats

to Congress. In the context of such a sweeping realignment of district boundaries, why was the Court so concerned about Bonilla's political situation? What, if anything, distinguished him from the many other officeholders who were dramatically affected by the new plan?

The answer might be the Court's intuition that Texas *intentionally* discriminated against the Latinos in the old District 23 by dividing them right when they were poised to oust Bonilla from office. According to the Court, this districting choice "bears the mark of intentional discrimination," especially "in light of evidence suggesting that the State intentionally drew [the new] District 23 to have a nominal Latino voting-age majority (without a citizen voting-age majority) for political reasons." 548 U.S. at 440-41. But why would this fact pattern suggest purposeful *racial* as opposed to *partisan* discrimination? After all, it was Latino *Democrats* who were Bonilla's most dedicated opponents.

4. Twelve years after *LULAC*, the Court again addressed the issue of intentional racial discrimination in the context of a dispute over redistricting in Texas. A district court found that Texas deliberately discriminated against Latino voters when it originally passed its congressional and state legislative plans in 2011. The district court then "attributed this same intent to the 2013 Legislature" when it enacted new plans that corresponded to interim court-drawn maps "because it had 'failed to engage in a deliberative process to ensure that the 2013 plans cured any taint from the 2011 plans.'" *Abbott v. Perez*, 138 S. Ct. 2305, 2318 (2018). This was legal error, in the view of the Supreme Court. As Justice Alito wrote for five Justices:

> The allocation of the burden of proof and the presumption of legislative good faith are not changed by a finding of past discrimination. "[P]ast discrimination cannot, in the manner of original sin, condemn governmental action that is not itself unlawful." The "ultimate question remains whether a discriminatory intent has been proved in a given case." The "historical background" of a legislative enactment is "one evidentiary source" relevant to the question of intent. But we have never suggested that past discrimination flips the evidentiary burden on its head....
>
> ... Nor is this a case in which a law originally enacted with discriminatory intent is later reenacted by a different legislature. The 2013 Texas Legislature did not reenact the plan previously passed by its 2011 predecessor. Nor did it use criteria that arguably carried forward the effects of any discriminatory intent on the part of the 2011 Legislature. Instead, it enacted, with only very small changes, plans that had been developed by the Texas court pursuant to instructions from this Court "not to incorporate ... any legal defects."
>
> Under these circumstances, there can be no doubt about what matters: It is the intent of the 2013 Legislature. And it was the plaintiffs' burden to overcome the presumption of legislative good faith and show that the 2013 Legislature acted with invidious intent.

Id. at 2324–25 (internal citations omitted). Justice Sotomayor dissented vigorously, joined by Justices Ginsburg, Breyer, and Kagan. She argued that the lower court had not, in fact, shifted the burden to Texas to show that it had cured the taint of past discrimination. She also contended that the evidence in the record amply supported the lower court's finding of intentional discrimination:

> ... To start, there is no question as to the discriminatory impact of the 2013 plans, as the "specific portions of the 2011 plans that [the District Court] found to be discriminatory or unconstitutional racial gerrymanders continue unchanged in the 2013 plans, their harmful effects 'continu[ing] to this day.'" Texas, moreover, has a long "history of discrimination" against minority voters. "In the last four decades, Texas has found itself in court every redistricting cycle, and each time it has lost."
>
> There is also ample evidence that the 2013 Legislature knew of the discrimination that tainted its 2011 maps. "The 2013 plans were enacted by a substantially similar Legislature with the same leadership only two years after the original enactment." The Legislature was also well aware that "the D.C. court concluded that [its 2011] maps were tainted by evidence of discriminatory purpose," and despite the District Court having warned of the potential that the Voting Rights Act may require further changes to the maps, "the Legislature continued its steadfast refusal to consider [that] possibility." ...
>
> The absence of a true deliberative process was coupled with a troubling sequence of events leading to the enactment of the 2013 maps. Specifically, "the Legislature pushed the redistricting bills through quickly in a special session," despite months earlier having been urged by the Texas attorney general to take on redistricting during the regular session. By pushing the bills through a special session, the Legislature did not have to comply with "a two-thirds rule in the Senate or a calendar rule in the House," and it avoided the "full public notice and hearing" that would have allowed "'meaningful input' from all Texans, including the minority community."

Id. at 2346-48. Who has the better of this dispute? Is it fair to infer discriminatory intent when (1) a legislature is found guilty of intentional discrimination when it originally passes a map; (2) a court orders an interim remedial plan to be used; and (3) the legislature then enacts a new map that largely follows the contours of the interim remedial plan? Additionally, how common is this scenario? Especially now that Section 5 is a dead letter thanks to *Shelby County*, how often will legislatures find themselves in the position of deciding whether to ratify a court-drawn map?

5. The *LULAC* plaintiffs also challenged the elimination of the old District 24, a district with a 26 percent African American population in the Dallas area that reliably elected a liberal white Democrat to Congress. In a portion of the opinion not reproduced above, the Court rejected this challenge. The Court first agreed with the lower court that this liberal white Democrat was not the "candidate of choice" of the

black community. The old District 24 was thus not one in which minority members had the opportunity to elect their preferred candidate. Next, and more importantly, the Court held that Section 2 does not protect "influence districts" in which minority members may assist in the election of their second-choice candidate:

> That African-Americans had influence in the district does not suffice to state a § 2 claim in these cases. The opportunity "to elect representatives of their choice," [52 U.S.C. § 10301(b)], requires more than the ability to influence the outcome between some candidates, none of whom is their candidate of choice. There is no doubt African-Americans preferred Martin Frost to the Republicans who opposed him. The fact that African-Americans preferred Frost to some others does not, however, make him their candidate of choice. Accordingly, the ability to aid in Frost's election does not make the old District 24 an African-American opportunity district for purposes of § 2. If § 2 were interpreted to protect this kind of influence, it would unnecessarily infuse race into virtually every redistricting, raising serious constitutional questions.

Id. at 445-46. But while *LULAC* removed influence districts from Section 2's scope, it did not address the status of "crossover districts," in which minority voters make up a large minority of the population but *are* able to elect their candidates of choice with the help of white voters. The Court confronted that issue in the following case:

Bartlett v. Strickland

556 U.S. 1 (2009)

Justice KENNEDY announced the judgment of the Court and delivered an opinion, in which THE CHIEF JUSTICE and Justice ALITO join.

This case requires us to interpret § 2 of the Voting Rights Act of 1965. The question is whether the statute can be invoked to require state officials to draw election-district lines to allow a racial minority to join with other voters to elect the minority's candidate of choice, even where the racial minority is less than 50 percent of the voting-age population in the district to be drawn. To use election-law terminology: In a district that is not a majority-minority district, if a racial minority could elect its candidate of choice with support from crossover majority voters, can § 2 require the district to be drawn to accommodate this potential?

I

...

District 18 in its present form emerged from the General Assembly's third redistricting attempt, in 2003. By that time the African-American voting-age population had fallen below 50 percent in the district as then drawn, and the General Assembly no longer could draw a geographically compact majority-minority district. Rather than draw District 18 to keep Pender County whole, however, the General Assembly drew it by splitting portions of Pender and New Hanover counties. District 18 has an African-American voting-age population of 39.36 percent. Had it left Pender County whole, the General Assembly could have drawn District 18 with an African-American voting-age population of 35.33 percent. The General Assembly's reason for splitting Pender County was to give African-American voters the potential to join with majority voters to elect the minority group's candidate of its choice. Failure to do so, state officials now submit, would have diluted the minority group's voting strength in violation of § 2.

In May 2004, Pender County and the five members of its board of commissioners filed the instant suit in North Carolina state court against the Governor of North Carolina, the Director of the State Board of Elections, and other state officials. The plaintiffs alleged that the 2003 plan violated the Whole County Provision [a requirement in the North Carolina Constitution that counties not be divided by state legislative districts] by splitting Pender County into two House districts. The state-official defendants answered that dividing Pender County was required by § 2....

III

A

This case turns on whether the first *Gingles* requirement can be satisfied when the minority group makes up less than 50 percent of the voting-age population in the potential election district. The parties agree on all other parts of the *Gingles* analysis, so the dispositive question is: What size minority group is sufficient to satisfy the first *Gingles* requirement?

At the outset the answer might not appear difficult to reach, for the *Gingles* Court said the minority group must "demonstrate that it is sufficiently large and geographically compact to constitute a majority in a single-member district." This would seem to end the matter, as it indicates the minority group must demonstrate it can constitute "a majority." But in *Gingles* and again in *Growe* the Court reserved what it considered to be a separate question — whether, "when a plaintiff alleges that a voting practice or procedure impairs a minority's ability to influence, rather than alter, election results, a showing of geographical compactness of a minority group not sufficiently large to constitute a majority will suffice." ...

Petitioners argue that although crossover districts do not include a numerical majority of minority voters, they still satisfy the first *Gingles* requirement because they are "effective minority districts." Under petitioners' theory keeping Pender County whole would have violated § 2 by cracking the potential crossover district that they drew as District 18. So, petitioners contend, § 2 required them to override state law and split Pender County, drawing District 18 with an African-American voting-age population of 39.36 percent rather than keeping Pender County whole and leaving District 18 with an African-American voting-age population of 35.33 percent. We reject that claim.

First, we conclude, petitioners' theory is contrary to the mandate of § 2. The statute requires a showing that minorities "have less opportunity than other members of the electorate to ... elect representatives of their choice." But because they form only 39 percent of the voting-age population in District 18, African-Americans standing alone have no better or worse opportunity to elect a candidate than does any other group of voters with the same relative voting strength. That is, African-Americans in District 18 have the opportunity to join other voters—including other racial minorities, or whites, or both—to reach a majority and elect their preferred candidate. They cannot, however, elect that candidate based on their own votes and without assistance from others. Recognizing a § 2 claim in this circumstance would grant minority voters "a right to preserve their strength for the purposes of forging an advantageous political alliance." Nothing in § 2 grants special protection to a minority group's right to form political coalitions. "[M]inority voters are not immune from the obligation to pull, haul, and trade to find common political ground." . . .

Allowing crossover-district claims would require us to revise and reformulate the *Gingles* threshold inquiry that has been the baseline of our § 2 jurisprudence. Mandatory recognition of claims in which success for a minority depends upon crossover majority voters would create serious tension with the third *Gingles* requirement that the majority votes as a bloc to defeat minority-preferred candidates. It is difficult to see how the majority-bloc-voting requirement could be met in a district where, by definition, white voters join in sufficient numbers with minority voters to elect the minority's preferred candidate. (We are skeptical that the bloc-voting test could be satisfied here, for example, where minority voters in District 18 cannot elect their candidate of choice without support from almost 20 percent of white voters. We do not confront that issue, however, because for some reason respondents conceded the third *Gingles* requirement in state court.) . . .

We find support for the majority-minority requirement in the need for workable standards and sound judicial and legislative administration. The rule draws clear lines for courts and legislatures alike. The same cannot be said of a less exacting standard that would mandate crossover districts under § 2. Determining whether a § 2 claim would lie—i.e., determining whether potential districts could function as crossover districts—would place courts in the untenable position of predicting many political variables and tying them to race-based assumptions. The Judiciary would be directed to make predictions or adopt premises that even experienced polling analysts and political experts could not assess with certainty, particularly over the long term. For example, courts would be required to pursue these inquiries: What percentage of white voters supported minority-preferred candidates in the past? How reliable would the crossover votes be in future elections? What types of candidates have white and minority voters supported together in the past and will those trends continue? Were past crossover votes based on incumbency and did that depend on race? What are the historical turnout rates among white and minority voters and will they stay the same? Those questions are speculative, and the answers (if they could be supposed) would prove elusive. A requirement to draw election districts on answers to these and like inquiries ought not to be inferred from the text or purpose of § 2. Though courts are capable of making refined and exacting factual inquiries, they "are inherently ill-equipped" to "make decisions based on highly political judgments" of the sort that crossover-district claims would require. There is an underlying principle of fundamental importance: We must be most cautious before interpreting a statute to require courts to make inquiries based on racial classifications and race-based predictions. The statutory mandate petitioners urge us to find in § 2 raises serious constitutional questions.

Heightening these concerns even further is the fact that § 2 applies nationwide to every jurisdiction that must draw lines for election districts required by state or local law. Crossover-district claims would require courts to make predictive political judgments not only about familiar, two-party contests in large districts but also about regional and local jurisdictions that often feature more than two parties or candidates. Under petitioners' view courts would face the difficult task of discerning crossover patterns in nonpartisan contests for a city commission, a school board, or a local water authority. The political data necessary to make such determinations are nonexistent for elections in most of those jurisdictions. And predictions would be speculative at best given that, especially in the context of local elections, voters' personal affiliations with candidates and views on particular issues can play a large role.

Unlike any of the standards proposed to allow crossover-district claims, the majority-minority rule relies on an objective, numerical test: Do minorities make up more than 50 percent of the voting-age population in the relevant geographic area? That rule provides straightforward guidance to courts and to those officials charged with drawing district lines to comply with § 2. Where an election district could be drawn in which minority voters form a majority but such a district is not drawn, or where a majority-minority district is cracked by assigning some voters elsewhere, then—assuming the other *Gingles* factors are also satisfied—denial of the opportunity to elect a candidate of choice is a present and discernible wrong that is not subject to the high degree of speculation and prediction attendant upon the analysis of crossover claims. Not an arbitrary invention, the majority-minority rule has its foundation in principles of democratic governance. The special significance, in the democratic process, of a majority means it is a special wrong when a minority group has 50 percent or more of the voting population and could constitute a compact voting majority but, despite racially polarized bloc voting, that group is not put into a district....

B

...

To the extent there is any doubt whether § 2 calls for the majority-minority rule, we resolve that doubt by avoiding serious constitutional concerns under the Equal Protection Clause.... If § 2 were interpreted to require crossover districts throughout the Nation, "it would unnecessarily infuse race into virtually every redistricting, raising serious constitutional questions." That interpretation would result in a substantial increase in the number of mandatory districts drawn with race as "the predominant factor motivating the legislature's decision."

On petitioners' view of the case courts and legislatures would need to scrutinize every factor that enters into districting to gauge its effect on crossover voting. Injecting this racial measure into the nationwide districting process would be of particular concern with respect to consideration of party registration or party influence. The easiest and most likely alliance for a group of minority voters is one with a political party, and some have suggested using minority voters' strength within a particular party as the proper yardstick under the first *Gingles* requirement. That approach would replace an objective, administrable rule with a difficult "judicial inquiry into party rules and local politics" to determine whether a minority group truly "controls" the dominant party's primary process. More troubling still is the inquiry's fusion of race and party affiliation as a determinant when partisan considerations themselves may be suspect in the drawing of district lines. Disregarding the majority-minority rule and relying on a combination of race and party to presume an effective majority would involve the law and courts in a perilous enterprise. It would rest on judicial predictions, as a matter of law, that race and party would hold together as an effective majority over time—at least for the decennial apportionment cycles and likely beyond. And thus would the relationship between race and party further distort and frustrate the search for neutral factors and principled rationales for districting....

C

Our holding that §2 does not require crossover districts does not consider the permissibility of such districts as a matter of legislative choice or discretion. Assuming a majority-minority district with a substantial minority population, a legislative determination, based on proper factors, to create two crossover districts may serve to diminish the significance and influence of race by encouraging minority and majority voters to work together toward a common goal. The option to draw such districts gives legislatures a choice that can lead to less racial isolation, not more....

Our holding also should not be interpreted to entrench majority-minority districts by statutory command, for that, too, could pose constitutional concerns. States that wish to draw crossover districts are free to do so where no other prohibition exists. Majority-minority districts are only required if all three *Gingles* factors are met and if §2 applies based on a totality of the circumstances. In areas with substantial crossover voting it is unlikely that the plaintiffs would be able to establish the third *Gingles* precondition—bloc voting by majority voters. In those areas majority-minority districts would not be required in the first place; and in the exercise of lawful discretion States could draw crossover districts as they deemed appropriate. States can—and in proper cases should—defend against alleged §2 violations by pointing to crossover voting patterns and to effective crossover districts. Those can be evidence, for example, of diminished bloc voting under the third *Gingles* factor or of equal political opportunity under the § 2 totality-of-the-circumstances analysis. And if there were a showing that a State intentionally drew district lines in order to destroy otherwise effective crossover districts, that would raise serious questions under both the Fourteenth and Fifteenth Amendments....

IV

Some commentators suggest that racially polarized voting is waning—as evidenced by, for example, the election of minority candidates where a majority of voters are white. Still, racial discrimination and racially polarized voting are not ancient history. Much remains to be done to ensure that citizens of all races have equal opportunity to share and participate in our democratic processes and traditions; and § 2 must be interpreted to ensure that continued progress.

It would be an irony, however, if § 2 were interpreted to entrench racial differences by expanding a "statute meant to hasten the waning of racism in American politics." Crossover districts are, by definition, the result of white voters joining forces with minority voters to elect their preferred candidate. The Voting Rights Act was passed to foster this cooperation. We decline now to expand the reaches of § 2 to require, by force of law, the voluntary cooperation our society has achieved. Only when a geographically compact group of minority voters could form a majority in a single-member district has the first *Gingles* requirement been met.

The judgment of the Supreme Court of North Carolina is affirmed.

It is so ordered.

Justice SOUTER, with whom Justice STEVENS, Justice GINSBURG, and Justice BREYER join, dissenting.

The question in this case is whether a minority with under 50% of the voting population of a proposed voting district can ever qualify under § 2 of the Voting Rights Act of 1965 (VRA) as residents of a putative district whose minority voters would have an opportunity "to elect representatives of their choice." If the answer is no, minority voters in such a district will have no right to claim relief under § 2 from a statewide districting scheme that dilutes minority voting rights. I would hold that the answer in law as well as in fact is sometimes yes: a district may be a minority-opportunity district so long as a cohesive minority population is large enough to elect its chosen candidate when combined with a reliable number of crossover voters from an otherwise polarized majority.

In the plurality's view, only a district with a minority population making up 50% or more of the citizen voting age population (CVAP) can provide a remedy to minority voters lacking an opportunity "to elect representatives of their choice." This is incorrect as a factual matter if the statutory phrase is given its natural meaning; minority voters in districts with minority populations under 50% routinely "elect representatives of their choice." The effects of the plurality's unwillingness to face this fact are disturbing by any measure and flatly at odds with the obvious purpose of the VRA. If districts with minority populations under 50% can never count as minority-opportunity districts to remedy a violation of the States' obligation to provide equal electoral opportunity under § 2, States will be required under the plurality's rule to pack black voters into additional majority-minority districts, contracting the number of districts where racial minorities are having success in transcending racial divisions in securing their preferred representation. The object of the VRA will now be promoting racial blocs, and the role of race in districting decisions as a proxy for political identification will be heightened by any measure....

II

Though this case arose under the Constitution of North Carolina, the dispositive issue is one of federal statutory law: whether a district with a minority population under 50%, but large enough to elect its chosen candidate with the help of majority voters disposed to support the minority favorite, can ever count as a district where minority voters have the opportunity "to elect representatives of their choice" for purposes of § 2. I think it clear from the nature of a vote-dilution claim and the text of § 2 that the answer must be yes. There is nothing in the statutory text to suggest that Congress meant to protect minority opportunity to elect solely by the creation of majority-minority districts. On the contrary, § 2 "focuses exclusively on the consequences of apportionment," as Congress made clear when it explicitly prescribed the ultimate functional approach: a totality of the circumstances test. And a functional analysis leaves no doubt that crossover districts vindicate the interest expressly protected by § 2: the opportunity to elect a desired representative....

[W]hether a district with a minority population under 50% of the CVAP may redress a violation of § 2 is a question of fact with an obvious answer: of course minority voters constituting less than 50% of the voting population can have an opportunity to elect the candidates of their choice, as amply shown by empirical studies confirming that such minority groups regularly elect their preferred candidates with the help of modest crossover by members of the majority. The North Carolina Supreme Court, for example, determined that voting districts with a black voting age population of as little as 38.37% have an opportunity to elect black candidates, a factual finding that has gone unchallenged and is well supported by electoral results in North Carolina. Of the nine House districts in which blacks make up more than 50% of the voting age population (VAP), all but two elected a black representative in the 2004 election. Of the 12 additional House districts in which blacks are over 39% of the VAP, all but one elected a black representative in the 2004 election. It would surely surprise legislators in North Carolina to suggest that black voters in these 12 districts cannot possibly have an opportunity to "elect [the] representatives of their choice."

It is of course true that the threshold population sufficient to provide minority voters with an opportunity to elect their candidates of choice is elastic, and the proportions will likely shift in the future, as they have in the past. That is, racial polarization has declined, and if it continues downward the first *Gingles* condition will get easier to satisfy.

But this is no reason to create an arbitrary threshold; the functional approach will continue to allow dismissal of claims for districts with minority populations too small to demonstrate an ability to elect, and with "crossovers" too numerous to allow an inference of vote dilution in the first place. No one, for example, would argue based on the record of experience in this case that a district with a 25% black population would meet the first *Gingles* condition. And the third *Gingles* requirement, majority-bloc voting, may well provide an analytical limit to claims based on crossover districts. But whatever this limit may be, we have no need to set it here, since the respondent state officials have stipulated to majority-bloc voting. In sum, § 2 addresses voting realities, and for practical purposes a 39%-minority district in which we know minorities have the potential to elect their preferred candidate is every bit as good as a 50%-minority district.

In fact, a crossover district is better. Recognizing crossover districts has the value of giving States greater flexibility to draw districting plans with a fair number of minority-opportunity districts, and this in turn allows for a beneficent reduction in the number of majority-minority districts with their "quintessentially race-conscious calculus," thereby moderating reliance on race as an exclusive determinant in districting decisions. A crossover is thus superior to a majority-minority district precisely because it requires polarized factions to break out of the mold and form the coalitions that discourage racial divisions.

III

. . .

B

. . .

2

The plurality is also concerned that recognizing the "potential" of anything under 50% would entail an exponential expansion of special minority districting; the plurality goes so far as to suggest that recognizing crossover districts as possible minority-opportunity districts would inherently "entitl[e] minority groups to the maximum possible voting strength." But this conclusion again reflects a confusion of the gatekeeping function of the *Gingles* conditions with the ultimate test for relief under § 2.

As already explained, the mere fact that all threshold *Gingles* conditions could be met and a district could be drawn with a minority population sufficiently large to elect the candidate of its choice does not require drawing such a district. This case simply is about the first *Gingles* condition, not about the number of minority-opportunity districts needed under § 2, and accepting Bartlett's position would in no way imply an obligation to maximize districts with minority voter potential. Under any interpretation of the first *Gingles* factor, the State must draw districts in a way that provides minority voters with a fair number of districts in which they have an opportunity to elect candidates of their choice; the only question here is which districts will count toward that total.

3

The plurality's fear of maximization finds a parallel in the concern that treating crossover districts as minority-opportunity districts would "create serious tension" with the third *Gingles* prerequisite of majority-bloc voting. The plurality finds "[i]t . . . difficult to see how the majority-bloc-voting requirement could be met in a district where, by definition, white voters join in sufficient numbers with minority voters to elect the minority's preferred candidate."

It is not difficult to see. If a minority population with 49% of the CVAP can elect the candidate of its choice with crossover by 2% of white voters, the minority "by definition" relies on white support to elect its preferred candidate. But this fact alone would raise no doubt, as a matter of definition or otherwise, that the majority-bloc-voting requirement could be met, since as much as 98% of the majority may have voted against the minority's candidate of choice. As explained above, the third *Gingles* condition may well impose an analytical floor to the minority population and a ceiling on the degree of crossover allowed in a crossover district; that is, the concept of majority-bloc voting requires that majority voters tend to stick together in a relatively high degree. The precise standard for determining majority-bloc voting is not at issue in this case, however; to refute the plurality's 50% rule, one need only recognize that racial cohesion of 98% would be bloc voting by any standard.

4

The plurality argues that qualifying crossover districts as minority-opportunity districts would be less administrable than demanding 50%, forcing courts to engage with the various factual and predictive questions that would come up in determining what percentage of majority voters would provide the voting minority with a chance at electoral success. But claims based on a State's failure to draw majority-minority districts raise the same issues of judicial judgment; even when the 50% threshold is satisfied, a court will still have to engage in factually messy enquiries about the "potential" such a district may afford, the degree of minority cohesion and majority-bloc voting, and the existence of vote dilution under a totality of the circumstances. The plurality's rule, therefore, conserves an uncertain amount of judicial resources, and only at the expense of ignoring a class of § 2 claims that this Court has no authority to strike from the statute's coverage. . . .

6

Finally, the plurality tries to support its insistence on a 50% threshold by invoking the policy of constitutional avoidance, which calls for construing a statute so as to avoid a possibly unconstitutional result. The plurality suggests that allowing a lower threshold would "require crossover districts throughout the Nation," thereby implicating the principle of *Shaw v. Reno* that districting with an excessive reliance on race is unconstitutional ("excessive" now being equated by the plurality with the frequency of creating opportunity districts). But the plurality has it precisely backwards. A State will inevitably draw some crossover districts as the natural byproduct of districting based on traditional factors. If these crossover districts count as minority-opportunity districts, the State will be much closer to meeting its § 2 obligation without any reference to race, and fewer minority-opportunity districts will, therefore, need to be created purposefully. But if, as a matter of law, only majority-minority districts provide a minority seeking equality with the opportunity to elect its preferred candidates, the State will have much further to go to create a sufficient number of minority-opportunity districts, will be required to bridge this gap by creating exclusively majority-minority districts, and will inevitably produce a districting plan that reflects a greater focus on race. The plurality, however, seems to believe that any reference to race in districting poses a constitutional concern, even a State's decision to reduce racial blocs in favor of crossover districts. A judicial position with these consequences is not constitutional avoidance.

IV

More serious than the plurality opinion's inconsistency with prior cases construing § 2 is the perversity of the results it portends. Consider the effect of the plurality's rule on North Carolina's districting scheme. Black voters make up approximately 20% of North Carolina's VAP and are distributed throughout 120 State House districts. As noted before, black voters constitute more than 50% of the VAP in 9 of these districts and over 39% of the VAP in an additional 12. Under a functional approach to § 2, black voters in North Carolina have an opportunity to elect (and regularly do elect) the representative of their choice in as many as 21 House districts, or 17.5% of North Carolina's total districts. North Carolina's districting plan is therefore close to providing black voters with proportionate electoral opportunity. According to the plurality, however, the remedy of a crossover district cannot provide opportunity to minority voters who lack it, and the requisite opportunity must therefore be lacking for minority voters already living in districts where they must rely on crossover. By the plurality's reckoning, then, black voters have an opportunity to elect representatives of their choice in, at most, nine North Carolina House districts. In the plurality's view, North Carolina must have a long way to go before it satisfies the § 2 requirement of equal electoral opportunity.

A State like North Carolina faced with the plurality's opinion, whether it wants to comply with § 2 or simply to avoid litigation, will, therefore, have no reason to create crossover districts. Section 2 recognizes no need for such districts, from which it follows that they can neither be required nor be created to help the State meet its obligation of equal electoral opportunity under § 2. And if a legislature were induced to draw a crossover district by the plurality's encouragement to create them voluntarily, it would open itself to attack by the plurality based on the pointed suggestion that a policy favoring crossover districts runs counter to *Shaw*. The plurality has thus boiled § 2 down to one option: the best way to avoid suit under § 2, and the only way to comply with § 2, is by drawing district lines in a way that packs minority voters into majority-minority districts, probably eradicating crossover districts in the process.

Perhaps the plurality recognizes this aberrant implication, for it eventually attempts to disavow it. It asserts that "§ 2 allows States to choose their own method of complying with the Voting Rights Act, and we have said that may include drawing crossover districts.... [But] § 2 does not mandate creating or preserving crossover districts." But this is judicial fiat, not legal reasoning; the plurality does not even attempt to explain how a crossover district can be a minority-opportunity district when assessing the compliance of a districting plan with § 2, but cannot be one when sought as a remedy to a § 2 violation. The plurality cannot have it both ways. If voluntarily drawing a crossover district brings a State into compliance with § 2, then requiring creation of a crossover district must be a way to remedy a violation of § 2, and eliminating a crossover district must in some cases take a State out of compliance with the statute. And when the elimination of a crossover district does cause a violation of § 2, I cannot fathom why a voter in that district should not be able to bring a claim to remedy it.

In short, to the extent the plurality's holding is taken to control future results, the plurality has eliminated the protection of § 2 for the districts that best vindicate the goals of the statute, and has done all it can to force the States to perpetuate racially concentrated districts, the quintessential manifestations of race consciousness in American politics.

I respectfully dissent.

Notes and Questions

1. In an important passage, the plurality states: "But because they form only 39 percent of the voting-age population in District 18, African-Americans standing alone have no better or worse opportunity to elect a candidate than does any other group of voters with the same relative voting strength." 556 U.S. at 14 (plurality opinion). Is this true? What if (as is likely) there is racially polarized voting between blacks and whites—but *not* between a different 39 percent minority (say blondes) and the majority?

2. The plurality contends that if crossover district claims were permitted, then "serious tension" would ensue between *Gingles*'s first and third prongs. To see why, suppose that a potential district is 25 percent black and 75 percent white, that black voters are perfectly cohesive, and that both groups turn out to vote at the same rate. Then for the black voters' candidate of choice to prevail, she would have to receive their 25 percent of the vote, plus another 25 percent (plus one) from white voters. The latter 25 percent represents one-third of the white vote, that is, a crossover rate of 33 percent. A crossover rate this high arguably means there is insufficient white bloc voting to satisfy *Gingles*'s third prong.

Justice Souter responds with a different numerical example: If minority voters comprise 49 percent of a potential district, then a crossover rate as low as 2 percent (and white bloc voting as high as 98 percent) would be enough to enable the election of the minority-preferred candidate. Is the point of this example to show that it is more common than other scenarios? Or to establish that friction between *Gingles*'s first and third prongs is not inevitable in crossover districts?

3. Perhaps the strongest argument for a strict 50 percent threshold is administrability; it is easy to tell whether a potential district falls above or below this line, but harder to determine when a minority group is large enough—given variations in turnout, minority cohesiveness, and white bloc voting—to elect the candidate of its choice. For how much should this consideration count given that it is not mentioned in the statutory text? Given that courts must *already* grapple with turnout, the extent of racial polarization, the correlation between race and party, and several other thorny issues in *subsequent* stages of the Section 2 analysis?

In his dissent, Justice Breyer proposes an alternative to the plurality's 50 percent threshold:

> Suppose we pick a numerical ratio that requires the minority voting age population to be twice as large as the percentage of majority crossover votes needed to elect the minority's preferred candidate. We would calculate the latter (the percentage of majority crossover votes the minority voters need) to take account of both the percentage of minority voting age population in the district and the cohesiveness with which they vote. Thus, if minority voters account for 45% of the voters in a district and 89% of those voters tend to vote cohesively as a group, then the minority needs a crossover vote of about 20% of the majority voters to elect its preferred candidate. (Such a district with 100 voters would have 45 minority voters and 55 majority voters; 40 minority voters would vote for the minority group's preferred candidate at election time; the minority voters would need 11 more votes to elect their preferred candidate; and 11 is about 20% of the majority's 55.)

Id. at 46 (Breyer, J., dissenting). How compelling is Justice Breyer's approach? Is it actually comparable in its administrability to the plurality's rule? In practice, given typical rates of minority cohesion and white bloc voting, Justice Breyer's approach would set a minority population floor in the 40-45 percent range.

4. The plurality argues that if crossover district claims were recognized, then race would become an even larger part of redistricting than it already is. The logic is the following: There are many areas in the country where reasonably compact *majority-minority* districts cannot be drawn, but reasonably compact *crossover* districts can be. In these areas, Section 2 claims cannot currently be brought. But these claims would become colorable if only the potential existence of crossover districts had to be shown. Thus Section 2—a provision that inherently requires the consideration of race—would become more broadly applicable.

Justice Souter's rebuttal is that crossover districts are less problematic from a racialization perspective than majority-minority districts. In the former, minority voters must band together with white voters to elect minority-preferred candidates. This interracial cooperation is highly desirable and conveys a message of collaborative rather than antagonistic racial politics. Who has the better of this debate? How should a smaller number of majority-minority districts (the likely outcome of the plurality's rule) be weighed against a larger number of crossover districts (the probable product of Justice Souter's approach)?

5. Suppose a jurisdiction decides to draw a crossover district in a region where a majority-minority district could have been drawn instead. Is the jurisdiction now vulnerable to a Section 2 challenge? As noted by Justice Souter, the reasoning of the plurality's opinion suggests the answer is yes. A plaintiff would be able to point to the existence of a potential majority-minority district, and the actual crossover district would not be deemed a valid remedy. However, the plurality balks at this implication, stating that "States can—and in proper cases should—defend against alleged § 2 violations by pointing to crossover voting patterns and to effective crossover districts." *Id.* at 24 (plurality opinion). The best reading of current law is therefore the following: *Plaintiffs* must always prove that an additional majority-minority district could have been designed. But *defendants* may respond to such proof by showing that a crossover district already exists in the same area as the putative majority-minority district.

What about the opposite scenario—a jurisdiction replacing old crossover districts with new majority-minority districts? North Carolina did exactly that in the 2010 redistricting cycle, converting two congressional, nine state senate, and fourteen state house crossover districts into majority-minority districts. When these plans were disputed on racial gerrymandering grounds, the state responded that it was simply trying to comply with *Bartlett*. In *Cooper v. Harris*, 137 S. Ct. 1455 (2017) (to which we return in Part III), the Supreme Court clarified that *Bartlett* does *not* require majority-minority districts to be created wherever Section 2 liability could otherwise be established. The Court described the state's position: "that if, as *Strickland* held, § 2 does not *require* crossover districts (for groups insufficiently large under *Gingles*), then § 2 also cannot be *satisfied by* crossover districts (for groups in fact meeting *Gingles*'s size condition)." *Id.* at 1472. This position, declared the Court, "is at war with our § 2 jurisprudence." *Id.* It turns "the third *Gingles* condition [into] no condition at all" and amounts to "a pure error of law." *Id.*

And what if a state has already drawn a majority-minority district, but minority voters are still unable to elect their preferred candidate (due to low turnout or less-than-perfect cohesion)? Can the state still be found liable under Section 2? The Fifth Circuit recently said yes, striking down a majority-minority Mississippi state senate district as dilutive. See *Thomas v. Bryant*, 938 F.3d 134 (5th Cir. 2019). In so ruling, the court rejected the idea that *Bartlett* barred Section 2 claims against majority-minority districts, explaining that "the Court did not hold . . . that if the district being challenged already contains a majority-minority population, then a § 2 claim is precluded." *Id.* at 157. However, Judge Willett dissented on this ground, arguing that the majority's "blinkered focus on outcomes rather than opportunity clashes with the VRA's express text and relevant caselaw, both of which underscore electoral participation and opportunity— not electoral success." *Id.* at 183 (Willett, J., dissenting). Sitting en banc, the Fifth Circuit also vacated the decision below on the ground that the case became moot after the 2019 election was held. See *Thomas v. Reeves*, 961 F.3d 800 (5th Cir. 2020) (en banc).

6. How should population be counted in determining whether the minority group in question can constitute a majority of a reasonably compact district? Should total population, voting age population (VAP), or citizen voting age population (CVAP) be used? When Latinos are in question, significant numbers are often recent immigrants, so the Latino percentage of citizens is likely to be substantially below their percentage of the total population or the voting age population.[j] The Supreme Court has not explicitly clarified the correct unit of analysis. In *LULAC*, however, the Court referred repeatedly to CVAP, leading most observers to think that was the relevant metric. See also *Cano v. Davis*, 211 F. Supp. 2d 1208, 1233 (C.D. Cal. 2002) ("The Ninth Circuit, along with every other circuit to consider the issue, has held that CVAP is the appropriate measure to use in determining whether an additional effective majority-minority district can be created.").

7. Suppose there is no single minority community that is large enough to satisfy the first *Gingles* prong, but that two such communities— African Americans and Latinos, for example, or Latinos and Asian Americans— would together be large enough, if combined in a district. Is the first prong satisfied? Most courts that have considered this question have admitted the possibility that a "rainbow coalition" can establish a Section 2 claim, but only if the component minorities can show that they in fact constitute an electoral coalition. See, *e.g.*, *Nixon v. Kent County*, 34 F.3d 369 (6th Cir. 1994); *Brewer v. Ham*, 876 F.2d 448, 454 (5th Cir. 1989); *Romero v. City of Pomona*, 883 F.2d 1418, 1426–27 (9th Cir. 1989). The Supreme Court conditionally endorsed this approach in *Growe v. Emison*, 507 U.S. 25, 41 (1993):

> Assuming (without deciding) that it was permissible for the District Court to combine distinct ethnic and language minority groups for purposes of assessing compliance with § 2, when dilution of the power of such an agglomerated political bloc is the basis for an alleged violation, proof of minority political cohesion is all the more essential.

What if no *two* minority communities are numerous enough to comprise a majority of a hypothetical district but *three* minority groups would be sufficiently numerous? In *Holloway v. City of Virginia Beach*, 2021 WL 1226554 (E.D. Va. Mar. 31, 2021), the district court ruled in favor of a claim brought by African American, Hispanic, and Asian American voters. Notably, the court found that these groups were politically cohesive because of not only their voting patterns but also their shared political advocacy. According to the court, "qualitative evidence can be used as a strong

---

j. The same could also be true if the plaintiff group consisted of Asian Americans. However, concentrations of Asian American populations large enough to be a majority in a legislative district are still relatively rare.

metric for determining the political cohesion of a minority group." *Id.* at *30. Do you agree that political cohesion can be ascertained based on qualitative as well as quantitative evidence?

8. Did *Bartlett* make a difference? Perhaps not, because prior to the decision, "no federal court of appeals . . . held that § 2 requires creation of coalition districts. Instead, all to consider the question . . . interpreted the first *Gingles* factor to require a majority-minority standard." 556 U.S. at 19 (plurality opinion). Thus before and after *Bartlett*, most plaintiffs tried to show that additional majority-minority districts could be drawn, and most jurisdictions remedied Section 2 violations by creating such districts. Justice Souter's vision of crossover districts steadily supplanting majority-minority districts largely remains a road not traveled.

9. Gingles*'s Second and Third Prongs.* As we have seen, while *Bartlett* is primarily about *Gingles*'s first prong, it also implicates the second and third prongs—in particular, how the size of the minority population and the rate of crossover voting by the white majority are related. Because no Supreme Court case since *Gingles* has focused on racial polarization in voting, this is an appropriate place to consider this important topic.

To begin with, why must minority political cohesion and white bloc voting be demonstrated in a Section 2 suit? Consider the answer given by Stephanopoulos, *Race, Place, and Power*, *supra*, 68 Stanford Law Review at 1338:

> Conceptually, there can be vote dilution only if there is racial polarization in voting. A minority group that is not politically cohesive has no *preferred* candidate, no candidate *of choice*, to rally behind. Likewise, a white majority that does not vote as a bloc also does not prevent the election of a minority-preferred candidate (if there is one). Such a candidate is able to compete freely, to appeal to voters of all stripes, without running into a wall of unyielding white opposition. As the Court reasoned in [*Growe*], "the 'minority political cohesion' and 'majority bloc voting' showings are needed to establish that the challenged districting thwarts a distinctive minority vote by submerging it in a larger white voting population. Unless these points are established, there neither has been a wrong nor can be a remedy."

Note that this discussion assumes that the purpose of Section 2 is to promote the election of minority-preferred candidates—and not, say, to address breakdowns of normal coalitional politics or to combat discriminatory attitudes held by white voters.

Next, how should racial polarization in voting be calculated? *Gingles* itself referred approvingly to two techniques: extreme case analysis and bivariate ecological regression. The former entails (1) identifying precincts that are highly (usually over 90 percent) racially homogeneous; (2) compiling election results involving a minority candidate of choice for these precincts; and (3) using these results to determine the extent of minority political cohesion and white bloc voting. Under bivariate ecological regression, on the other hand, *all* precincts are used (not just racially homogeneous ones). The share of the vote received by the minority-preferred candidate is then regressed on each precinct's minority population share. The fit of this regression indicates how well electoral preferences are explained by race, while the x- and y-intercepts denote the levels of minority political cohesion and white bloc voting. See Bernard Grofman et al., Minority Representation and the Quest for Voting Equality 82–108 (1992) (describing these techniques in detail); Gary King, A Solution to the Ecological Inference Problem: Reconstructing Individual Behavior from Aggregate Data (1997) (introducing a more sophisticated version of bivariate ecological regression, known as King's ecological inference); D. James Greiner, *Ecological Inference in Voting Rights Act Disputes: Where Are We Now, and Where Do We Want to Be?*, 47 Jurimetrics 115, 155–59 (2007) (exhaustively listing the dozens of lower court cases that have relied on these techniques).

While even this level of methodological detail may be too much for some readers, courts have also had to wrestle with several additional technical issues. For example, should quantitative cutoffs be set, below which minority political cohesion and white bloc voting should be deemed absent? Courts have generally refrained from trying to specify such thresholds. See Elmendorf et al., *Racially Polarized Voting, supra*, 83 University of Chicago Law Review at 611-12. Should "endogenous" elections for the institution at issue, or "exogenous" elections for other (statewide or national) offices, be used? Courts have tended to prefer endogenous races but still to consult exogenous ones. See *id.* at 613, 616. What about primary versus general elections? Here courts have been partial toward primary elections, on the ground that they are less affected by partisanship and so more indicative of the influence of race. See *id.* at 616-17. Who counts as a minority candidate of choice? The judicial penchant has been presumptively to include minority members, and sometimes to include white candidates when there is strong evidence of their support from minority voters. See *id.* at 621–24. Lastly, should precincts' racial composition be determined using Census data (which covers all eligible voters) or voter files (which can be used to zero in on actual voters only)? The vast majority of courts have relied on Census data, but the Second Circuit recently approved a technique known as Bayesian Improved Surname Geocoding that begins with voter files and then employs an algorithm to predict the race of each voter. See *Clerveaux v. East Ramapo Cent. Sch. Dist.*, 984 F.2d 213 (2d Cir. 2021).

The analysis of racial polarization in voting has been further complicated by two more problems—to which scholars have proposed innovative solutions. The first is that both extreme case analysis and ecological regression become less feasible when there are multiple minority groups (not just one) living in a more residentially integrated (rather than segregated) pattern. In response, D. James Greiner, *Re-Solidifying Racial Bloc Voting: Empirics and Legal Doctrine in the Melting Pot*, 86 Indiana Law Journal 447 (2011), has shown how election results can be combined with responses to an opinion survey to produce accurate polarization estimates even in the face of greater diversity and integration. The second, even more fundamental problem is that election results are only partly a function of voters' preferences. They are also inevitably a function of candidates' own characteristics: their race, ideology, competence, and so on. Consequently, *observed* levels of polarization are an ambiguous proxy for *underlying* levels, controlling for candidates' attributes. In response, Elmendorf et al., *Racially Polarized Voting*, *supra*, suggest clever experiments in which candidates' features are either set or varied randomly, and subjects are then asked which candidate they would vote for.

Turning back to questions that have occupied courts, should it matter what the *reasons* are for racial polarization in voting? A plurality in *Gingles* said no: "[O]nly the correlation between race of voter and selection of certain candidates, not the causes of the correlation, matters." 478 U.S. at 63 (plurality opinion). This position was implicitly ratified in *LULAC*, in which the Court thought it "evident that the second and third *Gingles* preconditions . . . are present" where "92% of Latinos voted against Bonilla . . . while 88% of non-Latinos voted for him" — without ever asking what might explain this divergence. 548 U.S. at 427. On the other hand, five Justices in *Gingles* expressed some unease about this approach to polarization. Several lower courts have also held that polarization that is attributable to non-racial factors — such as socioeconomic status or partisan preference — does not satisfy the second and third *Gingles* prongs. As the Fifth Circuit quipped in a major en banc decision, "§ 2 is implicated only where Democrats lose because they are black, not where blacks lose because they are Democrats." *LULAC v. Clements*, 999 F.2d 831, 854 (5th Cir. 1993) (en banc). See also, *e.g.*, *Uno v. City of Holyoke*, 72 F.3d 973, 981 (1st Cir. 1995) ("[P]laintiffs cannot prevail on a VRA § 2 claim if there is significantly probative evidence that whites voted as a bloc for reasons wholly unrelated to racial animus."); Richard L. Hasen, *Race or Party, Race as Party, or Party All the Time: Three Uneasy Approaches to Conjoined Polarization in Redistricting and Voting Cases*, 59 William & Mary Law Review 1837 (2018) (explaining how racial and partisan polarization are interrelated and how this link complicates Voting Rights Act doctrine).

Lastly, how has racial polarization in voting changed over time? In the 1990s and early 2000s, a wave of scholarship expressed optimism that white crossover voting was rising, and thus that polarization was declining. See, *e.g.*, Charles S. Bullock, III & Richard E. Dunn, *The Demise of Racial Districting and the Future of Black Representation*, 48 Emory Law Journal 1209 (1999); Bernard Grofman et al., *Drawing Effective Minority Districts: A Conceptual Framework and Some Empirical Evidence*, 79 North Carolina Law Review 1383 (2001). More recently, however, the tide has turned pessimistic again. When Congress reauthorized Section 5 in 2006, it heard testimony that white bloc voting remained high in virtually all covered jurisdictions. See S. Rep. No. 109-295, at 123 (2006). Similarly, Stephen Ansolabehere et al., *Race, Region, and Vote Choice in the 2008 Election: Implications for the Future of the Voting Rights Act*, 123 Harvard Law Review 1385 (2010), and Stephanopoulos, *Race, Place, and Power*, *supra*, both found that black-white and Latino-white polarization have stayed stable — and stark — for decades.

10. *Totality of Circumstances*. If plaintiffs satisfy *Gingles*'s three preconditions for liability, the analysis then progresses to the totality-of-circumstances stage. At this

stage, courts consider holistically the ten or so factors identified by the 1982 Senate Report. See S. Rep. No. 97-417, at 28–29 (1982); Katz et al., *Documenting Discrimination, supra*, 39 University of Michigan Journal of Law Reform at 675-730 (exhaustively surveying courts' findings with respect to these factors). As the following case makes clear, courts also take into account the proportionality of the representation that minority voters already enjoy in the jurisdiction.

Johnson v. De Grandy

512 U.S. 997 (1994)

Justice SOUTER delivered the opinion of the Court.

These consolidated cases are about the meaning of vote dilution and the facts required to show it, when § 2 of the Voting Rights Act of 1965 is applied to challenges to single-member legislative districts. We hold that no violation of § 2 can be found here, where, in spite of continuing discrimination and racial bloc voting, minority voters form effective voting majorities in a number of districts roughly proportional to the minority voters' respective shares in the voting-age population. While such proportionality is not dispositive in a challenge to single-member districting, it is a relevant fact in the totality of circumstances to be analyzed when determining whether members of a minority group have "less opportunity than other members of the electorate to participate in the political process and to elect representatives of their choice."

I

[After the State of Florida enacted new state house and state senate maps in April 1992, collectively known as SJR 2–G, the plaintiffs] charge[d] the new reapportionment plan with violating § 2. They claimed that SJR 2–G "'unlawfully fragments cohesive minority communities and otherwise impermissibly submerges their right to vote and to participate in the electoral process,'" and they pointed to areas around the State where black or Hispanic populations could have formed a voting majority in a politically cohesive, reasonably compact district (or in more than one), if SJR 2–G had not fragmented each group among several districts or packed it into just a few.

The Department of Justice filed a similar complaint, naming the State of Florida and several elected officials as defendants and claiming that SJR 2–G diluted the voting strength of blacks and Hispanics in two parts of the State in violation of § 2. The Government alleged that SJR 2–G diluted the votes of the Hispanic population in an area largely covered by Dade County (including Miami) and the black population in an area covering much of Escambia County (including Pensacola). . . .

III

On the merits of the vote dilution claims covering the House districts, the crux of the State's argument is the power of Hispanics under SJR 2–G to elect candidates of their choice in a number of districts that mirrors their share of the Dade County area's voting-age population (i.e., 9 out of 20 House districts); this power, according to the State, bars any finding that the plan dilutes Hispanic voting strength. The District Court is said to have missed that conclusion by mistaking our precedents to require the plan to maximize the number of Hispanic-controlled districts. . . .

B

We do, however, part company from the District Court in assessing the totality of circumstances. The District Court found that the three *Gingles* preconditions were satisfied, and that Hispanics had suffered historically from official discrimination, the social, economic, and political effects of which they generally continued to feel. Without more, and on the apparent assumption that what could have been done to create additional Hispanic supermajority districts should have been done, the District Court found a violation of § 2. But the assumption was erroneous, and more is required, as a review of *Gingles* will show.

1

. . . But if *Gingles* so clearly identified the three [preconditions] as generally necessary to prove a § 2 claim, it just as clearly declined to hold them sufficient in combination, either in the sense that a court's examination of relevant circumstances was complete once the three factors were found to exist, or in the sense that the three in combination necessarily and in all circumstances demonstrated dilution. This was true not only because bloc voting was a matter of degree, with a variable legal significance depending on other facts, but also because the ultimate conclusions about equality or inequality of opportunity were intended by Congress to be judgments resting on comprehensive, not limited, canvassing of relevant facts. Lack of electoral success is evidence of vote dilution, but courts must also examine other evidence in the totality of circumstances, including the extent of the opportunities minority voters enjoy to participate in the political processes. To be sure, some § 2 plaintiffs may have easy cases, but although lack of equal electoral opportunity may be readily imagined and unsurprising when demonstrated under circumstances that include the three essential *Gingles* factors, that conclusion must still be addressed explicitly, and without isolating any other arguably relevant facts from the act of judgment.

2

If the three *Gingles* factors may not be isolated as sufficient, standing alone, to prove dilution in every multimember district challenge, a fortiori they must not be when the challenge goes to a series of single-member districts, where dilution may be more difficult to grasp. Plaintiffs challenging single-member districts may claim, not total submergence, but partial submergence; not the chance for some electoral success in place of none, but the chance for more success in place of some. When the question thus comes down to the reasonableness of drawing a series of district lines in one combination of places rather than another, judgments about inequality may become closer calls. As facts beyond the ambit of the three *Gingles* factors loom correspondingly larger, factfinders cannot rest uncritically on assumptions about the force of the *Gingles* factors in pointing to dilution.

The cases now before us, of course, fall on this more complex side of the divide, requiring a court to determine whether provision for somewhat fewer majority-minority districts than the number sought by the plaintiffs was dilution of the minority votes. The District Court was accordingly required to assess the probative significance of the *Gingles* factors critically after considering the further circumstances with arguable bearing on the issue of equal political opportunity. We think that in finding dilution here the District Court misjudged the relative importance of the *Gingles* factors and of historical discrimination, measured against evidence tending to show that in spite of these facts, SJR 2–G would provide minority voters with an equal measure of political and electoral opportunity.

The District Court did not, to be sure, commit the error of treating the three *Gingles* conditions as exhausting the enquiry required by § 2. Consistently with *Gingles*, the court received evidence of racial relations outside the immediate confines of voting behavior and found a history of discrimination against Hispanic voters continuing in society generally to the present day. But the District Court was not critical enough in asking whether a history of persistent discrimination reflected in the larger society and its bloc-voting behavior portended any dilutive effect from a newly proposed districting scheme, whose pertinent features were majority-minority districts in substantial proportion to the minority's share of voting-age population. The court failed to ask whether the totality of facts, including those pointing to proportionality, showed that the new scheme would deny minority voters equal political opportunity.

Treating equal political opportunity as the focus of the enquiry, we do not see how these district lines, apparently providing political effectiveness in proportion to voting-age numbers, deny equal political opportunity. The record establishes that Hispanics constitute 50 percent of the voting-age population in Dade County and under SJR 2–G would make up supermajorities in 9 of the 18 House districts located primarily within the county. Likewise, if one considers the 20 House districts located at least in part within Dade County, the record indicates that Hispanics would be an effective voting majority in 45 percent of them (i.e., nine), and would constitute 47 percent of the voting-age population in the area. In other words, under SJR 2–G Hispanics in the Dade County area would enjoy substantial proportionality. On this evidence, we think the State's scheme would thwart the historical tendency to exclude Hispanics, not encourage or perpetuate it. Thus in spite of that history and its legacy, including the racial cleavages that characterize Dade County politics today, we see no grounds for holding in these cases that SJR 2–G's district lines diluted the votes cast by Hispanic voters.

The De Grandy plaintiffs urge us to put more weight on the District Court's findings of packing and fragmentation, allegedly accomplished by the way the State drew certain specific lines.... We would agree that where a State has split (or lumped) minority neighborhoods that would have been grouped into a single district (or spread among several) if the State had employed the same line-drawing standards in minority neighborhoods as it used elsewhere in the jurisdiction, the inconsistent treatment might be significant evidence of a § 2 violation, even in the face of proportionality. . . . But even if one imputed a greater significance to the accounts of testimony, they would boil down to findings that several of SJR 2–G's district lines separate portions of Hispanic neighborhoods, while another district line draws several Hispanic neighborhoods into a single district. This, however, would be to say only that lines could have been drawn elsewhere, nothing more. But some dividing by district lines and combining within them is virtually inevitable and befalls any population group of substantial size. Attaching the labels "packing" and "fragmenting" to these phenomena, without more, does not make the result vote dilution when the minority group enjoys substantial proportionality.

3

It may be that the significance of the facts under § 2 was obscured by the rule of thumb apparently adopted by the District Court, that anything short of the maximum number of majority-minority districts consistent with the *Gingles* conditions would violate § 2, at least where societal discrimination against the minority had occurred and continued to occur. But reading the first *Gingles* condition in effect to define dilution as a failure to maximize in the face of bloc voting (plus some other incidents of societal bias to be expected where bloc voting occurs) causes its own dangers, and they are not to be courted.

Assume a hypothetical jurisdiction of 1,000 voters divided into 10 districts of 100 each, where members of a minority group make up 40 percent of the voting population and voting is totally polarized along racial lines. With the right geographic dispersion to satisfy the compactness requirement, and with careful manipulation of district lines, the minority voters might be placed in control of as many as 7 of the 10 districts. Each such district could be drawn with at least 51 members of the minority group, and whether the remaining minority voters were added to the groupings of 51 for safety or scattered in the other three districts, minority voters would be able to elect candidates of their choice in all seven districts. The point of the hypothetical is not, of course, that any given district is likely to be open to such extreme manipulation, or that bare majorities are likely to vote in full force and strictly along racial lines, but that reading § 2 to define dilution as any failure to maximize tends to obscure the very object of the statute and to run counter to its textually stated purpose. One may suspect vote dilution from political famine, but one is not entitled to suspect (much less infer) dilution from mere failure to guarantee a political feast. However prejudiced a society might be, it would be absurd to suggest that the failure of a districting scheme to provide a minority group with effective political power 75 percent above its numerical strength indicates a denial of equal participation in the political process. Failure to maximize cannot be the measure of § 2.

4

While, for obvious reasons, the State agrees that a failure to leverage minority political strength to the maximum possible point of power is not definitive of dilution in bloc-voting societies, it seeks to impart a measure of determinacy by applying a definitive rule of its own: that as a matter of law no dilution occurs whenever the percentage of single-member districts in which minority voters form an effective majority mirrors the minority voters' percentage of the relevant population. Proportionality so defined would thus be a safe harbor for any districting scheme.

The safety would be in derogation of the statutory text and its considered purpose, however, and of the ideal that the Voting Rights Act of 1965 attempts to foster. An inflexible rule would run counter to the textual command of § 2, that the presence or absence of a violation be assessed "based on the totality of circumstances." . . . In a substantial number of voting jurisdictions, that past reality has included such reprehensible practices as ballot box stuffing, outright violence, discretionary registration, property requirements, the poll tax, and the white primary; and other practices censurable when the object of their use is discriminatory, such as at-large elections, runoff requirements, anti-single-shot devices, gerrymandering, the impeachment of office-holders, the annexation or deannexation of territory, and the creation or elimination of elective offices. Some of those expedients could occur even in a jurisdiction with numerically demonstrable proportionality; the harbor safe for States would thus not be safe for voters. It is, in short, for good reason that we have been, and remain, chary of entertaining a simplification of the sort the State now urges upon us.

Even if the State's safe harbor were open only in cases of alleged dilution by the manipulation of district lines, however, it would rest on an unexplored premise of highly suspect validity: that in any given voting jurisdiction (or portion of that jurisdiction under consideration), the rights of some minority voters under § 2 may be traded off against the rights of other members of the same minority class. Under the State's view, the most blatant racial gerrymandering in half of a county's single-member districts would be irrelevant under § 2 if offset by political gerrymandering in the other half, so long as proportionality was the bottom line.

Finally, we reject the safe harbor rule because of a tendency the State would itself certainly condemn, a tendency to promote and perpetuate efforts to devise majority-minority districts even in circumstances where they may not be necessary to achieve equal political and electoral opportunity. Because in its simplest form the State's rule would shield from § 2 challenge a districting scheme in which the number of majority-minority districts reflected the minority's share of the relevant population, the conclusiveness of the rule might be an irresistible inducement to create such districts. It bears recalling, however, that for all the virtues of majority-minority districts as remedial devices, they rely on a quintessentially race-conscious calculus aptly described as the "politics of second best." If the lesson of *Gingles* is that society's racial and ethnic cleavages sometimes necessitate majority-minority districts to ensure equal political and electoral opportunity, that should not obscure the fact that there are communities in which minority citizens are able to form coalitions with voters from other racial and ethnic groups, having no need to be a majority within a single district in order to elect candidates of their choice. Those candidates may not represent perfection to every minority voter, but minority voters are not immune from the obligation to pull, haul, and trade to find common political ground, the virtue of which is not to be slighted in applying a statute meant to hasten the waning of racism in American politics.

It is enough to say that, while proportionality in the sense used here is obviously an indication that minority voters have an equal opportunity, in spite of racial polarization, "to participate in the political process and to elect representatives of their choice," the degree of probative value assigned to proportionality may vary with other facts. No single statistic provides courts with a shortcut to determine whether a set of single-member districts unlawfully dilutes minority voting strength. . . .

IV

Having found insufficient evidence of vote dilution in the drawing of House districts in the Dade County area, we look now to the comparable districts for the state Senate. As in the case of House districts, we understand the District Court to have misapprehended the legal test for vote dilution when it found a violation of § 2 in the location of the Senate district lines. Because the court did not modify the State's plan, however, we hold the ultimate result correct in this instance.

SJR 2–G creates 40 single-member Senate districts, 5 of them wholly within Dade County. Of these five, three have Hispanic supermajorities of at least 64 percent, and one has a clear majority of black voters. Two more Senate districts crossing county lines include substantial numbers of Dade County voters, and in one of these, black voters, although not close to a majority, are able to elect representatives of their choice with the aid of cross-over votes.

Within this seven-district Dade County area, both minority groups enjoy rough proportionality. The voting-age population in the seven-district area is 44.8 percent Hispanic and 15.8 percent black. Hispanics predominate in 42.9 percent of the districts (three out of seven), as do blacks in 14.3 percent of them (one out of seven). While these numbers indicate something just short of perfect proportionality (42.9 percent against 44.8; 14.3 percent against 15.8), the opposite is true of the five districts located wholly within Dade County. . . .

We affirm the District Court's decision to leave the State's plan for Florida State Senate districts undisturbed. As in the case of the House districts, the totality of circumstances appears not to support a finding of vote dilution here, where both minority groups constitute effective voting majorities in a number of state Senate districts substantially proportional to their share in the population, and where plaintiffs have not produced evidence otherwise indicating that under SJR 2–G voters in either minority group have "less opportunity than other members of the electorate to participate in the political process and to elect representatives of their choice." . . .

It is so ordered.

Notes and Questions

1. After *Gingles* itself, *De Grandy* is probably the Supreme Court's most doctrinally significant decision regarding Section 2. It clarifies, first, that liability does not automatically follow when the three *Gingles* preconditions are satisfied. Second, in the words of Justice O'Connor's concurring opinion, it holds that the proportionality of a minority group's representation "is *always* relevant evidence in determining vote dilution, but is *never* itself dispositive." 512 U.S. at 1025 (O'Connor, J., concurring). And third, it explains how proportionality is to be determined. It is the number of districts in which minority voters are able to elect their preferred candidates divided by the total number of districts. If this proportion is below the minority share of the population, then a Section 2 claim that makes it to the totality-of-circumstances stage is strengthened. Conversely, if this proportion is near or above the minority share of the population, then a Section 2 claim is undermined.

2. Within which geographic area should proportionality be evaluated? In *De Grandy*, the Court considered the proportionality of Latino and African American representation in and around Dade County. In *LULAC*, however, the Court stated that this narrow focus was "[b]ased on the parties' apparent agreement that the proper frame of reference was the Dade County area." 548 U.S. at 436. Typically, though, "the answer in these cases is to look at proportionality statewide." *Id.* The Court elaborated:

> The role of proportionality is not to displace this local appraisal or to allow the State to trade off the rights of some against the rights of others. Instead, it provides some evidence of whether "the political processes leading to nomination or election in the State or political subdivision are not equally open to participation." For this purpose, the State's seven-district area is arbitrary. It just as easily could have included six or eight districts. Appellants have alleged statewide vote dilution based on a statewide plan, so the electoral opportunities of Latinos across the State can bear on whether the lack of electoral opportunity for Latinos in District 23 is a consequence of Plan 1374C's redrawing of lines or simply a consequence of the inevitable "win some, lose some" in a State with racial bloc voting. Indeed, several of the other factors in the totality of circumstances have been characterized with reference to the State as a whole. Particularly given the presence of racially polarized voting — and the possible submergence of minority votes — throughout Texas, it makes sense to use the entire State in assessing proportionality.
>
> Looking statewide, there are 32 congressional districts. The five reasonably compact Latino opportunity districts amount to roughly 16% of the total, while Latinos make up 22% of Texas' citizen voting-age population.... Latinos are, therefore, two districts shy of proportional representation....

Id. at 437-38. Why should regions of a state with few minority voters, in which no minority-opportunity districts can be constructed, be included in the proportionality inquiry?

3. Was *De Grandy* inevitable? Under the *Gingles* framework as it existed before *De Grandy*, Section 2 suits could seemingly be brought until every possible, reasonably compact, minority-opportunity district had been created—even if minority voters would enjoy disproportionately high representation as a result. Each such suit would be able to satisfy the *Gingles* preconditions (assuming racial polarization was present) and would receive the same support at the totality-of-circumstances stage from the list of Senate factors. But as the *De Grandy* Court notes, this is an absurd conclusion. "One may suspect vote dilution from political famine, but one is not entitled to suspect (much less infer) dilution from mere failure to guarantee a political feast." 512 U.S. at 1017. A ruling like *De Grandy* may thus have been necessary to cabin the reach of *Gingles* and to prevent it from mandating the maximization of minority representation.

4. Recall that Section 2 states that "nothing in this section establishes a right to have members of a protected class elected in numbers equal to their proportion in the population." This proviso was essential to the passage of the 1982 amendments, but is *De Grandy* consistent with it? In particular, how can *De Grandy*'s emphasis on the proportionality of a minority group's representation be squared with the proviso's disclaimer of proportionality as a goal? Here is the Court's response:

> "Proportionality" as the term is used here links the number of majority-minority voting districts to minority members' share of the relevant population. The concept is distinct from the subject of the proportional representation clause of § 2 . . . . This proviso speaks to the success of minority candidates, as distinct from the political or electoral power of minority voters. And the proviso also confirms what is otherwise clear from the text of the statute, namely, that the ultimate right of § 2 is equality of opportunity, not a guarantee of electoral success for minority-preferred candidates of whatever race.

Id. at 1014 n.11. Are you persuaded? Or is the Court's distinction between candidates who are themselves minority members and candidates who are preferred by minority voters too fine?

5. Was *De Grandy*'s fear of the maximization of minority representation justified? Stephanopoulos, *Race, Place, and Power, supra*, 68 Stanford Law Review at 1370-71, finds that at all relevant times, black and Latino voters have been underrepresented in state legislatures throughout America. In 1995, for example, just after *De Grandy* was decided, only about 14 percent of state house members were black in the typical state with a 20 percent black population, and only about 11 percent of state house members were Latino in the typical state with a 20 percent Latino population. These figures also changed only slightly between 1995 and 2015.

6. We have seen that in *Holder v. Hall* the Court ruled that a Section 2 claim could not be based on a contention that a single official was elected rather than a multi-member body. The plurality opinion by Justice Kennedy and a concurring opinion by Justice O'Connor worked within the *Gingles* framework. Justice Thomas, joined by Justice Scalia, made up the remainder of the majority in *Holder*, but concurred on much broader grounds. As Justice Thomas wrote, "I would hold that the size of a governing body is not a 'standard, practice, or procedure' within the terms of the Act. In my view, however, the only principle limiting the scope of the terms 'standard, practice, or procedure' that can be derived from the text of the Act would exclude, not only the challenge to size advanced today, but also challenges to allegedly dilutive election methods that we have considered within the scope of the Act in the past."

As Justice Thomas recognized, his approach would require overruling *Gingles* and several subsequent cases. His concurring opinion in *Holder* consists primarily of two long parts. Part II could be described as the "statutory" or "legal" portion of his opinion, in which he attempts to show that his narrow reading of Section 2 is justified by normal principles of statutory interpretation. Reprinted below are substantial excerpts from Part I of Justice Thomas' opinion, in which he addresses many of the broader issues raised by the attempt to proscribe minority vote dilution.

As you read Justice Thomas's provocative opinion, consider the following questions: With respect to his argument that the Supreme Court improperly is making judgments about political theory, is doing so actually illegitimate if Congress has *authorized* the Court to make these judgments? With respect to his preferred approach, which would limit Section 2 to claims of vote denial, doesn't this position also embrace a particular theory of representation—just a different one from the Court's? With respect to the alleged tensions produced by majority-minority districts, are they backed by any empirical evidence or merely speculative? And with respect to the alternatives to majority-minority districts mentioned by Justice Thomas (cumulative voting, limited voting, and the like), shouldn't he be *supportive* of them since they provide for minority representation in a less race-conscious fashion?

Holder v. Hall

512 U.S. 874 (1994) (concurring opinion)

Justice THOMAS, with whom Justice SCALIA joins, concurring in the judgment....

I

If one surveys the history of the Voting Rights Act, one can only be struck by the sea change that has occurred in the application and enforcement of the Act since it was passed in 1965. The statute was originally perceived as a remedial provision directed specifically at eradicating discriminatory practices that restricted blacks' ability to register and vote in the segregated South. Now, the Act has grown into something entirely different. In construing the Act to cover claims of vote dilution, we have converted the Act into a device for regulating, rationing, and apportioning political power among racial and ethnic groups. In the process, we have read the Act essentially as a grant of authority to the federal judiciary to develop theories on basic principles of representative government, for it is only a resort to political theory that can enable a court to determine which electoral systems provide the "fairest" levels of representation or the most "effective" or "undiluted" votes to minorities.

Before I turn to an analysis of the text of § 2 to explain why, in my view, the terms of the statute do not authorize the project that we have undertaken in the name of the Act, I intend first simply to describe the development of the basic contours of vote dilution actions under the Voting Rights Act. An examination of the current state of our decisions should make obvious a simple fact that for far too long has gone unmentioned: vote dilution cases have required the federal courts to make decisions based on highly political judgments—judgments that courts are inherently ill-equipped to make. A clear understanding of the destructive assumptions that have developed to guide vote dilution decisions and the role we have given the federal courts in redrawing the political landscape of the Nation should make clear the pressing need for us to reassess our interpretation of the Act.

A

As it was enforced in the years immediately following its enactment, the Voting Rights Act of 1965 was perceived primarily as legislation directed at eliminating literacy tests and similar devices that had been used to prevent black voter registration in the segregated South. . . .

The Act was immediately and notably successful in removing barriers to registration and ensuring access to the ballot. . . .

The Court's decision in *Allen*, however, marked a fundamental shift in the focal point of the Act. . . . The decision in *Allen* . . . ensured that the terms "standard, practice, or procedure" would extend to encompass a wide array of electoral practices or voting systems that might be challenged for reducing the potential impact of minority votes.

As a consequence, *Allen* also ensured that courts would be required to confront a number of complex and essentially political questions in assessing claims of vote dilution under the Voting Rights Act. The central difficulty in any vote dilution case, of course, is determining a point of comparison against which dilution can be measured. As Justice Frankfurter observed several years before *Allen*, "[t]alk of 'debasement' or 'dilution' is circular talk. One cannot speak of 'debasement' or 'dilution' of the value of a vote until there is first defined a standard of reference as to what a vote should be worth." *Baker v. Carr* (Frankfurter, J., dissenting). But in setting the benchmark of what "undiluted" or fully "effective" voting strength should be, a court must necessarily make some judgments based purely on an assessment of principles of political theory. As Justice Harlan pointed out in his dissent in *Allen*, the Voting Rights Act supplies no rule for a court to rely upon in deciding, for example, whether a multimember at-large system of election is to be preferred to a single-member district system; that is, whether one provides a more "effective" vote than another.... The choice is inherently a political one, and depends upon the selection of a theory for defining the fully "effective" vote—at bottom, a theory for defining effective participation in representative government. In short, what a court is actually asked to do in a vote dilution case is "to choose among competing bases of representation—ultimately, really, among competing theories of political philosophy." *Baker* (Frankfurter, J., dissenting).

Perhaps the most prominent feature of the philosophy that has emerged in vote dilution decisions since *Allen* has been the Court's preference for single-member districting schemes, both as a benchmark for measuring undiluted minority voting strength and as a remedial mechanism for guaranteeing minorities undiluted voting power. Indeed, commentators surveying the history of voting rights litigation have concluded that it has been the objective of voting rights plaintiffs to use the Act to attack multimember districting schemes and to replace them with single-member districting systems drawn with majority-minority districts to ensure minority control of seats.

It should be apparent, however, that there is no principle inherent in our constitutional system, or even in the history of the Nation's electoral practices, that makes single-member districts the "proper" mechanism for electing representatives to governmental bodies or for giving "undiluted" effect to the votes of a numerical minority. On the contrary, from the earliest days of the Republic, multimember districts were a common feature of our political systems. The Framers left unanswered in the Constitution the question whether congressional delegations from the several States should be elected on a general ticket from each State as a whole or under a districting scheme and left that matter to be resolved by the States or by Congress. It was not until 1842 that Congress determined that Representatives should be elected from single-member districts in the States....

The obvious advantage the Court has perceived in single-member districts, of course, is their tendency to enhance the ability of any numerical minority in the electorate to gain control of seats in a representative body. But in choosing single-member districting as a benchmark electoral plan on that basis the Court has made a political decision and, indeed, a decision that itself depends on a prior political choice made in answer to Justice Harlan's question in *Allen*. Justice Harlan asked whether a group's votes should be considered to be more "effective" when they provide *influence* over a greater number of seats, or *control* over a lesser number of seats. In answering that query, the Court has determined that the purpose of the vote—or of the fully "effective" vote—is controlling seats. In other words, in an effort to develop standards for assessing claims of dilution, the Court has adopted the view that members of any numerically significant minority are denied a fully effective use of the franchise unless they are able to control seats in an elected body. Under this theory, votes that do not control a representative are essentially wasted; those who cast them go unrepresented and are just as surely disenfranchised as if they had been barred from registering. Such conclusions, of course, depend upon a certain theory of the "effective" vote, a theory that is not inherent in the concept of representative democracy itself.

In fact, it should be clear that the assumptions that have guided the Court reflect only one possible understanding of effective exercise of the franchise, an understanding based on the view that voters are "represented" only when they choose a delegate who will mirror their views in the legislative halls. But it is certainly possible to construct a theory of effective political participation that would accord greater importance to voters' ability to influence, rather than control, elections. And especially in a two-party system such as ours, the influence of a potential "swing" group of voters composing 10%–20% of the electorate in a given district can be considerable. Even such a focus on practical influence, however, is not a necessary component of the definition of the "effective" vote. Some conceptions of representative government may primarily emphasize the formal value of the vote as a mechanism for participation in the electoral process, whether it results in control of a seat or not. Under such a theory, minorities unable to control elected posts would not be considered essentially without a vote; rather, a vote duly cast and counted would be deemed just as "effective" as any other. If a minority group is unable to control seats, that result may plausibly be attributed to the inescapable fact that, in a majoritarian system, numerical minorities lose elections.

In short, there are undoubtedly an infinite number of theories of effective suffrage, representation, and the proper apportionment of political power in a representative democracy that could be drawn upon to answer the questions posed in *Allen*. I do not pretend to have provided the most sophisticated account of the various possibilities; but such matters of political theory are beyond the ordinary sphere of federal judges. And that is precisely the point. The matters the Court has set out to resolve in vote dilution cases are questions of political philosophy, not questions of law. As such, they are not readily subjected to any judicially manageable standards that can guide courts in attempting to select between competing theories.

But the political choices the Court has had to make do not end with the determination that the primary purpose of the "effective" vote is controlling seats or with the selection of single-member districting as the mechanism for providing that control. In one sense, these were not even the most critical decisions to be made in devising standards for assessing claims of dilution, for in itself, the selection of single-member districting as a benchmark election plan will tell a judge little about the number of minority districts to create. Single-member districting tells a court "how" members of a minority are to control seats, but not "how many" seats they should be allowed to control.

But "how many" is the critical issue. Once one accepts the proposition that the effectiveness of votes is measured in terms of the control of seats, the core of any vote dilution claim is an assertion that the group in question is unable to control the "proper" number of seats — that is, the number of seats that the minority's percentage of the population would enable it to control in the benchmark "fair" system. The claim is inherently based on ratios between the numbers of the minority in the population and the numbers of seats controlled. As Justice O'CONNOR has noted, "any theory of vote dilution must necessarily rely to some extent on a measure of minority voting strength that makes some reference to the proportion between the minority group and the electorate at large." *Gingles* (opinion concurring in judgment). As a result, only a mathematical calculation can answer the fundamental question posed by a claim of vote dilution. And once again, in selecting the proportion that will be used to define the undiluted strength of a minority—the ratio that will provide the principle for decision in a vote dilution case—a court must make a political choice.

The ratio for which this Court has opted, and thus the mathematical principle driving the results in our cases, is undoubtedly direct proportionality. Indeed, four Members of the Court candidly recognized in *Gingles* that the Court had adopted a rule of roughly proportional representation, at least to the extent proportionality was possible given the geographic dispersion of minority populations. (O'CONNOR, J., concurring in judgment). While in itself that choice may strike us intuitively as the fairest or most just rule to apply, opting for proportionality is still a political choice, not a result required by any principle of law.

B

The dabbling in political theory that dilution cases have prompted, however, is hardly the worst aspect of our vote dilution jurisprudence. Far more pernicious has been the Court's willingness to accept the one underlying premise that must inform every minority vote dilution claim: the assumption that the group asserting dilution is not merely a racial or ethnic group, but a group having distinct political interests as well. Of necessity, in resolving vote dilution actions we have given credence to the view that race defines political interest. We have acted on the implicit assumption that members of racial and ethnic groups must all think alike on important matters of public policy and must have their own "minority preferred" representatives holding seats in elected bodies if they are to be considered represented at all.

It is true that in *Gingles* we stated that whether a racial group is "politically cohesive" may not be assumed, but rather must be proved in each case. But the standards we have employed for determining political cohesion have proved so insubstantial that this "precondition" does not present much of a barrier to the assertion of vote dilution claims on behalf of any racial group.[12] Moreover, it provides no test—indeed, it is not designed to provide a test—of whether race itself determines a distinctive political community of interest. According to the rule adopted in *Gingles*, plaintiffs must show simply that members of a racial group tend to prefer the same candidates.

---

12. Cf. *Citizens for a Better Gretna v. Gretna*, 834 F.2d 496, 501–02 (5th Cir. 1987) (emphasizing that political cohesion under *Gingles* can be shown where a "significant number" of minority voters prefer the same candidate, and suggesting that data showing that anywhere from 49% to 67% of the members of a minority group preferred the same candidate established cohesion), cert. denied, 492 U.S. 905 (1989).

There is no set standard defining how strong the correlation must be, and an inquiry into the cause for the correlation (to determine, for example, whether it might be the product of similar socioeconomic interests rather than some other factor related to race) is unnecessary. Thus, whenever similarities in political preferences along racial lines exist, we proclaim that the cause of the correlation is irrelevant, but we effectively rely on the fact of the correlation to assume that racial groups have unique political interests.

As a result, *Gingles'* requirement of proof of political cohesiveness, as practically applied, has proved little different from a working assumption that racial groups can be conceived of largely as political interest groups. And operating under that assumption, we have assigned federal courts the task of ensuring that minorities are assured their "just" share of seats in elected bodies throughout the Nation.

To achieve that result through the currently fashionable mechanism of drawing majority-minority single-member districts, we have embarked upon what has been aptly characterized as a process of "creating racially 'safe boroughs.'" We have involved the federal courts, and indeed the Nation, in the enterprise of systematically dividing the country into electoral districts along racial lines—an enterprise of segregating the races into political homelands that amounts, in truth, to nothing short of a system of "political apartheid." *Shaw*, [*infra,* Part III]. Blacks are drawn into "black districts" and given "black representatives"; Hispanics are drawn into Hispanic districts and given "Hispanic representatives"; and so on. Worse still, it is not only the courts that have taken up this project. In response to judicial decisions and the promptings of the Justice Department, the States themselves, in an attempt to avoid costly and disruptive Voting Rights Act litigation, have begun to gerrymander electoral districts according to race. That practice now promises to embroil the courts in a lengthy process of attempting to undo, or at least to minimize, the damage wrought by the system we created. The assumptions upon which our vote dilution decisions have been based should be repugnant to any nation that strives for the ideal of a color-blind Constitution. "The principle of equality is at war with the notion that District A must be represented by a Negro, as it is with the notion that District B must be represented by a Caucasian, District C by a Jew, District D by a Catholic, and so on." *Wright v. Rockefeller* (Douglas, J., dissenting). Despite Justice Douglas' warning sounded 30 years ago, our voting rights decisions are rapidly progressing towards a system that is indistinguishable in principle from a scheme under which members of different racial groups are divided into separate electoral registers and allocated a proportion of political power on the basis of race. Under our jurisprudence, rather than requiring registration on racial rolls and dividing power purely on a population basis, we have simply resorted to the somewhat less precise expedient of drawing geographic district lines to capture minority populations and to ensure the existence of the "appropriate" number of "safe minority seats."

That distinction in the practical implementation of the concept, of course, is immaterial. The basic premises underlying our system of safe minority districts and those behind the racial register are the same: that members of the racial group must think alike and that their interests are so distinct that the group must be provided a separate body of representatives in the legislature to voice its unique point of view. Such a "system, by whatever name it is called, is a divisive force in a community, emphasizing differences between candidates and voters that are irrelevant." *Id.* Justice Douglas correctly predicted the results of state sponsorship of such a theory of representation: "When racial or religious lines are drawn by the State . . . antagonisms that relate to race or to religion rather than to political issues are generated; communities seek not the best representative but the best racial or religious partisan." In short, few devices could be better designed to exacerbate racial tensions than the consciously segregated districting system currently being constructed in the name of the Voting Rights Act.

As a practical political matter, our drive to segregate political districts by race can only serve to deepen racial divisions by destroying any need for voters or candidates to build bridges between racial groups or to form voting coalitions. "Black-preferred" candidates are assured election in "safe black districts"; white-preferred candidates are assured election in "safe white districts." Neither group needs to draw on support from the other's constituency to win on election day.

[T]he system we have instituted affirmatively encourages a racially based understanding of the representative function. The clear premise of the system is that geographic districts are merely a device to be manipulated to establish "black representatives" whose real constituencies are defined, not in terms of the voters who populate their districts, but in terms of race. The "black representative's" function, in other words, is to represent the "black interest."

Perhaps not surprisingly, the United States has now adopted precisely this theory of racial group representation, as the arguments advanced in another case decided today, *Johnson v. De Grandy*, should show. The case involved a claim that an apportionment plan for the Florida Legislature should have provided another Hispanic district in Dade County. Florida responded to the claim of vote dilution by arguing that the plan already provided Dade County Hispanics with seats in proportion to their numbers. According to the Solicitor General, this claim of proportionality should have been evaluated, not merely on the basis of the population in the Dade County area where the racial gerrymandering was alleged to have occurred, but on a statewide basis. It did not matter, in the Solicitor General's view, that Hispanic populations elsewhere in the State could not meet the *Gingles* geographic compactness test and thus could not possibly have controlled districts of their own. After all, the Solicitor General reasoned, the Hispanic legislators elected from Hispanic districts in Dade County would represent, not just the interests of the Dade County Hispanics, but the interests of all the Hispanics in the State. As the argument shows, at least some careful observers have recognized the racial gerrymandering in our vote dilution cases for what it is: a slightly less precise mechanism than the racial register for allocating representation on the basis of race.

C

While the results we have already achieved under the Voting Rights Act might seem bad enough, we should recognize that our approach to splintering the electorate into racially designated single-member districts does not by any means mark a limit on the authority federal judges may wield to rework electoral systems under our Voting Rights Act jurisprudence. On the contrary, in relying on single-member districting schemes as a touchstone, our cases so far have been somewhat arbitrarily limited to addressing the interests of minority voters who are sufficiently geographically compact to form a majority in a single-member district. There is no reason *a priori*, however, that our focus should be so constrained. The decision to rely on single-member geographic districts as a mechanism for conducting elections is merely a political choice — and one that we might reconsider in the future. Indeed, it is a choice that has undoubtedly been influenced by the adversary process: in the cases that have come before us, plaintiffs have focused largely upon attacking multimember districts and have offered single-member schemes as the benchmark of an "undiluted" alternative.

But as the destructive effects of our current penchant for majority-minority districts become more apparent, courts will undoubtedly be called upon to reconsider adherence to geographic districting as a method for ensuring minority voting power. Already, some advocates have criticized the current strategy of creating majority-minority districts and have urged the adoption of other voting mechanisms — for example, cumulative voting or a system using transferable votes — that can produce proportional results without requiring division of the electorate into racially segregated districts. Cf., *e.g.*, [writings of Guinier, Karlan, and others].

Such changes may seem radical departures from the electoral systems with which we are most familiar. Indeed, they may be unwanted by the people in the several States who purposely have adopted districting systems in their electoral laws. But nothing in our present understanding of the Voting Rights Act places a principled limit on the authority of federal courts that would prevent them from instituting a system of cumulative voting as a remedy under § 2, or even from establishing a more elaborate mechanism for securing proportional representation based on transferable votes. [G]eographic districting is not a requirement inherent in our political system. Rather, districting is merely another political choice made by the citizenry in the drafting of their state constitutions. Like other political choices concerning electoral systems and models of representation, it too is presumably subject to a judicial override if it comes into conflict with the theories of representation and effective voting that we may develop under the Voting Rights Act.

Indeed, the unvarnished truth is that all that is required for districting to fall out of favor is for Members of this Court to further develop their political thinking. We should not be surprised if voting rights advocates encourage us to "revive our political imagination," Guinier, and to consider "innovative and nontraditional remedies" for vote dilution, Karlan, for under our Voting Rights Act jurisprudence, it is only the limits on our "political imagination" that place restraints on the standards we may select for defining undiluted voting systems. Once we candidly recognize that geographic districting and other aspects of electoral systems that we have so far placed beyond question are merely political choices, those practices, too, may fall under suspicion of having a dilutive effect on minority voting strength. And when the time comes to put the question to the test, it may be difficult indeed for a Court that, under *Gingles*, has been bent on creating roughly proportional representation for geographically compact minorities to find a principled reason for holding that a geographically dispersed minority cannot challenge districting itself as a dilutive electoral practice. In principle, cumulative voting and other non-district-based methods of effecting proportional representation are simply more efficient and straightforward mechanisms for achieving what has already become our tacit objective: roughly proportional allocation of political power according to race. . . .

D

Such is the current state of our understanding of the Voting Rights Act. That our reading of the Act has assigned the federal judiciary the task of making the decisions I have described above should suggest to the Members of this Court that something in our jurisprudence has gone awry. We would be mighty Platonic guardians indeed if Congress had granted us the authority to determine the best form of local government for every county, city, village, and town in America. But under our constitutional system, this Court is not a centralized politburo appointed for life to dictate to the provinces the "correct" theories of democratic representation, the "best" electoral systems for securing truly "representative" government, the "fairest" proportions of minority political influence, or, as respondents would have us hold today, the "proper" sizes for local governing bodies. We should be cautious in interpreting any Act of Congress to grant us power to make such determinations. . . .

A full understanding of the authority that our current interpretation of the Voting Rights Act assigns to the federal courts, and of the destructive effects that our exercise of that authority is presently having upon our body politic, compels a single conclusion: a systematic reexamination of our interpretation of the Act is required.

II

. . . In my view, our current practice should not continue. Not for another Term, not until the next case, not for another day. The disastrous implications of the policies we have adopted under the Act are too grave; the dissembling in our approach to the Act too damaging to the credibility of the federal judiciary. The "inherent tension" — indeed, I would call it an irreconcilable conflict — between the standards we have adopted for evaluating vote dilution claims and the text of the Voting Rights Act [i.e., the proviso in Section 2 that proportional representation is not required,] would itself be sufficient in my view to warrant overruling the interpretation of § 2 set out in *Gingles*. When that obvious conflict is combined with the destructive effects our expansive reading of the Act has had in involving the federal judiciary in the project of dividing the Nation into racially segregated electoral districts, I can see no reasonable alternative to abandoning our current unfortunate understanding of the Act. . . .[k]

III. Racial Gerrymandering

The above materials on the Voting Rights Act referred at several points to a distinct cause of action for *racial gerrymandering* that courts have recognized under the Equal Protection Clause. We now consider this constitutional claim in more detail.

The claim has its antecedents in 1960s cases such as *Gomillion v. Lightfoot*, 364 U.S. 339 (1960), and *Wright v. Rockefeller*, 376 U.S. 52 (1964), in which allegations were made that political boundaries were drawn so as to segregate voters on racial grounds. In *Gomillion*, the Supreme Court agreed that the borders of the City of Tuskegee had unconstitutionally been changed to exclude nearly all black voters from the jurisdiction. In *Wright*, on the other hand, the Court concluded that plaintiffs had failed to prove that congressional district lines in Manhattan were "the product of a state contrivance to segregate on the basis of race or place of origin." 376 U.S. at 57.

The Court's next early confrontation with racial gerrymandering came in *United Jewish Organizations, Inc. v. Carey*, 430 U.S. 144 (1977). To comply with Section 5 of the Voting Rights Act, New York drew seven state house districts and three state senate districts with nonwhite majorities in Kings County (i.e., Brooklyn), a covered jurisdiction. New York also drew many more districts with white majorities; "the 1974 plan left approximately 70% of the senate and assembly districts in Kings County with white majorities, [while] only 65% of the population of the county was white." *Id.* at 154. Additionally, the plan divided a Hasidic Jewish community of about 30,000 in the Williamsburgh area. This community has previously been placed in a single district; now, though, it was split between two state house and state senate districts.

A fractured Court rejected a claim by the Hasidic Jews that they had been harmed by unconstitutional racial gerrymandering. First, the plurality held that there is no "per se rule against using racial factors in districting and apportionment." *Id.* at 161 (plurality opinion). Second, the plurality ruled that New York had done no more than what was required by Section 5; it had not *increased* minority representation relative to the previous plan. Third, and most importantly, the plurality grouped the Hasidic Jews with other white voters, and concluded that their electoral influence had not been improperly diluted by the new plan:

---

k. For a study supporting Justice Thomas' position, see Anthony A. Peacock, Deconstructing the Republic: Voting Rights, the Supreme Court, and the Founders' Republicanism Reconsidered (2008) — Eds.

> [T]here was no fencing out the white population from participation in the political processes of the county, and the plan did not minimize or unfairly cancel out white voting strength.... As the Court of Appeals observed, the plan left white majorities in approximately 70% of the assembly and senate districts in Kings County, which had a countywide population that was 65% white. Thus, even if voting in the county occurred strictly according to race, whites would not be underrepresented relative to their share of the population.
>
> ... [A]s long as whites in Kings County, as a group, were provided with fair representation, we cannot conclude that there was a cognizable discrimination against whites or an abridgment of their right to vote on the grounds of race. Furthermore, the individual voter in the district with a nonwhite majority has no constitutional complaint merely because his candidate has lost out at the polls and his district is represented by a person for whom he did not vote. Some candidate, along with his supporters, always loses.

Id. at 165-66 (plurality opinion). The plurality thus seemed to treat racial gerrymandering as a claim indistinguishable from racial vote dilution. In both cases, the only relevant injuries were exclusion from the political process and disproportionately low representation. Since white voters in Kings County suffered neither of these harms, there was no constitutional violation.

In the wake of *United Jewish Organizations*, racial vote dilution (under both the Constitution and Section 2 of the Voting Rights Act) was the only game in town for almost two decades. That changed in 1993, when the Supreme Court issued the first of its modern racial gerrymandering decisions, *Shaw v. Reno*. The political background to *Shaw* is described by Michael Barone and Grant Ujifusa, The Almanac of American Politics 1994, at 942 (1993):

> North Carolina's robust growth in the 1980s gave it a new 12th congressional district in the 1990 Census, its first new seat in 60 years. It had one of the most turbulent districting processes in the nation, thanks to application of the Voting Rights Act, whose 1982 amendments were interpreted by the Justice Department as requiring the creation of not one but two black-majority districts in a state that had none before. Thus in December 1991 was struck down the first Democratic plan, which would have created a new black-majority 1st District in east Carolina, but would have left Charlie Rose's 7th District with a large number of blacks and created a Republican-leaning new seat in the central Piedmont.
>
> Republicans chortled, hoping for the creation of a black-Lumbee Indian majority district that would cost Rose his majority, but the last laugh was on them. Clever Democratic districters drew up a plan with a second black district consisting of a thin line of territory, in some places no wider than I-85,

linking black precincts from Durham west to Charlotte; the new Republican 12th District disappeared, and the marginal 5th and 8th Districts were made more Democratic—pretty ingenious work. It violated the age-old principle of contiguity, but it was accepted by the Justice Department in 1992. Nevertheless, it was widely attacked for its extremely irregular district lines (its only competitor for this was Texas, a plan also drawn by Democrats to preserve their own seats while complying with the Voting Rights Act), and in June 1993, a case was pending in the U.S. Supreme Court on the future of the plan.

Shaw v. Reno

509 U.S. 630 (1993)

Justice O'CONNOR delivered the opinion of the Court.

This case involves two of the most complex and sensitive issues this Court has faced in recent years: the meaning of the constitutional "right" to vote, and the propriety of race-based state legislation designed to benefit members of historically disadvantaged racial minority groups. As a result of the 1990 census, North Carolina became entitled to a twelfth seat in the United States House of Representatives. The General Assembly enacted a reapportionment plan that included one majority-black congressional district. After the Attorney General of the United States objected to the plan pursuant to §5 of the Voting Rights Act of 1965, the General Assembly passed new legislation creating a second majority-black district. Appellants allege that the revised plan, which contains district boundary lines of dramatically irregular shape, constitutes an unconstitutional racial gerrymander. The question before us is whether appellants have stated a cognizable claim.

I

The voting age population of North Carolina is approximately 78% white, 20% black, and 1% Native American; the remaining 1% is predominantly Asian. The black population is relatively dispersed; blacks constitute a majority of the general population in only 5 of the State's 100 counties.... The largest concentrations of black citizens live in the Coastal Plain, primarily in the northern part. The General Assembly's first redistricting plan contained one majority-black district centered in that area of the State.

Forty of North Carolina's one hundred counties are covered by §5 of the Voting Rights Act of 1965....

The Attorney General ... interposed a formal objection to the General Assembly's plan. The Attorney General specifically objected to the configuration of boundary lines drawn in the south-central to southeastern region of the State. In the Attorney General's view, the General Assembly could have created a second majority-minority district "to give effect to black and Native American voting strength in this area" by using boundary lines "no more irregular than [those] found elsewhere in the proposed plan," but failed to do so for "pretextual reasons."

[T]he General Assembly enacted a revised redistricting plan that included a second majority-black district. The General Assembly located the second district not in the south-central to southeastern part of the State, but in the north-central region along Interstate 85.

The first of the two majority-black districts contained in the revised plan, District 1, is somewhat hook shaped. Centered in the northeast portion of the State, it moves southward until it tapers to a narrow band; then, with finger-like extensions, it reaches far into the southern-most part of the State near the South Carolina border. District 1 has been compared [by a judge in the lower court] to a "Rorschach ink-blot test," and [by the *Wall Street Journal* to] a "bug splattered on a windshield."

The second majority-black district, District 12, is even more unusually shaped. It is approximately 160 miles long and, for much of its length, no wider than the I-85 corridor. It winds in snake-like fashion through tobacco country, financial centers, and manufacturing areas "until it gobbles in enough enclaves of black neighborhoods." Northbound and southbound drivers on I-85 sometimes find themselves in separate districts in one county, only to "trade" districts when they enter the next county. Of the 10 counties through which District 12 passes, five are cut into three different districts; even towns are divided. At one point the district remains contiguous only because it intersects at a single point with two other districts before crossing over them. One state legislator has remarked that "[i]f you drove down the interstate with both car doors open, you'd kill most of the people in the district." . . .

The Attorney General did not object to the General Assembly's revised plan. But numerous North Carolinians did. . . .

. . . Appellants alleged not that the revised plan constituted a political gerrymander, nor that it violated the "one person, one vote" principle, see *Reynolds*, but that the State had created an unconstitutional *racial* gerrymander. [The lower court dismissed the case. Plaintiffs appealed.]

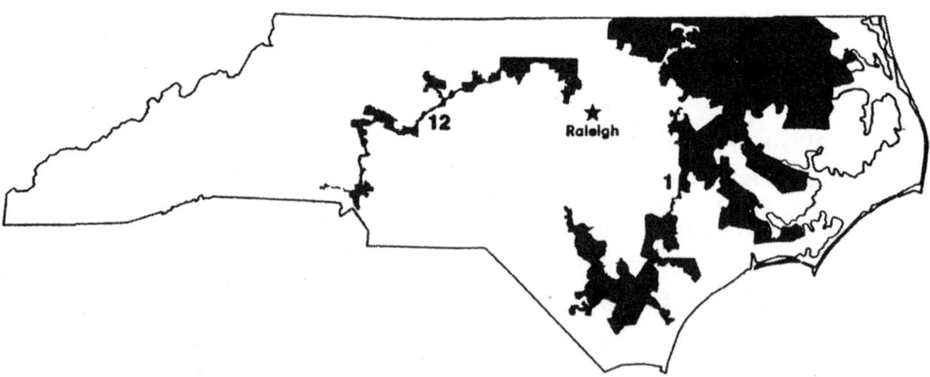

Source: CQ Press, Congressional Districts in the 1990s: A Portrait of America (1993). Reprinted by permission.

II

. . .

B

. . . Our focus is on appellants' claim that the State engaged in unconstitutional racial gerrymandering. That argument strikes a powerful historical chord: It is unsettling how closely the North Carolina plan resembles the most egregious racial gerrymanders of the past.

An understanding of the nature of appellants' claim is critical to our resolution of the case. In their complaint, appellants did not claim that the General Assembly's reapportionment plan unconstitutionally "diluted" white voting strength. They did not even claim to be white. Rather, appellants' complaint alleged that the deliberate segregation of voters into separate districts on the basis of race violated their constitutional right to participate in a "color-blind" electoral process.

Despite their invocation of the ideal of a "color-blind" Constitution, appellants appear to concede that race-conscious redistricting is not always unconstitutional. That concession is wise: This Court never has held that race-conscious state decisionmaking is impermissible in all circumstances. What appellants object to is redistricting legislation that is so extremely irregular on its face that it rationally can be viewed only as an effort to segregate the races for purposes of voting, without regard for traditional districting principles and without sufficiently compelling justification. For the reasons that follow, we conclude that appellants have stated a claim upon which relief can be granted under the Equal Protection Clause.

III

A

. . . No inquiry into legislative purpose is necessary when the racial classification appears on the face of the statute. Express racial classifications are immediately suspect because, "[a]bsent searching judicial inquiry . . . there is simply no way of determining what classifications are 'benign' or 'remedial' and what classifications are in fact motivated by illegitimate notions of racial inferiority or simple racial politics." *Richmond v. J.A. Croson Co.*

Classifications of citizens solely on the basis of race "are by their very nature odious to a free people whose institutions are founded upon the doctrine of equality." *Hirabayashi v. United States.* They threaten to stigmatize individuals by reason of their membership in a racial group and to incite racial hostility. Accordingly, we have held that the Fourteenth Amendment requires state legislation that expressly distinguishes among citizens because of their race to be narrowly tailored to further a compelling governmental interest.

These principles apply not only to legislation that contains explicit racial distinctions, but also to those "rare" statutes that, although race-neutral, are, on their face, "unexplainable on grounds other than race." *Arlington Heights v. Metropolitan Housing Development Corp.* . . .

B

Appellants contend that redistricting legislation that is so bizarre on its face that it is "unexplainable on grounds other than race," *Arlington Heights*, *supra*, demands the same close scrutiny that we give other state laws that classify citizens by race. Our voting rights precedents support that conclusion. [The Court reviewed past cases inquiring into whether boundaries had been drawn with the purpose of segregating or otherwise distinguishing between voters on the basis of race.] ...

Wright illustrates the difficulty of determining from the face of a single-member districting plan that it purposefully distinguishes between voters on the basis of race. A reapportionment statute typically does not classify persons at all; it classifies tracts of land, or addresses. Moreover, redistricting differs from other kinds of state decisionmaking in that the legislature always is *aware* of race when it draws district lines, just as it is aware of age, economic status, religious and political persuasion, and a variety of other demographic factors. That sort of race consciousness does not lead inevitably to impermissible race discrimination. As *Wright* demonstrates, when members of a racial group live together in one community, a reapportionment plan that concentrates members of the group in one district and excludes them from others may reflect wholly legitimate purposes. The district lines may be drawn, for example, to provide for compact districts of contiguous territory, or to maintain the integrity of political subdivisions.

The difficulty of proof, of course, does not mean that a racial gerrymander, once established, should receive less scrutiny under the Equal Protection Clause than other state legislation classifying citizens by race. Moreover, it seems clear to us that proof sometimes will not be difficult at all. In some exceptional cases, a reapportionment plan may be so highly irregular that, on its face, it rationally cannot be understood as anything other than an effort to "segregat[e] ... voters" on the basis of race. *Gomillion v. Lightfoot*, in which a tortured municipal boundary line was drawn to exclude black voters, was such a case. So, too, would be a case in which a State concentrated a dispersed minority population in a single district by disregarding traditional districting principles such as compactness, contiguity, and respect for political subdivisions. We emphasize that these criteria are important not because they are constitutionally required—they are not—but because they are objective factors that may serve to defeat a claim that a district has been gerrymandered on racial lines.

Put differently, we believe that reapportionment is one area in which appearances do matter. A reapportionment plan that includes in one district individuals who belong to the same race, but who are otherwise widely separated by geographical and political boundaries, and who may have little in common with one another but the color of their skin, bears an uncomfortable resemblance to political apartheid. It reinforces the perception that members of the same racial group—regardless of their age, education, economic status, or the community in which they live—think alike, share the same political interests, and will prefer the same candidates at the polls. We have rejected such perceptions elsewhere as impermissible racial stereotypes. By perpetuating such notions, a racial gerrymander may exacerbate the very patterns of racial bloc voting that majority-minority districting is sometimes said to counteract.

The message that such districting sends to elected representatives is equally pernicious. When a district obviously is created solely to effectuate the perceived common interests of one racial group, elected officials are more likely to believe that their primary obligation is to represent only the members of that group, rather than their constituency as a whole. This is altogether antithetical to our system of representative democracy. . . .

For these reasons, we conclude that a plaintiff challenging a reapportionment statute under the Equal Protection Clause may state a claim by alleging that the legislation, though race-neutral on its face, rationally cannot be understood as anything other than an effort to separate voters into different districts on the basis of race, and that the separation lacks sufficient justification. . . .

C

The dissenters consider the circumstances of this case "functionally indistinguishable" from multimember districting and at-large voting systems, which are loosely described as "other varieties of gerrymandering." We have considered the constitutionality of these practices in other Fourteenth Amendment cases and have required plaintiffs to demonstrate that the challenged practice has the purpose and effect of diluting a racial group's voting strength. See, *e.g.*, *Rogers v. Lodge*; *Mobile v. Bolden*; *White v. Regester*; *Whitcomb v. Chavis*. At-large and multimember schemes, however, do not classify voters on the basis of race. Classifying citizens by race, as we have said, threatens special harms that are not present in our vote-dilution cases. It therefore warrants different analysis.

Justice SOUTER apparently believes that racial gerrymandering is harmless unless it dilutes a racial group's voting strength. As we have explained, however, reapportionment legislation that cannot be understood as anything other than an effort to classify and separate voters by race injures voters in other ways. It reinforces racial stereotypes and threatens to undermine our system of representative democracy by signaling to elected officials that they represent a particular racial group rather than their constituency as a whole. Justice SOUTER does not adequately explain why these harms are not cognizable under the Fourteenth Amendment.

The dissenters make two other arguments that cannot be reconciled with our precedents. First, they suggest that a racial gerrymander of the sort alleged here is functionally equivalent to gerrymanders for nonracial purposes, such as political gerrymanders. This Court has held political gerrymanders to be justiciable under the Equal Protection Clause. See *Davis v. Bandemer*. But nothing in our case law compels the conclusion that racial and political gerrymanders are subject to precisely the same constitutional scrutiny. In fact, our country's long and persistent history of racial discrimination in voting—as well as our Fourteenth Amendment jurisprudence, which always has reserved the strictest scrutiny for discrimination on the basis of race—would seem to compel the opposite conclusion.

Second, Justice STEVENS argues that racial gerrymandering poses no constitutional difficulties when district lines are drawn to favor the minority, rather than the majority. We have made clear, however, that equal protection analysis "is not dependent on the race of those burdened or benefited by a particular classification." Indeed, racial classifications receive close scrutiny even when they may be said to burden or benefit the races equally. . . .

IV

. . . [T]he very reason that the Equal Protection Clause demands strict scrutiny of all racial classifications is because without it, a court cannot determine whether or not the discrimination truly is "benign." Thus, if appellants' allegations of a racial gerrymander are not contradicted on remand, the District Court must determine whether the General Assembly's reapportionment plan satisfies strict scrutiny. We therefore consider what that level of scrutiny requires in the reapportionment context.

The state appellees suggest that a covered jurisdiction may have a compelling interest in creating majority-minority districts in order to comply with the Voting Rights Act. The States certainly have a very strong interest in complying with federal antidiscrimination laws that are constitutionally valid as interpreted and as applied. But in the context of a Fourteenth Amendment challenge, courts must bear in mind the difference between what the law permits, and what it requires.

For example, on remand North Carolina might claim that it adopted the revised plan in order to comply with the § 5 "nonretrogression" principle. Under that principle, a proposed voting change cannot be precleared if it will lead to "a retrogression in the position of racial minorities with respect to their effective exercise of the electoral franchise." *Beer v. United States*. . . .

Although the Court concluded that the redistricting scheme at issue in *Beer* was nonretrogressive, it did not hold that the plan, for that reason, was immune from constitutional challenge. The Court expressly declined to reach that question. Indeed, the Voting Rights Act and our case law make clear that a reapportionment plan that satisfies § 5 still may be enjoined as unconstitutional. Thus, we do not read *Beer* or any of our other § 5 cases to give covered jurisdictions *carte blanche* to engage in racial gerrymandering in the name of nonretrogression. A reapportionment plan would not be narrowly tailored to the goal of avoiding retrogression if the State went beyond what was reasonably necessary to avoid retrogression. . . .

Before us, the state appellees contend that the General Assembly's revised plan was necessary not to prevent retrogression, but to avoid dilution of black voting strength in violation of § 2, as construed in *Thornburg v. Gingles*. . . .

Appellants maintain that the General Assembly's revised plan could not have been required by § 2. They contend that the State's black population is too dispersed to support two geographically compact majority-black districts, as the bizarre shape of District 12 demonstrates, and that there is no evidence of black political cohesion. They also contend that recent black electoral successes demonstrate the willingness of white voters in North Carolina to vote for black candidates. Appellants point out that blacks currently hold the positions of State Auditor, Speaker of the North Carolina House of Representatives, and chair of the North Carolina State Board of Elections. They also point out that in 1990 a black candidate defeated a white opponent in the Democratic Party run-off for a United States Senate seat before being defeated narrowly by the Republican incumbent in the general election. Appellants further argue that if § 2 did require adoption of North Carolina's revised plan, § 2 is to that extent unconstitutional. These arguments were not developed below, and the issues remain open for consideration on remand.

The state appellees alternatively argue that the General Assembly's plan advanced a compelling interest entirely distinct from the Voting Rights Act. We previously have recognized a significant state interest in eradicating the effects of past racial discrimination. But the State must have a "strong basis in evidence for [concluding] that remedial action [is] necessary." *Croson.*

. . . This question also need not be decided at this stage of the litigation. . . .

V

Racial classifications of any sort pose the risk of lasting harm to our society. They reinforce the belief, held by too many for too much of our history, that individuals should be judged by the color of their skin. Racial classifications with respect to voting carry particular dangers. Racial gerrymandering, even for remedial purposes, may balkanize us into competing racial factions; it threatens to carry us further from the goal of a political system in which race no longer matters — a goal that the Fourteenth and Fifteenth Amendments embody, and to which the Nation continues to aspire. It is for these reasons that race-based districting by our state legislatures demands close judicial scrutiny.

In this case, the Attorney General suggested that North Carolina could have created a reasonably compact second majority-minority district in the south-central to southeastern part of the State. We express no view as to whether appellants successfully could have challenged such a district under the Fourteenth Amendment. . . . Today we hold only that appellants have stated a claim under the Equal Protection Clause by alleging that the North Carolina General Assembly adopted a reapportionment scheme so irrational on its face that it can be understood only as an effort to segregate voters into separate voting districts because of their race, and that the separation lacks sufficient justification. If the allegation of racial gerrymandering remains uncontradicted, the District Court further must determine whether the North Carolina plan is narrowly tailored to further a compelling governmental interest. Accordingly, we reverse the judgment of the District Court and remand the case for further proceedings consistent with this opinion.

It is so ordered.

Justice WHITE, with whom Justice BLACKMUN and Justice STEVENS join, dissenting.

.... [T]he notion that North Carolina's plan, under which whites remain a voting majority in a disproportionate number of congressional districts, and pursuant to which the State has sent its first black representatives since Reconstruction to the United States Congress, might have violated appellants' constitutional rights is both a fiction and a departure from settled equal protection principles. Seeing no good reason to engage in either, I dissent.

I

A

The grounds for my disagreement with the majority are simply stated: Appellants have not presented a cognizable claim, because they have not alleged a cognizable injury. To date, we have held that only two types of state voting practices could give rise to a constitutional claim. The first involves direct and outright deprivation of the right to vote, for example by means of a poll tax or literacy test. Plainly, this variety is not implicated by appellants' allegations and need not detain us further. The second type of unconstitutional practice is that which "affects the political strength of various groups," *Bolden* (STEVENS, J., concurring in judgment), in violation of the Equal Protection Clause. As for this latter category, we have insisted that members of the political or racial group demonstrate that the challenged action have the intent and effect of unduly diminishing their influence on the political process. Although this severe burden has limited the number of successful suits, it was adopted for sound reasons.

The central explanation has to do with the nature of the redistricting process. As the majority recognizes, "redistricting differs from other kinds of state decisionmaking in that the legislature always is aware of race when it draws district lines, just as it is aware of age, economic status, religious and political persuasion, and a variety of other demographic factors." "Being aware," in this context, is shorthand for "taking into account," and it hardly can be doubted that legislators routinely engage in the business of making electoral predictions based on group characteristics—racial, ethnic, and the like.... Because extirpating such considerations from the redistricting process is unrealistic, the Court has not invalidated all plans that consciously use race, but rather has looked at their impact.

Redistricting plans also reflect group interests and inevitably are conceived with partisan aims in mind. To allow judicial interference whenever this occurs would be to invite constant and unmanageable intrusion. Moreover, a group's power to affect the political process does not automatically dissipate by virtue of an electoral loss. Accordingly, we have asked that an identifiable group demonstrate more than mere lack of success at the polls to make out a successful gerrymandering claim. See, *e.g.*, *White v. Regester*; *Whitcomb v. Chavis*.

... Indeed, as a brief survey of decisions illustrates, the Court's gerrymandering cases all carry this theme — that it is not mere suffering at the polls but discrimination in the polity with which the Constitution is concerned....

To distinguish a claim that alleges that the redistricting scheme has discriminatory intent and effect from one that does not has nothing to do with dividing racial classifications between the "benign" and the malicious — an enterprise which, as the majority notes, the Court has treated with skepticism. Rather, the issue is whether the classification based on race discriminates against anyone by denying equal access to the political process....

B

.... [I]t strains credulity to suggest that North Carolina's purpose in creating a second majority-minority district was to discriminate against members of the majority group by "impair[ing] or burden[ing their] opportunity ... to participate in the political process." *United Jewish Organizations v. Carey* (Stewart, J., concurring in judgment). The State has made no mystery of its intent, which was to respond to the Attorney General's objections, by improving the minority group's prospects of electing a candidate of its choice. I doubt that this constitutes a discriminatory purpose as defined in the Court's equal protection cases — i.e., an intent to aggravate "the unequal distribution of electoral power." But even assuming that it does, there is no question that appellants have not alleged the requisite discriminatory effects. Whites constitute roughly 76 percent of the total population and 79 percent of the voting age population in North Carolina. Yet, under the State's plan, they still constitute a voting majority in 10 (or 83 percent) of the 12 congressional districts. Though they might be dissatisfied at the prospect of casting a vote for a losing candidate — a lot shared by many, including a disproportionate number of minority voters — surely they cannot complain of discriminatory treatment.

II

...

B

Lacking support in any of the Court's precedents, the majority's novel type of claim also makes no sense. As I understand the theory that is put forth, a redistricting plan that uses race to "segregate" voters by drawing "uncouth" lines is harmful in a way that a plan that uses race to distribute voters differently is not, for the former "bears an uncomfortable resemblance to political apartheid." The distinction is untenable.

Racial gerrymanders come in various shades: At-large voting schemes; the fragmentation of a minority group among various districts "so that it is a majority in none," otherwise known as "cracking"; the "stacking" of "a large minority population concentration ... with a larger white population"; and, finally, the "concentration of [minority voters] into districts where they constitute an excessive majority," also called "packing." In each instance, race is consciously utilized by the legislature for electoral purposes; in each instance, we have put the plaintiff challenging the district lines to the burden of demonstrating that the plan was meant to, and did in fact, exclude an identifiable racial group from participation in the political process.

Not so, apparently, when the districting "segregates" by drawing odd-shaped lines.[7] In that case, we are told, such proof no longer is needed. Instead, it is the *State* that must rebut the allegation that race was taken into account, a fact that, together with the legislators' consideration of ethnic, religious, and other group characteristics, I had thought we practically took for granted. Part of the explanation for the majority's approach has to do, perhaps, with the emotions stirred by words such as "segregation" and "political apartheid." But their loose and imprecise use by today's majority has, I fear, led it astray. The consideration of race in "segregation" cases is no different than in other race-conscious districting; from the standpoint of the affected groups, moreover, the line-drawings all act in similar fashion. A plan that "segregates" being functionally indistinguishable from any of the other varieties of gerrymandering, we should be consistent in what we require from a claimant: Proof of discriminatory purpose and effect.

The other part of the majority's explanation of its holding is related to its simultaneous discomfort and fascination with irregularly shaped districts. Lack of compactness or contiguity, like uncouth district lines, certainly is a helpful indicator that some form of gerrymandering (racial or other) might have taken place and that "something may be amiss." Disregard for geographic divisions and compactness often goes hand in hand with partisan gerrymandering.

But while district irregularities may provide strong indicia of a potential gerrymander, they do no more than that. In particular, they have no bearing on whether the plan ultimately is found to violate the Constitution. Given two districts drawn on similar, race-based grounds, the one does not become more injurious than the other simply by virtue of being snake-like, at least so far as the Constitution is concerned and absent any evidence of differential racial impact. The majority's contrary view is perplexing in light of its concession that "compactness or attractiveness has never been held to constitute an independent federal constitutional requirement for state legislative districts." *Gaffney*. It is shortsighted as well, for a regularly shaped district can just as effectively effectuate racially discriminatory gerrymandering as an odd-shaped one. By focusing on looks rather than impact, the majority "immediately casts attention in the wrong direction—toward superficialities of shape and

7. I borrow the term "segregate" from the majority, but, given its historical connotation, believe that its use is ill-advised. Nor is it a particularly accurate description of what has occurred. The majority-minority district that is at the center of the controversy is, according to the State, 54.71% African-American. Even if racial distribution was a factor, no racial group can be said to have been "segregated"—i.e., "set apart" or "isolate[d]." Webster's Collegiate Dictionary 1063 (9th ed. 1983).

size, rather than toward the political realities of district composition." R. Dixon, Democratic Representation: Reapportionment in Law and Politics 459 (1968).

Limited by its own terms to cases involving unusually-shaped districts, the Court's approach nonetheless will unnecessarily hinder to some extent a State's voluntary effort to ensure a modicum of minority representation. This will be true in areas where the minority population is geographically dispersed. It also will be true where the minority population is not scattered but, for reasons unrelated to race—for example incumbency protection—the State would rather not create the majority-minority district in its most "obvious" location.[10] When, as is the case here, the creation of a majority-minority district does not unfairly minimize the voting power of any other group, the Constitution does not justify, much less mandate, such obstruction....

III

Although I disagree with the holding that appellants' claim is cognizable, the Court's discussion of the level of scrutiny it requires warrants a few comments. I have no doubt that a State's compliance with the Voting Rights Act clearly constitutes a compelling interest. Here, the Attorney General objected to the State's plan on the ground that it failed to draw a second majority-minority district for what appeared to be pretextual reasons. Rather than challenge this conclusion, North Carolina chose to draw the second district.... [A] State is entitled to take such action.

The Court, while seemingly agreeing with this position, warns that the State's redistricting effort must be "narrowly tailored" to further its interest in complying with the law. It is evident to me, however, that what North Carolina did was precisely tailored to meet the objection of the Attorney General to its prior plan. Hence,

10. This appears to be what has occurred in this instance. In providing the reasons for the objection, the Attorney General noted that "[f]or the south-central to southeast area, there were several plans drawn providing for a second majority-minority congressional district" and that such a district would have been no more irregular than others in the State's plan. North Carolina's decision to create a majority-minority district can be explained as an attempt to meet this objection. Its decision not to create the more compact southern majority-minority district that was suggested, on the other hand, was more likely a result of partisan considerations. Indeed, in a suit brought prior to this one, different plaintiffs charged that District 12 was "grossly contorted" and had "no logical explanation other than incumbency protection and the enhancement of Democratic partisan interests.... The plan... ignores the directive of the [Department of Justice] to create a minority district in the southeastern portion of North Carolina since any such district would jeopardize the reelection of... the Democratic incumbent." With respect to this incident, one writer has observed that "understanding why the configurations are shaped as they are requires us to know at least as much about the interests of incumbent Democratic politicians, as it does knowledge of the Voting Rights Act." Grofman, *Would Vince Lombardi Have Been Right If He Had Said: "When It Comes to Redistricting, Race Isn't Everything, It's the Only Thing"?*, 14 Cardozo L.Rev. 1237, 1258 (1993). The District Court in *Pope* [*v. Blue*] dismissed appellants' claim, reasoning in part that "plaintiffs do not allege, nor can they, that the state's redistricting plan has caused them to be "shut out of the political process."

I see no need for a remand at all, even accepting the majority's basic approach to this case.

Furthermore, how it intends to manage this standard, I do not know. Is it more "narrowly tailored" to create an irregular majority-minority district as opposed to one that is compact but harms other State interests such as incumbency protection or the representation of rural interests? Of the following two options — creation of two minority influence districts or of a single majority-minority district — is one "narrowly tailored" and the other not? Once the Attorney General has found that a proposed redistricting change violates §5's nonretrogression principle in that it will abridge a racial minority's right to vote, does "narrow tailoring" mean that the most the State can do is preserve the *status quo*? Or can it maintain that change, while attempting to enhance minority voting power in some other manner? This small sample only begins to scratch the surface of the problems raised by the majority's test. But it suffices to illustrate the unworkability of a standard that is divorced from any measure of constitutional harm. In that, State efforts to remedy minority vote dilution are wholly unlike what typically has been labeled "affirmative action." To the extent that no other racial group is injured, remedying a Voting Rights Act violation does not involve preferential treatment. It involves, instead, an attempt to *equalize* treatment, and to provide minority voters with an effective voice in the political process. The Equal Protection Clause of the Constitution, surely, does not stand in the way.

IV

Since I do not agree that petitioners alleged an Equal Protection violation and because the Court of Appeals faithfully followed the Court's prior cases, I dissent and would affirm the judgment below.

[Separate dissenting opinions by Justices Blackmun, Stevens, and Souter are omitted.]

Notes and Questions

1. A number of writers have criticized *Shaw*, but none more strongly than A. Leon Higginbotham, Jr. et al., Shaw v. Reno*: A Mirage of Good Intentions with Devastating Racial Consequences*, 62 Fordham Law Review 1593, 1603 (1994):

> With plaintiffs' urging, the Court has created law that could make *Shaw v. Reno* equivalent for the civil rights jurisprudence of our generation to what *Plessy v. Ferguson* and *Dred Scott v. Sandford* were for prior generations.

Critics have questioned not only Justice O'Connor's constitutional doctrine, but her rhetoric.

> However race-conscious the General Assembly had been, and it concededly had drawn the plan with the intent to create two majority-black districts, it had not in fact segregated the races into separate districts.

> Consider the racial composition of the two districts in which the *Shaw* plaintiffs lived. House District 2's population was 76.23 percent white and 21.94 percent black; House District 12's population was 41.80 percent white and 56.63 percent black. To say that either district even remotely resembles "political apartheid"—especially given that House District 2, where a majority of the *Shaw* plaintiffs lived, was a nearly perfect mirror of the state's overall racial makeup—would be risible if it were not so pernicious.

Pamela S. Karlan, *All Over the Map: The Supreme Court's Voting Rights Trilogy*, 1993 Supreme Court Review 245, 282. See also, *e.g.*, T. Alexander Aleinikoff & Samuel Issacharoff, *Race and Redistricting: Drawing Constitutional Lines After* Shaw v. Reno, 92 Michigan Law Review 588, 651 (1993) ("*Shaw* does not adequately instruct lower courts as to how they should review subsequent claims, it does not resolve the ongoing claims of the filler people [that is, the white voters in majority-minority districts], and it does not answer the more troubling questions that lie close to heart of any system of districting.").

A few scholars have praised *Shaw*. James F. Blumstein, *Racial Gerrymandering and Vote Dilution:* Shaw v. Reno *in Doctrinal Context*, 26 Rutgers Law Journal 517 (1995), argues that the Court rightly applied the paradigm of racial discrimination it had developed in other contexts to racial redistricting. Katharine Inglis Butler, *Affirmative Racial Gerrymandering: Fair Representation for Minorities or a Dangerous Recognition of Group Rights?*, 20 Rutgers Law Journal 595 (1995), applauds *Shaw* as valuing individual rather than group-based rights while arguing that racial gerrymandering is neither required by the Voting Rights Act nor justified to remedy past discrimination. Melissa L. Saunders, *The Dirty Little Secrets of* Shaw, 24 Harvard Journal of Law & Public Policy 141 (2000), contends that racial gerrymandering doctrine does not fulfill the goals favored by writers such as Blumstein and Butler.

2. What kind of claim does *Shaw* recognize? One explanation is suggested by Richard H. Pildes and Richard G. Niemi, *Expressive Harms, "Bizarre Districts," and Voting Rights: Evaluating Election-District Appearances After* Shaw v. Reno, 92 Michigan Law Review 483, 506–09 (1993):

> One can only understand *Shaw*, we believe, in terms of a view that what we call *expressive* harms are constitutionally cognizable. An expressive harm is one that results from the ideas or attitudes expressed through a governmental action, rather than from the more tangible or material consequences the action brings about. On this view, the *meaning* of a governmental action is just as important as what that action *does*. Public policies can violate the Constitution not only because they bring about concrete costs, but because the very meaning they convey demonstrates inappropriate respect for relevant public values. On this unusual conception of constitutional harm, when a governmental action expresses disrespect for such values, it can violate the Constitution.

> [*Shaw*] becomes intelligible only if one recognizes that it rests on just this concern for expressive harms. *Shaw* validates such harms as constitutionally cognizable, along with more familiar, concrete, material injuries. Indeed, close attention to the language of Justice O'Connor's opinion reveals a constant struggle to articulate exactly these sorts of expressive harms. Thus, the opinion is laden with references to the social perceptions, the messages, and the governmental reinforcement of values that the Court believes North Carolina's districting scheme conveys. There is simply no way to make sense of these references, which give the opinion its character and are central to its holding, without recognizing that the decision is grounded in concern for expressive harms. This conception of constitutionally cognizable harms explains why the Court is adamant that "reapportionment is one area in which appearances do matter." If they do, it must be because, even apart from any concrete harm to individual voters, such appearances themselves express a value structure that offends constitutional principles.
>
> *Shaw* therefore rests on the principle that, when government appears to use race in the redistricting context in a way that subordinates all other relevant values, the state has impermissibly endorsed too dominant a role for race. The constitutional harm must lie in this endorsement itself: the very expression of this kind of value reductionism becomes the constitutional violation.

Expressive harm as a rationale for *Shaw* has not gone without criticism:

> Normatively, the expressive harm explanation is vulnerable to the charge that law based on "appearances" rather than reality can have no firm grounding and, more generally, conflicts with one of the great truths in the western tradition: that actions and understandings based on appearances rather than reality are morally and intellectually deficient. In addition, the empirical assumptions on which the expressive harm explanation is based are probably implausible and certainly undemonstrated.

Daniel Hays Lowenstein, *You Don't Have to Be Liberal to Hate the Racial Gerrymandering Cases*, 50 Stanford Law Review 779, 797 (1998). On the last point, Pamela S. Karlan, *Just Politics? Five Not So Easy Pieces of the 1995 Term*, 34 Houston Law Review 289 (1997), shows that in later racial gerrymandering cases decided in 1996, the Court ignored evidence that the types of expressive harm assumed to accompany racial gerrymandering were not actually occurring. She observes: "It seems to be enough that the Court has perceived a pernicious message, regardless of whether voters or elected representatives have received one." In an empirical study, similarly, Stephen Ansolabehere and Nathaniel Persily, *Testing* Shaw v. Reno*: Do Majority-Minority Districts Cause Expressive Harms?*, 90 New York University Law Review 1041 (2015), investigate whether there are differences in voters' racial attitudes between compact and noncompact majority-minority districts. There are not; black,

Latino, and white voters' racial resentment and approval of their representatives do not appreciably vary based on whether these voters happen to live in compact or noncompact majority-minority districts.

Notwithstanding these criticisms, a plurality of the Court adopted Pildes and Niemi's terminology, referring in a subsequent case to "the nature of the expressive harms with which we are dealing." *Bush v. Vera*, 517 U.S. 952, 984 (1996) (plurality opinion). The plurality also relied on Pildes and Niemi's ranking of congressional districts' compactness in striking down three majority-minority districts in Texas. See *id.* at 960.

3. *Shaw* is generally regarded as a "conservative" decision. The five-member majority was composed of the justices generally regarded as conservatives, and the insistence on treating "benign" and malignant racial classifications as equally suspect is consistent with a prominent theme of contemporary conservatism. Nevertheless, *Shaw* is by no means a pure gain, measured by conservative values. One such value is the preservation of the role of the states in the federal structure. The Voting Rights Act in general, and amended Section 2 as interpreted in *Gingles* in particular, intrude into the crucial realm of the state's freedom to structure its own political system.[1] Most Americans would now agree that the intrusion was justified by the overriding need to assure the extension of voting rights, though there remains sharp disagreement over the appropriate degree of that intrusion. The intrusion is limited, however, in the sense that so long as the state complies, it is otherwise free to structure its political system as it chooses. After *Shaw*, however, race-based districting is *required* up to the point mandated by federal law, but sharply *restricted* beyond the federal mandate. Thus, the zone of state discretion with respect to one important factor in districting is narrowed. Is this really a conservative decision?

With respect to partisanship, similarly, *Shaw* arguably barred states from drawing highly convoluted districts with supermajorities of minority voters. Such districts, though, are usually preferred by *Republican*, not *Democratic*, mapmakers. This is because the districts "pack" or overconcentrate minority voters, thus wasting many of their (heavily Democratic) votes and benefiting Republican candidates in the rest of the state. By preventing the creation of the districts, *Shaw* may have stopped Republicans from implementing their most advantageous redistricting strategy. See Adam B. Cox & Richard T. Holden, *Reconsidering Racial and Partisan Gerrymandering*, 78 University of Chicago Law Review 553, 590 (2011) ("If a legal rule added a ceiling to the VRA's floor—that is, a prohibition against assembling districts with large supermajorities of minority voters—the ceiling could suppress the second-best strategy for Republicans of packing minority voters.").

---

1. Admittedly, the congressional districts under challenge in *Shaw* are part of the national system of government, not that of the state, and the federalism concerns expressed in this Note are perhaps minimal. However, *Shaw* is equally applicable to districting at the state and local levels.

4. The majority in *Shaw* acknowledged that the plaintiffs were not alleging that their votes were diluted. The only harm they claimed to suffer was that the state had "segregate[d] citizens into separate voting districts on the basis of race." It is at least plausible to suggest that the harm alleged is suffered by all citizens as citizens, not by particular citizens as individuals. When such generalized harms are alleged, the Court ordinarily begins by asking whether the plaintiffs have "standing" to assert the claim in a judicial proceeding. We shall not review the intricacies of standing doctrine, which is complex and beyond the scope of this book, but it is striking that the issue of standing appears to have been overlooked by both the majority and the dissenters in *Shaw*.

In 1995, on the same day the Court decided *Miller v. Johnson*, excerpted below, it addressed the standing issue in *Hays v. Louisiana*, 515 U.S. 737 (1995), in which it held that only residents of the district being challenged have standing to bring a racial gerrymandering action. Commentators have struggled to find a rationale for this ruling. If the harm is the separation of racial groups into voting districts without regard to dilution of votes or other disadvantaging of a group, why are those who fall on one side of the separation more aggrieved than those who fall on the other side? John Hart Ely, *Standing to Challenge Pro-Minority Gerrymanders*, 111 Harvard Law Review 576 (1997), suggests that only residents of the district in question who are not members of the racial group for whose benefit the district was created should have standing. Samuel Issacharoff and Pamela S. Karlan, *Standing and Misunderstanding in Voting Rights Law*, 111 Harvard Law Review 2276, 2278 (1997), argue that Ely's suggestion is inconsistent with the theory of the racial gerrymandering cause of action as the Supreme Court has articulated it.

5. The implementation of *Shaw* raised a number of difficult questions. First and most basically, what must a plaintiff demonstrate to show a prima facie violation of the Equal Protection Clause? The majority acknowledged that "race-conscious" districting is not always unconstitutional. Does "race-conscious" mean "race-motivated"? The Court also said that districting "unexplainable on grounds other than race" is prima facie unconstitutional. If a districting plan is at all race-motivated, does it not follow that it cannot be *entirely* explained on grounds other than race? Is that sufficient? Or does "unexplainable on grounds other than race" mean that a plan is prima facie unconstitutional only if nothing *other* than race enters into the explanation?

One problem with the *Shaw* approach was that the irregular shape of the Twelfth Congressional District in North Carolina resulted from the state legislature's determination to comply with the Justice Department's insistence on a second majority-minority district at the expense of the Republicans rather than the Democrats. More generally, it is virtually impossible that race or any other single consideration could be the *sole* cause of a district's configuration, especially if the districting plan is enacted through a political process. The unrealistic but repeated reference to race as a sole cause undoubtedly reflected Justice O'Connor's awareness of the difficulty of answering this question: If a plan only partially explainable by race can be unconstitutional and yet race-conscious districting is not always unconstitutional, how can a line be drawn?

Together with what constitutes a prima facie violation, the other important question left open by *Shaw* was what compelling state interests could defend a plan shown to be presumptively unconstitutional. Of particular importance was whether compliance with the Voting Rights Act would count as a compelling state interest sufficient to justify a plan. Bear in mind that the plans attacked in the cases that reached the Supreme Court were from states that were covered by the Voting Rights Act. Legislatures in these states knew that if they did not create a sufficient number of majority-minority districts to satisfy the Justice Department, their plans would not be precleared and could not be put into effect. Indeed, in North Carolina and Georgia, the challenged districts were drawn only after the Justice Department had rejected earlier plans that created only one majority-minority district in North Carolina and only two in Georgia. Furthermore, these and other states knew that in many instances they would be vulnerable to Section 2 actions unless they created new majority-minority districts. Would the desire to comply with Section 5 or Section 2 of the Voting Rights Act count as a compelling state interest?

As you read the following materials, consider how these questions were resolved in post-*Shaw* decisions.

Post-*Shaw* Decisions

After the 1990 census, Georgia's population entitled it to go from ten to eleven congressional districts. One of the ten old districts was a majority-minority district. The Georgia legislature (the General Assembly) passed and sought preclearance for a new plan containing two majority-minority districts and a third district in which African Americans made up 35 percent of the voting age population. Despite the increase from one majority-minority district to two and an absence of evidence of an intent to discriminate, preclearance was denied. A second plan was also rejected, as Justice Department lawyers pointed to a so-called "max-black" plan that had been developed by the American Civil Liberties Union, containing three majority-minority districts. The General Assembly then adopted a plan based on the ACLU proposal, containing three majority-minority districts. Black representatives were elected from each of the three majority-minority districts.

One of these, the Eleventh District, was challenged by five white residents of the district as an unconstitutional racial gerrymander. The Eleventh District was described by the *Almanac of American Politics*: "Geographically, it is a monstrosity, stretching from Atlanta to Savannah. Its core is the plantation country in the center of the state, lightly populated, but heavily black. It links by narrow corridors the black neighborhoods in Augusta, Savannah and southern DeKalb County." In *Miller v. Johnson*, 515 U.S. 900 (1995) (from which the above characterizations are taken), the Supreme Court struck down the Eleventh District as violative of the Equal Protection Clause.

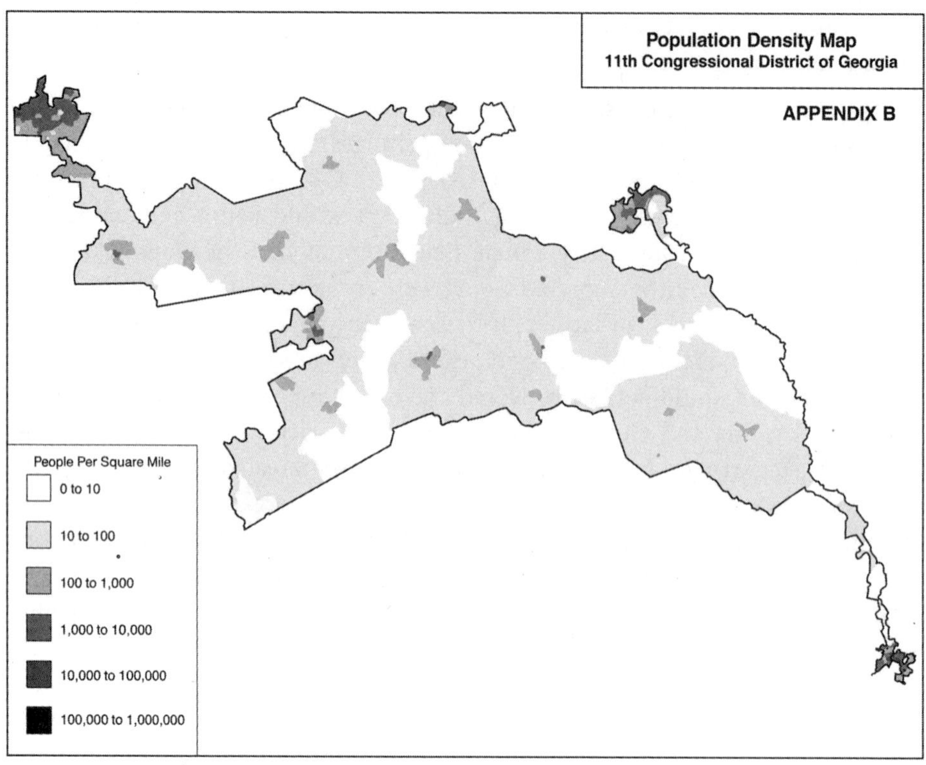

The district court had found and the state did not deny that "race was the predominant, overriding factor in drawing the Eleventh District." Rather, the state contended that "regardless of the legislature's purposes, a plaintiff must demonstrate that a district's shape is so bizarre that it is unexplainable other than on the basis of race." It may seem to the uninitiated that the shape of the Georgia district is pretty bizarre, but veterans of redistricting will see nothing unusual in the district's outline. Comparison of the Georgia district with the North Carolina district in *Shaw* or the Texas districts displayed later in this chapter will show that the Georgia Eleventh is pretty low on the bizarreness scale. What the district court and the Supreme Court found remarkable about the district was the enclosure of black neighborhoods in distant cities.

Justice Kennedy, writing for a majority that included Chief Justice Rehnquist and Justices O'Connor, Scalia, and Thomas, responded that the appellants' "conception of the constitutional violation misapprehends our holding in *Shaw*."

> Our observation in *Shaw* of the consequences of racial stereotyping was not meant to suggest that a district must be bizarre on its face before there is a constitutional violation. Nor was our conclusion in *Shaw* that in certain instances a district's appearance (or, to be more precise, its appearance in combination with certain demographic evidence) can give rise to an equal protection claim, a holding that bizarreness was a threshold showing, as

appellants believe it to be. Our circumspect approach and narrow holding in *Shaw* did not erect an artificial rule barring accepted equal protection analysis in other redistricting cases. Shape is relevant not because bizarreness is a necessary element of the constitutional wrong or a threshold requirement of proof, but because it may be persuasive circumstantial evidence that race for its own sake, and not other districting principles, was the legislature's dominant and controlling rationale in drawing its district lines. The logical implication, as courts applying *Shaw* have recognized, is that parties may rely on evidence other than bizarreness to establish race-based districting....

... Electoral districting is a most difficult subject for legislatures, and so the States must have discretion to exercise the political judgment necessary to balance competing interests. Although race-based decisionmaking is inherently suspect, until a claimant makes a showing sufficient to support that allegation the good faith of a state legislature must be presumed. The courts, in assessing the sufficiency of a challenge to a districting plan, must be sensitive to the complex interplay of forces that enter a legislature's redistricting calculus. Redistricting legislatures will, for example, almost always be aware of racial demographics; but it does not follow that race predominates in the redistricting process. *Shaw*. The distinction between being aware of racial considerations and being motivated by them may be difficult to make. This evidentiary difficulty, together with the sensitive nature of redistricting and the presumption of good faith that must be accorded legislative enactments, requires courts to exercise extraordinary caution in adjudicating claims that a state has drawn district lines on the basis of race. The plaintiff's burden is to show, either through circumstantial evidence of a district's shape and demographics or more direct evidence going to legislative purpose, that race was the predominant factor motivating the legislature's decision to place a significant number of voters within or without a particular district. To make this showing, a plaintiff must prove that the legislature subordinated traditional race-neutral districting principles, including but not limited to compactness, contiguity, respect for political subdivisions or communities defined by actual shared interests, to racial considerations. Where these or other race-neutral considerations are the basis for redistricting legislation, and are not subordinated to race, a state can "defeat a claim that a district has been gerrymandered on racial lines." *Shaw*....

[The district court found] "it was 'exceedingly obvious' from the shape of the Eleventh District, together with the relevant racial demographics, that the drawing of narrow land bridges to incorporate within the District outlying appendages containing nearly 80% of the district's total black population was a deliberate attempt to bring black populations into the district. Although by comparison with other districts the geometric shape of the Eleventh District may not seem bizarre on its face, when its shape is considered in conjunction with its racial and population densities, the story of racial gerrymandering seen by the District Court becomes much clearer. [This evidence was confirmed by evidence that the Justice Department would accept "nothing less than abject surrender to its maximization agenda" and that the General Assembly "was driven by its overriding desire to comply."]

Race was, as the District Court found, the predominant, overriding factor explaining the General Assembly's decision to attach to the Eleventh District various appendages containing dense majority-black populations. As a result, Georgia's congressional redistricting plan cannot be upheld unless it satisfies strict scrutiny, our most rigorous and exacting standard of constitutional review.

. . . Whether or not in some cases compliance with the Voting Rights Act, standing alone, can provide a compelling interest independent of any interest in remedying past discrimination, it cannot do so here. As we suggested in *Shaw*, compliance with federal antidiscrimination laws cannot justify race-based districting where the challenged district was not reasonably necessary under a constitutional reading and application of those laws. The congressional plan challenged here was not required by the Voting Rights Act under a correct reading of the statute.

[It is] safe to say that the congressional plan enacted in the end was required in order to obtain preclearance. It does not follow, however, that the plan was required by the substantive provisions of the Voting Rights Act.

We do not accept the contention that the State has a compelling interest in complying with whatever preclearance mandates the Justice Department issues. When a state governmental entity seeks to justify race-based remedies to cure the effects of past discrimination, we do not accept the government's mere assertion that the remedial action is required. Rather, we insist on a strong basis in evidence of the harm being remedied. See, e.g., *Shaw*. . . . Our presumptive skepticism of all racial classifications prohibits us as well from accepting on its face the Justice Department's conclusion that racial districting is necessary under the Voting Rights Act. Where a State relies on the Department's determination that race-based districting is necessary to comply with the Voting Rights Act, the judiciary retains an independent obligation in adjudicating consequent equal protection challenges to ensure that the State's actions are narrowly tailored to achieve a compelling interest. Were we to accept the Justice Department's objection itself as a compelling interest adequate to insulate racial districting from constitutional review, we would be surrendering to the Executive Branch our role in enforcing the constitutional limits on race-based official action. We may not do so. . . .

> Georgia's drawing of the Eleventh District was not required under the Act because there was no reasonable basis to believe that Georgia's earlier enacted plans violated § 5. Wherever a plan is "ameliorative," a term we have used to describe plans increasing the number of majority-minority districts, it "cannot violate § 5 unless the new apportionment itself so discriminates on the basis of race or color as to violate the Constitution." *Beer.* Georgia's first and second proposed plans increased the number of majority-black districts from 1 out of 10 (10%) to 2 out of 11 (18.18%). These plans were "ameliorative" and could not have violated § 5's nonretrogression principle. Acknowledging as much, the United States now relies on the fact that the Justice Department may object to a state proposal either on the ground that it has a prohibited purpose or a prohibited effect. The Government justifies its preclearance objections on the ground that the submitted plans violated § 5's purpose element. The key to the Government's position, which is plain from its objection letters if not from its briefs to this Court, is and always has been that Georgia failed to proffer a nondiscriminatory purpose for its refusal in the first two submissions to take the steps necessary to create a third majority-minority district.
>
> The Government's position is insupportable. . . . The State's policy of adhering to other districting principles instead of creating as many majority-minority districts as possible does not support an inference that the plan "so discriminates on the basis of race or color as to violate the Constitution," *Beer,* and thus cannot provide any basis under § 5 for the Justice Department's objection.
>
> Instead of grounding its objections on evidence of a discriminatory purpose, it would appear the Government was driven by its policy of maximizing majority-black districts. Although the Government now disavows having had that policy and seems to concede its impropriety, the District Court's well-documented factual finding was that the Department did adopt a maximization policy and followed it in objecting to Georgia's first two plans. . . .

Id. at 912-25. Justice O'Connor wrote a short concurring opinion. Justices Ginsburg, joined by Justices Stevens, Breyer and Souter, dissented. Justice Stevens also wrote a dissenting opinion arguing that the plaintiffs lacked standing.

Miller places less emphasis than *Shaw* on the shape of a district as an element of the constitutional violation and more emphasis on the underlying racial motivation, with shape being significant primarily as an indicator of the existence of racial motivation. *Miller* requires a plaintiff to prove "that race was the *predominant* factor motivating the legislature's decision to place a significant number of voters within or without a particular district. To make this showing, a plaintiff must prove that the legislature subordinated traditional race-neutral districting principles, including but not limited to compactness, contiguity, respect for political subdivisions or communities defined by actual shared interests, to racial considerations." 515 U.S. at 916 (emphasis added).

Many scholars have commented on the difficulty of attributing a predominant motive to a body as complex as a legislature engaged in as complex an enterprise as redistricting. John Hart Ely, *Gerrymanders: The Good, the Bad, and the Ugly*, 50 Stanford Law Review 607, 612 (1998), summarizes these views pithily:

> Drawing a voting district involves an infinity of choices, each of which is similarly likely to be influenced by a number of considerations. The boundaries zig and zag, shuck and jive, sidle like sidewinders. And each spasm has at least one story of its own: How in the name of heaven could one suppose the whole monstrosity to have a "dominant purpose," unless it's to accommodate as many little purposes as possible?

The "predominant factor" test has also been criticized as fundamentally misconceived in the context of a racial gerrymandering case:

> To ask whether one factor "predominates" over others is to imply that the districting process consists of a weighing or balancing of factors. But that is not what occurs with race in redistricting. Under the VRA, race is not a "factor" at all, but a prior requirement in a lexical ordering. In John Rawls' definition of a lexical (or serial) ordering:
>
>> This is an order which requires us to satisfy the first principle in the ordering before we can move on to the second, the second before we consider the third, and so on. A principle does not come into play until those previous to it are either fully met or do not apply. A serial ordering avoids, then, having to balance principles at all; those earlier in the ordering have an absolute weight, so to speak with respect to later ones, and hold without exception.
>
> A consideration that is lexically prior is a *privileged* consideration. It is a necessary precondition of what comes afterward, and aside from that, there is little that can be said about how it is "weighted" against the rest....
>
> Because the racial quotas imposed under the VRA were *privileged* considerations, debate over their "predominance" is inevitably uncertain and arbitrary. Although the majority and the dissenters in the racial gerrymandering cases debated numerous aspects of the complex factual records, there was no serious disagreement between them over what actually happened. In each case, the state was forced to create a minimum number of [majority-minority districts]. Subject to that constraint, the state produced its districting plan by a normal political process of competition and negotiation. The majority on the Court and the dissenters debated the artificial question of whether to characterize the privileged consideration as predominant, when they all knew that the privileged consideration was never balanced against other considerations at all.

Lowenstein, *You Don't Have to Be Liberal to Hate the Racial Gerrymandering Cases, supra*, 50 Stanford Law Review at 806–07.

If the evidence shows that the legislature gave very little attention to traditional principles, some attention to race, and lots of attention to political goals, has the plaintiff proven a prima facie case under *Miller*?

* * *

In the next two major racial gerrymandering decisions, the Court struck down congressional districts in Texas and North Carolina.

In the Texas case, *Bush v. Vera*, 517 U.S. 952 (1996), Justice O'Connor wrote the lead opinion, which was joined only by Chief Justice Rehnquist and Justice Kennedy. Three congressional districts were challenged: the 30th, a majority-black district in the Dallas area, and two districts in the Houston area, the 29th, which was majority-Hispanic, and the 18th, which was majority-black. A majority of justices concluded that all three were unconstitutional, although there was no opinion for the Court. Justice O'Connor's lead opinion viewed this as a "mixed motive case," given that race was not the only consideration in drawing these districts. On the level of scrutiny, she wrote:

> Strict scrutiny would not be appropriate if race-neutral, traditional districting considerations predominated over racial ones. We have not subjected political gerrymandering to strict scrutiny. See *Bandemer*. And we have recognized incumbency protection, at least in the limited form of

Texas' 18th Congressional District

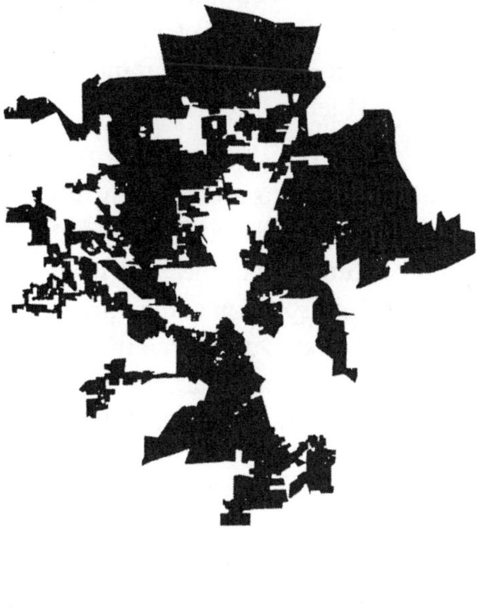

Texas' 30th Congressional District

> "avoiding contests between incumbent[s]," as a legitimate state goal. See *Karcher*; *White v. Weiser*; *Burns v. Richardson*. Because it is clear that race was not the only factor that motivated the legislature to draw irregular district lines, we must scrutinize each challenged district to determine whether the District Court's conclusion that race predominated over legitimate districting considerations, including incumbency, can be sustained.

Id. at 964. Following lengthy discussion of the three districts, Justice O'Connor's lead opinion upheld the district court's conclusion that race was the predominant factor. The evidence supporting this conclusion included the districts highly irregular shapes; the ways in which their boundaries corresponded to concentrations of minority voters; and the use of redistricting software enabling race, and only race, to be analyzed at the census block level. The opinion then turned to the state's asserted interest in complying with Section 2's results test. The opinion assumed without deciding that compliance with the results test could be a compelling interest, but concluded that the districts were not narrowly tailored to serve this interest because of their extreme noncompactness:

> A § 2 district that is *reasonably* compact and regular, taking into account traditional districting principles such as maintaining communities of interest and traditional boundaries, may pass strict scrutiny without having to defeat rival compact districts designed by plaintiffs' experts in endless "beauty contests." . . .
>
> . . . We have, however, already found that all three districts are bizarrely shaped and far from compact, and that those characteristics are predominantly attributable to gerrymandering that was racially motivated and/or achieved by the use of race as a proxy. District 30, for example, reaches out to grab small and apparently isolated minority communities which, based on the evidence presented, could not possibly form part of a compact majority-minority district, and does so in order to make up for minority populations closer to its core that it shed in a further suspect use of race as a proxy to further neighboring incumbents' interests.
>
> These characteristics defeat any claim that the districts are narrowly tailored to serve the State's interest in avoiding liability under § 2, because § 2 does not require a State to create, on predominantly racial lines, a district that is not "reasonably compact." If, because of the dispersion of the minority population, a reasonably compact majority-minority district cannot be created, § 2 does not require a majority-minority district; if a reasonably compact district can be created, nothing in § 2 requires the race-based creation of a district that is far from compact.

Id. at 977-79.

Although Justice O'Connor was the author of the lead opinion from which the foregoing excerpts were taken, she also added a *concurring* opinion, in which she spoke only for herself. This opinion was significant because Justice O'Connor stated firmly her view that compliance with Section 2 is a compelling state interest. Thus "if a State pursues that compelling interest by creating a district that 'substantially addresses' the potential liability, and does not deviate substantially from a hypothetical court-drawn § 2 district for predominantly racial reasons, its districting plan will be deemed narrowly tailored." *Id.* at 994 (O'Connor, J., concurring).

The remaining two votes to strike down the Texas districts were explained in a concurring opinion by Justice Thomas, joined by Justice Scalia, who found the level of scrutiny question not close because "[s]trict scrutiny applies to all governmental classifications based on race, and we have expressly held that there is no exception for race-based redistricting," *Id.* at 1000 (Thomas, J., concurring in the judgment). Dissenting opinions by Justices Stevens and Souter were each joined by Justices Ginsburg and Breyer.

The North Carolina case, *Shaw v. Hunt*, 517 U.S. 899 (1996) (*Shaw II*), was part of the same litigation as *Shaw v. Reno*. On remand, the District Court found that North Carolina's 12th congressional district, described in *Shaw I*, was constitutional. Chief Justice Rehnquist wrote an opinion for the Court reversing the district court and striking down the 12th district.

The most significant portions of *Shaw II* were the discussions of the state's asserted interests. The Court rejected the state's argument that avoiding litigation under the Voting Rights Act was a compelling interest. While assuming *arguendo* that compliance with "the properly interpreted Voting Rights Act" was a compelling interest, the majority held that "a State must also have a 'strong basis in evidence' for believing that it is violating the Act. It has no such interest in avoiding meritless lawsuits." *Id.* at 908 n.4. The Court went on to conclude that the 12th district was not narrowly tailored to comply with the VRA. It rejected the state's argument that "once a legislature has a strong basis in evidence for concluding that a § 2 violation exists in the State, it may draw a majority-minority district anywhere, even if the district is in no way coincident with the compact *Gingles* district, as long as racially polarized voting exists where the district is ultimately drawn," reasoning that:

> If a § 2 violation is proven for a particular area, it flows from the fact that individuals in this area "have less opportunity than other members of the electorate to participate in the political process and to elect representatives of their choice." The vote dilution injuries suffered by these persons are not remedied by creating a safe majority-black district somewhere else in the State. For example, if a geographically compact, cohesive minority population lives in south-central to southeastern North Carolina, as the Justice Department's objection letter suggested, District 12 which spans the Piedmont Crescent would not address that § 2 violation. The black voters of the south-central to southeastern region would still be suffering precisely the same injury that they suffered before District 12 was drawn. District 12 would not address the professed interest of relieving the vote dilution, much less be narrowly tailored to accomplish the goal.

> Arguing, as appellees do and the District Court did, that the State may draw the district anywhere derives from a misconception of the vote-dilution claim. To accept that the district may be placed anywhere implies that the claim, and hence the coordinate right to an undiluted vote (to cast a ballot equal among voters), belongs to the minority as a group and not to its individual members. It does not.

Id. at 917. Justice Stevens, joined by Justices Ginsburg and Breyer, wrote a dissenting opinion. Justice Souter, also joined by Ginsburg and Breyer, dissented on the grounds stated in Souter's opinion in *Bush v. Vera*.

* * *

Like some monster in a popular movie series, North Carolina's 12th District kept coming back. The legislature drew new lines in response to *Shaw II*, and the new district was challenged as a racial gerrymander. The district court concluded that it was unconstitutional, and granted summary judgment for the plaintiffs. The Supreme Court reversed and ordered the district court to hold a trial. *Hunt v. Cromartie*, 526 U.S. 541 (1999). It did, and again found the 12th District unconstitutional. And again, the Supreme Court reversed in *Easley v. Cromartie*, 532 U.S. 234 (2001). Justice Breyer wrote for the majority, but the key vote was Justice O'Connor, who for the first time voted to uphold a plan against a racial gerrymandering challenge. All of the other justices voted as they had in *Shaw I*, *Miller*, *Vera*, and *Shaw II*.

As Justice Breyer said at the outset of his opinion, "The issue in this case is evidentiary." Acknowledging that the question was whether the District Court had committed "clear error" in finding that the predominant reason for the new District 12 was race, Justice Breyer wrote:

> The critical District Court determination — the matter for which we remanded this litigation — consists of the finding that race *rather than* politics *predominantly* explains District 12's 1997 boundaries. That determination rests upon three findings (the district's shape, its splitting of towns and counties, and its high African-American voting population) that we previously found insufficient to support summary judgment. Given the undisputed evidence that racial identification is highly correlated with political affiliation in North Carolina, these facts in and of themselves cannot, as a matter of law, support the District Court's judgment. The District Court rested, however, upon five new subsidiary findings to conclude that District 12's lines are the product of no "mer[e] correlat[ion]," but are instead a result of the predominance of race in the legislature's line-drawing process. . . .
>
> The District Court primarily based its "race, not politics," conclusion upon its finding that "the legislators excluded many heavily-Democratic precincts from District 12, even when those precincts immediately border the Twelfth and would have established a far more compact district." . . .

> [T]he problem with this evidence is that it focuses upon party registration, not upon voting behavior.... [W]hite voters registered as Democrats "cross-over" to vote for a Republican candidate more often than do African-Americans, who register and vote Democratic between 95% and 97% of the time. A legislature trying to secure a safe Democratic seat is interested in Democratic voting behavior. Hence, a legislature may, by placing reliable Democratic precincts within a district without regard to race, end up with a district containing more heavily African-American precincts, but the reasons would be political rather than racial....
>
> The District Court's final citation is to [the expert witness's] assertion that there are other ways in which the legislature could have created a safely Democratic district without placing so many primarily African-American districts within District 12.... But, unless the evidence also shows that these hypothetical alternative districts would have better satisfied the legislature's other nonracial political goals as well as traditional nonracial districting principles, this fact alone cannot show an improper legislative motive. After all, the Constitution does not place an *affirmative* obligation upon the legislature to avoid creating districts that turn out to be heavily, even majority, minority. It simply imposes an obligation not to create such districts for predominantly racial, as opposed to political or traditional, districting motivations.
>
> We concede the record contains a modicum of evidence offering support for the District Court's conclusion.... The evidence taken together, however, does not show that racial considerations predominated in the drawing of District 12's boundaries. That is because race in this case correlates closely with political behavior. The basic question is whether the legislature drew District 12's boundaries because of race *rather than* because of political behavior (coupled with traditional, nonracial districting considerations).... We can put the matter more generally as follows: In a case such as this one where majority-minority districts (or the approximate equivalent) are at issue and where racial identification correlates highly with political affiliation, the party attacking the legislatively drawn boundaries must show at the least that the legislature could have achieved its legitimate political objectives in alternative ways that are comparably consistent with traditional districting principles. That party must also show that those districting alternatives would have brought about significantly greater racial balance. Appellees failed to make any such showing here. We conclude that the District Court's contrary findings are clearly erroneous.

Id. at 243-58. Justice Thomas, joined by Chief Justice Rehnquist and Justices Kennedy and Scalia, dissented on the ground that the findings of the District Court were not clearly erroneous.

Notes and Questions

1. All of the previous racial gerrymandering cases whose merits had been given more than summary attention by the Supreme Court had been decided in favor of the plaintiffs by a 5–4 vote, with the same five justices constituting the majority. Why did Justice O'Connor cast her deciding vote to uphold the plan in *Easley*?

The justices' factual analyses are long and have not been fully set forth here, but major factual differences are not readily apparent to the naked eye. Except, perhaps, for these two: First, the other racial gerrymandering cases that were resolved by the Court on the merits were attacks on majority-minority districts that were either required as a condition of preclearance or that the states could anticipate would be required for that purpose. State legislatures set out to meet quotas for majority-minority districts because they had no choice. But after *Shaw II*, there was no realistic possibility that a chastened Justice Department would deny preclearance for failure to create a second majority-minority congressional district in North Carolina. Thus, the legislature at least had the option of being motivated by other considerations than race, such as partisanship.

Second, in addition to being strangely shaped, the districts in *Shaw I*, *Miller*, *Vera*, and *Shaw II* paid little heed to geographic communities of interest. They fused urban and rural African American communities hundreds of miles apart, they separated members of the same urban community on racial grounds, and so on. In contrast, the district at issue in *Easley* was substantially more respectful of community boundaries. As the majority put it, the district "joined three major cities in a manner legislators regarded as reflecting 'a real commonality of urban interests, with inner city schools, urban health care ... problems, public housing problems." *Id.* at 250. See also Stephanopoulos, *Redistricting and the Territorial Community*, *supra*, 160 University of Pennsylvania Law Review at 1419-21 (advancing this argument).

2. In the last paragraph of his opinion for the Court, Justice Breyer says that a plaintiff in a racial gerrymandering case should show, among other things, that an alternative plan could be devised that would bring about "significantly greater racial balance." What does he mean by racial balance? Is a district racially unbalanced if a majority of its residents are African American? Why? If so, is a district in which a majority of residents are white racially unbalanced? Why not? What does racial balance have to do with the premises of the racial gerrymandering doctrine as set forth in *Shaw v. Reno* and the later cases?

3. Plaintiffs won almost no racial gerrymandering claims in the post-2000 round of redistricting.[m] For an analysis of the failed *Shaw/Miller* challenges in that decade, see Jocelyn Friedrichs Benson, *A Shared Existence: The Current Compatibility of the Equal Protection Clause and Section 5 of the Voting Rights Act*, 88 Nebraska Law Review 124 (2009).

---

m. A rare exception is *Clark v. Putnam County*, 293 F.3d 1261 (11th Cir. 2002).

Does this mean *Easley* made it much more difficult for plaintiffs to win these cases? Perhaps. Or perhaps the racial gerrymandering cases of the 1990s represented a judicial reaction (perhaps a ham-handed one) to the Justice Department's extremely aggressive enforcement of Section 5 of the Voting Rights Act, which provoked some state legislatures to take liberties with district shapes beyond what they typically had done previously to obtain preclearance without abandoning their other political objectives. The chastisement the Court administered to the Justice Department in the 1990s may have been sufficient to prevent a repetition of these events in the 2000s.

Still another explanation for the lull in racial gerrymandering litigation is advanced by Richard H. Pildes, *The Constitutionalization of Democratic Politics*, 118 Harvard Law Review 28, 68–69 (2004), who argues that it reflected the internalization of new redistricting norms by line-drawers in the 2000s:

> [S]tate legislators and other actors internalized the vague legal constraints of *Shaw* in ways that generated a stable equilibrium. Though the law itself could not generate that stability ex ante by establishing necessary and sufficient criteria for the application of *Shaw*, political practice nonetheless became stable. Risk-averse politicians otherwise in control of redistricting turned out to have strong incentives to avoid having redistricting plans challenged in litigation; courts might impose their own remedial districts, or the political landscape might shift before a judicially invalidated plan came back for legislative revision. In the 2000 round of redistricting, legislators and their counsels recognized the obligation to comply with the VRA, but they also internalized a sense of constraint from *Shaw*; the prevailing view was that minority districts were required when they could be created in a manner consistent with the design of other districts, but that exceptionally contorted minority districts were neither required nor constitutional. Thus, legislators correctly internalized *Shaw*, not as barring them from intentionally creating minority districts, but as imposing general, extrinsic limits on the extent to which districts could be noncompact.... Predictions notwithstanding, vague law was transformed into settled practice.

4. Recall two of the districts that were at issue in *LULAC v. Perry* (discussed above in Section 2): District 23, which had been redrawn to protect the vulnerable Republican incumbent, Henry Bonilla, and District 25, which merged Latino communities in Austin and along the Mexican border and was deemed an invalid Section 2 remedy by the Court. Due to his view that Section 2 does not extend to vote dilution, Justice Scalia, joined by Justice Thomas, had to reach the plaintiffs' racial gerrymandering challenges to those districts. With respect to District 23, Justice Scalia agreed with the district court that incumbent protection, not race, was its predominant purpose:

> The District Court found that the goal of the map drawers was to adjust the lines of that district to protect the imperiled incumbent: "The record presents undisputed evidence that the Legislature desired to increase the

> number of Republican votes cast in Congressional District 23 to shore up Bonilla's base and assist in his reelection." To achieve this goal, the legislature extended the district north to include counties in the central part of the State with residents who voted Republican, adding 100,000 people to the district. Then, to comply with the one-person, one-vote requirement, the legislature took one-half of heavily Democratic Webb County, in the southern part of the district, and included it in the neighboring district....
>
> I cannot find, under the clear error standard, that the District Court was required to reach a different conclusion.

548 U.S. at 513, 516 (Scalia, J., concurring in the judgment in part and dissenting in part). With respect to District 25, Justice Scalia argued that strict scrutiny was triggered because, "[i]n [his] view... when a legislature intentionally creates a majority-minority district, race is necessarily its predominant motivation." *Id.* at 518. Applying strict scrutiny, however, he concluded that the district was narrowly tailored to comply with Section 5 of the Voting Rights Act:

> I would hold that compliance with § 5 of the Voting Rights Act can be such a [compelling] interest. We long ago upheld the constitutionality of § 5 as a proper exercise of Congress's authority under § 2 of the Fifteenth Amendment to enforce that Amendment's prohibition on the denial or abridgment of the right to vote. If compliance with § 5 were not a compelling state interest, then a State could be placed in the impossible position of having to choose between compliance with § 5 and compliance with the Equal Protection Clause. Moreover, the compelling nature of the State's interest in § 5 compliance is supported by our recognition in previous cases that race may be used where necessary to remedy identified past discrimination. Congress enacted § 5 for just that purpose, and that provision applies only to jurisdictions with a history of official discrimination. In the proper case, therefore, a covered jurisdiction may have a compelling interest in complying with § 5....
>
> ... [A]ppellants [do not] charge that in creating District 25 the State did more than what was required by § 5. In light of these concessions, I do not believe a remand is necessary, and I would affirm the judgment of the District Court.

Id. at 520. Can Justice Scalia's reasoning be squared with his vote in *Shelby County* holding Section 5 unconstitutional?

5. While there was little successful racial gerrymandering litigation in the 2000s, a number of suits were victorious in the 2010 redistricting cycle. The backdrop to all of these suits was similar: In full control of redistricting, Republican mapmakers either froze the minority percentages of existing majority-minority districts or increased these percentages using specific racial targets. Minority plaintiffs then challenged these districts, and the states defended them as being necessary to comply with either Section 2 or Section 5 of the Voting Rights Act. *Alabama*

Legislative Black Caucus v. Alabama, excerpted below, marked the Supreme Court's first engagement with this new generation of racial gerrymandering claims.

Alabama Legislative Black Caucus v. Alabama

575 U.S. 254 (2015)

Justice BREYER delivered the opinion of the Court....

I

The Alabama Constitution requires the legislature to reapportion its State House and Senate electoral districts following each decennial census. In 2012 Alabama redrew the boundaries of the State's 105 House districts and 35 Senate districts. In doing so, Alabama sought to achieve numerous traditional districting objectives, such as compactness, not splitting counties or precincts, minimizing change, and protecting incumbents. But it placed yet greater importance on achieving two other goals.

First, it sought to minimize the extent to which a district might deviate from the theoretical ideal of precisely equal population. In particular, it set as a goal creating a set of districts in which no district would deviate from the theoretical, precisely equal ideal by more than 1% — i.e., a more rigorous deviation standard than our precedents have found necessary under the Constitution. No one here doubts the desirability of a State's efforts generally to come close to a one-person, one-vote ideal.

Second, it sought to ensure compliance with federal law, and, in particular, the Voting Rights Act of 1965. At the time of the redistricting Alabama was a covered jurisdiction under that Act. Accordingly § 5 of the Act required Alabama to demonstrate that an electoral change, such as redistricting, would not bring about retrogression in respect to racial minorities' "ability . . . to elect their preferred candidates of choice." Specifically, Alabama believed that, to avoid retrogression under § 5, it was required to maintain roughly the same black population percentage in existing majority-minority districts.

Compliance with these two goals posed particular difficulties with respect to many of the State's 35 majority-minority districts (8 in the Senate, 27 in the House). That is because many of these districts were (compared with the average district) underpopulated. In order for Senate District 26, for example, to meet the State's no-more-than-1% population-deviation objective, the State would have to add about 16,000 individuals to the district. And, prior to redistricting, 72.75% of District 26's population was black. Accordingly, Alabama's plan added 15,785 new individuals, and only 36 of those newly added individuals were white....

II

We begin by considering the geographical nature of the racial gerrymandering claims. The District Court repeatedly referred to the racial gerrymandering claims as claims that race improperly motivated the drawing of boundary lines of the State *considered as a whole*.

A racial gerrymandering claim, however, applies to the boundaries of individual districts. It applies district-by-district. It does not apply to a State considered as an undifferentiated "whole." We have consistently described a claim of racial gerrymandering as a claim that race was improperly used in the drawing of the boundaries of one or more *specific electoral districts.*

Our district-specific language makes sense in light of the nature of the harms that underlie a racial gerrymandering claim. Those harms are personal. They include being "personally . . . subjected to [a] racial classification," *Vera*, as well as being represented by a legislator who believes his "primary obligation is to represent only the members" of a particular racial group, *Shaw I.* They directly threaten a voter who lives in the district attacked. But they do not so keenly threaten a voter who lives elsewhere in the State. Indeed, the latter voter normally lacks standing to pursue a racial gerrymandering claim.

Voters, of course, can present statewide *evidence* in order to prove racial gerrymandering in a particular district. And voters might make the claim that *every* individual district in a State suffers from racial gerrymandering. But this latter claim is not the claim that the District Court, when using the phrase "as a whole," considered here. Rather, the concept as used here suggests the existence of a legal unicorn, an animal that exists only in the legal imagination. . . .

We recognize that the plaintiffs relied heavily upon statewide evidence to prove that race predominated in the drawing of individual district lines. And they also sought to prove that the use of race to draw the boundaries of the majority-minority districts affected the boundaries of other districts as well. Such evidence is perfectly relevant. . . . That Alabama expressly adopted and applied a policy of prioritizing mechanical racial targets above all other districting criteria (save one-person, one-vote) provides evidence that race motivated the drawing of particular lines in multiple districts in the State. And neither the use of statewide evidence nor the effort to show widespread effect can transform a racial gerrymandering claim about a set of individual districts into a separate, general claim that the legislature racially gerrymandered the State "as" an undifferentiated "whole." . . .

IV

The District Court held in the alternative that the claims of racial gerrymandering must fail because "[r]ace was not the predominant motivating factor" in the creation of any of the challenged districts. In our view, however, the District Court did not properly calculate "predominance." In particular, it judged race to lack "predominance" in part because it placed in the balance, among other nonracial factors, legislative efforts to create districts of approximately equal population.

[A]n equal population goal is not one factor among others to be weighed against the use of race to determine whether race "predominates." Rather, it is part of the redistricting background, taken as a given, when determining whether race, or other factors, predominate in a legislator's determination as to *how* equal population objectives will be met.

To understand this conclusion, recall what "predominance" is about: A plaintiff pursuing a racial gerrymandering claim must show that "race was the predominant factor motivating the legislature's decision to place a significant number of voters within or without a particular district." To do so, the "plaintiff must prove that the legislature subordinated *traditional race-neutral districting principles* . . . to racial considerations."

Now consider the nature of those offsetting "traditional race-neutral districting principles." We have listed several, including "compactness, contiguity, respect for political subdivisions or communities defined by actual shared interests," incumbency protection, and political affiliation.

But we have not listed equal population objectives. And there is a reason for that omission. The reason that equal population objectives do not appear on this list of "traditional" criteria is that equal population objectives play a different role in a State's redistricting process. That role is not a minor one. Indeed, in light of the Constitution's demands, that role may often prove "predominant" in the ordinary sense of that word. But, as the United States points out, "predominance" in the context of a racial gerrymandering claim is special. It is not about whether a legislature believes that the need for equal population takes ultimate priority. Rather, it is, as we said, whether the legislature "placed" race "above traditional districting considerations in determining *which* persons were placed *in appropriately apportioned districts*." In other words, if the legislature must place 1,000 or so additional voters in a particular district in order to achieve an equal population goal, the "predominance" question concerns *which* voters the legislature decides to choose, and specifically whether the legislature predominately uses race as opposed to other, "traditional" factors when doing so.

Consequently, we agree with the United States that the requirement that districts have approximately equal populations is a background rule against which redistricting takes place. It is not a factor to be treated like other nonracial factors when a court determines whether race predominated over other, "traditional" factors in the drawing of district boundaries. . . .

All this is to say that, with respect to District 26 and likely others as well, had the District Court treated equal population goals as background factors, it might have concluded that race was the predominant boundary-drawing consideration. Thus, on remand, the District Court should reconsider its "no predominance" conclusions with respect to Senate District 26 and others to which our analysis is applicable. . . .

V

The District Court, in a yet further alternative holding, found that "[e]ven if the [State] subordinated traditional districting principles to racial considerations," the racial gerrymandering claims failed because, in any event, "the Districts would satisfy strict scrutiny." In the District Court's view, the "Acts are narrowly tailored to comply with Section 5" of the Voting Rights Act. That provision "required the Legislature to maintain, where feasible, the existing number of majority-black districts and *not substantially reduce the relative percentages of black voters in those districts*." And, insofar as the State's redistricting embodied racial considerations, it did so in order to meet this §5 requirement.

In our view, however, this alternative holding rests upon a misperception of the law. Section 5, which covered particular States and certain other jurisdictions, does not require a covered jurisdiction to maintain a particular numerical minority percentage. It requires the jurisdiction to maintain a minority's ability to elect a preferred candidate of choice. That is precisely what the language of the statute says. It prohibits a covered jurisdiction from adopting any change that "has the purpose of or will have the effect of diminishing the ability of [the minority group] to elect their preferred candidates of choice." . . .

Consistent with this view, the United States tells us that "Section 5" does not "requir[e] the State to maintain the same percentage of black voters in each of the majority-black districts as had existed in the prior districting plans." Rather, it "prohibits only those diminutions of a minority group's proportionate strength that strip the group within a district of its existing ability to elect its candidates of choice." We agree. Section 5 does not require maintaining the same population percentages in majority-minority districts as in the prior plan. Rather, §5 is satisfied if minority voters retain the ability to elect their preferred candidates. . . .

The record makes clear that both the District Court and the legislature relied heavily upon a mechanically numerical view as to what counts as forbidden retrogression. And the difference between that view and the more purpose-oriented view reflected in the statute's language can matter. Imagine a majority-minority district with a 70% black population. Assume also that voting in that district, like that in the State itself, is racially polarized. And assume that the district has long elected to office black voters' preferred candidate. Other things being equal, it would seem highly unlikely that a redistricting plan that, while increasing the numerical size of the district, reduced the percentage of the black population from, say, 70% to 65% would have a significant impact on the black voters' ability to elect their preferred candidate. And, for that reason, it would be difficult to explain just why a plan that uses racial criteria predominately to maintain the black population at 70% is "narrowly tailored" to achieve a "compelling state interest," namely the interest in preventing §5 retrogression. . . .

. . . [W]e conclude that the District Court and the legislature asked the wrong question with respect to narrow tailoring. They asked: "How can we maintain present minority percentages in majority-minority districts?" But given §5's language, its purpose, the Justice Department Guidelines, and the relevant precedent, they should have asked: "To what extent must we preserve existing minority percentages in order to maintain the minority's present ability to elect the candidate of its choice?" Asking the wrong question may well have led to the wrong answer. Hence, we cannot accept the District Court's "compelling interest/narrow tailoring" conclusion. . . .

The cases are remanded for further proceedings consistent with this opinion.

It is so ordered.

[Justice Scalia and Justice Thomas dissented separately, with Chief Justice Roberts and Justices Alito and Thomas joining Justice Scalia's dissent.]

Notes and Questions

1. *Alabama Legislative Black Caucus* is doctrinally notable for several reasons. First, the Supreme Court emphatically confirms what had been implicit in earlier cases, namely, that racial gerrymandering claims are inherently district-specific, not statewide, in scope. Is this a sensible position even when mapmakers design all of the districts in a plan pursuant to a single statewide strategy? Second, the Court clarifies that equal population is not an objective that might predominate over a racial purpose; rather, it is a background constitutional requirement that must be satisfied by every plan. But what if (as here) a state chooses to make its districts *more* equal in population than the Constitution compels? Why can *that* goal not predominate over racial considerations?

Third, the Court construes the post-2006 version of Section 5 of the Voting Rights Act for the first time. Like the district court in *Texas v. United States* (discussed above in Section 1), the Court concludes that Section 5 bars any reduction in the number of districts in which minority voters are able to elect their preferred candidates. But Section 5 does *not* prohibit all decreases in districts' minority percentages. To the contrary, such decreases are perfectly acceptable if they do not cause minority voters to lose their ability to elect their candidates of choice. Why is the Court willing to wrestle with Section 5's meaning even after the provision was neutered by *Shelby County*? What if the Court's hypothetical district had its black population reduced from 70% to 45% but there was evidence that black voters could still elect their preferred candidate more than half the time? Then would Section 5 be violated?

2. On remand from the Supreme Court, the district court held that twelve state senate and state house districts were unconstitutional gerrymanders, and that twenty-four other challenged districts were lawful. The stricken districts had nearly identical percentages of black voters as their predecessors in the 2000s maps, *and* there was evidence that the racial targets were met at the expense of other redistricting criteria. In contrast, the sustained districts either had more different demographics from their antecedents or could attribute their similar black percentages to compliance with non-racial criteria. See *Alabama Legislative Black Caucus v. Alabama*, 231 F. Supp. 3d 1026 (M.D. Ala. 2017). Did the district court faithfully follow the Supreme Court's instructions?

3. While no other state seems to have employed Alabama's exact strategy of *freezing* districts' minority percentages, several states relied on close variants. North Carolina, for example, converted all districts in which minority voters had been electing their candidates of choice into *majority-minority* districts, while Virginia

used a 55% racial floor when it redrew its existing ability districts. In a series of cases, courts ultimately held that many of the resulting districts in these states were unconstitutional racial gerrymanders. See *Bethune-Hill v. Va. State Bd. of Elections*, 326 F. Supp. 3d 128 (E.D. Va. 2018) (striking down eleven Virginia state house districts); *Covington v. North Carolina*, 316 F.R.D. 117 (M.D.N.C. 2016) (striking down twenty-eight North Carolina state house and senate districts); *Harris v. McCrory*, 159 F. Supp. 3d 600 (M.D.N.C. 2016) (striking down two North Carolina congressional districts); *Page v. Va. State Bd. of Elections*, 2015 WL 3604029 (E.D. Va. June 5, 2015) (striking down one Virginia congressional district). Under the logic of *Alabama Legislative Black Caucus*, is race the predominant factor when a state uses a racial floor but allows ability districts' minority percentages to vary significantly above that threshold? If so, how are states supposed to comply with their obligations under the Voting Rights Act? See Justin Levitt, *Quick and Dirty: The New Misreading of the Voting Rights Act*, 43 Florida State University Law Review 573 (2016) (addressing these issues and also arguing that many covered states misconstrued their obligations under Section 5).

4. In *Bethune-Hill v. Virginia State Bd. of Elections*, 137 S. Ct. 788 (2017), the Supreme Court vacated most of a district court judgment that had upheld twelve Virginia state house districts against a racial gerrymandering challenge. The district court had emphasized the districts' compliance with traditional districting criteria. The Supreme Court made clear that such compliance does not shield districts from attack. After all, noncompliance with traditional criteria is simply one way in which a predominant racial motivation may be shown; it is not an element of the claim itself:

> . . . The Equal Protection Clause does not prohibit misshapen districts. It prohibits unjustified racial classifications.
>
> . . . The racial predominance inquiry concerns the actual considerations that provided the essential basis for the lines drawn, not post hoc justifications the legislature in theory could have used but in reality did not.
>
> Traditional redistricting principles, moreover, are numerous and malleable. The District Court here identified no fewer than 11 race-neutral redistricting factors a legislature could consider, some of which are "surprisingly ethereal" and "admi[t] of degrees." By deploying those factors in various combinations and permutations, a State could construct a plethora of potential maps that look consistent with traditional, race-neutral principles. But if race for its own sake is the overriding reason for choosing one map over others, race still may predominate.
>
> For these reasons, a conflict or inconsistency between the enacted plan and traditional redistricting criteria is not a threshold requirement or a mandatory precondition in order for a challenger to establish a claim of racial gerrymandering. Of course, a conflict or inconsistency may be persuasive circumstantial evidence tending to show racial predomination, but

> there is no rule requiring challengers to present this kind of evidence in every case.

Id. at 798–99. What is left, at this point, of the expressive harm theory that scholars thought underlay *Shaw*? What racial message can districts that are compact and compliant with traditional districting criteria convey?

On remand from the Supreme Court, the lower court held that eleven Virginia state house districts were unconstitutional racial gerrymanders. The lower court based its conclusion that race predominated in the construction of these districts on the state's use of a 55 percent black voting age population target as well as extensive district-specific evidence. The court also ruled that the districts could not survive strict scrutiny because, above all, the 55 percent target was unnecessary for compliance with either Section 2 or Section 5 of the Voting Rights Act. See *Bethune-Hill*, 326 F. Supp. 3d at 143-81.

Virginia's Attorney General decided not to appeal the district court's decision. However, the Virginia House of Delegates, which had intervened as a defendant at the trial stage, chose to continue the litigation. In *Virginia House of Delegates v. Bethune-Hill*, 139 S. Ct. 1945 (2019), the Supreme Court held that the House lacked standing and thus avoided commenting on the merits of the racial gerrymandering claims:

> To begin with, the House has not identified any legal basis for its claimed authority to litigate on the State's behalf. Authority and responsibility for representing the State's interests in civil litigation, Virginia law prescribes, rest exclusively with the State's Attorney General. . . . Virginia has thus chosen to speak as a sovereign entity with a single voice. In this regard, the State has adopted an approach resembling that of the Federal Government, which "centraliz[es]" the decision whether to seek certiorari by "reserving litigation in this Court to the Attorney General and the Solicitor General." Virginia, had it so chosen, could have authorized the House to litigate on the State's behalf, either generally or in a defined class of cases. . . . But the choice belongs to Virginia, and the House's argument that it has authority to represent the State's interests is foreclosed by the State's contrary decision.
>
> . . . Aside from its role in enacting the invalidated redistricting plan, the House, echoed by the dissent, asserts that the House has standing because altered district boundaries may affect its composition. . . .
>
> . . . [A]lthough redrawing district lines indeed may affect the membership of the chamber, the House as an institution has no cognizable interest in the identity of its members. Although the House urges that changes to district lines will "profoundly disrupt its day-to-day operations," it is scarcely obvious how or why that is so. As the party invoking this Court's jurisdiction, the House bears the burden of doing more than "simply alleg[ing] a nonobvious harm."

> Analogizing to "group[s] other than a legislative body," the dissent insists that the House has suffered an "obvious" injury. But groups like the string quartet and basketball team posited by the dissent select their own members. Similarly, the political parties involved in the cases the dissent cites select their own leadership and candidates. In stark contrast, the House does not select its own members. Instead, it is a representative body composed of members chosen by the people. Changes to its membership brought about by the voting public thus inflict no cognizable injury on the House.

Id. at 1951-55. Justice Alito, joined by Chief Justice Roberts, Justice Breyer, and Justice Kavanaugh, dissented. In an interesting passage, he argued that how district lines are drawn has significant implications for the behavior of both individual legislators and the legislature as a whole. As to individual legislators, "[w]hen the boundaries of a district are changed, the constituents and communities of interest present within the district are altered, and this is likely to change the way in which the district's representative does his or her work." *Id.* at 1956. And as to the legislature as a whole, "it matters a lot how voters with shared interests and views are concentrated or split up." "The cumulative effects of all the decisions that go into a districting plan have an important impact on the overall work of the body." *Id.*

Does *Virginia House of Delegates* create opportunities for gamesmanship? Suppose that a district plan is enacted under conditions of unified government, that the minority party captures the attorney general position later in the decade, and that plaintiffs then successfully challenge the plan in federal district court. If the attorney general (who may be aligned politically with the plaintiffs) declines to appeal, is the plan then doomed, even if the Supreme Court would likely reverse the district court? Assuming the answer is yes, is this a sensible rule? It would seem to allow the invalidation of district maps, without possibility of appeal, when an initially unified government is replaced by a divided government. But maybe this is actually desirable if one posits that unified governments typically pass gerrymandered maps. Then making it easier for these maps to be struck down could be a net positive.

Virginia House of Delegates rests, in part, on the fact that Virginia had authorized the Attorney General to make decisions for the state in litigation. Could states circumvent the case's holding by simply authorizing *multiple* parties, or *other* parties, to represent the state? Wisconsin Republicans may have done just that when, after losing the races for governor and attorney general in 2018, they passed a lame duck law that enabled the legislature (still under Republican control) to instruct the attorney general how to proceed. "If requested by the governor or either house of the legislature," the attorney general must "appear for and represent the state" and "prosecute or defend in any court . . . any cause or matter, civil or criminal." Wis. Stat. § 165.25(1m).

Perhaps the most interesting portions of *Virginia House of Delegates* address the very nature of a legislature (and thus whether it is harmed by the invalidation of a district map). The majority has a thin conception of a legislature, under which its only function is formally to represent the people of a state. On this view, it doesn't matter who composes the legislature or what the legislature does; only the official provision of representation is relevant. The dissent, on the other hand, has a much thicker understanding of a legislature, under which its membership and output are every bit as significant as its nominal representation of the people. On this account, a legislature necessarily has an interest in the preservation of its current district map, because any change to the map would affect its makeup and policies. Which theory do you find more persuasive? If a legislature only has an interest in its formal representation of the people, as the majority opinion maintains, then why should it matter whether one chamber or both are appellants? Even if both chambers appeal, isn't their grievance still not judicially cognizable?

5. In *Cooper v. Harris* (to which we also referred in Part II), the Supreme Court affirmed a district court judgment that had invalidated two North Carolina congressional districts as racial gerrymanders. Unsurprisingly, given its rulings in *Alabama Legislative Black Caucus* and *Bethune-Hill*, the Court held that race predominated when "the State's mapmakers, in considering District 1, purposefully established a racial target: African Americans should make up no less than a majority of the voting-age population." 137 S. Ct. at 1468. More interesting was the Court's rejection of the state's argument that District 1 had to be made a majority-minority district in order to comply with Section 2 of the Voting Rights Act. This argument's fatal flaw, according to the Court, was that there was insufficient evidence of white bloc voting, meaning that the third *Gingles* precondition was not satisfied:

> Here, electoral history provided no evidence that a § 2 plaintiff could demonstrate the third *Gingles* prerequisite—effective white bloc-voting. For most of the twenty years prior to the new plan's adoption, African-Americans had made up less than a majority of District 1's voters; the district's BVAP usually hovered between 46% and 48%. Yet throughout those two decades, as the District Court noted, District 1 was "an extraordinarily safe district for African-American preferred candidates." In the *closest* election during that period, African-Americans' candidate of choice received 59% of the total vote; in other years, the share of the vote garnered by those candidates rose to as much as 70%. . . .

Id. at 1470. Note that if slightly less than half of District 1's voters were African Americans, and if their preferred candidate usually won around two-thirds of the vote, then approximately one-third of white voters typically supported that candidate—and approximately two-thirds opposed him. Is white vote bloc voting really absent when two-thirds of white voters oppose the minority candidate of choice?

All eight participating Justices agreed that District 1 was unconstitutional. But the Court splintered, five to three, on the lawfulness of District 12. As in *Easley v. Cromartie* (which involved the same district and the same issue), the dispute was over whether race or partisanship predominated in the district's creation. This time, though, the majority found that race predominated, based on (1) statements by the legislative architects of the plan that they were converting District 12 into a majority-minority district; (2) similar statements by the plan's key line-drawer; (3) testimony by the member of Congress who represented District 12; (4) expert analysis showing that black Democrats were disproportionately added to District 12 relative to white Democrats; and (5) the fact that District 12 was, in fact, made a majority-minority district. *Id.* at 1474-78. The majority also stressed that its conclusion was based on the highly deferential standard of review it applied; it was "far from having a 'definite and firm conviction' that the District Court made a mistake." *Id.* at 1478.

Justice Alito's dissent downplayed the significance of this evidence and emphasized instead the extent to which District 12 had been packed with Democrats in order to benefit Republicans in adjacent districts. *Id.* at 1491–1504 (Alito, J., concurring in the judgment in part and dissenting in part). More importantly, the majority and the dissent disagreed as to whether it is a plaintiff's obligation in a racial gerrymandering case to present a demonstration plan that is more racially balanced but that still achieves the State's political goals equally well. Echoing language to this effect in *Easley*, the dissent argued that this was indeed a requirement. The majority, on the other hand, held that while "an alternative districting plan . . . can serve as key evidence in a race-versus-politics dispute," "it is hardly the *only* means." *Id.* at 1479. "A plaintiff's task . . . is simply to persuade the trial court—without any special evidentiary prerequisite—that race (not politics) was the 'predominant consideration.'" *Id.*

Who has the better of this debate over what *Easley* required? If the plaintiffs in *Cooper* had needed to present a demonstration plan, what would it have looked like? In particular, would it have had to include ten Republican districts and three Democratic districts (mirroring the partisan breakdown of the actual map)? What if the actual map was also suspect on *partisan* gerrymandering grounds—would the plaintiffs have had to submit a plan that was equally legally dubious?

6. After its two majority-minority districts were struck down by the district court, North Carolina responded by redrawing its congressional map without considering racial data *at all*, and by openly announcing its intention to advantage Republican candidates. One of the state's explicit criteria for its new plan was: "The partisan makeup of the congressional delegation under the enacted plan [shall be] 10 Republicans and 3 Democrats." Is there any possible racial gerrymandering objection to this plan? Is there a Section 2 violation if minority-preferred candidates continue to prevail in two districts? And if these claims are unavailable (as seems likely), then what was the point of the original lawsuit? Even though it succeeded, after all, it did not meaningfully alter either the political or the racial composition of North Carolina's districts. As we discussed at length in Chapter Four, North Carolina's remedial congressional plan was the subject of partisan gerrymandering litigation that culminated in the Supreme Court's ruling in *Rucho v. Common Cause* that all such claims are nonjusticiable.

The fact that North Carolina redrew its congressional map in a supposedly race-blind manner raises the question: What would be the practical implications if states generally did not consider race in the redistricting process (perhaps because some future Supreme Court decision forbade them from doing so)? To answer this question, Jowei Chen and Nicholas O. Stephanopoulos, *The Race-Blind Future of Voting Rights*, 130 Yale Law Journal 862 (2021), used a computer algorithm to simulate large numbers of district maps for nineteen states. The algorithm was instructed to ignore race but to match or beat existing plans' scores on all nonracial, nonpartisan criteria. The authors found that, in most states, nonracial redistricting would yield substantially fewer districts where minority voters are able to elect their preferred candidates. The authors also showed that the minority opportunity districts that do arise when lines are drawn randomly are more likely to be crossover and coalition districts and less likely to have very large minority population shares. Lastly, contradicting the conventional wisdom about how minority and partisan representation are related, the authors concluded that the elimination of some opportunity districts due to nonracial redistricting would benefit Republicans, not Democrats, especially in the deep South.

Chapter 6

Election Administration and Remedies

Over the past two decades, public, legislative, and scholarly interest in the "nuts and bolts" of elections has increased dramatically. Among the subjects receiving prominent attention are voting technology, voter identification, voter registration, provisional ballots, challenges to voter eligibility, polling place operations, and post-election disputes. There has also been increasing concern over the institutions and people who are responsible for running elections, including the possibility of election results being subverted by party-aligned officials. We collectively refer to this set of topics as election administration. The U.S. has seen numerous controversies over the rules and institutions governing elections administration since the 2000 election, many of which have wound up in court. These disputes tend to have a partisan flavor, with Democrats generally concerned about the need to ensure voter access and Republicans more worried about election integrity. For detailed accounts of post-2000 election administration controversies, see Richard L. Hasen, The Voting Wars: From Florida 2000 to the Next Meltdown (2012), and Richard L. Hasen, Election Meltdown: Dirty Tricks, Distrust, and the Threat to American Democracy (2020).

To understand this set of issues, it is important to be aware of two distinctive features of election administration in the United States. One is the pronounced *decentralization* of our system. For the most part, responsibility for the conduct of elections rests with local officials. While it is common to speak of the "election system," there is not just one election system or even fifty systems in the U.S., but thousands of systems—comprised of the various county and municipal entities charged with running elections. While Congress imposed some requirements on the states and provided some federal funding through the Help America Vote Act of 2002 ("HAVA") (discussed in Part III.C below), American election administration remains primarily a state and local matter, much more decentralized than in other countries. Daniel P. Tokaji, *The Future of Election Reform: From Rules to Institutions*, 28 Yale Law & Policy Review 125, 137–42 (2009). Some of these rules and practices become the subject of federal court litigation when they are challenged under the U.S. Constitution or federal statutes like the Voting Rights Act of 1965.

The other distinctive feature of American election administration is *partisanship*. In over 30 states, the chief election official—typically the Secretary of State—is selected through a partisan electoral process, while in other states, the chief election official is appointed by an official (such as a governor) elected as a representative of his or her party. National Conference of State Legislatures, *Election Administration at State and Local Levels* (Feb. 3, 2020), https://perma.cc/597F-9ZV3; Martha Kropf & David Kimball, Helping America Vote: The Limits of Election Reform 98 (2012). At the local level, election officials are elected in roughly two-thirds of all jurisdictions, and party-affiliated officials run elections in almost half of all local jurisdictions.

These features of American election administration raise important questions regarding the appropriate role of courts. The decentralization of elections introduces the possibility that different jurisdictions will adopt different practices, which may in turn deny equal treatment to some voters. Should courts intervene to ensure that voters in different parts of a state are treated equally, for example, when it comes to what equipment they use for voting or how their votes are counted? Partisanship in the administration of elections may also furnish an argument for judicial intervention—for example, where a Secretary of State adopts a rule for counting provisional ballots that tends to advantage his or her party. Should courts closely scrutinize such a rule? What about a voter identification law that may make it more difficult for some groups of citizens to vote? Alternatively, should courts leave the regulation of elections to Congress, state legislatures, and election officials at the state and local level?

Part I of this Chapter discusses constitutional questions surrounding the counting of votes and burdens on voting. Part II addresses claims of race discrimination arising from election administration rules or practices. Part III considers federal laws that are designed to improve access to the voting, as well as empirical research on how election administration rules affect turnout. Part IV considers the remedies that a court might order for violation of election laws.

I. Constitutional Claims

A. Counting and Recounting Votes

To what extent should courts ensure that votes are counted using uniform standards? This issue attained national prominence following the 2000 presidential election, which was so close that the final outcome depended on the State of Florida. The initial count showed Bush leading by 1,784 votes out of millions of votes cast in the state. Many previously ignored problems with election administration came to light as a result of the controversy. For example, Democrats focused on the "butterfly ballot" (see Figure 6.1) used in Palm Beach County, a ballot that listed candidates for president on two pages facing each other with a punch-card vote to be cast along the ballot's spine. Democrats claimed that ballot design made it unduly likely that voters would cast votes for someone other than their preferred candidate. Reform Party candidate Pat Buchanan received 3,704 votes in Palm Beach County, nearly 2,700 more than he received in any of Florida's other counties; in addition, approximately 19,000 ballots were thrown out as "overvotes" (ballots containing votes for

Figure 6-1 The Palm Beach County "Butterfly Ballot"

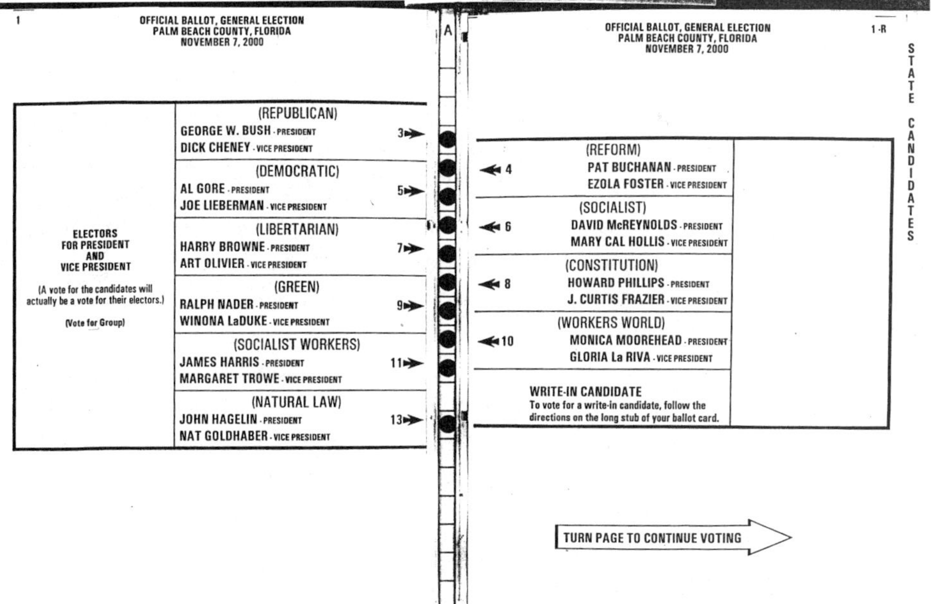

1

OFFICIAL BALLOT, GENERAL ELECTION
PALM BEACH COUNTY, FLORIDA
NOVEMBER 7, 2000

ELECTORS
FOR PRESIDENT
AND
VICE PRESIDENT

(A vote for the candidates will actually be a vote for their electors.)

(Vote for Group)

(REPUBLICAN)
GEORGE W. BUSH - PRESIDENT
DICK CHENEY - VICE PRESIDENT 3

(DEMOCRATIC)
AL GORE - PRESIDENT
JOE LIEBERMAN - VICE PRESIDENT 5

(LIBERTARIAN)
HARRY BROWNE - PRESIDENT
ART OLIVIER - VICE PRESIDENT 7

(GREEN)
RALPH NADER - PRESIDENT
WINONA LaDUKE - VICE PRESIDENT 9

(SOCIALIST WORKERS)
JAMES HARRIS - PRESIDENT
MARGARET TROWE - VICE PRESIDENT 11

(NATURAL LAW)
JOHN HAGELIN - PRESIDENT
NAT GOLDHABER - VICE PRESIDENT 13

A

OFFICIAL BALLOT, GENERAL ELECTION
PALM BEACH COUNTY, FLORIDA
NOVEMBER 7, 2000

1-R

STATE CANDIDATES

4 (REFORM)
PAT BUCHANAN - PRESIDENT
EZOLA FOSTER - VICE PRESIDENT

6 (SOCIALIST)
DAVID McREYNOLDS - PRESIDENT
MARY CAL HOLLIS - VICE PRESIDENT

8 (CONSTITUTION)
HOWARD PHILLIPS - PRESIDENT
J. CURTIS FRAZIER - VICE PRESIDENT

10 (WORKERS WORLD)
MONICA MOOREHEAD - PRESIDENT
GLORIA La RIVA - VICE PRESIDENT

WRITE-IN CANDIDATE
To vote for a write-in candidate, follow the directions on the long stub of your ballot card.

TURN PAGE TO CONTINUE VOTING

Photo courtesy of Election Data Services.

more than one presidential candidate). Although legal challenges to the butterfly ballot eventually went nowhere, the issue energized many Democrats into supporting strong efforts by Gore to overturn the preliminary results.

As an automatic machine recount provided for by Florida law was proceeding, Gore filed an election "protest" asking for a manual recount of the vote in four counties, three of which used punch-card voting systems. When it seemed the recounts could not be finished in time to meet state deadlines, Gore sought an extension of time for the manual recounts. Republicans argued against the extension and contended that the law did not allow for manual recounts absent a machine error in counting the votes. The Florida Supreme Court, however, allowed the recounts and extended the time to complete them, based upon its interpretation of Florida election statutes. In interpreting the statutes, the Florida court made background reference to provisions of the Florida Constitution that the Florida court characterized as calling for fair elections. *Palm Beach County Canvassing Board v. Harris*, 772 So. 2d 1220 (Fla. 2000). The Supreme Court issued a brief, unanimous, *per curiam* (unsigned) opinion remanding the case to the Florida Supreme Court for clarification as to whether it was relying solely on Florida statutes or also on the state's constitution, which would raise issues under Article II of the U.S. Constitution. *Bush v. Palm Beach County Canvassing Bd.*, 531 U.S. 70 (2000).

Despite Gore's victory in the first round of litigation, he still trailed Bush after the extended deadline the Florida Supreme Court had set. Gore then filed a separate election "contest," asking for a selective manual recount of nearly 10,000 undervotes from Miami-Dade County and approximately 4,000 votes set aside in Palm Beach County. (Undervotes are ballots that fail to record a valid vote for any candidate.) The trial court held that Gore failed to meet the statutory standard for a contest, and Gore appealed to the Florida Supreme Court.

The Florida Supreme Court, in a 4–3 vote, reversed the trial court. The court held that the trial court had applied the wrong legal standards in judging the merits of Gore's claim. *Gore v. Harris*, 772 So. 2d 1243 (Fla. 2000). The court ordered that certain recounts, completed after the deadline it had set in the earlier case, be included in the totals and that a manual recount of undervotes in all the remaining counties in the state, not just the counties singled out by Gore, go forward. However, the recounts requested by Gore that had already been conducted would be grandfathered in. These recounts, unlike the new ones ordered by the court, had included all ballots, not just undervoted ballots. The court further held that in examining the undervotes to determine whether the ballots indeed contained a valid vote for a presidential candidate, the counters should use a "clear intent of the voter" standard, as indicated in Florida statutes. The court failed to be more specific, perhaps out of fear that a more specific standard would violate the U.S. Supreme Court's understanding of Article II of the U.S. Constitution suggested in its earlier *per curiam* opinion.

While a state court judge was organizing the recount process, Bush filed a petition for a writ of certiorari and a stay in the U.S. Supreme Court. As the recounts began on Saturday, December 9, the Supreme Court, by a 5–4 vote, stayed the Florida Supreme Court's order, thereby suspending the recount. *Bush v. Gore*, 531 U.S. 1046 (2000). On the evening of December 12, the Supreme Court issued this opinion:

Bush v. Gore

531 U.S. 98 (2000)

PER CURIAM.

I

[The Court summarized the facts and procedural posture of the case. Bush's] petition presents the following questions: whether the Florida Supreme Court established new standards for resolving Presidential election contests, thereby violating Art. II, §1, cl. 2, of the United States Constitution and failing to comply with 3 U.S.C. §5, and whether the use of standardless manual recounts violates the Equal Protection and Due Process Clauses. With respect to the equal protection question, we find a violation of the Equal Protection Clause.

II

A

The closeness of this election, and the multitude of legal challenges which have followed in its wake, have brought into sharp focus a common, if heretofore unnoticed, phenomenon. Nationwide statistics reveal that an estimated 2% of ballots cast do not register a vote for President for whatever reason, including deliberately choosing no candidate at all or some voter error, such as voting for two candidates or insufficiently marking a ballot. In certifying election results, the votes eligible for inclusion in the certification are the votes meeting the properly established legal requirements.

This case has shown that punch card balloting machines can produce an unfortunate number of ballots which are not punched in a clean, complete way by the voter. After the current counting, it is likely legislative bodies nationwide will examine ways to improve the mechanisms and machinery for voting.

B

The individual citizen has no federal constitutional right to vote for electors for the President of the United States unless and until the state legislature chooses a statewide election as the means to implement its power to appoint members of the Electoral College. U.S. Const., Art. II, §1. This is the source for the statement in *McPherson v. Blacker*, 146 U.S. 1, 35 (1892), that the State legislature's power to select the manner for appointing electors is plenary; it may, if it so chooses, select the electors itself, which indeed was the manner used by State legislatures in several States for many years after the Framing of our Constitution. History has now favored the voter, and in each of the several States the citizens themselves vote for Presidential electors. When the state legislature vests the right to vote for President in its people, the right to vote as the legislature has prescribed is fundamental; and one source of its fundamental nature lies in the equal weight accorded to each vote and the equal dignity owed to each voter. The State, of course, after granting the franchise in the special context of Article II, can take back the power to appoint electors. See *id.* ("[T]here is no doubt of the right of the legislature to resume the power at any time, for it can neither be taken away nor abdicated") (quoting S.Rep. No. 395, 43d Cong., 1st Sess.).

The right to vote is protected in more than the initial allocation of the franchise. Equal protection applies as well to the manner of its exercise. Having once granted the right to vote on equal terms, the State may not, by later arbitrary and disparate treatment, value one person's vote over that of another. See, *e.g., Harper v. Virginia Bd. of Elections*, 383 U.S. 663, 665 (1966) ("[O]nce the franchise is granted to the electorate, lines may not be drawn which are inconsistent with the Equal Protection Clause of the Fourteenth Amendment"). It must be remembered that "the right of suffrage can be denied by a debasement or dilution of the weight of a citizen's vote just as effectively as by wholly prohibiting the free exercise of the franchise." *Reynolds v. Sims*.

There is no difference between the two sides of the present controversy on these basic propositions. Respondents say that the very purpose of vindicating the right to vote justifies the recount procedures now at issue. The question before us, however, is whether the recount procedures the Florida Supreme Court has adopted are consistent with its obligation to avoid arbitrary and disparate treatment of the members of its electorate.

Much of the controversy seems to revolve around ballot cards designed to be perforated by a stylus but which, either through error or deliberate omission, have not been perforated with sufficient precision for a machine to count them. In some cases a piece of the card—a chad—is hanging, say by two corners. In other cases there is no separation at all, just an indentation.

The Florida Supreme Court has ordered that the intent of the voter be discerned from such ballots. For purposes of resolving the equal protection challenge, it is not necessary to decide whether the Florida Supreme Court had the authority under the legislative scheme for resolving election disputes to define what a legal vote is and to mandate a manual recount implementing that definition. The recount mechanisms implemented in response to the decisions of the Florida Supreme Court do not satisfy the minimum requirement for non-arbitrary treatment of voters necessary to secure the fundamental right. Florida's basic command for the count of legally cast votes is to consider the "intent of the voter." *Gore* v. *Harris*. This is unobjectionable as an abstract proposition and a starting principle. The problem inheres in the absence of specific standards to ensure its equal application. The formulation of uniform rules to determine intent based on these recurring circumstances is practicable and, we conclude, necessary.

The law does not refrain from searching for the intent of the actor in a multitude of circumstances; and in some cases the general command to ascertain intent is not susceptible to much further refinement. In this instance, however, the question is not whether to believe a witness but how to interpret the marks or holes or scratches on an inanimate object, a piece of cardboard or paper which, it is said, might not have registered as a vote during the machine count. The factfinder confronts a thing, not a person. The search for intent can be confined by specific rules designed to ensure uniform treatment.

The want of those rules here has led to unequal evaluation of ballots in various respects. See *Gore* v. *Harris* (Wells, J., dissenting) ("Should a county canvassing board count or not count a 'dimpled chad' where the voter is able to successfully dislodge the chad in every other contest on that ballot? Here, the county canvassing boards disagree"). As seems to have been acknowledged at oral argument, the standards for accepting or rejecting contested ballots might vary not only from county to county but indeed within a single county from one recount team to another.

The record provides some examples. A monitor in Miami-Dade County testified at trial that he observed that three members of the county canvassing board applied different standards in defining a legal vote. And testimony at trial also revealed that at least one county changed its evaluative standards during the counting process. Palm Beach County, for example, began the process with a 1990 guideline which precluded counting completely attached chads, switched to a rule that considered a vote to be legal if any light could be seen through a chad, changed back to the 1990 rule, and then abandoned any pretense of a *per se* rule, only to have a court order that the county consider dimpled chads legal. This is not a process with sufficient guarantees of equal treatment.

An early case in our one person, one vote jurisprudence arose when a State accorded arbitrary and disparate treatment to voters in its different counties. *Gray v. Sanders*, 372 U.S. 368 (1963). The Court found a constitutional violation. We relied on these principles in the context of the Presidential selection process in *Moore v. Ogilvie*, 394 U.S. 814 (1969), where we invalidated a county-based procedure that diluted the influence of citizens in larger counties in the nominating process. There we observed that "[t]he idea that one group can be granted greater voting strength than another is hostile to the one man, one vote basis of our representative government."

The State Supreme Court ratified this uneven treatment. It mandated that the recount totals from two counties, Miami-Dade and Palm Beach, be included in the certified total. The court also appeared to hold *sub silentio* that the recount totals from Broward County, which were not completed until after the original November 14 certification by the Secretary of State, were to be considered part of the new certified vote totals even though the county certification was not contested by Vice President Gore. Yet each of the counties used varying standards to determine what was a legal vote. Broward County used a more forgiving standard than Palm Beach County, and uncovered almost three times as many new votes, a result markedly disproportionate to the difference in population between the counties.

In addition, the recounts in these three counties were not limited to so-called undervotes but extended to all of the ballots. The distinction has real consequences. A manual recount of all ballots identifies not only those ballots which show no vote but also those which contain more than one, the so-called overvotes. Neither category will be counted by the machine. This is not a trivial concern. At oral argument, respondents estimated there are as many as 110,000 overvotes statewide. As a result, the citizen whose ballot was not read by a machine because he failed to vote for a candidate in a way readable by a machine may still have his vote counted in a manual recount; on the other hand, the citizen who marks two candidates in a way discernible by the machine will not have the same opportunity to have his vote count, even if a manual examination of the ballot would reveal the requisite indicia of intent. Furthermore, the citizen who marks two candidates, only one of which is discernible by the machine, will have his vote counted even though it should have been read as an invalid ballot. The State Supreme Court's inclusion of vote counts based on these variant standards exemplifies concerns with the remedial processes that were under way.

That brings the analysis to yet a further equal protection problem. The votes certified by the court included a partial total from one county, Miami-Dade. The Florida Supreme Court's decision thus gives no assurance that the recounts included in a final certification must be complete. Indeed, it is respondent's submission that it would be consistent with the rules of the recount procedures to include whatever partial counts are done by the time of final certification, and we interpret the Florida Supreme Court's decision to permit this. This accommodation no doubt results from the truncated contest period established by the Florida Supreme Court in *Bush I*, at respondents' own urging. The press of time does not diminish the constitutional concern. A desire for speed is not a general excuse for ignoring equal protection guarantees.

In addition to these difficulties the actual process by which the votes were to be counted under the Florida Supreme Court's decision raises further concerns. That order did not specify who would recount the ballots. The county canvassing boards were forced to pull together ad hoc teams comprised of judges from various Circuits who had no previous training in handling and interpreting ballots. Furthermore, while others were permitted to observe, they were prohibited from objecting during the recount.

The recount process, in its features here described, is inconsistent with the minimum procedures necessary to protect the fundamental right of each voter in the special instance of a statewide recount under the authority of a single state judicial officer. Our consideration is limited to the present circumstances, for the problem of equal protection in election processes generally presents many complexities.

The question before the Court is not whether local entities, in the exercise of their expertise, may develop different systems for implementing elections. Instead, we are presented with a situation where a state court with the power to assure uniformity has ordered a statewide recount with minimal procedural safeguards. When a court orders a statewide remedy, there must be at least some assurance that the rudimentary requirements of equal treatment and fundamental fairness are satisfied.

Given the Court's assessment that the recount process underway was probably being conducted in an unconstitutional manner, the Court stayed the order directing the recount so it could hear this case and render an expedited decision. The contest provision, as it was mandated by the State Supreme Court, is not well calculated to sustain the confidence that all citizens must have in the outcome of elections. The State has not shown that its procedures include the necessary safeguards. The problem, for instance, of the estimated 110,000 overvotes has not been addressed, although Chief Justice Wells called attention to the concern in his dissenting opinion.

Upon due consideration of the difficulties identified to this point, it is obvious that the recount cannot be conducted in compliance with the requirements of equal protection and due process without substantial additional work. It would require not only the adoption (after opportunity for argument) of adequate statewide standards for determining what is a legal vote, and practicable procedures to implement them, but also orderly judicial review of any disputed matters that might arise. In addition, the Secretary of State has advised that the recount of only a portion of the ballots requires that the vote tabulation equipment be used to screen out undervotes, a function for which the machines were not designed. If a recount of overvotes were also required, perhaps even a second screening would be necessary. Use of the equipment for this purpose, and any new software developed for it, would have to be evaluated for accuracy by the Secretary of State, as required by Fla. Stat. § 101.015 (2000).

The Supreme Court of Florida has said that the legislature intended the State's electors to "participat[e] fully in the federal electoral process," as provided in 3 U.S.C. § 5. That statute, in turn, requires that any controversy or contest that is designed to lead to a conclusive selection of electors be completed by December 12. That date is upon us, and there is no recount procedure in place under the State Supreme Court's order that comports with minimal constitutional standards. Because it is evident that any recount seeking to meet the December 12 date will be unconstitutional for the reasons we have discussed, we reverse the judgment of the Supreme Court of Florida ordering a recount to proceed.

Seven Justices of the Court agree that there are constitutional problems with the recount ordered by the Florida Supreme Court that demand a remedy.[a] See *post* (SOUTER, J., dissenting); *post* (BREYER, J., dissenting). The only disagreement is as to the remedy. Because the Florida Supreme Court has said that the Florida Legislature intended to obtain the safe-harbor benefits of 3 U.S.C. § 5, Justice BREYER's proposed remedy—remanding to the Florida Supreme Court for its ordering of a constitutionally proper contest until December 18—contemplates action in violation of the Florida election code, and hence could not be part of an "appropriate" order authorized by Fla. Stat. § 102.168(8) (2000).

* * *

None are more conscious of the vital limits on judicial authority than are the members of this Court, and none stand more in admiration of the Constitution's design to leave the selection of the President to the people, through their legislatures, and to the political sphere. When contending parties invoke the process of the courts, however, it becomes our unsought responsibility to resolve the federal and constitutional issues the judicial system has been forced to confront.

The judgment of the Supreme Court of Florida is reversed, and the case is remanded for further proceedings not inconsistent with this opinion....

It is so ordered.

CHIEF Justice REHNQUIST, with whom Justice SCALIA and Justice THOMAS join, concurring.

We join the *per curiam* opinion. We write separately because we believe there are additional grounds that require us to reverse the Florida Supreme Court's decision.

---

a. This statement in the opinion has been a source of some controversy. Dissenting opinions of Justices Breyer and Souter appear below. Is the Court correct that those justices agree that there is a constitutional problem?—Eds.

[The concurring opinion began by setting forth the view that Article II gave the state *legislature* the sole power to set the rules for choosing presidential electors.]

II

Acting pursuant to its constitutional grant of authority, the Florida Legislature has created a detailed, if not perfectly crafted, statutory scheme that provides for appointment of Presidential electors by direct election. . . .

The state legislature has also provided mechanisms both for protesting election returns and for contesting certified election results. Section 102.166 governs protests. Any protest must be filed prior to the certification of election results by the county canvassing board. Once a protest has been filed, "[t]he county canvassing board may authorize a manual recount." If a sample recount conducted pursuant to § 102.166(5) "indicates an error in the vote tabulation which could affect the outcome of the election," the county canvassing board is instructed to: "(a) Correct the error and recount the remaining precincts with the vote tabulation system; (b) Request the Department of State to verify the tabulation software; or (c) Manually recount all ballots." In the event a canvassing board chooses to conduct a manual recount of all ballots, § 102.166(7) prescribes procedures for such a recount.

Contests to the certification of an election, on the other hand, are controlled by § 102.168. The grounds for contesting an election include "[r]eceipt of a number of illegal votes or rejection of a number of legal votes sufficient to change or place in doubt the result of the election." Any contest must be filed in the appropriate Florida circuit court, and the canvassing board or election board is the proper party defendant. Section 102.168(8) provides that "[t]he circuit judge to whom the contest is presented may fashion such orders as he or she deems necessary to ensure that each allegation in the complaint is investigated, examined, or checked, to prevent or correct any alleged wrong, and to provide any relief appropriate under such circumstances." In Presidential elections, the contest period necessarily terminates on the date set by 3 U.S.C. § 5 for concluding the State's "final determination" of election controversies.

In its first decision, *Palm Beach Canvassing Bd. v. Harris* (*Harris I*), the Florida Supreme Court extended the 7-day statutory certification deadline established by the legislature. This modification of the code, by lengthening the protest period, necessarily shortened the contest period for Presidential elections. Underlying the extension of the certification deadline and the shortchanging of the contest period was, presumably, the clear implication that certification was a matter of significance: The certified winner would enjoy presumptive validity, making a contest proceeding by the losing candidate an uphill battle. In its latest opinion, however, the court empties certification of virtually all legal consequence during the contest, and in doing so departs from the provisions enacted by the Florida Legislature.

The court determined that canvassing boards' decisions regarding whether to recount ballots past the certification deadline (even the certification deadline established by *Harris I*) are to be reviewed *de novo*, although the Election Code clearly vests discretion whether to recount in the boards, and sets strict deadlines subject to the Secretary's rejection of late tallies and monetary fines for tardiness. See Fla. Stat. Ann. § 102.112 (Supp. 2001). Moreover, the Florida court held that all late vote tallies arriving during the contest period should be automatically included in the certification regardless of the certification deadline (even the certification deadline established by *Harris I*), thus virtually eliminating both the deadline and the Secretary's discretion to disregard recounts that violate it.

Moreover, the court's interpretation of "legal vote," and hence its decision to order a contest-period recount, plainly departed from the legislative scheme. Florida statutory law cannot reasonably be thought to *require* the counting of improperly marked ballots. Each Florida precinct before election day provides instructions on how properly to cast a vote; each polling place on election day contains a working model of the voting machine it uses; and each voting booth contains a sample ballot. In precincts using punch-card ballots, voters are instructed to punch out the ballot cleanly:

> "AFTER VOTING, CHECK YOUR BALLOT CARD TO BE SURE YOUR VOTING SELECTIONS ARE CLEARLY AND CLEANLY PUNCHED AND THERE ARE NO CHIPS LEFT HANGING ON THE BACK OF THE CARD."

No reasonable person would call it "an error in the vote tabulation," Fla. Stat. Ann. § 102.166(5), or a "rejection of . . . legal votes," Fla. Stat. Ann. § 102.168(3)(c), when electronic or electromechanical equipment performs precisely in the manner designed, and fails to count those ballots that are not marked in the manner that these voting instructions explicitly and prominently specify. The scheme that the Florida Supreme Court's opinion attributes to the legislature is one in which machines are *required* to be "capable of correctly counting votes," § 101.5606(4), but which nonetheless regularly produces elections in which legal votes are predictably *not* tabulated, so that in close elections manual recounts are regularly required. This is of course absurd. The Secretary, who is authorized by law to issue binding interpretations of the Election Code, rejected this peculiar reading of the statutes. The Florida Supreme Court, although it must defer to the Secretary's interpretations, rejected her reasonable interpretation and embraced the peculiar one. See *Palm Beach County Canvassing Board* v. *Harris* (*Harris II*).

But as we indicated in our remand of the earlier case, in a Presidential election the clearly expressed intent of the legislature must prevail. And there is no basis for reading the Florida statutes as requiring the counting of improperly marked ballots, as an examination of the Florida Supreme Court's textual analysis shows. We will not parse that analysis here, except to note that the principal provision of the election code on which it relied, § 101.5614(5), was, as Chief Justice Wells pointed out in his dissent in *Harris II*, entirely irrelevant. The State's Attorney General (who was supporting the Gore challenge) confirmed in oral argument here that never before the present election had a manual recount been conducted on the basis of the contention that "undervotes" should have been examined to determine voter intent. For the court to step away from this established practice, prescribed by the Secretary, the state official charged by the legislature with "responsibility to . . . [o]btain and maintain uniformity in the application, operation, and interpretation of the election laws," was to depart from the legislative scheme.

[The concurrence concluded in Part III that "[t]he scope and nature of the remedy ordered by the Florida Supreme Court jeopardizes the 'legislative wish' to take advantage of the safe harbor provided by 3 U.S.C. § 5."]

Justice STEVENS, with whom Justice GINSBURG and Justice BREYER join, dissenting.

The Constitution assigns to the States the primary responsibility for determining the manner of selecting the Presidential electors. See Art. II, § 1, cl. 2. When questions arise about the meaning of state laws, including election laws, it is our settled practice to accept the opinions of the highest courts of the States as providing the final answers. On rare occasions, however, either federal statutes or the Federal Constitution may require federal judicial intervention in state elections. This is not such an occasion.

The federal questions that ultimately emerged in this case are not substantial. [Justice Stevens rebutted the concurring opinion's interpretation of Article II and argued that Congress in enacting 3 U.S.C. § 5 "did not impose any affirmative duties upon the States that their governmental branches could 'violate.'"]

Nor are petitioners correct in asserting that the failure of the Florida Supreme Court to specify in detail the precise manner in which the "intent of the voter," Fla. Stat. § 101.5614(5) (Supp. 2001), is to be determined rises to the level of a constitutional violation.[2] We found such a violation when individual votes within the same State were weighted unequally, see, *e.g., Reynolds,* but we have never before called into question the substantive standard by which a State determines that a vote has been legally cast. And there is no reason to think that the guidance provided to the factfinders, specifically the various canvassing boards, by the "intent of the voter" standard is any less sufficient—or will lead to results any less uniform—than, for example, the "beyond a reasonable doubt" standard employed everyday by ordinary citizens in courtrooms across this country.

Admittedly, the use of differing substandards for determining voter intent in different counties employing similar voting systems may raise serious concerns. Those concerns are alleviated—if not eliminated—by the fact that a single impartial magistrate will ultimately adjudicate all objections arising from the recount process. Of course, as a general matter, "[t]he interpretation of constitutional principles must not be too literal. We must remember that the machinery of government would not

---

2. The Florida statutory standard is consistent with the practice of the majority of States, which apply either an "intent of the voter" standard or an "impossible to determine the elector's choice" standard in ballot recounts. . . .

work if it were not allowed a little play in its joints." *Bain Peanut Co. of Tex. v. Pinson*, 282 U.S. 499, 501 (1931) (Holmes, J.). If it were otherwise, Florida's decision to leave to each county the determination of what balloting system to employ—despite enormous differences in accuracy[4]—might run afoul of equal protection. So, too, might the similar decisions of the vast majority of state legislatures to delegate to local authorities certain decisions with respect to voting systems and ballot design.

Even assuming that aspects of the remedial scheme might ultimately be found to violate the Equal Protection Clause, I could not subscribe to the majority's disposition of the case. As the majority explicitly holds, once a state legislature determines to select electors through a popular vote, the right to have one's vote counted is of constitutional stature. As the majority further acknowledges, Florida law holds that all ballots that reveal the intent of the voter constitute valid votes. Recognizing these principles, the majority nonetheless orders the termination of the contest proceeding before all such votes have been tabulated. Under their own reasoning, the appropriate course of action would be to remand to allow more specific procedures for implementing the legislature's uniform general standard to be established.

In the interest of finality, however, the majority effectively orders the disenfranchisement of an unknown number of voters whose ballots reveal their intent—and are therefore legal votes under state law—but were for some reason rejected by ballot-counting machines. It does so on the basis of the deadlines set forth in Title 3 of the United States Code. But, as I have already noted, those provisions merely provide rules of decision for Congress to follow when selecting among conflicting slates of electors. They do not prohibit a State from counting what the majority concedes to be legal votes until a bona fide winner is determined.... As the majority notes, "[a] desire for speed is not a general excuse for ignoring equal protection guarantees." ...

What must underlie petitioners' entire federal assault on the Florida election procedures is an unstated lack of confidence in the impartiality and capacity of the state judges who would make the critical decisions if the vote count were to proceed. Otherwise, their position is wholly without merit. The endorsement of that position by the majority of this Court can only lend credence to the most cynical appraisal of the work of judges throughout the land. It is confidence in the men and women who administer the judicial system that is the true backbone of the rule of law. Time will one day heal the wound to that confidence that will be inflicted by today's decision. One thing, however, is certain. Although we may never know with complete certainty the identity of the winner of this year's Presidential election, the identity of

4. The percentage of nonvotes in this election in counties using a punch-card system was 3.92%; in contrast, the rate of error under the more modern optical-scan systems was only 1.43%. Put in other terms, for every 10,000 votes cast, punch-card systems result in 250 more nonvotes than optical-scan systems. A total of 3,718,305 votes were cast under punch-card systems, and 2,353,811 votes were cast under optical-scan systems.

the loser is perfectly clear. It is the Nation's confidence in the judge as an impartial guardian of the rule of law.

I respectfully dissent.

Justice SOUTER, with whom Justice BREYER joins and with whom Justice STEVENS and Justice GINSBURG join with regard to all but Part C, dissenting.

The Court should not have reviewed either [*Bush I*], or this case, and should not have stopped Florida's attempt to recount all undervote ballots by issuing a stay of the Florida Supreme Court's orders during the period of this review. If this Court had allowed the State to follow the course indicated by the opinions of its own Supreme Court, it is entirely possible that there would ultimately have been no issue requiring our review, and political tension could have worked itself out in the Congress following the procedure provided in 3 U.S.C. § 15. The case being before us, however, its resolution by the majority is another erroneous decision. [Justice Souter expresses his disagreement with the concurrence's interpretations of Article II and 3 U.S.C. § 5.]

C

It is only on the third issue before us that there is a meritorious argument for relief, as this Court's *Per Curiam* opinion recognizes. It is an issue that might well have been dealt with adequately by the Florida courts if the state proceedings had not been interrupted, and if not disposed of at the state level it could have been considered by the Congress in any electoral vote dispute. But because the course of state proceedings has been interrupted, time is short, and the issue is before us, I think it sensible for the Court to address it.

Petitioners have raised an equal protection claim (or, alternatively, a due process claim, see generally *Logan v. Zimmerman Brush Co.*, 455 U.S. 422 (1982)), in the charge that unjustifiably disparate standards are applied in different electoral jurisdictions to otherwise identical facts. It is true that the Equal Protection Clause does not forbid the use of a variety of voting mechanisms within a jurisdiction, even though different mechanisms will have different levels of effectiveness in recording voters' intentions; local variety can be justified by concerns about cost, the potential value of innovation, and so on. But evidence in the record here suggests that a different order of disparity obtains under rules for determining a voter's intent that have been applied (and could continue to be applied) to identical types of ballots used in identical brands of machines and exhibiting identical physical characteristics (such as "hanging" or "dimpled" chads). I can conceive of no legitimate state interest served by these differing treatments of the expressions of voters' fundamental rights. The differences appear wholly arbitrary.

In deciding what to do about this, we should take account of the fact that electoral votes are due to be cast in six days. I would therefore remand the case to the courts of Florida with instructions to establish uniform standards for evaluating the several types of ballots that have prompted differing treatments, to be applied within and among counties when passing on such identical ballots in any further recounting (or successive recounting) that the courts might order.

Unlike the majority, I see no warrant for this Court to assume that Florida could not possibly comply with this requirement before the date set for the meeting of electors, December 18. Although one of the dissenting justices of the State Supreme Court estimated that disparate standards potentially affected 170,000 votes, the number at issue is significantly smaller. The 170,000 figure apparently represents all uncounted votes, both undervotes (those for which no Presidential choice was recorded by a machine) and overvotes (those rejected because of votes for more than one candidate). But as Justice BREYER has pointed out, no showing has been made of legal overvotes uncounted, and counsel for Gore made an uncontradicted representation to the Court that the statewide total of undervotes is about 60,000. To recount these manually would be a tall order, but before this Court stayed the effort to do that the courts of Florida were ready to do their best to get that job done. There is no justification for denying the State the opportunity to try to count all disputed ballots now.

I respectfully dissent.

Justice GINSBURG, with whom Justice STEVENS joins, and with whom Justice SOUTER and Justice BREYER join as to Part I, dissenting.

I

[In this part, Justice Ginsburg provides a lengthy explanation for her disagreement with Chief Justice Rehnquist's concurring opinion.]

II

I agree with Justice STEVENS that petitioners have not presented a substantial equal protection claim. Ideally, perfection would be the appropriate standard for judging the recount. But we live in an imperfect world, one in which thousands of votes have not been counted. I cannot agree that the recount adopted by the Florida court, flawed as it may be, would yield a result any less fair or precise than the certification that preceded that recount. See, *e.g.*, *McDonald v. Board of Election Comm'rs of Chicago*, 394 U.S. 802, 807 (1969) (even in the context of the right to vote, the state is permitted to reform "'one step at a time'").

Even if there were an equal protection violation, I would agree with Justice STEVENS, Justice SOUTER, and Justice BREYER that the Court's concern about "the December 12 deadline" is misplaced.... Equally important, as Justice BREYER explains, the December 12 "deadline" for bringing Florida's electoral votes into 3 U.S.C. § 5's safe harbor lacks the significance the Court assigns it....

I dissent.

Justice BREYER, with whom Justice STEVENS and Justice GINSBURG join except as to Part I-A-1, and with whom Justice SOUTER joins as to Part I, dissenting.

The Court was wrong to take this case. It was wrong to grant a stay. It should now vacate that stay and permit the Florida Supreme Court to decide whether the recount should resume.

I

The political implications of this case for the country are momentous. But the federal legal questions presented, with one exception, are insubstantial.

A

1

The majority raises three Equal Protection problems with the Florida Supreme Court's recount order: first, the failure to include overvotes in the manual recount; second, the fact that *all* ballots, rather than simply the undervotes, were recounted in some, but not all, counties; and third, the absence of a uniform, specific standard to guide the recounts. As far as the first issue is concerned, petitioners presented no evidence, to this Court or to any Florida court, that a manual recount of overvotes would identify additional legal votes. The same is true of the second, and, in addition, the majority's reasoning would seem to invalidate any state provision for a manual recount of individual counties in a statewide election.

The majority's third concern does implicate principles of fundamental fairness. The majority concludes that the Equal Protection Clause requires that a manual recount be governed not only by the uniform general standard of the "clear intent of the voter," but also by uniform subsidiary standards (for example, a uniform determination whether indented, but not perforated, "undervotes" should count). . . . I agree that, in these very special circumstances, basic principles of fairness may well have counseled the adoption of a uniform standard to address the problem. In light of the majority's disposition, I need not decide whether, or the extent to which, as a remedial matter, the Constitution would place limits upon the content of the uniform standard.

2

Nonetheless, there is no justification for the majority's remedy, which is simply to reverse the lower court and halt the recount entirely. An appropriate remedy would be, instead, to remand this case with instructions that, even at this late date, would permit the Florida Supreme Court to require recounting *all* undercounted votes in Florida, including those from Broward, Volusia, Palm Beach, and Miami-Dade Counties, whether or not previously recounted prior to the end of the protest period, and to do so in accordance with a single-uniform substandard.

The majority justifies stopping the recount entirely on the ground that there is no more time. In particular, the majority relies on the lack of time for the Secretary to review and approve equipment needed to separate undervotes. But the majority reaches this conclusion in the absence of *any* record evidence that the recount could not have been completed in the time allowed by the Florida Supreme Court. The majority finds facts outside of the record on matters that state courts are in a far better position to address. Of course, it is too late for any such recount to take place by December 12, the date by which election disputes must be decided if a State is to take advantage of the safe harbor provisions of 3 U.S.C. § 5. Whether there is time to conduct a recount prior to December 18, when the electors are scheduled to meet, is a matter for the state courts to determine. And whether, under Florida law, Florida could or could not take further action is obviously a matter for Florida courts, not this Court, to decide.

By halting the manual recount, and thus ensuring that the uncounted legal votes will not be counted under any standard, this Court crafts a remedy out of proportion to the asserted harm. And that remedy harms the very fairness interests the Court is attempting to protect. The manual recount would itself redress a problem of unequal treatment of ballots. As Justice STEVENS points out, the ballots of voters in counties that use punch-card systems are more likely to be disqualified than those in counties using optical-scanning systems. According to recent news reports, variations in the undervote rate are even more pronounced. Thus, in a system that allows counties to use different types of voting systems, voters already arrive at the polls with an unequal chance that their votes will be counted. I do not see how the fact that this results from counties' selection of different voting machines rather than a court order makes the outcome any more fair. Nor do I understand why the Florida Supreme Court's recount order, which helps to redress this inequity, must be entirely prohibited based on a deficiency that could easily be remedied.

B

The remainder of petitioners' claims, which are the focus of THE CHIEF JUSTICE's concurrence, raise no significant federal questions. . . .

II

Despite the reminder that this case involves "an election for the President of the United States," no preeminent legal concern, or practical concern related to legal questions, required this Court to hear this case, let alone to issue a stay that stopped Florida's recount process in its tracks. . . .

Of course, the selection of the President is of fundamental national importance. But that importance is political, not legal. And this Court should resist the temptation unnecessarily to resolve tangential legal disputes, where doing so threatens to determine the outcome of the election.

The Constitution and federal statutes themselves make clear that restraint is appropriate. They set forth a road map of how to resolve disputes about electors, even after an election as close as this one. That road map foresees resolution of electoral disputes by *state* courts. See 3 U.S.C. § 5 (providing that, where a "State shall have provided, by laws enacted prior to [election day], for its final determination of any controversy or contest concerning the appointment of . . . electors . . . by judicial or other methods," the subsequently chosen electors enter a safe harbor free from congressional challenge). But it nowhere provides for involvement by the United States Supreme Court.

To the contrary, the Twelfth Amendment commits to Congress the authority and responsibility to count electoral votes. A federal statute, the Electoral Count Act, enacted after the close 1876 Hayes-Tilden Presidential election, specifies that, after States have tried to resolve disputes (through "judicial" or other means), Congress is the body primarily authorized to resolve remaining disputes. See Electoral Count Act of 1887, 3 U.S.C. §§ 5, 6, and 15.

The legislative history of the Act makes clear its intent to commit the power to resolve such disputes to Congress, rather than the courts. [Justice Breyer recounts the legislative history.]

Given this detailed, comprehensive scheme for counting electoral votes, there is no reason to believe that federal law either foresees or requires resolution of such a political issue by this Court. Nor, for that matter, is there any reason to that think the Constitution's Framers would have reached a different conclusion. Madison, at least, believed that allowing the judiciary to choose the presidential electors "was out of the question." Madison, July 25, 1787 (reprinted in 5 Elliot's Debates on the Federal Constitution 363 (2d ed. 1876)).

The decision by both the Constitution's Framers and the 1886 Congress to minimize this Court's role in resolving close federal presidential elections is as wise as it is clear. However awkward or difficult it may be for Congress to resolve difficult electoral disputes, Congress, being a political body, expresses the people's will far more accurately than does an unelected Court. And the people's will is what elections are about....

...I think it not only legally wrong, but also most unfortunate, for the Court simply to have terminated the Florida recount. Those who caution judicial restraint in resolving political disputes have described the quintessential case for that restraint as a case marked, among other things, by the "strangeness of the issue," its "intractability to principled resolution," its "sheer momentousness,... which tends to unbalance judicial judgment," and "the inner vulnerability, the self-doubt of an institution which is electorally irresponsible and has no earth to draw strength from." Bickel, *supra*. Those characteristics mark this case.

At the same time, as I have said, the Court is not acting to vindicate a fundamental constitutional principle, such as the need to protect a basic human liberty. No other strong reason to act is present. Congressional statutes tend to obviate the need. And, above all, in this highly politicized matter, the appearance of a split decision runs the risk of undermining the public's confidence in the Court itself. That confidence is a public treasure. It has been built slowly over many years, some of which were marked by a Civil War and the tragedy of segregation. It is a vitally necessary ingredient of any successful effort to protect basic liberty and, indeed, the rule of law itself. We run no risk of returning to the days when a President (responding to this Court's efforts to protect the Cherokee Indians) might have said, "John

Marshall has made his decision; now let him enforce it." Loth, Chief Justice John Marshall and The Growth of the American Republic 365 (1948). But we do risk a self-inflicted wound—a wound that may harm not just the Court, but the Nation.

I fear that in order to bring this agonizingly long election process to a definitive conclusion, we have not adequately attended to that necessary "check upon our own exercise of power," "our own sense of self-restraint." *United States v. Butler*, 297 U.S. 1, 79 (1936) (Stone, J., dissenting). Justice Brandeis once said of the Court, "The most important thing we do is not doing." Bickel, *supra*. What it does today, the Court should have left undone. I would repair the damage done as best we now can, by permitting the Florida recount to continue under uniform standards.

I respectfully dissent.

Notes and Questions

1. *Why* Bush v. Gore *Matters. Bush v. Gore* is the first Supreme Court case applying equal protection analysis to the "nuts and bolts" of elections. It is therefore important on a doctrinal level, a subject explored in the Notes below. In addition, *Bush v. Gore* is important because it signaled that federal courts were "open for business" with respect to election administration claims. Samuel Issacharoff, *Judge John R. Brown Memorial Lecture: Judging in the Time of the Extraordinary*, 47 Houston Law Review 533, 540–41 (2010). Since 2000, there have been many constitutional challenges to election administration practices in the lower courts, although the Supreme Court itself has avoided citing *Bush v. Gore*. Why do you suppose that is?

2. *The Equal Protection Holding*. What is the holding of *Bush v. Gore*? The Court says that Florida's recount process violated equal protection, but why? Because of the arbitrary and disparate treatment of voters? The differential treatment of similarly situated voters across counties? The broad discretion that Florida law gave in discerning the intent of the voter? The fact that there was disparate treatment of identical ballots in a recount conducted as part of a single judicial proceeding? Note that there are broader and narrower ways of characterizing the holding (which is not to say that all of them are equally good).

3. *The Level of Scrutiny*. In its discussion of the merits, the majority relies upon *Harper* and *Reynolds* (*supra* Chapters 2 and 3 respectively). These cases establish that voting is a fundamental right, burdens on which are subject to heightened scrutiny. Did the Court apply strict scrutiny? If so, why did the "safe harbor" provision of 3 U.S.C. §5 trump the right of every voter to have each vote counted? Consider what the Court itself said earlier in *Bush v. Gore*: "The press of time does not diminish the constitutional concern. A desire for speed is not a general excuse for ignoring equal protection guarantees."

The level of scrutiny in election administration cases is discussed further in *Crawford v. Marion County Board of Elections* (2008) and the notes that follow, in Section C below.

4. *Other Constitutional Theories.* Was the essence of the problem in *Bush v. Gore* really one of due process rather than equal protection? See Roy A. Schotland, *In* Bush v. Gore: *Whatever Happened to the Due Process Ground?*, 34 Loyola University of Chicago Law Journal 211 (2002); Einer Elhauge, *The Lessons of Florida 2000*, Policy Review, Dec. 1 2001, at 15–36. Should the Court's decision be understood in light of First Amendment cases, which sharply limit the state's ability to rely on vague or ambiguous standards in regulating speech acts? See Abner S. Greene, *Is There a First Amendment Defense for* Bush v. Gore?, 80 Notre Dame Law Review 1643 (2005); Daniel P. Tokaji, *First Amendment Equal Protection*, 101 Michigan Law Review 2409, 2487–95 (2003). Part of the justification for these First Amendment cases is that government officials cannot be trusted to implement such standards in an evenhanded fashion. Is the result in *Bush v. Gore* best explained by the Supreme Court's doubt of the neutrality of local election officials counting the ballots, or of the Florida Supreme Court? See Richard H. Pildes, *Foreword: The Constitutionalization of Democratic Politics*, 118 Harvard Law Review 28, 49 (2004) (suggesting that *Bush v. Gore* may best be understood as concerned with the "unconstitutional risk of partisan manipulation in the recount and hence the election itself").

5. *The Remedy.* Perhaps the most controversial part of the Court's opinion was its decision to end the recount rather than allowing recounts to resume under a uniform standard. After the opinion in *Bush v. Gore* was released, Gore's lawyers initially considered but quickly rejected the possibility of asking the Florida Supreme Court to order recounts pursuant to a uniform standard, and Gore conceded the election. He had little choice, given that the U.S. Supreme Court's opinion said that "any recount seeking to meet the December 12 [safe harbor] date will be unconstitutional."

The Court reached this conclusion after stating that the Florida Supreme Court indicated that the Florida legislature wished to take advantage of the safe harbor provision of 3 U.S.C. § 5. According to the Court, the Florida court demonstrated this intention when it stated in *Palm Beach County Canvassing Board v. Harris* that Florida's Secretary of State could ignore late returns only if accepting them would "preclud[e] Florida voters from participating fully in the federal electoral process." Was that enough evidence of the Florida Supreme Court's interpretation of Florida law?

We shall return to the question of election remedies in Part IV of this Chapter.

6. *Federalism.* The five Justices in the Supreme Court majority were well-known for their support protecting the power of state governments from interference by the federal government. Critics charge that the *Bush v. Gore* decision is inconsistent with state sovereignty principles. As we saw in Chapter 5, the Rehnquist Court's decisions establishing the constitutional claim of an "unconstitutional racial gerrymander" similarly have been criticized for deviating from federalism principles. Those cases may have something else in common with *Bush v. Gore*: "Whatever interest the Supreme Court's opinion [in *Bush v. Gore*] vindicated, it was not the interest of an

identifiable individual voter. Rather[,] it was a perceived systemic interest in having recounts conducted according to a uniform standard or not at all. It was structural equal protection, just as the [racial gerrymandering] cases have been." Pamela S. Karlan, *Nothing Personal: The Evolution of the Newest Equal Protection from* Shaw v. Reno *to* Bush v. Gore, 79 North Carolina Law Review 1345, 1364 (2001).

7. *A Constitutional Crisis Avoided?* The *Bush v. Gore* opinion was sharply criticized by liberals and even some conservatives as result-oriented jurisprudence. But Richard Posner, a prominent conservative scholar and judge, justified the result in *Bush v. Gore* as "rough justice" if not "legal justice": "I cannot see the case for precipitating a political and constitutional crisis merely in order to fuss with a statistical tie that, given the inherent subjectivity involved in hand counting spoiled ballots, can never be untied." Richard A. Posner, *Florida 2000: A Legal and Statistical Analysis of the Election Deadlock and Ensuing Litigation*, 2000 Supreme Court Review 1, 46. If the Supreme Court had not intervened, the recounts would have gone forward. If Gore indeed won the recount (something that was far from assured), it was probable that the Florida Legislature would have sent a competing slate of electors to Congress. Congress then would have used one of a series of complicated rules to determine who was President. Under most of the scenarios, Bush would have been declared the President. Is that a crisis? For criticism of Judge Posner's crisis rationale, see Richard L. Hasen, *A "Tincture of Justice": Judge Posner's Failed Rehabilitation of* Bush v. Gore, 80 Texas Law Review 137 (2001) (book review); Ward Farnsworth, *"To Do a Great Right, Do a Little Wrong": A User's Guide to Judicial Lawlessness*, 86 Minnesota Law Review 227 (2001).

8. *The Article II Rationale.* Richard A. Epstein has defended the Article II rationale, set forth in Chief Justice Rehnquist's concurring opinion but not adopted by a majority of the Court. Calling the majority's equal protection rationale "a confused nonstarter at best, which deserves much of the scorn that has been heaped upon it," Epstein argues that a constitutional violation occurs when "the state court's interpretation [of the legislative provisions governing the choosing of presidential electors] does not fall within the boundaries of acceptable interpretation, but rather represents what must be called, for want of a better term, a gross deviation from the scheme outlined in the statute." Richard A. Epstein, *"In Such Manner as the Legislature Thereof May Direct": The Outcome in* Bush v Gore *Defended*, in The Vote: Bush, Gore and the Supreme Court 13, 20 (Cass R. Sunstein & Richard A. Epstein, eds., 2001). Is this a persuasive argument? For a different perspective, see Harold J. Krent, *Judging: The Problem of Second-Guessing State Judges' Interpretation of State Law in* Bush v. Gore, 29 Florida State University Law Review 493, 497 (2001).

9. *Increased Election Litigation.* Election litigation has increased substantially since 2000. Consider Figure 6.2, which shows that the number of election-related cases in a sample of cases on Lexis in the pre-2000 period was just 94 per year, compared to an average of 270 cases per year from 2000–2018. And the 2020 election shattered the old record, with 424 cases.

Figure 6-2 "Election Challenge" Cases per Year: 1996–2020

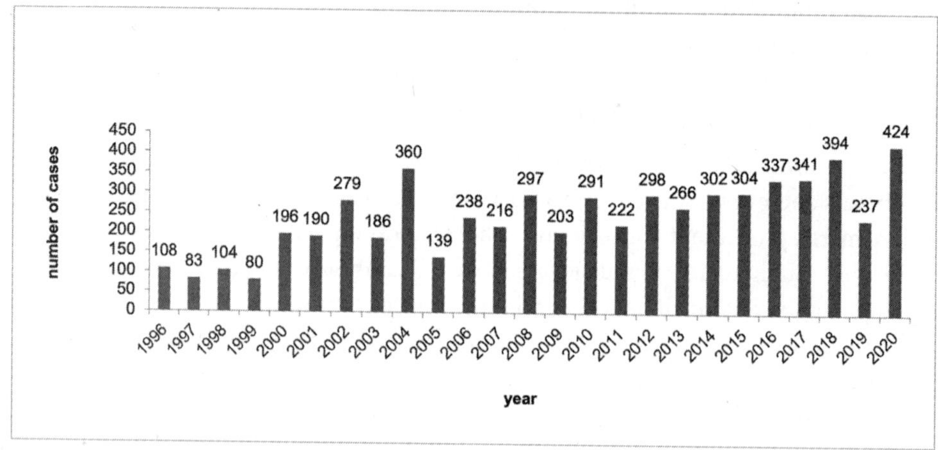

Source: Richard L. Hasen, Election Challenge Litigation, 1996-2020, https://electionlawblog.org/wp-content/uploads/Election-Litigation-1996-2020.xlsx.

We discuss two of the most active subjects of litigation — voting technology and voter identification — in Sections B and C below.

10. *The 2020 Election and the Independent State Legislature Doctrine.* In some ways, the 2020 election was remarkably successful. In the midst of an unprecedented global pandemic that caused a massive shift in how people vote, state and local election officials managed to conduct a secure presidential election that was free from any reasonable doubt over the outcome. See Nathaniel Persily & Charles Stewart III, *The Miracle and Tragedy of the 2020 Election*, 32 Journal of Democracy 159 (2021). Yet President Trump's baseless claims that he was denied victory due to electoral fraud — sometimes known as Trump's "Big Lie" — cast a dark cloud over the election and pose a continuing challenge to our democracy.

2020 was an especially active year for election litigation. The Stanford-MIT Healthy Elections Project found over 500 cases and appeals arising from 46 states plus the District of Columbia and Puerto Rico. Stanford-MIT Healthy Elections Project, *COVID-Related Election Litigation Tracker*, https://perma.cc/7FYS-GHJR (accessed July 13, 2021). In general, these cases can be broken down into two broad categories. The first encompasses cases seeking to compel states to liberalize their voting rules in response to the pandemic, mostly brought by Democrats and their allies. The second are cases challenging the liberalization of voting rules or alleging electoral fraud, mostly brought by Republicans or their allies.

A prominent subject of litigation in the first category was absentee voting. Given the risks of contracting COVID through in-person contact, the country saw a massive shift in how people vote, with millions choosing to vote by mail rather than in person. One survey found that the fraction of people voting by mail more than doubled (going from 21% to 46%), while the percentage of people voting in person on election day fell by more than half (going from 60% to 28%). Charles Stewart III,

How We Voted in 2020: A Topical Look at the Survey of the Performance of American Elections 6 (March 2021). There was a dramatic difference by party affiliation, with many more Democrats (60%) than Republicans (32%) opting to vote by mail. *Id.* at 9. In 2020, 34 states and D.C. had no-excuse absentee voting, which allows people to cast their votes through the mail without providing a reason. National Conference of State Legislators, *Voting Outside the Polling Place Report*, Table 1: States with No-Excuse Absentee Voting (May 1, 2020), https://perma.cc/EA6T-WLLQ.

In recent years, the Supreme Court has looked with disfavor at federal court injunctions issued close to Election Day. This trend continued in 2020. On a 5-4 vote, the Court stayed a preliminary injunction requiring Wisconsin to accept absentee ballots postmarked after election day. *Republican National Committee v. Democratic National Committee*, 140 S. Ct. 1205 (2020); see also *Merrill v. People First of Alabama*, 141 S. Ct. 190 (2020) (staying preliminary injunction issued by a federal court in Alabama, which would have relaxed the requirements for absentee voting and made curbside voting available). Before the general election, the Court upheld a stay of yet another injunction, which would have extended the deadline for the receipt of mail-in ballots in Wisconsin. *Democratic National Committee v. Wisconsin State Legislature*, 141 S. Ct. 28 (2020). These decisions, which are driven by the Court's skepticism of federal court last-minute election injunctions close to an election, are discussed further in Part IV of this chapter.

Other cases seeking to make voting easier were brought in state court. Prominent among the was a case in Pennsylvania, a pivotal swing state, seeking to require the state to count absentee and mail-in ballots received up to three days after Election Day. The Pennsylvania Supreme Court issued a pre-election injunction requiring that these ballots be counted, so long as they were not clearly postmarked after that date. *Pennsylvania Democratic Party v. Boockvar*, 238 A.3d 345, 371-72, 386 (Penn. 2020). Its ruling was partly predicated on the "Free and Equal Elections Clause" of the Pennsylvania State Constitution, which it understood to require that the electoral process be kept open to the extent possible. *Id.* at 369-70. But the state court denied an order requiring that so-called "naked ballots"—that is, ballots that were returned without a secrecy envelope to ensure the voter's anonymity—be counted. *Id.* at 380, 386.

Republicans sought U.S. Supreme Court review of the Pennsylvania Supreme Court's ruling. The main issue before the U.S. Supreme Court was whether a state court, relying on its state constitution, may alter the rules for conducting a presidential election. Republicans' argument relied on the "independent state legislature" doctrine, which holds that state *legislatures* have the authority to set rules governing presidential election, which state courts may not alter. Article II, Section 1 of the U.S. Constitution provides "the Legislature" of each state has authority to determine how presidential electors are appointed. Supporters of the independent state legislature theory contend that the term "the Legislature" means what it says. On their reading, state courts are powerless to alter or strike down state election statutes in presidential elections on the ground that they violate a state constitution (which was not written by the state legislature). On the other hand, the Supreme Court has interpreted the term "the Legislature," which also appears in the Elections Clause of Article I, Section 4, to include the state's entire lawmaking power. *Arizona State Legislature v. Arizona Independent Redistricting Commission*, 576 U.S. 787 (2015) (*infra* Chapter 7, Part III.D.). That would include constitution-makers and state courts interpreting state constitutions.

The Supreme Court denied relief in the Pennsylvania case and subsequently declined to rule on the merits, over the dissents of Justice Thomas and Justice Alito (joined by Justice Gorsuch). *Republican Party of Pennsylvania v. DeGraffenreid*, 141 S. Ct. 732 (2021). Four of the Court's nine justices (Thomas, Alito, Gorsuch, and Kavanaugh), however, have signaled their agreement with the independent state legislature doctrine. Richard L. Hasen, *Trump's Legal Farce Is Having Tragic Results*, N.Y. Times, Nov. 23, 2020. For a scholarly defense of this doctrine, see Michael T. Morley, *The Independent State Legislature Doctrine, Federal Elections, and State Constitutions*, 55 Georgia Law Review 1 (2020). For a rebuttal, see Vikram D. Amar, *Federal Court Review of State Court Interpretations of State Laws that Regulate Federal Elections: Debunking the 'Independent State Legislature' Notion Once and for all, and Keeping Federal Judges to Their Important but Limited Lanes* (November 16, 2020), https://perma.cc/RSU6-UDL4. Is the independent state legislature a "ticking time bomb," waiting to go off in some future election? See Rick Hasen, *Breaking and Analysis: Supreme Court Refuses to Hear Cases Over Conduct of Election in Pennsylvania, With Justices Alito, Gorsuch and Thomas Dissenting: A Ticking Time Bomb to Go Off in a Later Case*, Election Law Blog, Feb. 22, 2021, https://perma.cc/4DQP-5EB9.

The second category of cases involve challenges to the liberalization of voting rules or allegations of electoral fraud, mostly brought by Republicans and their supporters. Some of these cases were brought before the election. In New Jersey, for example, the Trump campaign and RNC challenged a state executive order and subsequent legislation facilitating mail-in voting. A federal district court denied preliminary injunctive relief. *Donald J. Trump for President, Inc. v. Way*, 492 F. Supp. 3d 354 (D.N.J. 2020). In Texas, Republicans brought suit shortly before Election Day to challenge approximately 127,000 ballots cast at drive-through voting sites in the Houston area. The federal courts denied a preliminary injunction and dismissed the lawsuit. *Hotze v. Hollins*, 2020 WL 6437668 (S.D. Tex. Nov. 2, 2020); *Hotze v. Hollins*, 2020 WL 6440440 (5th Cir. Nov. 2, 2020).

After Election Day, President Trump's most ardent supporters went to court in several states seeking to have him declared the winner. Their main argument rested on claims of electoral fraud, most of them lacking in substantial evidence. Courts in Michigan, Wisconsin, Pennsylvania, and other states rejected lawsuits by Trump and his allies. In the most prominent of these cases, the Supreme Court rejected for lack of standing a lawsuit by the State of Texas against certification of election results in four states that Joe Biden won. *Texas v. Pennsylvania*, 141 S. Ct. 1230 (2020).

The Trump camp's scorched-earth litigation strategy was unsuccessful in reversing the result of the 2020 presidential election, given the scant evidence of significant fraud, and the willingness of most election officials—many of them Republicans—to defend the results and the integrity of our election system. Still, the Big Lie achieved some of its intended effects. Many Trump supporters continue to believe his claim that the election was stolen from him, despite the lack of credible evidence. Does this pose an ongoing threat to the stability of American democracy? See Hasen, *Trump's Legal Farce Is Having Tragic Results*, N.Y. Times, Nov. 23, 2020. Consider the growing partisan pressure on state and local election officials, discussed in the next note.

11. *Partisan Pressure on Election Officials.* State chief election officials—in most states, the Secretary of State—play a central role in running elections. See Jocelyn Friedrichs Benson, *Democracy and the Secretary: The Crucial Role of State Election Administrators in Promoting Accuracy and Access to Democracy*, 27 St. Louis University Public Law Review 343 (2008). Yet most states continue to elect their chief election officials on a partisan basis, and many local jurisdictions do the same. A consistent theme of the election administration controversies since 2000 has been allegations of partisanship on the part of state and local election officials. There is some empirical support for the proposition that officials tend to exercise their discretion in a way that benefits their party. Martha Kropf & David Kimball, Helping America Vote: The Limits of Election Reform 98, 104–07 (2012). For a discussion of the problems associated with partisan oversight of elections, see Christian M. Sande, *Where Perception Meets Reality: The Elusive Goal of Impartial Election Oversight*, 34 William Mitchell Law Review 729 (2008). Does the fact that most state chief election officials have partisan affiliations warrant closer judicial scrutiny of their decisions? For an argument that it does, see Daniel P. Tokaji, *The Future of Election Reform: From Rules to Institutions*, 28 Yale Law & Policy Review at 149–53.

State and local election officials are facing greater threats to their impartiality than ever, in the wake of the false claims of widespread election fraud in 2020. After Election Day, President Trump exerted intense public and private pressure on Republican-aligned election officials in key swing states, even after it was clear he had lost. The most egregious example was phone call to Georgia's Republican Secretary of State Brad Raffensperger, which was recorded. Amy Gardner, *'I Just Want to Find 11,780 Votes': In Extraordinary Hour-Long Call, Trump Pressures Georgia Secretary of State to Recalculate the Vote in His Favor*, Wash. Post, Jan. 3, 2021. In that call, the President embraced various disproven conspiracy theories, based on which he claimed to have won the state. At one point, the President said:

> So look. All I want to do is this. I just want to find 11,780 votes, which is one more than we have. Because we won the state.

And later:

> So what are we going to do here, folks? I only need 11,000 votes. Fellas, I need 11,000 votes. Give me a break.

Secretary of State Raffensperger resisted President Trump's entreaties. In response, Trump and his allies have attacked Raffensperger mercilessly. The state Republican party even censured Raffensperger. He is running for reelection as Georgia's Secretary of State in 2022, but faces a challenge from a Trump loyalist and is given a slim chance of winning the Republican primary. Russell Berman, *Trump's Revenge Begins in Georgia*, The Atlantic, July 12, 2021. What implications does all this have for future attempts at election subversion? Will election officials perform their jobs conscientiously if they risk losing those jobs for doing so?

The risk of election subversion does not end with the possibility that election officials will be voted out of office for resisting political pressure. Since the 2020 election, supporters of former President Trump have taken aggressive steps to assert control over the administration of elections. For example, a new Georgia election law allows the state legislature to suspend county election officials and gives it greater control over the state election board. Some county election board members have already been stripped of their positions, most of them Democrats and several people of color. According to one report, there have been 216 bills in 41 states to give state legislatures more power over election officials, 24 of which have been enacted into law in 14 states. Nick Corasaniti & Reid J. Epstein, *How Republican States Are Expanding Their Power Over Elections*, N.Y. Times, June 19, 2021. Many state and local election officials have received threats of violence. Some have left their jobs, while those who remain face increasing pressure to put partisan interests above their responsibility to administer elections evenhandedly. Brennan Center for Justice, *Election Officials Under Attack*, June 16, 2021, https://perma.cc/9834-6AGK; Michael Wines, *After a Nightmare Year, Election Officials Are Quitting*, N.Y. Times, July 2, 2021.

What can be done to safeguard the impartiality of those charged with running our elections? See Richard L. Hasen, *Identifying and Minimizing the Risk of Election Subversion and Stolen Elections in the Contemporary United States*, 135 Harvard Law Review Forum (forthcoming 2022).

B. Voting Technology

Exercising the right to vote effectively requires that voters' intentions be recorded and counted accurately. Yet the issue of voting technology was not much on the public's radar screen before the 2000 presidential election. During and after that election, a great deal of evidence emerged regarding disparities in the accuracy of the various vote-counting technologies, resulting especially from deficiencies of the punch-card voting machines used in Florida and in many other parts of the country at the time.

A number of post-Florida commissions recommended changes to voting technology and ballot design. Perhaps the most influential study is the July 2001 Report of the Caltech-MIT Voting Technology Project, *Voting—What Is, What Could Be*. The study estimated that between 4 and 6 million votes for president were lost for a variety of reasons including faulty equipment and confusing ballots (1.5 to 2 million votes), registration mix-ups (1.5 to 3 million votes), polling place problems (up to 1 million votes), and absentee ballot problems (number of lost votes unknown). One of the report's main findings was that punch card technology was among the worst technologies. Other empirical studies found a "racial gap" in the number of lost votes resulting from punch card technologies, with more invalid votes cast in heavily African-American precincts. Michael Tomz & Robert P. Van Houweling, *How Does Voting Equipment Affect the Racial Gap in Voided Ballots?*, 47 American Journal of Political Science 46 (2003). For summaries of the post-2000 empirical research concerning disparities in the number of lost votes resulting from different types of voting equipment, see Daniel P. Tokaji, *The Paperless Chase: Electronic Voting and Democratic Values*, 73 Fordham Law Review 1712, 1754–68 (2005) and Richard B. Saphire & Paul Moke, *Litigating* Bush v. Gore *in the States: Dual Voting Systems and the Fourteenth Amendment*, 51 Villanova Law Review 229, 238–42 (2006).

As a result of the Help America Vote Act of 2002 ("HAVA"), discussed in Part II.C, punch card voting systems were virtually extinct by 2006. Attention turned to the security of new voting technology, most notably paperless direct record electronic (DRE) systems such as touchscreens. The switch to new voting systems has reduced the number of ballots that do not register a valid vote. Charles Stewart III, *Residual Vote in the 2004 Election*, 5 Election Law Journal 158 (2006), estimates that improvements in voting technology and procedures from 2000 to 2004 "saved" approximately one million votes. DRE supporters argued that they are easier to use and less error-prone than other voting systems, and that they are more accessible to voters with certain types of disabilities. See Paul S. Herrnson et al., Voting Technology: The Not-So-Simple Act of Casting a Ballot(2008); R. Michael Alvarez & Thad E. Hall, Electronic Elections: The Perils and Promises of Digital Democracy (2008); Robert M. Stein, et al., *Voting Technology, Election Administration, and Voter Performance*, 7 Election Law Journal 123 (2008). DRE critics claimed that the new technology had serious security flaws.

Another round of litigation challenged DRE systems on constitutional grounds. Courts have generally rejected these challenges. The decision in *Wexler v. Anderson*, 452 F.3d 1226 (11th Cir. 2006), is typical. Plaintiffs in that case, including U.S. Congressman Robert Wexler, argued that voters using paperless touchscreen machines were disadvantaged relative to other voters, because they were at greater risk of not having their votes count in the event of a recount. The Eleventh Circuit rejected Plaintiffs' argument, reasoning:

> [Plaintiffs] have avoided the question that is of constitutional dimension: Are voters in touchscreen counties less likely to cast an effective vote than voters in optical scan counties? It is this question, and not the question of whether uniform procedures have been followed across a state regardless of differences in voting technology, that the Supreme Court consistently has emphasized in its voting jurisprudence. *See, e.g., Bush* ("Having once granted the right to vote on equal terms, the state may not, by later arbitrary treatment, value one person's vote over that of another."); *Dunn v. Blumstein* ("[A] citizen has a constitutionally protected right to participate in

> elections on an equal basis with other citizens in the jurisdiction."); *Reynolds v. Sims* ("Weighting the votes of citizens differently, by any method or means, merely because of where they happen to reside, hardly seems justifiable."); *Wesberry v. Sanders* ("[A]s nearly as is practicable[,] one man's vote in a congressional election is to be worth as much as another's.").
>
> The right to vote is fundamental, forming the bedrock of our democracy. Nevertheless, states are entitled to burden that right to ensure that elections are fair, honest and efficient. *See Burdick v. Takushi*; *Anderson v. Celebrezze*; *Storer v. Brown* [these cases are discussed in Section C below and in Chapter 9—Eds.] Recognizing that "[e]lection laws will invariably impose some burden upon individual voters," the Supreme Court has explained that the level of scrutiny courts apply to state voting regulations should vary with the degree to which a regulation burdens the right to vote....
>
> [I]f voters in touchscreen counties are burdened at all, that burden is the mere possibility that should they cast residual ballots, those ballots will receive a different, and allegedly inferior, type of review in the event of a manual recount. Such a burden, borne of a reasonable, nondiscriminatory regulation, is not so substantial that strict scrutiny is appropriate.... Thus, we review Florida's manual recount procedures to determine if they are justified by the State's "important regulatory interests." *See Burdick*.
>
> Here, Florida has important reasons for employing different manual recount procedures according to the type of voting system a county uses. The differences between these procedures are necessary given the differences in the technologies themselves and the types of errors voters are likely to make in utilizing those technologies. Voters casting optical scan ballots can make a variety of mistakes that will cause their ballots not to be counted. For example, a voter casting an optical scan ballot might leave a stray pencil mark or circle a candidate's name rather than filling in the appropriate bubble. Thus, although an optical scan tabulation machine may register an undervote for a particular race on a particular ballot, there may be sufficient indicia on the ballot that the voter actually chose a candidate in that race such that the vote would be counted in a manual recount. In contrast, a voter in a touchscreen county either chooses a candidate for a particular race or does not; the touchscreen machines do not record ambiguous indicia of voter intent that can later be reviewed during a manual recount.

For other examples, see *Weber v. Shelley*, 347 F.3d 1101 (9th Cir. 2003); *Schade v. Maryland State Board of Elections*, 930 A.2d 304 (Md. 2007); *Andrade v. NAACP of Austin*, 345 S.W.3d 1 (Tex. 2011).

The American electoral infrastructure, including our voting technology, received renewed attention in the wake of the Russian government's interference with the 2016 election. One aspect of that interference was the targeting of election websites in at least 21 states, according to the Department of Homeland Security. See Michael McFaul & Bronte Kass, *Understanding Putin's Intentions and Actions in the 2016 U.S. Presidential Election*, in Securing American Elections: Prescriptions for Enhancing the Integrity and Independence of the 2020 U.S. Presidential Election and Beyond (2019). The Mueller Report documented Russian attempts to interfere with state and local election systems, as well as the private firms servicing them. Those efforts included the placement of malware within the software of a voter registration vendor. While there is no evidence to date that such hacking affected any actual votes in the 2016 election, the incidents have prompted increased concern about the security of voting technology. Recent reports by Stanford's Cyber Policy Center and the National Academies of Sciences, Engineering, and Medicine recommend another overhaul of the United States' electoral infrastructure. Herbert Lin et al., *Increasing the Security of the U.S. Election Infrastructure*, in Securing American Elections: Prescriptions for Enhancing the Integrity and Independence of the 2020 U.S. Presidential Election and Beyond (2019); National Academies of Sciences, Engineering, and Medicine, Securing the Vote: Protecting American Democracy (2018). The Stanford report's recommendations include requiring a voter-verifiable paper audit trail and auditing of all elections, securing election technology through independent code inspection and "white-hat" attacks, and committing regular funding streams to strengthen election cybersecurity.

The State of Georgia has faced especially serious problems with its voting systems. In 2018, a federal district court found that the state had failed to address the "mounting tide of evidence of the inadequacy and security risks" posed by its direct record electronic (DRE) voting system but declined to order an immediate rollout of a paper-based system. *Curling v. Kemp*, 334 F. Supp. 3d 1303, 1307 (N.D. Ga. 2018). As the 2020 election approached, the court found that the state's DRE machines, election software, and voter databases were "antiquated, seriously flawed, and vulnerable to failure, breach, contamination, and attack," posing "imminent threats of contamination, dysfunction, and attacks on State and county voting systems." *Curling v. Raffensperger*, 397 F. Supp. 3d 1334, 1339-40 (N.D. Ga. 2019). In response, the district court issued a preliminary injunction requiring the state to stop using its current voting system and software. *Id.* at 1410. In its June 2020 primary, the state attempted to roll out a new ballot-marking device, a voting system that prints out a ballot with a bar code that can be read by an electronic scanner. *Id.* at 1341 n. 10.

The rollout of Georgia's new voting system did not go well. Problems with the delivery and activation of equipment caused some voters to wait for hours, which polling places — understaffed due to the COVID-19 pandemic — struggled to troubleshoot. Nick Corasanti & Stephanie Saul, *Georgia Havoc Raises New Doubts on Pricey Voting Machines*, N.Y Times, June 11, 2020. What's the lesson from the Georgia fiasco? That state and local election officials should be more careful and deliberate when implementing new voting technology? That courts should hesitate to order technologically complex changes to a state's voting system? Perhaps both?

C. Voter Identification and Other Burdens on Voting

No election administration issue has been more contentious than voter identification. The Help America Vote Act ("HAVA") imposed a limited voter identification requirement, applicable to first-time voters who had registered by mail, but allowed either a photo ID or other documents (like a utility bill or bank statement). A number of states have enacted requirements that go beyond HAVA. The most stringent of these state laws require voters to show government-issued *photo* identification in order to have their votes counted. Supporters, primarily Republicans, argue that stricter voter identification laws are needed to preserve the reality and appearance of election integrity, by ensuring that only eligible citizens may participate. Opponents, primarily Democrats, argue that the requirements impede participation by eligible voters, especially those who are poor, elderly, disabled, or minorities. Each side also disputes the other's claims, Democrats arguing that photo ID requirements prevent little or no voter fraud and Republicans arguing that the requirements prevent few if any eligible voters from voting. Why do Republicans support strict voter identification laws? Why do Democrats oppose them? See Hasen, The Voting Wars, *supra*, at 1–72.

Several states' voter identification laws have been challenged as unconstitutional. In the following case, the Supreme Court upheld Indiana's voter identification law, probably the strictest law in the nation at the time the case was decided:

Crawford v. Marion County Election Board

553 U.S. 181 (2008)

Justice STEVENS announced the judgment of the Court and delivered an opinion in which THE CHIEF JUSTICE and Justice KENNEDY join.

At issue in these cases is the constitutionality of an Indiana statute requiring citizens voting in person on election day, or casting a ballot in person at the office of the circuit court clerk prior to election day, to present photo identification issued by the government.

Referred to as either the "Voter ID Law" or "SEA 483," the statute applies to in-person voting at both primary and general elections. The requirement does not apply to absentee ballots submitted by mail, and the statute contains an exception for persons living and voting in a state-licensed facility such as a nursing home. A voter who is indigent or has a religious objection to being photographed may cast a provisional ballot that will be counted only if she executes an appropriate affidavit before the circuit court clerk within 10 days following the election. A voter who has photo identification but is unable to present that identification on election day may file a provisional ballot that will be counted if she brings her photo identification to the circuit county clerk's office within 10 days. No photo identification is required in order to register to vote, and the State offers free photo identification to qualified voters able to establish their residence and identity.

Promptly after the enactment of SEA 483 in 2005, the Indiana Democratic Party and the Marion County Democratic Central Committee (Democrats) filed suit in the Federal District Court for the Southern District of Indiana against the state officials responsible for its enforcement, seeking a judgment declaring the Voter ID Law invalid and enjoining its enforcement. A second suit seeking the same relief was brought on behalf of two elected officials and several nonprofit organizations representing groups of elderly, disabled, poor, and minority voters. The cases were consolidated, and the State of Indiana intervened to defend the validity of the statute.

The complaints in the consolidated cases allege that the new law substantially burdens the right to vote in violation of the Fourteenth Amendment; that it is neither a necessary nor appropriate method of avoiding election fraud; and that it will arbitrarily disfranchise qualified voters who do not possess the required identification and will place an unjustified burden on those who cannot readily obtain such identification.

[The district court granted defendants' motion for summary judgment, a divided panel of the Seventh Circuit affirmed, and the Seventh Circuit denied en banc review.]

I

In *Harper v. Virginia State Bd. of Elections* [*supra* Chapter 2] the Court held that Virginia could not condition the right to vote in a state election on the payment of a poll tax of $1.50. We rejected the dissenters' argument that the interest in promoting civic responsibility by weeding out those voters who did not care enough about public affairs to pay a small sum for the privilege of voting provided a rational basis for the tax. Applying a stricter standard, we concluded that a State "violates the Equal Protection Clause of the Fourteenth Amendment whenever it makes the affluence of the voter or payment of any fee an electoral standard." We used the term "invidiously discriminate" to describe conduct prohibited under that standard, noting that we had previously held that while a State may obviously impose "reasonable residence restrictions on the availability of the ballot," it "may not deny the opportunity to vote to a bona fide resident merely because he is a member of the armed services." Although the State's justification for the tax was rational, it was invidious because it was irrelevant to the voter's qualifications.

Thus, under the standard applied in *Harper*, even rational restrictions on the right to vote are invidious if they are unrelated to voter qualifications. In *Anderson v. Celebrezze*, 460 U.S. 780 (1983), however, we confirmed the general rule that "evenhanded restrictions that protect the integrity and reliability of the electoral process itself" are not invidious and satisfy the standard set forth in *Harper*. Rather than applying any "litmus test" that would neatly separate valid from invalid restrictions, we concluded that a court must identify and evaluate the interests put forward by the State as justifications for the burden imposed by its rule, and then make the "hard judgment" that our adversary system demands.

In later election cases we have followed *Anderson*'s balancing approach.... [I]n *Burdick v. Takushi*, 504 U.S. 428 (1992), we applied *Anderson*'s standard for "'reasonable, nondiscriminatory restrictions,'" and upheld Hawaii's prohibition on write-in voting despite the fact that it prevented a significant number of "voters from participating in Hawaii elections in a meaningful manner." (Kennedy, J., dissenting). We reaffirmed *Anderson*'s requirement that a court evaluating a constitutional challenge to an election regulation weigh the asserted injury to the right to vote against the "'precise interests put forward by the State as justifications for the burden imposed by its rule.'"[8]

In [none of the cases] did we identify any litmus test for measuring the severity of a burden that a state law imposes on a political party, an individual voter, or a discrete class of voters. However slight that burden may appear, as *Harper* demonstrates, it must be justified by relevant and legitimate state interests "sufficiently weighty to justify the limitation." *Norman v. Reed*. We therefore begin our analysis of the constitutionality of Indiana's statute by focusing on those interests.

II

The State has identified several state interests that arguably justify the burdens that SEA 483 imposes on voters and potential voters. While petitioners argue that the statute was actually motivated by partisan concerns and dispute both the significance of the State's interests and the magnitude of any real threat to those interests, they do not question the legitimacy of the interests the State has identified. Each is unquestionably relevant to the State's interest in protecting the integrity and reliability of the electoral process.

The first is the interest in deterring and detecting voter fraud. The State has a valid interest in participating in a nationwide effort to improve and modernize election procedures that have been criticized as antiquated and inefficient. The State also argues that it has a particular interest in preventing voter fraud in response to a problem that is in part the product of its own maladministration—namely, that Indiana's voter registration rolls include a large number of names of persons who are either deceased or no longer live in Indiana. Finally, the State relies on its interest in safeguarding voter confidence. Each of these interests merits separate comment.

Election Modernization

Two recently enacted federal statutes have made it necessary for States to reexamine their election procedures. Both contain provisions consistent with a State's

8. Contrary to Justice SCALIA's suggestion, our approach remains faithful to *Anderson* and *Burdick*. The *Burdick* opinion was explicit in its endorsement and adherence to *Anderson*, and repeatedly cited *Anderson*. To be sure, *Burdick* rejected the argument that strict scrutiny applies to all laws imposing a burden on the right to vote; but in its place, the Court applied the "flexible standard" set forth in *Anderson*. *Burdick* surely did not create a novel "deferential 'important regulatory interests' standard." [These cases are discussed *infra* Chapter 9, Part I, in Note 1 following *Munro v. Socialist Workers Party*.—Eds.]

choice to use government-issued photo identification as a relevant source of information concerning a citizen's eligibility to vote.

In the National Voter Registration Act of 1993 (NVRA), Congress established procedures that would both increase the number of registered voters and protect the integrity of the electoral process. The statute requires state motor vehicle driver's license applications to serve as voter registration applications. While that requirement has increased the number of registered voters, the statute also contains a provision restricting States' ability to remove names from the lists of registered voters. These protections have been partly responsible for inflated lists of registered voters. For example, evidence credited by [the district court] estimated that as of 2004 Indiana's voter rolls were inflated by as much as 41.4%, and data collected by the Election Assistance Committee in 2004 indicated that 19 of 92 Indiana counties had registration totals exceeding 100% of the 2004 voting-age population.

In HAVA, Congress required every State to create and maintain a computerized statewide list of all registered voters. HAVA also requires the States to verify voter information contained in a voter registration application and specifies either an "applicant's driver's license number" or "the last 4 digits of the applicant's social security number" as acceptable verifications. If an individual has neither number, the State is required to assign the applicant a voter identification number.

HAVA also imposes new identification requirements for individuals registering to vote for the first time who submit their applications by mail. If the voter is casting his ballot in person, he must present local election officials with written identification, which may be either "a current and valid photo identification" or another form of documentation such as a bank statement or paycheck. If the voter is voting by mail, he must include a copy of the identification with his ballot. A voter may also include a copy of the documentation with his application or provide his driver's license number or Social Security number for verification. Finally, in a provision entitled "Fail-safe voting," HAVA authorizes the casting of provisional ballots by challenged voters.

Of course, neither HAVA nor NVRA required Indiana to enact SEA 483, but they do indicate that Congress believes that photo identification is one effective method of establishing a voter's qualification to vote and that the integrity of elections is enhanced through improved technology. That conclusion is also supported by a report issued shortly after the enactment of SEA 483 by the Commission on Federal Election Reform chaired by former President Jimmy Carter and former Secretary of State James A. Baker III, which is a part of the record in these cases. In the introduction to their discussion of voter identification, they made these pertinent comments:

> A good registration list will ensure that citizens are only registered in one place, but election officials still need to make sure that the person arriving at a polling site is the same one that is named on the registration list. In the old days and in small towns where everyone knows each other, voters did not need to identify themselves. But in the United States, where 40

million people move each year, and in urban areas where some people do not even know the people living in their own apartment building let alone their precinct, some form of identification is needed.

There is no evidence of extensive fraud in U.S. elections or of multiple voting, but both occur, and it could affect the outcome of a close election. The electoral system cannot inspire public confidence if no safeguards exist to deter or detect fraud or to confirm the identity of voters. Photo identification cards currently are needed to board a plane, enter federal buildings, and cash a check. Voting is equally important.

Voter Fraud

The only kind of voter fraud that SEA 483 addresses is in-person voter impersonation at polling places. The record contains no evidence of any such fraud actually occurring in Indiana at any time in its history. Moreover, petitioners argue that provisions of the Indiana Criminal Code punishing such conduct as a felony provide adequate protection against the risk that such conduct will occur in the future. It remains true, however, that flagrant examples of such fraud in other parts of the country have been documented throughout this Nation's history by respected historians and journalists,[11] that occasional examples have surfaced in recent years,[12] and that Indiana's own experience with fraudulent voting in the 2003 Democratic primary for East Chicago Mayor—though perpetrated using absentee ballots and not in-person fraud—demonstrate that not only is the risk of voter fraud real but that it could affect the outcome of a close election.

There is no question about the legitimacy or importance of the State's interest in counting only the votes of eligible voters. Moreover, the interest in orderly

---

11. One infamous example is the New York City elections of 1868. William (Boss) Tweed set about solidifying and consolidating his control of the city. One local tough who worked for Boss Tweed, "Big Tim" Sullivan, insisted that his "repeaters" (individuals paid to vote multiple times) have whiskers:

> When you've voted 'em with their whiskers on, you take 'em to a barber and scrape off the chin fringe. Then you vote 'em again with the side lilacs and a mustache. Then to a barber again, off comes the sides and you vote 'em a third time with the mustache. If that ain't enough and the box can stand a few more ballots, clean off the mustache and vote 'em plain face. That makes every one of 'em good for four votes.

A. Callow, The Tweed Ring 210 (1966) (quoting M. Werner, Tammany Hall 439 (1928)).

12. The district court cited record evidence containing examples from California, Washington, Maryland, Wisconsin, Georgia, Illinois, Pennsylvania, Missouri, Miami, and St. Louis. The Brief of *Amici Curiae* Brennan Center for Justice et al. in Support of Petitioners addresses each of these examples of fraud. While the brief indicates that the record evidence of in-person fraud was overstated because much of the fraud was actually absentee ballot fraud or voter registration fraud, there remain scattered instances of in-person voter fraud. For example, after a hotly contested gubernatorial election in 2004, Washington conducted an investigation of voter fraud and uncovered 19 "ghost voters." After a partial investigation of the ghost voting, one voter was confirmed to have committed in-person voting fraud. Le & Nicolosi, *Dead Voted in Governor's Race*, Seattle Post-Intelligencer, Jan. 7, 2005, p. A1.

administration and accurate recordkeeping provides a sufficient justification for carefully identifying all voters participating in the election process. While the most effective method of preventing election fraud may well be debatable, the propriety of doing so is perfectly clear.

In its brief, the State argues that the inflation of its voter rolls provides further support for its enactment of SEA 483. The record contains a November 5, 2000, newspaper article asserting that as a result of NVRA and "sloppy record keeping," Indiana's lists of registered voters included the names of thousands of persons who had either moved, died, or were not eligible to vote because they had been convicted of felonies. The conclusion that Indiana has an unusually inflated list of registered voters is supported by the entry of a consent decree in litigation brought by the Federal Government alleging violations of NVRA. Even though Indiana's own negligence may have contributed to the serious inflation of its registration lists when SEA 483 was enacted, the fact of inflated voter rolls does provide a neutral and nondiscriminatory reason supporting the State's decision to require photo identification.

Safeguarding Voter Confidence

Finally, the State contends that it has an interest in protecting public confidence "in the integrity and legitimacy of representative government." While that interest is closely related to the State's interest in preventing voter fraud, public confidence in the integrity of the electoral process has independent significance, because it encourages citizen participation in the democratic process. As the Carter-Baker Report observed, the "electoral system cannot inspire public confidence if no safeguards exist to deter or detect fraud or to confirm the identity of voters."

III

States employ different methods of identifying eligible voters at the polls. Some merely check off the names of registered voters who identify themselves; others require voters to present registration cards or other documentation before they can vote; some require voters to sign their names so their signatures can be compared with those on file; and in recent years an increasing number of States have relied primarily on photo identification. A photo identification requirement imposes some burdens on voters that other methods of identification do not share. For example, a voter may lose his photo identification, may have his wallet stolen on the way to the polls, or may not resemble the photo in the identification because he recently grew a beard. Burdens of that sort arising from life's vagaries, however, are neither so serious nor so frequent as to raise any question about the constitutionality of SEA 483; the availability of the right to cast a provisional ballot provides an adequate remedy for problems of that character.

The burdens that are relevant to the issue before us are those imposed on persons who are eligible to vote but do not possess a current photo identification that complies with the requirements of SEA 483. The fact that most voters already possess a valid driver's license, or some other form of acceptable identification, would not save the statute under our reasoning in *Harper,* if the State required voters to pay a tax or a fee to obtain a new photo identification. But just as other States provide free voter registration cards, the photo identification cards issued by Indiana's BMV are also free. For most voters who need them, the inconvenience of making a trip to the BMV, gathering the required documents, and posing for a photograph surely does not qualify as a substantial burden on the right to vote, or even represent a significant increase over the usual burdens of voting.[17]

Both evidence in the record and facts of which we may take judicial notice, however, indicate that a somewhat heavier burden may be placed on a limited number of persons. They include elderly persons born out-of-state, who may have difficulty obtaining a birth certificate; persons who because of economic or other personal limitations may find it difficult either to secure a copy of their birth certificate or to assemble the other required documentation to obtain a state-issued identification; homeless persons; and persons with a religious objection to being photographed. If we assume, as the evidence suggests, that some members of these classes were registered voters when SEA 483 was enacted, the new identification requirement may have imposed a special burden on their right to vote.

The severity of that burden is, of course, mitigated by the fact that, if eligible, voters without photo identification may cast provisional ballots that will ultimately be counted. To do so, however, they must travel to the circuit court clerk's office within 10 days to execute the required affidavit. It is unlikely that such a requirement would pose a constitutional problem unless it is wholly unjustified. And even assuming that the burden may not be justified as to a few voters,[19] that conclusion is by no means sufficient to establish petitioners' right to the relief they seek in this litigation.

IV

Given the fact that petitioners have advanced a broad attack on the constitutionality of SEA 483, seeking relief that would invalidate the statute in all its applications, they bear a heavy burden of persuasion. Only a few weeks ago we held that the Court of Appeals for the Ninth Circuit had failed to give appropriate weight to the magnitude of that burden when it sustained a preelection, facial attack on a Washington statute regulating that State's primary election procedures. *Washington State Grange v. Washington State Republican Party* [discussed *infra*, Chapter 8—Eds]. Our reasoning in that case applies with added force to the arguments advanced by petitioners in these cases.

---

17. To obtain a photo identification card a person must present at least one "primary" document, which can be a birth certificate, certificate of naturalization, U.S. veterans photo identification, U.S. military photo identification, or a U.S. passport. Indiana, like most States, charges a fee for obtaining a copy of one's birth certificate. This fee varies by county and is currently between $3 and $12. Some States charge substantially more.

19. Presumably most voters casting provisional ballots will be able to obtain photo identifications before the next election. It is, however, difficult to understand why the State should require voters with a faith-based objection to being photographed to cast provisional ballots subject to later verification in every election when the BMV is able to issue these citizens special licenses that enable them to drive without any photo identification.

Petitioners ask this Court, in effect, to perform a unique balancing analysis that looks specifically at a small number of voters who may experience a special burden under the statute and weighs their burdens against the State's broad interests in protecting election integrity. Petitioners urge us to ask whether the State's interests justify the burden imposed on voters who cannot afford or obtain a birth certificate and who must make a second trip to the circuit court clerk's office after voting. But on the basis of the evidence in the record it is not possible to quantify either the magnitude of the burden on this narrow class of voters or the portion of the burden imposed on them that is fully justified.

First, the evidence in the record does not provide us with the number of registered voters without photo identification; Judge Barker found petitioners' expert's report to be "utterly incredible and unreliable." Much of the argument about the numbers of such voters comes from extrarecord, postjudgment studies, the accuracy of which has not been tested in the trial court.

Further, the deposition evidence presented in the District Court does not provide any concrete evidence of the burden imposed on voters who currently lack photo identification. The record includes depositions of two case managers at a day shelter for homeless persons and the depositions of members of the plaintiff organizations, none of whom expressed a personal inability to vote under SEA 483. A deposition from a named plaintiff describes the difficulty the elderly woman had in obtaining an identification card, although her testimony indicated that she intended to return to the BMV since she had recently obtained her birth certificate and that she was able to pay the birth certificate fee.

Judge Barker's opinion makes reference to six other elderly named plaintiffs who do not have photo identifications, but several of these individuals have birth certificates or were born in Indiana and have not indicated how difficult it would be for them to obtain a birth certificate. One elderly named plaintiff stated that she had attempted to obtain a birth certificate from Tennessee, but had not been successful, and another testified that he did not know how to obtain a birth certificate from North Carolina. The elderly in Indiana, however, may have an easier time obtaining a photo identification card than the nonelderly, and although it may not be a completely acceptable alternative, the elderly in Indiana are able to vote absentee without presenting photo identification.

The record says virtually nothing about the difficulties faced by either indigent voters or voters with religious objections to being photographed. While one elderly man stated that he did not have the money to pay for a birth certificate, when asked if he did not have the money or did not wish to spend it, he replied, "both." From this limited evidence we do not know the magnitude of the impact SEA 483 will have on indigent voters in Indiana. The record does contain the affidavit of one homeless woman who has a copy of her birth certificate, but was denied a photo identification card because she did not have an address. But that single affidavit gives no indication of how common the problem is.

In sum, on the basis of the record that has been made in this litigation, we cannot conclude that the statute imposes "excessively burdensome requirements" on any class of voters. See *Storer v. Brown*.[20] A facial challenge must fail where the statute has a "plainly legitimate sweep." *Washington State Grange*. When we consider only the statute's broad application to all Indiana voters we conclude that it "imposes only a limited burden on voters' rights." *Burdick*. The "precise interests" advanced by the State are therefore sufficient to defeat petitioners' facial challenge to SEA 483.

Finally we note that petitioners have not demonstrated that the proper remedy—even assuming an unjustified burden on some voters—would be to invalidate the entire statute. When evaluating a neutral, nondiscriminatory regulation of voting procedure, "[w]e must keep in mind that [a] ruling of unconstitutionality frustrates the intent of the elected representatives of the people." *Washington State Grange*.

V

In their briefs, petitioners stress the fact that all of the Republicans in the General Assembly voted in favor of SEA 483 and the Democrats were unanimous in opposing it. In her opinion rejecting petitioners' facial challenge, Judge Barker noted that the litigation was the result of a partisan dispute that had "spilled out of the state house into the courts." It is fair to infer that partisan considerations may have played a significant role in the decision to enact SEA 483. If such considerations had provided the only justification for a photo identification requirement, we may also assume that SEA 483 would suffer the same fate as the poll tax at issue in *Harper*.

But if a nondiscriminatory law is supported by valid neutral justifications, those justifications should not be disregarded simply because partisan interests may have provided one motivation for the votes of individual legislators. The state interests identified as justifications for SEA 483 are both neutral and sufficiently strong to

---

20. Three comments on Justice SOUTER's speculation about the non-trivial burdens that SEA 483 may impose on "tens of thousands" of Indiana citizens are appropriate. First, the fact that the District Judge estimated that when the statute was passed in 2005, 43,000 citizens did not have photo identification tells us nothing about the number of free photo identification cards issued since then. Second, the fact that public transportation is not available in some Indiana counties tells us nothing about how often elderly and indigent citizens have an opportunity to obtain a photo identification at the BMV, either during a routine outing with family or friends or during a special visit to the BMV arranged by a civic or political group such as the League of Women Voters or a political party. Further, nothing in the record establishes the distribution of voters who lack photo identification. To the extent that the evidence sheds any light on that issue, it suggests that such voters reside primarily in metropolitan areas, which are served by public transportation in Indiana (the majority of the plaintiffs reside in Indianapolis and several of the organizational plaintiffs are Indianapolis organizations). Third, the indigent, elderly, or disabled need not "journey all the way to their county seat each time they wish to exercise the franchise," if they obtain a free photo identification card from the BMV. While it is true that obtaining a birth certificate carries with it a financial cost, the record does not provide even a rough estimate of how many indigent voters lack copies of their birth certificates. Supposition based on extensive Internet research is not an adequate substitute for admissible evidence subject to cross-examination in constitutional adjudication.

require us to reject petitioners' facial attack on the statute. The application of the statute to the vast majority of Indiana voters is amply justified by the valid interest in protecting "the integrity and reliability of the electoral process." *Anderson.*

The judgment of the Court of Appeals is affirmed.

Justice SCALIA, with whom Justice THOMAS and Justice ALITO join, concurring in the judgment.

The lead opinion assumes petitioners' premise that the voter-identification law "may have imposed a special burden on" some voters, but holds that petitioners have not assembled evidence to show that the special burden is severe enough to warrant strict scrutiny, That is true enough, but for the sake of clarity and finality (as well as adherence to precedent), I prefer to decide these cases on the grounds that petitioners' premise is irrelevant and that the burden at issue is minimal and justified.

To evaluate a law respecting the right to vote—whether it governs voter qualifications, candidate selection, or the voting process—we use the approach set out in *Burdick.* This calls for application of a deferential "important regulatory interests" standard for nonsevere, nondiscriminatory restrictions, reserving strict scrutiny for laws that severely restrict the right to vote. The lead opinion resists the import of *Burdick* by characterizing it as simply adopting "the balancing approach" of *Anderson v. Celebrezze.* Although *Burdick* liberally quoted *Anderson, Burdick* forged *Anderson*'s amorphous "flexible standard" into something resembling an administrable rule. Since *Burdick,* we have repeatedly reaffirmed the primacy of its two-track approach. See *Timmons v. Twin Cities Area New Party*; *Clingman v. Beaver.* "[S]trict scrutiny is appropriate only if the burden is severe." *Id.* Thus, the first step is to decide whether a challenged law severely burdens the right to vote. Ordinary and widespread burdens, such as those requiring "nominal effort" of everyone, are not severe. Burdens are severe if they go beyond the merely inconvenient.

Of course, we have to identify a burden before we can weigh it. The Indiana law affects different voters differently, but what petitioners view as the law's several light and heavy burdens are no more than the different *impacts* of the single burden that the law uniformly imposes on all voters. To vote in person in Indiana, *everyone* must have and present a photo identification that can be obtained for free. The State draws no classifications, let alone discriminatory ones, except to establish *optional* absentee and provisional balloting for certain poor, elderly, and institutionalized voters and for religious objectors. Nor are voters who already have photo identifications exempted from the burden, since those voters must maintain the accuracy of the information displayed on the identifications, renew them before they expire, and replace them if they are lost.

The Indiana photo-identification law is a generally applicable, nondiscriminatory voting regulation, and our precedents refute the view that individual impacts are relevant to determining the severity of the burden it imposes. In the course of concluding that the Hawaii laws at issue in *Burdick*" impose[d] only a limited burden on voters' rights to make free choices and to associate politically through the vote," we considered the laws and their reasonably foreseeable effect on *voters generally.* We did not discuss whether the laws had a severe effect on Mr. Burdick's own right to vote, given his particular circumstances. . . . Subsequent cases have followed *Burdick*'s generalized review of nondiscriminatory election laws. Indeed, *Clingman*'s holding that burdens are not severe if they are ordinary and widespread would be rendered meaningless if a single plaintiff could claim a severe burden.

Not all of our decisions predating *Burdick* addressed whether a challenged voting regulation severely burdened the right to vote, but when we began to grapple with the magnitude of burdens, we did so categorically and did not consider the peculiar circumstances of individual voters or candidates. . . .

Insofar as our election-regulation cases rest upon the requirements of the Fourteenth Amendment, weighing the burden of a nondiscriminatory voting law upon each voter and concomitantly requiring exceptions for vulnerable voters would effectively turn back decades of equal-protection jurisprudence. A voter complaining about such a law's effect on him has no valid equal-protection claim because, without proof of discriminatory intent, a generally applicable law with disparate impact is not unconstitutional. The Fourteenth Amendment does not regard neutral laws as invidious ones, *even when their burdens purportedly fall disproportionately on a protected class. A fortiori* it does not do so when, as here, the classes complaining of disparate impact are not even protected.*

Even if I thought that *stare decisis* did not foreclose adopting an individual-focused approach, I would reject it as an original matter. This is an area where the dos and don'ts need to be known in advance of the election, and voter-by-voter examination of the burdens of voting regulations would prove especially disruptive. A case-by-case approach naturally encourages constant litigation. Very few new election regulations improve everyone's lot, so the potential allegations of severe burden are endless. A State reducing the number of polling places would be open to the complaint it has violated the rights of disabled voters who live near the closed stations. Indeed, it may even be the case that some laws already on the books are especially burdensome for some voters, and one can predict lawsuits demanding that a State adopt voting over the Internet or expand absentee balloting.

That sort of detailed judicial supervision of the election process would flout the Constitution's express commitment of the task to the States. See Art. I, § 4. It is for state legislatures to weigh the costs and benefits of possible changes to their election codes, and their judgment must prevail unless it imposes a severe and unjustified

* A number of our early right-to-vote decisions, purporting to rely upon the Equal Protection Clause, strictly scrutinized nondiscriminatory voting laws requiring the payment of fees. See, *e.g.*, *Harper v. Virginia Bd. of Elections* (1966) (poll tax); *Bullock v. Carter* (1972) (ballot-access fee); *Lubin v. Panish* (1974) (ballot-access fee). To the extent those decisions continue to stand for a principle that *Burdick* does not already encompass, it suffices to note that we have never held that legislatures must calibrate *all* election laws, even those totally unrelated to money, for their impacts on poor voters or must otherwise accommodate wealth disparities.

overall burden upon the right to vote, or is intended to disadvantage a particular class. Judicial review of their handiwork must apply an objective, uniform standard that will enable them to determine, *ex ante,* whether the burden they impose is too severe.

The lead opinion's record-based resolution of these cases, which neither rejects nor embraces the rule of our precedents, provides no certainty, and will embolden litigants who surmise that our precedents have been abandoned. There is no good reason to prefer that course.

* * *

The universally applicable requirements of Indiana's voter-identification law are eminently reasonable. The burden of acquiring, possessing, and showing a free photo identification is simply not severe, because it does not "even represent a significant increase over the usual burdens of voting." And the State's interests are sufficient to sustain that minimal burden. That should end the matter. That the State accommodates some voters by permitting (not requiring) the casting of absentee or provisional ballots, is an indulgence—not a constitutional imperative that falls short of what is required.

Justice SOUTER, with whom Justice GINSBURG joins, dissenting.

Indiana's "Voter ID Law" threatens to impose nontrivial burdens on the voting right of tens of thousands of the State's citizens, and a significant percentage of those individuals are likely to be deterred from voting. The statute is unconstitutional under the balancing standard of *Burdick*: a State may not burden the right to vote merely by invoking abstract interests, be they legitimate, or even compelling, but must make a particular, factual showing that threats to its interests outweigh the particular impediments it has imposed. The State has made no such justification here, and as to some aspects of its law, it has hardly even tried. I therefore respectfully dissent from the Court's judgment sustaining the statute.

I

Voting-rights cases raise two competing interests, the one side being the fundamental right to vote. The Judiciary is obliged to train a skeptical eye on any qualification of that right. See *Reynolds.*

As against the unfettered right, however, lies the "[c]ommon sense, as well as constitutional law . . . that government must play an active role in structuring elections; 'as a practical matter, there must be a substantial regulation of elections if they are to be fair and honest and if some sort of order, rather than chaos, is to accompany the democratic processes.'" *Burdick* (quoting *Storer v. Brown*).

Given the legitimacy of interests on both sides, we have avoided pre-set levels of scrutiny in favor of a sliding-scale balancing analysis: the scrutiny varies with the effect of the regulation at issue. And whatever the claim, the Court has long made a careful, ground-level appraisal both of the practical burdens on the right to vote and of the State's reasons for imposing those precise burdens. . . .

The lead opinion does not disavow these basic principles. But I think it does not insist enough on the hard facts that our standard of review demands.

II

Under *Burdick*, "the rigorousness of our inquiry into the propriety of a state election law depends upon the extent to which a challenged regulation burdens First and Fourteenth Amendment rights," upon an assessment of the "character and magnitude of the asserted [threatened] injury," and an estimate of the number of voters likely to be affected.

A

The first set of burdens shown in these cases is the travel costs and fees necessary to get one of the limited variety of federal or state photo identifications needed to cast a regular ballot under the Voter ID Law. The travel is required for the personal visit to a license branch of the Indiana Bureau of Motor Vehicles (BMV), which is demanded of anyone applying for a driver's license or nondriver photo identification. The need to travel to a BMV branch will affect voters according to their circumstances, with the average person probably viewing it as nothing more than an inconvenience. Poor, old, and disabled voters who do not drive a car, however, may find the trip prohibitive,[4] witness the fact that the BMV has far fewer license branches in each county than there are voting precincts. . . .

The burden of traveling to a more distant BMV office rather than a conveniently located polling place is probably serious for many of the individuals who lack photo identification. They almost certainly will not own cars, and public transportation in Indiana is fairly limited. . . .

Although making voters travel farther than what is convenient for most and possible for some does not amount to a "severe" burden under *Burdick*, that is no reason to ignore the burden altogether. It translates into an obvious economic cost (whether in work time lost, or getting and paying for transportation) that an Indiana voter must bear to obtain an ID.

For those voters who can afford the roundtrip, a second financial hurdle appears: in order to get photo identification for the first time, they need to present "'a birth certificate, a certificate of naturalization, U.S. veterans photo identification, U.S. military photo identification, or a U.S. passport.'" As the lead opinion says, the two most common of these documents come at a price: Indiana counties charge

---

4. The State asserts that the elderly and disabled are adequately accommodated through their option to cast absentee ballots, and so any burdens on them are irrelevant. But as petitioners' *amici* AARP and the National Senior Citizens Law Center point out, there are crucial differences between the absentee and regular ballot. . . .

It is one thing (and a commendable thing) for the State to make absentee voting available to the elderly and disabled; but it is quite another to suggest that, because the more convenient but less reliable absentee ballot is available, the State may freely deprive the elderly and disabled of the option of voting in person.

anywhere from $3 to $12 for a birth certificate (and in some other States the fee is significantly higher), and that same price must usually be paid for a first-time passport, since a birth certificate is required to prove U.S. citizenship by birth. The total fees for a passport, moreover, are up to about $100. So most voters must pay at least one fee to get the ID necessary to cast a regular ballot. As with the travel costs, these fees are far from shocking on their face, but in the *Burdick* analysis it matters that both the travel costs and the fees are disproportionately heavy for, and thus disproportionately likely to deter, the poor, the old, and the immobile.

B

To be sure, Indiana has a provisional-ballot exception to the ID requirement for individuals the State considers "indigent" as well as those with religious objections to being photographed, and this sort of exception could in theory provide a way around the costs of procuring an ID. But Indiana's chosen exception does not amount to much relief.

The law allows these voters who lack the necessary ID to sign the poll book and cast a provisional ballot. As the lead opinion recognizes, though, that is only the first step; to have the provisional ballot counted, a voter must then appear in person before the circuit court clerk or county election board within 10 days of the election, to sign an affidavit attesting to indigency or religious objection to being photographed (or to present an ID at that point). Unlike the trip to the BMV (which, assuming things go smoothly, needs to be made only once every four years for renewal of nondriver photo identification), this one must be taken every time a poor person or religious objector wishes to vote, because the State does not allow an affidavit to count in successive elections. And unlike the trip to the BMV (which at least has a handful of license branches in the more populous counties), a county has only one county seat. Forcing these people to travel to the county seat every time they try to vote is particularly onerous for the reason noted already, that most counties in Indiana either lack public transportation or offer only limited coverage.

That the need to travel to the county seat each election amounts to a high hurdle is shown in the results of the 2007 municipal elections in Marion County, to which Indiana's Voter ID Law applied. Thirty-four provisional ballots were cast, but only two provisional voters made it to the County Clerk's Office within the 10 days. All 34 of these aspiring voters appeared at the appropriate precinct; 33 of them provided a signature, and every signature matched the one on file; and 26 of the 32 voters whose ballots were not counted had a history of voting in Marion County elections.

All of this suggests that provisional ballots do not obviate the burdens of getting photo identification. And even if that were not so, the provisional-ballot option would be inadequate for a further reason: the indigency exception by definition offers no relief to those voters who do not consider themselves (or would not be considered) indigent but as a practical matter would find it hard, for nonfinancial reasons, to get the required ID (most obviously the disabled).

C

Indiana's Voter ID Law thus threatens to impose serious burdens on the voting right, even if not "severe" ones, and the next question under *Burdick* is whether the number of individuals likely to be affected is significant as well. Record evidence and facts open to judicial notice answer yes.

Although the District Court found that petitioners failed to offer any reliable empirical study of numbers of voters affected, we may accept that court's rough calculation that 43,000 voting-age residents lack the kind of identification card required by Indiana's law. The District Court made that estimate by comparing BMV records reproduced in petitioners' statistician's report with U.S. Census Bureau figures for Indiana's voting-age population in 2004, and the State does not argue that these raw data are unreliable. . . .

The upshot is this. Tens of thousands of voting-age residents lack the necessary photo identification. A large proportion of them are likely to be in bad shape economically.[25] The Voter ID Law places hurdles in the way of either getting an ID or of voting provisionally, and they translate into nontrivial economic costs. There is accordingly no reason to doubt that a significant number of state residents will be discouraged or disabled from voting.

Petitioners, to be sure, failed to nail down precisely how great the cohort of discouraged and totally deterred voters will be, but empirical precision beyond the foregoing numbers has never been demanded for raising a voting-rights claim. While of course it would greatly aid a plaintiff to establish his claims beyond mathematical doubt, he does enough to show that serious burdens are likely.

Thus, petitioners' case is clearly strong enough to prompt more than a cursory examination of the State's asserted interests. And the fact that Indiana's photo identification requirement is one of the most restrictive in the country makes a critical examination of the State's claims all the more in order.

III

Because the lead opinion finds only "limited" burdens on the right to vote, it avoids a hard look at the State's claimed interests. But having found the Voter ID Law burdens far from trivial, I have to make a rigorous assessment of "the precise interests put forward by the State as justifications for the burden imposed by its rule, [and] the extent to which those interests make it necessary to burden the plaintiff's rights." *Burdick*.

As this quotation from *Burdick* indicates, the interests claimed to justify the regulatory scheme are subject to discount in two distinct ways. First, the generalities raised by the State have to be shaved down to the precise "aspect[s of claimed interests] addressed by the law at issue." *California Democratic Party v. Jones,* 530

---

25. Studies in other States suggest that the burdens of an ID requirement may also fall disproportionately upon racial minorities. See Overton, *Voter Identification*, 105 Mich. L. Rev. 631 (2007). . . .

U.S. 567, 584 (2000) (emphasis omitted). And even if the State can show particularized interests addressed by the law, those interests are subject to further discount depending on "the extent to which [they] make it necessary to burden the plaintiff's rights." *Burdick*.

As the lead opinion sees it, the State has offered four related concerns that suffice to justify the Voter ID Law: modernizing election procedures, combating voter fraud, addressing the consequences of the State's bloated voter rolls, and protecting public confidence in the integrity of the electoral process. On closer look, however, it appears that the first two (which are really just one) can claim modest weight at best, and the latter two if anything weaken the State's case . . .

[T]he State's interest in deterring a voter from showing up at the polls and claiming to be someone he is not must . . . be discounted for the fact that the State has not come across a single instance of in-person voter impersonation fraud in all of Indiana's history. Neither the District Court nor the Indiana General Assembly that passed the Voter ID Law was given any evidence whatsoever of in-person voter impersonation fraud in the State. . . .

The antifraud rationale is open to skepticism on one further ground, what *Burdick* spoke of as an assessment of the degree of necessity for the State's particular course of action. Two points deserve attention, the first being that the State has not even tried to justify its decision to implement the photo identification requirement immediately on passage of the new law. A phase-in period would have given the State time to distribute its newly designed licenses, and to make a genuine effort to get them to individuals in need, and a period for transition is exactly what the Commission on Federal Election Reform, headed by former President Carter and former Secretary of State Baker, recommended in its report. See Building Confidence in U.S. Elections § 2.5 (Sept.2005). . . . Although Indiana claims to have adopted its ID requirement relying partly on the Carter-Baker Report, the State conspicuously rejected the Report's phase-in recommendation aimed at reducing the burdens on the right to vote, and just as conspicuously fails even to try to explain why.

What is left of the State's claim must be downgraded further for one final reason: regardless of the interest the State may have in adopting a photo identification requirement as a general matter, that interest in no way necessitates the particular burdens the Voter ID Law imposes on poor people and religious objectors. Individuals unable to get photo identification are forced to travel to the county seat every time they wish to exercise the franchise, and they have to get there within 10 days of the election. Nothing about the State's interest in fighting voter fraud justifies this requirement of a post-election trip to the county seat instead of some verification process at the polling places. . . .

[I]f it is true that the State's fear of in-person voter impersonation fraud arises from its bloated voter checklist, the answer to the problem is in the State's own hands. The claim that the State has an interest in addressing a symptom of the problem (alleged impersonation) rather than the problem itself (the negligently maintained bloated rolls) is thus self-defeating; it shows that the State has no justifiable need to burden the right to vote as it does, and it suggests that the State is not as serious about combating fraud as it claims to be.

The State's final justification, its interest in safeguarding voter confidence, similarly collapses. The problem with claiming this interest lies in its connection to the bloated voter rolls; the State has come up with nothing to suggest that its citizens doubt the integrity of the State's electoral process, except its own failure to maintain its rolls. The answer to this problem is not to burden the right to vote, but to end the official negligence. . . .

Without a shred of evidence that in-person voter impersonation is a problem in the State, much less a crisis, Indiana has adopted one of the most restrictive photo identification requirements in the country. The State recognizes that tens of thousands of qualified voters lack the necessary federally issued or state-issued identification, but it insists on implementing the requirement immediately, without allowing a transition period for targeted efforts to distribute the required identification to individuals who need it. The State hardly even tries to explain its decision to force indigents or religious objectors to travel all the way to their county seats every time they wish to vote, and if there is any waning of confidence in the administration of elections it probably owes more to the State's violation of federal election law than to any imposters at the polling places. It is impossible to say, on this record, that the State's interest in adopting its signally inhibiting photo identification requirement has been shown to outweigh the serious burdens it imposes on the right to vote.

If more were needed to condemn this law, our own precedent would provide it, for the calculation revealed in the Indiana statute crosses a line when it targets the poor and the weak. If the Court's decision in *Harper v. Virginia Bd. of Elections* stands for anything, it is that being poor has nothing to do with being qualified to vote. *Harper* made clear that "[t]o introduce wealth or payment of a fee as a measure of a voter's qualifications is to introduce a capricious or irrelevant factor." The State's requirements here, that people without cars travel to a motor vehicle registry and that the poor who fail to do that get to their county seats within 10 days of every election, likewise translate into unjustified economic burdens uncomfortably close to the outright $1.50 fee we struck down 42 years ago. Like that fee, the onus of the Indiana law is illegitimate just because it correlates with no state interest so well as it does with the object of deterring poorer residents from exercising the franchise.

* * *

The Indiana Voter ID Law is thus unconstitutional: the state interests fail to justify the practical limitations placed on the right to vote, and the law imposes an unreasonable and irrelevant burden on voters who are poor and old. I would vacate the judgment of the Seventh Circuit, and remand for further proceedings.

[A dissenting opinion from Justice BREYER is omitted. Like Justice Souter, he concluded that the burdens imposed by Indiana's law outweighed the state's interests.]

Notes and Questions

1. *What Is the Constitutional Standard?* Six justices voted to uphold Indiana's voter ID law against a facial challenge under the Fourteenth Amendment, but no opinion commands a majority. Justice Stevens's opinion (for himself and two other justices) embraces a balancing test for laws alleged to impede participation, under which the burden on voter participation is weighed against the state's asserted justifications. Rather than strict scrutiny being triggered by certain practices, with all others being subjected to rational basis review, the lead opinion suggests that courts should require a stronger justification from the state as the burdens on voters increase. As one commentator put it, the test is less like a "light switch" and "more like a dimmer." Justin Levitt, *Crawford—More Rhetorical Bark Than Legal Bite?*, May 2, 2008, https://perma.cc/FB2E-G9RW. Justice Scalia (also writing for himself and two other justices) criticized the balancing approach of the lead opinion, and would instead apply a "two-track approach" that would function like a light switch rather than a dimmer. Under his test, a court should first determine whether the challenged practice imposes a "severe" burden, which he characterizes as one that "go[es] beyond the merely inconvenient." If it does, then he would apply strict scrutiny; if not, then he would apparently uphold them so long as they are reasonable, a standard he describes as imposing a "minimal burden." Justice Scalia also argued that courts should look at the effect on "*voters generally*" rather than the particular individuals suing, who may be especially vulnerable. Is this a more appropriate (or at least more administrable) legal standard than the one embraced by Justice Stevens' lead opinion?

2. *The Poll Tax Comparison.* The plaintiffs and dissenters in *Crawford* sought to compare Indiana's photo identification requirement to the $1.50 poll tax struck down in *Harper v. Virginia Board of Elections*, based on its effect on poor voters. Even though Indiana provided photo ID cards free of charge, the argument goes, voters lacking identification are required to expend money to obtain the primary documents needed to obtain ID, such as a birth certificate or certificate of naturalization. Additionally, voters lacking ID would be put to the burden of either collecting these documents and going to the BMV to obtain photo ID, or of appearing at the county seat within 10 days after each election to sign an affidavit of indigency. Does the poll tax comparison hold? Should a "tax on the voter's time" be considered a severe burden, sufficient to trigger strict scrutiny? If so, what is the logical stopping point? Do all election practices that may incidentally burden poor people violate equal protection? For example, it is presumably more burdensome for voters lacking an automobile—who are likely to be less affluent than other voters—to get to their polling places. Does the poll tax analogy mean that the government might be required to provide additional polling places in poor neighborhoods, or even to subsidize transportation for poor voters? Presumably not, although some courts have required states to make it easier for people to obtain ID and otherwise to mitigate the burden on less affluent voters. See Richard L. Hasen, *Softening Voter ID Laws Through Litigation: Is It Enough?*, 2016 Wis. L. Rev. Forward 100.

3. *Facial vs. As-Applied Challenges.* Note that the lead opinion rejects plaintiffs' facial challenge to Indiana's law, but leaves the door open to a later as-applied challenge. For example, someone who objects to being photographed on religious grounds could argue that the law imposes an unconstitutional burden on his or her right to vote. Will this encourage case-by-case litigation, as Justice Scalia suggests? If the plaintiffs and dissenters are correct that the Indiana requirements will prevent significant numbers of eligible people from voting, will the availability of case-by-case relief be sufficient to prevent the requirements from operating as prerequisites for voting in practice?

Consider the posture in which this type of issue might be litigated. After a close election, the losing candidate might argue that the votes of religious objectors who came to the polls without photo ID should be counted. Those voters would likely have cast provisional ballots, as the lead opinion explains. The losing candidate would then be in the position of arguing that Indiana's law is unconstitutional, as applied to those voters. This introduces the possibility of a post-election dispute over whether particular ballots should be counted. Is this the best posture in which to resolve election administration disputes? For an argument that pre-election litigation is preferable to post-election litigation, see Richard L. Hasen, *Beyond the Margin of Litigation: Reforming U.S. Election Administration to avoid Electoral Meltdown*, 62 Washington & Lee Law Review 937, 991 (2005). Note that the opinion does not preclude pre-election as-applied litigation by plaintiffs who can demonstrate a particularized burden they would face under the identification requirement. In our hypothetical case, should the court decline to hear the issue posed after the election when the candidate or the voters could have raised the issue beforehand?

Suppose that a law imposes a large burden on a small segment of the voting population. Is such a law susceptible to a facial challenge after *Crawford*, or only an as-applied challenge? Take for example a law that required all newly registered voters without a fixed address to produce their birth certificates the first time they appear at the polls. Could a homeless voter affected by this law bring a facial challenge to it? Alternatively, could such a voter bring a claim alleging that the law is unconstitutional as applied to *all* homeless voters? One commentator offers a qualified defense of *Crawford*'s preference for as-applied challenges, noting that it may refocus the judicial inquiry on the individual right to vote:

> *Crawford* opened up the possibility of a different and more productive form of litigation by inviting future litigants to bring as-applied rather than facial challenges. Here, *Crawford* may have done the court system, and litigants, a service. It nudged courts' role away from the broad structural evaluation and redesign of election administration regimes and toward a clear focus on whether individual voters are being excluded. To be sure, this narrower role will involve courts deeply in adjudicating—critics would say micromanaging—the burdens regulations place on particular voters and groups of voters. Judges will continue to see these issues through lenses somewhat colored by partisanship, which is probably inevitable. But litigants will be

> able to step away from broad policy arguments such as those focused on increasing turnout, with all the social-scientific uncertainty such arguments entail, in favor of a clear focus on the burdens on individual voters' rights.

Joseph Fishkin, *Equal Citizenship and the Individual Right to Vote*, 86 Indiana Law Journal 1289 (2011).

In a postscript to *Crawford*, the Indiana Supreme Court rejected a state constitutional challenge to Indiana's voter identification law. *League of Women Voters of Indiana v. Rokita*, 929 N.E.2d 758 (Ind. 2010). Like Justice Stevens' lead opinion in *Crawford*, the Indiana Supreme Court rested heavily on the facial/as-applied distinction, pointing out that no individual voter had alleged that the law impaired his or her ability to vote, and leaving the door open to future as-applied challenges.

4. *Other State ID Laws*. Indiana, Georgia, and Missouri were the first states to enact laws requiring government-issued photo ID. Since *Crawford*, several other states have followed suit—including Kansas, Pennsylvania, South Carolina, Texas, and Wisconsin. For the most part, the legislative battle has been fought along party lines. For competing perspectives on voter ID and other alleged barriers to voting, see Hans von Spakovsky, *Protecting the Integrity of the Election Process*, 11 Election Law Journal 90 (2012), and Justin Levitt, *Election Deform: The Pursuit of Unwarranted Electoral Regulation*, 11 Election Law Journal 97 (2012).

In addition to challenges under the U.S. Constitution, there have been *state* constitutional challenges to some of the state laws requiring government-issued photo ID. The Missouri Supreme Court held that a photo ID statute violated the equal protection clause of that state's constitution. *Weinschenk v. State of Missouri*, 203 S.W.3d 201 (Mo. 2006). But the Georgia Supreme Court rejected a state constitutional challenge to that state's photo ID law. *Democratic Party of Georgia v. Perdue*, 707 S.E.2d 67 (Ga. 2011). Pennsylvania's ID law was enjoined during the 2012 election cycle on state law grounds, although the state supreme court left open the possibility that it might be implemented in the future if access to voter identification cards were improved. See *Applewhite v. Commonwealth of Pennsylvania*, 54 A.3d 1 (Pa. 2012). On remand, a state trial court permanently enjoined Pennsylvania's voter ID law, because the process for distributing free ID fell short of the "liberal access" required by state law and because the ID law violated the fundamental right to vote under the state constitution. *Applewhite v. Commonwealth of Pennsylvania*, 2014 WL 184988 (Pa. Comm. Ct. 2014). A Wisconsin state court enjoined that state's voter ID law during the 2012 election cycle, but the court of appeals ultimately rejected a state constitutional challenge to the law. *League of Women Voters of Wisconsin Educ. Network v. Walker*, 834 N.W. 2d 393 (Wis. Ct. App. 2013).

Missouri adopted a law requiring most voters to present photo ID, while providing an exception allowing voters to provide non-photo ID if they submit an affidavit that meets certain requirements. The Missouri Supreme Court concluded that this law was too burdensome on voters. The court therefore affirmed an order enjoining the state from requiring an affidavit from voters using non-photo ID and from disseminating materials indicating that photo ID is required—a decision that effectively eliminates the photo ID requirement. *Priorities USA v. State of Missouri*, 591 S.W.3d 448 (Mo. 2020). In Iowa, a state trial court upheld that state's ID law, while striking down a provision that would make it more difficult to get a voter ID card. Anna Spoerre, *Judge Upholds ID Requirement at Polls but Strikes down Other Parts of 2017 Iowa Voting Reform Law*, Des Moines Register, Oct. 1, 2019.

5. *Empirical Research on Voter ID.* The legal and policy debates over voter identification depend in large measure on disputed factual questions, including the effect of identification laws on participation, the prevalence of voting fraud, and the likelihood that identification laws will curb fraud. In *Crawford*, the evidence of both the benefits and the burdens of Indiana's law was quite weak. As the lead opinion notes, the only type of fraud that Indiana's law would prevent is in-person voter impersonation fraud, yet there was "no evidence of any such fraud actually occurring in Indiana at any time in its history." On the other hand, the lead opinion notes that plaintiffs' evidence of the Indiana law's burden on voters was also very weak. What is the appropriate course for a court to take under the circumstances?

There have been many efforts to measure the benefits and burdens associated with voter identification laws. It is difficult to measure the incidence of voter fraud with precision, though most observers agree that voter impersonation at the polling place—the type of fraud that Indiana-type ID laws are most likely to prevent—is quite rare. See Lorraine Minnite, The Myth of Voter Fraud (2010). What about the claim that the *perception* of widespread illegal voting, even if inaccurate, may depress participation by eligible citizens? The evidence for this proposition is weak, according to Stephen Ansolabehere and Nathaniel Persily, *Vote Fraud in the Eye of the Beholder: The Role of Public Opinion in the Challenge to Voter Identification Requirements*, 121 Harvard Law Review 1737 (2008).

On the other side, there is lingering uncertainty over the extent to which voter ID laws actually affect turnout. One article on the subject concludes that: "We should be wary of claims—from all sides of the controversy—regarding turnout effects from voter ID laws.... [T]he data are not up to the task of making a compelling statistical argument." Robert S. Erikson & Lorraine C. Minnite, *Modeling Problems in the Voter Identification—Voter Turnout Debate*, 8 Election Law Journal 85 (2009). One study, however, finds that states with strict voter ID law have seen substantial drops in Latino, Asian American, and African American turnout, with Democrats more likely to be affected than Republicans. Zoltan Hajnal, Nazita Lajevardi & Lindsay Nielson, *Voter Identification Laws and the Suppression of Minority Votes*, 79 Journal of Politics 363 (2017). Other studies have shown that between 84 and 95 percent of registered voters have state-issued ID, but that racial minorities are less likely to have such ID. See U.S. Government Accountability Office, *Issues Related to State Voter Identification Laws* 21–28 (2014). Some of the most recent voter ID laws are even stricter than the one upheld in *Crawford*. Thus, even if the effects of

Indiana's law are modest, it is possible that other states' laws will have a greater effect on turnout.

Can voter mobilization efforts successfully counter the effects of voter ID laws? A recent empirical study finds evidence that they can. Jacob R. Neiheisel & Rich Horner, *Voter Identification Requirements and Aggregate Turnout in the U.S.: How Campaigns Offset the Costs of Turning Out When Voting Is Made More Difficult*, 18 Election Law Journal 227 (2019). The authors find that while new voter ID laws decreased turnout by about two percentage points in counties without a corresponding increase in campaign activity, there was no effect in counties with more campaign activity, presumably including voter mobilization.

6. *Other Burdens on Voting.* Voter identification laws are just one of several types of burdens on voting that have been challenged on equal protection grounds. Others include restrictions on the counting of provisional ballots, early and absentee voting, and voter registration. For the most part, courts have applied the *Anderson-Burdick* balancing test set forth in Justice Stevens's lead opinion in *Crawford.* One example is *Obama for America v. Husted*, 697 F.3d 423 (6th Cir. 2012), which found a likely equal protection violation arising from Ohio's rules for in-person early voting. Other courts have looked with skepticism on such claims. The Fifth Circuit, for example, stayed an injunction against a Texas rule that allowed only one location per county at which mail-in ballots could be dropped off. *Texas League of United Latin American Citizens v. Hughs*, 978 F.3d 136 (5th Cir. 2020). Plaintiffs argued that this would make it more difficult for them to vote during the pandemic. The court determined that this limitation on voting was justified under the *Anderson-Burdick* test, because any burden on voting was minimal and outweighed by the state's interest in fraud prevention and the orderly administration of elections. Other courts have denied or stayed relief under the *Purcell* doctrine (discussed *infra* Part IV of this Chapter), which generally prohibits federal courts from issuing an injunction against election rules close to an election. For a summary and criticism of lower court rulings deferring to state administrative interests, see Joshua Douglas, *Undue Deference to States in the 2020 Election Litigation*, 30 William & Mary Bill of Rights Journal __ (forthcoming).

II. Race Discrimination

One way of challenging an election law or practice is to demonstrate that it burdens the right to vote without a constitutionally sufficient justification. As set forth in Part I.C above, a majority of justices in *Crawford* adopted the *Anderson-Burdick* balancing standard for assessing the constitutionality of challenged laws or practices under the Equal Protection Clause. There is another way of challenging an election law or practice: by showing that it is racially discriminatory, in violation of the Voting Rights Act of 1965 (VRA) or the U.S. Constitution. Voting rights advocates have challenged voter ID laws and various other burdens on voting as discriminating against people of color, particularly African Americans and Latinos. Such claims may be based either on a discriminatory *purpose* or discriminatory *results.*

The Fourteenth Amendment, the Fifteenth Amendment, and the VRA forbid all voting laws or practices that have a racially discriminatory purpose. Such discrimination was common in the mid-Twentieth Century, when many states had laws that were designed to prevent Blacks or other racial groups from exercising their right to vote. A racially discriminatory purpose is more difficult to prove today, but such claims are sometimes made and occasionally succeed.

Impermissible race discrimination may also be shown by demonstrating a racially discriminatory *result.* Section 2 of the VRA states in pertinent part:

> (a) No voting qualification or prerequisite to voting or standard, practice, or procedure shall be imposed or applied by any State or political subdivision in a manner which *results in* a denial or abridgement of the right of any citizen of the United States to vote on account of race or color. . . .
>
> (b) A violation of subsection (a) is established if, based on the totality of circumstances, it is shown that the political processes leading to nomination or election in the State or political subdivision are not equally open to participation by members of a class of citizens protected by subsection (a) of this section in that its members have less opportunity than other members of the electorate to participate in the political process and to elect representatives of their choice.

52 U.S.C. § 10301 (emphasis added).

Congress adopted the "results" language in subsection (a) and the "totality of the circumstances" language in subsection (b) in 1982, through amendments to the VRA. These amendments were in response to Supreme Court precedent requiring that a discriminatory purpose be shown. Chapter 5 addressed the standard that applies under Section 2 when considering *vote dilution* claims—that is, a claim that a law or practice, like a redistricting plan or at-large election scheme, weakens the voting strength of a particular racial group. Section 2's results test may also be applied to *vote denial* claims—that is, a claim that a law or practice makes it more difficult for member of a particular racial group to vote at all. See Daniel P. Tokaji, *The New Vote Denial: Where Election Reform Meets the Voting Rights Act*, 57 South Carolina Law Review 689 (2006).

For many years, there was uncertainty about how Section 2 should be applied to vote denial claims. Until 2013, the preclearance process under Section 5 of the Voting Rights Act was sometimes used to stop allegedly discriminatory voting laws from taking effect. The Supreme Court struck down the VRA's coverage formula in *Shelby County v. Holder*, 570 U.S. 529 (2013) (Chapter 5, *supra*), effectively ending Section 5 preclearance. Advocates then turned to Section 2 of the VRA. There was reason to believe that Section 2 would be a less potent weapon against racially discriminatory vote denial than was Section 5. See Nicholas Stephanopoulos, *The South after* Shelby County, 2013 Supreme Court Review 55 (2014). Nevertheless, voting rights advocates had some success in lower courts, using Section 2 to stop practices alleged to impose a disproportionate burden on people of color.

In the following case, however, the U.S. Supreme Court rejected a Section 2 challenge to Arizona rules alleged to make it more difficult for Latinos, African Americans, and Native Americans to vote. Consider the legal standard the Court applies to Section 2 vote denial claims, and how difficult it will be for future voters to challenge practices that have a disparate impact on people of color.

Brnovich v. Democratic National Committee

141 S. Ct. 2321 (2021)

Justice ALITO delivered the opinion of the Court.

In these cases, we are called upon for the first time to apply § 2 of the Voting Rights Act of 1965 to regulations that govern how ballots are collected and counted. Arizona law generally makes it very easy to vote. All voters may vote by mail or in person for nearly a month before election day, but Arizona imposes two restrictions that are claimed to be unlawful. First, in some counties, voters who choose to cast a ballot in person on election day must vote in their own precincts or else their ballots will not be counted. Second, mail-in ballots cannot be collected by anyone other than an election official, a mail carrier, or a voter's family member, household member, or caregiver. After a trial, a District Court upheld these rules, as did a panel of the United States Court of Appeals for the Ninth Circuit. But an en banc court, by a divided vote, found them to be unlawful. It relied on the rules' small disparate impacts on members of minority groups, as well as past discrimination dating back to the State's territorial days. And it overturned the District Court's finding that the Arizona Legislature did not adopt the ballot-collection restriction for a discriminatory purpose. We now hold that the en banc court misunderstood and misapplied § 2 and that it exceeded its authority in rejecting the District Court's factual finding on the issue of legislative intent.

I

A

Congress enacted the landmark Voting Rights Act of 1965, 52 U.S.C. § 10301 et seq., in an effort to achieve at long last what the Fifteenth Amendment had sought to bring about 95 years earlier: an end to the denial of the right to vote based on race. Ratified in 1870, the Fifteenth Amendment provides in § 1 that "[t]he right of citizens of the United States to vote shall not be denied or abridged by the United States or by any State on account of race, color, or previous condition of servitude." Section 2 of the Amendment then grants Congress the "power to enforce [the Amendment] by appropriate legislation."

Despite the ratification of the Fifteenth Amendment, the right of African-Americans to vote was heavily suppressed for nearly a century. States employed a variety of notorious methods, including poll taxes, literacy tests, property qualifications, "white primar[ies]," and "grandfather clause[s]." Challenges to some blatant efforts reached this Court and were held to violate the Fifteenth Amendment. But as late as the mid-1960s, black registration and voting rates in some States were appallingly low.

Invoking the power conferred by §2 of the Fifteenth Amendment, Congress enacted the Voting Rights Act (VRA) to address this entrenched problem. The Act and its amendments in the 1970s specifically forbade some of the practices that had been used to suppress black voting. Sections 4 and 5 of the VRA imposed special requirements for States and subdivisions where violations of the right to vote had been severe. And §2 addressed the denial or abridgment of the right to vote in any part of the country.

As originally enacted, §2 closely tracked the language of the Amendment it was adopted to enforce. Section 2 stated simply that "[n]o voting qualification or prerequisite to voting, or standard, practice, or procedure shall be imposed or applied by any State or political subdivision to deny or abridge the right of any citizen of the United States to vote on account of race or color."

Unlike other provisions of the VRA, §2 attracted relatively little attention during the congressional debates and was "little-used" for more than a decade after its passage. But during the same period, this Court considered several cases involving "vote-dilution" claims asserted under the Equal Protection Clause of the Fourteenth Amendment. See *Whitcomb v. Chavis*, 403 U.S. 124 (1971); *Burns v. Richardson*, 384 U.S. 73 (1966); *Fortson v. Dorsey*, 379 U.S. 433 (1965). In these and later vote-dilution cases, plaintiffs claimed that features of legislative districting plans, including the configuration of legislative districts and the use of multi-member districts, diluted the ability of particular voters to affect the outcome of elections....

[T]he question whether a VRA §2 claim required discriminatory purpose or intent came before this Court in *Mobile v. Bolden*, 446 U.S. 55 (1980) [see Chapter 5]. The plurality opinion for four Justices concluded first that §2 of the VRA added nothing to the protections afforded by the Fifteenth Amendment. The plurality then observed that prior decisions "ha[d] made clear that action by a State that is racially neutral on its face violates the Fifteenth Amendment only if motivated by a discriminatory purpose." The obvious result of those premises was that facially neutral voting practices violate §2 only if motivated by a discriminatory purpose....

Shortly after *Bolden* was handed down, Congress amended §2 of the VRA. The oft-cited Report of the Senate Judiciary Committee accompanying the 1982 Amendment stated that the amendment's purpose was to repudiate *Bolden* and establish a new vote-dilution test.... The bill that was initially passed by the House of Representatives included what is now §2(a). In place of the phrase "to deny or abridge the right ... to vote on account of race or color," the amendment substituted "in a manner which results in a denial or abridgement of the right ... to vote on account of race or color." ...

What is now § 2(b) was added, and that provision sets out what must be shown to prove a § 2 violation. It requires consideration of "the totality of circumstances" in each case and demands proof that "the political processes leading to nomination or election in the State or political subdivision are not *equally open* to participation" by members of a protected class "*in that its members have less opportunity* than other members of the electorate to participate in the political process and to elect representatives of their choice." (emphasis added). . . .

This concentration on the contentious issue of vote dilution reflected the results of the Senate Judiciary Committee's extensive survey of what it regarded as Fifteenth Amendment violations that called out for legislative redress. That survey listed many examples of what the Committee took to be unconstitutional vote dilution, but the survey identified only three isolated episodes involving the outright denial of the right to vote, and none of these concerned the equal application of a facially neutral rule specifying the time, place, or manner of voting. These sparse results were presumably good news. They likely showed that the VRA and other efforts had achieved a large measure of success in combating the previously widespread practice of using such rules to hinder minority groups from voting.

This Court first construed the amended § 2 in *Thornburg v. Gingles*, 478 U.S. 30 (1986) [see Chapter 5]—another vote-dilution case. Justice Brennan's opinion for the Court set out three threshold requirements for proving a § 2 vote-dilution claim, and, taking its cue from the Senate Report, provided a non-exhaustive list of factors to be considered in determining whether § 2 had been violated. "The essence of a § 2 claim," the Court said, "is that a certain electoral law, practice, or structure interacts with social and historical conditions to cause an inequality in the opportunities" of minority and non-minority voters to elect their preferred representatives.

In the years since *Gingles*, we have heard a steady stream of § 2 vote-dilution cases, but until today, we have not considered how § 2 applies to generally applicable time, place, or manner voting rules. In recent years, however, such claims have proliferated in the lower courts.

B

The present dispute concerns two features of Arizona voting law, which generally makes it quite easy for residents to vote. All Arizonans may vote by mail for 27 days before an election using an "early ballot." No special excuse is needed, and any voter may ask to be sent an early ballot automatically in future elections. In addition, during the 27 days before an election, Arizonans may vote in person at an early voting location in each county. And they may also vote in person on election day. . . .

The regulations at issue in this suit govern precinct-based election-day voting and early mail-in voting. Voters who choose to vote in person on election day in a county that uses the precinct system must vote in their assigned precincts. If a voter goes to the wrong polling place, poll workers are trained to direct the voter to the right location. If a voter finds that his or her name does not appear on the register at what the voter believes is the right precinct, the voter ordinarily may cast a provisional ballot. That ballot is later counted if the voter's address is determined to be within the precinct. But if it turns out that the voter cast a ballot at the wrong precinct, that vote is not counted.

For those who choose to vote early by mail, Arizona has long required that "[o]nly the elector may be in possession of that elector's unvoted early ballot." In 2016, the state legislature enacted House Bill 2023 (HB 2023), which makes it a crime for any person other than a postal worker, an elections official, or a voter's caregiver, family member, or household member to knowingly collect an early ballot—either before or after it has been completed.

In 2016, the Democratic National Committee and certain affiliates brought this suit and named as defendants (among others) the Arizona attorney general and secretary of state in their official capacities. Among other things, the plaintiffs claimed that both the State's refusal to count ballots cast in the wrong precinct and its ballot-collection restriction "adversely and disparately affect Arizona's American Indian, Hispanic, and African American citizens," in violation of § 2 of the VRA. In addition, they alleged that the ballot-collection restriction was "enacted with discriminatory intent" and thus violated both § 2 of the VRA and the Fifteenth Amendment. . . .

II

[The Court concluded that Attorney General Brnovich had standing to appeal.]

[W]e think it prudent to make clear at the beginning that we decline in these cases to announce a test to govern all VRA § 2 claims involving rules, like those at issue here, that specify the time, place, or manner for casting ballots. Each of the parties advocated a different test, as did many amici and the courts below. . . . All told, no fewer than 10 tests have been proposed. But as this is our first foray into the area, we think it sufficient for present purposes to identify certain guideposts that lead us to our decision in these cases.

III

A

We start with the text of VRA § 2. [The majority quoted the text of subsections (a) and (b), set forth above in this Section.]

In *Gingles*, our seminal § 2 vote-dilution case, the Court quoted the text of amended § 2 and then jumped right to the Senate Judiciary Committee Report, which focused on the issue of vote dilution. Our many subsequent vote-dilution cases have largely followed the path that *Gingles* charted. But because this is our first § 2 time, place, or manner case, a fresh look at the statutory text is appropriate. Today, our statutory interpretation cases almost always start with a careful consideration of the text, and there is no reason to do otherwise here.

B

Section 2(a), as noted, omits the phrase "to deny or abridge the right . . . to vote on account of race or color," which the *Bolden* plurality had interpreted to require proof of discriminatory intent. In place of that language, § 2(a) substitutes the phrase "in a manner which *results in* a denial or abridgement of the right . . . to vote on account of race or color." (Emphasis added.) We need not decide what this text would mean if it stood alone because § 2(b), which was added to win Senate approval, explains what must be shown to establish a § 2 violation. Section 2(b) states that § 2 is violated only where "the political processes leading to nomination or election" are not "*equally open* to participation" by members of the relevant protected group "*in that its members have less opportunity* than other members of the electorate to participate in the political process and to elect representatives of their choice." (Emphasis added.)

The key requirement is that the political processes leading to nomination and election (here, the process of voting) must be "equally open" to minority and non-minority groups alike, and the most relevant definition of the term "open," as used in § 2(b), is "without restrictions as to who may participate," Random House Dictionary of the English Language (J. Stein ed. 1966), or "requiring no special status, identification, or permit for entry or participation," Webster's Third New International Dictionary (1976).

What § 2(b) means by voting that is not "equally open" is further explained by this language: "in that its members have less opportunity than other members of the electorate to participate in the political process and to elect representatives of their choice." The phrase "in that" is "used to specify the respect in which a statement is true." Thus, equal openness and equal opportunity are not separate requirements. Instead, equal opportunity helps to explain the meaning of equal openness. And the term "opportunity" means, among other things, "a combination of circumstances, time, and place suitable or favorable for a particular activity or action." *Id.*

Putting these terms together, it appears that the core of § 2(b) is the requirement that voting be "equally open." The statute's reference to equal "opportunity" may stretch that concept to some degree to include consideration of a person's ability to use the means that are equally open. But equal openness remains the touchstone.

C

One other important feature of § 2(b) stands out. The provision requires consideration of "the totality of circumstances." Thus, any circumstance that has a logical bearing on whether voting is "equally open" and affords equal "opportunity" may be considered. We will not attempt to compile an exhaustive list, but several important circumstances should be mentioned.

1

1. First, the size of the burden imposed by a challenged voting rule is highly relevant. The concepts of "open[ness]" and "opportunity" connote the absence of

obstacles and burdens that block or seriously hinder voting, and therefore the size of the burden imposed by a voting rule is important. After all, every voting rule imposes a burden of some sort. Voting takes time and, for almost everyone, some travel, even if only to a nearby mailbox. Casting a vote, whether by following the directions for using a voting machine or completing a paper ballot, requires compliance with certain rules. But because voting necessarily requires some effort and compliance with some rules, the concept of a voting system that is "equally open" and that furnishes an equal "opportunity" to cast a ballot must tolerate the "usual burdens of voting." *Crawford v. Marion County Election Bd.* (opinion of Stevens, J.). Mere inconvenience cannot be enough to demonstrate a violation of § 2.[11]

2. For similar reasons, the degree to which a voting rule departs from what was standard practice when § 2 was amended in 1982 is a relevant consideration. Because every voting rule imposes a burden of some sort, it is useful to have benchmarks with which the burdens imposed by a challenged rule can be compared. The burdens associated with the rules in widespread use when § 2 was adopted are therefore useful in gauging whether the burdens imposed by a challenged rule are sufficient to prevent voting from being equally "open" or furnishing an equal "opportunity" to vote in the sense meant by § 2. Therefore, it is relevant that in 1982 States typically required nearly all voters to cast their ballots in person on election day and allowed only narrow and tightly defined categories of voters to cast absentee ballots. As of January 1980, only three States permitted no-excuse absentee voting. We doubt that Congress intended to uproot facially neutral time, place, and manner regulations that have a long pedigree or are in widespread use in the United States. We have no need to decide whether adherence to, or a return to, a 1982 framework is necessarily lawful under § 2, but the degree to which a challenged rule has a long pedigree or is in widespread use in the United States is a circumstance that must be taken into account.

3. The size of any disparities in a rule's impact on members of different racial or ethnic groups is also an important factor to consider. Small disparities are less likely than large ones to indicate that a system is not equally open. To the extent that minority and non-minority groups differ with respect to employment, wealth, and education, even neutral regulations, no matter how crafted, may well result in some predictable disparities in rates of voting and noncompliance with voting rules.

---

11. There is a difference between openness and opportunity, on the one hand, and the absence of inconvenience, on the other. For example, suppose that an exhibit at a museum in a particular city is open to everyone free of charge every day of the week for several months. Some residents of the city who have the opportunity to view the exhibit may find it inconvenient to do so for many reasons—the problem of finding parking, dislike of public transportation, anticipation that the exhibit will be crowded, a plethora of weekend chores and obligations, etc. Or, to take another example, a college course may be open to all students and all may have the opportunity to enroll, but some students may find it inconvenient to take the class for a variety of reasons. For example, classes may occur too early in the morning or on Friday afternoon; too much reading may be assigned; the professor may have a reputation as a hard grader; etc.

But the mere fact there is some disparity in impact does not necessarily mean that a system is not equally open or that it does not give everyone an equal opportunity to vote. The size of any disparity matters. And in assessing the size of any disparity, a meaningful comparison is essential. What are at bottom very small differences should not be artificially magnified.

4. Next, courts must consider the opportunities provided by a State's entire system of voting when assessing the burden imposed by a challenged provision. This follows from § 2(b)'s reference to the collective concept of a State's "political processes" and its "political process" as a whole. Thus, where a State provides multiple ways to vote, any burden imposed on voters who choose one of the available options cannot be evaluated without also taking into account the other available means.

5. Finally, the strength of the state interests served by a challenged voting rule is also an important factor that must be taken into account. As noted, every voting rule imposes a burden of some sort, and therefore, in determining "based on the totality of circumstances" whether a rule goes too far, it is important to consider the reason for the rule. Rules that are supported by strong state interests are less likely to violate § 2.

One strong and entirely legitimate state interest is the prevention of fraud. Fraud can affect the outcome of a close election, and fraudulent votes dilute the right of citizens to cast ballots that carry appropriate weight. Fraud can also undermine public confidence in the fairness of elections and the perceived legitimacy of the announced outcome....

2

While the factors set out above are important, others considered by some lower courts are less helpful in a case like the ones at hand. First, it is important to keep in mind that the *Gingles* or "Senate" factors grew out of and were designed for use in vote-dilution cases. Some of those factors are plainly inapplicable in a case involving a challenge to a facially neutral time, place, or manner voting rule. Factors three and four concern districting and election procedures like "majority vote requirements," "anti-single shot provisions," and a "candidate slating process." Factors two, six, and seven (which concern racially polarized voting, racially tinged campaign appeals, and the election of minority-group candidates), have a bearing on whether a districting plan affects the opportunity of minority voters to elect their candidates of choice. But in cases involving neutral time, place, and manner rules, the only relevance of these and the remaining factors is to show that minority group members suffered discrimination in the past (factor one) and that effects of that discrimination persist (factor five). We do not suggest that these factors should be disregarded. After all, § 2(b) requires consideration of "the totality of circumstances." But their relevance is much less direct.

We also do not find the disparate-impact model employed in Title VII and Fair Housing Act cases useful here. The text of the relevant provisions of Title VII and the Fair Housing Act differ from that of VRA §2, and it is not obvious why Congress would conform rules regulating voting to those regulating employment and housing. For example, we think it inappropriate to read §2 to impose a strict "necessity requirement" that would force States to demonstrate that their legitimate interests can be accomplished only by means of the voting regulations in question. Stephanopoulos, *Disparate Impact, Unified Law*, 128 Yale L.J. 1566, 1617–1619 (2019) (advocating such a requirement). Demanding such a tight fit would have the effect of invalidating a great many neutral voting regulations with long pedigrees that are reasonable means of pursuing legitimate interests. It would also transfer much of the authority to regulate election procedures from the States to the federal courts. For those reasons, the Title VII and Fair Housing Act models are unhelpful in §2 cases.

D

The interpretation set out above follows directly from what §2 commands: consideration of "the totality of circumstances" that have a bearing on whether a State makes voting "equally open" to all and gives everyone an equal "opportunity" to vote. The dissent, by contrast, would rewrite the text of §2 and make it turn almost entirely on just one circumstance—disparate impact.

That is a radical project, and the dissent strains mightily to obscure its objective. To that end, it spends 20 pages discussing matters that have little bearing on the questions before us. [The majority cited the historical background to the VRA and "points of law that nobody disputes."]

Only after this extended effort at misdirection is the dissent's aim finally unveiled: to undo as much as possible the compromise that was reached between the House and Senate when §2 was amended in 1982. Recall that the version originally passed by the House did not contain §2(b) and was thought to prohibit any voting practice that had "discriminatory effects," loosely defined. That is the freewheeling disparate-impact regime the dissent wants to impose on the States. But the version enacted into law includes §2(b), and that subsection directs us to consider "the totality of circumstances," not, as the dissent would have it, the totality of just one circumstance. There is nothing to the dissent's charge that we are departing from the statutory text by identifying some of those considerations. . . .

Section 2 of the Voting Rights Act provides vital protection against discriminatory voting rules, and no one suggests that discrimination in voting has been extirpated or that the threat has been eliminated. But §2 does not deprive the States of their authority to establish non-discriminatory voting rules, and that is precisely what the dissent's radical interpretation would mean in practice. The dissent is correct that the Voting Rights Act exemplifies our country's commitment to democracy, but there is nothing democratic about the dissent's attempt to bring about a wholesale transfer of the authority to set voting rules from the States to the federal courts.

IV

A

In light of the principles set out above, neither Arizona's out-of-precinct rule nor its ballot-collection law violates § 2 of the VRA. Arizona's out-of-precinct rule enforces the requirement that voters who choose to vote in person on election day must do so in their assigned precincts. Having to identify one's own polling place and then travel there to vote does not exceed the "usual burdens of voting." *Crawford* (opinion of Stevens, J.). On the contrary, these tasks are quintessential examples of the usual burdens of voting.

Not only are these unremarkable burdens, but the District Court's uncontested findings show that the State made extensive efforts to reduce their impact on the number of valid votes ultimately cast. The State makes accurate precinct information available to all voters. When precincts or polling places are altered between elections, each registered voter is sent a notice showing the voter's new polling place. Arizona law also mandates that election officials send a sample ballot to each household that includes a registered voter who has not opted to be placed on the permanent early voter list, and this mailing also identifies the voter's proper polling location. In addition, the Arizona secretary of state's office sends voters pamphlets that include information (in both English and Spanish) about how to identify their assigned precinct.

Polling place information is also made available by other means. The secretary of state's office operates websites that provide voter-specific polling place information and allow voters to make inquiries to the secretary's staff. Arizona's two most populous counties, Maricopa and Pima, provide online polling place locators with information available in English and Spanish. Other groups offer similar online tools. Voters may also identify their assigned polling place by calling the office of their respective county recorder. And on election day, poll workers in at least some counties are trained to redirect voters who arrive at the wrong precinct.

The burdens of identifying and traveling to one's assigned precinct are also modest when considering Arizona's "political processes" as a whole.... [E]ven if it is marginally harder for Arizona voters to find their assigned polling places, the State offers other easy ways to vote. Any voter can request an early ballot without excuse. Any voter can ask to be placed on the permanent early voter list so that an early ballot will be mailed automatically. Voters may drop off their early ballots at any polling place, even one to which they are not assigned. And for nearly a month before election day, any voter can vote in person at an early voting location in his or her county. The availability of those options likely explains why out-of-precinct votes on election day make up such a small and apparently diminishing portion of overall ballots cast—0.47% of all ballots in the 2012 general election and just 0.15% in 2016.

Next, the racial disparity in burdens allegedly caused by the out-of-precinct policy is small in absolute terms. The District Court accepted the plaintiffs' evidence that, of the Arizona counties that reported out-of-precinct ballots in the 2016 general election, a little over 1% of Hispanic voters, 1% of African-American voters, and 1% of Native American voters who voted on election day cast an out-of-precinct ballot. For non-minority voters, the rate was around 0.5%. A policy that appears to work for 98% or more of voters to whom it applies—minority and non-minority alike—is unlikely to render a system unequally open. . . .

The Court of Appeals' decision . . . failed to give appropriate weight to the state interests that the out-of-precinct rule serves. Not counting out-of-precinct votes induces compliance with the requirement that Arizonans who choose to vote in-person on election day do so at their assigned polling places. And as the District Court recognized, precinct-based voting furthers important state interests. It helps to distribute voters more evenly among polling places and thus reduces wait times. It can put polling places closer to voter residences than would a more centralized voting-center model. In addition, precinct-based voting helps to ensure that each voter receives a ballot that lists only the candidates and public questions on which he or she can vote, and this orderly administration tends to decrease voter confusion and increase voter confidence in elections. And the policy of not counting out-of-precinct ballots is widespread. . . .

Section 2 does not require a State to show that its chosen policy is absolutely necessary or that a less restrictive means would not adequately serve the State's objectives. . . .

In light of the modest burdens allegedly imposed by Arizona's out-of-precinct policy, the small size of its disparate impact, and the State's justifications, we conclude the rule does not violate § 2 of the VRA.

B

HB 2023 likewise passes muster under the results test of § 2. Arizonans who receive early ballots can submit them by going to a mailbox, a post office, an early ballot drop box, or an authorized election official's office within the 27-day early voting period. They can also drop off their ballots at any polling place or voting center on election day, and in order to do so, they can skip the line of voters waiting to vote in person. Making any of these trips—much like traveling to an assigned polling place—falls squarely within the heartland of the "usual burdens of voting." *Crawford* (opinion of Stevens, J.). And voters can also ask a statutorily authorized proxy—a family member, a household member, or a caregiver—to mail a ballot or drop it off at any time within 27 days of an election.

Arizona also makes special provision for certain groups of voters who are unable to use the early voting system. Every county must establish a special election board to serve voters who are "confined as the result of a continuing illness or physical disability," are unable to go to the polls on election day, and do not wish to cast an early vote by mail. At the request of a voter in this group, the board will deliver a ballot in person and return it on the voter's behalf. Arizona law also requires employers to give employees time off to vote when they are otherwise scheduled to work certain shifts on election day.

The plaintiffs were unable to provide statistical evidence showing that HB 2023 had a disparate impact on minority voters. Instead, they called witnesses who testified that third-party ballot collection tends to be used most heavily in disadvantaged communities and that minorities in Arizona—especially Native Americans—are disproportionately disadvantaged. But from that evidence the District Court could conclude only that prior to HB 2023's enactment, "minorities generically were more likely than non-minorities to return their early ballots with the assistance of third parties." How much more, the court could not say from the record. Neither can we. And without more concrete evidence, we cannot conclude that HB 2023 results in less opportunity to participate in the political process.

Even if the plaintiffs had shown a disparate burden caused by HB 2023, the State's justifications would suffice to avoid § 2 liability. "A State indisputably has a compelling interest in preserving the integrity of its election process." *Purcell v. Gonzalez*, 549 U.S. 1 (2006). Limiting the classes of persons who may handle early ballots to those less likely to have ulterior motives deters potential fraud and improves voter confidence....

[P]revention of fraud is not the only legitimate interest served by restrictions on ballot collection.... [T]hird-party ballot collection can lead to pressure and intimidation. And it should go without saying that a State may take action to prevent election fraud without waiting for it to occur and be detected within its own borders.... Fraud is a real risk that accompanies mail-in voting even if Arizona had the good fortune to avoid it. Election fraud has had serious consequences in other States. For example, the North Carolina Board of Elections invalidated the results of a 2018 race for a seat in the House of Representatives for evidence of fraudulent mail-in ballots. The Arizona Legislature was not obligated to wait for something similar to happen closer to home.

As with the out-of-precinct policy, the modest evidence of racially disparate burdens caused by HB 2023, in light of the State's justifications, leads us to the conclusion that the law does not violate § 2 of the VRA.

V

We also granted certiorari to review whether the Court of Appeals erred in concluding that HB 2023 was enacted with a discriminatory purpose. The District Court found that it was not, and appellate review of that conclusion is for clear error....

The court noted, among other things, that HB 2023's enactment followed increased use of ballot collection as a Democratic get-out-the-vote strategy and came "on the heels of several prior efforts to restrict ballot collection, some of which were spearheaded by former Arizona State Senator Don Shooter." Shooter's own election in 2010 had been close and racially polarized. Aiming in part to frustrate the Democratic Party's get-out-the-vote strategy, Shooter made what the court termed "unfounded and often far-fetched allegations of ballot collection fraud." But what came after the airing of Shooter's claims and a "racially-tinged" video created by a private party was a serious legislative debate on the wisdom of early mail-in voting.

That debate, the District Court concluded, was sincere and led to the passage of HB 2023 in 2016. Proponents of the bill repeatedly argued that mail-in ballots are more susceptible to fraud than in-person voting. The bill found support from a few minority officials and organizations, one of which expressed concern that ballot collectors were taking advantage of elderly Latino voters. And while some opponents of the bill accused Republican legislators of harboring racially discriminatory motives, that view was not uniform. One Democratic state senator pithily described the "problem" HB 2023 aimed to "solv[e]" as the fact that "one party is better at collecting ballots than the other one."

We are more than satisfied that the District Court's interpretation of the evidence is permissible. The spark for the debate over mail-in voting may well have been provided by one Senator's enflamed partisanship, but partisan motives are not the same as racial motives. See *Cooper v. Harris*, 581 U. S. ___ (2017) [see Notes following *Bartlett v. Strickland* and *Alabama Legislative Black Caucus* in Chapter 5]. The District Court noted that the voting preferences of members of a racial group may make the former look like the latter, but it carefully distinguished between the two. And while the District Court recognized that the "racially-tinged" video helped spur the debate about ballot collection, it found no evidence that the legislature as a whole was imbued with racial motives.

The Court of Appeals did not dispute the District Court's assessment of the sincerity of HB 2023's proponents . . . The Court of Appeals nevertheless concluded that the District Court committed clear error by failing to apply a "'cat's paw'" theory sometimes used in employment discrimination cases. A "cat's paw" is a "dupe" who is "used by another to accomplish his purposes." Webster's New International Dictionary 425 (2d ed. 1934). A plaintiff in a "cat's paw" case typically seeks to hold the plaintiff's employer liable for "the animus of a supervisor who was not charged with making the ultimate [adverse] employment decision." *Staub v. Proctor Hospital*, 562 U.S. 411, 415 (2011).

The "cat's paw" theory has no application to legislative bodies. The theory rests on the agency relationship that exists between an employer and a supervisor, but the legislators who vote to adopt a bill are not the agents of the bill's sponsor or proponents. Under our form of government, legislators have a duty to exercise their judgment and to represent their constituents. It is insulting to suggest that they are mere dupes or tools.

* * *

Arizona's out-of-precinct policy and HB 2023 do not violate § 2 of the VRA, and HB 2023 was not enacted with a racially discriminatory purpose. The judgment of the Court of Appeals is reversed, and the cases are remanded for further proceedings consistent with this opinion.

It is so ordered.

[Justice GORSUCH's concurring opinion is omitted.]

Justice KAGAN, with whom Justice BREYER and Justice SOTOMAYOR join, dissenting.

If a single statute represents the best of America, it is the Voting Rights Act. It marries two great ideals: democracy and racial equality. And it dedicates our country to carrying them out. Section 2, the provision at issue here, guarantees that members of every racial group will have equal voting opportunities. Citizens of every race will have the same shot to participate in the political process and to elect representatives of their choice. They will all own our democracy together — no one more and no one less than any other.

If a single statute reminds us of the worst of America, it is the Voting Rights Act. Because it was — and remains — so necessary. Because a century after the Civil War was fought, at the time of the Act's passage, the promise of political equality remained a distant dream for African American citizens. Because States and localities continually "contriv[ed] new rules," mostly neutral on their face but discriminatory in operation, to keep minority voters from the polls. *South Carolina v. Katzenbach*. Because "Congress had reason to suppose" that States would "try similar maneuvers in the future" — "pour[ing] old poison into new bottles" to suppress minority votes. *Ibid.* Because Congress has been proved right.

The Voting Rights Act is ambitious, in both goal and scope. When President Lyndon Johnson sent the bill to Congress, ten days after John Lewis led marchers across the Edmund Pettus Bridge, he explained that it was "carefully drafted to meet its objective — the end of discrimination in voting in America." He was right about how the Act's drafting reflected its aim. "The end of discrimination in voting" is a far-reaching goal. And the Voting Rights Act's text is just as far-reaching. A later amendment, adding the provision at issue here, became necessary when this Court construed the statute too narrowly. And in the last decade, this Court assailed the Act again, undoing its vital Section 5. See *Shelby County v. Holder* [*supra* Chapter 5.] But Section 2 of the Act remains, as written, as expansive as ever — demanding that every citizen of this country possess a right at once grand and obvious: the right to an equal opportunity to vote.

Today, the Court undermines Section 2 and the right it provides. The majority fears that the statute Congress wrote is too "radical" — that it will invalidate too many state voting laws. So the majority writes its own set of rules, limiting Section 2 from multiple directions. Wherever it can, the majority gives a cramped reading to broad language. And then it uses that reading to uphold two election laws from Arizona that discriminate against minority voters. I could say — and will in the following pages—that this is not how the Court is supposed to interpret and apply statutes. But that ordinary critique woefully undersells the problem. What is tragic here is that the Court has (yet again) rewritten—in order to weaken—a statute that stands as a monument to America's greatness, and protects against its basest impulses. What is tragic is that the Court has damaged a statute designed to bring about "the end of discrimination in voting." I respectfully dissent.

I

The Voting Rights Act of 1965 is an extraordinary law. Rarely has a statute required so much sacrifice to ensure its passage. Never has a statute done more to advance the Nation's highest ideals. And few laws are more vital in the current moment. Yet in the last decade, this Court has treated no statute worse. To take the measure of today's harm, a look to the Act's past must come first. The idea is not to recount, as the majority hurriedly does, some bygone era of voting discrimination. It is instead to describe the electoral practices that the Act targets—and to show the high stakes of the present controversy.

A

Democratic ideals in America got off to a glorious start; democratic practice not so much. The Declaration of Independence made an awe-inspiring promise: to institute a government "deriving [its] just powers from the consent of the governed." But for most of the Nation's first century, that pledge ran to white men only. The earliest state election laws excluded from the franchise African Americans, Native Americans, women, and those without property. In 1855, on the precipice of the Civil War, only five States permitted African Americans to vote. And at the federal level, our Court's most deplorable holding made sure that no black people could enter the voting booth. See *Dred Scott v. Sandford*, 19 How. 393 (1857).

But the "American ideal of political equality . . . could not forever tolerate the limitation of the right to vote" to whites only. *Mobile v. Bolden* (Marshall, J., dissenting). And a civil war, dedicated to ensuring "government of the people, by the people, for the people," brought constitutional change. In 1870, after a hard-fought battle over ratification, the Fifteenth Amendment carried the Nation closer to its founding aspirations. "The right of citizens of the United States to vote shall not be denied or abridged by the United States or by any State on account of race, color, or previous condition of servitude." Those words promised to enfranchise millions of black citizens who only a decade earlier had been slaves. Frederick Douglass held that the Amendment "means that we are placed upon an equal footing with all other men"—that with the vote, "liberty is to be the right of all."

Momentous as the Fifteenth Amendment was, celebration of its achievements soon proved premature. The Amendment's guarantees "quickly became dead letters in much of the country." . . . Many States, especially in the South, suppressed the black vote through a dizzying array of methods: literacy tests, poll taxes, registration requirements, and property qualifications. Most of those laws, though facially neutral, gave enough discretion to election officials to prevent significant effects on poor or uneducated whites. . . .

"After a century's failure to fulfill the promise" of the Fifteenth Amendment, "passage of the VRA finally led to signal improvement." *Shelby County* (Ginsburg, J., dissenting). In the five years after the statute's passage, almost as many African Americans registered to vote in six Southern States as in the entire century before 1965. The crudest attempts to block voting access, like literacy tests and poll taxes, disappeared. Legislatures often replaced those vote denial schemes with new measures — mostly to do with districting — designed to dilute the impact of minority votes. But the Voting Rights Act, operating for decades at full strength, stopped many of those measures too. As a famed dissent assessed the situation about a half-century after the statute's enactment: The Voting Rights Act had become "one of the most consequential, efficacious, and amply justified exercises of federal legislative power in our Nation's history." *Shelby County* (Ginsburg, J., dissenting).

B

Yet efforts to suppress the minority vote continue. No one would know this from reading the majority opinion. It hails the "good news" that legislative efforts had mostly shifted by the 1980s from vote denial to vote dilution. And then it moves on to other matters, as though the Voting Rights Act no longer has a problem to address — as though once literacy tests and poll taxes disappeared, so too did efforts to curb minority voting. But as this Court recognized about a decade ago, "racial discrimination and racially polarized voting are not ancient history." *Bartlett v. Strickland*, 556 U.S. 1, 25 (2009). Indeed, the problem of voting discrimination has become worse since that time — in part because of what this Court did in *Shelby County*. Weaken the Voting Rights Act, and predictable consequences follow: yet a further generation of voter suppression laws.

Much of the Voting Rights Act's success lay in its capacity to meet ever-new forms of discrimination. [Justice Kagan went on to discuss Section 5 of the VRA and the decision in *Shelby County*, which relieved covered jurisdictions of the requirement that they preclear voting changes with the federal government.]

The rashness of the act soon became evident. Once Section 5's strictures came off, States and localities put in place new restrictive voting laws, with foreseeably adverse effects on minority voters. On the very day *Shelby County* issued, Texas announced that it would implement a strict voter-identification requirement that had failed to clear Section 5. Other States — Alabama, Virginia, Mississippi — fell like dominoes, adopting measures similarly vulnerable to preclearance review. The North Carolina Legislature, starting work the day after *Shelby County*, enacted a sweeping election bill eliminating same-day registration, forbidding out-of-precinct voting, and reducing early voting, including souls-to-the-polls Sundays. . . .

And that was just the first wave of post-*Shelby County* laws. In recent months, State after State has taken up or enacted legislation erecting new barriers to voting.

Those laws shorten the time polls are open, both on Election Day and before. They impose new prerequisites to voting by mail, and shorten the windows to apply for and return mail ballots. They make it harder to register to vote, and easier to purge voters from the rolls. Two laws even ban handing out food or water to voters standing in line. Some of those restrictions may be lawful under the Voting Rights Act. But chances are that some have the kind of impact the Act was designed to prevent—that they make the political process less open to minority voters than to others.

So the Court decides this Voting Rights Act case at a perilous moment for the Nation's commitment to equal citizenship. It decides this case in an era of voting-rights retrenchment—when too many States and localities are restricting access to voting in ways that will predictably deprive members of minority groups of equal access to the ballot box. . . . [A]fter *Shelby County*, the vitality of Section 2—a "permanent, nationwide ban on racial discrimination in voting"—matters more than ever. For after *Shelby County*, Section 2 is what voters have left.

II

Section 2, as drafted, is well-equipped to meet the challenge. Congress meant to eliminate all "discriminatory election systems or practices which operate, designedly or otherwise, to minimize or cancel out the voting strength and political effectiveness of minority groups." S. Rep. No. 97–417, p. 28 (1982) (S. Rep.). And that broad intent is manifest in the provision's broad text. As always, this Court's task is to read that language as Congress wrote it—to give the section all the scope and potency Congress drafted it to have. So I start by showing how Section 2's text requires courts to eradicate voting practices that make it harder for members of some races than of others to cast a vote, unless such a practice is necessary to support a strong state interest. I then show how far from that text the majority strays. Its analysis permits exactly the kind of vote suppression that Section 2, by its terms, rules out of bounds.

A

Section 2, as relevant here, has two interlocking parts. [Justice Kagan quoted the language of subsections (a) and (b).]

Those provisions have a great many words, and I address them further below. But their essential import is plain: Courts are to strike down voting rules that contribute to a racial disparity in the opportunity to vote, taking all the relevant circumstances into account.

The first thing to note about Section 2 is how far its prohibitory language sweeps. The provision bars any "voting qualification," any "prerequisite to voting," or any "standard, practice, or procedure" that "results in a denial or abridgement of the right" to "vote on account of race." The overlapping list of covered state actions makes clear that Section 2 extends to every kind of voting or election rule. . . . So, for example, the provision "covers all manner of registration requirements, the practices surrounding registration," the "locations of polling places, the times polls are open, the use of paper ballots as opposed to voting machines, and other similar aspects of the voting process that might be manipulated to deny any citizen the right to cast a ballot and have it properly counted." All those rules and more come within the statute—so long as they result in a race-based "denial or abridgement" of the voting right....

The "results in" language, connecting the covered voting rules to the prohibited voting abridgement, tells courts that they are to focus on the law's effects. Rather than hinge liability on state officials' motives, Congress made it ride on their actions' consequences.... Congress ... saw an intent test as imposing "an inordinately difficult burden for plaintiffs." Even if state actors had purposefully discriminated, they would likely be "ab[le] to offer a non-racial rationalization," supported by "a false trail" of "official resolutions" and "other legislative history eschewing any racial motive." So only a results-focused statute could prevent States from finding ways to abridge minority citizens' voting rights.

But when to conclude—looking to effects, not purposes—that a denial or abridgment has occurred? Again, answering that question is subsection (b)'s function. It teaches that a violation is established when, "based on the totality of circumstances," a State's electoral system is "not equally open" to members of a racial group. And then the subsection tells us what that means. A system is not equally open if members of one race have "less opportunity" than others to cast votes, to participate in politics, or to elect representatives. The key demand, then, is for equal political opportunity across races.

That equal "opportunity" is absent when a law or practice makes it harder for members of one racial group, than for others, to cast ballots. When Congress amended Section 2, the word "opportunity" meant what it also does today: "a favorable or advantageous combination of circumstances" for some action. See American Heritage Dictionary. In using that word, Congress made clear that the Voting Rights Act does not demand equal outcomes. If members of different races have the same opportunity to vote, but go to the ballot box at different rates, then so be it—that is their preference, and Section 2 has nothing to say. But if a law produces different voting opportunities across races—if it establishes rules and conditions of political participation that are less favorable (or advantageous) for one racial group than for others—then Section 2 kicks in. It applies, in short, whenever the law makes it harder for citizens of one race than of others to cast a vote.

And that is so even if (as is usually true) the law does not single out any race, but instead is facially neutral.... Those laws, Congress thought, would violate Section 2, though they were not facially discriminatory, because they gave voters of different races unequal access to the political process.

Congress also made plain, in calling for a totality-of-circumstances inquiry, that equal voting opportunity is a function of both law and background conditions—in other words, that a voting rule's validity depends on how the rule operates in conjunction with facts on the ground. . . . [S]ometimes government officials enact facially neutral laws that leverage—and become discriminatory by dint of—pre-existing social and economic conditions. The classic historical cases are literacy tests and poll taxes. A more modern example is . . . limited registration hours. Congress knew how those laws worked: It saw that "inferior education, poor employment opportunities, and low incomes"—all conditions often correlated with race—could turn even an ordinary-seeming election rule into an effective barrier to minority voting in certain circumstances. . . . "The essence of a §2 claim," we have said, is that an election law "interacts with social and historical conditions" in a particular place to cause race-based inequality in voting opportunity. *Gingles* (majority opinion). That interaction is what the totality inquiry is mostly designed to discover.

At the same time, the totality inquiry enables courts to take into account strong state interests supporting an election rule. . . . Among the "balance of considerations" a court is to weigh is a State's need for the challenged policy. *Houston Lawyers' Assn. v. Attorney General of Tex.*, 501 U.S. 419, 427 (1991). But in making that assessment of state interests, a court must keep in mind—just as Congress did—the ease of "offer[ing] a non-racial rationalization" for even blatantly discriminatory laws. S. Rep., at 37. State interests do not get accepted on faith. And even a genuine and strong interest will not suffice if a plaintiff can prove that it can be accomplished in a less discriminatory way. As we have put the point before: When a less racially biased law would not "significantly impair[] the State's interest," the discriminatory election rule must fall. *Houston Lawyers' Assn.*

So the text of Section 2, as applied in our precedents, tells us the following, every part of which speaks to the ambition of Congress's action. Section 2 applies to any voting rule, of any kind. The provision prohibits not just the denial but also the abridgment of a citizen's voting rights on account of race. The inquiry is focused on effects: It asks not about why state officials enacted a rule, but about whether that rule results in racial discrimination. The discrimination that is of concern is inequality of voting opportunity. That kind of discrimination can arise from facially neutral (not just targeted) rules. There is a Section 2 problem when an election rule, operating against the backdrop of historical, social, and economic conditions, makes it harder for minority citizens than for others to cast ballots. And strong state interests may save an otherwise discriminatory rule, but only if that rule is needed to achieve them—that is, only if a less discriminatory rule will not attain the State's goal.

That is a lot of law to apply in a Section 2 case. Real law—the kind created by Congress. . . . Section 2 was indeed meant to do something important—crucial to the operation of our democracy. The provision tells courts—however "radical" the majority might find the idea—to eliminate facially neutral (as well as targeted) electoral rules that unnecessarily create inequalities of access to the political process. That is the very project of the statute, as conceived and as written—and now as damaged by this Court.

B

The majority's opinion mostly inhabits a law-free zone. It congratulates itself in advance for giving Section 2's text "careful consideration." And then it leaves that language almost wholly behind. . . . So too the majority barely mentions this Court's precedents construing Section 2's text. On both those counts, you can see why. As just described, Section 2's language is broad. To read it fairly, then, is to read it broadly. And to read it broadly is to do much that the majority is determined to avoid. . . . It only grudgingly accepts — and then apparently forgets — that the provision applies to facially neutral laws with discriminatory consequences. And it hints that as long as a voting system is sufficiently "open," it need not be equally so. In sum, the majority skates over the strong words Congress drafted to accomplish its equally strong purpose: ensuring that minority citizens can access the electoral system as easily as whites.

The majority instead founds its decision on a list of mostly made-up factors, at odds with Section 2 itself. To excuse this unusual free-form exercise, the majority notes that Section 2 authorizes courts to conduct a "totality of circumstances" analysis. But as described above, Congress mainly added that language so that Section 2 could protect against "the demonstrated ingenuity of state and local governments in hobbling minority voting power." *De Grandy*. The totality inquiry requires courts to explore how ordinary-seeming laws can interact with local conditions — economic, social, historical — to produce race-based voting inequalities. That inquiry hardly gives a court the license to devise whatever limitations on Section 2's reach it would have liked Congress to enact. But that is the license the majority takes. The "important circumstances" it invents all cut in one direction — toward limiting liability for race-based voting inequalities. (Indeed, the majority gratuitously dismisses several factors that point the opposite way.) Think of the majority's list as a set of extra-textual restrictions on Section 2 — methods of counteracting the law Congress actually drafted to achieve the purposes *Congress* thought "important." The list — not a test, the majority hastens to assure us, with delusions of modesty — stacks the deck against minority citizens' voting rights. Never mind that Congress drafted a statute to protect those rights — to prohibit any number of schemes the majority's non-test test makes it possible to save. . . .

The majority objects to an excessive "transfer of the authority to set voting rules from the States to the federal courts." It even sees that transfer as "[un]democratic." But maybe the majority should pay more attention to the "historical background" that it insists "does not tell us how to decide this case." That history makes clear the incongruity, in interpreting this statute, of the majority's paean to state authority — and conversely, its denigration of federal responsibility for ensuring non-discriminatory voting rules. The Voting Rights Act was meant to replace state and local election rules that needlessly make voting harder for members of one race than for others. The text of the Act perfectly reflects that objective. The "democratic" principle it upholds is not one of States' rights as against federal courts. The democratic principle it upholds is the right of every American, of every race, to have equal access to the ballot box. The majority today undermines that principle as it refuses to apply the terms of the statute. By declaring some racially discriminatory burdens inconsequential, and by refusing to subject asserted state interests to serious means-end scrutiny, the majority enables voting discrimination.

III

Just look at Arizona. Two of that State's policies disproportionately affect minority citizens' opportunity to vote. The first — the out-of-precinct policy — results in Hispanic and African American voters' ballots being thrown out at a statistically higher rate than those of whites. And whatever the majority might say about the ordinariness of such a rule, Arizona applies it in extra-ordinary fashion: Arizona is *the* national outlier in dealing with out-of-precinct votes, with the next-worst offender nowhere in sight. The second rule — the ballot-collection ban — makes voting meaningfully more difficult for Native American citizens than for others. And nothing about how that ban is applied is "usual" either — this time because of how many of the State's Native American citizens need to travel long distances to use the mail. Both policies violate Section 2, on a straightforward application of its text. Considering the "totality of circumstances," both "result in" members of some races having "less opportunity than other members of the electorate to participate in the political process and to elect a representative of their choice." § 10301(b). The majority reaches the opposite conclusion because it closes its eyes to the facts on the ground.[10]

A

Arizona's out-of-precinct policy requires discarding any Election Day ballot cast elsewhere than in a voter's assigned precinct. Under the policy, officials throw out every choice in every race — including national or statewide races (*e.g.*, for President or Governor) that appear identically on every precinct's ballot. The question is whether that policy unequally affects minority citizens' opportunity to cast a vote.

Although the majority portrays Arizona's use of the rule as "unremarkable," the State is in fact a national aberration when it comes to discarding out-of- precinct ballots. In 2012, about 35,000 ballots across the country were thrown out because they were cast at the wrong precinct. Nearly one in three of those discarded votes — 10,979 — was cast in Arizona. As the Court of Appeals concluded, and the chart below indicates, Arizona threw away ballots in that year at 11 times the rate of the second-place discarder (Washington State). Somehow the majority labels that difference "marginal[]," but it is anything but. . . . [A]cross the five elections at issue in this litigation (2008–2016), Arizona threw away far more out-of-precinct votes — almost 40,000 — than did any other State in the country.

---

10. Because I would affirm the Court of Appeals' holding that the effects of these policies violate Section 2, I need not pass on that court's alternative holding that the laws were enacted with discriminatory intent.

Votes in such numbers can matter—enough for Section 2 to apply. The majority obliquely suggests not, comparing the smallish number of thrown-out votes (minority and non-minority alike) to the far larger number of votes cast and counted. But elections are often fought and won at the margins—certainly in Arizona. Consider the number of votes separating the two presidential candidates in the most recent election: 10,457. That is fewer votes than Arizona discarded under the out-of-precinct policy in two of the prior three presidential elections. . . . [T]he out-of-precinct policy—which discards thousands upon thousands of ballots in every election—affects more than sufficient votes to implicate Section 2's guarantee of equal electoral opportunity.

And the out-of-precinct policy operates unequally: Ballots cast by minorities are more likely to be discarded. In 2016, Hispanics, African Americans, and Native Americans were about twice as likely—or said another way, 100% more likely—to have their ballots discarded than whites. . . . The record does not contain statewide figures for 2012. But in Maricopa and Pima Counties, the percentages were about the same as in 2016. Assessing those disparities, the plaintiffs' expert found, and the District Court accepted, that the discriminatory impact of the out-of-precinct policy was statistically significant—meaning, again, that it was highly unlikely to occur by chance. . . .

Facts also undermine the State's asserted interests, which the majority hangs its hat on. A government interest, as even the majority recognizes, is "merely one factor to be considered" in Section 2's totality analysis. Here, the State contends that it needs the out-of-precinct policy to support a precinct-based voting system. But 20 other States combine precinct-based systems with mechanisms for partially counting out-of-precinct ballots (that is, counting the votes for offices like President or Governor). And the District Court found that it would be "administratively feasible" for Arizona to join that group. Arizona—echoed by the majority—objects that adopting a partial-counting approach would decrease compliance with the vote-in-your-precinct rule (by reducing the penalty for a voter's going elsewhere). But there is more than a little paradox in that response. We know from the extraordinary number of ballots Arizona discards that its current system fails utterly to "induce[] compliance." Presumably, that is because the system—most notably, its placement and shifting of polling places—sows an unparalleled level of voter confusion. A State that makes compliance with an election rule so unusually hard is in no position to claim that its interest in "induc[ing] compliance" outweighs the need to remedy the race-based discrimination that rule has caused.

B

Arizona's law mostly banning third-party ballot collection also results in a significant race-based disparity in voting opportunities. The problem with that law again lies in facts nearly unique to Arizona—here, the presence of rural Native American communities that lack ready access to mail service. Given that circumstance, the Arizona statute discriminates in just the way Section 2 proscribes. The majority once more comes to a different conclusion only by ignoring the local conditions with which Arizona's law interacts.

The critical facts for evaluating the ballot-collection rule have to do with mail service. Most Arizonans vote by mail. But many rural Native American voters lack access to mail service, to a degree hard for most of us to fathom. Only 18% of Native voters in rural counties receive home mail delivery, compared to 86% of white voters living in those counties. And for many or most, there is no nearby post office. Native Americans in rural Arizona "often must travel 45 minutes to 2 hours just to get to a mailbox." And between a quarter to a half of households in these Native communities do not have a car. So getting ballots by mail and sending them back poses a serious challenge for Arizona's rural Native Americans.

For that reason, an unusually high rate of Native Americans used to "return their early ballots with the assistance of third parties." As the District Court found: "[F]or many Native Americans living in rural locations," voting "is an activity that requires the active assistance of friends and neighbors." So in some Native communities, third-party collection of ballots—mostly by fellow clan members—became "standard practice." And stopping it, as one tribal election official testified, "would be a huge devastation."

Arizona has always regulated these activities to prevent fraud. State law makes it a felony offense for a ballot collector to fail to deliver a ballot. It is also a felony for a ballot collector to tamper with a ballot in any manner. And as the District Court found, "tamper evident envelopes and a rigorous voter signature verification procedure" protect against any such attempts. For those reasons and others, no fraud involving ballot collection has ever come to light in the State....

Put all of that together, and Arizona's ballot-collection ban violates Section 2. The ban interacts with conditions on the ground—most crucially, disparate access to mail service—to create unequal voting opportunities for Native Americans. Recall that only 18% of rural Native Americans in the State have home delivery; that travel times of an hour or more to the nearest post office are common; that many members of the community do not have cars. Given those facts, the law prevents many Native Americans from making effective use of one of the principal means of voting in Arizona. What is an inconsequential burden for others is for these citizens a severe hardship. And the State has shown no need for the law to go so far. Arizona, as noted above, already has statutes in place to deter fraudulent collection practices. Those laws give every sign of working. Arizona has not offered any evidence of fraud in ballot collection, or even an account of a harm threatening to happen. And anyway, Arizona did not have to entirely forego a ballot-collection restriction to comply with Section 2. It could, for example, have added an exception to the statute for Native clan or kinship ties, to accommodate the special, "intensely local" situation of the rural Native American community. *Gingles*. That Arizona did not do so shows, at best, selective indifference to the voting opportunities of its Native American citizens.

The majority's opinion fails to acknowledge any of these facts.... Like the rest of today's opinion, the majority's treatment of the collection ban thus flouts what Section 2 commands: the eradication of election rules resulting in unequal opportunities for minority voters.

IV

Congress enacted the Voting Rights Act to address a deep fault of our democracy—the historical and continuing attempt to withhold from a race of citizens their fair share of influence on the political process. For a century, African Americans had struggled and sacrificed to wrest their voting rights from a resistant Nation. The statute they and their allies at long last attained made a promise to all Americans. From then on, Congress demanded, the political process would be equally open to every citizen, regardless of race....

This Court has no right to remake Section 2. Maybe some think that vote suppression is a relic of history—and so the need for a potent Section 2 has come and gone. Cf. *Shelby County* ("[T]hings have changed dramatically"). But Congress gets to make that call. Because it has not done so, this Court's duty is to apply the law as it is written. The law that confronted one of this country's most enduring wrongs; pledged to give every American, of every race, an equal chance to participate in our democracy; and now stands as the crucial tool to achieve that goal. That law, of all laws, deserves the sweep and power Congress gave it. That law, of all laws, should not be diminished by this Court.

Notes and Questions

1. *Statutory Text and Legislative History.* As noted above, there are two ways of showing a violation of Section 2 of the VRA. One is by showing that the challenged law or practice has a discriminatory *result.* The other is by showing that it was motivated by racially discriminatory *purpose.* The majority concludes that plaintiffs had shown neither a discriminatory result nor a discriminatory purpose. The dissent concludes that there was a discriminatory result, and therefore finds it unnecessary to address the question of discriminatory purpose.

Starting with the results prong, both sides claim to rely on the text of Section 2, using dictionaries to bolster their arguments. Does the text provide meaningful guidance on how Section 2 should be interpreted? See Nicholas Stephanopoulos, *The Supreme Court Showcased Its 'Textualist' Double Standard on Voting Rights*, Washington Post, July 1, 2021. What about the legislative history of the 1982 amendments to Section 2, particularly the Senate Report upon which the dissent relies? The dissent also relies on the history preceding the enactment of the VRA, including the shameful history of suppressing the votes of Black Americans after the enactment of the Fifteenth Amendment. Of what relevance is this history to the interpretation of the statute?

2. *The Standard for Vote Denial Claims.* Part II of Justice Alito's opinion for the majority states that it "decline[s] in these cases to announce a test to govern all VRA

§ 2 claims involving rules . . . that specify the time, place, or manner for casting ballots." But the majority does seem to announce a test in Part III.C.1 of its opinion, setting forth five factors that courts should consider in determining whether there is a racially discriminatory result. Where do these factors come from? The dissent characterizes the majority of "inhabit[ing] a law-free zone." The majority, for its part, accuses the dissent of adopting a "radical" interpretation of Section 2. Are either of these rather harsh criticisms warranted?

Prior to the Court's decision in *Brnovich*, some lower courts had applied a two-part test for determining whether Section 2's results standard had been violated, looking to whether (1) there was a disparate impact on racial minorities, and (2) whether the challenged practice interacts with social and historical conditions to cause that disparate impact. Is that test more faithful to the text and purpose of Section 2 than the one the majority adopts? For pre-*Brnovich* academic commentary on the standard that should govern Section 2 vote denial cases, see Nicholas O. Stephanopoulos, *Disparate Impact, Unified Law*, 128 Yale Law Journal 1566 (2019); Joshua S. Sellers, *Election Law and White Identity Politics*, 87 Fordham Law Review 1515, 1546–51 (2019); Jamelia N. Morgan, *Disparate Impact and Voting Rights: How Objections to Impact-Based Claims Prevent Plaintiffs from Prevailing in Cases Challenging New Forms of Disenfranchisement*, 9 Alabama Civil Rights & Civil Liberties Law Review 93 (2018); Pamela S. Karlan, *Turnout, Tenuousness, and Getting Results in Section 2 Vote Denial Claims*, 77 Ohio State Law Journal 763 (2016); Daniel P. Tokaji, *Applying Section 2 to the New Vote Denial*, 50 Harvard Civil Rights—Civil Liberties Law Review 439 (2015); Janai Nelson, *The Causal Context of Disparate Vote Denial*, 54 Boston College Law Review 579 (2013); and Christopher Elmendorf, *Making Sense of Section 2: Of Biased Votes, Unconstitutional Elections, and Common Law Statutes*, 160 University of Pennsylvania Law Review 377 (2012).

Democrats in Congress have already introduced legislation that would overrule *Brnovich*'s interpretation of Section 2. One provision of the John Lewis Voting Rights Advancement Act of 2021 (JLVRAA) (discussed in Chapter 5, Note 4 following *Shelby County v. Holder*) would adopt a new standard for vote denial claims. Specifically, it would replace the five-factor standard with a two-prong test like that which several lower courts had adopted prior to *Brnovich*. Do you favor such a standard? Are there reasons to be concerned about its constitutionality? For arguments in favor of adding a third prong that considers the state's interests, partly to allay constitutional concerns, see Nicholas Stephanopoulos, *Observations about the JLVRAA*, Election Law Blog, Aug. 18, 2021, https://perma.cc/4X7T-QAWM and Tokaji, *Applying Section 2 to the New Vote Denial*, *supra*, at 473-74, 484-89.

3. *Future Vote Denial Claims.* Turning to the specifics of Arizona's challenged practices, the majority upholds them partly because it finds that they imposed a minimal burden on voters. But isn't the central question whether they imposed racial disparities, rather than the magnitude of the burden imposed? Does the majority conflate disparities and burdens? See Nicholas Stephanopoulos, Brnovich *and the*

Conflation of Disparities and Burdens, Election Law Blog, July 6, 2021, https://perma.cc/JG47-2MK2.

How difficult will *Brnovich* make it for future plaintiffs to succeed in Section 2 vote denial claims? Professor Hasen argues:

> Thanks to *Brnovich*, a state can now assert an interest in preventing fraud to justify a law without proving that fraud is actually a serious risk, but at the same time, minority voters have a high burden: They must show that the state has imposed more than the "usual burdens of voting."

Richard L. Hasen, *The Supreme Court Is Putting Democracy at Risk*, N.Y. Times, July 1, 2021.

Consider too the majority's emphasis on whether the challenged practice "departs from what was standard practice when § 2 was amended in 1982." Given that absentee and early voting laws were much stricter in 1982 than they are today, can challenges to any new restrictions on these methods of voting succeed? What about challenges to strict voter ID laws, which were not common in 1982? For differing perspectives on this question, see Richard L. Hasen, *The Supreme Court's Latest Voting Rights Opinion Is Even Worse Than It Seems*, Slate, July 8, 2021 (arguing that the majority offers "a new and impossible test for plaintiffs to meet to show a Section 2 vote denial claim"), and Nicholas Stephanopoulos, *Strong and Weak Claims After* Brnovich, Election Law Blog, July 1, 2021, https://perma.cc/6TS8-9A8G ("challenges to relatively novel restrictions," such as voter ID laws, "will be more likely to prevail" than challenges to practices that were common in 1982).

4. *Racially Discriminatory Purpose.* After dispensing with plaintiffs' results-based argument, Justice Alito's majority opinion concludes that they had also failed to show racially discriminatory *purpose*. According to the majority, partisan motives aren't the same as racial ones. Does that argument hold up in an era where there is a strong correlation between race and party affiliation? Is it possible to disentangle racial motivations from partisan ones? For discussion of this problem, see Richard L. Hasen, *Race or Party, Race as Party, or Party All the Time: Three Uneasy Approaches to Conjoined Polarization in Redistricting and Voting Cases*, 59 William & Mary Law Review 1837 (2018), and Bruce E. Cain and Emily R. Zhang, *Blurred Lines: Conjoined Polarization and Voting Rights*, 77 Ohio State Law Journal 867 (2016).

Nowadays, it is unusual for courts to find that a voting law was enacted with racially discriminatory purpose, but the Fourth Circuit found that this showing had been made in a pre-*Brnovich* case, *North Carolina State Conference of the NAACP v. McCrory*, 831 F.3d 204 (4th Cir. 2017), cert. denied, 137 S. Ct. 1399 (2017). Shortly after the Supreme Court's decision in *Shelby County,* North Carolina adopted an omnibus voting law that included a voter ID requirement, limits on early voting, the elimination of same-day registration, and restrictions on the counting of provisional ballots. Finding that these restrictions "target[ed] African Americans with almost surgical precision," the Fourth Circuit held that they were adopted with discriminatory intent. *Id.* at 214. Expert testimony in that case showed that African

American race was a better predictor of whether someone would vote Democratic than being registered as a Democrat. *Id.* at 225. The Fourth Circuit issued its decision before *Brnovich*. Would this evidence be enough to show an impermissible discriminatory purpose after *Brnovich*?

A few days before the decision in *Brnovich*, the U.S. Department of Justice brought a lawsuit challenging a new law in Georgia. The complaint alleges that the Georgia law was adopted with the purpose of making it more difficult for African Americans to vote. See U.S. Department of Justice, *Justice Department Files Lawsuit Against the State of Georgia to Stop Racially Discriminatory Provisions of New Voting Law*, June 25, 2021, https://perma.cc/WGZ5-9QW9. What are the chances of this lawsuit succeeding after *Brnovich*?

For more on voting rights litigators' shift toward discriminatory intent claims, see Danielle Lang and J. Gerald Hebert, *A Post-*Shelby *Strategy: Exposing Discriminatory Intent in Voting Rights Litigation*, 127 Yale Law Journal Forum 779 (2018). For a discussion of the difficulties and limitations inherent in an approach focused on discriminatory intent, see Franita Tolson, *Election Law "Federalism" and the Limits of the Antidiscrimination Framework*, 59 William & Mary Law Review 2211 (2018).

5. *Ballot Security Programs.* Another area in which concerns of race discrimination have arisen is with so-called "ballot security" programs. In 1981, the Democratic National Committee filed a complaint against the Republican National Committee, alleging that the latter sent out mailings to predominantly minority precincts and created a list of voters whose mail was returned as undeliverable, so that those voters could be challenged at the polls. Critics sometimes refer to this practice as "caging." That lawsuit was settled through a nationwide consent decree restricting ballot security programs, which the district court declined to lift. *Democratic National Committee v. Republican National Committee*, 671 F. Supp. 2d 575 (D.N.J. 2009). The district court rejected the Republican National Committee's argument that changed factual circumstances—including an increased risk of voter fraud—warranted dissolution of the consent decree. After reviewing "mountains of documentary evidence" from both sides, the court concluded that "[v]oter intimidation presents an ongoing threat to the participation of minority individuals in the political process, and continues to pose a far greater danger to the integrity of the process than the type of vote fraud the RNC is prevented from addressing by the Decree." The Third Circuit affirmed, rejecting the RNC's argument that the increase in minority registration and turnout showed that voter suppression was no longer a problem and noting that the "increase in minority voter registration and voter turnout could be evidence that the Decree is necessary and effective." 673 F.3d 192, 208–09 (3d Cir. 2012).

The *DNC v. RNC* consent decree yet again became an issue during the 2016 presidential election. The Democratic Party claimed that the RNC was colluding with the Trump campaign to engage in prohibited ballot security efforts. The district court denied the DNC's motion for sanctions and its request to extend the consent decree. *Democratic National Committee v. Republican National Committee*, 2016

WL 6584915 (D.N.J. 2016). Then in 2018, the court terminated the consent decree against Republican ballot security measures. The Third Circuit affirmed. *Democratic Nat'l Comm. v. Republican Nat'l Comm.*, __ Fed. Appx. ___, 2019 WL 117555 (3d Cir. Jan. 7, 2019).

After the 2020 election, there are heightened worries that "election integrity" programs will be used to make it more difficult for some people, especially racial minorities, to vote. Did the court pull the plug on the *DNC v. RNC* consent decree too soon?

6. *A Voter Impact Statement.* One commentator argues that existing laws are insufficient to protect racial minorities and other vulnerable voters, suggesting that jurisdictions be required to provide a "Voter Impact Statement" (analogous to an Environmental Impact Statement) before election administration rules can take effect. Gilda R. Daniels, *A Vote Delayed Is a Vote Denied: A Preemptive Approach to Eliminating Election Administration That Disenfranchises Unwanted Voters,* 47 University of Louisville Law Review 57 (2008). Is it a good idea to require a Voter Impact Statement? Would it discourage states from adopting laws that have the purpose or effect of discouraging voting by certain groups?

III. Law and Turnout

To what extent do laws regulating election administration affect voter turnout? That question underlies many of the cases discussed in Parts I and II of this chapter. There is often sharp disagreement over whether and to what extent a rule or practice will affect participation, as well as the extent to which it serves other values like the orderly and secure administration of elections. In court, these battles will often come down to a battle of the experts, with each side presenting its evidence on the impact that the challenged rule or practice will have.

Litigation is one means by which to try to improve access to the ballot. Legislation is another. A number of federal and state statutes are designed to enhance access and thus to increase the number of people who will exercise the right to vote. In this Part, we examine three federal laws that are designed, at least in part, to expand access: (1) the language access provisions of the Voting Rights Act, (2) the National Voter Registration Act of 1993 (NVRA), and (3) the Help America Vote Act of 2002 (HAVA). We then survey some of the empirical research on the impact that these and other election laws have on turnout, considering reforms that have been proposed or that might be adopted to improve access.

A. Language Assistance

In 1975, Congress amended the Voting Rights Act to mandate that certain jurisdictions provide assistance to non-English proficient voters. The impetus for these amendments was Congress' finding of relatively low registration and participation rates among certain ethnic minority groups. For example, a congressional committee found that only 44.4 percent of Latino citizens, compared to 73.4 percent of other citizens, were registered to vote in 1972. S. Rep. No. 94-295, *reprinted in* 1975 U.S.C.C.A.N 774 (1975). Congress also found educational inequalities affecting Latino, Asian American, and American Indian groups that limited access to the electoral process:

> Through the use of various practices and procedures, citizens of language minorities have been effectively excluded from participation in the electoral process. Among other factors, the denial of the right to vote of such minority group citizens is ordinarily directly related to the unequal educational opportunities afforded them, resulting in high illiteracy and low voting participation.

52 U.S.C. § 10503(a). The language assistance provisions of the VRA are temporary, but have been extended three times since their enactment, in 1982, 1992 and again in 2006.

The key provisions of the VRA pertaining to language assistance are Sections 4(f)(4) and Section 203. Section 4(f)(4) expanded the VRA's coverage formula, to include jurisdictions with low registration and participation rates, in which more than 5 percent are of a language-minority group and in which English-only election materials had been provided in the 1972 election. Covered jurisdictions are required to provide election materials in the language of the relevant minority group, and to comply with the other VRA requirements applicable to covered jurisdictions, including preclearance of electoral changes. Section 203 applies to jurisdictions with high concentrations of non-English proficient voters. Under the current threshold, a jurisdiction is required to comply with the requirements of Section 203 if more than 5 percent of the voting-age population or more than 10,000 citizens of voting age are members of a language minority group and are of limited English proficiency.

Section 203 jurisdictions, like those covered by Section 4(f)(4), are required to provide all election materials in the languages of the relevant language minority groups. That includes registration forms, instructions, oral assistance, and ballots. For more detailed descriptions of the requirements of Sections 4(f)(4) and 203, see James Thomas Tucker, *Enfranchising Language Minority Citizens: The Bilingual Election Provisions of the Voting Rights Act*, 10 New York University Journal of Legislation & Public Policy 195 (2006/2007), and Jocelyn Friedrichs Benson, *Su Voto Es Su Voz: Incorporating Voters of Limited English Proficiency into American Democracy*, 48 Boston College Law Review 251 (2007).

Are the language assistance provisions of the VRA justified? With the significant exception of Puerto Ricans, nearly all native-born American citizens grow up learning to speak and read English. Immigrants are expected to learn some English as a condition of naturalization. Putting aside Puerto Ricans, are voters unable to understand English entitled to foreign language assistance in registering and voting? One commentator analogizes language assistance requirements to laws like the Americans with Disabilities Act, which require that people with disabilities be accommodated:

> The accommodation of group differences is already an established principle that operates in a number of areas of anti-discrimination law, particularly in federal laws requiring "reasonable accommodations" to address religious discrimination and disability discrimination in the workplace. The voter who is unable to understand an English-only ballot, but who could exercise a meaningful vote if the election materials were available in another language, is not unlike the disabled individual who can perform the essential functions of a job if office practices or equipment are modified, or who can cast a vote if provided access to polling sites and offered appropriate voting technologies to accommodate the disability.
>
> Accommodation laws function as a form of anti-discrimination enforcement distinct from traditional civil rights laws because they embody a "difference" model rather than the more common "sameness" model that prohibits differentiation on the basis of a group characteristic or trait. A difference model "assumes that individuals who possess the quality or trait at issue are different in a relevant respect from individuals who don't and that "treating them similarly can itself become a form of oppression." Accommodations are also bounded by cost-benefit considerations affecting both the individual requiring an accommodation and the entity providing the accommodation. Once a group-based difference is recognized, there is a legal duty to provide an appropriate accommodation, but only up to the point that the provider faces no undue hardship.

Angelo Ancheta, *Language Assistance and Local Voting Rights Law*, 44 Indiana Law Review 161 (2010). Do you agree that language accommodation is analogous to disability accommodation?

The efficacy of the VRA's language assistance provisions remains the subject of considerable debate. Supporters of the VRA's language assistance provisions argue that they have significantly increased registration and participation rates among Latino, Asian American, and Native American voters. A GAO report found few quantitative data on the utility of the VRA's language assistance requirements, though it noted that most election officials who were asked supported bilingual voting assistance. Government Accountability Office, *Bilingual Voting Assistance: Selected Jurisdictions' Strategies for Identifying Needs and Providing Assistance* (2008). Another study found that language assistance is widely used where it is available, but is frequently inadequate. James Thomas Tucker & Rodolfo Espino, *Government Effectiveness and Efficiency? The Minority Language Assistance Provisions of the VRA*, 12 Texas Journal on Civil Liberties & Civil Rights 163, 229–30, 231 (2007). For more on the benefits of language assistance in voting, see Spencer

Overton, Stealing Democracy: The New Politics of Voter Suppression 121–47 (2006), and James Thomas Tucker, The Battle over Bilingual Ballots: Language Minorities and Political Access under the Voting Rights Act (2009).

Congress extended the language assistance provisions of the VRA in 2006. This proved to be one of the more controversial aspects of the VRA reauthorization process, with some members of Congress disputing the need for bilingual language assistance. Questions were also raised about Congress' constitutional authority to require state and local governments to provide language assistance. In *Katzenbach v. Morgan*, 384 U.S. 641 (1966), the Supreme Court upheld a related provision of the original VRA, Section 4(e), which prohibited enforcement of state literacy requirements against those who had been educated in non-English speaking schools in Puerto Rico. The Court deferred to Congress' judgment that this requirement was needed to ensure that Puerto Ricans in the states would receive "nondiscriminatory treatment" with respect to voting and other public services. In later cases starting with *City of Boerne v. Flores*, 521 U.S. 507 (1997), however, the Court has adopted a much less deferential posture with respect to legislation enacted to enforce constitutional rights. It has required "congruence and proportionality" between the means used and the ends that Congress seeks to achieve. But while striking down several laws as exceeding the proper scope of Congress' enforcement authority, the Court has distinguished its cases upholding various provisions of the VRA. (These cases are discussed in Chapter 5, Part I.)

Are the language assistance provisions of the VRA constitutional, under the test articulated in *Boerne* and later cases? What constitutional right do these provisions "enforce"? Are the provisions congruent and proportional to those rights? Should the Court adopt a more deferential posture when considering legislation aimed at protecting a fundamental right like voting? For discussion of these issues, see James Thomas Tucker, *The Battle over "Bilingual Ballots" Shifts to the Courts: A Post-*Boerne *Assessment of Section 203 of the Voting Rights Act*, 45 Harvard Journal on Legislation 507 (2008), and Daniel P. Tokaji, *Intent and Its Alternatives: Defending the New Voting Rights Act*, 58 Alabama Law Review 349 (2006).

May English-speaking voters challenge a *Spanish-only* election system? One court concluded that they may. *Diffenderfer v. Gomez-Colon*, 587 F. Supp. 2d 338 (D.P.R. 2008), vacated as moot 587 F.3d 445 (1st Cir. 2009). The district court in *Diffenderfer* found Puerto Rico in violation of Section 2 of the Voting Rights Act, the Equal Protection Clause, and the First Amendment for failing to provide English-language ballots. While on appeal, the case became moot because the law was changed to require bilingual ballots, thus precluding the First Circuit from reaching the merits. The district court's holding on the Section 2 issue is nevertheless interesting given that the VRA defines a "language minority" as encompassing "persons who are American Indian, Asian American, Alaskan Natives or of Spanish heritage." 52 U.S.C. § 10310(c)(3). Was the district court's interpretation of the statute plausible? Was it necessary to avoid an unconstitutional result?

B. The National Voter Registration Act (and the Elections Clause)

In 1993, Congress enacted the National Voter Registration Act (NVRA), 52 U.S.C. § 20501 *et seq.*, sometimes called the "Motor Voter" law, because it ties voter registration to applying for or renewing one's driver's license. The law is much broader, however, providing that the state must designate as voter registration agencies all offices in the state that provide public assistance or state-funded programs for persons with disabilities. The law also requires each state to accept registration forms by mail and includes a number of other requirements. There is a substantial body of empirical research on the impact of the NVRA.[b] This evidence tends to show that the NVRA was successful in increasing voter registration, but it is less clear whether the NVRA increased turnout.

The NVRA's requirements apply only to registration of voters in federal elections. However, in order to avoid dual systems of voter registration, almost all states use the procedures mandated by the Motor Voter law for registration to vote in state and local as well as federal elections. Illinois initially attempted to maintain a dual registration system, but as of 1997, Mississippi was the only state doing so. In that year, the Supreme Court ruled that Mississippi's dual registration system could not be kept in effect without preclearance under Section 5 of the Voting Rights Act. *Young v. Fordice*, 520 U.S. 273 (1997).

One requirement of the NVRA is that states are required to "accept and use" a nationally uniform voter application form, referred to as the "Federal Form," that applicants can use to register by mail. 52 U.S.C. § 20505(a)(1). The Federal Form is developed by the Election Assistance Commission (discussed *infra*, in connection with the Help America Vote Act of 2002), in consultation with the states. This form does not require voters to provide proof of their identity or citizenship when they register. In 2004, however, voters in the State of Arizona approved a ballot initiative (Proposition 200), which among other things requires voters to provide "evidence of U.S. citizenship" at the time they register. Arizona argued that the NVRA should not be understood to prevent states from requiring voters to prove their eligibility in order to register, notwithstanding the NVRA's requirement that states "accept and use" the Federal Form. The Supreme Court rejected that argument in *Arizona v. Inter Tribal Council of Arizona*, 570 U.S. 1 (2013), by a 7-2 vote. Justice Scalia's opinion for the majority concluded that the "accept and use" language of the NVRA

---

b. See Robert D. Brown & Justin Wedeking, *People Who Have Their Tickets But Do Not Use Them: "Motor Voter," Registration, and Turnout Revisited*, 34 American Politics Research 479 (2006); Raymond E. Wolfinger & Jonathan Hoffman, *Registering and Voting with Motor Voter*, 34 PS: Political Science and Politics 85 (2001); Stephen Knack, *Drivers Wanted: Motor Voter and the Election of 1996*, 32 PS: Political Science and Politics 237 (1999); and Michael D. Martinez & David Hill, *Did Motor Voter Work?*, 27 American Politics Quarterly 296 (1999).

pre-empted Arizona's law requiring that election officials "reject" federal voter registration forms if not accompanied by proof of citizenship.

The most important part of the opinion in *Arizona v. Inter Tribal Council of Arizona* is its discussion of Congress' power to regulate congressional elections under the Elections Clause in Article I, Section 4 of the U.S. Constitution. The Elections Clause allows states to make regulations governing the "times, places and manner of holding elections" for the U.S. House and Senate, but provides that Congress "may at any time by law make or alter such regulations."

After explaining why the text of the NVRA is best understood to pre-empt the state law, Justice Scalia addressed Arizona's reliance on "the presumption against pre-emption sometimes invoked in our Supremacy Clause cases." In Supremacy Clause cases, the Court has sometimes required a clear statement of Congress' intent to override state law. The majority in *Arizona v. Inter Tribal Council* explained why this presumption does not apply in cases where Congress acts pursuant to its Elections Clause power:

> There is good reason for treating Elections Clause legislation differently: The assumption that Congress is reluctant to pre-empt does not hold when Congress acts under that constitutional provision, which empowers Congress to "make or alter" state election regulations. Art. I, § 4, cl. 1. When Congress legislates with respect to the "Times, Places and Manner" of holding congressional elections, it *necessarily* displaces some element of a pre-existing legal regime erected by the States. Because the power the Elections Clause confers is none other than the power to pre-empt, the reasonable assumption is that the statutory text accurately communicates the scope of Congress's pre-emptive intent. Moreover, the federalism concerns underlying the presumption in the Supremacy Clause context are somewhat weaker here. Unlike the States' "historic police powers," the States' role in regulating congressional elections — while weighty and worthy of respect — has always existed subject to the express qualification that it "terminates according to federal law." *Buckman Co. v. Plaintiffs' Legal Comm.*, 531 U.S. 341 (2001). *In sum, there is no compelling reason not to read Elections Clause legislation simply to mean what it says.*
>
> We conclude that the fairest reading of the statute is that a state-imposed requirement of evidence of citizenship not required by the Federal Form is "inconsistent with" the NVRA's mandate that States "accept and use" the Federal Form. If this reading prevails, the Elections Clause requires that Arizona's rule give way.

The majority opinion then described a limitation on Congress' power under the Elections Clause. Article I, Section 2 and the Seventeenth Amendment provide that the qualifications for voting in congressional elections shall be the same as the qualifications for the larger branch of the state legislature. The Constitution thus gives states the power to set qualifications for voting in congressional elections.

The majority opinion recognized that "it would raise serious constitutional doubts if a federal statute precluded a State from obtaining the information necessary to enforce its voting qualifications," but concluded that its interpretation of the NVRA raised no such difficulties. That is because states may request that changes to the federal registration form "include information the State deems necessary to determine eligibility," and seek judicial review if the U.S. Election Assistance Commission (EAC) refuses to make the requested changes. Arizona could seek changes to the federal form that would allow it to enforce its proof-of-citizenship requirement, so there was no conflict with the constitutional provisions giving states the power to set qualifications for voting. Justice Kennedy concurred in the judgment and all of the majority opinion except its discussion of the presumption against pre-emption. Justices Thomas and Alito dissented, both disagreeing with the majority's broad understanding of Congress' pre-emptive power under the Elections Clause.

The majority in *Arizona v. Inter Tribal Council of Arizona* suggested that, while Congress has broad authority to regulate the time, place, and manner of conducting congressional elections, states have the power to set qualifications for voting in those elections. A recent article by Professor Tolson takes issue with that presumption, arguing that Congress has broad authority to limit state voter qualification standards under the Elections Clause:

> Using the Elections Clause as its focal point, this Article argues that the Court should interpret federal election laws, and their underlying legislative record, within the broader scope of authority that the U.S. Constitution delegates to Congress over elections. The Elections Clause, which gives the states the power to "choose the Times, Places and Manner of . . . [federal] Elections," is power that the states exercise freely, so long as Congress does not assert its authority to "make or alter" state regulations. In essence, Congress has a veto power over certain state electoral practices, a veto that is present in the VRA's suspension of regulations that govern federal elections in targeted states. Thus, to interpret broadly means that the Court credits the authority that Congress has across constitutional provisions—here, the Elections Clause and the Fourteenth and Fifteenth Amendments—in assessing the legislative record underlying voting rights legislation. This multi-clause analysis shows how the Elections Clause complicates the federalism narrative that scholars and courts embrace in describing our election system because federalism is not a barrier to aggressive federal action under the Elections Clause seeking to protect the fundamental right to vote.

Franita Tolson, *The Spectrum of Congressional Authority over Elections*, 99 Boston University Law Review 317, 321–22 (2019). Is such broad congressional power to regulate elections consistent with Article I, Section 2, which gives the *states* power to set qualifications for voting in congressional elections? For more recent scholarship on Congress's authority under the Elections Clause, see Nicholas Stephanopoulos, *The Sweep of the Electoral Power*, Const. Comment. (forthcoming), Eliza Sweren-Becker and Michael Waldman, *The Meaning, History, and Importance of the Elections*

Clause, 96 Wash. L. Rev. __ (forthcoming), and Franita Tolson, *The Elections Clause and the Underenforcement of Federal Law*, 129 Yale L.J. Forum 171, 177 (2019).

Can Congress use its Elections Clause power to enact new legislation protecting voting rights? In *Shelby County v. Holder* (Chapter 5), the Supreme Court struck down the coverage formula in Section 4(b) of the Voting Rights Act, effectively ending preclearance under Section 5. Does the Elections Clause furnish an alternative source of congressional power to regulate state election practices used in congressional elections? Does it give Congress the power to regulate election practices that discriminate based on race? For commentary on the scope of congressional power over voting rights under the Elections Clause, see Samuel Issacharoff, *Beyond the Discrimination Model on Voting*, 127 Harvard Law Review 95 (2013), Derek T. Muller, *The Play in the Joints of the Elections Clauses*, 13 Election Law Journal 310 (2014), and Franita Tolson, *Congressional Power to Protect Voting Rights after* Shelby County *and* Arizona Inter Tribal, 13 Election Law Journal 322 (2014). For analyses of the states' powers and obligations under the Qualifications Clause in Article I, Section 2 of the Constitution, see Franita Tolson, *Protecting Political Participation Through the Voter Qualifications Clause of Article I*, 56 Boston College Law Review 159 (2015), and Derek T. Muller, *Scrutinizing Federal Electoral Qualifications*, 90 Indiana Law Journal 559 (2015).

Another issue that has arisen under the NVRA concerns the state's authority to remove voters from the rolls. The NVRA imposes certain limits on a state's authority to remove voters from state registration lists, a practice that critics sometimes refer to as "purging" the rolls. The relevant section of the NVRA provides that "[a]ny State program or activity to protect the integrity of the electoral process . . . shall not result in the removal of the name of any person from the official list of voters . . . by reason of the person's failure to vote. . . ." 52 U.S.C. § 20507(b). This provision includes an exception for voter removal programs relying on change-of-address information from the U.S. Post Office and the failure to vote after a notice from election authorities.

In *Husted v. A. Philip Randolph Institute*, 138 S. Ct. 1833 (2018), a 5-4 majority of the U.S. Supreme Court upheld Ohio's practice of using the failure to vote as a basis for initiating the removal of voters. Under Ohio's process, registered voters are sent a notice if they do not vote during a two-year period. Voters who fail to either respond to that notice or to vote in the next two federal election cycles are then removed from the rolls. Writing for the five-justice majority in *Husted*, Justice Alito explained:

> We reject [plaintiffs'] argument because the Failure-to-Vote Clause . . . simply forbids the use of nonvoting as the sole criterion for removing a registrant, and Ohio does not use it that way. Instead, . . . Ohio removes registrants only if they have failed to vote *and* have failed to respond to a notice. . . .
>
> [Ohio's system] does not strike any registrant solely by reason of the failure to vote. Instead, as expressly permitted by federal law, it removes

registrants only when they have failed to vote *and* have failed to respond to a change-of-residence notice.

Husted, 138 S. Ct. at 1842–43.

Four justices dissented. Writing for the dissenters, Justice Breyer expressed the view that Ohio's process violated the NVRA because "under it, a registrant who fails to vote in a single federal election, fails to respond to a forwardable notice, and fails to vote for another four years may well be purged. If the registrant had voted at any point, the registrant would not have been removed." *Id.* at 1854 (Breyer, J., dissenting) (internal citation omitted).

For an argument that the voter purge in *Husted* should be understood as an intentional—and therefore unconstitutional—effort to keep eligible people from voting, see Lisa Marshall Manheim and Elizabeth G. Porter, *The Elephant in the Room: Intentional Vote Suppression*, 2019 Supreme Court Review 213.

C. The Help America Vote Act

After the contested presidential election of 2002, Congress passed the Help America Vote Act of 2002, 52 U.S.C. § 20901 *et seq.* The Act, now commonly known as HAVA, represents the federal government's most significant intervention to date in the "nuts and bolts" of election administration.

In the deliberations leading up to HAVA's enactment, Congress attempted to balance the values of access and integrity. As Representative Steny Hoyer, one of HAVA's most prominent supporters, put it: "Everyone agrees that we should make it easier to vote . . . and we should make it harder to cheat." David Nather, *Election Overhaul May Have to Wait in Line Behind Other 'Crisis' Issues*, CQ Weekly, July 27, 2002, at 2034. The difficulty was reaching agreement on how to promote these ends, with Democrats tending to emphasize access and Republicans integrity.

HAVA contained both carrots and sticks to induce states to improve the administration of elections. Informed by the empirical research on voting technology that occurred in the wake of the 2000 election, Title I of HAVA authorized substantial federal funds for states to upgrade their voting technology and make other improvements in the administration of elections. 52 U.S.C. § 20902. Title II of HAVA set up a new agency, the Election Assistance Commission (EAC), to distribute these federal funds and to oversee implementation of the Act's requirements. 52 U.S.C. § 20921. Through Title III of HAVA, Congress imposed certain limited requirements upon states, including voting equipment standards, a statewide registration database, a limited identification requirement for first-time voters who registered by mail, and provisional voting. 52 U.S.C. §§ 21081–83.

An empirical analysis of HAVA concludes that the statute was responsible for some significant improvements in election administration, but also some unintended consequences. Martha Kropf & David Kimball, Helping America Vote: The Limits of Election Reform 98, 104–07 (2012). Professors Kropf and Kimball find that

HAVA improved voting technology, while also increasing the costs of administering elections. Moreover, the authors conclude that HAVA did not sufficiently address the "human side" of election administration, including the prevalence of partisanship at the state and local level.

There have also been serious problems with the federal agency created to oversee election administration reform. From the beginning, the EAC encountered significant problems in performing its duties under HAVA. Congress delayed in approving sufficient funds and in confirming the EAC commissioners. More fundamentally, as one commentator put it: "The EAC was designed to have as little regulatory authority as possible." Leonard Shambon, *Implementing the Help America Vote Act*, 3 Election Law Journal 424, 428 (2004). It is denied the power to issue rules and regulations, except to implement certain provisions of the NVRA. 52 U.S.C. § 20508(a). The structure of the EAC—which is composed of four members, two from each major party, with a majority required for the Commission to act—also imposes a barrier to action. For more on the EAC's problems, see Daniel P. Tokaji, *The Future of Election Reform*, *supra*, at 134–36, and Jennifer Nou, *Sub-Regulating Elections*, 2013 Supreme Court Review 135, 144–46, 152–54 (2014). Going into the 2012 election, the EAC had no commissioners, even though some of the agency's functions were continuing. Legislation has been introduced to end the EAC and transfer some of its functions to the Federal Election Commission.

Another area where HAVA has had some unintended consequences is provisional ballots. HAVA requires that provisional ballots be made available to certain voters—in particular, those who appear at the polls and find that their names are not on the registration list, and those who appear at the polls without required identification. 52 U.S.C. §§ 21082(a)(1), 21083(b)(2)(B). The idea behind this requirement is to provide a backstop, so that voters are not turned away without being able to cast a ballot due to an administrative error.

HAVA's provisional ballot mandate has provided fertile ground for litigation, with opposing candidates in close races sometimes disagreeing over whether and how those ballots should be counted. During the 2004 election season, the question arose whether voters should be allowed to cast a provisional ballot and have those ballots counted, if they mistakenly show up to vote at the wrong precinct. The operative language of HAVA provides that a voter

> shall be permitted to cast a provisional ballot at that polling place upon the execution of a written affirmation by the individual before an election official at the polling place stating that the individual is . . . a registered voter in the jurisdiction in which the individual desires to vote. . . .

52 U.S.C. § 21082(a)(2). The dispute turned on whether "jurisdiction" meant the *precinct* at which the voter appeared (in which case voters at the wrong precinct need not be given a provisional ballot), or the *county or municipality* in which the voter resided (in which case voters were entitled to receive provisional ballots and, at least arguably, to have those ballots counted). Lower courts concluded that HAVA did

not require states to count provisional ballots cast in the wrong precinct. See *Sandusky County Democratic Party v. Blackwell*, 387 F.3d 565 (6th Cir. 2004). For further discussion of HAVA's provisional voting requirements, see Leonard Shambon & Keith Abouchar, *Trapped by Precincts? The Help America Vote Act's Provisional Ballots and the Problem of Precincts*, 10 New York University Journal of Legislation & Public Policy 133 (2006–2007), and Edward B. Foley, *The Promise and Problems of Provisional Voting*, 73 George Washington Law Review 1193 (2005). To minimize the likelihood of post-election disputes over provisional ballots, Foley recommends "development of clear rules for determining when provisional ballots are to be counted."

Another aspect of HAVA that has led to court battles is its requirement that every state have in place a statewide voter registration list and that information in voter registration databases be "matched" against other records. Specifically, HAVA requires that:

> The chief State election official and the official responsible for the State motor vehicle authority of a State shall enter into an agreement to match information in the database of the statewide voter registration system with information in the database of the motor vehicle authority to the extent required to enable each such official to verify the accuracy of the information provided on applications for voter registration.

52 U.S.C. § 21083(a)(5)(B)(i).

One of the cases involving voter registration lists found its way to the U.S. Supreme Court. In a case brought by the Ohio Republican Party, a federal district court issued a temporary restraining order against Ohio's Secretary of State for failing to comply with HAVA's matching requirement, and the Sixth Circuit affirmed. The Supreme Court reversed in a unanimous *per curiam* opinion, which concluded that Congress had not authorized federal courts to enforce the above-quoted provision of HAVA in suits brought by private parties. *Brunner v. Ohio Republican Party*, 555 U.S. 5 (2008). Private litigants are thus unable to bring actions alleging a failure to comply with this requirement.

D. Empirical Research on Turnout

Although this Chapter has mainly focused on *federal* constitutional and statutory law, most of the rules governing election administration come from the states. State laws vary dramatically, so much so that each state may be viewed as its own election ecosystem. See Steven F. Huefner et al., From Registration to Recounts: The Election Ecosystems of Five Midwestern States 177 (2007). For example, each state has its own set of rules governing voter identification, voter registration, early and absentee voting, provisional voting, and the process by which recounts and other post-election proceedings are conducted. It is not possible to examine all these laws in this Casebook. It is, however, worth considering what effect election administration rules have on whether people vote. To answer this question, we review the empirical literature on voter turnout, including the composition of the electorate and factors that are associated with a propensity to vote. Next, we consider how different voting rules affect turnout.

The proportion of Americans eligible to vote who actually *do* vote is generally thought to be low. In comparison to other industrialized democracies, turnout among the voting age population in the U.S. is generally low.[c] This disparity is at least partly attributable to the prevalence of single member districts in the U.S., in which the candidate receiving the most votes in a district wins the election. Political scientists general attribute the lower turnout in winner-take-all systems to the fact that they tend to result in more "wasted votes," in comparison with proportional representation systems.[d] (See Chapter 5, *supra*, for more on the distinction between winner-take-all and proportional representation systems.)

Turnout in the U.S. in recent decades is also lower in comparison to some previous periods of U.S. history. In the fifteen presidential elections from 1840 to 1896 (the peak period in American history), turnout is estimated to have averaged 78 percent.[e] This period was associated with intense competition between the parties and strong party machines.[f] Turnout among the voting age population declined precipitously during the period from around 1896 to 1920, especially in southern states where African Americans were denied their right to vote.[g] It increased somewhat during the 1920s and 1930s, then declined outside the South in subsequent decades before leveling off in the 1980s and 1990s.[h] Turnout increased slightly at the beginning of the current century, climbing from 52 percent in 1996 to 62 percent in 2008.[i] It was around 60 percent in the 2012 and 2016 presidential elections.[j] Despite the COVID pandemic, roughly two-third of eligible citizens voted in 2020, the highest turnout in well over a century.[k]

The turnout information in the preceding paragraph is based on the *voting eligible population* rather than the *voting age population*. The voting age population includes many people who are not eligible to vote. The people ineligible to vote include non-citizens as well as many felons (see Chapter 2). In addition, population

---

c. David Hill, American Voter Turnout: An Institutional Perspective 2 (2006)

d. *Id.* at 64–66.

e. These figures were calculated using the table in Ruy A. Teixeira, The Disappearing American Voter 9, tbl. 1–3 (1992).

f. Michael McDonald, *American Voter Turnout in Historical Perspective*, in The Oxford Handbook of American Elections and Political Behavior 125, 131–32 (2010).

g. Harold W. Stanley & Richard G. Niemi, Vital Statistics on American Politics 2015–2016, at 7, fig. 1-2.

h. *Id.*

i. *Id.* at 4-5, tbl. 1-1.

j. *Id.*

k. Nathaniel Persily & Charles Stewart III, *The Miracle and Tragedy of the 2020 Election*, 32 J. Democracy 165 (2021).

figures are based upon the United States census, which does not produce a perfectly accurate count. When considering voter turnout using percentages of *eligible voters* and adjusting for errors in the census, McDonald and Popkin found no significant change outside the South in *eligible* voter turnout rates between 1972 and 2000. In the South, eligible voter turnout *increased* during that period.[l]

U.S. voter turnout is therefore not as low as commonly thought, when measured as a percentage of the voting eligible population and compared to other elections in recent decades. Still, when one recalls the long struggle outlined in Chapter 2 to extend the suffrage to increased segments of the American population and the importance placed on the right to vote in the American civic culture, one may well be puzzled why so many citizens—at least one-third of eligible voters in presidential election years, and a higher percentage in other election years—do not exercise their right to vote. Why do not all citizens seek a voice in the decisions that affect their own lives? If people are dissatisfied with the performance of government, why do they abandon their best opportunity to enforce improvement? Given the elimination of poll taxes, how can so many people not find voting worth the minimal expenditure of time and effort required?

Empirical research on turnout shows significant differences between those who vote and those who don't, when it comes to their views about government and politics. Not surprisingly, the intensity of one's political preferences is associated with the likelihood of coming out to vote. People with strong feelings about candidates or parties have a much higher propensity to vote. So too, interest in the election campaign and concern over its outcome are strongly correlated with voting. Citizens with a strong sense of political efficacy (that is, those who think that government can be understood and influenced by ordinary citizens), as well as those with a sense of civic responsibility, are more likely to vote. The perception that the election will be close, and therefore that one's vote is likely to matter, is also correlated with higher turnout.

Perhaps low turnout would not be a cause for public concern if those who voted mirrored those who did not vote, but voters tend not to be a random distribution of the population. In a landmark study, Raymond E. Wolfinger and Steven J. Rosenstone examined the socioeconomic factors correlated with the propensity to vote, finding that that *education* was the factor most highly correlated with voting.[m] Three decades later, another comprehensive study was published by Jan E. Leighley and Jonathan Nagler.[n] The authors examines voter turnout in presidential elections between 1972 and 2008, including the demographics of the voting population, the

l. Michael P. McDonald & Samuel L. Popkin, *The Myth of the Vanishing Voter*, 95 American Political Science Review 963 (2001).

m. Raymond E. Wolfinger & Steven J. Rosenstone, Who Votes? 23–25 (1980).

n. Jan E. Leighley & Jonathan Nagler, Who Votes Now?: Demographics, Issues, Inequality, and Turnout in the United States (2014).

consequences of electoral reforms, and the differences between voters and nonvoters. The following findings are of special interest to students of election law:

- Voter turnout has not declined systematically since 1972. Although there have been variations in turnout in different presidential elections, these appear to reflect political context as much as citizens' motivation to participate in the electoral process.[o]
- The correlation between socioeconomic status and turnout remains strong, with better educated and higher income individuals more likely to vote. But despite the significant increase in economic inequality during the 1972–2008 period, the authors do not find a significant increase in income bias among the electorate as a whole.[p]
- Leighley and Nagler analyze the "representativeness" of voters — that is, how closely their policy views correspond to those of nonvoters. They find that voters are more liberal than nonvoters on some issues but more conservative than nonvoters on other issues. But voters consistently hold more conservative policy views than nonvoters on issues relating to economic inequality.[q]

Although there has historically been a significant racial gap in turnout, white and non-Hispanic black citizens turned out at almost the same rate in the 2008 and 2012 presidential elections.[r] That is largely attributable to Barack Obama being on the ballot both years. In 2016 and 2020, the turnout gap between white and nonwhite voters was around 12.5%.[s]

What legal changes to voting might be adopted to increase or enhance voter participation and increase the representativeness of the electorate? Here are three of many possibilities:

Compulsory voting. If more participation in U.S. elections is desirable, then why not simply pass a law requiring that people vote or face a penalty? The idea is not as far-fetched as it might sound to American readers. Australia, Belgium, Italy and a number of other countries with high voter turnout have such laws.

Studies show that, controlling for other factors, turnout is about 10–15 percentage points higher in countries with compulsory voting. The range of penalties for nonvoting range from Australia's $50 fine to Greece's penalty of imprisonment for up to one year, to Italy's posting of the names of nonvoters on the communal notice board. Despite this wide range of stated penalties, lack of enforcement is ubiquitous.[t]

---

o. *Id.* at 45.

p. *Id.* at 45-46.

q. *Id.* at 176.

r. Daniel P. Tokaji, *Responding to* Shelby County*: A Grand Election Bargain*, 8 Harvard Law & Policy Review 71, 86 (2014).

s. Kevin Morris, Large Racial Turnout Gap Persisted in 2020 Election, Aug. 6, 2021, https://perma.cc/564L-MSYE.

t. See Richard L. Hasen, *Voting Without Law?*, 144 University of Pennsylvania Law Review 2135 (1996). For arguments in favor of compulsory voting, see Arend Lijphart, *Unequal Participation:*

Should compulsory voting be adopted in the United States? There do not appear to be any constitutional barriers against it. If the state can force you to serve on a jury, enlist in the army, and separate your trash for recycling purposes, the state can presumably make you show up and vote. A compulsory voting law allows you to cast a blank ballot, so it does not appear that you would be forced to choose from available candidates. Still, it seems highly doubtful that compulsory voting will be adopted in the United States in the near future given the lack of public support for it. What explains the resistance to compulsory voting in the U.S. when it is accepted in some other democratic countries?[u]

Easing Registration. One way to increase turnout might be to reduce the cost of voting. The barrier most often discussed is the registration requirement. The United States is one of the few if not the only major democracy in the world that requires advance registration as a prerequisite to voting without the government assuming responsibility for seeing to it that all eligible people are registered. Registration requirements have not always been imposed in the United States. Most were put in place around the turn of the century, possibly for the very purpose of discouraging voting by immigrants, workers, and others who were regarded by some as too ignorant to vote, though this is a point of contention among historians.[v]

Neither elimination of registration requirements nor universal registration is likely in the foreseeable future, but easing of barriers to registration is feasible. Though every state but North Dakota requires voters to register, states vary considerably in their registration requirements. Several states allow election day registration (EDR), which allows voters to appear at the polling place and vote on election day without having registered in advance. Social science research shows that EDR is associated with higher turnout.[w] Presumably, this is because EDR lowers the cost

---

Democracy's Unresolved Dilemma, 91 American Political Science Review 1 (1997), and Lisa Hill, *On the Reasonableness of Compelling Citizens to 'Vote': the Australian Case*, 50 Political Studies 80 (2002).

u. See also Nicholas O. Stephanopoulos, *A Feasible Roadmap to Compulsory Voting*, The Atlantic, Nov. 2, 2015 (arguing that the most likely path to compulsory voting in the United States might be for Democratic-leaning cities in swing states to adopt the policy at the municipal level).

v. See Dayna L. Cunningham, *Who Are to Be the Electors? A Reflection on the History of Voter Registration in the United States*, 9 Yale Law & Policy Review 370, 380–85 (1991).

w. See Barry C. Burden & Jacob C. Neiheisel, *The Impact of Election Day Registration on Voter Turnout and Election Outcomes*, 30 American Politics Research 634 (2012); Elizabeth Rigby & Melanie J. Springer, *Does Electoral Reform Increase (or Decrease) Political Equality?* 64 Political Research Quarterly 420, 427–29 (2011); Roger Larocca & John S. Klemanski, *U.S. State Election Reform and Turnout in Presidential Elections*, 11 State Politics & Policy Quarterly 76, 90, 93–94 (2011); Craig Leonard Brians & Bernard Grofman, *Election Day Registration's Effect on U.S. Voter Turnout*, 82 Social Science Quarterly 161, 170, 176–77 (2001); Benjamin Highton, *Easy Registration and Voter Turnout*, 59 Journal of Politics 565, 568 (1997); Mark J. Fenster, *The Impact of Allowing Day of Registration Voting on Turnout in U.S. Elections From 1960 to 1992: A Research Note*, 22 American Political Research 74, 80, 84 (1994).

of voting and because some people become interested in voting as the election nears and the campaign intensifies.[x]

Other differences in registration procedures that affect turnout, though not as much as the closing date, are whether the registration offices are open evenings or weekends; whether the registration offices are open full-time during business hours; whether registration by mail is permitted for persons who are sick, disabled, or absent from home; and how quickly voters are "purged" from the registration lists for not voting in one or more elections. One study found that "registration portability"—the practice of allowing registrants who have moved within a state to change their registration and vote on election day at their new polling place—significantly increased turnout among people who had recently moved.[y]

Perhaps surprisingly, the general availability of registration by mail and the availability of "deputy registrars" (private citizens who are deputized to register voters at homes, workplaces, shopping malls, etc.) do *not* appear to measurably increase turnout. But political scientists estimate that if all states had the most liberal registration procedures of the sort that have been shown to make a difference—i.e., voters can register up to election day; registration offices keep regular hours including being open evenings or weekends; people who are sick, disabled, or absent can register by mail; and voters are not purged without checks to confirm that they have either died or moved—then national turnout might increase by about seven to nine percentage points.[z] Consistent with prior evidence, Leighley and Nagler find that EDR is associated with higher turnout.[aa]

Convenience Voting. Laws easing voter registration are only one way of lowering the costs of voting. Other possible methods include weekend voting, early voting (that is, giving voters the option of voting during a short period before the election), absentee voting, vote-by-mail, and internet voting. Each method makes it easier at least for some voters to cast ballots. These other methods have costs as well as benefits, however. For example, weekend voting and early voting occur at polling places and require poll workers. Weekend voting might discourage some voters who are unwilling to sacrifice their recreational time.

Does convenience voting really increase turnout, or merely cause people who would vote anyways to shift to an alternative method. A study of absentee balloting concluded that "[l]iberal absentee laws do appear to help stimulate turnout among certain groups, such as persons with disabilities and students. Yet, the extent to which overall turnout can be increased beyond these groups is uncertain. More

---

x. Another advantage of EDR is that it tends to reduce reliance on provisional ballots. Eligible voters who do not appear on the registration list when they go to vote may, in EDR states, cast a regular ballot rather than voting provisionally. See Steven F. Huefner et al., From Registration to Recounts: The Election Ecosystems of Five Midwestern States 177 (2007).

y. Michael P. McDonald, *Portable Voter Registration*, 30 Political Behavior 491 (2008).

z. See Wolfinger & Rosenstone, *supra*, at 71–77; Teixeira, *supra*, at 107–12.

aa. Leighley & Nagler, *supra*, at 117.

likely, only those who are politically motivated (and thus likely to vote) will make plans in advance to vote absentee."[bb] One study found that early voting is associated with *lower* turnout, at least when implemented by itself.[cc] Some have gone even further, suggesting that expanding convenience voting may have "perverse consequences" by increasing participation by those already most likely to vote, thus skewing the electorate even further toward better educated, more affluent, and white voters.[dd] On the other hand, another study found that email messages combined with a user-friendly electronic absentee ballot delivery system increased the likelihood of overseas voters participating.[ee] Leighley and Nagler likewise found that no-excuse absentee had a positive effect on turnout, although the effects of early voting were less certain.[ff] Convenience voting may have a greater effect when combined with increasingly sophisticated get-out-the-vote efforts.[gg]

Several states (Colorado, Hawaii, Nevada, Oregon, Utah, Vermont, and Washington) now have elections in which almost all voting is conducted by mail. Rather than having designated polling places, all registered voters are automatically sent a ballot that they may complete at home and return by mail or other means. Research on Oregon has revealed that this system has increased turnout, particularly in local elections in which turnout is typically low. There is some evidence that turnout has disproportionately increased among those already most likely to vote, specifically "those who are white, educated, older, and have higher incomes."[hh] Thus, Oregon's vote-by-mail system seems to improve turnout, but may also increase the socioeconomic bias of the electorate. On the other hand, a recent study found that Colorado's all-mail voting system both increased turnout and increased equity, with the largest gains among low-propensity voting groups.[ii]

Absentee voting, vote-by-mail, and internet voting raise another concern: the potential for electoral fraud, which President Trump played up during and after the

---

bb. Jeffrey A. Karp & Susan A. Banducci, *Absentee Voting, Mobilization, and Participation*, 29 American Politics Research 183, 191 (2001).

cc. Barry C. Burden, David T. Canon, Kenneth R. Mayer & Donald P. Moynihan, *Election Laws, Mobilization, and Turnout: The Unanticipated Consequences of Election Reform*, 58 American Journal of Political Science 95 (2014).

dd. Adam J. Berinsky, *The Perverse Consequences of Electoral Reform in the United States*, 33 American Political Research 471 (2005).

ee. Michael Hanmer, Paul S. Herrnson & Claire Smith, *The Impact of E-mail on the Use of New Convenience Voting Methods and Turnout by Overseas Voters*, 14 Election Law Journal 1 (2015).

ff. Leighley & Nagler, *supra*, at 117.

gg. For a discussion of contemporary means of getting out the vote, see Sasha Issenberg, The Victory Lab: The Secret Science of Winning Campaigns (2013).

hh. Jeffrey A. Karp & Susan A. Banducci, *Going Postal: How All-Mail Elections Influence Turnout*, 22 Political Behavior 223, 233 (2000). Adam J. Berinsky et al., *Who Votes by Mail? A Dynamic Model of the Individual-Level Consequences of Voting-by-Mail Systems*, 65 Public Opinion Quarterly 178, 191 (2001) found that vote-by-mail "mobilizes older voters, those who are well educated, and those with substantial amounts of campaign interest."

ii. Adam Bonica, Jacob M. Grumbach, Charlotte Hill & Hakeem Jefferson, *All-Mail Voting in Colorado Increases Turnout and Reduces Turnout Inequality*, 72 Electoral Studies 102363 (2021).

2020 election. While it is easy to exaggerate the prevalence of fraud, these concerns are not completely imaginary. North Carolina recently witnessed the most egregious example of absentee voting fraud in many years, which led the State Board of Elections to order a new election for the state's Ninth Congressional District. The 2019 election for that seat was closely contested between Republican Mark Harris and Democrat Dan McCready. On Election Night, Harris appeared to have won by a narrow margin. Some weeks afterwards, it came to light that a Republican operative named L. McCrae Dowless, Jr. had engaged in some old-fashioned ballot stuffing using absentee ballots. According to published reports, Dowless and his agents would request absentee ballots and then go to voters' homes when the ballots were sent. After collecting the ballots, they would mark them for return. It was estimated that over 1,200 ballots were illegally marked in this way, more than the approximately 900 votes separating the candidates. There was also evidence that absentee ballot fraud was not new to this part of North Carolina, but had been going on for years. David A. Graham, *North Carolina Had No Choice: A House Election Tainted by Fraud Gets Its Inevitable Do-Over*, The Atlantic, Feb. 22, 2019.

Notes and Questions

1. Most public discussions of turnout assume that increasing the rate of voting is a desirable public goal. Why should this be so? If registration barriers screen out people who are less well informed and have less education, without actually preventing many people from voting who are highly motivated to do so, might this be regarded as a desirable state of affairs? Would the quality of public decision making be improved by greater participation by people who are less interested and less informed? If not, does it follow that higher turnout is a goal that ought to be abandoned? Does your answer depend upon whether you consider an election to be like an examination in which there is a "right" answer rather than as a means for dividing power among political equals? Does it depend on whether the policy preferences of nonvoters are different from those of voters?

2. Democratic and Republican political operatives have less interest in increasing turnout overall than in increasing turnout of likely supporters. Suppose you wanted to increase the vote of a particular segment of the population. How would you do it? Perhaps you would like to pay people to vote. Of course, it is illegal in every state and in federal elections to pay people to vote for a particular candidate or for or against a particular ballot issue. But what about payments to increase turnout? Federal law prohibits the practice, but at least three states—Alaska, California, and Mississippi—allow it when there are no federal candidates on the ballot. Should such a practice be illegal, legal but discouraged, or encouraged? For a collection of statutes on vote buying and commentary on these issues, see Richard L. Hasen, *Vote Buying*, 88 California Law Review 1323 (2000).

3. Most of the responsibility for running elections—including federal elections—rests with local officials in counties, cities, and towns throughout the United States. Is this a desirable state of affairs? Should we consider centralizing the administration

of American elections? If so, what sort of structure might be implemented to promote fair and effective administration? The experience of the EAC in implementing HAVA's modest requirements might suggest that increasing federal responsibility over elections is not a panacea.

4. Are there other means to enhance participation and improve the administration of elections, without the creation of a new agency or the imposition of statutory mandates? Heather Gerken has proposed one possible solution. She suggests a "Democracy Index" that would measure the performance of the states in registering voters, allowing them to cast their ballots, and counting their votes properly. See Heather K. Gerken, The Democracy Index: Why Our Election System Is Failing and How to Fix It (2009). The idea is to create a healthy competition among the states, providing an incentive for them to improve their relative performance. She analogizes her proposal to the *U.S. News* rankings of colleges and professional schools, which has had a significant (though not uniformly positive) impact on higher education. This idea has become a reality. The MIT Election Data & Science Lab maintains an index that measures election administration in the states using seventeen indicators, which may be found at https://elections.mit.edu/#/data/map.

A recent article develops and applies a new index for assessing state election administration. Quan Li, Michael J. Pomante II & Scot Schraufnagel, *Cost of Voting in the American States*, 17 Election Law Journal 234 (2018). The authors develop a "Cost of Voting Index" (COVI), designed to measure the "totality of time and effort associated with casting a vote" in every state, by looking at rules regarding voter registration, convenience voting, voter ID, and polling hours. The authors rank Mississippi, Virginia, Tennessee, Indiana, and Texas (in that order) as the worst states in 2016, and Oregon, Colorado, California, North Dakota, Iowa, and Maine (again in order) as the best. The authors updated the index in 2020. Quan Li, Michael J. Pomante II & Scot Schraufnagel, *Cost of Voting in the American States: 2020*, 19 Election Law Journal 503 (2020). Oregon maintained its #1 position in the rankings, due in part to its liberal voter registration and mail-voting processes. Virginia showed the most dramatic improvement, going from 49th to 12th due to registration reforms and other changes, while Michigan jumped from 45th to 13th due to changes in its voter registration and absentee voting processes. *Id.* at 508. Texas was deemed to have the most restrictive electoral processes, after having reduced the number of polling stations in some parts of the state and adopting "the most restrictive pre-registration law in the country." *Id.*

5. After the 2012, election, President Obama created the Presidential Commission on Election Administration, sometimes referred to as "Bauer-Ginsberg," after its two co-chairs: Democratic lawyer Bob Bauer and Republican lawyer Ben Ginsberg. The Bauer-Ginsberg Commission released its findings and recommendations in January 2014. *The American Voting Experience: Report and Recommendations of the Presidential Commission on Election Administration* (Jan. 2014). Its key recommendations include online voter registration, expanded interstate exchanges of voter registration information, electronic pollbooks, expanded opportunities for early

and absentee voting, reform of the certification process for voting equipment, and regular audits of voting equipment. Are these reforms likely to improve the voting process? What changes would you recommend?

Upon taking control of the U.S. House in early 2019, the Democratic leadership made election reform its first legislative priority. The "For the People Act of 2019" (H.R. 1), proposed major changes to federal election administration, as well as redistricting, campaign finance, and ethics. Among its changes to election administration were expansion of early voting, automatic voter registration, limits on voter purges, and making Election Day a federal holiday. The bill also included provisions regarding election security, including the sharing of intelligence information on threats with state election officials. The bill passed on a party-line vote in the House, but had no chance in the Senate (which had a Republican majority) and would surely have been vetoed by President Trump in any event.

Democrats introduced a revised version of the For the People Act in 2021. H.R. 1, 117th Cong. (2021). Democrats had gained a majority in the House and the slenderest of majorities in the Senate—split 50-50, with Vice President Kamala Harris holding the tiebreaking vote. Senate rules require a three-fifths majority (60 of 100 votes) to break a filibuster. As long as that rule remains in place, there is no chance of the For the People Act getting through the Senate. Should Democrats eliminate the filibuster, or adopt a special exception to it, to get voting reforms passed? What precedent would that set for future efforts by the dominant party to remake federal election law?

IV. Judicial Remedies

What should courts do when they conclude that federal or state election laws have been violated? Much depends on the posture and timing of the litigation. A distinction may be drawn between *pre-election* and *post-election* litigation. When a lawsuit is brought and injunctive relief is sought well in advance of election day, it is sometimes possible to stop the challenged practice from taking effect. For example, if a voter identification law is enacted and challenged many months before the next election and a court decides that the law is likely unconstitutional, then it may enjoin the law. If time is short, then plaintiffs will sometimes seek an emergency temporary restraining order or a preliminary injunction. In deciding whether to order such preliminary relief, courts typically consider the likelihood of success on the merits, irreparable injury, the balance of hardships, and the public interest.

Litigants who wait too long to file suit may find it difficult to obtain relief before election day. Before *Crawford*, the Supreme Court had considered a challenge to an Arizona voter identification requirement in *Purcell v. Gonzalez*, 549 U.S. 1 (2006). Arizona's Proposition 200 required voters to show either one form of photo identification, or two forms of non-photo identification. Without deciding on Proposition 200's constitutionality, the Court's *per curiam* opinion vacated an injunction against the law that had been issued by the Ninth Circuit. The opinion in *Purcell* suggests that lower federal courts should be cautious in issuing injunctions against state election procedures shortly before an election:

> Faced with an application to enjoin operation of voter identification procedures just weeks before an election, the Court of Appeals was required to weigh, in addition to the harms attendant upon issuance or nonissuance of an injunction, considerations specific to election cases and its own institutional procedures. Court orders affecting elections, especially conflicting orders, can themselves result in voter confusion and consequent incentive to remain away from the polls. As an election draws closer, that risk will increase.

Is it prudent for courts to exercise particular restraint when deciding whether to issue an injunction shortly before an election? Is it better for courts to wait until after an election has been conducted, to see if the anticipated problems actually materialize? Are there advantages to resolving constitutional issues through pre-election litigation rather than post-election litigation? For criticism of *Purcell*, see Richard L. Hasen, *The Untimely Death of* Bush v. Gore, 60 Stanford Law Review 1, 28–43 (2007).

The limitations imposed by *Purcell* came to the fore during the 2014 election cycle, which saw cases challenging voting restrictions in North Carolina, Ohio, Texas, and Wisconsin. All these cases involve claims under both the Fourteenth Amendment and Section 2 of the VRA. In all four states, at least one lower court had ordered an injunction against challenged voting rules. The Supreme Court allowed all but one of the state laws to take effect in the 2014 election cycle. *Ohio State Conference of the NAACP v. Husted*, 768 F.3d 524 (6th Cir. 2014), stayed by *Husted v. Ohio State Conference of NAACP*, 573 U.S. 988 (2014); *League of Women Voters of N.C. v. North Carolina*, 769 F.3d 224 (4th Cir. 2014), stayed by *North Carolina v. League of Women Voters of N.C.*, 574 U.S. 927 (2014); *Veasey v. Perry*, 71 F. Supp. 3d 627 (S.D. Tex. 2014), stayed 769 F.3d. 890, 893 (5th Cir. 2014), affirmed *Perry v. Veasey*, 135 S. Ct. 9 (2014). The one restriction the Court stopped was Wisconsin's voter ID law, which the Seventh Circuit had reinstated very close to the election. The Supreme Court issued a stay that effectively prevented Wisconsin's law from taking effect in 2014, though it later denied review of the Seventh Circuit's opinion, thus allowing it to be implemented in later elections. *Frank v. Walker*, 17 F. Supp. 3d 837 (E.D. Wis. 2014), stayed and reversed 768 F.3d 744 (7th Cir. 2014), stay vacated 574 U.S. 929 (2014), cert. denied 575 U.S. 913 (2015).

What are we to make of these cases? It is difficult to say for sure, given there were no opinions for the Court in any of them. One lesson is that lower courts should be wary of changing election rules close to election day. Professor Hasen explains:

> The orders appeared contradictory, for example by allowing strict voter identification requirements to be used on Election Day 2014 in Texas but not Wisconsin. But the apparent common thread . . . was the Supreme Court's

> application of "the *Purcell* principle:" the idea that courts should not issue orders which change election rules in the period just before the election. This idea has appeared in earlier Supreme Court cases, most prominently in *Purcell v. Gonzalez*, a 2006 short *per curiam* case in which the Court vacated a Ninth Circuit injunction which had temporarily blocked use of Arizona's strict new voter identification law. The Court in *Purcell* criticized the Ninth Circuit both for not explaining its reasoning and for issuing an order just before an election which could cause voter confusion and problems for those administering elections. In the 2014 election cases, the Court consistently voted against changing the electoral status quo just before the election. Ironically, given the Court's criticism of the Ninth Circuit for not giving reasons in *Purcell*, the Court did not explain its reasons in any of the 2014 election orders.

Richard L. Hasen, *Reining in the* Purcell *Principle*, 43 Florida State University Law Review 427 (2016). Professor Hasen argues that the concern with the disruption arising from an injunction close to an election should not be paramount, but just one of several factors that courts consider when determining whether to grant injunctive relief. He also suggests that the Supreme Court should issue opinions that explain the majority's reasoning, even if not until weeks after the election is over, so that litigants and lower courts are not left guessing about the Court's reasoning.

One provision of the proposed John Lewis Voting Rights Advancement Act of 2021 (JLVRAA) (discussed in Chapter 5, Note 4 following *Shelby County v. Holder*) would partly overrule *Purcell*, or at least the expansive gloss that the Court has given it in recent decisions. The bill provides that a state or locality's inability to enforce its election laws "standing alone, shall not be deemed to constitute irreparable harm to the public interest" in cases under federal voting laws, including the Constitution. It also provides that:

> [P]roximity of the action to an election shall not be a valid reason to deny [injunctive] relief, or stay the operation of or vacate the issuance of such relief, unless the party opposing the issuance or continued operation of relief meets the burden of proving by clear and convincing evidence that the issuance of the relief would be so close in time to the election as to cause irreparable harm to the public interest or that compliance with such relief would impose serious burdens on the party opposing relief.

Should Congress instruct courts on the equitable factors that it should consider in determining whether to issue an injunction or stay in election cases? Does it unduly intrude on the authority of courts to make those determinations?

In some cases, it is impossible or impracticable for courts to issue an injunction before the election. Sometimes, the alleged legal problem with an election does not occur until on or after voting has begun. Where a pre-election remedy is impossible or undesirable, a different set of remedial possibilities comes into play. One possibility is to order that ballots be recounted or included in vote totals, as the

Florida Supreme Court did in the state court litigation leading up to *Bush v. Gore*. A court may also order that certain ballots *not* be counted, where there is fraud or some other serious problem. An example is a case arising from Miami's 1997 mayoral election, *In re the Matter of the Protest of Election Returns and Absentee Ballots*, 707 So. 2d 1170 (Fla. App. 3d Dist. 1998). Facing evidence of fraudulent absentee ballots, the court ordered that absentee ballots be voided and that the election be determined based on ballots cast at the polls. In rare cases, a court may even order a do-over—voiding the election and ordering that a new one be conducted. The following is one of those unusual cases.

Pabey v. Pastrick

816 N.E.2d 1138 (Ind. 2004)

DICKSON, Justice.

Plaintiff/appellant George Pabey is appealing from a judgment denying relief in an election contest. We reverse.

The primary election for the Democratic nomination for the office of mayor of the city of East Chicago, Indiana, took place on May 6, 2003. The candidates were incumbent Robert Pastrick and challengers George Pabey and Lonnie Randolph. The results of that election were:

Pastrick	4,083
Pabey	3,805
Randolph	2,289

At trial, Pabey sought to have all of the absentee ballots declared invalid or, in the alternative, to have the election invalidated and a new election ordered. . . .

Of the 8,227 votes personally cast on election day, Pabey received 199 more votes than Pastrick. But of the 1,950 absentee ballots, Pastrick defeated Pabey by 477 votes, producing a 278-vote final victory for Pastrick. The trial court concluded that Pabey had proven "that a deliberate series of actions occurred" that "perverted the absentee voting process and compromised the integrity and results of that election." The judge found "direct, competent, and convincing evidence that established the pervasive fraud, illegal conduct, and violations of elections law" and proved the "voluminous, widespread and insidious nature of the misconduct."

Notwithstanding the overwhelming evidence of election misconduct, however, [the trial judge] was cautious regarding his authority to order a special election under the circumstances. . . . The judge perceived that he was not authorized by statute to order a special election because Pabey's evidence was only able to prove the invalidity of 155 actual votes, and because this was 123 votes short of the 278-vote difference that separated Pabey and Pastrick, [the trial judge] reluctantly concluded that Pabey had failed to adequately establish that the proven deliberate series of actions "make it impossible to determine which candidate received the highest number of votes.". . . . [Pabey appealed, but the Court of Appeals dismissed the appeal for lack of jurisdiction. Pabey's motion to transfer the case to the Indiana Supreme Court was then granted.]

I

[The court rejected Pastrick's procedural and jurisdictional arguments for dismissing the appeal.]

II

Pabey argues that "the pervasive fraud, illegal conduct, and violations of elections law" identified by the trial court are sufficient as a matter of law to establish the requisite "deliberate act or series of actions occurred making it impossible to determine the candidate who received the highest number of votes cast in the election." Ind. Code § 3-12-8-2. Under the circumstances, he asks that the results of the primary election be vacated and a special election be ordered.

The evidentiary hearing in the trial court spanned eight and one-half days and included the testimony of 165 witnesses. Among the findings and conclusions included in the trial court's judgment are the following:

> Petitioner George Pabey has satisfied his burden to establish that a deliberate series of actions occurred in the May 6, 2003 primary election to determine the Democrat nominee for the office of Mayor of the City of East Chicago, Indiana. Those actions perverted the absentee voting process and compromised the integrity and results of that election.
>
> [Those] deliberate series of actions included *but are not limited* to the following:
>
> a) a predatory pattern exercised by Pastrick supporters of inducing voters that were first-time voters or otherwise less informed or lacking in knowledge of the voting process, the infirm, the poor, and those with limited skills in the English language, to engage in absentee voting;
>
> b) the numerous actions of Pastrick supporters of providing compensation and/or creating the expectation of compensation to induce voters to cast their ballot via the absentee process. Those actions primarily—but not exclusively—involved the payment of money to voters to be present outside the polls on Election Day. The extensive evidence presented established that, at the least thirty-nine separate individuals . . . fell within the ambit of those activities that engaged cash incentives to encourage absentee voting;
>
> c) the actions of various Pastrick supporters who directed applicants for absentee ballots to contact that Pastrick supporter when the applicant received his or her absent[ee] ballot and, once called, to proceed to their home and, though not authorized by law to do so, "assist" the voter in completing the ballot;
>
> d) the use of vacant lots or former residences of voters on applications for absentee ballots;

> e) the possession of unmarked absentee ballots by Pastrick supporters and the delivery of those ballots to absentee voters;
>
> f) the possession of completed and signed ballots by Pastrick supporters who were not authorized by law to have such possession;
>
> g) the routine completion of substantive portions of absentee ballot applications by Pastrick supporters to which applicants simply affixed their signature;
>
> h) the routine use of false representations—usually the indication that the applicant "expected" to be absent from Lake County on May 6, 2003—by those Pastrick supporters who filled out the substantive portions of applications and by votes solicited by Pastrick supporters to vote absentee to complete absentee ballot applications;
>
> i) votes cast by employees of the City of East Chicago who simply did not reside in East Chicago; and
>
> j) a zealotry to promote absentee voting that was motivated by the personal financial interests of Pastrick supporters and, in particular, city employees.
>
> [T]he series of deliberate actions set forth in [the above items (a) through (j)] implicate various state laws concerning absentee ballots [therein detailing various election and criminal laws implicated, including various violations constituting class D felonies]....
>
> [T]he commission of criminal acts by Pastrick supporters that included such activity as their unauthorized possession of completed ballots ..., the unauthorized possession of unmarked ballots ..., their presence while voters marked and completed their absentee ballots ..., and the *direct* solicitation of a vote for cash all yielded absentee votes which respondent Pastrick concedes are invalid.
>
> The East Chicago Democrat mayoral primary may be a "textbook" example of the chicanery that can attend the absentee vote cast by mail: examples of instances where the supervision and monitoring of voting by Pastrick supporters and the subsequent possession of ballots by those malefactors are common herein. Those illegalities came with a side order of predation in which the naïve, the neophytes, the infirm and the needy were subjected to the unscrupulous election tactics so extensively discussed.
>
> [I]t is apparent that a political subculture exists in Lake County which views the political machinations at issue with a "wink and a smile" and "business as usual."

The trial court was also cognizant of the difficulties faced by Pabey in discovering and presenting evidence to support his claims.

> Given the voluminous, widespread and insidious nature of the misconduct proven, together with the sheer number of voters impacted by that

> misconduct, petitioner Pabey, his legal counsel, and amateur investigators faced a herculean task of locating and interviewing absentee voters, visiting multi-family dwellings and housing projects, gathering and combing through voluminous election documents, and analyzing, comparing, sifting and assembling the information necessary to present their case.... In short, the time constraints that govern election contests, primarily designed to serve important interests and needs of election officials and the public interest in finality, simply do not work well in those elections where misconduct is of the dimension and multi-faceted variety present here.....

The Election Contest Statute provides that "[t]he court shall determine the issues raised by the petition and answer to the petition." Ind.Code § 3-12-8-17(b). As relevant to the issue before us, both section 2 of the statute, which prescribes the grounds upon which an election may be contested, and section 6 [specifies] that an election may be contested on [several grounds including]:

> ... A deliberate act or series of actions occurred making it impossible to determine the candidate who received the highest number of votes cast in the election.

Ind.Code § 3-12-8-2. Pabey contested the results of the East Chicago mayoral primary pursuant to subsection (5), that is, that a deliberate series of actions had occurred that made it impossible to determine the candidate who had received the highest number of votes cast in the primary, to which we will refer hereafter as the "Deliberate Actions" ground....

[T]his Court has long held that statutes providing for contesting elections "should be liberally construed in order that the will of the people in the choice of public officers may not be defeated by any merely formal or technical objections." Tombaugh v. Grogg, 146 Ind. 99 (1896); *see also* Hadley v. Gutridge, 58 Ind. 302, 309 (1877)....

The statutory language ... requires that the deliberate acts or series of actions must result in "making it impossible to determine the candidate who received the highest number of votes cast in the election." Interpreting the phrase "deliberate act or series of actions" so as to have the purpose and meaning intended, we conclude that it requires the acts or series of actions to be deliberate in the sense of being purposeful in that the actor or actors knew or reasonably should have known that such conduct would "make it impossible" to determine the candidate receiving the most votes.

As to the phrase "votes cast in the election" used in the statute, the plain meaning demonstrates that the legislature meant to restrict this ground to votes actually cast and not to include potential votes that were not actually cast. However, by the word "votes," the legislature could not have meant it to include votes *illegally* cast. To impose such a meaning would render ineffectual the purpose of the statute. More than a century ago, this Court recognized that the "true gravamen of the case, whatever may be the ground of contest, is 'the highest number of legal votes.'" Dobyns v. Weadon, 50 Ind. 298, 302 (1875) (emphasis omitted). We hold that the word "votes," as used in the phrase "highest number of votes," means *legal* votes.

The last and most challenging issue relating to the Deliberate Acts ground is the application and methodology intended by the phrase "impossible to determine." The trial judge focused on individual ballots to determine whether Pabey proved to a mathematical certainty that there existed a number of invalid votes cast that equaled or exceeded Pastrick's margin of victory ... [T]he trial court believed:

> [A] court is not free to engage in speculation as to whether the will of the electorate has been served or to impose ... its *subjective* determination as to whether it is "impossible" to determine which candidate received the most votes in an election. Objective factors established by the evidence must guide that determination.

The trial court declared 155 votes to be invalid but concluded "that those invalid votes were the result of a series of deliberate actions that do not make it impossible to determine which of the candidates" received the most votes. This construction is unnecessarily restrictive and incorrect....

[T]he disruptive effects of deliberate conduct committed with the express purpose of obscuring the election outcome based on legal votes cast is likely to be more invidious and its results difficult to ascertain and quantify. Schemes that seek to discourage proper and confidential voting or that endeavor to introduce unintended or illegal votes into the outcome will inevitably produce outcome distortions that defy precise quantification. Furthermore, the grounds of mistake and malfunction are distinguished by the absence of deliberate human efforts to thwart true election results, and are generally not obscured by the material witnesses' self-interest or desire to avoid criminal self-incrimination. With its enactment of the Deliberate Actions ground in the Election Contest Statute, the legislature expressly intended to provide the remedy of a special election not merely for inadvertent mistakes and malfunctions, but also for deliberate conduct. In construing the language of these subsections, we must interpret and apply them in such a manner as to achieve the effect intended. As to the Deliberate Actions ground, the legislature could not reasonably have intended to immunize obviously corrupt elections where the resulting distortion of an election outcome could not be precisely traced and mathematically determined.

On the other hand, the mere occurrence of conduct by one or more persons who knew or reasonably should have known that the conduct would make it impossible to determine the candidate receiving the most valid votes, but which deliberate conduct does not affect the outcome of an election, would be inconsistent with the language "makes it impossible to determine the candidate who received the highest number of votes" and thus cannot be a valid ground requiring a special election. We are convinced that this language was intended to require that the results of an election contested under the Deliberate Actions ground may not be set aside and a special election ordered unless the deliberate acts or series of actions succeed in substantially undermining the reliability of the election and the trustworthiness of its outcome.

We therefore hold that the burden upon a challenger seeking a special election under the Deliberate Actions ground . . . of the Election Contest statute is to conclusively demonstrate (a) the occurrence of an act or series of actions by one or more persons who knew or reasonably should have known that such conduct would make it impossible to determine which candidate receives the most legal votes cast in the election, and (b) the deliberate act or series of actions so infected the election process as to profoundly undermine the integrity of the election and the trustworthiness of its outcome.[4] A special election should be ordered only in rare and exceptional cases. . . .

In the present case, the undisputed trial court findings establish the occurrence of a deliberate series of actions that "perverted the absentee voting process and compromised the integrity and results of that election." The court found that this scheme subjected "the naïve, the neophytes, the infirm and the needy" to "unscrupulous election tactics," that there was "convincing evidence that established the pervasive fraud, illegal conduct, and violations of elections law," and that the misconduct was "voluminous, widespread and insidious."

When as here an election is characterized by a widespread and pervasive pattern of deliberate conduct calculated to cast unlawful and deceptive ballots, the election results are inherently deceptive and unreliable. Widespread corruption of this nature has a high probability of producing untold improper votes and unreliable election results by coercing or intimidating citizens to vote in disregard of their own preferences and by manipulating them into voting when they would otherwise not vote at all. The effectiveness and breadth of such a scheme is inherently difficult to quantify. The opportunities for positive proof of individual ballot improprieties will inevitably be relatively few in comparison with the actual impact of such efforts.

. . . . The magnitude, pervasiveness, and widespread effect of the deliberate series of actions found in this case leads to but one conclusion. The Pastrick campaign certainly knew or consciously intended that the results of their conduct would so inhibit opposing votes and inject invalid favorable votes as to profoundly undermine the integrity of the election and the trustworthiness of its outcome. And this objective was clearly achieved. Given the exceptional facts and circumstances of this case, any other conclusion is inconceivable.

In view of the uncontested factual findings of the trial court, we conclude that Pabey has established that a deliberate series of actions occurred making it impossible to determine the candidate who received the highest number of legal votes cast in the election and that the trial court erred in denying Pabey's request for a special election. While this remedy will be appropriate only rarely and under the most egregious circumstances, it is compelled by the facts of this case.

---

4. Under these subsections, a contestor need not prove to a mathematical certainty that the number of invalid votes equaled or exceeded the contestee's margin of victory, but such proof would of course be sufficient to warrant relief.

III

[The court reviewed the legislative history and judicial interpretations of Indiana's election contest statute, concluding that it gave courts the authority to order a special election if deliberate actions make it impossible to determine who won.]

IV

[The court rejected the Lake County Election Board's cross appeal asserting that the trial court erred as to some of the 155 absentee ballots that it determined to be invalid.]

As discussed in Part II above, our ultimate resolution of this case does not rest on the mathematical comparison of votes invalidated to Pastrick's final victory margin. Instead, it rests on the trial court's unchallenged findings and conclusions of pervasive and widespread deliberate conduct that "perverted the absentee voting process and compromised the integrity and results of that election." The total number of absentee votes invalidated by the trial court is not determinative. Our conclusion is not altered whether the number of invalidated absentee ballots is 155 as found by the trial court, or 100, as urged by the Lake County Election Board.

Conclusion

We reverse the trial court's determination denying a special election and remand to the trial court with directions to promptly order a special election by issuing a writ of election pursuant to Indiana Code § 3-10-8-3, and for all further proceedings consistent with this opinion. . . .

BOEHM, J., dissenting [joined by SULLIVAN, J.].

I respectfully dissent. In my view, the controlling question is not whether election law violations occurred. The trial court found they did, and that finding was plainly supported by the evidence. But the central issue here is whether the corruption was the cause of the election result. The presence of corruption, even if "widespread," is no basis to upset an election and nullify the votes of the electorate if a majority of untainted votes supported the winning candidate. As the majority opinion spells out in some detail, the trial court found election law violations, and they were not limited to a few isolated instances. But the standard set forth in Indiana law for overturning an election it is that it is "impossible to determine the candidate who received the highest number of votes." The trial court, like the majority, read "the highest number of votes" to mean legitimate votes. The trial court, despite the portions of the judgment quoted by the majority, found that the plaintiffs failed to carry their burden of establishing that.

The trial court's finding, like any fact determination, is reversible only if clearly erroneous. I believe that the trial court carefully analyzed these complex facts, and its finding is correct on this record. The trial court found the statute to require that the plaintiffs establish, by a preponderance of the evidence, that the "deliberate acts" rendered it "impossible" to determine who got the most legitimate votes. I think that is the correct reading of the statute, and I believe it is the same reading the majority gives it. I also believe that reading makes sense. If corruption is widespread but has no effect on the election result, neither the public nor the parties should be put to the trouble of redoing the election. This does not mean the plaintiffs had to prove enough individual instances of unlawful votes to tip the election. It does mean that they needed to prove that the unlawful practices made it more likely than not that the result of the election, measured by lawful votes, was unknowable. There are a number of ways that a statistician might attempt to establish that it was a more probable than not that the deliberate acts affected the result. Here the trial court's judgment turned on its finding that there was no such showing. Neither plaintiffs nor the majority show how, on this record, the trial court was incorrect, much less clearly erroneous. . . .

I also believe the majority's standard for judicial intervention in an election is problematic. The statute as written provides a relatively objective standard: are enough votes tainted that it is more likely than not that the result of the election, measured by lawful ballots, is unknown. The majority puts an essentially subjective patina on this test and calls for a new election whenever wrongdoing "profoundly undermines the integrity of the election and the trustworthiness of its outcome." This seems to me to invite courts to exercise essentially discretionary authority to alter election results that they deem undermined. Given that many Indiana trial judges are selected by partisan election, it seems an unwise expansion of the quite limited standard selected by the legislature, and one calculated to lead to claims of improper judicial interference with the electoral process. . . .

The difficulties the plaintiffs faced in proving their case were substantial, but are in my view no reason to upset an election. To be sure, plaintiffs here labored under severe constraints, but those constraints are imposed by statute and are designed to prevent judicial interference with electoral results except in the most extreme circumstances. Indiana law requires an election contest, as opposed to a recount, to be filed within seven days after the election. I.C. § 3-12-8-5 (1998). The matter is to be heard within twenty days after notice of a contest is served. I.C. § 3-12-8-16. This very short timetable undoubtedly imposes limits on the access to information and discovery that is available in more conventional lawsuits. But there is a very good reason why the election laws require this very expedited resolution of election disputes, even at the cost of sacrificing the court's normal opportunities for fact finding. There are many other remedies for the actions complained of in addition to setting aside an election. These include criminal prosecution of those who violate the law. As the entire nation painfully learned in the 2000 presidential contest, protracted election disputes leave the leadership and governance of the body politic in question. Upsetting an election thus visits a penalty on all citizens of the affected electorate, not just the wrongdoers.

In sum, the legislature has provided that the election stands if, after disregarding the votes shown to be tainted, there is no showing that the result is unknown. The majority cites authorities under other statutes that suggest a lower threshold of proof may be sufficient to overturn an election. I believe under our statutes Indiana courts have no business imposing a higher standard on the electorate. The trial court faithfully carried out the charge given to it by the legislature and found that the plaintiffs' case fell short of establishing the need for a new primary election. There is no doubt that the plaintiffs proved old-style election fraud in some cases, and highly inappropriate behavior in others. But our disapproval of the conduct of some of the participants in the election is no basis to change its result without proof that the ultimate result was altered by the wrongdoing.

Notes and Questions

1. Who has the better of the argument between the majority and the dissent? The statute allows for an election to be contested where it is "impossible" to determine which candidate received the most votes. Was it really impossible to make that determination? Note that the number of votes determined to have been cast illegally was less than the margin of victory.

2. Consider too the costs of requiring a do-over. Where a special election is ordered, the composition of those voting in the new election will inevitably be different than that of the original election. Some people who came out to vote the first time will not show up for the second, and vice-versa. Should this reality determine a court's judgment about whether to order a new election?

3. One example of a case in which the court reached a different judgment from the *Pabey* court is the challenge to Florida's butterfly ballot, shown in Part I of this chapter. Despite evidence that many voters who intended to vote for then-Vice-President Gore mistakenly voted for Reform Party candidate Pat Buchanan, the Florida courts declined to void the election and order a new one, citing the heavy burden on those seeking such a remedy. *Fladell v. Palm Beach County Canvassing Board*, 772 So. 2d 1240 (Fla. 2000). Reconsider whether that was the correct result.

4. Adjusting vote totals and ordering a new election are not the only possible remedies where state or federal law have been violated. Civil damages and criminal penalties may also be available. While litigants in voting rights cases usually seek injunctive relief, damages may be an appropriate remedy in some cases. See *Taylor v. Howe*, 225 F.3d 993 (8th Cir. 2000) (awarding damages for harassment and deliberate denial of the vote on account of race). Criminal penalties may also be available, especially in a case like *Pabey* where there is evidence of intentional violations of the law. For a detailed discussion of the remedies available to courts in election cases, see Steven F. Huefner, *Remedying Election Wrongs*, 44 Harvard Journal of Legislation 265 (2007). Should the availability of such after-the-fact civil and criminal remedies inform the court's judgment of whether to order a new election?

5. The American Law Institute, a well-respected group of leading lawyers, judges, and law professors, writes "Restatements" and "Principles" across a number of areas of the law. The ALI recently undertook a project to state certain principles related to election administration, led by Professors Foley and Huefner. "This project has three parts. The first part concerns the rules for 'non-precinct voting'—the casting of

ballots by means other than the traditional polling place on election day. The second part concerns general principles for the resolution of disputed elections and is applicable to both presidential and nonpresidential elections. The third part concerns presidential election disputes specifically and establishes procedures to complete the resolution of a disputed presidential election within the unique and challenging time constraints established by Congress." American Law Institute, Principles of the Law, Election Administration: Non-Precinct Voting and Resolution of Ballot-Counting Disputes (2019). For any states in the market for a set of rules decided in advance by a bipartisan group of lawyers, judges, and scholars, the ALI principles are available for adoption and consultation.

6. A recurrent question in election administration is what should be done when a natural disaster, terrorist attack, pandemic, or other emergency disrupts an election that has already begun. A recent article finds that, when such events occur, courts are often asked to intervene without clear standards to guide them. Michael T. Morley, *Election Emergencies: Voting in the Wake of Natural Disasters and Terrorist Attacks*, 67 Emory Law Journal 545 (2018). Professor Morley argues that courts should generally be reluctant to extend voting hours for run-of-the-mill problems like bad weather or power outages. The better approach, he suggests, is for states to adopt laws providing clear criteria for when election officials should take remedial action in response to emergencies.

These questions became very real and pressing during the early days of the COVID-19 pandemic, which caused some states to make last-minute changes to their 2020 primaries and is certain to cause additional disruption in the general election (see Note 10 following *Bush v. Gore, supra*). One affected state was Wisconsin. The state had its presidential primary on April 7, 2020, in the midst of the pandemic lockdown. To accommodate voters who were concerned about voting in person, a federal district court issued an order allowing absentee ballots to be mailed and postmarked *after* election day, so long last they were received within one week. By a 5-4 vote, the U.S. Supreme Court stayed that court order, with Justice Kavanaugh writing for the majority:

> Extending the date by which ballots may be cast by voters—not just received by the municipal clerks but cast by voters—for an additional six days after the scheduled election day fundamentally alters the nature of the election. And again, the plaintiffs themselves did not even ask for that relief in their preliminary injunction motions. Our point is not that the argument is necessarily forfeited, but is that the plaintiffs themselves did not see the need to ask for such relief. By changing the election rules so close to the election date and by affording relief that the plaintiffs themselves did not ask for in their preliminary injunction motions, the District Court contravened this Court's precedents and erred by ordering such relief. This Court has repeatedly emphasized that lower federal courts should ordinarily not alter the election rules on the eve of an election. See *Purcell v. Gonzalez*, 549

U.S. 1 (2006) (per curiam); *Frank v. Walker*, 574 U.S. 929 (2014); *Veasey v. Perry*,135 S. Ct. 9 (2014).

> The unusual nature of the District Court's order allowing ballots to be mailed and postmarked after election day is perhaps best demonstrated by the fact that the District Court had to issue a subsequent order enjoining the public release of any election results for six days after election day. In doing so, the District Court in essence enjoined nonparties to this lawsuit. It is highly questionable, moreover, that this attempt to suppress disclosure of the election results for six days after election day would work. And if any information were released during that time, that would gravely affect the integrity of the election process. The District Court's order suppressing disclosure of election results showcases the unusual nature of the District Court's order allowing absentee ballots mailed and postmarked after election day to be counted. And all of that further underscores the wisdom of the *Purcell* principle, which seeks to avoid this kind of judicially created confusion.

Republican National Committee v. Democratic National Committee, 140 S. Ct. 1205 (2020).

Justice Ginsburg wrote a dissenting opinion, joined by Justices Breyer, Sotomayor, and Kagan. The dissenters expressed concern that "massive disenfranchisement" would result from the Court's order, because some voters who timely requested absentee ballots would not receive them by election day. *Id.* at 1209. Those voters, she argued, faced a Hobson's Choice of "brav[ing] the polls, endangering their own and others' safety," or "los[ing] their right to vote." *Id.* at 1211.

Three months later, the Supreme Court again issued a stay of a district court order liberalizing voting rules in response to the pandemic. *Merrill v. People First of Alabama*, 2020 WL 3604049 (July 2, 2020). In that case, a federal district court had enjoined Alabama's witness requirement and photo ID rules for at-risk voters, as well as the state's de facto ban on curbside voting. This time, there was no published opinion, but the vote was again 5-4. As in the Wisconsin case, the Republican-appointed justices voted to stay the lower court's order, while the Democratic-appointed justices would have denied the stay.

The Court's skepticism of late-issued federal court injunctions continued in the general election. The Court affirmed the *Purcell*-based stay of a district court injunction in a case arising out of Wisconsin. *Democratic National Committee v. Wisconsin State Legislature*, 141 S. Ct. 28 (2020). Justice Kavanaugh's concurring opinion offered an especially strong version of the *Purcell* doctrine:

> Even seemingly innocuous late-in-the-day judicial alterations to state election laws can interfere with administration of an election and cause unanticipated consequences. If a court alters election laws near an election, election administrators must first understand the court's injunction,

> then devise plans to implement that late-breaking injunction, and then determine as necessary how best to inform voters, as well as state and local election officials and volunteers, about those last-minute changes. It is one thing for state legislatures to alter their own election rules in the late innings and to bear the responsibility for any unintended consequences. It is quite another thing for a federal district court to swoop in and alter carefully considered and democratically enacted state election rules when an election is imminent.
>
> That important principle of judicial restraint not only prevents voter confusion but also prevents election administrator confusion—and thereby protects the State's interest in running an orderly, efficient election and in giving citizens (including the losing candidates and their supporters) confidence in the fairness of the election.

Id. at 31 (Kavanaugh, J., concurring). For a contrasting view, see *id.* at 42 (Kagan, J. dissenting) (arguing that *Purcell* should be understood as directing courts to "consider all relevant factors, not just the calendar," consistent with the "usual rules of equity").

Two Supreme Court justices have even suggested that the presumption against injunctions close to an election be extended to *state* courts. *Moore v. Cirsota*, 141 S. Ct. 46, 48 (2020) (Gorsuch, J., joined by Alito, J. dissenting) (agreeing with lower court dissenters who "thoughtfully explained... the broader problems with last-minute election-law-writing-by-lawsuit"). *But see Democratic National Committee v. Wisconsin State Legislature*, 141 S. Ct. at 28 (Roberts, C.J., concurring) (distinguishing state court and federal court election injunctions).

The Court's decisions in *RNC v. DNC*, *Merrill*, and *DNC v. Wisconsin State Legislature* send an unambiguous message that a majority of justices will look skeptically on federal court injunctions altering voting procedures shortly before election day, even in the middle of a crisis. Has the *Purcell* principle hardened into an ironclad rule against such injunctions? What impact are these decisions likely to have on future election litigation? Should we be concerned about the seemingly partisan character of the Court's decisionmaking, with all nine justices voting consistent with the preferences of the political party of the President who appointed them? See Richard L. Hasen, *Three Pathologies of American Voting Rights Illuminated by the COVID-19 Pandemic, and How to Treat and Cure Them,* 19 Election Law Journal 263 (2020). For more criticism of the Court's reliance on *Purcell*, see Wilfred U. Codrington III, Purcell *in Pandemic*, 96 New York University Law Review (forthcoming 2021).

Chapter 7

Ballot Propositions

Most of this book, like American political thought generally, centers around institutions of representative democracy, in which the people elect representatives who are empowered either directly or through their appointees to make governmental decisions. In most states, representative democracy has long been supplemented by direct votes on propositions. For example, every state but Delaware requires a vote of the people to amend the state constitution. However, near the end of the nineteenth century, the Populists and later the Progressives urged the extension of direct democracy to further supplement the ordinary legislative process. The three mechanisms most often advanced by the Progressives were the initiative, the referendum, and the recall.[a]

The *initiative* is a mechanism that permits a specified number of voters to propose a statute (and, in many states, a constitutional amendment) by signing petitions. Once the petitions qualify by receiving enough signatures the proposal is placed on the ballot, and it is enacted if the voters approve it. The initiative is the direct democracy device that usually receives by far the most public attention and debate.

The *referendum* permits voters to challenge a statute passed by the legislature. If a referendum petition qualifies, the challenged statute does not go into effect unless it is approved by the voters at the next election.[b] Some confusion is engendered by the fact that the word "referendum" sometimes is used as a generic term, referring to any type of ballot proposition.[c] In this chapter we use "referendum" in the more

a. For a colorful account of the adoption of the initiative and referendum in Oregon, see David Schuman, *The Origin of State Constitutional Direct Democracy: William Simon U'Ren and "The Oregon System,"* 67 Temple Law Review 947 (1994). More generally, see Nathaniel A. Persily, *The Peculiar Geography of Direct Democracy: Why the Initiative, Referendum and Recall Developed in the American West*, 2 Michigan Law & Policy Review 11 (1997).

b. Suppose a petition referring a legislatively-enacted redistricting statute to the voters qualifies for the ballot. According to the procedures governing the referendum process, the law is ineffective until and unless the voters approve it. If the first available election at which the referendum can be put to the voters occurs at the statewide primary, at which districts are needed for the nomination of candidates for Congress and the state legislature, what districts should be used? See *Assembly v. Deukmejian*, 639 P.2d 939 (Cal. 1982). What if the initiative has not yet qualified but seems likely to qualify? See Vandermost v. Bowen, 269 P.3d 446 (Cal. 2012).

c. Although "referenda" is often used as the plural for "referendum," "referendums" is the more correct term, according to the Oxford English Dictionary. "Plebiscite" is another term sometimes used generically to refer to any type of ballot measure.

specific sense and use terms such as "ballot proposition" and "ballot measure" as generic terms for the direct democracy procedures.

The *recall* is a device whereby voters may attempt to unseat an elected official whose term has not expired. Logically, the recall might best be categorized as a part of the system of representative democracy, but it is customarily listed with the devices of direct democracy.

Another category of ballot propositions consists of measures submitted to the voters by the state legislature. Most often this is done because voter approval is required, as in the case of constitutional amendments and bond authorizations in most states. Occasionally, a state legislature will voluntarily pass a statute whose going into effect is conditional on voter approval.

Although ballot measure elections do not occur at the national level in the United States,[d] about half the states have adopted one or more of the above devices. All but five of these states did so before or during the first two decades of the twentieth century. Since 1978 only Mississippi, whose supreme court in 1922 had struck down an initiative law on procedural grounds,[e] has adopted (or, as in Mississippi's case, readopted) the initiative. But see *In re Initiative Measure No. 65*, 2021 WL 1940821 (Miss. May 14, 2021) (invalidating Mississippi's ballot initiative process on a technicality).

Despite the relative stability in availability of the initiative and referendum, a continuing controversy swirls around direct democracy. Even after nearly a century of experience, observers offer sharply differing assessments of the initiative, the most frequently used device. This chapter begins with background and an evaluation by Richard Ellis, a political scientist. Ensuing sections consider some limits on the content of initiative proposals and judicial oversight of the initiative process.

---

d. The United States is one of five major democracies that have never had a nationwide referendum. The others are India, Israel, Japan, and the Netherlands. See David Butler & Austin Ranney, *Conclusion*, in Referendums around the World 258 (1994).

e. *Power v. Robinson*, 93 So. 769 (Miss. 1922). This ruling was reaffirmed in *Moore v. Molpus*, 578 So.2d 624 (Miss. 1991), a decision that prompted the readoption of the initiative in 1992.

I. Pros and Cons

Richard J. Ellis, Democratic Delusions: The Initiative Process in America

26–43 (2002)[f]

The Initiative's Radical Past

Arguably the single most important event in the birth of the initiative and referendum in America was the publication, early in 1892, of a small book with the awkward title *Direct Legislation by the Citizenship through the Initiative and Referendum.* So electric was its impact that the title page of the 1893 edition boasted that it was "the book that started the Referendum Movement." Its author, James W. Sullivan, a member of the New York Typographers' Union, explicitly addressed the volume to the "radical world." In the mid-1880s Sullivan, who at the time was a devotee of Henry George and the single tax, had become interested in the Swiss model of direct legislation, and in 1888 he took a leave of absence from his job as editor of a reform weekly to visit Switzerland and investigate the impact direct legislation had had on the nation's economics and politics. Sullivan was not the first to describe the Swiss experience, but he was the first to make the Swiss model seem relevant to the United States. Sullivan's message to American workers was simple and appealing: by empowering the wage-working majority, direct legislation would destroy "the American plutocracy." ... Introduce the initiative and the referendum, Sullivan preached, and the walls of the citadel would come crumbling down. The "straightforward politics of direct legislation" had peacefully and simply transformed Switzerland, and there was no reason it could not usher in a similarly bloodless social revolution in the United States.

Among the many American radicals to be captivated by Sullivan's message, none was more important than the founding father of Oregon's initiative and referendum, the blacksmith-turned-lawyer William Simon U'Ren.... Although U'Ren had come across the idea of the initiative and referendum a year or two earlier, Sullivan's study fired his imagination. U'Ren felt the veil lift from his eyes. "I forgot, for the time, all about Henry George and the single tax. All these I now saw to be details. The one important thing was to restore the law-making power where it belonged—into the hands of the people. Once give us that, we could get anything we wanted—single tax, anything."

[U'Ren's efforts led to creation of a Joint Committee on Direct Legislation, consisting of five farm and labor organizations,] with U'Ren, the Farmers' Alliance representative, as secretary. The committee spearheaded a massive propaganda campaign designed to mobilize popular support for direct democracy. Its rhetoric was unabashedly radical and populist: the legislature was a bastion of "the monied and monopolistic classes," and only direct legislation would "make it impossible for corporations and boodlers to obtain unjust measures by which to profit at the expense of the people." More than just the rhetoric was radical, for the organization also demanded a mandatory referendum that would require all legislation passed at the state, county, or municipal level [to be] approved by voters before becoming law. U'Ren also pressed the direct democracy agenda from within the Populist party. After joining the party in 1893, he was soon selected secretary of the Populist state committee and then chair of the 1894 Populist state convention. In 1896 he carried the battle directly to the Oregon state legislature as a Populist state legislator.

From the Margins to the Mainstream

. . .

Since the mid-1880s radicals in the labor movement and agrarian protest movements had been attracted to direct legislation for its transformative promise. It would enable farmers and workers to turn the tables on corporate power and economic privilege, using numbers to defeat money. But so long as the vision was revolutionary or tied to a specific policy agenda—such as progressive taxation on land, income, and inheritances, or higher wages and shorter working days—it was difficult if not impossible to gain the support of the establishment: publishers and editors, bankers, lawyers, professionals, the comfortable middle class, and party politicians. The widespread economic distress and discontent of the early 1890s had created a window of opportunity for economic radicalism, but by 1896 the window was fast closing. If direct legislation were to be established across the country, it would need to appeal to more than just disaffected laborers and intellectuals; it would have to dance not just with those who brought it but with those who had initially spurned and spat upon it. After 1896 the initiative and referendum movement increasingly became a political movement divorced from any particular economic vision.

. . . U'Ren's rhetoric and position also shifted during this period. Through 1895 he had vigorously advocated a mandatory referendum on all or nearly all laws. . . . In 1896, however, U'Ren suddenly abandoned the mandatory referendum in favor of an optional referendum. Moreover, he began to downplay direct legislation's transformative powers. By the end of 1897, after the state legislature had again failed to act on the initiative and referendum, U'Ren stressed that direct legislation would be used infrequently. Far from citizens becoming political animals, the initiative would allow Oregonians to "give our time to our business and only touch politics occasionally as an incidental duty—and yet do vastly more effective work than was ever done by any amount of labor under the present system." The threat of the initiative and referendum would be sufficient to force the politicians to clean up their act and prevent them from passing wasteful, pernicious, or unjust laws. Direct legislation would be the "gun behind the door."

[I]n 1902, . . . Oregon voters . . . overwhelmingly approved [a] constitutional amendment establishing the initiative and referendum, making Oregon the third state to adopt direct legislation. (South Dakota was the first, and in Utah, the second, the initiative and referendum did not take effect until decades later because the legislature refused to pass enabling legislation.) In 1904 two initiatives qualified for the Oregon ballot, making it the first state to try out the new tools of direct democracy. Immediately thereafter the floodgates opened: over the next decade Oregonians voted on over one hundred statewide initiatives and popular referenda. Many longstanding friends of the initiative now worried that direct legislation was being abused. Even before the flood had begun, in January 1906, the *Oregon Journal* reminded Oregonians that "the real friends of the initiative law will be slow to invoke its aid, and when they do it will be to remedy a manifest evil that it is ordinarily difficult if not impossible to reach." . . .

As states debated whether to adopt the initiative and referendum in the opening decades of the twentieth century, proponents continued to rely upon both millennial and minimalist justifications. The minimalist rationale appealed to those who feared that direct legislation made utopian demands upon the citizenry and subverted representative democracy, or who worried that the initiative process would be used to launch a class war against the rich and well-to-do or to wage a moral crusade against unpopular minorities. Direct legislation, Woodrow Wilson reassured the doubters, was not "a substitute for representative institutions, but only . . . a means of stimulation and control . . . a sobering means of obtaining genuine representative action on the part of legislative bodies." In this minimalist conception, which typically privileged the referendum over the initiative, direct legislation was just another "safeguard of politics," one which citizens would only need to deploy infrequently to keep politicians in check. The minimalist rationale effectively assuaged fears, but the millennial rationale spoke more directly to people's hopes and dreams. Although the Populist party had long since faded away, the Populist vision — which imagined that the initiative and referendum could usher in a radically transformed world "in which equal rights to all shall live on forever, and special privileges shall be known no more" — was still very much alive in the Progressive era. Direct legislation, in this view, would do more than just add another check on the behavior of legislators; it would, in the words of the *Boston Common*, transform politics by enabling "the rising tide of sentiment for social justice" to sweep away "the special interests which now play for delay." . . .

A mixture of minimalist and millennial arguments helped to enact the initiative and referendum in nineteen states in the two decades between 1898 and 1918, but neither set of expectations proved a reliable guide to the subsequent history of the initiative. Certainly the initiative and referendum, despite notable and undeniable accomplishments, did little to justify the utopian, emancipatory hopes of radical transformation with which so many early advocates began. True, in some states Populist-backed governmental reforms, from direct election of senators to woman suffrage, were achieved through the initiative, but for the most part these reforms came about the old-fashioned way: through the legislative process. Useful reforms in working conditions (especially shorter hours) were sometimes enacted by initiative, but the more sweeping radical panaceas like the single tax were consistently defeated by voters. Moreover, far from disappearing, money, lobbyists, and powerful special interests continued to play a leading role in every state in the nation, whether the state possessed direct legislation or not. Indeed money and special interests usually played at least as prominent a part in initiative campaigns as they did in candidate campaigns.

The early years of direct legislation did little to vindicate the minimalists either. In Oregon in 1912 there were twenty-eight statewide initiatives on the November ballot, a national record that still stands to this day.... Activists in other states rushed to follow Oregon's lead. Coloradans voted on twenty initiatives in 1912, while in 1914 California's electorate faced seventeen initiatives and Arizona's fifteen. In 1920–21 North Dakota, which enacted the initiative in 1914, voted on sixteen initiatives, a record that the state eclipsed a decade later when citizens were asked to vote on eighteen in 1932. Outside of these hotbeds of initiative activity, the minimalist argument often fared much better. In states like Arkansas, Maine, Massachusetts, Michigan, Nebraska, and Nevada, for instance, the initiative was used sparingly in the first few decades of its existence....

The minimalist prediction was particularly relevant in the 1950s and 1960s as Figure 7.1 attests. [Even in] Oregon, the state that used the initiative more often than any other, citizens finally appeared to have learned to use direct democracy with discretion. Between 1956 and 1969 Oregonians voted on only nine initiatives and never faced more than two initiatives on the same ballot. Meanwhile, Oregonians took great pride in their government, turned out to vote in large numbers and had high levels of trust in their public officials. Elsewhere in the nation the story was much the same. In the thirty years between 1942 and 1971, nearly 350 statewide

Figure 7-1 Average Number of Initiatives per Two-Year Election Cycle

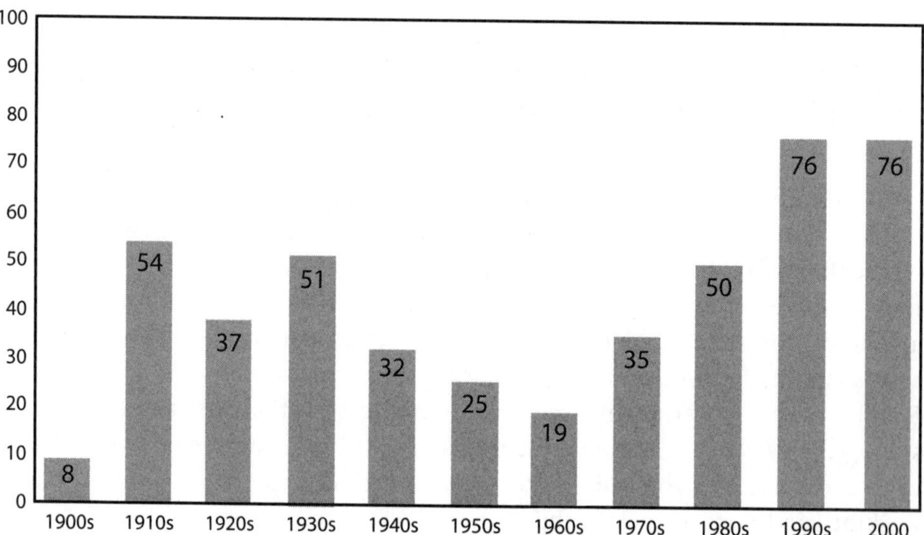

initiatives made it to the ballot, an average of about one initiative every two years for each of the initiative states. During these three decades, direct legislation did indeed seem to be the gun behind the door that the minimalists had promised, something more valuable for its potential than for its use.

The Silent Revolution

Between 1990 and 2000 there were 458 initiatives nationwide. That is over three times the rate at which initiatives appeared on the ballot in the 1940s, 1950s, and 1960s. Today the initiative can no longer be plausibly portrayed as a gun behind the door, at least not in the states that have come to rely most heavily on the initiative process, particularly Oregon, California, Colorado, Washington, and Arizona. In these five states the gun is now madly brandished about and fired in almost every conceivable direction. Politicians scatter, running for cover, desperately trying to keep their heads down. Citizens appear bewildered, unsure what to think. The gunmen cry "power to the people," but few of the people seem to feel more empowered by the blaze of gunfire. To be sure, citizens take a certain delight at the occasional shot lodged in the politicians' posterior, but the gunslingers are not content to threaten only the political class. Vulnerable minorities are at least as likely to be the targets of the shootings as are the rich and powerful. To some it appears that beneath their populist masks, the gunslingers are the very same special interest groups and politicians from which the gun behind the door had promised to protect us.

When was the initiative transformed from a gun behind the door to a weapon of choice for interest groups and politicians? Many observers credit (or blame) California's Proposition 13, the 1978 property tax-cutting initiative that was spearheaded by Howard ("I'm mad as hell") Jarvis. Proposition 13, which passed by an overwhelming majority despite the opposition of virtually every major politician and newspaper in the state, dramatically illustrated direct legislation's enormous power to make public policy as well as to transform the political agenda. And yet Proposition 13 was as much symptom as it was cause. Increased reliance on the initiative, both in California and the nation, was already discernible even before Proposition 13 appeared on the June, 1978 ballot. In 1976–77 there were fifty-two initiatives across the nation, the highest number since the 1938–39 election cycle. Californians themselves had voted on ten initiatives in 1972–73; one has to go back a half century to 1922–23 to find more statewide initiatives on the California ballot. Even more telling evidence against the Proposition 13 explanation is that it was not until 1988 that initiative use shifted up into a higher gear nationwide (see Table 7.1). For almost a decade after Proposition 13, the average number of initiatives on the ballot nationally was actually less than the number of initiatives in the two-year election cycle immediately preceding Proposition 13.

Although no single event or year can be unambiguously identified as beginning the modern initiative revolution, there is little doubt about the magnitude of the change. [M]ore initiatives were approved by California in the last two decades of the twentieth century than were passed in the preceding sixty-eight years dating back

Table 7-1 Number of Initiatives per Two-Year Election

	Mean	High	Low
1952–1971	20	31	10
1972–1975	32	39	25
1976–1987	48	58	42
1988–2001	75	103	61

to the initiative's adoption in 1912. Initiative-made law, once a minor feature of the California political landscape, has become its dominant and defining feature.

California and Oregon have been the clear leaders in initiative use, but there have been plenty of followers in the past two decades. Even states without a strong tradition of initiative use have increasingly gotten into the act. Idaho, Maine, Nevada, South Dakota, and Utah had more initiatives on the ballot in the 1980s and 1990s than in the previous eight decades of the century combined. Citizens in Maine, for instance, voted on twenty-six initiatives between 1980 and 2000, which is over double the number they had cast judgment on in the previous seventy years. . . . Across the nation, 35 percent of the approximately two thousand initiatives that have reached the ballot since 1904 qualified in the past two decades. More dramatically still, each of the past seven election cycles rank among the top ten election cycles in initiative use (see Table 7.2).

Initiative use indisputably became more widespread in the 1980s and 1990s than it had been in previous decades, but this national pattern is not reproduced in every state. In fact, Arkansas, North Dakota, and Oklahoma used the initiative less often in the 1980s and 1990s than they had in the preceding half century. For a few states it is the 1950s and 1960s that are exceptional, with the 1980s and 1990s representing something of a return to normalcy. In Missouri, for instance, there was only one initiative on the ballot in the 1950s and 1960s, but throughout the rest of the century, including the 1980s and 1990s, the state has consistently averaged about nine initiatives per decade. In other states the absolute number of initiatives remains small despite the increase in initiative use in recent decades. In Utah, for example, almost two-thirds of the state's initiatives appeared on the ballot between 1980 and 2000, but the total number of initiatives in those two decades was only eleven. . . . These statistics help to remind us that when we talk about an initiative revolution we are talking about a phenomenon that has transformed some states while leaving others relatively untouched.

Heavy initiative use remains concentrated in a relatively few states. Between 1980 and 2000 three states (California, Oregon, and Colorado) accounted for 40 percent of the total number of statewide initiatives in the nation. Indeed, Oregon and California alone accounted for 30 percent of statewide initiatives in the 1980s and 1990s and about the same percentage during the rest of the twentieth century. In 2000 these two pace-setting states accounted for close to 40 percent of the nation's

Table 7-2 Ranking of the Top Ten Election Cycles in Initiative Use, 1904–2001

Rank	Election Cycle	No. of Initiatives
1	1996–1997	103
2	1914–1915	92
3	2000–2001	79
4	1932–1933	76
5	1994–1995	75
6	1990–1991	70
7	1992–1993	68
8	1912–1913	67
9	1998–1999	66
10	1988–1989	61

initiatives. Six in ten initiatives between 1990 and 2000 came from six states (Arizona, California, Colorado, North Dakota, Oregon, and Washington), and those same six states account for better than 60 percent of the initiatives in the twentieth century. In short, although initiatives are more numerous today than ever before, a handful of high-use states continue to experience the effects of direct legislation in a way that is qualitatively different from other initiative states.

A Populist Paradox

Among the most striking features of the contemporary period is that increased reliance on the initiative has not been accompanied by a rush to adopt direct legislation in other states. This stands in marked contrast to the first two decades of the twentieth century, when high rates of initiative use were accompanied by a rush of states enacting the initiative. In the sixteen years between 1902 and 1918, over two-fifths of the states then in the union adopted the initiative. Only five states have adopted the initiative since then, and four of those (Alaska [1959], Wyoming [1968], Florida [1968], and Illinois [1970]) adopted the initiative between 1959 and 1970, a period in which the initiative was little used across the country. Ironically, only one state has adopted the initiative during the decades of the initiative's greatest popularity. That state is Mississippi, which enacted the initiative in 1992.

More paradoxical still [are] the antipopulist constraints Mississippi placed upon the initiative power. The brand of direct democracy enacted in Mississippi bears little resemblance to the populist instrument used in California or in Oregon. To begin with, Mississippi established that no more than five initiatives could appear on any one ballot. The state also refused to permit statutory initiatives or popular referenda. Although voters can change the state constitution by means of an initiative petition, they cannot make laws through the initiative process, nor can they directly negate laws passed by the state legislature. Further constraining voters' ability to utilize the initiative process is a requirement that one-fifth of the petition signatures must come from each of the five congressional districts. The Mississippi initiative process also permits the legislature to place an alternative measure on the same ballot, thereby giving the voters a choice between two bills. To make things even more difficult, the legislature required that the majority in favor of an initiative must comprise at least 40 percent of the number of all voters who cast ballots in that election. Moreover, every initiative that has revenue implications must identify the amount and source of revenue required to implement it; if the initiative reduces revenues or reallocates funding it must specify which programs will be affected. Finally, Mississippi prohibits initiatives that would change the initiative process or alter either the state's bill of rights or its constitutional right-to-work guarantee.

Mississippi's emasculated initiative power resulted from intense opposition by an unlikely legislative alliance of rural conservatives and African-American liberals. Both saw themselves as minority groups who could be harmed by a purely majoritarian system. Blacks feared that whites would use the initiative power to discriminate against them, and legislators from rural districts feared that densely populated urban areas would be advantaged by the initiative. This coalition succeeded in defeating the initiative proposal no fewer than three times in the lower house, and with each defeat the proponents watered down the original proposal still further.

Not surprisingly, persuading legislatures to adopt the initiative process has proved a hard sell, but it is not only legislators who are responsible for the glacial pace of change. Legislators have been able to halt adoption of the initiative precisely because, unlike at the outset of the twentieth century, there has not been a deafening popular outcry in favor of adopting direct legislation. . . .

The increased use of the initiative in the 1980s and 1990s is thus only half the story. If we are to understand the late-twentieth century initiative process, we must also understand the dog that didn't bark. In the last two decades of the twentieth century, bills to enact the initiative and referendum have been introduced in virtually every state in the nation, but with the exception of Mississippi no state has added the initiative to its democratic arsenal. The initiative's failure to spread to other states has come as a surprise to many political analysts [who predicted] that a substantial number of states would adopt the initiative and referendum before the end of the [twentieth] century. . . . Why have [their] predictions failed to come to pass even while direct legislation is used with increasing frequency in those states that possess the power?

Some initiative proponents might not see this development as paradoxical. In both cases the cause is the same: professional legislators looking out for their own interests or doing the bidding of powerful special interests. In states with the initiative power, this argument goes, the increase in initiative use is attributable to the legislature consistently ignoring popular demands and preferences. And in states without the initiative power, the failure to adopt direct legislation is also a result of the legislature ignoring the popular will. But there is an alternative explanation, namely that the explosion in initiative use in states like California has scared off many who were originally sympathetic to the idea. Certainly that is how many legislators explain their opposition to direct legislation. . . .

In the late 1970s and early 1980s virtually every state that lacked the initiative was giving serious thought to adopting it. In 1977 the United States Senate held hearings on the possibility of adopting the initiative at the national level, which helped put the idea of a nationwide initiative and referendum on the national agenda for the next decade. But at the beginning of the twenty-first century, the idea of a national initiative has dropped almost completely off the national radar. . . .

This is not to say that the initiative and referendum will not spread to other states in the coming years. Throughout the nation, particularly in the South, there are groups and politicians lobbying for the initiative and referendum. Republican governors in Louisiana and New York have come out in support of the initiative. And some antigovernment and antitax groups continue to push the initiative because they believe it is "a great tool for putting handcuffs on the government." But both the left and the right, Democrats and Republicans, are deeply divided over the desirability of the initiative. For every conservative who salivates at the thought of using direct legislation to cut taxes or end affirmative action, there are others who fear it may be used to further the liberal agenda. In Louisiana, for instance, business interests strongly opposed the Republican governor's direct legislation proposal, fearing it would be used to increase the minimum wage or enact environmental regulations that would increase the cost of doing business. And in Texas, the Christian Coalition resisted the initiative and referendum because they feared it would be used to legalize gambling. Among liberals, too, fears outnumber hopes. Apart from environmentalists, who have had some notable successes in initiative campaigns—particularly in the 1970s and 1980s (their record in recent years, however, has been decidedly poor)—much of the rest of the left fears that direct legislation will be used to cripple the government's capacity to provide much-needed social services. These kinds of fears were not absent in the early twentieth century, but for the most part they were limited to the business groups. As a result, the early-twentieth-century movement to pass direct legislation could plausibly be dramatized as a conflict between powerful special interests and the people. At the beginning of a new century, with groups from all sides of the political spectrum fearful of the initiative's enormous power to make sudden and drastic changes, that populist morality play no longer works as well.

If this analysis is correct, the initiative and referendum will at best be slow to spread across the country, particularly so long as high-use initiative states continue to dramatize the winner-take-all character of direct legislation politics. For most groups, so long as they have a reasonable chance of being heard in the legislature, the thought of what they might lose from direct legislation seems to far outweigh dreams of what they might gain. The Mississippi experience suggests that if another state does adopt the initiative process, intense pressure from interest groups will dilute and restrict the process in ways that make it unlikely that the state would have a large number of initiatives. In short, for the foreseeable future it is unlikely that direct legislation will become an important, let alone dominant force in the political life of those twenty-six states that do not currently have the initiative. Those critics who fear that direct legislation will spread across the country like a cancer are probably as misguided as the enthusiasts who anticipate national redemption through direct legislation's glorious march from sea to shining sea.

Supply-Side Politics

If it is possible to speak about the future spread of direct legislation to non-initiative states with a modicum of certainty, it is more difficult to predict the future course of the initiative and referendum within those states that already possess the power. Is the current popularity of direct legislation just a fad or phase the nation is passing through, or is it here to stay as a permanent feature of a transformed political landscape? . . .

Our predictions of the future can only be as good as our explanations of the past. To forecast what will happen in the coming decades, we need to understand what has been driving initiative use over the past several decades. Probably the most common explanation of initiative use focuses on the mood of the voters. When the voters are angry and discontented, the number of initiatives increases. . . . Certainly trust in government has declined at roughly the same time that initiative use has increased. But although trust in government has an intuitive appeal as an explanation, the trust theory loses some its luster when it is inspected more closely. Trust in government after all has fluctuated substantially over the past several decades, but initiative use has remained relatively immune to those fluctuations. When trust has rebounded, as it did in the mid-1980s and again in the mid-1990s, initiative use has not declined. Nor has anyone provided any evidence that trust in government is lower in states that use the initiative more often. Although popular anger and distrust may have played an important role in triggering the renaissance of the initiative, it is much less clear that continued reliance on the initiative is closely related to levels of popular trust or discontent.

If initiative use seems to remain relatively constant in the face of wide swings in popular mood, we may be better off looking not at the demand side of the equation but rather at the supply side. A supply-side model of initiative use turns our attention away from the mood of the voters and toward those who produce the initiatives. According to this theory, the number of initiatives on the ballot is determined not by the demands of the people but by the suppliers of initiatives: the initiative activists and professionals who place initiatives on the ballot. The professionalization of signature gathering is particularly important in insulating initiative use from popular mood. If anyone with enough money can qualify an initiative for the ballot, then initiative use will vary independently of public demand. If we wish to predict the future of the initiative process in the United States, we must start by understanding the business of signature gathering.

Notes and Questions

1. Debate over the desirability of direct democracy has waxed and waned in the United States since the late nineteenth century. Thomas E. Cronin, Direct Democracy 224–32 (1989), evaluates empirically many of the pro and con arguments. Supportive arguments that he assesses include:

a. Direct democracy enhances government responsiveness and accountability.

b. It provides a safety valve "when legislators prove timid, corrupt, or dominated by special interests."

c. It protects against bossism.

d. It brings about rule by the common people.

e. It reduces the influence of special interests.

f. It permits less well-represented groups to bring their ideas before the public.

g. It stimulates educational debate on important policy issues.

h. It stimulates voter interest in public issues and stimulates turnout.

i. It promotes trust in government.

Cronin also evaluates arguments raised by opponents:

a. Direct democracy undermines representative democracy.

b. It produces unsound legislation.

c. It endangers minority rights.

d. It depends on voters who are not capable of competent policy judgments.

e. It amplifies special interest influence.

f. It lacks accountability because it is not subject to the usual checks and balances.

Cronin finds some merit in a couple of the supportive arguments, that direct democracy provides a safety valve and that it helps some less-represented groups find a forum. The opponents, he concludes, raise a serious objection with respect to the lack of checks and balances. Mostly, though, he finds that empirical support for the arguments on both sides ranges from none to mixed. "Both proponents and opponents have too often overstated their positions," he concludes. "The existing direct democracy processes have both virtues and liabilities."

Another study of the initiative process that reaches relatively balanced conclusions is Elisabeth R. Gerber, The Populist Paradox: Interest Group Influence and the Promise of Direct Legislation (1999). Gerber finds that in general, citizen groups are better able than economic groups to use the initiative successfully to pass new laws. However, she does not contend that her conclusion necessarily supports the process:

> I do *not* say that citizen group dominance of the direct legislation process is necessarily good. The normative value one attributes to this finding depends very strongly on one's assessment of whether majoritarian interests already receive sufficient representation in modern American government. Certainly, the early Populist and Progressive advocates of direct legislation took the position that minority interests, especially those of certain powerful industries, were overrepresented in state legislatures at the expense of broader middle-class interests. To the extent that one agrees that those same sorts of narrow economic interests are overrepresented in state legislatures today, the normative implication of citizen group dominance is favorable. In contrast, to those who believe that business or economic interests are limited in their ability to influence state legislatures or that they hold appropriate levels of power in the state legislative process, the shift of power toward majoritarian interests may be interpreted as bad. Most important, to those who believe the state legislative process facilitates compromise between competing interests, empowering the majority through the direct legislation process threatens to upset the delicate balance between majority and minority interests.

Id. at 142.

In contrast to Ellis, Cronin, and Gerber, all of whom take a relatively balanced view, most students of the initiative process approach the subject from a distinctly supportive or negative perspective. Recent decades have seen a flurry of books hostile to the initiative, including David S. Broder, Democracy Derailed (2000); Peter Schrag, Paradise Lost (1998); Joseph F. Zimmerman, The Initiative: Citizen Law-Making (1999). Supportive views are put forward in Shaun Bowler and Todd Donovan, Demanding Choices: Opinion, Voting, and Direct Democracy (1998).

2. Recall that in *Federalist No. 10*, contained in Chapter 1 of this book, James Madison distinguished between what he called republics and democracies. The former, which Madison preferred, embrace large populations and the representative system. The latter consist of small populations that meet and act directly. The initiative, at least at the state level, is a mixture of these forms. It is used by a large population—relative, that is, to a group that could meet together as a single assembly—but it operates directly rather than through representatives.

Although Madison's terminology distinguishing between republics and democracies is no longer widespread, serious debates still occur about the role of majorities in a democracy. Almost everyone agrees that majorities will and should be able to make public decisions. Within that broad agreement, however, there are many controversial issues. The two that are most relevant are the limits, if any, on the scope of majority rule and the process by which majority rule should be manifested.[g]

---

g. For a good overview of many of the theoretical issues surrounding majority rule, see Elaine Spitz, Majority Rule (1984).

Limits on the scope of majority rule. Recall that in *Federalist No. 10*, Madison wrote that a faction, which by definition is a group working adversely to the rights of some citizens or to the permanent and aggregate interests of the community, can be either a minority or a majority of the population. Fear of "majority tyranny" or, less starkly, that majorities will treat minorities unfairly, has been a major theme of American political thought since Madison's time.[h] Some political philosophers have invoked various conceptions of natural rights in furtherance of the view that there are some things majorities are not entitled to do. In American law and politics, the Bills of Rights in federal and state constitutions have been intended to limit the power of majorities.

Majoritarian processes. Aside from whatever limits on majority rule may exist, American political thought divides over how immediate the control of the majority over public policy should be. One view, sometimes referred to, especially by its detractors, as the plebiscitary view of democracy, holds that the most democratic procedures are those that facilitate the immediate conversion of a policy favored by a majority into law. Madison and many of his contemporaries opposed the majorities empowered by such procedures as "transient majorities"—as do many of our contemporaries. Their idea is that dramatic events or skillful propaganda may create a temporary public frenzy causing a majority to favor ill-considered measures that, given a chance for greater reflection, the majority would oppose. Aside from the problem of the transient majority, those opposed to plebiscitary democracy maintain that representation and other devices that mediate the transformation of majority preferences into law will result in better deliberation and wiser policies. Such mediation arises from what Americans refer to as the system of checks and balances.

Although, as was said above, nearly all Americans believe in some form of majority rule, there are considerable differences on the desirability of substantive and procedural limits or checks on majorities. Proposals and devices that will tend to reduce these limits are often referred to as majoritarian. Not surprisingly, the initiative is often thought of as the supremely majoritarian device. Debates on the desirability of the initiative are therefore often surrogates for debates on majoritarianism itself.

This is fair enough, but it is subject to two possible qualifications. The first, which is pointed to by some supporters of the initiative, is that even in the states identified by Ellis as using the initiative most widely, it remains the exception and not the rule. The overwhelming majority of laws in those states are enacted in the ordinary way by the state legislatures.[i] Thus, although the initiative is majoritarian with respect to

h. Two classics of American thought—though one was written by a Frenchman!—concerned themselves in significant part with this question. See Alexis de Tocquevelle, Democracy in America (Harvey C. Mansfield & Delba Winthrop, trs., 2000) [1835, 1840]; John C. Calhoun, A Disquisition on Government (1993) [1853].

i. Of course, just counting laws can give a misleading picture, because the matters contained in initiatives are often of great importance.

whatever specific issue is being voted on at a particular time, it can also be thought of as part of the overall system of checks and balances. Groups that for one reason or another find it difficult to pursue their objectives in the ordinary legislative process have the opportunity to see if they can do better by taking their proposal to the electorate. For what may be the best defense of the initiative on this ground, see Maimon Schwarzschild, *Popular Initiatives and American Federalism, Or, Putting Direct Democracy In Its Place*, 13 Journal of Contemporary Legal Issues 531 (2004).

The second possible qualification attacks the premise that the initiative actually is a majoritarian institution. We consider that qualification in the following Note.

3. Although majoritarianism in its stronger forms has many critics among students of American government, its precepts often receive a favorable public reaction. Therefore, many supporters of the initiative eschew Schwarzschild's approach of emphasizing the compatibility of the initiative with checks and balances. Instead, they employ populist rhetoric declaring that the initiative embodies the true voice of the people, who can initiate and enact legislation free of the influence of interest groups.

In response to such rhetoric, some opponents of the initiative have sought to turn the tables by contending that the initiative is not majoritarian at all but is instead manipulated and controlled by special interests. The opponents point to the large amounts often spent by interest groups in initiative campaigns and, more generally, contend that the process has been captured by what is often referred to as the "initiative industry." That a high degree of professionalization has surrounded the initiative process in at least some of the high-use states is unquestionably true. See, for example, Jack Citrin, *Who's the Boss? Direct Democracy and Popular Control of Government*, in Broken Contract? Changing Relationships Between Americans and Their Government (Stephen C. Craig, ed., 1996). Sometimes the professionalization is described in somewhat breathless terms:

> Increasingly, initiative proponents hire members of an "initiative industry," composed of professional campaign consultants who often specialize in direct democracy, to aid in this process. The proponents and their consultants are capable of conducting sophisticated research on the existing legal landscape in order to draft the measures to achieve their intended results with an eye toward future judicial review. Moreover, it is not unusual for them to use focus groups and conduct polls to determine how most effectively to promote or "spin" their measures to the voters.

Glen Staszewski, *Rejecting the Myth of Popular Sovereignty and Applying an Agency Model to Direct Democracy*, 56 Vanderbilt Law Review 395, 422 (2003).

Such language can perhaps serve as a corrective to excessive rhetoric extolling the initiative as a pure reflection of the public will. However, those who deny that the initiative works as a majoritarian device run into difficulties. The effects of campaign spending in initiative campaigns will be considered in Chapter 13. For present purposes we can mention that most studies have concluded that one-sided big spending can be quite effective when used in opposition to an initiative proposal but is remarkably ineffective when used to pass a measure. Because large economic resources can often stop the enactment of initiatives, the effectiveness of campaign spending can be said to limit the majoritarian effect of the initiative. But the more important point is that, by virtue of the usual ineffectiveness of spending to secure passage of proposals, spending does not bring into question the majoritarian nature of the initiative when it is used successfully.[j]

The suggestion that the rise of the initiative industry has permitted special interest groups to capture the initiative is subject to two objections. First, the initiative industry arose because the division of labor reduces costs, so that the services become more widely available, not less so. If it were generally true that the process is dominated by narrow interests, then a large percentage of initiatives would be supported by narrow interests and opposed by dispersed interests. There are such initiatives, but according to a recent study they amount to a small percentage—7.8 percent were of this type, and less than a third of these were approved by the voters.[k]

A second difficulty for those who deny the majoritarian nature of the initiative process is evidence suggesting that by and large, public policy is more in tune with majority preferences in initiative states than in other states. Recently, researchers have assumed that in addition to the direct effects of successful initiative measures that go into effect, the availability of the process also has indirect effects. Legislators, interest groups, and others anticipate the possibility of an initiative being proposed and perhaps enacted, and adjust their actions accordingly. Therefore, instead of attempting to measure direct democracy's effects only by considering successful initiatives, these researchers compare policies in states that have the initiative with policies in states that do not.[l] Thus, John G. Matsusaka, in For the Many or for the Few (2004), compares fiscal policy in states with and without the initiative and concludes that fiscal policy is closer to majority opinion in initiative states. A more recent study yielded similar findings on several social issues in initiative and non-initiative states.[m] Matsusaka summarizes his findings:

---

j. A similar conclusion applies to another problem with the initiative that has been documented in recent years, namely that by reason of resistance from legislatures, executive agencies, or courts, many initiatives fail to be implemented, either entirely or in part. See Elisabeth R. Gerber, Arthur Lupia, Mathew D. McCubbins & D. Roderick Kiewiet, Stealing the Initiative: How State Government Responds to Direct Democracy (2001). To the extent that enacted initiative measures are thus blocked, the majoritarian effect of the initiative is limited. But this does not detract from the majoritarian nature of initiatives to the extent they are implemented.

k. Howard R. Ernst, *The Historical Role of Narrow-Material Interests in Initiative Politics*, in Larry J. Sabato, Howard R. Ernst & Bruce A. Larson, Dangerous Democracy? The Battle over Ballot Initiatives in America (2001).

l. For commentary on this research method, see Daniel H. Lowenstein, *Book Review: Competition and Competitiveness in American Elections*, 6 Election Law Journal 278 (2007).

m. John G. Matsusaka, *Popular Control of Public Policy: A Quantitative Approach*, 5 Quarterly Journal of Political Science 133 (2010). See also John G. Matsusaka, Let the People Rule: How

> The evidence turns out to tell a remarkably consistent story. For every policy I am able to examine, the initiative pushes policy in the direction a majority of people say they want to go. I am unable to find *any* evidence that the majority dislikes the policy changes caused by the initiative, as implied by the special interest subversive view.

For the Many or for the Few, at xi–xii (emphasis in original). Matsusaka's conclusion has been disputed, however. Jeffrey Lax and Justin Phillips measured state public opinion on a host of issues and compared it to whether the public's preferred policies had, in fact, been adopted. They found that the availability of the initiative does *not* improve the congruence of public opinion and public policy. See Jeffrey R. Lax & Justin H. Phillips, *The Democratic Deficit in the States*, 56 American Journal of Political Science 148 (2012). See also James Monogan et al., *Public Opinion, Organized Interests, and Policy Congruence in Initiative and Noninitiative U.S. States*, 9 State Politics and Policy Quarterly 304 (2009) (also finding no difference in how public opinion is linked to public policy in initiative versus non-initiative states).

4. Ellis notes that the initiative originally won leftist support during the Populist era but achieved success when it won more moderate support in the Progressive period. Kenneth P. Miller, *Constraining Populism: The Real Challenge of Initiative Reform*, 41 Santa Clara Law Review 1037 (2001), argues that current supporters of the initiative are divided between progressivism and populism, two distinct and contradictory strains of thought. Populists, he asserts, are hostile to representative democracy and seek to displace it to the extent possible. Progressives seek to use the initiative to supplement and reinforce representative democracy. Miller argues that proposed reforms to the initiative process should be evaluated with this distinction in mind. In his view, only progressive-oriented reforms should be adopted. For further elaboration of these views, see Bruce E. Cain and Kenneth P. Miller, *The Populist Legacy: Initiatives and the Undermining of Representative Government*, in Dangerous Democracy? The Battle over Ballot Initiatives in America 33 (Larry J. Sabato, Howard R. Ernst & Bruce A. Larson, eds., 2001).

If initiatives are supported, possibly for different reasons, by populists and progressives, what about pluralists? Is it clear that those inclined to pluralism should oppose direct democracy? For that matter, is it so clear that progressivists should support the initiative process? The author of one study summarized the values at stake in the controversy over direct democracy as follows:

> Not only do direct and indirect forms of democracy differ in the institutional arrangements they advocate but they pursue quite different ends and values as well. Direct democracy values participation, open access, and

---

Direct Democracy Can Meet the Populist Challenge (2020) (arguing that, properly designed, direct democracy can alleviate populist tensions and make governments more responsive to their constituents).

> political equality. It tends to deemphasize compromise, continuity, and consensus. In short, direct democracy encourages conflict and competition and attempts to expand the base of participants. Indirect democracy values stability, consensus, and compromise and seeks institutional arrangements that insulate fundamental principles from momentary passions or fluctuations in opinion.

David Magleby, Direct Legislation 181 (1984). Although Magleby recognizes the legitimacy of both sets of values, he reaches conclusions generally critical of direct democracy, because he believes the benefits of the initiative and referendum are largely illusory, while some of their impairment of the values of representative democracy is real. For example, he writes:

> Essential to the claim that more democratic government results from direct legislation is the assumption that the issues placed on ballots are representative of the issues people have on their minds and would like submitted to a public vote. Very few voters, however, can spontaneously name any particular issues on which they would like to see the public vote. Those issues that do appear on the ballot are typically not the same issues that voters list as the most important problems facing the state or the nation....
>
> Because of voter disinterest and the signature threshold requirement, the agenda of issues to be decided is determined by proponents' capacity to hire professional signature-gathering firms or by the dedication of issue activists or single-issue groups who desire to place measures on the ballot.

Id. at 182.

Magleby's conclusions are criticized by Richard Briffault, *Distrust of Democracy*, 63 Texas Law Review 1347 (1985), who believes Magleby interprets the data in an unduly negative manner. For example, on the agenda-setting question, Briffault writes:

> Although Magleby's analysis of the high hurdles tending to limit access to the initiative agenda to special interest organizations is difficult to refute, a significant number of ballot measures have been the product of forces outside the power elite who are not usually successful at the ordinary politics of working the lobbies of the State House. In the last decade, such outside groups have qualified proposals to control handguns, restrict indoor smoking, ban nonreturnable beverage containers, limit nuclear power plants, and legalize the possession and use of marijuana.

Id. at 1357. More generally, Briffault contends that

> although [Magleby's] discussion of direct democracy is well informed by an understanding of its defects in practice, his analysis of legislatures is at the abstract level of the textbook model. When direct legislation "in the field" is set against an idealized construct of the legislative process, it is bound to fall short.

Id. at 1350. Briffault points out that a high percentage of initiative proposals deal with areas such as governmental processes or taxation, in which legislatures may sometimes be prone to subordinate the public interest to their own interests or those of special interest supporters. Briffault gives a number of examples and concludes:

> In these cases, the initiative served as a remedy for legislative failure—much as the Progressives had envisioned. Direct legislation did not serve as a substitute for the legislative process but as a complement when the legislature had displayed prolonged indifference to the wishes of a significant portion of the public. The initiative was an effective device for getting the legislature's attention and reminding representatives of the public outside the community of political insiders.

Id. at 1371.

In recent years in California, Republican leaders have often voiced more support for the initiative process than Democratic leaders. Could this be related to the fact that there are many more Democrats than Republicans in the state legislature, and consequently the initiative process may be a plausible way to bypass the Democratic legislature?

5. In Chapter 1 we considered the view of some that the pluralist system reflects the intensity of voters' wishes in addition to the sheer number of voters who favor or oppose a particular policy. Some writers have criticized the initiative process for failing to take account of intensity. For example, Sherman J. Clark, *A Populist Critique of Direct Democracy*, 112 Harvard Law Review 434, 465–66 (1998), writes:

> Representation lets each individual allocate that power where it matters most. Putting an issue to a direct vote by contrast, does two things. First, it prevents voters who care deeply about that particular issue from demonstrating the intensity of their concern. Second, it prevents voters who do *not* care deeply about that particular issue from using it as a vehicle for expressing the intensity of their concern about issues that matter more to them.

See also Sherman J. Clark, *The Character of Direct Democracy*, 13 Journal of Contemporary Legal Issues 341 (2004). For the view that representative legislatures are not necessarily better than the initiative for recording the intensity of voter preferences, see Lynn A. Baker, *Preferences, Priorities, and Plebiscites*, 13 Journal of Contemporary Legal Issues 313 (2004). For a proposal to reform initiatives to make them better able to capture voter intensity, see Eric A. Posner and Nicholas O. Stephanopoulos, *Quadratic Election Law*, 172 Public Choice 265 (2017). Posner and Stephanopoulos suggest giving each voter the same number of credits, which the voter could then convert into votes at a quadratic rate (one credit for one vote, four credits for two votes, and so on) across all races. They argue that this system, unlike one-person, one-vote, would register voter intensity and avert scenarios where tepid majorities prevail over passionate minorities.

6. Citrin, *supra*, makes an assertion that is widespread in the literature on initiatives, that "turnout rates generally are lower in American ballot proposition elections than in candidate elections." Such claims are based on data collected by David Magleby, Direct Legislation 83–87 (1984), showing the dropoff rates in elections in California, Massachusetts, and Washington during the 1970s and early 1980s. "Dropoff" refers to the percentage of voters who cast a ballot but do not cast a vote for a particular office or on a particular proposition. Citrin's statement is accurate only because it is based on Magleby's data for *all* propositions and for *all* candidates. However, there is no controversy over the majority of ballot propositions, which are placed on the ballot by the state legislatures. The public officials who enact state laws and therefore provide an alternative to initiatives are the state legislators. Therefore, the relevant comparison is between the dropoff for initiatives and the dropoff in races for state legislators. Unfortunately, Magleby gives no data on dropoff in state legislative elections for Massachusetts and Washington. For California, he gives data for the Assembly, and the dropoff rate in California for the years he covers was an average of eight percent for both the Assembly and for initiatives. One could wish for data covering additional states and more recent elections, but at present the evidence available does not support a claim of superiority for either representative democracy or direct democracy with respect to participation rates.

A more important though less frequently discussed question relating to participation results from the fact that some states, including California, vote on statewide initiatives at primaries as well as at general elections. Turnout is substantially lower at primaries. Perhaps even more of a problem is that depending on whether there is a hot contest for president, governor, or senator in one party or the other, turnout at the primary may be skewed in favor of Democratic (and therefore liberal) or Republican (and therefore conservative) voters. The skewing is not likely to be decisive in an initiative election unless that election is very close, but clearly it would be preferable, all else being equal, for initiatives to be voted on at high-turnout general elections. The greatest resistance to eliminating initiative voting at primaries results from the fear that concentrating all the initiatives for an election year into the general election would compound the problem of burdening voters with too many matters to vote on. For discussion of that problem, see Philip L. Dubois and Floyd Feeney, Lawmaking by Initiative 153–58 (1998).

7. As we have seen, one of the most prominent criticisms of direct democracy has been that it will facilitate tyranny of the majority over minorities. Derrick A. Bell, Jr., *The Referendum: Democracy's Barrier to Racial Equality*, 54 Washington Law Review 1, 16 (1978), contends that "the growing reliance on the referendum and initiative poses a threat to individual rights in general and in particular creates a crisis for the rights of racial and other discrete minorities." *Id.* at 2. He contends that the danger of majority tyranny in direct democracy exceeds the danger in representative democracy:

> Public officials, even those elected on more or less overtly racist campaigns, may prove responsive to minority pressures for civil rights measures

> once in office or, at least, be open to the negotiation and give-and-take that constitutes much of the political process. Thus, legislators may vote for, or executive officials may sign, a civil rights or social reform bill with full knowledge that a majority of their constituents oppose the measure. They are in the spotlight and do not wish publicly to advocate racism; they cannot openly attribute their opposition to "racist constituents." The more neutral reasons for opposition are often inadequate in the face of serious racial injustices, particularly those posing threats not confined to the minority community.
>
> When the legislative process is turned back to the citizenry either to enact laws by initiative or to review existing laws through the referendum, few of the concerns that can transform the "conservative" politician into a "moderate" public official are likely to affect the individual voter's decision. No political factors counsel restraint on racial passions emanating from long held and little considered beliefs and fears. Far from being the pure path to democracy . . . , direct democracy, carried out in the privacy of the voting booth, has diminished the ability of minority groups to participate in the democratic process. Ironically, because it enables the voters' racial beliefs and fears to be recorded and tabulated in their pure form, the referendum has been a most effective facilitator of that bias, discrimination, and prejudice which has marred American democracy from its earliest day.

Id. at 13–15.

Bell's criticism is probably on its strongest ground when directed against procedures that single out for referendum certain decisions, such as civil rights ordinances or land use regulations, that have particular effect on racial or other minorities. The Supreme Court has struck down procedures that require referendums before adoption of measures designed to benefit racial minorities, such as the adoption of fair housing ordinances or the imposition of school integration devices. See *Hunter v. Erickson*, 393 U.S. 385 (1969); *Washington v. Seattle School District No. 1*, 458 U.S. 457 (1982). However, it has permitted referendum requirements that apply only to measures benefiting poor people, such as approval of low-cost housing projects. See *James v. Valtierra*, 402 U.S. 137 (1971). The Court has also recently backed away from *Hunter* and *Seattle*, holding in *Schuette v. Coalition to Defend Affirmative Action*, 572 U.S. 291 (2014), that a voter initiative barring Michigan universities from adopting race-conscious affirmative action policies — and thus requiring proponents of affirmative action to change the state constitution to implement their agenda — was valid under the United States Constitution.

Defenders have contested the validity of Bell's charges as applied to initiatives, especially at the state level. Thus, Briffault, *supra*, 63 Texas Law Review at 1364–66, writes:

> [I]t is difficult to argue that historically minorities — in particular, blacks and other racial minorities did all that well in state legislatures. Racial

> discrimination was largely a product of state legislative action, not initiative votes. Nor are the great advances of minorities in recent decades attributable to state legislative action. The initial successes of the civil rights movement were won in the courts or on the streets. The legislatures resisted and delayed and became more responsive only under extraordinary political and legal pressures. Even today, in times of fiscal stringency, states may be more prone to cut programs that help minorities and the poor than those that serve more politically powerful groups.
>
> At another level, the challenge to the initiative for lack of sensitivity to minority interests is misguided; the initiative, like other devices of direct democracy, was designed as a *majoritarian* tool, to be used when the legislature failed to act on a program the majority desires. The appropriate question here is whether the initiative is more likely than the legislature to be a source of measures that discriminate against minorities or infringe upon the rights of the politically powerless. Without offering a firm answer, I suggest that there are two institutions that tend to mitigate the antiminority potential of direct legislation: the judiciary and the initiative process itself.
>
> The electorate-as-legislature can no more infringe upon constitutionally protected rights than can the representative legislature. Although the courts frequently bestow rhetorical plaudits on direct democracy, they have not hesitated to invalidate initiative measures as unconstitutional....
>
> The second constraint on majoritarian abuse lies in the nature of the initiative process. [I]t is difficult to get measures on the ballot and it is difficult to get them passed. Minority groups benefit from the "negative bias" in the system. A minority group that intensely opposes a measure can seek to block ballot qualification and it can mount a campaign that generates doubts and uncertainties about the proposition, exploiting the electorate's innate caution and reinforcing the tendency to reject initiatives even if the proposition appeals to antiminority prejudices. The "negative bias," although a barrier to "good" legislation, functions equally as a shield against "bad" legislation: a defect of direct democracy may also prevent its abuse.

In recent years, opponents of certain initiatives have revived the claim that the process may be abused by majorities against unpopular minorities. These initiatives include California's Proposition 187 in the 1994 general election, which sought to exclude illegal immigrants from various public benefits including education and non-emergency medical care, and initiatives in numerous states that have sought to ban same-sex marriage or prevent municipalities from prohibiting discrimination based on sexual orientation. For criticism of the "anti-gay" initiatives, see Hans A. Linde, *When Initiative Lawmaking Is Not "Republican Government": The Campaign Against Homosexuality*, 72 Oregon Law Review 19 (1993); *Symposium: The Bill of Rights vs. the Ballot Box: Constitutional Implications of Anti-Gay Ballot Initiatives*, 55 Ohio State Law Journal 491 (1994). As it happened, Briffault's claim that the judiciary constitutes an effective shield for minority groups against the initiative process was largely if not entirely vindicated in each of these instances. Most of Proposition 187 was struck down as either unconstitutional or preempted by federal law in *League of Latin American Citizens v. Wilson*, 997 F. Supp. 1244 (C.D. Cal. 1997). In *Romer v. Evans*, 517 U.S. 620 (1995), the Supreme Court struck down a Colorado initiative that would have barred state and local antidiscrimination protections based on sexual orientation. And in *Obergefell v. Hodges*, 576 U.S. 644 (2015), the Court invalidated Kentucky, Michigan, Ohio, and Tennessee measures that limited marriage to one man and one woman.

In any event, the debate continues. Barbara Gamble, *Putting Civil Rights to a Popular Vote*, 41 American Journal of Political Science 244 (1997), offers empirical evidence in favor of the view that initiatives jeopardize minority rights:

> By examining over three decades of civil rights laws that have appeared on state and local ballots across the nation, I find strong evidence that the majority has indeed used its direct legislative powers to deprive political minorities of their civil rights. In five issue areas — housing and public accommodations for racial minorities, school desegregation, gay rights, English language laws, and AIDS policies — the majority has been extraordinarily successful at using the ballot box to repeal existing legislative protections and to pass laws that block elected representatives from creating new laws. Furthermore, the judicial system, with its deference to the direct democratic process, provides only partial protection to the minorities whose rights have been taken away by popular vote.

Id. at 244–45. See also Zoltan L. Hajnal et al., *Minorities and Direct Legislation: Evidence from California Ballot Proposition Elections*, 64 Journal of Politics 154 (2002) (finding that, across all California initiatives over a thirty-year period, minority voters were systematically more likely than white voters to find themselves on the losing side); Daniel C. Lewis, *Bypassing the Representational Filter? Minority Rights Policies Under Direct Democracy Institutions in the U.S. States*, 11 State Politics and Policy Quarterly 198 (2011) (finding that initiative states are significantly more likely than non-initiative states to enact anti-minority measures).

But Todd Donovan and Shaun Bowler, *Responsive or Responsible Government?*, *in* Citizens as Legislators: Direct Democracy in the United States 249, 265 (Shaun Bowler et al., eds., 1998), argue that Gamble's and others' criticism may be valid at the local level, but "is overstated and not supported by data when examined at the state level." Donovan and Bowler claim that most of the initiatives in Gamble's study are local and that they are non-randomly selected. They also point out that in *The Federalist Papers*, Madison and Hamilton relied not only on representative democracy as a means of protecting minorities, but also on decision-making in large, diverse jurisdictions. By focusing on *statewide* initiatives hostile to minorities, Donovan and Bowler find that a much smaller percentage passed and that all the important ones that did pass were struck down by the courts. They cite another study finding that city councils are more likely to pass anti-discrimination ordinances for gays in large than in small jurisdictions, and conclude that the most important variable affecting how well minorities fare is not the existence of the initiative process but the size and diversity of the jurisdiction. *Id.* at 264–70.

8. While the above criticism of voter initiatives is that they may be used to discriminate against minorities, in recent years, statewide *majorities* have sought to limit initiatives. In particular, Republican majorities have tried to make it more difficult to place measures on the ballot, presumably because initiatives can circumvent Republican-dominated legislatures and pursue progressive goals that could never be achieved legislatively in these states. For example, South Dakota restricted the window for collecting petition signatures to winter months. Florida enacted a stringent cap on contributions to initiative campaigns. Idaho required measures to obtain signatures from six percent of residents in every legislative district in the state. And in Mississippi, the state supreme court nullified the entire initiative process because the relevant constitutional provision refers to five congressional districts while the state now only has four districts. See Reid J. Epstein & Nick Corasaniti, *Republicans Move to Limit a Grass-Roots Tradition of Direct Democracy*, N.Y. Times, May 22, 2021, at A1.

9. Another long-standing device of direct democracy that suddenly came into national prominence several years ago is the *recall*. In California, Governor Gray Davis was recalled from office in October 2003 and replaced by actor Arnold Schwarzenegger. This was the first time a governor had been recalled in any state since 1921. In Wisconsin, Governor Scott Walker narrowly survived a recall attempt in June 2012. Current California Governor Gavin Newsom also survived a recall election in 2021.

Should those who favor the initiative process also favor the recall? What differences might there be between the two processes?

The United States Constitution does not provide for the recall of United States Senators, or Members of Congress. Instead, the Constitution provides only that each House of Congress has the power to judge the qualifications of its own members or to expel them. Or at least this is how the Constitution traditionally has been understood. New Jersey law nonetheless provides a procedure for the recall of federal officials. In *Committee to Recall Robert Menendez from the Office of U.S. Senator v. Wells*, 7 A.3d 720 (N.J. 2010), plaintiff sought to recall a sitting U.S. Senator from New Jersey, Robert Menendez. The Secretary of State, as chief elections officer of the state, refused to accept the recall petition for filing, a condition necessary before recall proponents could being circulating signatures. The Secretary refused to accept the petition relying upon the state Attorney General's determination that the circulation of recall petitions for United States Senator would have no legal effect.

The New Jersey Supreme Court, in a lengthy opinion examining historical practice and numerous provisions of the Constitution, concluded on a 4–2 vote that the New Jersey recall provision violated the U.S. Constitution when applied to a recall of U.S. Senators: "[W]e find that the case is ripe for review and that the Federal

Constitution does not allow States the power to recall U.S. Senators. That conclusion is faithful to the rule of law. It is faithful to the written words in the Constitution, as illuminated by the Framers who debated its text and those who participated in the state ratifying conventions. It is guided by relevant case law and informed by thoughtful scholarship. It is also faithful to the enduring form of our constitutional democracy, which the Framers established more than 200 years ago." *Id.* at 751-52.

The dissenters differed sharply:

> [T]he majority would tell the citizenry of New Jersey that it cannot recall one of its U.S. Senators even if he or she is indicted, convicted and incarcerated but not impeached; in those circumstances, the majority would conclude that the people of New Jersey have no means to avoid being disenfranchised.
>
> When hundreds of thousands of our fellow citizens voted to create a recall mechanism by constitutional amendment, they set a high standard for bringing that machinery to bear. They did so intentionally, to reserve recall for only those infrequent cases in which it is truly warranted. As we have seen, in this circumstance, those who would invoke the remedy of recall would need, in a short time span, to amass signatures of more voters than it took to elect the Senator in the first place. Nothing in the record, nothing in history, and nothing in our common shared experience suggests that recall will so threaten the work of the Senate, or of the federal government, or even the life of the one who now holds that office, that it should be denied. Nothing suggests that the people gave up that right when joining together as a Republic and binding themselves to the Federal Constitution. Indeed, it is only by lifting up a narrow and historically unsupportable view of the federal system that the majority can argue for the result it reaches.
>
> In effect, the majority sees the Senate as an institution immune from criticism, even of the most profound and fundamental kind; it sees not a part of a federal system, but an elitist institution the members of which should not have to be troubled by what the people they represent believe, save for the necessity of having to return and convince the people to vote them back into office every six years.

Id. at 776-77 (Rivera-Soto & Hoens, JJ., dissenting).

10. In order for an initiative, referendum, or recall to appear on the ballot, its proponents must gather enough signatures within a set amount of time. These rules are specific to state and local law. The COVID-19 pandemic, and accompanying closures of public places, made signature gathering substantially more difficult. Ballot measure proponents asked federal and state courts to relax requirements, such as by reducing the number of signatures required to qualify a measure, lengthening the time for the collection of ballots, and allowing signatures submitted electronically rather than signed in ink on a physical paper. Most courts were reluctant to loosen such rules, even during the pandemic. See *Arizonans for Fair Elections v. Hobbs*,

474 F. Supp. 3d 910 (D. Ariz. 2020); *Bambenek v. White*, 2020 WL 2123951 (C.D. Ill. May 1, 2020); *Morgan v. White*, No. 1-20-cv-02189 (N.D. Ill. May 18, 2020); *Thompson v. DeWine*, 959 F.3d 804 (6th Cir. 2020); *Fight for Nevada v. Cegavske*, 460 F. Supp. 3d 1049 (D. Nev. 2020); *Miller v. Thurston*, 967 F.3d 727 (8th Cir. 2020).

Courts were more willing during the pandemic to loosen signature requirements for *candidates* to qualify for the ballot. See, for example, *Esshaki v. Whitmer*, 813 Fed. Appx. 830 (6th Cir. 2020), requiring the state of Michigan to make reasonable accommodations for candidates seeking ballot access. These rulings can help minor parties and independent candidates, who often are not afforded automatic ballot access like Democratic and Republican candidates. *Libertarian Party v. Pritzker*, 455 F. Supp. 3d 738 (N.D. Ill. 2020) (loosening Illinois ballot access rules during the pandemic for Illinois minor parties).

For an argument that courts should not treat ballot measure proponents worse than candidates when it comes to loosening qualifying rules during exigent circumstances, see Richard L. Hasen, *Direct Democracy Denied: The Right to Initiative During a Pandemic*, University of Chicago Law Review Online, June 26, 2020, https://perma.cc/9N48-VYYF. Chief Justice Roberts disagreed with this position in a short opinion concurring in the grant of a stay of a district court's order in *Little v. Reclaim Idaho*, 140 S. Ct. 2616 (2020). He observed that "nothing in the Constitution requires Idaho or any other State to provide for ballot initiatives." *Id.* at 2617 (Roberts, C.J., concurring in the grant of stay). He added that "reasonable, nondiscretionary restrictions" of ballot access for voter initiatives "are almost certainly justified by the important regulatory interests in combating fraud and ensuring that ballots are not cluttered with initiatives that have not demonstrated sufficient grassroots support." *Id.*

II. Content Restrictions

People's Advocate v. Superior Court

226 Cal. Rptr. 640 (Cal. App. 1986)

THE COURT:

At the June 5, 1984, election the people adopted a statutory initiative measure entitled the "Legislative Reform Act of 1983" (the Act). [The Act] makes sweeping changes in the organization and operation of the Assembly and Senate and limits the content of future legislation which appropriates money for their operations. Petitioners, [who were supporters of the initiative,] sought a declaration that the Act was valid and an order compelling compliance with its terms.

The real parties [in interest, i.e., the state legislature and others who opposed the initiative,] moved for judgment on the pleadings, challenging the provisions of the Act which regulate the internal rules, the selection of officers and employees, the selection and powers of committees of the houses of the Legislature and which limit prospectively the content of budget legislation as violative of the California Constitution; real parties challenged the remaining provisions as inseverable from the invalid provisions. The superior court granted the motion and entered judgment declaring the entire Act unconstitutional and of no force or effect. . . .

We shall deny relief as to those provisions of the Act found by the trial court to be violative of the Constitution. However, the remaining provisions of the Act relating to secrecy in legislative proceedings are severable and as to those we shall issue a writ directing the trial court to vacate its judgment declaring their invalidity.

Discussion

It is well to be clear at the outset what this case is and is not about. First, the issue before this court is one of law, not policy; it is whether the Act is constitutional, not whether it is necessary or wise. We address that issue and that issue alone. Second, this case is not about whether the will of the people shall be heeded. The Act is not the only relevant expression of popular sentiment in this case. The provisions of the California Constitution (art. IV, § 7) which empower the houses of the Legislature to govern their own proceedings were first enacted almost 150 years ago and have twice been reenacted by the electorate. They are part of a constitutional structure of government by which the people have made statutes — even initiative statutes — subordinate to the Constitution, and have empowered the courts of this state in the exercise of the judicial power to interpret the state's fundamental charter. We are not presented with a conflict between the voice of the people expressed directly and through their elected representatives, but between two conflicting directives from the electorate: the Act and the California Constitution.

The powers challenged by the Act are deeply rooted in constitutional soil. Since the inception of our state the power of a legislative body to govern its own internal workings has been viewed as essential to its functioning except as it may have been expressly constrained by the California Constitution. The fundamental charter of our state government was enacted by the people against a history of parliamentary common law. That law is implicit in the Constitution's structure and its separation of powers. As was said by the California Supreme Court over one hundred years ago: "A legislative assembly, when established, becomes vested with all the powers and privileges which are necessary and incidental to a free and unobstructed exercise of its appropriate functions. These powers and privileges are derived not from the Constitution; on the contrary, they arise from the very creation of a legislative body, and are founded upon the principle of self preservation.[n] The Constitution is not a grant, but a restriction upon the power of the Legislature, and hence an express enumeration of legislative powers and privileges in the Constitution cannot be considered as the exclusion of others not named unless accompanied by negative terms. A

n. Does this sentence suggest that the Legislative Reform initiative would have been void even if it had been a constitutional amendment? — Eds.

legislative assembly has, therefore, all the powers and privileges which are necessary to enable it to exercise in all respects, in a free, intelligent, and impartial manner, its appropriate functions, except so far as it may be restrained by the express provisions of the Constitution, or by some express law made unto itself, regulating and limiting the same." (*Ex parte D.O. McCarthy* (1866) 29 Cal. 395, 403.)

McCarthy recognized as an integral part of this parliamentary common law the power of a house of the Legislature to "choose its own officers, and remove them at pleasure," to "establish its own rules of proceeding," and "[t]o be secret in its proceedings and debates." However, it is unnecessary for us to found our decision on that law for these powers have been made an express part of the California Constitution. They are to be found in article IV, sections 7 and 11 of the Constitution. The real parties claim that, with the exception of [certain] sections[,] each section of the Act facially violates these constitutional provisions. We agree with the claim.

I

Article IV, section 7, subdivision (a), directs that "[e]ach house shall choose its officers and adopt rules for its proceedings." Article IV, section 11, provides that the "Legislature or either house may by resolution provide for the selection of committees necessary for the conduct of its business. . . ."

The . . . Act regulates the appointments of the Speaker of the Assembly and the President pro tempore of the Senate. It also seeks to regulate the appointment and powers of the standing, select, joint and interim committees of the houses. The Act would also regulate the method of adoption of rules for the conduct of the houses both generally and as applied to specific subject matters. It further provides that these statutory provisions may not be amended or modified except as permitted by the Act. The First part of the Act repeals the existing provisions of the Government Code which relate to these subjects These provisions of the Act manifestly invade one or more of the powers of the houses over their committees, staff and internal proceedings as expressly delegated to them by article IV, sections 7 and 11 of the Constitution.

A

Petitioners respond that the Act is within a coordinate power of the people granted them by the Constitution, i.e. the initiative "power of the electors to propose statutes . . . and to adopt or reject them." (Art. II, § 8.) This power is shared with the Legislature and the Governor. See art. IV, §§ 8, 10; *Carlson v. Cory* 189 Cal. Rptr. 185 (Cal.App. 1983). A rule or resolution is solely the product of the house or houses which adopted it. The petitioners claim that a statute is superior to a rule or resolution and hence may supersede and control the subject matters of the rule making powers vested in the two houses by article IV, sections 7 and 11. Thus, so the petitioners' argument goes, there is no conflict between the Act and the Constitution. The claim presupposes that these *subject matters* are among those which may be regulated by statute. Therein lies the fallacy.

The subjects of statutes are categorically different from the subjects of the rule-making powers of article IV, sections 7 and 11. The subjects of statutes are laws. (Art. IV, § 8: "The Legislature may make no law except by statute. . . .") The kinds of rules and principles which are subsumed under the statutory "law" are addressed to the world outside the Legislature. Conversely, the internal rules of the Legislature do not have the force of law except as they may bind the house which adopted them. Since the subjects of statutory laws and rules of internal proceedings *categorically* differ, a statute may not control a rule of internal proceeding.

These subject matters are the prerogatives of different governmental entities. Laws, as expressed in statutes, are the prerogatives of the Legislature, together with the Governor, and of the electorate. Rules or resolutions which affect the selection of the officers of the houses or their rules of proceeding or rules for their committees or their employees are the exclusive prerogative of "[e]ach house" of the Legislature or the combined houses. (Art. IV, § 7, subd. (a).) The people's initiative statutory power, being limited to the subject matter of statutes, does not extend to these matters.

There is one exception to this separation of powers, and it underscores this reading. Article IV, section 7, subdivision (c) (a part of the rule-making section at issue), provides that "[t]he proceedings of each house and the committees thereof shall be public except as provided by *statute or* by *concurrent resolution* . . . adopted by a two-thirds vote . . . of each house, provided, that if there is a conflict between such a statute and concurrent resolution, the last adopted shall prevail." (Emphasis added.) This is the only constitutional provision which authorizes the *statutory* control of a rule or resolution of internal proceeding and that authority is subject to revocation by resolution. The unmistakable implication is that none other was intended.

In sum, the people through the electorate have been given the power to make statutes, i.e. the power to make laws for all the people, but not the power to make rules for the selection of officers or rules of proceeding or rules which regulate the committees or employees of either or both houses of the Legislature. These powers (with the exception noted) are exclusively the province of the houses affected by them.

B

Petitioners also defend the constitutionality of the Act by pointing to the apparent anomaly that the Legislature has in fact adopted statutes which purport to regulate the internal proceedings of its houses.

Petitioners offer no reasons why this practice is legally significant. There are none. The *form* (statute or rule or resolution) chosen by a house to exercise its rule-making power cannot preempt or estop a house from employing its *substantive* powers under Article IV, sections 7 and 11.[12] A rule of internal proceeding made in the guise of a

---

12. The houses have no doubt been encouraged to choose the statutory form for rule making because its parliamentary authority (Mason, Manual of Legis. Proc. (1979)) has told them that they may do so without precluding a subsequent change in the statute by *rule*. "The constitutional right

statute is nonetheless a *rule* "adopted" by the house and may be changed by an internal rule. "The enactment of statutes relating to internal proceedings was obviously accomplished by the voluntary participation of each of the two Houses. Thus each House was essentially engaged in its rule-making function." *Paisner v. Attorney General*, 458 N.E.2d 734, 739–740 (Mass. 1983). A rule of proceeding adopted by the Legislature by statute is, notwithstanding its means of adoption or label, a rule or resolution within the provisions of article IV, sections 7 and 11. It is not the form by which the rule is adopted but its substance which measures its place in the constitutional scheme. The people wholly lack this power whatever the form of its application.

Nor could a house estop itself or a future house by use of the statutory form from adopting any rule the substance of which is within the powers exclusively delegated to it by the Constitution. "The long indulgence in [a] custom cannot create a right in the legislature, or either house thereof, to do that which it has no power or authority to do." *Special Assembly Int. Com. v. Southard*, 90 P.2d 304 (Cal. 1939)....

Lastly, the petitioners seek to trade upon an assumption about the extent of the legislative power of the people. They assume that the initiative power includes the whole of the legislative power within which they locate the rule-making power. The assumption is incorrect. "The legislative power of this State is vested in the California Legislature which consists of the Senate and Assembly, but the people reserve to themselves the powers of initiative and referendum." (Art. IV, § 1.) Such reserved powers are exclusively specified in article II, section 8, and are limited to that which has been specifically delegated. They do not include the power to regulate the internal workings of the houses....

To accomplish the purposes attempted by the Act, a constitutional amendment is required. Only by means of an initiative constitutional amendment may the people modify or impinge upon the freedom of the Legislature to exercise its constitutionally granted powers.

II

Section 9934 is invalid for different reasons. It seeks to govern the content of future legislation by limiting the amount of monies appropriated for the support of the Legislature. It provides that "within 30 days following the enactment . . . the total amount of monies appropriated for the support of the Legislature, . . . shall be reduced by an amount equal to thirty percent of the total amount of monies appropriated for support of the Legislature for the 1983–84 fiscal year, and the amount so reduced shall revert to the General Fund. For each fiscal year thereafter, the total amount of monies appropriated . . . shall not exceed an amount equal to that

---

of a state legislature to control its own procedure cannot be withdrawn or restricted by statute, but statutes may control procedure insofar as they do not conflict with the rules of the houses or with the rules contained in the constitution." (Mason, p. 35.) Pursuant to this advice, a statute adopted by the *Legislature* may govern an internal proceeding in the *absence* of a rule. It may not preclude a contrary rule.

expended for support in the preceding fiscal year" adjusted up or down by the percentage increase or decrease in the general fund spending for the same year.

Real parties argue that section 9934 runs afoul of the "familiar principle of law that no legislative board, by normal legislative enactment, may divest itself or future boards of the power to enact legislation within its competence." *City and County of San Francisco v. Cooper* 120 Cal.Rptr. 707 (Cal. 1975). We agree.

Neither house of the Legislature may bind its own hands or those of future Legislatures by adopting rules not capable of change. "[T]he power of the electorate to enact legislation by use of the initiative process is circumscribed by the same limitations as the legislative powers resting in the legislative body concerned." *Mueller v. Brown*, 34 Cal.Rptr. 474 (Cal.App. 1963).

This principle has special application here. What is at issue is not the authority to amend a statute, however adopted, but the power to say what content a future statute may have. The authority to enact statutes which appropriate money for the support of the state government, including the Legislature, is set forth in article 4, section 12 of the California Constitution. It provides for the appropriation of such monies through the adoption of the budget bill. It also provides for special appropriations measures which may be adopted outside of the budget bill process. (Art. IV, §12, subd. (c).) Although either vehicle may be used to provide for the support of the Legislature, the budget bill is the vehicle historically used for the adoption of the Legislative budget.

The budget process takes special form. The Governor submits a budget bill accompanied by a budget document which supplies the budgetary detail for the budget bill. (Art. IV, §12, subds. (a) and (c). The Legislature is given the power inter alia to "control the . . . enforcement of budgets. . . ." (Art. IV, §12, subd. (e).)

Section 9934 limits the amount of monies that may be "appropriated" by statute for the support of the Legislature in each fiscal year beginning with the fiscal year 1984–1985. The limitation is based upon a formula tied to the budget bill enacted for the fiscal year 1982–1983. Section 9934 thus seeks to operate upon and condition the content of future statutes, appropriations statutes. In so doing it invades not only the *content* of the Governor's budget bill but displaces the process (budget and budget bill) by which article IV, section 12, commands the adoption and enforcement of the budget. It also affects any alternative means of appropriation by placing limits upon the content of any Legislative appropriations bill. By these means, section 9934 "divest[s] [the Legislature] of the power to enact legislation within its competence" and violates the specific injunctions of article IV, section 12 of the Constitution. (See *City and County of San Francisco v. Cooper, supra.*) Since the Legislature is denied such a statutory power, so are the people.[13] For these reasons section 9934 is invalid.

PUGLIA, P.J., and EVANS and BLEASE, JJ., concur.

---

13. The limitation imposed by section 9934 upon the content of a budget measure must be distinguished from the constitutional authorization to appropriate money by statute by measures other than the budget bill. That power is specifically recognized in article IV, section 12. It authorizes the

Notes and Questions

1. In footnote n, we asked whether the proposition would have been struck down if it had been circulated and enacted as a constitutional amendment. Assume the answer to that question is no. The only difference between enactment of an initiative statute and enactment of an initiative constitutional amendment in California, as well as in many other states, is that the constitutional amendment requires more signatures. Other than striking down the particular proposition, does *People's Advocate* have much significance if the same result can be reached by a group willing to spend the extra money needed to obtain enough signatures to qualify a constitutional amendment? Would you support a constitutional provision putting legislative rules beyond the reach of the initiative process altogether? Is it abusive to use the initiative to change legislative rules? To the contrary, might it be argued that changing legislative rules is an especially appropriate use of the initiative process? With respect to the last question, consider the Illinois constitutional provisions described in the following note.

2. In Illinois, the initiative is permitted *only* for the purpose of altering the legislative process.

> Amendments to Article IV [the legislative article] of this Constitution may be proposed by a petition signed by a [specified number of electors]. Amendments shall be limited to structural and procedural subjects contained in Article IV....

Illinois Constitution, art. 14, § 3. The rationale for this very limited scope of the initiative process has been explained as follows:

> Section 3 recognizes that the General Assembly is unlikely to propose any changes in its basic structure, but that some changes may appear to be necessary. Thus, a method of constitutional revision other than through the General Assembly is necessary.

Robert A. Helman & Wayne W. Whalen, *Constitutional Commentary*, in Smith-Hurd Compiled Statutes Annotated, Const., art. 14, § 3 (1993).

Paisner v. Attorney General, 458 N.E.2d 734 (Mass. 1983), was cited by the California court because it interpreted the Massachusetts Constitution to place the

---

Legislature and hence the people to provide by statute for a continuing appropriation to pay for some specified program. However, the power so recognized does not authorize the placement of a *legal* limit upon the power of the Legislature to enact future appropriations legislation.

Although as a practical fiscal matter, a statute containing a continuous appropriation may limit the Legislature's *financial choices* in other appropriations measures, such a limitation is not one imposed by *law*. That is not the case here. The limitation mandated by section 9934 places legal limits upon the content of the legislation by which the Legislature is given the money to conduct its operations. That restriction exceeds the Legislature's own statutory power and hence exceeds the power of the people to do the same thing.

legislature's power over its own rules and procedures beyond control by statutes, including initiative statutes. *Paisner* and *People's Advocate* could be crudely paraphrased as saying that the initiative can address most subjects but not the legislative process itself. Does the Illinois constitution take exactly the opposite approach? If so, which is better?

The Illinois provision for the initiative, narrow to begin with, has been interpreted strictly by the Illinois courts. In *Coalition for Political Honesty v. State Board of Elections*, 359 N.E.2d 138 (Ill. 1976), the Illinois Supreme Court ruled that an Illinois initiative must make both structural *and* procedural changes to the legislative process. On this basis it struck down three initiative proposals, including one that prohibited legislators from voting on bills in which they had conflicts of interest. Presumably, the court regarded that as a procedural but not as a structural change. In *Chicago Bar Association v. State Board of Elections*, 561 N.E.2d 50 (Ill. 1990), the court struck down a proposal that would have required a three-fifths vote in each house for any bill that would increase revenues and would have required a special revenue committee to be created in each house, with detailed specifications regarding number of members, method of appointment, and so on. The court explained:

> The [proponent] argues that the proposed Amendment does affect structural and procedural subjects of article IV, and thus complies with section 3 of article XIV. Even assuming that the [proponent] is correct in this regard, we find that the proposed Amendment is not *limited to* the structural and procedural subjects of article IV. Wrapped up in this structural and procedural package is a substantive issue not found in article IV — the subject of increasing State revenue or increasing taxes.

Id. at 55. See also *Hooker v. Illinois State Board of Elections*, 63 N.E.3d 824 (Ill. 2016) (striking down an initiative that would have created an independent redistricting commission because it changed the responsibilities of the Auditor General, an official whose duties are not a structural and procedural subject of article IV). If an initiative like the one in *People's Advocate* were proposed in Illinois, would the Illinois courts permit it to go on the ballot?

3. The cases described above show that courts will often protect the legislature's autonomy from interference through the initiative process. Will they do so consistently and will they extend similar protection to the other two branches of government?

In *Citizens Coalition for Tort Reform v. McAlpine*, 810 P.2d 162 (Alaska 1991), the Supreme Court of Alaska struck from the ballot an initiative proposal to limit contingent attorney's fees in personal injury cases. The Alaska Constitution, art. XI, §7, barred initiative proposals to "create courts, define the jurisdiction of courts or prescribe their rules." The initiative in *Citizens Coalition* limited fees "regardless of whether the recovery is by settlement, arbitration, or judgment." The Alaska

Supreme Court reasoned that since the regulation of the practice of law, including regulation of fees, was within its own power, the proposed initiative was an effort to prescribe a court rule.

In *Yute Air Alaska v. McAlpine*, 698 P.2d 1173 (1985), the Alaska court approved an initiative proposal that provided in part:

> The governor shall use best efforts and all appropriate means to persuade the United States Congress to repeal . . . the Jones Act[, which required the use of United States vessels for shipping goods between United States ports]. Until that Act is repealed, the governor shall publish an annual report documenting the harmful effects of the Act on Alaska commerce, and progress made towards its repeal.

The court rejected a contention that this provision was not a "law" that could be enacted by the initiative process. What if this proposal were enacted and the governor did not favor repeal of the Jones Act? What if the Jones Act were still in effect and the governor or staff or consultants employed by the governor to prepare the required annual report concluded from the evidence that harm to Alaska commerce from the Jones Act either did not exist or could not be documented?

4. In some states the initiative may be used to "amend" the state constitution but not to "revise" it. See, *e.g.*, *McFadden v. Jordan*, 196 P.2d 787 (Cal. 1948), cert. denied 336 U.S. 918 (1949); *Holmes v. Appling*, 392 P.2d 636 (Or. 1964). This distinction is said to be "based on the principle that 'comprehensive changes' to the Constitution require more formality, discussion and deliberation than is available through the initiative process." See *Raven v. Deukmejian*, 801 P.2d 1077 (Cal. 1990).

Not surprisingly, California's famous Proposition 13 was challenged on the ground that it revised rather than amended the California Constitution. Proposition 13 has been described

> as a revolutionary measure for reducing the level and growth of state and local government expenditure as well as sharply restricting the use of the property tax as a source of government revenue. [Proposition 13] 1) restricts the property tax rate to no more than 1 percent of assessed value; 2) sets assessed value for a property that has not been transferred since 1975–76 equal to its fair market value in that year plus 2 percent per year (compounded); in the event that the property has been transferred since 1975–76, the market value at the time of sale is used (plus the 2 percent growth factor); and 3) requires that new taxes or increases in existing taxes (except property taxes) receive a two-thirds approval of the legislature in the case of state taxes, or of the electorate, in the case of local taxes.
>
> The potential fiscal impact of these provisions is enormous. . . .
>
> There are, among others, implications for financial markets; taxpayer equity; efficiency of the housing market; the structure of state and local

> government; and perhaps, most dramatically, for other governments, including the federal government.

William H. Oakland, *Proposition 13: Genesis and Consequences*, in The Property Tax Revolt: The Case of Proposition 13, 31, 31–32 (1981).[o] In *Amador Valley Joint Union High School District v. State Board of Equalization*, 583 P.2d 1281, 1286 (Cal. 1978), the California Supreme Court ruled that Proposition 13 was valid as a constitutional "amendment." The court stated that

> our analysis in determining whether a particular constitutional enactment is a revision or an amendment must be both quantitative and qualitative in nature. For example, an enactment which is so extensive in its provisions as to change directly the "substantial entirety" of the Constitution by the deletion or alteration of numerous existing provisions may well constitute a revision thereof. However, even a relatively simple enactment may accomplish such far reaching changes in the nature of our basic governmental plan as to amount to a revision also.

Proposition 13 was not a revision under this analysis, because its "changes operate functionally within a relatively narrow range to accomplish a new system of taxation which may provide substantial tax relief for our citizens."

However, in *Raven, supra*, the court ruled that a provision in an initiative known as Proposition 115 was void because it purported to revise the constitution. The provision in question required that various procedural rights of defendants in criminal cases

> shall be construed by the courts of this state in a manner consistent with the Constitution of the United States. This Constitution shall not be construed by the courts to afford greater rights to criminal defendants than those afforded by the Constitution of the United States....

This provision admittedly was not a revision on quantitative grounds. Despite the fact that the California Supreme Court had a "general principle or policy" of being guided in its construction of state constitutional rights by the United States Supreme Court's interpretation of corresponding federal rights, the California court had departed from this policy on a number of occasions. Accordingly, from a qualitative standpoint, "the effect of Proposition 115 is devastating," because as to the rights in question, "California courts in criminal cases would no longer have authority to

---

o. The effects of Proposition 13 have been described less neutrally by Julian N. Eule, *Crocodiles in the Bathtub: State Courts, Voter Initiatives and the Threat of Electoral Reprisal*, 65 University of Colorado Law Review 733 (1994):

> Proposition 13 has left education, welfare, public safety, the economy, and the infrastructure in shambles. California, which once ranked as the nation's leader in primary and secondary education, now relishes a year in which it finishes forty-eighth rather than fiftieth. The University of California may still be a gem among public institutions of higher learning, but too often it is less a diamond than a zirconium.

interpret the state Constitution in a manner more protective of defendants' rights than extended by the federal Constitution. . . ." 801 P.2d at 1087.

Less than a year later the California court upheld Proposition 140 against a claim that it revised the state constitution. Proposition 140 imposed term limits on state legislators and other elected state officials; reduced the state legislature's budget by about 38 percent; and eliminated pensions for future state legislators. The court distinguished *Raven* as follows:

> As indicated in *Raven*, a qualitative revision includes one that involves a change in the basic plan of California government, i.e., a change in its fundamental structure or the foundational powers of its branches. *Raven* invalidated a portion of Proposition 115 because it deprived the state judiciary of its foundational power to decide cases by independently interpreting provisions of the state Constitution, and delegated that power to the United States Supreme Court.
>
> By contrast, Proposition 140 on its face does not affect either the structure or the foundational powers of the Legislature, which remains free to enact whatever laws it deems appropriate. The challenged measure alters neither the content of those laws nor the process by which they are adopted. No legislative power is diminished or delegated to other persons or agencies. The relationships between the three governmental branches, and their respective powers, remain untouched.

Legislature v. Eu, 816 P.2d 1309 (Cal. 1991), cert. denied 503 U.S. 919 (1992).

Amador Valley, *Raven*, and *Legislature* involved, respectively: Proposition 13, which dramatically lowered property taxes, greatly increased the difficulty of increasing taxes in the future, and predictably effected a major shift of power from local to state governments; Proposition 115, which converted a general principle of interpretation of certain rights into a mandatory principle; and Proposition 140, which adopted term limits and slashed the legislative budget. Which of these propositions brought about the most "comprehensive changes" in the California system of governance? Which brought about the least "comprehensive changes"?

Do the decisions summarized in this Note and in Note 3 suggest the possibility that courts are more sensitive to intrusions on their own powers than on those of the coordinate branches of government?

5. The issue of amendment versus revision of the California Constitution arose in a very high-profile case involving the question of a ban on gay marriage. In 2008, the California Supreme Court held that the state's voter initiated statutory ban on same-sex marriage violated various provisions of the California Constitution. *In re Marriage Cases*, 43 Cal. 4th 757 (2008). In response, voters passed Proposition 8, an initiated constitutional amendment changing the state Constitution to provide that: "Only marriage between a man and a woman is valid or recognized in California." Opponents of Proposition 8 then challenged the measure in the state Supreme Court as an unconstitutional revision of the state constitution.

In *Strauss v. Horton*, 46 Cal. 4th 364, 440–44 (2009), the California Supreme Court rejected the argument that Proposition 8 was an impermissible revision of the Constitution:

> Proposition 8 adds a single section—section 7.5—to article I of the California Constitution, a section that provides, in its entirety, that "Only marriage between a man and a woman is valid or recognized in California." Pursuant to the analysis prescribed in our past decisions, we examine "both the quantitative and qualitative effects of the measure on our constitutional scheme." *Raven.*
>
> From a quantitative standpoint, it is obvious that Proposition 8 does not amount to a constitutional revision. The measure adds one 14-word section (§ 7.5) to article I—a section that affects two other sections of article I (§§ 1, 7) by creating an exception to the privacy, due process, and equal protection clauses contained in those two sections as interpreted in the majority opinion in the *Marriage Cases.* Quantitatively, Proposition 8 unquestionably has much less of an effect on the preexisting state constitutional scheme than virtually any of the previous constitutional changes that our past decisions have found to constitute amendments rather than revisions. Indeed, petitioners do not even advance the argument that Proposition 8 constitutes a revision under the quantitative prong of the amendment/revision analysis.
>
> Instead, petitioners rest their claim that Proposition 8 constitutes a constitutional revision solely upon the qualitative prong of the amendment/revision analysis. The constitutional change embodied in Proposition 8, however, differs fundamentally from those that our past cases have identified as the kind of qualitative change that may amount to a revision of the California Constitution.
>
> As we have seen, the numerous past decisions of this court that have addressed this issue all have indicated that the type of measure that may constitute a revision of the California Constitution is one that makes "far reaching changes in the nature *of our basic governmental plan*" (*Amador*), or, stated in slightly different terms, that "substantially alter[s] *the basic governmental framework set forth in our Constitution.*" *Legislature v. Eu*, italics added. Thus, for example, our decision in *Amador,* in providing an example of the type of "relatively simple enactment" that may constitute a revision, posed a hypothetical enactment "which purported to vest *all judicial power in the Legislature.*" (*Amador,* italics added.) Similarly, in *Raven*—the *only* case to find that a measure constituted a revision of the California Constitution because of the qualitative nature of the proposed change—the court relied upon the circumstance that the provision there at issue "would substantially alter the substance and integrity of the state Constitution as a document of independent force and effect" (*Raven*) by implementing "a broad attack on state court authority to exercise independent judgment in

construing a wide spectrum of important rights under the state Constitution." (*Id.*) . . .

Proposition 8 works no such fundamental change in the *basic governmental plan or framework* established by the preexisting provisions of the California Constitution—that is, "in [the government's] fundamental structure or the foundational powers of its branches." (*Legislature v. Eu.*) Instead, Proposition 8 simply changes the substantive content of a state constitutional rule in one specific subject area—the rule relating to access to the designation of "marriage." Contrary to petitioners' contention, the measure does not transform or undermine the judicial function: California courts will continue to exercise their basic and historic responsibility to enforce *all* of the provisions of the California Constitution, which now include the new section added by the voters' approval of Proposition 8.

Petitioners contend, however, that even if Proposition 8 does not make a fundamental change in the basic *governmental plan* or *framework* established by the Constitution, the measure nonetheless should be found to constitute a revision because it allegedly "strike[s] directly at the foundational constitutional principle of equal protection . . . by establishing that an unpopular group may be selectively stripped of fundamental rights by a simple majority of voters." Petitioners' argument rests, initially, on the premise that a measure that abrogates a so-called *foundational constitutional principle of law,* no less than a measure that makes a fundamental change in the basic governmental structure or in the foundational power of its branches as established by the state Constitution, should be viewed as a constitutional revision rather than as a constitutional amendment. Petitioners suggest that their position is not inconsistent with our past amendment/revision decisions, on the theory that none of those decisions *explicitly* held that *only* a measure that makes a fundamental change in the state's governmental plan or framework can constitute a constitutional revision. . . .

In our view, a fair and full reading of this court's past amendment/revision decisions demonstrates that those cases stand for the proposition that in deciding whether or not a constitutional change constitutes a qualitative revision, a court must determine whether the change effects a substantial change in the governmental plan or structure established by the Constitution. As we have seen, a number of our past amendment/revision decisions have involved initiative measures that made very important substantive changes in fundamental state constitutional principles such as the right not to be subjected to cruel or unusual punishment and the right to be protected against unlawful searches and seizures—initiative measures that, like the current Proposition 8, cut back on the greater level of protection afforded by preceding court decisions and were challenged as constitutional revisions on the ground that the constitutional changes they effected deprived

> individuals of important state constitutional protections they previously enjoyed and left courts unable to fully protect such rights. Nonetheless, in each case this court did not undertake an evaluation of the relative importance of the constitutional right at issue or the degree to which the protection of that right had been diminished, but instead held that the measure did not amount to a qualitative revision *because it did not make a fundamental change in the nature of the governmental plan or framework established by the Constitution*. . . .
>
> Although petitioners seize upon isolated passages in a few decisions as assertedly supporting their position that a change other than a modification in the governmental plan or framework may constitute a revision, a fair reading of those decisions in their entirety discloses that they do not provide such support but instead affirmatively reiterate and apply the established rule that, in order to constitute a qualitative revision, a constitutional measure must make a far reaching change in the fundamental governmental structure or the foundational power of its branches as set forth in the Constitution. Under this standard, which has been applied repeatedly and uniformly in the precedents that govern this court's jurisprudence, it is evident that because Proposition 8 works no change of that nature in the California Constitution, it does not constitute a constitutional revision. . . .
>
> Furthermore, even if, as petitioners urge, our past decisions were to be interpreted as not precluding the possibility that a constitutional change other than a change in the governmental plan or framework could, under some circumstances, constitute a constitutional revision rather than a constitutional amendment, petitioners' contention that Proposition 8 represents a constitutional revision still would lack merit. As is revealed by the foregoing history of the amendment/revision distinction, and as our past cases demonstrate in applying that distinction, a change in the California Constitution properly is viewed as a constitutional revision only if it embodies a change of such *far reaching scope* that is fairly comparable to the example set forth in the *Amador* decision, namely, a change that "vests all judicial power in the Legislature." It is only a qualitative change *of that kind of far reaching scope* that the framers of the 1849 and 1879 Constitutions plausibly intended to be proposed *only* by *a new constitutional convention*, and *not* through the ordinary amendment process. As we shall explain, the constitutional change embodied in Proposition 8—although without question of great importance to the affected individuals—by no means makes such a far reaching change in the California Constitution as to amount to a constitutional revision.

Whatever one thinks of the merits of the court's ruling in *Strauss*, it stands as a clearer (and apparently stricter) view of the meaning of constitutional revisions than has been expressed in some earlier California cases. The upshot is that revision challenges to initiated constitutional amendments in California will be harder to win.

6. In Part II of *People's Advocate*, the court strikes down the portion of the initiative purporting to restrict future appropriations to cover the expenses of the legislature. The court's holding is a narrow one. It could be evaded if proponents qualified an initiative constitutional amendment rather than an initiative statute. Furthermore, as the court makes clear in its footnote 13, nothing prevents use of initiative statutes in California for appropriations, including appropriations extending permanently into the future. As the following excerpt explains, initiatives containing appropriations have become a common practice in California, though budgeting by initiative is restricted by the constitutions of some other states:

> Nine states place restrictions on the extent to which taxes can be levied or appropriations made through the initiative process. Even more states prohibit the use of the referendum to block or alter tax and appropriation measures....
>
> California is one of the states that does not impose restriction on the use of the initiative to raise revenue or spend money. One consequence is that a large proportion of the state's budget is now permanently subject to control by initiatives adopted in the past. Some believe that this not only creates annual budgeting problems but also encourages interest groups that lack the protected status conferred by the prior initiatives to seek protection for themselves....
>
> California, like many other states, subjects its normal appropriations to a number of important processes. The budget must be balanced. Appropriations, except those for the public schools, must be passed by two-thirds of the membership of each house, and all appropriations are subject to an item veto by the governor. No bill except the budget bill may contain more than one item of appropriation, "and that for one certain, expressed purpose." Appropriations contained in initiative measures are subject to none of these processes. This seems unduly lax, making it easier in some instances to secure appropriations through the initiative than through the legislative process. Because the appropriations process necessarily involves comparisons among programs, it also seems unwise and ultimately unworkable to allow a great proportion of a state's resources to be appropriated through the initiative process.

Philip L. Dubois & Floyd Feeney, Lawmaking by Initiative 83 (1998). See also Jessica A. Levinson & Robert M. Stern, *Ballot Box Budgeting in California: The Bane of the Golden State or an Overstated Problem?*, 37 Hastings Constitutional Law Quarterly 689 (2010) (proposing that all voter initiatives that affect the state budget identify their funding sources or spending cuts).

7. Numerous additional subject-matter restrictions on the content of initiatives exist in one or more states. Following is a sampling:

In many jurisdictions, initiatives may not resolve "administrative" as opposed to "legislative" questions. This issue most commonly arises in connection with initiative proposals at the local level. For example, in *Foster v. Clark*, 790 P.2d 1 (Or. 1990), the Portland City Council had changed the name of a street from "Union Avenue" to "Martin Luther King, Jr. Boulevard." An initiative proposal to change the name of the street back to "Union Avenue" was struck off the ballot on the ground that it dealt with an administrative issue.

A few jurisdictions prohibit the reversal by initiative of a decision that already has been made by the legislative body. See, *e.g.*, *Schaefer v. Village Board*, 501 N.W.2d 901 (Wis. 1993).

In at least some states, courts will remove from the ballot initiatives that declare an opinion on some question of public policy without legislating on the subject. The California Supreme Court adopted this view in *AFL-CIO v. Eu*, 686 P.2d 609 (Cal. 1984), while acknowledging that there may be value to permitting the people by direct vote not only to adopt statutes, but also to adopt resolutions, declare policy, and make known their views upon matters of statewide, national, or even international concern. Such initiatives, while not having the force of law, could nevertheless guide the lawmakers in future decisions. Indeed it may well be that the declaration of broad statements of policy is a more suitable use for the initiative than the enactment of detailed and technical statutes. Under the terms of the California Constitution, however, the initiative does not serve these hortatory objectives; it functions instead as a reserved legislative power, a method of enacting statutory law. But see *Howard Jarvis Taxpayers Association v. Padilla*, 363 P.3d 486 (Cal. 2016) (holding that while advisory *initiatives* are not permitted, the *legislature* may place non-binding questions on the ballot, such as whether the United States Supreme Court's campaign finance jurisprudence should be reversed through a constitutional amendment).

8. *Dueling Initiatives.* The final issue in *People's Advocate* was whether the unchallenged portions of the proposition could survive after other provisions were declared unconstitutional. The answer to that question, which arises frequently with respect to initiatives as well as legislatively-enacted statutes in an era of active judicial review, depends on whether the unchallenged provisions, or those held to be constitutional, are "severable" from the provisions that are struck down.

A different issue of severability arises when two initiatives are adopted at the same election covering the same general subject matter. In the past one or two decades it has become increasingly common for interest groups threatened by an initiative to qualify one or more competing initiatives more to their liking. In general this has not been an effective technique, but it gives rise to the possibility of competing initiatives both being approved. This occurred in 1988 when the voters of California approved both Proposition 68 and Proposition 73, competing campaign finance initiatives. Although both propositions received a majority of affirmative votes, Proposition 73 received more votes than Proposition 68. Article II, section 10(b) of the California constitution provides: "If the provisions of 2 or more measures approved at the same election conflict, those of the measure receiving the highest affirmative vote shall prevail." In *Taxpayers to Limit Campaign Spending v. Fair Political Practices Commission*, 799 P.2d 1220 (Cal. 1990), the California Supreme Court stated the question and answered it as follows: "Does section 10(b) contemplate enforcement of any provisions of an initiative that receives a majority of the votes cast when another initiative on the same ballot, directed to the same subject and offered as a competing regulatory scheme, receives a greater majority? We conclude that it does not." The court relied in part on historical and textual analyses of section 10(b) and related provisions. The court also offered these more general observations:

> In order to further the fundamental right of the electorate to enact legislation through the initiative process, this court must on occasion indulge in a presumption that the voters thoroughly study and understand the content of complex initiative measures. Relying on this presumption we attempt to ascertain and implement the purposes of the measure. No case has been called to our attention, however, in which the court has assumed that voters not only recognized that they were approving initiatives with fundamentally conflicting provisions intended to regulate the same subject, but also analyzed the remaining provisions in order to predict which would be implemented if either measure received a lesser affirmative vote. A construction of section 10(b) that obligates the court to implement a fictitious electoral intent would be unreasonable and unjustified.
>
> In concluding that section 10(b) mandates an attempt to reconcile these competing initiatives, each of which offers a comprehensive but fundamentally different regulatory scheme, the dissent and the Court of Appeal apparently assume that a majority of the same voters cast their votes for both Proposition 73 and Proposition 68, and thus enforcement of parts of Proposition 68 will carry out the intent of the electorate. [H]owever, there is no sound basis for the predicate assumption. The parties concede that the court cannot determine whether a majority of the voters intended that both measures become effective if both passed. Absent some basis for such a determination, the court cannot logically conclude that it was the intent of a majority of the electorate that both propositions be implemented to the extent possible, or that the voters anticipated the amalgam created by the Court of Appeal.
>
> When competing initiatives are on the ballot, it is possible, if not probable, that many of the votes in favor of each measure were cast by the voters who cast votes against the alternative proposition. The arguments for and against the initiatives here asked the voters to do just that—to choose between the two measures. A construction of section 10(b) that invites judicial reconciliation of competing initiatives in these circumstances would lead as easily to thwarting the will of the electorate as to carrying it out.[p]

p. Suppose the arguments in support of two initiatives dealing with the same subject urged voters to vote in favor of both. Would the California Supreme Court uphold the non-conflicting provisions of the measure that received fewer votes?—Eds.

> [Supporters of Proposition 68] argue that a construction of section 10(b) that does not permit implementation of individual, non-conflicting provisions of initiative measures will "eviscerate" the initiative process, and will make it possible for opponents of an initiative to defeat it even when it has been adopted by an overwhelming majority of the voters. The opponents will be able to do so, they argue, by placing another, less complex, but conflicting, measure, on the same ballot in the hope that it will receive a greater vote.
>
> The possibility of abuse of the initiative, however, does not offset the equally serious threat to the process that may occur when courts and regulatory agencies attempt to enforce provisions of conflicting initiatives in the absence of any assurance that the electorate anticipated the resulting regulatory scheme.
>
> The process is better served by presentation at a subsequent election of a new initiative measure which the voters can consider in light of the scheme established by the measure that prevailed in the earlier election. We do not denigrate the conscientious efforts of the voters to familiarize themselves with ballot measures. The increasing number and complexity of statewide and local initiative measures, however, supports our conclusions that we should not read section 10(b) as mandating what constitutes judicial legislation in which portions of one regulatory scheme are excised and attached to another, quite different scheme. Nor should we assume . . . that the voters would have approved incorporation of these several Proposition 68 provisions into the regulatory scheme created by Proposition 73.

Id. at 1235-36. See also Michael D. Gilbert, *Interpreting Initiatives*, 97 Minnesota Law Review 1621 (2013) (arguing that courts should interpret initiatives, both when dueling measures pass and generally, by trying to determine the intent of the median voter in the relevant election).

9. One content restriction that exists in most initiative states and that has been the subject of considerable litigation is the "single subject rule." For example, California Constitution, art. II, § 8(d) provides: "An initiative measure embracing more than one subject may not be submitted to the electors or have any effect." Even in states whose constitutions contain no express single subject rule for initiatives, courts sometimes extend to initiatives the single subject rule that is explicitly applicable to the legislature. *E.g., Washington Federation of State Employees v. State*, 901 P.2d 1028 (Wash. 1995); *Montana Automobile Association v. Greely*, 632 P.2d 300, 311 (Mont. 1981).

For many years, challenges to initiatives on single-subject grounds had the greatest success in Florida, as the following case illustrates.

In re Advisory Opinion to the Attorney General

632 So.2d 1018 (Fla. 1994)

McDONALD, Justice.

[T]he Attorney General has petitioned this Court for an advisory opinion on the validity of an initiative petition....

The petition seeks to amend article I, section 10 of the Florida Constitution, which provides:

> No bill of attainder, ex post facto law or law impairing the obligation of contracts shall be passed.

The petition would amend the above provision in the following manner:

> 1) Article I, section 10 of the Constitution of the State of Florida is hereby amended by ... adding a new subsection "(b)" at the end thereof to read:
>
> (b) The state, political subdivisions of the state, municipalities or any other governmental entity shall not enact or adopt any law regarding discrimination against persons which creates, establishes or recognizes any right, privilege or protection for any person based upon any characteristic, trait, status, or condition other than race, color, religion, sex, national origin, age, handicap, ethnic background, marital status, or familial status. As used herein the term 'sex' shall mean the biological state of either being a male person or a female person; 'marital status' shall mean the state of being lawfully married to a person of the opposite sex, separated, divorced, widowed or single; and 'familial status' shall mean the state of being a person domiciled with a minor, as defined by law, who is the parent or person with legal custody of such minor or who is a person with written permission from such parent or person with legal custody of such minor.
>
> (2) All laws previously enacted which are inconsistent with this provision are hereby repealed to the extent of such inconsistency....

Our advisory opinion is limited to determining whether the proposed amendment complies with article XI, section 3 of the Florida Constitution and section 101.161, Florida Statutes (1993). Article XI, section 3 of the Florida Constitution requires that a proposed amendment "shall embrace but one subject and matter directly connected therewith." The Attorney General concluded that "on its face," the amendment appeared to satisfy the single-subject requirement. Looking beyond the surface, however, we find that the proposed amendment touches upon more than one subject and therefore violates the single-subject provision of the constitution.

Florida's state constitution reflects a consensus on the issues and values that the electorate has declared to be of fundamental importance. When voters are asked to consider a modification to the constitution, they should not be forced to "accept part of an initiative proposal which they oppose in order to obtain a change in the constitution which they support." *Fine v. Firestone*, 448 So.2d 984, 988 (Fla.1984). The single-subject rule is a constitutional restraint placed on proposed amendments to prevent voters from being trapped in such a predicament. Thus, to comply with the single-subject requirement, the proposed amendment must manifest a "logical and natural oneness of purpose." *Id.*

To ascertain whether the necessary "oneness of purpose" exists, we must consider whether the proposal affects separate functions of government and how the proposal affects other provisions of the constitution. *Id.* In support of the validity of the proposed amendment, the American Family Political Committee argues that discrimination is the sole subject of the proposed amendment. This Court has emphasized, however, that "enfolding disparate subjects within the cloak of a broad generality does not satisfy the single-subject requirement." *Evans v. Firestone*, 457 So.2d 1351, 1353 (Fla. 1984). In *Fine*, we disapproved a proposed amendment that characterized the provisions as affecting the single subject of revenues because it actually affected the government's ability to tax, government user-fee operations, and funding of capital improvements through revenue bonds. Similarly, we find that the subject of discrimination in the proposed amendment is an expansive generality that encompasses both civil rights and the power of all state and local governmental bodies. By including the language "any other governmental entity," the proposed amendment encroaches on municipal home rule powers and on the rulemaking authority of executive agencies and the judiciary. In addition, the amendment modifies article I, section 2 of the Florida Constitution, dealing with the basic rights of all natural persons, and also affects article I, section 6 of the Florida Constitution, dealing with the right of employees to bargain collectively.

The proposed amendment also violates the single-subject requirement because it enumerates ten classifications of people that would be entitled to protection from discrimination if the amendment were passed. The voter is essentially being asked to give one "yes" or "no" answer to a proposal that actually asks ten questions. For example, a voter may want to support protection from discrimination for people based on race and religion, but oppose protection based on marital status and familial status. Requiring voters to choose which classifications they feel most strongly about, and then requiring them to cast an all or nothing vote on the classifications listed in the amendment, defies the purpose of the single-subject limitation. Therefore, the proposed amendment fails the single-subject requirement of article IV, section 3 of the Florida Constitution.

[The court also ruled that an additional reason for striking the measure from the ballot was that the proposed ballot title and summary were misleading. A concurring opinion by Justice Kogan is omitted.]

Notes and Questions

1. The initiative power was first inserted into the Florida Constitution in 1968, and is limited to constitutional amendments.[q] In 1970, the Florida Supreme Court ruled

---

q. For a good account of the history of the initiative in Florida, see Joseph W. Little, *Does Direct Democracy Threaten Constitutional Governance in Florida?*, 24 Stetson Law Review 393 (1995).

that an initiative proposal for a unicameral legislature was improper as a constitutional revision rather than a constitutional amendment. *Adams v. Gunter*, 238 So.2d 824 (1970). The legislature and the voters responded by amending the constitution to allow revisions as well as amendments by initiative, but also by inserting a single subject rule applicable to initiatives. Presumably, the purpose of the amendment was to assure greater leeway for changing the constitution through the initiative. Initially, the Florida Supreme Court interpreted the single subject rule in that spirit, applying the rule in the same deferential manner that it had long used in interpreting the single subject rule applicable to the legislature. See *Weber v. Smathers*, 338 So. 2d 819 (Fla. 1976); *Floridians Against Casino Takeover v. Let's Help Florida*, 363 So. 2d 337 (Fla. 1978).

In *Fine v. Firestone*, 448 So. 2d 984 (Fla. 1984), cited in *In re Advisory Opinion*, the Florida Supreme Court "receded" from earlier decisions interpreting the two single subject rules to establish the same standard. The court concluded that

> we should take a broader view of the legislative provision because any proposed law must proceed through legislative debate and public hearing. Such a process allows change in the content of any law before its adoption. This process is, in itself, a restriction on the drafting of a proposal which is not applicable to the scheme for constitutional revision or amendment by initiative.

Id. at 989. Additional reasons, more specific to Florida, for applying the rule more strictly to initiatives than to legislative enactments, depended on the specific language used in the constitutional provisions and on the fact that the single-subject rule for the legislature applied only to statutes while the rule for initiatives applied only to constitutional amendments and revisions.

Most states that have considered the issue at least purport to apply the single subject rule identically to the legislature and to the initiative process. Indeed, the Oregon Supreme Court canvassed decisions in a number of states on this point and concluded that "[i]t does appear . . . that the Florida court stands alone." *Oregon Education Association v. Phillips*, 727 P.2d 602 (Or. 1986).[r]

The Florida Supreme Court continues to implement the single subject rule with a heavy hand. In 2005, redistricting reformers in Ohio and California placed proposals on the ballot to impose new redistricting criteria and to entrust the enactment of redistricting plans to commissions. Both proposals were decisively defeated, but the reformers had their day before the voters. In Florida, a similar effort was stifled by the Supreme Court, which ruled in *Advisory Opinion to the Attorney General*, 926

Thomas Rutherford, *The People Drunk or the People Sober? Direct Democracy Meets the Supreme Court of Florida*, 15 St. Thomas Law Review 61 (2002), provides an exhaustive analysis of the Florida court's activism in its treatment of initiatives.

r. Footnote 4 of *Oregon Education Association* contains references to initiative single subject decisions from several states. A concurring opinion by Judge Hans Linde, a distinguished scholar on the initiative process, contains a thoughtful discussion of the single subject rule.

So. 2d 1218, 1225-26 (Fla. 2006), that the redistricting initiative violated the single subject rule:

> Not only would the proposed amendment create a new redistricting commission, but it would also change the standards applicable to the districts that are created by the commission....
>
> The other provisions of the proposed amendment exhibit "a natural relation and connection as component parts or aspects of" the new method proposed for apportionment. These provisions explain the composition of the commission, specify the apportionment process, and provide for judicial apportionment if the commission fails to complete its duty. However, the creation of new standards to be used in apportioning the districts is not a component part of this apportionment plan and results in logrolling. A voter who advocates apportionment by a redistricting commission may not necessarily agree with the change in the standards for drawing legislative and congressional districts. Conversely, a voter who approves the change in district standards may not want to change from the legislative apportionment process currently in place. Thus, a voter would be forced to vote in the "all or nothing" fashion that the single subject requirement safeguards against.

2. What is the purpose of the single subject rule, as applied to initiatives? Two purposes are commonly articulated: to prevent voter confusion and, as the Florida court stated, to prevent logrolling. At least two types of logrolling are theoretically possible. The first type would combine two or more provisions, none of which alone would command majority support. Suppose, for example, a proposal contains provisions *A* and *B*, each of which is supported by one-third of the voters and opposed by two-thirds. The supporters of *A* are different voters from the supporters of *B*. The proponents hope that each group of voters will care more about the provision they support than the one they oppose, and vote for the proposal, which would then receive two-thirds of the total vote. The second type of logrolling occurs when a majority of voters supports *A* and opposes *B*. The proponents hope that they will care more about their support for *A* than their opposition to *B* and vote for the proposal. *B* in this example is known as a "rider," because if the proponents are successful, *B*, though opposed by a majority of voters, will ride to victory on the popularity of *A*.

Is the single subject rule well suited to accomplish its anti-confusion and anti-logrolling purposes? See Clayton P. Gillette, *Expropriation and Institutional Design in State and Local Government Law*, 80 Virginia Law Review 625, 664–70 (1994) (arguing that the single subject rule serves an anti-logrolling function); Daniel H. Lowenstein, *California Initiatives and the Single-Subject Rule*, 30 UCLA Law Review 936, 954–65 (1983) (arguing that the rule serves neither purpose, but proposing an alternative rationale for the rule); John G. Matsusaka & Richard L. Hasen, *Aggressive Enforcement of the Single Subject Rule*, 9 Election Law Journal 399 (2010) (rejecting both arguments for single subject rule).

3. Although Florida may be the only state that expressly applies the single subject rule more rigorously to initiatives than to acts of the state legislature, for some time there have been other states that articulate relatively strict interpretations of the rule. For example, in Arizona, the rule is described as follows:

> If the different changes contained in the proposed amendment all cover matters necessary to be dealt with in some manner, in order that the Constitution, as amended, shall constitute a consistent and workable whole on the general topic embraced in that part which is amended, and if, logically speaking, they should stand or fall as a whole, then there is but one amendment submitted. But, if any one of the propositions, although not directly contradicting the others, does not refer to such matters, or if it is not such that the voter supporting it would reasonably be expected to support the principle of the others, then there are in reality two or more amendments to be submitted, and the proposed amendment falls within the constitutional prohibition.

Tilson v. Mofford, 737 P.2d 1367 (Ariz. 1987) (quoting *Kerby v. Luhrs*, 36 P.2d 549 (Ariz. 1934)). Nevertheless, at least until recently, no state other than Florida seems to have applied the rule strictly with any consistency.

Most states do not follow Arizona in requiring that all the provisions in an initiative be "necessary." For example, in Alaska, the "standard is that the 'act should embrace some one general subject; and by this is meant, merely, that all matters treated of should fall under some one general idea, be so connected with or related to each other, either logically or in popular understanding, as to be parts of, or germane to, one general subject.'" *Yute Air Alaska v. McAlpine*, 698 P.2d 1173 (Alaska 1985) (quoting from earlier decisions applying the single subject rule to legislatures). In California, likewise, the courts have applied the single subject rule liberally in order to sustain "statutes and initiatives which fairly disclose a reasonable and common sense relationship among their various components in furtherance of a common purpose." *Brosnahan v. Brown*, 651 P.2d 274, 284 (Cal. 1982).

One writer criticizes the liberal application of the rule in California on these grounds:

> The supreme court uses several artifices to avoid invalidating initiatives under the single-subject rule. Indeed, with these methods it can avoid altogether a meaningful application of the rule. These artifices include the broad manner of defining "subject," the loose relationship allowed between the measure's provisions and its "subject," the failure to distinguish between a measure's subject and objective, and the preference for delaying review until after an election. These artifices allow the court to sidestep serious review of complex initiative measures.

Marilyn E. Minger, Comment, *Putting the "Single" Back in the Single-Subject Rule: A Proposal for Initiative Reform in California*, 24 U.C. Davis Law Review 879, 899–900 (1991). For a defense of the liberal interpretation, see Lowenstein, *supra*.

4. Even in a state that interprets the rule liberally, anyone drafting an initiative—and anyone looking for a way to invalidate an initiative—should bear the single subject rule in mind. During the heyday of liberal interpretation of the rule by the California Supreme Court, lower courts nevertheless employed the rule to strike down two initiatives in 1988 and 1991. *California Trial Lawyers Association v. Eu*, 200 Cal. App.3d 351 (1988); *Chemical Specialties Manufacturers Assn., Inc. v. Deukmejian*, 227 Cal. App.3d 663 (1991). More importantly, as the following materials will show, a sea change may be taking place in the interpretation of the initiative single subject rule.

5. A good example of the liberal interpretation of the single subject rule that long prevailed in California is *Fair Political Practices Commission v. Superior Court*, 599 P.2d 46 (Cal. 1979). California's Political Reform Act, also known as Proposition 9, had been adopted by initiative in June, 1974. The court described Proposition 9 as follows:

> Chapters 1 and 2 contain general provisions and definitions, including a severability provision. Chapter 3 establishes the [Fair Political Practices Commission]. Chapter 4 establishes disclosure requirements for candidates' significant financial supporters. Chapter 5 places limitations on campaign spending. Chapter 6 regulates lobbyist activities. Chapter 7 establishes rules relating to conflict of interest. Chapter 8 establishes rules relating to voter pamphlet summaries of arguments on proposed ballot measures. Chapter 9 regulates ballot position of candidates. Chapter 10 establishes auditing procedures to aid enforcement of the law, and Chapter 11 imposes penalties for violations of the act.

Id. at 47. The court applied its established test under the single subject rule and upheld Proposition 9 because its provisions were "reasonably germane" to the general subject of "elections and different methods for preventing corruption and undue influence in political campaigns and governmental activities." *Id.* at 41, 47. A membership group of California lobbyists urged the court to abandon the "reasonably germane" test, which the group contended was not sufficient to serve the rule's alleged purposes of allaying voter confusion and avoiding logrolling.

The court rejected this proposal: "Consistent with our duty to uphold the people's right to initiative process, we adhere to the reasonably germane test and, in doing so, find that the measure before us complies with the one subject requirement." *Id.* at 41. The court responded to the lobbying group's contentions on the purposes of the rule:

> Although the initiative measure before us is wordy and complex, there is little reason to expect that claimed voter confusion could be eliminated or substantially reduced by dividing the measure into four or ten separate propositions.[s] Our society being complex, the rules governing it whether

s. One of the editors of this volume wrote most of Proposition 9. He cheerfully concedes complexity but takes umbrage at wordiness.—Eds.

> adopted by legislation or initiative will necessarily be complex. Unless we are to repudiate or cripple use of the initiative, risk of confusion must be borne.
>
> Nor does the possibility that some voters might vote for the measure—while objecting to some parts—warrant rejection of the reasonably germane test. Such risk is inherent in any initiative containing more than one sentence or even an "and" in a single sentence unless the provisions are redundant.

Id. at 42.

6. The *FPPC* court concluded that there is no single subject violation because the provisions of the Political Reform Act "are reasonably germane to the subject of political practices." It would be hard to argue that the measure was not confined to "political practices," and "political practices" presumably constitute a subject, albeit a broad one. The California constitution restricts initiatives to a single subject, but it does not say the subject has to be a narrow one. Does it follow that the court's conclusion is irrebuttably correct? Plainly not, because that argument proves too much. If *any* subject would do, then no measure could ever violate the single subject rule. Consider, for example, the initiative proposal that gave rise to the California single subject rule. Qualified for the ballot in 1948, it was the last of a series of initiatives sponsored in the 1930s and 1940s by the "ham and eggs" movement, so called because it favored public pensions that would put ham and eggs on the plates of senior citizens. The contents of the 1948 initiative were summarized as follow by the California Attorney General:

> Establishes 2 percent tax on gross receipts of all kinds. Legalizes, licenses and taxes bookmaking and other gambling. Abolishes all other State and local taxes and fees. Provides minimum monthly retirement pensions of $100 until July 1952, $130 thereafter, plus increases proportioned to cost-of-living increases since 1944, payable to aged persons, permanently disabled persons, widows, clergymen, teachers. Provides temporary disability and burial benefits. Regulates oleomargarine, certain healing arts, civic centers, public lands, water pollution, surface mining. Reapportions State Senate. Prohibits primary election cross-filing.

Relying on either common sense or on the legislative history of the single subject rule, we may take as a given that whatever else it may mean, the rule in California must at least rule out a repeat of the 1948 initiative. Yet, the above argument could be employed to vindicate the 1948 initiative just as easily as the 1974 Political Reform Act. All the provisions of the 1948 proposal, we might say, "are reasonably germane to the subject of public policy." True, public policy is an even broader subject than political practices, but it is still a subject. There has to be a limit on how broad the subject can be, if the rule is to have any meaning at all. The difficulty is that the rule gives no guidance as to what the limit should be.

The *FPPC* majority's approach, based on a case decided the year after the rule's adoption, allows broad subjects such as "political practices," but would prohibit measures approaching the 1948 ham and eggs measure in the disparateness of its provisions. Justice Wiley Manuel dissented, proposing that all the provisions in a measure should be functionally related to each other. Which interpretation is better as a matter of policy? Does the *Jones* case that follows employ the majority's interpretation of the single subject rule in *FPPC*, Justice Manuel's interpretation, or a different approach altogether?

7. *Senate of the State of California v. Jones*, 988 P.2d 1089 (Cal. 1999), was a 5–1 decision in which the California Supreme Court removed Proposition 24, an initiative, from the ballot because it violated the single subject rule. Proposition 24 contained four substantive provisions:

> a. It changed the method for setting salaries for state legislators. Instead of a state commission *setting* the salary changes, the commission would *recommend* changes, which had to be approved by both the legislature and the voters.
>
> b. It set restrictions on reimbursement of legislators for travel and living expenses.
>
> c. It imposed penalties on legislators if the budget was not approved each year by the deadline.
>
> d. It took the power of redistricting away from the legislature. Districting plans were to be adopted by the California Supreme Court, subject to approval by the voters.

The court reaffirmed previous decisions holding that a measure is consistent with the single subject rule if, "despite its varied collateral effects, all of its parts are 'reasonably germane' to each other, and to the general purpose or object of the initiative."[t] *Id.* at 1098. The court said the rule does not require that an initiative's provisions "interlock in a functional relationship." *Id.* The provisions merely had to be "reasonably related to a common theme or purpose." *Id.* But the court claimed that the precedents "clearly recognize that the single-subject requirement serves an important role in preserving the integrity and efficacy of the initiative process." *Id.* at 1099.

The court acknowledged that the first three provisions described above were reasonably germane to one another, but found that the fourth, the redistricting provision, caused the violation. "[W]hen viewed from a realistic and commonsense perspective, the provisions of Proposition 24 appear to embrace at least two distinct subjects—state officers' compensation and reapportionment." *Id.* at 1101.

The initiative proponent claimed that because each of the four provisions called for voter approval of certain actions, "voter involvement" provided a single subject. The court rejected that proposed subject as too broad, observing that if it were

t. Emphasis is removed in this and other quotations in this paragraph.

accepted, it would validate a proposal calling for voter approval of matters as disparate as "fisheries, student class-size reduction, and securities fraud." *Id.* at 1102. The court then turned to a more serious defense of the measure, that all the provisions related to the problem of "legislative self-interest."

Without resolving the question whether remedying legislative self-interest would itself be too broad a "subject" for an initiative measure, the court rejected the argument because it found that the provision relating to legislative salaries was unrelated to that subject. The court emphasized that under the existing system, set up in 1990, the salaries were set entirely by the commission, which was appointed by the governor without legislative confirmation. Because it would turn that commission into a body that only recommended salaries rather than establishing them, and would "reinvest legislators with a direct role in the process," albeit subject to further approval by the voters, Proposition 24 could not "be defended as involving the single subject or theme of imposing a voter-approval requirement in areas in which legislators may act in their own self-interest." *Id.* at 1103. The court was unimpressed with arguments that by setting up the commission in 1990 the legislators had made salary increases politically feasible by removing themselves from political accountability for the increases and that as a result legislative salaries had more than doubled from $49,000 to $99,000 in eight years. That increase might "simply reflect that the current figure is a fairer and more accurate measure of the appropriate compensation for such officers."[u] *Id.* at 1103. The proponent of Proposition 24 might disagree, but the fact remains that the salary provision was not aimed at a legislative conflict of interest. Therefore, although the provision "can be viewed as reasonably related to the objective of minimizing legislators' salaries, this argument does not establish that the provision is reasonably germane to the subject or objective of providing a check upon legislator self-interest." *Id.* at 1104.

Not surprisingly, the proponent relied heavily on *FPPC*, among other precedents. The court responded:

> In *FPPC*, the initiative at issue embodied a broad and comprehensive reform of campaign contributions and other political practices and activities, among other things creating a new entity—the Fair Political Practices Commission—to regulate and oversee political campaign activity. In concluding that the measure did not violate the single-subject rule, the court in *FPPC* found that the provisions of the measure were "reasonably germane to the subject of political practices," explaining that "the voters may not be limited to brief general statements but may deal comprehensively and in detail with an area of the law." Unlike Proposition 24, the measure

u. Many readers of this book and, for that matter, its editors, may agree that a doubling of salary from $49,000 to $99,000 over the course of the relatively noninflationary 1990s made the legislative salaries "fairer and more accurate." Supporters of Proposition 24 presumably thought otherwise. Is the court improperly smuggling its disagreement with the premises and policies of Proposition 24 into the question of whether the measure contains more than a single subject?—Eds.

> challenged in *FPPC* did not seek to combine one major structural change in the state constitutional framework (such as the transfer of the reapportionment power from the legislative to the judicial branch) with unrelated measures (such as those reducing and revising the pay of legislators and other state officers), but instead embodied a comprehensive package of provisions that were reasonably related to a common theme of reforming political campaign practices and related activities of candidates, lobbyists, and proponents of ballot measures.

Id. at 1104-05. The court concluded:

> In sum, we conclude that the initiative measure challenged in this case violates the single-subject rule. The portion of Proposition 24 that proposes to transfer the power of reapportionment from the Legislature, where it traditionally has resided, to the Supreme Court, itself involves a most fundamental and far-reaching change in the law. Assuming . . . that the transfer of this traditional legislative power to this court does not rise to the level of a constitutional revision that never may be accomplished by initiative but only by a constitutional convention or legislative submission, the proposal to adopt such a significant change nonetheless clearly represents a separate "subject" within the meaning of the single-subject rule upon which a clear expression of the voters' intent is essential. To permit the drafters of an initiative petition to combine a provision transferring the power of reapportionment from the Legislature to this court with unrelated provisions relating to legislators' pay would inevitably create voter confusion and obscure the electorate's intent with regard to each of the separate subjects included within the initiative, undermining the basic objectives sought to be achieved by the single-subject rule.

Id. at 1105.

8. To repeat the questions raised earlier, does *Jones* change the standard relied upon by the majority in *FPPC* for applying the single subject rule to initiatives? Does the majority in *Jones* adopt the standard favored by Justice Manuel in his *FPPC* dissent? And a new question: After *Jones*, is the single subject rule for initiatives applied in the same manner as the single subject rule applicable to statutes enacted by the legislature?

9. *Jones* distinguishes *FPPC* on the ground that the "comprehensive package of provisions" in the Political Reform Act of 1974 "were reasonably related to a common theme of reforming political campaign practices and related activities of candidates, lobbyists, and proponents of ballot measures." Is that an accurate characterization of the Political Reform Act or of the rationale given by the *FPPC* court? One major provision of the Political Reform Act limits personal gifts by lobbyists to a variety of elected and non-elected state officials. Other provisions require thousands of state and local officials and civil servants to disclose their personal economic interests and to disqualify themselves from governmental decisions when the

decisions conflict with their personal economic interests. How closely "related" are these regulated activities to "political campaign practices"? Are they more closely related to campaign practices than the provisions of Proposition 24 are to legislative self interest?

More generally, why did the California Supreme Court uphold the Political Reform Act of 1974 and strike down Proposition 24?

10. The *Jones* court's rejection of the "legislative self-interest" defense of Proposition 24 has been criticized by Daniel H. Lowenstein, *Initiatives and the New Single Subject Rule*, 1 Election Law Journal 35, 40 (2002):

> The court's reasoning is either thick-headed politically, disingenuous, or both. As the proponent of Proposition 24 argued to the court, control over salaries was transferred from the legislature to a commission precisely to enable salary increases. Legislators were afraid of voter retaliation if they voted to increase their own salaries, so they passed the job to a commission that was electorally unaccountable. In fact, under the commission system, legislative salaries doubled during an eight-year period of low inflation, from $49,000 to $99,000. . . .
>
> [The court displayed] its utter inability or unwillingness to acknowledge the political impulse behind a measure like Proposition 24. As is very well known and very well documented, distrust of government is widespread, as is the belief that public officials care more about themselves and about special interests than about ordinary people. The many people who hold such beliefs are not simply concerned with particular conflicts of interest, narrowly defined. Their concern is that the system as a whole is set up to favor insiders. For those who share that perception of politics, a system for increasing legislators' salaries without requiring legislators to put their fingerprints on the increases is worse than a system that requires legislators to pay a political price for increases, even if the Supreme Court might characterize that system as one of conflict of interest. A proposal that *in practice* reduces legislators' pecuniary benefits, reduces their control over their own districts, and punishes them for late enactment of a budget is a coherent and unified measure animated by a single purpose.

11. In a portion of the *Jones* opinion not reprinted above, the majority described how the proponents of Proposition 24 drafted several different versions of the proposal, each combining the redistricting provision with various additional provisions. The inference the majority drew was that the proponents were motivated exclusively to change redistricting procedures and that the additional provisions—the legislative compensation provisions in the version that was finally proposed—were intended as "sweeteners" to attract voter support. Assuming the truth of the court's inference regarding the proponents' motivation, what relevance does it have, if any, to the single subject determination? Gerald Uelmen, *Handling Hot Potatoes: Judicial Review of California Initiatives After* Senate v. Jones, 41 Santa Clara Law

Review 999, 1010 (2001), finds the court's discussion of the proponents' purposes significant and predicts that in future single subject cases, "the court will look to the alternative drafts and other evidence of 'manipulation,' which support a claim that 'logrolling' is going on."

12. In *Manduley v. Superior Court*, 41 P.3d 3 (Cal. 2002), the California Supreme Court upheld a lengthy initiative that addressed sentencing of repeat criminal offenders (by amending California's "three-strikes" law), gang-related crime, and the juvenile justice system. The common purpose was said to be addressing the problem of juvenile and gang-related crime, but not "simply to reduce crime generally." *Id.* at 29. The court then said that this was a subject or goal that "clearly is not so broad that an unlimited array of provisions could be considered relevant thereto. Indeed, . . . in previous decisions we have upheld initiatives containing various provisions related to even broader goals in the criminal justice system." *Id.* at 29. The court was willing to overlook the fact that the juvenile procedure provisions applied to juveniles who were not members of gangs, that the majority of gang members affected by the gang provisions were not juveniles, and that changes to the three-strikes law applied equally to adults and juveniles.

Does *Manduley* represent a retreat from *Jones*? Not overtly, but then *Jones* did not overtly represent a departure from *FPPC* and other California cases. It is undoubtedly too early to say, especially in light of the criticism offered by some that aggressive application of the single subject rule inevitably entails inconsistent and even arbitrary results. One possible clue to the different results in *Jones* and *Manduley* is the court's statement that the provisions in the latter case do not "comprise 'a most fundamental and far-reaching change in the law' that clearly represents a single subject upon which a clear expression of the voters' intent is essential," quoting from *Jones*. *Id.* at 32-33. If initiatives are more likely to violate the single subject rule because one or more of their provisions are "fundamental and far-reaching," then the single subject rule will come to resemble the constitutional revision doctrine, discussed above.

13. If *Manduley* notwithstanding, *Jones* was more than an aberration, then it marked a dramatic change from a half century of deferential application of the single subject rule by the California Supreme Court. In Florida also, as we have seen, aggressive application of the rule began only after early decisions construed the rule liberally. Indeed, the only state whose Supreme Court appears to have applied the rule aggressively from the start is Colorado. Colorado has permitted initiatives for both statutes and constitutional amendments since 1910, but the single subject rule for initiatives was not added to the state constitution until 1994. Colorado Constitution art. V, § 1(5.5). The most distinctive feature of the rule in Colorado is the procedure established for single subject review. A Ballot Title Setting Board, consisting of the Secretary of State and representatives of the Attorney General and Legislative Legal Services Office, rules on whether each initiative that is filed complies with the single subject rule, a determination that is reviewable by the state supreme court before the petition is circulated. The result is that an inordinate number of single

subject cases come before the court. In the words of Anne Campbell, *In the Eye of the Beholder: The Single Subject Rule for Ballot Initiatives*, in The Battle Over Citizen Lawmaking 131, 159 (M. Dane Waters, ed., 2001):

> Literally dozens of initiated measures have been challenged on single subject grounds since the restriction first went into effect in 1995. In the vast majority of the cases the Title Setting Board's title and judgment that an initiative encompasses a single subject are overturned. Either the Attorney General, the Secretary of State, and the Deputy for Legislative Legal Services are uncharacteristically inept when it comes to determining the validity of initiatives, or the Colorado Supreme Court is extremely strict in its scrutiny of initiatives.

The Separate Vote Requirement and Academic Criticisms of the Single Subject Rule

In Oregon and Montana, the state supreme courts have strengthened their single subject review at least as dramatically as in California, but they have done so under a distinct rule, known as the "separate vote" requirement. Oregon, which in 1902 became the third state to adopt the initiative, added a single subject rule in 1968. Oregon Constitution art. IV, § 1(2)(d). When the Oregon Supreme Court first had occasion to apply the rule to an initiative, it adopted the same deferential standard that was applicable to laws passed by the legislature. *Oregon Education Association v. Phillips*, 727 P.2d 602 (Or. 1986), and that standard was reiterated as recently as 1997. See *State ex rel. Caleb v. Beesley*, 949 P.2d 724 (Or. 1997). The following year, in *Armatta v. Kitzhaber*, 959 P.2d 49 (Or. 1998), the Oregon Supreme Court struck down a "victims' rights" constitutional amendment that had been approved by voters in 1996. The measure embraced a single subject under the standards set forth in the cases just mentioned. Therefore, instead of relying on Article IV, § 1(2)(d), the Oregon court invoked the substantially overlapping separate vote requirement. Oregon Constitution art. XVII, § 1. That section requires that when "two or more amendments shall be submitted . . . to the voters of this state at the same election, they shall be so submitted that each amendment shall be voted on separately." Such provisions are common in state constitutions, but no court before *Armatta* appears to have given them separate significance when there was also an applicable single subject rule. Nevertheless, the Oregon court stated that the separate vote requirement imposes a more restrictive requirement than the single subject rule.

According to *Armatta*, a proposed constitutional amendment violates the separate vote requirement if the proposal "would make two or more changes to the constitution that are substantive and that are not closely related." 959 P.2d at 64. The court acknowledged that the purposes of the single subject rule and the separate vote requirement are similar. "Both serve to ensure that the voters will not be compelled to vote upon multiple 'subjects' or multiple constitutional changes in a single vote." *Id.* at 63. Why should there be two rules serving the same purpose? Is the separate vote requirement easier to apply than the single subject rule? Consider the following:

> The only discernible "purpose" behind *Armatta*'s construal of the separate vote requirement as more restrictive than the single subject rule was that doing so enabled the Oregon Supreme Court to strike down an initiative constitutional amendment that its members did not like while pretending not to reverse its long string of precedents liberally interpreting both the legislative and initiative single subject rules. In addition, the court's conjuring up of the separate vote doctrine permitted it to throw out a constitutional amendment while avoiding rewriting the single subject rule as applied to initiative and legislatively-enacted statutes. But this advantage is paid for at the cost of greatly confusing the law as it applies to constitutional amendments. For what is the difference between saying that provisions belong to the same "subject" and that they are "closely related"? Provisions belong to the same subject *because* they are related. [The two formulations] use different words to describe the same concept. The establishment of two rules applicable to constitutional amendments, purporting to be distinct but delineated with words having the same meaning, can only muddy the waters considerably. And on top of this problem, the court's new rule requires it to decide the obscure questions whether provisions in a constitutional amendment make one change or several, and whether such changes as are made are "substantive."

Lowenstein, *Initiatives and the New Single Subject Rule, supra.*

Has the Oregon Supreme Court backed away from uniformly applying the separate vote requirement with rigor? In *Lehman v. Bradbury*, 37 P.3d 989 (Or. 2002), it struck down an initiative that had been approved ten years earlier (!) purporting to impose term limits on executive and legislative elected officials in state government as well as on members of Congress elected from Oregon. But over a dissent the Oregon Supreme Court rejected a separate vote challenge in *Meyer v. Bradbury*, 142 P.3d 1031, 1038 (2006):

> [The challenged initiative] does not change different constitutional provisions that confer different fundamental rights on different groups of persons. See *Armatta* (changes to constitutional provisions involving separate constitutional rights granted to different persons not closely related for separate-vote requirement); see also *Lehman* (when separate constitutional provisions conferring separate rights on different groups are affected by proposed amendment, it is "strong indication" that provisions not closely related for separate-vote requirement).
>
> Second, [the challenged initiative] is not a complicated measure. If adopted, [it] will do essentially two things: (1) create a general authority for both the people and the legislature to enact laws regulating campaign finances; but (2) condition the legislature's ability in that regard through

> a supermajority procedural requirement. The supermajority requirement that [the measure] would place on the legislature both carries out and limits the general authority to enact contribution and expenditure laws that the measure would create. In other words, the supermajority requirement is a procedural condition on which the right to exercise substantive authority is predicated. Viewed in that manner, the constitutional changes proposed by [the challenged initiative] are "closely related" and therefore do not offend the Article XVII, section 1, separate-vote requirement.

Is this a weakening of the Oregon separate-vote rule?

The Montana Supreme Court also has breathed life into the separate-vote rule. As in Oregon, the single subject rule was applied to initiatives as deferentially as to statutes passed by the legislature. See *Martin v. State Highway Commission*, 88 P.2d 41 (Mont. 1939). In *Marshall v. Cooney*, 975 P.2d 325 (Mont. 1999), the Montana Supreme Court relied expressly on *Armatta* and invoked the separate vote requirement for constitutional amendments to strike down an initiative approved by the voters the previous year, requiring new taxes and tax increases to be subject to voter approval. However, the Montana court does not seem to have adopted the *Armatta* standard for applying the separate vote requirement. The reason it gave for striking down the tax initiative was that it would have changed or affected several different provisions of the Montana constitution. In Oregon, that would not have been sufficient. Assuming that the effect on each constitutional provision constituted a separate "change," in Oregon it would still have to be shown that the changes were substantive and that they were not "closely related." The Montana standard appears to be easier than the Oregon standard to apply, but it may encourage drafters of amendments to ignore loose ends that might be serious but that could only be tied up by referring to two or more existing constitutional articles or sections.

Numerous commentators have called for more aggressive judicial review of initiatives under the single-subject and separate-vote rules. *E.g.*, Dubois & Feeney, *supra*, at 148–49. Until a few years ago, only the Florida Supreme Court had heeded that call with any consistency. The foregoing materials show that recently California, Colorado, Montana, Oregon, and Washington have joined the ranks, though Montana and Oregon have done so under the guise of the separate vote requirement. No one can say whether these recent developments will prove to be an aberration or an enduring trend. For the time being, those who draft initiatives would be well advised to pay close attention to the single subject requirements. Even in states that have not yet shown signs of aggressive review, a state Supreme Court that for any reason is unsympathetic to a measure may find that the recent developments in the states mentioned make it both easy and tempting to follow suit.

In criticizing aggressive judicial use of the single subject rule, Lowenstein argued that when judges are forced to make highly subjective decisions, it is hard for their reasoning not to be influenced by their belief systems, values, and ideologies. In an empirical study of the single subject rule, John G. Matsusaka and Richard L. Hasen found strong support for Lowenstein's claim. The authors examined votes of state appellate court judges on single subject cases in five states during the period 1997–2006 (more than 150 cases and more than 700 individual votes). They found that judges are more likely to uphold an initiative against a single subject challenge if their partisan affiliations suggest they would be sympathetic to the policy proposed by the initiative. More important, they found that partisan affiliation was extremely important in states with aggressive enforcement of the single subject rule—the rate of upholding an initiative jumped from 42 percent when a judge disagreed with the policy to 83 percent when he agreed—but not very important in states with restrained enforcement. Matsusaka & Hasen, *supra*.

In Robert D. Cooter and Michael D. Gilbert, *A Theory of Direct Democracy and the Single Subject Rule*, 110 Columbia Law Review 687 (2010), the authors offer a new gloss on the single subject rule, the "separable preferences" criterion. Under this criterion, if a voter could decide whether one provision of a proposed measure should pass without knowing if the other passes, then voter preferences are separable and the measure should be found to violate the single subject rule. When voter preferences are not separable, there is no rational way to consider the individual issues in isolation, and it is proper for the voters to consider the issues as a package. The authors claim that this approach will minimize logrolling and the use of riders.

If California courts implemented the Cooter-Gilbert separable preferences test, would these courts be more inclined or less inclined to strike down initiatives on single subject grounds? See Richard L. Hasen & John G. Matsusaka, *Some Skepticism About the "Separable Preferences" Approach to the Single Subject Rule: A Comment on Cooter & Gilbert*, 110 Columbia Law Review Sidebar 35 (2010), (positing California courts would be more inclined); Cooter & Gilbert, *Reply*, 110 Columbia Law Review Sidebar 59 (2010), (disagreeing with Hasen & Matsusaka).[v]

III. Procedural Requirements and Judicial Review

Laws passed by the initiative process are subject to judicial review under the state and federal constitutions, and state constitutional amendments passed by initiative are reviewed under the United States Constitution. One contention has been that the initiative process itself violates Article IV, § 4 of the Constitution, which provides in part: "The United States shall guarantee to every state in this union a republican form of government, and shall protect each of them against invasion...." Those who believe the initiative process violates this "Guaranty Clause" maintain, relying in part on Madison's *Federalist No. 10*, that the "republican form of government" that is guaranteed must consist of a representative government, in contrast with a

v. Aside from its merits, does the single subject rule violate the First Amendment rights or other constitutional rights of initiative proponents or voters? For an opinion rejecting such a challenge to Nevada's single subject rule, see *Pest Committee v. Miller*, 626 F.3d 1097 (9th Cir. 2010).

"democratic" form relying on direct action by the voters. The constitutionality of a tax adopted by initiative in Oregon was challenged on this theory in *Pacific States Tel. & Tel. Co. v. Oregon*, 223 U.S. 118 (1912). The Supreme Court declined to reach the merits of this challenge, holding instead that questions raised under the Guaranty Clause are nonjusticiable.

State courts generally have followed *Pacific States* and declined to pass on whether the initiative process violates the Guaranty Clause. A former member of the Oregon Supreme Court has argued that state courts should not be bound by the federal nonjusticiability doctrine. He contends that if state courts are unwilling to strike down the initiative process as a whole, they should declare that the submission to the voters of certain types of measures, particularly those that stigmatize particular groups, may violate the requirement of a republican form of government. See Hans A. Linde, *When Initiative Lawmaking Is Not "Republican Government": The Campaign Against Homosexuality*, 72 Oregon Law Review 19 (1993); Hans A. Linde, *Who Is Responsible for Republican Government?*, 65 University of Colorado Law Review 709 (1994). However, Linde's theory was rejected by an Oregon appellate court, which refused to remove from the ballot an "anti-gay" initiative:

> [P]laintiffs claim that Article IV, section 4 of the United States Constitution, which guarantees to the states a republican form of government, prohibits the use of the initiative for various purposes, including, among others, to enact a state constitutional amendment that "imposes unique disabilities on an identifiable group of citizens," and to propose a measure that asks voters to act on the basis of passion and interest. Plaintiffs assert that the Guaranty Clause forbids states from holding an election by popular vote on any "proposed laws aimed at restricting the substantive rights of unpopular minority groups." . . .
>
> Plaintiffs . . . do not cite *Pacific States* or make any argument about why we are not bound by the United States Supreme Court's interpretation of the federal constitution. . . . [W]e conclude that the United States Supreme Court's interpretation of the Guaranty Clause as presenting a purely political question that is exclusively for Congress and not the courts to decide, precludes the courts of this state from entering any declaration about compliance with the Guaranty Clause.

Lowe v. Keisling, 882 P.2d 91, 100-01 (Or. App. 1994). For criticism of the Linde approach, see Jesse H. Choper, *Observations on the Guarantee Clause—As Thoughtfully Addressed by Justice Linde and Professor Eule*, 65 University of Colorado Law Review 741, 744–46 (1994).

Although court challenges to the initiative process itself have been stymied to date, it is not surprising that specific measures enacted through a process designed to produce innovative and controversial laws should stimulate numerous judicial challenges. One type of challenge, considered in the preceding Part, contends that the measure is not one that may be adopted by the initiative process. The other most common types of challenges are those charging a failure to comply with procedural requirements and those claiming that the measure or some portion of it is substantively unconstitutional under either the federal or (in the case of an initiative statute) state constitution. Following a brief overview of the procedural requirements for initiatives, we discuss the difficult question of how strictly procedural requirements should be enforced against initiative proponents—and in election law generally—and other questions distinctive to substantive judicial review of initiatives.

Recall that Richard Ellis, in the excerpt that opened this chapter, noted the strong differences in the frequency of use of the initiative among the states that allow for it. The differences may be influenced by the fact that the procedural requirements for qualification vary considerably from state to state. Some of the more common requirements are described by David B. Magleby, *Direct Legislation in the States*, in Referendums around the World 218, 225–29 (David Butler & Austin Ranney, eds., 1994):

> One of the most important legal requirements in all direct legislation processes is the signature threshold and related requirements.[w] All forms of the initiative and popular referendum require that petitioners gather sufficient signatures from registered voters to meet a signature threshold, typically set as a proportion of the vote for governor in the previous gubernatorial election. Signature requirements range from a low of 2 percent in North Dakota for statutory initiatives to a high of 15 percent in Wyoming for statutory initiatives and [referendums.]
>
> The stringency of a state's signature threshold is inversely related to the frequency of measures qualifying for the ballot. Thirteen states have a geographic distribution requirement for signatures on direct legislation petitions. The intent of this requirement is to force petitioners to demonstrate support for their measure outside a few highly populated counties. The presence of a geographic distribution requirement appears to hamper proponents in getting their measures on the ballot.[x] . . .
>
> Other important procedural rules include the time period a measure can remain in circulation, the process whereby the measure is given its official title and summary, limitations on the subject matter that may be part of the measure, and whether the vote necessary for success is a simple majority

w. Aside from the number of signatures required, the requirement that most affects the number of initiatives that qualify appears to be the time period allowed for circulation. These two requirements can be stated in combined form as the number of signatures required per day. According to Susan A. Banducci, *Direct Legislation: When Is It Used and When Does It Pass?* in Citizens as Legislators, *supra*, at 109, 116, each reduction of 2,000 required signatures per day results, on average, in an additional three initiatives that qualify in an election cycle.—Eds.

x. But will such provisions bear constitutional scrutiny? Not according to *Idaho Coalition United for Bears v. Cenarrussa*, 342 F.3d 1073 (9th Cir. 2003), which struck down as a violation of the one person, one vote principle an Idaho requirement that initiative proponents obtain signatures from at least six percent of voters in at least half Idaho's counties.—Eds.

of those voting on the measure, a majority of those voting in the election, or a supermajority of 60 percent or more of those voting in the election. Initiative petitions typically may circulate for up to 120 days, but the time limitation can be as short as 50 days or as long as 360 days. [R]eferendum petitions typically have a shorter time period for circulation, averaging about 90 to 120 days.

Because initiatives are proposed laws or constitutional amendments, they can be very lengthy and technical in their wording. All states provide a short summary of the proposal, and most states give a short title as well. In some states, the proponents are permitted to title and summarize their own measures, but in most states this task is left to election officials. The process of summarizing and titling initiatives is often challenged in court....

The vote needed for enactment of direct legislation also varies among the states. Some states require a majority of those voting on the measure, others a majority of those voting in the election, and still others an extraordinary majority of those voting in the election. At least one state requires a majority vote in two consecutive elections for a constitutional initiative to take effect. In 1988 and 1990, for instance, Nevada voters approved a constitutional initiative banning income taxes. When Minnesota voted on whether to adopt the initiative process in 1980, 53.2 percent of those voting on the question voted for the proposal, but a quarter of a million persons who voted in the election failed to vote on the question. Hence the affirmative vote was only 46.7 percent of all voters in the election. Since Minnesota law requires that a majority of those voting in the election vote affirmatively for changes in the state constitution, the proposal for a statewide initiative failed.

Only registered voters may sign petitions, except in North Dakota, which does not have voter registration. There is a wide variation in how states verify petition signatures, ranging from verifying each signature to verifying random samples of signatures. States routinely check for duplicate signatures and evidence of petition fraud.

For valuable commentary on a variety of issues relating to implementation of the initiative process, see Philip L. Dubois and Floyd Feeney, Lawmaking by Initiative (1998). A good source for the procedural requirements in any given state, as well as for much other information about direct democracy in the United States, is the web site of the Initiative and Referendum Institute of the University of Southern California, https://www.iandrinstitute.org. See also *Protect Marriage Illinois v. Orr*, 463 F.3d 604 (7th Cir. 2006) (rejecting a challenge to a signature requirement for placing an advisory question on the Illinois ballot because states have the authority to regulate ballot access as they see fit).

In California (and increasingly in some other states that use the initiative process) the reliance on professional circulators to qualify initiatives has become immense. Consider the following from a report issued by a non-profit research organization:

> Professional signature-gathering firms now boast that they can qualify *any* measure for the ballot (one "guarantees" qualification) if paid enough money for cadres of individual signature gatherers, and their statement is probably true. Any individual, corporation or organization with approximately $1 million to spend can now place any issue on the ballot and at least have a chance of enacting a state law. Qualifying an initiative for the statewide ballot is thus no longer so much a measure of general citizen interest as it is a test of fundraising ability. Instead of waging volunteer petition campaigns for broad-based grassroots support, initiative proponents now engage in intense searches for large contributors willing to fund increasingly expensive paid circulation drives.

California Commission on Campaign Financing, Democracy By Initiative 265 (1992).

Elizabeth Garrett, *Money, Agenda Setting, and Direct Democracy*, 77 Texas Law Review 1845 (1999), argues that the widespread reliance on professional circulators for the qualification of initiatives in many states turns the initiative into a preserve for well-funded groups. But Daniel H. Lowenstein, *Election Law Miscellany: Enforcement, Access to Debates, Qualification of Initiatives*, 77 Texas Law Review 2001, 2002–08 (1999), criticizes the system's reliance on professional circulation firms for the opposite reason, that the efficiency of the firms and the consequent low cost of qualifying a measure result in qualification of proposals that have not demonstrated widespread support.

A. Strict Enforcement or Substantial Compliance?

Proponents of a redistricting initiative in California filed their petitions for what became known as Proposition 77 in early May, 2005. In mid-May, an attorney for the proponents discovered that there were differences between the text of the proposal filed with the Attorney General (and provided by the Attorney General to the legislature and to the public via the internet) and the version that was circulated. The attorney did not disclose the discrepancies to anyone except an attorney for Republican Governor Schwarzenegger, who was supporting the initiative. On June 10, a Friday, the Secretary of State certified that Proposition 77 had qualified for the ballot. The following Monday, the attorney for the proponents disclosed the discrepancies to the Secretary of State. The latter, also a Republican, waited until early July before reporting the problem to the Attorney General, a Democrat, who promptly made the problem known to the public and later joined in a challenge to the placement of Proposition 77 on the ballot. In the meantime, the governor called a special election for November to vote on Proposition 77 and several other initiatives.

Opponents of Proposition 77, joined by the Attorney General, sought removal of the proposal from the ballot. The trial judge ruled in their favor and a divided appellate court affirmed. In the appellate court, both the majority and the dissenter issued long and thoughtful opinions. Several days later, the California Supreme Court restored Proposition 77, saying in a two-paragraph decision that in "the absence of a showing that the discrepancies . . . were likely to have misled the persons who signed the initiative petition, we conclude that it would not be appropriate to deny the electorate the opportunity to vote on Proposition 77 at the special election to be held on November 8, 2005, on the basis of such discrepancies." *Costa v. S. C. (Lockyer)*, 128 P.3d 149 (Cal. 2005).

In taking that action, did the Supreme Court overrule the appellate court on the merits, or simply rule that the merits should be decided after the election? Apparently the latter. As we shall see, the court issued an opinion on the merits long after Proposition 77 had been defeated. Is pre-election review appropriate in cases such as this one when there is a procedural question whether the measure is properly qualified for the ballot? One reason for denying pre-election review, which will be stronger in some cases and weaker in others, is that shortness of time may preclude a thorough review of the issues raised. To the extent that was true in the Proposition 77 case, were the delays caused by the proponents' failure to disclose the discrepancies relevant?

As mentioned, the Supreme Court resolved the merits after Proposition 77 had been defeated at the polls. The court reaffirmed the correctness of keeping the initiative on the ballot. *Costa v. Superior Court*, 128 P.3d 675 (Cal. 2006). Although there were a few opponents who thought otherwise, most observers agreed that the differences between the two versions of the proposal were unlikely to affect anyone's support or opposition. On the other hand, they were more than mere typographical errors or trivial changes. The version circulated accidentally failed to reflect a final edit that had been performed by the attorney for the proponents. In addition to a large number of wording changes, a paragraph of the statement of purposes was omitted, and a deadline was changed. Should changes of this order — neither insignificant nor politically salient — have resulted in removal of the proposition from the ballot? The court wrote:

> Although it has been suggested that the issue before us turns on whether the controlling decisions require "strict" or "substantial" compliance with the applicable election laws, in some respects such an approach presents a potentially misleading dichotomy. . . .
>
> [T]he governing cases . . . have recognized that an unreasonably literal or inflexible application of constitutional or statutory requirements that fails to take into account the purpose underlying the particular requirement at issue would be inconsistent with the fundamental nature of the people's constitutionally enshrined initiative power . . .

Id. at 689. Whether or not the terminology is potentially misleading, the question of substantial compliance comes up in a wide variety of settings in election law and poses a difficult jurisprudential question that is worth serious consideration. An orderly electoral system requires a wide variety of deadlines, thresholds, and specific rules of all types. Those rules make it possible for all actors in the system to know what they must do to accomplish their objectives. Because humans are fallible, failure to comply with the rules in various ways and to various degrees is inevitable. Most such failures will be inadvertent but some will be calculated, and it usually will be difficult for outsiders to tell the difference.

Should a candidate or a proposition lose a position on the ballot, or should some other valuable right be lost, because of failure to comply with rules? As the California Supreme Court said, an overly literal or inflexible application of rules can lead to a system that sets traps and barriers for the unwary. But bending the rules can be unfair to those who have complied and can lead to a state of affairs in which requirements are more impressionistic than defined. Furthermore, when a court decides important electoral questions on the basis of "substantial compliance" rather than the rules, the judges face the serious danger that their judgment will be affected by their political preferences. Judges are not likely to say to themselves that they will let this proposition or this candidate on the ballot because they support the proposition or because the candidate belongs to the judges' party. But judges who are favorably disposed to a candidate or proposition are likely to be more receptive to the idea that removal is unreasonable. It did not escape notice that the majority of justices who kept Governor Schwarzenegger's redistricting initiative on the ballot were Republicans.

B. Pre-Election Judicial Review

Challenges to initiative measures may be brought on a variety of grounds, which are likely to fall into three categories: the proposal violates a substantive provision of the United States Constitution or, if it is a proposed statute, of the state constitution; the proposal is not one that can be enacted by initiative, for example, because it violates the single subject rule; or the measure did not receive enough signatures or otherwise did not satisfy the procedural requirements to qualify for the ballot, as the respondents claimed in *Costa*. The challenge may be brought before the election, seeking to have the measure removed from the ballot, or after the election, seeking to have it declared void. The question arises whether a case brought before the election is premature.

The California Supreme Court sought to clarify its policy on pre-election review in terms of the three categories just set forth. Presumptively, substantive constitutional challenges are not to be heard until and unless the measure is approved by the voters. Challenges, such as *Costa*, to the procedures by which the measure qualified for the ballot should be heard before the election, if feasible. Challenges based not on substantive constitutionality but on the assertion that the proposal is not the type of measure that can be adopted as an initiative are in-between cases. Unlike a claim that the measure has not properly qualified, there is no likelihood that such a challenge will be moot after the election. Thus, such a claim is "susceptible to resolution either before or after the election." *Independent Energy Producers Association v. McPherson*, 136 P.3d 178, 181 (Cal. 2006).

In *Wyoming National Abortion Rights Action League v. Karpan*, 881 P.2d 282 (Wyo. 1994), pro-choice groups challenged an initiative containing provisions apparently unconstitutional under abortion rulings of the United States Supreme Court. The Wyoming court cited cases from a number of states holding that review of such substantive constitutional issues would have to wait until after the election. For example, the Arizona Supreme Court had written:

> Just as under the separation of powers doctrine the courts are powerless to predetermine the constitutionality of legislation, so also they are powerless to predetermine the validity of the substance of an initiated measure....
>
> In the absence of any constitutional or statutory directive to the contrary, the proper place to argue about the potential impact of an initiative is in the political arena, in speeches, newspaper articles, advertisements and other forums. The constitutionality of the interpretation or application of the proposed amendment will be considered by this court only after the amendment is adopted and the issue is presented by litigants whose rights are affected.

Tilson v. Mofford, 737 P.2d 1367, 1369, 1372 (Ariz. 1987). The Wyoming court acknowledged that Arizona's position was that of the majority of states and was supported by the pragmatic consideration that the constitutional issue could be avoided if the initiative measure were defeated at the polls. Nevertheless, the Wyoming court declined to follow the majority rule:

> We hold that an initiative statute that contravenes direct constitutional language, or constitutional language as previously interpreted by the highest court of a state or of the United States, is subject to review under the declaratory judgment statutes.... [I]f such a measure were clearly unconstitutional, there would be no purpose in submitting it to the electorate under the initiative process. The initiative process was designed and intended for a different purpose than simply providing a formal straw vote.

Wyoming National Abortion Rights Action League, 881 P.2d at 288. On the other hand, the court said it would remove a measure from the ballot only if it were unconstitutional in its entirety. The anti-abortion initiative had some provisions that were constitutional and therefore remained on the ballot.

Proposition 187 was a controversial California initiative in 1994. One of its provisions was to prohibit children who are undocumented noncitizens in the United States from attending public schools. Virtually everyone, including most knowledgeable supporters of Proposition 187, agreed that the public school provision violated the Equal Protection Clause as interpreted in *Plyler v. Doe*, 457 U.S. 202 (1982). Some supporters of Proposition 187 hoped that if the prohibition were enacted, a majority on the Supreme Court might be persuaded to reverse *Plyler*. Other provisions of

Proposition 187, denying various public services to undocumented noncitizens, did not obviously violate existing constitutional doctrine. Would the Wyoming court that decided *Wyoming National Abortion Rights League* have ruled Proposition 187 off the ballot? Would it have done so if Proposition 187 had contained only the public school provision and had been proposed solely for the purpose of challenging *Plyler*? Does this hypothetical suggest that state courts should or should not provide pre-election constitutional review of initiatives?

Suppose you are consulted by a group in Wyoming that has drafted a law to bar undocumented noncitizens from public schools, in the belief that a majority on the Supreme Court would be willing to reverse *Plyler v. Doe*. The group proposes to circulate the proposed law as an initiative. How would you advise them to draft their law to assure that the Wyoming courts will permit it to go on the ballot?

In *Nasberg v. City of Augusta*, 662 A.2d 227 (Me. 1995), the Supreme Judicial Court of Maine upheld the refusal of a city to place an initiative proposal on the ballot. A statute provided that after a public hearing, municipal officers were to file with the city clerk

> a report containing the final draft of the proposed amendment and a written opinion by an attorney admitted to the bar of this State that the proposed amendment does not contain any provision prohibited by the general laws, the United States Constitution or the Constitution of Maine.

The city attorney believed the charter amendment in question violated a provision of the Maine Constitution and the City Council voted not to place the proposal on the ballot unless the proponents obtained a written opinion by an attorney upholding the proposal's constitutionality. The court stated that the intent of requiring an attorney's letter was "to prevent clearly unconstitutional provisions from being placed on municipal ballots." *Id.* at 229. Suppose, under a requirement similar to Maine's, a group collected sufficient signatures to qualify an initiative whose sole purpose was to deny the ability of undocumented noncitizens to enroll in public schools. Suppose it is your belief that the proposal is plainly unconstitutional under *Plyler v. Doe*, but that there is a substantial chance that the Supreme Court would overrule *Plyler v. Doe* and that therefore the proposal would be upheld. Under these circumstances, would you sign an opinion letter of the sort called for by the Maine statute? What if you did not think it likely that the Supreme Court would overrule *Plyler v. Doe* but you believed that the Court misinterpreted the Constitution in that decision?

Like the state courts, commentators are divided on the desirability of pre-election review of substantive constitutional questions. Opponents of pre-election review contend that it "involves issuing an advisory opinion, violates ripeness requirements, undermines the policy of avoiding unnecessary constitutional questions, and constitutes unwarranted judicial interference with a legislative process." James D. Gordon III & David B. Magleby, *Pre-Election Judicial Review of Initiatives and Referendums*, 64 Notre Dame Law Review 298 (1989). Gordon and Magleby elaborate on their ripeness point:

> Suits attacking the substantive validity of ballot measures involve a double contingency which renders any injury speculative and uncertain. First, the measure may not pass; only a minority do. . . . Second, even if the measure passes, there may be no threat of enforcement. Prosecutors and other government officials often exercise their discretion not to enforce a law because of their doubts about its constitutionality, their perception of its social disutility, or their allocation of resources to other tasks. Also, there is often the possibility that if enacted, the law may be applied in a constitutional manner. Therefore, the uncertainty about the measure's passage and the government's implementation of it creates a double contingency which makes suits attacking the substantive constitutionality of ballot measures unripe for review.

Id. at 310.

William E. Adams, Jr., *Pre-Election Anti-Gay Ballot Initiative Challenges: Issues of Electoral Fairness, Majoritarian Tyranny, and Direct Democracy*, 55 Ohio State Law Journal 583, 626 (1994), calls for pre-election substantive review, at least where necessary to protect groups such as the targets of "anti-gay" initiatives from oppression:

> In response to the argument that the judicial system would be subjected to criticism for removing a measure before an election, one should consider the alternatives. If a court strikes a measure passed by the electorate, the criticism of the judicial system certainly will not be less. Going through the charade of an election to pass a measure that cannot withstand legal scrutiny not only wastes time, energy, and other resources, it also mocks the electoral system it supposedly honors. Voters are given the option of either choosing what is constitutionally permissible or having their choice rejected for its illegality. Further, holding these elections has a harmful impact upon those whom the courts should be protecting. The controversy and animosity surrounding these measures has generated violent acts against the groups they target. This should not be surprising because the attempt to give discrimination an official sanction simply reinforces the bigoted notion that the persons being denied protection are worthy of the scorn and abuse they receive.

Most of the controversy involves judicial review of initiatives for substantive constitutionality. Courts typically will engage in pre-election review of procedural questions relating to the qualification of an initiative. See Douglas Michael, Comment, *Judicial Review of Initiative Constitutional Amendments*, 14 U.C. Davis Law Review 461, 468–74 (1980). "Indeed," according to one court, "the procedures leading up to an election cannot be questioned after the people have voted, but instead the procedures must be challenged before the election is held." *Tilson v. Mofford*, 737 P.2d 1367, 1369 (Ariz. 1987). It is questionable how many states follow the Arizona rule that approval of an initiative by the electorate obviates post-election challenges to procedural inadequacies. For example, a Nebraska term-limits initiative was voided because under an unexpected interpretation of the state constitution, the proponents had collected too few signatures to qualify the measure. See *Duggan v. Beermann*, 515 N.W.2d 788 (Neb. 1994).

C. Hard Looks?

Some critics of the initiative process, including Derrick Bell, whose writings were quoted in Part I of this chapter, have proposed that when initiatives are challenged for substantive unconstitutionality, they should be subjected to particularly rigorous review. In the words of another proponent of this view, challenged initiatives should receive a "hard look." Julian N. Eule, *Judicial Review of Direct Democracy*, 99 Yale Law Journal 1503 (1990). Eule bases his argument on the constitutional system of checks and balances, which he contends is largely circumvented by the initiative process:

> Where courts are but *one* of many checks on majority preferences, they serve predominantly as a safety net to catch those grains of tyrannical majoritarianism that slip through when the constitutional filtering system malfunctions. Most arguments for judicial restraint, I shall suggest, ought not to be perceived as pro-majoritarian. They are more on the order of "everything in its place." The claim is not that majorities do not need checking, but that courts are just one of several "solutions" to majority factions. The delicate balance put in place by the Framers is disturbed as much by judicial hyperactivity as by judicial dormancy. Where, however, the filtering system has been removed, courts must play a larger role — not because direct democracy is unconstitutional, nor because it frequently produces legislation that we may find substantively displeasing or short sighted, but because the judiciary stands *alone* in guarding against the evils incident to transient, impassioned majorities that the Constitution seeks to dissipate.

Id. at 1525. Eule does not propose that the "hard look" should be applied to all initiatives:

> Because the harder look is prompted by a concern for individual rights and equal application of laws, it is principally in these areas that the courts should treat [initiatives] with particular suspicion. Where, on the other hand, the electorate acts to improve the processes of legislative representation, the justification for judicial vigilance is absent. Measures to enforce ethics in government, regulate lobbyists, or reform campaign finance practices pose no distinctive threat of majoritarian tyranny. These measures install new filters rather than seeking to bypass the existing ones....
>
> I am unwilling, however, to group alterations of government structure and reapportionment efforts in the category of governmental reform. Too often these "reforms" are a facade for disenfranchising minorities; courts should be watchful of such chicanery. Neither do I ignore the threat of majority tyranny in fiscal measures like taxation and spending limitations.

> The beneficiaries of these so-called taxpayer revolts are principally upper and upper-middle class white citizens. The brunt of the burdens, in contrast, is borne by the underrepresented poor and by racial minorities.

Id. at 1559–60. Even where the "hard look" is applicable, Eule would apply it in a flexible manner:

> I do not perceive the concept of a hard judicial look to be a rigid one. Unlike "strict scrutiny" — a standard which on paper at least can be reduced to precise formulation — it is not intended to take on a unitary form. What I have in mind is more a general notion that courts should be willing to examine the realities of [initiatives] — that the unspoken assumptions about the legislative process that so often induce judicial restraint deserve less play in a setting where they are more fanciful. Sometimes a hard judicial look will take the form . . . of a candid "We know what's going on here and we won't allow any of it." In other situations[,] recognition that the burden of plebiscitary action falls on political actors able to defend their interests in the popular arena, combined with a need to conserve limited judicial capital, will appropriately lead to a more modest form of review.

Id. at 1572–73.

Eule concedes that, to date at least, courts addressing the question almost invariably have said that for purposes of substantive constitutional review, it makes no difference whether a law was passed by the legislature or by initiative. *Id.* at 1505–06. Furthermore, his call for a "hard judicial look" has been criticized by some scholars. Lynn Baker, *Direct Democracy and Discrimination: A Public Choice Perspective*, 67 Chicago-Kent Law Review 707, 756 (1991), argues that the "hard look" is unnecessary:

> [From Eule's discussion,] one might expect the United States Reports to be littered with instances in which the Court has upheld arguably racially discriminatory legislation enacted by plebiscites. In fact, the Court has heard only four cases in which plebiscitary legislation was challenged as racially discriminatory in violation of the Fourteenth Amendment. Applying the same equal protection standards that it applies to the enactments of representative bodies, the Court found that three of the four plebiscitary enactments violated the Equal Protection Clause.

Eule responds that although the Court *purported* to use the same equal protection standards it applies to laws produced by legislatures, in fact it may silently have been giving the initiatives in question a hard look. See Julian N. Eule, *Representative Government: The People's Choice*, 67 Chicago-Kent Law Review 777, 780–82 (1991).

The "hard look" approach is also criticized by Robin Charlow, *Judicial Review, Equal Protection and the Problem with Plebiscites*, 79 Cornell Law Review 527 (1994), who contends that heightened judicial review is a misplaced remedy for the defects that critics find in the initiative process:

> [T]he real problem that proponents of special judicial review have with plebiscites lies with the plebiscitary process, not with plebiscitary results. But, having concluded that the process, although undesirable, is constitutional, they are left with no constitutional recourse but to attack the results.
>
> Either state and local plebiscitary processes are constitutional forms of lawmaking or they are not. If they are constitutional, dissatisfaction with the perceived efficacy of these processes for particular groups should not, in and of itself, warrant different constitutional treatment of the products of such processes. In other words, if plebiscitary lawmaking does not violate the Guarantee Clause, it should not matter whether state and local plebiscitary schemes fulfill the structural goals of the system prescribed for federal decisionmaking. That federal structure, and its tripartite, minority-protective safeguards, could have been, but was not, imposed on the states. In terms of the structure of state governments, the federal constitution imposes no limits beyond those contained in the Guarantee Clause. If that clause condemns only the extremes of state government excess (pure democracy and monarchy), then that is all the structural protection against state and local majoritarianism that minorities were intended to receive under the Constitution.

Id. at 556–57. Furthermore, Charlow contends that heightened judicial review of initiatives may hinder rather than further the constitutional system of checks and balances:

> It could be said that the implementation of plebiscites was motivated by a desire to have the populace perform in a new power-checking capacity. Plebiscites grew out of the populist Progressive reform movement of the late 19th and early 20th centuries. According to conventional historical analyses, public lawmaking was approved in an effort to break the perceived stranglehold that certain minority, monied interests—in particular, wealthy corporations—had managed to secure over elected state and local legislatures. The plebiscitary institution, therefore, like conventional branches of government, has a tradition of serving a distinct part in assuring against the overconcentration of power in one governmental body.
>
> ... One purpose of separating power among the three branches of government was to diminish the influence of majoritarian faction expressed in the politically responsive legislative branch. The special review thesis seems to conclude that the populace must be checked by the judiciary precisely because it presents a similar and even more exceptional threat of majoritarian tyranny. Thus, with regard to the peril of majoritarian tyranny, plebiscites are supposedly worse than legislatures, and therefore more in need of judicial oversight or, conversely, less deserving of judicial deference.
>
> However, it could also be said that separation of powers was adopted to prevent minoritarian tyranny, for example, in the unelected judicial branch.

> This would support the separation of powers explanation for the judiciary's deference to the will of the majoritarian legislative branch. Plebiscites were likewise instituted to allay minority faction, albeit in the usually majoritarian legislative body rather than in the judiciary. Therefore, if courts are supposed to defer to legislatures in order to guard against an excessive concentration of their own minoritarian power, perhaps they ought likewise defer to the electorate in the case of plebiscites in order to ensure against the overconcentration of minoritarian power within the usually majoritarian legislature. Indeed, in theory plebiscites embody the will of the ultimate politically responsive body—the electorate itself—so courts should defer to them even more readily than they do to legislative action in order to avoid minority tyranny.

Id. at 580–82. In her conclusion, Charlow says that she agrees with Bell, Eule, and other critics, that the initiative process creates dangers for some groups, but she contends that heightened substantive constitutional review of initiatives is neither called for nor an adequate solution. She proposes instead that the initiative process be improved or, if it is perceived to be sufficiently dangerous, that it be scrapped. Alternatively, she suggests that remedies may be found within the political process, by defeating oppressive initiative proposals, or repealing those that are enacted. Finally, she suggests that if discriminatory laws still survive, the solution is in improvement of equal protection doctrine generally, rather than heightened application of the Equal Protection Clause only to laws that were enacted by initiative. *Id.* at 625–30.

D. "The Legislature Thereof"

As the above discussion makes clear, voter initiatives, like conventional statutes, may be invalidated when they violate the United States Constitution. There is, however, language in the Constitution that might be understood to threaten certain initiatives precisely because they are *not* statutes. The Elections Clause of Article I, Section 4 states: "The Times, Places and Manner of holding Elections for Senators and Representatives, shall be prescribed in each State *by the Legislature thereof*; but the Congress may at any time by Law make or alter such Regulations." The italicized language—*by the Legislature thereof*—raises the possibility that initiatives relating to congressional elections may be unconstitutional because they are enacted by the electorate rather than by the state legislature. On this view, "Legislature" refers to the state's institutional legislative body, and does not encompass any other form of lawmaking, such as direct democracy. Similar language appears in Article II, Section 1, concerning the process through which presidential electors are selected: "Each state shall appoint, *in such manner as the Legislature thereof may direct*, a number of electors, equal to the whole number of Senators and Representatives to which the State may be entitled in the Congress." See *Bush v. Gore*, 531 U.S. 98, 112–22 (2000) (Rehnquist, J., concurring) (arguing that this provision barred Florida courts from tackling issues relating to the state's 2000 contested presidential election in ways disfavored by the Florida legislature).

In a pair of cases in the early twentieth century, the Supreme Court hinted, but did not hold outright, that initiatives do not violate the Elections Clause merely because they regulate congressional elections. In *Ohio ex rel. Davis v. Hildebrant*, 241 U.S. 565 (1916), the Court upheld an Ohio referendum in which voters rejected a congressional district map passed by the legislature. According to the Court, it was immaterial that voters are distinct from the legislature, because "the referendum constituted a part of the state Constitution and laws, and was contained within the legislative power." *Id.* at 567. Similarly, in *Smiley v. Holm*, 285 U.S. 355 (1932), the Court sustained a Minnesota governor's veto of a legislatively enacted plan for congressional elections. Again, the governor's involvement was unobjectionable, even though the governor is not the legislature either, because his veto was "in accordance with the method which the state has prescribed for legislative enactments." *Id.* at 367.

The Court finally addressed the validity of initiatives (rather than referenda or vetoes) that regulate congressional elections in *Arizona State Legislature v. Arizona Independent Redistricting Commission*, 576 U.S. 787 (2015). In 2000, Arizona voters passed an initiative, Proposition 106, that transferred redistricting authority for congressional and state legislative maps from the legislature to an independent commission. In 2012, angry with the commission's maps due to their supposed pro-Democratic bias, the Republican-dominated legislature challenged the commission's constitutionality under the Elections Clause. A closely divided Court rejected this challenge, in the process affirming that "Legislature" refers to any kind of lawmaking that is authorized by a state's constitution. Writing for the Court, Justice Ginsburg began by considering the definition of "Legislature":

> We note, preliminarily, that dictionaries, even those in circulation during the founding era, capaciously define the word "legislature." Samuel Johnson defined "legislature" simply as "[t]he power that makes laws." 2 A Dictionary of the English Language (1st ed. 1755); *ibid.* (6th ed. 1785); *ibid.* (10th ed. 1792); *ibid.* (12th ed. 1802). Thomas Sheridan's dictionary defined "legislature" exactly as Dr. Johnson did: "The power that makes laws." 2 A Complete Dictionary of the English Language (4th ed. 1797). Noah Webster defined the term precisely that way as well. Compendious Dictionary of the English Language 174 (1806). And Nathan Bailey similarly defined "legislature" as "the Authority of making Laws, or Power which makes them." An Universal Etymological English Dictionary (20th ed. 1763).
>
> As to the "power that makes laws" in Arizona, initiatives adopted by the voters legislate for the State just as measures passed by the representative body do. See Ariz. Const., Art. IV, pt. 1, §1 ("The legislative authority of the state shall be vested in the legislature, consisting of a senate and a house of representatives, but the people reserve the power to propose laws and amendments to the constitution and to enact or reject such laws and amendments at the polls, independently of the legislature."). . . . As well in Arizona, the people may delegate their legislative authority over

> redistricting to an independent commission just as the representative body may choose to do.

Id. at 813-14. Justice Ginsburg next emphasized that states are generally free to structure their governments as they see fit and that initiatives are democratically legitimate because of their popular involvement:

> [I]t is characteristic of our federal system that States retain autonomy to establish their own governmental processes. See *Alden v. Maine*, 527 U.S. 706, 752 (1999) ("A State is entitled to order the processes of its own governance.").... Arizona engaged in definition of that kind when its people placed both the initiative power and the AIRC's redistricting authority in the portion of the Arizona Constitution delineating the State's legislative authority....
>
> We resist reading the Elections Clause to single out federal elections as the one area in which States may not use citizen initiatives as an alternative legislative process. Nothing in that Clause instructs, nor has this Court ever held, that a state legislature may prescribe regulations on the time, place, and manner of holding federal elections in defiance of provisions of the State's constitution....
>
> The Framers may not have imagined the modern initiative process in which the people of a State exercise legislative power coextensive with the authority of an institutional legislature. But the invention of the initiative was in full harmony with the Constitution's conception of the people as the font of governmental power. As Madison put it: "The genius of republican liberty seems to demand ... not only that all power should be derived from the people, but that those intrusted with it should be kept in dependence on the people." ...
>
> In this light, it would be perverse to interpret the term "Legislature" in the Elections Clause so as to exclude lawmaking by the people, particularly where such lawmaking is intended to check legislators' ability to choose the district lines they run in, thereby advancing the prospect that Members of Congress will in fact be "chosen ... by the People of the several States," Art. I, § 2.

Id. at 817-18. Lastly, Justice Ginsburg pointed out that if Proposition 106 was unconstitutional, so too must be many other initiatives that pertained to congressional elections. Avoiding such disruption was another argument in favor of her reading of the Elections Clause:

> Banning lawmaking by initiative to direct a State's method of apportioning congressional districts would do more than stymie attempts to curb partisan gerrymandering, by which the majority in the legislature draws district lines to their party's advantage. It would also cast doubt on numerous other election laws adopted by the initiative method of legislating.

> The people, in several States, functioning as the lawmaking body for the purpose at hand, have used the initiative to install a host of regulations governing the "Times, Places and Manner" of holding federal elections. Art. I, § 4. For example, the people of California provided for permanent voter registration, specifying that "no amendment by the Legislature shall provide for a general biennial or other periodic reregistration of voters." Cal. Elec. Code Ann. § 2123 (West 2003). The people of Ohio banned ballots providing for straight-ticket voting along party lines. Ohio Const., Art. V, § 2a. The people of Oregon shortened the deadline for voter registration to 20 days prior to an election. Ore. Const., Art. II, § 2. None of those measures permit the state legislatures to override the people's prescriptions. The Arizona Legislature's theory—that the lead role in regulating federal elections cannot be wrested from "the Legislature," and vested in commissions initiated by the people—would endanger all of them.

Id. at 822. Is Justice Ginsburg correct that all of these initiatives would have been jeopardized by a ruling in favor of the Arizona legislature? In his dissent, Chief Justice Roberts commented that "none of them purports to do what the Arizona Constitution does here: set up an unelected, unaccountable institution that permanently and totally displaces the legislature from the redistricting process." *Id.* at 848 (Roberts, C.J., dissenting). Moreover, even if the other initiatives were invalid, how great would the resulting disruption be? Wouldn't the law just revert to its pre-initiative form, leaving the legislature free to amend it if it deemed such amendment advisable?

Chief Justice Roberts's core contention was that "Legislature" had at the Framing, and continues to have, an "unambiguous meaning," namely "the representative body which makes the laws of the people." *Id.* at 827. In developing this argument, he relied heavily on an analysis of the Constitution's *other* references to "Legislature." "The Constitution includes seventeen provisions referring to a State's 'Legislature.' . . . [M]any of them are only consistent with an institutional legislature—and flatly incompatible with the majority's reading of 'the Legislature' to refer to the people as a whole." *Id.* at 2680. For an academic version of this intratextualist claim, see Michael T. Morley, *The Intratextual Independent "Legislature" and the Elections Clause*, 109 Northwestern University Law Review Online 847 (2015). Does "Legislature" need to have the same meaning every time the Constitution uses the term, or may its definition vary by context? Is there a difference between the legislature as *institution* and the legislature as *lawmaker*?

Chief Justice Roberts also criticized the majority for its "naked appeals to public policy," 576 U.S. at 825 (Roberts, C.J., dissenting), in particular its endorsement of independent commissions as a way "to curb the practice of gerrymandering," *id.* at 824. Is there anything wrong with deciding a constitutional case based in part on policy considerations? As to these considerations, Chief Justice Roberts suggested they were overblown; despite "the high motives that inspired the Arizona Commission," "partisanship . . . affected the Commission on issues ranging from staffing decisions to drawing the district lines." *Id.* at 848 (Roberts, C.J., dissenting). In making this claim, though, Chief Justice Roberts relied exclusively on a lower court decision that *upheld* the Commission's district maps. See *id.* at 821. There is also abundant academic evidence that, in America and abroad, commissions do a better job than legislatures at promoting democratic values such as partisan fairness, electoral competitiveness, and congruent representation. See Nicholas O. Stephanopoulos, *Arizona and Anti-Reform*, 2015 University of Chicago Legal Forum 477 (summarizing this literature and confirming its findings through a new empirical study).

Note that *Arizona State Legislature* was a 5-4 decision and that one of the Justices in the majority, Justice Kennedy, recently retired from the Supreme Court. What is the likelihood that the case will remain good law going forward? There will be no shortage of opportunities to challenge it soon, since we are rapidly approaching the next redistricting cycle, in which an array of commissions with responsibility for congressional plans will release new maps.

Interestingly, plaintiffs attacking Michigan's new independent redistricting commission (also adopted via voter initiative) did not argue that it violates the "Legislature thereof" language of the Elections Clause. Instead, they objected on First Amendment grounds to its eligibility criteria for commissioners, which excluded certain partisan officials and mandated a particular partisan composition (four Democrats, four Republicans, and five independents). The Sixth Circuit recently rejected this challenge. See *Daunt v. Benson*, 999 F.3d 299 (6th Cir. 2021). Why did these litigants not make a "Legislature thereof" argument? Could it be because this claim is relevant only to *congressional* redistricting while Michigan's commission is responsible for drawing congressional *and state legislative* maps?

Chapter 8

Major Political Parties

Political parties play a central role in the working of electoral systems in every national democracy (and, for that matter, in most dictatorships). Some countries, such as Italy and Israel, rely on a multi-party, coalition-building system. Mexico and Japan were examples of a system characterized by a single party that dominated the government with a fractured opposition for many years, until the ruling party fell from power. In the United States, at least since the 1830s, politics has centered around two major political parties.

For most of our history, the national parties in the United States were essentially federations of state organizations. Since the mid-20th Century, the national parties have grown in importance as independent organizations, though this development came about by different means in the two major parties. Growth of the Republican National Committee began after the Republican disaster in the 1964 presidential election, as the national party organization became increasingly important as a provider of administrative and fundraising support for Republican candidates and state organizations. In the Democratic Party, beginning in 1968, the national organization successfully began to assert power over state organizations on various matters, especially the procedures for selecting delegates to national nominating conventions. Later, the national Democratic organizations increased their fundraising and administrative support activities.[a]

At the national level, law has played comparatively little role in creating or shaping the parties, which have been thought of as autonomous, private organizations to be kept free from legal regulation. Yet the activities of political parties—nominating candidates for office, building and reflecting support for legislation—are central to the actual working of government. A tension reflected in a variety of legal issues thus arises between the private nature of party organizations and the essential political functions they perform. To what extent should the parties be subject to the same constitutional constraints as the government? To what extent should party activities be regulated in the public interest? To the extent regulation is necessary or desirable, should it be a matter of federal law or should it be left to the states? To what extent do parties have constitutional protection from regulation? More

---

a. See generally John F. Bibby, *Party Renewal in the National Republican Party*, in Party Renewal in America: Theory and Practice (Gerald M. Pomper, ed., 1980); James A. Reichley, *The Rise of National Parties*, in The New Direction in American Politics (J. Chubb & P. Peterson, eds., 1985).

generally, how does the party system, particularly in presidential elections, relate to the federal system? How active or restrained should the courts be in party affairs?

At the state level, parties went similarly unregulated through most of the nineteenth century. During the twentieth century there was a strong tendency toward regulation of the parties by state law. The centerpiece in this movement was the state-mandated direct primary election for choosing party candidates, but party activities have been regulated in many other significant respects as well. To some extent, regulation of parties is self-regulation, as party members in state legislatures codify by statute the governing arrangements the parties choose. Alternatively, regulation may put into effect the interests or opinions of some elements of a party over other elements. When the legislature governs the major parties, it is never entirely external to the entities it regulates, as it is when it regulates, say, businesses or labor unions. Sometimes the parties are regulated by initiatives, over which they have less control. Even then, however, the major parties are rarely helpless, and sometimes they use initiatives as a means of pursuing their objectives.[b]

Like federal non-regulation, state law regulation gives rise to many questions: Do the particular regulations serve the interests of the parties? Of the public? Would a different system of regulation be preferable? Would it be better to deregulate the parties and let them decide on their own structure? Do parties have a constitutional right to deregulation? If parties are to be deregulated, who should be able to set the rules for the parties? Party members (i.e., voters)? Party activists? Party officials? Partisan elected officials? Should the allocation of power within the party be determined by law?

This chapter considers these and other questions relating to the major political parties. Issues more important to minor parties and independent candidates are addressed in Chapter 9.

I. The Party and the Political System

The role parties do and should play in American politics has long been a subject of controversy among political scientists, party activists, government officials, lawyers and, at times, the general public. In reading the following materials, consider whether law has much to do with the controversy or should have much to do with it.

The Constitution does not mention political parties. The framers of the Constitution, of course, recognized the power of organized groups and public opinion and took steps to curb them through the indirect election of the Senate, the Electoral College, and the system of checks and balances described by Madison in *Federalist*

b. See Richard L. Hasen, *Parties Take the Initiative (and Vice Versa)*, 100 Columbia Law Review 731 (2000).

Nos. 10 and 51. None of these measures, however, seems directed expressly against political parties as opposed to other types of associations formed for political purposes. The majority of the framers, if asked, probably would have included political parties in the "factions" the constitutional system should guard against. See Richard Hofstadter, The Idea of a Party System 40–73 (1969).

Despite their relegation to a constitutional no-man's land, political parties arose quickly in America for reasons described by Justice Reed in *Ray v. Blair*, 343 U.S. 214, 220–21 (1952):

> As is well known, political parties in the modern sense were not born with the Republic. They were created by necessity, by the need to organize the rapidly increasing population, scattered over our Land, so as to coordinate efforts to secure needed legislation and oppose that deemed undesirable.

Political parties are, to some extent, an anomaly engrafted onto a constitutional system that did not plan for them.[c]

The boundaries of a political party are less clear than might appear at first glance. Political scientist V.O. Key famously characterized parties as having three distinct aspects: the party-in-government, the party leadership, and the party-in-the-electorate.[d] A central and enduring controversy is how ideologically-oriented or "disciplined" the parties *should* be. One's position on the proper scope of legal regulation of political parties may well turn on one's view of the propriety or impropriety of "party discipline" and of means to achieve party ideological unity and coherence.

The most disciplined political party is one whose leaders pick the candidates for office on the basis of fealty to the party's positions and have the capacity to discipline non-adherents. It is probably also the party whose members—the voters—have the least to say about who the candidates should be. A disciplined party is thus arguably less democratic in organization and structure and more "boss" dominated than a looser ideological coalition. It is also the party whose structure arguably can produce the clearest ideological choice for voters at the general election.[e] A leading school of thought among students of political parties holds that parties serve the public best when they are firmly controlled by leaders, not voters. Joseph Schlesinger, a proponent of this view, remarked that definitions of parties "must exclude the voters. Voters are choosers among parties, not components of them."[f]

---

c. For an important analysis by a social scientist of the process by which parties arose and evolved, see John H. Aldrich, Why Parties? The Origin and Transformation of Party Politics in America (1995). For a lively historical summary of the rise of the American parties and their fortunes down through the 1950s, see James MacGregor Burns, The Deadlock of Democracy 8–203 (1963).

d. V.O. Key, Politics, Parties, and Pressure Groups 163-65 (4th ed. 1958).

e. For a careful analysis of leading American theories of party government, see Austin Ranney, The Doctrine of Responsible Party Government (1954). For a useful account that is more concise and more up-to-date, see Leon Epstein, Political Parties in the American Mold 9–39 (1986).

f. Joseph Schlesinger, *On the Theory of Party Organizations*, 46 Journal of Politics 369, 377 (1984). See also Gerald M. Pomper, *The Alleged Decline of American Parties*, in Politicians and Party

Relatively weak party discipline was long a defining characteristic of the American system. A prominent political scientist writing in 1901 found very little incidence of strong party-line voting in Congress or in state legislatures, and he gave this explanation:

> If in England a member of the majority in the House of Commons refuses to support an important measure upon which the cabinet insists, and if enough of his colleagues share his opinion to turn the scale, the consequence must be a change of ministry or a dissolution; but under similar circumstances in America no such dire results will follow. The measure will simply be lost, but the member can retain his seat undisturbed till the end of his term, and the administration will go on as before. Hence the difficulty in carrying out party platforms, and the discredit into which they have fallen in consequence.[g]

Nevertheless, the history of American political parties has been to give voters more, not less direct control over party candidates and positions. No doubt this trend is strongly related to the ascendancy of progressivist ideas in American politics. To quote Justice Reed again:

> The party conventions of locally chosen delegates, from the county to the national level, succeeded the caucuses of self-appointed legislators or other interested individuals. Dissatisfaction with the manipulation of conventions caused that system to be largely superseded by the direct primary.

Ray v. Blair, 343 U.S. at 221. Direct primaries, which have become by far the most common method of selecting party nominees, allow candidates to appeal over the heads of party leaders directly to the voters. Their ascendance played an important role in weakening the control over party leaders.

American major parties usually have been ideologically loose confederations of people of varying political persuasions, seeking to moderate their position on issues so as to attract the maximum number of voters. In 1950, the Committee on Political Parties of the American Political Science Association submitted a seminal report called *Toward a More Responsible Two Party System*,[h] criticizing the lack of ideological coherence within the major parties. The thesis of the report was:

> Historical and other factors have caused the American two-party system to operate as two loose associations of state and local organizations, with very

---

Politics 14, 18 (John G. Geer, ed., 1998). An important forerunner of these views was Part IV of the celebrated book by Joseph Schumpeter, Capitalism, Socialism and Democracy (1942). Schumpeter rejected as unrealistic the "classical doctrine" of democracy, in which the public set policies that were then carried out by elected officials. Rather, he saw elections as opportunities for parties and leaders to compete with each other for public support.

g. A. Lawrence Lowell, *The Influence of Party upon Legislation in England and America*, 1 Annual Report of the American Historical Association for the Year 1901, at 321, 346.

h. The report was reprinted as a supplement to 44 American Political Science Review No. 3, Part 2 (1950).

> little national machinery and very little national cohesion. As a result, either major party, when in power, is ill-equipped to organize its members in the legislative and the executive branches into a government held together and guided by the party program. Party responsibility at the polls thus tends to vanish. This is a very serious matter, for it affects the very heartbeat of American democracy. It also poses grave problems of domestic and foreign policy in an era when it is no longer safe for the nation to deal piecemeal with issues that can be disposed of only on the basis of coherent programs.

The Committee argued that "an effective party system requires, first, that the parties are able to bring forth programs to which they commit themselves and, second, that the parties possess sufficient internal cohesion to carry out these programs."[i] The Committee made a number of recommendations to bring about centralized, ideologically coherent parties. One typical recommendation would have given the national party the right to exclude ideologically disloyal state organizations from party deliberations (such as refusing to seat them at the national convention).

Morris Fiorina sums up the developments that had contributed to the weakening of party leadership over the decades:

> Several long-term trends have served to undercut old-style party organizations. The patronage system has been steadily chopped back since passage of the Civil Service Act of 1883. The social welfare functions of the parties have passed to the government as the modern welfare state developed. And, less concretely, the entire ethos of the old-style party organization is increasingly at odds with modern ideas of government based on rational expertise. These longterm trends spawned specific attacks on the old party organizations. In the late nineteenth and early twentieth centuries the Populists, Progressives, and assorted other reformers fought electoral corruption with the Australian Ballot and personal registration systems. They attempted to break the hold of the party bosses over nominations by mandating the direct primary. They attacked the urban machines with drives for nonpartisan at-large elections and nonpartisan city managers. None of these reforms destroyed the parties; they managed to live with the reforms better than most reformers had hoped. But the reforms reflected changing popular attitudes toward the parties and accelerated the secular decline in the influence of the party organizations. . . .
>
> In the 1970s two series of reforms further weakened the influence of organized parties in American national politics. The first was a series of legal changes deliberately intended to lessen organized party influence in the presidential nominating process. In the Democratic party, "New Politics" activists captured the national party apparatus and imposed a series of rules changes designed to "open up" the politics of presidential nominations.

---

i. *Id.* at 17–18.

> The Republican party—long more amateur and open than the Democratic party—adopted weaker versions of the Democratic rule changes. In addition, modifications of state electoral laws to conform to the Democratic rule changes (enforced by the federal courts) stimulated Republican rules changes as well. [T]he presidential nominating process has indeed been opened up. In little more than a decade after the disastrous 1968 Democratic conclave, the number of primary states has more than doubled, and the number of delegates chosen in primaries has increased from little more than a third to three-quarters. Moreover, the remaining delegates emerge from caucuses far more open to mass citizen participation, and the delegates themselves are more likely to be amateurs, than previously....
>
> A second series of 1970s reforms lessened the role of formal party organizations in the conduct of political campaigns. These are financing regulations growing out of the Federal Election Campaign Act of 1971 as amended in 1974 and 1976. In this case the reforms were aimed at cleaning up corruption in the financing of campaigns; their effects on the parties were a by-product, though many individuals accurately predicted its nature....
>
> The ultimate results of such reforms are easy to predict. A lesser party role in the nominating and financing of candidates encourages candidates to organize and conduct independent campaigns, which further weakens the role of parties.[j]

Although party leaders still have limited control over their members, partisan polarization has increased dramatically in succeeding decades, as the ideological coherence of the parties and their members has increased. Democratic and Republican legislators have increasingly diverged ideologically on a wide range of issues, and voters have also sorted themselves into the two major parties in accordance with their ideology. There is a large body of research on polarization of the parties.[k] Although ideological polarization has increased, the parties themselves are as diffused as ever. As Joey Fishkin and Heather Gerken put it: "a party today is best understood as a loose coalition of diverse entities, some official and some not,

---

j. Morris P. Fiorina, *The Decline of Collective Responsibility in American Politics*, 109 Daedalus 25 (1980).

k. For examples, see Solutions to Political Polarization in America 15 (Nathaniel Persily, ed., 2015); Alan I. Abramowitz, The Disappearing Center: Engaged Citizens, Polarization, and American Democracy (2010); Sean M. Theriault, Party Polarization in Congress (2008); Nolan McCarty, Keith T. Poole & Howard Rosenthal, Polarized America: The Dance of Ideology and Unequal Riches (2006); Richard H. Pildes, *Why the Center Does Not Hold: The Causes of Hyperpolarized Democracy in America*, 99 California Law Review 273, 276–81 (2011); Boris Shor & Nolan McCarty, *The Ideological Mapping of American Legislatures*, 105 American Political Science Review 530 (2011); Gary C. Jacobson, *Party Polarization in National Politics: The Electoral Connection*, in Polarized Politics: Congress and the President in a Partisan Era (Jon R. Bond & Richard Fleisher, eds., 2000).

organized around a popular national brand."[l] There is strong evidence that partisan polarization has compromised the functioning of our system of government, especially the legislative branch.[m]

At first glance, it might seem strange that intensified partisan polarization would accompany the weakening of party leadership, but an emerging body of literature suggests that these two developments are linked. A group of scholars, sometimes referred to as "political realists," argue that weaker party organizations have led to political dysfunction. The theory is that party leaders have a strong incentive to make deals that require moderation of strong ideological positions. Rick Pildes argues that an overly romantic view of democratic politics, one that disregards the important role that party leaders play in reining in dissenting factions, has contributed to a debilitating political fragmentation that makes it difficult to govern.[n] As Jonathan Rauch puts it, "government cannot govern unless political machines are something like them exist and work, because machines are uniquely willing and able to negotiate compromises and make them stick."[o] Bruce Cain similarly argues that populist reforms aimed at increasing public participation have often been counterproductive, increasing the influence of those with the most intense preferences while weakening party leaders with the strongest interest in tacking toward the center.[p] On the other hand, Tom Mann and E.J. Dionne argue that the so-called "political realists" actually have an overly nostalgic view of what democracy was like in the days before political reform, when deals were made in smoke-filled rooms and many people were excluded from politics.[q]

Given the increased polarization of the parties and the electorate, divided government may make governance more difficult than ever in the present era. An example are the persistent stalemates over raising the debt limit, with many Republicans unwilling to do so, at least when a Democrat is President. Is divided government a bigger problem in the present era of hyperpolarization?

One area in which party discipline is relatively strong is the Electoral College. Occasionally electors will vote for someone other than the candidate they were

---

l. Joseph Fishkin & Heather K. Gerken, *The Party's Over:* McCutcheon, *Shadow Parties, and the Future of the Party System*, 2014 Supreme Court Review 175, 187 (2014). For more on the relationship between polarization and the weakening of political parties, see Seth E. Masket, No Middle Ground: How Informal Party Organizations Control Nominations and Polarize Legislatures (2011).

m. See, e.g., Nolan McCarty, *Polarization, Dysfunction, and Constitutional Change*, 50 Indiana Law Journal 223 (2016).

n. Richard Pildes, *Romanticizing Democracy, Political Fragmentation, and the Decline of American Government*, 124 Yale Law Journal 804 (2014).

o. Jonathan Rauch, *Political Realism: How Hacks, Machines, Big Money, and Back-Room Deals Can Strengthen American Democracy* 2 (May 2015), at https://perma.cc/9LJL-HG5Y.

p. Bruce E. Cain, Democracy More or Less: America's Political Reform Quandary (2014).

q. Thomas E. Mann & E.J. Dionne, Jr., *The Futility of Nostalgia and the Romanticism of the New Political Realists: Why Praising the 19th-Century Political Machine Won't Solve the 21st Century's Problems* (2015), https://perma.cc/U4RC-RTGE.

elected to support, but such incidents have been rare.[r] One example was the 2016 election, there were two defections among the 306 electors pledged to vote for Republican candidate Donald Trump, and five defections among the 227 electors pledged to Democratic candidate Hillary Clinton.[s] More broadly, the success of anti-establishment candidates may reveal the weakness of today's major parties. Trump won the Republican nomination and ultimately the Presidency, and Senator Bernie Sanders did surprisingly well on the Democratic side, despite the fact that party insiders vigorously opposed both candidates. Some argue that their success is testament to the major party leaders' loss of control over basic organizational functions, including the presidential nomination process.[t]

Suppose you wanted to strengthen the Republican and Democratic parties. What steps would you take to do it? Consider the pros and cons of the following proposals and, to the extent you believe they are desirable, consider whether they should be adopted by state or national party organizations or by state or national law:

A. Allocating a fixed number of seats for elected officials and other party leaders as delegates to the national convention.

B. Requiring all candidates in a party's primary for national, state, and local office to sign a pledge under oath that if elected they will faithfully adhere to and attempt to enact the party's platform as adopted at its convention. (If you agree with this proposal, would there be some system of discipline and punishment if the promise were broken?)

C. Requiring all candidates in a party's primary for national, state, and local office to sign a pledge that they will support the candidate of the party chosen in the primary even if they are defeated.

D. Providing public funding for any or all of a party's internal operations.

E. Requiring a candidate for statewide office who is not the designee of a party convention to obtain the signatures of 5 or 10 percent of registered party members in order to qualify for the ballot in the upcoming primary.

F. Requiring voters who want to switch parties to wait out one primary election before they could reregister. See *Kusper v. Pontikes*, 414 U.S. 51 (1973). Cf. *Rosario v. Rockefeller*, 410 U.S. 752 (1973).

Some of the foregoing proposals might raise substantial constitutional and legal questions, especially if they were implemented by state or federal statute. The materials that follow should help you identify some of these questions.

---

r. See Jack W. Peltason, *Constitutional Law for Political Parties*, in On Parties: Essays Honoring Austin Ranney 9, 11–13 (Nelson W. Polsby & Raymond F. Wolfinger, eds., 1999).

s. Kiersten Schmidt & Wilson Andrews, *A Historic Number of Electors Defected, and Most Were Supposed to Vote for Clinton*, New York Times, Dec. 19, 2016.

t. Samuel Issacharoff, *Outsourcing Politics: The Hostile Takeovers of Our Hollowed Out Political Parties*, 54 Houston Law Review 845 (2017).

II. Obligations of Parties under the Constitution

For a long time, courts treated political parties as private associations, subject only to the comparatively minimal legal restraints imposed on purely private groups. See *Developments in the Law—Judicial Control of Actions of Private Associations*, 76 Harvard Law Review 983, 1020–37 (1963). The courts' reluctance to intervene in the internal operations of political parties was influenced by the view that their functions of compromise, negotiation, and conciliation between competing political factions would be hampered by deciding disputes through litigation. See Comment, *Judicial Intervention in Political Party Disputes: The Political Thicket Reconsidered*, 22 UCLA Law Review 622, 625 (1975).

The scope of state regulation of political party operations increased dramatically, however, beginning in 1903 when Wisconsin mandated that parties choose candidates through the direct primary and established procedures for conducting the primary. The primary quickly became a critical locus of party activity and a battlefront in the courts. Once state government began to direct the way political parties were to operate, legal questions inevitably arose as to the extent parties thus became subject to a higher standard of constitutional constraint than a purely private association. In recent decades, the Supreme Court has understood the Constitution to impose significant limits on state regulation of political parties.[u]

In the remainder of this part, we shall consider the extent to which the courts have imposed or should impose constraints on the parties in the name of protecting constitutional rights. In Part III, we shall consider the extent to which parties are immune under the First Amendment from regulation by state legislatures. In Part IV of this chapter we shall consider the constitutional limits on patronage, a practice that for much of this country's history was an important means for the parties to maintain power and influence.

A. The Federal Interest in Regulating Party Primaries

Before the constitutional constraints on parties could be explored, the initial question whether the federal constitution had any impact on the party primary had to be answered. As previously mentioned, the Constitution makes no mention of parties or primaries. Article I, § 4 of the Constitution gives state legislatures the power to prescribe the "Times, Places and Manner of holding Elections for Senators

u. For an overview of the history of legal regulation of political parties, see John W. Epperson, The Changing Legal Status of Political Parties in the United States (1986). For a more detailed account of a crucial period including the initial adoption of direct primaries, see Adam Winkler, *Voters' Rights and Parties' Wrongs: Early Political Party Regulation in the State Courts, 1886–1915*, 100 Columbia Law Review 873 (2000).

and Representatives," subject to Congress's power to "make or alter such Regulations." The Fifteenth and Nineteenth Amendments prohibit discrimination on grounds of race or sex in extension of the right to vote. Was a state party primary an "election" under Article I, § 4 subject to federal regulation? Were the antidiscrimination guarantees of the Fifteenth and Nineteenth Amendments applicable to the right to vote in primaries of political parties, which many viewed as purely private associations?

By a 5–4 decision in *Newberry v. United States*, 256 U.S. 232 (1921), the Supreme Court temporarily delayed the application of federal statutory and constitutional constraints to state party primaries. The defendants in *Newberry*—a candidate for Michigan's Republican nomination for Senate and his supporters—were charged with violating federal statutes that limited campaign expenditures. Newberry's lawyer, former Justice and future Chief Justice Charles Evans Hughes, argued that Congress' power under Article I, § 4 extended only to general elections, not primaries, and thus the statute did not apply to his clients. The Court held that the statute was inapplicable, but only four justices agreed with Hughes' position. They concluded that primaries "are in no sense elections for office, but merely methods by which party adherents agree upon candidates." 256 U.S. at 740. The virtual necessity of party nomination for election did not impress these four justices. "Birth must precede, but it is no part of either funeral or apotheosis," reasoned the plurality. *Id.* at 757. The fifth vote was supplied by Justice McKenna, who reasoned that Congress might have the power to regulate senatorial primaries in the future because of the passage of the Seventeenth Amendment, which provided for the direct election of senators. Four justices dissented.

B. The White Primary Cases and the State Action Doctrine

The *Newberry* holding could not long withstand the increasing use of the primary as the main method of selecting candidates, or the necessity of a federal role in protecting the voting rights of African Americans, particularly in the then one-party southern states where victory in the Democratic primary was tantamount to election. The Texas Democratic primary became the main constitutional battleground over a quarter of a century as the state party tried a variety of increasingly sophisticated devices to exclude African-American participation and as African Americans responded with court challenges.

In *Nixon v. Herndon*, 273 U.S. 536 (1927), the Court unanimously held that Texas's state law expressly disqualifying African Americans from voting in the Democratic primary denied African-American voters equal protection under the *Fourteenth* Amendment. The Court did not discuss whether the *Fifteenth* Amendment right to vote extended to a primary election. Texas then repealed the statute, but gave the party's executive committee the right to determine who was qualified to vote in the primary. The executive committee promptly obliged by passing a resolution prohibiting African Americans from participating.

In *Nixon v. Condon*, 286 U.S. 73 (1932), the Court invalidated the executive committee's resolution on the ground that the state had, by statute, given the executive committee a power it never had previously held. The executive committee thereby acted as an agent of the state and the result was the same as in *Nixon v. Herndon*. Again, the Fourteenth Amendment's Equal Protection Clause was the ground for decision.

Undaunted, the Texas Democratic Party in convention then adopted a resolution restricting party membership to whites. No legislation authorized this resolution. The issue of the constitutional power of the party to do something the state could not do itself was squarely presented. In *Grovey v. Townsend*, 295 U.S. 45 (1935), the Court temporarily stepped back from the principle that racial discrimination in party affairs was unconstitutional. It held unanimously that the Texas party's resolution did not violate federally guaranteed constitutional rights. The philosophy of *Newberry*, that the party was a private association and its primary not a subject of federal constitutional interest, was temporarily reaffirmed.

The landmark decision in *United States v. Classic*, 313 U.S. 299 (1941), though not involving issues of racial discrimination, resumed the course of placing party primaries under the restraint of federal constitutional law. The indictment in *Classic* charged several Louisiana election officials with dishonest practices in a primary election for Congress. The district court dismissed the indictment on the ground that no federal statutory right was violated by a dishonest count in a state-administered congressional primary. The Supreme Court reversed, and overruled *Newberry* explicitly. The Court held Congress had the power to regulate primary elections under Article I, § 4. The new thinking of the Court on Congress's expansive powers in the elections area was analogous to its new thinking regarding the power of the federal government in economic regulation, inspired by Franklin Roosevelt's abortive Court packing plan and his recent appointees.

Grovey v. Townsend also succumbed to this new trend, in *Smith v. Allwright*, 321 U.S. 649 (1944), decided three years after *Classic*. In *Allwright* the Court emphasized the *Fifteenth* Amendment as the source of the voter's right to be free from racial discrimination in casting a ballot in a party primary. The Court stated that *Classic* "fused the primary and general elections into a single instrumentality." Texas's detailed regulation and involvement in the primary process turned that process into a state function, even though it was conducted by the ostensibly private Democratic Party.

The Court's new activism in protecting African-American voting rights in party primaries took its final step in *Terry v. Adams*, 345 U.S. 461 (1953). The Jaybird Democratic Association of Fort Bend County, Texas, a group founded in 1889, held a straw vote every year several months before the official Democratic primary. The Jaybird vote was open to any white voter. The Jaybird election victor had no special official status under state law and had to compete on an equal basis with every other candidate in the primary.[v] In practice, however, the Jaybird victor always won the primary and general elections. In a result reached by a majority that was split between three separate opinions, the Court held that the Jaybird action excluding African Americans from the straw vote violated the Fifteenth Amendment.

Justice Black, writing for three justices, noted that the Fifteenth Amendment clearly includes "any election in which public issues are decided or public officials selected," but just as clearly excludes social or business clubs. He also noted that the qualifications for voting in the Jaybird straw vote were identical to those for voting in the Democratic primary, with the one additional proviso of race. He concluded:

> For a state to permit such a duplication of its election processes is to permit a flagrant abuse of those processes to defeat the purposes of the Fifteenth Amendment. The use of the county-operated primary to ratify the result of the prohibited election merely compounds the offense. It violates the Fifteenth Amendment for a state, by such circumvention, to permit within its borders the use of any device that produces an equivalent of the prohibited election.

Justice Frankfurter said he found the case "by no means free of difficulty. Whenever the law draws a line between permissive and forbidden conduct cases are bound to arise which are not obviously on one side or the other." Crucial to his decision was his view that "[a]s the action of the entire white voting community, the Jaybird primary is as a practical matter the instrument of those few in this small county who are politically active—the officials of the local Democratic party and, we may assume, the elected officials of the county." In particular, those officials "participate by voting in the Jaybird primary," and they "join the white voting community in proceeding with elaborate formality, in almost all respects parallel to the procedures dictated by Texas law for the primary itself, to express their preferences in a wholly successful effort to withdraw significance from the State-prescribed primary, to subvert the operation of what is formally the law of the State for primaries in this county." He then concluded that the state had "entered into a comprehensive scheme of regulation of political primaries, including procedures by which election officials shall be chosen.... If the Jaybird Association, although not a political party, is a device to defeat the law of Texas regulating primaries, and if the electoral officials, clothed with State power in the county, share in that subversion, they cannot divest themselves of the State authority and help as participants in the scheme."

Justice Clark, writing for four justices, found that the Jaybird Association was a political party for purposes of the Fifteenth Amendment, and therefore covered by *Smith v. Allwright*:

v. The Jaybird Association had a rule barring candidates who had already served more than two consecutive terms, though no such term limit appeared in state law.

> Not every private club, association or league organized to influence public candidacies or political action must conform to the Constitution's restrictions on political parties. Certainly a large area of freedom permits peaceable assembly and concerted private action for political purposes to be exercised separately by white and colored citizens alike. More, however, is involved here....
>
> Quite evidently the Jaybird Democratic Association operates as an auxiliary of the local Democratic Party organization, selecting its nominees and using its machinery for carrying out an admitted design of destroying the weight and effect of Negro ballots in Fort Bend County. To be sure, the Democratic primary and the general election are nominally open to the colored elector. But his must be an empty vote cast after the real decisions are made. And because the Jaybird-indorsed nominee meets no opposition in the Democratic primary, the Negro minority's vote is nullified at the sole stage of the local political process where the bargaining and interplay of rival political forces could make it count.

Justice Minton dissented.

Terry held that Texas "violated the Fifteenth Amendment by permitting within its borders a private device that would have been forbidden in a public election," according to Ronald D. Rotunda, *Constitutional and Statutory Restrictions on Political Parties in the Wake of* Cousins v. Wigoda, 53 Texas Law Review 935, 954 (1975). Rotunda adds that the "logic of the *White Primary Cases* supports the conclusion that an election for public office is a public function and that any integral part of that function must be constitutional." *Id.* at 955.

Suppose a hypothetical Jaybird Association never conducts straw votes, but consists of a handful of local leaders who publicize their recommendations to the voters before each primary election. If this small group's recommended candidates always or nearly always win in the primaries, and if the group's members are all whites, would their activities violate the Fifteenth Amendment? If the group includes members of all races and all ethnic groups but are all males, would their activities violate the Nineteenth Amendment? What if the members are all white males, but the candidates they endorse come from all racial and ethnic groups and both sexes? What if their recommendations appear to be influential but fall way short of being decisive? What if they do not publicize their recommendations at all, but contribute substantial campaign funds to the candidates they support?

Do the *White Primary Cases* impair parties' associational rights, by subjecting parties and even non-party groups like the Jaybird Association as subject to constitutional constraints? Consider the following perspective:

Daniel Hays Lowenstein, *Associational Rights of Major Political Parties: A Skeptical Inquiry*

71 Texas Law Review 1741, 1747–54 (1993)

Nearly everyone who has written about the constitutional rights or obligations of parties seems to have assumed that whether parties or their activities are to be classified as "private" or "public" is a crucial issue. . . .

To the uninitiated, this must seem odd. Parties are not government agencies. In ordinary conversation, to suggest that they are would be bizarre. However, the Supreme Court's continued adherence to the state action doctrine has forced the Justices to depart from ordinary conceptions of what entities are "public." Under the doctrine, unless an entity's actions affecting others are regarded as "public," the entity need not conform to the requirements of due process of law, equal protection, freedom of speech, or other provisions of the Bill of Rights. Accordingly, when the Supreme Court was confronted in the *White Primary Cases* with the question of whether the Texas Democratic Party could exclude African-Americans from voting in its primaries, the only way it could find to prohibit such an exclusion was to declare that parties, at least when they nominate candidates in primary elections, are acting as public agencies.

The difficulty created by the *White Primary Cases* for proponents of freedom of association for political parties is that the public/private distinction is generally perceived as governing not only whether an entity must conform to constitutional requirements in its treatment of others, but also whether the entity itself enjoys constitutional rights against the government. Thus, by declaring parties to be "public," the *White Primary Cases* not only prohibited them from depriving racial minorities of their right to vote but also seemed to deprive the parties of the protections of the Bill of Rights. If instead parties were declared to be "private," they would enjoy constitutional rights, but the foundation for the *White Primary Cases* would be undercut.

One response to this dilemma would be to disavow the *White Primary Cases* and treat parties as purely private in nature. The proposal is not monstrous, because the *White Primary Cases* had only modest success in extending the franchise to African-Americans in the southern states and, more importantly, because federal voting rights legislation and greatly changed mores make it extremely unlikely that the parties would seek to exclude primary voters on grounds of race in the foreseeable future. Renunciation now of the *White Primary Cases* would have no tangible cost in racial discrimination, would bring constitutional doctrine into accord with the common sense notion that parties are not government agencies, and would clear the way for a full extension of constitutional freedoms to parties. However, the *White Primary Cases*, despite their limited effectiveness, are rightly remembered as one of the bright spots in the history of the Supreme Court and the struggle for racial equality. For the Supreme Court now to declare that the cases were wrong would be unpleasant, even disillusioning. Most of us would never believe the Court anyway. Furthermore, it is always possible that at some time in the future the parties will act in a manner perceived to deny fundamental rights to some group of Americans. The possibility of constitutional relief, won so painstakingly from the 1920s to the 1950s, should not be tossed away lightly. In any event, few commentators and no courts have suggested the disavowal of the *White Primary Cases.*

At the opposite extreme is the position that the parties are public, pure and simple. [But this position is not viable after the cases considered in Part III of the present chapter. Therefore,] as the Justices like to say, it is "too late in the day" for the argument to succeed. Nor should it. The idea of parties as "public" is in tension not only with the everyday recognition that parties are not government agencies, but also with the need to assure that the party system maintains a basic autonomy from the state so that the parties may serve as vehicles for expressing the public's needs and sentiments. Such autonomy distinguishes democracies from authoritarian systems, and our constitutional law may as well recognize this fact. It is one thing to argue about the nature of the protection accorded to parties by the First Amendment, but to argue that the parties are entitled to *no* such protection has an incongruous ring to it.

A third approach is the middle ground that parties are a mixture of public and private elements or that some of their activities are public and others private. Leon Epstein captures this idea by analogizing parties to public utilities.[45] Of course, the key question for any middle-ground approach is: When is the party private, and when is it public? The most common answer has been that it is the election process that is a governmental activity; therefore, when parties nominate candidates or engage in other activities directly connected with the conduct of elections, their activities are public. Other activities, such as internal governance and the adoption of platforms, are private.

... A middle ground allows for both possibilities by dividing party activities into two categories. But within the "public" category it must still be the case that the parties bear no constitutional rights, and within the "private" category the party will be free to deny equal protection, freedom of speech, and other constitutional protections to others.

The final approach is to ignore the problem. Thus, the *White Primary Cases* are limited to their "unusual context: a state-mandated racially discriminatory primary scheme in a one-party state where nomination is tantamount to election."[48] If we take the public/private distinction seriously, this will not do. To suggest that political parties act as agents of the government when and only when they violate the fundamental rights of citizens is to do violence to the English language, if the terms "public" and "private" are taken to have any descriptive meaning whatever.

---

45. Leon D. Epstein, Political Parties in the American Mold 155–59 (1986).

48. San Francisco County Democratic Cent. Comm. v. Eu, 826 F.2d 814, 826 n.21 (9th Cir. 1987), *aff'd*, 489 U.S. 214 (1989).

But should we take the public/private distinction seriously? If we set the distinction aside momentarily, we are free simply to conclude . . . that parties bear constitutional rights *and* that they act unconstitutionally when they deprive any group of citizens of the opportunity for political participation. Surely this is the result most of us want. We can obtain this result by recognizing that the question of whether a party action is public or private is not a tool of analysis used in deciding a constitutional controversy, but is instead the attachment, after the fact, of a more or less superfluous label to a result reached for other reasons. For example, the reason parties are prohibited from excluding African-Americans from primaries is not that they act in a public capacity when they exclude. Rather, the action of excluding African-Americans is labeled a state action because we have chosen to interpret the Constitution as prohibiting it. . . .

Thus the terms "public" and "private" (like many similar terms in the law) actually function as *post hoc* labels, rather than as the *a priori* analytical devices that conventional doctrine supposes them to be. They do so because the world is too diverse for all its phenomena to fit comfortably within a small set of categories that can suffice for an acceptable normative ordering. A dichotomy such as the public/private distinction is devised because it is found to be a useful way of ordering some range of activities, but it is an artificial categorization. . . . As such, it is susceptible to manipulation, and it is virtually certain to be manipulated for at least two reasons. First, different people (such as different Justices) who apply the categories will be guided by different values and life experiences. Second, although the categories may be straightforward and acceptable within a range of problems, outside of that range their application will be obscure or even perverse.

So it is with the public/private distinction as applied to political parties. We have seen that the distinction leads to perverse results, for it permits parties either to be subject to constitutional rights or to bear them, but not both (at least with respect to any given party activity). However, the greatest harm caused by fixation on the public/private distinction is not that it requires an embarrassing and illogical confinement of the *White Primary Cases* "to their facts," but that it tends to preclude consideration of the actual relationship between the government and major political parties. That relationship does not justify denying First Amendment Rights to parties, but it significantly affects the way in which those rights should be applied.

As this excerpt reflects, considerable attention has been given to the tension that may exist between the constitutional *rights* of parties and the constitutional *obligations* of parties. Similar tension may exist between parties' *constitutional* rights and their *statutory* obligations. Consider, for example, the requirement of Section 5 of the Voting Rights Act that a covered "State or political subdivision" was required to seek preclearance before implementing changed voting procedures. If eligibility for voting in primaries in a covered jurisdiction is set by parties and a party wishes to change the requirements, must it seek preclearance? By the logic of *Smith v. Allwright*, if the primary and general elections are "fused," then preclearance must be required to prevent the state from evading Section 5 by handing control of the primaries to the parties. See, *e.g.*, *MacGuire v. Amos*, 343 F. Supp. 119 (M.D. Ala. 1972). However, suppose candidates are nominated at party conventions rather than at primaries. Was a change in the method of selecting delegates to the convention subject to preclearance under the Voting Rights Act?

This question was answered affirmatively in a 5–4 decision in *Morse v. Republican Party*, 517 U.S. 186 (1996). Virginia law assured the candidates of the two major parties a position on the ballot and left it to the parties to determine how to nominate their candidates. The Republicans had used various nomination methods, but for 1994 they adopted a "convention" method under which any Republican could be a delegate and have a vote upon payment of a fee up to $45. There was no opinion for the Court, but a majority of justices concluded that the party's adoption of the fee was subject to preclearance. In a lengthy opinion, Justice Stevens, joined by Justice Ginsburg, cited Congress's intent when it passed the Voting Rights Act to assure effective enforcement of the Fifteenth Amendment as a factor. The *White Primary Cases*, and the persistent efforts in southern states to set up nomination processes that blocked African Americans from voting, were well known to the Congress that passed the Voting Rights Act. Justice Breyer, joined by Justices O'Connor and Souter, also relied heavily on this point. But he recognized the burden on parties' associational rights that could result from overly broad application of the preclearance requirement to parties. He noted that: "First Amendment questions about the extent to which the Federal Government, through preclearance procedures, can regulate the workings of a political party convention, are difficult ones, as are those about the limits imposed by the state action cases." Is this an area in which it's simply impossible to draw clear lines? What principles should guide the determination about whether party activities are subject to regulation or, alternatively, immune from regulation? The cases and materials in Part III grapple with that problem.

III. Associational Rights of Parties

A. Presidential Nominations

For most of our history party organization was centered at the state and local levels. National parties were confederations of these state organizations, and for the most part were inactive except during the quadrennial periods of presidential nomination and campaigning. Since the 1830s, presidential candidates have been nominated at national party conventions, which, until the 1970s, were dominated by the state organizations.

Each state could decide for itself by what means its delegation to the convention would be selected. When disputes arose over who could properly represent a state party at the National Convention, these disputes were referred to the Credentials Committee, whose decisions were subject to appeal to the Convention as a whole.

Often these disputes were treated more as ploys in the competition for the nomination than as matters to be resolved on the basis of principle or legal propriety.

Since there were few restrictions on the manner in which states could select delegates, state legislatures could regulate the process without much danger of coming into conflict with national party rules or requirements. Dating from the Progressive period in the early twentieth century, some states used presidential primaries, but these states were not close to a majority at the conventions. Although the presidential primaries provided a test of the popularity of competing candidates, they were not the predominant factor in the parties' nomination decisions. The great majority of delegates at the conventions were more or less selected and controlled by the state party leaders and organizations, and it was the *state* leaders who ultimately had the greatest say in who would be the presidential candidates.

Because of the controversies attending their troubled 1968 convention in Chicago, the Democrats created a commission to propose reformed delegate selection procedures. The commission was originally chaired by Senator George McGovern, who later became a candidate for President and was succeeded by Representative Donald Fraser. The reforms proposed by the McGovern-Fraser commission and later adopted almost intact by the Democratic National Committee had three major thrusts.

First, whether the state used a primary or a caucus system,[w] the procedure had to be open to all registered Democrats and held at a time and in a manner that would permit each participant to vote for a specific presidential candidate. Previously, in many states, delegates or those empowered to name the delegates were selected long before the presidential campaign began, or otherwise in a manner calculated to discourage participation by anyone but supporters of the dominant party organization.

Second, the tallying of voter preferences had to be roughly though not necessarily precisely proportional. In other words, "winner-take-all" primaries or caucus procedures would be prohibited. However, in a compromise, states were permitted to retain winner-take-all primaries through the 1972 election. As we shall see shortly, this compromise helped trigger the first round of litigation under the new rules.

Third, the demographic makeup of the delegation, especially with respect to race and sex, but also with respect to characteristics such as age and income, must not depart excessively from the population of the states. By 1980 the Democratic

---

w. "Caucuses," in this context, are meetings held simultaneously across the state in each neighborhood. Participants in each caucus select representatives, usually chosen according to the presidential candidates they support, to a higher level caucus or convention. A pyramidal process eventuates in a statewide convention of representatives whose selection is ultimately traceable to the preferences expressed at the original caucuses. The statewide convention selects the actual presidential nominating delegation.

Convention required that each delegation include equal numbers of men and women.[x]

One important consequence of the adoption of the reforms was that there was a dramatic increase in the number of states that selected their delegates by holding a presidential primary. This was not required by the new rules, and it probably was not even desired by many of the reformers, who consisted primarily of liberal activists who undoubtedly expected to be overrepresented among voters turning out at caucuses held in accordance with the new requirements. However, the caucus requirements were complex, and many states found it easier to assure compliance with the new rules by opting for a primary election. Furthermore, those state parties that were still dominated by old-line organizations may have preferred a presidential primary to a caucus proceeding that could spread the new "democratization" to state party governance. See Byron E. Shafer, Quiet Revolution: The Struggle for the Democratic Party and the Shaping of Post-Reform Politics (1983); Nelson W. Polsby, Consequences of Party Reform (1983).

Although the Republican Party did not adopt all the reforms that the Democrats adopted, the Republicans were influenced significantly by them. They did adopt some of the reforms, though usually in a more moderate version. In addition, when the reforms were adopted via state legislation, the new laws often applied to the Republicans as well. This was especially true in the case of the adoption of presidential primaries, which with very few exceptions was done either for both parties or for neither.

By inducing greatly increased use of presidential primaries, the new rules helped bring about a basic change in the method of selecting the president. As we have seen, success in primaries was only a part of a campaign for the nomination prior to 1972. Its major significance was to demonstrate to party leaders that an aspirant would make a strong candidate. For example, John Kennedy's victory over Hubert Humphrey in the West Virginia primary in 1960 went a long way toward overcoming doubts of some party leaders as to whether a Roman Catholic could win votes in heavily Protestant parts of the country. But the final decision was determined not by primaries, but by negotiations between state delegation leaders at the convention. In contrast, since 1972, the nominee of each party has been the candidate who could win a majority of delegate votes in the primaries and state caucuses.

The parties, especially the Democrats, continued to tinker with the delegate selection rules after 1972. More and more states have moved to primaries as the means of selecting delegates to presidential conventions. Of greater consequence to us in this section are the constitutional questions presented by changes to delegate selection rules. State parties have sometimes resisted those changes. Since the state party is likely to have influence over the state legislature on such matters, the state

x. For a detailed history of the McGovern-Fraser proposals, see Byron E. Shafer, Quiet Revolution: The Struggle for the Democratic Party and the Shaping of Post-Reform Politics (1983).

party's resistance sometimes is buttressed by state law. When such conflicts arise, they raise the question whether the national party rules, state party rules, or state legislation should be supreme with respect to the selection of the state party delegation to a national convention.[y] When such conflicts are brought to court, they present an additional question: Should the conflicts be resolved by the judiciary at all, or should they be left to the political process for resolution?

Brown v. O'Brien, 409 U.S. 1 (1972), went to the Supreme Court on the eve of the 1972 Democratic National Convention. The Credentials Committee, whose rulings would be subject to review by the convention delegates, had upheld challenges to the California and Illinois delegations. The California challenge was based on the fact that California had conducted a winner-take-all primary. George McGovern, who had won the primary, virtually was assured the nomination if he received all the California delegates, whereas the nomination might be up for grabs if the California delegation were divided among the candidates in proportion to their vote percentages. The Illinois delegation, which was controlled by Chicago Mayor Richard Daley, was challenged for underrepresenting women, minorities, and young people.

The D.C. Circuit, while rejecting the Illinois claim, held the credentials committee ruling unseating the California McGovern delegates violated due process, since those delegates were selected in accordance with then existing state law. The losing sides both applied to the Supreme Court for stays of the D.C. Circuit's orders. Three days before the Convention opened, the Court granted those requests, in part because of the "grave doubts" it had about the action of the D.C. Circuit. In the *per curiam* opinion in *O'Brien*, 409 U.S. at 4, the Court said:

> It has been understood since our national political parties first came into being as voluntary associations of individuals that the convention itself is the proper forum for determining intra-party disputes as to which delegates shall be seated. Thus, these cases involve claims of the federal judiciary to review actions heretofore thought to lie in the control of political parties. Highly important questions are presented concerning justiciability, whether the action of the Credentials Committee is state action, and if so, the reach of the Due Process Clause in this unique context. Vital rights of association guaranteed by the Constitution are also involved.

The Court did not, however, definitively resolve the issues it identified, because of the lack of time for adequate briefing of them and "the availability of the Convention as a forum to review the recommendations of the Credentials Committee." The

---

y. One constitutional question that has not been tested is the degree to which Congress has the power to regulate the national conventions or other national or state party processes. To date, Congress has withheld its legislative hand. For discussion of constitutional issues that would be raised by congressional efforts to regulate, see William Mayer and Andrew E. Busch, The Front-Loading Problem in Presidential Elections 131–40 (2004); Daniel Lowenstein, *Presidential Nomination Reform: Legal Restraints and Procedural Possibilities*, in Reforming the Presidential Nomination Process 173 (Steven S. Smith & Melanie J. Springer, eds., 2009).

Convention did ultimately uphold the Credentials Committee on the Illinois challenge but reversed its decision on the California challenge, thus assuring the nomination for Senator McGovern.

Meanwhile, the Daley delegation (also called the Wigoda delegation) had obtained an injunction from an Illinois state judge prohibiting the challengers (the Cousins delegation) from acting as delegates. The Cousins delegation ignored the injunction and participated in the Convention as the delegates from Illinois. The Illinois state judge who had issued the injunction then held the Cousins delegation in contempt of court for violating it. The issue was thus clearly joined over the power of state election law to govern the conduct of a national party's convention. The Supreme Court ultimately held that the Illinois judge had no power to control the actions of the Convention. *Cousins v. Wigoda*, 419 U.S. 477 (1975).

The Democratic National Committee's call for the 1980 Democratic National Convention required that participation in the delegate selection process must be limited to Democrats only. Wisconsin had employed an "open" primary since 1903, when it became one of the first states to adopt the direct primary system for nominating candidates. An open primary is one in which each voter may request to vote in the primary of whichever party he or she chooses on election day, without regard to party membership or affiliation. Wisconsin Democrats defied the national Democratic Party by conducting an open primary in 1980. A Wisconsin court ordered the national party to seat Wisconsin's delegates at the convention, despite the violation of the national party rules. In *Democratic Party of the United States v. Wisconsin ex rel. La Follette*, 450 U.S. 107 (1981), the Supreme Court reversed the state court's order.

Justice Stewart's opinion for the majority emphasized that the Court was not ruling that the national Democrats could prevent Wisconsin from conducting an open primary. He wrote that Wisconsin had an interest in conducting its elections as it chose and that the national Democrats had an interest in how the delegates to their convention were selected. He went on:

> But these interests are not incompatible, and to the limited extent they clash in this case, both interests can be preserved. The National Party rules do not forbid Wisconsin to conduct an open primary. But if Wisconsin does open its primary, it cannot require that Wisconsin delegates to the National Party Convention vote there in accordance with the primary results, if to do so would violate Party rules.

Justice Powell, joined by Justices Blackmun and Rehnquist, dissented.

Notes and Questions

1. Justice Stewart emphasized the National Democratic Party's constitutional right to freedom of association as an important reason for the result he reached in *La Follette*. Yet, the Wisconsin Democratic Party strongly supported the open primary and attempted to defend it in the litigation. Is the majority's ruling an infringement

on the state party's freedom of association? Why is the state party's right to select delegates to the National Convention by the process it chooses of less constitutional weight than the National Party's right to decide which delegates to seat?

2. At first glance, the passage from *La Follette* quoted above seems silly. The purpose of holding a primary is to determine how much support the competing presidential candidates will receive from the state's delegation to the national convention. What good does it do to tell the state that it is perfectly free to run its primary any way it chooses, but that the primary will count only if it is run the way the national party orders? Justice Powell made this seemingly telling point in dissent.

But first glances can be deceiving, and subsequent events showed that Justice Stewart was right and Justice Powell was wrong. *La Follette* left Wisconsin with more leverage than at first appeared. In 1980, the Democratic National Convention seated the Wisconsin delegation despite the fact that the state's open primary violated the national rules and despite the fact that the Supreme Court had stayed the lower court order requiring that the delegates be seated. In 1984, the Wisconsin Democrats yielded by selecting delegates at caucuses open only to Democrats, but by 1988 the national Democrats had given in, revising the national rules to permit Wisconsin to use an open primary.

The law of *Cousins* and *La Follette* is that although the states may select delegates pretty much as they choose within their own borders, the national party at its convention is free to accept or reject the delegates sent by the state and may choose to replace these delegates with substitutes selected using any method it cares to honor. This *seems* to be a victory for the national party because it has the last word. But the last word that the national party actually will utter will be determined politically, and in the political process the states carry considerable weight.

Despite increasing disenchantment with the national conventions, they still draw considerable attention and are regarded as significant events in the presidential election campaign. Let us imagine what would happen if the national Democratic rulemakers and the State of Wisconsin each decided to press their respective positions on the open primary to the hilt. Wisconsin would send its delegation, and the credentials committee, if it adhered to the rules, would recommend that the delegation not be seated. The matter would then be decided in an open vote on the floor of the convention. In the typical modern convention, this would be one of the few newsworthy events in a week of intensive news coverage. Would the delegates vote to exclude a state's democratically elected delegation because of an obscure technicality, poorly understood by most of the delegates themselves, not to mention millions of television viewers? The person being nominated for president at the convention would be unlikely to permit the matter to go to a floor vote, and the nominee would be even less likely to permit the exclusion of a state's elected delegation, an action that could only mystify the public.

The national party's ultimate weapon in rules conflicts with state parties and state governments was protected in *La Follette*, but the states can make that weapon very costly to use by sending to the convention a delegation clothed with the aura of having been selected democratically and legitimately. The result is that each side has a strong incentive to accommodate the other. The give-and-take that occurred between the national Democrats and the Wisconsin Democrats over the open primary suggests that consigning such controversies to the political process is unlikely to lead to one-sided results.

The foregoing discussion assumes that by the time of the convention, the presidential candidate has been determined by the primaries and the caucuses, as was the case in both parties in every election after 1972 through 2020. But what if the contest is still undecided and a controversy like the ones described above in Wisconsin were to arise? That possibility almost came to pass in 2008. The nomination battle in the Democratic Party between Hillary Clinton and Barack Obama was close through the last primaries, and some of Clinton's supporters hoped she would bring the contest to the convention. Two states, Michigan and Florida, held presidential primaries on January 29, 2008, in violation of Democratic party rules prohibiting those states from holding primaries before February 5. According to the party rules, no delegates selected in such primaries would be seated at the convention. The precise details varied in the two states, but roughly speaking Clinton campaigned much more actively than Obama in the two states, in primaries that, at the time, seemed only symbolic. Clinton won significant majorities of the "delegates" in both Florida and Michigan, though if the rules were followed, no actual delegates would be seated.

As the possibility arose that the primaries and caucuses might fail to produce a clear winner between Clinton and Obama, it was not surprising that Clinton proposed that the Florida and Michigan delegates should be seated, the party rules to the contrary notwithstanding. State party leaders from both states joined in. Frantic efforts were made, unsuccessfully, to arrange some sort of "do-over" primary on short notice. Ultimately, after it became clear that Obama would prevail regardless of how the dispute over Florida and Michigan was resolved, the full delegations of both seats were seated with full voting rights. Kevin J. Coleman, Congressional Research Service, *Presidential Nominating Process: Current Issues* 5 (2012), *available at* https://perma.cc/BG4K-2QHP. Had the nomination been uncertain at the convention, the Florida and Michigan issues would have been resolved by a political battle between the Clinton and Obama forces. The incident was a reminder that the national party's power to determine which state delegations will be seated is profoundly subject to political influence.

3. Would the result in *La Follette* have been different if Congress had passed a statute allowing state legislatures to choose between an open and closed primary and Wisconsin had opted for an open primary in opposition to national party rules? Would it be relevant that the great majority of Democrats in the House and Senate voted for the bill and that it was signed by a Democratic president?

Could Congress require the political parties to hold their primaries in every state on a single day? Should it? In the absence of any such action by Congress, New

Hampshire has a statute that sets its primary date one week earlier than the next earliest state. What would happen if Vermont passed the same statute?

If one of the national parties stated it would not seat delegates selected in primaries unless the primary were held on a date specified, would its refusal to seat the delegates be constitutionally protected under *La Follette*? Would such a rule be materially different for constitutional purposes than a rule that states not hold their primaries before a specified date? What if the state required by the national party to vote on a particular date proved (1) that it had traditionally held its primary on a different date; (2) that change in the date was strongly resisted by the other major party; and (3) that holding the two parties' primaries on separate dates would entail considerable public expense and would be likely to reduce turnout, not only in the presidential primaries but in other elections held concurrently, such as state and local primaries and ballot measure elections?

4. *La Follette* does not really answer the question of the extent to which the decision of a national political party in allocation and selection of delegates is "state action" subject to constitutional restraint. See generally the numerous cases and secondary sources cited in *Cousins v. Wigoda*, 419 U.S. at 483, n.4. Consider the following:

A. Can the party require all candidates for president to swear in advance of the nomination to support and abide by its platform with the sanction of withdrawal of the nomination if the candidate deviates? If so, is the victorious candidate who allegedly deviates entitled to a trial where he or she can challenge the allegations and evidence? Before whom? Under what procedures?

B. Is allocation of delegates to states at national party conventions subject to the principles of the redistricting decisions? Suppose, for example, the Republicans decide to award substantial numbers of extra delegates at their next convention to states carried by Republican candidates for President or Senator or that elected a majority of Republicans to the seats in the House allocated to their state. The Republicans' theory is that the bonus allocation will encourage state organizations to work harder to get out the Republican vote. What are the practical consequences of such a system, compared to apportionment of delegates strictly by population?

C. Is it constitutional for a party to require that a state's delegation to a nominating convention must contain women, identified racial minorities, and young people in the exact percentage that those groups are present in the population of the state? See *Bachur v. Democratic National Party*, 836 F.2d 837 (4th Cir. 1987), holding that Maryland rules to implement policies of the national Democratic Party, requiring individuals to vote for equal numbers of men and women for delegate to the convention, did not infringe on the right to vote. See generally John G. Kester, *Constitutional Restrictions on Political Parties*, 60 Virginia Law Review 735, 770–72 (1974).

D. Is your answer to any of the above questions affected by the fact that the major parties receive public funds to finance their conventions? Would your answer be influenced if Congress appropriated funds to pay for the parties' internal operations? Their public relations activities?

E. Is your view of when a political party's action is state action different for the national, state, and local parties? Suppose, for example, that in a given state, trial court judges are not nominated in primaries but by the party county committees. A party committee in a given county is taken over by a reform faction. Assume further that the party's nomination for trial court judge in that county is tantamount to election. Wholly on its own volition, the party committee establishes a screening committee of distinguished lawyers and non-lawyers to recommend nominees for judge to it, and the party committee agrees to be bound by the screening committee's choice. A candidate for judge rejected by the screening committee sues the county party, alleging that the screening committee considered hearsay statements of unidentified lawyers and former clients in rejecting the candidate and did not give the rejected candidate the opportunity to confront accusers and be heard on the charges. The candidate alleges the screening committee is in effect an arm of the county party, whose nomination of the candidate endorsed by the screening committee is state action subject to the due process clause of the Fourteenth Amendment. What result, and why?

5. As we have seen, the controversies that raised questions of parties' associational freedoms in the 1970s centered on presidential nominations. In the ensuing decades, the legal battles more often have pitted competing viewpoints within particular states. Before we move to those developments, it is worth pausing to note two additional areas of controversy around presidential elections. In this Note we mention the timing of presidential primaries. In the next three we will discuss the Electoral College.

As we have seen, the 1968 reforms in the Democratic Party's nominating process had the unanticipated consequence of altering the process in both parties to one dominated by primaries. Even the states that declined to adopt presidential primaries have used caucuses that are closer in nature to primaries than to the old processes dominated by state party leaders. Caucuses, like primaries, are open to voters who choose among the contenders for the party's nominations.

It has become a modern tradition that the first decisive event in the nomination process is the Iowa caucus in each party, followed by the New Hampshire primary. After these events, states have been free to schedule their primaries and caucuses whenever they wished. At first the nominating events were fairly evenly spread out between February and June. However, a pattern began to emerge. Going into Iowa and New Hampshire, there were typically anywhere up to ten or so reasonably serious candidates in each party—with the exception of a party in which an incumbent president was seeking reelection. Of these, two or three would be regarded as front-runners and the rest as "dark horses." Iowa and New Hampshire would winnow the field down, usually to two or at the most three candidates. One or two of these might be dark horses who had done unexpectedly well in Iowa or, especially, New Hampshire. The surviving candidates would then fight it out in the ensuing primaries and caucuses. Often, for one reason or another, attention would be focused on one or a small number of primaries that were regarded as crucial. Eventually — often before many states had conducted their primaries or caucuses — it would become clear that a particular candidate was going to win. Usually the other candidates withdrew from the race, so that the later contests were purely pro forma.

Whatever the merits of this system as a method of choosing a pair of finalists in the competition to be President of the United States, it began to draw the ire of partisan activists in states that were holding their primaries and caucuses late in the process. Many of these people thought that their states were being frozen out, as the contests were over for all practical purposes by the time their citizens had a chance to vote. Gradually, states began to move their primary and caucus dates earlier. And then not so gradually.

All this came to a head as the 2008 election approached. States sought to hold their contests earlier and earlier. It began to appear that Iowa and New Hampshire, determined to retain their positions at the head of the line, might have to hold their contests before Christmas. The parties responded to complaints about the non-representative quality of Iowa and New Hampshire by extending to two additional states — Nevada and South Carolina — an early place in line. All other states were prohibited by both parties from acting before February 5. The Republicans would penalize a state that breached the February 5 limit by seating only half the state's delegates. The Democrats would not seat any delegates from a state in violation. As we have already seen in Note 2, above, two large states — Florida and Michigan — defied the national parties by holding their primaries on January 29. Other states all complied, but twenty states, including such large ones as California, New York, and Illinois, set their primaries on the first legal date, February 5, "Super-Tuesday." After the 2008 election, both parties modified their rules in an effort to discourage front-loading. The Republican and Democratic rules for 2012 prohibited states from holding primaries or caucuses before the first Tuesday in March in the calendar year of the national convention with exemptions for Iowa, New Hampshire, Nevada, and South Carolina. *Delegate Selection Rules for the 2012 Democratic Convention*, Rule 11.A; *The Rules of the Republican Party*, Rule 15(b)(1). This marked the first time that the Republican Party had imposed a timing rule for delegate selection events. Coleman, *supra*, at 6. In an effort to encourage states to hold later primaries and caucuses, the Republican Party rules were amended to require that states holding primaries before April (other than the four exempt states) allocate their delegates proportionally. Thus, states wishing to have a statewide winner-take-all primary or caucus would have to push it back until at least April. This tended to make the later contests more significant. The Democratic Party modified its rules for 2012 to eliminate one category of superdelegates, require other superdelegates to declare their candidate preference within 10 days of their state's primary or caucus, and encourage states to hold regional primaries.

The Democratic nomination was not contested in 2012 because President Obama was seeking reelection, but there was a vigorous contest for the Republican presidential nomination. Three states (Arizona, Florida, and Michigan) chose to hold their primaries before March, notwithstanding party rules to the contrary. This could potentially have created a fight at the convention, had the contest for the Republican nomination wound up being close. But that did not happen. An initially crowded field was quickly winnowed down to four candidates: Mitt Romney, Rick Santorum, Newt Gingrich, and Ron Paul. The rule changes appear to have had their desired effect, as a number of states moved back the dates on which their primaries and caucuses were held. This probably left the race for the Republican nomination in doubt for longer than would otherwise have been the case.

In 2016, a crowded field on the Republican side eventually narrowed to three candidates: Texas U.S. Senator Ted Cruz, Ohio Governor John Kasich, and Donald Trump. For much of the spring, it appeared possible that no candidate would secure the 1,237 delegates necessary to ensure his nomination on the first ballot. Had that transpired, a furious battle to persuade delegates might well have unfolded on the convention floor. See Benjamin Ginsberg, *The Path to Convention Chaos*, Politico, March 12, 2016. That possibility was eliminated after Trump's resounding victories in several East Coast primaries. Cruz and Kasich dropped out of the race in early May after Trump's resounding victory in Indiana, which left him a clear path to an outright majority of delegates. The Republican Party's delegate selection rules, which allow winner-take-all and winner-take-most primaries, helped Trump secure a majority of delegates and thus avoid a contested convention.

The Democratic rules, which require the proportional allocation of delegates, resulted in a more drawn-out contest. Hillary Clinton led the race from start to finish, though she faced an unexpectedly formidable challenge from Vermont U.S. Senator Bernie Sanders. She did not clinch a majority of the delegates necessary to ensure the nomination until June. DNC Chair Debbie Wasserman-Schultz was forced to resign her post just before the convention, after leaked emails showed that party officials had been working behind the scenes to help Clinton. Sanders did especially well in states with caucuses, where turnout tends to be much lower than in primaries, bringing out the most devoted party voters. Caucuses have had some significant problems, like long lines, ballot shortages, and the failure to transmit accurate results. On the other hand, supporters of caucuses argue that they encourage participatory democracy and encourage party activism.

In 2020, spurred by the Democratic National Committee, the states of Washington, Minnesota, and Colorado (the three largest caucus states) moved to primaries, along with Utah, Idaho, and Nebraska. Nate Cohn, *Fewer States Will Have Caucuses in 2020. Will It Matter?*, N.Y. Times, Apr. 12, 2019. What effects does the move away from caucuses have? Is it a good thing? Consider that more people participate in primaries, while highly motivated voters tend to dominate the caucus process.

The Democratic Party has reduced the influence of so-called "superdelegates," political insiders who played a prominent role in the 2008 process. Astead W. Herndon, *Democrats Overhaul Controversial Superdelegate System*, N.Y. Times, Aug. 25, 2018. For a skeptical view of such "populist" reforms, designed to decrease the influence of party insiders and increase the voice of the people, see Stephen Gardbaum and Richard H. Pildes, *Populism and Institutional Design: Methods of Selecting Candidates for Chief Executive*, 93 New York University Law Review 647 (2018). Professors Gardbaum and Pildes "challenge the unexamined notion that our current populist system of candidate selection is the best way to choose the nominees who then compete in the general election for President." They argue in favor of institutional mechanisms providing more influence to party insiders, on the ground that they furnish a kind of "peer review" that helps prevent the party from being captured by extreme and even anti-democratic forces. Do you agree? For more suggestions on how the presidential selection process might be improved, see Symposium, *The Presidential Nominations Process*, 93 New York University Law Review 589 (2018).

The 2020 presidential nominations were decided fairly quickly once primaries began. President Donald Trump secured the Republican nomination without serious opposition, and former Vice-President Joe Biden emerged as the preferred candidate among an initially crowded field of Democrats after South Carolina's February primary. By early April, all of Biden's opponents had suspended their campaigns. In a close race, the COVID-19 pandemic might have caused significant disruption to the presidential nominating process.

Even without a contested presidential nomination, there was still litigation in New York, over that state's decision to cancel its Democratic primary after all the candidates except Biden had dropped out. On March 28, 2020, Governor Andrew Cuomo issued an executive order rescheduling the April primary for June 23, 2020. The state legislature subsequently enacted a statute authorizing the New York State Board of Elections—and specifically, commissioners affiliated with the major party holding a primary—to omit candidates who had suspended their campaigns or publicly announced their withdrawal. Then on April 27, 2020, the Board's two Democratic commissioners removed the names of the ten candidates who had done so. With only Biden remaining, the commissioners cancelled New York's primary, which they described as nothing more than a "beauty contest," citing the COVID-19 pandemic as the reason for their decision.

Supporters of two presidential candidates, Andrew Yang and Bernie Sanders, disagreed with the Board's decision. At their request, a federal district court ordered that the removed candidates be restored to the ballot and that the Democratic presidential primary take place. The Second Circuit affirmed, applying the *Anderson-Burdick* balancing standard (see *infra*) and concluding the burden on voters and delegates outweighed the state's interests. *Yang v. Kosinski*, 960 F.3d 119 (2d Cir. 2020). Addressing the central question of what purpose a presidential primary would serve after the nominee had effectively been chosen, the Second Circuit explained:

> Yang wants an opportunity to compete for delegates. And so does Sanders. . . . By the same token, the Yang and Sanders delegates also want to compete for an opportunity to attend the Democratic National Convention. These are not trivial interests. Those familiar with the internal structure of the Democratic Party and the history of its National Convention will have no difficulty appreciating their significance.
>
> At the Democratic National Convention, delegates have many important responsibilities, some with long-term consequences. In addition to participating in the selection of the presidential nominee, they vote on the procedural rules of the Convention; the National Democratic Party electoral platform; issues of party governance; and not insignificantly, the selection of the vice-presidential nominee. Furthermore, the power of the elected delegates extends beyond the quadrennial national convention. The delegates of the National Convention remain "the highest authority [and governing body] of the Democratic Party" until new delegates are selected. Accordingly, the programs and policies adopted at the Democratic National Convention will continue to influence state party rules or actions of the Democratic National Committee.

Id. at 130-31.

Do you agree that voters and would-be delegates have an important interest in having a primary take place, even after all but one of the candidates has dropped out? Was it appropriate for a federal court to intervene in this intra-party dispute, especially during a pandemic? Why didn't the *Purcell v. Gonzalez* doctrine, which generally counsels against federal court injunctions just before a scheduled election, apply here? See Chapter 6, Part IV.

6. Under Article II, Section 1 of the U.S. Constitution: "Each state shall appoint, in such manner as the Legislature thereof may direct, a number of electors, equal to the whole number of Senators and Representatives to which the State may be entitled in the Congress. . . ." Those electors then cast their votes on an assigned day in each of the states, with the totals sent to Congress to be counted. In the first two elections, George Washington was the consensus candidate and the only serious question was who would be chosen as vice-president. Under the original Constitution, each elector voted for two people, with no differentiation between president and vice-president. If one candidate received votes equal to a majority of the electors that candidate was elected president and the candidate with the next highest number of votes was vice-president. If no candidate received votes from a majority of the electors, the president was selected by the House of Representatives, with each state having one vote.

Beginning with the election of 1796, the electors began to divide between two national parties, a development not anticipated by the authors of the Constitution. This created no particular problem in 1796, but in 1800, when the Republican Thomas Jefferson defeated the Federalist John Adams, each Republican elector cast one vote for Jefferson and one for his running mate Aaron Burr, with the result that they each received the same number of electoral votes and the election was thrown into the House. The Federalists, hostile to Jefferson, sought to elect Burr as president. A deadlock arose that was finally broken when the sole Representative from Delaware, a Federalist, withheld his state's vote from Burr, enabling Jefferson to win. In the aftermath of this constitutional crisis, the Twelfth Amendment was passed. In effect it adapted the Electoral College to the party system by requiring electors to specify the presidential and vice-presidential candidates they were voting for, so that votes for the two offices could be counted separately.

Article II, Section 1 permits "the Legislature" of each state to decide the manner in which the state will appoint its electors. In early elections two methods were used predominantly, selection by the legislature and popular election. Popular election took place in districts in some states and on a statewide, winner-take-all basis in others. Over time, nearly all the states settled on the statewide popular vote. All but two states use that method. Maine and Nebraska pick two electors, corresponding to their two senators, by statewide election, and their remaining electors in their congressional districts.

The Electoral College has long been criticized, usually by people who favor a national popular election. Most of the time, the candidate who receives the highest number of votes nationwide also prevails in the Electoral College. But not always. In two of the last six presidential elections, the winner of the popular vote did not receive the highest number of electoral votes and thus lost the election. In 2000, Al Gore received 48.4 percent of the popular vote to George W. Bush's 47.9 percent, but lost by a narrow margin of five votes in the Electoral College (271-266). In 2016, Hillary Clinton won 48.0 percent of the popular vote to Donald Trump's 45.9 percent, winning 2.9 million more votes nationwide. Yet Clinton lost the electoral vote by a substantial margin, winning only 232 electors to Trump's 306. The final vote in the Electoral College was 304 to 227 in favor of Trump, because seven electors voted for someone other than the candidate to whom they were pledged. Most states require electors to vote for the candidate to whom they are pledged, with some of them providing by law that the failure to do so cancels the elector's vote and requires her replacement. One of the questions that emerged is whether the law permits states to enforce their rules against "faithless electors" or, alternatively, whether the Constitution requires them to exercise their independent judgment when casting their electoral votes. Despite a concerted effort to persuade Trump electors to vote for someone else, only two electors from Texas ultimately did so (one voting for libertarian Republican Ron Paul, the other for Ohio Governor John Kasich), while five Democratic electors voted for someone other than Hillary Clinton.

Seemingly, changing the method for selecting a president prescribed by the Constitution requires a constitutional amendment. At least, that is what has been generally assumed. For several years, a group of reformers has espoused a plan, known as the National Popular Vote Plan, intended to get around the Electoral College without amending the Constitution. The idea is that state legislatures should adopt a procedure that would select electors pledged not to the presidential candidate winning the most votes within the states, but to the candidate winning the national popular vote. The plan does not go into effect until and unless states representing a majority of the Electoral College sign on. At that point, the popular vote in non-cooperating states would be taken into account but the electoral votes from non-cooperating states would become irrelevant. Supporters have produced a volume that opponents of the plan as well as supporters will find a useful reference work, John R. Koza et al., Every Vote Equal: A State-Based Plan for Electing the President by National Popular Vote (2006). As of 2021, a total of 16 jurisdictions collectively having 195 electoral votes have signed on to the national popular vote plan.

If they succeed in obtaining states with a majority of the electoral votes to sign up for the plan, they can anticipate two constitutional challenges. The first will be that the plan is an interstate compact of the sort that requires congressional approval. For divergent views on this question, see Jennings "Jay" Wilson, *Bloc Voting in the Electoral College: How the Ignored States Can Become Relevant and Implement Popular Election Along the Way*, 5 Election Law Journal 384 (2006); Derek T. Muller, *The Compact Clause and the National Popular Vote Interstate Compact*, 6 Election Law Journal 372 (2007); Jennifer Hendricks, *Popular Election of the President: Using or Abusing the Electoral College?*, 7 Election Law Journal 218 (2008); and Derek T. Muller, *More Thoughts on the Compact Clause and the National Popular Vote: A Response to Professor Hendricks*, 7 Election Law Journal 227 (2008). The second will be that although under Article I, Section 1, the legislature is authorized to determine the manner of appointing the electors, it is the state that must do the appointing. The contention will be that determining the identity of the electors by the national popular vote is not appointment by the state.

Should the Electoral College be changed or eliminated? Is a constitutional amendment required to move to a national popular vote?

7. Under the Electoral College system, each state's voters actually select a slate of electors, who in turn for vote for presidential candidates. Most of the time, those electors vote for the candidate whom they agreed to support, consistent with the wishes of their state's voters. But not always. In 2016, three of the State of Washington's electors violated their pledge to support Hillary Clinton, in an unsuccessful effort to persuade Donald Trump's electors to do the same.

Electors who don't vote for the presidential candidate they are pledged to support are called "faithless electors." Washington is one of 15 states that imposes sanctions on faithless electors, and the three electors who violated their pledge to support Clinton were each fined $1000. They challenged their fines on the ground that the Constitution allows members of the Electoral College to vote as they wish. The U.S. Supreme court unanimously disagreed. In *Chiafalo v. Washington*, 140 S. Ct. 2316 (2020), an opinion for eight justices (all but Justice Thomas), Justice Kagan concluded that the Constitution allows states to sanction faithless electors:

> Article II, §1's appointments power gives the States far-reaching authority over presidential electors, absent some other constitutional constraint. [E]ach State may appoint electors "in such Manner as the Legislature thereof may direct." This Court has described that clause as "conveying the broadest power of determination" over who becomes an elector. *McPherson v. Blacker*, 146 U.S. 1, 27 (1892). And the power to appoint an elector (in any manner) includes power to condition his appointment—that is, to say what the elector must do for the appointment to take effect....
>
> The Electors argue that three simple words stand in for more explicit language about discretion. Article II, §1 first names the members of the Electoral College: "electors." The Twelfth Amendment then says that electors shall "vote" and that they shall do so by "ballot." The "plain meaning" of those terms, the Electors say, requires electors to have "freedom of choice." If the States could control their votes, "the electors would not be 'Electors,' and their 'vote by Ballot' would not be a 'vote.'"
>
> But those words need not always connote independent choice. Suppose a person always votes in the way his spouse, or pastor, or union tells him to. We might question his judgment, but we would have no problem saying that he "votes" or fills in a "ballot." In those cases, the choice is in someone else's hands, but the words still apply because they can signify a mechanical act....
>
> The Electors' constitutional claim has neither text nor history on its side. Article II and the Twelfth Amendment give States broad power over electors, and give electors themselves no rights. Early in our history, States decided to tie electors to the presidential choices of others, whether legislatures or citizens. Except that legislatures no longer play a role, that practice has continued for more than 200 years. Among the devices States have long used to achieve their object are pledge laws, designed to impress on electors their role as agents of others. A State follows in the same tradition if, like Washington, it chooses to sanction an elector for breaching his promise. Then too, the State instructs its electors that they have no ground for reversing the vote of millions of its citizens. That direction accords with the Constitution—as well as with the trust of a Nation that here, We the People rule.

Is the Court right that the Constitution's use of the word "vote" need not be understood to imply an independent choice? Would we understand citizens to have a right to vote, if they were ordered to vote for a particular candidate on pain of monetary sanctions? Of what relevance is the consistent practice of states, which have long tied the members of the Electoral College to the preferences of state voters?

8. A federal statute, the Electoral Count Act of 1887, governs the process by which electoral votes are cast and counted. Among its key provisions are that states have 35 days after Election Day to resolve any disputes over the election result, if they want to avail themselves of the "safe harbor" date for ensuring that their determinations are conclusive. 3 U.S.C. § 5. Six days later, in mid-December, the electors meet in each of the states to cast their electoral votes. 3 U.S.C. § 7. Congress then meets to count the votes on January 6. 3 U.S.C. § 15. The President is then inaugurated on January 20.

Most years, the main drama is on Election Night, and the casting and counting of electoral votes is a soporific affair. Not in 2020.

President Trump refused to concede defeat, continuing to press his false claims of election fraud in court and in public statements (see *supra*, Chapter 6). Many of his supporters believed him. With his attempts to overturn the election results in court failing, President Trump appealed to state legislatures in key states to overturn the result. Kyle Cheney, *Trump Calls on GOP State Legislatures to Overturn Election Results*, Politico, Nov. 21, 2020. He also tried to assemble a group of "alternative electors" who might try to keep him in office. Nicholas Riccardi, *Why Trump's Latest Electoral College Ploy Is Doomed to Fail*, AP, Dec. 14, 2020. When all that failed, he delivered a lengthy but impassioned speech to supporters on January 6, 2020, the date that Congress was to meet to count the electoral votes. He claimed that the election had been "rigged" against him and, toward the end, said the following:

> We fight like hell. And if you don't fight like hell, you're not going to have a country anymore. . . .
>
> So we're going to, we're going to walk down Pennsylvania Avenue. I love Pennsylvania Avenue. And we're going to the Capitol, and we're going to try and give.
>
> The Democrats are hopeless — they never vote for anything. Not even one vote. But we're going to try and give our Republicans, the weak ones because the strong ones don't need any of our help. We're going to try and give them the kind of pride and boldness that they need to take back our country.
>
> So let's walk down Pennsylvania Avenue.

Walk down Pennsylvania Avenue they did. That afternoon, a mob of President Trump's supporters stormed the U.S. Capitol, disrupting the joint session of Congress as which the electoral votes were to be counted. Members of the mob occupied and looted the Capitol, some of them assaulting police officers and reporters. Members of Congress were evacuated. It took hours for the Capitol building to be cleared of the rioters after which the session to count the electoral votes recommenced. Senate Majority Leader Mitch McConnell, a Republican, referred to the events of that day as a "failed insurrection." Early on the morning of January 7, after rejecting objections to some of the electoral votes, Congress finished counting the electoral votes and certified President-elect Joe Biden and Vice President-elect Kamala Harris as the winners.

The events of January 6, 2021, and the weeks-long drama that preceded it, reveal several vulnerable points in the Electoral College process. Even after all lawsuits have been resolved, a partisan Secretary of State might refuse to certify the result. A Governor might refuse to prepare and send the Certificates of Ascertainment after certification. State legislatures might overturn the vote of the people, as President Trump attempted to convince some of them to do. And Congress might ultimately refuse to count the electoral votes presented to it. What if anything can be done to address the vulnerabilities in this process?

B. State Parties

1. Establishing the Right

In the *White Primary Cases*, constitutional rights of voters were asserted successfully against political parties. In *Cousins* and *La Follette*, parties were able to assert their own associational rights to defend national party control of the national conventions against state judicial interference. We now turn to cases in which state parties, or individuals claiming to act on a party's behalf, assert associational rights under the First Amendment as a means of striking down state regulation.

Tashjian v. Republican Party of Connecticut

479 U.S. 208 (1986)

Justice MARSHALL delivered the opinion of the Court.

Appellee Republican Party of the State of Connecticut (Party) in 1984 adopted a Party rule which permits independent voters—registered voters not affiliated with any political party—to vote in Republican primaries for federal and state-wide offices. Appellant Julia Tashjian, the Secretary of the State of Connecticut, is charged with the administration of the State's election statutes, which include a provision requiring voters in any party primary to be registered members of that party. Conn. Gen. Stat. § 9-431 (1985). Appellees, who in addition to the Party include the Party's federal officeholders and the Party's state chairman, challenged this eligibility provision on the ground that it deprives the Party of its First Amendment right to enter into political association with individuals of its own choosing. The District Court granted summary judgment in favor of appellees. The Court of Appeals affirmed. We . . . now affirm.

I

In 1955, Connecticut adopted its present primary election system. For major parties, the process of candidate selection for federal and statewide offices requires a statewide convention of party delegates; district conventions are held to select candidates for seats in the state legislature. The party convention may certify as the party-endorsed candidate any person receiving more than 20% of the votes cast in a roll-call vote at the convention. Any candidate not endorsed by the party who received 20% of the vote may challenge the party-endorsed candidate in a primary election, in which the candidate receiving the plurality of votes becomes the party's nominee. Candidates selected by the major parties, whether through convention or primary, are automatically accorded a place on the ballot at the general election. . . .

Motivated in part by the demographic importance of independent voters in Connecticut politics,[3] in September 1983 the Party's Central Committee recommended calling a state convention to consider altering the Party's rules to allow independents to vote in Party primaries. In January 1984 the state convention adopted the Party rule now at issue, which provides:

> Any elector enrolled as a member of the Republican Party and any elector not enrolled as a member of a party shall be eligible to vote in primaries for nomination of candidates for the offices of United States Senator, United States Representative, Governor, Lieutenant Governor, Secretary of the State, Attorney General, Comptroller and Treasurer.

During the 1984 session, thc Republican leadership in the state legislature, in response to the conflict between the newly enacted Party rule and § 9-431, proposed to amend the statute to allow independents to vote in primaries when permitted by Party rules. The proposed legislation was defeated, substantially along party lines, in both houses of the legislature, which at that time were controlled by the Democratic Party. . . .[4]

II

. . . The nature of appellees' First Amendment interest is evident. "It is beyond debate that freedom to engage in association for the advancement of beliefs and ideas is an inseparable aspect of the 'liberty' assured by the Due Process Clause of the Fourteenth Amendment, which embraces freedom of speech." *NAACP v. Alabama ex rel. Patterson*, 357 U.S. 449 (1958). The freedom of association protected by the First and Fourteenth Amendments includes partisan political organization. "The right to associate with the political party of one's choice is an integral part of this basic constitutional freedom." *Kusper.*

The Party here contends that § 9-431 impermissibly burdens the right of its members to determine for themselves with whom they will associate, and whose support they will seek, in their quest for political success. The Party's attempt to broaden the base of public participation in and support for its activities is conduct undeniably central to the exercise of the right of association. As we have said, the freedom to

3. The record shows that in October 1983 there were 659,268 registered Democrats, 425,695 registered Republicans, and 532,723 registered and unaffiliated voters in Connecticut.

4. In the November 1984 elections, the Republicans acquired a majority of seats in both houses of the state legislature, and an amendment to § 9-431 was passed, but was vetoed by the Democratic Governor.

join together in furtherance of common political beliefs "necessarily presupposes the freedom to identify the people who constitute the association." *La Follette.*

A major state political party necessarily includes individuals playing a broad spectrum of roles in the organization's activities. Some of the Party's members devote substantial portions of their lives to furthering its political and organizational goals, others provide substantial financial support, while still others limit their participation to casting their votes for some or all of the Party's candidates. Considered from the standpoint of the Party itself, the act of formal enrollment or public affiliation with the Party is merely one element in the continuum of participation in Party affairs, and need not be in any sense the most important.

Were the State to restrict by statute financial support of the Party's candidates to Party members, or to provide that only Party members might be selected as the Party's chosen nominees for public office, such a prohibition of potential association with nonmembers would clearly infringe upon the rights of the Party's members under the First Amendment to organize with like-minded citizens in support of common political goals. As we have said, "'[a]ny interference with the freedom of a party is simultaneously an interference with the freedom of its adherents.'" *La Follette* (quoting *Sweezy v. New Hampshire*, 354 U.S. 234 (1957)).[6] The statute here places limits upon the group of registered voters whom the Party may invite to participate in the "basic function" of selecting the Party's candidates. *Kusper.* The State thus limits the Party's associational opportunities at the crucial juncture at which the appeal to common principles may be translated into concerted action, and hence to political power in the community.[7]

---

6. It is this element of potential interference with the rights of the Party's members which distinguishes the present case from others in which we have considered claims by nonmembers of a party seeking to vote in that party's primary despite the party's opposition. In this latter class of cases, the nonmember's desire to participate in the party's affairs is overborne by the countervailing and legitimate right of the party to determine its own membership qualifications. See *Rosario.* Similarly, the Court has upheld the right of national political parties to refuse to seat at their conventions delegates chosen in state selection processes which did not conform to party rules. See *La Follette*; *Cousins.* These situations are analytically distinct from the present case, in which the Party and its members seek to provide enhanced opportunities for participation by willing nonmembers. Under these circumstances, there is no conflict between the associational interests of members and nonmembers.

7. Appellant contends that any infringement of the associational right of the Party or its members is de minimis, because Connecticut law, as amended during the pendency of this litigation, provides that any previously unaffiliated voter may become eligible to vote in the Party's primary by enrolling as a Party member as late as noon on the last business day preceding the primary. Thus, appellant contends, any independent voter wishing to participate in any Party primary may do so.

This is not a satisfactory response to the Party's contentions for two reasons. First, as the Court of Appeals noted, the formal affiliation process is one which individual voters may employ in order to associate with the Party, but it provides no means by which the members of the Party may choose to broaden opportunities for joining the association by their own act, without any intervening action by potential voters. Second, and more importantly, the requirement of public affiliation with the Party in order to vote in the primary conditions the exercise of the associational right upon

It is, of course, fundamental to appellant's defense of the State's statute that this impingement upon the associational rights of the Party and its members occurs at the ballot box, for the Constitution grants to the States a broad power to prescribe the "Times, Places and Manner of holding Elections for Senators and Representatives," Art. I, §4, cl. 1, which power is matched by state control over the election process for state offices. But this authority does not extinguish the State's responsibility to observe the limits established by the First Amendment rights of the State's citizens. The power to regulate the time, place, and manner of elections does not justify, without more, the abridgment of fundamental rights, such as the right to vote, see *Wesberry*, or, as here, the freedom of political association. We turn then to an examination of the interests which appellant asserts to justify the burden cast by the statute upon the associational rights of the Party and its members.

III

Appellant contends that §9-431 is a narrowly tailored regulation which advances the State's compelling interests by ensuring the administrability of the primary system, preventing raiding, avoiding voter confusion, and protecting the responsibility of party government.

A

[Appellant argues] that the administrative burden imposed by the Party rule is a sufficient ground on which to uphold the constitutionality of §9-431. Appellant contends that the Party's rule would require the purchase of additional voting machines, the training of additional poll workers, and potentially the printing of additional ballot materials specifically intended for independents voting in the Republican primary. In essence, appellant claims that the administration of the system contemplated by the Party rule would simply cost the State too much.

Even assuming the factual accuracy of these contentions . . . , the possibility of future increases in the cost of administering the election system is not a sufficient basis here for infringing appellees' First Amendment rights. Costs of administration would likewise increase if a third major party should come into existence in Connecticut, thus requiring the State to fund a third major-party primary. Additional voting machines, poll workers, and ballot materials would all be necessary under these circumstances as well. But the State could not forever protect the two existing major parties from competition solely on the ground that two major parties are all the public can afford. While the State is of course entitled to take administrative and financial considerations into account in choosing whether or not to have a primary system at all, it can no more restrain the Republican Party's freedom of association

---

the making of a public statement of adherence to the Party which the State requires regardless of the actual beliefs of the individual voter. As counsel for appellees conceded at oral argument, a requirement that independent voters merely notify state authorities of their intention to vote in the Party primary would be acceptable as an administrative measure, but "[t]he problem is that the State is insisting on a public act of affiliation . . . joining the Republican Party as a condition of this association."

for reasons of its own administrative convenience than it could on the same ground limit the ballot access of a new major party.

B

Appellant argues that § 9-431 is justified as a measure to prevent raiding, a practice "whereby voters in sympathy with one party designate themselves as voters of another party so as to influence or determine the results of the other party's primary." *Rosario.* While we have recognized that "a State may have a legitimate interest in seeking to curtail 'raiding,' since that practice may affect the integrity of the electoral process," *Kusper*; *Rosario*, that interest is not implicated here. The statute as applied to the Party's rule prevents independents, who otherwise cannot vote in any primary, from participating in the Republican primary. Yet a raid on the Republican Party primary by independent voters, a curious concept only distantly related to the type of raiding discussed in *Kusper* and *Rosario*, is not impeded by § 9-431; the independent raiders need only register as Republicans and vote in the primary. Indeed, under Conn.Gen.Stat. § 9-56 (1985), which permits an independent to affiliate with the Party as late as noon on the business day preceding the primary, the State's election statutes actually *assist* a "raid" by independents, which could be organized and implemented at the 11th hour. The State's asserted interest in the prevention of raiding provides no justification for the statute challenged here.

C

Appellant's next argument in support of § 9-431 is that the closed primary system avoids voter confusion. Appellant contends that "[t]he legislature could properly find that it would be difficult for the general public to understand what a candidate stood for who was nominated in part by an unknown amorphous body outside the party, while nevertheless using the party name." Appellees respond that the State is attempting to act as the ideological guarantor of the Republican Party's candidates, ensuring that voters are not misled by a "Republican" candidate who professes something other than what the State regards as true Republican principles.

As we have said, "[t]here can be no question about the legitimacy of the State's interest in fostering informed and educated expressions of the popular will in a general election." *Anderson v. Celebrezze*, 460 U.S. 780 (1983). To the extent that party labels provide a shorthand designation of the views of party candidates on matters of public concern, the identification of candidates with particular parties plays a role in the process by which voters inform themselves for the exercise of the franchise. Appellant's argument depends upon the belief that voters can be "misled" by party labels. But "[o]ur cases reflect a greater faith in the ability of individual voters to inform themselves about campaign issues." *Id.* Moreover, appellant's concern that candidates selected under the Party rule will be the nominees of an "amorphous" group using the Party's name is inconsistent with the facts. The Party is not proposing that independents be allowed to choose the Party's nominee without Party participation; on the contrary, to be listed on the Party's primary ballot continues to require, under a statute not challenged here, that the primary candidate have obtained at least 20% of the vote at a Party convention, which only Party members may attend. Conn. Gen. Stat. § 9-400 (1985). If no such candidate seeks to challenge the convention's nominee in a primary, then no primary is held, and the convention nominee becomes the Party's nominee in the general election without any intervention by independent voters. Even assuming, however, that putative candidates defeated at the Party convention will have an increased incentive under the Party's rule to make primary challenges, hoping to attract more substantial support from independents than from Party delegates, the requirement that such challengers garner substantial minority support at the convention greatly attenuates the State's concern that the ultimate nominee will be wedded to the Party in nothing more than a marriage of convenience.

In arguing that the Party rule interferes with educated decisions by voters, appellant also disregards the substantial benefit which the Party rule provides to the Party and its members in seeking to choose successful candidates. Given the numerical strength of independent voters in the State, one of the questions most likely to occur to Connecticut Republicans in selecting candidates for public office is how can the Party most effectively appeal to the independent voter? By inviting independents to assist in the choice at the polls between primary candidates selected at the Party convention, the Party rule is intended to produce the candidate and platform most likely to achieve that goal. The state statute is said to decrease voter confusion, yet it deprives the Party and its members of the opportunity to inform themselves as to the level of support for the Party's candidates among a critical group of electors. "A State's claim that it is enhancing the ability of its citizenry to make wise decisions by restricting the flow of information to them must be viewed with some skepticism." *Anderson*. The State's legitimate interests in preventing voter confusion and providing for educated and responsible voter decisions in no respect "make it necessary to burden the [Party's] rights." *Id.*

D

Finally, appellant contends that § 9-431 furthers the State's compelling interest in protecting the integrity of the two-party system and the responsibility of party government. Appellant argues vigorously and at length that the closed primary system chosen by the state legislature promotes responsiveness by elected officials and strengthens the effectiveness of the political parties.

The relative merits of closed and open primaries have been the subject of substantial debate since the beginning of this century, and no consensus has as yet emerged.[11] Appellant invokes a long and distinguished line of political scientists and public officials who have been supporters of the closed primary. But our role is not

---

11. At the present time, 21 States provide for "closed" primaries of the classic sort, in which the primary voter must be registered as a member of the party for some period of time prior to the holding of the primary election. Sixteen States allow a voter previously unaffiliated with any party to vote in a party primary if he affiliates with the party at the time of, or for the purpose of, voting in the primary. Four States provide for nonpartisan primaries in which all registered voters may

to decide whether the state legislature was acting wisely in enacting the closed primary system in 1955, or whether the Republican Party makes a mistake in seeking to depart from the practice of the past 30 years.[12]

We have previously recognized the danger that "splintered parties and unrestrained factionalism may do significant damage to the fabric of government." *Storer v. Brown*, 415 U.S. 724 (1974). We upheld a California statute which denied access to the ballot to any independent candidate who had voted in a party primary or been registered as a member of a political party within one year prior to the immediately preceding primary election. We said:

> [T]he one-year disaffiliation provision furthers the State's interest in the stability of its political system. We also consider that interest as not only permissible, but compelling and as outweighing the interest the candidate and his supporters may have in making a late rather than an early decision to seek independent ballot status.

The statute in *Storer* was designed to protect the parties and the party system against the disorganizing effect of independent candidacies launched by unsuccessful putative party nominees. This protection, like that accorded to parties threatened by raiding in *Rosario*, is undertaken to prevent the disruption of the political parties from without, and not, as in this case, to prevent the parties from taking internal steps affecting their own process for the selection of candidates. The forms of regulation upheld in *Storer* and *Rosario* imposed certain burdens upon the protected First and Fourteenth Amendment interests of some individuals, both voters and potential candidates, in order to protect the interests of others. In the present case, the state statute is defended on the ground that it protects the integrity of the Party against the Party itself.

Under these circumstances, the views of the State, which to some extent represent the views of the one political party transiently enjoying majority power, as to the optimum methods for preserving party integrity lose much of their force. The State argues that its statute is well designed to save the Republican Party from undertaking a course of conduct destructive of its own interests. But on this point "even if the State were correct, a State, or a court, may not constitutionally substitute its own judgment for that of the Party." *La Follette*. The Party's determination of the boundaries of its own association, and of the structure which best allows it to pursue its political goals, is protected by the Constitution. "And as is true of all expressions of

---

participate, while nine States have adopted classical "open" primaries, in which all registered voters may choose in which party primary to vote.

12. We note that appellant's direst predictions about destruction of the integrity of the election process and decay of responsible party government are not borne out by the experience of the 29 States which have chosen to permit more substantial openness in their primary systems than Connecticut has permitted heretofore.

First Amendment freedoms, the courts may not interfere on the ground that they view a particular expression as unwise or irrational." *Id.*[13]

We conclude that the State's enforcement, under these circumstances, of its closed primary system burdens the First Amendment rights of the Party. The interests which the appellant adduces in support of the statute are insubstantial, and accordingly the statute, as applied to the Party in this case, is unconstitutional.

IV

[In Part IV, the Court considered and rejected a different defense of the statute, based on provisions in the Constitution requiring that the qualifications for voters be the same in elections for Congress as they are for voters in elections for the more numerous branch of the state legislature. Art. 1, § 2; Seventeenth Amendment. The state argued that since the Republican Party rule allowed independents to vote in congressional but not state legislative primaries, different qualifications for voting in the two types of election were being imposed, contrary to the dictate of the Constitution. The Court agreed with the state that the constitutional provisions apply to voter qualifications in primaries as well as in general elections, but concluded that the Constitution was intended to prevent congressional voter qualifications from being *more* restrictive than the qualifications for state legislative voting but not to prevent *less* restrictive qualifications. Justice Stevens, in an opinion joined by Justice Scalia, dissented from this latter conclusion.]

V

We conclude that § 9-431 impermissibly burdens the rights of the Party and its members protected by the First and Fourteenth Amendments. The interests asserted by appellant in defense of the statute are insubstantial. The judgment of the Court of Appeals is

Affirmed.

Justice SCALIA, with whom THE CHIEF JUSTICE and Justice O'CONNOR join, dissenting....

In my view, the Court's opinion exaggerates the importance of the associational interest at issue, if indeed it does not see one where none exists. There is no question here of restricting the Republican Party's ability to recruit and enroll Party

---

13. Our holding today does not establish that state regulation of primary voting qualifications may never withstand challenge by a political party or its membership. A party seeking, for example, to open its primary to all voters, including members of other parties, would raise a different combination of considerations. Under such circumstances, the effect of one party's broadening of participation would threaten other parties with the disorganization effects which the statutes in *Storer* and *Rosario* were designed to prevent. We have observed on several occasions that a State may adopt a "policy of confining each voter to a single nominating act," a policy decision which is not involved in the present case. See *Anderson*; *Storer*. The analysis of these situations derives much from the particular facts involved....

members by offering them the ability to select Party candidates; Conn. Gen. Stat. § 9-56 (1985) permits an independent voter to join the Party as late as the day before the primary. Nor is there any question of restricting the ability of the Party's members to select whatever candidate they desire. Appellees' only complaint is that the Party cannot leave the selection of its candidate to persons who are not members of the Party, and are unwilling to become members. It seems to me fanciful to refer to this as an interest in freedom of association between the members of the Republican Party and the putative independent voters. The Connecticut voter who, while steadfastly refusing to register as a Republican, casts a vote in the Republican primary, forms no more meaningful an "association" with the Party than does the independent or the registered Democrat who responds to questions by a Republican Party pollster. If the concept of freedom of association is extended to such casual contacts, it ceases to be of any analytic use. . . .

The ability of the members of the Republican Party to select their own candidate, on the other hand, unquestionably implicates an associational freedom—but it can hardly be thought that that freedom is unconstitutionally impaired here. The Party is entirely free to put forward, if it wishes, that candidate who has the highest degree of support among Party members and independents combined. The State is under no obligation, however, to let its party primary be used, instead of a party-funded opinion poll, as the means by which the party identifies the relative popularity of its potential candidates among independents. Nor is there any reason apparent to me why the State cannot insist that this decision to support what might be called the independents' choice be taken *by the party membership in a democratic fashion*, rather than through a process that permits the members' votes to be diluted—and perhaps even absolutely outnumbered—by the votes of outsiders.

The Court's opinion characterizes this, disparagingly, as an attempt to "protec[t] the integrity of the Party against the Party itself." There are two problems with this characterization. The first, and less important, is that it is not true. We have no way of knowing that a majority of the Party's members is in favor of allowing ultimate selection of its candidates for federal and statewide office to be determined by persons outside the Party. That decision was not made by democratic ballot, but by the Party's state convention—which, for all we know, may have been dominated by officeholders and office seekers whose evaluation of the merits of assuring election of the Party's candidates, vis-à-vis the merits of proposing candidates faithful to the Party's political philosophy, diverged significantly from the views of the Party's rank and file. I had always thought it was a major purpose of state-imposed party primary requirements to protect the general party membership against this sort of minority control. Second and more important, however, *even if* it were the fact that the majority of the Party's members wanted its candidates to be determined by outsiders, there is no reason why the State is bound to honor that desire—any more than it would be bound to honor a party's democratically expressed desire that its candidates henceforth be selected by convention rather than by primary, or by the party's executive committee in a smoke-filled room. In other words, the validity of the state-imposed primary requirement itself, which we have hitherto considered "too plain for argument," *American Party of Texas v. White*, 415 U.S. 767 (1974), presupposes that the State *has* the right "to protect the Party against the Party itself." Connecticut may lawfully require that significant elements of the democratic election process be democratic — whether the Party wants that or not. It is beyond my understanding why the Republican Party's delegation of its democratic choice to a Republican Convention can be proscribed, but its delegation of that choice to nonmembers of the Party cannot.

In the case before us, Connecticut has said no more than this: Just as the Republican Party may, if it wishes, nominate the candidate recommended by the Party's executive committee, so long as its members select that candidate by name in a democratic vote; so also it may nominate the independents' choice, so long as its members select him by name in a democratic vote. That seems to me plainly and entirely constitutional.

I respectfully dissent.

Notes and Questions

1. Connecticut law was changed to allow the parties to open their primaries to nonmembers, but the rules of both major parties now allow only registered members to vote. See Elizabeth Garrett, *Is the Party Over? Courts and the Political Process*, 2002 Supreme Court Review 95, 120.

2. Suppose state law requires the selection of nominees for state office by party primary, but the leaders of one of the major parties decide they would prefer to select the party's nominees by means of a state convention. The party therefore brings an action challenging the statutory requirement that the party choose its nominees in primary elections. What result? See generally Stephen E. Gottlieb, *Rebuilding the Right of Association: The Right to Hold a Convention as a Test Case*, 11 Hofstra Law Review 191 (1982). Relying on dicta in a number of Supreme Court cases, Professor Hasen has argued that Congress could well have the constitutional power to require states to use primaries rather than caucuses or conventions to choose party presidential nominees. Richard L. Hasen,*"Too Plain for Argument?" The Uncertain Congressional Power to Require Parties to Choose Presidential Nominees Through Direct and Equal Primaries*, 102 Northwestern University Law Review 2009 (2008). The Ninth Circuit, relying on the same dicta, held that a minor party in Alaska could be required to use a primary rather than a convention to choose its party nominees for state offices. *Alaskan Independence Party v. State of Alaska*, 545 F.3d 1173 (9th Cir. 2008),

3. The Elections Clause, Article I, § 4, cl. 1 of the United States Constitution, referred to in *Tashjian*, provides:

> The times, places and manner of holding elections for Senators and Representatives, shall be prescribed in each state by the legislature thereof; but the Congress may at any time by law make or alter such regulations. . . .

If Congress passed a law requiring that party nominations in congressional elections be determined by nominating conventions, could the law be enforced over the objection of a state party that preferred to select its nominees in primaries? Would it matter in this dispute whether the state statutes provided for primaries, provided for conventions, or were silent? Would the result be different in the opposite case: Congress requires primaries, and a state party prefers nominating conventions? If a federal statute required that only persons registered in the party be permitted to vote in congressional primaries, would this requirement be enforceable against the Republican Party of Connecticut?

4. Suppose the Democratic Party of Connecticut decided to adopt the same rule as the Republicans. In that event, registered Democrats would vote only in the Democratic primary, registered Republicans would vote only in the Republican primary, and independent voters would be permitted to vote in whichever party's primary they chose at any given election. This type of primary is described as "semi-closed," as we shall see shortly in connection with *Clingman v. Beaver.* What incentive would a voter have to register as a party member under this system? Does the state have a legitimate interest in encouraging voters to affiliate with parties? Is the political system better off if voters are so encouraged?

If the open primary validated in *Tashjian* had the effect of weakening the party system by reducing incentives for voters to affiliate with parties, should a supporter of strong parties accept this setback as the price of the increased associational freedom *Tashjian* recognizes in parties? On the whole, how are parties likely to use such associational freedom? Will the choices they make be more or less likely than choices made by state legislatures to promote a stronger party system?

5. The Court relied on *Tashjian* in *Eu v. San Francisco County Democratic Central Committee*, 489 U.S. 214 (1989), to strike down numerous California statutes regulating parties. One of the statutes prohibited the parties from endorsing candidates in primaries.

Recall the view of political scientists, summarized in Part I, that parties consist of at least three parts: the party in the electorate, the party in elective office, and the party organization. Why should the latter of these be able to speak for the party in endorsing candidates in the primary? If the party organization really does speak for the party, what is the point in holding the primary at all? Would a statute be constitutional that permitted state and county central committees to endorse candidates and to publicize those endorsements, but required that such publicity refer to the endorsement as that of the committee, not of the party? Consider footnote 19 of the Justice Marshall's opinion for the Court in *Eu*:

> The State suggested at oral argument that the endorsement ban prevents fraud by barring party officials from misrepresenting that they speak for the party. To the extent that the State suggests that only the primary election results can constitute a party endorsement, it confuses an endorsement

from the official governing bodies that may influence election results with the results themselves....

The other statutes struck down in *Eu* were detailed provisions for internal governance of the parties, dealing with such matters as the term of office for party chairs. In the California Elections Code, there were separate chapters setting governance rules and procedures for each of the two major parties, as well as for certain of the minor parties. The practice in California was that Democrats would go along with any changes the Republican members of the legislature wanted to make in the Republican chapter, and vice versa. The plaintiffs in *Eu* were a handful of county central committees, candidates, and party activists. At their behest, the Court struck down the statutes that had been enacted by the parties' elected representatives in the legislature. The Court did so to protect the parties' freedom of association. As between the plaintiffs in *Eu* and the elected legislators from either the Democratic or Republican Party, which had a better claim to speak for the party? For criticism of *Tashjian* and *Eu*, see Daniel Hays Lowenstein, *Associational Rights of Major Political Parties: A Skeptical Inquiry*, 71 Texas Law Review 1741 (1993).

6. *Rosario v. Rockefeller*, 410 U.S. 752 (1973), and *Kusper v. Pontikes*, 414 U.S. 51 (1973), both involved waiting periods before voters who switched parties could vote in the primary of their new party. In *Rosario*, voters challenged a New York requirement that in order to vote in a party's primary, they must affiliate with the party 30 days before the previous general election. For example, a Republican voter who wanted to switch to the Democratic Party would have to have enrolled as a Democrat by early October of an election year in order to vote in the next Democratic primary held in the state. The Court upheld this long waiting period, in part because it protected parties against "raiding" by supporters of an opposing party. Raiding would occur if there were an uncontested primary in Party *A* and supporters of Party *A* therefore decided to vote in the primary of Party *B*, where their votes might prove decisive. Because few voters could anticipate this situation prior to the preceding general election, the waiting period was expected to make raiding impossible. However, this anti-raiding purpose was insufficient to justify Illinois' longer waiting period of 23 months in *Kusper*. Illinois conducted primaries each year, so that the 23-month waiting period meant that voters who wished to switch parties would have to go through at least one primary election without being able to vote within either party. The Court regarded this denial of the right to vote as unnecessary and as outweighing the state's anti-raiding purpose.

No political party participated as a litigant in either *Rosario* or *Kusper*. Yet the Court was willing to assume that the statutes being challenged were intended to protect the associational integrity of the political parties. Why shouldn't the same assumption be made in *Eu*? The obvious answer would seem to be that in disputes like *Rosario* and *Kusper* between individual voters and the state it can be assumed that the state is in accord with the wishes of the parties, but that this assumption would obviously be inappropriate in a dispute such as *Eu* between one or more parties and the state. But on what basis can we characterize *Eu* as a dispute between the major parties and the state? Recall that neither the Democratic nor the Republican State Central Committee was a plaintiff. Even if the state committees had been plaintiffs, why should the "party organization" be regarded as speaking for "the Democratic Party" or "the Republican Party" more than the Democratic and Republican elected officials who enacted the statutes under attack?

7. Under *Tashjian,* states may not bar independents from *voting* in a party primary when the party wants them to be able to participate. But what about a state bar on independents *running as candidates* in a party primary, when the party wants those independents to be able to run? In *State of Alaska v. Alaska Democratic Party,* 426 P.3d 901 (2018), the Alaska Supreme Court held that such a law violates the party's freedom of association. Applying a balancing test, the Alaska Supreme Court found that the law imposed a "substantial" burden on the party's rights. It then applied strict scrutiny, requiring that the law be narrowly tailored to the state's compelling interests. The court rejected the state's proffered interests in ensuring public support for the Democratic Party, ensuring that candidates have strong public support, and preventing voter confusion, and therefore held that the state-imposed burden on the party's associational rights was unjustified. Isn't it reasonable to require that people running for office as a nominee of a political party be a member of that party? Should it matter that the party alleging a violation of its associational rights (the Alaska Democratic Party) is the minority party in the state?

2. *The Scope of the Right*

In 1996, California voters approved an initiative measure, Proposition 198, over the opposition of Democratic and Republican party leaders as well as several minor parties. Proposition 198 changed California's historic closed primary to a form of open primary known as a "blanket primary." In the usual open primary, voters may select a ballot of whichever party they choose, but must vote in that party's primary for each office. In a blanket primary, the voter may vote in one party's primary for one office and a different party's primary for another office. For example, in the 1998 California primary, many voters voted for a Democrat for governor and a Republican for U.S. senator, because the Republican nomination for governor and the Democratic nomination for senator were essentially uncontested.

The Democratic and Republican parties and two minor parties filed an action contending that under *Tashjian*, they could not be forced by state law to nominate their candidates through a blanket primary. The United States District Court and the Ninth Circuit upheld the imposition of the blanket primary on the parties, but the Supreme Court struck it down in *California Democratic Party v. Jones*, 530 U.S. 567 (2000).

Justice Scalia (who dissented in *Tashjian*) wrote for the Court:

> [We have not held] that the processes by which political parties select their nominees are, as respondents would have it, wholly public affairs that

States may regulate freely. To the contrary, we have continually stressed that when States regulate parties' internal processes they must act within limits imposed by the Constitution. See, *e.g., Eu; La Follette.* In this regard, respondents' reliance on *Smith v. Allwright* and *Terry v. Adams* is misplaced. In *Allwright,* we invalidated the Texas Democratic Party's rule limiting participation in its primary to whites; in *Terry,* we invalidated the same rule promulgated by the Jaybird Democratic Association, a "self-governing voluntary club." These cases held only that, when a State prescribes an election process that gives a special role to political parties, it "endorses, adopts and enforces the discrimination against Negroes," that the parties (or, in the case of the Jaybird Democratic Association, organizations that are "part and parcel" of the parties, (Clark, J., concurring)) bring into the process—so that the parties' discriminatory action becomes state action under the Fifteenth Amendment. They do not stand for the proposition that party affairs are public affairs, free of First Amendment protections—and our later holdings make that entirely clear. See, *e.g., Tashjian.* . . .

In no area is the political association's right to exclude more important than in the process of selecting its nominee. That process often determines the party's positions on the most significant public policy issues of the day, and even when those positions are predetermined it is the nominee who becomes the party's ambassador to the general electorate in winning it over to the party's views. . . .

Proposition 198 forces political parties to associate with—to have their nominees, and hence their positions, determined by—those who, at best, have refused to affiliate with the party, and, at worst, have expressly affiliated with a rival. In this respect, it is qualitatively different from a closed primary. Under that system, even when it is made quite easy for a voter to change his party affiliation the day of the primary, and thus, in some sense, to "cross over," at least he must formally *become a member of the party*; and once he does so, he is limited to voting for candidates of that party.[8]

[The Court cited statistics seeming to show that the votes of non-party members in major-party primaries could often be decisive.] The impact of voting by nonparty members is much greater upon minor parties, such as the Libertarian Party and the Peace and Freedom Party. In the first primaries these parties conducted following California's implementation of Proposition 198, the total votes cast for party candidates in some races was more than *double* the total number of *registered party members.* . . .

8. In this sense, the blanket primary also may be constitutionally distinct from the open primary, in which the voter is limited to one party's ballot. This case does not require us to determine the constitutionality of open primaries.

[T]he deleterious effects of Proposition 198 are not limited to altering the identity of the nominee. Even when the person favored by a majority of the party members prevails, he will have prevailed by taking somewhat different positions — and, should he be elected, will continue to take somewhat different positions in order to be renominated. As respondents' own expert concluded, "[t]he policy positions of Members of Congress elected from blanket primary states are . . . more moderate, both in an absolute sense and relative to the other party, and so are more reflective of the preferences of the mass of voters at the center of the ideological spectrum" (expert report of Elisabeth R. Gerber). It is unnecessary to cumulate evidence of this phenomenon, since, after all, the whole purpose of Proposition 198 was to favor nominees with "moderate" positions. It encourages candidates — and officeholders who hope to be renominated — to curry favor with persons whose views are more 'centrist' than those of the party base. In effect, Proposition 198 has simply moved the general election one step earlier in the process, at the expense of the parties' ability to perform the 'basic function' of choosing their own leaders. *Kusper*. . . .

In sum, Proposition 198 forces petitioners to adulterate their candidate-selection process — the "basic function of a political party" — by opening it up to persons wholly unaffiliated with the party. Such forced association has the likely outcome — indeed, in this case the intended outcome — of changing the parties' message. We can think of no heavier burden on a political party's associational freedom. Proposition 198 is therefore unconstitutional unless it is narrowly tailored to serve a compelling state interest. . . .

[The Court considered and rejected seven suggested state interests. One of these was] that the blanket primary is the only way to ensure that disenfranchised persons enjoy the right to an effective vote. By "disenfranchised," respondents do not mean those who cannot vote; they mean simply independents and members of the minority party in "safe" districts. These persons are disenfranchised, according to respondents, because under a closed primary they are unable to participate in what amounts to the determinative election — the majority party's primary; the only way to ensure they have an "effective" vote is to force the party to open its primary to them. This also appears to be nothing more than reformulation of an asserted state interest we have already rejected — recharacterizing nonparty members' keen desire to participate in selection of the party's nominee as "disenfranchisement" if that desire is not fulfilled. We have said, however, that a "nonmember's desire to participate in the party's affairs is overborne by the countervailing and legitimate right of the party to determine its own membership qualifications." *Tashjian*. The voter's desire to participate does not become more weighty simply because the State supports it. Moreover, even if it were accurate to describe the plight of the non-party-member in a safe district as "disenfranchisement," Proposition 198 is not needed to solve the problem. The voter who feels himself disenfranchised should simply join the party. That may put him to a hard choice, but it is not a state-imposed restriction upon his freedom of association, whereas compelling party members to accept his selection of their nominee is a state-imposed restriction upon theirs....

Finally, we may observe that even if all these state interests were compelling ones, Proposition 198 is not a narrowly tailored means of furthering them. Respondents could protect them all by resorting to a nonpartisan blanket primary. Generally speaking, under such a system, the State determines what qualifications it requires for a candidate to have a place on the primary ballot—which may include nomination by established parties and voter-petition requirements for independent candidates. Each voter, regardless of party affiliation, may then vote for any candidate, and the top two vote getters (or however many the State prescribes) then move on to the general election. This system has all the characteristics of the partisan blanket primary, save the constitutionally crucial one: Primary voters are not choosing a party's nominee.[z] Under a nonpartisan blanket primary, a State may ensure more choice, greater participation, increased "privacy," and a sense of "fairness"—all without severely burdening a political party's First Amendment right of association....

Justice Kennedy wrote a concurring opinion and Justices Stevens and Ginsburg dissented.

Notes and Questions

1. Was the result in *Jones* dictated by *Tashjian*?

2. Some of the language in Justice Scalia's opinion may give the impression that the Court's decision had the effect of striking down blanket primaries in the two additional states (Alaska and Washington) that then used them and of jeopardizing open primaries in the much larger number of states that use them. That impression is just as misleading as it would be to say that *Tashjian* jeopardizes closed primaries. What both decisions do is give the parties rather than the state legislatures the last word. However, the state legislature usually will provide for the type of primary favored by the major parties. *Tashjian* arose because the Democratic-controlled

z. Justice Scalia's statement that a nonpartisan primary has all the characteristics of a partisan blanket primary save that voters are not selecting a party's nominee may be misleading. The difference is by no means a conceptual one alone. In a nonpartisan primary, which is the electoral procedure followed in Louisiana, all candidates are running against each other in the primary. In a partisan blanket primary such as the one struck down in this case, Republican candidates run against Republicans, Democratic candidates against Democrats, and so on. Thus, in the partisan blanket primary, there will always be a general election with one candidate from each party. In a nonpartisan primary, as conducted in Louisiana and at the local level in many states, there will not be a general election if one candidate gets a majority of the votes in the primary. Even if there is a general (or run-off) election, the candidates might both be members of the same party.—Eds.

legislature refused to permit the Republicans to modify their primary. *Jones* arose because of an initiative. Thus, not many states had to change their primary systems because of *Jones*.

3. Even in a blanket primary, Republicans run against Republicans and Democrats run against Democrats for their parties' nominations. As is discussed in *Jones*, Louisiana goes one step further, by eliminating even this feature from primary elections. In Louisiana, all candidates from all parties run against each other, and if one gets a majority of the vote, he or she is elected. If no candidate gets a majority, there is a run-off between the two top vote-getters, even if they are both from the same party.

The Louisiana system has run into a snag as applied to congressional elections. Its "primary," or first-round election, is held in October. The run-off is held on the Tuesday following the first Monday in November, which is required to be the date for federal elections by 2 U.S.C. §§1 and 7. However, the Supreme Court ruled that the possibility of a candidate being elected in the primary violates the statutory requirement of a uniform nationwide date for electing the members of Congress. *Foster v. Love*, 522 U.S. 67 (1997).

4. Professor Hasen criticized *Jones* in *Do the Parties or the People Own the Electoral Process?*, 149 University of Pennsylvania Law Review 815 (2001). Hasen maintains that parties' right to control their internal affairs is protected by the First Amendment, but that nominating candidates is not an internal matter. "Rather, primaries are a means for voters to structure the electoral process by winnowing down candidates to a list of finalists to run in the general election. Voters through the initiative process or the state legislature should be allowed to dictate the form of that winnowing process...." He argues that if members of party organizations object to losing control of the nomination process to voters, their real complaint is with the direct primary itself, not with the particular form of the blanket primary. "Yet," he points out, "the Supreme Court in *Jones* rejected the idea that the direct primary is unconstitutional...." Finally, he questions the empirical premises put forth by opponents of the blanket primary:

> The evidence we have on the effect of the form in which primary elections are held on the strength of parties does not demonstrate that parties are in great danger from more open primaries. Despite the existence of the blanket primary in the State of Washington for many years, the Republican Party there is among the strongest party organizations in the nation. More generally, during the same period that almost half of the states had open or blanket primaries, party cohesion in Congress reached high levels unprecedented in American history. It appears that the openness of the primaries has not caused candidates to become so moderate that they cannot engage in party-line voting most of the time.

An even broader attack on the Court's application of the First Amendment to political parties is contained in Gregory P. Magarian, *Regulating Political Parties Under a "Public Rights" First Amendment*, 44 William & Mary Law Review 1939 (2003).

What effect does the Court's strong commitment to parties' associational rights, evident in *Jones*, have on political discourse more generally? James Gardner argues that the expressive association cases are founded in the responsible party model, which prescribes a "highly circumscribed role . . . in the electoral process for engagement and persuasion of individual voters":

> According to the model, democracy does not consist in unconstrained reflection and deliberation by the people followed by a popular choice among candidates competing to do the people's bidding. It involves instead something much less: unconstrained reflection and deliberation by political elites, organized by competing parties, followed by approval or disapproval by the electorate of the parties' proposed political programs. . . . An election, on this view, is not—or certainly need not be—an occasion for serious public reflection, deliberation, and debate; it is instead nothing more than a very gross kind of referendum on the performance of the party currently in power.

James A. Gardner, What Are Campaigns for? The Role of Persuasion in Electoral Law and Politics 64 (2009). Is Gardner right about the limited function that elections serve? Can they realistically be expected to do more? How much of this is attributable to the associational rights that the Court has conferred on parties under the First Amendment?

Bruce E. Cain has defended *Jones* in *Party Autonomy and Two Party Electoral Competition*, 149 University of Pennsylvania Law Review 793 (2001):

> As decades of political science research amply demonstrates, the party label has enormous informational value—indeed since a majority of the electorate tends to vote predictably along the lines of party label, it is the most important resource that the party possesses. Giving up control of that label is a significant blow to the party's capacity to determine its nominees. . . .

Cain believes that the threat to the party's control of its nominations is real:

> Studies of the 1998 California primary revealed two main types of strategic voters: hedgers who had no competitive race in their own primary and therefore voted for the most preferred candidate in another party's primary (thereby ensuring that they at least get their second favorite candidate in November), and raiders/saboteurs who voted for the weakest candidate in order to help their own party's candidate in the fall. While the number of raiders/saboteurs is small and the total number of strategic voters will normally be less than the total number of sincere crossover voters, it is clear that a party's nomination in the spring may be determined by a significant number of voters who will not support the nominee in November. This raises serious questions about the authenticity and legitimacy of party nominees made under a blanket system and about the system's vulnerability to strategic manipulation.

For additional commentary on this subject, see Samuel Issacharoff, *Political Parties with Public Purposes: Political Parties, Associational Freedoms, and Partisan Competition*, 101 Columbia Law Review 274 (2001); Nathaniel Persily, *Toward a Functional Defense of Political Party Autonomy*, 76 New York University Law Review 750 (2001). For empirical studies of the blanket primary, see Voting at the Political Fault Line: California's Experiment with the Blanket this Primary (Bruce E. Cain & Elisabeth R. Gerber, eds., 2002).

5. One of the arguments for an open primary is that it might reduce polarization. Allowing non-party members to participate in the primary process could, on this theory, result in more moderate voters participating and more moderate candidates making it to the general election. However, there is little evidence that opening primaries will decrease polarization. Eric McGhee, Seth Masket, Boris Shor, Steven Rogers & Nolan McCarty, *A Primary Cause of Partisanship? Nomination Systems and Legislator Ideology*, 58 American Journal of Political Science 337 (2014).

Oklahoma uses a "semiclosed" primary. Only members of a party may vote in primaries, unless the party permits independent voters to participate. In *Clingman v. Beaver*, 544 U.S. 581 (2005), the Court rejected a challenge to these rules brought by the Libertarian Party, which wanted to allow any voters, including those who were members of other parties, to vote in its primaries.[aa]

Writing for a plurality that included Chief Justice Rehnquist and Justices Kennedy and Scalia, Justice Thomas wrote that there was no real "association" being denied by the Oklahoma rules, because any of the voters who wanted to significantly associate with the Libertarians were free to do so by disaffiliating from their other party. Alternatively, if there was a burden on association, it was a minimal one.

In the rest of Justice Thomas's opinion he spoke for the Court, as he was joined by Justices O'Connor and Breyer.[bb] He rejected the plaintiffs' reliance on *Tashjian*, writing that:

> As our cases since *Tashjian* have clarified, strict scrutiny is appropriate only if the burden is severe. In *Tashjian* itself, independent voters could join the Connecticut Republican Party as late as the day before the primary. As explained above, requiring voters to register with a party prior to participating in the party's primary minimally burdens voters' associational rights.

Justice Thomas also said *Tashjian* was distinguishable, primarily on the obvious ground that in *Clingman*, unlike *Tashjian*, the state was not requiring voters to

---

aa. The plaintiffs also included Republican and Democratic voters who wanted to vote in the Libertarian primary.

bb. There was a procedural issue in the case, not discussed here, on which Justice Breyer declined to join the majority.

register as Libertarians in order to vote in the Libertarian primary. Is *Tashjian* a viable precedent after *Clingman*?

The foregoing reasoning led Justice Thomas to the conclusion that because of the lack of a severe burden on associational rights, strict scrutiny was not compelled. Several government interests justified the restrictions under less severe scrutiny. First was the state's interest in preserving the parties as "visible and identifiable interest groups." Allowing members of other parties to vote could result in the nomination of candidates out of accord with the preference of Libertarian members. Although the party might be willing to take this risk in exchange for possible electoral benefit, the state had an interest in avoiding confusion. The state could believe democracy would be facilitated when voters classify themselves by party affiliations. Removing the connection between affiliation and voting in primaries could disrupt that system.

Second, the state could seek to facilitate efficient campaigning and party-building, which would be difficult without advance identification of which voters were likely to vote in the party's primary. Third, the state could seek to prevent party switching, or what political scientists call "strategic voting" (i.e., a vote cast for a candidate in order to give another candidate or party a tactical advantage). For example, if there were no competitive race in the Democratic Party, some Democrats might vote in the Libertarian Primary to try to nominate a candidate they thought would draw Republican votes in the general election.

In a concurring opinion, joined in part by Justice Breyer, Justice O'Connor wrote that when the state prohibits a party from allowing voters to participate in its primaries it implicates important associational interests. But she agreed with the Court that these interests were not seriously burdened in the Oklahoma case. Justice Stevens, joined by Justices Ginsburg and Souter, dissented.

The most recent case in the line beginning with *Tashjian* is *Washington State Grange v. Washington State Republican Party*, 552 U.S. 442 (2008). Since 1935, Washington had been using blanket primaries similar to the one struck down in *California Democratic Party v. Jones*, *supra*. That case gave parties the right to opt out of a mandatory blanket primary, and the parties in Washington rapidly exercised that option.[cc] You will recall that in *Jones*, the Court suggested a "less restrictive alternative" that states could use, a nonpartisan blanket primary. This device, which has been used in Louisiana, consists of primary elections that avoid party nominations altogether. As it works in Louisiana, all candidates for an office appear on the ballot in the primary. Any candidate who receives a majority of votes is elected. If no candidate gets a majority, the two top candidates oppose each other in the general election, which is a run-off election. Typically, these two candidates would be a Democrat and a Republican, but they might be two Democrats or two Republicans, and occasionally they might include an independent or a member of a third party.

cc. See *Democratic Party of Washington State v. Reed*, 343 F.3d 1198 (2003).

Because the candidates are not categorized by party, the primary does not result in any official party nominees, even if it does result in a run-off between one candidate who is a Republican and one who is a Democrat.

If Washington had adopted the Louisiana system, apparently it would have had clear sailing. Instead, an initiative approved by Washington's voters, called I-872, adopted what the state called a nonpartisan blanket primary system, but with a partisan wrinkle. Candidates can list a "party preference" on the ballot.[dd] The parties objected to the system on the ground that if the name of a party appeared next to each candidate's name on the ballot, the primaries would for all practical purposes result in a party nomination so far as most voters would be concerned. The party would thus end up with a *de facto* nominee selected in part by voters with no affiliation with the party, which under *Jones* is what the parties are entitled to object to.[ee] The Ninth Circuit accepted this argument and ruled that the parties were entitled to opt out of the system.

The Supreme Court, in an opinion by Justice Thomas, upheld the Washington system against a facial challenge. "The State has had no opportunity to implement I-872, and its courts have had no occasion to construe the law in the context of actual disputes arising from the electoral context, or to accord the law a limiting construction to avoid constitutional questions." Facial challenges are disfavored, in part because they "often rest on speculation."

The Court did not accept the parties' and the Ninth Circuit's contention that candidates in the general election would be *de facto* party nominees.

> The flaw in this argument is that, unlike the California primary [in *Jones*], the I-872 primary does not, by its terms, choose parties' nominees. The essence of nomination — the choice of a party representative — does not occur under I-872. The law never refers to the candidates as nominees of any party, nor does it treat them as such.... The top two candidates from the primary election proceed to the general election regardless of their party preferences.

The Court added in a footnote:

> It is true that parties may no longer indicate their nominees on the ballot, but that is unexceptionable: The First Amendment does not give political parties a right to have their nominees designated as such on the ballot. Parties do not gain such a right simply because the State affords candidates the opportunity to indicate their party preferences on the ballot.

---

dd. Another difference between the Louisiana and Washington systems was that in Washington, the two top candidates run against each other in the general election, even if one of them won a majority in the primary. This difference is not material to the constitutional question.

ee. Indeed, there was not even a requirement that candidates be members of the party they listed as their "party preference."

The Court continued:

> Respondents counter that, even if the I-872 primary does not actually choose parties' nominees, it nevertheless burdens their associational rights because voters will assume that candidates on the general election ballot are the nominees of their preferred parties. This brings us to the heart of respondents' case—and to the fatal flaw in their argument. At bottom, respondents' objection to I-872 is that voters will be confused by candidates' party-preference designations. Respondents' arguments are largely variations on this theme. Thus, they argue that even if voters do not assume that candidates on the general election ballot are the nominees of their parties, they will at least assume that the parties associate with, and approve of, them. This, they say, compels them to associate with candidates they do not endorse, alters the messages they wish to convey, and forces them to engage in counterspeech to disassociate themselves from the candidates and their positions on the issues.
>
> We reject each of these contentions for the same reason: They all depend, not on any facial requirement of I-872, but on the possibility that voters will be confused as to the meaning of the party-preference designation. But respondents' assertion that voters will misinterpret the party-preference designation is sheer speculation. It "depends upon the belief that voters can be 'misled' by party labels...."
>
> Of course, it is *possible* that voters will misinterpret the candidates' party-preference designations as reflecting endorsement by the parties. But these cases involve a facial challenge, and we cannot strike down I-872 on its face based on the mere possibility of voter confusion. Because respondents brought their suit as a facial challenge, we have no evidentiary record against which to assess their assertions that voters will be confused. Indeed, because I-872 has never been implemented, we do not even have ballots indicating how party preference will be displayed. It stands to reason that whether voters will be confused by the party-preference designations will depend in significant part on the form of the ballot....
>
> As long as we are speculating about the form of the ballot—and we can do no more than speculate in this facial challenge—we must, in fairness to the voters of the State of Washington who enacted I-872 and in deference to the executive and judicial officials who are charged with implementing it, ask whether the ballot could conceivably be printed in such a way as to eliminate the possibility of widespread voter confusion and with it the perceived threat to the First Amendment.
>
> It is not difficult to conceive of such a ballot. For example, petitioners propose that the actual I-872 ballot could include prominent disclaimers explaining that party preference reflects only the self-designation of the

> candidate and not an official endorsement by the party. They also suggest that the ballots might note preference in the form of a candidate statement that emphasizes the candidate's personal determination rather than the party's acceptance of the candidate, such as "my party preference is the Republican Party." Additionally, the State could decide to educate the public about the new primary ballots through advertising or explanatory materials mailed to voters along with their ballots. We are satisfied that there are a variety of ways in which the State could implement I-872 that would eliminate any real threat of voter confusion. And without the specter of widespread voter confusion, respondents' arguments about forced association and compelled speech fall flat....
>
> Because we have concluded that I-872 does not severely burden respondents, the State need not assert a compelling interest. The State's asserted interest in providing voters with relevant information about the candidates on the ballot is easily sufficient to sustain I-872.

Chief Justice Roberts, joined by Justice Alito, added a concurring opinion. Justice Scalia, joined by Justice Kennedy, dissented.

Notes and Questions

1. If you were an attorney advising the Washington officials charged with implementing I-872, how would you advise them to proceed? Suppose what may or may not be true, that the groups supporting I-872 want the Washington primaries to be as close as possible to the former partisan blanket primaries that Washington conducted from 1935 until *Jones*. In other words, suppose these groups *do* want the surviving Democratic and Republican candidates in the general election to be *de facto* nominees of their parties. If you were counsel to those groups and you were consulted about what their lobbying efforts on the implementation of I-872 should be directed toward, how would you advise them?

After the Supreme Court decision, Washington implemented 1-872 by including the following disclaimer on its ballot:

> READ: Each candidate for partisan office may state a political party that he or she prefers. A candidate's preference does not imply that the candidate is nominated or endorsed by the party, or that the party approves of or associates with that candidate.

Wash. Admin. Code § 434-230-015(4)(a). In addition, the ballot indicates candidates' preferences with "(Prefers Democratic Party)" or "(Prefers Republican Party)," instead of just "R" or "D." The state mails explanatory materials to all voters, indicating that candidates may state their party preference, but that this does not imply endorsement by the parties.

On remand in *Washington State Grange*, the federal district court upheld the constitutionality of I-872's implementation, concluding that it "eliminate[d] the possibility of widespread confusion among the reasonable, well-informed electorate."

2011 WL 92032 (W.D. Wash. 2011). The Ninth Circuit affirmed that I-872 as implemented did not violates the parties' rights. 676 F.3d 784 (9th Cir. 2012).

2. One aspect of *Washington State Grange* that is worth considering is its formalism. At least for purposes of a facial challenge, the Court is unreceptive to claims of the *de facto* effect of I-872. Rather, the law is taken on its own terms, which do not include the concept of party nomination, whatever the actual political effect of the system created by the law may be. Formalism also seemed conspicuous in another election law case the Supreme Court decided in the same term, *New York State Board of Elections v. López Torres*, 552 U.S. 196 (2008). In *López Torres*, plaintiffs objected to the system for party nominations of candidates for the New York Supreme Court, which despite its name is a trial court of general jurisdiction. The judicial candidates are nominated through a complex system of election of delegates to nominating conventions. The Second Circuit struck down the system on the ground that, as a practical matter, it assured party insiders almost complete control of the nominating process. As in *Washington State Grange*, the *López Torres* Court overruled the lower court and upheld the nominating system, offering a formalist reliance on the system "on paper" rather than on the system's practical effects. Here, Justice Scalia, who dissented in *Washington State Grange*, wrote for the Court:[ff]

> Our cases invalidating ballot-access requirements have focused on the requirements themselves, and not on the manner in which political actors function under those requirements. Here respondents complain not of the state law, but of the voters' (and their elected delegates') preference for the choices of the party leadership.
>
> To be sure, we have . . . permitted States to set their faces against "party bosses" by requiring party-candidate selection through processes more favorable to insurgents, such as primaries. But to say that the State can require this is a far cry from saying that the Constitution demands it. None of our cases establishes that an individual's constitutional right is to have a "fair shot" at winning the party's nomination. And with good reason. What constitutes a "fair shot" is a reasonable enough question for legislative judgment, which we will accept so long as it does not too much infringe upon the party's associational rights. But it is hardly a manageable constitutional question for judges — especially for judges in our legal system, where traditional electoral practice gives no hint of even the existence, much less the content, of a constitutional requirement of a "fair shot" at party nomination.

Do *Washington State Grange* and *López Torres* embody election law formalism? If so, is that a good or a bad thing?

3. One of the arguments for a "top two" primary like that upheld in *Washington State Grange* is that it could mitigate political polarization. The theory is that

---

ff. The Court was unanimous on the result but Justice Kennedy, joined in part by Justice Breyer, concurred in the result only.

moderate candidates are more likely to make it out of a top two primary than a traditional party primary. A recent study, however, finds mixed evidence on whether a top two primary system actually promotes moderation. Eric McGee & Boris Shor, *Has the Top Two Primary Elected More Moderates?*, 15 Perspectives on Politics 1053 (2017). Looking at California and Washington, two states which use a top-two primary, the authors find an "inconsistent effect." There was greater evidence of moderation in California than in Washington, but that could be explained by a contemporaneous policy change: the use of an independent redistricting commission to draw district lines, which resulted in more competitive districts. For an overview of research, finding that congressional primaries have a modest impact in driving polarization, see Lee Drutman, *What We Know about Congressional Primaries and Congressional Primary Reform* (July 1, 2021), https://www.newamerica.org/political-reform/reports/what-we-know-about-congressional-primaries-and-congressional-primary-reform/.

4. A recent Tenth Circuit case addresses the extent to which a state political party has a constitutional right to determine how its candidates are selected. The Utah Republican Party has traditionally begun its candidate selection process with a convention. If one candidate gained over 60 percent of the convention vote, then that candidate would appear on the general election ballot as the party's nominee. If no candidate reached that threshold, then the top two vote-getters at the party convention would appear on the primary ballot.

In 2014, Utah's overwhelmingly Republican legislature approved an alternative pathway to the primary ballot. Under this new law, candidates may now qualify by gathering a prescribed number of signatures. The Utah Republican Party challenged this law, alleging that it infringed on its First Amendment right of association. A majority of the Tenth Circuit rejected the Utah Republican Party's challenge, concluding that the state's interests in managing elections—increasing participation and enhancing access to the ballot—outweighed the "minimal" burden on political parties' associational rights. *Utah Republican Party v. Cox*, 892 F.3d 1085 (10th Cir. 2018). Chief Judge Tymkovich dissented in part, finding evidence that the 2014 law was intended to "change the *substantive type* of candidates the Party nominates, all the while masquerading as mere *procedural* reform." *Id.* at 1095 (Tymkovich, C.J., concurring in part and dissenting in part). The Tenth Circuit subsequently denied rehearing en banc, with Chief Judge Tymkovich urging that the U.S. Supreme Court reconsider its approach to major parties' associational rights embodied in cases like *California Democratic Party v. Jones*:

> The behemoth, corrupt party machines we imagine to have caused the progressive era's turn to primaries are now, in many respects, out of commission. In important ways, the party system is the weakest it has ever been—a sobering reality given parties' importance to our republic's stability. And given new evidence of the substantial associational burdens, even distortions, caused by forcibly expanding a party's nomination process, a closer look seems in order. The time appears ripe for the Court to

> reconsider (or rather, as I see it, consider for the first time) the scope of government regulation of political party primaries and the attendant harms to associational rights and substantive ends.

Id. at 1072 (concurring in denial of rehearing en banc). The Supreme Court denied certiorari. 139 S. Ct. 1290 (2019).

Do you agree that a reconsideration of major parties' associational rights is in order? If so, how should courts think about those rights?

You may at this point wish to think in general terms about the pros and cons of judicial oversight of political parties and the laws regulating them. Consider this criticism of the U.S. Supreme Court's approach to the associational rights of major parties:

> The Court has long determined that, with respect to political parties, First Amendment rights ought to be allocated in ways that promote democratic values and good governance. Unfortunately, in doing so, it has adopted a set of theoretical assumptions that do not hold true in the real world of contemporary politics. Known in the literature as "responsible party government," the theory, which, as it happens, also accounts for the specifics of the recent calls for party reform, presumes that electoral accountability emerges from the choice between ideologically distinct political parties during competitive elections.
>
> Responsible party government theory underpins the Court's jurisprudence on the First Amendment rights of political parties. It is responsible party government that explains not only why current constitutional doctrine entrenches the two-party system but also why it invariably sides with the leaders of the two major parties when internal disputes arise. . . .
>
> The commitment to responsible party government in the Court's jurisprudence, and also among party reformers, is a colossal mistake. Responsible party government has not panned out. The political parties are stronger and more ideologically distinct than in any prior era. Yet, responsible party government has not emerged. . . .

Tabatha Abu El-Haj, *Networking the Party: First Amendment Rights and the Pursuit of Responsive Party Government*, 118 Columbia Law Review 1225 (2018).

Professor Abu El-Haj advocates a different kind of constitutional analysis, under which courts would focus on "a party's capacity to mobilize broad and representative political participation and facilitate a two-way street of information transmission through party activists." *Id.* at 1234. The idea is to enhance the political parties' ability to function as effective civic associations, allowing for interaction between party elites and the broader electorate. *Id.* at 1300. Is Professor Abu El-Haj's critique of the Court's jurisprudence persuasive? Is her alternative vision realistic? For an argument that Professor Abu El-Haj's diagnosis is accurate, but that legislative and party-based solutions are likely to be more productive than focusing on the courts, see Michael Kang, *The Problem of Irresponsible Party Government*, 119 CLR Forum, No. 1, https://columbialawreview.org/content/the-problem-of-irresponsible-party-government/. Professor Abu El-Haj responds in *The Possibilities for Responsive Party Government*, 119 CLR Forum, No. 4, https://columbialawreview.org/content/the-possibilities-for-responsive-party-government/.

IV. Parties and Patronage

"Patronage" refers to the practice of awarding governmental benefits to allies of the party or the individuals in power. Broadly speaking the term can refer to a variety of governmental benefits, such as the awarding of profitable contracts or of government franchises, loans, or grants. Commonly, the term is used more narrowly to refer to the providing of government jobs to allies and party loyalists. These jobs can run the spectrum from very high level positions, such as ambassadorships and judgeships, to the lowest level manual or clerical positions. They can be full-time jobs or particular assignments, such as, in many states, inheritance tax appraisers.

Patronage, and the controversy it arouses, has played a conspicuous part in American history and even in American culture. Mention of a few highlights will illustrate the point. After Republican Thomas Jefferson defeated Federalist incumbent John Adams in the 1800 presidential election, Adams appointed as many Federalists as possible to a variety of offices, including the notorious "midnight judges," one of whom was the great Chief Justice John Marshall. Jefferson later wrote:

> I can say with truth that one act of Mr. Adams's life, and one only, ever gave me a moment's personal displeasure. I did consider his last appointments to office as personally unkind. They were from among my most ardent political enemies, from whom no faithful cooperation could ever be expected, and laid me under the embarrassment of acting thro' men whose views were to defeat mine; or to encounter the odium of putting others in their places. It seemed but common justice to leave a successor free to act by instruments of his own choice.[gg]

Upon taking office, Jefferson seemed to promise a new policy, when he declared:

> [E]very difference of opinion is not a difference of principle. We have called by different names brethren of the same principle. We are all Republicans, we are all Federalists.[hh]

Nevertheless, within a few months, Jefferson was forced to explain his replacement of Federalist officeholders with Republicans:

---

gg. Letter from Thomas Jefferson to Abigail Adams, June 13, 1804, in Thomas Jefferson, *Writings* 1144, 1145–46 (Library of America, 1984).

hh. Thomas Jefferson, First Inaugural Address, March 4, 1801, *id.* at 492, 493.

> Declarations of myself in favor of *political tolerance*, exhortations to *harmony* and affection in social intercourse, and to respect for the *equal rights* of the minority, have, on certain occasions, been quoted & misconstrued into assurances that the tenure of offices was to be undisturbed. But could candor apply such a construction? . . . When it is considered, that during the late administration, those who were not of a particular sect of politics were excluded from all office; when, by a steady pursuit of this measure, nearly the whole offices of the U S were monopolized by that sect; when the public sentiment at length declared itself, and burst open the doors of honor and confidence to those whose opinions they more approved, was it to be imagined that this monopoly of office was still to be continued in the hands of the minority? Does it violate their *equal rights*, to assert some rights in the majority also? Is it *political intolerance* to claim a proportionate share in the direction of the public affairs? Can they not *harmonize* in society unless they have everything in their own hands?[ii]

During the so-called "era of good feelings" that followed, partisan patronage was not an issue at the national level, since national politics was dominated by a single party. During the 1820s, the Democratic-Republican Party split between the supporters, respectively, of John Quincy Adams and Andrew Jackson. The Jacksonians, finally victorious in the 1828 election, openly declared their policy of filling offices by partisan criteria. In the ensuing decades, there was alternation in the presidency between the Democrats and the Whigs and, after 1860, between the Democrats and the Republicans. Each time the presidency was transferred from one party to the other, federal officeholders were swept out of office to be replaced by adherents of the newly victorious party.

Even during its heyday, the practice of federal patronage did not go without criticism. The otherwise routine firing of the manager of the Salem, Massachusetts, custom-house in 1848, by the Whigs after the victory of their candidate, Zachary Taylor, became immortalized because its victim, Nathaniel Hawthorne, recorded the incident in his introductory essay to one of America's greatest novels. "[I]t is a strange experience," Hawthorne wrote:

> to a man of pride and sensibility, to know that his interests are within the control of individuals who neither love nor understand him, and by whom, since one or the other must needs happen, he would rather be injured than obliged. Strange, too, for one who has kept his calmness throughout the contest, to observe the bloodthirstiness that is developed in the hour of triumph, and to be conscious that he is himself among its objects! There are few uglier traits of human nature than this tendency—which I now witnessed in men no worse than their neighbours—to grow cruel, merely

ii. Thomas Jefferson, Letter to Elias Shipman and Others, a Committee of the Merchants of New Haven, July 12, 1801, *id.* at 497, 498 (emphasis in original).

> because they possessed the power of inflicting harm. If the guillotine, as applied to office-holders, were a literal fact, instead of one of the most apt of metaphors, it is my sincere belief, that the active members of the victorious party were sufficiently excited to have chopped off all our heads, and have thanked Heaven for the opportunity![jj]

Opposition to patronage at the federal level grew, especially after the Civil War, and came to a head when a disappointed office seeker assassinated President James Garfield in 1881. The Pendleton Act, introducing the federal civil service system and sharply reducing the number of federal positions subject to patronage appointments, was enacted in 1883.

Patronage played a more important role and lasted longer in state and local politics. Patronage, in both the narrow and the broad senses, was the mainstay of party "machines" in state and, most notoriously, in big city politics around the country. Patronage and the corruption many people associated with it were a prime target of the "muckraking" journalists of the turn of the century and of the early twentieth century Progressive movement. The result was a gradual displacement of a great deal of patronage in state and local governments with civil service systems over the course of most of the twentieth century.

The best known strong patronage systems to survive into the 1970s were those of the state of Illinois and the city of Chicago, the latter controlled by then Mayor Richard Daley.[kk] By 1976, when the Supreme Court decided *Elrod v. Burns*, patronage in the narrow sense had declined considerably in most of the country, so that the significance of the Court's patronage cases may not be as great as the justices in both the majority and the minority in *Elrod* and subsequent cases seem to have believed. However, patronage in the narrow sense has by no means entirely disappeared, and patronage in the broader sense is likely to endure in one form or another so long as democracy as we know it exists.[ll] One question you might bear in mind, as you read the patronage cases that follow, is to what extent their conclusions ought to be applicable to other types of government benefits, such as the awarding of franchises or contracts, or even broader policy matters such as the adoption of legislation. Does it violate the First Amendment for government officials to base such decisions in whole or in part on the party affiliation of interested persons? On whether or not interested persons have made campaign contributions to the right party or the right candidates?

---

jj. Nathaniel Hawthorne, *The Custom-House*, in The Scarlet Letter 4, 31 (3d Norton Critical Edition, 1988).

kk. See generally Cynthia Grant Bowman, *"We Don't Want Anybody Anybody Sent": The Death of Patronage Hiring in Chicago*, 86 Northwestern University Law Review 57 (1991).

ll. See generally Raymond E. Wolfinger, *Why Political Machines Have Not Withered Away and Other Revisionist Thoughts*, 34 Journal of Politics 365 (1972).

Elrod v. Burns

427 U.S. 347 (1976)

Mr. Justice BRENNAN announced the judgment of the Court and delivered an opinion in which Mr. Justice WHITE and Mr. Justice MARSHALL joined.

This case presents the question whether public employees who allege that they were discharged or threatened with discharge solely because of their partisan political affiliation or nonaffiliation state a claim for deprivation of constitutional rights secured by the First and Fourteenth Amendments....

In December 1970, the Sheriff of Cook County, a Republican, was replaced by Richard Elrod, a Democrat. At that time, respondents, all Republicans, were employees of the Cook County Sheriff's Office. They were non-civil-service employees and, therefore, not covered by any statute, ordinance, or regulation protecting them from arbitrary discharge....

It has been the practice of the Sheriff of Cook County, when he assumes office from a Sheriff of a different political party, to replace non-civil-service employees of the Sheriff's Office with members of his own party when the existing employees lack or fail to obtain requisite support from, or fail to affiliate with, that party. Consequently, subsequent to Sheriff Elrod's assumption of office, respondents, with the exception of Buckley, were discharged from their employment solely because they did not support and were not members of the Democratic Party and had failed to obtain the sponsorship of one of its leaders. Buckley is in imminent danger of being discharged solely for the same reasons....

The Cook County Sheriff's practice of dismissing employees on a partisan basis is but one form of the general practice of political patronage. The practice also includes placing loyal supporters in government jobs that may or may not have been made available by political discharges. Nonofficeholders may be the beneficiaries of lucrative government contracts for highway construction, buildings, and supplies. Favored wards may receive improved public services. Members of the judiciary may even engage in the practice through the appointment of receiverships, trusteeships, and refereeships. Although political patronage comprises a broad range of activities, we are here concerned only with the constitutionality of dismissing public employees for partisan reasons.

Patronage practice is not new to American politics. It has existed at the federal level at least since the Presidency of Thomas Jefferson, although its popularization and legitimation primarily occurred later, in the Presidency of Andrew Jackson. The practice is not unique to American politics. It has been used in many European countries, and in darker times, it played a significant role in the Nazi rise to power in Germany and other totalitarian states. More recent times have witnessed a strong decline in its use, particularly with respect to public employment. Indeed, only a few decades after Andrew Jackson's administration, strong discontent with the corruption and inefficiency of the patronage system of public employment eventuated in the Pendleton Act, the foundation of modern civil service. And on the state and local levels, merit systems have increasingly displaced the practice.[8] . . .

The decline of patronage employment is not, of course relevant to the question of its constitutionality. It is the practice itself, not the magnitude of its occurrence, the constitutionality of which must be determined. Nor for that matter does any unacceptability of the practice signified by its decline indicate its unconstitutionality. Our inquiry does not begin with the judgment of history, though the actual operation of a practice viewed in retrospect may help to assess its workings with respect to constitutional limitations. . . .

The cost of the practice of patronage is the restraint it places on freedoms of belief and association. In order to maintain their jobs, respondents were required to pledge their political allegiance to the Democratic Party, work for the election of other candidates of the Democratic Party, contribute a portion of their wages to the Party, or obtain the sponsorship of a member of the Party, usually at the price of one of the first three alternatives. Regardless of the incumbent party's identity, Democratic or otherwise, the consequences for association and belief are the same. An individual who is a member of the out-party maintains affiliation with his own party at the risk of losing his job. He works for the election of his party's candidates and espouses its policies at the same risk. The financial and campaign assistance that he is induced to provide to another party furthers the advancement of that party's policies to the detriment of his party's views and ultimately his own beliefs, and any assessment of his salary is tantamount to coerced belief. . . .

It is not only belief and association which are restricted where political patronage is the practice. The free functioning of the electoral process also suffers. Conditioning public employment on partisan support prevents support of competing political interests. Existing employees are deterred from such support, as well as the multitude seeking jobs. As government employment, state or federal, becomes more pervasive, the greater the dependence on it becomes, and therefore the greater becomes the power to starve political opposition by commanding partisan support, financial and otherwise. Patronage thus tips the electoral process in favor of the incumbent party, and where the practice's scope is substantial relative to the size of the electorate, the impact on the process can be significant.

[The practice of patronage firings] unavoidably confronts decisions by this Court either invalidating or recognizing as invalid government action that inhibits belief and association through the conditioning of public employment on political faith. . . .

---

8. See *Broadrick v. Oklahoma*, 413 U.S. 601, 604–605 n.2 (1973). Factors contributing to the declining use of patronage have not been limited to the proliferation of merit systems. New methods of political financing, the greater necessity of job expertise in public employment, growing issue orientation in the elective process, and new incentives for political campaigners have also contributed.

Particularly pertinent to the constitutionality of the practice of patronage dismissals are *Keyishian v. Board of Regents*, 385 U.S. 589 (1967), and *Perry v. Sindermann*, 408 U.S. 593 (1972). In *Keyishian*, the Court invalidated New York statutes barring employment merely on the basis of membership in "subversive" organizations. *Keyishian* squarely held that political association alone could not, consistently with the First Amendment, constitute an adequate ground for denying public employment. In *Perry*, the Court broadly rejected the validity of limitations on First Amendment rights as a condition to the receipt of a governmental benefit....

Patronage practice falls squarely within the prohibitions of *Keyishian* and *Perry*. Under that practice, public employees hold their jobs on the condition that they provide, in some acceptable manner, support for the favored political party. The threat of dismissal for failure to provide that support unquestionably inhibits protected belief and association, and dismissal for failure to provide support only penalizes its exercise. The belief and association which government may not ordain directly are achieved by indirection....

Although the practice of patronage dismissals clearly infringes First Amendment interests, our inquiry is not at an end, for the prohibition on encroachment of First Amendment protections is not an absolute. Restraints are permitted for appropriate reasons....

It is firmly established that a significant impairment of First Amendment rights must survive exacting scrutiny....

One interest which has been offered in justification of patronage is the need to insure effective government and the efficiency of public employees. It is argued that employees of political persuasions not the same as that of the party in control of public office will not have the incentive to work effectively and may even be motivated to subvert the incumbent administration's efforts to govern effectively. We are not persuaded. The inefficiency resulting from the wholesale replacement of large numbers of public employees every time political office changes hands belies this justification. And the prospect of dismissal after an election in which the incumbent party has lost is only a disincentive to good work. Further, it is not clear that dismissal in order to make room for a patronage appointment will result in replacement by a person more qualified to do the job since appointment often occurs in exchange for the delivery of votes, or other party service, not job capability. More fundamentally, however, the argument does not succeed because it is doubtful that the mere difference of political persuasion motivates poor performance; nor do we think it legitimately may be used as a basis for imputing such behavior. The Court has consistently recognized that mere political association is an inadequate basis for imputing disposition to ill-willed conduct.... At all events, less drastic means for insuring government effectiveness and employee efficiency are available to the State. Specifically, employees may always be discharged for good cause, such as insubordination or poor job performance, when those bases in fact exist.

Even if the first argument that patronage serves effectiveness and efficiency be rejected, it still may be argued that patronage serves those interests by giving the employees of an incumbent party the incentive to perform well in order to insure their party's incumbency and thereby their jobs. Patronage, according to the argument, thus makes employees highly accountable to the public. But the ability of officials more directly accountable to the electorate to discharge employees for cause and the availability of merit systems, growth in the use of which has been quite significant, convince us that means less intrusive than patronage still exist for achieving accountability in the public work force and, thereby, effective and efficient government. The greater effectiveness of patronage over these less drastic means, if any, is at best marginal, a gain outweighed by the absence of intrusion on protected interests under the alternatives.

The lack of any justification for patronage dismissals as a means of furthering government effectiveness and efficiency distinguishes this case from *CSC v. Letter Carriers*, 413 U.S. 548 (1973), and *United Public Workers v. Mitchell*, 330 U.S. 75 (1949). In both of those cases, legislative restraints on political management and campaigning by public employees were upheld despite their encroachment on First Amendment rights because, *inter alia*, they did serve in a necessary manner to foster and protect efficient and effective government. Interestingly, the activities that were restrained by the legislation involved in those cases are characteristic of patronage practices. As the Court observed in *Mitchell*, "The conviction that an actively partisan governmental personnel threatens good administration has deepened since [1882]. Congress recognizes danger to the service in that political rather than official effort may earn advancement and to the public in that governmental favor may be channeled through political connections."

A second interest advanced in support of patronage is the need for political loyalty of employees, not to the end that effectiveness and efficiency be insured, but to the end that representative government not be undercut by tactics obstructing the implementation of policies of the new administration, policies presumably sanctioned by the electorate. The justification is not without force, but is nevertheless inadequate to validate patronage wholesale. Limiting patronage dismissals to policymaking positions is sufficient to achieve this governmental end. Nonpolicymaking individuals usually have only limited responsibility and are therefore not in a position to thwart the goals of the in-party.

No clear line can be drawn between policymaking and nonpolicymaking positions. While nonpolicymaking individuals usually have limited responsibility, that is not to say that one with a number of responsibilities is necessarily in a policymaking position. The nature of the responsibilities is critical. Employee supervisors, for example, may have many responsibilities, but those responsibilities may have only limited and well-defined objectives. An employee with responsibilities that are not well defined or are of broad scope more likely functions in a policymaking position. In determining whether an employee occupies a policymaking position, consideration should also be given to whether the employee acts as an adviser or formulates plans for the implementation of broad goals. Thus, the political loyalty "justification is a matter of proof, or at least argument, directed at particular kinds of jobs." *Illinois State Employees Union v. Lewis*, 473 F.2d 561 (7th Cir. 1972). Since, as we have noted, it is the government's burden to demonstrate an overriding interest in order to validate an encroachment on protected interests, the burden of establishing this justification as to any particular respondent will rest on the petitioners on remand, cases of doubt being resolved in favor of the particular respondent.

It is argued that a third interest supporting patronage dismissals is the preservation of the democratic process. According to petitioners, "we have contrived no system for the support of party that does not place considerable reliance on patronage. The party organization makes a democratic government work and charges a price for its services."[21] The argument is thus premised on the centrality of partisan politics to the democratic process.

Preservation of the democratic process is certainly an interest protection of which may in some instances justify limitations on First Amendment freedoms. But however important preservation of the two-party system or any system involving a fixed number of parties may or may not be, we are not persuaded that the elimination of patronage practice or, as is specifically involved here, the interdiction of patronage dismissals, will bring about the demise of party politics. Political parties existed in the absence of active patronage practice prior to the administration of Andrew Jackson, and they have survived substantial reduction in their patronage power through the establishment of merit systems.

Patronage dismissals thus are not the least restrictive alternative to achieving the contribution they may make to the democratic process. The process functions as well without the practice, perhaps even better, for patronage dismissals clearly also retard that process. Patronage can result in the entrenchment of one or a few parties to the exclusion of others. And most indisputably, as we recognized at the outset, patronage is a very effective impediment to the associational and speech freedoms which are essential to a meaningful system of democratic government. Thus, if patronage contributes at all to the elective process, that contribution is diminished by the practice's impairment of the same. Indeed, unlike the gain to representative government provided by the Hatch Act in *CSC v. Letter Carriers, supra*, and *United Public Workers v. Mitchell, supra*, the gain to representative government provided by the practice of patronage, if any, would be insufficient to justify its sacrifice of First Amendment rights.

To be sure, *Letter Carriers* and *Mitchell* upheld Hatch Act restraints sacrificing political campaigning and management, activities themselves protected by the First Amendment. But in those cases it was the Court's judgment that congressional subordination of those activities was permissible to safeguard the core interests of

---

21. Brief for Petitioners, quoting V.O. Key, Politics, Parties and Pressure Groups 369 (5th ed. 1964).

individual belief and association. Subordination of some First Amendment activity was permissible to protect other such activity. Today, we hold that subordination of other First Amendment activity, that is, patronage dismissals, not only is permissible, but also is mandated by the First Amendment. And since patronage dismissals fall within the category of political campaigning and management, this conclusion irresistibly flows from *Mitchell* and *Letter Carriers*. For if the First Amendment did not place individual belief and association above political campaigning and management, at least in the setting of public employment, the restraints on those latter activities could not have been judged permissible in *Mitchell* and *Letter Carriers*.

It is apparent that at bottom we are required to engage in the resolution of conflicting interests under the First Amendment. The constitutional adjudication called for by this task is well within our province. The illuminating source to which we turn in performing the task is the system of government the First Amendment was intended to protect, a democratic system whose proper functioning is indispensably dependent on the unfettered judgment of each citizen on matters of political concern. Our decision in obedience to the guidance of that source does not outlaw political parties or political campaigning and management. Parties are free to exist and their concomitant activities are free to continue. We require only that the rights of every citizen to believe as he will and to act and associate according to his beliefs be free to continue as well.

In summary, patronage dismissals severely restrict political belief and association. Though there is a vital need for government efficiency and effectiveness, such dismissals are on balance not the least restrictive means for fostering that end. There is also a need to insure that policies which the electorate has sanctioned are effectively implemented. That interest can be fully satisfied by limiting patronage dismissals to policymaking positions. Finally, patronage dismissals cannot be justified by their contribution to the proper functioning of our democratic process through their assistance to partisan politics since political parties are nurtured by other, less intrusive and equally effective methods. More fundamentally, however, any contribution of patronage dismissals to the democratic process does not suffice to override their severe encroachment on First Amendment freedoms. We hold, therefore, that the practice of patronage dismissals is unconstitutional under the First and Fourteenth Amendments, and that respondents thus stated a valid claim for relief....

The judgment of the Court of Appeals is

Affirmed.

Mr. Justice STEVENS did not participate in the consideration or decision of this case.

Mr. Justice STEWART, with whom Mr. Justice BLACKMUN joins, concurring in the judgment.

Although I cannot join the plurality's wide-ranging opinion, I can and do concur in its judgment.

This case does not require us to consider the broad contours of the so-called patronage system, with all its variations and permutations. In particular, it does not require us to consider the constitutional validity of a system that confines the hiring of some governmental employees to those of a particular political party, and I would intimate no views whatever on that question.

The single substantive question involved in this case is whether a nonpolicymaking, nonconfidential government employee can be discharged or threatened with discharge from a job that he is satisfactorily performing upon the sole ground of his political beliefs. I agree with the plurality that he cannot. See *Perry v. Sindermann.*

[A short dissenting opinion by Chief Justice BURGER is omitted.]

Mr. Justice POWELL, with whom THE CHIEF JUSTICE and Mr. Justice REHNQUIST join, dissenting.

The Court holds unconstitutional a practice as old as the Republic, a practice which has contributed significantly to the democratization of American politics. This decision is urged on us in the name of First Amendment rights, but in my view the judgment neither is constitutionally required nor serves the interest of a representative democracy. It also may well disserve rather than promote core values of the First Amendment. I therefore dissent.

The Cook County Sheriff's Office employs approximately 3,000 people. Roughly half of these employees are "merit" employees given various protections from discharge. The other half of the employees have no such protection. Customary Illinois political practice has allowed such "non-merit" positions to be awarded on "patronage" grounds. This tradition has entitled newly elected officeholders to replace incumbent nonmerit employees with patronage appointments.

[Patronage] in employment played a significant role in democratizing American politics. Before patronage practices developed fully, an "aristocratic" class dominated political affairs, a tendency that persisted in areas where patronage did not become prevalent. Patronage practices broadened the base of political participation by providing incentives to take part in the process, thereby increasing the volume of political discourse in society. Patronage also strengthened parties, and hence encouraged the development of institutional responsibility to the electorate on a permanent basis. Parties became "instrument(s) through which discipline and responsibility may be achieved within the Leviathan." Sorauf, "Patronage and Party," 3 *Midwest J. Pol. Sci.* 115 (1959).

In many situations patronage employment practices also entailed costs to government efficiency. These costs led eventually to reforms placing most federal and state civil service employment on a nonpatronage basis. But the course of such reform is of limited relevance to the task of constitutional adjudication in this case. It is pertinent to note, however, that a perceived impingement on employees' political beliefs by the patronage system was not a significant impetus to such reform. Most advocates of reform were concerned primarily with the corruption and inefficiency that patronage was thought to induce in civil service and the power that patronage practices were thought to give the "professional" politicians who relied on them. Moreover, it generally was thought that elimination of these evils required the imposition both of a merit system and of restrictions on First Amendment activities by government employees.

[In this case we] have complaining employees who apparently accepted patronage jobs knowingly and willingly, while fully familiar with the "tenure" practices long prevailing in the Sheriff's Office. Such employees have *benefited* from their political beliefs and activities; they have not been penalized for them. In these circumstances, I [believe] that beneficiaries of a patronage system may not be heard to challenge it when it comes their turn to be replaced....

It is difficult to disagree with the view, as an abstract proposition, that government employment ordinarily should not be conditioned upon one's political beliefs or activities. But we deal here with a highly practical and rather fundamental element of our political system, not the theoretical abstractions of a political science seminar. In concluding that patronage hiring practices are unconstitutional, the plurality seriously underestimates the strength of the government interest—especially at the local level—in allowing some patronage hiring practices, and it exaggerates the perceived burden on First Amendment rights.

As indicated above, patronage hiring practices have contributed to American democracy by stimulating political activity and by strengthening parties, thereby helping to make government accountable. It cannot be questioned seriously that these contributions promote important state interests....

The complaining parties are or were employees of the Sheriff. In many communities, the sheriff's duties are as routine as process serving, and his election attracts little or no general public interest. In the States, and especially in the thousands of local communities, there are large numbers of elective offices, and many are as relatively obscure as that of the local sheriff or constable. Despite the importance of elective offices to the ongoing work of local governments, election campaigns for lesser offices in particular usually attract little attention from the media, with consequent disinterest and absence of intelligent participation on the part of the public. Unless the candidates for these offices are able to dispense the traditional patronage that has accrued to the offices, they also are unlikely to attract donations of time or money from voluntary groups. In short, the resource pools that fuel the intensity of political interest and debate in "important" elections frequently "could care less" about who fills the offices deemed to be relatively unimportant. Long experience teaches that at this local level traditional patronage practices contribute significantly to the democratic process. The candidates for these offices derive their support at the precinct level, and their modest funding for publicity, from cadres of friends and political associates who hope to benefit if their "man" is elected. The activities of the latter are often the principal source of political information for the voting public. The "robust" political discourse that the plurality opinion properly emphasizes is furthered—not restricted—by the time-honored system.

Patronage hiring practices also enable party organizations to persist and function at the local level. Such organizations become visible to the electorate at large only at election time, but the dull periods between elections require ongoing activities: precinct organizations must be maintained; new voters registered; and minor political "chores" performed for citizens who otherwise may have no practical means of access to officeholders. In some communities, party organizations and clubs also render helpful social services.

It is naive to think that these types of political activities are motivated at these levels by some academic interest in "democracy" or other public service impulse. For the most part, as every politician knows, the hope of some reward generates a major portion of the local political activity supporting parties. It is difficult to overestimate the contributions to our system by the major political parties, fortunately limited in number compared to the fractionalization that has made the continued existence of democratic government doubtful in some other countries. Parties generally are stable, high-profile, and permanent institutions. When the names on a long ballot are meaningless to the average voter, party affiliation affords a guidepost by which voters may rationalize a myriad of political choices. Voters can and do hold parties to long-term accountability, and it is not too much to say that, in their absence, responsive and responsible performance in low-profile offices, particularly, is difficult to maintain.

It is against decades of experience to the contrary, then, that the plurality opinion concludes that patronage hiring practices interfere with the "free functioning of the electoral process." . . . One would think that elected representatives of the people are better equipped than we to weigh the need for some continuation of patronage practices in light of the interests above identified, and particularly in view of local conditions. . . .

Notes and Questions

1. In *CSC v. Letter Carriers*, 413 U.S. 548 (1973), and *United Public Workers v. Mitchell*, 330 U.S. 75 (1949), the Court upheld the constitutionality of the Hatch Act. The Hatch Act prohibited most partisan political activity by the great majority of federal employees. In *Elrod*, Justice Brennan distinguishes the Hatch Act cases in part by saying, "in those cases it was the Court's judgment that congressional subordination of those activities was permissible to safeguard the core interests of individual belief and association." The belief that the individual is the fundamental unit in democratic politics is central to the school of thought known as progressivism. In Chapter 1 of this book, we were introduced to a competing school of thought, pluralism, which views the group as the fundamental unit. Of all the groups involved in American politics, none play a more central role than political parties.

In the Hatch Act cases, as Justice Brennan wrote, severe restriction of public employees' political freedom was permitted in order to promote the value of political individualism. In *Elrod*, the state's desire to promote the value of collective activity through political parties is held insufficient to justify an equally severe restriction on public employees' political freedom. Read together, do the Hatch Act cases and *Elrod* suggest that progressivism is preferred by the Constitution over competing beliefs such as pluralism and party government? Should progressivism be a constitutionally preferred value? Are there special characteristics of patronage and public employment that might distinguish these cases from others in which competing progressivist and pluralist or party government values might be in conflict?

2. In *Branti v. Finkel*, 445 U.S. 507 (1980), a public defender appointed by a newly-elected county legislature quickly proceeded to fire several attorneys in the public defender's office, allegedly because they were Republicans. The public defender sought to defend the firings, in part, on the ground that attorneys were "policymakers," and therefore not protected by *Elrod*. Justice Stevens, writing for the Court, disagreed:

> As Mr. Justice Brennan noted in *Elrod*, it is not always easy to determine whether a position is one in which political affiliation is a legitimate factor to be considered.... Under some circumstances, a position may be appropriately considered political even though it is neither confidential nor policymaking in character. As one obvious example, if a State's election laws require that precincts be supervised by two election judges of different parties, a Republican judge could be legitimately discharged solely for changing his party registration. That conclusion would not depend on any finding that the job involved participation in policy decisions or access to confidential information. Rather, it would simply rest on the fact that party membership was essential to the discharge of the employee's governmental responsibilities.
>
> It is equally clear that party affiliation is not necessarily relevant to every policymaking or confidential position. The coach of a state university's football team formulates policy, but no one would seriously claim that Republicans make better coaches than Democrats, or vice versa, no matter which party is in control of the state government. On the other hand, it is equally clear that the governor of a state may appropriately believe that the official duties of various assistants who help him write speeches, explain his views to the press, or communicate with the legislature cannot be performed effectively unless those persons share his political beliefs and party commitments. In sum, the ultimate inquiry is not whether the label "policymaker" or "confidential" fits a particular position; rather the question is whether the hiring authority can demonstrate that party affiliation is an appropriate requirement for the effective performance of the public office involved.

Since "whatever policymaking occurs in the public defender's office must relate to the needs of individual clients and not to any partisan political interests," Justice Stevens concluded that the attorneys in the public defender's office were protected by the *Elrod* doctrine. He added, in footnote 13, that "an official such as a prosecutor" has broader public responsibilities, and that the Court was expressing no opinion on whether "the deputy of such an official could be dismissed on grounds of political party affiliation or loyalty." Justices Powell, Rehnquist, and Stewart dissented in *Branti*.

How would you advise a newly-elected district attorney who wishes to fire all deputies who are not members of his or her party? May a party membership test be a condition of employment in the civil division of a state attorney general's office?

Could Branti, the public defender, fire Finkel if Finkel made a speech criticizing Branti's management of the public defender's office? If he made a speech criticizing the county legislature for providing too low a budget to the public defender's office? If he made a speech criticizing the county legislature for actions unrelated to the public defender's office? Reconsider this question after reading the excerpts from the *Umbehr* and *O'Hare* cases below.

3. *Branti* seems to have modified *Elrod*'s exception for "policymaking" employees, by stating that the question is whether party affiliation is "an appropriate requirement" for the position. Justice Stevens's examples of a football coach (inappropriate) and an assistant to the governor (appropriate) may seem intuitively obvious, but what is the standard of "appropriateness"? Would it be appropriate to fire a prison warden on grounds of partisan affiliation? The head of a city construction project? The director of an agency that enforces the state's campaign finance laws? The personal secretary to the mayor? With respect to the last of these questions, see *Faughender v. City of North Olmsted*, 927 F.2d 909 (6th Cir. 1991), holding the mayor's personal secretary could be fired on political grounds. What about the personal secretary to the head of a city department? What about a receptionist in the mayor's office?

* * *

Elrod bars firing non-policymaking employees on grounds of their partisan affiliation. In *Rutan v. Republican Party of Illinois*, 497 U.S. 62 (1990), the Supreme Court extended the *Elrod* rule to patronage hiring and transfer decisions. Justice Brennan, writing for the Court, saw no constitutional difference between hiring and firing:

> The same First Amendment concerns that underlay our decisions in *Elrod* and *Branti* are implicated here. Employees who do not compromise their beliefs stand to lose the considerable increases in pay and job satisfaction attendant to promotions, the hours and maintenance expenses that are consumed by long daily commutes, and even their jobs if they are not rehired after a "temporary" layoff. These are significant penalties and are imposed for the exercise of rights guaranteed by the First Amendment. Unless these patronage practices are narrowly tailored to further vital government interests, we must conclude that they impermissibly encroach on First Amendment freedoms.
>
> We find, however, that our conclusions in *Elrod* and *Branti* are equally applicable to the patronage practices at issue here. A government's interest

in securing effective employees can be met by discharging, demoting, or transferring staff members whose work is deficient. A government's interest in securing employees who will loyally implement its policies can be adequately served by choosing or dismissing certain high-level employees on the basis of their political views. Likewise, the "preservation of the democratic process" is no more furthered by the patronage promotions, transfers, and rehires at issue here than it is by patronage dismissals. First, "political parties are nurtured by other, less intrusive and equally effective methods." *Elrod*. Political parties have already survived the substantial decline in patronage employment practices in this century. Second, patronage decidedly impairs the elective process by discouraging free political expression by public employees. Respondents, who include the Governor of Illinois and other state officials, do not suggest any other overriding government interest in favoring Republican Party supporters for promotion, transfer, and rehire.

We therefore determine that promotions, transfers, and recalls after layoffs based on political affiliation or support are an impermissible infringement on the First Amendment rights of public employees. . . .

Petitioner James W. Moore presents the closely related question whether patronage hiring violates the First Amendment. Patronage hiring places burdens on free speech and association similar to those imposed by the patronage practices discussed above. A state job is valuable. Like most employment, it provides regular paychecks, health insurance, and other benefits. In addition, there may be openings with the State when business in the private sector is slow. There are also occupations for which the government is a major (or the only) source of employment, such as social workers, elementary school teachers, and prison guards. Thus, denial of a state job is a serious privation. . . .

Justice Scalia wrote a dissenting opinion. He talked about the demise of patronage in American politics and what this meant for the party system:

It may well be that the Good Government Leagues of America were right, and that Plunkitt, James Michael Curley, and their ilk were wrong; but that is not entirely certain. As the merit principle has been extended and its effects increasingly felt; as the Boss Tweeds, the Tammany Halls, the Pendergast Machines, the Byrd Machines, and the Daley Machines have faded into history; we find that political leaders at all levels increasingly complain of the helplessness of elected government, unprotected by "party discipline," before the demands of small and cohesive interest groups.

The choice between patronage and the merit principle—or, to be more realistic about it, the choice between the desirable mix of merit and patronage principles in widely varying federal, state, and local political contexts—is not so clear that I would be prepared, as an original matter, to chisel a single, inflexible prescription into the Constitution. Fourteen years ago, in *Elrod*, the Court did that. *Elrod* was limited however, as was the later decision of *Branti*, to patronage firings, leaving it to state and federal legislatures to determine when and where political affiliation could be taken into account in hirings and promotions. Today the Court makes its constitutional civil service reform absolute, extending to all decisions regarding government employment. Because the First Amendment has never been thought to require this disposition, which may well have disastrous consequences for our political system, I dissent....

The whole point of my dissent is that the desirability of patronage is a policy question to be decided by the people's representatives; I do not mean, therefore, to endorse that system. But in order to demonstrate that a legislature could reasonably determine that its benefits outweigh its "coercive" effects, I must describe those benefits as the proponents of patronage see them: As Justice Powell discussed at length in his *Elrod* dissent, patronage stabilizes political parties and prevents excessive political fragmentation—both of which are results in which States have a strong governmental interest....

The Court simply refuses to acknowledge the link between patronage and party discipline, and between that and party success.... It is unpersuasive to claim, as the Court does, that party workers are obsolete because campaigns are now conducted through media and other money-intensive means. Those techniques have supplemented but not supplanted personal contacts. Certainly they have not made personal contacts unnecessary in campaigns for the lower level offices that are the foundations of party strength, nor have they replaced the myriad functions performed by party regulars not directly related to campaigning. And to the extent such techniques have replaced older methods of campaigning (partly in response to the limitations the Court has placed on patronage), the political system is not clearly better off. Increased reliance on money-intensive campaign techniques tends to entrench those in power much more effectively than patronage—but without the attendant benefit of strengthening the party system. A challenger can more easily obtain the support of party workers (who can expect to be rewarded even if the candidate loses—if not this year, then the next) than the financial support of political action committees (which will generally support incumbents, who are likely to prevail).

It is self-evident that eliminating patronage will significantly undermine party discipline; and that as party discipline wanes, so will the strength of the two-party system. But, says the Court, "[p]olitical parties have already survived the substantial decline in patronage employment practices in this century." This is almost verbatim what was said in *Elrod*. Fourteen years later it seems much less convincing. Indeed, now that we have witnessed, in 18 of the last 22 years, an Executive Branch of the Federal Government under the control of one party while the Congress is entirely or (for two years) partially within the control of the other party; now that we have undergone the most recent federal election, in which 98% of the incumbents, of whatever party, were returned to office; and now that we have seen elected officials changing their political affiliation with unprecedented readiness, the statement that "political parties have already survived" has a positively whistling-in-the-graveyard character to it. Parties have assuredly survived—but as what? As the forges upon which many of the essential compromises of American political life are hammered out? Or merely as convenient vehicles for the conducting of national Presidential elections?

The patronage system does not, of course, merely foster political parties in general; it fosters the two-party system in particular. When getting a job, as opposed to effectuating a particular substantive policy, is an available incentive for party workers, those attracted by that incentive are likely to work for the party that has the best chance of displacing the "ins," rather than for some splinter group that has a more attractive political philosophy but little hope of success. Not only is a two-party system more likely to emerge, but the differences between those parties are more likely to be moderated, as each has a relatively greater interest in appealing to a majority of the electorate and a relatively lesser interest in furthering philosophies or programs that are far from the mainstream. The stabilizing effects of such a system are obvious. . . .

Equally apparent is the relatively destabilizing nature of a system in which candidates cannot rely upon patronage-based party loyalty for their campaign support, but must attract workers and raise funds by appealing to various interest groups. There is little doubt that our decisions in *Elrod* and *Branti*, by contributing to the decline of party strength, have also contributed to the growth of interest-group politics in the last decade. See, e.g., Fitts, *The Vice of Virtue*, 136 University of Pennsylvania Law Review 1567, 1603–1607 (1988). Our decision today will greatly accelerate the trend. It is not only campaigns that are affected, of course, but the subsequent behavior of politicians once they are in power. The replacement of a system firmly based in party discipline with one in which each office-holder comes to his own accommodation with competing interest groups produces "a dispersion of political influence that may inhibit a political party from enacting its programs into law." *Branti* (Powell, J., dissenting).

Patronage, moreover, has been a powerful means of achieving the social and political integration of excluded groups. By supporting and ultimately dominating a particular party "machine," racial and ethnic minorities have—on the basis of their politics rather than their race or ethnicity—acquired the patronage awards the machine had power to confer. No one disputes the historical accuracy of this observation, and there is no reason to think that patronage can no longer serve that function. The abolition of patronage, however, prevents groups that have only recently obtained political power, especially blacks, from following this path to economic and social advancement. . . .

While the patronage system has the benefits argued for above, it also has undoubted disadvantages. It facilitates financial corruption, such as salary kickbacks and partisan political activity on government-paid time. It reduces the efficiency of government, because it creates incentives to hire more and less-qualified workers and because highly qualified workers are reluctant to accept jobs that may only last until the next election. And, of course, it applies some greater or lesser inducement for individuals to join and work for the party in power.

To hear the Court tell it, this last is the greatest evil. That is not my view, and it has not historically been the view of the American people. Corruption and inefficiency, rather than abridgement of liberty, have been the major criticisms leading to enactment of the civil service laws — for the very good reason that the patronage system does not have as harsh an effect upon conscience, expression, and association as the Court suggests. As described above, it is the nature of the pragmatic, patronage-based, two-party system to build alliances and to suppress rather than foster ideological tests for participation in the division of political "spoils." What the patronage system ordinarily demands of the party worker is loyalty to, and activity on behalf of, the organization itself rather than a set of political beliefs. He is generally free to urge *within the organization* the adoption of any political position; but if that position is rejected he must vote and work for the party nonetheless. The diversity of political expression (other than expression of party loyalty) is channeled, in other words, to a different stage — to the contests for party endorsement rather than the partisan elections. It is undeniable, of course, that the patronage system entails some constraint upon the expression of views, particularly at the partisan-election stage, and considerable constraint upon the employee's right to associate with the other party. It greatly exaggerates these, however, to describe them as a general "coercion of belief." Indeed, it greatly exaggerates them to call them "coercion" at all; since we generally make a distinction between inducement and compulsion. . . . In sum, I do not deny that the patronage system influences or redirects, perhaps to a substantial degree, individual political expression and political association. But like the many generations of Americans that have preceded us, I do not consider that a significant impairment of free speech or free association.

In emphasizing the advantages and minimizing the disadvantages (or at least minimizing one of the disadvantages) of the patronage system, I do not mean to suggest that that system is best. It may not always be; it may never be. To oppose our *Elrod-Branti* jurisprudence, one need not believe that the patronage system is *necessarily* desirable; nor even that it is always

> and everywhere *arguably* desirable; but merely that it is a political arrangement that may sometimes be a reasonable choice, and should therefore be left to the judgment of the people's elected representatives. The choice in question, I emphasize, is not just between patronage and a merit-based civil service, but rather among various combinations of the two that may suit different political units and different eras: permitting patronage hiring, for example, but prohibiting patronage dismissal; permitting patronage in most municipal agencies but prohibiting it in the police department; or permitting it in the mayor's office but prohibiting it everywhere else. I find it impossible to say that, always and everywhere, all of these choices fail our "balancing" test.

Notes and Questions

1. The most famous patronage-based machine to survive into the 1970s was the Chicago Democratic organization headed by Mayor Richard Daley. One commentator contends that, in practice, patronage has not brought about the benefits attributed to it by Justices Powell and Scalia in their dissents in *Elrod* and *Rutan*. Cynthia Grant Bowman, *"We Don't Want Anybody Anybody Sent": The Death of Patronage Hiring in Chicago*, 86 Northwestern University Law Review 57 (1991). Addressing the contention that patronage helps disadvantaged groups to begin their climb up the societal ladder, Professor Bowman writes:

> Machines clearly did function to bring in *some* new groups during *some* historical periods. The early Chicago machine is an example of a patronage party which did in fact incorporate a series of ethnic groups into political life, but it did so only because it faced substantial competition both from the Republican Party and from factions within the Democratic Party. Thus, as Republican Thompson reached out to newer ethnic groups, including Blacks, and [Democrat] Cermak struggled with the Irish for control of the Democratic party, the machine competed for Polish, Czech, Jewish, and Italian votes in addition to those of the older Irish immigrants.
>
> In other cities, however, the classic urban machine did not perform a democratizing function on any consistent basis. Recent studies show that the typical Irish machine was slow to incorporate the Southern and Eastern European immigrants who arrived after the Irish. In cities other than Chicago, where Irish machines succeeded in putting together a 'minimal winning electoral coalition' without appealing to newer immigrants who might compete with the Irish for jobs and political power, urban machines had no incentive to mobilize the more recently arrived ethnic groups, and did not do so. In Boston, for example, where the Irish comprised a majority of the population and could thus control city government without relying upon the votes of any of the newer groups, the machine played virtually no role in integrating those other ethnic groups into political life. Thus, the more a machine was able to consolidate its power by use of patronage, the

> less likely it was to fulfill the function of broadening the number of groups involved in the political process.
>
> It is not difficult to understand why mature urban political machines did not consistently perform the democratizing functions Scalia and Powell have alleged that they did. A patronage party depends on the allocation of a scarce resource—public jobs. After the initial spurts in the growth of public employment in the late nineteenth and early twentieth centuries, it was simply not possible to increase the supply of municipal jobs without limit. Hence, the only workable strategy for a patronage party was to "deflate" the demand for this scarce resource so that it would not exceed the supply of employment opportunities. If new groups continually entered the process, this delicate economy would be destroyed. Thus, patronage parties which have consolidated power generally have not sought to maximize participation of new groups in the political process. Instead, they are highly selective mobilizers and have emphasized the deliverability and controllability of votes over vote-maximization.

If such criticism is sound empirically, to what extent does it undermine the Powell-Scalia position? How would you expect Justice Scalia to have responded to Professor Bowman?

2. Professor Bowman observes that "Contract patronage was the route taken when other forms of patronage were foreclosed by the Court; this trend was exacerbated by the decrease in government employment after 1980 and the privatization of many functions previously performed by government workers. From 1982 to 1992, for example, the rate of increase in Illinois state employment declined, while spending on government contracts doubled." Cynthia Grant Bowman, *The Supreme Court's Patronage Decisions and the Theory and Practice of Politics*, in The U.S. Supreme Court and the Electoral Process 124, 138 (David K. Ryden, ed., 2000).

The Court addressed the question of patronage contracting in two companion cases, extending the First Amendment rights of public employees that had been protected in the *Elrod* and *Pickering* lines of cases (see Note 2 following *Elrod*) to independent contractors that do business with government agencies. In *Board of County Commissioners, Wabaunsee County v. Umbehr*, 518 U.S. 668 (1996), Umbehr had a contract with the county for hauling trash. The contract had been renewed on an annual basis, until Umbehr sharply criticized the County Board of Commissioners on various matters. Allegedly in retaliation for the criticism, the Board voted to terminate the contract. The Supreme Court held that Umbehr was entitled to relief for violation of his speech rights under the First Amendment if he proved that the termination was indeed retaliatory and that under a balancing analysis taken from *Pickering*, his free speech interests outweighed the County's "legitimate interests as contractor, deferentially viewed...."

In *O'Hare Truck Service v. City of Northlake*, 518 U.S. 712 (1996), the city had a list of towing services that it called upon by a rotation system. O'Hare allegedly was dropped from the list when its owner declined to make a campaign contribution in response to a request from the mayor, who was running for reelection. The Court ruled that the *Elrod-Branti-Rutan* line of cases was applicable, notwithstanding that O'Hare provided services to the city as an independent contractor, whereas the plaintiffs in the earlier cases were individuals who were or desired to be government employees.

The tests applied in these cases were not the same. In *Umbehr*, the Court balanced the interests in free speech against the government's interests. In *O'Hare* by contrast, the Court held that retaliation for a disfavored party affiliation was unconstitutional under the *Elrod-Branti-Rutan* line, unless party affiliation was an "appropriate requirement" for the position in question. There was no balancing, except to determine the propriety of conditioning the job on the basis of partisan affiliation. The Court in *O'Hare* attempted to define the circumstances under which one approach or the other would be employed. After describing the *Elrod-Branti-Rutan* affiliation test, the Court went on:

> Our cases call for a different, though related, inquiry where a government employer takes adverse action on account of an employee or service provider's right of free speech. There, we apply the balancing test from *Pickering. Elrod* and *Branti* involved instances where the raw test of political affiliation sufficed to show a constitutional violation, without the necessity of an inquiry more detailed than asking whether the requirement was appropriate for the employment in question. There is an advantage in so confining the inquiry where political affiliation alone is concerned, for one's beliefs and allegiances ought not to be subject to probing or testing by the government. It is true, on the other hand . . . , that the inquiry is whether the affiliation requirement is a reasonable one, so it is inevitable that some case-by-case adjudication will be required even where political affiliation is the test the government has imposed. A reasonableness analysis will also accommodate those many cases, perhaps including the one before us, where specific instances of the employee's speech or expression, which require balancing in the *Pickering* context, are intermixed with a political affiliation requirement. In those cases, the balancing *Pickering* mandates will be inevitable. This case-by-case process will allow the courts to consider the necessity of according to the government the discretion it requires in the administration and awarding of contracts over the whole range of public works and the delivery of governmental service.

Do you find these distinctions clear and persuasive?

3. Can a public employee sue when adverse action is taken against him based on a *mistaken* belief that he seeks to exercise his right to free speech in connection with an election campaign? Yes, the Supreme Court held in *Heffernan v. City of Paterson*, 136 S. Ct. 1412 (2016). Jeffrey Heffernan was a police officer in Paterson, New Jersey. He worked in the office of the Chief of Police, who had been appointed by the incumbent mayor. One day, Office Heffernan went to the campaign office

of a rival candidate for mayor, where he was spotted by another police officer. In retaliation, Heffernan alleged, he was demoted. Heffernan claimed he had no intent to support anyone for mayor but was simply picking up the yard sign for his infirm mother. Nevertheless, in an opinion by Justice Breyer, the Supreme Court held that Heffernan could make a First Amendment retaliation claim under the *Elrod* line of cases. The Court reasoned that it was the government's politically-motivated reason for demoting the employee that counts, not whether the public employee actually intended to engage in protected political activity. Justice Thomas (joined by Justice Alito) dissented, on the ground that Heffernan was not engaged in protected speech or assembly.

4. Justice Scalia's dissent in *Rutan* attributes a decline in the power of political parties to the Supreme Court's prohibition on patronage. An alternative hypothesis is that the Court has followed, rather than created, a trend. Consider the following: "In part, the debate over the virtues of patronage comes too late. The replacement of party-centered, labor intensive political campaigns with candidate-centered, capital-intensive ones has lessened politicians' demand for patronage employment. Politicians want money for media campaigns, not precinct workers. This increased demand for campaign contributions puts pressure on politicians to exchange government favors, including contracts, for such contributions." Richard L. Hasen, *Patronage*, in 4 Encyclopedia of the American Constitution 1885 (Leonard W. Levy & Kenneth L. Karst, eds., 2d ed. 2000). Consider the argument, discussed in Part I of this Chapter, that good government reforms have contributed to partisan polarization. With fewer tools at their disposal to rein in dissident members, the argument goes, party leaders lack the tools to forge compromise and advance centrist policies. Would bringing back patronage help?

5. *Elrod* was among the cases cited in Justice Kennedy's concurring opinion in *Vieth v. Jubelirer* (Chapter 4), which suggested that partisan gerrymandering might be challenged on First Amendment grounds. According to Justice Kennedy, this line of cases bars the government from "burdening or penalizing citizens because of their participation in the electoral process, their voting history, their association with a political party, or their expression of political views." Do you agree with this characterization of the patronage cases? Is partisan gerrymandering analogous?

Chapter 9

Third Parties and Independent Candidates

In Chapter 8 we gave extended attention to legal questions affecting the major political parties because, for most of its history, the national politics of the United States have been dominated by two parties—since 1856, the Democrats and the Republicans. Somewhat less uniformly, politics at the state and local levels also have been dominated by the two major parties. Questions about the rights and obligations of the major parties therefore have the most direct and obvious influence on the functioning of democratic government.

Despite two-party dominance, third parties and independent candidates sometimes have played a significant role in American politics. For example, in seven presidential elections since 1856, more than ten percent of the votes cast have gone to a candidate who was not a Democrat or Republican. The most recent example is the 1992 election, in which 18.9% of the votes were cast for independent candidate H. Ross Perot.[a] Independent and third party candidates may also affect elections by taking votes away from major party candidates. In 2016, the number of votes collectively received by the Libertarian and Green Party candidates exceeded the difference between the major party candidates in several key states, including Michigan, Pennsylvania, and Wisconsin. Republican candidate Donald Trump won these three states. Had Hillary Clinton won all of these states, she would have won the presidency, though it is far from certain that the third-party candidates actually affected the outcome in any of them. Some of those third party voters given a choice of Clinton or Trump would have voted for Trump, and some would have stayed home. See Edward B. Foley, *Third-Party and Independent Presidential Candidates: The Need for a Runoff Mechanism*, 85 Fordham Law Review 993 (2016) (discussed below, at the end of Part I of this Chapter).

Below the level of the presidency, third-party and independent candidates are occasionally elected. Bernie Sanders, who identifies as a Democratic Socialist, was elected as an independent candidate to represent Vermont in the House of Representatives starting in 1991 and in the Senate starting in 2006. Two current U.S. Senators (Angus King of Maine and Sanders) are formally independent, although both

a. When Perot ran for President in 1996, he received about 8 percent of the vote.

caucus with the Democrats. When Sanders ran for president in 2016 and 2020, he chose to run as a Democrat rather than as an independent candidate. Why?

Despite their limited role in American politics, third parties and independent candidates account for more than their share of litigation. This is not surprising, because the major parties are far more likely to be able to resolve their problems through legislation or other political means.[b] In addition, major parties control the legislature and at best have little reason to ease burdens facing third parties and independent candidates. The most persistent form of litigation brought by third parties and independent candidates concerns barriers to being listed on the ballot. The first principal case in this chapter, *Munro v. Socialist Workers Party*, is an example. Part I of this chapter covers ballot access and related ballot issues, such as write-in votes and "fusion" candidacies. Part II covers third parties' and independent candidates' challenges to alleged discrimination in access to state benefits.

A natural question to consider at the beginning of this chapter is whether election laws are responsible for the mostly peripheral role played by third parties and independent candidates in American politics. The probable answer is that election laws *are* of overriding importance, but not the laws that are the focus of this chapter. Instead, what is decisive is the use of *single-member districts* combined with *first-past-the-post elections*, under which the candidate with the most votes wins (even if that candidate receives less than a majority). This system makes it very difficult for third party candidates to win legislative seats. Unless its support is concentrated regionally, a third party cannot ordinarily win a plurality in any given district and therefore cannot win any legislative seats. In presidential elections, the Electoral College works to the same effect, as the example of H. Ross Perot indicates. In 1992, Perot won 18.9% of the popular vote, but because he did not win a plurality in any state, he did not win any electoral votes.

In other countries with *proportional representation* systems, parties can win legislative representation with relatively small proportions of the total vote, much less than a majority. Since that usually does not occur in the U.S. system, it is difficult for third parties to attract strong candidates, who will recognize the small likelihood of winning office under a third-party banner. The lack of strong candidates makes it even more difficult to attract support from voters, who may already be predisposed not to "waste" their votes on candidates and parties with no realistic chance of winning. Again, presidential elections illustrate the problem facing third parties. In 2000, consumer group activist Ralph Nader ran as a candidate for the Green Party. Nader's support in public opinion polls slipped in the days before the election, amid the charges of some Democrats that Nader's candidacy would "spoil" Democratic candidate Al Gore's chances and lead to the election of Republican George W. Bush. A third party candidate often faces charges of being a "spoiler" from backers

b. For a comparison and analysis of the use of litigation by major and minor parties in cases that reach the Supreme Court, see Lee Epstein and Charles D. Hadley, *On the Treatment of Political Parties in the U.S. Supreme Court, 1900–1986*, 52 Journal of Politics 413 (1990).

of the major party candidate who appears likely to lose support to the third party candidate.

The strong tendency of single-member districting to yield a two-party system was first demonstrated in a classic work of American political science by E.E. Schattschneider:

> The system does not operate to destroy the defeated major party because the defeated major party is able to retain a *monopoly of the opposition.* The cutting edge of the two-party system is precisely at the point of contact of the second major party and the third party (or the first minor party aspiring to become [the] third major party). What it amounts to is this: the advantage of the second party over the third is overwhelming. It usually wins all seats or very nearly all seats not won by the first party. Among all the opposition parties in the field it has by a very wide margin the best chance of displacing the party in power. Because this is true it is extremely likely that it can assemble about its banner nearly all of the elements in the country seriously opposed to the party in power and seriously interested in an early party overturn. *The monopoly of the opposition* is the most important asset of the second major party. As long as it can monopolize the movement to overthrow the party in power, the second party is important; any party able to monopolize the opposition is certain to come into power sooner or later. The second major party is able to argue, therefore, that people who vote for minor opposition parties dissipate the opposition, that the supporters of the minor parties *waste their votes.* All who oppose the party in power are made to feel a certain need for concentrating their support behind the party most likely to lead a successful opposition. As a consequence the tendency to support minor parties is checked. The tendency of the single-member district system to give the second major party a great advantage over all minor parties is extremely important. In this way it is possible to explain the *longevity* of the major parties and the instability of the minor parties. Thus, while the major parties seem to go on forever, what has become of, and who remembers a long series of Labor, Farmer-Labor, Workers', United Labor, Socialist-Labor, Peoples', Union, and American parties launched since the Civil War?
>
> Why are third parties with highly sectional support unable to survive? In this case, the single-member district system operates in favor of the third party and against one or the other of the major parties within the section. A third party ought therefore to be able to entrench itself in a region and maintain itself permanently. Obviously, the system of representation cannot account for the tendency of sectional third parties to fade away; the explanation must be found elsewhere. As a matter of fact, it is not necessary to go far afield for an explanation. Even more important than congressional elections are presidential elections, which might properly be described as the focus of American politics.... Now it is clear that a purely sectional

> party can never win a presidential election. Presidents can be elected only by combinations of sections, by parties that cross sectional lines. An exclusively sectional party is doomed to permanent futility, therefore, in the pursuit of the most important single objective of party strategy. Sooner or later exclusively sectional parties are likely to lose even their sectional support in favor of a major party which has a real chance of winning the supreme prize. For this reason narrowly sectional parties cannot displace the traditional type of major party, even though the single-member district system of electing representatives might sometimes give them an advantage.

E.E. Schattschneider, Party Government 81–83 (1942). Maurice Duverger later showed that single-member districting leads to two-party systems while more proportional systems lead to multi-party systems across a great number of democracies. Maurice Duverger, Political Parties 216–28 (2d English ed. 1959). This principle has therefore come to be known as Duverger's Law.[c] On the other hand, single-member districts do not inexorably lead to two-party systems, at least not in parliamentary systems like the United Kingdom and Canada, where third parties may sometimes enjoy regional success on a sustained basis. See David Schleicher, *Things Aren't Going That Well Over There Either: Party Polarization and Election Law in Comparative Perspective*, 2015 University of Chicago Legal Forum 433.

Another election law that makes it difficult for third parties to prosper is the nomination of major party candidates through direct primary elections. Primaries are intended to increase the ability of voters to control the ideological direction of the major parties. If primaries in fact accomplish this purpose then they are likely to harm third parties, whose chances of winning votes depend primarily on voter dissatisfaction with the major parties. As explained in a leading empirical study of third party voting:

> The story of why people vote for third parties is a story of major party deterioration. To be sure, third parties can help their own causes by selecting high caliber candidates or by building a loyal following over the years. But, overwhelmingly, it is the failure of the major parties to do what the electorate expects of them—reflect the issue preferences of voters, manage the economy, select attractive and acceptable candidates, and build voter loyalty to the parties and the political system—that most increases the likelihood of voters backing a minor party. Citizens by and large cast third party

c. For additional commentary, see, *e.g.*, Douglas W. Rae, The Political Consequences of Electoral Laws 87–103 (1967); William H. Riker, *The Number of Political Parties: A Reexamination of Duverger's Law*, 9 Comparative Politics 93 (1976). Duverger's Law has greater empirical validity if it is modified, in the way suggested by Schattschneider, by recognizing that regionally concentrated third parties can survive in a single-member district system when there is no presidential election creating pressure for a two-party system. Canada and India are examples of countries in which regional third parties have had some success. See Jae-On Kim & Mahn-Geum Ohn, *A Theory of Minor-Party Persistence: Election Rules, Social Cleavage, and the Number of Political Parties*, 70 Social Forces 575 (1992).

> ballots because they are dissatisfied with the major parties, not because they are attracted to the alternatives.

Steven J. Rosenstone, Roy L. Behr & Edward H. Lazarus, Third Parties in America 162 (2d ed. 1996).

Ballot access requirements and the exclusion of minor parties from public benefits probably have a slight impact on third parties' chances of electoral success, compared to single-member districts, first-past-the-post elections, the Electoral College, and the primary system. Nevertheless, ballot access is unquestionably of crucial importance to any independent candidate or third party, as well as for those who believe that the presence of third parties makes an important contribution to American democracy. In the words of Rosenstone, Behr and Lazarus:

> [T]he power of third parties lies in their capacity to affect the content and range of political discourse, and ultimately public policy, by raising issues and options that the two major parties have ignored. In so doing, they not only promote their cause but affect the very character of the two-party system.

For a recent argument that our two-party system is profoundly dysfunctional and that the development of third parties should be encouraged, see Lee Drutman, Breaking the Two-Party Doom Loop: The Case for Multiparty Democracy in America 2-3 (2020):

> America now has a genuine, fully sorted, two-party system. This is a new and significant development. While we've always had a two-party system in name, for most of our history the two parties have been capacious, incoherent, and overlapping. This overlap lent a certain stability to American national politics, because it worked with, rather than against, our compromise-oriented political institutions.
>
> This new era is qualitatively different: two distinct, national party coalitions organized around two distinct visions of American national identity, each claiming to represent a true majority. Only one other time in American history has the party system resembled this arrangement: the 1860s, when the United States fought a civil war and then tried to recover from one.
>
> A fully divided two-party system without any overlap is probably unworkable in any democracy, given what it does to our minds. It leads us to see our fellow citizens not as political opponents to politely disagree with but as enemies to delegitimize and destroy. It turns politics from a forum where we resolve disagreements into a battlefield where we must win and they must lose.
>
> A fully divided two-party system is decidedly unworkable in America, given our political institutions. We have separation-of-powers government designed to make narrow majority rule difficult to impossible. And yet we

have a party system where both sides attempt to impose narrow majority rule on each other. The mismatch is unsustainable.

Finally, a fully divided two-party system is completely unworkable when the partisan divide is over the character of national identity, as it is today. This raises the stakes impossibly high and makes compromise impossible. It poses an existential threat to the future of American democracy.

Drutman advocates reforms that he thinks would weaken the grip of the two major parties and allow multiple parties to flourish. One of his proposals is ranked-choice voting (discussed *infra*, Note 7 following *Timmons v. Twin Cities Area New Party*). He also proposes adopting multi-member districts, expanding the size of the House, and getting rid of primaries. Do you agree that the time has come for major structural reforms that would weaken the two-party system? Would these reforms achieve that objective? Are they realistically achievable? Are there others that should be considered?

I. Ballot Access

The issue of ballot access for parties and candidates did not arise in the 19th century, because before the introduction of the secret (or "Australian") ballot around the end of that century, the state did not typically provide a ballot at all. It was the responsibility of the voter to supply a ballot. In practice, this usually meant that the parties provided printed ballots, each containing the names of their own candidates, and each distinctively colored so that observers could easily tell which party's ballot an individual was casting. This system made it relatively difficult for voters to "split their tickets," and it also made it difficult to support a party that was not sufficiently well organized to print and distribute its own ballots.

To permit secret voting, states had to print their own ballots with the names of competing candidates, so that voters could choose in private. This meant that the state had to set rules for the eligibility of parties and candidates to be listed on the state-supplied ballots. For parties and candidates who qualified, the Australian ballot was a considerable boon, because the obstacles that hindered voters wishing to depart from the major parties were removed. But for parties and candidates who did not qualify, the Australian ballot made a bad situation worse. Although most states permit write-in votes,[d] it is easier to vote for a listed candidate, and unlisted candidates typically are not considered serious ones. For a wealth of information on past and current ballot access requirements, see Richard Winger, *How Ballot Access Laws Affect the U.S. Party System*, 16 American Review of Politics 321 (1996).

---

d. In *Burdick v. Takushi*, 504 U.S. 428 (1992), discussed *infra*, Note 1 following *Munro*, the Supreme Court ruled that the Constitution does not necessarily require a state to permit write-in votes.

Until 1968, the states were free to set whatever ballot qualifications they chose. In that year, a strong challenge to the Democrats and Republicans was mounted by George Wallace, running under the banner of the American Independent Party. Wallace was able to satisfy the petition requirements for listing on the ballot for every state but one, Ohio. Even in Ohio, Wallace was able to satisfy the relatively stiff fifteen percent signature requirement, but he was not able to do so by the early deadline of February 7 of the election year. Such an early deadline can be particularly difficult for third party and independent challenges, which often develop in response to the candidates chosen by the major parties.

In *Williams v. Rhodes*, 393 U.S. 23 (1968), the Supreme Court ordered Wallace to be placed on the Ohio ballot. Ohio's laws, according to the Court, made it "virtually impossible for any party to qualify on the ballot except the Republican and Democratic Parties," which retained automatic ballot status by receiving at least ten percent of the votes in gubernatorial elections. The Court has not relied on a constitutional right to be a candidate for public office, in *Williams* or in subsequent cases. Rather, the Court said that Ohio's restrictions placed burdens on "two different, although overlapping, kinds of rights—the right of individuals to associate for the advancement of political beliefs, and the right of qualified voters, regardless of their political persuasion, to cast their votes effectively."

The Court rejected Ohio's claim that its strict requirements could be justified under the Equal Protection Clause by its interest in promoting a two-party system.

> The fact is ... that the Ohio system does not favor a "two-party system"; it favors two particular parties—the Republicans and the Democrats—and in effect tends to give them a complete monopoly.... New parties struggling for their place must have the time and opportunity to organize in order to meet reasonable requirements for ballot position, just as the old parties have had in the past.
>
> ... Concededly, the State does have an interest in attempting to see that the election winner be the choice of a majority of its voters. But to grant the State power to keep all political parties off the ballot until they have enough members to win would stifle the growth of all new parties working to increase their strength from year to year.

This language in *Williams* indicated that the Court was willing to concede a state interest in requiring some demonstration of support for a candidate or party as a prerequisite to ballot access. In *Jenness v. Fortson*, 403 U.S. 431 (1971), the Court made it clear that more than token support could be required. *Jenness* upheld Georgia's requirement that independent candidates obtain signatures from electors equal in number to five percent of the number of registered voters in the jurisdiction. The deadline was the same as that for candidates who wished to be listed on the ballot as candidates in party primaries. The Court regarded the Georgia requirements as significantly less onerous than the ones struck down in *Williams*.

> Unlike Ohio, Georgia does not require every candidate to be the nominee of a political party, but fully recognizes independent candidacies. Unlike Ohio, Georgia does not fix an unreasonably early filing deadline for candidates not endorsed by established parties. Unlike Ohio, Georgia does not impose upon a small party or a new party the Procrustean requirement of establishing elaborate primary election machinery. Finally, and in sum, Georgia's election laws, unlike Ohio's, do not operate to freeze the political status quo....
>
> There is surely an important state interest in requiring some preliminary showing of a significant modicum of support before printing the name of a political organization's candidate on the ballot—the interest, if no other, in avoiding confusion, deception, and even frustration of the democratic process at the general election. The 5% figure is, to be sure, apparently somewhat higher than the percentage of support required to be shown in many States as a condition for ballot position, but this is balanced by the fact that Georgia has imposed no arbitrary restrictions whatever upon the eligibility of any registered voter to sign as many nominating petitions as he wishes.

Although the Court viewed the Georgia requirements in *Jenness* as less onerous than the Ohio requirements in *Williams*, in fact the Georgia requirements—by keying to the number of *registered*, rather than *actual* voters—may have been much more onerous. See Richard Winger, *The Supreme Court and the Burial of Ballot Access: A Critical Review of* Jenness v. Fortson, 1 Election Law Journal 235, 242 (2002).

Numerous cases involving ballot access and related issues, like write-in voting and fusion candidacies, have found their way to the Supreme Court. The Court has generally adhered to the pattern set in *Williams* and *Jenness*: It will uphold ballot access requirements that are difficult for many minor parties and independent candidates to satisfy, but will intervene when it believes the requirements are so severe that they pose obstacles even to parties and candidates that can demonstrate significant electoral support.

Munro v. Socialist Workers Party

479 U.S. 189 (1986)

Justice WHITE delivered the opinion of the Court.

The State of Washington requires that a minor-party candidate for partisan office receive at least 1% of all votes cast for that office in the State's primary election before the candidate's name will be placed on the general election ballot. The question for decision is whether this statutory requirement, as applied to candidates for statewide offices, violates the First and Fourteenth Amendments to the United States Constitution. The Court of Appeals for the Ninth Circuit declared the provision unconstitutional. We reverse.

In 1977, the State of Washington enacted amendments to its election laws, changing the manner in which candidates from minor political parties qualify for placement on the general election ballot. Before the amendments, a minor-party candidate did not participate in the State's primary elections, but rather sought his or her party's nomination at a party convention held on the same day as the primary election for "major" parties. The convention-nominated, minor-party candidate secured a position on the general election ballot upon the filing of a certificate signed by at least 100 registered voters who had participated in the convention and who had not voted in the primary election. The 1977 amendments retained the requirement that a minor-party candidate be nominated by convention, but imposed the additional requirement that, as a precondition to general ballot access, the nominee for an office appear on the primary election ballot and receive at least 1% of all votes cast for that particular office at the primary election.

Washington conducts a "blanket primary" at which registered voters may vote for any candidate of their choice, irrespective of the candidates' political party affiliation. . . .[e]

The events giving rise to this action occurred in 1983, after the state legislature authorized a special primary election to be held on October 11, 1983, to fill a vacancy in the office of United States Senator. Appellee Dean Peoples qualified to be placed on the primary election ballot as the nominee of appellee Socialist Workers Party. Also appearing on that ballot were 32 other candidates. At the primary, Mr. Peoples received approximately nine one-hundredths of one percent of the total votes cast for the office,[9] and, accordingly, the State did not place his name on the general election ballot. . . .

Restrictions upon the access of political parties to the ballot impinge upon the rights of individuals to associate for political purposes, as well as the rights of qualified voters to cast their votes effectively, *Williams*, and may not survive scrutiny under the First and Fourteenth Amendments. . . . These associational rights, however, are not absolute and are necessarily subject to qualification if elections are to be run fairly and effectively. *Storer v. Brown*, 415 U.S. 724, 730 (1974).

While there is no "litmus-paper test" for deciding a case like this, *ibid.*, it is now clear that States may condition access to the general election ballot by a minor-party or independent candidate upon a showing of a modicum of support among the potential voters for the office. In *Jenness*, the Court unanimously rejected a challenge to Georgia's election statutes that required independent candidates and minor-party candidates, in order to be listed on the general election ballot, to submit petitions signed by at least 5% of the voters eligible to vote in the last election for the office in question. Primary elections were held only for those political organizations whose

---

e. This system was similar to the one in California that was later struck down in *California Democratic Party v. Jones*, 530 U.S. 567 (2000). After *Jones*, the State of Washington switched to a nonpartisan blanket primary with candidates' party preference listed on the ballot, upheld against a facial challenge in *Washington State Grange v. Washington State Republican Party*, 552 U.S. 442 (2008). Both *Jones* and *Washington State Grange* are discussed in Chapter 8, Part III.B.2. — Eds.

9. Mr. Peoples received 596 of the 681,690 votes cast in the primary.

candidate received 20% or more of the vote at the last gubernatorial or Presidential election. The Court's opinion observed that "[t]here is surely an important state interest in requiring some preliminary showing of a significant modicum of support before printing the name of a political organization's candidate on the ballot—the interest, if no other, in avoiding confusion, deception, and even frustration of the democratic process at the general election." And, in *American Party of Texas v. White*, 415 U.S. 767 (1974), candidates of minor political parties in Texas were required to demonstrate support by persons numbering at least 1% of the total vote cast for Governor at the last preceding general election. Candidates could secure the requisite number of petition signatures at precinct nominating conventions and by supplemental petitions following the conventions. Voters signing these supplemental petitions had to swear under oath that they had not participated in another party's primary election or nominating process. In rejecting a First Amendment challenge to the 1% requirement, we asserted that the State's interest in preserving the integrity of the electoral process and in regulating the number of candidates on the ballot was compelling and reiterated the holding in *Jenness* that a State may require a preliminary showing of significant support before placing a candidate on the general election ballot.

Jenness and *American Party* establish with unmistakable clarity that States have an "undoubted right to require candidates to make a preliminary showing of substantial support in order to qualify for a place on the ballot. . . ." *Anderson v. Celebrezze*, 460 U.S. 780, 788–789, n. 9 (1983) [discussed in Note 1 following this case—Eds.] We reaffirm that principle today.

The Court of Appeals determined that Washington's interest in insuring that candidates had sufficient community support did not justify the enactment of [the 1% requirement] because "Washington's political history evidences no voter confusion from ballot overcrowding." We accept this historical fact, but it does not require invalidation. . . .

We have never required a State to make a particularized showing of the existence of voter confusion, ballot overcrowding, or the presence of frivolous candidacies prior to the imposition of reasonable restrictions on ballot access. . . .

To require States to prove actual voter confusion, ballot overcrowding, or the presence of frivolous candidacies as a predicate to the imposition of reasonable ballot access restrictions would invariably lead to endless court battles over the sufficiency of the "evidence" marshaled by a State to prove the predicate. Such a requirement would necessitate that a State's political system sustain some level of damage before the legislature could take corrective action. Legislatures, we think, should be permitted to respond to potential deficiencies in the electoral process with foresight rather than reactively, provided that the response is reasonable and does not significantly impinge on constitutionally protected rights.

In any event, the record here suggests that [imposition of the 1% requirement] was, in fact, linked to the state legislature's perception that the general election ballot was becoming cluttered with candidates from minor parties who did not command significant voter support. In 1976 . . . , the largest number of minor political parties in Washington's history—12—appeared on the general election ballot. The record demonstrates that at least part of the legislative impetus for [the 1% requirement] was concern about minor parties having such easy access to Washington's general election ballot.

The primary election in Washington . . . is "an integral part of the entire election process . . . [that] functions to winnow out and finally reject all but the chosen candidates." *Storer v. Brown*, 415 U.S. 724, 735 (1974). We think that the State can properly reserve the general election ballot "for major struggles," *ibid.*, by conditioning access to that ballot on a showing of a modicum of voter support. In this respect, the fact that the State is willing to have a long and complicated ballot at the primary provides no measure of what it may require for access to the general election ballot. The State of Washington was clearly entitled to raise the ante for ballot access, to simplify the general election ballot, and to avoid the possibility of unrestrained factionalism at the general election.

Neither do we agree with the Court of Appeals and appellees that the burdens imposed on appellees' First Amendment rights by the 1977 amendments are far too severe to be justified by the State's interest in restricting access to the general ballot. Much is made of the fact that prior to 1977, virtually every minor-party candidate who sought general election ballot position so qualified, while since 1977 only 1 out of 12 minor-party candidates has appeared on that ballot. Such historical facts are relevant, but they prove very little in this case, other than the fact that [the 1% requirement] does not provide an insuperable barrier to minor-party ballot access.[11] It is hardly a surprise that minor parties appeared on the general election ballot before [the requirement was imposed]; for, until then, there were virtually no restrictions on access. Under our cases, however, Washington was not required to afford such automatic access and would have been entitled to insist on a more substantial showing of voter support. Comparing the actual experience before and after 1977 tells us nothing about how minor parties would have fared in those earlier years had Washington conditioned ballot access to the maximum extent permitted by the Constitution.

Appellees urge that this case differs substantially from our previous cases because requiring primary votes to qualify for a position on the general election ballot is qualitatively more restrictive than requiring signatures on a nominating petition. In effect, their submission would foreclose any use of the primary election to determine a minor party's qualification for the general ballot. We are unpersuaded, however, that the differences between the two mechanisms are of constitutional dimension. Because Washington provides a "blanket primary," minor party candidates

11. [The requirement] apparently poses an insubstantial obstacle to minor-party candidates for non-statewide offices and independent candidates for statewide offices. Since 1977, 36 out of 40 such minor-party candidates have qualified for the general election ballot and 4 out of 5 independent candidates for statewide office have so qualified.

can campaign among the entire pool of registered voters. Effort and resources that would otherwise be directed at securing petition signatures can instead be channeled into campaigns to "get the vote out," foster candidate name recognition, and educate the electorate. To be sure, candidates must demonstrate, through their ability to secure votes at the primary election, that they enjoy a modicum of community support in order to advance to the general election. But requiring candidates to demonstrate such support is precisely what we have held States are permitted to do.

Appellees argue that voter turnout at primary elections is generally lower than the turnout at general elections, and therefore . . . the pool of potential supporters from which Party candidates can secure 1% of the vote [is reduced]. We perceive no more force to this argument than we would with an argument by a losing candidate that his supporters' constitutional rights were infringed by their failure to participate in the election. Washington has created no impediment to voting at the primary elections; every supporter of the Party in the State is free to cast his or her ballot for the Party's candidates. . . . States are not burdened with a constitutional imperative to reduce voter apathy or to "handicap" an unpopular candidate to increase the likelihood that the candidate will gain access to the general election ballot. As we see it, Washington has done no more than to visit on a candidate a requirement to show a "significant modicum" of voter support, and it was entitled to require that showing in its primary elections.

We also observe that [Washington's statute] is more accommodating of First Amendment rights and values than were the statutes we upheld in *Jenness*, *American Party*, and *Storer*. Under each scheme analyzed in those cases, if a candidate failed to satisfy the qualifying criteria, the State's voters had no opportunity to cast a ballot for that candidate and the candidate had no ballot-connected campaign platform from which to espouse his or her views; the unsatisfied qualifying criteria served as an absolute bar to ballot access. Undeniably, such restrictions raise concerns of constitutional dimension, for the "exclusion of candidates . . . burdens voters' freedom of association, because an election campaign is an effective platform for the expression of views on the issues of the day. . . ." *Anderson*. Here, however, Washington virtually guarantees what the parties challenging the Georgia, Texas, and California election laws so vigorously sought — candidate access to a statewide ballot. This is a significant difference. Washington has chosen a vehicle by which minor-party candidates must demonstrate voter support that serves to promote the very First Amendment values that are threatened by overly burdensome ballot access restrictions. It can hardly be said that Washington's voters are denied freedom of association because they must channel their expressive activity into a campaign at the primary as opposed to the general election. It is true that voters must make choices as they vote at the primary, but there are no state-imposed obstacles impairing voters in the exercise of their choices. . . .

The judgment of the Court of Appeals for the Ninth Circuit is therefore reversed.

It is so ordered.

Justice MARSHALL, with whom Justice BRENNAN joins, dissenting.

... The minor party's often unconventional positions broaden political debate, expand the range of issues with which the electorate is concerned, and influence the positions of the majority, in some instances ultimately becoming majority positions. And its very existence provides an outlet for voters to express dissatisfaction with the candidates or platforms of the major parties. Notwithstanding the crucial role minor parties play in the American political arena, the Court holds today that the associational rights of minor parties and their supporters are not unduly burdened by a ballot access statute that, in practice, completely excludes minor parties from participating in statewide general elections.

I

The Court fails to articulate the level of scrutiny it applies in holding that the Washington 1% primary vote requirement is not an unconstitutional ballot access restriction. . . .

By contrast, the standard of review set forth in our prior decisions is clear: Whether viewed as a burden on the right to associate or as discrimination against minor parties, a provision that burdens minor-party access to the ballot must be necessary to further a compelling state interest, and must be narrowly tailored to achieve that goal. The necessity for this approach becomes evident when we consider that major parties, which by definition are ordinarily in control of legislative institutions, may seek to perpetuate themselves at the expense of developing minor parties. The application of strict scrutiny to ballot access restrictions ensures that measures taken to further a State's interest in keeping frivolous candidates off the ballot do not incidentally impose an impermissible bar to minor-party access.

Appellant argues that there is no ballot access limitation here at all, and thus no need for the application of heightened scrutiny, because minor parties can appear on a primary ballot simply by meeting reasonable petition requirements. I cannot accept, however, as a general proposition, that access to any ballot is always constitutionally adequate. The Court, in concluding here that the State may reserve the general election ballot for "major struggles," appears to acknowledge that, because of its finality, the general election is the arena where issues are sharpened, policies are hotly debated, and the candidates' positions are clarified. Nonetheless, the Court deems access to the primary adequate to satisfy minor-party rights to ballot access, even though we have characterized the primary election principally as a "forum for continuing intraparty feuds," *Storer v. Brown*, 415 U.S. 724, 735 (1974), rather than an arena for debate on the issues. Access to a primary election ballot is not, in my view, all the access that is due when minor parties are excluded entirely from the general election.

The Court's conclusion stems from a fundamental misconception of the role minor parties play in our constitutional scheme. To conclude that access to a primary ballot is adequate ballot access presumes that minor-party candidates seek only to get elected. But, as discussed earlier, minor-party participation in electoral politics serves to expand and affect political debate.... That contribution cannot be realized if they are unable to participate meaningfully in the phase of the electoral process in which policy choices are most seriously considered. A statutory scheme that excludes minor parties entirely from this phase places an excessive burden on the constitutionally protected associational rights of those parties and their adherents....

I am unconvinced that the Washington statute serves the asserted justification for the law: avoiding ballot overcrowding and voter confusion. The statute streamlines the general election, where overcrowding and confusion appear never to have been much of a problem before the 1977 amendments, at the expense of an already cumbersome primary ballot. Between 1907 and 1977, no more than six minor party candidates ever appeared on the general election ballot for any statewide office, and no more than four ever ran for any statewide office other than Governor, suggesting that the ballot was never very crowded. But in the 1983 special election that prompted this lawsuit, appellee Peoples, instead of being placed on the general election ballot with 2 other candidates, was placed on the primary ballot along with *32* other candidates: 18 Democrats and 14 Republicans.

The Court notes that we have not previously required a State seeking to impose reasonable ballot access restrictions to make a particularized showing that voter confusion in fact existed before those restrictions were imposed. But where the State's solution exacerbates the very problem it claims to solve, the State's means cannot be even rationally related to its asserted ends....

Additionally, while a State may have an interest in eliminating frivolous candidates by requiring candidates to demonstrate "a significant modicum of support" to qualify for a place on the ballot, Washington already had a mechanism that required minor-party candidates to show such support, which it retained after its imposition of the 1% primary vote requirement in 1977. Appellees did not challenge the legitimacy of the convention and petition requirements in this case, but the fact that a mechanism for requiring some showing of support previously existed casts doubt on the need for the imposition of still another requirement on minor-party candidates. Moreover, the application of the 1% requirement suggests it is overbroad, avoiding frivolous candidacies only by excluding virtually all minor-party candidates from general elections for statewide office.

The only purpose this statute seems narrowly tailored to advance is the impermissible one of protecting the major political parties from competition precisely when that competition would be most meaningful. Because the statute burdens appellees' First Amendment interests, it must be subjected to strict scrutiny; because it fails to pass such scrutiny, it is unconstitutional.

II

Even if I were prepared to adopt the nebulous logic the Court employs in preference to the mandatory strict standard of review in this case, I could not reach the majority's result. While this Court has in the past acknowledged that limits on minor-party access to the ballot may in some circumstances be appropriate, we have made equally clear that States may not employ ballot access limitations which result in the exclusion of minor parties from the ballot. . . .

Under this reasoning, the validity of ballot access limitations is a function of empirical evidence: A minor party is not impermissibly burdened by ballot access restrictions when "a reasonably diligent independent candidate" could be expected to satisfy the ballot access requirement. *Storer*. . . .

Washington's primary law acts as an almost total bar to minor-party access to statewide general election ballots. . . . The Court of Appeals found that by 1984, only one minor-party candidate had been able to surmount the 1% barrier and earn the right to participate in the general election. The legislation leading to this substantial elimination of minor parties from the political arena in Washington's general elections should not be sustained as a legitimate requirement of a demonstration of significant support.

Notes and Questions

1. *The* Anderson-Burdick *Standard.* In *Williams*, the Court required a compelling state interest to justify the burden on voting and associational rights. In *Munro*, however, the majority is not very clear on the level of scrutiny it applies (as Justice Marshall points out in dissent), though it does cite *Anderson v. Celebrezze*, 460 U.S. 780 (1983). In *Anderson*, the Court articulated a flexible standard for reviewing restrictions on ballot access under the First and Fourteenth Amendments:

> Although [the] rights of voters are fundamental, not all restrictions imposed by the States on candidates' eligibility for the ballot impose constitutionally suspect burdens on voters' rights to associate or to choose among candidates. We have recognized that, "as a practical matter, there must be a substantial regulation of elections if they are to be fair and honest and if some sort of order, rather than chaos, is to accompany the democratic processes." *Storer v. Brown*, 415 U.S. 724, 730 (1974). To achieve these necessary objectives, States have enacted comprehensive and sometimes complex election codes. Each provision of these schemes, whether it governs the registration and qualifications of voters, the selection and eligibility of candidates, or the voting process itself, inevitably affects — at least to some degree — the individual's right to vote and his right to associate with others for political ends. Nevertheless, the State's important regulatory interests are generally sufficient to justify reasonable, nondiscriminatory restrictions.
>
> Constitutional challenges to specific provisions of a State's election laws therefore cannot be resolved by any "litmus-paper test" that will separate valid from invalid restrictions. *Storer*. Instead, a court must resolve such a challenge by an analytical process that parallels its work in ordinary litigation. It must first consider the character and magnitude of the asserted

> injury to the rights protected by the First and Fourteenth Amendments that the plaintiff seeks to vindicate. It then must identify and evaluate the precise interests put forward by the State as justifications for the burden imposed by its rule. In passing judgment, the Court must not only determine the legitimacy and strength of each of those interests, it also must consider the extent to which those interests make it necessary to burden the plaintiff's rights. Only after weighing all these factors is the reviewing court in a position to decide whether the challenged provision is unconstitutional. The results of this evaluation will not be automatic; as we have recognized, there is "no substitute for the hard judgments that must be made." *Storer.*

The Court further elaborated on this standard in *Burdick v. Takushi*, 504 U.S. 428, 433–34 (1992), which upheld Hawaii's prohibition on write-in voting under the First and Fourteenth Amendment:

> Election laws will invariably impose some burden upon individual voters. Each provision of a code, "whether it governs the registration and qualifications of voters, the selection and eligibility of candidates, or the voting process itself, inevitably affects-at least to some degree-the individual's right to vote and his right to associate with others for political ends." *Anderson*. Consequently, to subject every voting regulation to strict scrutiny and to require that the regulation be narrowly tailored to advance a compelling state interest . . . would tie the hands of States seeking to assure that elections are operated equitably and efficiently. Accordingly, the mere fact that a State's system "creates barriers . . . tending to limit the field of candidates from which voters might choose . . . does not of itself compel close scrutiny." *Bullock v. Carter*, 405 U.S. 134, 143 (1972); *Anderson*; *McDonald v. Board of Election Comm'rs of Chicago*, 394 U.S. 802 (1969).
>
> Instead, as the full Court agreed in *Anderson*, a more flexible standard applies. A court considering a challenge to a state election law must weigh "the character and magnitude of the asserted injury to the rights protected by the First and Fourteenth Amendments that the plaintiff seeks to vindicate" against "the precise interests put forward by the State as justifications for the burden imposed by its rule," taking into consideration "the extent to which those interests make it necessary to burden the plaintiff's rights." *Id.*
>
> Under this standard, the rigorousness of our inquiry into the propriety of a state election law depends upon the extent to which a challenged regulation burdens First and Fourteenth Amendment rights. Thus, as we have recognized when those rights are subjected to "severe" restrictions, the regulation must be "narrowly drawn to advance a state interest of compelling importance." *Norman v. Reed*, 502 U.S. 279, 289 (1992). But when a state election law provision imposes only "reasonable, nondiscriminatory restrictions" upon the First and Fourteenth Amendment rights of voters, "the State's important regulatory interests are generally sufficient to justify" the restrictions. *Anderson.*

The standard articulated in *Anderson* and *Burdick* has become increasingly important in recent years, because it has been used in constitutional challenges to other kinds of election laws, including challenges to blanket primaries (see *Washington State Grange*, Chapter 8, Part III.B.2), and burdens on voting like ID requirements (see *Crawford v. Marion County Election Board*, Chapter 6, Part I.C). Under this standard, "severe" burdens on voting and associational rights are subject to strict scrutiny, while "reasonable, nondiscriminatory restrictions" may be justified by important regulatory interests. This standard is not a model of precision. What does it take for a burden to be severe? And what sort of regulatory interests may justify non-severe restrictions on voting and association? This standard may be thought of as a sliding scale: the heavier the burden on voters, the stronger the state's interests must be; conversely, the lighter the burden on voters, the less weighty the state justification must be.

Despite the uncertainty that may exist regarding the constitutional standard, if we look at the results in the ballot access cases that have reached the Supreme Court, the pattern does not seem particularly unclear. With the assistance of the Court in *Williams*, George Wallace was able to appear on every state's ballot in the 1968 presidential election. John Anderson, an independent candidate in 1980, also appeared on the ballot in all states, again with the help of the Court, which in *Anderson v. Celebrezze* repeated its 1968 performance by striking down overly restrictive Ohio requirements.[f] In 1992 and 1996, Ross Perot appeared on the ballot of every state, without the necessity for Supreme Court intervention.[g] It thus appears that under the Court's present doctrine, states cannot enforce requirements whose effect is to bar from the ballot candidates or parties with enough support to make a substantial showing in the election. The Court has been much more likely to allow the exclusion of third party and independent candidates who are unlikely to make a substantial showing.

Lower court decisions are somewhat more difficult to predict, given the fact-intensive balancing test that applies to ballot access cases. For an example of an appellate court decision deferring to state interests, upholding a rule that denied ballot access to parties that get less than three percent of the vote, see *Green Party of Arkansas v. Martin*, 649 F.3d 675 (8th Cir. 2011). Likewise, in *Tripp v. Scholz*, 872 F.3d 857 (7th Cir. 2017), the Seventh Circuit rejected Green Party members' constitutional challenge to Illinois's law requiring that new political parties' candidates obtain petition signatures equal to five percent of the total number of votes cast in the last state legislative district election to appear on the general election ballot.

---

f. More precisely, the district court ordered that Anderson's name be placed on the ballot in Ohio, and this ruling was vindicated by the Supreme Court in 1983. Anderson also required judicial assistance to reach the ballot in Maine and Maryland.

g. Green Party candidate Ralph Nader appeared on the ballot in 43 states in 2000 but only appeared on the ballot in 34 states in 2004, in the face of a concerted effort by Democrats to keep him off the ballot. See *infra* Note 3. In 2008, Nader appeared on the ballot in 45 states, in some of them as the candidate of the Peace & Freedom Party.

Even considered alongside additional requirements that petition sheets be notarized and that petitions be gathered in a 90-day period, the court found that Illinois's signature requirement did not impose a severe burden. The court went on to conclude that the state's interests in preventing ballot overcrowding, voter confusion, and circulator fraud justified these requirements.

Lower courts are not always so deferential to state interests. In *Green Party of Tennessee v. Hargett*, 791 F.3d 684 (6th Cir. 2015), the Sixth Circuit struck down a state requirement that minor parties have at least one candidate for statewide office obtain votes equal to five percent of the votes cast for governor in the last gubernatorial election, in order to retain ballot access. The Eleventh Circuit upheld a lower court ruling that struck down Georgia's ballot access requirements for third-party presidential candidates. *Green Party of Georgia v. Kemp*, 171 F. Supp. 3d 1340 (N.D. Ga. 2016), *aff'd*, 674 Fed. Appx. 974 (11th Cir. 2017) (per curiam). That court again ruled in favor of a third party and its candidates challenging Georgia's ballot-access laws in *Cowen v. Georgia Secretary of State,* 960 F.3d 1339 (11th Cir. 2020). That case challenged the state's qualification requirements for congressional candidates. The Eleventh Circuit reversed the district court's decision granting summary judgment to the state, on the ground that it had failed to apply the contextual balancing standard mandated by *Anderson*. See also *Gill v. Scholz*, 962 F.3d 360 (7th Cir. 2020) (ruling in favor of an independent candidate challenging Illinois's ballot access requirements, on the ground that the district court had granted summary judgment to the state without applying *Anderson-Burdick* balancing standard).

2. *Broadening Political Debate.* What constitutional interests are served by having third party and independent candidates on the ballot when they have little chance of winning? In his dissenting opinion, Justice Marshall asserts:

> The minor party's often unconventional positions broaden political debate, expand the range of issues with which the electorate is concerned, and influence the positions of the majority, in some instances ultimately becoming majority positions. And its very existence provides an outlet for voters to express dissatisfaction with the candidates or platforms of the major parties.

It is undoubtedly the case that many third party and independent candidates recognize that they have no chance of being elected and therefore are running for other reasons. For the government, however, the function served by elections — determining who shall hold public office — is the crucial one. In designing election procedures, should the government be permitted to exalt its own purpose over other uses to which parties and candidates may wish to put elections?

Some scholars have contended that the right to vote has expressive elements — one can send a message by the vote one casts. See Adam Winkler, Note, *Expressive Voting*, 68 New York University Law Review 330 (1993). In *Burdick*, the Supreme Court rejected such a role for voting, holding that "[a]ttributing to elections a more generalized expressive function would undermine the ability of States to operate elections fairly and efficiently." Was the Court right to reject the idea that voting serves an expressive function?

3. *Competition.* Should judicial review of ballot access rules consider their impact upon political competition? Consider the 2004 cases involving presidential candidate Ralph Nader, who unsuccessfully sought injunctive relief to get his name on the ballot in six states. The issues included the constitutionality of state rules regarding the deadline for petitions, the number of signatures required to get on the ballot, and the use of out-of-state petition circulators. See Richard Winger, *An Analysis of the 2004 Nader Ballot Access Federal Court Cases*, 32 Fordham Urban Law Journal 567 (2005).

In one of those cases, *Nader v. Keith*, 385 F.3d 729, 732–34 (7th Cir. 2004), Judge Posner wrote the following in regard to Nader's attempt to get on the Illinois ballot, despite having gathered insufficient signatures by the filing deadline:

> [T]he barriers to the entry of third parties must not be set too high; yet the two major parties, who between them exert virtually complete control over American government, are apt to collude to do just that. For like other duopolists they would prefer not to be challenged by some upstart—although if a major party believes that a third party will take more votes from the other party than from itself, it will support that third party (surreptitiously, because it's supporting an ideological opponent), and the other party will oppose it (also surreptitiously, because it's opposing an ideological ally). . . .
>
> It doesn't follow from what we said about the importance of preserving opportunities for the entry of new parties into the political arena that it would be a good thing if there were no barriers at all to third-party candidacies. A multiplication of parties would make our politics more ideological by reducing the influence of the median voter (who in a two-party system determines the outcome of most elections), and this could be a very bad thing. More mundanely, terminal voter confusion might ensue from having a multiplicity of Presidential candidates on the ballot—for think of the confusion caused by the "butterfly" ballot used in Palm Beach County, Florida in the 2000 Presidential election. That fiasco was a consequence of the fact that the ballot listed ten Presidential candidates. The butterfly ballot was a folded punchcard ballot in which the ten candidates for President were listed on facing pages. [The butterfly ballot is depicted in Chapter 6, Figure 6.1.—Eds.] . . .
>
> Less obviously, third-party candidates would themselves be harmed if there were no barriers to including such candidates on the ballot. It is to the Libertarian Party's advantage that if Nader's challenge fails, its candidate will be the only independent candidate for President on the ballot. If there were 98 independent candidates, none could hope for a nontrivial vote.

> So there have to be hurdles to getting on the ballot and the requirement of submitting a minimum number of nominating petitions is a standard one. In a state the size of Illinois—the population exceeds 12 million, of whom more than 7 million are registered voters—requiring a third-party candidate to obtain 25,000 signed nominating petitions cannot be thought excessive. *Jenness* upheld a Georgia law that required petitions from 5 percent of the registered voters—in Illinois that would mean 350,000 petitions! Equally stringent requirements have been upheld in other cases. . . .

For a criticism of Judge Posner's analysis of the third party issues in *Nader v. Keith*, see Richard Winger, *How Many Parties Ought to Be on the Ballot?: An Analysis of* Nader v. Keith, 5 Election Law Journal 170 (2006). See also Dmitri Evseev, *A Second Look at Third Parties: Correcting the Supreme Court's Understanding of Elections*, 85 Boston University Law Review 1277 (2005). For further discussion of the scholarly debate regarding competition and competitiveness, see Chapter 4.

In 2008, two circuit courts struck down state restrictions on Nader's attempt to get on the ballot. *Nader v. Blackwell*, 545 F.3d 459 (6th Cir. 2008); *Nader v. Brewer*, 531 F.3d 1028 (9th Cir. 2008). For an analysis of the effect of partisan affiliation on judicial decisions in Nader's ballot access lawsuits, see Kyle C. Kopko, *Partisanship Suppressed: Judicial Decision-Making in Ralph Nader's 2004 Ballot Access Litigation*, 7 Election Law Journal 301 (2008). Nader's former campaign manager has written a book recounting the barriers the campaign experienced and, more broadly, arguing that the two major parties have made it extremely difficult for third party and independent campaigns to compete in U.S. elections. Theresa Amato, Grand Illusion: The Myth of Voter Choice in a Two-Party Tyranny (2009).

Do ballot ordering laws requiring that major-party candidates appear first on the ballot violate the Constitution? These laws arguably disadvantage third-party and independent candidates because candidates at the top of the ballot generally receive more votes, all other things being equal. This phenomenon is referred to as the "primacy effect," and is generally understood to arise from voters choosing the first satisfactory candidate on the list—or, as some social scientists put it, "satisficing." See Mary Beth Beazley, *Ballot Design as Fail-Safe: An Ounce of Rotation is Worth a Pound of Litigation*, 12 Election Law Journal 18 (2013). In *Green Party of Tennessee v. Hargett*, 700 F.3d 816, 826 (6th Cir. 2012), the court rejected a facial constitutional challenge to a state law requiring that "on general election ballots, the name of each political party having nominees on the ballot shall be listed in the following order: majority party, minority party, and recognized minor party, if any." The Sixth Circuit cited evidence disfavoring facial challenges, while leaving the door open for an as-applied challenge based on evidence that the state law disadvantages third-party candidates.

4. *Bad Legislative Intent?* Why did the Washington legislature adopt the system challenged in *Munro*? Apparently, to avoid becoming a "laughing stock" and to save money. In the 1976 elections, a Jazz musician named Red Kelly formed the OWL

Party, which stood for "Out With Logic; On With Lunacy," which ran a series of joke candidates to mock the political system. For example, "Fast" Lucie Griswold ran for secretary of state as an OWL candidate. She advocated that the next secretary be able to "take shorthand or do typing." She also took "unequivocal stands" against "(1) The heartbreak of psoriasis; (2) Bed wetting; (3) The big 'O'; [and] (4) Post nasal drip." The legislature may have been motivated, at least in part, to save the expense of having the OWL Party's statements appear in ballot materials printed at public expense. If that more benign explanation of the legislature's intent is correct, should it have any bearing on the constitutionality of its ballot access law? For an argument in the negative, see Richard L. Hasen, *Bad Legislative Intent*, 2006 Wisconsin Law Review 843.

5. *Top-Two Primaries.* Consider the State of Washington's top-two primary system, which the Supreme Court upheld against a facial challenge in *Washington State Grange v. Washington State Republican Party*, 552 U.S. 442 (2008) (discussed at greater length in Chapter 8). In Washington, all voters may now vote for candidates of any party in the primary election, but only the top two vote-getters (regardless of party) proceed to the general election. This makes it very unlikely that any third-party candidates will make it to the general election ballot. Does this present a serious problem, to the extent one believes that elections should provide a forum for citizens to express dissatisfaction with the major parties? Should Washington's system be struck down as applied to third-party candidates repeatedly frustrated in their efforts to obtain access to the general election ballot?

Recall that Washington allows candidates to list their party preference on the primary ballot. What if candidates preferring a third party may not have that preference listed on the ballot, unless the party gets a prescribed number of votes, registered voters, or petition signatures? That is currently the law in California, which adopted a top-two primary like Washington's in 2010. See Jessica Levinson, *Is the Party Over? Examining the Constitutionality of Proposition 14 as It Relates to Ballot Access for Minor Parties*, 44 Loyola of Los Angeles Law Review 463 (2011). Levinson argues that strict scrutiny should apply to a restriction on a third-party preference being listed on a ballot. In *Chamness v. Bowen*, 722 F.3d 1110 (9th Cir. 2013), the Ninth Circuit rejected a candidate's argument that the state should allow him to be designated as "Independent" rather than "No Party Preference" on the ballot. Applying the *Anderson-Burdick* standard, the Ninth Circuit concluded that the state's rule was viewpoint-neutral and imposed "only a slight burden on speech," which was justified by its important regulatory interests in preventing confusion and in managing its ballots.

6. *Filing Fees.* While the Court has generally been deferential to ballot access rules, it has been intolerant of state laws conditioning ballot appearance on the payment of filing fees. In *Bullock v. Carter*, 405 U.S. 134 (1972), the Court struck down filing fees for local offices in Texas as violative of equal protection. The decision was based in part of the excessive size of the filing fees:

> Unlike a filing-fee requirement that most candidates could be expected to fulfill from their own resources or at least through modest contributions, the very size of the fees imposed under the Texas system gives it a patently exclusionary character. Many potential office seekers lacking both personal wealth and affluent backers are in every practical sense precluded from seeking the nomination of their chosen party, no matter how broad or enthusiastic their popular support. The effect of this exclusionary mechanism on voters is neither incidental nor remote. Not only are voters substantially limited in their choice of candidates, but also there is the obvious likelihood that this limitation would fall more heavily on the less affluent segment of the community, whose favorites may be unable to pay the large costs required by the Texas system.... [W]e would ignore reality were we not to recognize that this system falls with unequal weight on voters, as well as candidates, according to their economic status.

Two years later, the Court considered a challenge to a filing fee of $701.60 for candidates for the Los Angeles County Board of Supervisors. Considering that the supervisorial districts had populations close to two million people, the filing fee surely qualified as nominal. Nevertheless, the Court struck it down in *Lubin v. Panish*, 415 U.S. 709 (1974), finding that because there was no alternative way of qualifying for the ballot, the filing fee "inevitably renders the California system exclusionary as to some aspirants." The Court added that the state could require a candidate unable to pay the filing fee to "demonstrate the 'seriousness' of his candidacy by persuading a substantial number of voters to sign a petition in his behalf." Is *Lubin* consistent with cases like *Jenness v. Fortson*? Is it of much benefit to third parties and independent candidates?

While filing fees tend to impede both major-party and third-party candidates from running for office, there is empirical evidence that they have a greater impact on the latter. See Thomas Stratmann, *Ballot Access Restrictions and Candidate Entry in Elections*, 21 European Journal of Political Economy 59 (2005). For an argument that filing fees for federal elected office violate the Qualification Clauses of the U.S. Constitution, see Mark R. Brown, *Ballot Fees as Impermissible Qualifications for Federal Office*, 54 American University Law Review 1283 (2005).

7. *Ballot Access in Major Party Primaries.* Ballot access laws occasionally pose difficulties for major party candidates, as well as third party and independent candidates. In 2014, Representative John Conyers, Jr. of Detroit, who had served in the U.S. House since 1964, was declared ineligible for the August primary for failure to gather the requisite 1000 petition signatures. The Wayne County Clerk ruled that hundreds of the signatures submitted by Rep. Conyers were invalid because they were collected by petition circulators who were not registered to vote in Michigan as required by state law. Conyers and his supporters promptly sued, and a federal district court issued a preliminary injunction putting him on the primary ballot. *Moore v. Johnson*, 2014 WL 4924409 (E.D. Mich. 2014). The district court found the Michigan statute "in all material respects, indistinguishable" from the Ohio statute

struck down in *Nader v. Blackwell*, 545 F.3d 459 (6th Cir. 2008). Applying strict scrutiny, the district rejected Michigan's argument that the in-state registration requirement was justified by the interest in preventing fraud—specifically, the risk that out-of-state petition circulators could not be forced to testify in a dispute over the authenticity of signatures. While recognizing that fraud prevention is a compelling interest, the district court concluded that this interest can be served by requiring petition circulators to submit to legal process in Michigan—as the state already did with respect to other offices. The state chose not to appeal.

8. *"Sore Loser" Laws.* To what extent should state election laws be upheld on the ground that they prevent candidates who lose major-party primaries from running in the general election as independent or third-party candidates? A recent example of such a candidacy is that of U.S. Senator Joe Lieberman. After having served in the Senate since 1988, Senator Lieberman ran for reelection in 2006 but lost the Democratic Party's primary to Ned Lamont. Targeting the Democratic Party's base, Lamont campaigned in vigorous opposition to the War in Iraq, which Lieberman had strongly supported. Because Connecticut does not have a "sore-loser" law, Lieberman was able to run as an independent candidate in the general election and retained his seat, defeating both Lamont and a Republican challenger, Alan Schlesinger. Does this example strengthen the argument for upholding laws that limit the ability of primary-election losers to run in the general election? Alternatively, does it furnish an argument *against* "sore loser" laws, given that Senator Lieberman won reelection in the general election by appealing to moderate voters of both major parties? Is it possible that allowing "sore loser" candidacies may improve the electoral process by facilitating the election of more centrist candidates?

In *Storer v. Brown*, 415 U.S. 724 (1974), the Court indicated it would uphold statutes designed to prevent "sore loser" candidacies. One of the statutes at issue in *Storer*, California Elections Code § 6830(d), broadly prohibited a candidate from running in the general election as an independent if he or she had been affiliated with a party that was qualified to appear on the ballot within a year prior to that party's primary. The Court explained:

> The direct party primary in California is not merely an exercise or warm-up for the general election but an integral part of the entire election process, the initial stage in a two-stage process by which the people choose their public officers. It functions to winnow out and finally reject all but the chosen candidates. The State's general policy is to have contending forces within the party employ the primary campaign and primary election to finally settle their differences. The general election ballot is reserved for major struggles; it is not a forum for continuing intraparty feuds. The provision against defeated primary candidates running as independents effectuates this aim, the visible result being to prevent the losers from continuing the struggle and to limit the names on the ballot to those who have won the primaries and those independents who have properly qualified.

> The people, it is hoped, are presented with understandable choices and the winner in the general election with sufficient support to govern effectively.
>
> Section 6830(d) . . . carries very similar credentials. It protects the direct primary process by refusing to recognize independent candidates who do not make early plans to leave a party and take the alternative course to the ballot. It works against independent candidacies prompted by short-range political goals, pique, or personal quarrel. It is also a substantial barrier to a party fielding an "independent" candidate to capture and bleed off votes in the general election that might well go to another party.

Today, sore loser laws are nearly ubiquitous in congressional elections and common in presidential elections (although there is some room for disagreement as to whether they apply to those elections in some states). Michael S. Kang & Barry C. Burden, *Sore Loser Laws in Presidential and Congressional Elections*, in Routledge Handbook of Primary Elections (2018). Professor Michael Kang argues that sore loser laws should be repealed, because of the salutary effect that independent and third-party candidacies have on the *major* parties. Michael S. Kang, *Sore Loser Laws and Democratic Contestation*, 99 Georgetown Law Journal 1013 (2011). Professor Kang notes: "Sore loser laws existed in roughly half the states twenty years ago, but now only three states permit a losing primary election candidate subsequently to file to appear on the ballot in the general election as the nominee of another party or as an independent candidate." Citing the Lieberman example, he argues that repealing these laws would reduce political polarization:

> Sore loser laws close off exit opportunities for moderate candidates and thereby remove the strongest threat that rejected candidates possess in intraparty politics—the option of breaking up the party coalition and running against the party's nominee in the general election. For this reason, sore loser laws give great leverage to the ideologically demanding party base over politically moderate dissenters. They therefore preempt the natural incentives for the controlling elements within the party to compromise with their parties' more moderate dissenters and move the parties toward the political center. . . .
>
> Sore loser laws should be removed, not as a constitutional matter by courts, but as a matter of party reform by states seeking to encourage greater centrism from the major parties and their candidates. Primary elections regularly embody and play out intraparty conflicts that are inherent in major party politics. However, sore loser laws grant primary winners a nearly absolute legal trump in the form of exclusive ballot access in the general election. The primary winner not only wins the major party nomination for the general election, but also effectively becomes the only primary candidate even permitted to appear on the general election ballot. As a result, primary winners have less incentive to compromise with primary losers in their political disagreements, and internal party dissent can become bottled up without sufficient accommodation. Sore loser laws,

> though conceived as a way of strengthening party politics, actually may stall the natural process of conflict and compromise inherent in a process of democratic contestation and discourage primary winners from accounting properly for dissent, to the detriment of the party.

Do you agree that sore loser laws should be repealed? Do you think many legislators of either major party are likely to support the repeal of sore loser laws? Do the anti-competitive effects of sore loser laws provide a basis for declaring them unconstitutional? One study finds that sore loser laws account for as much as one tenth of the ideological division between the major parties. Barry C. Burden, Bradley M. Jones & Michael S. Kang, *Sore Loser Laws and Congressional Polarization*, 39 Legislative Studies Quarterly 299 (2014). Another study, however, finds that sore loser laws improve ideological alignment between the median legislator and the median voter. Nicholas O. Stephanopoulos, Eric M. McGhee & Steven Rogers, *The Realities of Electoral Reform*, 68 Vanderbilt Law Review 761 (2015).

9. *Qualifications and Ballot Access.* The line of cases that has been described in this section assumes that the candidate is eligible to be elected to and serve in the office in question. States typically have leeway to set actual qualifications for state and local office, though not without limit. Thus, in *Turner v. Fouche*, 396 U.S. 346 (1970), the Court ruled that a requirement that appointed school board members be freeholders had no rational basis and therefore violated the Equal Protection Clause.

A plurality of the Supreme Court may have obscured the distinction between qualifications for office and requirements for access to the ballot in *Clements v. Fashing*, 457 U.S. 957 (1982). The issues in this case included an equal protection challenge to a Texas constitutional provision that disqualified judges from serving in the state legislature during the judicial term for which they had been elected, even if they were willing to resign their judicial offices. Justice Rehnquist, writing for a four-member plurality, summarized the holdings of the ballot access cases and observed that "[n]ot all ballot access restrictions require 'heightened' equal protection scrutiny." Because the disqualification in question did not impose "special burdens" based on political affiliation or viewpoint, and because the plurality regarded it as imposing merely a reasonable "waiting period" on judges who wanted to run for the legislature, the provision needed only a rational basis to be upheld. That rational basis was found in Texas's interest in discouraging judges from vacating their terms of office.

Was the plurality correct to regard this issue as controlled by the ballot access decisions? (Justice Stevens provided a fifth vote to uphold the Texas provision, but without referring to any of the *Williams* line of cases.) If Texas permitted judges to run for and serve in the state legislature before their judicial terms expired, but required that they run as write-in candidates, would the exclusion from the ballot be upheld on the authority of *Clements*?

10. *Fusion Candidacies.* In New York, the Liberal Party since the 1940s and the Conservative Party since the 1960s have played a more prominent role than third

parties in other states. An important reason is that in New York, individuals may appear on the ballot as the candidate of more than one party. Thus, in New York, the Liberal Party often nominates the same candidate as the Democrats and the Conservative Party often nominates the same candidate as the Republicans. These minor parties typically receive enough votes so that major party politicians have some incentive to prove themselves sufficiently "pure" ideologically to retain the support of the relevant minor party.

Most states have "anti-fusion" laws that either prevent candidates from appearing on the ballot under the label of more than one party or otherwise prevent minor parties from following the New York strategy. See generally Daniel A. Mazmanian, Third Parties in Presidential Elections 115–35 (1974); Howard A. Scarrow, *Duverger's Law, Fusion, and the Decline of American "Third" Parties*, 39 Western Political Quarterly 634 (1986). In 1997, the Supreme Court considered a constitutional attack on Minnesota's anti-fusion law, and in the process made some broad pronouncements about law favoring the two-party system.

Timmons v. Twin Cities Area New Party

520 U.S. 351 (1997)

CHIEF JUSTICE REHNQUIST delivered the opinion of the Court.

Most States prohibit multiple-party, or "fusion," candidacies for elected office.[1] The Minnesota laws challenged in this case prohibit a candidate from appearing on the ballot as the candidate of more than one party. Minn. Stat. §§ 204B.06, subd. 1(b) and 204B.04, subd. 2 (1994). We hold that such a prohibition does not violate the First and Fourteenth Amendments to the United States Constitution.

Respondent is a chartered chapter of the national New Party. Petitioners are Minnesota election officials. In April 1994, Minnesota State Representative Andy Dawkins was running unopposed in the Minnesota Democratic-Farmer-Labor Party's (DFL) primary.[2] That same month, New Party members chose Dawkins as their candidate for the same office in the November 1994 general election. Neither Dawkins nor the DFL objected,[h] and Dawkins signed the required affidavit of candidacy for the New Party. Minnesota, however, prohibits fusion candidacies. Because

---

1. "Fusion," also called "cross-filing" or "multiple-party nomination," is "the electoral support of a single set of candidates by two or more parties." Argersinger, "A Place on the Ballot": Fusion Politics and Antifusion Laws, 85 American History Review 287, 288 (1980).

2. The DFL is the product of a 1944 merger between Minnesota's Farmer-Labor Party and the Democratic Party, and is a "major party" under Minnesota law.

h. Is the constitutional attack on the anti-fusion law stronger if the DFL consents to Dawkins being both its own candidate and that of the New Party? If so, should the fact that the DFL, as Chief Justice Rehnquist says, did not object, be regarded as the equivalent of consent? Since the statute prohibited the fusion candidacy in any event, there was neither a reason for nor a mechanism for the DFL to register a formal objection. — Eds.

Dawkins had already filed as a candidate for the DFL's nomination, local election officials refused to accept the New Party's nominating petition....

Fusion was a regular feature of Gilded Age of American politics. Particularly in the West and Midwest, candidates of issue-oriented parties like the Grangers, Independents, Greenbackers, and Populists often succeeded through fusion with the Democrats, and vice versa. Republicans, for their part, sometimes arranged fusion candidacies in the South, as part of a general strategy of encouraging and exploiting divisions within the dominant Democratic Party.

Fusion was common in part because political parties, rather than local or state governments, printed and distributed their own ballots. These ballots contained only the names of a particular party's candidates, and so a voter could drop his party's ticket in the ballot box without even knowing that his party's candidates were supported by other parties as well. But after the 1888 presidential election, which was widely regarded as having been plagued by fraud, many States moved to the "Australian ballot system." Under that system, an official ballot, containing the names of all the candidates legally nominated by all the parties, was printed at public expense and distributed by public officials at polling places. By 1896, use of the Australian ballot was widespread. During the same period, many States enacted other election-related reforms, including bans on fusion candidacies. Minnesota banned fusion in 1901. This trend has continued and, in this century, fusion has become the exception, not the rule. Today, multiple-party candidacies are permitted in just a few States, and fusion plays a significant role only in New York....

When deciding whether a state election law violates First and Fourteenth Amendment associational rights, we weigh the "character and magnitude" of the burden the State's rule imposes on those rights against the interests the State contends justify that burden, and consider the extent to which the State's concerns make the burden necessary. *Burdick.* Regulations imposing severe burdens on plaintiffs' rights must be narrowly tailored and advance a compelling state interest. Lesser burdens, however, trigger less exacting review, and a State's "important regulatory interests" will usually be enough to justify "reasonable, nondiscriminatory restrictions." *Burdick.* No bright line separates permissible election-related regulation from unconstitutional infringements on First Amendment freedoms. *Storer.*

The New Party's claim that it has a right to select its own candidate is uncontroversial, so far as it goes. See, *e.g.*, *Cousins.* That is, the New Party, and not someone else, has the right to select the New Party's "standard bearer." It does not follow, though, that a party is absolutely entitled to have its nominee appear on the ballot as that party's candidate. A particular candidate might be ineligible for office, unwilling to serve, or, as here, another party's candidate. That a particular individual may not appear on the ballot as a particular party's candidate does not severely burden that party's association rights.

The New Party relies on *Eu* and *Tashjian* [*supra*, Chapter 8—Eds.] ... But while *Tashjian* and *Eu* involved regulation of political parties' internal affairs and core associational activities, Minnesota's fusion ban does not. The ban, which applies to major and minor parties alike, simply precludes one party's candidate from appearing on the ballot, as that party's candidate, if already nominated by another party. Respondent is free to try to convince Representative Dawkins to be the New Party's, not the DFL's, candidate. Whether the party still wants to endorse a candidate who, because of the fusion ban, will not appear on the ballot as the party's candidate, is up to the party.

The Court of Appeals also held that Minnesota's laws "keep the New Party from developing consensual political alliances and thus broadening the base of public participation in and support for its activities." The burden on the party was, the court held, severe because "[h]istory shows that minor parties have played a significant role in the electoral system where multiple party nomination is legal, but have no meaningful influence where multiple party nomination is banned." In the view of the Court of Appeals, Minnesota's fusion ban forces members of the New Party to make a "no-win choice" between voting for "candidates with no realistic chance of winning, defect[ing] from their party and vot[ing] for a major party candidate who does, or declin[ing] to vote at all."

But Minnesota has not directly precluded minor political parties from developing and organizing. Nor has Minnesota excluded a particular group of citizens, or a political party, from participation in the election process. The New Party remains free to endorse whom it likes, to ally itself with others, to nominate candidates for office, and to spread its message to all who will listen.

The Court of Appeals emphasized its belief that, without fusion-based alliances, minor parties cannot thrive. This is a predictive judgment which is by no means self-evident.[9] But, more importantly, the supposed benefits of fusion to minor parties does not require that Minnesota permit it. Many features of our political system—*e.g.*, single-member districts, "first past the post" elections, and the high costs of campaigning—make it difficult for third parties to succeed in American politics. But the Constitution does not require States to permit fusion any more than it

9. Between the First and Second World Wars, for example, various radical, agrarian, and labor-oriented parties thrived, without fusion, in the Midwest. See generally R. Vallely, Radicalism in the States (1989). One of these parties, Minnesota's Farmer-Labor Party, displaced the Democratic Party as the Republicans' primary opponent in Minnesota during the 1930's. As one historian has noted: "The Minnesota Farmer-Labor Party elected its candidates to the governorship on four occasions, to the U.S. Senate in five elections, and to the U.S. House in twenty-five campaigns.... Never less than Minnesota's second strongest party, in 1936 Farmer-Laborites dominated state politics.... The Farmer-Labor Party was a success despite its independence of America's two dominant national parties and despite the sometimes bold anticapitalist rhetoric of its platforms." J. Haynes, Dubious Alliance 9 (1984). It appears that factionalism within the Farmer-Labor Party, the popular successes of New Deal programs and ideology, and the gradual movement of political power from the States to the National Government contributed to the party's decline. Eventually, a much-weakened Farmer-Labor Party merged with the Democrats, forming what is now Minnesota's Democratic-Farmer-Labor Party, in 1944.

requires them to move to proportional-representation elections or public financing of campaigns.

The New Party contends that the fusion ban burdens its "right ... to communicate its choice of nominees on the ballot on terms equal to those offered other parties, and the right of the party's supporters and other voters to receive that information," and insists that communication on the ballot of a party's candidate choice is a "critical source of information for the great majority of voters ... who ... rely upon party 'labels' as a voting guide."

It is true that Minnesota's fusion ban prevents the New Party from using the ballot to communicate to the public that it supports a particular candidate who is already another party's candidate. In addition, the ban shuts off one possible avenue a party might use to send a message to its preferred *candidate* because, with fusion, a candidate who wins an election on the basis of two parties' votes will likely know more—if the parties' votes are counted separately—about the particular wishes and ideals of his constituency. We are unpersuaded, however, by the party's contention that it has a right to use the ballot itself to send a particularized message, to its candidate and to the voters, about the nature of its support for the candidate. Ballots serve primarily to elect candidates, not as forums for political expression. See *Burdick*. Like all parties in Minnesota, the New Party is able to use the ballot to communicate information about itself and its candidate to the voters, so long as that candidate is not already someone else's candidate. The party retains great latitude in its ability to communicate ideas to voters and candidates through its participation in the campaign, and party members may campaign for, endorse, and vote for their preferred candidate even if he is listed on the ballot as another party's candidate.

In sum, Minnesota's laws do not restrict the ability of the New Party and its members to endorse, support, or vote for anyone they like. The laws do not directly limit the party's access to the ballot. They are silent on parties' internal structure, governance, and policymaking. Instead, these provisions reduce the universe of potential candidates who may appear on the ballot as the party's nominee only by ruling out those few individuals who both have already agreed to be another party's candidate and also, if forced to choose, themselves prefer that other party. They also limit, slightly, the party's ability to send a message to the voters and to its preferred candidates. We conclude that the burdens Minnesota imposes on the party's First and Fourteenth Amendment associational rights—though not trivial—are not severe.

The Court of Appeals determined that Minnesota's fusion ban imposed "severe" burdens on the New Party's associational rights, and so it required the State to show that the ban was narrowly tailored to serve compelling state interests. We disagree; given the burdens imposed, the bar is not so high. Instead, the State's asserted regulatory interests need only be "sufficiently weighty to justify the limitation" imposed on the party's rights. *Norman v. Reed*, 502 U.S. 279, 288–289 (1992). Nor do we require elaborate, empirical verification of the weightiness of the State's asserted justifications. See *Munro*.

... Minnesota argues here that its fusion ban is justified by its interests in avoiding voter confusion, promoting candidate competition (by reserving limited ballot space for opposing candidates), preventing electoral distortions and ballot manipulations, and discouraging party splintering and "unrestrained factionalism."

States certainly have an interest in protecting the integrity, fairness, and efficiency of their ballots and election processes as means for electing public officials. Petitioners contend that a candidate or party could easily exploit fusion as a way of associating his or its name with popular slogans and catchphrases. For example, members of a major party could decide that a powerful way of "sending a message" via the ballot would be for various factions of that party to nominate the major party's candidate as the candidate for the newly-formed "No New Taxes," "Conserve Our Environment," and "Stop Crime Now" parties. In response, an opposing major party would likely instruct its factions to nominate that party's candidate as the "Fiscal Responsibility," "Healthy Planet," and "Safe Streets" parties' candidate.

Whether or not the putative "fusion" candidates' names appeared on one or four ballot lines, such maneuvering would undermine the ballot's purpose by transforming it from a means of choosing candidates to a billboard for political advertising. The New Party responds to this concern, ironically enough, by insisting that the State could avoid such manipulation by adopting more demanding ballot-access standards rather than prohibiting multiple-party nomination. However, as we stated above, because the burdens the fusion ban imposes on the party's associational rights are not severe, the State need not narrowly tailor the means it chooses to promote ballot integrity. The Constitution does not require that Minnesota compromise the policy choices embodied in its ballot-access requirements to accommodate the New Party's fusion strategy.

Relatedly, petitioners urge that permitting fusion would undercut Minnesota's ballot-access regime by allowing minor parties to capitalize on the popularity of another party's candidate, rather than on their own appeal to the voters, in order to secure access to the ballot. That is, voters who might not sign a minor party's nominating petition based on the party's own views and candidates might do so if they viewed the minor party as just another way of nominating the same person nominated by one of the major parties. Thus, Minnesota fears that fusion would enable minor parties, by nominating a major party's candidate, to bootstrap their way to major-party status in the next election and circumvent the State's nominating-petition requirement for minor parties. The State surely has a valid interest in making sure that minor and third parties who are granted access to the ballot are bona fide and actually supported, on their own merits, by those who have provided the statutorily required petition or ballot support.

States also have a strong interest in the stability of their political systems. This interest does not permit a State to completely insulate the two-party system from minor parties' or independent candidates' competition and influence, nor is it a paternalistic license for States to protect political parties from the consequences of their own internal disagreements. That said, the States' interest permits them to enact reasonable election regulations that may, in practice, favor the traditional two-party system, and that temper the destabilizing effects of party-splintering and excessive factionalism. The Constitution permits the Minnesota Legislature to decide that political stability is best served through a healthy two-party system. And while an interest in securing the perceived benefits of a stable two-party system will not justify unreasonably exclusionary restrictions, States need not remove all of the many hurdles third parties face in the American political arena today.

In *Storer,* we upheld a California statute that denied ballot positions to independent candidates who had voted in the immediately preceding primary elections or had a registered party affiliation at any time during the year before the same primary elections. After surveying the relevant caselaw, we "ha[d] no hesitation in sustaining" the party-disaffiliation provisions. We recognized that the provisions were part of a "general state policy aimed at maintaining the integrity of . . . the ballot," and noted that the provision did not discriminate against independent candidates. We concluded that while a "State need not take the course California has, . . . California apparently believes with the Founding Fathers that splintered parties and unrestrained factionalism may do significant damage to the fabric of government. See The Federalist No. 10 (Madison). It appears obvious to us that the one-year disaffiliation provision furthers the State's interest in the stability of its political system."[12]

Our decision in *Burdick v. Takushi* is also relevant. There, we upheld Hawaii's ban on write-in voting against a claim that the ban unreasonably infringed on citizens' First and Fourteenth Amendment rights. In so holding, we rejected the petitioner's argument that the ban "deprive[d] him of the opportunity to cast a meaningful ballot," emphasizing that the function of elections is to elect candidates and that "we have repeatedly upheld reasonable, politically neutral regulations that have the effect of channeling expressive activit[ies] at the polls."

Minnesota's fusion ban is far less burdensome than the disaffiliation rule upheld in *Storer,* and is justified by similarly weighty state interests. . . . Under the California disaffiliation statute at issue in *Storer, any* person affiliated with a party at any time during the year leading up to the primary election was absolutely precluded from appearing on the ballot as an independent or as the candidate of another party. Minnesota's fusion ban is not nearly so restrictive; the challenged provisions say nothing about the previous party affiliation of would-be candidates but only require that, in order to appear on the ballot, a candidate not be the nominee of more than one party. California's disaffiliation rule limited the field of candidates by thousands; Minnesota's precludes only a handful who freely choose to be so limited.

---

12. [The dissent] insists that New York's experience with fusion politics undermines Minnesota's contention that its fusion ban promotes political stability. California's experiment with cross-filing, on the other hand, provides some justification for Minnesota's concerns. In 1946, for example, Earl Warren was the nominee of both major parties, and was therefore able to run unopposed in California's general election. It appears to be widely accepted that California's cross-filing system stifled electoral competition and undermined the role of distinctive political parties.

It is also worth noting that while California's disaffiliation statute absolutely banned many candidacies, Minnesota's fusion ban only prohibits a candidate from being named twice.

We conclude that the burdens Minnesota's fusion ban imposes on the New Party's associational rights are justified by "correspondingly weighty" valid state interests in ballot integrity and political stability. In deciding that Minnesota's fusion ban does not unconstitutionally burden the New Party's First and Fourteenth Amendment rights, we express no views on the New Party's policy-based arguments concerning the wisdom of fusion. It may well be that, as support for new political parties increases, these arguments will carry the day in some States' legislatures. But the Constitution does not require Minnesota, and the approximately 40 other States that do not permit fusion, to allow it. The judgment of the Court of Appeals is reversed.

It is so ordered.

JUSTICE STEVENS, with whom JUSTICE GINSBURG joins, and with whom JUSTICE SOUTER joins as to Parts I and II, dissenting.

... The Court's conclusion that the Minnesota statute prohibiting multiple-party candidacies is constitutional rests on three dubious premises: (1) that the statute imposes only a minor burden on the Party's right to choose and to support the candidate of its choice; (2) that the statute significantly serves the State's asserted interests in avoiding ballot manipulation and factionalism; and (3) that, in any event, the interest in preserving the two-party system justifies the imposition of the burden at issue in this case. I disagree with each of these premises.

I

The members of a recognized political party unquestionably have a constitutional right to select their nominees for public office and to communicate the identity of their nominees to the voting public. Both the right to choose and the right to advise voters of that choice are entitled to the highest respect.

The Minnesota statutes place a significant burden on both of those rights. The Court's recital of burdens that the statute does not inflict on the Party does nothing to minimize the severity of the burdens that it does impose. The fact that the Party may nominate its second choice surely does not diminish the significance of a restriction that denies it the right to have the name of its first choice appear on the ballot. Nor does the point that it may use some of its limited resources to publicize the fact that its first choice is the nominee of some other party provide an adequate substitute for the message that is conveyed to every person who actually votes when a party's nominees appear on the ballot....

II

... [E]ven accepting the majority's view that the burdens imposed by the law are not weighty, the State's asserted interests must at least bear some plausible relationship to the burdens it places on political parties. Although the Court today suggests that the State does not have to support its asserted justifications for the fusion ban with evidence that they have any empirical validity, we have previously required more than a bare assertion that some particular state interest is served by a burdensome election requirement.[3]

While the State describes some imaginative theoretical sources of voter confusion that could result from fusion candidacies, in my judgment the argument that the burden on First Amendment interests is justified by this concern is meritless and severely underestimates the intelligence of the typical voter. . . .

The State's concern about ballot manipulation, readily accepted by the majority, is similarly farfetched. The possibility that members of the major parties will begin to create dozens of minor parties with detailed, issue-oriented titles for the sole purpose of nominating candidates under those titles is entirely hypothetical. The majority dismisses out-of-hand the Party's argument that the risk of this type of ballot manipulation and crowding is more easily averted by maintaining reasonably stringent requirements for the creation of minor parties. In fact, though, the Party's point merely illustrates the idea that a State can place some kinds—but not every kind—of limitation on the abilities of small parties to thrive. If the State wants to make it more difficult for any group to achieve the legal status of being a political party, it can do so within reason and still not run up against the First Amendment. *Anderson*; *Jenness*. But once the State has established a standard for achieving party status, forbidding an acknowledged party from putting on the ballot its chosen candidate clearly frustrates core associational rights.[5]

The State argues that the fusion ban promotes political stability by preventing intraparty factionalism and party raiding. States do certainly have an interest in maintaining a stable political system. *Eu*. But the State has not convincingly articulated how the fusion ban will prevent the factionalism it fears. Unlike the law at issue in *Storer*, for example, this law would not prevent sore-loser candidates from

3. In any event, the parade of horribles that the majority appears to believe might visit Minnesota should fusion candidacies be allowed is fantastical, given the evidence from New York's experience with fusion. Thus, the evidence that actually is available diminishes, rather than strengthens, Minnesota's claims. The majority asserts [in n.12] that California's cross-filing system, in place during the first half of this century, provides a compelling counterexample. But cross-filing, which "allowed candidates to file in the primary of any or all parties without specifying party affiliation," D. Mazmanian, Third Parties in Presidential Elections 132–133 (1974), is simply not the same as fusion politics, and the problems suffered in California do not provide empirical support for Minnesota's position.

5. A second "ballot manipulation" argument accepted by the majority is that minor parties will attempt to "capitalize on the popularity of another party's candidate, rather than on their own appeal to the voters, in order to secure access to the ballot." What the majority appears unwilling to accept is that *Andy Dawkins was the New Party's chosen candidate*. The Party was not trying to capitalize on his status as someone else's candidate, but to identify him as their own choice.

[Is Justice Stevens correct that the New Party was not trying to capitalize on Dawkins' status as the DFL nominee? Doesn't the fusion strategy for minor parties crucially depend on nominating the candidates of major parties, at least in many cases?—Eds.]

defecting with a disaffected segment of a major party and running as an opposition candidate for a newly formed minor party. Nor does this law, like those aimed at requiring parties to show a modicum of support in order to secure a place on the election ballot, prevent the formation of numerous small parties. Indeed, the activity banned by Minnesota's law is the formation of coalitions, not the division and dissension of "splintered parties and unrestrained factionalism."

As for the State's argument that the fusion ban encourages candidate competition, this claim treats "candidates" as fungible goods, ignoring entirely each party's interest in nominating not just any candidate, but the candidate who best represents the party's views. Minnesota's fusion ban simply cannot be justified with reference to this or any of the above-mentioned rationales. I turn, therefore, to what appears to be the true basis for the Court's holding—the interest in preserving the two-party system.

III

... In most States, perhaps in all, there are two and only two major political parties. It is not surprising, therefore, that most States have enacted election laws that impose burdens on the development and growth of third parties. The law at issue in this case is undeniably such a law. The fact that the law was both intended to disadvantage minor parties and has had that effect is a matter that should weigh against, rather than in favor of, its constitutionality.

Our jurisprudence in this area reflects a certain tension: On the one hand, we have been clear that political stability is an important state interest and that incidental burdens on the formation of minor parties are reasonable to protect that interest, see *Storer*; on the other, we have struck down state elections laws specifically because they give "the two old, established parties a decided advantage over any new parties struggling for existence," *Williams*. Between these boundaries, we have acknowledged that there is "no litmus-paper test for separating those restrictions that are valid from those that are invidious ... The rule is not self-executing and is no substitute for the hard judgments that must be made." *Storer.*

Nothing in the Constitution prohibits the States from maintaining single-member districts with winner-take-all voting arrangements. And these elements of an election system do make it significantly more difficult for third parties to thrive. But these laws are different in two respects from the fusion bans at issue here. First, the method by which they hamper third-party development is not one that impinges on the associational rights of those third parties; minor parties remain free to nominate candidates of their choice, and to rally support for those candidates. The small parties' relatively limited likelihood of ultimate success on election day does not deprive them of the right to try. Second, the establishment of single-member districts correlates directly with the States' interests in political stability. Systems of proportional representation, for example, may tend toward factionalism and fragile coalitions that diminish legislative effectiveness. In the context of fusion candidacies, the risks to political stability are extremely attenuated. Of course, the reason minor parties so ardently support fusion politics is because it allows the parties to build up a greater base of support, as potential minor party members realize that a vote for the smaller party candidate is not necessarily a "wasted" vote. Eventually, a minor party might gather sufficient strength that—were its members so inclined—it could successfully run a candidate not endorsed by any major party, and legislative coalition-building will be made more difficult by the presence of third-party legislators. But the risks to political stability in that scenario are speculative at best.

In some respects, the fusion candidacy is the best marriage of the virtues of the minor party challenge to entrenched viewpoints and the political stability that the two-party system provides. The fusion candidacy does not threaten to divide the legislature and create significant risks of factionalism, which is the principal risk proponents of the two-party system point to. But it does provide a means by which voters with viewpoints not adequately represented by the platforms of the two major parties can indicate to a particular candidate that—in addition to his support for the major party views—he should be responsive to the views of the minor party whose support for him was demonstrated where political parties demonstrate support—on the ballot.

The strength of the two-party system—and of each of its major components—is the product of the power of the ideas, the traditions, the candidates, and the voters that constitute the parties. It demeans the strength of the two-party system to assume that the major parties need to rely on laws that discriminate against independent voters and minor parties in order to preserve their positions of power....

In my opinion legislation that would otherwise be unconstitutional because it burdens First Amendment interests and discriminates against minor political parties cannot survive simply because it benefits the two major parties. Accordingly, I respectfully dissent.

JUSTICE SOUTER, dissenting.

[Justice Souter did not believe that the defense that an anti-fusion law helped strengthen the two-party system was properly before the Court, a question addressed by Chief Justice Rehnquist and Justice Stevens in portions of their opinions that have been omitted above. Justice Souter added these paragraphs:]

I am, however, unwilling to go the further distance of considering and rejecting the majority's "preservation of the two-party system" rationale. For while Minnesota has made no such argument before us, I cannot discount the possibility of a forceful one. There is considerable consensus that party loyalty among American voters has declined significantly in the past four decades. In the wake of such studies, it may not be unreasonable to infer that the two-party system is in some jeopardy.

Surely the majority is right that States "have a strong interest in the stability of their political systems," that is, in preserving a political system capable of governing effectively. If it could be shown that the disappearance of the two-party system would undermine that interest, and that permitting fusion candidacies poses a substantial threat to the two-party scheme, there might well be a sufficient predicate for recognizing the constitutionality of the state action presented by this case. Right now, however, no State has attempted even to make this argument, and I would therefore leave its consideration for another day.

Notes and Questions

1. The Democratic-Farmer-Labor Party enjoyed a comfortable majority in both houses of the Minnesota legislature. If it is true that the DFL did not object to its candidates being endorsed by other parties, then why didn't the legislature repeal the sections that the New Party is challenging?

2. Suppose the Supreme Court had struck down the Minnesota anti-fusion laws and the DFL passed a rule prohibiting its candidates from appearing on the ballot additionally as the candidate of other parties. Would the DFL have the right to enforce this rule under *Tashjian*, *Eu*, and *California Democratic Party v. Jones* (discussed in Chapter 8, Part III.B)?

3. If Justice Stevens's dissenting view had prevailed, would the role of third parties have been enhanced? For an argument that fusion would enhance competitiveness (a topic discussed in Chapter 4, Part III), see Samuel Issacharoff and Richard H. Pildes, *Politics as Markets: Partisan Lockups of the Democratic Process*, 50 Stanford Law Review 643 (1998). Some third party activists have suggested that a constitutional right to engage in fusion would help third parties grow. See, *e.g.*, John B. Anderson & Jeffrey L. Freeman, *Taking the First Steps Towards a Multiparty System in the United States*, 21 Fletcher Forum of World Affairs 73, 81 (1997). Other commentators take the opposite view, arguing that New York's experience demonstrates that fusion relegates third parties to a permanent secondary pressure group role. James Gray Pope, *Fusion,* Timmons v. Twin Cities Area New Party, *and the Future of Third Parties in the United States*, 50 Rutgers Law Review 473 (1998). A third view holds that the fusion ban should have little marginal effect on the power of third parties in the United States, given Duverger's Law. See Richard L. Hasen, *Entrenching the Duopoly: Why the Supreme Court Should Not Allow the States to Protect the Democrats and Republicans from Political Competition*, 1997 Supreme Court Review 331, 367–71.

One study supports the claim that fusion candidacies help third parties. Bernard Tamas & Matthew Dean Hindman, *Ballot Access Laws and the Decline of American Third-Parties*, 13 Election Law Journal 260 (2014). In general, Tamas and Hindman find that ballot access laws have little effect on third parties' ability to get U.S. House candidates on the ballot or on their share of the vote. Thus, the authors conclude, ballot access laws were probably not a major factor in the decline of third parties in the twentieth century. But when third parties actively participate in fusion, they are more likely to get their candidates on the ballot and that third-party candidates get more votes. Does this finding help or hurt the constitutional case against anti-fusion laws? Another commentator finds that California's legislature was less polarized when candidates could cross-list under more than one party, a form of fusion. Seth Masket, No Middle Ground: How Informal Party Organizations Control Nominations and Polarize Legislatures 74-75 (2011).

4. According to Hasen, *supra*, the real significance of *Timmons* is that it marks the first time the Supreme Court has recognized preservation of the two-party system as a legitimate state interest that may justify a state regulation against constitutional attack. Compare *Timmons* ("the States' interest permits them to enact reasonable election regulations that may, in practice, favor the traditional two-party system") with *Williams v. Rhodes*, *supra* ("The fact is, however, that the Ohio system does not merely favor a 'two-party system'; it favors two particular parties—the Republicans and the Democrats—and in effect tends to give them a complete monopoly. . . . New parties struggling for their place must have the time and opportunity to organize in order to meet reasonable requirements for ballot position, just as the old parties have had in the past."). Hasen argues that this newly-recognized interest might allow states to further limit the ability of third parties to serve as pressure groups as well as limiting information available to voters through the third party labels. This first assertion is borne out by post-*Timmons* cases such as *Wood v. Meadows*, 207 F.3d 708, 712 (4th Cir. 2000), in which the Fourth Circuit cited *Timmons*' statements regarding state promotion of the two-party system as a justification for a 150-day filing deadline for independent candidates.

But consider this:

> The scholarly opposition to *Timmons* was led by Richard Hasen, who read the case as permitting infringement of First Amendment rights in furtherance of the state's interest in preserving the two-party system. He based his interpretation primarily on the Court's statement that "the Constitution permits the Minnesota Legislature to decide that political stability is best served through a healthy two-party system." . . .
>
> Hasen's reading is a possible one, but it is not the most plausible reading and certainly not the friendliest. He emphasizes the term "two-party" in the final phrase of the quoted passage. The phrase takes on a different meaning if instead we emphasize "healthy." So read, the Court's statement does not suggest that *preservation* of the two-party system is a state interest that can justify constitutional infringements, but rather that *given* the existence of a two-party system, the state has an interest in keeping it healthy.

Daniel H. Lowenstein, *Legal Regulation and Protection of American Parties*, in Handbook of Party Politics 456, 464 (Richard S. Katz & William Crotty, eds., 2006). Lowenstein adds that in the quotation following the reference to Hasen's article in the previous paragraph, the Court says that the state may pursue valid interests in a manner that will benefit the two-party system, not that the preservation of the two-party system is itself an interest that would justify infringement of First Amendment rights.

5. Pennsylvania generally banned cross-party candidacies, but it made an exception for certain local elections. Presumably in order to encourage but not require non-partisan politics in those local elections, cross-party candidacies were permitted, but only among the major parties. Thus, a candidate could appear on the general election ballot as the candidate of the Democratic and Republican parties. However, the minor parties were not permitted to participate in the cross-party candidacies. A federal court had struck down this disparity before the Supreme Court decided *Timmons*. After *Timmons*, that ruling was reaffirmed in *Reform Party of Allegheny County v. Department of Elections*, 174 F.3d 305 (3d Cir. 1999):

> Nothing in the *Timmons* opinion itself weakens the equal protection analysis of [the former ruling], because no equal protection claim was asserted or considered by the Court in *Timmons*. The statutory scheme in *Timmons* differs from the Pennsylvania scheme in a manner crucial for the equal protection analysis. *Timmons* involved an across-the-board ban on fusion by both major and minor parties. In contrast, the Pennsylvania statutes involve a ban on cross-nomination that facially discriminates against minor parties by allowing major parties, but not minor parties, to cross-nominate in certain circumstances. The Supreme Court in *Timmons* did not hold that states can treat minor parties in a discriminatory way.

Id. at 312.

6. The Supreme Court now applies the *Anderson-Burdick* balancing standard to laws that allegedly infringe the associational rights of parties, including major parties and third parties. Does that make sense? Nicholas Stephanopoulos argues that courts should focus on whether the challenged practice produces *misalignment*, in the sense that they result in voter preferences that are not congruent with those of elected representatives:

> Under the alignment approach, . . . judicial review of party regulations would vary based on the type of rule at issue. If a rule is potentially misaligning (such as a sore loser law), courts would engage in precisely the same congruence-and-interests balancing as in the franchise restriction context. The greater the likelihood of misalignment, the more compelling the state's interests would need to be for the rule to be sustained (and the tighter the rule's tailoring), and vice versa. Conversely, if a rule is potentially aligning (such as a mandatory inclusive primary or a measure that restricts third-party ballot qualification), courts would balance the rule's potential benefit in congruence against its attendant burden on parties' associational rights. The rule would be upheld if its aligning benefit were deemed to outweigh its rights burden, and struck down if not. Alignment would be treated as an additional state interest that could justify the encumbrance of parties' rights. Under either sort of inquiry, of course, accurate data about the alignment or misalignment that is likely to ensue would be crucial.

Nicholas O. Stephanopoulos, *Elections and Alignment*, 114 Columbia Law Review 283, 333-34 (2014). Is this approach preferable to the one the court current employs? What would be the result in cases like *Munro* and *Timmons*?

7. Fusion ballots are one way of allowing third parties to get on the ballot without becoming spoilers. Another is to institute instant runoff voting ("IRV"), sometimes referred to as ranked-choice voting ("RCV"). Under this system, voters rank the candidates in their order of preference. Each ballot's top choice is then counted. If no candidate has a majority, the last-place candidate is removed and the top remaining choice on the ballots counted, with the process continuing until one of the candidates has a majority of votes. One advantage of instant runoff voting is that it would allow supporters of third-party and independent candidates to vote for their most-preferred candidate without the spoiler effect. For example, in the 2016 presidential election, a supporter of Green Party candidate Jill Stein could have ranked her #1 and Hillary Clinton #2, while a supporter of Libertarian Party candidate Gary Johnson could have ranked him #1 and Donald Trump #2. This would allow the third party candidates' supporters to select their favorite candidates without the risk of inadvertently helping their least favorite candidate win. For an argument to this effect, see Edward B. Foley, *Third-Party and Independent Presidential Candidates: The Need for a Runoff Mechanism*, 85 Fordham Law Review 993 (2016).

II. Public Benefits

Ballot access may be the issue most frequently litigated by third parties and independent candidates in recent decades, but it is not the only one. We shall now consider the extent to which such parties and candidates may be entitled to a share of other benefits sometimes provided by the government.

In 1974, Congress passed comprehensive amendments to the previously enacted Federal Election Campaign Act (FECA). The amended FECA provided for campaign disclosure, a variety of limits on campaign contributions and expenditures, and public financing of presidential campaigns. Nearly every significant provision of the Act was quickly challenged in *Buckley v. Valeo*. In later chapters we shall consider in some detail both the amended FECA and the *Buckley* decision. In this chapter, we consider only the portion of *Buckley* responding to the claim that the presidential public financing provisions unconstitutionally discriminated against third parties and independent candidates.

Buckley v. Valeo

424 U.S. 1, 85–109 (1976)

PER CURIAM . . .

III. Public Financing of Presidential Election Campaigns

A series of statutes for the public financing of Presidential election campaigns produced the scheme now found in 26 U.S.C. § 6096 and Subtitle H of the Internal Revenue Code of 1954. . . .

A. Summary of Subtitle H

Section 9006 establishes a Presidential Election Campaign Fund (Fund), financed from general revenues in the aggregate amount designated by individual taxpayers, under § 6096, who on their income tax returns may authorize payment to the Fund of one dollar of their tax liability in the case of an individual return or two dollars in the case of a joint return.[i] The Fund consists of three separate accounts to finance (1) party nominating conventions, (2) general election campaigns, and (3) primary campaigns.

Chapter 95 of Title 26, which concerns financing of party nominating conventions and general election campaigns, distinguishes among "major," "minor," and "new" parties. A major party is defined as a party whose candidate for President in the most recent election received 25% or more of the popular vote. A minor party is defined as a party whose candidate received at least 5% but less than 25% of the vote at the most recent election. All other parties are new parties, including both newly created parties and those receiving less than 5% of the vote in the last election.

Major parties are entitled to $2,000,000 to defray their national committee Presidential nominating convention expenses, must limit total expenditures to that amount, and may not use any of this money to benefit a particular candidate or delegate. A minor party receives a portion of the major-party entitlement determined by the ratio of the votes received by the party's candidate in the last election to the average of the votes received by the major parties' candidates. The amounts given to the parties and the expenditure limit are adjusted for inflation, using 1974 as the base year. No financing is provided for new parties, nor is there any express provision for financing independent candidates or parties not holding a convention.

For expenses in the general election campaign, § 9004(a)(1) entitles each major-party candidate to $20,000,000. This amount is also adjusted for inflation. To be eligible for funds the candidate must pledge not to incur expenses in excess of the entitlement under § 9004(a)(1) and not to accept private contributions. . . . Minor-party candidates are also entitled to funding, again based on the ratio of the vote received by the party's candidate in the preceding election to the average of the

i. Since the 1994 tax year, taxpayers have been able to designate three dollars on an individual return and six dollars on a joint return. — Eds.

major-party candidates. Minor-party candidates must certify that they will not incur campaign expenses in excess of the major-party entitlement and that they will accept private contributions only to the extent needed to make up the difference between that amount and the public funding grant. New-party candidates receive no money prior to the general election, but any candidate receiving 5% or more of the popular vote in the election is entitled to post-election payments according to the formula applicable to minor-party candidates. Similarly, minor-party candidates are entitled to post-election funds if they receive a greater percentage of the average major-party vote than their party's candidate did in the preceding election; the amount of such payments is the difference between the entitlement based on the preceding election and that based on the actual vote in the current election. A further eligibility requirement for minor- and new-party candidates is that the candidate's name must appear on the ballot, or electors pledged to the candidate must be on the ballot, in at least 10 States.

Chapter 96 establishes a third account in the Fund, the Presidential Primary Matching Payment Account. This funding is intended to aid campaigns by candidates seeking Presidential nomination "by a political party" in "primary elections." The threshold eligibility requirement is that the candidate raise at least $5,000 in each of 20 States, counting only the first $250 from each person contributing to the candidate. In addition, the candidate must agree to abide by [overall campaign spending limits]. Funding is provided according to a matching formula: each qualified candidate is entitled to a sum equal to the total private contributions received, disregarding contributions from any person to the extent that total contributions to the candidate by that person exceed $250. Payments to any candidate under Chapter 96 may not exceed 50% of the overall expenditure ceiling accepted by the candidate.

B. Constitutionality of Subtitle H

Appellants argue that Subtitle H is invalid [among other reasons] because Subtitle H invidiously discriminates against certain interests in violation of the Due Process Clause of the Fifth Amendment. We find no merit in these contentions....

Equal protection analysis in the Fifth Amendment area is the same as that under the Fourteenth Amendment. In several situations concerning the electoral process, the principle has been developed that restrictions on access to the electoral process must survive exacting scrutiny. The restriction can be sustained only if it furthers a "vital" governmental interest, *American Party of Texas v. White*, that is "achieved by a means that does not unfairly or unnecessarily burden either a minority party's or an individual candidate's equally important interest in the continued availability of political opportunity." *Lubin v. Panish*. These cases, however, dealt primarily with state laws requiring a candidate to satisfy certain requirements in order to have his name appear on the ballot. These were, of course, direct burdens not only on the candidate's ability to run for office but also on the voter's ability to voice preferences regarding representative government and contemporary issues. In contrast, the denial of public financing to some Presidential candidates is not restrictive of voters' rights and less restrictive of candidates'.[128] Subtitle H does not prevent any candidate from getting on the ballot or any voter from casting a vote for the candidate of his choice; the inability, if any, of minor-party candidates to wage effective campaigns will derive not from lack of public funding but from their inability to raise private contributions. Any disadvantage suffered by operation of the eligibility formulae under Subtitle H is thus limited to the claimed denial of the enhancement of opportunity to communicate with the electorate that the formulae afford eligible candidates. But eligible candidates suffer a countervailing denial. As we more fully develop later, acceptance of public financing entails voluntary acceptance of an expenditure ceiling. Noneligible candidates are not subject to that limitation.[129] Accordingly, we conclude that public financing is generally less restrictive of access to the electoral process than the ballot-access regulations dealt with in prior cases. In any event, Congress enacted Subtitle H in furtherance of sufficiently important governmental interests and has not unfairly or unnecessarily burdened the political opportunity of any party or candidate.

It cannot be gainsaid that public financing as a means of eliminating the improper influence of large private contributions furthers a significant governmental interest. In addition, the limits on contributions necessarily increase the burden of fundraising, and Congress properly regarded public financing as an appropriate means of relieving major-party Presidential candidates from the rigors of soliciting private contributions. The States have also been held to have important interests in limiting places on the ballot to those candidates who demonstrate substantial popular support. Congress' interest in not funding hopeless candidacies with large sums of public money necessarily justifies the withholding of public assistance from candidates without significant public support. Thus, Congress may legitimately require "some preliminary showing of a significant modicum of support," *Jenness*, as an eligibility requirement for public funds. This requirement also serves the important public interest against providing artificial incentives to "splintered parties and unrestrained factionalism." *Storer*.

At the same time Congress recognized the constitutional restraints against inhibition of the present opportunity of minor parties to become major political entities

---

128. Appellants maintain that denial of funding is a more severe restriction than denial of access to the ballot, because write-in candidates can win elections, but candidates without funds cannot. New parties will be unfinanced, however, only if they are unable to get private financial support, which presumably reflects a general lack of public support for the party. Public financing of some candidates does not make private fundraising for others any more difficult; indeed, the elimination of private contributions to major-party Presidential candidates might make more private money available to minority candidates.

129. Appellants dispute the relevance of this answer to their argument on the ground that they will not be able to raise money to equal major-party spending. As a practical matter, however, Subtitle H does not enhance the major parties' ability to campaign; it substitutes public funding for what the parties would raise privately and additionally imposes an expenditure limit. If a party cannot raise funds privately, there are legitimate reasons not to provide public funding, which would effectively facilitate hopeless candidacies.

if they obtain widespread support. As the Court of Appeals said, "provisions for public funding of Presidential campaigns . . . could operate to give an unfair advantage to established parties, thus reducing, to the nation's detriment, . . . the 'potential fluidity of American political life.'"

1. General Election Campaign Financing

Appellants insist that Chapter 95 falls short of the constitutional requirement in that its provisions supply larger, and equal, sums to candidates of major parties, use prior vote levels as the sole criterion for pre-election funding, limit new-party candidates to post-election funds, and deny any funds to candidates of parties receiving less than 5% of the vote. These provisions, it is argued, are fatal to the validity of the scheme, because they work invidious discrimination against minor and new parties in violation of the Fifth Amendment. We disagree.[131]

As conceded by appellants, the Constitution does not require Congress to treat all declared candidates the same for public financing purposes. As we said in *Jenness*, "there are obvious differences in kind between the needs and potentials of a political party with historically established broad support, on the one hand, and a new or small political organization on the other. . . . Sometimes the grossest discrimination can lie in treating things that are different as though they were exactly alike, a truism well illustrated in *Williams*." Since the Presidential elections of 1856 and 1860, when the Whigs were replaced as a major party by the Republicans, no third party has posed a credible threat to the two major parties in Presidential elections. Third parties have been completely incapable of matching the major parties' ability to raise money and win elections. Congress was, of course, aware of this fact of American life, and thus was justified in providing both major parties full funding and all other parties only a percentage of the major-party entitlement.[133] Identical treatment of all parties, on the other hand, "would not only make it easy to raid the United States Treasury, it would also artificially foster the proliferation of splinter parties." The Constitution does not require the Government to "finance the efforts of every nascent political group," *American Party of Texas*, merely because Congress chose to finance the efforts of the major parties.

Furthermore, appellants have made no showing that the election funding plan disadvantages nonmajor parties by operating to reduce their strength below that

131. The allegations of invidious discrimination are based on the claim that Subtitle H is facially invalid; since the public financing provisions have never been in operation, appellants are unable to offer factual proof that the scheme is discriminatory in its effect. In rejecting appellants' arguments, we of course do not rule out the possibility of concluding in some future case, upon an appropriate factual demonstration, that the public financing system invidiously discriminates against nonmajor parties.

133. Appellants suggest that a less discriminatory formula would be to grant full funding to the candidate of the party getting the most votes in the last election and then give money to candidates of other parties based on their showing in the last election relative to the "leading" party. That formula, however, might unfairly favor incumbents, since their major-party challengers would receive less financial assistance.

attained without any public financing. First, such parties are free to raise money from private sources, and by our holding today new parties are freed from any expenditure limits, although admittedly those limits may be a largely academic matter to them. But since any major-party candidate accepting public financing of a campaign voluntarily assents to a spending ceiling, other candidates will be able to spend more in relation to the major-party candidates. The relative position of minor parties that do qualify to receive some public funds because they received 5% of the vote in the previous Presidential election is also enhanced. Public funding for candidates of major parties is intended as a substitute for private contributions; but for minor-party candidates such assistance may be viewed as a supplement to private contributions since these candidates may continue to solicit private funds up to the applicable spending limit. Thus, we conclude that the general election funding system does not work an invidious discrimination against candidates of nonmajor parties.

Appellants challenge reliance on the vote in past elections as the basis for determining eligibility. That challenge is foreclosed, however, by our holding in *Jenness*, that popular vote totals in the last election are a proper measure of public support. And Congress was not obliged to select instead from among appellants' suggested alternatives. Congress could properly regard the means chosen as preferable, since the alternative of petition drives presents cost and administrative problems in validating signatures, and the alternative of opinion polls might be thought inappropriate since it would involve a Government agency in the business of certifying polls or conducting its own investigation of support for various candidates, in addition to serious problems with reliability.

Appellants next argue, relying on the ballot-access decisions of this Court, that the absence of any alternative means of obtaining pre-election funding renders the scheme unjustifiably restrictive of minority political interests. Appellants' reliance on the ballot-access decisions is misplaced. To be sure, the regulation sustained in *Jenness*, for example, incorporated alternative means of qualifying for the ballot, and the lack of an alternative was a defect in the scheme struck down in *Lubin*. To suggest, however, that the constitutionality of Subtitle H therefore hinges solely on whether some alternative is afforded overlooks the rationale of the operative constitutional principles. Our decisions finding a need for an alternative means turn on the nature and extent of the burden imposed in the absence of available alternatives. We have earlier stated our view that Chapter 95 is far less burdensome upon and restrictive of constitutional rights than the regulations involved in the ballot-access cases. Moreover, expenditure limits for major parties and candidates may well improve the chances of nonmajor parties and their candidates to receive funds and increase their spending. Any risk of harm to minority interests is speculative due to our present lack of knowledge of the practical effects of public financing and cannot overcome the force of the governmental interests against use of public money to foster frivolous candidacies, create a system of splintered parties, and encourage unrestrained factionalism.

Appellants' reliance on the alternative-means analyses of the ballot-access cases generally fails to recognize a significant distinction from the instant case. The primary goal of all candidates is to carry on a successful campaign by communicating to the voters' persuasive reasons for electing them. In some of the ballot-access cases the States afforded candidates alternative means for qualifying for the ballot, a step in any campaign that, with rare exceptions, is essential to successful effort. Chapter 95 concededly provides only one method of obtaining pre-election financing; such funding is, however, not as necessary as being on the ballot. Plainly, campaigns can be successfully carried out by means other than public financing; they have been up to this date, and this avenue is still open to all candidates. And, after all, the important achievements of minority political groups in furthering the development of American democracy were accomplished without the help of public funds. Thus, the limited participation or nonparticipation of nonmajor parties or candidates in public funding does not unconstitutionally disadvantage them.

Of course, nonmajor parties and their candidates may qualify for post-election participation in public funding and in that sense the claimed discrimination is not total. Appellants contend, however, that the benefit of any such participation is illusory due to § 9004(c), which bars the use of the money for any purpose other than paying campaign expenses or repaying loans that had been used to defray such expenses. The only meaningful use for post-election funds is thus to repay loans; but loans, except from national banks, are "contributions" subject to the general limitations on contributions. Further, they argue, loans are not readily available to nonmajor parties or candidates before elections to finance their campaigns. Availability of post-election funds therefore assertedly gives them nothing. But in the nature of things the willingness of lenders to make loans will depend upon the pre-election probability that the candidate and his party will attract 5% or more of the voters. When a reasonable prospect of such support appears, the party and candidate may be an acceptable loan risk since the prospect of post-election participation in public funding will be good.

Finally, appellants challenge the validity of the 5% threshold requirement for general election funding. They argue that, since most state regulations governing ballot access have threshold requirements well below 5%, and because in their view the 5% requirement here is actually stricter than that upheld in *Jenness*, the requirement is unreasonable. We have already concluded that the restriction under Chapter 95 is generally less burdensome than ballot-access regulations. Further, the Georgia provision sustained in *Jenness* required the candidate to obtain the signatures of 5% of all eligible voters, without regard to party. To be sure, the public funding formula does not permit anyone who voted for another party in the last election to be part of a candidate's 5%. But under Chapter 95 a Presidential candidate needs only 5% or more of the actual vote, not the larger universe of eligible voters. As a result, we cannot say that Chapter 95 is numerically more, or less, restrictive than the regulation in *Jenness*. In any event, the choice of the percentage requirement that best accommodates the competing interests involved was for Congress to make. Without any doubt a range of formulations would sufficiently protect the public fisc and not foster factionalism, and would also recognize the public interest in the fluidity of our political affairs. We cannot say that Congress' choice falls without the permissible range.

2. Nominating Convention Financing

The foregoing analysis and reasoning sustaining general election funding apply in large part to convention funding under Chapter 95 and suffice to support our rejection of appellants' challenge to these provisions. Funding of party conventions has increasingly been derived from large private contributions, and the governmental interest in eliminating this reliance is as vital as in the case of private contributions to individual candidates.... We therefore conclude that appellants' constitutional challenge to the provisions for funding nominating conventions must also be rejected.

3. Primary Election Campaign Financing

Appellants' final challenge is to the constitutionality of Chapter 96, which provides funding of primary campaigns. They contend that these provisions are constitutionally invalid (1) because they do not provide funds for candidates not running in party primaries and (2) because the eligibility formula actually increases the influence of money on the electoral process. In not providing assistance to candidates who do not enter party primaries, Congress has merely chosen to limit at this time the reach of the reforms encompassed in Chapter 96.... The choice to limit matching funds to candidates running in primaries may reflect that concern about large private contributions to candidates centered on primary races and that there is no historical evidence of similar abuses involving contributions to candidates who engage in petition drives to qualify for state ballots. Moreover, assistance to candidates and nonmajor parties forced to resort to petition drives to gain ballot access implicates the policies against fostering frivolous candidacies, creating a system of splintered parties, and encouraging unrestrained factionalism.

The eligibility requirements in Chapter 96 are surely not an unreasonable way to measure popular support for a candidate, accomplishing the objective of limiting subsidization to those candidates with a substantial chance of being nominated....

For the reasons stated, we reject appellants' claims that Subtitle H is facially unconstitutional.

Notes and Questions

1. Should the Court have struck down the public financing system on the ground that it was unfair to new parties? See Marlene Arnold Nicholson, Buckley v. Valeo: *The Constitutionality of the Federal Election Campaign Act Amendments of 1974*, 1977 Wisconsin Law Review 323:

> One of the most persuasive arguments against the allocation formula is its discrimination against new political parties. A new party could have the

> support of 5 percent of the electorate, or even much more, but would receive no funding from the government because of the lack of a showing of support at the previous general presidential election. Although the new party may be entitled to a grant after the election, funds will only be dispersed to such a party in the amount of outstanding debts. Therefore, the new party must gamble that it will obtain 5 percent of the vote and find creditors also willing to gamble. The new party is thus caught in what has been described as a "Catch-22" situation: it cannot obtain public funding without a showing of electoral support, but it may not be able to get electoral support without public funding.

Nicholson also challenges what the Court described as "the important public interest against providing artificial incentives to 'splintered parties and unrestrained factionalism'":

> Evidently it was thought that the availability of funds on a more liberal basis to third parties would encourage persons to split from the major parties and form their own parties in situations where, but for the availability of funds, such factionalization would not take place. However, it seems more likely that the present statute is an artificial influence which actually discourages factionalization, because of burdens upon parties not qualifying for public subsidies. A more liberal funding formula might merely compensate for the disincentives to factionalization created by contribution limitations and disclosure laws. It seems clear from the legislative history of the Act that at least some members of Congress purposely sought to protect the two-party system not just from artificial incentives to factionalism, but also from the old fashioned natural factionalism, which has disturbed the major parties at infrequent intervals in the past....
>
> The only concern voiced by the majority opinion with respect to third parties was that the subsidies must not inhibit "the present opportunity of minority parties to become major political entities if they obtain widespread support." Apparently the Court concluded that it had not been proven that the subsidy provisions would function in such a manner. It should be noted, however, that the Court showed no solicitude for parties and candidates who have no realistic chance of gaining widespread support. The Court ignored the fact that even "hopeless candidacies" serve important first amendment functions and are also subject to other restraints under the 1974 legislation which inhibit the performance of such functions.

2. Should the Court have struck down the matching requirement for eligibility to receive public funding in presidential primaries? Writing before the *Buckley* decision, Joel L. Fleishman, *The 1974 Federal Election Campaign Act Amendments: The Shortcomings of Good Intentions*, 1975 Duke Law Journal 851, 886–89, argued that the matching requirement was unconstitutional in the absence of an alternative method of qualification, such as petition signatures:

> Despite its simplicity and reliability . . . , a monetary eligibility criterion has a serious constitutional flaw. Instead of manifesting general public support for a contender, it reflects a candidate's support among those who can afford to spend discretionary income or capital on politics—a sizable, but nonetheless minority, proportion of the population. In view of the Court's holdings and language in the filing fee cases[,] it is difficult to see how an exclusively monetary eligibility criterion could be sustained against an equal protection attack. . . .
>
> The Court's heavy reliance [in the filing fee cases] on the interests of a candidate's prospective supporters and on their socio-economic background is even more appropriate with respect to the subsidy-qualifying mechanism than it is to filing fees. To qualify for the subsidy, a candidate must raise the necessary funds from his supporters. If his supporters are without means sufficient to contribute, it is *their* indigency which is being discriminated against in the political arena, not *his*.

Nicholson, *supra*, at 351, adds:

> Certainly matching grants are an effective means of screening frivolous candidates from public funding, but they are grossly overinclusive. Also screened out in the process are candidates supported by the poor.

3. When state statutes have authorized provision of voter registration lists to the major parties for use in campaigning and get-out-the-vote drives, federal courts have ruled that election officials are constitutionally required to provide the lists to minor parties on the same terms. See *Libertarian Party of Indiana v. Marion County Board of Voter Registration*, 778 F. Supp. 1458 (S.D. Ind. 1991); *Socialist Workers Party v. Rockefeller*, 314 F. Supp. 984 (S.D.N.Y. 1970), aff'd., 400 U.S. 806 (1970).

A statute passed by Congress in 1978 permitted national and state committees of political parties to send mail at subsidized postage rates. In 1980, Congress amended the statute so that only parties whose presidential candidate in the most recent election had received at least five percent of the vote were eligible for the subsidy. In *Greenberg v. Bolger*, 497 F. Supp. 756 (E.D.N.Y. 1980), this exclusion of small parties from the postal subsidy was found to violate both the First Amendment and the Equal Protection Clause.

Is *Greenberg* consistent with *Buckley*? The *Greenberg* opinion pointed out some salient differences between the two cases:

> The definitions [establishing eligibility for the postal subsidy] are derived from the Campaign Fund Act. . . . But, unlike the Campaign Fund Act, the 1978 Act [as amended in 1980] does not require major or minor parties to accept expenditure or contribution limitations as a condition of the receipt of public funds in the form of a postal subsidy. Moreover, the 1978 Act unlike the Campaign Fund Act makes no provision for the possible

reimbursement of a political party unable to qualify for advance funds given past results (or the lack of results in the case of a newly created party), but making the requisite showing in a current election. In addition, the 5 percent requirement reflects a concern for nationwide impact neglecting the local or statewide success that some third parties enjoy.

4. Campaign finance laws are not the only practices that may (intentionally or not) benefit or hinder third party and independent candidates. Major party candidates receive a number of additional benefits, including invitations to speak or debate. When the state is involved in organizing debates, may it exclude independent candidates? The Supreme Court considered that question in *Arkansas Educational Television Commission v. Forbes*, 523 U.S. 666 (1998). Justice Kennedy's opinion for the Court upheld the exclusion of independent congressional candidate Ralph Forbes. The majority first concluded that a debate sponsored by a public television agency was not a "public forum" to which rights of access generally exist under the First Amendment. The Court then explained and applied the standard applicable to exclusions from the state-sponsored debate:

> The debate's status as a nonpublic forum . . . did not give AETC unfettered power to exclude any candidate it wished. . . . To be consistent with the First Amendment, the exclusion of a speaker from a nonpublic forum must not be based on the speaker's viewpoint and must otherwise be reasonable in light of the purpose of the property. *Cornelius* . . .
>
> There is no substance to Forbes' suggestion that he was excluded because his views were unpopular or out of the mainstream. His own objective lack of support, not his platform, was the criterion. Indeed, the very premise of Forbes' contention is mistaken. A candidate with unconventional views might well enjoy broad support by virtue of a compelling personality or an exemplary campaign organization. By the same token, a candidate with a traditional platform might enjoy little support due to an inept campaign or any number of other reasons.
>
> Nor did AETC exclude Forbes in an attempted manipulation of the political process. The evidence provided powerful support for the jury's express finding that AETC's exclusion of Forbes was not the result of "political pressure from anyone inside or outside [AETC]." There is no serious argument that AETC did not act in good faith in this case. AETC excluded Forbes because the voters lacked interest in his candidacy, not because AETC itself did.
>
> The broadcaster's decision to exclude Forbes was a reasonable, viewpoint-neutral exercise of journalistic discretion consistent with the First Amendment.

Assume Justice Kennedy is right that Forbes was excluded in the exercise of reasonable journalistic discretion. Is it inherently wrong for public broadcasters to pick and choose among parties and candidates to participate in debates? If so, can public broadcasters be good journalists? For an examination of these issues, see Daniel H. Lowenstein, *Election Law Miscellany: Enforcement, Access to Debates, Qualification of Initiatives*, 77 Texas Law Review 2001, 2012–13 (1999). For an argument that the real reason for Forbes' exclusion was that he had been a "thorn in the side of the Arkansas political establishment for years—not a pest or a gadfly, but a serious rival to better-financed politicians," see Jamin B. Raskin, *The Debate Gerrymander*, 77 Texas Law Review 1943, 1956 (1999).

Justice Stevens, joined by Justices Souter and Ginsburg, dissented in *AETC* on the ground that the state lacked "narrow, objective, and definite standards" to guide its decision on whom should be included in the debate:

> The importance of avoiding arbitrary or viewpoint-based exclusions from political debates militates strongly in favor of requiring the controlling state agency to use (and adhere to) preestablished, objective criteria to determine who among qualified candidates may participate. When the demand for speaking facilities exceeds supply, the State must "ration or allocate the scarce resources on some acceptable neutral principle." *Rosenberger.* A constitutional duty to use objective standards—*i.e.*, "neutral principles"—for determining whether and when to adjust a debate format would impose only a modest requirement that would fall far short of a duty to grant every multiple-party request. Such standards would also have the benefit of providing the public with some assurance that state-owned broadcasters cannot select debate participants on arbitrary grounds.

Is Justice Stevens right? How can we know whether a candidate's exclusion was really based on his viewpoint or lack of popular support, absent clear standards set in advance? As an example of such standards, Justice Stevens cited FEC rules that require private broadcasters and corporations sponsoring debates to use "pre-established objective criteria to determine which candidates may participate in [the] debate." 11 C.F.R. § 110.13(c). Would such rules help avoid viewpoint-based exclusion of candidates from debates?

More recently, the Green Party, Libertarian Party, and others filed administrative complaints with the FEC, alleging that the Commission on Presidential Debates—which has staged every general election presidential debate since 1988—is not a "nonpartisan staging organization" as required by federal law. The complainants also sought a rulemaking that would prohibit a polling threshold (currently set at 15 percent) as the sole criterion for access to presidential debates. A district court recently concluded that the FEC acted arbitrarily and capriciously in denying the administrative complaints and refusing the initiate rulemaking, sending the matter back to the agency for reconsideration. *Level the Playing Field v. Federal Election Commission*, 232 F. Supp. 3d 130 (D.D.C. 2017). The D.C. Circuit ultimately concluded that the FEC did not act arbitrary and capriciously, in determining that the Commission on Presidential Debates was not overtly partisan. *Level the Playing Field v. Federal Election Commission*, 961 F.3d 462 (D.C. Cir. 2020).

5. In this chapter, we have considered cases in which third parties and independent candidates have sought things — like ballot access, public funding, and participation in broadcast debates — that were being provided to major party candidates. In these cases, the third parties and independent candidates claim a constitutional right to be treated the same as major parties. In other cases, third parties or independent candidates seek to be relieved of burdens that are imposed on major party candidates. In such cases, third parties and independent candidates claim a right to differential treatment.

An important example is the claim of some third parties to exemption from campaign financial disclosure requirements. In *Buckley v. Valeo, supra*, the Supreme Court upheld generally the constitutionality of disclosure requirements. However, the Court stated that where a third party could show that disclosure might subject it, its contributors, or its vendors to public or private harassment, the third party could be entitled to a constitutional exemption from the requirement of itemizing contributions and expenditures. In *Brown v. Socialist Workers '74 Campaign Committee*, 459 U.S. 87 (1982), the Court ruled that the Socialist Workers Party had made a sufficient showing and must be granted an exemption. Chapter 16 considers *Brown* and more recent decisions in this line.

Chapter 10

Campaigns

In almost any theory of democracy, the election plays a central role in assuring that government policy will bear some relationship to popular sentiment. For elections to play this role, voters must have information regarding the choices that appear on the ballot. The election campaign is the concentrated and purposive communication of information with the specific objective of influencing voter choice. While campaigns are neither the only nor necessarily the most important source of information for voters, few would deny their importance in the American political system.

This chapter considers some of the laws related to campaigning. We necessarily focus on just a few questions, but candidates considering a run for office must negotiate a maze of laws regulating their campaigns. For example, state and local laws often require that candidates for office be residents of the district or area in which they run, and sometimes candidates are prosecuted for violating such laws. Indiana Secretary of State Charlie White was convicted for serving in a prior city council role while not being a resident of the city. He also resigned his position as Secretary of State. Kristine Guerra, *Former Indiana Secretary of State Charlie White Begins Home Detention Sentence*, Indianapolis Star, Oct. 5, 2015, https://bit.ly/3ga7bCW.[a]

Nuts-and-bolts legal issues become very important even as potential candidates explore whether to run for election; the first thing a prudent potential candidate should do is hire a lawyer and an accountant. In many states, the law will require filing regular reports on campaign finances with appropriate administrative agencies. Those who fail to file proper reports may face fines, or at least face embarrassment when the matter comes to light. Chapter 16 considers campaign finance disclosure rules in some detail.

---

a. Under the Constitution's Qualifications Clauses, members of the United States Senate and the House of Representatives must be residents of the state they represent. See U.S. Const., Art. I, § 2, cl. 2; § 3, cl. 1. Numerous courts have struck down state statutes attempting to impose additional requirements such as that a candidate for the House be a resident of the Congressional district. See Daniel H. Lowenstein, *Are Congressional Term Limits Constitutional?*, 18 Harvard Journal of Law and Public Policy 1, 43–44 (1994) (collecting cases). See also *Schaefer v. Townsend*, 215 F.3d 1031 (9th Cir. 2000), cert denied *sub nom. Jones v. Schaefer*, 532 U.S. 904 (2001), in which the Ninth Circuit held that "California's requirement that candidates to the House of Representatives reside within the state *before* election violates the Constitution by handicapping the class of nonresident candidates who otherwise satisfy the Qualifications Clause."

This chapter considers other legal issues related to the law of campaigns. To inform the legal debate, we begin in Part I with a brief review of the political science of campaigns. How, if at all, does negative speech affect campaigns? How does media coverage influence voter choice? Do party conventions and presidential debates affect how voters choose a presidential candidate?

We then turn to two issues. First, many people are concerned about the content of campaigns. Some view campaigns as full of negative, misleading, and false speech, a problem that may have been exacerbated by social media. Part II considers whether campaign speech may be regulated. Part III explores special rules which have developed around judicial elections, a topic of much interest in recent years.

I. What We Know about American Political Campaigns

A common theme of the political science literature is that not all campaigns are created equal. The dynamics differ depending upon the office sought, whether or not the election is a party primary, a partisan general election (in which candidates run under a party label) or a nonpartisan general election, and whether or not the candidates are running for an open seat or in an election in which an incumbent seeks reelection.

Given their importance in American political life, presidential elections have received a great deal of political scientists' attention. More money and national media attention are spent on presidential races than on any other race for public office. Political scientists have noted an apparent paradox in presidential elections: they can accurately "forecast" the Democratic and Republican candidates' share of the presidential vote based upon a statistical model that considers only a few factors, most importantly the state of the economy in the months before the election. Models that ignore issues related to the campaign, including major campaign "events" such as conventions or debates,[b] were at least until recently highly accurate in predicting the outcome of most presidential races. The accuracy of forecasting suggests that presidential election campaigns do not matter. The paradox is that polls of voters' preferences for president are volatile, and fluctuate in response to events as they occur during the campaign, suggesting that campaigns do matter to election outcomes.

---

b. Wlezien and Erikson find that more than half the reported post-convention "bounce"—whereby a presidential candidate receives additional support in polls after the candidate's party convention—is due not to increase in a candidate's support but to sampling error in the polls. Christopher Wlezien & Robert S. Erikson, *Campaign Effects in Theory and Practice*, 29 American Politics Research 419, 426 (2001). Nonetheless, the authors believe that "events that happen during the campaign cause voters preferences to change.... The problem is empirically identifying those effects." *Id.* at 419.

Two political scientists have sought to resolve this paradox by hypothesizing that voters typically pay little attention to a presidential campaign until shortly before the election. In the period when voters are ignorant, there may be a considerable gap (or disequilibrium) between their presidential candidate preferences expressed to pollsters in the months before the election and how these voters ultimately vote on election day. During the campaign period, voters receive information through the media that helps them to make decisions consistent with their enlightened self-interest, eventually lining up voter preferences with those predicted by the forecasting models. Andrew Gelman & Gary King, *Why Are American Election Campaign Polls So Variable When Votes are So Predictable?*, 23 British Journal of Political Science 409 (1993).

In this understanding, presidential campaigns matter in a peculiar way. Both presidential campaigns are likely to be well-funded and well-run, leading to a situation where neither major-party candidate can gain a political advantage by campaigning. But a candidate could not abandon campaigning because doing so would allow the other campaign to gain an advantage with voters. Thomas M. Holbrook, Do Campaigns Matter? 147 (1996). To what extent does the 2016 election and the choice of Republican Donald Trump over Hillary Clinton upend thinking about the importance of traditional campaigns? Clinton vastly outspent Trump (though not in the critical last weeks of the campaign), and Trump used his celebrity status, social media, and an unorthodox campaign message to garner a great deal of free press coverage. A fluke or the wave of the future? The 2020 election saw candidates Trump and Joe Biden more closely matched financially, so the role of money and campaigning is hard to untangle. We return to this issue in Chapter 12.

How do campaigns impart information to voters? Some campaign messages come directly from candidates or campaigns, such as through campaign appearances, debates, and campaign advertising (whether on television or radio, or by mail, phone, or, increasingly, the internet and social media). These messages often contain appeals to emotions, either to impart positive feelings about the candidate or fear about the candidates' opponent. Though some have derided such emotional appeals as distracting voters from making good decisions about whom to vote for, others defend such emotional appeals as providing a sound basis for voter choice. Ted Brader, Campaigning for Hearts and Minds (2006). Somewhat surprisingly, Brader found "the most knowledgeable or 'sophisticated' citizens are also the most responsive to emotional appeals." *Id.* at 183. Brader believes voters can make sound decisions about which candidates to vote for by relying on their emotional responses.

If campaign advertising appeals to emotions, is it manipulative, causing voters to vote against their true preferences? Ansolabehere and Iyengar do not think so: "In the end, political advertising does not produce wholesale manipulation and deception of the electorate. Rather, it leads partisans to cast 'informed' votes. Exposure to advertising induces less-informed Democrats and Republicans to vote like their fellow partisans, who are more knowledgeable about the candidates and public affairs." Stephen Ansolabehere & Shanto Iyengar, Going Negative: How Political

Advertisements Shrink and Polarize the Electorate 66 (1995). Indeed, "Democrats and Republicans tend to reject messages from the opposing party, and liberals and conservatives reject persuasive communications that are inconsistent with their ideologies." John R. Zaller, The Nature and Origin of Mass Public Opinion 267 (1992).

Other information on campaigns comes through media coverage of the candidates. There seems little question that much of the news media coverage aims to make politics entertaining to viewers—after all, newspaper publishers want to sell newspapers and television executives want to sell advertising. Media coverage typically focuses on the "horserace" aspect of the campaign (who's ahead in the polls) as well as "gaffe" coverage, such as when a candidate makes a mistake in a debate or elsewhere. There is much less coverage of the candidates' various positions on issues and policies, a fact often lamented by some civic minded activists.

Political scientists are divided, however, on whether this media coverage has a negative influence on voter choices. Thomas Patterson, for example, believes that media coverage deprives voters of valuable information on the candidates, and leads to the choosing of candidates who are telegenic and can speak in sound bites. Thomas E. Patterson, Out of Order (1994). Samuel Popkin, in contrast, believes that media coverage can give voters the information they need to make choices consistent with their interests. Samuel L. Popkin, The Reasoning Voter: Communication and Persuasion in Presidential Campaigns (1991). For example, Popkin defends "gaffe" coverage. He points to President Ford's 1976 campaign gaffe when he tried to take a bite of the inedible husk of a Mexican tamale. Popkin explains that Ford's unfamiliarity with the tamale told Latino voters that he was unfamiliar with their culture and unlikely to be sympathetic to their interests. *Id.* at 111. Because the gaffe coverage was entertaining, voters had a rational incentive to obtain the information.

Gelman and King, *supra*, at 449, find horserace coverage largely irrelevant: "[J]ournalists should realize that they can report the polls all they want, and continue to make incorrect causal inferences about them, but they are not helping to predict or even influence the election."

Campaigns for other offices differ in significant ways from presidential campaigns. Some campaigns for lower office will be lopsided (for example, because one campaign will have more resources than the other, or a more competent campaign staff), and a superior campaign organization could be a decisive factor in some elections. Other elections may be swayed by national events (such as a pandemic or corruption scandals) beyond the message control of ordinary campaigns.

Unlike presidential and U.S. Senate campaigns, which rely heavily on television advertising, about one-third of U.S. House campaigns (and fewer campaigns in expensive media markets) rely on means other than television to get their messages out. Gary C. Jacobson, The Politics of Congressional Elections 88 (6th ed. 2004.) In state elections, statewide campaigns in large states such as California may depend heavily on television advertisements and direct mail; in smaller states, and in district races even in larger states, in-person contact, radio, phone, and mail are likely to be much more important than television.

Increasingly, voters are turning to the internet and social media for campaign information. With many campaigns sending opposition researchers to record the opposing candidate, a controversial remark or gaffe made on the campaign trail can mushroom into a major campaign issue when the video is posted on the internet. Consider Virginia U.S. Senator George Allen, who was considered a shoo-in for reelection to the Senate in 2006 until his "macaca moment." Allen was being recorded by an opposition researcher from the campaign of his opponent, James Webb. On video quickly posted on the internet's YouTube website, "[h]e called a Webb volunteer of Indian descent 'macaca' and welcomed him to 'America and the real world of Virginia.'" Michael D. Shear & Tim Craig, *After 2 Decades in Ascent, A Stunning Breakdown*, Washington Post, Nov. 10, 2006, at A01. His campaign tumbled after that moment. What, if anything, did Virginia voters learn about Allen from the extensive gaffe coverage of the so-called "macaca moment"?

In low salience races, such as races for superior court judge or local dog catcher, voters may have seen no advertising and know nothing about the candidate before entering the voting booth, and will rely upon various voting cues in deciding how to vote.[c] A party label is a useful cue for voters — knowing the candidate is a Republican or Democrat may be all the voter needs to know. In the absence of a party label (be it in a party primary or nonpartisan election), voters may rely upon the candidate's listed occupation, whether or not the candidate is the incumbent, and even the likely ethnic background of the candidate based upon the candidate's surname to choose how to vote. See Richard L. Hasen, *"High Court Wrongly Elected:" A Public Choice Model of Judging and Its Implications for the Voting Rights Act*, 75 North Carolina Law Review 1305, 1316 (1997) (collecting citations to the political science literature). With the increasing nationalization of the party "brand," do party labels help or hurt the creation of coherent policy on the local level? See Christopher S. Elmendorf & David Schleicher, *Informing Consent: Voter Ignorance, Political Parties, and Election Law*, 2013 University of Illinois Law Review 363.

There is also evidence, though it is disputed across different types of races, that being listed first on a ballot can benefit a candidate, particularly in a low salience race. See J.A. Krosnick, J.M. Miller, & M.P. Tichy, *An Unrecognized Need For Ballot Reform: Effects of Candidate Name Order*, in Rethinking the Vote: The Politics and Prospects of American Election Reform 51 (A.N. Crigler, M.R. Just & E.J. McCaffery, eds., 2004); Jonathan GS Koppell & Jennifer A. Steen, *The Effects of Ballot Position*

---

c. That is, if they do vote. Voters are more likely to vote for more prominent races (the "top of the ticket") than in less salient local races, even though the chances of affecting the outcome of larger races are much smaller. For roll-off figures in judicial retention elections, see Philip L. Dubois, From Ballot to Bench 48 tbl. 2 (1980).

on Election Outcomes, 66 Journal of Politics 267 (2004); R. Michael Alvarez, Betsy Sinclair & Richard L. Hasen, *How Much is Enough? The "Ballot Order Effect" and the Use of Social Science Research in Election Law Disputes*, 5 Election Law Journal 40 (2006); Mary Beth Beazley, *Ballot Design as a Fail-Safe: An Ounce of Rotation is Worth a Pound of Litigation*, 12 Election Law Journal 18, 30-33 (2013).

Though voters typically express disapproval of the job done by many state legislatures and Congress, being an incumbent is a decided advantage for both state and federal officeholders.

Political scientists have also studied a number of popular perceptions about campaigns. Many in the public believe that campaigns, especially presidential campaigns, are too long. Some believe that there is too much negative campaigning, which increases voter cynicism about the political process. Some political scientists defend negative campaigning as imparting valuable information to voters. John G. Geer, In Defense of Negativity: Attack Ads in Presidential Campaigns (2006). Others counter that negative campaigning can demobilize voters, especially independent voters, leading to a decline in voter turnout. Ansolabehere & Iyengar, *supra*, ch. 5. The effect of negative campaigning on turnout continues to be debated. For a summary and critique, see Deborah Jordan Brooks, *The Resilient Voter: Moving Toward Closure in the Debate over Negative Campaigning and Turnout*, 68 Journal of Politics 684 (2006).

In sum, political scientists appear to have moved beyond the question of "Do campaigns matter" to the question of "When and how do campaigns matter? Campaign effects are themselves quite variable, and therefore we must identify which conditions narrow or broaden the scope for manipulation." Henry Brady, Richard Johnston, & John Sides, *The Study of Political Campaigns*, in Capturing Campaign Effects 1, 12 (Henry Brady & Richard Johnston, eds., 2006).

Notes and Questions

1. Depending upon how one diagnoses the problems, if any, of American political campaigns, it is possible to imagine a whole series of laws that might be passed to regulate campaigns, some of which have been adopted in other democracies. For example, laws might seek to shorten the campaign period, require candidates to participate in a number of debates, bar candidate television advertising except for free air time provided by the government, prevent false or negative campaign speech, require newscasts to broadcast campaign conventions and cover issues, not "horserace" coverage or campaign gaffes, require candidates to run in elections with party labels, limit fundraising by independent groups that are more likely to run negative advertisements, and require candidates to abide by an oath of civility. Many, if not most, of these proposed laws would run afoul of the First Amendment of the U.S. Constitution, as we will see in Parts II and III of this Chapter. Putting aside the constitutional issue for a moment, would you favor adopting any of these laws? Why or why not?

Considering existing law, James A. Gardner, *Deliberation or Tabulation? The Self Undermining Constitutional Architecture of Election Campaigns*, 54 Buffalo Law Review 1413 (2007), argues that American law purports to understand campaigns to be about reasoned deliberation, but that campaign finance laws, ballot access laws, and other current election laws discourage such deliberation:

> Sometimes the law delivers what it promises, sometimes not. In the case of election campaigns, the law publicly proclaims a strong commitment to a widely held social conception of what election campaigns ought to be. In that understanding, campaigns ought to be deliberative in that their characteristic activity should be the practice of thoughtful and reasoned persuasion. Instead, the laws and jurisprudential doctrines structuring American election campaigns are built around a very different assumption: that the purpose of campaigns is primarily to tabulate exogenous voter preferences, and that political actors cannot reasonably expect, and therefore need not by law enjoy, meaningful opportunities during the campaign period to persuade voters to their points of view. Reasoned persuasion, in this environment, can thus be expected to play at most a minor, supporting role in most campaigns. Nothing in the law affirmatively prevents persuasion from occurring, but certainly the architecture of campaign law does nothing to facilitate it, and in some cases throws up obstacles to persuasion that may well be significant.

Id. at 1481. For a book-length development of this idea, see James A. Gardner, What Are Campaigns For?: The Role of Persuasion in Electoral Law and Politics (2009). What changes to election law might facilitate more deliberation? Should election law be changed to facilitate more deliberation?

2. Dirty tricks have always been a part of campaigns. Recent examples include New Hampshire Republican Party officials jamming the phone lines of an election day assistance program of the Democratic Party and Democrats in Milwaukee slashing tires of vans taking Republican voters to the polls. See Thomas B. Edsall, *GOP Official Faces Sentence in Phone Jamming Case*, Washington Post, May 17, 2006, at A10; Meg Jones, *4 Get Jail in Election Day Tire Slashing*, Milwaukee Journal-Sentinel, April 26, 2006.

Many of these practices are already illegal under state and local law, and some under federal law as well. Should a new federal law be passed to deal specifically with campaign dirty tricks? Bills have been proposed to expand coverage or increase penalties, but none have yet passed. For an example, see the Deceptive Practices and Voter Intimidation Act of 2007, S. 453, 110th Cong., 1st session. Among other provisions, the bill would prohibit any person, whether acting under color of law or otherwise, from knowingly deceiving any other person regarding: (1) the time, place, or manner of conducting any federal election; or (2) the qualifications for or restrictions on voter eligibility in such an election. Assuming such laws are constitutional (they well may not be), are they advisable? See Richard L. Hasen, Cheap Speech (2022).

3. *Campaign Hang-Ups.* In recent years, many campaigns have turned to automated, prerecorded telephone calls (or "robocalls") to voters to get out the vote, even though it is not clear that robocalls are effective as a voter mobilization tool. See Donald P. Green & Alan S. Gerber, Get Out the Vote! How to Increase Voter Turnout (2004). Indeed, voters have complained about the frequency of these calls and a number of states have considered legislation to ban the practice. See Susan Saulny, *Limits Sought on "Robocalls" in Campaigns*, N.Y. Times, April 25, 2007.

A less reputable practice is "push polling:" "Push polls are not really polls at all; their object is not to measure public opinion, but to manipulate it by providing as many 'respondents' as possible, with hypothetical, sometimes blatantly false information about candidates, political parties, or initiatives." Evan Gerstmann & Matthew J. Streb, *Putting an End to Push Polling: Why It Should Be Banned and Why the First Amendment Lets Congress Ban It*, 3 Election Law Journal 37 (2004). Do you agree with Gerstmann and Streb that banning push polling is a good idea? Consider the constitutional question of banning the practice after you have reviewed the material in Part II.

II. Regulating Campaign Speech

281 Care Committee v. Arneson

766 F.3d 774 (8th Cir. 2014), *cert. denied*, 575 U.S. 912 (2015)

Before SMITH, BEAM, and BENTON, Circuit Judges.

BEAM, Circuit Judge.

[Two Minnesota-based, grassroots advocacy organizations founded to oppose school-funding ballot initiatives and their leaders filed a suit arguing that a provision of the Minnesota Fair Campaign Practices Act (FCPA) inhibited their ability to speak freely against these ballot initiatives and, thereby, violated their First Amendment rights. The case went from the federal district court to the appeals court back to the district court, which upheld the constitutionality of the law. It is now before the appeals court a second time.]

I. Background

In relevant part, the challenged provision of the FCPA provides:

> A person is guilty of a gross misdemeanor who intentionally participates in the preparation, dissemination, or broadcast of paid political advertising or campaign material . . . with respect to the effect of a ballot question, that is designed or tends to . . . promote or defeat a ballot question, that is false, and that the person knows is false or communicates to others with reckless disregard of whether it is false.

Minn. Stat. § 211B.06, subd. 1. Other than a source protected by the FCPA exemption for "news items or editorial comments by the news media," anyone can lodge a claim under § 211B.06 with the Minnesota Office of Administrative Hearings (OAH) within one year after the alleged occurrence of the act that is the subject of the complaint. The OAH immediately assigns an administrative law judge (ALJ) to the matter, who then determines if there is a prima facie violation and, if so, probable cause supporting the complaint. If the complaint alleging a § 211B.06 violation is filed "within 60 days before the primary or special election or within 90 days before the general election to which the complaint relates, the ALJ must conduct an expedited probable cause hearing." If a complaint survives a probable cause assessment, the chief ALJ assigns the complaint to a three-judge panel for an evidentiary hearing, which could realistically necessitate the employment of legal counsel by the accused. A final decision and/or civil penalty (up to $5,000) imposed by an ALJ panel is subject to judicial review. Only when a complaint is finally disposed of by the OAH, is it subject to further prosecution by the county attorney. One possible resolution by the ALJ panel is to refer the complaint to the appropriate county attorney without rendering its own opinion on the matter, or in addition to its own resolution.

As noted in [the appeals court's first opinion in this case]:

> Minnesota has a long history of regulating knowingly false speech about political candidates; it has criminalized defamatory campaign speech since 1893. However, the FCPA's regulation of issue-related political speech is a comparatively recent innovation. Minnesota did not begin regulating knowingly false speech about ballot initiatives until 1988. Between 1988 and 2004, the FCPA's regulation of speech regarding ballot initiatives allowed for only one enforcement mechanism: mandatory criminal prosecution of alleged violators by county attorneys. In 2004, the Minnesota legislature amended the FCPA to provide that alleged violations of section 211B.06 initially be dealt with through civil complaints filed with the [OAH].

Upon remand from [the appeals court, the district court upheld the constitutionality of the law.] Regarding the appropriate level of scrutiny to apply in this action, even though this court [in the first appeal] directed the district court to apply strict scrutiny upon remand, the district court determined that the intervening Supreme Court opinion, *United States v. Alvarez*, 567 U.S. 709 (2012), altered the landscape. Discussing *Alvarez*, the district court noted that the four-Justice plurality, led by Justice Kennedy, applied strict scrutiny and found the Stolen Valor Act unconstitutional. The district court accurately noted that Justice Breyer wrote a concurring opinion in *Alvarez*, joined by Justice Kagan, in which he agreed that the Stolen Valor Act was unconstitutional but arrived at that holding applying intermediate, not strict, scrutiny. Appellees argued to the district court that Justice Breyer's concurrence controlled in *Alvarez* because when "a fragmented Court decides a case and no single rationale explaining the result enjoys the assent of five Justices, the holding of the Court may be viewed as that position taken by those Members who concurred in the judgments on the narrowest grounds." *Marks v. United States*, 430 U.S. 188, 193 (1977). Accordingly, applying the *Marks* rule, Appellees argued that the appropriate level of scrutiny to apply in this case is intermediate scrutiny. The district court agreed that intermediate scrutiny applied according to *Alvarez*, but conducted its determinative analysis applying strict scrutiny because the court held that no matter the level of scrutiny, Minnesota Statute § 211B.06 survives even the most stringent.

Applying a strict scrutiny analysis to the instant facts, the district court held § 211B.06 serves a "compelling interest" (i.e., preserving fair and honest elections and preventing a fraud upon the electorate through the deliberate spreading of material, false information) and that, on balance, that interest was important enough to justify the speech § 211B.06 has restricted in pursuit of that interest. This appeal followed.

II. Discussion

[The court held that the trial court directly determined that the plaintiffs had standing to bring their case.]

C. Scrutiny

"As a general matter, the First Amendment means that government has no power to restrict expression because of its message, its ideas, its subject matter, or its content." *Alvarez* (plurality opinion). To evaluate whether a statute violates the First Amendment, the first step is to articulate the level of scrutiny to apply in this court's analysis — i.e., the standard on which this court examines the fit between the statutory ends and means. The parties hotly dispute the level of scrutiny to apply here, including a vibrant discussion as to whether, and how, *Alvarez* applies. The district court and now Appellees advocate that *Alvarez* is the guidepost for our analysis regarding the constitutionality of § 211B.06, and instructs that we apply intermediate scrutiny in this case. However, while *Alvarez* dealt with a content-based restriction on protected speech, the restriction at issue in *Alvarez* did not regulate political speech, the key factor in the instant analysis. Accordingly, *Alvarez* is not dispositive.

In *Alvarez*, the Supreme Court analyzed a First Amendment challenge to the Stolen Valor Act, which criminalized false claims about the receipt of military decorations or medals. Specifically, the defendant, Alvarez, lied in announcing he held the Congressional Medal of Honor and he was indicted under the Stolen Valor Act for doing so. In arriving at the conclusion that the Stolen Valor Act as written violated the First Amendment, four Justices applied strict scrutiny and the two concurring Justices applied intermediate scrutiny. Despite the disagreement over the level of scrutiny to apply, however, all six Justices in *Alvarez* agreed that false statements do not represent a category of speech altogether exempt from First Amendment protection. Simply stated, false statements, as a general proposition, are not beyond constitutional protection. Like the Stolen Valor Act, § 211B.06 targets falsity, as opposed to the legally cognizable harms associated with a false statement. In this arena, the Court makes clear that there is no free pass around the First Amendment.

The key today, however, is that although *Alvarez* dealt with a regulation proscribing false speech, it did not deal with legislation regulating false political speech. This distinction makes all the difference and is entirely the reason why *Alvarez* is not the ground upon which we tread. Justice Breyer in his concurring opinion in *Alvarez* recognized the significant difference between the false speech regulated by the Stolen Valor Act and other areas of false speech, including false political speech, acknowledging that strict scrutiny is often the test to apply, and noting that almost no amount of fine tailoring could achieve a similar government interest in a political context:

> I recognize that in some contexts, particularly political contexts, such a narrowing will not always be easy to achieve. In the political arena a false statement is more likely to make a behavioral difference (say, by leading the listeners to vote for the speaker) but at the same time criminal prosecution is particularly dangerous (say, by radically changing a potential election result) and consequently can more easily result in censorship of speakers and their ideas.

(Breyer, J., concurring). *Alvarez*, of course, guides our analysis to the extent it discusses the regulation of false speech in light of general First Amendment protections, but the Court's pronouncements in the myriad other cases discussing the regulation of political speech dictate the level of scrutiny to apply to our analysis.

So, again, it is key that the regulatory scheme at play in *Alvarez* dealt entirely, and only, with false speech. In fact, it was largely (if not solely) because the regulation at issue in *Alvarez* concerned false statements about easily verifiable facts that did not concern subjects often warranting greater protection under the First Amendment, that the concurring Justices applied intermediate scrutiny. Here, because the speech at issue occupies the core of the protection afforded by the First Amendment, we apply strict scrutiny to legislation attempting to regulate it. Accordingly, because *Alvarez* does not alter the landscape on this issue, the scrutiny directed in [the earlier appeals court decision] endures.

D. Regulation of Political Speech

The First Amendment of the United States Constitution states: "Congress shall make no law . . . abridging the freedom of speech." U.S. Const. amend. I. The regulation of political speech or expression is, and always has been, at the core of the protection afforded by the First Amendment. "Political speech is the primary object of First Amendment protection and the lifeblood of a self-governing people." *McCutcheon v. Federal Election Commission* [see Chapter 14—Eds.] (Thomas, J. concurring). . . .

Much legal discourse has taken place regarding the special place held for political discussion in our system of government, and the application of these principles, usually discussed in the context of speech surrounding candidates for office, "extend[s] equally to issue-based elections such as [political campaigns on a ballot issue]." *McIntyre v. Ohio Elections Commission* [see Chapter 16—Eds.]. So,

> [d]iscussion of public issues and debate on the qualifications of candidates are integral to the operation of the system of government established by our Constitution. The First Amendment affords the broadest protection to such political expression in order to assure the unfettered interchange of ideas for the bringing about of political and social changes desired by the people. Although First Amendment protections are not confined to the exposition of ideas, there is practically universal agreement that a major purpose of that Amendment was to protect the free discussion of governmental affairs, of course including discussions of [political campaigns on a ballot issue]. This no more than reflects our profound national commitment to the principle that debate on public issues should be uninhibited, robust, and wide-open.

Id. Applying strict scrutiny, the burden on Appellees in this matter is to demonstrate that the interest advanced in support of the § 211B.06 is narrowly tailored to meet a compelling government interest.

E. Statutory Ends and Means

The county attorneys are unable to meet their burden in this case. Even if we were to assume that the asserted compelling interests discussed herein pass muster for purposes of this constitutional analysis, no amount of narrow tailoring succeeds because § 211B.06 is not necessary, is simultaneously overbroad and underinclusive, and is not the least restrictive means of achieving any stated goal. We explain.

1. Compelling Interest

"Precisely what constitutes a 'compelling interest' is not easily defined. Attempts at definition generally use alternative, equally superlative language: 'interest[] of the highest order,' 'overriding state interest,' 'unusually important interest.'" *Republican Party of Minn. v. White*, 416 F.3d 738, 749 (8th Cir.2005) (en banc) (*White II*) (quoting *Wisconsin v. Yoder*, 406 U.S. 205, 215 (1972); *McIntyre*; *Goldman v. Weinberger*, 475 U.S. 503, 530 (1986) (O'Connor, J., dissenting)). Too, the discussion regarding whether a state interest is compelling or not bottoms on other considerations in the strict scrutiny analysis, such as the impact of the regulation itself. . . .

The district court concluded that the major purpose of § 211B.06 is to preserve fair and honest elections and prevent a fraud on the electorate. The district court additionally articulated that the purpose of § 211B.06 is to "implement[] minimal, narrowly tailored safeguards against campaigns of misinformation," and to "[l]imit[] the dissemination of knowingly or recklessly false statements about the effects of ballot initiatives," because "[d]eliberate or reckless efforts to mislead the public and change the outcome of a ballot measure not only have an adverse impact on the issue being decided, [they] undermine the premises of democratic government, including the necessity of free but fair debates."

Despite the strong protection for political speech under the First Amendment, the Supreme Court has acknowledged that a state interest in preventing fraud "carries special weight during election campaigns when false statements, if credited, may have serious adverse consequences for the public at large.: *McIntyre*. . . .

Directly regulating what is said or distributed during an election, as § 211B.06 does, goes beyond an attempt to control the process to enhance the fairness overall so as to carefully protect the right to vote. We concede that regulating falsity in the political realm definitely exemplifies a stronger state interest than, say, regulating the dissemination and content of information generally, given the importance of the electoral process in the United States. *McIntyre*. Even in that context, however, the state does not have carte blanche to regulate the dissemination of false statements during political campaigns and the Supreme Court has yet to specifically weigh in on the balancing of interests when it does.

Today we need not determine whether, on these facts, preserving fair and honest elections and preventing fraud on the electorate comprise a compelling state interest because the narrow tailoring that must juxtapose that interest is absent here. Again, "[a] law cannot be regarded as protecting an interest of the highest order, and thus as justifying a restriction upon speech, when it leaves appreciable damage to that supposedly vital interest unprohibited." *White II*. Accordingly, we turn to the "narrow tailoring" examination of § 211B.06.

2. Narrowly Tailored

Even if we conclude that Minnesota has a compelling state interest in preserving "fair and honest" elections and preventing a "fraud upon the electorate," § 211B.06 fails under strict scrutiny. Under such inquiry, the requisite tailoring is determinative as to the statute's constitutionality because those making the laws may pursue stated interests "only so long as [they do] not unnecessarily infringe an individual's right to freedom of speech." *McCutcheon* (plurality).

[T]o survive strict scrutiny, Appellees must do more than assert a compelling state interest — they must demonstrate that § 211B.06 is narrowly tailored.

The county attorneys claim that § 211B.06 is indeed "actually necessary" to preserve fair and honest elections in Minnesota. They do so, however, without confirming that there is an actual, serious threat of individuals disseminating knowingly false statements concerning ballot initiatives. The county attorneys instead claim that empirical evidence is not required to support this legislative judgment. Rather, they assert that common sense dictates "that political advertising aimed at voters and intentionally designed to induce a particular vote through the use of false facts impacts voters' understanding and perceptions; can influence their vote; and ultimately change an election." Because American elections employ secret ballots, Appellees continue (adopting the district court's reasoning), the effects of knowingly false statements do not lend themselves easily to empirical evidence. Accordingly, they argue, the statute is justified, reasonably, by its purpose in preventing fraud on the electorate through minimal regulations on knowingly false statements of fact.

Continuing in their defense of § 211B.06, the county attorneys argue that § 211B.06 is also not overbroad because it is narrowly tailored through its mens rea requirement of actual malice, achieved through the "knowingly false or reckless disregard of falsity" limitation. This mens rea requirement, they claim with reference to the district court's analysis of *Garrison v. La.*, 379 U.S. 64, 75 (1964), provides the "breathing space" necessary to protect free speech, while narrowly tailoring the prohibition to further the state's interest. In that same vein, the county attorneys additionally claim that § 211B.06 is not underinclusive because it exempts "news items or editorial comments by the news media," and is limited to "paid political advertising or campaign material" Again, as did the district court, the county attorneys deduce that such an exemption is not only viewpoint neutral but recognizes the countervailing interests in a free press and keeps the government out of the editorial rooms while simultaneously targeting the problem—ballot-question advocates and opponents who pose a greater threat than the news media of disseminating intentionally false statements regarding the effect of a ballot question. This, too, according to the district court, allows for oral statements made in debates or "on the street corner soap box," made spontaneously or in the heat of the moment, such that these speakers "need never curb their unscripted oral statements to avoid violating § 211B.06." And, finally, the county attorneys (as did the district court) conclude that § 211B.06 is the least restrictive alternative because even though counterspeech could be used, it is not as effective in achieving the legitimate purpose § 211B.06 was enacted to serve, especially after an election is over or towards the end of a campaign, when, apparently, the county attorneys believe § 211B.06 best serves the state's interest.

Each of these arguments fail under the required scrutiny. Previously stated, § 211B.06 is not narrowly tailored. First, because § 211B.06 perpetuates fraud, as discussed below, it is not actually necessary. It is also simultaneously overbroad and underinclusive. And, finally, it is not the least restrictive means of achieving the stated goals it allegedly advances. We address all of the areas. . . .

Stated most simply, § 211B.06 does not survive strict scrutiny because it tends to perpetuate the very fraud it is allegedly designed to prohibit. For this reason, among others, the restriction is neither narrowly tailored nor necessary. In fact, it illustrates that the asserted compelling interest falls short. If § 211B.06 is truly intended, in part, to ensure "campaigns of decency" and "election of candidates to office[s] of honor and trust," as the county attorneys claim (in reliance upon Minnesota case law), the statute wholly misses the mark. In fact, looking to the similar statutory scheme in Ohio, the Supreme Court in *Susan B. Anthony List v. Driehaus*, 134 S. Ct. 2334 (2014) (*SBA List*) illuminated the many abuses that emanate from such an endeavor. Just having a statute like § 211B.06 on the books creates an environment fraught with problems.

In *SBA List*, the Ohio Attorney General himself (Ohio AG), though charged simultaneously with the zealous representation of the Ohio Elections Commission in the same action, took the unique and rare step of filing an amicus brief as a "friend of the Court and the legal process" and as Ohio's "chief law officer" to enlighten the

Court as to the "actual workings and effect of the Ohio false statements statute in practice." Many of the concerns expressed by the Ohio AG made headway with the Court and resonate here as well.

First, as a practical matter, it is immensely problematic that anyone may lodge a complaint with the OAH alleging a violation of § 211B.06. There is no promise or requirement that the power to file a complaint will be used prudently. "Because the universe of potential complainants is not restricted to state officials who are constrained by explicit guidelines or ethical obligations, there is a real risk of complaints from, for example, political opponents." *Id.* Complaints can be filed at a tactically calculated time so as to divert the attention of an entire campaign from the meritorious task at hand of supporting or defeating a ballot question, possibly diffusing public sentiment and requiring the speaker to defend a claim before the OAH, thus inflicting political damage. Just as the Court explained in the context of the Ohio false statements statute, section § 211B.06 makes anyone speaking out about a ballot question "easy targets." *Id.*

As previously noted, the county attorneys claim that empirical evidence is not needed to establish that § 211B.06 is actually necessary. However, their reliance upon "common sense" to establish that the use of false statements impacts voters' understanding, influences votes and ultimately changes elections, is not enough on these facts to establish a direct causal link between § 211B.06 and an interest in preserving fair and honest elections. Even though the effect of election fraud or detecting the fraud itself, arguably, is a bit more amorphous and difficult to detect, only relying upon common sensibilities to prove it is taking place still falls short. In *Alvarez*, the Court took the government to task for relying upon "common sense" to establish that its stated interest was at risk. (plurality). Certainly, it must be acknowledged that allowing an individual to disseminate political advertising that contains knowing falsehoods does not advance a fair and honest election. Yet merely relying upon common sense does not satisfy the heavy burden when protected speech is regulated. *Id.* We "have never accepted mere conjecture as adequate to carry a First Amendment burden." [*Nixon v.*] *Shrink Mo. Gov't PAC* [see Chapter 14 — Eds.]. Appellees defend the statute's ability to dissuade fraud with common sense, but is there such a problem that this infringement on protected speech must occur in the first instance? They argue that the law itself has been construed by Minnesota courts countless times but how often, in practice, is it put to use? Such conjecture about the effects and dangers of false statements equates to implausibility as far as this analysis goes, because, when the statute infringes core political speech, we tend to not take chances. . . .

The Ohio AG [in *SBA List*] addressed the reality of the problem head on and explained that by its nature, the "statutory scheme pulls within its ambit much protected speech."

> Few respondents contest an adverse Commission finding in court because the election will be over, won or lost, by the time any judicial hearing takes place, and so the remedy is largely meaningless. Even if the speaker is

> ultimately victorious, that speaker gets little or nothing for his or her efforts but additional legal bills. Nevertheless, the few challenges that do take place demonstrate that the State administrative apparatus affects a good deal of speech that is well within the ambit of constitutionally protected speech, and that the remedy is rarely, if ever, a timely one.

Between 2001 and 2010 in Ohio, for example, their Commission (the body in Ohio charged with similar duties as Minnesota's OAH to review these complaints) found violations of their respective false statements statute in 90 cases. Additionally,

> the Commission dismissed another forty-eight cases after a hearing, and 112 were dismissed because the complainant withdrew the complaint or failed to prosecute (typically after the election—a further indication that the goal may often be less an ultimate finding of a violation than a probable-cause finding before the election). Two hundred sixty were dismissed with findings of "no probable cause."

The Ohio AG included such figures to illuminate that in reality "numerous speakers who have not made a false statement even under the modest burden of proof for 'probable cause,' are forced to devote time, resources, and energy defending themselves before the Elections Commission, typically in the late stages of a campaign."

We do not cite to the Ohio AG statistical offerings to imply that just such empirical evidence is required to establish the causal link between § 211B.06 and the interests it is in place to protect. Nor do we cite the Ohio AG's explanation of how that state's false statements statutes are working in practice to imply that, in fact, the exact same reality must exist in Minnesota. The Ohio AG's explanation, however, clearly exemplifies the potential for abuse and an absence of narrow tailoring of the Minnesota law—and thus, a lack of necessity.

An affidavit submitted by the county attorneys in this matter avers that the Hennepin County Attorney's Office has not commenced any criminal prosecutions under § 211B.06 for false political and campaign material. The county attorneys have likewise filed copies of OAH decisions that have followed evidentiary hearings concerning § 211B.06 complaints, with varying findings concerning the challenged statements—some successful, some not. These exhibits, however, do not provide us with the bigger picture and thus we are at a loss to deduce any significance from their inclusion in the record except to establish that the OAH receives some complaints under § 211B.06, some of which are meritorious and others not. If anything, the sampling of orders exemplify that protected speech is being swept in by § 211B.06 unnecessarily, further establishing the chilling nature of this statute, as well as its overbreadth, which we turn to next.

For all practical purposes, the real potential damage is done at the time a complaint is filed, no matter the possibility of criminal prosecution down the line. The burdens of the OAH proceedings themselves greatly impact electoral speech and are cause for concern. Even before a probable cause hearing, the allegation of the falsity itself likely makes the news circuit and creates a stir in the ongoing political discourse. Practically, should probable cause be found by the ALJ when the complaint is filed close to an election, no judicial review can take place to effect any relief prior to the impending election. So, the damage is inflicted at the point of filing, even if the complainant is ultimately unable to prove up the allegations of falsity under the clear and convincing standard required during a resulting evidentiary hearing that would occur after a finding of probable cause. Essentially, then, this damage (or injury) occurs quite easily, at the whim of "anyone" willing to file a complaint under oath. Not only does this injury occur upon filing, it only deepens upon the finding of probable cause. At bottom, then, this core political speech is penalized using a burden of proof even lower than a preponderance of the evidence, with few, if any, safeguards to protect this "zenith" of First Amendment-protected political speech. See *Meyer v. Grant*, 486 U.S. 414 (1988). . . .

Notwithstanding its overbreadth, the lack of a causal link between the advanced interests and § 211B.06 is not the only way in which § 211B.06 is not actually necessary to achieve the stated interests. A second consideration in our analysis as to whether § 211B.06 is narrowly tailored to achieve Minnesota's asserted compelling interest in preserving fair and honest elections and preventing a fraud on the electorate, is that the county attorneys have not offered persuasive evidence to dispel the generally accepted proposition that counterspeech may be a logical solution to the interest advanced in this case. "[W]hen the Government seeks to regulate protected speech, the restriction must be the least restrictive means among available, effective alternatives." *Alvarez* (plurality). There is no reason to presume that counterspeech would not suffice to achieve the interests advanced and is a less restrictive means, certainly, to achieve the same end goal.

> The remedy for speech that is false is speech that is true. This is the ordinary course in a free society. The response to the unreasoned is the rational; to the uninformed, the enlightened; to the straight-out lie, the simple truth. . . . The First Amendment itself ensures the right to respond to speech we do not like, and for good reason. Freedom of speech and thought flows not from the beneficence of the state but from the inalienable rights of the person. And suppression of speech by the government can make exposure of falsity more difficult, not less so. Society has the right and civic duty to engage in open, dynamic, rational discourse. These ends are not well served when the government seeks to orchestrate public discussion through content-based mandates.

Id. (plurality).

Possibly there is no greater arena wherein counterspeech is at its most effective. It is the most immediate remedy to an allegation of falsity. "The theory of our Constitution is that the best test of truth is the power of the thought to get itself accepted in the competition of the market." *Id.* It is the citizenry that can discern for themselves what the truth is, not an ALJ behind doors. "The preferred First Amendment remedy of more speech, not enforced silence . . . has special force." *Brown v. Hartlage*, 456 U.S. 45, 61 (1982). Especially as to political speech, counterspeech is the tried and true buffer and elixir. Putting in place potential criminal sanctions and/or the possibility of being tied up in litigation before the OAH, or both, at the mere whim and mention from anyone who might oppose your view on a ballot question is wholly overbroad and overburdensome and chills otherwise protected speech. That counterspeech confronts these asserted compelling interests and is a less restrictive means of countering the concern leads us again to deduce that the interests are less compelling than touted and the statute is not narrowly tailored to achieve the goal.

Outside of counterspeech it is difficult at this point to envision other, less restrictive means to abate the alleged interest. No matter, however, because counterspeech, alone, establishes a viable less restrictive means of addressing the preservation of fair and honest elections in Minnesota and preventing fraud on the electorate. The county attorneys claim that counterspeech is not good enough to adequately address the concern because it cannot change the outcome of an election, nor can it effectively counter targeted communications with voters at the end of a campaign. The district court added that counterspeech may not be effective in the "David and Goliath" scenario when one group may so greatly outmatch a political opponent that the message, or correction, offered in response goes largely unheard. But these claims do not sufficiently respond to the use of counterspeech on these facts. The county attorneys simply do not acknowledge that if counterspeech does not suffice, § 211B.06 does not either. We have already pointed out the practical problems inherent with § 211B.06 and the reality regarding how it could actually perpetuate fraud in an election. Such realities cannot be ignored. If the genuine concern is to preserve fair and honest elections and prevent a fraud on the electorate, then it would seem that they, too, could not continue to keep § 211B.06 as part of a legislative scheme when the realities of its possible abuse are exposed. Section 211B.06 thus plainly fails the test of being the least restrictive means to serve the state's interest.

Another basis advanced by the county attorneys to demonstrate the narrow tailoring of § 211B.06 falls short. The mens rea requirement in § 211B.06 does not effectively narrow the statute to limit its reach as intended. The risk of chilling otherwise protected speech is not eliminated or lessened by the mens rea requirement because, as we have already noted, a speaker might still be concerned that someone will file a complaint with the OAH, or that they might even ultimately be prosecuted, for a careless false statement or possibly a truthful statement someone deems false, no matter the speaker's veracity. Or, most cynically, many might legitimately fear that no matter what they say, an opponent will utilize § 211B.06 to simply tie them up in litigation and smear their name or position on a particular matter, even if the speaker never had the intent required to render him liable. See *Alvarez* (Breyer, J., concurring) (discussing the similar chill inherent in the Stolen Valor Act, rendered unconstitutional by the Court). The mens rea requirement in this context does not safeguard the statute's constitutionality nor deter someone from filing a complaint challenging statements involving exaggeration, rhetoric, figurative language, and unfavorable, misleading or illogical statements or opinions. There is nothing in place to realistically stop the potential for abuse of § 211B.06' s mechanisms.

Finally, the exemption for "news items or editorial comments by the news media," from the FCPA, § 211B.01 subd. 2, as well as § 211B.06's limitation to "paid political advertising or campaign material," actually exemplify that § 211B.06 is underinclusive. The former, the county attorneys argue, protects the countervailing interests in a free press, and the latter, the district court points out, allows for oral statements in debates and on television, along with spontaneous soapbox pronouncements and other such speech that includes "unscripted oral statements," without fear of reprisal. First, to claim that a statement made during a debate is spontaneous and unscripted, and thus should receive greater leeway, is disingenuous at best, in a day when many political speakers take the greatest pains to be politically correct at all times, carefully crafting, in advance, every statement they make in the political arena. Applying their logic regarding the effect of such speech, to allow the "dissemination" (albeit orally) of these statements outside the confines of § 211B.06 leaves equally injurious speech untouched, although it is capable of inflicting the same harm, say, as that included in a published campaign pamphlet. Appellants' example of the hypocrisy that can occur under this scheme perhaps best illustrates the problem, although we alter their example slightly. Overlaying the press exemption with the statutory restrictions, we envision a newspaper opinion section which, on the same day, prints the very same "false" information regarding the effects of a ballot question twice—once as an editorial and again in a paid advertisement from a local group opposing the initiative. One is exempt from prosecution and the other is not. Such a result does not advance a stated interest in preventing a fraud on the electorate.

It is in the political arena where robust discourse must take place. And although there are certain outright falsities one could envision in the discussion of a proposed ballot question, especially when considering there are hotly debated sides to every issue, it seems that too often in that situation, the "falsity" deemed by one person actionable under § 211B.06 will be a statement of conjecture about the future state of affairs should the ballot question pass or fail. Despite the certainty of conjecture, however, the state may not prevent others from "resort[ing] to exaggeration, to vilification of men who have been, or are, prominent in church or state, and even to false statement." *Cantwell v. Conn.*, 310 U.S. 296, 310 (1940). Such "back and forth" is the way of the world in election discourse. "[S]ome false statements are inevitable if there is to be an open and vigorous expression of views in public and private conversation. . . ." *Alvarez* (plurality). We therefore leave room for the rough and tumble of political discourse for the farfetched. "[P]olitical speech by its nature will sometimes have unpalatable consequences, and, in general, our society accords greater weight to the value of free speech than to the dangers of its misuse." *McIntyre.*

The county attorneys claim that § 211B.06 actually serves its purpose most fervently at the end of a campaign or even after an election is over. This claim is wholly without merit. Given the information exposed by the Ohio AG and our own analysis of § 211B.06, it is possible that it is at that point that § 211B.06 can be utilized to induce the most damage to the state interest it is designed to serve. As asserted by the Ohio AG, who is charged with the task of enforcing the similar statutory scheme, these laws "allow [] the State's legal machinery to be used extensively by private actors to gain political advantage in circumstances where malicious falsity cannot ultimately be established."

Given these realities, the county attorneys have failed to demonstrate that § 211B.06 is either narrowly tailored or necessary to preserve fair and honest elections and prevent a fraud on the electorate. The mens rea requirement established in the statute, and any other alleged narrowing safeguards that Appellees claim render this statute constitutional, have little effect in abating the advanced concern of the state. Citing Minnesota law, the county attorneys claim that the legislative intent of § 211B.06 is to prevent corrupt campaign practices that would "mislead the public and permit close elections . . . to be won by fraud." *In re Contest of Gen. Election*, 264 N.W.2d 401, 406 (Minn.1978) (Otis, J., dissenting). But as we have discussed, the practical application of § 211B.06 only opens the door to more fraud. The statute itself actually opens a Pandora's box to disingenuous politicking itself.

While we would like to agree with the district court that because § 211B.06 employs "the force and impartiality of law," it "serves to check the unfair use of disparate advantage during a campaign," we do not have the luxury of indulging that scenario given the abridgement of core political speech at risk. With such abridgement left unregulated, not only is § 211B.06 not narrowly tailored but likely does not rise to the level of explicating a "compelling" interest. The citizenry, not the government, should be the monitor of falseness in the political arena. Citizens can digest and question writings or broadcasts in favor or against ballot initiatives just as they are equally poised to weigh counterpoints. *McIntyre* ("People are intelligent enough to evaluate the source of an anonymous writing. They can see it is anonymous. They know it is anonymous. They can evaluate its anonymity along with its message, as long as they are permitted, as they must be, to read that message. And then, once they have done so, it is for them to decide what is responsible, what is valuable, and what is truth.").

[A portion of the opinion concerning the immunity of the state attorney general under the Eleventh Amendment is omitted.]

III. Conclusion

For the reasons stated herein, we . . . reverse and remand for further proceedings consistent with this opinion.

Notes and Questions

1. The case settled on remand, but the Minnesota statute is still on the books. If you were advising a candidate for office in Minnesota about whether the candidate is free to lie in a campaign, what would you say? Note that *281 Care Committee* applied in the context of ballot measure elections not candidate elections. Should that matter?

There apparently have been no attempted criminal prosecutions since this case, and no further court decisions on whether any part of the statute survives. But complaints made by individuals about candidates making purportedly false statements have been rejected by Administrative Law Judges on constitutional grounds, citing *281 Care Committee*. *Yelena Kurdyumova v. Susan Pha*, Minn. OAH, 82-0325-33963, 2016 WL 7462521, at *2 (Nov. 28, 2016); *Mark Osland v. Rick Greene, Committee To Re-elect Rick Greene, District 2 Commissioner*, Minn. OAH, 80-0325-33972, 2016 WL 6921576, at *4 (Nov. 14, 2016).

Wholly apart from potential liability under the statute, a person still may be liable for the common law tort of defamation if the person makes a false statement injurious to reputation. The Supreme Court in a series of cases beginning with *New York Times v. Sullivan*, 376 U.S. 254 (1964), held that the First Amendment bars defamation cases involving statements made about public officials or public figures, unless the plaintiff proves by the higher evidentiary standard of "clear and convincing evidence" that the statements were made with "actual malice." That means plaintiff must offer proof that the defendant knew the statement was false or was made with reckless disregard as to its truth or falsity. The actual malice standard did not save the Minnesota statute. Should it have? Does *281 Care Committee* call into question the constitutionality of defamation cases about issues in elections?

2. In undertaking its strict scrutiny analysis, the court punted on whether the state's interest in "preserving fair and honest elections and preventing fraud on the electorate" is compelling. Why? What's the counterargument?

3. The court instead decided the case on the issue of whether the law is narrowly tailored, arguing among other things that the law facilitates fraud by allowing people to bring unfounded charges that opponents are violating the statute. That seemed to be a problem under a separate statute in Ohio, according to a brief filed by Ohio's attorney general in a separate case, *SBA List*, and relied upon by the appeals court in *281 Care Committee*. Why not rely upon the risk of fraud *in Minnesota* in a case about Minnesota's law? The court also wrote that counterspeech is a more narrowly tailored remedy than a law barring false campaign speech. Such an argument assumes that counterspeech will be more successful than a claim under the false campaign statute for ferreting out the truth and assisting voters. On what basis does the court reach this empirical conclusion?

4. In *SBA List*, the Supreme Court unanimously held that a group which had been the subject of a complaint for false campaign speech before the Ohio Elections Commission had standing to raise a claim that Ohio's law is unconstitutional. On remand, the trial court, applying strict scrutiny, struck down Ohio's law as a violation of the First Amendment. *Susan B. Anthony List v. Ohio Elections Commission*, 45 F. Supp. 3d 765 (S.D. Ohio 2014). The Sixth Circuit affirmed: "Ohio's political false-statements laws are content-based restrictions targeting core political speech that are not narrowly tailored to serve the state's admittedly compelling interest in conducting fair elections. Accordingly, we affirm the district court's judgment

finding the laws unconstitutional." 814 F.3d 466 (6th Cir. 2016). Note that the Sixth Circuit, unlike the Eighth Circuit, did accept the conduct of fair elections as a compelling interest. It saw many problems with the Ohio law's lack of tailoring. Is it possible to write an appropriately tailored false campaign speech law that could sustain constitutional attack?

Minn. Stat. § 211B.02, not considered in *281 Care Committee*, prohibits "a false claim stating or implying that a candidate or ballot question has the support or endorsement of a major political party or party unit or of an organization." A state appeals court upheld it, finding it narrowly tailored. *Linert v. MacDonald*, 901 N.W.2d 664, 670 (Minn. Ct. App. 2017) (section 211B.02 "is narrowly tailored to serve the state's compelling interest in promoting informed voting and protecting the political process and does not substantially sweep outside the statute's legitimate aim").

5. South Africa's Constitutional Court decided a high-profile case involving an allegation of a false political statement about the country's president. A public investigation revealed that renovations of the president's house had cost much more money than expected due to poor management. In response, South Africa's main opposition party, the Democratic Alliance, texted the following message to its supporters: "The [inspector's] report shows how [President] Zuma stole your money to build his R246m home. Vote DA on 7 May to beat corruption. Together for change." South Africa's ruling party, the African National Congress, then filed a complaint claiming that the message was false and therefore unlawful under the country's Electoral Act.

A majority of the Constitutional Court ruled against the African National Congress. Five justices deemed the message an "interpretation" of the inspector's report, and thus not a factual statement capable of being true or false. Two more justices thought the message was actually true. In dissent, three justices argued that the message was false (because the report did not, in fact, find that President Zuma "stole" any money) and hence subject to liability. Interestingly, none of the justices addressed the lurking constitutional question: If the Electoral Act applies to all false political statements, is it consistent with the South African Constitution's protection of free speech? See *Democratic Alliance v. African National Congress* [2015] ZACC 1 (CC); Nicholas O. Stephanopoulos, *Liable Lies*, 7 Constitutional Court Review 1 (2017) (criticizing the Electoral Act for its overbroad coverage and suggesting a normatively defensible proscription of political lies).

6. We have focused thus far on the campaign speech of candidates, parties, committees, and others who are involved in promoting or opposing candidates or ballot measures. Campaigns end when voters cast their ballots, and many state laws bar certain forms of electioneering in or near polling places in the moments before that ballot is cast. The idea is that voters should have a chance to cast their ballot free from undue pressure or intimidation.

In *Burson v. Freeman*, 504 U.S. 191 (1992), a case cited in a few of the principal cases in this chapter, the Supreme Court rejected a First Amendment challenge to Tennessee's ban on certain forms of electioneering within 100 feet of polling place entrances. This was a rare case in which (a plurality of) the Court upheld the constitutionality of a law under strict scrutiny review.

The Court applied *Burson* and struck down a Minnesota ban on "political" apparel in polling places in *Minnesota Voters Alliance v. Mansky*, 138 S. Ct. 1876 (2018). Among other things, the state law provided that a "political badge, political button, or other political insignia may not be worn at or about the polling place on primary or election day." The case arose from a complaint of a Tea Party group, the Minnesota Voters Alliance, that in 2010 sent its members to vote wearing political paraphernalia, including T-shirts containing Tea Party messages such as "Don't tread on me" and a button saying "Please I.D. Me," even though Minnesota has no voter-ID law. Poll workers asked the voters to cover up their political messages because of a state law banning electioneering at and around polling places.

The Court recognized that the state "may reasonably take steps to ensure that partisan discord not follow the voter up to the voting booth, and distract from a sense of shared civic obligation at the moment it counts the most." *Id.* at 1888. But it held the Minnesota statute unconstitutionally overbroad, viewing the great discretion afforded election officials to determine what was improper apparel as a violation of the First Amendment. The Court asked, "Would a 'Support Our Troops' shirt be banned, if one of the candidates or parties had expressed a view on military funding or aid for veterans? What about a '#MeToo' shirt, referencing the movement to increase awareness of sexual harassment and assault?" *Id.* at 1890.

Mansky affirmed that a state "may prohibit messages intended to mislead voters about voting requirements and procedures," but noted that the state excluded the "Please I.D. Me" buttons because they were political, not because they were misleading. *Id.* at 1889 n.4.The Court offered as permissible alternatives other, rather broad state laws that prohibit electioneering, including a Texas statute banning "a badge, insignia, emblem, or other similar communicative device relating to a candidate, measure, or political party appearing on the ballot, or to the conduct of the election" at polling places and within 100 feet of them. Texas Elections Code § 61.010. The Court added that such laws do not necessarily set the "outer limit" of what states may proscribe. *Mansky*, 138 S. Ct. at 1891.

As we will see in Chapters 12-14, the "relating to" language used in the Texas statute to separate campaign speech from non-campaign speech is much broader than the language the Court has demanded of campaign finance laws to comply with the First Amendment. Why the more permissive approach to laws regulating campaign speech as opposed to campaign spending?

7. Does *Mansky*'s recognition of the state's right to "prohibit messages intended to mislead voters about voting requirements and procedures" give states the ability consistent with the First Amendment to pass laws against false *election* speech about when, where, and how people vote? For an argument in the affirmative, see Richard L. Hasen, Cheap Speech ch. 3 (2022). What about misleading *election* speech? Or would that be too vague to be consistent with the First Amendment interests in

robust political speech recognized in *281 Care Committee*, *SBA List*, and *Mansky*? If such laws are constitutional, are they advisable?

8. In recent years, technology has facilitated the creation of "deep fakes," videos that can make it appear that a politician (or anyone else) is doing or saying something that could be embarrassing and that could potentially affect election outcomes. See Danielle K. Citron & Robert Chesney, *Deep Fakes: A Looming Challenge for Privacy, Democracy, and National Security*, 107 Calif. L. Rev. 1753 (2019). Can such deep fakes be banned consistent with the First Amendment? If not, will counterspeech serve as an adequate response? What about a law requiring the labeling of deep fakes posted on the Internet as "altered"? See Hasen, *supra*; Rebecca Green, *Counterfeit Campaign Speech*, 70 Hastings Law Journal 1445, 1447-48 (2019).

9. Some people complain that negative campaigning and a lack of civility between opponents, rather than false statements, are the greatest problems with campaigns. Laws purporting to regulate truthful (or non-malicious) negative or uncivil statements violate the First Amendment. One commentator has proposed that candidates targeted in negative television or radio advertisements be given the right to a contemporaneous equal time response, which would air immediately after the negative ad. "Unless the candidate himself speaks about an opponent in a negative ad, the sponsor of the negative ad would be required to share the media cost of a response ad." Michael Kimmel, *A Proposal to Strengthen the Right of Response to Negative Campaign Commercials*, 49 Catholic University Law Review 89, 91 (1999). What should be considered a "negative" ad to trigger the statute? Is it constitutional to require candidates to pay for their opposing candidates' advertisements?

III. Judicial Elections

A. Why Judicial Elections?

In the federal courts, judges are nominated by the President and face United States Senate confirmation for a life appointment (subject to impeachment). States, however, use a variety of mechanisms for choosing judges. Justice O'Connor, in her concurring opinion in *Republican Party of Minnesota v. White*, 536 U.S. 765 (2002), (excerpted below), described the various judicial selection mechanisms:

> ... 39 States currently employ some form of judicial elections for their appellate courts, general jurisdiction trial courts, or both. American Judicature Society, Judicial Selection in the States: Appellate and General Jurisdiction Courts (Apr.2002). ... Judicial elections were not always so prevalent. The first 29 States of the Union adopted methods for selecting judges that did not involve popular elections. [H]owever, beginning with Georgia in 1812, States began adopting systems for judicial elections. From the 1830's until the 1850's, as part of the Jacksonian movement toward greater popular control of public office, this trend accelerated, and by the Civil War, 22 of the 34 States elected their judges. By the beginning of the 20th century, however,

> elected judiciaries increasingly came to be viewed as incompetent and corrupt, and criticism of partisan judicial elections mounted. In 1906, Roscoe Pound gave a speech to the American Bar Association in which he claimed that "compelling judges to become politicians, in many jurisdictions has almost destroyed the traditional respect for the bench."
>
> In response to such concerns, some States adopted a modified system of judicial selection that became known as the Missouri Plan (because Missouri was the first State to adopt it for most of its judicial posts). Under the Missouri Plan, judges are appointed by a high elected official, generally from a list of nominees put together by a nonpartisan nominating commission, and then subsequently stand for unopposed retention elections in which voters are asked whether the judges should be recalled. If a judge is recalled, the vacancy is filled through a new nomination and appointment. This system obviously reduces threats to judicial impartiality, even if it does not eliminate all popular pressure on judges. See Grodin, Developing a Consensus of Constraint: A Judge's Perspective on Judicial Retention Elections, 61 S. Cal. L.Rev.1969, 1980 (1988) (admitting that he cannot be sure that his votes as a California Supreme Court Justice in "critical cases" during 1986 were not influenced subconsciously by his awareness that the outcomes could affect his chances in the retention elections being conducted that year). The Missouri Plan is currently used to fill at least some judicial offices in 15 States.
>
> Thirty-one States, however, still use popular elections to select some or all of their appellate and/or general jurisdiction trial court judges, who thereafter run for reelection periodically. Of these, slightly more than half use nonpartisan elections, and the rest use partisan elections. Most of the States that do not have any form of judicial elections choose judges through executive nomination and legislative confirmation.

Once a state decides to conduct judicial elections, a whole new set of questions arise. Are judicial elections subject to the one person, one vote rule? (No. *Wells v. Edwards*, 409 U.S. 1095 (1973).) To the Voting Rights Act? (Yes, *Chisom v. Roemer*, 501 U.S. 380 (1991), but courts might apply the Act differently to judicial elections. *Houston Lawyers' Association v. Attorney General of Texas*, 501 U.S. 419 (1991).) Why the divergent answers to these questions?

In the sections below, we consider special judicial speech and conduct rules, as well as special campaign finance and recusal rules, which some states have put in place alongside their judicial election systems. As we shall see some of these provisions have been challenged as violating the free speech and association protections of the First Amendment of the U.S. Constitution.

Before turning to these rules, consider — in light of the material on the nature elections and representation in the earlier chapters of this book — two perspectives on whether or not judges *should* be selected through elections.

Charles Gardner Geyh:

For years, court defenders have called attention to differences between the judiciary and the political branches of government. Judges are supposed to be impartial; governors and legislators are not. Governors and legislators are supposed to represent the views of their constituents; judges are not. Judges are subject to ethical restrictions that limit their ability to clarify their positions or comment on their decisions; governors and legislators are not. These distinctions are routinely trotted out in defense of the incremental.... Seemingly lost in the incremental reform shuffle, is the obvious point that the fundamental differences between the judiciary and the other branches undermine the legitimacy of judicial elections altogether.

In *Marbury v. Madison*, Chief Justice Marshall declared that it is the province of the judiciary to say what the law is. It is the courts that must bring the law to bear in individual cases, clarify disagreements between private citizens as to what the law requires, analyze the legislature's handiwork and tell us what statutes mean, and tell the political branches when their interpretations of the Constitution, as embodied in legislation or executive action, are wrong and must be invalidated.

In other words, we need some entity to arbitrate the law's meaning, and those who make, execute and live under the laws of the state and nation, depend on the specialized expertise of judges to perform that function. Governors need not be lawyers and often are not. The same may be said of legislators. With respect to judges, however, virtually every state with an elective judiciary has embedded in its constitution or statutes the requirement that judges be licensed to practice law in that state.

It is one thing to expect voters with no training in the law to decide whether the policies favored by senators and governors (who may not be lawyers either) coincide with their own positions, and quite another to expect them to decide whether the rulings of judges coincide with the law. If we suspend disbelief and assume that voters can actually acquire the expertise needed to assess a judge's familiarity with and fidelity to innumerable laws as reflected in the myriad cases she has decided, then the learning curve will be considerably steeper than that required to divine a political branch candidate's position on the major issues of the day, and decide whether the candidate will be receptive to the concerns of constituents.

Historically, however, it has been impossible for voters to gather the information they need to make intelligent decisions from the candidates themselves....

In short, if voters are expected to second-guess the decisions of a judge who brings years of specialized training to bear in deciding complex, subtly nuanced issues of law, they need more information than would be required to assess the performance of political branch officials for whom

> no professional training is required. And yet, voters have had access to far less information from judicial candidates than their political branch counterparts.

Charles Gardner Geyh, *Why Judicial Elections Stink*, 64 Ohio State Law Journal 43, 59 (2003).

Chris W. Bonneau:

> Powerful opponents of judicial elections — which include the American Bar Association, Justice at Stake and the American Judicature Society, as well as former Supreme Court justice Sandra Day O'Connor — have spent countless hours and funds to eradicate elections ... Critics tend to cloak their activity in "good government" rhetoric, arguing that the election process erodes public confidence in the courts by injecting politics into the judicial process and threatens judicial independence as judges are dependent on the public to retain their jobs. But political scientists have been examining judicial elections for some time and have amassed considerable empirical evidence in this area. The data suggest ... [t]here is no evidence that elections cause voters to view judicial institutions as less legitimate.... [T]here is no difference, other things being equal, in the quality of judges who emerge from elections as opposed to appointments.... Campaign spending makes elections more competitive.... There is no proof that elected judges are for sale.... More generally, there is no systematic evidence to date that judges' votes are influenced by campaign contributions.
>
> Little has also been said about the biases in the systems with which critics would like to replace elections. No method is perfect. But, unlike the "merit" commission process most frequently offered as an alternative — in which judges are selected by the governor off a list formulated by political and legal elites and then retain their jobs simply by receiving a majority of "Yes" votes in an uncompetitive election — elections are at least transparent processes open to the public.
>
> In the debate so far, many of the arguments have been based on rhetoric, not fact. It is important to remember that efforts to maximize judicial "independence" from the electorate can also maximize independence from the law and the Constitution. Without a mechanism for effectively holding judges accountable, judges are free to "go rogue" and make decisions based solely on their political views. Is that better than a campaign season every now and then?

Chris W. Bonneau, *Why We Should Keep Judicial Elections*, Washington Post, May 26, 2011. See also Chris W. Bonneau & Melinda Gann Hall, In Defense of Judicial Elections (2009); Jed Handelsman Shugermen, The People's Court (2012) (arguing that states moved to judicial elections to reduce the corruption associated with political patronage and judicial appointment).

Notes and Questions

1. In 2010, Iowa voters ousted from office three state Supreme Court justices who had held that the state constitution guaranteed a right to same-sex marriage. No Iowa judge had ever been voted out of office in a retention election before, and the vote came after a major campaign against the judges by opponents of same-sex marriage. A.G. Sulzberger, *Voters Moving to Oust Judges over Decisions*, N.Y. Times, Sept. 25, 2010, at A1.

Is this a result to be celebrated as an example of judicial accountability or to be condemned as an affront to judicial independence? See David E. Pozen, *Judicial Elections as Popular Constitutionalism*, 110 Columbia Law Review 2047 (2010); Nicole Mansker & Neal Devins, *Do Judicial Elections Facilitate Popular Constitutionalism; Can They?*, 111 Columbia Law Review Sidebar 27 (2011), http://columbialawreview.org/assets/sidebar/volume/111/27_Mansker.pdf; David E. Pozen, *What Happened in Iowa?*, 111 Columbia Law Review Sidebar 90 (2011), http://www.columbialawreview.org/assets/sidebar/volume/111/90_Pozen.pdf.

2. As Bonneau notes, many opponents of judicial elections assume that judicial elections, especially in today's era of more politicized judicial elections, will undermine voters' confidence in the judiciary. James L. Gibson tested the empirical assumption through a poll of Kentucky voters and concluded that things are not so simple:

> Two notable theoretical conclusions stand out from this analysis. First, citizens vary in their expectations of judicial campaigns and this variability must be considered when assessing how campaign activities affect the legitimacy of courts. The assumption that all of the courts' constituents expect strong judicial independence with nonpartisan and nonideological decision making is clearly wrong. Whether it is desirable or undesirable, a sizable portion of Americans expect a politicized judiciary and therefore is not off-put by politicized campaigns.
>
> Second, the effect of campaigns on citizens must be calculated as a net effect, after taking into consideration the many dimensions on which campaigns are perceived and evaluated. Experimental research examining campaign effects in isolation is certainly useful. But the oversight of most research lies in the failure to understand that elections, by themselves, provide a significant boost to the legitimacy of courts. Elections may be (and almost certainly are) a mixed bag, with some positive influences on citizens but with negative consequences as well. Only when we gauge whether the positive outweighs the negative can we draw proper verdicts about the institutional consequences of elections.
>
> These conclusions have important policy implications, the most obvious of which is that those who base their criticisms of elections on unseemly campaign activity must consider as well that simply being able to vote for judges makes courts more legitimate. Presumably, we care most about

> whether elections add to or subtract from the legitimacy of courts in toto, not whether a particular ad campaign is churlish. Opponents of elections cannot in the future ignore that fact that the rough and tumble of judicial campaigns may be doing little more than denying courts the full benefits of elections, rather than creating a deficit in institutional legitimacy.

James L. Gibson, Electing Judges: The Surprising Effects of Campaigning on Judicial Legitimacy 127 (2012).

3. Bonneau says that there is little evidence judicial elections affect judicial behavior. For some contrary evidence, see Sanford C. Gordon and Gregory A. Huber, *The Effect of Electoral Competitiveness on Judicial Behavior* 2 Quarterly Journal of Political Science 107 (2007) (finding judges elected through partisan elections sentence more severely than judges standing in retention elections); Michael S. Kang & Joanna M. Shepherd, *Partisanship in State Supreme Courts: The Empirical Relationship Between Party Campaign Contributions and Judicial Decisionmaking*, 44 Journal of Legal Studies S161 (2015) (finding correlation between extent of party campaign contributions and judicial votes).

4. Despite certain high-profile, nasty, and expensive judicial races, most judicial elections hardly attract the attention of the public, and often even lawyers do not know whom to vote for in judicial elections. In one episode in California, a well-respected trial court judge was defeated in office by an inexperienced challenger, likely because the judge had a foreign sounding name. The governor then reappointed the ousted incumbent to an open judicial position. Jessica Garrison, *Gov. is the Judge: Janavs Back to the Bench*, Los Angeles Times, June 10, 2006. What efforts, if any, should states make to ensure that voters are informed about judicial candidates?

5. As judicial elections have become, in the words of Professor Schotland, "nastier, noisier, and costlier," some of the best lawyers may be declining to run for judge. See Roy A. Schotland, *Six Fatal Flaws: A Comment on Bopp and Neeley*, 86 Denver University Law Review 233, 242–45 (2008). Do concerns about the candidate pool affect the desirability of judicial elections?

6. Is the pro-con debate a waste of time, because voters are unlikely to give up their right to vote for judges, and no states in the last few decades have rejected elections in favor of alternative means of appointment? Consider Roy A. Schotland, *A Plea for Reality*, 74 Missouri Law Review 507, 517 (2009): "Let us put aside the endless debate and focus on feasible changes to reduce the problematic aspects of judicial elections. The debate distracts severely and concretely: In any state where events (or reform energies) stir dissatisfaction with judicial elections, the first response is to work toward ending contestable elections. Understandable as that response is, its supporters ignore (or, more likely, do not realize) that for the past generation that route has gone nowhere, and, consequently, they have failed to even try for feasible improvements—which get little to no attention, leaving the problems to continue or even worsen." Taking Schotland's point seriously, what improvements, if any, would you suggest? Are such improvements constitutional? See the next two sections.

B. Judicial Candidate Speech and Conduct Codes

Republican Party of Minnesota v. White

536 U.S. 765 (2002)

Justice SCALIA delivered the opinion of the Court.

The question presented in this case is whether the First Amendment permits the Minnesota Supreme Court to prohibit candidates for judicial election in that State from announcing their views on disputed legal and political issues.

I

Since Minnesota's admission to the Union in 1858, the State's Constitution has provided for the selection of all state judges by popular election. Since 1912, those elections have been nonpartisan. Since 1974, they have been subject to a legal restriction which states that a "candidate for a judicial office, including an incumbent judge," shall not "announce his or her views on disputed legal or political issues." Minn. Code of Judicial Conduct, Canon 5(A)(3)(d)(i) (2000). This prohibition, promulgated by the Minnesota Supreme Court and based on Canon 7(B) of the 1972 American Bar Association (ABA) Model Code of Judicial Conduct, is known as the "announce clause." Incumbent judges who violate it are subject to discipline, including removal, censure, civil penalties, and suspension without pay. Lawyers who run for judicial office also must comply with the announce clause. Minn. Rule of Professional Conduct 8.2(b) (2002) ("A lawyer who is a candidate for judicial office shall comply with the applicable provisions of the Code of Judicial Conduct"). Those who violate it are subject to, *inter alia,* disbarment, suspension, and probation.

In 1996, one of the petitioners, Gregory Wersal, ran for associate justice of the Minnesota Supreme Court. In the course of the campaign, he distributed literature criticizing several Minnesota Supreme Court decisions on issues such as crime, welfare, and abortion. A complaint against Wersal challenging, among other things, the propriety of this literature was filed with the Office of Lawyers Professional Responsibility, the agency which, under the direction of the Minnesota Lawyers Professional Responsibility Board, investigates and prosecutes ethical violations of lawyer candidates for judicial office. The Lawyers Board dismissed the complaint; with regard to the charges that his campaign materials violated the announce clause, it expressed doubt whether the clause could constitutionally be enforced. Nonetheless, fearing that further ethical complaints would jeopardize his ability to practice law, Wersal withdrew from the election. In 1998, Wersal ran again for the same office. Early in that race, he sought an advisory opinion from the Lawyers Board with regard to whether it planned to enforce the announce clause. The Lawyers Board responded equivocally, stating that, although it had significant doubts about the constitutionality of the provision, it was unable to answer his question because he had not submitted a list of the announcements he wished to make.

Shortly thereafter, Wersal filed this lawsuit in Federal District Court against respondents, seeking, *inter alia,* a declaration that the announce clause violates the

First Amendment and an injunction against its enforcement. Wersal alleged that he was forced to refrain from announcing his views on disputed issues during the 1998 campaign, to the point where he declined response to questions put to him by the press and public, out of concern that he might run afoul of the announce clause. Other plaintiffs in the suit, including the Minnesota Republican Party, alleged that, because the clause kept Wersal from announcing his views, they were unable to learn those views and support or oppose his candidacy accordingly. The parties filed cross-motions for summary judgment, and the District Court found in favor of respondents, holding that the announce clause did not violate the First Amendment. Over a dissent by Judge Beam, the United States Court of Appeals for the Eighth Circuit affirmed. We granted certiorari.

II

Before considering the constitutionality of the announce clause, we must be clear about its meaning. Its text says that a candidate for judicial office shall not "announce his or her views on disputed legal or political issues."

We know that "announc[ing] . . . views" on an issue covers much more than *promising* to decide an issue a particular way. The prohibition extends to the candidate's mere statement of his current position, even if he does not bind himself to maintain that position after election. All the parties agree this is the case, because the Minnesota Code contains a so-called "pledges or promises" clause, which *separately* prohibits judicial candidates from making "pledges or promises of conduct in office other than the faithful and impartial performance of the duties of the office," — a prohibition that is not challenged here and on which we express no view.

There are, however, some limitations that the Minnesota Supreme Court has placed upon the scope of the announce clause that are not (to put it politely) immediately apparent from its text. The statements that formed the basis of the complaint against Wersal in 1996 included criticism of past decisions of the Minnesota Supreme Court. One piece of campaign literature stated that "[t]he Minnesota Supreme Court has issued decisions which are marked by their disregard for the Legislature and a lack of common sense." It went on to criticize a decision excluding from evidence confessions by criminal defendants that were not tape-recorded, asking "[s]hould we conclude that because the Supreme Court does not trust police, it allows confessed criminals to go free?" It criticized a decision striking down a state law restricting welfare benefits, asserting that "[i]t's the Legislature which should set our spending policies." And it criticized a decision requiring public financing of abortions for poor women as "unprecedented" and a "pro-abortion stance." Although one would think that all of these statements touched on disputed legal or political issues, they did not (or at least do not now) fall within the scope of the announce clause. The Judicial Board issued an opinion stating that judicial candidates may criticize past decisions, and the Lawyers Board refused to discipline Wersal for the foregoing statements because, in part, it thought they did not violate the announce clause. The Eighth Circuit relied on the Judicial Board's opinion in upholding the announce clause, and the Minnesota Supreme Court recently embraced the Eighth Circuit's interpretation.

There are yet further limitations upon the apparent plain meaning of the announce clause: In light of the constitutional concerns, the District Court construed the clause to reach only disputed issues that are likely to come before the candidate if he is elected judge. The Eighth Circuit accepted this limiting interpretation by the District Court, and in addition construed the clause to allow general discussions of case law and judicial philosophy. The Supreme Court of Minnesota adopted these interpretations as well when it ordered enforcement of the announce clause in accordance with the Eighth Circuit's opinion.

It seems to us, however, that—like the text of the announce clause itself—these limitations upon the text of the announce clause are not all that they appear to be. First, respondents acknowledged at oral argument that statements critical of past judicial decisions are *not* permissible if the candidate also states that he is against *stare decisis*. Thus, candidates must choose between stating their views critical of past decisions and stating their views in opposition to *stare decisis*. Or, to look at it more concretely, they may state their view that prior decisions were erroneous only if they do not assert that they, if elected, have any power to eliminate erroneous decisions. Second, limiting the scope of the clause to issues likely to come before a court is not much of a limitation at all. One would hardly expect the "disputed legal or political issues" raised in the course of a state judicial election to include such matters as whether the Federal Government should end the embargo of Cuba. Quite obviously, they will be those legal or political disputes that are the proper (or by past decisions have been made the improper) business of the state courts. And within that relevant category, "[t]here is almost no legal or political issue that is unlikely to come before a judge of an American court, state or federal, of general jurisdiction." *Buckley v. Illinois Judicial Inquiry Bd.*, 997 F.2d 224, 229 (C.A.7 1993). Third, construing the clause to allow "general" discussions of case law and judicial philosophy turns out to be of little help in an election campaign. At oral argument, respondents gave, as an example of this exception, that a candidate is free to assert that he is a "strict constructionist." But that, like most other philosophical generalities, has little meaningful content for the electorate unless it is exemplified by application to a particular issue of construction likely to come before a court—for example, whether a particular statute runs afoul of any provision of the Constitution. Respondents conceded that the announce clause would prohibit the candidate from exemplifying his philosophy in this fashion. Without such application to real-life issues, all candidates can claim to be "strict constructionists" with equal (and unhelpful) plausibility.

In any event, it is clear that the announce clause prohibits a judicial candidate from stating his views on any specific nonfanciful legal question within the province of the court for which he is running, except in the context of discussing past decisions—and in the latter context as well, if he expresses the view that he is not bound by *stare decisis*.[5]

---

5. In 1990, in response to concerns that its 1972 Model Canon—which was the basis for Minnesota's announce clause—violated the First Amendment, the ABA replaced that canon with a

Respondents contend that this still leaves plenty of topics for discussion on the campaign trail. These include a candidate's "character," "education," "work habits," and "how [he] would handle administrative duties if elected." Indeed, the Judicial Board has printed a list of preapproved questions which judicial candidates are allowed to answer. These include how the candidate feels about cameras in the courtroom, how he would go about reducing the caseload, how the costs of judicial administration can be reduced, and how he proposes to ensure that minorities and women are treated more fairly by the court system. Whether this list of preapproved subjects, and other topics not prohibited by the announce clause, adequately fulfill the First Amendment's guarantee of freedom of speech is the question to which we now turn.

III

As the Court of Appeals recognized, the announce clause both prohibits speech on the basis of its content and burdens a category of speech that is "at the core of our First Amendment freedoms"—speech about the qualifications of candidates for public office. The Court of Appeals concluded that the proper test to be applied to determine the constitutionality of such a restriction is what our cases have called strict scrutiny; the parties do not dispute that this is correct. Under the strict-scrutiny test, respondents have the burden to prove that the announce clause is (1) narrowly tailored, to serve (2) a compelling state interest. *E.g., Eu.* In order for respondents to show that the announce clause is narrowly tailored, they must demonstrate that it does not "unnecessarily circumscrib[e] protected expression." *Brown v. Hartlage.*

The Court of Appeals concluded that respondents had established two interests as sufficiently compelling to justify the announce clause: preserving the impartiality of the state judiciary and preserving the appearance of the impartiality of the state judiciary. Respondents reassert these two interests before us, arguing that the first is compelling because it protects the due process rights of litigants, and that the second is compelling because it preserves public confidence in the judiciary.[6] Respondents are rather vague, however, about what they mean by "impartiality." Indeed,

---

provision that prohibits a judicial candidate from making "statements that commit or appear to commit the candidate with respect to cases, controversies or issues that are likely to come before the court." ABA Model Code of Judicial Conduct, Canon 5(A)(3)(d)(ii) (2000). At oral argument, respondents argued that the limiting constructions placed upon Minnesota's announce clause by the Eighth Circuit, and adopted by the Minnesota Supreme Court, render the scope of the clause no broader than the ABA's 1990 canon. This argument is somewhat curious because, based on the same constitutional concerns that had motivated the ABA, the Minnesota Supreme Court was urged to replace the announce clause with the new ABA language, but, unlike other jurisdictions, declined. The ABA, however, agrees with respondents' position. We do not know whether the announce clause (as interpreted by state authorities) and the 1990 ABA canon are one and the same. No aspect of our constitutional analysis turns on this question.

6. Although the Eighth Circuit also referred to the compelling interest in an "independent" judiciary, both it and respondents appear to use that term, as applied to the issues involved in this case, as interchangeable with "impartial."

although the term is used throughout the Eighth Circuit's opinion, the briefs, the Minnesota Code of Judicial Conduct, and the ABA Codes of Judicial Conduct, none of these sources bothers to define it. Clarity on this point is essential before we can decide whether impartiality is indeed a compelling state interest, and, if so, whether the announce clause is narrowly tailored to achieve it.

A

One meaning of "impartiality" in the judicial context—and of course its root meaning—is the lack of bias for or against either *party* to the proceeding. Impartiality in this sense assures equal application of the law. That is, it guarantees a party that the judge who hears his case will apply the law to him in the same way he applies it to any other party. This is the traditional sense in which the term is used. See Webster's New International Dictionary 1247 (2d ed.1950) (defining "impartial" as "[n]ot partial; esp., not favoring one more than another; treating all alike; unbiased; equitable; fair; just"). It is also the sense in which it is used in the cases cited by respondents and *amici* for the proposition that an impartial judge is essential to due process. *Tumey v. Ohio,* 273 U.S. 510, 523, 531–534 (1927) (judge violated due process by sitting in a case in which it would be in his financial interest to find against one of the parties); *Aetna Life Ins. Co. v. Lavoie,* 475 U.S. 813, 822–825 (1986) (same); *Ward v. Monroeville,* 409 U.S. 57, 58–62 (1972) (same); *Johnson v. Mississippi,* 403 U.S. 212, 215–216 (1971) (*per curiam*) (judge violated due process by sitting in a case in which one of the parties was a previously successful litigant against him); *Bracy v. Gramley,* 520 U.S. 899, 905 (1997) (would violate due process if a judge was disposed to rule against defendants who did not bribe him in order to cover up the fact that he regularly ruled in favor of defendants who did bribe him); *In re Murchison,* 349 U.S. 133, 137–139 (1955) (judge violated due process by sitting in the criminal trial of defendant whom he had indicted).

We think it plain that the announce clause is not narrowly tailored to serve impartiality (or the appearance of impartiality) in this sense. Indeed, the clause is barely tailored to serve that interest *at all,* inasmuch as it does not restrict speech for or against particular *parties,* but rather speech for or against particular *issues.* To be sure, when a case arises that turns on a legal issue on which the judge (as a candidate) had taken a particular stand, the party taking the opposite stand is likely to lose. But not because of any bias against that party, or favoritism toward the other party. *Any* party taking that position is just as likely to lose. The judge is applying the law (as he sees it) evenhandedly.

B

It is perhaps possible to use the term "impartiality" in the judicial context (though this is certainly not a common usage) to mean lack of preconception in favor of or against a particular *legal view.* This sort of impartiality would be concerned, not with guaranteeing litigants equal application of the law, but rather with guaranteeing them an equal chance to persuade the court on the legal points in their case. Impartiality in this sense may well be an interest served by the announce clause, but it is not a *compelling* state interest, as strict scrutiny requires. A judge's lack of predisposition regarding the relevant legal issues in a case has never been thought a necessary component of equal justice, and with good reason. For one thing, it is virtually impossible to find a judge who does not have preconceptions about the law. As then-Justice REHNQUIST observed of our own Court: "Since most Justices come to this bench no earlier than their middle years, it would be unusual if they had not by that time formulated at least some tentative notions that would influence them in their interpretation of the sweeping clauses of the Constitution and their interaction with one another. It would be not merely unusual, but extraordinary, if they had not at least given opinions as to constitutional issues in their previous legal careers." *Laird v. Tatum,* 409 U.S. 824, 835 (1972) (memorandum opinion). Indeed, even if it were possible to select judges who did not have preconceived views on legal issues, it would hardly be desirable to do so. "Proof that a Justice's mind at the time he joined the Court was a complete *tabula rasa* in the area of constitutional adjudication would be evidence of lack of qualification, not lack of bias." The Minnesota Constitution positively forbids the selection to courts of general jurisdiction of judges who are impartial in the sense of having no views on the law ("Judges of the supreme court, the court of appeals and the district court shall be learned in the law"). And since avoiding judicial preconceptions on legal issues is neither possible nor desirable, pretending otherwise by attempting to preserve the "appearance" of that type of impartiality can hardly be a compelling state interest either.

C

A third possible meaning of "impartiality" (again not a common one) might be described as open-mindedness. This quality in a judge demands, not that he have no preconceptions on legal issues, but that he be willing to consider views that oppose his preconceptions, and remain open to persuasion, when the issues arise in a pending case. This sort of impartiality seeks to guarantee each litigant, not an *equal* chance to win the legal points in the case, but at least *some* chance of doing so. It may well be that impartiality in this sense, and the appearance of it, are desirable in the judiciary, but we need not pursue that inquiry, since we do not believe the Minnesota Supreme Court adopted the announce clause for that purpose.

Respondents argue that the announce clause serves the interest in open-mindedness, or at least in the appearance of openmindedness, because it relieves a judge from pressure to rule a certain way in order to maintain consistency with statements the judge has previously made. The problem is, however, that statements in election campaigns are such an infinitesimal portion of the public commitments to legal positions that judges (or judges-to-be) undertake, that this object of the prohibition is implausible. Before they arrive on the bench (whether by election or otherwise) judges have often committed themselves on legal issues that they must later rule upon. See, *e.g., Laird, supra* (describing Justice Black's participation in several cases construing and deciding the constitutionality of the Fair Labor Standards Act, even though as a Senator he had been one of its principal authors; and Chief Justice Hughes's authorship of the opinion overruling *Adkins v. Children's Hospital of D. C.,*

261 U.S. 525, (1923), a case he had criticized in a book written before his appointment to the Court). More common still is a judge's confronting a legal issue on which he has expressed an opinion while on the bench. Most frequently, of course, that prior expression will have occurred in ruling on an earlier case. But judges often state their views on disputed legal issues outside the context of adjudication-in classes that they conduct, and in books and speeches. Like the ABA Codes of Judicial Conduct, the Minnesota Code not only permits but encourages this. See Minn. Code of Judicial Conduct, Canon 4(B) (2002) ("A judge may write, lecture, teach, speak and participate in other extra-judicial activities concerning the law . . ."); Minn. Code of Judicial Conduct, Canon 4(B), Comment. (2002) ("To the extent that time permits, a judge is encouraged to do so . . ."). That is quite incompatible with the notion that the need for open-mindedness (or for the appearance of open-mindedness) lies behind the prohibition at issue here.

The short of the matter is this: In Minnesota, a candidate for judicial office may not say "I think it is constitutional for the legislature to prohibit same-sex marriages." He may say the very same thing, however, up until the very day before he declares himself a candidate, and may say it repeatedly (until litigation is pending) after he is elected. As a means of pursuing the objective of open-mindedness that respondents now articulate, the announce clause is so woefully underinclusive as to render belief in that purpose a challenge to the credulous. See *City of Ladue v. Gilleo,* 512 U.S. 43, 52–53 (1994) (noting that underinclusiveness "diminish[es] the credibility of the government's rationale for restricting speech"); *Florida Star v. B.J.F.,* 491 U.S. 524, 541–542 (1989) (SCALIA, J., concurring in judgment) ("[A] law cannot be regarded as protecting an interest of the highest order, and thus as justifying a restriction upon truthful speech, when it leaves appreciable damage to that supposedly vital interest unprohibited" (internal quotation marks and citation omitted)).

Justice STEVENS asserts that statements made in an election campaign pose a special threat to open-mindedness because the candidate, when elected judge, will have a *particular* reluctance to contradict them. That might be plausible, perhaps, with regard to campaign *promises.* A candidate who says "If elected, I will vote to uphold the legislature's power to prohibit same-sex marriages" will positively be breaking his word if he does not do so (although one would be naive not to recognize that campaign promises are — by long democratic tradition — the least binding form of human commitment). But, as noted earlier, the Minnesota Supreme Court has adopted a separate prohibition on campaign "pledges or promises," which is not challenged here. The proposition that judges feel significantly greater compulsion, or appear to feel significantly greater compulsion, to maintain consistency with *nonpromissory* statements made during a judicial campaign than with such statements made before or after the campaign is not self-evidently true. It seems to us quite likely, in fact, that in many cases the opposite is true. We doubt, for example, that a mere statement of position enunciated during the pendency of an election will be regarded by a judge as more binding — or as more likely to subject him to popular disfavor if reconsidered — than a carefully considered holding that the judge set forth in an earlier opinion denying some individual's claim to justice. In any event, it suffices to say that respondents have not carried the burden imposed by our strict-scrutiny test to establish this proposition (that campaign statements are uniquely destructive of open-mindedness) on which the validity of the announce clause rests.

Moreover, the notion that the special context of electioneering justifies an *abridgment* of the right to speak out on disputed issues sets our First Amendment jurisprudence on its head. "[D]ebate on the qualifications of candidates" is "at the core of our electoral process and of the First Amendment freedoms," not at the edges. *Eu.* "The role that elected officials play in our society makes it all the more imperative that they be allowed freely to express themselves on of current public importance." *Wood v. Georgia,* 370 U.S. 375, 395 (1962). "It is simply not the function of government to select which issues are worth discussing or debating in the course of a political campaign." *Brown.* We have never allowed the government to prohibit candidates from communicating relevant information to voters during an election.

Justice GINSBURG would do so — and much of her dissent confirms rather than refutes our conclusion that the purpose behind the announce clause is not open-mindedness in the judiciary, but the undermining of judicial elections. She contends that the announce clause must be constitutional because due process would be denied if an elected judge sat in a case involving an issue on which he had previously announced his view. She reaches this conclusion because, she says, such a judge would have a "direct, personal, substantial, and pecuniary interest" in ruling consistently with his previously announced view, in order to reduce the risk that he will be "voted off the bench and thereby lose [his] salary and emoluments," But elected judges — regardless of whether they have announced any views beforehand — *always* face the pressure of an electorate who might disagree with their rulings and therefore vote them off the bench. Surely the judge who frees Timothy McVeigh places his job much more at risk than the judge who (horror of horrors!) reconsiders his previously announced view on a disputed legal issue. So if, as Justice GINSBURG claims, it violates due process for a judge to sit in a case in which ruling one way rather than another increases his prospects for reelection, then — quite simply — the practice of electing judges is itself a violation of due process. It is not difficult to understand how one with these views would approve the election-nullifying effect of the announce clause. They are not, however, the views reflected in the Due Process Clause of the Fourteenth Amendment, which has coexisted with the election of judges ever since it was adopted.

Justice GINSBURG devotes the rest of her dissent to attacking arguments we do not make. For example, despite the number of pages she dedicates to disproving this proposition, we neither assert nor imply that the First Amendment requires campaigns for judicial office to sound the same as those for legislative office. What we do assert, and what Justice GINSBURG ignores, is that, *even if* the First Amendment allows greater regulation of judicial election campaigns than legislative election campaigns, the announce clause still fails strict scrutiny because it is woefully underinclusive, prohibiting announcements by judges (and would-be judges) only at certain times and in certain forms. We rely on the cases involving speech during elections, *supra*, only to make the obvious point that this underinclusiveness cannot be explained by resort to the notion that the First Amendment provides less protection during an election campaign than at other times.

But in any case, Justice GINSBURG greatly exaggerates the difference between judicial and legislative elections. She asserts that "the rationale underlying unconstrained speech in elections for political office—that representative government depends on the public's ability to choose agents who will act at its behest—does not carry over to campaigns for the bench." This complete separation of the judiciary from the enterprise of "representative government" might have some truth in those countries where judges neither make law themselves nor set aside the laws enacted by the legislature. It is not a true picture of the American system. Not only do state-court judges possess the power to "make" common law, but they have the immense power to shape the States' constitutions as well. Which is precisely why the election of state judges became popular.

IV

To sustain the announce clause, the Eighth Circuit relied heavily on the fact that a pervasive practice of prohibiting judicial candidates from discussing disputed legal and political issues developed during the last half of the 20th century. It is true that a "universal and long-established" tradition of prohibiting certain conduct creates "a strong presumption" that the prohibition is constitutional: "Principles of liberty fundamental enough to have been embodied within constitutional guarantees are not readily erased from the Nation's consciousness." *McIntyre* [*infra* Chapter 16—Eds]. The practice of prohibiting speech by judicial candidates on disputed issues, however, is neither long nor universal....

* * *

There is an obvious tension between the article of Minnesota's popularly approved Constitution which provides that judges shall be elected, and the Minnesota Supreme Court's announce clause which places most subjects of interest to the voters off limits. (The candidate-speech restrictions of all the other States that have them are also the product of judicial fiat.) The disparity is perhaps unsurprising, since the ABA, which originated the announce clause, has long been an opponent of judicial elections. See ABA Model Code of Judicial Conduct, Canon 5(C)(2), Comment (2000) ("[M]erit selection of judges is a preferable manner in which to select the judiciary"); An Independent Judiciary: Report of the ABA Commission on Separation of Powers and Judicial Independence 96 (1997) ("The American Bar Association strongly endorses the merit selection of judges, as opposed to their election.... Five times between August 1972 and August 1984 the House of Delegates has approved recommendations stating the preference for merit selection and encouraging bar associations in jurisdictions where judges are elected ... to work for the adoption of merit selection and retention"). That opposition may be well taken (it certainly had the support of the Founders of the Federal Government), but the First Amendment does not permit it to achieve its goal by leaving the principle of elections in place while preventing candidates from discussing what the elections are about. "[T]he greater power to dispense with elections altogether does not include the lesser power to conduct elections under conditions of state-imposed voter ignorance. If the State chooses to tap the energy and the legitimizing power of the democratic process, it must accord the participants in that process . . . the First Amendment rights that attach to their roles." *Renne v. Geary*, 501 U.S. 312, 349 (1991) (Marshall, J., dissenting); accord, *Meyer v. Grant* (rejecting argument that the greater power to end voter initiatives includes the lesser power to prohibit paid petition-circulators).

The Minnesota Supreme Court's canon of judicial conduct prohibiting candidates for judicial election from announcing their views on disputed legal and political issues violates the First Amendment. Accordingly, we reverse the grant of summary judgment to respondents and remand the case for proceedings consistent with this opinion.

It is so ordered.

Justice O'CONNOR, concurring.

I join the opinion of the Court but write separately to express my concerns about judicial elections generally. Respondents claim that "[t]he Announce Clause is necessary . . . to protect the State's compelling governmental interes[t] in an actual and perceived . . . impartial judiciary." I am concerned that, even aside from what judicial candidates may say while campaigning, the very practice of electing judges undermines this interest.

We of course want judges to be impartial, in the sense of being free from any personal stake in the outcome of the cases to which they are assigned. But if judges are subject to regular elections they are likely to feel that they have at least some personal stake in the outcome of every publicized case. Elected judges cannot help being aware that if the public is not satisfied with the outcome of a particular case, it could hurt their reelection prospects. See Eule, Crocodiles in the Bathtub: State Courts, Voter Initiatives and the Threat of Electoral Reprisal, 65 U. Colo. L. Rev. 733, 739 (1994) (quoting former California Supreme Court Justice Otto Kaus' statement that ignoring the political consequences of visible decisions is "'like ignoring a crocodile in your bathtub'"); Bright & Keenan, Judges and the Politics of Death: Deciding Between the Bill of Rights and the Next Election in Capital Cases, 75 B.U. L. Rev. 759, 793–794 (1995) (citing statistics indicating that judges who face elections are far more likely to override jury sentences of life without parole and impose the death penalty than are judges who do not run for election). Even if judges were able to suppress their awareness of the potential electoral consequences of their decisions and refrain from acting on it, the public's confidence in the judiciary could be undermined simply by the possibility that judges would be unable to do so.

Moreover, contested elections generally entail campaigning. And campaigning for a judicial post today can require substantial funds. See Schotland, Financing Judicial Elections, 2000: Change and Challenge, 2001 L. Rev. Mich. State U. Detroit

College of Law 849, 866 (reporting that in 2000, the 13 candidates in a partisan election for 5 seats on the Alabama Supreme Court spent an average of $1,092,076 on their campaigns); American Bar Association, Report and Recommendations of the Task Force on Lawyers' Political Contributions, pt. 2 (July 1998) (reporting that in 1995, one candidate for the Pennsylvania Supreme Court raised $1,848,142 in campaign funds, and that in 1986, $2,700,000 was spent on the race for Chief Justice of the Ohio Supreme Court). Unless the pool of judicial candidates is limited to those wealthy enough to independently fund their campaigns, a limitation unrelated to judicial skill, the cost of campaigning requires judicial candidates to engage in fundraising. Yet relying on campaign donations may leave judges feeling indebted to certain parties or interest groups. See Thomas, National L. J., Mar. 16, 1998, p. A8, col. 1 (reporting that a study by the public interest group Texans for Public Justice found that 40 percent of the $9,200,000 in contributions of $100 or more raised by seven of Texas' nine Supreme Court justices for their 1994 and 1996 elections "came from parties and lawyers with cases before the court or contributors closely linked to these parties"). Even if judges were able to refrain from favoring donors, the mere possibility that judges' decisions may be motivated by the desire to repay campaign contributors is likely to undermine the public's confidence in the judiciary. See Greenberg Quinlan Rosner Research, Inc., and American Viewpoint, National Public Opinion Survey Frequency Questionnaire 4 (2001) (available at https://perma.cc/3G6R-C47Z) (describing survey results indicating that 76 percent of registered voters believe that campaign contributions influence judicial decisions); *id.* (describing survey results indicating that two-thirds of registered voters believe individuals and groups who give money to judicial candidates often receive favorable treatment); Barnhizer, "On the Make": Campaign Funding and the Corrupting of the American Judiciary, 50 Cath. U. L.Rev. 361, 379 (2001) (relating anecdotes of lawyers who felt that their contributions to judicial campaigns affected their chance of success in court).

Despite these significant problems, 39 States currently employ some form of judicial elections for their appellate courts, general jurisdiction trial courts, or both. . . .

Minnesota has chosen to select its judges through contested popular elections instead of through an appointment system or a combined appointment and retention election system along the lines of the Missouri Plan. In doing so the State has voluntarily taken on the risks to judicial bias described above. As a result, the State's claim that it needs to significantly restrict judges' speech in order to protect judicial impartiality is particularly troubling. If the State has a problem with judicial impartiality, it is largely one the State brought upon itself by continuing the practice of popularly electing judges.

Justice KENNEDY, concurring.

. . . Minnesota may choose to have an elected judiciary. It may strive to define those characteristics that exemplify judicial excellence. It may enshrine its definitions in a code of judicial conduct. It may adopt recusal standards more rigorous than due process requires, and censure judges who violate these standards. What

Minnesota may not do, however, is censor what the people hear as they undertake to decide for themselves which candidate is most likely to be an exemplary judicial officer. Deciding the relevance of candidate speech is the right of the voters, not the State. See *Brown v. Hartlage*. The law in question here contradicts the principle that unabridged speech is the foundation of political freedom. . . .

[The dissenting opinion of Justice STEVENS is omitted.]

Justice GINSBURG, with whom Justice STEVENS, Justice SOUTER, and Justice BREYER join, dissenting.

Whether state or federal, elected or appointed, judges perform a function fundamentally different from that of the people's elected representatives. Legislative and executive officials act on behalf of the voters who placed them in office; "judge[s] represen[t] the Law." *Chisom v. Roemer* (SCALIA, J., dissenting). Unlike their counterparts in the political branches, judges are expected to refrain from catering to particular constituencies or committing themselves on controversial issues in advance of adversarial presentation. Their mission is to decide "individual cases and controversies" on individual records, *Plaut v. Spendthrift Farm, Inc.,* 514 U.S. 211, 266, (1995) (STEVENS, J., dissenting), neutrally applying legal principles, and, when necessary, "stand[ing] up to what is generally supreme in a democracy: the popular will," Scalia, The Rule of Law as a Law of Rules, 56 U. Chi. L. Rev. 1175, 1180 (1989).

A judiciary capable of performing this function, owing fidelity to no person or party, is a "longstanding Anglo-American tradition," *United States v. Will,* 449 U.S. 200, (1980), an essential bulwark of constitutional government, a constant guardian of the rule of law. The guarantee of an independent, impartial judiciary enables society to "withdraw certain subjects from the vicissitudes of political controversy, to place them beyond the reach of majorities and officials and to establish them as legal principles to be applied by the courts." *West Virginia Bd. of Ed. v. Barnette,* 319 U.S. 624, 638 (1943). "Without this, all the reservations of particular rights or privileges would amount to nothing." The Federalist No. 78.

The ability of the judiciary to discharge its unique role rests to a large degree on the manner in which judges are selected. The Framers of the Federal Constitution sought to advance the judicial function through the structural protections of Article III, which provide for the selection of judges by the President on the advice and consent of the Senate, generally for lifetime terms. Through its own Constitution, Minnesota, in common with most other States, has decided to allow its citizens to choose judges directly in periodic elections. But Minnesota has not thereby opted to install a corps of political actors on the bench; rather, it has endeavored to preserve the integrity of its judiciary by other means. Recognizing that the influence of political parties is incompatible with the judge's role, for example, Minnesota has designated all judicial elections nonpartisan. And it has adopted a provision, here called the Announce Clause, designed to prevent candidates for judicial office from "publicly making known how they would decide issues likely to come before them as judges."

The question this case presents is whether the First Amendment stops Minnesota from furthering its interest in judicial integrity through this precisely targeted speech restriction.

I

The speech restriction must fail, in the Court's view, because an electoral process is at stake; if Minnesota opts to elect its judges, the Court asserts, the State may not rein in what candidates may say.

I do not agree with this unilocular, "an election is an election," approach. Instead, I would differentiate elections for political offices, in which the First Amendment holds full sway, from elections designed to select those whose office it is to administer justice without respect to persons. Minnesota's choice to elect its judges, I am persuaded, does not preclude the State from installing an election process geared to the judicial office.

Legislative and executive officials serve in representative capacities. They are agents of the people; their primary function is to advance the interests of their constituencies. Candidates for political offices, in keeping with their representative role, must be left free to inform the electorate of their positions on specific issues. Armed with such information, the individual voter will be equipped to cast her ballot intelligently, to vote for the candidate committed to positions the voter approves. Campaign statements committing the candidate to take sides on contentious issues are therefore not only appropriate in political elections; they are "at the core of our electoral process," *Williams v. Rhodes*, for they "enhance the accountability of government officials to the people whom they represent," *Brown v. Hartlage*.

Judges, however, are not political actors. They do not sit as representatives of particular persons, communities, or parties; they serve no faction or constituency. "[I]t is the business of judges to be indifferent to popularity." *Chisom*. They must strive to do what is legally right, all the more so when the result is not the one "the home crowd" wants. Rehnquist, Dedicatory Address: Act Well Your Part: Therein All Honor Lies, 7 Pepperdine L.Rev. 227, 229–300 (1980). Even when they develop common law or give concrete meaning to constitutional text, judges act only in the context of individual cases, the outcome of which cannot depend on the will of the public.

Thus, the rationale underlying unconstrained speech in elections for political office-that representative government depends on the public's ability to choose agents who will act at its behest—does not carry over to campaigns for the bench. As to persons aiming to occupy the seat of judgment, the Court's unrelenting reliance on decisions involving contests for legislative and executive posts is manifestly out of place. In view of the magisterial role judges must fill in a system of justice, a role that removes them from the partisan fray, States may limit judicial campaign speech by measures impermissible in elections for political office.

The Court sees in this conclusion, and in the Announce Clause that embraces it, "an obvious tension": The Minnesota electorate is permitted to select its judges by popular vote, but is not provided information on "subjects of interest to the voters"—in particular, the voters are not told how the candidate would decide controversial cases or issues if elected. This supposed tension, however, rests on the false premise that by departing from the federal model with respect to who *chooses* judges, Minnesota necessarily departed from the federal position on the *criteria* relevant to the exercise of that choice....

Minnesota did not choose a judicial selection system with all the trappings of legislative and executive races. While providing for public participation, it tailored judicial selection to fit the character of third branch office holding. The balance the State sought to achieve—allowing the people to elect judges, but safeguarding the process so that the integrity of the judiciary would not be compromised—should encounter no First Amendment shoal.

II

Proper resolution of this case requires correction of the Court's distorted construction of the provision before us for review. According to the Court, the Announce Clause "prohibits a judicial candidate from stating his views on any specific nonfanciful legal question within the province of the court for which he is running, except in the context of discussing past decisions—and in the latter context as well, if he expresses the view that he is not bound by *stare decisis.*" In two key respects, that construction misrepresents the meaning of the Announce Clause as interpreted by the Eighth Circuit and embraced by the Minnesota Supreme Court.

First and most important, the Court ignores a crucial limiting construction placed on the Announce Clause by the courts below. The provision does not bar a candidate from generally "stating [her] views" on legal questions it prevents her from "publicly making known how [she] would *decide*" disputed issues. That limitation places beyond the scope of the Announce Clause a wide range of comments that may be highly informative to voters. Consistent with the Eighth Circuit's construction, such comments may include, for example, statements of historical fact ("As a prosecutor, I obtained 15 drunk driving convictions"); qualified statements ("Judges should use *sparingly* their discretion to grant lenient sentences to drunk drivers"); and statements framed at a sufficient level of generality ("Drunk drivers are a threat to the safety of every driver"). What remains within the Announce Clause is the category of statements that essentially commit the candidate to a position on a specific issue, such as "I think all drunk drivers should receive the maximum sentence permitted by law.

Second, the Court misportrays the scope of the Clause as applied to a candidate's discussion of past decisions. Citing an apparent concession by respondents at argument, the Court concludes that "statements critical of past judicial decisions are not permissible if the candidate also states that he is against *stare decisis*" (emphasis deleted). That conclusion, however, draws no force from the meaning attributed to the Announce Clause by the Eighth Circuit. In line with the Minnesota Board on Judicial Standards, the Court of Appeals stated without qualification that the Clause "does not prohibit candidates from discussing appellate court decisions." . . .

The Court's characterization of the Announce Clause as "election-nullifying," "plac[ing] most subjects of interest to the voters off limits," is further belied by the facts of this case. In his 1996 bid for office, petitioner Gregory Wersal distributed literature sharply criticizing three Minnesota Supreme Court decisions. Of the court's holding in the first case — that certain unrecorded confessions must be suppressed — Wersal asked, "Should we conclude that because the Supreme Court does not trust police, it allows confessed criminals to go free?" Of the second case, invalidating a state welfare law, Wersal stated: "The Court should have deferred to the Legislature. It's the Legislature which should set our spending policies." And of the third case, a decision involving abortion rights, Wersal charged that the court's holding was "directly contrary to the opinion of the U.S. Supreme Court," "unprecedented," and a "pro-abortion stance."

When a complaint was filed against Wersal on the basis of those statements, the Lawyers Professional Responsibility Board concluded that no discipline was warranted in part because it thought the disputed campaign materials did not violate the Announce Clause. And when, at the outset of his 1998 campaign, Wersal sought to avoid the possibility of sanction for future statements, he pursued the option, available to all Minnesota judicial candidates, of requesting an advisory opinion concerning the application of the Announce Clause. In response to that request, the Board indicated that it did not anticipate any adverse action against him. Wersal has thus never been sanctioned under the Announce Clause for any campaign statement he made. On the facts before us, in sum, the Announce Clause has hardly stifled the robust communication of ideas and views from judicial candidate to voter.

III

Even as it exaggerates the reach of the Announce Clause, the Court ignores the significance of that provision to the integrated system of judicial campaign regulation Minnesota has developed. Coupled with the Announce Clause in Minnesota's Code of Judicial Conduct is a provision that prohibits candidates from "mak[ing] pledges or promises of conduct in office other than the faithful and impartial performance of the duties of the office." Although the Court is correct that this "pledges or promises" provision is not directly at issue in this case, the Court errs in overlooking the interdependence of that prohibition and the one before us. In my view, the constitutionality of the Announce Clause cannot be resolved without an examination of that interaction in light of the interests the pledges or promises provision serves.

A

All parties to this case agree that, whatever the validity of the Announce Clause, the State may constitutionally prohibit judicial candidates from pledging or promising certain results.

The reasons for this agreement are apparent. Pledges or promises of conduct in office, however commonplace in races for the political branches, are inconsistent "with the judge's obligation to decide cases in accordance with his or her roles." This judicial obligation to avoid prejudgment corresponds to the litigant's right, protected by the Due Process Clause of the Fourteenth Amendment, to "an impartial and disinterested tribunal in both civil and criminal cases," *Marshall v. Jerrico, Inc.*, 446 U.S. 238, 242, (1980). . . .

B

The constitutionality of the pledges or promises clause is thus amply supported; the provision not only advances due process of law for litigants in Minnesota courts, it also reinforces the authority of the Minnesota judiciary by promoting public confidence in the State's judges. The Announce Clause, however, is equally vital to achieving these compelling ends, for without it, the pledges or promises provision would be feeble, an arid form, a matter of no real importance. . . .

* * *

This Court has recognized in the past, as Justice O'CONNOR does today, a "fundamental tension between the ideal character of the judicial office and the real world of electoral politics," *Chisom*. We have no warrant to resolve that tension, however, by forcing States to choose one pole or the other. Judges are not politicians, and the First Amendment does not require that they be treated as politicians simply because they are chosen by popular vote. Nor does the First Amendment command States that wish to promote the integrity of their judges in fact and appearance to abandon systems of judicial selection that the people, in the exercise of their sovereign prerogatives, have devised.

For more than three-quarters of a century, States like Minnesota have endeavored, through experiment tested by experience, to balance the constitutional interests in judicial integrity and free expression within the unique setting of an elected judiciary. P 5. The Announce Clause, borne of this long effort, "comes to this Court bearing a weighty title of respect." I would uphold it as an essential component in Minnesota's accommodation of the complex and competing concerns in this sensitive area. Accordingly, I would affirm the judgment of the Court of Appeals for the Eighth Circuit.

Notes and Questions

1. On remand, the Eighth Circuit, sitting en banc, went further than the Supreme Court in *White*, striking down both a clause limiting judges' partisan political activities and their personal solicitation of campaign contributions. *Republican Party of Minnesota v. White*, 416 F.3d 738 (8th Cir. 2005) (en banc), cert. denied *sub. nom. Dimick v. Republican Party of Minnesota*, 546 U.S. 1157 (2006).

More recently, a divided Eighth Circuit, sitting en banc rejected Wersal's challenge to three Minnesota judicial campaign rules. *Wersal v. Sexton*, 674 F.3d 1010

(8th Cir. 2012) (en banc). The court majority held one of the three challenges was not ripe and rejected the other two on the merits:

> [The endorsement clause states a judge or a judicial candidate shall not "publicly endorse or, except for the judge or candidate's opponent, publicly oppose another candidate for public office."] Like the district court, we conclude the endorsement clause serves the compelling interests of preserving impartiality and avoiding the appearance of impropriety.... When a judge or judicial candidate endorses another candidate, it creates a risk of partiality toward the endorsed party and his or her supporters, as well as a risk of partiality against other candidates opposing the endorsed party. The endorsement clause is directly aimed at this speech about parties, as it prevents potential litigants in a case from the risk of having an unfair trial. At the very least, the clause serves the State's interest in avoiding the appearance of impropriety. Namely, even if a particular endorsement does not serve to create an actual bias toward or against a particular party, the act of endorsement itself undermines the judiciary's appearance of impartiality because the public may perceive the judge to be beholden to political interests....
>
> We next address the solicitation clause, which bars judges and candidates from "personally solicit[ing] or accept[ing] campaign contributions other than as authorized by Rules 4.2 and 4.4." 52 Minn. Stat. Ann., Code of Judicial Conduct, Canon 4.1(A)(6).... Rules 4.2 and 4.4 allow candidates to solicit funds through a campaign committee, although the committee is not to disclose the identity of contributors to the candidate.... [D]irect personal solicitation creates a situation where potential contributors must choose to either contribute to the candidate, or decline to contribute, with a resulting risk of retribution. *See In re Dunleavy*, 838 A.2d 338, 351 (Me.2003) ("If a contribution is made, a judge might subsequently be accused of favoring the contributor in court. If a contribution is declined, a judge might be accused of punishing a contributor in court."). In either scenario, the candidate is more likely to decipher whether the potential donor chooses to make a contribution, which gives rise to a greater risk of a quid pro quo.... We must emphasize once more Minnesota's separate interest in avoiding the appearance of impropriety. Regardless of whether a potential donor chooses to make a contribution — and whether a candidate ultimately learns of the donor's choice — the appearance of impartiality is attenuated.

Two judges concurred in the result, and five dissented. The Supreme Court declined to hear the case. *Wersal v. Sexton*, 568 U.S. 823 (2012).

2. *Wersal* was one of a number of conflicting lower court rulings, disagreeing both about the constitutionality of particular judicial campaign rules as well as the level of scrutiny to apply. See *Siefert v. Alexander*, 608 F.3d 974 (7th Cir. 2010), cert. denied 563 U.S. 983 (2011); *Bauer v. Shepard*, 620 F.3d 704 (7th Cir. 2010), cert. denied

563 U.S. 983 (2011); *Carey v. Wolnitzek*, 614 F.3d 189 (6th Cir. 2010); *Sanders County Republican Central Committee v. Bullock*, 698 F.3d 741 (9th Cir. 2012).

In the following case, the Supreme Court weighed in on the issue in the context of a Florida rule on personal solicitations of campaign contributions by judicial candidates.

Williams-Yulee v. Florida Bar

575 U.S. 433 (2015)

Chief Justice ROBERTS delivered the opinion of the Court, except as to Part II.

Our Founders vested authority to appoint federal judges in the President, with the advice and consent of the Senate, and entrusted those judges to hold their offices during good behavior. The Constitution permits States to make a different choice, and most of them have done so. In 39 States, voters elect trial or appellate judges at the polls. In an effort to preserve public confidence in the integrity of their judiciaries, many of those States prohibit judges and judicial candidates from personally soliciting funds for their campaigns. We must decide whether the First Amendment permits such restrictions on speech.

We hold that it does. Judges are not politicians, even when they come to the bench by way of the ballot. And a State's decision to elect its judiciary does not compel it to treat judicial candidates like campaigners for political office. A State may assure its people that judges will apply the law without fear or favor—and without having personally asked anyone for money. We affirm the judgment of the Florida Supreme Court.

I

A

When Florida entered the Union in 1845, its Constitution provided for trial and appellate judges to be elected by the General Assembly. Florida soon followed more than a dozen of its sister States in transferring authority to elect judges to the voting public. The experiment did not last long in the Sunshine State. The war came, and Florida's 1868 Constitution returned judicial selection to the political branches. Over time, however, the people reclaimed the power to elect the state bench: Supreme Court justices in 1885 and trial court judges in 1942.

In the early 1970s, four Florida Supreme Court justices resigned from office following corruption scandals. Florida voters responded by amending their Constitution again. Under the system now in place, appellate judges are appointed by the Governor from a list of candidates proposed by a nominating committee—a process known as "merit selection." Then, every six years, voters decide whether to retain incumbent appellate judges for another term. Trial judges are still elected by popular vote, unless the local jurisdiction opts instead for merit selection.

Amid the corruption scandals of the 1970s, the Florida Supreme Court adopted a new Code of Judicial Conduct. In its present form, the first sentence of Canon 1 reads, "An independent and honorable judiciary is indispensable to justice in our society." Canon 1 instructs judges to observe "high standards of conduct" so that "the integrity and independence of the judiciary may be preserved." Canon 2 directs that a judge "shall act at all times in a manner that promotes public confidence in the integrity and impartiality of the judiciary." Other provisions prohibit judges from lending the prestige of their offices to private interests, engaging in certain business transactions, and personally participating in soliciting funds for nonprofit organizations.

Canon 7C(1) governs fundraising in judicial elections. The Canon, which is based on a provision in the American Bar Association's Model Code of Judicial Conduct, provides:

> A candidate, including an incumbent judge, for a judicial office that is filled by public election between competing candidates shall not personally solicit campaign funds, or solicit attorneys for publicly stated support, but may establish committees of responsible persons to secure and manage the expenditure of funds for the candidate's campaign and to obtain public statements of support for his or her candidacy. Such committees are not prohibited from soliciting campaign contributions and public support from any person or corporation authorized by law.

Florida statutes impose additional restrictions on campaign fundraising in judicial elections. Contributors may not donate more than $1,000 per election to a trial court candidate or more than $3,000 per retention election to a Supreme Court justice. Fla. Stat. § 106.08(1)(a) (2014). Campaign committee treasurers must file periodic reports disclosing the names of contributors and the amount of each contribution.

Judicial candidates can seek guidance about campaign ethics rules from the Florida Judicial Ethics Advisory Committee. The Committee has interpreted Canon 7 to allow a judicial candidate to serve as treasurer of his own campaign committee, learn the identity of campaign contributors, and send thank you notes to donors.

Like Florida, most other States prohibit judicial candidates from soliciting campaign funds personally, but allow them to raise money through committees. According to the American Bar Association, 30 of the 39 States that elect trial or appellate judges have adopted restrictions similar to Canon 7C(1).

B

Lanell Williams-Yulee, who refers to herself as Yulee, has practiced law in Florida since 1991. In September 2009, she decided to run for a seat on the county court for Hillsborough County, a jurisdiction of about 1.3 million people that includes the city of Tampa. Shortly after filing paperwork to enter the race, Yulee drafted a letter announcing her candidacy. The letter described her experience and desire to "bring fresh ideas and positive solutions to the Judicial bench." The letter then stated:

> An early contribution of $25, $50, $100, $250, or $500, made payable to 'Lanell Williams-Yulee Campaign for County Judge', will help raise the

> initial funds needed to launch the campaign and get our message out to the public. I ask for your support [i]n meeting the primary election fund raiser goals. Thank you in advance for your support.

Yulee signed the letter and mailed it to local voters. She also posted the letter on her campaign Web site.

Yulee's bid for the bench did not unfold as she had hoped. She lost the primary to the incumbent judge. Then the Florida Bar filed a complaint against her. As relevant here, the Bar charged her with violating Rule 4–8.2(b) of the Rules Regulating the Florida Bar. That Rule requires judicial candidates to comply with applicable provisions of Florida's Code of Judicial Conduct, including the ban on personal solicitation of campaign funds in Canon 7C(1).

Yulee admitted that she had signed and sent the fundraising letter. But she argued that the Bar could not discipline her for that conduct because the First Amendment protects a judicial candidate's right to solicit campaign funds in an election. The Florida Supreme Court appointed a referee, who held a hearing and recommended a finding of guilt. As a sanction, the referee recommended that Yulee be publicly reprimanded and ordered to pay the costs of the proceeding ($1,860).

The Florida Supreme Court adopted the referee's recommendations. The court explained that Canon 7C(1) "clearly restricts a judicial candidate's speech" and therefore must be "narrowly tailored to serve a compelling state interest." The court held that the Canon satisfies that demanding inquiry. First, the court reasoned, prohibiting judicial candidates from personally soliciting funds furthers Florida's compelling interest in "preserving the integrity of [its] judiciary and maintaining the public's confidence in an impartial judiciary." (internal quotation marks omitted; alteration in original). In the court's view, "personal solicitation of campaign funds, even by mass mailing, raises an appearance of impropriety and calls into question, in the public's mind, the judge's impartiality." Second, the court concluded that Canon 7C(1) is narrowly tailored to serve that compelling interest because it "insulate[s] judicial candidates from the solicitation and receipt of funds while leaving open, ample alternative means for candidates to raise the resources necessary to run their campaigns."

The Florida Supreme Court acknowledged that some Federal Courts of Appeals—"whose judges have lifetime appointments and thus do not have to engage in fundraising"—had invalidated restrictions similar to Canon 7C(1). But the court found it persuasive that every State Supreme Court that had considered similar fundraising provisions—along with several Federal Courts of Appeals—had upheld the laws against First Amendment challenges. Florida's chief justice and one associate justice dissented. We granted certiorari.

II

The First Amendment provides that Congress "shall make no law ... abridging the freedom of speech." The Fourteenth Amendment makes that prohibition applicable to the States. The parties agree that Canon 7C(1) restricts Yulee's speech on the basis of its content by prohibiting her from soliciting contributions to her election campaign. The parties disagree, however, about the level of scrutiny that should govern our review.

We have applied exacting scrutiny to laws restricting the solicitation of contributions to charity, upholding the speech limitations only if they are narrowly tailored to serve a compelling interest. See *Riley v. National Federation of Blind of N.C., Inc.*, 487 U.S. 781, 798 (1988); *id.*, at 810 (Rehnquist, C.J., dissenting). As we have explained, noncommercial solicitation "is characteristically intertwined with informative and perhaps persuasive speech." *Id.*, (majority opinion) (quoting *Schaumburg v. Citizens for Better Environment,* 444 U.S. 620, 632 (1980)). Applying a lesser standard of scrutiny to such speech would threaten "the exercise of rights so vital to the maintenance of democratic institutions." *Schneider v. State (Town of Irvington),* 308 U.S. 147, 161 (1939).

The principles underlying these charitable solicitation cases apply with even greater force here. Before asking for money in her fundraising letter, Yulee explained her fitness for the bench and expressed her vision for the judiciary. Her stated purpose for the solicitation was to get her "message out to the public." As we have long recognized, speech about public issues and the qualifications of candidates for elected office commands the highest level of First Amendment protection. See *Eu*. Indeed, in our only prior case concerning speech restrictions on a candidate for judicial office, this Court and both parties assumed that strict scrutiny applied. *White.*

Although the Florida Supreme Court upheld Canon 7C(1) under strict scrutiny, the Florida Bar and several *amici* contend that we should subject the Canon to a more permissive standard: that it be "closely drawn" to match a "sufficiently important interest." *Buckley,* The "closely drawn" standard is a poor fit for this case. The Court adopted that test in *Buckley* to address a claim that campaign contribution limits violated a contributor's "freedom of political association." Here, Yulee does not claim that Canon 7C(1) violates her right to free association; she argues that it violates her right to free speech. And the Florida Bar can hardly dispute that the Canon infringes Yulee's freedom to discuss candidates and public issues—namely, herself and her qualifications to be a judge. The Bar's call to import the "closely drawn" test from the contribution limit context into a case about solicitation therefore has little avail.

As several of the Bar's *amici* note, we applied the "closely drawn" test to solicitation restrictions in *McConnell v. FEC,* 540 U.S. 93, 136 (2003), overruled in part by *Citizens United v. FEC,* 558 U.S. 310 (2010). But the Court in that case determined that the solicitation restrictions operated primarily to prevent circumvention of the contribution limits, which were the subject of the "closely drawn" test in the first place. *McConnell* offers no help to the Bar here, because Florida did not adopt Canon 7C(1) as an anticircumvention measure.

In sum, we hold today what we assumed in *White*: a State may restrict the speech of a judicial candidate only if the restriction is narrowly tailored to serve a compelling interest.

III

The Florida Bar faces a demanding task in defending Canon 7C(1) against Yulee's First Amendment challenge. We have emphasized that "it is the rare case" in which a State demonstrates that a speech restriction is narrowly tailored to serve a compelling interest. *Burson v. Freeman,* 504 U.S. 191, 211 (1992) (plurality opinion). But those cases do arise. See *ibid.*; *Holder v. Humanitarian Law Project,* 561 U.S. 1, 25–39 (2010); *McConnell* (opinion of KENNEDY, J.); cf. *Adarand Constructors, Inc. v. Pena,* 515 U.S. 200, 237 (1995) ("we wish to dispel the notion that strict scrutiny is 'strict in theory, but fatal in fact' "). Here, Canon 7C(1) advances the State's compelling interest in preserving public confidence in the integrity of the judiciary, and it does so through means narrowly tailored to avoid unnecessarily abridging speech. This is therefore one of the rare cases in which a speech restriction withstands strict scrutiny.

A

The Florida Supreme Court adopted Canon 7C(1) to promote the State's interests in "protecting the integrity of the judiciary" and "maintaining the public's confidence in an impartial judiciary." The way the Canon advances those interests is intuitive: Judges, charged with exercising strict neutrality and independence, cannot supplicate campaign donors without diminishing public confidence in judicial integrity. This principle dates back at least eight centuries to Magna Carta, which proclaimed, "To no one will we sell, to no one will we refuse or delay, right or justice." The same concept underlies the common law judicial oath, which binds a judge to "do right to all manner of people . . . without fear or favour, affection or ill-will," 10 Encyclopaedia of the Laws of England 105 (2d ed. 1908), and the oath that each of us took to "administer justice without respect to persons, and do equal right to the poor and to the rich," 28 U.S.C. § 453. Simply put, Florida and most other States have concluded that the public may lack confidence in a judge's ability to administer justice without fear or favor if he comes to office by asking for favors.

The interest served by Canon 7C(1) has firm support in our precedents. We have recognized the "vital state interest" in safeguarding "public confidence in the fairness and integrity of the nation's elected judges." *Caperton v. Massey* [*infra*, this Chapter] (internal quotation marks omitted). The importance of public confidence in the integrity of judges stems from the place of the judiciary in the government. Unlike the executive or the legislature, the judiciary "has no influence over either the sword or the purse; . . . neither force nor will but merely judgment." The Federalist No. 78, p. 465 (C. Rossiter ed. 1961) (A. Hamilton) (capitalization altered). The judiciary's authority therefore depends in large measure on the public's willingness to respect and follow its decisions. As Justice Frankfurter once put it for the Court, "justice must satisfy the appearance of justice." *Offutt v. United States,* 348 U.S. 11, 14 (1954). It follows that public perception of judicial integrity is "a state interest of the highest order." *Caperton* (quoting *White*).

The principal dissent observes that bans on judicial candidate solicitation lack a lengthy historical pedigree. We do not dispute that fact, but it has no relevance here. As the precedent cited by the principal dissent demonstrates, a history and tradition of regulation are important factors in determining whether to recognize "new categories of unprotected speech." *Brown v. Entertainment Merchants Assn.*, 131 S. Ct. 2729, 2734 (2011). But nobody argues that solicitation of campaign funds by judicial candidates is a category of unprotected speech. As explained above, the First Amendment fully applies to Yulee's speech. The question is instead whether that Amendment permits the particular regulation of speech at issue here.

The parties devote considerable attention to our cases analyzing campaign finance restrictions in political elections. But a State's interest in preserving public confidence in the integrity of its judiciary extends beyond its interest in preventing the appearance of corruption in legislative and executive elections. As we explained in *White*, States may regulate judicial elections differently than they regulate political elections, because the role of judges differs from the role of politicians. *White* (GINSBURG, J., dissenting). Politicians are expected to be appropriately responsive to the preferences of their supporters. Indeed, such "responsiveness is key to the very concept of self-governance through elected officials." *McCutcheon* [*infra*, Chapter 14—Eds.] (plurality opinion). The same is not true of judges. In deciding cases, a judge is not to follow the preferences of his supporters, or provide any special consideration to his campaign donors. A judge instead must "observe the utmost fairness," striving to be "perfectly and completely independent, with nothing to influence or controul him but God and his conscience." Address of John Marshall, in Proceedings and Debates of the Virginia State Convention of 1829–1830, p. 616 (1830). As in *White*, therefore, our precedents applying the First Amendment to political elections have little bearing on the issues here.

The vast majority of elected judges in States that allow personal solicitation serve with fairness and honor. But "[e]ven if judges were able to refrain from favoring donors, the mere possibility that judges' decisions may be motivated by the desire to repay campaign contributions is likely to undermine the public's confidence in the judiciary." *White* (O'Connor, J., concurring). In the eyes of the public, a judge's personal solicitation could result (even unknowingly) in "a possible temptation . . . which might lead him not to hold the balance nice, clear and true." *Tumey v. Ohio*, 273 U.S. 510, 532 (1927). That risk is especially pronounced because most donors are lawyers and litigants who may appear before the judge they are supporting. See A. Bannon, E. Velasco, L. Casey, & L. Reagan, The New Politics of Judicial Elections: 2011–12, p. 15 (2013).

The concept of public confidence in judicial integrity does not easily reduce to precise definition, nor does it lend itself to proof by documentary record. But no one denies that it is genuine and compelling. In short, it is the regrettable but unavoidable appearance that judges who personally ask for money may diminish their integrity that prompted the Supreme Court of Florida and most other States to sever the direct link between judicial candidates and campaign contributors. As the Supreme Court of Oregon explained, "the spectacle of lawyers or potential litigants directly handing over money to judicial candidates should be avoided if the public is to have faith in the impartiality of its judiciary." *In re Fadeley,* 310 Ore. 548, 565 (1990). Moreover, personal solicitation by a judicial candidate "inevitably places the solicited individuals in a position to fear retaliation if they fail to financially support that candidate." *Simes,* 368 Ark. at 585. Potential litigants then fear that "the integrity of the judicial system has been compromised, forcing them to search for an attorney in part based upon the criteria of which attorneys have made the obligatory contributions." *Ibid.* A State's decision to elect its judges does not require it to tolerate these risks. The Florida Bar's interest is compelling.

B

Yulee acknowledges the State's compelling interest in judicial integrity. She argues, however, that the Canon's failure to restrict other speech equally damaging to judicial integrity and its appearance undercuts the Bar's position. In particular, she notes that Canon 7C(1) allows a judge's campaign committee to solicit money, which arguably reduces public confidence in the integrity of the judiciary just as much as a judge's personal solicitation. Yulee also points out that Florida permits judicial candidates to write thank you notes to campaign donors, which ensures that candidates know who contributes and who does not.

It is always somewhat counterintuitive to argue that a law violates the First Amendment by abridging *too little* speech. We have recognized, however, that underinclusiveness can raise "doubts about whether the government is in fact pursuing the interest it invokes, rather than disfavoring a particular speaker or viewpoint." *Brown.* In a textbook illustration of that principle, we invalidated a city's ban on ritual animal sacrifices because the city failed to regulate vast swaths of conduct that similarly diminished its asserted interests in public health and animal welfare. *Church of Lukumi Babalu Aye, Inc. v. Hialeah,* 508 U.S. 520, 543–547 (1993).

Underinclusiveness can also reveal that a law does not actually advance a compelling interest. For example, a State's decision to prohibit newspapers, but not electronic media, from releasing the names of juvenile defendants suggested that the law did not advance its stated purpose of protecting youth privacy. *Smith v. Daily Mail Publishing Co.,* 443 U.S. 97, 104–105 (1979).

Although a law's underinclusivity raises a red flag, the First Amendment imposes no freestanding "underinclusiveness limitation." *R.A.V. v. St. Paul,* 505 U.S. 377, 387 (1992) (internal quotation marks omitted). A State need not address all aspects of a problem in one fell swoop; policymakers may focus on their most pressing concerns. We have accordingly upheld laws — even under strict scrutiny — that conceivably could have restricted even greater amounts of speech in service of their stated interests.

Viewed in light of these principles, Canon 7C(1) raises no fatal underinclusivity concerns. The solicitation ban aims squarely at the conduct most likely to undermine public confidence in the integrity of the judiciary: personal requests for money by judges and judicial candidates. The Canon applies evenhandedly to all judges and judicial candidates, regardless of their viewpoint or chosen means of solicitation.

And unlike some laws that we have found impermissibly underinclusive, Canon 7C(1) is not riddled with exceptions. Indeed, the Canon contains zero exceptions to its ban on personal solicitation.

Yulee relies heavily on the provision of Canon 7C(1) that allows solicitation by a candidate's campaign committee. But Florida, along with most other States, has reasonably concluded that solicitation by the candidate personally creates a categorically different and more severe risk of undermining public confidence than does solicitation by a campaign committee. The identity of the solicitor matters, as anyone who has encountered a Girl Scout selling cookies outside a grocery store can attest. When the judicial candidate himself asks for money, the stakes are higher for all involved. The candidate has personally invested his time and effort in the fundraising appeal; he has placed his name and reputation behind the request. The solicited individual knows that, and also knows that the solicitor might be in a position to singlehandedly make decisions of great weight: The same person who signed the fundraising letter might one day sign the judgment. This dynamic inevitably creates pressure for the recipient to comply, and it does so in a way that solicitation by a third party does not. Just as inevitably, the personal involvement of the candidate in the solicitation creates the public appearance that the candidate will remember who says yes, and who says no.

In short, personal solicitation by judicial candidates implicates a different problem than solicitation by campaign committees. However similar the two solicitations may be in substance, a State may conclude that they present markedly different appearances to the public. Florida's choice to allow solicitation by campaign committees does not undermine its decision to ban solicitation by judges.

Likewise, allowing judicial candidates to write thank you notes to campaign donors does not detract from the State's interest in preserving public confidence in the integrity of the judiciary. Yulee argues that permitting thank you notes heightens the likelihood of actual bias by ensuring that judicial candidates know who supported their campaigns, and ensuring that the supporter knows that the candidate knows. Maybe so. But the State's compelling interest is implicated most directly by the candidate's personal solicitation itself. A failure to ban thank you notes for contributions not solicited by the candidate does not undercut the Bar's rationale.

In addition, the State has a good reason for allowing candidates to write thank you notes and raise money through committees. These accommodations reflect Florida's effort to respect the First Amendment interests of candidates and their contributors—to resolve the "fundamental tension between the ideal character of the judicial office and the real world of electoral politics." *Chisom*. They belie the principal dissent's suggestion that Canon 7C(1) reflects general "hostility toward judicial campaigning" and has "nothing to do with the appearances created by judges' asking for money." Nothing?

The principal dissent also suggests that Canon 7C(1) is underinclusive because Florida does not ban judicial candidates from asking individuals for personal gifts or loans. But Florida law treats a personal "gift" or "loan" as a campaign contribution if the donor makes it "for the purpose of influencing the results of an election," and Florida's Judicial Qualifications Commission has determined that a judicial candidate violates Canon 7C(1) by personally soliciting such a loan. In any event, Florida can ban personal solicitation of campaign funds by judicial candidates without making them obey a comprehensive code to leading an ethical life. Underinclusivity creates a First Amendment concern when the State regulates one aspect of a problem while declining to regulate a different aspect of the problem that affects its stated interest *in a comparable way.* The principal dissent offers no basis to conclude that judicial candidates are in the habit of soliciting personal loans, football tickets, or anything of the sort. Even under strict scrutiny, "[t]he First Amendment does not require States to regulate for problems that do not exist." *Burson* (State's regulation of political solicitation around a polling place, but not charitable or commercial solicitation, was not fatally underinclusive under strict scrutiny).

Taken to its logical conclusion, the position advanced by Yulee and the principal dissent is that Florida may ban the solicitation of funds by judicial candidates only if the State bans *all* solicitation of funds in judicial elections. The First Amendment does not put a State to that all-or-nothing choice. We will not punish Florida for leaving open more, rather than fewer, avenues of expression, especially when there is no indication that the selective restriction of speech reflects a pretextual motive.

C

After arguing that Canon 7C(1) violates the First Amendment because it restricts too little speech, Yulee argues that the Canon violates the First Amendment because it restricts too much. In her view, the Canon is not narrowly tailored to advance the State's compelling interest through the least restrictive means.

By any measure, Canon 7C(1) restricts a narrow slice of speech. A reader of Justice KENNEDY's dissent could be forgiven for concluding that the Court has just upheld a latter-day version of the Alien and Sedition Acts, approving "state censorship" that "locks the First Amendment out," imposes a "gag" on candidates, and inflicts "dead weight" on a "silenced" public debate. But in reality, Canon 7C(1) leaves judicial candidates free to discuss any issue with any person at any time. Candidates can write letters, give speeches, and put up billboards. They can contact potential supporters in person, on the phone, or online. They can promote their campaigns on radio, television, or other media. They cannot say, "Please give me money." They can, however, direct their campaign committees to do so. Whatever else may be said of the Canon, it is surely not a "wildly disproportionate restriction upon speech." (SCALIA, J., dissenting).

Indeed, Yulee concedes—and the principal dissent seems to agree—that Canon 7C(1) is valid in numerous applications. Yulee acknowledges that Florida can prohibit judges from soliciting money from lawyers and litigants appearing before them. In addition, she says the State "might" be able to ban "direct one-to-one solicitation of lawyers and individuals or businesses that could reasonably appear in the court for which the individual is a candidate." She also suggests that the Bar could forbid "in person" solicitation by judicial candidates. But Yulee argues that the Canon cannot constitutionally be applied to her chosen form of solicitation: a letter posted online and distributed via mass mailing. No one, she contends, will lose confidence in the integrity of the judiciary based on personal solicitation to such a broad audience.

This argument misperceives the breadth of the compelling interest that underlies Canon 7C(1). Florida has reasonably determined that personal appeals for money by a judicial candidate inherently create an appearance of impropriety that may cause the public to lose confidence in the integrity of the judiciary. That interest may be implicated to varying degrees in particular contexts, but the interest remains whenever the public perceives the judge personally asking for money.

Moreover, the lines Yulee asks us to draw are unworkable. Even under her theory of the case, a mass mailing would create an appearance of impropriety if addressed to a list of all lawyers and litigants with pending cases. So would a speech soliciting contributions from the 100 most frequently appearing attorneys in the jurisdiction. Yulee says she might accept a ban on one-to-one solicitation, but is the public impression really any different if a judicial candidate tries to buttonhole not one prospective donor but two at a time? Ten? Yulee also agrees that in person solicitation creates a problem. But would the public's concern recede if the request for money came in a phone call or a text message?

We decline to wade into this swamp. The First Amendment requires that Canon 7C(1) be narrowly tailored, not that it be "perfectly tailored." *Burson*. The impossibility of perfect tailoring is especially apparent when the State's compelling interest is as intangible as public confidence in the integrity of the judiciary. Yulee is of course correct that some personal solicitations raise greater concerns than others. A judge who passes the hat in the courthouse creates a more serious appearance of impropriety than does a judicial candidate who makes a tasteful plea for support on the radio. But most problems arise in greater and lesser gradations, and the First Amendment does not confine a State to addressing evils in their most acute form. Here, Florida has concluded that all personal solicitations by judicial candidates create a public appearance that undermines confidence in the integrity of the judiciary; banning all personal solicitations by judicial candidates is narrowly tailored to address that concern.

In considering Yulee's tailoring arguments, we are mindful that most States with elected judges have determined that drawing a line between personal solicitation by candidates and solicitation by committees is necessary to preserve public confidence in the integrity of the judiciary. These considered judgments deserve our respect, especially because they reflect sensitive choices by States in an area central to their own governance—how to select those who "sit as their judges." *Gregory v. Ashcroft*, 501 U.S. 452, 460 (1991).

Finally, Yulee contends that Florida can accomplish its compelling interest through the less restrictive means of recusal rules and campaign contribution limits. We disagree. A rule requiring judges to recuse themselves from every case in which a lawyer or litigant made a campaign contribution would disable many jurisdictions. And a flood of postelection recusal motions could "erode public confidence in judicial impartiality" and thereby exacerbate the very appearance problem the State is trying to solve. *Caperton* (ROBERTS, C.J., dissenting). Moreover, the rule that Yulee envisions could create a perverse incentive for litigants to make campaign contributions to judges solely as a means to trigger their later recusal — a form of peremptory strike against a judge that would enable transparent forum shopping.

As for campaign contribution limits, Florida already applies them to judicial elections. A State may decide that the threat to public confidence created by personal solicitation exists apart from the amount of money that a judge or judicial candidate seeks. Even if Florida decreased its contribution limit, the appearance that judges who personally solicit funds might improperly favor their campaign donors would remain. Although the Court has held that contribution limits advance the interest in preventing *quid pro quo* corruption and its appearance in political elections, we have never held that adopting contribution limits precludes a State from pursuing its compelling interests through additional means. And in any event, a State has compelling interests in regulating judicial elections that extend beyond its interests in regulating political elections, because judges are not politicians.

In sum, because Canon 7C(1) is narrowly tailored to serve a compelling government interest, the First Amendment poses no obstacle to its enforcement in this case. As a result of our decision, Florida may continue to prohibit judicial candidates from personally soliciting campaign funds, while allowing them to raise money through committees and to otherwise communicate their electoral messages in practically any way. The principal dissent faults us for not answering a slew of broader questions, such as whether Florida may cap a judicial candidate's spending or ban independent expenditures by corporations. Yulee has not asked these questions, and for good reason — they are far afield from the narrow regulation actually at issue in this case.

We likewise have no cause to consider whether the citizens of States that elect their judges have decided anything about the "oracular sanctity of judges" or whether judges are due "a hearty helping of humble pie." The principal dissent could be right that the decision to adopt judicial elections "probably springs," at least in part, from a desire to make judges more accountable to the public, although the history on this matter is more complicated. In any event, it is a long way from general notions of judicial accountability to the principal dissent's view, which evokes nothing so much as Delacroix's painting of Liberty leading a determined band of *citoyens,* this time against a robed aristocracy scurrying to shore up the ramparts of the judicial castle through disingenuous ethical rules. We claim no similar insight into the People's passions, hazard no assertions about ulterior motives of those who promulgated Canon 7C(1), and firmly reject the charge of a deceptive "pose of neutrality" on the part of those who uphold it.

* * *

The desirability of judicial elections is a question that has sparked disagreement for more than 200 years. Hamilton believed that appointing judges to positions with life tenure constituted "the best expedient which can be devised in any government to secure a steady, upright, and impartial administration of the laws." The Federalist No. 78 at 465. Jefferson thought that making judges "dependent on none but themselves" ran counter to the principle of "a government founded on the public will." 12 The Works of Thomas Jefferson 5 (P. Ford ed. 1905). The federal courts reflect the view of Hamilton; most States have sided with Jefferson. Both methods have given our Nation jurists of wisdom and rectitude who have devoted themselves to maintaining "the public's respect . . . and a reserve of public goodwill, without becoming subservient to public opinion." Rehnquist, Judicial Independence, 38 University of Richmond Law Review 579, 596 (2004).

It is not our place to resolve this enduring debate. Our limited task is to apply the Constitution to the question presented in this case. Judicial candidates have a First Amendment right to speak in support of their campaigns. States have a compelling interest in preserving public confidence in their judiciaries. When the State adopts a narrowly tailored restriction like the one at issue here, those principles do not conflict. A State's decision to elect judges does not compel it to compromise public confidence in their integrity.

The judgment of the Florida Supreme Court is

Affirmed.

[A concurring opinion by Justice BREYER is omitted.]

Justice GINSBURG, with whom Justice BREYER joins as to Part II, concurring in part and concurring in the judgment.

I

I join the Court's opinion save for Part II. As explained in my dissenting opinion in *White*, I would not apply exacting scrutiny to a State's endeavor sensibly to "differentiate elections for political offices . . . , from elections designed to select those whose office it is to administer justice without respect to persons."

II

I write separately to reiterate the substantial latitude, in my view, States should possess to enact campaign-finance rules geared to judicial elections. . . .

The Court's recent campaign-finance decisions, trained on political actors, should not hold sway for judicial elections. . . . For reasons spelled out in the dissenting opinions in *Citizens United* and *McCutcheon,* I would have upheld the legislation there at issue. But even if one agrees with those judgments, they are geared to elections for representative posts, and should have "little bearing" on judicial elections. . . .

States may therefore impose different campaign-finance rules for judicial elections than for political elections. Experience illustrates why States may wish to do so. When the political campaign-finance apparatus is applied to judicial elections, the distinction of judges from politicians dims. Donors, who gain audience and influence through contributions to political campaigns, anticipate that investment in campaigns for judicial office will yield similar returns. Elected judges understand this dynamic. As Ohio Supreme Court Justice Paul Pfeifer put it: "Whether they succeed or not," campaign contributors "mean to be buying a vote." Liptak & Roberts, *Campaign Cash Mirrors a High Court's Rulings*, N.Y. Times, Oct. 1, 2006, pp. A1, A22 (internal quotation marks omitted).

In recent years, moreover, issue-oriented organizations and political action committees have spent millions of dollars opposing the reelection of judges whose decisions do not tow a party line or are alleged to be out of step with public opinion. Following the Iowa Supreme Court's 2009 invalidation of the State's same-sex marriage ban, for example, national organizations poured money into a successful campaign to remove three justices from that Court. J. Shugerman, The People's Courts: Pursuing Judicial Independence in America 3 (2012). Attack advertisements funded by issue or politically driven organizations portrayed the justices as political actors; they lambasted the Iowa Supreme Court for "usurp[ing] the will of voters." A. Skaggs, M. da Silva, L. Casey, & C. Hall, The New Politics of Judicial Elections 2009–10, p. 9 (C. Hall ed. 2011) (internal quotation marks omitted).

Similarly portraying judges as belonging to another political branch, huge amounts have been spent on advertisements opposing retention of judges because they rendered unpopular decisions in favor of criminal defendants. D. Goldberg, S. Samis, E. Bender, & R. Weiss, The New Politics of Judicial Elections 2004, pp. 5, 10–11 (J. Rutledge ed. 2005) (hereinafter Goldberg). In North Carolina, for example, in 2014, a political action committee aired "a widely condemned TV spot accusing [North Carolina Supreme Court Justice Robin] Hudson of being 'soft' on child-molesters." James Oliphant, *When Judges Go Courting*, National Journal Magazine, Oct. 18, 2014, p. 28. And in West Virginia, as described in *Caperton*, coal executive Don Blankenship lavishly funded a political action committee called "And For The Sake Of The Kids." That group bought advertisements accusing Justice Warren McGraw of freeing a "child rapist" and allowing that "rapist" to "work as a janitor at a West Virginia school." Goldberg 4; see A. Bannon, E. Velasco, L. Casey, & L. Reagan, The New Politics of Judicial Elections 2011–12, p. 22 (L. Kinney and P. Hardin Eds.. 2013) (reporting that in 2011 and 2012, interest-oriented groups were 22 times more likely to purchase an "attack" advertisement than were judicial candidates themselves).

Disproportionate spending to influence court judgments threatens both the appearance and actuality of judicial independence. Numerous studies report that the money pressure groups spend on judicial elections "can affect judicial decision-making across a broad range of cases." J. Shepherd & M. Kang, Skewed Justice 1 (2014), https://perma.cc/7PQD-LPWC (finding that a recent "explosion in spending on television attack advertisements . . . has made courts less likely to rule in favor of defendants in criminal appeals").

How does the electorate perceive outsized spending on judicial elections? Multiple surveys over the past 13 years indicate that voters overwhelmingly believe direct contributions to judges' campaigns have at least "some influence" on judicial decision making. . . .

"A State's decision to elect its judges does not require it to tolerate these risks." *Ante.* What may be true of happy families, L. Tolstoy, Anna Karenina 1 (R. Pevear and L. Volokhonsky trans. 2000) ("All happy families are alike"), or of roses, Gertrude Stein, Sacred Emily, in Geography and Plays 178, 187 (1922) (reprint 1968) ("Rose is a rose is a rose is a rose"), does not hold true in elections of every kind. States should not be put to the polar choices of either equating judicial elections to political elections, or else abandoning public participation in the selection of judges altogether. Instead, States should have leeway to "balance the constitutional interests in judicial integrity and free expression within the unique setting of an elected judiciary." *White* (GINSBURG, J., dissenting).

Justice SCALIA, with whom Justice THOMAS joins, dissenting.

An ethics canon adopted by the Florida Supreme Court bans a candidate in a judicial election from asking anyone, under any circumstances, for a contribution to his campaign. Faithful application of our precedents would have made short work of this wildly disproportionate restriction upon speech. Intent upon upholding the Canon, however, the Court flattens one settled First Amendment principle after another.

I

The first axiom of the First Amendment is this: As a general rule, the state has no power to ban speech on the basis of its content. One need not equate judges with politicians to see that this principle does not grow weaker merely because the censored speech is a judicial candidate's request for a campaign contribution. Our cases hold that speech enjoys the full protection of the First Amendment unless a widespread and longstanding tradition ratifies its regulation. *Brown.* No such tradition looms here. Georgia became the first State to elect its judges in 1812, and judicial elections had spread to a large majority of the States by the time of the Civil War. *White.* Yet there appears to have been no regulation of judicial candidates' speech throughout the 19th and early 20th centuries. . . . The American Bar Association first proposed ethics rules concerning speech of judicial candidates in 1924, but these rules did not achieve widespread adoption until after the Second World War.

Rules against soliciting campaign contributions arrived more recently still. The ABA first proposed a canon advising against it in 1972, and a canon prohibiting it only in 1990. Even now, 9 of the 39 States that elect judges allow judicial candidates to ask for campaign contributions. In the absence of any long-settled custom about judicial candidates' speech in general or their solicitations in particular, we have no basis for relaxing the rules that normally apply to laws that suppress speech because of content.

One likewise need not equate judges with politicians to see that the electoral setting calls for all the more vigilance in ensuring observance of the First Amendment. When a candidate asks someone for a campaign contribution, he tends (as the principal opinion acknowledges) also to talk about his qualifications for office and his views on public issues. This expression lies at the heart of what the First Amendment is meant to protect. In addition, banning candidates from asking for money personally "favors some candidates over others—incumbent judges (who benefit from their current status) over non-judicial candidates, the well-to-do (who may not need to raise any money at all) over lower-income candidates, and the well-connected (who have an army of potential fundraisers) over outsiders." *Carey v. Wolnitzek*, 614 F.3d 189, 204 (6th Cir. 2010). This danger of legislated (or judicially imposed) favoritism is the very reason the First Amendment exists.

Because Canon 7C(1) restricts fully protected speech on the basis of content, it presumptively violates the First Amendment. We may uphold it only if the State meets its burden of showing that the Canon survives strict scrutiny—that is to say, only if it shows that the Canon is narrowly tailored to serve a compelling interest. I do not for a moment question the Court's conclusion that States have different compelling interests when regulating judicial elections than when regulating political ones. Unlike a legislator, a judge must be impartial—without bias for or against any party or attorney who comes before him. I accept for the sake of argument that States have a compelling interest in ensuring that its judges are *seen* to be impartial. I will likewise assume that a judicial candidate's request to a litigant or attorney presents a danger of coercion that a political candidate's request to a constituent does not. But Canon 7C(1) does not narrowly target concerns about impartiality or its appearance; it applies even when the person asked for a financial contribution has no chance of ever appearing in the candidate's court. And Florida does not invoke concerns about coercion, presumably because the Canon bans solicitations regardless of whether their object is a lawyer, litigant, or other person vulnerable to judicial pressure. So Canon 7C(1) fails exacting scrutiny and infringes the First Amendment. This case should have been just that straightforward.

II

The Court concludes that Florida may prohibit personal solicitations by judicial candidates as a means of preserving "public confidence in the integrity of the judiciary." It purports to reach this destination by applying strict scrutiny, but it would be more accurate to say that it does so by applying the appearance of strict scrutiny.

A

The first sign that mischief is afoot comes when the Court describes Florida's compelling interest. The State must first identify its objective with precision before one can tell whether that interest is compelling and whether the speech restriction narrowly targets it. In *White*, for example, the Court did not allow a State to invoke hazy concerns about judicial impartiality in justification of an ethics rule against judicial candidates' announcing their positions on legal issues. The Court instead separately analyzed the State's concerns about judges' bias against parties, preconceptions on legal issues, and openmindedness, and explained why each concern (and each for a different reason) did not suffice to sustain the rule.

In stark contrast to *White,* the Court today relies on Florida's invocation of an ill-defined interest in "public confidence in judicial integrity." The Court at first suggests that "judicial integrity" involves the "ability to administer justice without fear or favor." As its opinion unfolds, however, today's concept of judicial integrity turns out to be "a mere thing of wax in the hands of the judiciary, which they may twist, and shape into any form they please." 12 The Works of Thomas Jefferson 137 (P. Ford ed. 1905). When the Court explains how solicitation undermines confidence in judicial integrity, integrity starts to sound like saintliness. It involves independence from any "*possible* temptation" that "*might* lead" the judge, "even unknowingly," to favor one party (emphasis added). When the Court turns to distinguishing in-person solicitation from solicitation by proxy, the any-possible-temptation standard no longer helps and thus drops out. The critical factors instead become the "pressure" a listener feels during a solicitation and the "appearance that the candidate will remember who says yes, and who says no." But when it comes time to explain Florida's decision to allow candidates to write thank-you notes, the "appearance that the candidate . . . remember[s] who says yes" gets nary a mention. And when the Court confronts Florida's decision to prohibit mass-mailed solicitations, concern about pressure fades away. More outrageous still, the Court at times molds the interest in the perception that judges have integrity into an interest in the perception that judges do not solicit — for example when it says, "all personal solicitations by judicial candidates create a public appearance that undermines confidence in the integrity of the judiciary; banning all personal solicitations by judicial candidates is narrowly tailored to address that concern." *Ante.* This is not strict scrutiny; it is sleight of hand.

B

The Court's twistifications have not come to an end; indeed, they are just beginning. In order to uphold Canon 7C(1) under strict scrutiny, Florida must do more than point to a vital public objective brooding overhead. The State must also meet a difficult burden of demonstrating that the speech restriction substantially advances the claimed objective. The State "bears the risk of uncertainty," so "ambiguous proof will not suffice." *Brown.* In an arresting illustration, this Court held that a law punishing lies about winning military decorations like the Congressional Medal of Honor failed exacting scrutiny, because the Government could not satisfy its "heavy burden" of proving that "the public's general perception of military awards is diluted by false claims." *United States v. Alvarez* (plurality opinion).

Now that we have a case about the public's perception of judicial honor rather than its perception of military honors, the Justices of this Court change the rules. The Court announces, on the basis of its "intuiti[on]," that allowing personal solicitations will make litigants worry that " 'judges' decisions may be motivated by the desire to repay campaign contributions.' " But this case is not about whether Yulee has the right to receive campaign contributions. It is about whether she has the right to *ask* for campaign contributions that Florida's statutory law already allows her to receive. Florida bears the burden of showing that banning *requests* for lawful contributions will improve public confidence in judges—not just a little bit, but significantly, because "the Government does not have a compelling interest in each marginal percentage point by which its goals are advanced." *Brown.*

Neither the Court nor the State identifies the slightest evidence that banning requests for contributions will substantially improve public trust in judges. Nor does common sense make this happy forecast obvious. The concept of judicial integrity "dates back at least eight centuries," and judicial elections in America date back more than two centuries—but rules against personal solicitations date back only to 1972. The peaceful coexistence of judicial elections and personal solicitations for most of our history calls into doubt any claim that allowing personal solicitations would imperil public faith in judges. Many States allow judicial candidates to ask for contributions even today, but nobody suggests that public confidence in judges fares worse in these jurisdictions than elsewhere. And in any event, if candidates' appeals for money are "characteristically intertwined" with discussion of qualifications and views on public issues (plurality opinion), how can the Court be so sure that the public will regard them as improprieties rather than as legitimate instances of campaigning? In the final analysis, Florida comes nowhere near making the convincing demonstration required by our cases that the speech restriction in this case substantially advances its objective.

C

But suppose we play along with the premise that prohibiting solicitations will significantly improve the public reputation of judges. Even then, Florida must show that the ban restricts no more speech than necessary to achieve the objective.

Canon 7C(1) falls miles short of satisfying this requirement. The Court seems to accept Florida's claim that solicitations erode public confidence by creating the perception that judges are selling justice to lawyers and litigants. Yet the Canon prohibits candidates from asking for money from *anybody*—even from someone who is neither lawyer nor litigant, even from someone who (because of recusal rules) cannot possibly appear before the candidate as lawyer or litigant. Yulee thus may not call up an old friend, a cousin, or even her parents to ask for a donation to her campaign. The State has not come up with a plausible explanation of how soliciting someone who has no chance of appearing in the candidate's court will diminish public confidence in judges.

No less important, Canon 7C(1) bans candidates from asking for contributions even in messages that do not target any listener in particular—mass-mailed letters, flyers posted on telephone poles, speeches to large gatherings, and Web sites addressed to the general public. Messages like these do not share the features that lead the Court to pronounce personal solicitations a menace to public confidence in the judiciary. Consider online solicitations. They avoid "the spectacle of lawyers or potential litigants directly handing over money to judicial candidates," *ante*. People who come across online solicitations do not feel "pressure" to comply with the request. Nor does the candidate's signature on the online solicitation suggest "that the candidate will remember who says yes, and who says no." Yet Canon 7C(1) prohibits these and similar solicitations anyway. This tailoring is as narrow as the Court's scrutiny is strict.

Perhaps sensing the fragility of the initial claim that *all* solicitations threaten public confidence in judges, the Court argues that "the lines Yulee asks [it] to draw are unworkable." That is a difficulty of the Court's own imagination. In reality, the Court could have chosen from a whole spectrum of workable rules. It could have held that States may regulate no more than solicitation of participants in pending cases, or solicitation of people who are likely to appear in the candidate's court, or even solicitation of any lawyer or litigant. And it could have ruled that candidates have the right to make fundraising appeals that are not directed to any particular listener (like requests in mass-mailed letters), or at least fundraising appeals plainly directed to the general public (like requests placed online). The Supreme Court of Florida has made similar accommodations in other settings. It allows sitting judges to solicit memberships in civic organizations if (among other things) the solicitee is not "likely ever to appear before the court on which the judge serves." Code of Judicial Conduct for the State of Florida 23 (2014). And it allows sitting judges to accept gifts if (among other things) "the donor is not a party or other person . . . whose interests have come or are likely to come before the judge." *Id.* It is not too much to ask that the State show election speech similar consideration.

The Court's accusation of unworkability also suffers from a bit of a pot-kettle problem. Consider the many real-world questions left open by today's decision. Does the First Amendment permit restricting a candidate's appearing at an event where somebody *else* asks for campaign funds on his behalf? Does it permit prohibiting the candidate's *family* from making personal solicitations? Does it allow prohibiting the candidate from participating in the creation of a Web site that solicits funds, even if the candidate's name does not appear next to the request? More broadly, could Florida ban thank-you notes to donors? Cap a candidate's campaign spending? Restrict independent spending by people other than the candidate? Ban independent spending by corporations? And how, by the way, are judges supposed to decide whether these measures promote public confidence in judicial integrity, when the Court does not even have a consistent theory about what it means by "judicial integrity"? For the Court to wring its hands about workability under these circumstances is more than one should have to bear.

D

Even if Florida could show that banning all personal appeals for campaign funds is necessary to protect public confidence in judicial integrity, the Court must overpower one last sentinel of free speech before it can uphold Canon 7C(1). Among its other functions, the First Amendment is a kind of Equal Protection Clause for ideas.

The state ordinarily may not regulate one message because it harms a government interest yet refuse to regulate other messages that impair the interest in a comparable way. . . .

The Court's decision disregards these principles. The Court tells us that "all personal solicitations by judicial candidates create a public appearance that undermines confidence in the integrity of the judiciary." But Canon 7C(1) does not restrict *all* personal solicitations; it restricts only personal solicitations related to campaigns. The part of the Canon challenged here prohibits personal pleas for "campaign funds," and the Canon elsewhere prohibits personal appeals to attorneys for "publicly stated support." Judicial Conduct Code 38. So although Canon 7C(1) prevents Yulee from asking a lawyer for a few dollars to help her buy campaign pamphlets, it does not prevent her asking the same lawyer for a personal loan, access to his law firm's luxury suite at the local football stadium, or even a donation to help her fight the Florida Bar's charges. What could possibly justify these distinctions? Surely the Court does not believe that requests for campaign favors erode public confidence in a way that requests for favors unrelated to elections do not. Could anyone say with a straight face that it looks *worse* for a candidate to say "please give my campaign $25" than to say "please give *me* $25"?

Fumbling around for a fig-leaf, the Court says that "the First Amendment imposes no freestanding 'underinclusiveness limitation.'" This analysis elides the distinction between selectivity on the basis of content and selectivity on other grounds. Because the First Amendment does not prohibit underinclusiveness as such, lawmakers may target a problem only at certain times or in certain places. Because the First Amendment *does* prohibit content discrimination as such, lawmakers may *not* target a problem only in certain messages. Explaining this distinction, we have said that the First Amendment would allow banning obscenity "only in certain media or markets" but would preclude banning "only that obscenity which includes offensive political messages." *R.A.V. v. St. Paul,* 505 U.S. 377, 387–88 (1992) (emphasis deleted). This case involves selectivity on the basis of content. The Florida Supreme Court has decided to eliminate the appearances associated with "personal appeals for money," when the appeals seek money for a campaign but not when the appeals seek money for other purposes. That distinction violates the First Amendment.

Even on the Court's own terms, Canon 7C(1) cannot stand. The Court concedes that "underinclusiveness can raise 'doubts about whether the government is in fact pursuing the interest it invokes.'" Canon 7C(1)'s scope suggests that it has nothing to do with the appearances created by judges' asking for money, and everything to do with hostility toward judicial campaigning. How else to explain the Florida Supreme Court's decision to ban *all* personal appeals for campaign funds (even when the solicitee could never appear before the candidate), but to tolerate appeals for other kinds of funds (even when the solicitee will surely appear before the candidate)? It should come as no surprise that the ABA, whose model rules the Florida Supreme Court followed when framing Canon 7C(1), opposes judicial elections — preferring instead a system in which (surprise!) a committee of lawyers proposes candidates from among whom the Governor must make his selection. *See White.*

The Court tries to strike a pose of neutrality between appointment and election of judges, but no one should be deceived. A Court that sees impropriety in a candidate's request for *any* contributions to his election campaign does not much like judicial selection by the people. One cannot have judicial elections without judicial campaigns, and judicial campaigns without funds for campaigning, and funds for campaigning without asking for them. When a society decides that its judges should be elected, it necessarily decides that selection by the people is more important than the oracular sanctity of judges, their immunity from the (shudder!) indignity of begging for funds, and their exemption from those shadows of impropriety that fall over the proletarian public officials who must run for office. A free society, accustomed to electing its rulers, does not much care whether the rulers operate through statute and executive order, or through judicial distortion of statute, executive order, and constitution. The prescription that judges be elected probably springs from the people's realization that their judges can become their rulers—and (it must be said) from just a deep-down feeling that members of the Third Branch will profit from a hearty helping of humble pie, and from a severe reduction of their great remove from the (ugh!) People. (It should not be thought that I myself harbor such irreverent and revolutionary feelings; but I think it likely—and year by year more likely—that those who favor the election of judges do so.) In any case, hostility to campaigning by judges entitles the people of Florida to amend their Constitution to replace judicial elections with the selection of judges by lawyers' committees; it does not entitle the Florida Supreme Court to adopt, or this Court to endorse, a rule of judicial conduct that abridges candidates' speech in the judicial elections that the Florida Constitution prescribes.

* * *

This Court has not been shy to enforce the First Amendment in recent Terms—even in cases that do not involve election speech. It has accorded robust protection to depictions of animal torture, sale of violent video games to children, and lies about having won military medals. Who would have thought that the same Court would today exert such heroic efforts to save so plain an abridgement of the freedom of speech? It is no great mystery what is going on here. The judges of this Court, like the judges of the Supreme Court of Florida who promulgated Canon 7C(1), evidently consider the preservation of public respect for the courts a policy objective of the highest order. So it is—but so too are preventing animal torture, protecting the innocence of children, and honoring valiant soldiers. The Court did not relax the Constitution's guarantee of freedom of speech when legislatures pursued those goals; it should not relax the guarantee when the Supreme Court of Florida pursues this one. The First Amendment is not abridged for the benefit of the Brotherhood of the Robe.

I respectfully dissent.

Justice KENNEDY, dissenting.

The dissenting opinion by Justice SCALIA gives a full and complete explanation of the reasons why the Court's opinion contradicts settled First Amendment principles. This separate dissent is written to underscore the irony in the Court's having concluded that the very First Amendment protections judges must enforce should be lessened when a judicial candidate's own speech is at issue. It is written to underscore, too, the irony in the Court's having weakened the rigors of the First Amendment in a case concerning elections, a paradigmatic forum for speech and a process intended to protect freedom in so many other manifestations....

Justice ALITO, dissenting.

I largely agree with what I view as the essential elements of the dissents filed by Justices SCALIA and KENNEDY. The Florida rule before us regulates speech that is part of the process of selecting those who wield the power of the State. Such speech lies at the heart of the protection provided by the First Amendment. The Florida rule regulates that speech based on content and must therefore satisfy strict scrutiny. This means that it must be narrowly tailored to further a compelling state interest. Florida has a compelling interest in making sure that its courts decide cases impartially and in accordance with the law and that its citizens have no good reason to lack confidence that its courts are performing their proper role. But the Florida rule is not narrowly tailored to serve that interest.

Indeed, this rule is about as narrowly tailored as a burlap bag. It applies to all solicitations made in the name of a candidate for judicial office—including, as was the case here, a mass mailing. It even applies to an ad in a newspaper. It applies to requests for contributions in any amount, and it applies even if the person solicited is not a lawyer, has never had any interest at stake in any case in the court in question, and has no prospect of ever having any interest at stake in any litigation in that court. If this rule can be characterized as narrowly tailored, then narrow tailoring has no meaning, and strict scrutiny, which is essential to the protection of free speech, is seriously impaired.

When petitioner sent out a form letter requesting campaign contributions, she was well within her First Amendment rights. The Florida Supreme Court violated the Constitution when it imposed a financial penalty and stained her record with a finding that she had engaged in unethical conduct. I would reverse the judgment of the Florida Supreme Court.

Notes and Questions

1. After *Williams-Yulee*, does strict scrutiny apply to review of the anti-solicitation rules? To other judicial conduct and speech rules? How does the Court define the state interests that it deems sufficiently compelling to satisfy strict scrutiny?

In *Wolfson v. Concannon*, 811 F.3d 1176 (9th Cir. 2016) (en banc), cert. denied 137 S. Ct. 296 (2016), the Ninth Circuit, sitting en banc, agreed with the *Williams-Yulee* plurality to apply strict scrutiny to review of three Arizona judicial conduct rules. It unanimously upheld a ban on the personal solicitation of campaign funds by judicial candidates as well as rules prohibiting judicial candidates from raising funds for, or publicly endorsing, other candidates. The court held these laws were justified by the state's compelling interest in promoting judicial impartiality.

Judge Berzon, concurring, took issue with nature of the state's compelling interest:

> The main opinion supports *all three* of Arizona's challenged restrictions on judicial candidates' behavior during judicial election campaigns on the basis of the same governmental interest—judicial impartiality. But three different species of speech regulation of judicial candidates are here at issue, not one. And while one of the regulations—the ban on personal solicitation—is closely related to the restriction considered in *Williams-Yulee,* two—the bans on endorsements and campaigning for nonjudicial candidates and causes—are quite different. As to the latter two bans, I am not at all sure that the governmental interest in preventing biased judicial decisionmaking survives the compelling interest/narrowly tailored standard we are required to apply. I am convinced, however, that there is a societal interest underlying those two restrictions—maintaining an independent judiciary—that more accurately captures the reasons to limit judicial candidates' endorsements and campaigning activity, and that does meet the compelling interest/narrow tailoring requirements.

How, if at all, is the interest in maintaining an independent judiciary different from the interest in judicial impartiality? Does *Williams-Yulee* recognize the former interest as compelling or only the latter?

2. Declaring that "*Williams-Yulee* marked a palpable change in the approach to state regulations of judicial-campaign speech—a change perhaps best exemplified by our unanimous en banc decision in *Wolfson,*" a unanimous Ninth Circuit panel in *French v. Jones*, 876 F.3d 1228, 1235 (9th Cir. 2017), cert. denied, 138 S. Ct. 1598 (2018), rejected a judicial candidate's challenge to a Montana rule barring such candidates from seeking, accepting, or using political endorsements in their campaigns. (Montana did not bar political parties from endorsing those candidates.) Applying post-*Williams-Yulee* strict scrutiny, the court held that two compelling interests justified Montana's rule:

> The first is an interest in both actual and perceived judicial impartiality. . . . [The rule] furthers a second interest that might be more compelling still: a related but distinct interest in a structurally independent judiciary. See *Wolfson*, 811 F.3d at 1186–88 (Berzon, J., concurring). If judicial candidates, including sitting judges running for reelection, regularly solicit and use endorsements from political parties, the public might view the judiciary as indebted to, dependent on, and in the end not different from the political branches.

French, 876 F.3d at 1237–38. The court rejected the candidate's under-inclusiveness and overbreadth arguments in light of *Williams-Yulee* and *Wolfson*, suggesting they would have fared better if analyzed solely under *White*. The Supreme Court declined to hear the case. 138 S. Ct. 1598 (2018).

Along similar lines, the Sixth Circuit rejected First Amendment and Equal Protection challenges to six provisions of the Ohio Code of Judicial conduct. These provisions included those: barring judicial candidates from making speeches on behalf of a political party or another candidate; endorsing or opposing a candidate for another public office; with three exceptions, preventing them from personally soliciting campaign contributions; and limiting the window for fundraising to 120 days before a primary and 120 days after a general election. Citing *Williams-Yulee*, the court applied strict scrutiny in upholding the provisions. *Platt v. Bd. of Comm'rs on Griev s. & Discipline*, 894 F.3d 235 (6th Cir. 2018).

A federal district court in Alabama tentatively barred enforcement of another judicial canon in *Parker v. Judicial Inquiry Commission of Alabama*, 295 F. Supp. 3d 1292 (M.D. Ala. 2018). A member of the Alabama Supreme Court and candidate for that court's chief justice challenged an Alabama rule which provided, among other things, that "a judge should abstain from public comment about a pending or impending proceeding in any court." Ala. Canon of Judicial Ethics 3A(6). A complaint had been filed against the state justice for making comments on a talk radio program about legal questions then pending before his court concerning the effects of the U.S. Supreme Court's decision on same-sex marriage in *Obergefell v. Hodges*, 576 U.S. 644 (2015).

Citing the Ninth Circuit's claim in *French* that *Williams-Yulee* significantly changed the constitutional calculus, the Alabama Court said *Williams-Yulee* was not a "reversal" of *White* and that *White* and *Williams-Yulee*, while in tension, must be read together. *Parker*, 295 F. Supp. 3d at 1301–02. The court agreed the government had a compelling interest in preserving public confidence in the integrity and impartiality of the state's judiciary. But it found the Alabama rule impermissibly over-inclusive and overbroad because the rule barred discussion of pending and impending judicial proceedings in any court, and it was not clear that discussion of issues pending in other courts would affect public confidence in the Alabama judiciary.

The court issued a preliminary injunction enjoining Alabama from enforcing the rule "to the extent that it proscribes public comment by a judge that cannot reasonably be expected to affect the outcome or impair the fairness of a proceeding in Alabama." Doesn't the federal court order raise its own vagueness problems? Can a judicial candidate in Alabama speak about a pending U.S. Supreme Court case on LGBT rights and religious liberties, when cases involving that issue could well be before Alabama courts in the near future?

Meanwhile, the Third Circuit concluded that a provision of the Delaware Constitution requiring that judicial candidates be members of the Democratic or Republican parties violated the First Amendment rights of a candidate who was neither. The Supreme Court ducked the issue in *Carney v. Adams*, 141 S. Ct. 493 (2020), holding that the candidate challenging the law lacked standing because he did not show he was ready and able to run for the office in the future.

3. The *Williams-Yulee* majority reads *White* as recognizing that judicial elections are different from ordinary elections. Did *White* so recognize? If not, doesn't *William-Yulee* do so?

4. The majority does not decide whether other rules, such as limits on spending in judicial campaigns can satisfy the strict scrutiny standard. Consider this question after reading the campaign finance materials later in this book.

5. In the next case, *Caperton v. Massey*, the vote was also 5-4, with Justice Kennedy in the majority holding that due process requires recusal of a judge in a case in which one of the litigants was a major funder of a campaign to get that judge elected. Chief Justice Roberts strongly dissented on First Amendment grounds. In this case, the two Justices' roles were reversed. What explains their divergent positions in these two cases? Richard L. Hasen, *Election Law's Path in the Roberts Court's First Decade: A Sharp Right Turn but with Speed Bumps and Surprising Twists*, 68 Stanford Law Review 1597 (2016), suggests that "Chief Justice Roberts, perhaps for institutional reasons or a different view of the problems with an elected judiciary, broke with his conservative colleagues in *Williams-Yulee*."

C. Judicial Elections and Campaign Money: Limits or Recusal?

As we saw in the last section, some judicial conduct codes bar judicial candidates from personal solicitation of campaign contributions to their judicial campaigns. This rule is but one of many campaign finance rules which have been proposed, or implemented in judicial elections, including contribution limitations, public financing of judicial campaigns, and proposals to keep the identity of judicial campaign contributors secret from judicial candidates. In addition, until recently some have suggested imposition of spending limits in judicial campaigns, such as limits on corporate spending in judicial elections.

The spending limit proposals came to a grinding halt after the Supreme Court's decision in *Citizens United v. Federal Election Commission*, described in detail in Chapter 13. That case held that spending limits violate the First Amendment in any campaign. The Court had an opportunity to distinguish spending limits in judicial campaigns, but it declined to do so.

What is the likely effect of *Citizens United* on judicial campaigns? Consider Sample, *Retention Elections 2.010*, *supra*, at 391–93:

> The dire predictions regarding *Citizens United*'s impact on judicial elections benefit from a contextual background that almost assures their infallibility—spending in judicial elections seems as likely to *decrease* over the near term as does gravity over the same period. A recent empirical study of campaign spending in judicial elections found that "[f]rom

2000–09, Supreme Court candidates raised $206.9 million nationally, more than double the $83.3 million raised from 1990–1999 (by comparison, the consumer price index rose only 25% from 2000–2009)." The overall national aggregate increase may actually understate the degree to which, on a state-by-state basis, expensive court campaigns have become the norm, rather than the exception. As the study notes, "[d]uring the earlier decade, 26 Supreme Court campaigns raised $1 million or more, and all but two came from three states: Alabama, Pennsylvania and Texas. In 2000–09, by contrast, there were 66 '"million dollar'" campaigns, in a dozen states."

However, these figures tell only a partial story, and one that is becoming decreasingly complete with each passing election cycle. This is because the figures account only for direct contributions to court campaigns. Yet, even the most conservative measurements of television advertising—by far the biggest driver of campaign costs—reflect that "[s]pecial-interest groups and party organizations accounted for . . . more than 40 percent of the estimated TV air time purchases in 2000–09." In 2008, special-interest groups and political parties accounted for fifty-two percent of all TV spending nationally—the first time that noncandidate groups outspent the candidates on the ballot.

A substantial portion of the noncandidate spending is being fueled by a concentrated few, who are investing in court races in a disproportionately large manner. In the prior decade, the top five spenders in twenty-nine state high court campaigns in the nation's ten costliest judicial election states—a total of 145—spent an average of $473,000 each. The result is that "a large number of justices in those states owe their elections to a few key benefactors." . . . .

The practical effect of [*Citizens United*] as applied to judicial races is that of a one-way ratchet—eliminating the general treasury bans where they existed and maintaining the status quo where they did not. As such, it is distinctly possible that some multistate corporations, faced with a complex and constantly changing patchwork of inconsistent state-by-state regulation, and who may have previously considered substantial spending in judicial races to be an inefficient proposition, will now decide that it is in their interests to take advantage of the across-the-board simplicity of a deregulated, post-*Citizens United* landscape. Viewed from the perspective of the general counsel's office in a multistate corporation, the clarity and uniformity following *Citizens United* surely makes substantial engagement in judicial election spending, at the very least, less of a legal and logistical burden than it was prior to the decision. If that perspective on reduced burdens holds sway, then *Citizens United* will increase corporate judicial election expenditures even in states where such expenditures were not legally curtailed in the past. In such a scenario, despite an in-state *de jure* status quo, court races will be dramatically different *de facto*. And the dire predictions will prove correct.

The data cited by Sample on contributions to judicial candidates indeed show a rise decade over decade, but since 2000 the pattern seems to be one of stasis, with periodic bouts of large spending activity, especially in states with partisan elections where partisan control of the state Supreme Court is at stake. Out-of-state money flows through independent groups into the most important and contested races, especially when there is a highly salient issue on which to run the campaign. Is this problem of punctuated, intense campaigns a greater or lesser danger to judicial independence than an overall increase in the amounts raised in judicial campaigns?

With judicial speech codes of uncertain constitutionality, and with limits on judicial campaign spending likely foreclosed by the First Amendment (for reasons made clear in later chapters), critics of judicial elections have argued for stronger recusal rules. They received support for this position in this case decided by the Supreme Court.

Caperton v. Massey

556 U.S. 868 (2009)

JUSTICE KENNEDY delivered the opinion of the Court.

In this case the Supreme Court of Appeals of West Virginia reversed a trial court judgment, which had entered a jury verdict of $50 million. Five justices heard the case, and the vote to reverse was 3 to 2. The question presented is whether the Due Process Clause of the Fourteenth Amendment was violated when one of the justices in the majority denied a recusal motion. The basis for the motion was that the justice had received campaign contributions in an extraordinary amount from, and through the efforts of, the board chairman and principal officer of the corporation found liable for the damages.

Under our precedents there are objective standards that require recusal when "the probability of actual bias on the part of the judge or decisionmaker is too high to be constitutionally tolerable." *Withrow v. Larkin*, 421 U.S. 35, 45 (1975). Applying those precedents, we find that, in all the circumstances of this case, due process requires recusal.

I

In August 2002 a West Virginia jury returned a verdict that found respondents A.T. Massey Coal Co. and its affiliates (hereinafter Massey) liable for fraudulent misrepresentation, concealment, and tortious interference with existing contractual relations. The jury awarded petitioners Hugh Caperton, Harman Development Corp., Harman Mining Corp., and Sovereign Coal Sales (hereinafter Caperton) the sum of $50 million in compensatory and punitive damages.

In June 2004 the state trial court denied Massey's post-trial motions challenging the verdict and the damages award, finding that Massey "intentionally acted in utter disregard of [Caperton's] rights and ultimately destroyed [Caperton's] businesses because, after conducting cost-benefit analyses, [Massey] concluded it was in its financial interest to do so." In March 2005 the trial court denied Massey's motion for judgment as a matter of law.

Don Blankenship is Massey's chairman, chief executive officer, and president. After the verdict but before the appeal, West Virginia held its 2004 judicial elections. Knowing the Supreme Court of Appeals of West Virginia would consider the appeal in the case, Blankenship decided to support an attorney who sought to replace Justice McGraw. Justice McGraw was a candidate for reelection to that court. The attorney who sought to replace him was Brent Benjamin.

In addition to contributing the $1,000 statutory maximum to Benjamin's campaign committee, Blankenship donated almost $2.5 million to "And For The Sake Of The Kids," a political organization formed under 2 U.S.C. § 527. The § 527 organization opposed McGraw and supported Benjamin. Blankenship's donations accounted for more than two-thirds of the total funds it raised. This was not all. Blankenship spent, in addition, just over $500,000 on independent expenditures—for direct mailings and letters soliciting donations as well as television and newspaper advertisements—"'to support ... Brent Benjamin.'" (quoting Blankenship's state campaign financial disclosure filings).

To provide some perspective, Blankenship's $3 million in contributions were more than the total amount spent by all other Benjamin supporters and three times the amount spent by Benjamin's own committee. Caperton contends that Blankenship spent $1 million more than the total amount spent by the campaign committees of both candidates combined.

Benjamin won. He received 382,036 votes (53.3%), and McGraw received 334,301 votes (46.7%).

In October 2005, before Massey filed its petition for appeal in West Virginia's highest court, Caperton moved to disqualify now-Justice Benjamin under the Due Process Clause and the West Virginia Code of Judicial Conduct, based on the conflict caused by Blankenship's campaign involvement. Justice Benjamin denied the motion in April 2006. He indicated that he "carefully considered the bases and accompanying exhibits proffered by the movants." But he found "no objective information ... to show that this Justice has a bias for or against any litigant, that this Justice has prejudged the matters which comprise this litigation, or that this Justice will be anything but fair and impartial." In December 2006 Massey filed its petition for appeal to challenge the adverse jury verdict. The West Virginia Supreme Court of Appeals granted review.

In November 2007 that court reversed the $50 million verdict against Massey. The majority opinion, authored by then-Chief Justice Davis and joined by Justices Benjamin and Maynard, found that "Massey's conduct warranted the type of judgment rendered in this case." It reversed, nevertheless, based on two independent grounds—first, that a forum-selection clause contained in a contract to which Massey was not a party barred the suit in West Virginia, and, second, that res judicata barred the suit due to an out-of-state judgment to which Massey was not a party. Justice Starcher dissented, stating that the "majority's opinion is morally and legally wrong." Justice Albright also dissented, accusing the majority of "misapplying the law and introducing sweeping 'new law' into our jurisprudence that may well come back to haunt us."

Caperton sought rehearing, and the parties moved for disqualification of three of the five justices who decided the appeal. Photos had surfaced of Justice Maynard vacationing with Blankenship in the French Riviera while the case was pending. Justice Maynard granted Caperton's recusal motion. On the other side Justice Starcher granted Massey's recusal motion, apparently based on his public criticism of Blankenship's role in the 2004 elections. In his recusal memorandum Justice Starcher urged Justice Benjamin to recuse himself as well. He noted that "Blankenship's bestowal of his personal wealth, political tactics, and 'friendship' have created a cancer in the affairs of this Court." Justice Benjamin declined Justice Starcher's suggestion and denied Caperton's recusal motion.

The court granted rehearing. Justice Benjamin, now in the capacity of acting chief justice, selected Judges Cookman and Fox to replace the recused justices. Caperton moved a third time for disqualification, arguing that Justice Benjamin had failed to apply the correct standard under West Virginia law—*i.e.,* whether "a reasonable and prudent person, knowing these objective facts, would harbor doubts about Justice Benjamin's ability to be fair and impartial." Caperton also included the results of a public opinion poll, which indicated that over 67% of West Virginians doubted Justice Benjamin would be fair and impartial. Justice Benjamin again refused to withdraw, noting that the "push poll" was "neither credible nor sufficiently reliable to serve as the basis for an elected judge's disqualification."

In April 2008 a divided court again reversed the jury verdict, and again it was a 3-to-2 decision. Justice Davis filed a modified version of his prior opinion, repeating the two earlier holdings. She was joined by Justice Benjamin and Judge Fox. Justice Albright, joined by Judge Cookman, dissented: "Not only is the majority opinion unsupported by the facts and existing case law, but it is also fundamentally unfair. Sadly, justice was neither honored nor served by the majority." The dissent also noted "genuine due process implications arising under federal law" with respect to Justice Benjamin's failure to recuse himself.

Four months later—a month after the petition for writ of certiorari was filed in this Court—Justice Benjamin filed a concurring opinion. He defended the merits of the majority opinion as well as his decision not to recuse. He rejected Caperton's challenge to his participation in the case under both the Due Process Clause and West Virginia law. Justice Benjamin reiterated that he had no "'direct, personal, substantial, pecuniary interest' in this case.'" Adopting "a standard merely of 'appearances,'" he concluded, "seems little more than an invitation to subject West Virginia's justice system to the vagaries of the day—a framework in which predictability and stability yield to supposition, innuendo, half-truths, and partisan manipulations."

We granted certiorari.

II

[Justice Kennedy reviewed existing Supreme Court precedent on when the constitutional guarantee of due process mandates judicial recusal. "The early and leading case on the subject is *Tumey v. Ohio*, 237 U.S. 510 (1927).... The *Tumey* Court concluded that the Due Process Clause incorporated the common-law rule that a judge must recuse himself when he has 'a direct, personal, substantial, pecuniary interest' in a case. This rule reflects the maxim that '[n]o man is allowed to be a judge in his own cause; because his interest would certainly bias his judgment, and, not improbably, corrupt his integrity.' The Federalist No. 10, p. 59 (J. Cooke ed.1961) (J. Madison); see Frank, Disqualification of Judges, 56 Yale L.J. 605, 611–612 (1947) (same)." Justice Kennedy then reviewed cases in which the Court held there was a due process problem created by judges (or others charged with a judicial-function) with a financial interest, either personal or for the benefit of a local government, in the outcome of the litigation. He also described criminal contempt recusal cases in which "a judge had no pecuniary interest in the case but was challenged because of a conflict arising from his participation in an earlier proceeding.... This Court set aside the convictions [of those moving for judicial recusal] on grounds that the judge had a conflict of interest at the trial stage because of his earlier participation followed by his decision to charge them."]

III

Based on the principles described in these cases we turn to the issue before us. This problem arises in the context of judicial elections, a framework not presented in the precedents we have reviewed and discussed.

Caperton contends that Blankenship's pivotal role in getting Justice Benjamin elected created a constitutionally intolerable probability of actual bias. Though not a bribe or criminal influence, Justice Benjamin would nevertheless feel a debt of gratitude to Blankenship for his extraordinary efforts to get him elected. That temptation, Caperton claims, is as strong and inherent in human nature as was the conflict the Court confronted in [the earlier recusal cases in which] a mayor-judge (or the city) benefited financially from a defendant's conviction, as well as the conflict... when a judge was the object of a defendant's contempt.

Justice Benjamin was careful to address the recusal motions and explain his reasons why, on his view of the controlling standard, disqualification was not in order. In four separate opinions issued during the course of the appeal, he explained why no actual bias had been established. He found no basis for recusal because Caperton failed to provide "objective evidence" or "objective information," but merely "subjective belief" of bias. Nor could anyone "point to any actual conduct or activity on [his] part which could be termed 'improper.'" In other words, based on the facts presented by Caperton, Justice Benjamin conducted a probing search into his actual motives and inclinations; and he found none to be improper. We do not question his subjective findings of impartiality and propriety. Nor do we determine whether there was actual bias.

Following accepted principles of our legal tradition respecting the proper performance of judicial functions, judges often inquire into their subjective motives and purposes in the ordinary course of deciding a case. This does not mean the inquiry is a simple one. "The work of deciding cases goes on every day in hundreds of courts throughout the land. Any judge, one might suppose, would find it easy to describe the process which he had followed a thousand times and more. Nothing could be farther from the truth." B. Cardozo, The Nature of the Judicial Process 9 (1921).

The judge inquires into reasons that seem to be leading to a particular result. Precedent and *stare decisis* and the text and purpose of the law and the Constitution; logic and scholarship and experience and common sense; and fairness and disinterest and neutrality are among the factors at work. To bring coherence to the process, and to seek respect for the resulting judgment, judges often explain the reasons for their conclusions and rulings. There are instances when the introspection that often attends this process may reveal that what the judge had assumed to be a proper, controlling factor is not the real one at work. If the judge discovers that some personal bias or improper consideration seems to be the actuating cause of the decision or to be an influence so difficult to dispel that there is a real possibility of undermining neutrality, the judge may think it necessary to consider withdrawing from the case.

The difficulties of inquiring into actual bias, and the fact that the inquiry is often a private one, simply underscore the need for objective rules. Otherwise there may be no adequate protection against a judge who simply misreads or misapprehends the real motives at work in deciding the case. The judge's own inquiry into actual bias, then, is not one that the law can easily superintend or review, though actual bias, if disclosed, no doubt would be grounds for appropriate relief. In lieu of exclusive reliance on that personal inquiry, or on appellate review of the judge's determination respecting actual bias, the Due Process Clause has been implemented by objective standards that do not require proof of actual bias. In defining these standards the Court has asked whether, "under a realistic appraisal of psychological tendencies and human weakness," the interest "poses such a risk of actual bias or prejudgment that the practice must be forbidden if the guarantee of due process is to be adequately implemented." *Withrow*.

We turn to the influence at issue in this case. Not every campaign contribution by a litigant or attorney creates a probability of bias that requires a judge's recusal, but this is an exceptional case. We conclude that there is a serious risk of actual bias — based on objective and reasonable perceptions — when a person with a personal stake in a particular case had a significant and disproportionate influence in placing the judge on the case by raising funds or directing the judge's election campaign when the case was pending or imminent. The inquiry centers on the contribution's relative size in comparison to the total amount of money contributed to the campaign, the total amount spent in the election, and the apparent effect such contribution had on the outcome of the election.

Applying this principle, we conclude that Blankenship's campaign efforts had a significant and disproportionate influence in placing Justice Benjamin on the case. Blankenship contributed some $3 million to unseat the incumbent and replace him with Benjamin. His contributions eclipsed the total amount spent by all other Benjamin supporters and exceeded by 300% the amount spent by Benjamin's campaign committee. Caperton claims Blankenship spent $1 million more than the total amount spent by the campaign committees of both candidates combined.

Massey responds that Blankenship's support, while significant, did not cause Benjamin's victory. In the end the people of West Virginia elected him, and they did so based on many reasons other than Blankenship's efforts. Massey points out that every major state newspaper, but one, endorsed Benjamin. It also contends that then-Justice McGraw cost himself the election by giving a speech during the campaign, a speech the opposition seized upon for its own advantage.

Justice Benjamin raised similar arguments. . . .

Whether Blankenship's campaign contributions were a necessary and sufficient cause of Benjamin's victory is not the proper inquiry. Much like determining whether a judge is actually biased, proving what ultimately drives the electorate to choose a particular candidate is a difficult endeavor, not likely to lend itself to a certain conclusion. This is particularly true where, as here, there is no procedure for judicial factfinding and the sole trier of fact is the one accused of bias. Due process requires an objective inquiry into whether the contributor's influence on the election under all the circumstances "would offer a possible temptation to the average . . . judge to . . . lead him not to hold the balance nice, clear and true." *Tumey.* Blankenship's campaign contributions — in comparison to the total amount contributed to the campaign, as well as the total amount spent in the election — had a significant and disproportionate influence on the electoral outcome. And the risk that Blankenship's influence engendered actual bias is sufficiently substantial that it "must be forbidden if the guarantee of due process is to be adequately implemented." *Withrow.*

The temporal relationship between the campaign contributions, the justice's election, and the pendency of the case is also critical. It was reasonably foreseeable, when the campaign contributions were made, that the pending case would be before the newly elected justice. The $50 million adverse jury verdict had been entered before the election, and the Supreme Court of Appeals was the next step once the state trial court dealt with post-trial motions. So it became at once apparent that, absent recusal, Justice Benjamin would review a judgment that cost his biggest donor's company $50 million. Although there is no allegation of a *quid pro quo* agreement, the fact remains that Blankenship's extraordinary contributions were made at a time when he had a vested stake in the outcome. Just as no man is allowed to be a judge in his own cause, similar fears of bias can arise when — without the consent of the other parties — a man chooses the judge in his own cause. And applying this principle to the judicial election process, there was here a serious, objective risk of actual bias that required Justice Benjamin's recusal.

Justice Benjamin did undertake an extensive search for actual bias. But, as we have indicated, that is just one step in the judicial process; objective standards may also require recusal whether or not actual bias exists or can be proved. Due process "may sometimes bar trial by judges who have no actual bias and who would do their very best to weigh the scales of justice equally between contending parties." *In re Murchison*, 349 U.S. 133, 136 (1955). The failure to consider objective standards requiring recusal is not consistent with the imperatives of due process. We find that Blankenship's significant and disproportionate influence—coupled with the temporal relationship between the election and the pending case—"offer a possible temptation to the average . . . judge to . . . lead him not to hold the balance nice, clear and true." [quoting cases quoting *Tumey*]. On these extreme facts the probability of actual bias rises to an unconstitutional level.

IV

Our decision today addresses an extraordinary situation where the Constitution requires recusal. Massey and its *amici* predict that various adverse consequences will follow from recognizing a constitutional violation here-ranging from a flood of recusal motions to unnecessary interference with judicial elections. We disagree. The facts now before us are extreme by any measure. The parties point to no other instance involving judicial campaign contributions that presents a potential for bias comparable to the circumstances in this case.

It is true that extreme cases often test the bounds of established legal principles, and sometimes no administrable standard may be available to address the perceived wrong. But it is also true that extreme cases are more likely to cross constitutional limits, requiring this Court's intervention and formulation of objective standards. This is particularly true when due process is violated. . . .

This Court's recusal cases are illustrative. . . . In this case we do nothing more than what the Court has done before. . . .

One must also take into account the judicial reforms the States have implemented to eliminate even the appearance of partiality. Almost every State—West Virginia included—has adopted the American Bar Association's objective standard: "A judge shall avoid impropriety and the appearance of impropriety." ABA Annotated Model Code of Judicial Conduct, Canon 2 (2004). The ABA Model Code's test for appearance of impropriety is "whether the conduct would create in reasonable minds a perception that the judge's ability to carry out judicial responsibilities with integrity, impartiality and competence is impaired." Canon 2A, Commentary.

The West Virginia Code of Judicial Conduct also requires a judge to "disqualify himself or herself in a proceeding in which the judge's impartiality might reasonably be questioned." Canon 3E(1); see also 28 U.S.C. § 455(a) ("Any justice, judge, or magistrate judge of the United States shall disqualify himself in any proceeding in which his impartiality might reasonably be questioned"). . . .

These codes of conduct serve to maintain the integrity of the judiciary and the rule of law. The Conference of the Chief Justices has underscored that the codes are "[t]he principal safeguard against judicial campaign abuses" that threaten to imperil "public confidence in the fairness and integrity of the nation's elected judges." Brief for Conference of Chief Justices as *Amicus Curiae*. This is a vital state interest:

"Courts, in our system, elaborate principles of law in the course of resolving disputes. The power and the prerogative of a court to perform this function rest, in the end, upon the respect accorded to its judgments. The citizen's respect for judgments depends in turn upon the issuing court's absolute probity. Judicial integrity is, in consequence, a state interest of the highest order." *White* (KENNEDY. J., concurring).

It is for this reason that States may choose to "adopt recusal standards more rigorous than due process requires." *Id.* see also *Bracy v. Gramley*, 520 U.S. 899, 904 (1997) (distinguishing the "constitutional floor" from the ceiling set "by common law, statute, or the professional standards of the bench and bar").

"The Due Process Clause demarks only the outer boundaries of judicial disqualifications. Congress and the states, of course, remain free to impose more rigorous standards for judicial disqualification than those we find mandated here today." *Aetna Life Ins. Co. v. Lavoie*, 475 U.S. 813, 828 (1986). Because the codes of judicial conduct provide more protection than due process requires, most disputes over disqualification will be resolved without resort to the Constitution. Application of the constitutional standard implicated in this case will thus be confined to rare instances.

* * *

The judgment of the Supreme Court of Appeals of West Virginia is reversed, and the case is remanded for further proceedings not inconsistent with this opinion.

It is so ordered.

Chief Justice ROBERTS, with whom Justice SCALIA, Justice THOMAS, and Justice ALITO join, dissenting.

I, of course, share the majority's sincere concerns about the need to maintain a fair, independent, and impartial judiciary—and one that appears to be such. But I fear that the Court's decision will undermine rather than promote these values.

Until today, we have recognized exactly two situations in which the Federal Due Process Clause requires disqualification of a judge: when the judge has a financial interest in the outcome of the case, and when the judge is trying a defendant for certain criminal contempts. Vaguer notions of bias or the appearance of bias were never a basis for disqualification, either at common law or under our constitutional precedents. Those issues were instead addressed by legislation or court rules.

Today, however, the Court enlists the Due Process Clause to overturn a judge's failure to recuse because of a "probability of bias." Unlike the established grounds for disqualification, a "probability of bias" cannot be defined in any limited way. The Court's new "rule" provides no guidance to judges and litigants about when recusal will be constitutionally required. This will inevitably lead to an increase in allegations that judges are biased, however groundless those charges may be. The end result will do far more to erode public confidence in judicial impartiality than an isolated failure to recuse in a particular case. . . .

II

In departing from this clear line between when recusal is constitutionally required and when it is not, the majority repeatedly emphasizes the need for an "objective" standard. The majority's analysis is "objective" in that it does not inquire into Justice Benjamin's motives or decisionmaking process. But the standard the majority articulates — "probability of bias" — fails to provide clear, workable guidance for future cases. At the most basic level, it is unclear whether the new probability of bias standard is somehow limited to financial support in judicial elections, or applies to judicial recusal questions more generally.

But there are other fundamental questions as well. With little help from the majority, courts will now have to determine:

1. How much money is too much money? What level of contribution or expenditure gives rise to a "probability of bias"?

2. How do we determine whether a given expenditure is "disproportionate"? Disproportionate *to what*?

3. Are independent, non-coordinated expenditures treated the same as direct contributions to a candidate's campaign? What about contributions to independent outside groups supporting a candidate?

4. Does it matter whether the litigant has contributed to other candidates or made large expenditures in connection with other elections?

5. Does the amount at issue in the case matter? What if this case were an employment dispute with only $10,000 at stake? What if the plaintiffs only sought non-monetary relief such as an injunction or declaratory judgment?

6. Does the analysis change depending on whether the judge whose disqualification is sought sits on a trial court, appeals court, or state supreme court?

7. How long does the probability of bias last? Does the probability of bias diminish over time as the election recedes? Does it matter whether the judge plans to run for reelection?

8. What if the "disproportionately" large expenditure is made by an industry association, trade union, physicians' group, or the plaintiffs' bar? Must the judge recuse in all cases that affect the association's interests? Must the judge recuse in all cases in which a party or lawyer is a member of that group? Does it matter how much the litigant contributed to the association?

9. What if the case involves a social or ideological issue rather than a financial one? Must a judge recuse from cases involving, say, abortion rights if he has received "disproportionate" support from individuals who

feel strongly about either side of that issue? If the supporter wants to help elect judges who are "tough on crime," must the judge recuse in all criminal cases?

10. What if the candidate draws "disproportionate" support from a particular racial, religious, ethnic, or other group, and the case involves an issue of particular importance to that group?

11. What if the supporter is not a party to the pending or imminent case, but his interests will be affected by the decision? Does the Court's analysis apply if the supporter "chooses the judge" not in *his* case, but in someone else's?

12. What if the case implicates a regulatory issue that is of great importance to the party making the expenditures, even though he has no direct financial interest in the outcome (*e.g.*, a facial challenge to an agency rulemaking or a suit seeking to limit an agency's jurisdiction)?

13. Must the judge's vote be outcome determinative in order for his nonrecusal to constitute a due process violation?

14. Does the due process analysis consider the underlying merits of the suit? Does it matter whether the decision is clearly right (or wrong) as a matter of state law?

15. What if a lower court decision in favor of the supporter is affirmed on the merits on appeal, by a panel with no "debt of gratitude" to the supporter? Does that "moot" the due process claim?

16. What if the judge voted against the supporter in many other cases?

17. What if the judge disagrees with the supporter's message or tactics? What if the judge expressly *disclaims* the support of this person?

18. Should we assume that elected judges feel a "debt of hostility" towards major *opponents* of their candidacies? Must the judge recuse in cases involving individuals or groups who spent large amounts of money trying unsuccessfully to defeat him?

19. If there is independent review of a judge's recusal decision, *e.g.*, by a panel of other judges, does this completely foreclose a due process claim?

20. Does a debt of gratitude for endorsements by newspapers, interest groups, politicians, or celebrities also give rise to a constitutionally unacceptable probability of bias? How would we measure whether such support is disproportionate?

21. Does close personal friendship between a judge and a party or lawyer now give rise to a probability of bias?

22. Does it matter whether the campaign expenditures come from a party or the party's attorney? If from a lawyer, must the judge recuse in every case involving that attorney?

23. Does what is unconstitutional vary from State to State? What if particular States have a history of expensive judicial elections?

24. Under the majority's "objective" test, do we analyze the due process issue through the lens of a reasonable person, a reasonable lawyer, or a reasonable judge?

25. What role does causation play in this analysis? The Court sends conflicting signals on this point. The majority asserts that "[w]hether Blankenship's campaign contributions were a necessary and sufficient cause of Benjamin's victory is not the proper inquiry." But elsewhere in the opinion, the majority considers "the apparent effect such contribution had on the outcome of the election," and whether the litigant has been able to "choos[e] the judge in his own cause." If causation is a pertinent factor, how do we know whether the contribution or expenditure had any effect on the outcome of the election? What if the judge won in a landslide? What if the judge won primarily because of his opponent's missteps?

26. Is the due process analysis less probing for incumbent judges—who typically have a great advantage in elections—than for challengers?

27. How final must the pending case be with respect to the contributor's interest? What if, for example, the only issue on appeal is whether the court should certify a class of plaintiffs? Is recusal required just as if the issue in the pending case were ultimate liability?

28. Which cases are implicated by this doctrine? Must the case be pending at the time of the election? Reasonably likely to be brought? What about an important but unanticipated case filed shortly after the election?

29. When do we impute a probability of bias from one party to another? Does a contribution from a corporation get imputed to its executives, and vice-versa? Does a contribution or expenditure by one family member get imputed to other family members?

30. What if the election is nonpartisan? What if the election is just a yes-or-no vote about whether to retain an incumbent?

31. What type of support is disqualifying? What if the supporter's expenditures are used to fund voter registration or get-out-the-vote efforts rather than television advertisements?

32. Are contributions or expenditures in connection with a primary aggregated with those in the general election? What if the contributor supported a different candidate in the primary? Does that dilute the debt of gratitude?

33. What procedures must be followed to challenge a state judge's failure to recuse? May *Caperton* claims only be raised on direct review? Or may such claims also be brought in federal district court under 42 U.S.C. § 1983, which allows a person deprived of a federal right by a state official to sue for

damages? If § 1983 claims are available, who are the proper defendants? The judge? The whole court? The clerk of court?

34. What about state-court cases that are already closed? Can the losing parties in those cases now seek collateral relief in federal district court under § 1983? What statutes of limitation should be applied to such suits?

35. What is the proper remedy? After a successful *Caperton* motion, must the parties start from scratch before the lower courts? Is any part of the lower court judgment retained?

36. Does a litigant waive his due process claim if he waits until after decision to raise it? Or would the claim only be ripe after decision, when the judge's actions or vote suggest a probability of bias?

37. Are the parties entitled to discovery with respect to the judge's recusal decision?

38. If a judge erroneously fails to recuse, do we apply harmless-error review?

39. Does the *judge* get to respond to the allegation that he is probably biased, or is his reputation solely in the hands of the parties to the case?

40. What if the parties settle a *Caperton* claim as part of a broader settlement of the case? Does that leave the judge with no way to salvage his reputation?

These are only a few uncertainties that quickly come to mind. Judges and litigants will surely encounter others when they are forced to, or wish to, apply the majority's decision in different circumstances. Today's opinion requires state and federal judges simultaneously to act as political scientists (why did candidate X win the election?), economists (was the financial support disproportionate?), and psychologists (is there likely to be a debt of gratitude?).

The Court's inability to formulate a "judicially discernible and manageable standard" strongly counsels against the recognition of a novel constitutional right. See *Vieth* (plurality opinion) (holding political gerrymandering claims nonjusticiable based on the lack of workable standards); *id.* (Kennedy, J., concurring in judgment) ("The failings of the many proposed standards for measuring the burden a gerrymander imposes . . . make our intervention improper"). The need to consider these and countless other questions helps explain why the common law and this Court's constitutional jurisprudence have never required disqualification on such vague grounds as "probability" or "appearance" of bias.

III

A

To its credit, the Court seems to recognize that the inherently boundless nature of its new rule poses a problem. But the majority's only answer is that the present case is an "extreme" one, so there is no need to worry about other cases. The Court repeats this point over and over. . . .

But this is just so much whistling past the graveyard. Claims that have little chance of success are nonetheless frequently filed. The success rate for certiorari petitions before this Court is approximately 1.1%, and yet the previous Term some 8,241 were filed. Every one of the "*Caperton* motions" or appeals or § 1983 actions will claim that the judge is biased, or probably biased, bringing the judge and the judicial system into disrepute. And all future litigants will assert that their case is *really* the most extreme thus far.

Extreme cases often test the bounds of established legal principles. There is a cost to yielding to the desire to correct the extreme case, rather than adhering to the legal principle. That cost has been demonstrated so often that it is captured in a legal aphorism: "Hard cases make bad law." . . .

B

And why is the Court so convinced that this is an extreme case? It is true that Don Blankenship spent a large amount of money in connection with this election. But this point cannot be emphasized strongly enough: Other than a $1,000 direct contribution from Blankenship, *Justice Benjamin and his campaign had no control over how this money was spent.* Campaigns go to great lengths to develop precise messages and strategies. An insensitive or ham-handed ad campaign by an independent third party might distort the campaign's message or cause a backlash against the candidate, even though the candidate was not responsible for the ads. See *Buckley v. Valeo* [*infra,* Chapter 12 — Eds.] ("Unlike contributions, such independent expenditures may well provide little assistance to the candidate's campaign and indeed may prove counterproductive"); see also Brief for Conference of Chief Justices as Amicus Curiae (citing examples of judicial elections in which independent expenditures backfired and hurt the candidate's campaign). The majority repeatedly characterizes Blankenship's spending as "contributions" or "campaign contributions," but it is more accurate to refer to them as "independent expenditures." Blankenship only "contributed" $1,000 to the Benjamin campaign.

Moreover, Blankenship's independent expenditures do not appear "grossly disproportionate" compared to other such expenditures in this very election. "And for the Sake of the Kids" — an independent group that received approximately two-thirds of its funding from Blankenship — spent $3,623,500 in connection with the election. But large independent expenditures were also made in support of Justice Benjamin's opponent. "Consumers for Justice" — an independent group that received large contributions from the plaintiffs' bar — spent approximately $2 million in this race. And Blankenship has made large expenditures in connection with several previous West Virginia elections, which undercuts any notion that his involvement in this election was "intended to influence the outcome" of particular pending litigation.

It is also far from clear that Blankenship's expenditures affected the outcome of this election. Justice Benjamin won by a comfortable 7-point margin (53.3% to

46.7%). Many observers believed that Justice Benjamin's opponent doomed his candidacy by giving a well-publicized speech that made several curious allegations; this speech was described in the local media as "deeply disturbing" and worse. Justice Benjamin's opponent also refused to give interviews or participate in debates. All but one of the major West Virginia newspapers endorsed Justice Benjamin. Justice Benjamin just might have won because the voters of West Virginia thought he would be a better judge than his opponent. Unlike the majority, I cannot say with any degree of certainty that Blankenship "cho[se] the judge in his own cause." I would give the voters of West Virginia more credit than that.

* * *

It is an old cliché, but sometimes the cure is worse than the disease. I am sure there are cases where a "probability of bias" should lead the prudent judge to step aside, but the judge fails to do so. Maybe this is one of them. But I believe that opening the door to recusal claims under the Due Process Clause, for an amorphous "probability of bias," will itself bring our judicial system into undeserved disrepute, and diminish the confidence of the American people in the fairness and integrity of their courts. I hope I am wrong.

I respectfully dissent.

[Justice SCALIA's dissenting opinion is omitted.]

Notes and Questions

1. Chief Justice Roberts asks so many questions in his dissent (let a thousand law review notes bloom!) that it does not seem fair to pile on with even more. But we cannot resist a few points.

2. Chief Justice Roberts predicted a flood of *Caperton* litigation. Professor Roy Schotland, surveying the reaction to *Caperton* in the lower courts, found no flood of such litigation so far. Roy A. Schotland, Caperton*'s Capers: Comment on Four of the Articles*, 60 Syracuse Law Review 337, 340 n.18 (2010). Why not?

3. In Chapters 13 and 14, we will see that Justice Kennedy consistently voted against the constitutionality of spending limits in campaigns, and was skeptical of other campaign finance regulations as well. Under Justice Kennedy's view, what role does large campaign money play in (judicial) elections? To what extent does large campaign spending influence the elected official? Does the potential for such influence justify more campaign finance limits? Finally, as the Chief Justice points out in the dissent, almost all of the money spent by Mr. Blankenship came in the form of contributions to a group making independent expenditures (through an entity we would now call a "Super PAC"), and did not go to Justice Benjamin. Why then did Justice Kennedy in the *Caperton* introduction refer to this as a case in which Justice Benjamin "had received campaign contributions in an extraordinary amount from, and through the efforts of" Mr. Blankenship?

4. Does campaign money affect judicial decisionmaking? See Michael S. Kang & Joanna M. Shepherd, *The Partisan Price of Justice: An Empirical Analysis of*

Campaign Contributions and Judicial Decisions, 86 New York University Law Review 69 (2011) (finding an effect of campaign contributions in partisan, but not nonpartisan, judicial elections).

5. Meanwhile, the Supreme Court briefly revisited the issues in *White* and *Caperton* in *Nevada Commission on Ethics v. Carrigan*, 564 U.S. 117 (2011). In *Carrigan*, a city council member from Sparks, Nevada challenged application of a conflict of interest provision arising out of his vote on a development plan supported by his campaign manager, who served as a lobbyist for the developer.

The Supreme Court held that the First Amendment did not protect a legislator's vote, and remanded the case to consider other issues, such as whether the conflict-of-interest provision was unconstitutionally vague. In dicta, the Court stated: "There are of course differences between a legislator's vote and a judge's, and thus between legislative and judicial recusal rules; nevertheless, there do not appear to have been any serious challenges to judicial recusal statutes as having unconstitutionally restricted judges' First Amendment rights." This statement was of course news to the many lawyers that had been litigating such challenges. A footnote to the sentence distinguished the issues in *White*: "We have held that restrictions on judges' speech during elections are a different matter. See *White* (holding that it violated the First Amendment to prohibit announcement of views on disputed legal and political issues by candidates for judicial election)."

Justice Kennedy, in a separate opinion, gave further room to argue for the constitutionality of rules regulating judges which may be unconstitutional when applied to legislators:

> The Court has held that due process may require recusal in the context of certain judicial determinations, see *Caperton*; but as the foregoing indicates, it is not at all clear that a statute of this breadth can be enacted to extend principles of judicial impartiality to a quite different context. The differences between the role of political bodies in formulating and enforcing public policy, on the one hand, and the role of courts in adjudicating individual disputes according to law, on the other, may call for a different understanding of the responsibilities attendant upon holders of those respective offices and of the legitimate restrictions that may be imposed upon them.

Chapter 11

Bribery

Our primary concern in the remainder of this book will be the campaign finance system and problems related to that system. One of the main reasons campaign finance has become a prominent issue in American politics is the belief of many that the raising of campaign funds provides the occasion for conduct that is corrupt or otherwise improper. As we shall see in later chapters, whether and under what circumstances campaign contributions are corrupt is a point of practical and theoretical controversy. The law of bribery, which attempts to deal with the most obviously corrupt forms of political activity, thus provides an appropriate preface to our consideration of campaign finance. In addition, developments in recent decades have made the law of bribery of increasing practical importance to people in and around politics.

Bribery was a common law offense, applicable originally only to official actions of a judicial nature, but extended gradually during the eighteenth and nineteenth centuries to all official actions. See generally *State v. Ellis*, 33 N.J.L. 102 (1868). Today, bribery is generally a statutory offense. It is not only one of the oldest legal concepts developed to protect the integrity of government and politics, but also one of the most basic.[a] Most people probably would agree with the Supreme Court's characterization of bribery laws as dealing "with only the most blatant and specific attempts of those with money to influence governmental action." *Buckley v. Valeo*, 424 U.S. 1, 28 (1976). The bribe is at the heart of our concept of corruption, whatever other conduct may be included within that concept.

While bribery prosecutions are common and the appellate reports contain many bribery cases, the bribery laws have received surprisingly little attention, except by participants in specific bribery prosecutions. In this chapter we will be particularly concerned with bribery of policy-making officials, and with the question of what

---

a. For a comprehensive history of the evolution of the concept of bribery throughout the course of western civilization, see John T. Noonan, Jr., Bribes (1984). For a cross-section of social scientific research on bribery and corruption, see the anthology, Political Corruption: Concepts and Contexts (Arnold J. Heidenheimer & Michael Johnston, eds., 2002). For an economic analysis of corruption, see Susan Rose-Ackerman, Corruption: A Study in Political Economy (1978). A variety of approaches to corruption, including the historical and the literary as well as the legal, may be found in the essays collected in Public and Private Corruption (William C. Heffernan & John Kleinig, eds., 2004).

counts as a bribe in situations that may arise commonly in politics. As you read the chapter, think about these questions:

1. What are the elements of the crime of bribery? Which elements seem to depend on the specific language of the statutes and which elements, if any, seem to be intrinsic to the crime of bribery?

2. How accurate is the Supreme Court's characterization, quoted above, of the coverage of bribery laws as they are written and as they have been interpreted by the courts? Is bribery limited to the most "blatant and specific" conduct?

3. Are the bribery statutes too vague, either as a matter of constitutional law or as a matter of fairness and effectiveness? Can you think of ways to make them clearer? At what cost, if any?

4. What should be the precise role of the bribery laws, especially in relation to other laws seeking to promote the integrity of the political system, such as those regulating campaign finances, lobbying practices, and conflicts of interest? Should the bribery laws be used solely against individuals who obviously have violated widely accepted norms, or should prosecutors and judges employ them aggressively as instruments of reform, to eliminate practices that are questionable or worse but may be widespread?

5. In particular, should *federal* prosecutors and judges use federal bribery and related statutes as an instrument for the reform of *state* and *local* political practices? As we shall see, in recent decades federal prosecutors have vigorously pursued state and local officials in some states, but the United States Supreme Court has partially curtailed their ability to do so. Should federal prosecutorial oversight of state and local government be expanded? Or should the Supreme Court go even further to limit such prosecutions?

6. Do the bribery statutes prohibit those acts and only those acts that are most plainly corrupt from a common sense standpoint? Should they? Are you sure you have a non-vague sense of what is a plainly corrupt act? Are you confident that you know a corrupt act when you see one?

It is difficult to think of the meaning of corruption without relying on one's conception of how the democratic process ought to function. Indeed, perhaps the best reason for studying the law of bribery is that the subject provides a concrete setting for evaluating and applying democratic norms. As an illustration, Part I of this chapter deals with unusual and relatively simple cases in which bribery of a *candidate* is alleged. Competing conceptions of political competition can have a major influence on how one believes such cases should be resolved. In Part II we consider the far more common and far more complex case of bribery of a *public official.*

I. Bribery of Candidates

People v. Hochberg

62 App.Div.2d 239, 404 N.Y.S.2d 161 (1978)

MIKOLL, Justice.

The People charged that the defendant, Assemblyman Alan Hochberg, met with one, Charles Rosen, in January and February, 1976, to secure Rosen's promise not to run against him in the 1976 Primary for the Assembly in exchange for Hochberg's promise to give Rosen a $20,000 a year job in the Legislature, a session job for Rosen's brother-in-law paying approximately $3,000, and a $5,000 political campaign contribution. The defense contended that Hochberg's discussions with Rosen were for the purpose of establishing a working political coalition between Rosen, the political group in Co-op City which evolved during the rent strike and defendant's group in Pelham Park, as well as filling positions on his legislative staff with qualified persons.

The defendant was convicted of violating section 421 (subd. 5) of the Election Law (Penal Law, § 110.00) which prohibits the fraudulent or wrongful doing of any act tending to affect the result of a primary election;[b] section 448 of the Election Law which prohibits any person, while holding public office, from corruptly using or promising to use his official authority to secure public employment upon consideration that the person so to be benefited or any other person will give or use their political influence or action in behalf of any candidate, or upon any other corrupt condition or consideration; and section 77 of the Public Officers Law which makes it a felony for any member of the Legislature to ask, receive, consent or agree to receive "any money, property or thing of value or of personal advantage" for performing any discretionary act which he may exercise by virtue of his office. . . .

The People's evidence established that defendant was the State Assemblyman from the heavily Democratic 81st Assembly District (A.D.) located in the Bronx, New York. He was to be a candidate for re-election in the 1976 elections for the term of office commencing January 1, 1977. The district was divided into two sections, 81st A.D. West, which consisted of an area known as Pelham Parkway where defendant resided and which area he controlled and 81st A.D. East, known as Co-op City, a large housing development community of about 60,000 people, where Charles Rosen, Chairman of Steering Committee III, was the very popular leader of a rent strike supported by 86% of the residents. Co-op City was 99% Democratic in party affiliation and comprised about 40% of the Democratic primary vote in the district. Pelham Parkway supplied about 60% of that vote. Success in the Democratic primary was tantamount to election in the 81st A.D.

---

b. Does such a generally worded statute cover the defendant's conduct in this case? See *People v. Lang*, 329 N.E.2d 176 (N.Y. 1975). — Eds.

[In 1975–76, the Democratic Party in the 81st A.D. was split between regular and reform factions. Defendant Hochberg attempted to form an alliance with a Democratic leader, Larry Dolnick, who also was associated with Rosen as a leader of the rent strike. He informed Dolnick that he, Hochberg, wanted to be reelected to the Assembly in 1976 and then run for Civil Court Judge in 1977. He offered to support Dolnick to fill the Assembly vacancy that would result. When Dolnick said he was not interested in public office, Hochberg offered Dolnick either a legislative staff job at a salary of $19–20,000 or a job for less where "he wouldn't have to appear." Finally, Hochberg offered to contribute $750 to the New Democratic Club, of which Dolnick was a leader.]

Defendant told Dolnick that he did not want a primary in 1976 because it would be expensive. On different occasions he inquired of Dolnick whether Charles Rosen intended to run against him. Dolnick said Rosen did not. However, defendant said he wanted to hear it from "the horse's mouth" and wanted Dolnick to set up a meeting. He stated that Rosen would be a viable candidate, that a primary campaign for the Assembly would cost upwards of $25,000 and that he wanted to run for Civil Judge in 1977 and that that was the reason he wanted to be sure Rosen would not run. Dolnick thereafter advised Rosen that the defendant wanted to talk to him and told Rosen of the offers the defendant had made to him.

Charles Rosen testified that he visited the office of the Special Prosecutor for Nursing Homes in December, 1975, to discuss defendant's connection with the Nursing Home Industry. He mentioned what he characterized as defendant's "third party bribe" offer and the Special Prosecutor subsequently suggested that Rosen meet with the defendant to allow him to repeat the "bribe."

On January 27, 1976, Dolnick and Rosen went to the Special Prosecutor's office and arrangements were made to record the meeting defendant requested. The first tape recording played at trial revealed that Dolnick, Rosen and defendant met at Dolnick's apartment on January 30, 1976, where defendant stated he did not want a primary in 1976, that he wanted to run for the bench in 1977 and that he wanted their support for that office. The discussion included references to defendant's job offer to Dolnick and his proposed $750 contribution for the New Democratic Club campaign. At this meeting defendant stated that he was willing to help Rosen achieve his dreams because the $25,000 he would probably have to spend in a tough primary against Rosen would kill his judgeship race. Defendant stated that he would not have the resources for two campaigns. Defendant offered the $20,000 job on his staff to Rosen but said they would have to work it out with Dolnick first because he had offered the same job to him. Defendant also said he would raise $5,000 for Rosen's 1978 Special Election campaign for the Assembly by recommending that other people contribute to Rosen's campaign fund.

On February 5, 1976, Rosen and the defendant met alone at the Larchmont Diner. The tape recording of this meeting disclosed that defendant offered to place Rosen in a $3,000 job on his committee at the current session. It was agreed Rosen could not take it, but that any name would be acceptable to defendant as a "stand-in" for Rosen. That conversation went like this:

> ROSEN: Now, you talked about this job on your committee. I can't take that job.
>
> HOCHBERG: Who can? Is that a thought?
>
> ROSEN: That somebody would be a stand-in.
>
> HOCHBERG: Right. Does it look bad if your wife?
>
> ROSEN: What about my sister-in-law . . . or my brother-in-law[?]
>
> HOCHBERG: Matter of fact . . . as I told you, as of Monday, at least for the figure I had quoted you they can . . . come up and sign on. Immediately. . . .
>
> ROSEN: So who will know.
>
> HOCHBERG: That's right. All right. That's. That's that.

Defendant further stated in the taped conversation that he could guarantee Rosen $5,000 for his Special Election campaign and that the $3,000 session job was evidence of his good faith in that it would be completely paid before the primary. Rosen testified that in addition defendant said, "I will give you ___" and then proceeded to write on a napkin the figure $5,000, asking him to nod if it was acceptable.

He also said that if the rent strike was not over, Rosen's stand-in could be placed in the $20,000 job. When Rosen asked defendant not to put the stand-in's name on the payroll until Wednesday instead of the Monday, as planned, the defendant made reference to the stand-in losing. Rosen replied, "Schmuck, he's losing nothing, I'm getting the money." Defendant agreed, "But that's it, you're losing, why . . . ?" Rosen explained he had to talk the matter over with his wife.

At a subsequent recorded meeting on February 8, 1976, Rosen advised the defendant that the "stand-in" would be in Albany the following day. Rosen asked him when the arrangement regarding the $5,000 contribution which he had written on the napkin would be consummated. Defendant said that he had an "excellent mechanism to protect both of us." Rosen could set up a bank account in the name of a campaign committee and contributions could be made to that entity by defendant. "No problems, it's perfectly legal." he assured Rosen.

The stand-in for Rosen, his brother-in-law, Chris Johnson, who was equipped with a recording device, arrived in Albany the next day and defendant accompanied him to the necessary offices so that he could be put on the payroll. Defendant told Johnson that he would not have to come to Albany again but he would like Johnson to answer some mail at home.

The defense, through cross-examination of Rosen, and the testimony of defense witness, Philip Luce, sought to establish that Rosen was biased against defendant in that Rosen was a militant communist, out to destroy the government of the United States and in the process to destroy Assemblyman Hochberg as a political force in the community.[c] At the same time, through cross-examination of Dolnick and Rosen, the defense attempted to show that the discussions with Rosen were merely political in nature, made to establish a political coalition in the 81st Assembly District. The defendant also attempted to develop a basis for the defense of entrapment through cross-examination and the establishment of bias on the part of Rosen towards defendant. In addition, the defense offered the testimony of several character witnesses.

Defendant on this appeal first contends that there was a failure to prove beyond a reasonable doubt that the offers made by defendant were contingent on Rosen not running in the primary since they were made as part of a larger political accommodation involving the 81st Assembly District. We disagree. While certainly on this record a question of fact was created for the jury, there was sufficient evidence for the jury to find that the job offers were made on the condition that Rosen not run in the primary. Defendant said he did not want a primary against Rosen, that it would cost him $25,000 and would "kill his judgeship race," because he would not then have the financial resources for such a race. Defendant's knowledge that the offers were made contingent upon Rosen's not running in the primary appears from his statement in reference to the offer of the $3,000 session job, that: "That's my good faith . . . it is completely paid . . . before the petitions are filed." Further, the fact that the $20,000 and the $3,000 staff jobs were offered by defendant without regard to the duties to be performed or the skills required indicated the presence of an ulterior motive. Defendant's reference to their "agreement," their "deal" and "personal *quid pro quo*" during both meetings with Rosen, in connection with their discussions, along with his caution to Rosen to "deny everything" is sufficient to establish that defendant attempted to condition the job offers on Rosen's promise not to run in the primary.

It is also urged by defendant that the People failed to prove that he accepted "or thing of value or of personal advantage." This is without merit. Unlawful fees and payments (Public Officers Law, § 77) are obviously a form of bribery. The benefit accruing to the public official need not be tangible or monetary to constitute a bribe (*People v. Hyde*, 156 App.Div. 618, 141 N.Y.S. 1089; *People ex rel. Dickinson v. Van De Carr*, [*infra* Part II.B of this chapter]). Here, Rosen's agreement not to run in the 1976 Primary was a sufficiently direct benefit to the defendant to be included within the term "thing of personal advantage."

Defendant next claims that there was a failure to prove that he acted with a wrongful intent because the People failed to prove that he knew he was violating sections 421 (subd. 5) and 448 (subd. 1) of the Election Law. We find this contention is without merit. There are sufficient facts in the record from which the jury could find that defendant acted with a corrupt intent (*People v. Lang*, 36 N.Y.2d

---

c. Aside from the obvious drawbacks of this defense tactic, consider its effect on the more substantial defense described in the following sentence. — Eds.

366, 370–371, 368 N.Y.S.2d 492, 495–497, 329 N.E.2d 176, 179–180). The trial court charged that a corrupt intent involved "an intentional and knowing disregard of the law." "Intentional" requires a conscious objective to engage in the prohibited conduct while "knowing" requires an awareness that one's conduct is of such nature or that such circumstances exist (Penal Law, § 15.05, subds. 1 and 2). Here, evidence existed that defendant used or promised to use his authority as a legislator to secure staff jobs for Rosen and Johnson with the intent and purpose of obtaining Rosen's promise to refrain from entering the primary in violation of section 448 (subd. 1) of the Election Law. Likewise, evidence existed that defendant deliberately attempted to cause Rosen to refrain from entering the primary in exchange for the said jobs and offers of campaign contributions in violation of section 421 (subd. 5) of the Election Law.

Defendant urges that, at best, the evidence only supports attempted unlawful fees and payments and attempted corrupt use of position or authority, in that, Rosen testified that he never intended to run in the primary. The argument must be rejected since both crimes encompass an attempt. Unlawful fees and payments requires only the mere asking, consenting or agreeing to receive anything of value or personal advantage in exchange for performing a discretionary act. Corrupt use of position or authority includes only corruptly *promising* to use official authority in exchange for a promise not to enter the primary.

Further, defendant argues that because Rosen said he never had the intention to run in the primary, there could be no actual *effect* on the primary, as required by section 448 (subd. 1) of the Election Law, and that likewise, Rosen's promise not to run in the primary was not a thing of value as required under section 77 of the Public Officers Law. This argument is defeated by the fact that Rosen's state of mind was a present but transient state of mind at the time, subject to change and unbound by the obligations inherent in a promise not to run. Such a promise would take away his unfettered freedom to be a candidate and change the transitory nature of his state of mind to permanency. Thus, the promise not to run affected the primary by removing Rosen as a viable potential primary candidate and, also, consequently, was a thing of value or personal advantage to defendant.

Defendant contends that the statutes under which he was convicted are (1) unconstitutional in that they are overbroad and inhibit First Amendment activities relative to free political discussion; and (2) unconstitutionally vague in prohibiting the use of official position or authority in exchange for the benefit of another's "political influence or action" or "upon any other corrupt condition or consideration." We find the first contention is without merit. The statutes place reasonable restrictions on the use of official position and authority which is corruptive of a free elective process. No one has a constitutional right to corruptly use official position or authority to obtain political gain. Secondly, the statutes here under attack are sufficiently definite to give a reasonable person notice of the nature of the acts prohibited. They are generally aimed at corrupt bargaining to obtain public office and specifically at the use of the public payroll in such bargains. In view of the myriad ways in which the objects sought to be prohibited may be accomplished, laws framed with narrow particularity would afford easy circumvention of their purpose and be ineffectual. Thus, the statutes are neither impermissibly vague nor overbroad. A person of ordinary intelligence would realize that it is illegal to offer Assembly staff positions to another as a payoff not to run against him in an election for public office....

Judgment affirmed.

Notes and Questions

1. Hochberg's first contention was that there was insufficient proof "that the offers made by defendant were contingent on Rosen not running in the primary since they were made as part of a larger political accommodation involving the 81st Assembly District." Was the defendant arguing (a) that Rosen's not running played no part in the "larger accommodation," or (b) that a deal that includes Rosen's agreement not to run is permissible so long as the agreement is part of a "larger political accommodation"? How does the court interpret this contention? Why is the contention unsuccessful? If the second meaning is intended, is the contention persuasive?

2. The court states in response to one of Hochberg's claims that under the evidence the jury could have found "that defendant acted with a corrupt intent." In this passage, the court is referring to the convictions under both Sections 421 and 448 of the Election Law. The latter section states that a violator must act "corruptly," but Section 421(5) contains no such requirement. Was the court mistaken in assuming that the prosecutor had to prove that Hochberg acted "corruptly" in order to violate Section 421(5)? What does it mean to act "corruptly"? See *infra* Part II.A.

3. You are consulted by Assemblyman Alex Alvarez, the favored candidate in next year's Democratic primary for an open State Senate seat. Barbara Bell has been mentioned as a possible opponent who might give Alvarez a strong race. Yesterday Bell had a meeting with Alvarez, during which she offered to run in the primary for the Assembly seat Alvarez will be vacating instead of challenging Alvarez for the Senate, if Alvarez will agree to support Bell in the Assembly primary and help her to raise money. Alvarez anticipates a tough general election contest against the likely Republican candidate and therefore would like to avoid strong opposition in the primary. He has no strong feelings one way or the other about Bell as a candidate for the Assembly. All things considered, he would like to accept Bell's offer if he may do so legally. How would you advise him, in New York? What would your advice be in California, where Elections Code § 18205 provides:

> A person shall not... advance, pay, solicit, or receive... any money or other valuable consideration... in order to induce a person not to become or to withdraw as a candidate for public office....

Aside from whatever legal advice you would give, do you regard Bell's offer as improper? Would your legal or ethical judgment be different if the proposal was first made by the Democratic state chair, who thought that the proposed arrangement would improve the Democrats' chances of winning both the Senate and the Assembly seats?

If one purpose of the New York and California statutes is to encourage and promote electoral competition, which solution to the problem would best promote competition in primary elections? Which solution would best promote competition in general elections? See generally Daniel H. Lowenstein, *Political Bribery and the Intermediate Theory of Politics*, 32 UCLA Law Review 784, 791–95 (1985).

4. *A Personal Postscript from Professor Lowenstein.* The article just cited was theoretically oriented and stated that "many of the transactions identified in this Article as definite or likely bribes are engaged in by public officials and those who deal with them on virtually a daily basis, with only the remotest chance of triggering a bribery prosecution." *Id.* at 789. It was therefore a surprise to read in the *Los Angeles Times* only a few months after the article was published that Representative Bobbi Fiedler was being indicted on the basis of alleged facts resembling those of the Alvarez-Bell problem.

Fiedler was a California member of the House of Representatives who was planning to run in the 1986 Republican primary for the right to run against then Democratic Senator Alan Cranston. She and her aide, Paul Clarke, were accused of attempting to induce another potential candidate, Ed Davis, to withdraw from the Republican primary by offering Davis assistance in raising funds to pay off a considerable deficit that he had incurred. According to the indictment, this offer violated California Elections Code § 18205, quoted above.[d] So far as is known, it was the first time anyone had ever been prosecuted under the section, which had originally been enacted in 1893.

About a week after the indictment I was retained to serve on the defense team, in part because my article supported the position that the allegations against Fiedler and Clarke did not violate California law even if they were true. As it turned out, there was so little evidence against Fiedler that the Los Angeles District Attorney agreed to the charge against her being dismissed. Although we believed the evidence against Clarke was equally weak, the District Attorney disagreed and pursued the case against him. We moved to have the case dismissed on a variety of legal grounds, including our contention that an offer of *political* benefits such as assistance in raising funds to pay off a campaign deficit did not constitute "valuable consideration" under Section 18205.

The good news from my perspective was that the Superior Court granted the motion to dismiss, and the District Attorney decided not to appeal. The bad news was that instead of deciding whether the statute covered political benefits in exchange for a withdrawal of candidacy, the court ruled on the very narrow ground that the list of verbs in Section 18205 does not include "offer." Thus, although a candidate

d. The section had a different number in 1986, but its language has not been changed.

who *solicits* a benefit in exchange for withdrawing is covered, a person who *offers* a benefit to a candidate in exchange for a withdrawal is not.

The Fiedler-Clarke case was very widely publicized. Furthermore, the events just described took place shortly before the California deadline for candidates to file for public office. Consequently, I received inquiries from several politicians who asked whether they could engage in variations on the Alvarez-Bell problem. What advice would you have given? Would your advice have been influenced by the pendency of the Fiedler-Clarke case? By the result, once the Fiedler-Clarke case had been dismissed?

Prior to my joining the Fiedler-Clarke defense team, I was interviewed by a large number of reporters, because I was virtually the only person who had done any research on the issue who was not connected to either the prosecution or (at that time) the defense. One of the reporters was from the *New York Times*, and in that interview I pointed out that *Hochberg*, a New York decision, was the closest judicial precedent to the Fiedler-Clarke case. The next morning, among my phone messages was one from Alan Hochberg!

After trying to remember exactly what I had said to the *New York Times* and briefly wondering whether I ought to consult a specialist in the law of defamation, I returned Hochberg's call. Far from being offended, Hochberg expressed considerable interest in the Fiedler-Clarke case and offered his services if there were any way he could assist them. Hochberg told me that as a result of losing his appeal he had served a prison term and had also been disbarred. He found occupation as a taxi driver, but one day, while he was sitting in his parked cab, another vehicle ran into it and disabled him. A judicial decision that to me had previously been an abstract treatment of an interesting intellectual problem suddenly took on a very human face.[e]

5. In *Kaisner v. State*, 772 S.W.2d 528 (Tex. App. 1989), the defendant was an incumbent sheriff running in a Republican primary for reelection. Because his 41% share of the vote was less than a majority, Texas law called for a runoff against the second-place candidate, one Robinson. Defendant was convicted of bribery for offering Robinson the job of Chief Deputy Sheriff if Robinson withdrew from the runoff election. The bribery statute applied to a "public servant," which was defined in the Texas Penal Code as including "a candidate for nomination or election to public office." The Texas Court of Appeals affirmed the conviction, stating that the decision to withdraw as a candidate "would have been the exercise of discretion as a public servant." The court went on:

---

e. In 1995, I spoke with Hochberg again. He reported that in all respects his life had gotten back on track in the past decade and was offering him considerable satisfaction. Alas, one of the other principals in the *Hochberg* case, Charles Rosen, has run into legal difficulties of his own. See Sewell Chan, *Bronx Odyssey: From Rebel to Executive to Felon*, N.Y. Times, October 10, 2006. Those who are familiar with the medieval concept of the wheel of fortune will find these events unsurprising.

> Appellant's argument is that the offer of a job to a political opponent falls within the traditional notion of political patronage and is therefore outside the statutory prohibition. We disagree. No such exception, justification or defense was authorized by the legislature. While it may have been acceptable or traditional behavior in Texas or other jurisdictions to "buy off" opponents, it is certainly within the province of the legislature to criminalize such acts.

Perhaps a more remarkable example of a court reaching to find a legal basis for a conviction for bribery of candidates to withdraw is *State v. Woodward*, 689 A.2d 801 (N.J. Super. A.D. 1997), which appears to hold that paying a potential candidate not to run comes under a statute banning bribery of voters.

6. Hochberg was convicted of bribery both in his capacity as a public official *and* in his capacity as a candidate. The remainder of this chapter will concern itself with bribery of public officials. Most such bribery cases involve relatively lower level or even ministerial officials. We shall concentrate on bribery in connection with higher level public policymaking. At higher levels, most decisionmaking is inherently discretionary and officials are subject to various pressures. To the extent that it is unclear what counts as a bribe, does this reflect lack of an underlying consensus on what pressures on officials are desirable, or at least acceptable, in a democratic society?

II. Bribery of Public Officials

Bribery statutes in the United States vary in their wording, and sometimes these variations are significant. Nevertheless, the basic elements of the crime are generally similar. The federal statute, 18 U.S.C. § 201, is representative. Subsection (a), which contains definitions, is followed by subsections (b)(1) and (2), defining, respectively, bribery and acceptance of a bribe:

> (b) Whoever—
>
> (1) directly or indirectly, corruptly gives, offers or promises anything of value to any public official . . . or offers or promises any public official . . . to give anything to any other person or entity, with intent—
>
> (A) to influence any official act; or
>
> (B) to influence such public official . . . to commit . . . or allow, any fraud . . . on the United States; or
>
> (C) to induce such public official . . . to do or omit to do any act in violation of the lawful duty of such official or person . . . ;
>
> (2) being a public official . . . directly or indirectly, corruptly demands, seeks, receives, accepts, or agrees to receive or accept anything of value personally or for any other person or entity, in return for:

(A) being influenced in the performance of any official act;

(B) being influenced to commit . . . or allow, any fraud . . . on the United States; or

(C) being induced to do or omit to do any act in violation of the official duty of such official . . . ;

. . .

shall be fined . . . or imprisoned . . . or both. . . .

There are five elements to the crime defined in this and most other American bribery statutes:

1. There must be a *public official.*

2. The defendant must have a *corrupt intent.*

3. A benefit, *anything of value*, must redound to the public official.

4. There must be an *intent to influence* the public official (or to be influenced if the recipient of the bribe is the defendant).

5. That which is intended to be influenced must be an *official act.*

Of the five elements only the first, that the bribee must be a public official, is relatively straightforward. Section 201 defines "public official" to include federal officials but not state and local officials (though, as we shall see, state and local officials may be prosecuted under other federal statutes as well as state statutes).[f] It is true that the boundary between the public and private sectors is often unclear, and there can be difficult questions as to whether officials in entities that straddle both sectors are "public officials" within the meaning of a bribery statute. In addition, some state bribery statutes apply to persons who are not public officials, such as party officials or, as in *Hochberg*, candidates for public office. But this element of the crime is not often at issue. The materials that follow in this chapter therefore focus on the remaining four elements.

First, however, the elements of bribery should be contrasted with those of the lesser offense of giving or receiving an unlawful *gratuity*, prohibited by federal law and the laws of many states. The federal statute, 18 U.S.C. § 201(c), is again representative:

(c) Whoever—

(1) otherwise than as provided by law for the proper discharge of official duty—

---

f. The precise definition of "public official" is "Member of Congress, Delegate, or Resident Commissioner, either before or after such official has qualified, or an officer or employee or person acting for or on behalf of the United States, or any department, agency or branch of Government thereof, including the District of Columbia, in any official function, under or by authority of any such department, agency, or branch of Government, or a juror." 18 U.S.C. § 201(a)(1).

(A) directly or indirectly gives, offers, or promises anything of value to any public official . . . for or because of any official act performed or to be performed by such public official . . . ; or

(B) being a public official . . . otherwise than as provided by law for the proper discharge of official duty, directly or indirectly demands, seeks, receives, accepts, or agrees to receive or accept anything of value personally for or because of any official act performed or to be performed by such official . . . ;

. . .

shall be fined . . . or imprisoned . . . or both.

A comparison of the elements of the unlawful gratuity offense with bribery yields the following:

1. The requirement that there be a public official is substantially the same, except that a transaction involving a former official can be an unlawful gratuity but not a bribe. This is because a bribe must look forward to an official act, whereas an unlawful gratuity may look forward or backward.

2. The actions proscribed by the bribery subsection must be done "corruptly." There is no such requirement for an unlawful gratuity.

3. The gratuity statute's requirement that a benefit ("anything of value") redound to the benefit of the official is identical to the bribery requirement, except that under the bribery provision the benefit may be received by the official *or any other person*, while under the unlawful gratuity provision the benefit must be received by the official "personally."

4. While an unlawful gratuity requires an intent that the benefit pass to the official "for or because of" the official act, there need be no intent (as in bribery) that the official be influenced by the benefit.

5. The requirement of an official act is seemingly identical for bribes and unlawful gratuities.

If, during an election year, Victoria strongly favors a particular bill and therefore mails $25 campaign contributions to each of the three members of the U.S. House of Representatives from her state who voted in favor of the bill, is she guilty of making an unlawful gratuity?

A. Corrupt Intent

What does the word "corruptly" in 18 U.S.C. § 201(b) mean? Is a gift or benefit to a public official made with the expectation that the gift or benefit will influence the official's conduct in a manner beneficial to the donor *always* a bribe under the federal statute? Is the presence of such an expectation what is meant by "corrupt"? If so, is the word "corruptly" surplusage? Courts will read the requirement of a corrupt intent into a bribery statute where it is not stated expressly. *E.g., State v. O'Neill*, 700 P.2d 711 (Wash. 1985). Indeed, one court did so even when the bribery statute had been amended to omit the word "corruptly." *State v. Alfonsi*, 147 N.W.2d 550 (Wisc. 1967). What is the significance, if any, of these holdings?

Could there be a bribe without an expectation that the gift or benefit will influence the public official's conduct? Is such an expectation necessary for a violation of the unlawful gratuity offense, 18 U.S.C. § 201(c)?

Compare with the federal statute these definitions from the California Penal Code:

> *Section 7(6)*: The word "bribe" signifies anything of value or advantage, present or prospective, or any promise or undertaking to give any, asked, given, or accepted, with a corrupt intent to influence, unlawfully, the person to whom it is given, in his or her action, vote, or opinion, in any public or official capacity.
>
> *Section 7(3)*: The word "corruptly" imports a wrongful design to acquire or cause some pecuniary or other advantage to the person guilty of the act or omission referred to, or to some other person.

Does the definition of "corruptly" in Section 7(3) help you answer any of the questions above? What does the word "unlawfully" in Section 7(6) mean? What does the word "wrongful" in Section 7(3) mean?

Problem

Linda Lewis, a newly-elected president of the state labor federation, issues a public statement that is reported in the press to the effect that the most important item on labor's legislative agenda is to defeat Bill Number 100. Accordingly, the federation will support and contribute to those legislators and only those legislators who vote against the bill. Senator Sam Scott, who has been publicly uncommitted on Bill Number 100 and who is in a difficult struggle for reelection, has decided, after taking into account his need for a contribution from the labor federation as well as many other considerations, including the merits of the bill, that he would like to vote against the bill. He also would like to accept the contribution. How would you advise him?

Senator Suji Park, who was publicly and firmly opposed to the bill prior to Lewis' statement, also would like to vote against the bill and accept a contribution. How would you advise her?

If both senators vote against the bill and accept a contribution, is Lewis guilty of bribing either or both state senators under the language of the federal bribery statute? Under the California statute? Is she guilty of making one or more unlawful gratuities under the language of the federal statute? Should her conduct be prohibited?

Whether or not they have violated the law, is Lewis acting unethically? Senator Scott? Senator Park?

B. Anything of Value

The standard bribe, as it usually is thought of, consists of a payment of money to an official for the official's personal use. On the official's part, it is motivated by venality. However, it is clear from the language of the statutes ("anything of value") and numerous judicial decisions that bribery is not limited to the "standard" case. Still within the category of venality, loans to an official, business transactions resulting in a sales commission for the official, and numbers for the official in an illegal lottery are among the diverse personal benefits that have been held to be bribes. Some statutes, including 18 U.S.C. § 201(b), expressly include benefits provided to third persons.

The most interesting questions that arise regarding the benefit to the official under bribery laws involve benefits that are political rather than personal. Of central importance are campaign contributions. Without apparent exception, American courts have held that a campaign contribution is a "thing of value" for purposes of typical bribery statutes. See Lowenstein, *supra*, at 808–09. The difficult question is not *whether* a campaign contribution may be a bribe but *when* it is a bribe. We shall consider that question in the following section.

What about political benefits, other than campaign contributions, that are provided to influence an official act? Could an endorsement of a public official running for reelection be a bribe if it is given with intent to influence or in exchange for some official action? If the endorsing organization is very influential in the official's district, might not the endorsement have considerable value? Would you regard such an occurrence as improper? Would it depend on the surrounding circumstances? What if the endorsement were a prerequisite to a campaign contribution by the organization? See Lowenstein, *supra*, at 809–11.

Another type of political benefit can come in the form of official actions performed by other government officials. "Logrolling" is the term commonly used when legislators trade votes. For example, suppose Carol represents a corn-growing district and William represents a wheat-growing district. If Carol is sponsoring a corn bill and William a wheat bill and each agrees reciprocally to vote for the other's bill in committee, have they bribed each other? Which, if any, of the elements of bribery are not present? In the following case, the "logroll" is not between two legislators but between a legislator and an executive branch official.

People ex rel. Dickinson v. Van de Carr

87 App.Div. 386, 84 N.Y.S. 461 (1903)

LAUGHLIN, J.:

[Dickinson, the relator, was an alderman of New York City charged with violating Penal Code § 72, a bribery statute. Rather than plead guilty or innocent, he filed a "traverse," an old-fashioned means of seeking dismissal of the case without trial.] The testimony showed that John McGaw Woodbury, the commissioner of street cleaning of the city of New York, wrote a letter to the relator on the 23d day of September, 1902, saying: "In reply to your letter of September 20th, I would say that the department is so short of horses, particularly in the borough of Brooklyn, that we have been very strict with the drivers during the warm weather to prevent any possibility of overheating or damaging the stock. We are many behind our complement. Should, however, the Honorable Board grant me the moneys for new stock and plant, this would give employment to more drivers, and as the heavy season comes on, having made a note of your favorable recommendation, the case of Covino will be reconsidered;" that on the thirtieth day of the same month the relator wrote and mailed a letter to Commissioner Woodbury in reply saying: "If you will reinstate Antonio Covino, who I think was too severely punished by being dismissed from your department, I will vote and otherwise help you to obtain the money needed for a new plant in Brooklyn;" and at this time there was pending in the board of aldermen a bill to authorize an issue of corporate stock "for new stock or plant for Department of Street Cleaning, Borough of Brooklyn."

... Section 72 of the Penal Code provides as follows:

> Officer accepting bribe — A [public official] who asks, receives, or agrees to receive a bribe, or any money, property, or value of any kind, or any promise or agreement therefor, upon any agreement or understanding that his vote, opinion, judgment, action, decision, or other official proceeding, shall be influenced thereby, or that he will do or omit any act or proceeding, or in any way neglect or violate any official duty, is punishable by imprisonment ... or fine ... or both. ...

It will be observed that the clause "asks, receives or agrees to receive a bribe, or any money, property, or value of any kind, or any promise or agreement therefor," is disjunctive. It first specifically includes certain officers who ask, receive or agree to receive a *bribe*. In the absence of any statute defining a bribe, we must have recourse to the decisions and text writers to determine what was embraced in that term at common law. Bribery was an indictable offense at common law, and although in the early days it was limited to judicial officers and those engaged in the administration of justice, it was later extended to all public officers. It was variously defined as taking or offering an "*undue reward*" or a "*reward*" to influence official action. Bribery is defined in the American and English Encyclopaedical of Law to be "the giving, offering or receiving of anything of value, or any valuable service, intended to influence one in the discharge of a legal duty." The cases of bribery that have been before the courts of this State, so far as brought to our attention, have related to the offering or giving of property or something of intrinsic value. The relator claims that, inasmuch as no money or property was asked or agreed to be received by him to influence his official action, he has not violated this statute. In view of the circumstances disclosed his letter is open to the inference that he desired to obtain a political or other personal advantage from or by securing Covino's reinstatement in the public service, and that he took advantage of the known desire on the part of the street commissioner to obtain this appropriation of public moneys, to improperly influence the action of the street commissioner on the application of Covino for reinstatement, by offering, in case that were done, to vote for and further the desired ... appropriation, and impliedly threatening in case of refusal to withhold his support therefrom. The interests of the public service require that public officers shall act honestly and fairly upon propositions laid before them for consideration, and shall neither be influenced by nor receive pecuniary benefit from their official acts or enter into bargains with their fellow-legislators or officers or with others for the giving or withholding of their votes conditioned upon their receiving any valuable favor, political or otherwise, for themselves or others. It was the duty of the relator to act fairly and honestly and according to his judgment upon the proposition of the street commissioner. It does not appear to have been the mandatory duty of the board of aldermen to favor the recommendation of Commissioner Woodbury. In these circumstances it was the duty of relator to favor or oppose the recommendation according to its merits or demerits. If in his judgment it should have been disapproved, he should have opposed it, and he should not bargain to vote for it upon obtaining an agreement from the street commissioner to reinstate Covino. It is quite as demoralizing to the public service and as much against the spirit and intent of the statute for a legislator or other public official to bargain to sell his vote or official action for a political or other favor or reward as for money. Either is a bribe, and they only differ in degree. Nor should he, by holding out this inducement, have tempted the commissioner to act favorably upon Covino's application for reinstatement. This was undue influence and would be detrimental to the public service. In addition to the word "bribe" in section 72 of the Penal Code other words are employed sufficiently broad to reach this case. It is a violation of the statute for a public officer to ask, receive or agree to receive "property or value of any kind or any promise or agreement therefor" upon any agreement or understanding that his vote or official action shall be influenced thereby. It is clear that the words "value of any kind," as here used, are more comprehensive than "property." The benefit which the relator expected to receive from the reinstatement of his constituent would, we think, be embraced in the meaning of this clause and would also constitute a bribe. We are, therefore, of the opinion that the facts tend to show that the relator has offended against the provisions of section 72 of the Penal Code and that he was properly held to answer upon the charge. ...

Order affirmed.

Notes and Questions

1. American legislators at all levels see it as one of their primary functions to intercede on behalf of their constituents in dealings with executive agencies of the government. Whether or not they are usually as direct in their negotiations as was the defendant in *Van de Carr*, there is never any doubt that the basis of the legislator's influence with the agencies is the legislature's control over each agency's budget, programs, salaries, governing statutes and the like. Is such intercession by legislators wrong? What harm results? See generally Morris P. Fiorina, Congress: Keystone of the Washington Establishment (2d ed. 1989). Can it be argued that the practice is beneficial? In any event, is such intercession by a legislator a bribe?

A recent article argues that an agreement for an official act constitutes a bribe only when it is exchanged for something external to politics, see Deborah Hellman, *A Theory of Bribery*, 38 Cardozo Law Review 1947 (2017). Is this a sensible line? On which side of the line does *Van de Carr* fall?

2. Can a campaign contribution by one legislator to another be a bribe if given in exchange for or to influence a vote on a bill? What if the donor is a candidate for Speaker or Majority Leader and the contribution is in exchange for or to influence the recipient's vote on the donor's candidacy? What if the "donor" legislator does not actually make a contribution, but agrees to help the recipient raise money? Can it be a bribe for one legislator to vote for a bill favored by a second legislator in exchange for or to influence the second legislator's vote in a contest for a leadership position? Consider *People v. Montgomery*, 61 Cal. App. 3d 718 (1976), in which the bribery conviction of a city council member was upheld. The offense consisted of agreeing to give favorable consideration to another council member's favored projects in return for the other member's vote for the defendant for mayor, an office that was filled by vote of the city council. Defendant did not raise on appeal the question whether such an agreement could constitute a bribe. If he had, how should the court have ruled? Is *Van de Carr* relevant?

3. Consider again the problem of Carol and William, set forth above immediately before *Van de Carr*. Does *Van de Carr* suggest that "logrolling" in its most traditional form constitutes bribery? If so, would a current-day court be likely to reach the same conclusion?

Some states have constitutional or statutory provisions making logrolling unlawful. See, *e.g.*, California Penal Code § 86: "Every member of either of the houses composing the Legislature of this state who ... gives ... any official vote in consideration that another Member of the Legislature shall give any such vote either upon the same or another question, is punishable by imprisonment. . . ."

Such prohibitions are old and, to say the least, rarely enforced.

4. Elizabeth, a well-known businesswoman who would be a strong challenger for a city council seat, tells Francisco, the incumbent council member, that she will agree not to run against him if he helps her obtain a zoning variance for a

commercial development that she wants to build. Has Elizabeth offered Francisco a bribe? Is this problem identical to *Hochberg* and *Kaisner*? See Lowenstein, *supra*, at 812–13.

C. Intent to Influence

Bribery often is assumed to require a *quid pro quo*, an agreement that in exchange for such and such a benefit, the official will perform such and such an official act in the desired manner. It is often easy to accomplish a corrupt purpose while avoiding an express agreement and it is usually difficult to prove the existence of such an agreement even if it has occurred. As a result, bribery has a reputation as a crime of narrow scope.

However, the supposed *quid pro quo* requirement is equivocal. On its face, the typical bribery statute does not require an agreement. There are some statutes that require the benefit to be given as "consideration" for the desired official act. *E.g.*, Texas Penal Code Ann. § 36.02. This language could support an interpretation that an agreement is required. Most of the statutes, however, including the federal bribery statute, require only that the benefit be given (or received) with an intent to influence (or to be influenced on) the official action.

In this section we shall consider the "intent to influence" element of bribery, with particular focus on cases in which the "thing of value" is a campaign contribution. Many contributions are made in the hope that they will influence the recipient to act favorably to the donor. Explicit exchanges of contributions for particular official actions (such as favorable votes on legislation) are less common. We saw in the preceding section that courts generally hold that campaign contributions *may* be bribes. In this section we shall consider *when* they are bribes.

To help keep your bearings as you work through the material that follows, it may be helpful to consider the following hypothetical cases. In the first four cases, campaign contributions are made to incumbent legislators, each of whom is regarded as relatively safe in his or her district and none of whom knows of any likely strong challengers in the foreseeable future.

Case 1: The ABC Corporation contributes $10,000 to Larry.[g] ABC has a large, permanent lobbying staff, because it has numerous, ongoing legislative interests on matters such as taxation and regulation. At the time of the contribution, no particular issue dominates ABC's agenda. In none of the discussions between ABC and Larry relative to the contribution is there any allusion to legislative issues. ABC makes the contribution because it hopes and believes that it will influence Larry to support ABC's positions more often than he would do if ABC made no contribution.

g. We assume in each of these hypotheticals that the contribution is legal under any applicable campaign finance regulations and is properly disclosed.

Larry accepts the contribution with a similar expectation that when it is more or less costless for him to do so, he will support ABC in the future.

Case 2: The XYZ Corporation has no ongoing interest in legislation and has not previously engaged in either lobbying or contributing to campaigns. However, for the last year, XYZ has been intensively lobbying in support of a large public works project that, if approved by the legislature, is likely to result in large contracts for XYZ. Analysts inside and outside the company believe the continued solvency of XYZ depends on approval of the project, which is the only issue on which XYZ is lobbying. XYZ contributes $10,000 to Laura. In none of the discussions between XYZ and Laura relating to the contribution is there any allusion made to the project or any other legislative issue. XYZ makes the contribution because it hopes and believes it will increase the chances that Laura will vote for the project. Laura has been undecided on the project and continues to be undecided after receiving the contribution. However, she appreciates the contribution and she mentions to her legislative assistant that because of the contribution she has switched from a position of leaning against the project to leaning in favor, pending further debate and possible reactions to the proposal in her district or among other interest groups.

Case 3: ABC Corporation, situated as in Case 1 above, contributes $10,000 to Lenny. During the meeting in which the head of ABC's political action committee hands over the contribution, the following dialogue occurs:

> *Lenny*: You know, I can't promise to support you on every issue. Sometimes we're just on opposite sides. But I realize that $10,000 is a big contribution, and if you give it to me I guarantee you that I'll give you my support whenever I can, consistent with other commitments and with the situation in my district.
>
> *PAC Director*: That's all we can ask. Here's your check.

Case 4: XYZ Corporation, situated as in Case 2 above, contributes $10,000 to Lucy. During the meeting in which the head of XYZ's political action committee makes the contribution, the following dialogue occurs:

> *Lucy*: There is some vocal opposition to your project in my district, and up to now I have been planning to vote against it. But I'll support it if you contribute $10,000 to my campaign.
>
> *PAC Director*: It's a deal. Here's your check.

Case 5: An issue-oriented group makes campaign contributions out of funds it raises from individuals who support the group's ideology. The group does no lobbying. Rather, it seeks to influence policy by helping to elect candidates with compatible views and defeat candidates with opposing views. In a given legislative district, a candidate who avidly supports the group's ideology is challenging an incumbent who, from the group's point of view, has one of the worst voting records in the legislature. The group contributes $10,000 to the challenger's campaign but otherwise has no contact with the candidate.

In Case 5, the group follows an "electoral strategy," seeking to influence policy by enhancing the chances of candidates who are likely, if elected, to pursue the policies the contributor favors. Some would object to a campaign finance system in which electoral strategies are broadly effective, because of an equity objection that those with resources to devote to large contributions attain a disproportionate influence on public policy. Even if such an objection is accepted, most would agree that the problem is with the system, not with the conduct of the contributor or the recipient of the contribution. No one has contended that contributions made pursuant to an electoral strategy are corrupt or that they are bribes.

The contributors in Cases 1 through 4 pursue a "legislative strategy," consisting of contributing to a person presently in office or a candidate who is likely to be elected, in the hopes of influencing the recipient to pursue the favored policies by reason of gratitude, a desire to encourage future donations from the same or additional sources, or similar motivations. Interest group contributions in the United States are often, though by no means always, made partly or entirely in pursuit of a legislative strategy. They are often received by candidates who know why the contribution is made.

It may help you to organize Cases 1 through 4 in your mind to see that they differ along two dimensions. In Cases 1 and 3, the corporations contribute to promote their legislative agenda generally but not to influence any particular vote or other legislative action. In the other two cases, the contributions are targeted to a particular bill. Thus, one difference relates to the specificity of the influence sought by the contributor. In Cases 1 and 2, the contributor hopes for influence but receives no assurances. In Cases 3 and 4, there is an explicit agreement that the contributor will receive favorable official action in exchange for the contribution. Thus, the second difference relates to the explicitness (and therefore certainty) of the influence. As you read the statutes and cases in the following materials, consider which, if any, of Cases 1 through 4 would constitute a bribe or other offense under the legal doctrines being put forth. Would the result be affected if the transfer were a personal gift of money to the legislator rather than a campaign contribution?

State v. Agan

384 S.E.2d 863 (Georgia 1989)

HUNT, Justice.

We granted certiorari to the Court of Appeals in *Agan v. State*, 191 Ga.App. 92, 380 S.E.2d 757 (1989) to review that opinion, with emphasis upon "[t]he correct interpretation of the offering of a bribe, as prohibited by OCGA § 16-10-2(a)(1), and the acceptance of a 'campaign contribution,' as defined in OCGA § 21-5-3(6)."

The facts, more fully set forth in the Court of Appeals' opinion, are summarized as follows. Agan, the Honorary Turkish Consul in Atlanta, sought a building height variance for the construction of a hotel on his property. Agan and Sarper, an Emory University professor, had discussed with officials of the Emory Medical

Clinic a plan to bring Turkish patients to the Clinic who would stay at the hotel. The Dekalb County Commission had twice rejected Agan's application for a variance. Agan submitted a third application, and spoke with two Dekalb County commissioners, Lanier and Fletcher, inquiring what Agan could do to insure the approval of his application. Agan told Fletcher he had a number of friends in the local Turkish-American Association who wished to contribute to Fletcher's campaign. At a meeting between Agan and Fletcher, Agan urged Fletcher to support the variance application, then left Fletcher with four checks totaling $3,700.00, made to Fletcher personally, and marked "for campaign contribution," despite Fletcher's protests that he did not even have a campaign bank account. The checks were drawn on the accounts of Sarper and three others who testified they were reimbursed for the checks by Agan and believed Agan wanted contributions to come from different people in order to give the impression he enjoyed broad support in the Turkish community. After another meeting between Agan and Fletcher in which Agan reiterated his need for the variance, Agan presented Fletcher with a fifth check for $800.00 marked as a campaign contribution, from a third party. Agan, accompanied by Sarper, also met with Lanier to discuss the variance. As they left Lanier's office, Sarper gave Agan an envelope at Agan's request and, back in Lanier's office, without Sarper, Agan presented Lanier with the envelope containing Sarper's check to Lanier for $3,000.00 marked "campaign contribution," despite Lanier's statement to him that he was not up for re-election for three years....

Sufficiency of the Evidence

1(a). The Court of Appeals correctly determined ... that a rational trier of fact could have found the essential elements of the crime of bribery to have been established beyond a reasonable doubt in regard to Agan. There was ample evidence at trial that Agan gave payments to Lanier and Fletcher for the specific purpose of influencing their votes on his application for a building height variance, thus committing the crime of bribery....

The Charge

[Bribery is defined] in OCGA § 16-10-2(a)(1), which provides that:

> [a] person commits the offense of bribery when ... [h]e gives or offers to give to any person acting for or on behalf of the state or any political subdivision thereof ... any benefit, reward, or consideration to which he is not entitled with the purpose of influencing him in the performance of any act related to the functions of his office.

....

2(b). The Court of Appeals found the trial court's charge faulty for failing to read the bribery statute, OCGA § 16-10-2, in conjunction with the Ethics in Government Act, OCGA § 21-5-1 et seq., which defines political contributions and sets forth the manner in which they may be received and reported. In particular, the Court of Appeals held the language of the bribery statute prohibiting the giving or offering to a public officer of a benefit to which that officer "is not entitled," is to be read very narrowly to proscribe the giving or offering to a public official of a benefit to which that officer "*is not qualified or privileged to receive or has no grounds or right to seek, request, or receive.*" [Emphasis supplied]. The Court of Appeals further held

> a campaign contribution, whether made to a candidate in the heat of a campaign or to encourage or influence the official after he is elected, is something which a candidate or elected official is qualified or privileged to request or receive and thus something to which he is "entitled" within the meaning of OCGA § 16-10-2.

We interpret this holding as meaning, in effect, that if money given to an office holder qualifies as a campaign contribution, requiring reporting under the Ethics in Government Act, OCGA § 21-5-1 et seq., then it cannot be a bribe. With this conclusion we respectfully disagree.

The Ethics in Government Act has in no manner altered the bribery statute. The Act simply defines a campaign contribution and, having defined, requires disclosure. Specifically, nothing in the Act permits a public officeholder to request or receive anything of value "to which he is not entitled with the purpose of influencing him in the performance of any act related to the functions of his office or employment...." (OCGA § 16-10-2(a)). Nor is the term "entitled," as contained in the bribery statute, modified in any way by the Ethics in Government Act. Other than those emoluments of public office that are expressly authorized and established by law, no holder of public office is entitled to request or receive—from any source, directly or indirectly—anything of value in exchange for the performance of any act related to the functions of that office.[2] ....

Constitutionality of the Bribery Statute

Vagueness Challenge

3. We find no merit to Agan's contention that OCGA § 16-10-2(a) is unconstitutionally vague, hence void....

First Amendment Challenge

4. Agan contends the bribery statute must be interpreted as condemning only a payment to a public officer who agrees to a clearly delineated *quid quo pro*, i.e., an explicit purchase of an explicit official act. Were that not so, he insists, the bribery statute would be an impermissible restraint upon free speech under the First Amendment to the Constitution of the United States. He relies principally upon *Buckley v. Valeo*, 424 U.S. 1 (1976).

In *Buckley*, the Supreme Court examined the application of the First Amendment to limitations upon campaign expenditures by a candidate for public office,

---

2. Our holding means that a transfer that is a bribe as defined by OCGA § 16-10-2 also may come within the definition of "contribution" as contained in the third sentence of OCGA § 21-5-3(6). The fact that such a transfer must be reported does not change its character as a bribe.

and limitations upon amounts that might be contributed to a campaign, finding a violation of the right of free speech for the former, and none for the latter. The holdings in *Buckley* do not apply to the bribery statute, which places no limitation upon amounts of contributions or expenditures, but, rather, restricts the purposes for which any "benefit, reward or consideration" may be offered or given to, or solicited or accepted by, a public officer. Even assuming the First Amendment might relate to the purposes of political transfers, it cannot be understood to shield the bribing of a public officer.[3]

Citizens of Georgia have every right to try to influence their public officers—through petition and protest, promises of political support and threats of political reprisal. They do *not* have, nor have they ever had, the "right" to buy the official act of a public officer. OCGA § 16-10-2(a). Public officers are not prohibited from receiving legitimate financial aid in support of nomination or election to public office. They do *not* have, nor have they ever had, the "right" to sell the powers of their offices.[4] OCGA § 16-10-2(b). The bribery statute does not serve to weaken free speech. It serves to strengthen free government....

Notes and Questions

1. One of the conventional elements of bribery is "consideration," what is often referred to as a *quid pro quo*.[h] Does *Agan* require a *quid pro quo*? Does 18 U.S.C. § 201(b)? Should a *quid pro quo* be required? If not, what more than a gift to the official and an official act favorable to the donor should be required for a bribe?

---

3. "Where the letter of the statute results in absurdity or injustice or would lead to contradictions, the meaning of general language may be restrained by the spirit or reason of the statute." *Sirmans v. Sirmans*, 149 S.E.2d 101 (Ga. 1966). That logic should apply alike to all legal authorities, including the Constitution.

We decline to follow the "rule," as urged by Agan, of *People v. Brandstetter*, 430 N.E.2d 731 (Ill. App. 1982), that: "[P]ublic officials are 'authorized by law' to receive campaign contributions from those who might seek to influence the candidate's performance as long as no promise for or performance of a specific official act is given in exchange." In that case, a political activist was convicted of bribery for handing to a state legislator a note that read: "Mr. _____, the offer for help in your election & $1000 for your campaign for Pro ERA vote."

While Brandstetter's conviction was affirmed on appeal, we are concerned that its "rule" would proliferate corrupt practices. As an example, note this story in *The Atlanta Journal and Constitution* of July 8, 1989: "A millionaire who handed out $10,000 checks on the [Texas] Senate floor while legislation that interested him was pending said the checks were political contributions, not an attempt to bribe lawmakers. 'It would be difficult to make it into a bribery case,' said [the district attorney], who believes it's time to change Texas's loose campaign finance laws. 'In Texas, it's almost impossible to bribe a public official as long as you report it....'"

4. The acceptance of a bribe is an egregious conflict of interest, and will vitiate official acts that otherwise appear to be lawful. [The footnote goes on to refer to several Georgia decisions in which zoning and other decisions were set aside at the behest of private citizens because they were infected by corruption or conflict of interest.—Eds.]

h. This is a Latin phrase whose literal translation is "something for something." See David Mellinkoff, Mellinkoff's Dictionary of American Legal Usage 116 (1992).

2. Some significant interpretations of the federal bribery laws during the 1970s arose out of transactions between Senator Daniel Brewster of Maryland and lobbyist Cyrus Anderson. Brewster was a member of the Senate Post Office and Civil Service Committee, and Anderson's client, mail-order catalogue merchant Spiegel, Inc., had a strong interest in keeping postal rates as low as possible. Anderson made several payments to Brewster during a period when potential postal rate increases were either pending or foreseeable. In 1967, when these payments were made, campaign reporting and accounting requirements were minimal. The payments could reasonably have been characterized as either campaign contributions or personal payments to Brewster. Brewster and Anderson were accused of both bribes and unlawful gratuities.

The Supreme Court ruled that Brewster could be prosecuted notwithstanding the Speech or Debate Clause of the Constitution, *United States v. Brewster*, 408 U.S. 501 (1972). Brewster and Anderson subsequently stood trial. Anderson was convicted of bribery.[i] Brewster was convicted of accepting unlawful gratuities but was acquitted of the bribery charges. Brewster appealed on the grounds, among others, that the unlawful gratuity statute is unconstitutionally vague and overbroad, and that the trial judge's instructions to the jury were inadequate to distinguish conduct falling within three categories: (1) guilt of bribery, (2) guilt of unlawful gratuity, and (3) innocence. In a long and difficult opinion, the Court of Appeals upheld the constitutionality of the unlawful gratuity statute but reversed Brewster's conviction because of the jury instructions. *United States v. Brewster*, 506 F.2d 62 (D.C.Cir. 1974). The court summarized its view of the two offenses as follows:

> To accept a thing of value "*in return for*: (1) *being influenced* in [the] performance of any official act," [as required by the bribery offense,] appears to us to imply a higher degree of criminal intent than to accept the same thing of value "for or because of any official act performed or to be performed." Perhaps the difference in meaning is slight, but Congress chose different language in which to express comparable ideas. The bribery section makes necessary an explicit *quid pro quo* which need not exist if only an illegal gratuity is involved; the briber is the mover or producer of the official act, but the official act for which the gratuity is given might have been done without the gratuity, although the gratuity was produced because of the official act.

As we shall see later in this chapter, in the *Sun-Diamond* case, the Supreme Court ruled on the connection between a gift to an official and an official act that is necessary for a violation of Section 201(c), the gratuity offense. With respect to Section 201(b), the bribery offense, is the *Brewster* court correct that an "explicit *quid pro quo*" is required for a violation? More on this question below in the notes following *McCormick*, our next case.

---

i. For Anderson's appeal, see *United States v. Anderson*, 509 F.2d 312 (D.C.Cir. 1974).

The *Brewster* court seemed to rule out the possibility of campaign contributions violating the federal *gratuity* offense, at least as long as the contribution is made to a campaign committee rather than to the candidate directly, as is now invariably the case. Is this the correct reading of the federal gratuity statute?

3. Coming into the 1980s, the federal courts had no clear and uniform understanding of what was required by way of an "intent to influence" under federal or state bribery laws or when a campaign contribution could be a bribe or an unlawful gratuity. Since then, federal prosecutors have become increasingly aggressive in attempting to enforce anti-corruption laws against state and local elected officials and, in some cases, against members of Congress. For example, several officials and lobbyists in California and South Carolina were imprisoned in the early 1990s because of federal "sting" investigations of corruption in and around the state legislatures. Three cases decided by the Supreme Court—*McNally v. United States* (1987), *McCormick v. United States* (1991), and *Evans v. United States* (1992)—reflect an apparent desire upon the part of the Supreme Court to control the extent of federal engagement in anti-corruption activity in states and localities. Together with a fourth decision, *United States v. Sun-Diamond Growers* (1999), they may also reflect concern by the Court with possibly excessively broad interpretation of anti-corruption laws. All four decisions appear or are discussed below.

In order to understand the significance as well as the limits of these decisions, it will be helpful to bear in mind four possible situations in which bribes may be prosecuted.

(1) Federal prosecutors may bring charges against federal officials and those who attempt to influence them under federal bribery statutes, such as 18 U.S.C. § 201. *Brewster* and *Sun-Diamond* are examples of this type of case.

(2) Federal prosecutors may bring charges under federal statutes that establish federal standards that may be imposed, under specified circumstances, on state and local officials. The most commonly used statutes of this type have been the Hobbs Act, 18 U.S.C. § 1951 (at issue in *McCormick* and *Evans*), and the Mail and Wire Fraud statutes, 18 U.S.C. §§ 1341, 1343 and 1346 (at issue in *McNally*, and discussed further below, in Note 5 following *McCormick*).[j]

(3) Federal prosecutors may bring charges against state or local officials under federal statutes that, in effect, incorporate the standards of "predicate" statutes, including state bribery statutes. Under statutes of this type, violation of one or more predicate statutes, combined with certain additional circumstances, becomes

j. An additional statute, passed in 1984 and used increasingly by federal prosecutors against state and local officials after 1990, is referred to as the "federal program bribery" provision, 18 U.S.C. § 666. It prohibits bribery, and also embezzlement and other forms of theft, by employees of governmental entities that receive federal grants. The prohibition is applicable to bribes without regard to whether federal funds are demonstrably affected. See *Salinas v. United States*, 522 U.S. 52 (1997). For commentary on federal program bribery, see George D. Brown, *Stealth Statute—Corruption, The Spending Power, and the Rise of 18 U.S.C. § 666*, 73 Notre Dame Law Review 247 (1998).

a federal violation. The most important statutes under this heading are the Travel Act, 18 U.S.C. § 1952, and the Racketeer Influenced and Corrupt Organizations Act (RICO), 18 U.S.C. §§ 1961–68. Statutes of the second and third types require that the corrupt activity impinge on some federal interest, such as by affecting interstate commerce or involving use of the mail, but these requirements are often satisfied and therefore have little effect in restraining federal enforcement of corrupt activity.

(4) State prosecutors may prosecute state or local officials under state bribery laws.

Because *McNally*, *McCormick*, and *Evans* each were examples of the second situation, they did not entail interpretation of 18 U.S.C. § 201 or state bribery statutes. Nevertheless, the decisions are of considerable interest, both theoretical and practical. From a practical standpoint, various factors can inhibit anti-corruption investigations and prosecutions by state and local prosecutors. Federal prosecutions under the Hobbs Act and the Mail and Wire Fraud statutes are the most visible and possibly the most numerous anti-corruption actions affecting state and local government officials.[k] Furthermore, it is at least possible that these decisions will affect the interpretation of other statutes. The Supreme Court may bring similar views to bear when it comes to interpreting 18 U.S.C. § 201, and state courts may find the views of the Supreme Court persuasive when construing their own statutes.

McCormick v. United States

500 U.S. 257 (1991)

Justice WHITE delivered the opinion of the Court.

This case requires us to consider whether the Court of Appeals properly affirmed the conviction of petitioner, an elected public official, for extorting property under color of official right in violation of the Hobbs Act, 18 U.S.C. § 1951.

I

[McCormick was a member of the West Virginia state legislature who represented a district that had suffered from a shortage of doctors. In 1984, he supported legislation to permit foreign medical school graduates to practice under temporary permits while they were studying for the state licensing examinations. During his reelection campaign, McCormick told the lobbyist for an organization of the foreign medical graduates "that his campaign was expensive, that he had paid considerable sums out of his own pocket, and that he had not heard anything from the foreign doctors." The lobbyist raised some money from the members of his group and gave McCormick an envelope containing $900 in cash. West Virginia law prohibited cash contributions over $50, and neither McCormick nor the organization reported the gift as a campaign contribution.

---

k. By one count, nearly six thousand state and local officials were convicted of federal corruption charges between 1977 and 1987. See Kenneth J. Meier & Thomas M. Holbrook, *"I Seen My Opportunities and I Took 'Em:" Political Corruption in the American States*, 54 Journal of Politics 135, 136 (1992).

McCormick was convicted of extortion under the Hobbs Act, which provides:

> (a) Whoever in any way or degree obstructs, delays, or affects commerce ... by way of robbery or extortion ... in violation of this section shall be fined ... or imprisoned ... or both.
>
> (b) as used in this section—
>
> ...
>
> (2) The term "extortion" means the obtaining of property from another with his consent, induced by wrongful use of actual or threatened force, violence, or fear, or under color of official right.]

II

McCormick's challenge to the judgment below affirming his conviction is limited to ... his claim that the payments made to him by or on behalf of the doctors were campaign contributions, the receipt of which did not violate the Hobbs Act.... McCormick does not challenge any rulings of the courts below with respect to the application of the Hobbs Act to payments made to nonelected officials or to payments made to elected officials that are properly determined not to be campaign contributions. Hence, we do not consider how the "under color of official right" phrase is to be interpreted and applied in those contexts....

B

We agree with the Court of Appeals that in a case like this it is proper to inquire whether payments made to an elected official are in fact campaign contributions, and we agree that the intention of the parties is a relevant consideration in pursuing this inquiry. But we cannot accept the Court of Appeals' approach to distinguishing between legal and illegal campaign contributions. The Court of Appeals stated that payments to elected officials could violate the Hobbs Act without proof of an explicit *quid pro quo* by proving that the payments "were never intended to be *legitimate* campaign contributions." ...

Serving constituents and supporting legislation that will benefit the district and individuals and groups therein is the everyday business of a legislator. It is also true that campaigns must be run and financed. Money is constantly being solicited on behalf of candidates, who run on platforms and who claim support on the basis of their views and what they intend to do or have done. Whatever ethical considerations and appearances may indicate, to hold that legislators commit the federal crime of extortion when they act for the benefit of constituents or support legislation furthering the interests of some of their constituents, shortly before or after campaign contributions are solicited and received from those beneficiaries, is an unrealistic assessment of what Congress could have meant by making it a crime to obtain property from another, with his consent, "under color of official right." To hold otherwise would open to prosecution not only conduct that has long been thought to be well within the law but also conduct that in a very real sense is unavoidable so long as election campaigns are financed by private contributions or expenditures, as they have been from the beginning of the Nation. It would require statutory language more explicit than the Hobbs Act contains to justify a contrary conclusion.

This is not to say that it is impossible for an elected official to commit extortion in the course of financing an election campaign. Political contributions are of course vulnerable if induced by the use of force, violence, or fear. The receipt of such contributions is also vulnerable under the Act as having been taken under color of official right, but only if the payments are made in return for an explicit promise or undertaking by the official to perform or not to perform an official act. In such situations the official asserts that his official conduct will be controlled by the terms of the promise or undertaking. This is the receipt of money by an elected official under color of official right within the meaning of the Hobbs Act.

This formulation defines the forbidden zone of conduct with sufficient clarity. As the Court of Appeals for the Fifth Circuit observed in *United States v. Dozier*, 672 F.2d 531, 537 (1982):

> A moment's reflection should enable one to distinguish, at least in the abstract, a legitimate solicitation from the exaction of a fee for a benefit conferred or an injury withheld. Whether described familiarly as a payoff or with the Latinate precision of *quid pro quo*, the prohibited exchange is the same: a public official may not demand payment as inducement for the promise to perform (or not to perform) an official act.

The United States agrees that if the payments to McCormick were campaign contributions, proof of a *quid pro quo* would be essential for an extortion conviction and quotes the instruction given on this subject in 9 Department of Justice Manual § 9-85A.306, p. 9-1938.134 (Supp.1988-2): "[C]ampaign contributions will not be authorized as the subject of a Hobbs Act prosecution unless they can be proven to have been given in return for the performance of or abstaining from an official act; otherwise any campaign contribution might constitute a violation."

We thus disagree with the Court of Appeals' holding in this case that a *quid pro quo* is not necessary for conviction under the Hobbs Act when an official receives a campaign contribution.[10] By the same token, we hold, as McCormick urges, that the District Court's instruction to the same effect was error.

III

[I]t is true that the trial court instructed that the receipt of voluntary campaign contributions did not violate the Hobbs Act. But under the instructions a contribution was not "voluntary" if given with any expectation of benefit; and as we read the instructions, taken as a whole, the jury was told that it could find McCormick guilty of extortion if any of the payments, even though a campaign contribution,

---

10. As noted previously, McCormick's sole contention in this case is that the payments made to him were campaign contributions. Therefore, we do not decide whether a *quid pro quo* requirement exists in other contexts, such as when an elected official receives gifts, meals, travel expenses, or other items of value.

was made by the doctors with the expectation that McCormick's official action would be influenced for their benefit and if McCormick knew that the payment was made with that expectation. It may be that the jury found that none of the payments was a campaign contribution, but it is mere speculation that the jury convicted on this basis rather than on the impermissible basis that even though the first payment was such a contribution, McCormick's receipt of it was a violation of the Hobbs Act....

V

Accordingly we reverse the judgment of the Court of Appeals and remand for further proceedings consistent with this opinion.

Justice STEVENS, with whom Justice BLACKMUN and Justice O'CONNOR join, dissenting....

In my opinion there is no statutory requirement that illegal agreements, threats, or promises be in writing, or in any particular form. Subtle extortion is just as wrongful—and probably much more common—than the kind of express understanding that the Court's opinion seems to require.

Nevertheless, to prove a violation of the Hobbs Act, I agree with the Court that it is essential that the payment in question be contingent on a mutual understanding that the motivation for the payment is the payer's desire to avoid a specific threatened harm or to obtain a promised benefit that the defendant has the apparent power to deliver, either through the use of force or the use of public office. In this sense, the crime does require a "*quid pro quo*." ...

This Court's criticism of the District Court's instructions focuses on this single sentence:

> Voluntary is that which is freely given without expectation of benefit.

The Court treats this sentence as though it authorized the jury to find that a legitimate campaign contribution is involuntary and constitutes extortion whenever the contributor expects to benefit from the candidate's election. In my opinion this is a gross misreading of that sentence in the context of the entire set of instructions.

In context, the sentence in question advised the jury that a payment is voluntary if it is made without the expectation of a benefit that is specifically contingent upon the payment. An expectation that the donor will benefit from the election of a candidate who, once in office, would support particular legislation regardless of whether or not the contribution is made, would not make the payment contingent or involuntary in that sense; such a payment would be "voluntary" under a fair reading of the instructions, and the candidate's solicitation of such contributions from donors who would benefit from his or her election is perfectly legitimate. If, however, the donor and candidate know that the candidate's support of the proposed legislation is contingent upon the payment, the contribution may be found by a jury to have been involuntary or extorted.

In my judgment, the instructions, read as a whole, properly focused the jury's attention on the critical issue of the candidate's and contributor's intent at the time the specific payment was made....

I respectfully dissent.

[A concurring opinion by Justice SCALIA is omitted.]

Notes and Questions

1. Is Justice Stevens's conception of a *quid pro quo* the same as the majority's?

2. Should the same *quid pro quo* requirement apply to benefits that are not campaign contributions?

3. The Court offered a somewhat different statement of the *quid pro quo* requirement in *Evans v. United States*, 504 U.S. 255 (1992). The central issue in *Evans* was whether the word "induced" in paragraph (b)(2) of the Hobbs Act means that the official must ask for or in some other way initiate or actively bring about the forbidden transaction.[1] This time, Justice Stevens (dissenter in *McCormick*) wrote for the majority, beginning with the statement:

> We granted certiorari to resolve a conflict in the Circuits over the question whether an affirmative act of inducement by a public official, such as a demand, is an element of the offense of extortion "under color of official right" prohibited by the Hobbs Act. We agree with the Court of Appeals for the Eleventh Circuit that it is not, and therefore affirm the judgment of the court below.

Evans, a member of the Board of Commissioners of DeKalb County, Georgia, had numerous conversations over a period of a year-and-a-half with an undercover FBI agent posing as a real estate developer seeking to rezone a tract of land. All or nearly all of the conversations were initiated by the agent. Near the end of the period, the agent gave Evans $7,000 in cash and a campaign contribution of $1,000. The jury could have found that Evans

> accepted the cash knowing that it was intended to ensure that he would vote in favor of the rezoning application and that he would try to persuade his fellow commissioners to do likewise. Thus, although petitioner did not initiate the transaction, his acceptance of the bribe constituted an implicit promise to use his official position to serve the interests of the bribe-giver.

The jury instructions correctly anticipated *McCormick*, advising that a campaign contribution by a person with business pending before an official was not

---

1. Paragraph (b)(2), it will be recalled, reads:
The term "extortion" means the obtaining of property from another, with his consent, induced by wrongful use of actual or threatened force, violence, or fear, or under color of official right.

sufficient for a violation of the Hobbs Act. But if the official "demands or accepts money in exchange for [a] specific requested exercise of his or her official power, such a demand or acceptance does constitute a violation of the Hobbs Act regardless of whether the payment is made in the form of a campaign contribution." Evans's objection to the jury instruction was that it permitted a conviction based on a mere "acceptance" of money in exchange for favorable official action, without requiring a demand or any affirmative act of inducement.

Relying in large part on historical research and analysis by James Lindgren, *The Elusive Distinction Between Bribery and Extortion: From the Common Law to the Hobbs Act*, 35 UCLA Law Review 815 (1988), the *Evans* majority concluded that inducement by the official was *not* an element of the offense.

> At common law, extortion was an offense committed by a public official who took "by colour of his office" money that was not due to him for the performance of his official duties. Extortion by the public official was the rough equivalent of what we would now describe as "taking a bribe." It is clear that petitioner committed that offense.

Since a portion of the payment to Evans was a campaign contribution, the Court briefly addressed *McCormick*:

> We reject petitioner's criticism of the instruction and conclude that it satisfies the *quid pro quo* requirement of *McCormick*, because the offense is completed at the time when the public official receives a payment in return for his agreement to perform specific official acts;[m] fulfillment of the *quid pro quo* is not an element of the offense.... We hold today that the Government need only show that a public official has obtained a payment to which he was not entitled, knowing that the payment was made in return for official acts.[n]

Referring to the last sentence of this quotation, Justice Kennedy, concurring in *Evans*, said that "this language requires a *quid pro quo* as an element of the Government's case in a prosecution" under the "color of official right" portion of the Hobbs Act. In other words, Kennedy interpreted the majority opinion as extending *McCormick* to all "color of official right" cases, whether or not the payment to the official is a campaign contribution. Do you agree?[o]

4. Does there need to be an *explicit* promise or agreement to convict someone of bribery? *McCormick* said that there is a violation "only if the payments are made in return for an *explicit promise or undertaking* by the official to perform or not to

m. Note that in its description of what the jury presumably found, quoted above, the Court referred to an *implicit* promise. Compare this to *McCormick*'s requirement of an *explicit* promise or undertaking. — Eds.

n. Recall that the majority opinion in *Evans* was written by Justice Stevens, who had dissented in *McCormick*. — Eds.

o. Justice Thomas dissented in *Evans*, joined by Justice Scalia and Chief Justice Rehnquist.

perform an official act. In such situations the official asserts that his official conduct will be controlled by the terms of the promise or undertaking" (emphasis added). But in *Evans*, Justice Stevens's opinion for the Court said "that the Government need only show that a public official has obtained a payment to which he was not entitled, knowing that the payment was made in return for official acts." This might be taken to suggest something less than an explicit promise or agreement. Justice Kennedy's *Evans* concurrence was less ambiguous in renouncing any explicitness requirement, saying that the briber and bribee "need not state the *quid pro quo* in express terms ... for otherwise the law's effect could be frustrated by knowing winks and nods."

These cases suggest that the Court is torn between the desire to set forth clear standards for bribery-type offenses and the recognition that the only clear standard that suggests itself—the requirement of an explicit agreement between the parties that the gift or campaign contribution is made in exchange for favorable official action—fails to match normative intuitions about what is and isn't corrupt conduct. To borrow language from Justice Kennedy's concurring opinion in *Evans*, if "winks and nods" suffice to satisfy a *quid pro quo* requirement, then the standard of conduct imposed by the law can never be clear. But if something more explicit than winks and nods is required for a violation, then the law will punish only the most inept, not the most corrupt.

The Supreme Court briefly addressed the issue in *McDonnell v. United States*, 136 S. Ct. 2355 (2016), which appears in Part II.D below. On behalf of a unanimous Court, Chief Justice Roberts wrote: "The agreement need *not* be explicit, and the public official need not specify the means that he will use to perform his end of the bargain." This statement appears to resolve the question, although it might be characterized as dicta. See Daniel P. Tokaji, *Bribery and Campaign Finance*: McDonnell*'s Double-Edged Sword*, 14 Ohio State Journal of Criminal Law Amici Briefs 15 (2017).

5. In addition to the Hobbs Act, the federal Mail and Wire Fraud statutes (18 U.S.C. §§ 1341, 1343, and 1346) are often used to prosecute state and local officials accused of bribery or other forms of corruption. The development of this statute over time reflects a back-and-forth between the Supreme Court and Congress, with Congress taking a more aggressive posture toward corruption and the Court limiting the scope of the statute.

In *McNally v. United States*, 483 U.S. 350 (1987), Kentucky public officials and others who participated in a scheme to steer state insurance business to benefit either themselves or their political allies were convicted of violating the federal Mail Fraud statute, 18 U.S.C. § 1341, which read:

> Whoever, having devised or intending to devise any scheme or artifice to defraud, or for obtaining money or property by means of false or fraudulent pretenses, representations, or promises, ... for the purpose of executing such scheme or artifice [uses the mails or causes them to be used], shall be fined ... or imprisoned ... or both.

A similarly worded prohibition applies to wire fraud. 18 U.S.C. § 1343.

Although the diversion of insurance business for the *McNally* defendants' benefit did not actually cost the state any money, the defendants were convicted on an interpretation that had been accepted by several lower courts, holding that it extends to "schemes to defraud citizens of their intangible rights to honest and impartial government." In *McNally*, the Supreme Court rejected this interpretation, holding that the statute "does not refer to the intangible right of the citizenry to good government." Among several other reasons for this conclusion, the Court stated a preference to avoid an interpretation that "involves the Federal Government in setting standards of disclosure and good government for local and state officials."

The practical effect of *McNally* was short-lived, as Congress in 1988 adopted a new section stating that for purposes of the Mail and Wire Fraud statutes, "the term 'scheme or artifice to defraud' includes a scheme or artifice to deprive another of the intangible right of honest services." 18 U.S.C. § 1346. For commentary on *McNally* and the Mail Fraud law, see John C. Coffee, *Modern Mail Fraud: The Restoration of the Public/Private Distinction*, 35 American Criminal Law Review 427 (1998).

What exactly is "a scheme or artifice to deprive another of the intangible right of honest services"? The Supreme Court answered the question in *Skilling v. United States*, 561 U.S. 358 (2010): the statute prohibits bribery and kickbacks, period. While acknowledging that § 1346 had sometimes been interpreted to prohibit a broader range of conduct, such as the failure to disclose a conflict of interest, the Court adopted this narrowing interpretation to avoid constitutional vagueness concerns. Looking back at the history of the statute, Justice Ginsburg's opinion for the majority concluded that bribery and kickbacks were at the core of the pre-*McNally* case law that Congress intended to restore through its 1988 amendment. According to the majority, Section 1346 should be understood in light of other federal statutes defining bribery (18 U.S.C. § 201(b)) and kickbacks (41 U.S.C. § 52(2)). Concurring in the judgment, Justice Scalia (joined by Justices Thomas and Kennedy) argued that the Court should have struck down the statute as unconstitutionally vague. Was the Court right to limit "honest services" fraud to bribery and kickbacks? Does the majority's interpretation resolve the vagueness problem? Should the Court have struck down the statute on its face, leaving Congress to write a more precise statute if it chose?

6. The Supreme Court again addressed the meaning of a "scheme or artifice to defraud" in *Kelly v. United States*, 140 S. Ct. 1565 (2020). That case arose out of New Jersey's "Bridgegate" scandal. Employees in the office of then-Governor Chris Christie and the Port Authority of New York and New Jersey allegedly reallocated traffic lanes on the George Washington Bridge (which connects New Jersey and New York). This was allegedly done to create a massive traffic jam in Fort Lee, New Jersey, as political retaliation against the city's mayor for not supporting Governor Christie's reelection. Bridget Kelly was Deputy Chief of Staff in the Governor's Office, and

William Baroni was Deputy Executive Director of the Port Authority. Both Kelly and Baroni allegedly participated in this scheme.

The government alleged that this was a scheme to defraud, in violation of the federal wire fraud statute since electronic communications were used to accomplish the lane reallocation. It did not allege "honest services" fraud, as there was no evident bribery or kickback, as required under *Skilling*. Instead, the government's theory was that these public officials defrauded the Port Authority of property (lanes and toll booths) and money (wages of public employee who worked on the lane closure) through their scheme. Kelly and Baroni were convicted, and the Third Circuit accepted the government's theory on appeal. *United States v. Baroni*, 909 F.3d 550 (3d Cir. 2018).

The Supreme Court reversed, with Justice Kagan writing for a unanimous Court. While acknowledging that act could be characterized as "corrupt," 140 S. Ct. at 1574, the Court explained that the defendant public officials could not be convicted under the wire fraud statute merely on a showing that they lied about their reasons for the lane closure. *Id.* at 1572. Rather, the officials must have had the "object" of obtaining public money or property. *Id.* Kelly and Baroni may have misused their authority to regulate traffic over the bridge, and may even have wasted public resources on their scheme, but they did not have the object of obtaining public property. *Id.* at 1574.

Should public officials be subject to federal criminal prosecution where they allocate public resources based on false pretenses? Does the Court's narrow interpretation of the fraud statute open the door to government officials misusing public resources for political payback? Conversely, would a broader reading of the statute lead to a different type of political retaliation, in the form of prosecutions of public officials on the ground that they lied about the reasons for their actions? After all, some public money or property is likely to be used in just about any action that a public official might take.

7. Federal prosecutors now commonly use the Hobbs Act and the "Honest Services" fraud statute to prosecute bribery involving state and local officials. Is the setting of standards of good government for states and localities an appropriate function for the federal government? For a careful and thoughtful consideration of this question, see George D. Brown, *New Federalism's Unanswered Question: Who Should Prosecute State and Local Officials for Political Corruption?*, 60 Washington & Lee Law Review 417 (2003).

8. Reconsider again Cases 1 through 4 in the hypotheticals at the beginning of this section. Are the contributors and legislators guilty of bribery or related offenses? And consider again whether the result would be different if the payments in each case were a personal gift rather than a campaign contribution.

United States v. Sun-Diamond Growers of California

526 U.S. 398 (1999)

Justice SCALIA delivered the opinion of the Court.

Talmudic sages believed that judges who accepted bribes would be punished by eventually losing all knowledge of the divine law. The Federal Government, dealing with many public officials who are not judges, and with at least some judges for whom this sanction holds no terror, has constructed a framework of human laws and regulations defining various sorts of impermissible gifts, and punishing those who give or receive them with administrative sanctions, fines, and incarceration. One element of that framework is 18 U.S.C. § 201(c)(1)(A), the "illegal gratuity statute," which prohibits giving "anything of value" to a present, past, or future public official "for or because of any official act performed or to be performed by such public official." In this case, we consider whether conviction under the illegal gratuity statute requires any showing beyond the fact that a gratuity was given because of the recipient's official position.

I

Respondent is a trade association that engaged in marketing and lobbying activities on behalf of its member cooperatives, which were owned by approximately 5,000 individual growers of raisins, figs, walnuts, prunes, and hazelnuts. Petitioner United States is represented by Independent Counsel Donald Smaltz, who, as a consequence of his investigation of former Secretary of Agriculture Michael Espy, charged respondent with, *inter alia*, making illegal gifts to Espy in violation of § 201(c)(1)(A). That statute provides, in relevant part, that anyone who

> otherwise than as provided by law for the proper discharge of official duty ... directly or indirectly gives, offers, or promises anything of value to any public official, former public official, or person selected to be a public official, for or because of any official act performed or to be performed by such public official, former public official, or person selected to be a public official ... shall be fined under this title or imprisoned for not more than two years, or both.

Count One of the indictment charged Sun-Diamond with giving Espy approximately $5,900 in illegal gratuities: tickets to the 1993 U.S. Open Tennis Tournament (worth $2,295), luggage ($2,427), meals ($665), and a framed print and crystal bowl ($524). The indictment alluded to two matters in which respondent had an interest in favorable treatment from the Secretary at the time it bestowed the gratuities. [First, Sun-Diamond hoped for favorable regulations from the Secretary of Agriculture defining which agricultural entities would be eligible for export subsidies. Second, Sun-Diamond sought the Secretary's assistance in persuading the Environmental Protection Agency to abandon or soften a proposed rule regulating a certain pesticide, methyl bromide.]

Although describing these two matters before the Secretary in which respondent had an interest, the indictment did not allege a specific connection between either of them—or between any other action of the Secretary—and the gratuities conferred....

II

[Justice Scalia described the textual juxtaposition of the bribery offense in Section 201(b) and the gratuity offense in Section 201(c), as at the beginning of Part II of this chapter.]

The distinguishing feature of each crime is its intent element. Bribery requires intent "to influence" an official act or "to be influenced" in an official act, while illegal gratuity requires only that the gratuity be given or accepted "for or because of" an official act. In other words, for bribery there must be a *quid pro quo*—a specific intent to give or receive something of value *in exchange* for an official act. An illegal gratuity, on the other hand, may constitute merely a reward for some future act that the public official will take (and may already have determined to take), or for a past act that he has already taken....

The District Court's instructions in this case, in differentiating between a bribe and an illegal gratuity, correctly noted that only a bribe requires proof of a *quid pro quo*. The point in controversy here is that the instructions went on to suggest that § 201(c)(1)(A), unlike the bribery statute, did not require any connection between respondent's intent and a specific official act. It would be satisfied, according to the instructions, merely by a showing that respondent gave Secretary Espy a gratuity because of his official position—perhaps, for example, to build a reservoir of goodwill that might ultimately affect one or more of a multitude of unspecified acts, now and in the future....

In our view, this interpretation does not fit comfortably with the statutory text, which prohibits only gratuities given or received "for or because of *any official act* performed or to be performed" (emphasis added). It seems to us that this means "for or because of some particular official act of whatever identity"—just as the question "Do you like any composer?" normally means "Do you like some particular composer?" It is linguistically possible, of course, for the phrase to mean "for or because of official acts in general, without specification as to which one"—just as the question "Do you like any composer?" could mean "Do you like all composers, no matter what their names or music?" But the former seems to us the more natural meaning, especially given the complex structure of the provision before us here. Why go through the trouble of requiring that the gift be made "for or because of any official act performed or to be performed by such public official," and then defining "official act" (in § 201(a)(3)) to mean "any decision or action on any question, matter, cause, suit, proceeding or controversy, which may at any time be pending, or which may by law be brought before any public official, in such official's official capacity," when, if the Government's interpretation were correct, it would have sufficed to say "for or because of such official's ability to favor the donor in executing the functions of his office"? The insistence upon an "official act," carefully defined, seems pregnant with the requirement that some particular official act be identified and proved.

Besides thinking that this is the more natural meaning of § 201(c)(1)(A), we are inclined to believe it correct because of the peculiar results that the Government's alternative reading would produce. It would criminalize, for example, token gifts to the President based on his official position and not linked to any identifiable act—such as the replica jerseys given by championship sports teams each year during ceremonial White House visits. Similarly, it would criminalize a high school principal's gift of a school baseball cap to the Secretary of Education, by reason of his office, on the occasion of the latter's visit to the school. That these examples are not fanciful is demonstrated by the fact that counsel for the United States maintained at oral argument that a group of farmers would violate § 201(c)(1)(A) by providing a complimentary lunch for the Secretary of Agriculture in conjunction with his speech to the farmers concerning various matters of USDA policy—so long as the Secretary had before him, or had in prospect, matters affecting the farmers. Of course the Secretary of Agriculture *always* has before him or in prospect matters that affect farmers, just as the President always has before him or in prospect matters that affect college and professional sports, and the Secretary of Education matters that affect high schools.

It might be said in reply to this that the more narrow interpretation of the statute can also produce some peculiar results. In fact, in the above-given examples, the gifts could easily be regarded as having been conferred, not only because of the official's position as President or Secretary, but also (and perhaps principally) "for or because of" the official acts of receiving the sports teams at the White House, visiting the high school, and speaking to the farmers about USDA policy, respectively. The answer to this objection is that those actions—while they are assuredly "official acts" in some sense—are not "official acts" within the meaning of the statute, which, as we have noted, defines "official act" to mean "any decision or action on any question, matter, cause, suit, proceeding or controversy, which may at any time be pending, or which may by law be brought before any public official, in such official's official capacity, or in such official's place of trust or profit." 18 U.S.C. § 201(a)(3). Thus, when the violation is linked to a particular "official act," it is possible to eliminate the absurdities *through the definition of that term.* When, however, no particular "official act" need be identified, and the giving of gifts by reason of the recipient's mere tenure in office constitutes a violation, nothing but the Government's discretion prevents the foregoing examples from being prosecuted.

[We omit Justice Scalia's responses to additional statutory arguments tendered by the government. In Part III, Justice Scalia rejected the government's argument that the erroneous jury instruction was harmless error.]

We hold that, in order to establish a violation of 18 U.S.C. § 201(c)(1)(A), the Government must prove a link between a thing of value conferred upon a public official and a specific "official act" for or because of which it was given. . . .

Notes and Questions

1. The Court's interpretation of Section 201(c)(1)(A) in *Sun-Diamond* is narrower than the interpretation urged by the government and adopted by the lower courts. But is it narrow enough for the gratuities statute to be applied comfortably to campaign contributions? Consider again the hypothetical case of Victoria, presented earlier in this chapter. Victoria strongly favored a particular bill and mailed $25 campaign contributions to each of the three members of the House of Representatives from her state who voted in favor of the bill. Has she violated 18 U.S.C. § 201(c)? Does *Sun-Diamond* have any bearing on her case?

2. Consider Justice Scalia's statement relating to Section 201(b), the bribery offense:

> Bribery requires intent "to influence" an official act or "to be influenced" in an official act, while illegal gratuity requires only that the gratuity be given or accepted "for or because of" an official act. In other words, for bribery there must be a *quid pro quo*—a specific intent to give or receive something of value *in exchange* for an official act.

Is this statement dictum, or part of the *Sun-Diamond* holding? Does the second sentence simply paraphrase the quoted statutory phrases in the first sentence or does it change the meaning of those phrases? In this passage, does the Court apply the standard set up in *McCormick* for Hobbs Act campaign contribution cases to *all* cases arising under the main federal bribery statute? Recall that in *McCormick*, Justice White said the agreement had to be explicit. Under Justice Scalia's reading of the bribery statute, must the exchange be explicit? Would Justice Scalia find a violation if the exchange occurred through winks and nods?

3. The gratuity statute refers to a benefit conferred or received for or because of an official act "performed or to be performed." Charles B. Klein, *What Exactly Is an Unlawful Gratuity after* United States v. Sun-Diamond Growers?, 68 George Washington Law Review 117, 119 (1999), explains:

> A lobbyist commits a traditional "backward-looking gratuity" violation when giving a gift to a U.S. senator to reward (or thank) the senator for previously voting to pass a particular bill. A lobbyist commits a traditional forward-looking gratuity when giving a gift to a U.S. senator to reward (or thank) the senator for a vote the senator already has committed to make, but has not yet made.

What if a lobbyist makes a gift to a U.S. senator whose position on a particular bill is unclear, with the intent to influence the senator's vote? Assume that there is no discussion of the bill, much less an explicit agreement, between the lobbyist and senator. Is the lobbyist guilty of bribery, an unlawful gratuity, or neither?

4. Since the 1960s, scandal and corruption have played a more prominent role in American politics than had been true in the decades before. The press and activist groups such as Common Cause have played a major part in this development, but

one can find periods of similar activity earlier in American history. What is perhaps unprecedented in the past few decades is the extent to which numerous federal, state, and local regulations have been enacted to combat corruption and other forms of impropriety, real or imagined, and the amount of civil and criminal litigation to enforce such regulations. There has been some backlash against these developments. See, *e.g.*, Frank Anechiaricho & James B. Jacobs, The Pursuit of Absolute Integrity: How Corruption Control Makes Government Ineffective (1996); Steven G. Calabresi, *Some Structural Consequences of the Increased Use of Ethics Probes as Political Weapons*, 11 Journal of Law & Politics 521 (1995); Suzanne Garment, Scandal: The Culture of Mistrust in American Politics (1992); Benjamin Ginsberg & Martin Shefter, Politics by Other Means: Politicians, Prosecutors, and the Press from Watergate to Whitewater (1999); Peter W. Morgan & Glenn H. Reynolds, The Appearance of Impropriety: How the Ethics Wars Have Undermined American Government, Business, and Society (1997). In decisions like *McNally, McCormick*, and *Sun-Diamond*, has the Supreme Court brought its considerable weight to bear on the side of those reacting against what they see as the excesses of the post-Watergate era? A qualifiedly affirmative answer to this question is given by George D. Brown, *Putting Watergate Behind Us—* Salinas, Sun-Diamond, *and Two Views of the Anticorruption Model*, 74 Tulane Law Review 747 (2000). For more particular focus on the gratuity offense, see George D. Brown, *The Gratuities Debate and Campaign Reform: How Strong Is the Link?*, 52 Wayne Law Review 1371 (2006). For criticism of the Court from an economic standpoint, arguing that it has adopted too narrow an approach to public corruption in cases like *Sun-Diamond* and *Skilling*, see Alex Stein, *Corrupt Intentions: Bribery, Unlawful Gratuity, and Honest-Services Fraud*, 75 Law & Contemporary Problems 61 (2012).

D. Official Act

The federal bribery statute, 18 U.S.C. § 201, requires an "official act." The Hobbs Act, the honest services fraud statute, and state laws impose a similar requirement for bribery convictions. But what is an official act? The Supreme Court answered the question for purposes of federal law in the following case.

McDonnell v. United States

136 S. Ct. 2355 (2016)

Chief Justice ROBERTS delivered the opinion of the Court.

In 2014, the Federal Government indicted former Virginia Governor Robert McDonnell and his wife, Maureen McDonnell, on bribery charges. The charges related to the acceptance by the McDonnells of $175,000 in loans, gifts, and other benefits from Virginia businessman Jonnie Williams, while Governor McDonnell was in office. Williams was the chief executive officer of Star Scientific, a Virginia-based company that had developed a nutritional supplement made from anatabine, a compound found in tobacco. Star Scientific hoped that Virginia's public universities would perform research studies on anatabine, and Williams wanted Governor McDonnell's assistance in obtaining those studies.

To convict the McDonnells of bribery, the Government was required to show that Governor McDonnell committed (or agreed to commit) an "official act" in exchange for the loans and gifts. The parties did not agree, however, on what counts as an "official act." The Government alleged in the indictment, and maintains on appeal, that Governor McDonnell committed at least five "official acts." Those acts included "arranging meetings" for Williams with other Virginia officials to discuss Star Scientific's product, "hosting" events for Star Scientific at the Governor's Mansion, and "contacting other government officials" concerning studies of anatabine. The Government also argued more broadly that these activities constituted "official action" because they related to Virginia business development, a priority of Governor McDonnell's administration. Governor McDonnell contends that merely setting up a meeting, hosting an event, or contacting an official—without more—does not count as an "official act."

At trial, the District Court instructed the jury according to the Government's broad understanding of what constitutes an "official act," and the jury convicted both Governor and Mrs. McDonnell on the bribery charges. The Fourth Circuit affirmed Governor McDonnell's conviction, and we granted review to clarify the meaning of "official act."

I

A

On November 3, 2009, petitioner Robert McDonnell was elected the 71st Governor of Virginia. His campaign slogan was "Bob's for Jobs," and his focus in office was on promoting business in Virginia. As Governor, McDonnell spoke about economic development in Virginia "on a daily basis" and attended numerous "events, ribbon cuttings," and "plant facility openings." He also referred thousands of constituents to meetings with members of his staff and other government officials. According to longtime staffers, Governor McDonnell likely had more events at the Virginia Governor's Mansion to promote Virginia business than had occurred in "any other administration."

This case concerns Governor McDonnell's interactions with one of his constituents, Virginia businessman Jonnie Williams. Williams was the CEO of Star Scientific, a Virginia-based company that developed and marketed Anatabloc, a nutritional supplement made from anatabine, a compound found in tobacco. Star Scientific hoped to obtain Food and Drug Administration approval of Anatabloc as an anti-inflammatory drug. An important step in securing that approval was initiating independent research studies on the health benefits of anatabine. Star Scientific hoped Virginia's public universities would undertake such studies, pursuant to a grant from Virginia's Tobacco Commission.

[The Court described the interactions between Williams, Governor McDonnell, and Mrs. McDonnell between 2009 and 2012. Over this period, the McDonnells received various things from Williams, including transportation on Williams's private plane, dinners, designer clothing, vacations, use of Williams's Ferrari, a Rolex watch, and cash to help pay for the wedding of the McDonnells' daughter. Altogether, the McDonnells received over $175,000 in loans and gifts from Williams. During the same period, Governor McDonnell did several things to help Star Scientific's efforts with respect to Antabloc, often shortly before or after the McDonnells received something of value from Williams. Among Governor McDonnell's actions in support of Star Scientific were introducing Williams to public officials, hosting events at the Governor's Mansion, communicating with researchers at Virginia's public universities about Anatabloc, and recommending that public officials meet with Star Scientific executives.]

B

In January 2014, Governor McDonnell was indicted for accepting payments, loans, gifts, and other things of value from Williams and Star Scientific in exchange for "performing official actions on an as-needed basis, as opportunities arose, to legitimize, promote, and obtain research studies for Star Scientific's products." The charges against him comprised one count of conspiracy to commit honest services fraud, three counts of honest services fraud, one count of conspiracy to commit Hobbs Act extortion, [and] six counts of Hobbs Act extortion. . . . See 18 U. S. C. §§ 1343, 1349 (honest services fraud); § 1951(a) (Hobbs Act extortion). Mrs. McDonnell was indicted on similar charges. . . .

The theory underlying both the honest services fraud and Hobbs Act extortion charges was that Governor McDonnell had accepted bribes from Williams. See *Skilling v. United States*, 561 U.S. 358, 404 (2010) (construing honest services fraud to forbid "fraudulent schemes to deprive another of honest services through bribes or kickbacks"); *Evans v. United States*, 504 U.S. 255, 260, 269 (1992) (construing Hobbs Act extortion to include "taking a bribe").

The parties agreed that they would define honest services fraud with reference to the federal bribery statute, 18 U. S. C. § 201 . . . .

The parties also agreed that obtaining a "thing of value . . . knowing that the thing of value was given in return for official action" was an element of Hobbs Act extortion, and that they would use the definition of "official act" found in the federal bribery statute to define "official action" under the Hobbs Act.

As a result of all this, the Government was required to prove that Governor McDonnell committed or agreed to commit an "official act" in exchange for the loans and gifts from Williams.

The Government alleged that Governor McDonnell had committed at least five "official acts":

> (1) "arranging meetings for [Williams] with Virginia government officials, who were subordinates of the Governor, to discuss and promote Anatabloc";

(2) "hosting, and . . . attending, events at the Governor's Mansion designed to encourage Virginia university researchers to initiate studies of anatabine and to promote Star Scientific's products to doctors for referral to their patients";

(3) "contacting other government officials in the [Governor's Office] as part of an effort to encourage Virginia state research universities to initiate studies of anatabine";

(4) "promoting Star Scientific's products and facilitating its relationships with Virginia government officials by allowing [Williams] to invite individuals important to Star Scientific's business to exclusive events at the Governor's Mansion"; and

(5) "recommending that senior government officials in the [Governor's Office] meet with Star Scientific executives to discuss ways that the company's products could lower healthcare costs."

The case proceeded to a jury trial, which lasted five weeks. [The Court reviewed the trial testimony.]

Following closing arguments, the District Court instructed the jury that to convict Governor McDonnell it must find that he agreed "to accept a thing of value in exchange for official action." The court described the five alleged "official acts" set forth in the indictment, which involved arranging meetings, hosting events, and contacting other government officials. The court then quoted the statutory definition of "official act," and—as the Government had requested—advised the jury that the term encompassed "acts that a public official customarily performs," including acts "in furtherance of longer-term goals" or "in a series of steps to exercise influence or achieve an end." [The district court declined McDonnell's request for an instruction that an "official act" must be intended to or in fact influence a specific official decision the government actually makes.]

The jury convicted Governor McDonnell on the honest services fraud and Hobbs Act extortion charges. . . . Mrs. McDonnell was also convicted on most of the charges against her. Although the Government requested a sentence of at least ten years for Governor McDonnell, the District Court sentenced him to two years in prison. . . .

[The Fourth Circuit affirmed Governor McDonnell's conviction, while Ms. McDonnell's appeal is still before that court.]

II

The issue in this case is the proper interpretation of the term "official act." Section 201(a)(3) defines an "official act" as "any decision or action on any question, matter, cause, suit, proceeding or controversy, which may at any time be pending, or which may by law be brought before any public official, in such official's official capacity, or in such official's place of trust or profit."

According to the Government, "Congress used intentionally broad language" in § 201(a)(3) to embrace "*any* decision or action, on *any* question or matter, that may at *any time* be pending, or which may by law be brought before *any* public official, in such official's official capacity." . . . . In the Government's view, "official act" specifically includes arranging a meeting, contacting another public official, or hosting an event—without more—concerning any subject, including a broad policy issue such as Virginia economic development. . . .

Taking into account the text of the statute, the precedent of this Court, and the constitutional concerns raised by Governor McDonnell, we reject the Government's reading of § 201(a)(3) and adopt a more bounded interpretation of "official act." Under that interpretation, setting up a meeting, calling another public official, or hosting an event does not, standing alone, qualify as an "official act."

A

The text of § 201(a)(3) sets forth two requirements for an "official act": First, the Government must identify a "question, matter, cause, suit, proceeding or controversy" that "may at any time be pending" or "may by law be brought" before a public official. Second, the Government must prove that the public official made a decision or took an action "on" that question, matter, cause, suit, proceeding, or controversy, or agreed to do so. The issue here is whether arranging a meeting, contacting another official, or hosting an event—without more—can be a "question, matter, cause, suit, proceeding or controversy," and if not, whether it can be a decision or action on a "question, matter, cause, suit, proceeding or controversy."

The first inquiry is whether a typical meeting, call, or event is itself a "question, matter, cause, suit, proceeding or controversy." The Government argues that nearly any activity by a public official qualifies as a question or matter—from workaday functions, such as the typical call, meeting, or event, to the broadest issues the government confronts, such as fostering economic development. We conclude, however, that the terms "question, matter, cause, suit, proceeding or controversy" do not sweep so broadly.

The last four words in that list—"cause," "suit," "proceeding," and "controversy"—connote a formal exercise of governmental power, such as a lawsuit, hearing, or administrative determination. See, *e.g.*, Crimes Act of 1790, § 21, 1 Stat. 117 (using "cause," "suit," and "controversy" in a related statutory context to refer to judicial proceedings) . . . . Although it may be difficult to define the precise reach of those terms, it seems clear that a typical meeting, telephone call, or event arranged by a public official does not qualify as a "cause, suit, proceeding or controversy."

But what about a "question" or "matter"? A "question" could mean any "subject or aspect that is in dispute, open for discussion, or to be inquired into," and a "matter" any "subject" of "interest or relevance." Webster's Third New International Dictionary 1394, 1863 (1961). If those meanings were adopted, a typical meeting, call, or event would qualify as a "question" or "matter." A "question" may also be interpreted more narrowly, however, as "a subject or point of debate or a proposition being or to be voted on in a meeting," such as a question "before the senate." *Id.*, at 1863. Similarly, a "matter" may be limited to "a topic under active and usually serious or practical consideration," such as a matter that "will come before the committee." *Id.*, at 1394.

To choose between those competing definitions, we look to the context in which the words appear. Under the familiar interpretive canon *noscitur a sociis*, "a word is known by the company it keeps." *Jarecki v. G. D. Searle & Co.*, 367 U. S. 303, 307 (1961). While "not an inescapable rule," this canon "is often wisely applied where a word is capable of many meanings in order to avoid the giving of unintended breadth to the Acts of Congress." *Ibid.*...

[W]e conclude that a "question" or "matter" must be similar in nature to a "cause, suit, proceeding or controversy." Because a typical meeting, call, or event arranged by a public official is not of the same stripe as a lawsuit before a court, a determination before an agency, or a hearing before a committee, it does not qualify as a "question" or "matter" under § 201(a)(3) ....

Because a typical meeting, call, or event is not itself a question or matter, the next step is to determine whether arranging a meeting, contacting another official, or hosting an event may qualify as a "decision or action" *on* a different question or matter. That requires us to first establish what counts as a question or matter in this case.

In addition to the requirements we have described, § 201(a)(3) states that the question or matter must be "pending" or "may by law be brought" before "any public official." "Pending" and "may by law be brought" suggest something that is relatively circumscribed — the kind of thing that can be put on an agenda, tracked for progress, and then checked off as complete. In particular, "may *by law* be brought" conveys something within the specific duties of an official's position — the function conferred by the authority of his office. The word "any" conveys that the matter may be pending either before the public official who is performing the official act, or before another public official....

For its part, the Fourth Circuit found at least three questions or matters at issue in this case: (1) "whether researchers at any of Virginia's state universities would initiate a study of Anatabloc"; (2) "whether the state-created Tobacco Indemnification and Community Revitalization Commission" would "allocate grant money for the study of anatabine"; and (3) "whether the health insurance plan for state employees in Virginia would include Anatabloc as a covered drug." We agree that those qualify as questions or matters under § 201(a)(3). Each is focused and concrete, and each involves a formal exercise of governmental power that is similar in nature to a lawsuit, administrative determination, or hearing.

The question remains whether — as the Government argues — merely setting up a meeting, hosting an event, or calling another official qualifies as a decision or action on any of those three questions or matters. Although the word "decision," and especially the word "action," could be read expansively to support the Government's view, our opinion in *United States v. Sun-Diamond Growers of Cal.*, 526 U. S. 398 (1999) [*supra*, Part II.C—Eds.], rejects that interpretation.

In *Sun-Diamond*, the Court stated that it was not an "official act" under § 201 for the President to host a championship sports team at the White House, the Secretary of Education to visit a high school, or the Secretary of Agriculture to deliver a speech to "farmers concerning various matters of USDA policy." *Id.*, at 407. *We recognized* that "the Secretary of Agriculture *always* has before him or in prospect matters that affect farmers, just as the President always has before him or in prospect matters that affect college and professional sports, and the Secretary of Education matters that affect high schools." *Ibid.* But we concluded that the existence of such pending matters was not enough to find that any action related to them constituted an "official act." *Ibid.* It was possible to avoid the "absurdities" of convicting individuals on corruption charges for engaging in such conduct, we explained, "*through the definition of that term*," *i.e.*, by adopting a more limited definition of "official acts." *Id.*, at 408.

It is apparent from *Sun-Diamond* that hosting an event, meeting with other officials, or speaking with interested parties is not, standing alone, a "decision or action" within the meaning of § 201(a)(3), even if the event, meeting, or speech is related to a pending question or matter. Instead, something more is required: § 201(a)(3) specifies that the public official must make a decision or take an action *on* that question or matter, or agree to do so.

For example, a decision or action to initiate a research study—or a decision or action on a qualifying step, such as narrowing down the list of potential research topics—would qualify as an "official act." A public official may also make a decision or take an action on a "question, matter, cause, suit, proceeding or controversy" by using his official position to exert pressure on *another* official to perform an "official act." In addition, if a public official uses his official position to provide advice to another official, knowing or intending that such advice will form the basis for an "official act" by another official, that too can qualify as a decision or action for purposes of § 201(a)(3).

Under this Court's precedents, a public official is not required to actually make a decision or take an action on a "question, matter, cause, suit, proceeding or controversy"; it is enough that the official agree to do so. See *Evans*, 504 U. S., at 268. The agreement need not be explicit, and the public official need not specify the means that he will use to perform his end of the bargain. Nor must the public official in fact intend to perform the "official act," so long as he agrees to do so. A jury could, for example, conclude that an agreement was reached if the evidence shows that the public official received a thing of value knowing that it was given with the expectation that the official would perform an "official act" in return. It is up to the jury, under the facts of the case, to determine whether the public official agreed to perform an "official act" at the time of the alleged quid pro quo. The jury may consider a broad range of pertinent evidence, including the nature of the transaction, to answer that question.

Setting up a meeting, hosting an event, or calling an official (or agreeing to do so) merely to talk about a research study or to gather additional information, however, does not qualify as a decision or action on the pending question of whether to initiate the study. Simply expressing support for the research study at a meeting, event, or call—or sending a subordinate to such a meeting, event, or call—similarly does not qualify as a decision or action on the study, as long as the public official does not intend to exert pressure on another official or provide advice, knowing or intending such advice to form the basis for an "official act." Otherwise, if every action somehow related to the research study were an "official act," the requirement that the public official make a decision or take an action on that study, or agree to do so, would be meaningless.

Of course, this is not to say that setting up a meeting, hosting an event, or making a phone call is always an innocent act, or is irrelevant, in cases like this one. If an official sets up a meeting, hosts an event, or makes a phone call on a question or matter that is or could be pending before another official, that could serve as evidence of an agreement to take an official act. A jury could conclude, for example, that the official was attempting to pressure or advise another official on a pending matter. And if the official agreed to exert that pressure or give that advice in exchange for a thing of value, that would be illegal....

In sum, an "official act" is a decision or action on a "question, matter, cause, suit, proceeding or controversy." The "question, matter, cause, suit, proceeding or controversy" must involve a formal exercise of governmental power that is similar in nature to a lawsuit before a court, a determination before an agency, or a hearing before a committee. It must also be something specific and focused that is "pending" or "may by law be brought" before a public official. To qualify as an "official act," the public official must make a decision or take an action on that "question, matter, cause, suit, proceeding or controversy," or agree to do so. That decision or action may include using his official position to exert pressure on another official to perform an "official act," or to advise another official, knowing or intending that such advice will form the basis for an "official act" by another official. Setting up a meeting, talking to another official, or organizing an event (or agreeing to do so)—without more—does not fit that definition of "official act."

B

In addition to being inconsistent with both text and precedent, the Government's expansive interpretation of "official act" would raise significant constitutional concerns. Section 201 prohibits *quid pro quo* corruption—the exchange of a thing of value for an "official act." In the Government's view, nearly anything a public official accepts—from a campaign contribution to lunch—counts as a *quid*; and nearly anything a public official does—from arranging a meeting to inviting a guest to an event—counts as a *quo*.

But conscientious public officials arrange meetings for constituents, contact other officials on their behalf, and include them in events all the time. The basic compact underlying representative government *assumes* that public officials will hear from their constituents and act appropriately on their concerns—whether it is the union official worried about a plant closing or the homeowners who wonder why it took five days to restore power to their neighborhood after a storm. The Government's position could cast a pall of potential prosecution over these relationships if the union had given a campaign contribution in the past or the homeowners invited the official to join them on their annual outing to the ballgame. Officials might wonder whether they could respond to even the most commonplace requests for assistance, and citizens with legitimate concerns might shrink from participating in democratic discourse.

This concern is substantial. White House counsel who worked in every administration from that of President Reagan to President Obama warn that the Government's "breathtaking expansion of public-corruption law would likely chill federal officials' interactions with the people they serve and thus damage their ability effectively to perform their duties." . . . .

None of this, of course, is to suggest that the facts of this case typify normal political interaction between public officials and their constituents. Far from it. But the Government's legal interpretation is not confined to cases involving extravagant gifts or large sums of money, and we cannot construe a criminal statute on the assumption that the Government will "use it responsibly." *United States v. Stevens*, 559 U. S. 460, 480 (2010). *The Court in Sun-Diamond* declined to rely on "the Government's discretion" to protect against overzealous prosecutions under § 201, concluding instead that "a statute in this field that can linguistically be interpreted to be either a meat axe or a scalpel should reasonably be taken to be the latter." 526 U. S., at 408, 412.

A related concern is that, under the Government's interpretation, the term "official act" is not defined "with sufficient definiteness that ordinary people can understand what conduct is prohibited," or "in a manner that does not encourage arbitrary and discriminatory enforcement."; *Skilling*, 561 U. S., at 402-03 *(internal quotation* marks omitted). Under the " 'standardless sweep' " of the Government's reading, *Kolender v. Lawson*, 461 U. S. 352, 358 (1983), public officials could be subject to prosecution, without fair notice, for the most prosaic interactions. "Invoking so shapeless a provision to condemn someone to prison" for up to 15 years raises the serious concern that the provision "does not comport with the Constitution's guarantee of due process." *Johnson v. United States*, 576 U.S. 591 (2015). Our more constrained interpretation of § 201(a)(3) avoids this "vagueness shoal." *Skilling*, 561 U. S., at 368.

The Government's position also raises significant federalism concerns. A State defines itself as a sovereign through "the structure of its government, and the character of those who exercise government authority." *Gregory v. Ashcroft*, 501 U. S. 452, 460 (1991). That includes the prerogative to regulate the permissible scope of interactions between state officials and their constituents. Here, where a more limited interpretation of "official act" is supported by both text and precedent, we decline to "construe the statute in a manner that leaves its outer boundaries ambiguous and involves the Federal Government in setting standards" of "good government for local and state officials." *McNally v. United States*, 483 U. S. 350, 360 (1987) . . . .

III

A

[The Court explained why the district court's jury instructions were overly broad, requiring that Governor McDonnell's conviction be vacated.]

B

Governor McDonnell raises two additional claims. First, he argues that the charges against him must be dismissed because the honest services statute and the Hobbs Act are unconstitutionally vague. We reject that claim. For purposes of this case, the parties defined honest services fraud and Hobbs Act extortion with reference to § 201 of the federal bribery statute. Because we have interpreted the term "official act" in § 201(a)(3) in a way that avoids the vagueness concerns raised by Governor McDonnell, we decline to invalidate those statutes under the facts here.

Second, Governor McDonnell argues that the charges must be dismissed because there is insufficient evidence that he committed an "official act," or that he agreed to do so. Because the parties have not had an opportunity to address that question in light of the interpretation of § 201(a)(3) adopted by this Court, we leave it for the Court of Appeals to resolve in the first instance. If the court below determines that there is sufficient evidence for a jury to convict Governor McDonnell of committing or agreeing to commit an "official act," his case may be set for a new trial. If the court instead determines that the evidence is insufficient, the charges against him must be dismissed. We express no view on that question.

* * *

There is no doubt that this case is distasteful; it may be worse than that. But our concern is not with tawdry tales of Ferraris, Rolexes, and ball gowns. It is instead with the broader legal implications of the Government's boundless interpretation of the federal bribery statute. A more limited interpretation of the term "official act" leaves ample room for prosecuting corruption, while comporting with the text of the statute and the precedent of this Court.

The judgment of the Court of Appeals is vacated, and the case is remanded for further proceedings consistent with this opinion.

It is so ordered.

Notes and Questions

1. The *McDonnell* decision came down after Justice Scalia's death, but it bears his imprint. Professor Hasen explains:

> The Supreme Court's unanimous ruling throwing out the conviction of Gov. McDonnell (while leaving open the possibility of a retrial on

> a narrower theory of the case) is sensible and courageous, and shows the continuing important influence of Justice Scalia in this area of the law. It is hard to write an opinion letting off the hook someone whose actions were as odious as Gov. McDonnell, in taking Rolexes, funding for his daughter's wedding and more from someone who wanted the governor's assistance in marketing the equivalent of snake oil. But it was the right thing to do.

Rick Hasen, "Influence of Justice Scalia Felt in Unanimous Decision Throwing Out Gov. McDonnell Conviction," Election Law Blog, June 27, 2016, https://perma.cc/3G5V-8TUM. Do you agree that the Court did the right thing in this case?

2. Will *McDonnell* open the floodgates to more bribery and corruption? Consider this perspective:

> [A] public official may be convicted of bribery for exerting "pressure" or offering "advice" regarding such an official action. More specifically, the Court says that a public official may properly be convicted of bribery for "using his official position [1] to exert pressure on another official to perform an 'official act,' or [2] to advise another official, knowing or intending that such advice will form the basis for an 'official act' by another official." . . . .
>
> Good government advocates needn't worry that the decision will make it too hard to get bribery convictions. I suspect most juries won't have a hard time finding "pressure" or "advice" where evidence like that in Governor McDonnell's case is presented. By the same token, libertarians shouldn't be too heartened by *McDonnell*. The Court has clarified the legal requirements for bribery convictions, but juries may infer the exchange of material benefits for political favors even if there's no proof of an explicit agreement. And that means ethically challenged politicians like Governor McDonnell shouldn't feel too comfortable either.

Dan Tokaji, *The Overreaction to* McDonnell, Election Law Blog, June 28, 2016, https://perma.cc/7M3Q-FB5T. For further commentary on the limits of *McDonnell*'s holding, see Tokaji, *supra*, Ohio State Journal of Criminal Law Amici Briefs, at 17–21, and George D. Brown, McDonnell *and the Criminalization of Politics*, 5 Virginia Journal of Criminal Law 1 (2017).

The government abandoned its prosecution of the McDonnells after the Supreme Court's decision. Charges were later dropped in another high-profile bribery prosecution involving Senator Robert Menendez (D-NJ), who had been indicted for his interactions with a longtime friend, Dr. Salomon Melgen. The government alleged that Dr. Melgen made gifts and contributions to political committees in exchange for political favors from Senator Menendez. Their 2017 trial ended in a hung jury. Prosecutors announced their intention to retry the defendants, but changed their mind after a ruling from the district court that relied heavily on *McDonnell*. The court in *United States v. Menendez*, 291 F. Supp. 3d 606 (D.N.J. 2018), allowed some of the bribery counts to stand, but granted defendants' motion for acquittal on those involving political contributions, on the ground that there was insufficient evidence of a *quid pro quo*. In particular, the court concluded that a "close temporal relationship between political contributions and favorable official action, without more, is not sufficient" to prove a *quid pro quo*. *Id.* at 624. A few days later, the government announced it was dropping all charges against the defendants.

Yet another high-profile bribery conviction was reversed, on the ground that the question or matter to be influenced must be identified at the time of the promise to perform an official act. Former New York Assembly Speaker Sheldon Silver allegedly received referral fees through a law firm with which he was affiliated in exchange for taking official actions that benefitted a cancer researcher and real estate developers. The Second Circuit vacated his first conviction based on a jury instruction on "official acts" that resembled the one invalidated in *McDonnell*. *United States v. Silver*, 864 F.3d 102 (2d Cir. 2017). Silver was retried and, after a revised instruction on official action, was again convicted. The Second Circuit again reversed the bribery conviction, on the ground that the "particular *question* or *matter* to be influenced" must be identified at the time of the official's promise. *United States v. Silver*, 948 F.3d 538, 545 (2d Cir. 2020). Because the district court's post-*McDonnell* jury instruction did not require that the specific matter be identified at the time the bribe was allegedly accepted, the Second Circuit vacated the second bribery conviction.

Has *McDonnell* made it too hard to convict public officials of bribery?

3. What do you think about the federalism concerns raised at the end of the Court's opinion? Should it be left to state legislators and state prosecutors to determine the proper boundaries of state officials' conduct? Is there a good argument for using federal criminal law to police at least some forms of official misconduct by state and local officials? The Court's opinion notes that the parties agreed to define honest services fraud with reference to the federal bribery statute. But should the same definition of bribery apply?

4. The evidence at the McDonnells' trial showed that they received substantial material benefits from Williams, at the same time that Governor McDonnell was trying to help Williams's company. Even if one believes that the Court's decision in *McDonnell* was correct, these interactions might be thought to raise serious concerns. Are there other ways of addressing those concerns, aside from bribery prosecutions?

5. Does *McDonnell* provide a suitably bright line between impermissible bribery and the ordinary give-and-take of politics? If not, what, if anything, can be done to clarify that line?

Chapter 12

The *Buckley* Framework

I. Introduction: Basic Facts and Figures about Campaign Financing in the U.S.

The remainder of this casebook considers efforts to regulate and reform the system of campaign finance in American politics, as well as the constitutional constraints on such efforts. We will focus in this chapter on the Supreme Court's opinion in *Buckley v. Valeo*, the fountainhead of modern American campaign finance jurisprudence, as well as on arguments for and against regulation of money in politics.

Before turning to these readings, it is worth considering a few of the basic facts and figures relating to campaign finance in the United States. More information will be presented later in this chapter and in subsequent chapters. But we need not present a comprehensive description of the campaign finance system here, because nowadays there is a steady stream of books that do this very well. Among the worthy volumes published in recent years are Financing the 2016 Election (David B. Magleby, ed., 2019); Financing the 2012 Election (David B. Magleby, ed., 2014); Financing the 2008 Election (David B. Magleby & Anthony Corrado, eds., 2011); The Election After Reform: Money, Politics, and the Bipartisan Campaign Reform Act (Michael J. Malbin, ed., 2006); Financing the 2004 Election (David B. Magleby, Anthony Corrado & Kelly D. Patterson, eds., 2006); Financing the 2000 Election (David B. Magleby, ed., 2002); Financing the 1996 Election (John C. Green, ed., 1999); Herbert E. Alexander & Anthony Corrado, Financing the 1992 Election (1995); Herbert E. Alexander, Financing Politics: Money, Elections & Political Reform (4th ed. 1992); Frank J. Sorauf, Inside Campaign Finance: Myths and Realities (1992); Frank J. Sorauf, Money in American Elections (1988).

Campaign finance spending in the U.S. consistently grew each election period from the 1970s through the 1990s and into the 2010s. One estimate placed total spending for the 1976 elections at $540 million (about $2.54 billion in 2021 dollars), compared to $4.2 billion for the 1996 elections (about $ 7.1 billion in 2021 dollars). Another estimate pegs 2012 spending in all U.S. elections at $10 billion.[a] These num-

a. The nominal dollar figures are from Herbert E. Alexander, *Spending in the 1996 Elections*, 11, 15, in Financing the 1996 Election, *supra*. The editors of this book converted the figures in this chapter to 2021 dollars using the inflation calculator available at the Bureau of Labor Statistics website, http://www.bls.gov/data/inflation_calculator.htm. Using somewhat different methodology, Candice Nelson concluded that total spending on 1999–2000 election-related activity was just

bers are rough estimates; it is very difficult to get accurate figures on total spending in all elections across the country.

Compiling statistics on *federal* election activity (presidential and congressional) is easier, thanks to the uniform reporting requirements of the Federal Election Commission (FEC). These figures tell a story of accelerating growth. Total federal spending was about $3.9 billion in the 2000 election (about $6 billion in 2021 dollars), $4.6 billion in 2004 ($6.5 billion in 2021 dollars), $6 billion in 2008 ($7.4 billion in 2021 dollars), $8 billion in 2012 ($9.2 billion in 2021 dollars), $9.3 billion in 2016 ($10.3 billion in 2021 dollars), and a whopping $14.4 billion in 2020. David B. Magleby, *Change and Continuity in the Financing of the 2016 U.S. Federal Election*, in Financing the 2016 Elections, *supra,* at 1, 27 tbl. 1; Karl Evers-Hillstrom, *Most Expensive Ever: 2020 Elections Cost $14.4 Billion*, Opensecrets.org, Feb. 11, 2021, https://perma.cc/7YUL-V6LG.

Spending has increased significantly in the past two decades, and court rulings have helped shape where that money flows. As explained in more detail in Chapter 14, the amount of money flowing to political action committees (or PACs), including "Super PACs" that are subject to no contribution limits, has grown significantly. These groups, not officially connected to federal candidates or parties, saw spending of $320 million (PACs only) in 2000 compared to over $4.2 billion in spending (for PACs and super PACs combined) in 2016. Magleby, *Change and Continuity*, at 28 tbl. 1. That means outside spending made up about 45% of all spending on federal elections in 2016.

Changes in technology also have made it considerably cheaper for candidates, parties, and outside groups to raise money from small donors. Small donors giving under $200 to federal candidates made up 23 percent of donations in 2020, compared to 15 percent in 2016. Opensecrets.org, *supra*. But big donors mattered a lot: "The top 100 donors gave $1.6 billion to political committees in 2020, accounting for 9 percent of total fundraising." *Id.* One couple, Sheldon and Miriam Adelson, contributed a staggering $218 million in the 2020 election cycle. OpenSecrets.org, *Who Are the Biggest Donors?*, https://perma.cc/B7ZV-Q99F (data as of June 10, 2021). Before changes in the law beginning in the 2010 *Citizens United* case, such large contributions from individuals were unheard of in U.S. elections.

Scholars are still assessing how changes in campaign finance rules in recent years, especially the changes triggered by the Supreme Court's decision in *Citizens United v. FEC* and other cases (discussed in the next two chapters), have affected elections and fueled outside spending.

The increase in independent expenditures by non-candidate, non-party groups is well-documented. But what effect, if any, is all this outside spending having on campaigns and governance? A recent study attempts to answer this question by asking

---

under $4 billion. Candice J. Nelson, *Spending in the 2000 Election*, 22–24, in Financing the 2000 Election, *supra*. The 2012 figure appears in Richard K. Scher, Political Campaigns in the United States 89 (2016).

those in the best position to know: congressional candidates, campaign operatives, legislative staff, and other political insiders, including people from outside groups. Daniel P. Tokaji & Renata E.B. Strause, *The New Soft Money: Outside Spending in Congressional Campaigns* (2014), https://perma.cc/S6X4-U344. Tokaji and Strause found that:

- Outside groups aren't monolithic but encompass a variety of different types of groups with very different aims and strategies — some pursuing long-term legislative goals, others narrowly focused on a particular candidate.
- Outside groups are doing much of the dirty work in campaigns, particularly running negative ads.
- There is a high degree of cooperation between outside groups and congressional campaigns, often taking the form of publicly-transmitted signals — though very little illegal coordination, as defined by federal law.
- Members of Congress perceive outside spending as a threat — usually implied but occasionally express — for those who refuse to toe the line of outside groups.

Whether the money is being raised by candidates, parties, or outside groups, the desire for more of it remains insatiable. Why are campaigns so expensive? Television time and postage, which dominate many federal campaigns, have gone up more rapidly than the consumer price index. Some things purchased by campaigns have become cheaper, especially computer technology. But this has not lowered campaign costs; it has simply made it possible — and therefore necessary, because campaigning is a competitive enterprise — for campaigns to function at a level of sophistication that was not previously possible. For example, campaigns now routinely engage in polling activities that would not have been imaginable decades ago. Internet and social media campaigning are the latest targets for campaign consultants.

Many people regard high campaign spending as a problem in itself. Most politicians, journalists, academics, and other close observers of electoral politics do not share this view. They point out that the total amount spent on political campaigns is miniscule compared, say, to what is spent to advertise commercial goods and services, or to government budgets generally. They maintain that communication is central to a democratic system and there is no reason to assume that such communication will be costless.

Part of the public sentiment against the growth of campaign spending probably reflects disapproval of the content of political advertising, which is often negative, misleading, superficial, strident, or all of the above. Many close observers of politics share this disapproval, though no one seems to have come up with a very good idea for what can be done about it and, as Chapter 10 shows, the Constitution would permit very little regulation in this area.

Aside from the content of campaigning, close observers tend to be less concerned about the growth in spending in itself than about some of the stresses and strains accompanying that growth. As the following pages will show, there are many such concerns, and different observers have very different ideas about how important they are. Debate has centered primarily around the distribution of campaign resources and the implications that the distribution has for electoral competition, and on the pressures that are generated by the need to raise increasing amounts of campaign contributions.

This chapter and the ones that follow explore whether, why, and how campaign financing should be regulated. "Regulation" could be anything from disclosure of the source and use of campaign funds, to limits on amounts contributed or spent, to public financing of campaigns. Before you begin reading these materials, ask yourself whether you believe campaign financing should be regulated. Why or why not?

Consider the following non-exhaustive list of reasons some have suggested for regulating campaign finances:

1. Prevent corruption of elected officials
2. Promote political equality
3. Promote alignment between voters and policy outcomes
4. Enhance the competitiveness of elections
5. Instill public confidence in the democratic process
6. Free candidates from excessive time spent on fundraising

Note that these reasons may be at odds with one another. For example, imposing a low dollar limit on the amount individuals may contribute to candidate campaigns might serve the goals of preventing corruption or promoting equality, but such a limit almost surely will increase the time that candidates must spend raising funds. Note also that these reasons may not be as distinct from one another as they may first appear. For example, sometimes people speak of "corruption" when they really have a concern about equality.[b] In addition, campaign finance regulation would not instill "public confidence" in the democratic process unless the public was concerned about some other underlying problem, such as corruption or inequality. Finally, these reasons must be considered in light of concerns about the free speech and associational rights guaranteed by the First Amendment of the Constitution, an issue to which we now turn.

---

b. As we shall see, the Supreme Court has encouraged this practice—perhaps inadvertently—by recognizing corruption but not equality as a rationale to justify campaign finance laws.

II. *Buckley v. Valeo:* The Foundation of American Campaign Finance Jurisprudence

The modern era of campaign finance regulation began, at the federal level, with the Federal Election Campaign Act Amendments of 1974 (FECA), codified at 2 U.S.C. § 431 *et seq.*[c] There were four basic forms of regulation contained in the FECA, and with some variations, these have remained the basic elements of most debate on campaign finance regulation ever since: disclosure; limits on the size of campaign contributions; limits on campaign expenditures; and public financing of campaigns. In addition, the FECA retained older forms of federal election regulation, most prominently a ban on contributions and expenditures by corporations and labor unions.

The FECA applies to congressional and presidential elections, only a small fraction of the elections held in the United States. However, around the same period, most of the states adopted roughly comparable laws that included some or all of the same forms of regulation.

Congress was aware when it enacted the FECA that there would be serious challenges to the law's constitutionality. The FECA includes a provision, now codified at 52 U.S.C. § 30110, allowing such challenges to receive expedited consideration in the federal courts. Almost before the ink of the statute had dried, a comprehensive challenge to most of its provisions was filed by an ideologically diverse group of plaintiffs.[d] The Court of Appeals upheld the law in its entirety with one very minor exception, 519 F.2d 821 (D.C. Cir. 1975), and the case went to the Supreme Court under the name *Buckley v. Valeo*. For a look at the story behind the litigation of *Buckley* and its aftermath, see Richard L. Hasen, *The Nine Lives of* Buckley v. Valeo, in First Amendment Stories ch. 12 (Richard W. Garnett & Andrew Koppelman, eds., 2011, reprinted in revised form in Election Law Stories (Joshua Douglas & Eugene Mazo, eds., 2016)).

On three previous occasions, the Court had taken pains to avoid deciding constitutional controversies over congressional attempts to regulate campaign finances.[e] In *Buckley*, the Court showed no such restraint. The Court adjudicated the validity of many different provisions and attempted to write a virtual treatise setting forth both general principles and considerable doctrinal detail, delineating the limits of

---

c. The public financing provisions of FECA are codified separately, in the Internal Revenue Code. The entire text of the statute as it stood following the 1974 amendments is set forth as an appendix to *Buckley v. Valeo*, 424 U.S. 1, 144–235 (1976).

The Federal Election Campaign Act was originally enacted in 1971, but before most of its provisions were scheduled to go into effect, the 1971 system of regulation was replaced by the 1974 amendments.

d. The disclosure requirements were alleged to be overbroad. All the other major provisions were alleged to be unconstitutional in their entirety.

e. See *United States v. CIO*, 335 U.S. 106 (1948); *United States v. UAW-CIO*, 352 U.S. 567 (1957); *Pipefitters Local Union No. 562 v. United States*, 407 U.S. 385 (1972).

regulation in this contentious field. The result was a *per curiam* decision (a decision "by the Court," i.e., not signed by any one justice) extending over 138 pages of the United States Reports, almost certainly the longest *per curiam* opinion in the history of the Supreme Court. The opinion was drafted by a committee of Justices, with the portion reprinted in this chapter drafted primarily by Justice Potter Stewart. See Richard L. Hasen, *The Untold Drafting History of* Buckley v. Valeo, 2 Election Law Journal 241 (2003). In addition to the *per curiam* opinion, five of the eight justices who participated in the case added separate views, disagreeing with one aspect or another of the majority decision. These separate statements fill an additional 83 pages of the official reports.

Buckley's major rulings were as follows:

1. The campaign disclosure requirements, the least controversial portion of FECA, were upheld. However, the Court stated that it would be unconstitutional to impose the disclosure requirements on parties or candidates who could show that disclosure might subject themselves, their contributors, or their vendors to governmental or private harassment. In *Brown v. Socialist Workers '74 Campaign Committee*, 459 U.S. 87 (1982), the Court ruled that a party was entitled to an exemption from disclosure requirements on this ground. We return to disclosure issues in Chapter 16.

2. In the portion of the opinion that is reprinted in this chapter, the Court upheld the limits on the size of contributions but struck down the expenditure limits. There were three different expenditure limits in the FECA: limits on independent spending on behalf of a candidate; limits on how much of his or her own money the candidate could spend; and limits on the total spending of a candidate's campaign. Prior to *Buckley*, most supporters of the legislation probably would have characterized the first two as corollaries of the FECA's contribution limits. The limit on independent expenditures prevented evasion of the contribution limits and the limits on use of the candidate's own money prevented unfairness to a wealthy candidate's less wealthy opponents, for whom raising money might be made more difficult as a result of the contribution limits. As will be seen, the *Buckley* Court regarded all the expenditure limits as comprising a separate category, sharply distinct from the contribution limits. This chapter and the two that follow explore issues growing out of the constitutional structure set up in *Buckley*.

3. The FECA enacted public financing in presidential but not congressional campaigns. In presidential primaries, candidates can receive public funds on a matching basis for private contributions up to $250. In general elections, the presidential campaigns of candidates who opt for public financing are entirely publicly financed, and the major party candidates receive no private contributions. These public financing provisions were upheld in *Buckley*. Footnote 65, appended to the section on expenditure limits and reprinted below, stated that despite the unconstitutionality of such limits if they are mandatory, it is permissible to attach spending limits as a condition of acceptance of public financing, on the theory that the limits then become voluntary. Chapter 15 explores public financing issues. In Chapter 9 we considered

the question whether the public financing plan unconstitutionally infringed the rights of third party and independent candidates.

4. The FECA created a new agency, the Federal Election Commission, for the purpose of administering and enforcing the new legislation. In *Buckley*, the Court ruled that the manner in which the FEC was constituted—two members each were appointed by the President, the Senate, and the House—violated the system of separation of powers established by the Constitution. The last point required that the Act be amended in 1976, to reconstitute the FEC with all members appointed by the President. The Act was amended again in 1979 and 2002, and we will consider those amendments in later chapters. Even with those amendments, the basic framework of the FECA that emerged from *Buckley* continues to govern federal elections, although recent court decisions have eroded a number of its key provisions. That FECA is considerably different from the one passed by Congress, since it does not include expenditure limits in congressional elections. Indeed, Chief Justice Burger, in a separate opinion in *Buckley*, declared that he would have struck down the entire law rather than leave standing such a modified version of what Congress wrote:

> [T]he Court's result does violence to the intent of Congress in this comprehensive scheme of campaign finance. By dissecting the Act bit by bit, and casting off vital parts, the Court fails to recognize that the whole of this Act is greater than the sum of its parts. Congress intended to regulate all aspects of federal campaign finances, but what remains after today's holding leaves no more than a shadow of what Congress contemplated. I question whether the residue leaves a workable program.

424 U.S. at 235–36 (Burger, C.J., concurring in part and dissenting in part).

Buckley is therefore a crucially important case for its direct effect on federal campaign law. There are several additional reasons why the decision, and especially the portion that is reprinted in this chapter, must be mastered by the student of election law. First, as mentioned above, the Court's opinion attempts to define in general outline and in considerable detail the constitutional limits on campaign finance reform in the United States. To be sure, critics have questioned *Buckley*'s internal consistency and its consistency with subsequent campaign finance decisions. Nevertheless, *Buckley* is still the most basic text against which any existing or proposed federal, state, or local campaign finance regulation must be tested. Second, because the case covers so much conceptual, doctrinal, polemical and even empirical ground, it provides a useful starting point for discussion of legal and policy aspects of the campaign finance problem. Finally, because of its breadth, and the contrast between its interventionism and the Court's earlier restraint in campaign finance cases, *Buckley* is an important case study for consideration of the judiciary's role in coping with the campaign finance problem and, more broadly, the Court's exercise of its function of judicial review in general.

Buckley v. Valeo

424 U.S. 1, 12–59 (1976)

I. Contribution and Expenditure Limitations

The intricate statutory scheme adopted by Congress to regulate federal election campaigns includes restrictions on political contributions and expenditures that apply broadly to all phases of and all participants in the election process. The major contribution and expenditure limitations in the Act prohibit individuals from contributing more than $25,000 in a single year or more than $1,000 to any single candidate for an election campaign[12] and from spending more than $1,000 a year "relative to a clearly identified candidate." Other provisions restrict a candidate's use of personal and family resources in his campaign and limit the overall amount that can be spent by a candidate in campaigning for federal office.

The constitutional power of Congress to regulate federal elections is well established and is not questioned by any of the parties in this case.[16] Thus, the critical constitutional questions presented here go not to the basic power of Congress to legislate in this area, but to whether the specific legislation that Congress has enacted interferes with First Amendment freedoms or invidiously discriminates against nonincumbent candidates and minor parties in contravention of the Fifth Amendment.[f]

A. General Principles

The Act's contribution and expenditure limitations operate in an area of the most fundamental First Amendment activities. Discussion of public issues and debate on the qualifications of candidates are integral to the operation of the system of government established by our Constitution. The First Amendment affords the broadest protection to such political expression in order "to assure [the] unfettered interchange of ideas for the bringing about of political and social changes desired by the people." *Roth v. United States*, 354 U.S. 476, 484 (1957). Although

---

12. An organization registered as a political committee for not less than six months which has received contributions from at least 50 persons and made contributions to at least five candidates may give up to $5,000 to any candidate for any election. . . . [These are the organizations generally known as "political action committees," or "PACs." — Eds.]

16. Article I, § 4, of the Constitution grants Congress the power to regulate elections of members of the Senate and House of Representatives. See *Smiley v. Holm*, 285 U.S. 355 (1932); *Ex parte Yarbrough*, 110 U.S. 651 (1884). Although the Court at one time indicated that party primary contests were not "elections" within the meaning of Art. I, § 4, *Newberry v. United States*, 256 U.S. 232 (1921), it later held that primary elections were within the Constitution's grant of authority to Congress. *United States v. Classic*, 313 U.S. 299 (1941). The Court has also recognized broad congressional power to legislate in connection with the elections of the President and Vice President. *Burroughs v. United States*, 290 U.S. 534 (1934).

f. References to the Fifth Amendment in this opinion are to what is sometimes referred to as the "equal protection component" of the Fifth Amendment. The Equal Protection Clause itself, in the Fourteenth Amendment, restricts only the states. The Court has found, in the due process provisions of the Fifth Amendment, restrictions on the federal government that are virtually identical to those of the Equal Protection Clause. — Eds.

First Amendment protections are not confined to "the exposition of ideas," *Winters v. New York*, 333 U.S. 507, 510 (1948), "there is practically universal agreement that a major purpose of that Amendment was to protect the free discussion of governmental affairs, . . . of course includ[ing] discussions of candidates. . . ." *Mills v. Alabama*, 384 U.S. 214, 218 (1966). This no more than reflects our "profound national commitment to the principle that debate on public issues should be uninhibited, robust, and wide-open," *New York Times Co. v. Sullivan*, 376 U.S. 254, 270 (1964). In a republic where the people are sovereign, the ability of the citizenry to make informed choices among candidates for office is essential, for the identities of those who are elected will inevitably shape the course that we follow as a nation. As the Court observed in *Monitor Patriot Co. v. Roy*, 401 U.S. 265, 272 (1971), "it can hardly be doubted that the constitutional guarantee has its fullest and most urgent application precisely to the conduct of campaigns for political office."

The First Amendment protects political association as well as political expression. The constitutional right of association explicated in *NAACP v. Alabama*, 357 U.S. 449, 460 (1958), stemmed from the Court's recognition that "(e)ffective advocacy of both public and private points of view, particularly controversial ones, is undeniably enhanced by group association." Subsequent decisions have made clear that the First and Fourteenth Amendments guarantee "freedom to associate with others for the common advancement of political beliefs and ideas," a freedom that encompasses "[t]he right to associate with the political party of one's choice." *Kusper v. Pontikes*, 414 U.S. 51, 56, 57 (1973), quoted in *Cousins v. Wigoda*, 419 U.S. 477, 487 (1975).

It is with these principles in mind that we consider the primary contentions of the parties with respect to the Act's limitations upon the giving and spending of money in political campaigns. Those conflicting contentions could not more sharply define the basic issues before us. Appellees contend that what the Act regulates is conduct, and that its effect on speech and association is incidental at most. Appellants respond that contributions and expenditures are at the very core of political speech, and that the Act's limitations thus constitute restraints on First Amendment liberty that are both gross and direct.

In upholding the constitutional validity of the Act's contribution and expenditure provisions on the ground that those provisions should be viewed as regulating conduct, not speech, the Court of Appeals relied upon *United States v. O'Brien*, 391 U.S. 367 (1968). The *O'Brien* case involved a defendant's claim that the First Amendment prohibited his prosecution for burning his draft card because his act was "symbolic speech" engaged in as a "demonstration against the war and against the draft." On the assumption that "the alleged communicative element in O'Brien's conduct [was] sufficient to bring into play the First Amendment," the Court sustained the conviction because it found "a sufficiently important governmental interest in regulating the nonspeech element" that was "unrelated to the suppression of free expression" and that had an "incidental restriction on alleged First Amendment freedoms . . . no greater than [was] essential to the furtherance of that interest." The Court expressly emphasized that *O'Brien* was not a case "where the alleged governmental interest in regulating conduct arises in some measure because the communication allegedly integral to the conduct is itself thought to be harmful."

We cannot share the view that the present Act's contribution and expenditure limitations are comparable to the restrictions on conduct upheld in *O'Brien*. The expenditure of money simply cannot be equated with such conduct as destruction of a draft card. Some forms of communication made possible by the giving and spending of money involve speech alone, some involve conduct primarily, and some involve a combination of the two. Yet this Court has never suggested that the dependence of a communication on the expenditure of money operates itself to introduce a nonspeech element or to reduce the exacting scrutiny required by the First Amendment[g]. . . .

Even if the categorization of the expenditure of money as conduct was accepted, the limitations challenged here would not meet the *O'Brien* test because the governmental interests advanced in support of the Act involve "suppressing communication." The interests served by the Act include restricting the voices of people and interest groups who have money to spend and reducing the overall scope of federal election campaigns. Although the Act does not focus on the ideas expressed by persons or groups subject to its regulations, it is aimed in part at equalizing the relative ability of all voters to affect electoral outcomes by placing a ceiling on expenditures for political expression by citizens and groups. Unlike *O'Brien*, where the Selective Service System's administrative interest in the preservation of draft cards was wholly unrelated to their use as a means of communication, it is beyond dispute that the interest in regulating the alleged "conduct" of giving or spending money "arises in some measure because the communication allegedly integral to the conduct is itself thought to be harmful."

Nor can the Act's contribution and expenditure limitations be sustained, as some of the parties suggest, by reference to the constitutional principles reflected in [decisions such as *Kovacs v. Cooper*, 336 U.S. 77 (1949), standing] for the proposition that the government may adopt reasonable time, place, and manner regulations, which do not discriminate among speakers or ideas, in order to further an important governmental interest unrelated to the restriction of communication. In contrast to *O'Brien*, where the method of expression was held to be subject to

---

g. This passage is criticized by J. Skelly Wright, *Politics and the Constitution: Is Money Speech?*, 85 Yale Law Journal 1001, 1007–08 (1976): "I am bound to say that this passage performs a judicial sleight of hand. The real question in the case was: Can the use of money be regulated, by analogy to conduct such as draft-card burning, where there is an undoubted incidental effect on speech? However, what the Court asked was whether pure speech can be regulated where there is some incidental effect on money. Naturally the answer to the Court's question was 'No.' But this left untouched the real question in the case. The Court riveted its attention on what the money could buy—be it communication, or communication mixed with conduct. Yet the campaign reform law did not dictate what could be bought. It focused exclusively on the giving and spending itself. In short, the Court turned the congressional telescope around and looked through the wrong end."—Eds.

prohibition, [*Kovacs*, etc.] involved place or manner restrictions on legitimate modes of expression—picketing, parading, demonstrating, and using a soundtruck. The critical difference between this case and those time, place, and manner cases is that the present Act's contribution and expenditure limitations impose direct quantity restrictions on political communication and association by persons, groups, candidates, and political parties in addition to any reasonable time, place, and manner regulations otherwise imposed.[17]

A restriction on the amount of money a person or group can spend on political communication during a campaign necessarily reduces the quantity of expression by restricting the number of issues discussed, the depth of their exploration, and the size of the audience reached.[18] This is because virtually every means of communicating ideas in today's mass society requires the expenditure of money. The distribution of the humblest handbill or leaflet entails printing, paper, and circulation costs. Speeches and rallies generally necessitate hiring a hall and publicizing the event. The electorate's increasing dependence on television, radio, and other mass media for news and information has made these expensive modes of communication indispensable instruments of effective political speech.

The expenditure limitations contained in the Act represent substantial rather than merely theoretical restraints on the quantity and diversity of political speech. The $1,000 ceiling on spending "relative to a clearly identified candidate," 18 U.S.C. § 608(e)(1), would appear to exclude all citizens and groups except candidates, political parties, and the institutional press from any significant use of the most effective modes of communication.[20] Although the Act's limitations on expenditures by cam-

---

17. The nongovernmental appellees argue that just as the decibels emitted by a sound truck can be regulated consistently with the First Amendment, *Kovacs*, the Act may restrict the volume of dollars in political campaigns without impermissibly restricting freedom of speech. This comparison underscores a fundamental misconception. The decibel restriction upheld in *Kovacs* limited the manner of operating a soundtruck but not the extent of its proper use. By contrast, the Act's dollar ceilings restrict the extent of the reasonable use of virtually every means of communicating information. As the *Kovacs* Court emphasized, the nuisance ordinance only barred sound trucks from broadcasting "in a loud and raucous manner on the streets," and imposed "no restriction upon the communication of ideas or discussion of issues by the human voice, by newspapers, by pamphlets, by dodgers," or by soundtrucks operating at a reasonable volume.

[The Court's argument has been criticized by a number of commentators who analogize controlling the volume of a soundtruck to controlling the "volume" of monetary expenditures. Lillian R. BeVier, *Money and Politics: A Perspective on the First Amendment and Campaign Finance Reform*, 73 California Law Review 1045, 1060 n.72 (1985), argues that this analogy "is flawed because the evil created by too much sound is noise in a strictly physical sense, whereas that thought to be created by too many dollars is noise only in a normative sense—namely that, in the view of the person drawing the analogy, too many dollars permit certain messages to be heard too much."—Eds.]

18. Being free to engage in unlimited political expression subject to a ceiling on expenditures is like being free to drive an automobile as far and as often as one desires on a single tank of gasoline.

20. The record indicates that, as of January 1, 1975, one full-page advertisement in a daily edition of a certain metropolitan newspaper cost $6,971.04—almost seven times the annual limit on expenditures "relative to" a particular candidate imposed on the vast majority of individual citizens and associations by § 608(e)(1).

paign organizations and political parties provide substantially greater room for discussion and debate, they would have required restrictions in the scope of a number of past congressional and Presidential campaigns[21] and would operate to constrain campaigning by candidates who raise sums in excess of the spending ceiling.

By contrast with a limitation upon expenditures for political expression, a limitation upon the amount that any one person or group may contribute to a candidate or political committee entails only a marginal restriction upon the contributor's ability to engage in free communication. A contribution serves as a general expression of support for the candidate and his views, but does not communicate the underlying basis for the support. The quantity of communication by the contributor does not increase perceptibly with the size of his contribution, since the expression rests solely on the undifferentiated, symbolic act of contributing.[h] At most, the size of the contribution provides a very rough index of the intensity of the contributor's support for the candidate. A limitation on the amount of money a person may give to a candidate or campaign organization thus involves little direct restraint on his political communication, for it permits the symbolic expression of support evidenced by a contribution but does not in any way infringe the contributor's freedom to discuss candidates and issues. While contributions may result in political expression if spent by a candidate or an association to present views to the voters, the transformation of contributions into political debate involves speech by someone other than the contributor.

Given the important role of contributions in financing political campaigns, contribution restrictions could have a severe impact on political dialogue if the limitations prevented candidates and political committees from amassing the resources necessary for effective advocacy. There is no indication, however, that the contribution limitations imposed by the Act would have any dramatic adverse effect on the

---

21. The statistical findings of fact agreed to by the parties in the District Court indicate that 17 of 65 major-party senatorial candidates in 1974 spent more than the combined primary-election, general-election, and fundraising limitations imposed by the Act. The 1972 senatorial figures showed that 18 of 66 major-party candidates exceeded the Act's limitations. This figure may substantially underestimate the number of candidates who exceeded the limits provided in the Act, since the Act imposes separate ceilings for the primary election, the general election, and fundraising, and does not permit the limits to be aggregated. The data for House of Representatives elections are also skewed, since statistics reflect a combined $168,000 limit instead of separate $70,000 ceilings for primary and general elections with up to an additional 20% permitted for fundraising. Only 22 of the 810 major-party House candidates in 1974 and 20 of the 816 major-party candidates in 1972 exceeded the $168,000 figure. Both Presidential candidates in 1972 spent in excess of the combined Presidential expenditure ceilings.

h. One critic argues that the Court omitted "any discussion of the contributor who wished to delegate his speech to a more effective communicator, as he freely could under the Court's invalidation of spending limitations if he picked an ad agency rather than a candidate." L.A. Powe, Jr., *Mass Speech and the Newer First Amendment*, 1982 Supreme Court Review 243, 253. — Eds.

funding of campaigns and political associations.[23] The overall effect of the Act's contribution ceilings is merely to require candidates and political committees to raise funds from a greater number of persons and to compel people who would otherwise contribute amounts greater than the statutory limits to expend such funds on direct political expression, rather than to reduce the total amount of money potentially available to promote political expression.

The Act's contribution and expenditure limitations also impinge on protected associational freedoms. Making a contribution, like joining a political party, serves to affiliate a person with a candidate. In addition, it enables like-minded persons to pool their resources in furtherance of common political goals. The Act's contribution ceilings thus limit one important means of associating with a candidate or committee, but leave the contributor free to become a member of any political association and to assist personally in the association's efforts on behalf of candidates. And the Act's contribution limitations permit associations and candidates to aggregate large sums of money to promote effective advocacy. By contrast, the Act's $1,000 limitation on independent expenditures "relative to a clearly identified candidate" precludes most associations from effectively amplifying the voice of their adherents, the original basis for the recognition of First Amendment protection of the freedom of association. See *NAACP v. Alabama*. The Act's constraints on the ability of independent associations and candidate campaign organizations to expend resources on political expression "is simultaneously an interference with the freedom of (their) adherents," *Sweezy v. New Hampshire*, 354 U.S. 234, 250 (1957) (plurality opinion).

In sum, although the Act's contribution and expenditure limitations both implicate fundamental First Amendment interests, its expenditure ceilings impose significantly more severe restrictions on protected freedoms of political expression and association than do its limitations on financial contributions.

---

23. Statistical findings agreed to by the parties reveal that approximately 5.1% of the $73,483,613 raised by the 1,161 candidates for Congress in 1974 was obtained in amounts in excess of $1,000. In 1974, two major-party senatorial candidates, Ramsey Clark and Senator Charles Mathias, Jr., operated large-scale campaigns on contributions raised under a voluntarily imposed $100 contribution limitation.

[Compare this footnote with footnote 21, *supra*, in which the Court documents the proposition that campaign spending limits would have a substantial repressive effect on campaign speech. In footnote 21 the Court considers the ratio of campaigns that would have exceeded the limits to those that spent within the limits. In footnote 23, the Court considers the ratio of money contributed in excess of the limits to that of money contributed within the limits. Why consider apples (the number of campaigns over the limit) in one case and oranges (the amount of money contributed over the limit) in the other?

Whatever the ratio that may be selected, how large must the ratio be for the Court to regard it as indicating that the limits in question will have a "dramatic adverse effect on the funding of campaigns and political associations"? According to the figures the Court gives in footnote 21, a total of 4.38% of House and Senate campaigns in 1972 and 1974 spent amounts that would have exceeded the campaign spending limits. Why does this indicate a "dramatic adverse effect" while the 5.1% figure the Court gives in footnote 23 shows the absence of such an effect? — Eds.]

B. Contribution Limitations

1. The $1,000 Limitation on Contributions by Individuals and Groups to Candidates and Authorized Campaign Committees

Section 608(b) provides, with certain limited exceptions, that "no person shall make contributions to any candidate with respect to any election for Federal office which, in the aggregate, exceed $1,000." The statute defines "person" broadly to include "an individual, partnership, committee, association, corporation, or any other organization or group of persons." § 591(g). The limitation reaches a gift, subscription, loan, advance, deposit of anything of value, or promise to give a contribution, made for the purpose of influencing a primary election, a Presidential preference primary, or a general election for any federal office.[24] §§ 591(e)(1), (2).... The restriction applies to aggregate amounts contributed to the candidate for each election with primaries, run-off elections, and general elections counted separately, and all Presidential primaries held in any calendar year treated together as a single election campaign. § 608(b)(5).

Appellants contend that the $1,000 contribution ceiling unjustifiably burdens First Amendment freedoms, employs overbroad dollar limits, and discriminates against candidates opposing incumbent officeholders and against minor-party candidates in violation of the Fifth Amendment. We address each of these claims of invalidity in turn.

(a)

As the general discussion in Part I-A, *supra*, indicated, the primary First Amendment problem raised by the Act's contribution limitations is their restriction of one aspect of the contributor's freedom of political association. The Court's decisions involving associational freedoms establish that the right of association is a "basic constitutional freedom," *Kusper*, that is "closely allied to freedom of speech and a right which, like free speech, lies at the foundation of a free society." *Shelton v. Tucker*, 364 U.S. 479, 486 (1960). In view of the fundamental nature of the right to associate, governmental "action which may have the effect of curtailing the freedom to associate is subject to the closest scrutiny." *NAACP v. Alabama*. Yet, it is clear that "(n)either the right to associate nor the right to participate in political activities is absolute." *CSC v. Letter Carriers*, 413 U.S. 548, 567 (1973). Even a "'significant interference' with protected rights of political association" may be sustained if the State demonstrates a sufficiently important interest and employs means closely drawn to avoid unnecessary abridgment of associational freedoms. *Cousins*.

Appellees argue that the Act's restrictions on large campaign contributions are justified by three governmental interests. According to the parties and *amici*, the primary interest served by the limitations and, indeed, by the Act as a whole, is

---

24. The Act exempts from the contribution ceiling the value of all volunteer services provided by individuals to a candidate or a political committee and excludes the first $500 spent by volunteers on certain categories of campaign-related activities. §§ 591(e)(5)(A)–(D)....

the prevention of corruption and the appearance of corruption spawned by the real or imagined coercive influence of large financial contributions on candidates' positions and on their actions if elected to office. Two "ancillary" interests underlying the Act are also allegedly furthered by the $1,000 limits on contributions. First, the limits serve to mute the voices of affluent persons and groups in the election process and thereby to equalize the relative ability of all citizens to affect the outcome of elections. Second, it is argued, the ceilings may to some extent act as a brake on the skyrocketing cost of political campaigns and thereby serve to open the political system more widely to candidates without access to sources of large amounts of money.

It is unnecessary to look beyond the Act's primary purpose to limit the actuality and appearance of corruption resulting from large individual financial contributions in order to find a constitutionally sufficient justification for the $1,000 contribution limitation. Under a system of private financing of elections, a candidate lacking immense personal or family wealth must depend on financial contributions from others to provide the resources necessary to conduct a successful campaign. The increasing importance of the communications media and sophisticated mass-mailing and polling operations to effective campaigning make the raising of large sums of money an ever more essential ingredient of an effective candidacy. To the extent that large contributions are given to secure a political *quid pro quo* from current and potential office holders, the integrity of our system of representative democracy is undermined. Although the scope of such pernicious practices can never be reliably ascertained, the deeply disturbing examples surfacing after the 1972 election demonstrate that the problem is not an illusory one.

Of almost equal concern as the danger of actual *quid pro quo* arrangements is the impact of the appearance of corruption stemming from public awareness of the opportunities for abuse inherent in a regime of large individual financial contributions. In *CSC v. Letter Carriers, supra*, the Court found that the danger to "fair and effective government" posed by partisan political conduct on the part of federal employees charged with administering the law was a sufficiently important concern to justify broad restrictions on the employees' right of partisan political association. Here, as there, Congress could legitimately conclude that the avoidance of the appearance of improper influence "is also critical . . . if confidence in the system of representative Government is not to be eroded to a disastrous extent."

Appellants contend that the contribution limitations must be invalidated because bribery laws and narrowly drawn disclosure requirements constitute a less restrictive means of dealing with "proven and suspected *quid pro quo* arrangements." But laws making criminal the giving and taking of bribes deal with only the most blatant and specific attempts of those with money to influence governmental action.[i] And while disclosure requirements serve the many salutary purposes discussed

i. Is this an accurate statement of the scope of the law of bribery under federal and state laws? See Chapter 11, *supra*. — Eds.

elsewhere in this opinion, Congress was surely entitled to conclude that disclosure was only a partial measure, and that contribution ceilings were a necessary legislative concomitant to deal with the reality or appearance of corruption inherent in a system permitting unlimited financial contributions, even when the identities of the contributors and the amounts of their contributions are fully disclosed.

The Act's $1,000 contribution limitation focuses precisely on the problem of large campaign contributions — the narrow aspect of political association where the actuality and potential for corruption have been identified — while leaving persons free to engage in independent political expression, to associate actively through volunteering their services, and to assist to a limited but nonetheless substantial extent in supporting candidates and committees with financial resources.[31] Significantly, the Act's contribution limitations in themselves do not undermine to any material degree the potential for robust and effective discussion of candidates and campaign issues by individual citizens, associations, the institutional press, candidates, and political parties.

We find that, under the rigorous standard of review established by our prior decisions, the weighty interests served by restricting the size of financial contributions to political candidates are sufficient to justify the limited effect upon First Amendment freedoms caused by the $1,000 contribution ceiling.

(b)

Appellants' first overbreadth challenge to the contribution ceilings rests on the proposition that most large contributors do not seek improper influence over a candidate's position or an officeholder's action. Although the truth of that proposition may be assumed, it does not undercut the validity of the $1,000 contribution limitation. Not only is it difficult to isolate suspect contributions, but, more importantly, Congress was justified in concluding that the interest in safeguarding against the appearance of impropriety requires that the opportunity for abuse inherent in the process of raising large monetary contributions be eliminated.

A second, related overbreadth claim is that the $1,000 restriction is unrealistically low because much more than that amount would still not be enough to enable an unscrupulous contributor to exercise improper influence over a candidate or

---

31. While providing significant limitations on the ability of all individuals and groups to contribute large amounts of money to candidates, the Act's contribution ceilings do not foreclose the making of substantial contributions to candidates by some major special-interest groups through the combined effect of individual contributions from adherents or the proliferation of political funds each authorized under the Act to contribute to candidates. As a prime example, § 610 permits corporations and labor unions to establish segregated funds to solicit voluntary contributions to be utilized for political purposes. Corporate and union resources without limitation may be employed to administer these funds and to solicit contributions from employees, stockholders, and union members. Each separate fund may contribute up to $5,000 per candidate per election so long as the fund qualifies as a political committee under § 608(b)(2).

The Act places no limit on the number of funds that may be formed through the use of subsidiaries or divisions of corporations, or of local and regional units of a national labor union. . . .

officeholder, especially in campaigns for statewide or national office. While the contribution limitation provisions might well have been structured to take account of the graduated expenditure limitations for congressional and Presidential campaigns, Congress' failure to engage in such fine tuning does not invalidate the legislation. As the Court of Appeals observed, "(i)f it is satisfied that some limit on contributions is necessary, a court has no scalpel to probe, whether, say, a $2,000 ceiling might not serve as well as $1,000." Such distinctions in degree become significant only when they can be said to amount to differences in kind.

(c)

Apart from these First Amendment concerns, appellants argue that the contribution limitations work such an invidious discrimination between incumbents and challengers that the statutory provisions must be declared unconstitutional on their face. In considering this contention, it is important at the outset to note that the Act applies the same limitations on contributions to all candidates regardless of their present occupations, ideological views, or party affiliations. Absent record evidence of invidious discrimination against challengers as a class, a court should generally be hesitant to invalidate legislation which on its face imposes evenhanded restrictions.

There is no such evidence to support the claim that the contribution limitations in themselves discriminate against major-party challengers to incumbents. Challengers can and often do defeat incumbents in federal elections. Major-party challengers in federal elections are usually men and women who are well known and influential in their community or State. Often such challengers are themselves incumbents in important local, state, or federal offices. Statistics in the record indicate that major-party challengers as well as incumbents are capable of raising large sums for campaigning. Indeed, a small but nonetheless significant number of challengers have in recent elections outspent their incumbent rivals. And, to the extent that incumbents generally are more likely than challengers to attract very large contributions, the Act's $1,000 ceiling has the practical effect of benefiting challengers as a class. Contrary to the broad generalization drawn by the appellants, the practical impact of the contribution ceilings in any given election will clearly depend upon the amounts in excess of the ceilings that, for various reasons, the candidates in that election would otherwise have received and the utility of these additional amounts to the candidates. To be sure, the limitations may have a significant effect on particular challengers or incumbents, but the record provides no basis for predicting that such adventitious factors will invariably and invidiously benefit incumbents as a class. Since the danger of corruption and the appearance of corruption apply with equal force to challengers and to incumbents, Congress had ample justification for imposing the same fundraising constraints upon both.

The charge of discrimination against minor-party and independent candidates is more troubling, but the record provides no basis for concluding that the Act invidiously disadvantages such candidates. As noted above, the Act on its face treats all candidates equally with regard to contribution limitations. And the restriction would appear to benefit minor-party and independent candidates relative to their major-party opponents because major-party candidates receive far more money in large contributions. Although there is some force to appellants' response that minor-party candidates are primarily concerned with their ability to amass the resources necessary to reach the electorate rather than with their funding position relative to their major-party opponents, the record is virtually devoid of support for the claim that the $1,000 contribution limitation will have a serious effect on the initiation and scope of minor-party and independent candidacies. Moreover, any attempt to exclude minor parties and independents en masse from the Act's contribution limitations overlooks the fact that minor-party candidates may win elective office or have a substantial impact on the outcome of an election.

In view of these considerations, we conclude that the impact of the Act's $1,000 contribution limitation on major-party challengers and on minor-party candidates does not render the provision unconstitutional on its face.

2. The $5,000 Limitation on Contributions by Political Committees

Section 608(b)(2) permits certain committees, designated as "political committees" [and popularly known as political action committees, or PACs—Eds.], to contribute up to $5,000 to any candidate with respect to any election for federal office. In order to qualify for the higher contribution ceiling, a group must have been registered with the Commission as a political committee under [52 U.S.C. § 30103] for not less than six months, have received contributions from more than 50 persons, and, except for state political party organizations, have contributed to five or more candidates for federal office. Appellants argue that these qualifications unconstitutionally discriminate against *ad hoc* organizations in favor of established interest groups and impermissibly burden free association. The argument is without merit. Rather than undermining freedom of association, the basic provision enhances the opportunity of bona fide groups to participate in the election process, and the registration, contribution, and candidate conditions serve the permissible purpose of preventing individuals from evading the applicable contribution limitations by labeling themselves committees....

4. The $25,000 Limitation on Total Contributions During any Calendar Year

In addition to the $1,000 limitation on the nonexempt contributions that an individual may make to a particular candidate for any single election, the Act contains an overall $25,000 limitation on total contributions by an individual during any calendar year. § 608(b)(3). A contribution made in connection with an election is considered, for purposes of this subsection, to be made in the year the election is held. Although the constitutionality of this provision was drawn into question by appellants, it has not been separately addressed at length by the parties. The overall $25,000 ceiling does impose an ultimate restriction upon the number of candidates and committees with which an individual may associate himself by means of financial support. But this quite modest restraint upon protected political activity serves to prevent evasion of the $1,000 contribution limitation by a person who might otherwise contribute massive amounts of money to a particular candidate through the use of unearmarked contributions to political committees likely to contribute to that candidate, or huge contributions to the candidate's political party. The limited, additional restriction on associational freedom imposed by the overall ceiling is thus no more than a corollary of the basic individual contribution limitation that we have found to be constitutionally valid.

C. Expenditure Limitations

The Act's expenditure ceilings impose direct and substantial restraints on the quantity of political speech. The most drastic of the limitations restricts individuals and groups, including political parties that fail to place a candidate on the ballot, to an expenditure of $1,000 "relative to a clearly identified candidate during a calendar year." Other expenditure ceilings limit spending by candidates, their campaigns, and political parties in connection with election campaigns. It is clear that a primary effect of these expenditure limitations is to restrict the quantity of campaign speech by individuals, groups, and candidates. The restrictions, while neutral as to the ideas expressed, limit political expression "at the core of our electoral process and of the First Amendment freedoms." *Williams v. Rhodes.*

1. The $1,000 Limitation on Expenditures "Relative to a Clearly Identified Candidate"

Section 608(e)(1) provides that "[no] person may make any expenditure . . . relative to a clearly identified candidate during a calendar year which, when added to all other expenditures made by such person during the year advocating the election or defeat of such candidate, exceeds $1,000." The plain effect of § 608(e)(1) is to prohibit all individuals, who are neither candidates nor owners of institutional press facilities, and all groups, except political parties and campaign organizations, from voicing their views "relative to a clearly identified candidate" through means that entail aggregate expenditures of more than $1,000 during a calendar year. The provision, for example, would make it a federal criminal offense for a person or association to place a single one-quarter page advertisement "relative to a clearly identified candidate" in a major metropolitan newspaper.[j]

j. Consider Daniel D. Polsby, Buckley v. Valeo*: The Special Nature of Political Speech*, 1976 Supreme Court Review 1, 6: "Under the FECA amendments, a person who, independently and on his own initiative, placed a full-page advertisement in the Washington Post urging the defeat of an incumbent president . . . could be fined and sent to prison. Even granting the seriousness of the problem, solutions so rigorous give off a whiff of brimstone."

But a different concern is expressed by John S. Shockley, *Money in Politics: Judicial Roadblocks to Campaign Finance Reform*, 10 Hastings Constitutional Law Quarterly 679, 695–96 (1983): "In thus striking down limits on expenditures the Court freed the wealthy to engage in significant use of the most effective modes of communication. But what are the Justices saying about the great majority of the American people who cannot spend more than $1,000 on candidates they support? By the Court's own words, a majority of the American people are excluded from effective communication."—Eds.

Before examining the interests advanced in support of § 608(e)(1)'s expenditure ceiling, consideration must be given to appellants' contention that the provision is unconstitutionally vague. Close examination of the specificity of the statutory limitation is required where, as here, the legislation imposes criminal penalties in an area permeated by First Amendment interests. . . .

The key operative language of the provision limits "any expenditure . . . relative to a clearly identified candidate." Although "expenditure," "clearly identified," and "candidate" are defined in the Act, there is no definition clarifying what expenditures are "relative to" a candidate. The use of so indefinite a phrase as "relative to" a candidate fails to clearly mark the boundary between permissible and impermissible speech, unless other portions of § 608(e)(1) make sufficiently explicit the range of expenditures covered by the limitation. The section prohibits "any expenditure . . . relative to a clearly identified candidate during a calendar year which, *when added to all other expenditures . . . advocating the election or defeat of such candidate*, exceeds, $1,000." (Emphasis added.) This context clearly permits, if indeed it does not require, the phrase "relative to" a candidate to be read to mean "advocating the election or defeat of" a candidate.

But while such a construction of § 608(e)(1) refocuses the vagueness question, the Court of Appeals was mistaken in thinking that this construction eliminates the problem of unconstitutional vagueness altogether. For the distinction between discussion of issues and candidates and advocacy of election or defeat of candidates may often dissolve in practical application. Candidates, especially incumbents, are intimately tied to public issues involving legislative proposals and governmental actions. Not only do candidates campaign on the basis of their positions on various public issues, but campaigns themselves generate issues of public interest. . . .

[These] constitutional deficiencies . . . can be avoided only by reading § 608(e)(1) as limited to communications that include explicit words of advocacy of election or defeat of a candidate, much as the definition of "clearly identified" in § 608(e)(2) requires that an explicit and unambiguous reference to the candidate appear as part of the communication.[51] This is the reading of the provision suggested by the non-governmental appellees in arguing that "[f]unds spent to propagate one's views on issues without expressly calling for a candidate's election or defeat are thus not covered." We agree that in order to preserve the provision against invalidation on vagueness grounds, § 608(e)(1) must be construed to apply only to expenditures for

51. Section 608(e)(2) defines "clearly identified" to require that the candidate's name, photograph or drawing, or other unambiguous reference to his identity appear as part of the communication. Such other unambiguous reference would include use of the candidate's initials (e.g., FDR), the candidate's nickname (e.g., Ike), his office (e.g., the President or the Governor of Iowa), or his status as a candidate (e.g., the Democratic Presidential nominee, the senatorial candidate of the Republican Party of Georgia).

communications that in express terms advocate the election or defeat of a clearly identified candidate for federal office.[52]

We turn then to the basic First Amendment question whether § 608(e)(1), even as thus narrowly and explicitly construed, impermissibly burdens the constitutional right of free expression. The Court of Appeals summarily held the provision constitutionally valid on the ground that "section 608(e) is a loophole-closing provision only" that is necessary to prevent circumvention of the contribution limitations. We cannot agree.

The discussion in Part I-A, *supra*, explains why the Act's expenditure limitations impose far greater restraints on the freedom of speech and association than do its contribution limitations. The markedly greater burden on basic freedoms caused by § 608(e)(1) thus cannot be sustained simply by invoking the interest in maximizing the effectiveness of the less intrusive contribution limitations. Rather, the constitutionality of § 608(e)(1) turns on whether the governmental interests advanced in its support satisfy the exacting scrutiny applicable to limitations on core First Amendment rights of political expression.

We find that the governmental interest in preventing corruption and the appearance of corruption is inadequate to justify § 608(e)(1)'s ceiling on independent expenditures. First, assuming, *arguendo*, that large independent expenditures pose the same dangers of actual or apparent *quid pro quo* arrangements as do large contributions, § 608(e)(1) does not provide an answer that sufficiently relates to the elimination of those dangers. Unlike the contribution limitations' total ban on the giving of large amounts of money to candidates, § 608(e)(1) prevents only some large expenditures. So long as persons and groups eschew expenditures that in express terms advocate the election or defeat of a clearly identified candidate, they are free to spend as much as they want to promote the candidate and his views. The exacting interpretation of the statutory language necessary to avoid unconstitutional vagueness thus undermines the limitation's effectiveness as a loophole-closing provision by facilitating circumvention by those seeking to exert improper influence upon a candidate or office-holder. It would naively underestimate the ingenuity and resourcefulness of persons and groups desiring to buy influence to believe that they would have much difficulty devising expenditures that skirted the restriction on express advocacy of election or defeat but nevertheless benefited the candidate's campaign. Yet no substantial societal interest would be served by a loophole-closing provision designed to check corruption that permitted unscrupulous persons and

52. This construction would restrict the application of § 608(e)(1) to communications containing express words of advocacy of election or defeat, such as "vote for," "elect," "support," "cast your ballot for," "Smith for Congress," "vote against," "defeat," "reject." [Pay close attention to this footnote. The entire controversy regarding "issue advocacy" in federal elections, discussed in detail in Chapter 13, begins with an understanding of the footnote and the accompanying text. — Eds.]

organizations to expend unlimited sums of money in order to obtain improper influence over candidates for elective office.

Second, quite apart from the shortcomings of § 608(e)(1) in preventing any abuses generated by large independent expenditures, the independent advocacy restricted by the provision does not presently appear to pose dangers of real or apparent corruption comparable to those identified with large campaign contributions. The parties defending § 608(e)(1) contend that it is necessary to prevent would-be contributors from avoiding the contribution limitations by the simple expedient of paying directly for media advertisements or for other portions of the candidate's campaign activities. They argue that expenditures controlled by or coordinated with the candidate and his campaign might well have virtually the same value to the candidate as a contribution and would pose similar dangers of abuse. Yet such controlled or coordinated expenditures are treated as contributions rather than expenditures under the Act.[53] Section 608(b)'s contribution ceilings rather than § 608(e)(1)'s independent expenditure limitation prevent attempts to circumvent the Act through prearranged or coordinated expenditures amounting to disguised contributions. By contrast, § 608(e)(1) limits expenditures for express advocacy of candidates made totally independently of the candidate and his campaign. Unlike contributions, such independent expenditures may well provide little assistance to the candidate's campaign and indeed may prove counterproductive. The absence of prearrangement

---

53. Section 608(e)(1) does not apply to expenditures "on behalf of a candidate" within the meaning of § 608(c)(2)(B). The latter subsection provides that expenditures "authorized or requested by the candidate, an authorized committee of the candidate, or an agent of the candidate" are to be treated as expenditures of the candidate and contributions by the person or group making the expenditure. The House and Senate Reports provide guidance in differentiating individual expenditures that are contributions and candidate expenditures under § 608(c)(2)(B) from those treated as independent expenditures subject to the § 608(e)(1) ceiling. The House Report speaks of independent expenditures as costs "incurred without the request or consent of a candidate or his agent." The Senate report addresses the issue in greater detail. It provides an example illustrating the distinction between "authorized or requested" expenditures excluded from § 608(e)(1) and independent expenditures governed by § 608(e)(1):

> "[A] person might purchase billboard advertisements endorsing a candidate. If he does so completely on his own, and not at the request or suggestion of the candidate or his agent's [sic] that would constitute an 'independent expenditure on behalf of a candidate' under section 614(c) of the bill. The person making the expenditure would have to report it as such.
>
> "However, if the advertisement was placed in cooperation with the candidate's campaign organization, then the amount would constitute a gift by the supporter and an expenditure by the candidate just as if there had been a direct contribution enabling the candidate to place the advertisement himself. It would be so reported by both."

The Conference substitute adopted the provision of the Senate bill dealing with expenditures by any person "authorized or requested" to make an expenditure by the candidate or his agents. In view of this legislative history and the purposes of the Act, we find that the "authorized or requested" standard of the Act operates to treat all expenditures placed in cooperation with or with the consent of a candidate, his agents, or an authorized committee of the candidate as contributions subject to the limitations set forth in § 608(b).

and coordination of an expenditure with the candidate or his agent not only undermines the value of the expenditure to the candidate, but also alleviates the danger that expenditures will be given as a *quid pro quo* for improper commitments from the candidate. Rather than preventing circumvention of the contribution limitations, § 608(e)(1) severely restricts all independent advocacy despite its substantially diminished potential for abuse.[k]

While the independent expenditure ceiling thus fails to serve any substantial governmental interest in stemming the reality or appearance of corruption in the electoral process, it heavily burdens core First Amendment expression. For the First Amendment right to "speak one's mind ... on all public institutions" includes the right to engage in "'vigorous advocacy' no less than 'abstract discussion.'" *New York Times Co. v. Sullivan*, 376 U.S., at 269. Advocacy of the election or defeat of candidates for federal office is no less entitled to protection under the First Amendment than the discussion of political policy generally or advocacy of the passage or defeat of legislation.

It is argued, however, that the ancillary governmental interest in equalizing the relative ability of individuals and groups to influence the outcome of elections serves to justify the limitation on express advocacy of the election or defeat of candidates imposed by § 608(e)(1)'s expenditure ceiling. But the concept that government may restrict the speech of some elements of our society in order to enhance the relative voice of others is wholly foreign to the First Amendment, which was designed "to secure 'the widest possible dissemination of information from diverse and antagonistic sources,'" and "to assure unfettered interchange of ideas for the bringing about of political and social changes desired by the people." *New York Times Co.* The First Amendment's protection against governmental abridgment of free expression cannot properly be made to depend on a person's financial ability to engage in public discussion. Cf. *Eastern R. Conf. v. Noerr Motors*, 365 U.S. 127, 139 (1961).[55] . . . .

---

k. In Part I.B.4 of its opinion, the Court upheld the $25,000 limitation on total contributions by an individual on the ground that the individual could evade the $1,000 limit on contributions to candidates by making "massive" contributions to PACs likely to support such candidates or "huge" contributions to the candidates' political parties. Was the "potential for abuse" addressed by the $25,000 limit more of a danger than the potential addressed by the limit on independent expenditures? — Eds.

55. Neither the voting rights cases nor the Court's decision upholding the Federal Communications Commission's fairness doctrine lends support to appellees' position that the First Amendment permits Congress to abridge the rights of some persons to engage in political expression in order to enhance the relative voice of other segments of our society. Cases invalidating governmentally imposed wealth restrictions on the right to vote or file as a candidate for public office rest on the conclusion that wealth "is not germane to one's ability to participate intelligently in the electoral process" and is therefore an insufficient basis on which to restrict a citizen's fundamental right to vote. *Harper*. These voting cases and the reapportionment decisions serve to assure that citizens are accorded an equal right to vote for their representatives regardless of factors of wealth or geography. But the principles that underlie invalidation of governmentally imposed restrictions on the franchise do not justify governmentally imposed restrictions on political expression. Democracy

For the reasons stated, we conclude that § 608(e)(1)'s independent expenditure limitation is unconstitutional under the First Amendment.

2. Limitation on Expenditures by Candidates from Personal or Family Resources

The Act also sets limits on expenditures by a candidate "from his personal funds, or the personal funds of his immediate family, in connection with his campaigns during any calendar year." § 608(a)(1). These ceilings vary from $50,000 for Presidential or Vice Presidential candidates to $35,000 for senatorial candidates, and $25,000 for most candidates for the House of Representatives.

The ceiling on personal expenditures by candidates on their own behalf, like the limitations on independent expenditures contained in § 608(e)(1), imposes a substantial restraint on the ability of persons to engage in protected First Amendment expression.[1] The candidate, no less than any other person, has a First Amendment right to engage in the discussion of public issues and vigorously and tirelessly to advocate his own election and the election of other candidates. Indeed, it is of particular importance that candidates have the unfettered opportunity to make their views known so that the electorate may intelligently evaluate the candidates' personal qualities and their positions on vital public issues before choosing among them on election day. Mr. Justice Brandeis' observation that in our country "public discussion is a political duty," *Whitney v. California*, 274 U.S. 357, 375 (1927) (concurring opinion), applies with special force to candidates for public office. Section 608(a)'s ceiling on personal expenditures by a candidate in furtherance of his own candidacy thus clearly and directly interferes with constitutionally protected freedoms.

The primary governmental interest served by the Act — the prevention of actual and apparent corruption of the political process — does not support the limitation on the candidate's expenditure of his own personal funds. As the Court of Appeals concluded: "Manifestly, the core problem of avoiding undisclosed and undue influence on candidates from outside interests has lesser application when the monies involved come from the candidate himself or from his immediate family." Indeed, the use of personal funds reduces the candidate's dependence on outside contributions and thereby counteracts the coercive pressures and attendant risks of abuse to which the Act's contribution limitations are directed.

---

depends on a well-informed electorate, not a citizenry legislatively limited in its ability to discuss and debate candidates and issues. . . .

1. Shockley, *supra*, 10 Hastings Constitutional Law Quarterly at 694–95, asks: "If one agrees with the Court that being able to spend only $25,000 to $50,000 annually on campaigning is in fact a substantial restraint upon constitutional expression, what does this say about the rights of the ninety-nine percent of the American electorate who cannot expend even this 'substantially restrained' amount? Since their ability to speak is presumably restrained even more, where are they to look for the protection of their First Amendment rights?" — Eds.

The ancillary interest in equalizing the relative financial resources of candidates competing for elective office, therefore, provides the sole relevant rationale for § 608(a)'s expenditure ceiling. That interest is clearly not sufficient to justify the provision's infringement of fundamental First Amendment rights. First, the limitation may fail to promote financial equality among candidates. A candidate who spends less of his personal resources on his campaign may nonetheless outspend his rival as a result of more successful fundraising efforts. Indeed, a candidate's personal wealth may impede his efforts to persuade others that he needs their financial contributions or volunteer efforts to conduct an effective campaign. Second, and more fundamentally, the First Amendment simply cannot tolerate § 608(a)'s restriction upon the freedom of a candidate to speak without legislative limit on behalf of his own candidacy. We therefore hold that § 608(a)'s restriction on a candidate's personal expenditures is unconstitutional.

3. Limitations on Campaign Expenditures

Section 608(c) places limitations on overall campaign expenditures by candidates seeking nomination for election and election to federal office. Presidential candidates may spend $10,000,000 in seeking nomination for office and an additional $20,000,000 in the general election campaign. §§ 608(c)(1)(A), (B). The ceiling on senatorial campaigns is pegged to the size of the voting-age population of the State with minimum dollar amounts applicable to campaigns in States with small populations. In senatorial primary elections, the limit is the greater of eight cents multiplied by the voting-age population or $100,000, and in the general election the limit is increased to 12 cents multiplied by the voting-age population or $150,000. §§ 608(c)(1)(C), (D). The Act imposes blanket $70,000 limitations on both primary campaigns and general election campaigns for the House of Representatives with the exception that the senatorial ceiling applies to campaigns in States entitled to only one Representative. §§ 608(c)(1)(C)–(E). These ceilings are to be adjusted upwards at the beginning of each calendar year by the average percentage rise in the consumer price index for the 12 preceding months. § 608(d).

No governmental interest that has been suggested is sufficient to justify the restriction on the quantity of political expression imposed by § 608(c)'s campaign expenditure limitations. The major evil associated with rapidly increasing campaign expenditures is the danger of candidate dependence on large contributions. The interest in alleviating the corrupting influence of large contributions is served by the Act's contribution limitations and disclosure provisions rather than by § 608(c)'s campaign expenditure ceilings. The Court of Appeals' assertion that the expenditure restrictions are necessary to reduce the incentive to circumvent direct contribution limits is not persuasive. There is no indication that the substantial criminal penalties for violating the contribution ceilings combined with the political repercussion of such violations will be insufficient to police the contribution provisions. Extensive reporting, auditing, and disclosure requirements applicable to both contributions and expenditures by political campaigns are designed to facilitate the detection of illegal contributions. Moreover, as the Court of Appeals noted, the Act permits an officeholder or successful candidate to retain contributions in excess of the expenditure ceiling and to use these funds for "any other lawful purpose." This provision undercuts whatever marginal role the expenditure limitations might otherwise play in enforcing the contribution ceilings.

The interest in equalizing the financial resources of candidates competing for federal office is no more convincing a justification for restricting the scope of federal election campaigns. Given the limitation on the size of outside contributions, the financial resources available to a candidate's campaign, like the number of volunteers recruited, will normally vary with the size and intensity of the candidate's support.[63] There is nothing invidious, improper, or unhealthy in permitting such funds to be spent to carry the candidate's message to the electorate.[64] Moreover, the equalization of permissible campaign expenditures might serve not to equalize the opportunities of all candidates, but to handicap a candidate who lacked substantial name recognition or exposure of his views before the start of the campaign.

The campaign expenditure ceilings appear to be designed primarily to serve the governmental interests in reducing the allegedly skyrocketing costs of political campaigns. Appellees and the Court of Appeals stressed statistics indicating that spending for federal election campaigns increased almost 300% between 1952 and 1972 in comparison with a 57.6% rise in the consumer price index during the same period. Appellants respond that during these years the rise in campaign spending lagged behind the percentage increase in total expenditures for commercial advertising and the size of the gross national product. In any event, the mere growth in the cost of federal election campaigns in and of itself provides no basis for governmental restrictions on the quantity of campaign spending and the resulting limitation on the scope of federal campaigns. The First Amendment denies government the power to determine that spending to promote one's political views is wasteful, excessive, or unwise. In the free society ordained by our Constitution it is not the government, but the people individually as citizens and candidates and collectively as associations and political committees who must retain control over the quantity and range of debate on public issues in a political campaign.[65]

---

63. This normal relationship may not apply where the candidate devotes a large amount of his personal resources to his campaign.

64. As [Judge Tamm's] opinion dissenting in part from the decision below noted: "If a senatorial candidate can raise $1 from each voter, what evil is exacerbated by allowing that candidate to use all that money for political communication? I know of none."

65. For the reasons discussed in Part III, *infra*, Congress may engage in public financing of election campaigns and may condition acceptance of public funds on an agreement by the candidate to abide by specified expenditure limitations. Just as a candidate may voluntarily limit the size of the contributions he chooses to accept, he may decide to forgo private fundraising and accept public funding.

[This footnote, number 65, is cryptic but extremely important, as the tying of permissible campaign spending limits to public funding has profoundly shaped the politics of campaign finance regulation. In Part III of its opinion the Court does give reasons for the permissibility of public financing, but contrary to the statement in footnote 65, there is no explanation in Part III or

For these reasons we hold that § 608(c) is constitutionally invalid.

In sum, the provisions of the Act that impose a $1,000 limitation on contributions to a single candidate, § 608(b)(1), a $5,000 limitation on contributions by a political committee to a single candidate, § 608(b)(2), and a $25,000 limitation on total contributions by an individual during any calendar year, § 608(b)(3), are constitutionally valid. These limitations, along with the disclosure provisions, constitute the Act's primary weapons against the reality or appearance of improper influence stemming from the dependence of candidates on large campaign contributions. The contribution ceilings thus serve the basic governmental interest in safeguarding the integrity of the electoral process without directly impinging upon the rights of individual citizens and candidates to engage in political debate and discussion. By contrast, the First Amendment requires the invalidation of the Act's independent expenditure ceiling, § 608(e)(1), its limitation on a candidate's expenditures from his own personal funds, § 608(a), and its ceilings on overall campaign expenditures, § 608(c). These provisions place substantial and direct restrictions on the ability of candidates, citizens, and associations to engage in protected political expression, restrictions that the First Amendment cannot tolerate.

Notes and Questions on Buckley *and the First Amendment*

1. *Campaign Finance and the First Amendment.* Few are likely to quarrel with the majority's opening assertion that the contribution and spending limits "operate in an area of the most fundamental First Amendment activities." Yet most commentators agree that *Buckley* is characterized by "fluctuating deference to congressional determinations." Marlene Arnold Nicholson, Buckley v. Valeo: *The Constitutionality of the Federal Election Campaign Act Amendments of 1974*, 1977 Wisconsin Law Review 323, 325. One reason, no doubt, is that if the restrictions operate within the core of the First Amendment, the governmental interests at stake lie within the core of the democratic process. Supporters of campaign finance regulation often claim that the governmental interests furthered are not only important, but are themselves intended to further First Amendment values, by making the opportunity to participate effectively in political debate more widespread. Whether this is the case and the implications for constitutional doctrine if it is have been questions of continuing controversy.

---

elsewhere in *Buckley* why Congress may "condition acceptance of public funds on an agreement by the candidate to abide by . . . expenditure limitations."

The text in the opinion immediately prior to footnote 65 should not be overshadowed by the footnote itself. If, collectively, the people favor a lower level of campaign expenditures, is it realistic for the Court to suggest that they may control the "quantity and range of debate" by reducing the contributions they make (as individuals or through associations) or receive (as candidates or political committees)? Consider Harold Leventhal, *Courts and Political Thickets*, 77 Columbia Law Review 345, 368 (1977): "This answer ignores the possibility that the dynamics of some campaign problems are such that they cannot be solved by individual decisions; the race for campaign funds — like an arms race — requires global regulation." — Eds.]

Those who believe there were First Amendment values on both sides accuse the *Buckley* majority of excessive formalism or mechanical jurisprudence. Such views were expressed by a member of the Court of Appeals panel whose ruling in *Buckley* upholding virtually all of the FECA Amendments was partially overruled by the Supreme Court:

> By ritual incantation of the notion of absolute protection, by applying it to the quantity as well as the content of political expression, and by making the unexamined and unprecedented assertion that money is speech, the Court elevated dry formalism over substantive constitutional reasoning. Political discussion is indeed at the core of the first amendment's guarantees, but the very centrality of political speech calls for a thorough rather than a conclusory analysis.

J. Skelly Wright, *Money and the Pollution of Politics: Is the First Amendment an Obstacle to Political Equality?*, 82 Columbia Law Review 611, 633 (1982). Another member of the Court of Appeals panel in *Buckley* argued that the presence of First Amendment considerations on both sides required a more pragmatic approach than the Supreme Court had displayed:

> The first amendment works to promote an open market in ideas. But we restrict the freedom of monopolists controlling a market to enhance the freedom of others in the market. At a time when the liberty of contract had the constitutional preeminence today assigned to freedom of expression, Justice Holmes declared that principles of freedom cannot preclude government limits on the power of wealth in order to create a fair competition.... These examples ... are suggestive of a pragmatic mode of thinking, which avoids focusing on the initial impact of a law, as a restriction, and looks at its overall effect.

Harold Leventhal, *Courts and Political Thickets*, 77 Columbia Law Review 345, 373 (1977).

These critics have themselves drawn criticism from those who believe it is dangerous to give greater weight to "First Amendment values" than to what they regard as the First Amendment's direct command that the government not regulate political speech. Consider L.A. Powe, Jr., *Mass Speech and the Newer First Amendment*, 1982 Supreme Court Review 243, 245–46, 268–69, 280–84:

> [T]he possibility [exists] that even if differing viewpoints are present there may be so overwhelming a predominance of communication in support of some of them that other viewpoints simply do not have a chance to be considered on the merits. For those who believe this occurs there is the not unnatural conclusion that the prevailing viewpoint has done so in an unfair way. Had the issue been joined between equals, a differing viewpoint would (or might) have prevailed. Most typically such concerns are expressed in the context of elections, and over the past decade there have

been a variety of attempts to even up the potential clash of ideas through either contribution or expenditure limitations on candidates and their supporters.... The structure of argument in the campaign finance cases is fairly simple. Because any contribution or expenditure will be translated into media advertising, a legislative restriction will necessarily limit speech. This is valid only if the government offers very important reasons. Typically, the government has two reasons, both going to the perceived purity of the electoral process. The first is that citizens may view large contributions to candidates as akin to bribery. But this rationale has not been sufficient to sustain all of the legislation. Thus the second justification: an election ought to have the elements of a fair fight, and when one side grossly outspends the other for advertising, a fair fight is impossible. Accordingly the marketplace of ideas is better served, and freedom of speech is enhanced, when one side of an issue is prevented from being repeated so often that it overwhelms rational thought about the merits of the election. This second justification for limiting contributions and expenditures is what I call the enhancement theory of freedom of speech. The theory has developed over the years on foundations that are foreign to the First Amendment; the theory has no place in any sensible treatment of the First Amendment and should, in the future, be summarily rejected....

To surrender the interests of individual autonomy and to attempt to tone down a debate (or one side of it) in the interests of enhancing the marketplace is to give up something that is directly traceable to the First Amendment in order to achieve a speculative gain. It is attempted on the speculative basis that a legislature knows at what points the problem of market failure is likely to surface and that enhancement is an effective means of avoiding them.... Furthermore, it rests on an assumption that less speech may well be better than more, an assumption that appears wildly at odds with the normal First Amendment belief that more speech is better....

The fundamental tenet of enhancement theory that less speech is better at some points seems to rest on two assumptions: first, additional speech on the other side either will not be forthcoming or is not worth the effort, and second, the "reach" of modern mass communications is of such a new order that it needs a different theory to make it function "consistently with the ends and purposes of the First Amendment." Yet just as there is a problem with determining how much is too much, there is also a gap in the explanation of why there will be no further speech on the other side to counter the speech that is being repeated too often. And how "new" is the problem? But for the "mass" communications of newspapers, specifically Pulitzer's and Hearst's, there would not have been a Spanish American War in 1898 to make Theodore Roosevelt next in line to the Presidency in 1900.

> Enhancement has been articulated as a rationale only for dealing with the mass media. The soapbox orator, that classic and heroic lone dissenter of so much of the First Amendment case law, seems exempt. He does not fit within enhancement, because he cannot, from his soapbox, create the necessary imbalance. In his case we cannot shut him off because we dislike him, dislike his message, are sick and tired of being bothered, are angry that someone could be so wrongheaded, or feel that he creates such an imbalance in the marketplace that it would be unfair to let him continue. We are stuck with walking away from him or maybe even countering what he says with our own position.
>
> The traditional solution, more rather than less speech, is both possible and desirable in the mass speech area as well. [A]s Brandeis recognized over fifty years ago, speech is a part of political liberty. Public discussion is a citizen's duty. As a society we have more to fear from an inert than an active citizenry. Fear and repression menace stable government; speech does not.... It is not so much that we retain a naive belief that truth is knowable or that the electorate will rationally choose it, as that the simple recognition that no theory requiring people to stop speaking (or stop listening) better fits with our traditions than the one we have adopted. The theory that a speaker has the right to choose his message and the intensity and frequency of its delivery reflects the recognition that a free-for-all on public issues serves both the ideals [of] self-government and those of maximizing individual choices.... It is hard to dispute that the wealthy seem to enjoy tremendous influence—and not only in this country. But if this is the concern, I would suspect that the best way of dealing with the power of wealth would be to attack its source rather than its consequences. In other words, if the wealthy are too powerful, change the tax and inheritance laws to prevent accumulations of wealth. If that is too extreme, then significant additional public funding can be made available for electoral campaigns, so that the advantages of wealth can either be eliminated or minimized. These are neither easy nor cost-free choices, but by not seeking to operate directly on speech in one case and by adding more speech without limiting anyone in the other, both are consistent with the traditions of the First Amendment.

For other defenses similar to Powe's, see Daniel D. Polsby, Buckley v. Valeo: *The Special Nature of Political Speech*, 1976 Supreme Court Review 1, Kathleen M. Sullivan, *Political Money and Freedom of Speech*, 30 U.C. Davis Law Review 663 (1997), and Robert Post, *Regulating Election Speech Under the First Amendment*, 77 Texas Law Review 1837 (1999).

Consider as a retort Cass R. Sunstein, *Political Equality and Unintended Consequences*, 94 Columbia Law Review 1390, 1397 (1994). Sunstein argues that *Buckley* is the "modern-day analogue of the infamous and discredited case of *Lochner v.*

New York [198 U.S. 45 (1905)], in which the Court invalidated maximum hour laws." Sunstein explains:

> Just as the due process clause once forbade government "interference" with the outcomes of the economic marketplace [the holding of *Lochner*—Eds.], so too the First Amendment now bans government "interference" with the political marketplace, with the term "marketplace" understood quite literally. In this way *Buckley* replicates *Lochner*. . . .
>
> Because it involves speech, *Buckley* is in one sense even more striking than *Lochner*. As I have noted, the goal of political equality is time-honored in the American constitutional tradition, as the goal of economic equality is not. Efforts to redress economic inequalities, or to ensure that they are not turned to political inequalities, should not be seen as impermissible redistribution, or as the introduction of government regulation into a place where it did not exist before. A system of unlimited campaign expenditures should be seen as a regulatory decision to allow disparities in resources to be turned into disparities in political influence. That may be the best decision, all things considered; but why is it unconstitutional for government to attempt to replace this system with an alternative? The Court offered no answer. Its analysis was startlingly cavalier. Campaign finance laws should be evaluated not through axioms, but pragmatically in terms of their consequences for free expression.

Id. at 1398–99; see also John Rawls, Political Liberalism 362 (1993); Frank Michelman, *Political Truth and the Rule of Law*, 8 Tel Aviv University Studies in Law 281 (1988); Owen M. Fiss, *Free Speech and Social Structure*, 71 Iowa Law Review 1405, 1407 (1986). As you begin your consideration of these questions, who do you think has the stronger argument and why? Reconsider these questions after you have completed study of the next two chapters.

2. *Neutrality.* "Content neutrality" has emerged as a major component of the Supreme Court's doctrine in applying the First Amendment. "The Court applies 'the most exacting scrutiny' to regulations that discriminate among instances of speech based on its content." Laurence H. Tribe, American Constitutional Law 798 (2d ed. 1988) (quoting *Widmar v. Vincent*, 454 U.S. 263, 276 (1981)).

In *Buckley*, the majority conceded that the FECA did not "focus on the ideas expressed by persons or groups subject to its regulations," while noting that the Act was "aimed in part at equalizing the relative ability of all voters to affect electoral outcomes." Defenders of regulation assert that "the equal money limits are concededly neutral as to the content of ideas expressed—a crucial point." Leventhal, *supra*, 77 Columbia Law Review at 359. However, critics of regulation do not invariably concede this point.

> In no case will the effects upon individuals, interest groups, and other political actors be precisely evenhanded. Indeed, it is ironic that the most forceful

> argument supporting campaign finance legislation praises the FECA for depriving the wealthy of the advantage of their position. The argument implies that the chief *virtue* of reform measures is their lack of neutrality of impact. Statutes that are supported precisely because they deprive a particular group of its ability to engage relatively effectively in politics, therefore, may not be as "entirely content neutral" as they seem.

Lillian R. BeVier, *Money and Politics: A Perspective on the First Amendment and Campaign Finance Reform*, 73 California Law Review 1045, 1062 (1985); see also Bradley A. Smith, *Money Talks: Speech, Corruption, Equality, and Campaign Finance*, 86 Georgetown Law Journal 45, 54 (1997) ("To suggest that any [campaign finance] scheme could be content neutral is to misunderstand the purpose of the enterprise: People who favor campaign finance reform do so because they believe that the present system of finance gives some individuals too much influence, thus leading to disfavored electoral and legislative results."); Sanford Levinson, Book Review, *Regulating Campaign Activity: The New Road to Contradiction?*, 83 Michigan Law Review 939, 945 (1985) ("[I]t is worth considering to what extent we in fact support such restrictions because of tacit assumptions about the contents of the views held by the rich, who would obviously feel most of the burden of the restrictions."). Indeed, according to two of the attorneys who litigated *Buckley*, plaintiffs considered but rejected the idea of arguing that the regulations were not neutral:

> An argument plaintiffs decided against making in *Buckley*, in part on the ground that it sounded too political, is that restrictions on campaign financing generally favor Democrats over Republicans because the latter needed to exploit their generally greater access to substantial contributors or larger total contributions to overcome the Democrats' much larger registered membership. Moreover, it can be argued persuasively that so long as our social system is based on the premise that inequalities of wealth serve valid and useful purposes, the wealthy need means to exercise their financial power to defend themselves politically against the greater numbers who may believe that their economic interests militate toward leveling.

Brice M. Clagett & John R. Bolton, Buckley v. Valeo, *Its Aftermath, and Its Prospects: The Constitutionality of Government Restraints on Political Campaign Financing*, 29 Vanderbilt Law Review 1327, 1335 (1976).

As a matter of tactics, do you believe the plaintiffs were correct to withhold this argument in the *Buckley* case? Do you believe contribution and expenditure limits are content neutral? Viewpoint neutral?

3. *Is Money Speech?* The *Buckley* majority said that limiting campaign expenditures was tantamount to limiting speech, because such a limit "necessarily reduces the quantity of expression by restricting the number of issues discussed, the depth of their exploration, and the size of the audience reached." As a practical matter, a limit on spending by a major campaign may limit the *repetition* of the same message

to the same audience. Is a reduction of repetition the same as a reduction of the size of the audience? What if the reason for the repetition is that many or most people are inclined to "tune out" the message (if it is broadcast) or throw it away unopened (if it is mailed)?

Though the question was hotly debated in the period leading up to *Buckley*, many defenders of reform accepted the Court's conclusion that spending limits need to be treated as speech limitations though, as we have seen, they often contend that the limits also serve First Amendment goals. One writer who refused to concede the point was J. Skelly Wright, *Politics and the Constitution: Is Money Speech?*, 85 Yale Law Journal 1001, 1012 (1976):

> [T]he effectiveness of political speakers is not necessarily diminished by reasonable contribution and expenditure ceilings. The giving and spending restrictions may cause candidates and other individuals to rely more on less expensive means of communication. But there is no reason to believe that such a shift in means reduces the number of issues discussed in a campaign. And, by forcing candidates to put more emphasis on local organizing or leafletting or door-to-door canvassing and less on full-page ads and television spot commercials, the restrictions may well generate deeper exploration of the issues raised. Finally, even to the extent that smaller audiences result from diminished use of the most expensive and pervasive media—and the campaigning so far gives no substantial indication that this happens—the effectiveness of a given speaker does not decline in relation to that of his opponents. All similarly situated competitors face the same constraints. Within those limits effectiveness still depends on the creativity of the speaker—and on the soundness of his ideas.

How persuasive is Judge Wright's argument? When candidates are limited in the amount they can spend in their campaigns—either because of the limits in their fund-raising capabilities or because of legally imposed spending limits—they are likely to use their scarce economic resources in the manner they regard as most cost-effective. If mass media—especially television and direct mail—are perceived as the most cost-effective media, then the imposition of spending limits may cause campaigns to cut back on "grass roots" expenditures and thereby increase their overall dependence on mass media. Spending in the 1976 presidential campaign was limited, because the major candidates accepted public financing. The perception that the campaigns sharply cut back on grass roots expenditures, such as bumper stickers and campaign buttons, led to the adoption of amendments in 1979 that made it possible for parties to spend sums outside the regular spending limits for grass roots activities.

Even if spending limits did have the effect of diverting campaigns from reliance on mass media to reliance on volunteers, as Wright supposes, would this necessarily be desirable? Political spot advertising on television is widely reviled, but the message is one that is controlled by the candidate. Volunteers might engage in more extended dialogue with voters, but anyone who has ever "walked precincts" in campaigns is likely to have mastered a brief, "canned" statement and been acutely aware of the need not to spend more than a few moments at any one residence. In any event, the volunteer may not be accurately reflecting the views of the candidate, especially in presidential or statewide elections in which few volunteers are likely to have any significant acquaintance with the candidate.

Justice Stevens revived the question, if cryptically, in a short concurrence in *Nixon v. Shrink Missouri Government PAC*, 528 U.S. 377 (2000), discussed in Chapter 14. There, Stevens said that money was property, not speech. More recently, Deborah Hellman has reexamined the money-speech equation in Deborah Hellman, *Money Talks But It Isn't Speech*, 95 Minnesota Law Review 953, 956 (2011). She writes:

> Briefly, where the good used to effectuate the right is distributed via the market, then a right which depends on that good includes the right to spend money. For example, abortion services are distributed via the market. Thus the right to abort a previable fetus includes the right to spend money to obtain an abortion. Where the good used to effectuate the right is not distributed via the market, then a right which depends on that good does not include the right to spend money. For example, votes are not distributed via the market. Thus, the right to vote does not include the right to buy or sell votes or even to pay someone to vote. This analysis suggests that restrictions on campaign giving and spending may not be restrictions on speech. When Congress takes electioneering out of the market, especially if it does so by providing public funding of campaigns, then restrictions on giving and spending in elections do not restrict speech and thus do not require heightened judicial review.

For an additional argument that money should be considered property, not speech, see Spencer A. Overton, *Mistaken Identity: Unveiling the Property Characteristics of Political Money*, 53 Vanderbilt Law Review 1235, 1269 (2000). According to Overton, "Courts should recognize that, as in the property context, issues of scarcity and distribution of political money may result in situations in which those with abundant political money unfairly interfere with the interests of those with less political money, and legislatures should be able to enact laws to prevent these harms. Just as some landlords and large companies may have unfair bargaining power over tenants, employees, and small competitors, those with abundant political money often have unfair bargaining power over those without political money." Compare Eugene Volokh, *Freedom of Speech and Speech About Political Candidates: The Unintended Consequences of Three Proposals*, 24 Harvard Journal of Law & Public Policy 47, 57–58 (2000): "Now Justice Stevens's 'simple point' is literally true—money is not speech—but it doesn't show much by itself. After all, expenditure limits don't just bar the use of money; they single out the use of money *to speak*. A law restricting people from flying places to give speeches would be a speech restriction, not because 'flying is speech' but because giving a speech is speech and burdening such speech (you may not fly in order to do it) is a speech restriction. Likewise for restrictions on spending money for speech."

4. *Balancing the First Amendment with Concerns over Corruption or Equality.* In *Buckley*, the Court applied a *balancing test* to determine if the government's interest in preventing corruption, the appearance of corruption, or equality could trump First Amendment concerns. In your view, how should the proper balance be struck? You may wish to consider your answer in light of the readings in Part III of this chapter.

5. *The Standard of Review.* As we have seen in earlier chapters, since the 1960s the Supreme Court has devoted considerable time to elaborating the "standard of review" that will be employed to test the constitutionality of various government measures. To simplify, it is ordinarily assumed that regulation that impinges on First Amendment rights — especially when it is political speech and association that are at stake — will be reviewed under the most rigorous standard, often described as "strict scrutiny." The *Buckley* majority having concluded that both contribution limits and spending limits impinge on the freedom of political speech or association, it would seem to follow that they should be subjected to strict scrutiny. But did the *Buckley* majority test all the limits against the strictest standard? As we will see, the Court has subjected contribution limits to a lower "exacting scrutiny," and the Supreme Court has sometimes highlighted and sometimes downplayed the differences between this standard and the strict scrutiny standard applied to spending limits.

Notes and Questions on the Court's Differing Treatment of Contribution Limits and Spending Limits

1. The *Buckley* majority distinguished sharply between contribution limits and expenditure limits, treating the latter as more offensive to the First Amendment than the former. Chief Justice Burger, in his separate opinion concurring in part and dissenting in part, criticized this distinction, asserting that "contributions and expenditures are two sides of the same First Amendment coin." He explained:

> The Court's attempt to distinguish the communication inherent in political *contributions* from the speech aspects of political *expenditures* simply "will not wash." We do little but engage in word games unless we recognize that people — candidates and contributors — spend money on political activity because they wish to communicate ideas, and their constitutional interest in doing so is precisely the same whether they or someone else utters the words.
>
> The Court attempts to make the Act seem less restrictive by casting the problem as one that goes to freedom of association rather than freedom of speech. I have long thought freedom of association and freedom of expression were two peas from the same pod. The contribution limitations of the

> Act impose a restriction on certain forms of associational activity that are for the most part, as the Court recognizes, harmless in fact. And the restrictions are hardly incidental in their effect upon particular campaigns. Judges are ill-equipped to gauge the precise impact of legislation, but a law that impinges upon First Amendment rights requires us to make the attempt. It is not simply speculation to think that the limitations on contributions will foreclose some candidacies. The limitations will also alter the nature of some electoral contests drastically.

Justice Blackmun, concurring in part and dissenting in part, also said he was "not persuaded that the Court makes, or indeed is able to make, a principled constitutional distinction between the contribution limitations, on the one hand, and the expenditure limitations, on the other, that are involved here." In later cases, individual justices have occasionally rejected *Buckley*'s decisive distinction between contribution and expenditure limits, see *Federal Election Commission v. National Conservative Political Action Committee*, 470 U.S. 480, 518, 519 (1985) (Marshall, J., dissenting) ("Although I joined the portion of the *Buckley per curiam* that distinguished contributions from independent expenditures for First Amendment purposes, I now believe that the distinction has no constitutional significance."), or sought to limit the scope of the distinction. See *Austin v. Michigan Chamber of Commerce*, 494 U.S. 652, 678 (1990) (Stevens, J., concurring) ("In my opinion the distinction between individual expenditures and individual contributions that the Court identified in *Buckley* should have little, if any, weight in reviewing corporate participation in candidate elections."). Most recently, Justice Thomas has rejected the distinction between contributions and expenditures in *Shrink Missouri.*

The distinction has also come in for heavy criticism from commentators outside the Supreme Court. The viability of the distinction has been doubted both by those who favor more stringent review of campaign finance regulations, *e.g.*, BeVier, *supra*, 73 California Law Review at 1063; Clagett & Bolton, *supra*, 29 Vanderbilt Law Review at 1332, and by those who favor greater constitutional tolerance for such regulations. For example, Judge Leventhal, *supra*, 77 Columbia Law Review at 358–59, wrote:

> With a limitation of contributions, political freedom is rendered less than absolute. The conclusion that the limitations on these freedoms were supported by an overriding public interest was sound, in my view, but certainly debatable. What strikes a careful reader of the opinion, however, is the Court's acceptance for the present of the legislative judgment that the public interest in reform is overriding, while reserving for the future the possibility of reconsidering whether the provision operates in the real world not merely as a limitation but as an effective exclusion from the political process.
>
> Strikingly different from the pragmatic tone, experimental outlook, and fact-and-record oriented discussion of the passages upholding the foregoing provisions, are the virtually adjoining passages that invalidate ceilings

> on overall campaign expenditures in a campaign for federal office, on a candidate's expenditures from his own funds, and on amounts that can be expended by a supporter directly on behalf of a candidate rather than by contribution.
>
> A close look at these passages discloses that the Court rested its conclusions on undemonstrated, and possibly undemonstrable, assertions about the way the statute would affect political life.

The Court has continued to treat the distinction between contributions and expenditures as the cornerstone of First Amendment doctrine affecting campaign finance regulation of candidates. (As we will see, the Court reached a different conclusion in the context of ballot measures.) Attempting to benefit from hindsight, Daniel Lowenstein reviewed experience since 1976 and concluded:

> [T]here is *some* basis for the Court's preference of contribution limits over expenditure limits. Contribution limits address the conflict of interest problem more directly, though not necessarily more effectively, than campaign spending limits, whereas spending limits restrict speech more directly than contribution limits. Indirect effects can be equally or more serious than direct effects, but in a world of great empirical uncertainty, one may have a higher degree of confidence in judgments of causation when the causal chain is direct.... Although the jury of social scientists is still out, there is reason to believe that to the extent spending limits reduce spending more than contribution limits, this will tend to make spending limits more detrimental to electoral competition....
>
> These advantages of contribution limits over spending limits are modest, at best, and very much subject to changing circumstances. They do not support a general principle that expenditure limits are nearly always unconstitutional while contribution limits are nearly always valid.

Daniel Hays Lowenstein, *A Patternless Mosaic: Campaign Finance and the First Amendment After* Austin, 21 Capital University Law Review 381, 401–02 (1992). For a stronger defense of *Buckley*'s distinction between contributions and expenditures, see Volokh, *supra*, 24 Harvard Journal of Law & Public Policy at 65 ("Especially given the ability of many people to pool their independent expenditures—the expenditures would only have to be independent of the candidate, not of each other—a regime that allowed unlimited expenditures but only modest contributions would still leave people with considerable opportunities to speak.").

2. *The Validity of Contribution Limits.* The Court upheld the FECA contribution limits as an effort "to limit the actuality and appearance of corruption resulting from large individual financial contributions." Although the Court was willing to assume "that most large contributors do not seek improper influence over a candidate's position or an officeholder's action," the Court quoted approvingly the Court of Appeals' statement that "a court has no scalpel to probe, whether, say, a $2,000 ceiling might not serve as well as $1,000." Does this approach provide adequate

protection to First Amendment rights? BeVier, *supra*, 73 California Law Review at 1086–88, believes it does not:

> Campaign contributions are valuable first amendment activities which, in *most* instances, involve little genuine risk of corrupting public decision-making. Contribution limitations thus systematically restrict protected, *non*dangerous activities. . . .
>
> In contrast to its customary strategy of overprotecting speech in order to protect speech that matters, the Court's willingness to defer to corruption-prevention measures represents an apparent strategy of underprotecting speech in order to protect a governmental interest that matters. The Court, in effect, has permitted Congress to outlaw entirely political activity that presents no genuine danger of corruption — the substantive evil that Congress has the right to prevent. . . .
>
> The question that must be faced, then, is whether "where corruption is the evil feared," the Court should underprotect speech. Genuine corruption, of course, undermines the integrity of any government. Moreover, it is difficult to detect and difficult to define precisely in a statute. Therefore it arguably is impossible to prevent with narrowly drawn prohibitions. Thus, the argument would go, the Court can reasonably permit the legislature to treat the problem with broad prophylactic rules and need not impose any requirement that the government demonstrate either the rules' necessity or their efficacy.
>
> This argument is troublesome because it treats the nature of the government interest as the only variable that determines how the Court should deal with plainly overbroad legislative rules. There is, of course, another variable to be considered, namely the fact that rules deter and punish legitimate political behavior. Strict scrutiny of legislative means is the first amendment norm, and overprotection of speech rights is a substantively and procedurally defensible judicial practice. The fact that corruption is the evil to be feared does not render political activity itself intrinsically less valuable. Moreover, no one has ever tried to explain why legislatures should in principle have more leeway to infringe upon first amendment rights to prevent corruption than they have, for example, to prevent subversion.

3. *The Invalidity of Expenditure Limits.* If the purpose of preventing contributors from gaining improper influence over elected officials justifies contribution limits, why is the same purpose not also a justification of overall limits on how much a candidate's campaign may spend? One reason in *Buckley* was that spending limits are subject to more stringent review under the First Amendment. In addition, the *Buckley* majority regarded contribution limits as the primary weapon against undue influence, and spending limits as a redundancy. "The interest in alleviating the corrupting influence of large contributions is served by the Act's contribution limitations and disclosure provisions rather than by . . . campaign expenditure restrictions."

This conclusion, like so many others in *Buckley*, has come in for criticism:

> Sixteen years after *Buckley*, few would argue that the FECA contribution limits have prevented conflicts of interest arising from campaign contributions. The Court seems to have assumed that the contribution limits set by Congress were fixed solely for the purpose of preventing contributions that could exert improper pressure. If so, the Court's assumption was erroneous. Although limits could prevent the most flagrant and dangerous contributions, to set the limits low enough to remove the likelihood of pressure would have been to preclude the possibility of raising funds for an adequate campaign. Congress recognized that in the absence of public financing, realistic contribution limits without expenditure limits could not effectively prevent the campaign finance system from being a system of institutionalized conflict of interest.

Lowenstein, *supra*, 21 Capital University Law Review at 398–99. Even if this argument that campaign spending limits are not redundant as an anti-corruption device is accepted, a spending limit itself would not prevent receipt of a contribution large enough for potential improper influence to exist. On what theory could a campaign spending limit prevent "a system of institutionalized conflict of interest"?

The other major argument in favor of expenditure limits that was rejected by the *Buckley* majority is that such limits would equalize the opportunity to participate in electoral politics and to influence outcomes. Was this equalization rationale rejected in *Buckley* because it was insufficient or because it was not even a permissible objective under the Constitution? Probably the most frequently quoted statement in *Buckley* is that "the concept that government may restrict the speech of some elements of our society in order to enhance the relative voice of others is wholly foreign to the First Amendment." We will return to this question later in this Chapter and in the next.

4. *Footnote 65*. Footnote 65 of the *Buckley* majority opinion stated that "Congress may engage in public financing of election campaigns and may condition acceptance of public funds on an agreement by the candidate to abide by specified expenditure limitations." Footnote 65 is an important and controversial qualification of the otherwise comprehensive condemnation of spending limits. Critics of public financing conditioned on the acceptance of spending limits point out that the simultaneous enactment of contribution limits may put considerable pressure on candidates to accept the public financing/spending limits package. We return to this issue of voluntariness versus coercion in Chapter 15.

5. The Court's treatment of contribution and expenditure limits has become more complex since *Buckley*. Chapter 13 looks at post-*Buckley* developments on spending limits. Chapter 14 considers post-*Buckley* developments on contribution limits. The remainder of this chapter considers in greater depth both political science questions related to campaign financing and the corruption and equality rationales for campaign finance regulation.

III. Empirical Observations about, and Theoretical Justifications for, Campaign Finance Regulation

A. Empirical Observations

The Court in *Buckley* permitted Congress to impose individual contribution limits on the grounds that such limits can prevent corruption or the appearance of corruption. As we shall see, many opponents of campaign finance regulation believe that legislative bodies often pass campaign finance regulations not to prevent corruption, but to protect their members from political competition.

These kinds of arguments raise empirical questions. Do large campaign contributions buy votes or otherwise "corrupt" legislators? Do campaign finance regulations promote public confidence in the electoral process by diminishing the "appearance of corruption"? Do such regulations harm political competition? Political scientists have been examining these questions for many years, and here we briefly summarize some of their findings.

What Do Campaign Contributions and Expenditures Buy? One of the enduring questions considered by political scientists and others is the extent to which campaign contributions and spending affect the decisions made by lawmakers. Although popular sentiment leans toward viewing contributions as "buying votes," finding empirical support for this claim is more difficult than one might think. As Frank Sorauf summarizes the literature:

> First, and most important, there simply are no data in the systematic studies that would support the popular assertions about the "buying" of the Congress or about any other massive influence of money on the legislative process. Second, even taking the evidence selectively, there is at best a case for a modest influence of money, a degree of influence that puts it well behind the other major influences on congressional behavior. Third, in some of the studies with a time dimension, there is evidence that vote support for the PAC's legislative position leads to greater campaign contributions. They do not, however, answer the question whether the legislative votes changed in order to "earn" the reward of increased contributions.

Frank J. Sorauf, Money in American Elections (1988). Sorauf acknowledges that large campaign contributions might buy access to elected officials but he found "no systematic evidence" supporting even the access hypothesis.

Most of the studies Sorauf relied on attempt to find systematic causal relationships between campaign contributions and congressional *floor votes*. As Sorauf reports, the results are mixed. Some commentators have suggested that influence derived from campaign contributions, to the extent that it exists, would be more likely to manifest itself in committees and in other legislative activities with less visibility than floor votes. Unfortunately, most other activities are much more difficult to measure than floor votes. One study, published after Sorauf's book, found some evidence of influence from contributions over committee activity. See Richard L. Hall & Frank W. Wayman, *Buying Time: Moneyed Interests and the Mobilization of Bias in Congressional Committees*, 84 American Political Science Review 797 (1990). Following Hall and Wayman, another study found that the American Medical Association's PAC gives contributions to congressional candidates in a manner consistent with the PAC's presumed desire to secure access to Members of Congress. See John D. Wilkerson & David Carrell, *Money, Politics, and Medicine: The American Medical PAC's Strategy of Giving in U.S. House Races*, 24 Journal of Health Politics, Policy and Law 335 (1999).

For a more skeptical view of the idea the contributors give to influence legislation or secure access, see Stephen Ansolabehere, John M. de Figueiredo, and James M. Snyder, Jr., *Why Is There So Little Money in U.S. Politics?*, 17 Journal of Economic Perspectives 105 (2003):

> Much of the academic research and public discussion of campaign contributions appears to be starting from some misguided assumptions. Campaign spending, measured as a share of GDP, does not appear to be increasing. Most of the campaign money does not come from interest group PACs, but rather from individual donors. Most donors give substantially less than the current hard money limits. It doesn't seem accurate to view campaign contributions as a way of investing in political outcomes. Instead, aggregate campaign spending in the United States, we conjecture, mainly reflects the consumption value that individuals receive from giving to campaigns. In addition, individual contributors provide the average and marginal dollar to political campaigns. Because politicians can readily raise campaign funds from individuals, rent-seeking donors lack the leverage to extract large private benefits from legislation.

For a further exploration, see Stephen Ansolabehere, James M. Snyder, Jr., and Michiko Ueda, *Did Firms Profit From Soft Money?*, 3 Election Law Journal 193 (2004).

Other recent empirical work, summarized in Nicholas O. Stephanopoulos, *Aligning Campaign Finance Law*, 101 Virginia Law Review 1425 (2015), presents a more nuanced picture of the connection between donors' preferences and officeholders' policies, showing that while it is hard to connect individual votes to donations, it is easier to connect overall voting records to donors ideological preferences:

> At the federal level, campaign spending totaled $7.3 billion in 2012. Almost all of this funding came from individual donors, not corporations or unions. Individuals gave about half of their contributions to specific candidates, a quarter to political parties, and a quarter to Political Action Committees ("PACs") and Super PACs. These donors were in no way representative of the country as a whole. They were heavily old, white, male, and, of course, wealthy. They also were far more polarized in their political views than

> the general population. Most Americans were moderates in 2012, but most donors were staunch liberals or conservatives.
>
> However, there is no evidence that much of this money is traded explicitly for political favors. Proof of quid pro quo transactions is vanishingly rare, and studies that try to document a link between PACs' contributions and politicians' votes typically come up empty. But there *is* evidence that politicians' positions reflect the preferences of their donors to an uncanny extent. The ideal points of members of Congress—that is, the "unique set[s] of policies that they 'prefer' to all others"—have almost exactly the same bimodal distribution as the ideal points of individual contributors. They look nothing like the far more centrist distribution of the public at large.

For explorations of the alignment between donor and legislator preferences, see Michael J. Barber, *Representing the Preferences of Donors, Partisans, and Voters in the U.S. Senate*, 80 Public Opinion Quarterly 225 (2016); Martin Gilens & Benjamin I. Page, *Testing Theories of American Politics: Elites, Interest Groups, and Average Citizens*, 12 Perspectives on Politics 564 (2014); Adam Bonica et al., *Why Hasn't Democracy Slowed Rising Inequality?*, 27 Journal of Economic Perspectives 103 (2013); Martin Gilens, Affluence and Influence: Economic Inequality and Political Power in America (2012); Larry M. Bartels, Unequal Democracy: The Political Economy of the New Gilded Age (2008); Peter L. Francia et al., The Financiers of Congressional Elections: Investors, Ideologues, and Intimates 16 (2003); Joseph Bafumi & Michael C. Herron, *Leapfrog Representation and Extremism: A Study of American Voters and Their Members in Congress*, 104 American Political Science Review 519 (2010).

In a neat experiment, Joshua L. Kalla & David E. Broockman, *Campaign Contributions Facilitate Access to Congressional Officials: A Randomized Field Experiment*, 60 American Journal of Political Science 545 (2015), contacted congressional offices to arrange a meeting to discuss a policy issue. Senior policy makers were three to four times more likely to make themselves available for a meeting when the person requesting the meeting identified explicitly as a campaign donor.

A recent study by Gilens, Patterson, and Haines used changes in state laws following *Citizens United* and related cases to see if states adopted more pro-corporate strategies as money flowed more freely. "We estimate that the change in campaign finance regulations after *Citizens United* resulted in about a 4% reduction in treated states' top corporate income tax rate and about an 8% reduction in those states that had previously banned only corporate independent expenditures. We also find significant reductions in plaintiff-friendly civil litigation standards—a change consistent with corporate interests. We find no effects for policies without clear corporate interests at stake, namely abortion, gun control, and eminent domain laws." Martin Gilens, Shawn Patterson Jr. & Pavielle Haines, *Letter: Campaign Finance Regulations and Public Policy*, 115 American Political Science Review 1074, 1075 (2021), https://doi.org/10.1017/S0003055421000149.

As the foregoing analyses suggest, the goals of different contributors may vary. Contributors who seek to attain their goals by helping candidates who support the same goals are sometimes said to follow an "electoral strategy." Those who contribute to candidates they believe are likely to win anyway in an attempt to influence their policies follow a "legislative strategy." See generally Kay Lehman Schlozman & John T. Tierney, Organized Interests and American Democracy 206–08 (1986). Of course, a single contribution could be intended to serve both purposes. But a contributor following a predominantly electoral strategy would be likely to contribute primarily to candidates in competitive races, while a legislative strategy would point toward contributions to secure incumbents, particularly those in leadership positions or serving on committees of importance to the contributor.

That many interest group contributions are made in pursuit of a legislative strategy seems beyond doubt. Nevertheless, there are many contributions, including many interest group contributions, that are made in pursuit of an electoral strategy. Even when contributors follow a legislative strategy, they don't always succeed. Richard L. Hasen, writing in Plutocrats United: Campaign Money, the Supreme Court, and the Distortion of American Elections (2016), argues that the best analogy of the role of money in politics is to a lottery to choose representatives and determine public policy, in which those with the greatest wealth get to buy more lottery tickets. In other words, spending money on campaigns increases, but does not guarantee, getting one's preferences enacted into policy. Influence is probabilistic, with probabilities increasing with investments.

To what extent does and should one's views on the proper campaign finance policy turn upon empirical beliefs about the relationship of money to electoral and political outcomes?

For those donors who wish to pursue a legislative strategy, campaign contributions often work hand in hand with lobbying activities. Indeed businesses spend much more on lobbying than in making campaign donations. Lobbyists are hired to influence what legislators and those in the executive branch do (or refuse to do). Campaign contributions are one significant tool for lobbyists to secure access to make a policy pitch to an official. But lobbyists often rely on personal connections as well. Richard L. Hasen, *Lobbying, Rent-Seeking and the Constitution*, 64 Stanford Law Review 191, 221-23 (2012) describes the relevant literature on how lobbying helps secure access:

> Lobbyists gain access through the cultivation of relationships with legislators and staffers using a variety of tools permissible under the law, especially the raising of campaign contributions for legislators. Campaign contributions are a key part of a culture of reciprocity. Feelings of reciprocity are formed easily and without the outlay of considerable resources, but those who help out the most are likely to get the greatest access. It is a natural instinct to help someone who has helped you. In this context, why shouldn't a legislator help a lobbyist supporter by favoring her client's interests on an issue about which the legislator has no personal preference?

> Lobbyists typically do not raise campaign contributions for any and all legislators. Republican lobbyists raise funds for Republicans and Democratic lobbyists raise funds for Democrats—though often such lobbyists are in the same firm as a means of hedging against future political change and having the ability to work both sides of the aisle in Congress Lobbying and fundraising patterns follow the fortunes of the parties in Congress. Following the "K Street Project" period in which the House Republican leadership built close relationships with lobbyists who engaged in major fundraising for the party many Republican lobbyists lost their jobs in 2006 and 2008 as Democrats took control of the House, Senate, and executive branch and Democratic lobbyists had greater career opportunities. When it became clear in 2010 that Republicans were poised to retake control of the House, Republican lobbyists again grew in demand.
>
> Lobbyists often do much more than simply contribute money themselves to pivotal legislators; they have become prolific fundraisers and bundlers of campaign contributions for key legislators and party leaders. For example, during the 2010 period when Republicans appeared poised to retake control of the House, House Minority Leader Boehner provided special access to lobbyists who contributed the maximum $37,800 contribution to various committees supporting him or who raised at least $100,000 from other contributors.
>
> Another key means of securing legislative access is for clients to hire former legislators and staffers as lobbyists (through the so-called "revolving door"). Many prominent former senators and members of Congress have become lobbyists, and dozens of former staffers of sitting senators and members of Congress have done so as well. Indeed, half the senators who left office between 1998 and 2004 became lobbyists. These revolving-door lobbyists have preexisting reciprocal relationships with current legislators and staffers, which they can then use to gain access for their clients. Though it is no longer permissible for a former senator to use the Senate gym as a place for lobbying, and there is a waiting period for senators after leaving the Senate to engage in certain lobbying activities there is no question that a former senator or major House staffer who is lobbying for a client is likely to get a phone call returned and a chance to make the case for the lobbyist's clients. In fact, as evidence that who you know is more important than what you know, Bertrand et al. found that revolving-door lobbyists tend to follow their former legislative bosses from committee to committee, switching from lobbying on an issue such as health care to one such as defense. Expertise is secondary to personal contacts.

The Supreme Court has long upheld laws requiring the disclosure of lobbying activities, *United States v. Harriss*, 347 U.S. 612 (1954), but few contend that the government could limit funds spend on lobbying without violating the Constitution. *See* Hasen, *supra*. If lobbying activities cannot be limited, and lobbying has been shown to affect public policy, does it still make sense to limit campaign spending? Would it make sense, in an effort to level the playing field, for enactment of subsidies for public interest lobbying? Deniz Igan & Prachi Mishra, *Wall Street, Capitol Hill, and K Street: Political Influence and Financial Regulation*, 57 Journal of Law and Economics 1063 (2014), Heather K. Gerken & Alex Tausanovitch, *A Public Finance Model for Lobbying: Lobbying, Campaign Finance, and the Privatization of Democracy*, 13 Election Law Journal 75 (2014); Heather Gerken, *Keynote Address: Lobbying as the New Campaign Finance*, 27 Georgia State University Law Review 1155 (2011); Dorie Apollonio et al., *Access and Lobbying: Looking Beyond the Corruption Paradigm*, 36 Hastings Constitutional Law Quarterly 13, 46 (2008). Would legislatures enact such a provision?

The full range of lobbying laws and options for reform are beyond the scope of this course and often covered in a course on the legislative process. But one cannot fully think about the role of money in politics by considering only campaign finance rules and not lobbying rules.

Do Campaign Finance Laws Instill Public Confidence in the Democratic Process? In *Buckley*, the Court wrote that "Congress could legitimately conclude that the avoidance of the appearance of improper influence is also critical . . . if confidence in the system of representative Government is not to be eroded to a disastrous extent" (internal quotations omitted). The Court wrote those words in upholding FECA's contribution limits. But do campaign contribution limits instill public confidence in the democratic process?

Nathaniel Persily and Kelli Lammie, *Perceptions of Corruption and Campaign Finance: When Public Opinion Determines Constitutional Law*, 153 University of Pennsylvania Law Review 119, 121 (2004), argue that "the Court's invocation of this novel state interest has less to do with the importance of removing unsavory appearances and more to do with the difficulty of proving actual corruption. Reliance on combating the appearance or perception of impropriety serves as a fallback state interest in the likely event that one cannot make the difficult showing that campaign contributions have actually influenced a representative's vote or official conduct."

Looking empirically at public opinion polling on corruption over time, the authors conclude that "trends in general attitudes of corruption seem unrelated to anything happening in the campaign finance system (e.g., a rise in contributions or the introduction of a particular reform)." *Id.* at 122. Indeed, public perceptions of corruption *went up* after Congress passed the most important campaign finance law in decades, the Bipartisan Campaign Reform Act of 2002.

The authors conclude:

> While believing that campaign contributions corrupt parties and candidates and that campaign finance reform is desirable, a majority of Americans also agree that special interests will continue to have undue influence even once such reforms are passed. Moreover, available survey data suggest that Americans' perceptions of corruption are related to their views about

> their position in society, the incumbents in office, or their attitudes about how government ought to tax and spend.

Id. at 173.

In a more recent and exhaustive study looking at changes within states over 30 years, David Primo and Jeff Milyo find "no statistically or substantively significant positive effects of campaign finance reforms on trust in government." David M. Primo & Jeffrey D. Milyo, Campaign Finance & Democracy: What the Public Really Thinks and Why It Matters 137, 145 (2020). The authors also find that public opinion on the desirability of campaign spending and contribution limits is polarized, with Democrats more supportive of limits than Republicans. There was less polarization on disclosure, which was popular across the board, and public financing, which was not. *Id.* at 159.

Does evidence that there is no relationship between campaign finance laws and public trust in government mean that the Court should no longer rely on the "appearance of corruption" to justify campaign finance regulation?

Campaign Finance Regulation and Political Competition. Whether or not legislators pass campaign finance laws in order to stifle political competition, political scientists have considered whether limiting how much a candidate can spend to run for election (or limiting the contributions a candidate may raise, which in turn affects spending) can affect competition.

Gary Jacobson's influential work in this area, beginning with Gary C. Jacobson, *The Effects of Campaign Spending on Congressional Elections*, 72 American Political Science Review 469 (1978) has argued that, at least as to races for the U.S. House of Representatives, any campaign finance law restricting campaign spending will help incumbents and diminish electoral competition. See also Gary C. Jacobson, *Enough is Too Much: Money and Competition in House Elections*, in Elections in America 173 (Kay Lehman Schlozman, ed., 1987).

As Jacobson later explained it:

> Campaign spending is subject to diminishing returns; the more dollars spent, the less gained by each additional dollar. Congressional incumbents usually exploit their official resources reaching constituents so thoroughly that the additional increment of information about their virtues put forth during the campaign adds comparatively little to what is already known and felt about them. . . .
>
> In general, then, spending should matter more to nonincumbent candidates than to incumbents because they have yet to get their message out, and getting a message out costs money. Spending may also matter to incumbents if they have to get out a *new* message. That is, when an incumbent is in trouble for some reason. . . . Regardless of their potential, if challengers cannot raise lots of money, they can forget about winning. If incumbents are strongly challenged, raising and spending lots of money may not help them much, although there is no reason to think it hurts. . . .

> Plainly, though, spending huge sums of money does not ensure reelection.... This means that *the incumbent's most effective electoral strategy is to discourage serious opposition.*

Gary C. Jacobson, The Politics of Congressional Elections 46–47 (6th ed. 2004).

Some research has found that the benefits incumbents gain from increased spending are greater than Jacobson suggests. See, *e.g.*, Donald P. Green & Jonathan S. Krasno, *Salvation for the Spendthrift Incumbent: Reestimating the Effects of Campaign Spending in House Elections*, 32 American Journal of Political Science 884 (1988); Scott J. Thomas, *Do Incumbent Campaign Expenditures Matter?*, 51 Journal of Politics 965 (1989); Kevin B. Grier, *Campaign Spending and Senate Elections, 1974–84*, 63 Public Choice 201 (1989); Donald P. Green & Jonathan S. Krasno, *Rebuttal to Jacobson's "New Evidence for Old Arguments,"* 34 American Journal of Political Science 363 (1990). Jacobson and others continue to find that the effects of increased incumbent spending are slight (albeit potentially decisive in close elections). See, *e.g.*, Gary C. Jacobson, *The Effects of Campaign Spending in House Elections: New Evidence for Old Arguments*, 34 American Journal of Political Science 334 (1990); Alan I. Abramowitz, *Incumbency, Campaign Spending, and the Decline of Competition in U.S. House Elections*, 53 Journal of Politics 35 (1991).

Alan Gerber contests Jacobson's findings in *Estimating the Effect of Campaign Spending on Senate Election Outcomes Using Instrumental Variables*, 92 American Political Science Review 401 (1998). Gerber finds that in Senate elections, incumbent spending is as effective as challenger spending. One possible explanation for the discrepant findings is that Senate challengers tend to be better known than House challengers, so that the dynamics of the two types of races may be different. Gerber explains the significance of the empirical debate in terms that both sides would agree on:

> The finding that incumbent spending wins elections has important implications for recent American politics. Campaign finance, and specifically the level of incumbent spending, is a potentially critical factor in the competitiveness of congressional elections. The finding that incumbent spending effects are important also requires reconsideration of the consequences of campaign finance reform. The debate typically turns on what happens to challengers and neglects incumbents. Spending limits that apply to both are seen as severely biased in favor of incumbents. As Jacobson argues, "campaign spending does have an important effect on who wins [congressional elections] and it is the amount spent by challengers (and other disadvantaged candidates) that actually makes the difference. Spending limits, if they have any effect at all on competition, can only work to the detriment of the challenger." In a companion paper, I conduct simulations of policy alternatives and show that, when the new estimates of incumbent spending effects are used, the conclusions inspired by the traditional view of campaign spending need major revision.... For example, spending caps, even if set lower than some challengers'

campaign spending levels, can significantly increase the chances of challenger victory.

Id. at 410. For an argument that low contribution limits increase political competition, see Thomas Stratmann, *Do Low Contribution Limits Insulate Incumbents from Competition?* 9 Election Law Journal 125 (2010). For contrary evidence, and some evidence that full public financing and corporate spending limits help incumbents, see Jordan Butcher and Jeffrey Milyo, *Do Campaign Finance Reforms Insulate Incumbents from Competition? New Evidence from State Legislative Elections*, 53 PS: Political Science and Politics 460 (2020).

B. Preventing Corruption

Daniel Hays Lowenstein, *On Campaign Finance Reform: The Root of All Evil Is Deeply Rooted*

18 Hofstra Law Review 301, 322–29 (1989)

What Is Meant by Influence?

Ironically, the inability of the econometric studies to answer whether campaign contributions have measurable effects on legislators' actions may result, in part, from the single-mindedness with which they have asked the question. Apparently believing that the extent of such measurable effects is of overriding importance, econometric analysts have attempted to tease out answers from data and mathematical tools ill-suited for the task. These analysts might make greater progress if they conducted a more open-ended inquiry into the dynamics of how campaign contributions enter into the legislative process and how they interact with other influences, rules and institutional factors to guide the conduct of individual legislators and the legislature as a whole. They would be well-advised to do so, not only to produce better social science, but because the degree of measurable aggregate influence of campaign contributions over legislative activity does not have the crucial normative significance that they have assumed.

It is commonly observed that any influence over legislative behavior generated by campaign contributions is intertwined with other influences. Michael Malbin, for example, points out that it is "difficult to separate the importance of PAC contributions from the lobbying efforts they are supposedly meant to enhance."[97] Some

97. See Michael Malbin, *Looking Back at the Future of Campaign Finance Reform*, in Money and Politics in the United States 232, 249 (Malbin ed., 1984); see also Sorauf, *supra* (stating that "[i]t is . . . very hard to separate the effects of lobbying and of constituency pressures from the effects of a campaign contribution.").

John Kingdon quoted a House member who stated: "A close friend of mine, who's been associated with me for years and is an important campaign contributor, is in the oil business. I had no idea how this bill would affect the oil people until I heard from him." John Kingdon, Congressmen's Voting Decisions 34 (3d ed. 1989). Would the friendship have been sufficient to make this legislator pay such heed without the contributions? If so, why did the member mention the fact that the

writers conclude that because it is impossible to be confident that legislative actions favorable to contributors have been caused by contributions, concern over contributions may be minimized. Their premise of intertwining is correct and important, but the conclusion they draw from it is wrong by 180 degrees.

The conclusion is wrong because the question of campaign finance is a question of conflict of interest. [For present purposes, a] conflict of interest exists when the consequences of a decision made in the course of a relationship of trust are likely to have an effect, not implicit in the trust relationship, on . . . the decisionmaker's self-interest. . . .

Often, and in various contexts, we take institutional steps to minimize the occurrence of conflicts of interest, or we disqualify a person from acting when a conflict of interest arises. Why do we do so? Part of the reason, and not necessarily the most important part, is our concern that the individual may deliberately set aside his or her obligations of trust in favor of self-interest. Even if we were sure we could identify all such cases of overt dishonesty, we would continue to regulate conflicts of interest because of the probability that even an honest person's judgment will be impaired when in a position of conflict. Centuries before terms such as "selective perception" were current, it was understood that an individual whose own self-interest is at stake finds it difficult to view a situation dispassionately and objectively. That is why we refer to a person without conflict as "disinterested."

Some people in a conflict situation may be able to act in the position of trust without being the slightest bit moved by the potential effects on self-interest. Others may find that considerations of self-interest are present in their minds but may be able, nonetheless, to struggle through to a conclusion based only on proper considerations. Still other people may be biased in their judgments in situations not conventionally regarded as conflicts of interest. The reason these situations can, and commonly do exist, is that conflict of interest is a concept based on the average person. Sometimes individuals are unusually resistant to being moved by self-interest, sometimes they are unusually susceptible, and sometimes their goals and preferences are sufficiently idiosyncratic that what constitutes self-interest is unusual. Therefore, conflict of interest regulation sometimes disqualifies an individual who is *not* biased, while at other times it fails to disqualify an individual who *is* biased. This does not mean that the regulation is faulty. It happens because there is no alternative to regulating on the basis of what we believe are typical human reactions.

What is the significance of the fact that the campaign finance question is a question of conflict of interest? First consider this statement from one of the econometric studies: "It is useful to imagine that the exogenous variables [such as party, ideology and constituency] determine an 'initial position' on the issue for a candidate,

---

friend is a contributor? Would the friendship be as close without the contributions? Could the legislator answer these questions with certainty?

and that contributions cause shifts away from that position."[104] As a heuristic device, this is often a useful procedure. As a description of reality it is woefully inadequate because of the intertwining of campaign contributions with other influencing factors. From the beginning of an issue's life, legislators know of past contributions and the possibility of future ones from the interest groups that are affected, just as the legislators know of relevant constituency effects, party positions, various aspects of the merits of the issue and so on. All of these combine in a manner no one fully understands to form an initial predisposition in the legislator. Thereafter, the legislator may receive new information on any or all of these factors. The new information may modify the legislator's initial position, but the information that is received and the manner in which it is processed will themselves be influenced by the initial position.

In reality, then, the influence of campaign contributions is present from the start, and it interacts in the human mind with other influences in an unfathomable but complex dynamic. It affects the "chemistry" or the "mix" of the legislator's deliberations. It may or may not affect the legislator's ultimate actions, but setting aside the most flagrant cases, no one can be sure, perhaps not even the legislator in question. For this reason, to say that campaign contributions "taint" the legislative process is to use the language with precision. It is not that the entire legislative process or even a great deal of it is corrupt; rather, it is that the corrupt element is intermingled with the entire process, in a way that cannot be isolated.

The conflicts of interest caused by campaign contributions are illustrated routinely in nearly every daily newspaper. For instance, the following example appeared in the *Los Angeles Times* while these paragraphs were being written. It is from an article about six Democrats, mostly from the south, on the House Ways and Means Committee.[109] At the time of the article, it was believed that these six members of Congress might swing the committee to report out a reduction in the tax on capital gains, supported by President Bush and the Republicans but opposed by a majority of the Democrats:

> Whatever the outcome, Bush has laid bare a deep split between Democrats' traditional ideology of opposing special treatment for the wealthy and the party's growing dependence on contributions from a host of business special interest groups, particularly real estate developers, that would benefit from the tax cut.
>
> "We've got wealthy Democrats in this country too," said a longtime supporter of a capital gains cut, Beryl Anthony Jr. (D-Ark.), who is a key

104. Chappell, *Campaign Contributions and Congressional Voting: A Simultaneous Probit-Tobit Model*, 64 Review of Economics & Statistics 77, 78 (1982).

109. Redburn, "Six Democrats Backing Capital Gains Tax Cut," L.A. Times, July 25, 1989, pt. 1, at 1.

party fund-raiser as head of the Democratic Congressional Campaign Committee.

A common way of describing this type of situation is to say that there is an "appearance of impropriety." While not exactly wrong, discussion of the campaign finance question in terms of appearances is misleading. It suggests that there is an underlying reality that is either proper or not proper, and if we could only look behind the locked door or, perhaps, into the legislator's head, we would know. Used as a rationale for reform measures, the argument is that the appearance of impropriety is a sufficient justification for reform, because it undermines popular confidence in government. Depending on who is speaking and who is listening, there may be an implied wink to the effect that impropriety is really very unlikely but that some sop must be thrown to the ignorantly suspicious public. Alternatively, the implied wink may suggest that of course there is impropriety, but it would be impolitic to say so directly.

Rather than saying there is an *appearance of impropriety* in the Democrats' dependence on contributions from interests demanding a capital gains reduction or in similar situations, it is more precise to say that there is a *reality of conflict of interest*. There was no meeting, behind closed doors or otherwise, not even a moment in a single legislator's mind, in which a decision was made either to succumb to the contributors or not to succumb. The pressure from the contributors is simply part of the mix of considerations out of which a position evolves. At best, one can exercise a judgment as to whether the outcome would have been different if there had been no contributions and no possibility of contributions. Even if the hypothetical outcome would have been the same, however, it does not change the fact that the real outcome results from an actual, tainted process. That is why the question of how much contributions affect legislative outcomes, while surely important, is not normatively crucial.

It may be objected that the conflict of interest argument applies equally to many of the major influences on the legislative process other than campaign contributions. Legislators who are highly responsive to their constituents, for example, most likely act in that manner because they believe it will help them get reelected — a self-interested reason. Legislators who adhere to the party position or the wishes of influential colleagues may do so because they hope for reciprocity in the future, or for advancement within the legislative chamber. They also act out of self-interest.

The fallacy in this objection is its assumption that all considerations of self-interest are equal. No one ever claimed that systems are corrupt simply because they contain incentives. If this were the case, there would be a conflict of interest any time an employer paid an employee a salary, since the employee who did a good job in hopes of keeping the job or being promoted would be acting corruptly. Such incentives are not conflicts of interest because they are implicit in the relationship of trust, in this case between the employer and employee.

A variety of pressures characterize political life in America. Sorting out which pressures are proper and which are not is difficult. There are, however, some easy cases. Constituency influence is an example. One side of the Burkean debate maintains that while legislators should regard constituent opinions as relevant data for public policy, they should be guided only by their own best judgments. There is no consensus in favor of that position. Accordingly, some degree of responsiveness to constituents' views is at least permissible in legislative positions of trust in this country.

The paradigm case of improper influence is the payment of money to the official for the official's benefit. That is what a campaign contribution is. Indeed, the distinction between a campaign contribution and a payment for the recipient's personal use can be blurred or nonexistent. Nevertheless, there are some differences. Campaign contributions, under current conditions, are more likely to be indispensable to an elected official than personal payments. This makes campaign contributions the more dangerous, though not the more unethical practice. A second difference is that the contributor may be motivated not to influence the recipient but to promote a cause that the recipient represents. In other words, contributors may follow an electoral rather than a legislative strategy.... [T]he fact that many contributions are ideological may affect the way people think about all contributions.

Despite differences, it is clear that our culture regards it as inappropriate for public officials to be influenced by campaign contributions. We need not look to Common Cause, Elizabeth Drew, and Brooks Jackson to establish this point. Stronger evidence comes from the scholars with whom I have joined issue in this part. Frank Sorauf, Michael Malbin, and others with similar views would not be at such great pains to characterize the influence of campaign contributions as minimal if they did not believe that it would be wrong if the contributions were influential, or at least that the overwhelming majority of their fellow citizens believe that it would be wrong.

Further confirmation can be found in the fact that a campaign contribution made with the intent to influence official conduct constitutes bribery, as that crime is defined in most American jurisdictions. It is true that the typical special interest bribe in the form of a campaign contribution is very rarely prosecuted. I doubt that this reflects approval of the practice as much as recognition of its pervasiveness, which in turn results from the fact that the receipt of special interest contributions is more or less a practical necessity for most legislators. This necessity may constitute an excellent reason for not prosecuting such routine transactions as bribes, but it does not justify preservation of the system that creates the necessity.

It is a fact of our political culture that although a great variety of the pressures brought to bear on politicians embody forces that are regarded as more or less democratic and therefore legitimate, this is not true of pressure imposed by payments of money to politicians, either for their personal benefit or for campaign use. At best, the existence of such pressures is tolerated as a necessary evil. The evil is necessary within the existing campaign finance system, but the existence of the evil provides a compelling reason for reforming that system.

Notes and Questions

1. The symposium in which this article appeared included several commentaries, pertinent excerpts of which will be set forth in these notes. First, Gary C. Jacobson, *Campaign Finance and Democratic Control: Comments on Gottlieb and Lowenstein's Papers*, 18 Hofstra Law Review 369, 377–78 (1989):

> Reelection depends on many other things besides money, and actions that promote reelection do not always serve constituents or conscience. Elected officials routinely confront choices between doing what helps them stay in office and doing what they think is best for their constituents, their party or their country. To give some familiar examples, the prevalence in Congress [of] wasteful pork barrel politics, of vacuous position taking, and of endless self-promotion, suggests that money is by no means the only electoral necessity that promotes shirking. Lowenstein falls short of demonstrating that the current campaign finance system, which, after all, limits the amount of money supplied by any particular individual or political action committee (PAC), is an especially egregious source of shirking and, therefore, requires the sweeping reforms he proposes.

2. Martin Shapiro, *Corruption, Freedom and Equality in Campaign Financing*, 18 Hofstra Law Review 385, 387 (1989):

> Lowenstein ... operates as a cultural anthropologist and discovers that there is an anti-corruption norm in American society and that campaign financing legislation is an expression of that norm. The norm is legitimated by its existence and the statutes are legitimated by the norm. This approach is not entirely satisfactory from the standpoint of constitutional law. There is a cultural norm of racism in our society. Does the existence of such a norm give constitutional legitimacy to racist statutes? Such an argument would not appear terribly attractive or constitutional. Moreover, there is that old bromide of cultural anthropology. Is the best evidence of a norm profession or behavior? If there is an anti-corruption norm in American society, surely there is also a pro-corruption norm in the widespread proclivity of Americans to seek to influence the behavior of legislators by any means short of assassination.

3. Sanford Levinson, *Electoral Regulation: Some Comments*, 18 Hofstra Law Review 411, 412–13 (1989):

> I remain unpersuaded by any analysis that expresses justified worry about the impact of money on the behavior of public officials and, at the same time, wholly ignores the power of the media to influence these same public officials in part through the media's ability to structure public consciousness.

> Almost a decade ago my colleague, L.A. Powe, queried why Congress should be able to limit the ability to influence the outcomes of elections of everyone, except those fortunate enough to be owners of mass media. . . . The potential for conflicts of interests at the heart of Lowenstein's analysis is also present when a candidate confronts the owners and editors of major newspapers on issues and when such a candidate beseeches the same owners and editors to support . . . his or her campaign.

4. Does it help to reconsider the corruption problem using the metaphor of pollution? See John Copeland Nagle, *Corruption, Pollution, and Politics*, 110 Yale Law Journal 293, 322 (2000):

> To say that the political system is polluted avoids the implication that particular representatives are polluted. It also avoids the connotation of corruption that suggests that no corruption can be tolerated. By contrast, the law tolerates some environmental pollution. The law intervenes to regulate or prohibit pollution only when the amount of a particular type of pollutant has harmful effects. Under this view, campaign contributions and spending would be permissible up to the point where they begin to produce harmful effects, including but not limited to corruption.

5. Some scholars have argued that Lowenstein is concerned less with corruption than with equality. See Bruce E. Cain, *Moralism and Realism in Campaign Finance Reform*, 1995 University of Chicago Legal Forum 111, and David A. Strauss, *What is the Goal of Campaign Finance Reform?*, 1995 University of Chicago Legal Forum 141. Consider the following argument from Strauss:

> One way to set aside any concern with inequality is to assume, as a thought experiment, that everyone has an equal opportunity to "bribe" the official or candidate of his or her choice by making campaign contributions. This will isolate the problem of corruption. For example, one might assume that the law requires campaign contributions to be made in vouchers that are distributed according to some conception of equality. Or one might assume a scheme that equalizes people's ability to make contributions by multiplying contributions by a factor inversely related to the contributor's income.
>
> One could argue that even in such an "equal" world, the corrupting effects of campaign contributions will be a problem because officials will be unduly responsive to contributors. But the question, once inequality is removed from the picture, is why this is troubling. Elected officials also respond to the wishes of past and potential future voters. While that may sometimes be a problem, no one thinks it is the same kind of problem as bribery. If everyone had the same capacity to contribute to campaigns—that is, if equality were somehow secured (or if we decided it was not an issue)—the difference between contributions and votes would diminish sharply.

Id. at 143–44; see also Kathleen M. Sullivan, *Political Money and Freedom of Speech*, 30 U.C. Davis Law Review 663, 680 (1997). Is Strauss right that at bottom Lowenstein is concerned not with corruption, but inequality?

In response to Cain's and Strauss's criticism, Lowenstein offered a hypothetical of his own in which four legislators agree to vote for a bill for different reasons. The first legislator made her decision along Burkean lines. The second followed the public opinion in his district. The third followed the wishes of her party leadership. The fourth, however, gave the following answer to why he voted for the bill:

> It's true that my judgment of good public policy, the views of most of my constituents, and the demands of party loyalty all pointed toward voting against the bill. But these considerations, even in combination, were outweighed by my desire to raise funds to help me get reelected. Therefore, I agreed to vote for this bill in exchange for a large contribution from Barbara Bigbucks.

Daniel Hays Lowenstein, *Campaign Contributions and Corruption: Comments on Strauss and Cain*, 1995 University of Chicago Legal Forum 163, 171–72. Why, if at all, should we be concerned with this answer? Lowenstein remarks that "the unequivocal disapproval of this transaction in the American political culture cannot be explained by concerns about equality or structural problems of collective action. Americans disapprove of this transaction because they recognize it as corrupt." *Id.* at 172. If Barbara Bigbucks could give no more than anyone else to Demetrios, would Demetrios's answer still be a problem? Is the answer that under those conditions Bigbucks could no longer give a (relatively) "large" contribution?

C. Promoting Equality

As noted above, Lowenstein vigorously contends that corruption and equality concerns in campaign finance are analytically distinct. We turn now to consider equality on its own merits. Does a concern for political equality justify campaign finance regulation? If so, what kinds of regulation?

Edward B. Foley, *Equal-Dollars-Per-Voter: A Constitutional Principle of Campaign Finance*

94 Columbia Law Review 1204 (1994)

The Constitution of the United States should contain a principle, which I shall call "equal-dollars-per-voter," that would guarantee to each eligible voter equal financial resources for purposes of supporting or opposing any candidate or initiative on the ballot in any election held within the United States. The argument for adopting this principle is that wealthy citizens should not be permitted to have a greater ability to participate in the electoral process simply on account of their greater wealth. This argument, in turn, depends upon a belief that the electoral process must be wealth-neutral in order to be fair to rich and poor alike.

An important function of electoral politics is to determine how wealth should be distributed among society's members. The existing distribution of wealth at the time of any particular election should not affect the electorate's determination of what the distribution should be henceforth. Money, however, is an indispensable element of any electoral campaign because money pays for the publicity and advertising that attempt to convince the undecided voters to support the campaign on election day. Consequently, if rich citizens are free to spend their own money to support or oppose candidates or ballot initiatives, they will have a greater opportunity than poor citizens to attempt to persuade undecided voters to agree with their positions. In this way, then, permitting wealthy citizens to use their wealth in electoral politics biases the electoral process in favor of their political objectives and against the political objectives of the poor. This bias contradicts the premise, stated above, that the electoral process should not be affected by whatever distribution of wealth exists in society at election time. In order to eliminate this bias, the Constitution should guarantee that all voters receive equal financial resources for the purpose of participating in electoral politics....

I. An Explanation of Equal-Dollars-Per-Voter

A. What Equal-Dollars-Per-Voter Requires

The principle of equal-dollars-per-voter means that each eligible voter should receive the same amount of financial resources for the purpose of participating in electoral politics. In other words, pursuant to this principle, the government would provide all eligible voters with the same sum of money—the principle does not specify any particular amount—and the voters could then donate this money to the electoral organizations of their choice. Electoral organizations consist of three types: (1) a candidate's campaign organization; (2) a broad-based interest group, otherwise known as a political party; or (3) a more narrowly-focused "special interest" group.

The only money that voters would be permitted to donate to an electoral organization would be the money they receive from the government pursuant to the equal-dollars-per-voter principle. Voters would not be permitted to supplement the electoral funds they receive from the government with their own personal funds, no matter how extensive their wealth and no matter how strong their desire. In this way, the principle of equal-dollars-per-voter would prohibit affluent citizens from spending any more on electoral politics than impoverished citizens.

The same principle applies to candidates as well as voters. Candidates would be permitted to spend only the money they had received either directly from voters or indirectly through an interest group (either broad-based or narrowly-focused). The only money candidates would be permitted to contribute to their own campaigns would be the money they had received from the government pursuant to the equal-dollars-per-voter principle. Thus, the principle would prohibit affluent candidates from using their personal wealth to advance their own candidacies.

Likewise, the only money that interest groups (either broad-based or narrowly-focused) would be permitted to spend to support or oppose a candidate would be the money they had received from voters pursuant to the equal-dollars-per-voter principle. Interest groups could spend this money in either of two ways. First, as already indicated, they could hand it over to a candidate's campaign, thus acting as a conduit between voters and candidates. Voters might prefer to donate their electoral funds to an interest group, rather than to a candidate directly, because they trust the interest group's judgment about which candidate most deserves their support. Alternatively, the interest group might decide to keep some or all of the money it had received from voters to spend on its own independent activities in support of or opposition to a candidate (e.g., newspaper advertisements endorsing a candidate).

Either way, interest groups would spend only the money they receive from voters. They would not be permitted to receive electoral funds from any other source—neither from a corporation, nor from a labor union, nor from any other club or voluntary association that engages in nonelectoral activities. If individuals associated with corporations, labor unions, or other nonelectoral organizations wished to spend money in connection with a campaign, they would be required to set up separate electoral organizations with separate accounts. The only money that these individuals could give to these electoral organizations would be the money they had received as voters pursuant to the equal-dollars-per-voter principle.

Individual voters would also be free to make their own independent expenditures to support or oppose a candidate or ballot initiative. For example, a voter might photocopy several hundred leaflets to distribute among her neighbors, urging them to vote for or against a particular candidate. Or, if sufficient funds were available, a voter might purchase advertising space in a local newspaper to endorse a candidate. But the principle of equal-dollars-per-voter would still apply to these independent expenditures. The principle requires all voters to receive the same amount of funds for all their expenditures in support of, or in opposition to, an electoral campaign. For this reason, voters would not be permitted to use their own personal funds to make independent expenditures.

In sum, the principle of equal-dollars-per-voter calls for a closed system of electoral funds. Within the system, the money may flow freely—from voter to interest group to candidate or from voter to candidate directly. The money could even pass from one interest group to another, and to yet another, before it is given to a candidate's campaign or spent independently to support or oppose a candidate—just so long as all the money originates with the individual voters pursuant to the basic principle. The principle requires simply that all individuals start with the same amount and that no outside funds be introduced into the system....

II. Distributive Justice and the Anti-Plutocracy Principle

The argument for equal-dollars-per-voter consists of two parts. First, I shall argue that a citizen's wealth should have no bearing upon her opportunity to participate in the electoral process. This proposition I call the "anti-plutocracy principle," as a plutocracy is a system of government in which a citizen's ability to participate as an elector depends upon the amount of wealth belonging to the citizen. Second, I shall argue that this anti-plutocracy principle encompasses the more specific principle that a citizen's wealth should have no bearing on her opportunity to attempt to persuade fellow citizens of the merits of her views. This more specific principle, which I call "equal-opportunity-for-persuasion," necessarily entails equal-dollars-per-voter.[33]

My argument for the anti-plutocracy principle is based upon the premise that political philosophy cannot yield a definitive answer to the question of distributive justice (i.e., how should society's wealth be distributed among its various members?). Because philosophy cannot answer this question, the members of society must adopt a decision-making process in which they collectively choose whatever principles of distributive justice they wish to govern their society. No particular pattern of distribution carries a presumption of validity from the perspective of political philosophy — not even the pattern that happens to exist at the time the members of society gather together to choose the principles of distributive justice. Accordingly, the decision-making process should be structured in such a way that it is not affected by the existing distribution of wealth in society.

In section B of this Part, I shall elaborate upon this argument. But first, in section A, I shall explain the premise that the question of distributive justice has no philosophically definitive answer.

A. The Indeterminacy of Distributive Justice

The problem of distributive justice, simply put, is the problem of who should get what — which members of society should obtain property rights to which of society's resources. The problem of distributive justice is by no means the only problem that confronts the polity. On the contrary, the state must address many other sorts of problems, including those caused by the failure of a market economy to allocate goods and services efficiently. In this Article, however, I focus solely on the problem of distributive justice. Even if the other problems confronting the polity miraculously disappeared, there would still be the fundamental problem of who is entitled to what. Moreover, the conclusions that I reach about distributive justice have profound implications for the specific issue of campaign finance.

In thinking about distributive justice, I start with the basic premise that all persons have equal intrinsic worth, which I call the principle of intrinsic equality. This idea of equal intrinsic worth is widely recognized by contemporary political philosophers to be the first principle of a just society. Ronald Dworkin, for example, invokes this basic principle when he says that the most fundamental requirement of a constitutional democracy is that it treat its citizens *as equals*, with equal concern and respect.

Different religious and metaphysical traditions provide different justifications for this principle of intrinsic equality. . . .

---

33. In calling this principle "equal opportunity for persuasion," I do not mean to imply that it guarantees citizens an equal *ability* to persuade. On the contrary, as I shall repeatedly emphasize, it guarantees only an equal opportunity for *attempting* to persuade.

Perhaps at some future stage of human history, some philosopher will succeed in demonstrating that one of the ... competing principles of justice ... is the only one consistent with intrinsic equality, or else is the only reasonable one in light of other compelling considerations. But that day has not yet arrived. Until then, it is legitimate and reasonable for individual citizens to adopt whichever of these principles they prefer. Alternatively, individuals legitimately and reasonably might decide to adopt some sort of compromise among these principles. In any event, for the foreseeable future, philosophers will remain unable to identify a definitive principle of distributive justice that all reasonable individuals must accept as the only valid principle—and which they must acknowledge to be binding upon society as a fundamental postulate from which the polity must not deviate. Instead, because different citizens legitimately and reasonably may adopt different principles of distributive justice, society must adopt some sort of collective decision-making procedure in which each individual expresses her preferences concerning distributive justice. This decision-making procedure must then tally these conflicting preferences into a coherent social result.

B. The Anti-Plutocracy Principle

Whatever the particulars of the decision-making procedure society adopts to resolve the disputes concerning distributive justice, this decision-making procedure should comply with the anti-plutocracy principle. Society might decide to restrict participation in the decision-making process on a variety of reasonable grounds. For example, society might set a minimum age requirement or perhaps even some minimum competency requirement (e.g., no mental impairment so severe as to prevent a person from understanding what it means to cast a vote in an election). But all members of society should have an equal opportunity to participate in this decision-making process *without regard to the amount of wealth they have at the time the decision-making process occurs.*

In Part III, I explain why the equal opportunity to participate must mean more than just an equal vote at the end of the decision-making process. Instead, it must include an equal opportunity to attempt to persuade one's fellow citizens to agree with one's own views about distributive justice. In the meantime, however, there is no doubt that the anti-plutocracy principle encompasses the proposition that all citizens should have equal voting rights without regard to wealth. Thus, I will state the case for the anti-plutocracy principle by focusing on the specific subject of wealth qualifications for voting.

1. *Wealth Qualifications for Voting.*—Suppose the decision-making process for choosing society's principles of distributive justice provided each citizen with one vote for each dollar of income the citizen had received in the previous year. Most of us instinctively recoil at the idea, but why exactly is it wrong?

To give the rich more votes than the poor just because they are rich would be a form of elitism in violation of the principle of intrinsic equality. The interests of poor citizens must count the same as the interests of rich citizens. Thus, there must be a justification for unequal voting rights other than the elitist assertion that the interests of the rich are inherently more deserving of satisfaction because the rich are inherently better than the poor.

But no such justification is available. The rich cannot claim that they are more likely to espouse better views of distributive justice than the poor. As we have seen, there is no way to determine in advance of the collective decision-making process which views of distributive justice are better or worse for society. A poor person's views about distributive justice deserve to have just as much input into the decision-making process as a rich person's views because there is no independent standard for evaluating the relative merit of the different views.

Moreover, human nature being what it is (i.e., substantially self-interested), there is a significant chance that rich citizens will simply cast their votes to support policies that will permit them to retain their wealth and to pass it on to their own offspring. Giving the rich more votes per capita than the poor will build into the decision-making process a bias in favor of the interests of rich citizens and against the interests of poor citizens. But because the interests of the poor must count as much as the interests of the rich, and because their views about distributive justice are equally legitimate, this risk of built-in bias is unacceptable.

To be sure, poor citizens may vote for distributive policies that maximize the amount of wealth to be redistributed from the rich to the poor (and to their offspring). There is no reason to believe, however, that the vote of poor citizens will be more self-interested than the vote of rich citizens. Whatever else they may possess, the rich have no monopoly on moral virtue.

Thus, if rich and poor alike are likely to use their votes to advance their own self-interests, the decision-making process should be structured to give each citizen, regardless of wealth, an equal opportunity to do so. The consequence may be an unseemly contest of self-interest against self-interest, but at least it will be a contest in which no one has an inherent advantage just because she happens to be wealthier at the outset of the decision-making process. In short, the likelihood of self-interested voting, combined with the inability of philosophy to identify an independent standard of distributive justice, requires adherence to the anti-plutocracy principle.

The following question inevitably arises: how can I insist upon adherence to the anti-plutocracy principle when I say that philosophy cannot provide society with an unassailable principle of distributive justice? The answer is that the anti-plutocracy principle follows necessarily from the foundational principle of intrinsic equality, whereas none of the competing principles of distributive justice follows inevitably from intrinsic equality. Moreover, the anti-plutocracy principle follows necessarily from intrinsic equality *precisely because* none of the competing principles of distributive justice follows inevitably from intrinsic equality. It is the very indeterminacy of distributive justice (together with the fact that citizens largely vote their own self-interests) which yields the conclusion that all citizens should have equal voting rights regardless of their respective wealth. The premise of indeterminacy compels this conclusion once one has already accepted the elementary proposition that the interests of all citizens must count equally.

Now, the rich may argue that they need extra voting rights to protect their greater wealth from the self-interested designs of the poor but that the poor need less protection because they have so much less to lose. This argument, however, must fail because it presumes that the rich are entitled to protect their wealth against redistributivist efforts by the poor (and the middle class). Whether the rich have a valid claim to the wealth they possess is precisely the issue to be decided by the decision-making process. Given the philosophical indeterminacy of distributive justice, one cannot presume in advance of the decision-making process that the rich have any valid claim at all to the wealth in their possession.

To be sure, the legitimate property rights of rich and poor alike may be protected by constitutional devices, like the Takings Clause, that prohibit the government from demanding specific individual citizens to sacrifice their property for public benefit without just compensation. But such constitutional provisions should not be construed to prevent the electorate, by majority vote, from enacting tax laws that redistribute wealth from the rich, as a class, to the poor, as a class. What is more, the existence of such constitutional devices cannot justify giving rich citizens more voting rights than poor citizens, thereby granting to rich citizens a built-in check against the pursuit of redistributivist tax laws by poor citizens. On the contrary, when society votes on whether to pursue redistributivist tax legislation, rich citizens and poor citizens must be equal participants in the process, each with an equal vote regardless of wealth. The only legitimate presumption in favor of the existing distribution of wealth at the time of voting is contained within the principle of majority rule itself: a tie vote favors the status quo. Otherwise, the electorate must be free to adopt whatever distributive policies it wishes, as none has any intrinsic philosophical advantage.

The argument is also sometimes made that the poor outnumber the rich and, therefore, if everyone has an equal vote, the masses of poor will overwhelm the relatively few affluent citizens. But no matter what the distribution of income happens to be, each citizen should have an equal say in what the distribution ought to be. Under majority rule, both those above and those below the median must convince the median voter to side with them on issues of distributive justice. Consequently, if there is a small percentage of super-rich citizens, to obtain a majority they must form a coalition with enough of those less affluent than they. Likewise, if there is a small percentage of super-poor citizens, they must build a coalition with those more affluent. Requiring both the rich and poor to build these coalitions is surely preferable to an electoral system that gives either the rich or the poor extra votes to protect themselves from majority rule. Majority rule may be an imperfect procedure, but it remains the best available device to decide issues of distributive justice, given a commitment to the fundamental proposition that the interests of each citizen count equally.

2. *No Buying or Selling of Votes.*—Adherence to the anti-plutocracy principle requires that no one be permitted to buy or sell votes. If citizens were permitted to trade votes for dollars, rich citizens would buy votes from poor citizens, thereby disenfranchising the poor who had sold their votes. This result is inevitable because of the declining marginal utility of income. Even if a poor person has a greater desire to vote in an election than does a rich person, the poor person may sell his vote to the rich person because of a pressing need to feed his family. Thus, to permit the exchange of votes for dollars would make a person's ability to participate in electoral politics dependent upon the person's wealth, precisely the result that the anti-plutocracy principle condemns as invalid.

Libertarians may argue that the prohibition on vote-selling is an illegitimate restraint of liberty. After all, the transaction is voluntary: the poor person wants to sell, and the rich person wants to buy. The poor person, however, should not be put in a position of having to choose between the right to vote and other, more pressing goods. Even though a transaction is voluntary, the transaction may not be fair if conditions at the time the agreement is made are themselves unfair. A person who is starving to death may be willing to sell one of his kidneys in exchange for food, but should the person be forced to make this choice? This question is one of distributive justice and has no definitive answer. Suppose, for example, the person is starving because he squandered all of his inheritance, refuses to work for a living, and thinks society owes him a decent standard of living even if he refuses to work.

The very indeterminacy of distributive justice is, again, precisely the relevant point for our purposes. No one can say *in advance of the electoral process* that the existing distribution of wealth is fair, thereby making it legitimate to permit a poor person to sell her vote if she wishes. Rather, the only way to determine the fairness of the existing distribution of wealth is to ask for its ratification in an electoral process in which each poor citizen has the same amount of input as does each rich person. And the only way to ensure that poor citizens have equal input is to prohibit the poor from selling their votes....

III. The Anti-Plutocracy Principle and Campaign Finance

The case for the equal-dollars-per-voter principle depends upon the following crucial proposition: the equal opportunity to participate in electoral politics, which is guaranteed to all regardless of wealth, must be understood to encompass not only an equal vote, but also the equal opportunity to attempt to persuade one's fellow voters to share one's own views about distributive justice. Once this crucial proposition is established, the argument for equal-dollars-per-voter becomes relatively straightforward: the argument is essentially a repetition of the argument for the anti-plutocracy principle in general, of which equal-dollars-per-voter is now recognized to be an integral component. Thus, society must accept that equal-dollars-per-voter, like the anti-plutocracy principle, is an essential precondition of democratic government.

A. An Equal Vote Is Not Enough

Voting is only the final stage of the electoral process. It is preceded not only by the agenda-formation stage (in which matters to be voted upon are identified) but also by what might be called the "argumentative stage," in which competing factions of the electorate attempt to persuade the mass of undecided voters to agree with their positions. Even if we put aside the problem of agenda formation and thus define the electoral process as commencing once the items on the ballot have been determined, we must acknowledge that a citizen does not have equal input in the electoral process if she is denied an equal opportunity to participate in the argumentative stage of the process.

The importance of the argumentative stage must not be underestimated. Many voters do not enter the electoral process with fixed and intransigent views about distributive justice. On the contrary, they are open to persuasion. Consequently, other citizens, who do enter the electoral process with strong and firm opinions about distributive justice, must have an opportunity to attempt to persuade the undecided voters.[82] Some citizens will be committed egalitarians, attempting to convince the undecided to support higher taxes, which would be spent on redistributivist social policies. Other citizens will be equally committed libertarians, attempting to convince the undecided to oppose such taxes. If both groups of citizens are to have truly equal opportunities to participate in the electoral process, they both must have equal opportunities to attempt to persuade the undecided voters. They need more than just an equal vote on election day.

If one of these groups has a greater opportunity to attempt to persuade the undecided voters, the members of this group will have an inherent structural advantage in the electoral process. To be sure, this advantage may not result in victory on election day. Attempts to persuade often fail. Nonetheless, having a greater opportunity to attempt to persuade is still an inherent advantage because, by definition, it

82. Recall here that I am limiting my discussion of the electoral process to its decisions on issues of distributive justice. My argument does not apply to other kinds of issues that might be put before the electorate. But as long as voters make decisions about issues of distributive justice — as they must do in a democracy committed to the anti-plutocracy principle — then my argument pertains.

Voters in a democracy need not vote directly for or against propositions of distributive justice (although they may do so in referenda, as in the case of California's famous Proposition 13). Instead, voters may vote on candidates who act as proxies for propositions about distributive justice (as was true in the 1992 presidential election, Clinton being the candidate who favored higher taxes for the purpose of higher spending on redistributive policies, and Bush being the candidate who opposed these tax-and-spend measures). When the office to be voted upon has the authority to make policy decisions in additional areas besides distributive justice, then voters will be concerned about the candidates' views on these matters as well. Nonetheless, regardless of whatever other types of issues might come before the elective office, as long as this office addresses issues of distributive justice, then voters will be concerned about the candidates' views about distributive justice, and thus the election must be governed by the principle of equal-dollars-per-voter.

is denied to one's opponents. Thus, if the electoral process is to avoid this kind of structural bias, the electoral process must guarantee all citizens an equal opportunity for persuading one another on issues of distributive justice.

Guaranteeing this equal opportunity for persuasion requires adherence to the principle of equal-dollars-per-voter. This point, although perhaps obvious, is worth making explicit. The attempt to persuade voters of the merits of one's views requires considerable financial resources. To attempt to persuade, one must advertise and publicize one's views. This advertising and publicity require resources, whether in the form of television time, billboard space, or door-to-door distribution of campaign literature.

Consequently, if all citizens are to have a truly equal opportunity to attempt to persuade their fellow citizens, then all citizens must have equal financial resources for this purpose.

And thus the argument for equal-dollars-per-voter is complete. The anti-plutocracy principle requires an equal opportunity for persuasion regardless of wealth, which in turn entails equal-dollars-per-voter. . . .

Notes and Questions

1. Foley argues that equality requires each voter to have "the equal opportunity to attempt to persuade one's fellow voters to share one's own views about distributive justice." Thus, Foley attempts to regulate equality for those pursuing an "electoral strategy," as described in the notes above. Can one make an equality argument for those pursuing a "legislative strategy"? Consider Richard L. Hasen, *Campaign Finance Laws and the Rupert Murdoch Problem*, 77 Texas Law Review 1627, 1645–46 (1999):

> Many critics of equality-based campaign finance reform miss the crucial role of access, and assume that the *only* equality argument against unequal contributions to or expenditures in favor of political candidates is that such contributions or expenditures increase the chances of a politician gaining election—what Lowenstein terms an "electoral strategy." Because money alone usually cannot buy an election contest, the anti-reform argument goes, this concern over use of money to buy elections is overblown.
>
> However, the retort that money does not buy elections ignores the access argument. If corporate PACs truly were solely interested in influencing the outcome of elections, they would not give so evenhandedly to parties, or to candidates running against each other in the same electoral contest. The money buys access, giving the contributor (assuming the most benign purposes) a greater chance of gaining the ear of the politician to make an argument in favor of the contributor's position on legislation. This is an advantage that non-contributors are much less likely to have. Those buying access are using their campaign expenditures as part of a *legislative strategy* to influence the outcome of the legislative process.

> Equality demands that every individual be given, so far as practical, the same political capital, so that each individual has a roughly equal ability to pursue both an electoral strategy and a legislative strategy. The most important step to ensure such equality is preventing vastly unequal expenditures of money in campaigns.

Hasen expands on these ideas in Plutocrats United: Campaign Money, the Supreme Court, and the Distortion of American Elections (2016), arguing for a combination of campaign finance limits and public financing through campaign finance vouchers to promote political equality and robust political competition.

For an important egalitarian argument rejecting the premises of deliberative democracy, see Frank Pasquale, *Reclaiming Egalitarianism in the Political Theory of Campaign Finance Reform*, 2008 University of Illinois Law Review 599. Pasquale concludes:

> Trying to argue for effective campaign finance regulation within the confines of leading Supreme Court cases is like trying to compose an epic in a sestina: the form itself defeats the meaning one would give it. About twenty-five years ago, Skelly Wright realized that "[w]ithin the confines of *Buckley* and *Bellotti*, only limited reforms are permissible. More effective measures will be possible only if the Court reconsiders these unfortunate precedents." But to the extent the Court has done so, it has edged toward a First Amendment absolutism that many thought had died with Justice Black.
>
> A new egalitarianism in campaign reform advocacy has to focus on facts that have changed since *Buckley*, not on futile efforts to recharacterize spending limits as "neutral" with respect to rich and poor citizens. Significant empirical research has called into question the cognitive content of campaign advertising. The function of fundraising is less to inform the public than to signal wealth and power to donors, potential rivals, and media outlets. Campaign contribution and expenditure limits can help to alleviate the strategic importance of the "dollar primary" by compressing the range of situations where money can critically alter the balance of power.
>
> The *Buckley* Court's hostility to egalitarianism is increasingly inappropriate in an America riven by economic inequality, and its romantic view of campaign spending becomes ever more naïve as techniques for manipulating public opinion flourish. Nevertheless, a durable majority of justices appear to support *Buckley* to this day. Rather than engage in the Sisyphean task of convincing a hostile Court of the validity of reform in deliberativist terms, reformers would be wiser to advance the egalitarian vision that ultimately animates reform. A constitutional amendment overturning *Buckley* is a prerequisite for unifying the political philosophy and constitutional theory of campaign finance reform.

Id. at 659–60. How would the other writers on this question respond to Pasquale?

2. Critics of the equality rationale for campaign finance regulation make a number of counterarguments. As we saw in *Buckley* and in the notes following the case, perhaps the most important argument (at least to the courts) has been that regulating campaign finances to achieve equality conflicts with First Amendment's rights of freedom of speech and association.

In addition to the argument that regulating finances to achieve equality is unconstitutional under the First Amendment, anti-equality arguments fall into two broad categories.

(a) *It is unfair to single out money to be regulated when other inequalities would remain.* Consider Bradley A. Smith, *Money Talks: Speech, Corruption, Equality, and Campaign Finance*, 86 Georgetown Law Journal 45, 91–92 (1997): "[A] ban on private monetary contributions tends to favor those with volunteer time, such as students and retirees, over working people, who have less time but may have money. It favors persons skilled in producing political advertising over persons skilled in growing corn or building homes." Consider in response Burt Neuborne, *Is Money Different?*, 77 Texas Law Review 1609, 1613 (1999): "The power of . . . money would be less troubling if there existed substitutes that allowed persons without great wealth to exercise equivalent power. Talent can occasionally play that role, enabling extraordinary persons without great wealth to play significant roles in the political process. But the link between money and effective speech is so strong that, over time, I believe it overwhelms talent." Indeed it is the very fungibility of money which makes it so useful. See also Ronald Dworkin, Sovereign Virtue: The Theory and Practice of Equality 366–67 (2000) ("Experience has shown — and never more dramatically than in recent elections — that any group's political success is so directly related to the sheer magnitude of its expenditures, particularly on television and radio, that this factor dwarfs others in accounting for political success. That is the heart of the democratic argument for expenditure limits in political campaigns."). If Dworkin is correct, how is it that during the second half of the twentieth century, when campaign costs were growing rapidly, Congress enacted the Clean Air Act of 1970, the Tax Reform Act of 1986, and any number of additional major laws that were strenuously opposed by well-financed interests? Is Dworkin's assertion about what experience shows consistent with the empirical research described in Section III.A above?

(b) *It is unnecessary to regulate wealth in campaign financing to achieve equality.* This argument has three separate components: (i) Some critics argue that money spent on elections does not correlate with legislative votes. We considered this argument in connection with the Sorauf excerpt above. Even if wealth does not correlate with legislative votes, it may correlate with other legislative action, such as a committee's decision to amend or table a bill. Is that reason enough to regulate campaign finances?; (ii) Some critics argue that the views of the wealthy are distributed randomly: "[T]he views of the 'rich' are, it appears, much less homogeneous than many other groups with a large amount of political influence." Smith, *supra*, 86 Georgetown Law Journal at 94; but see Neuborne, *supra*, 77 Texas Law Review at 1613 ("While there are wealthy left-wing radicals, and impoverished right-wing conservatives, by and large, the wealthy are likely to cluster at given points on the political spectrum that do not overlap with the places where the poor cluster."); (iii) Others object to the idea that "the poor" and "the rich" are immutable categories. In this regard, consider Lillian R. BeVier, *Campaign Finance Reform: Specious Arguments, Intractable Dilemmas*, 94 Columbia Law Review 1258, 1263–64 (1994):

> Wealth is always unequally distributed in a market economy because not only are initial material endowments unequal but so are intangible ones such as intellectual skills, energy, personality, judgment, and luck. However, where free exchange and the opportunity to exploit or to squander one's initial endowment exists, no distribution is permanent. The familiar saying "three generations from shirtsleeves to shirtsleeves" is but a homely way of capturing this universal flux.... A static conception [of wealth distribution] provides at best an incomplete, and at worst an inaccurate and irrelevant, account of reality because it fails to credit the continual redistribution of rights and entitlements that takes place in an inherently dynamic world where private property rights are protected and free markets prevail.

BeVier provides no empirical support for her claim about redistribution of wealth across generations, and long-term longitudinal empirical studies (studying the same people or families over time) may not exist. In the shorter term, the empirical picture does not support BeVier. One study found that in 1983 non-Hispanic African-Americans had a mean net worth only 19% of whites ($43,700, compared to $232,300 in 1995 dollars), and in 1995 their mean net worth was a similar 17% of whites ($40,800, compared to $242,400 in 1995 dollars). Edward N. Wolff, *Recent Trends in the Size Distribution of Household Wealth*, Journal of Economic Perspectives Summer 1998, at 131, 141. The study concluded that:

> The only households that saw their mean net worth and financial wealth rise in absolute terms between 1983 and 1995 were those in the top 20 percent of their respective distributions and the gains were particularly strong for the top 1 percent. All other groups suffered real wealth or income losses, and the declines were particularly precipitous at the bottom. Slicing the numbers by black and white, or by young and old, only confirms the growth in inequality of wealth.

Id. at 150. See also Javier Diaz-Giménez, Vincenzo Quadrini & José-Víctor Ríos-Rull, *Dimensions of Inequality: Facts on the U.S. Distributions of Earnings, Income, and Wealth*, Federal Reserve Bank of Minneapolis Quarterly Review, Spring 1997, at 3, 14 (table 7) (finding that over 90% of those in the bottom fifth of net worth in 1984 were in the bottom two-fifths in 1989, and over 92% of those in the top fifth of net worth in 1984 were in the top two-fifths in 1989).

In considering these competing viewpoints, bear in mind that many of the resources that flow into campaigns come from organizations, not individuals. Thus, few teachers are especially wealthy, but teachers' unions are one of the major sources of campaign resources—financial and otherwise—in contemporary America.

Spencer Overton takes issue with BeVier's arguments as well. After noting that "Professor BeVier's focus on the *income* of taxpayers also overlooks the important role of *wealth* in measuring class mobility," Overton offers statistics showing that when measured by wealth, economic mobility is "dismal." He continues by noting some racial disparities:

> In a study of men who turned twenty-one after 1980, 47% of whites reached middle class earnings by age thirty, whereas only 19% of blacks had done so. African Americans are nearly five times more likely than whites to fall from the top income quartile to the bottom quartile, while African Americans born to the bottom quartile attain the top quartile at less than one-half the rate of whites. In a study of American wealth mobility over 15 years, 0% of African American males in the study rose from the lowest wealth decile to the highest.

Spencer Overton, *The Donor Class: Campaign Finance, Democracy, and Participation*, 153 University of Pennsylvania Law Review 73, 94–96 (2004).

3. Smith and BeVier are two of a number of prominent writers who have written in favor of deregulating campaign finance. Readers interested in this debate might wish to start with Bradley A. Smith, *Faulty Assumptions and Undemocratic Consequences of Campaign Finance Reform*, 105 Yale Law Journal 1049 (1996) and a response by a supporter of regulation, E. Joshua Rosenkranz, *Faulty Assumptions in "Faulty Assumptions": A Response to Professor Smith's Critiques of Campaign Finance Reform*, 30 Connecticut Law Review 867 (1998). For another debate, see Kathleen M. Sullivan, *Political Money and Freedom of Speech*, 30 U.C. Davis Law Review 663, 668–69 (1997) and Frank Askin, *Political Money and Freedom of Speech: Kathleen Sullivan's Seven Deadly Sins—An Antitoxin*, 31 U.C. Davis Law Review 1065 (1998). Other notable deregulationist works include: Bradley A. Smith, Unfree Speech: The Folly of Campaign Finance Reform (2001); Joel M. Gora, *Campaign Finance Reform: Still Searching Today for a Better Way*, 6 Journal of Law and Policy 137 (1997); and Stephen E. Gottlieb, *The Dilemma of Election Campaign Finance Reform*, 18 Hofstra Law Review 213 (1989). For a skeptical, though not necessarily deregulationist, view, see Roy A. Schotland, *Proposals for Campaign Finance Reform: An Article Dedicated to Being Less Dull Than Its Title*, 21 Capital University Law Review 429 (1992). Professors Issacharoff and Karlan argue that effective campaign finance regulation is simply impossible because the money will have to "flow" somewhere. Samuel Issacharoff & Pamela S. Karlan, *The Hydraulics of Campaign Finance Reform*, 77 Texas Law Review 1705 (1999).

4. Claiming that "[l]egal academics who call for campaign finance reform ... have overlooked the significance of race," Spencer Overton argues that a focus on race significantly bolsters the equality argument for such regulation. Spencer Overton, *But Some Are More Equal: Race, Exclusion, and Campaign Finance*, 80 Texas Law Review 987 (2002). According to Overton, "[e]xisting frameworks fail to acknowledge that past state-mandated discrimination against racial minorities

has shaped the current distribution of property, which in turn hinders the ability of many people of color to participate fully in a privately financed political system.... By using the First Amendment to undermine legislative restrictions on the use of political money, courts effectively enshrine the existing distribution of property as a baseline for political advantage." *Id.* See also Terry Smith, *Race and Money in Politics*, 79 North Carolina Law Review 1469 (2001). The Smith article is part of a symposium, *Democracy in a New America*, and includes commentaries on the article by Samuel Issacharoff, Daniel H. Lowenstein, and Spencer Overton.

5. Note that Foley does not argue that the Constitution requires equality in campaign finance. For an argument that the Constitution requires the public financing of campaigns, see Jamin Raskin and John Bonifaz, *The Constitutional Imperative and Practical Superiority of Democratically Financed Elections*, 94 Columbia Law Review 1160 (1994). For a criticism of Raskin and Bonifaz, see Smith, *supra*, 86 Georgetown Law Journal at 79–88. See also Sullivan, *supra*, 30 U.C. Davis Law Review at 672–73 (arguing that campaign finance is more analogous to political speech than voting, for which formal equality is the constitutional standard).

6. Looking to move beyond the corruption and equality paradigms, Professor Nicholas O. Stephanopoulos, *Aligning Campaign Finance Law*, 101 Virginia Law Review 1425 (2015) proposes that the government has a compelling interest in "alignment" to justify certain campaign finance laws:

> Suppose a jurisdiction is troubled by [the fact that "politicians' positions reflect the preferences of their donors to an uncanny extent"] and decides to enact some kind of campaign finance reform. What reason might it give? One option is preventing the corruption of elected officials. But the Supreme Court has recently narrowed the definition of corruption to quid pro quo exchanges, and, as just noted, such exchanges do not occur with any regularity in contemporary America. Another possibility is avoiding the distortion of electoral outcomes due to the heavy spending of affluent individuals (and groups). But the Court has emphatically rejected any governmental interest in ameliorating "the corrosive and distorting effects of immense aggregations of wealth." Yet another idea is equalizing the resources of candidates or the electoral influence of voters. But this equality interest has been deemed invalid in even more strident terms. "[T]he concept that government may restrict the speech of some elements of our society in order to enhance the relative voice of others is wholly foreign to the First Amendment."
>
> So is our reformist jurisdiction out of luck? Not quite. This Article's thesis is that there is an additional interest, of the gravest importance, that both is threatened by money in politics and is furthered by (certain) campaign finance regulation. This interest is the promotion of *alignment* between voters' policy preferences and their government's policy outputs. Alignment operates at the levels of both the individual constituency and the jurisdiction

> as a whole. Within the constituency, the views of the district's median voter and the district's representative should align. One step up, the preferences of the *jurisdiction's* median voter and the *legislature's* median member should correspond. Moreover, at the jurisdictional level, the median voter's views should be congruent not only with the median legislator's positions, but also with actual policy outcomes. *Preference alignment* refers to the former sort of congruence; *outcome alignment* to the latter.
>
> Alignment is a significant—indeed, compelling—interest because of its tight connection to core democratic values. At the district level, it follows closely from the delegate theory of representation. A delegate "must do what his principal would do, must act as if the principal himself were acting . . . must vote as a majority of his constituents would," as Hanna Pitkin wrote in her landmark work. In other words, a delegate must align his own positions with those of his constituents. Likewise, at the jurisdictional level, alignment is essentially another term for majoritarianism. To say that policy should be congruent with the preferences of the median voter is to say that it should be congruent with the preferences of the voting *majority*. Of course, majoritarianism is not our only democratic principle. But, as Jeremy Waldron has argued, it *is* "required as a matter of fairness to all those who participate in the social choice."

How, if at all, does Professor Stephanopoulos's alignment interest differ from an interest in promoting political equality?

7. Bertrall L. Ross, *Addressing Inequality in the Age of* Citizens United, 93 New York University Law Review 1120 (2018), argues that the lack of responsiveness to the interests of the poor and the resulting political inequality stems from the lack of voter mobilization of poor voters. He advocates for campaign finance vouchers, earmarked contributions, and a mobilization matching fund to create incentives for campaigns to mobilize poor voters. Under Ross's earmarking proposal, "campaign contributors would be encouraged to earmark their contributions for mobilizing the marginalized," *id.* at 1184, and under his matching funds program, a government public financing program would match, "up to a certain amount, contributions that campaigns designate for use in mobilizing the politically marginalized," *id.* at 1186. Would these reforms work to promote political equality?

8. A final note relevant not only to equality-based arguments for campaign finance regulation, but for campaign finance regulation as a whole: Beware of unintended consequences. Cass R. Sunstein, *Political Equality and Unintended Consequences*, 94 Columbia Law Review 1390, 1400-11 (1994), argues that campaign finance legislation may prove unhelpful or counterproductive. See also Issacharoff & Karlan, *supra*, 77 Texas Law Review at 1714: "We are particularly worried that reforms would exacerbate the already disturbing trend toward politics being divorced from the mediating influence of candidates and political parties."

Sunstein concludes that because of congressional self-dealing in campaign finance regulation, "considerable judicial suspicion . . . is justified." He states that "we might try to avoid rigid, command-and-control regulation, which poses special dangers, and move instead toward more flexible, incentive-based strategies." Sunstein, *supra*, 94 Columbia Law Review at 1400. Sunstein too tentatively endorses campaign finance vouchers, *id.* at 1412–13, discussed in more detail in Chapter 15.

Chapter 13

Spending Limits

In *Buckley v. Valeo*, the Supreme Court struck down several provisions of FECA limiting campaign spending, including limits on a candidate's own spending and a $1,000 limit on independent spending by an individual supporting or opposing candidates for federal office. The Court held the independent expenditure limit violated the First Amendment because it was not necessary to prevent corruption (the Court viewed the independence requirement as preventing any *quid pro quo*) and because it imposed a heavy burden on First Amendment rights of speech and association. The Court also held that the law would not be effective because, under *Buckley*'s footnote 52, the law would apply only to spending that "expressly advocated" the election or defeat of a candidate, and not to ads that avoided those words of advocacy. Finally, the Court rejected a political equality rationale for spending limits, ruling such a rationale "wholly foreign" to the First Amendment.

After *Buckley*, the biggest question mark in the spending limits area concerned the imposition of such limits on corporations and labor unions, an issue not addressed in *Buckley*. Federal law had long imposed such limits, as had many states. As we shall see, the Supreme Court's consideration of this question has been controversial and inconsistent.

I. Corporate Spending Limits in Ballot Measure Campaigns

First National Bank of Boston v. Bellotti

435 U.S. 765 (1978)

Mr. Justice POWELL delivered the opinion of the Court.

In sustaining a state criminal statute that forbids certain expenditures by banks and business corporations for the purpose of influencing the vote on referendum proposals, the Massachusetts Supreme Judicial Court held that the First Amendment rights of a corporation are limited to issues that materially affect its business, property, or assets. . . .

I

The statute at issue, Mass. Gen. Laws Ann., ch. 55, § 8, prohibits appellants, two national banking associations and three business corporations, from making contributions or expenditures "for the purpose of . . . influencing or affecting the vote on any question submitted to the voters, other than one materially affecting any of the property, business or assets of the corporation." The statute further specifies that "[n]o question submitted to the voters solely concerning the taxation of the income, property or transactions of individuals shall be deemed materially to affect the property, business or assets of the corporation." . . .

Appellants wanted to spend money to publicize their views on a proposed constitutional amendment that was to be submitted to the voters as a ballot question at a general election on November 2, 1976. The amendment would have permitted the legislature to impose a graduated tax on the income of individuals. [Appellants] brought this action seeking to have the statute declared unconstitutional. [The state court upheld the statute.][3] . . .

III

The court below framed the principal question in this case as whether and to what extent corporations have First Amendment rights. We believe that the court posed the wrong question. The Constitution often protects interests broader than those of the party seeking their vindication. The First Amendment, in particular, serves significant societal interests. The proper question therefore is not whether corporations "have" First Amendment rights and, if so, whether they are coextensive with those of natural persons. Instead, the question must be whether § 8 abridges expression that the First Amendment was meant to protect. We hold that it does.

A

The speech proposed by appellants is at the heart of the First Amendment's protection. . . .

---

3. This was not the first challenge to § 8. The statute's legislative and judicial history has been a troubled one. Its successive re-enactments have been linked to the legislature's repeated submissions to the voters of a constitutional amendment that would allow the enactment of a graduated tax.

The predecessor of § 8, § 7 . . . , did not dictate that questions concerning the taxation of individuals could not satisfy the "materially affecting" requirement. The Supreme Judicial Court construed § 7 not to prohibit a corporate expenditure urging the voters to reject a proposed constitutional amendment authorizing the legislature to impose a graduated tax on corporate as well as individual income.

[T]he legislature amended § 7 by adding the sentence: "No question submitted to the voters concerning the taxation of the income, property or transactions of individuals shall be deemed materially to affect the property, business or assets of the corporation." The statute was challenged in 1972 by four of the present appellants; they wanted to oppose a referendum proposal similar to the one submitted to and rejected by the voters in 1962. Again the expenditure was held to be lawful.

The most recent amendment was enacted on April 28, 1975, when the legislature further refined the second sentence of § 8 to apply only to ballot questions "solely" concerning the taxation of individuals. Following this amendment, the legislature on May 7, 1975, voted to submit to the voters on November 2, 1976, the proposed constitutional amendment authorizing the imposition of a graduated personal income tax. It was this proposal that led to the case now before us.

As the Court said in *Mills v. Alabama*, 384 U.S. 214 (1966), "there is practically universal agreement that a major purpose of [the First] Amendment was to protect the free discussion of governmental affairs." If the speakers here were not corporations, no one would suggest that the State could silence their proposed speech. It is the type of speech indispensable to decisionmaking in a democracy, and this is no less true because the speech comes from a corporation rather than an individual. The inherent worth of the speech in terms of its capacity for informing the public does not depend upon the identity of its source, whether corporation, association, union, or individual.

The court below nevertheless held that corporate speech is protected by the First Amendment only when it pertains directly to the corporation's business interests. In deciding whether this novel and restrictive gloss on the First Amendment comports with the Constitution and the precedents of this Court, we need not survey the outer boundaries of the Amendment's protection of corporate speech, or address the abstract question whether corporations have the full measure of rights that individuals enjoy under the First Amendment.'[13] The question in this case, simply put, is whether the corporate identity of the speaker deprives this proposed speech of what otherwise would be its clear entitlement to protection. We turn now to that question.

B

The court below found confirmation of the legislature's definition of the scope of a corporation's First Amendment rights in the language of the Fourteenth Amendment. Noting that the First Amendment is applicable to the States through the Fourteenth, and seizing upon the observation that corporations "cannot claim for themselves the liberty which the Fourteenth Amendment guarantees." *Pierce v. Society of Sisters*, 268 U.S. 510 (1925), the court concluded that a corporation's First Amendment rights must derive from its property rights under the Fourteenth.

This is an artificial mode of analysis, untenable under decisions of this Court.... Freedom of speech and the other freedoms encompassed by the First Amendment always have been viewed as fundamental components of the liberty safeguarded by the Due Process Clause, and the Court has not identified a separate source for the right when it has been asserted by corporations. In *Grosjean v. American Press Co.*, 297 U.S. 233 (1936), the Court rejected the very reasoning adopted by the Supreme Judicial Court and did not rely on the corporation's property rights under the Fourteenth Amendment in sustaining its freedom of speech.

Yet appellee suggests that First Amendment rights generally have been afforded only to corporations engaged in the communications business or through which individuals express themselves, and the court below apparently accepted the

13. Nor is there any occasion to consider in this case whether, under different circumstances, a justification for a restriction on speech that would be inadequate as applied to individuals might suffice to sustain the same restriction as applied to corporations, unions, or like entities.

"materially affecting" theory as the conceptual common denominator between appellee's position and the precedents of this Court. It is true that the "materially affecting" requirement would have been satisfied in the Court's decisions affording protection to the speech of media corporations and corporations otherwise in the business of communication or entertainment, and to the commercial speech of business corporations. In such cases, the speech would be connected to the corporation's business almost by definition. But the effect on the business of the corporation was not the governing rationale in any of these decisions. None of them mentions, let alone attributes significance to, the fact that the subject of the challenged communication materially affected the corporation's business.

The press cases emphasize the special and constitutionally recognized role of that institution in informing and educating the public, offering criticism, and providing a forum for discussion and debate. But the press does not have a monopoly on either the First Amendment or the ability to enlighten. Similarly, the Court's decisions involving corporations in the business of communication or entertainment are based not only on the role of the First Amendment in fostering individual self-expression but also on its role in affording the public access to discussion, debate, and the dissemination of information and ideas. Even decisions seemingly based exclusively on the individual's right to express himself acknowledge that the expression may contribute to society's edification....

C

We thus find no support in the First or Fourteenth Amendment, or in the decisions of this Court, for the proposition that speech that otherwise would be within the protection of the First Amendment loses that protection simply because its source is a corporation that cannot prove, to the satisfaction of a court, a material effect on its business or property. The "materially affecting" requirement is not an identification of the boundaries of corporate speech etched by the Constitution itself. Rather, it amounts to an impermissible legislative prohibition of speech based on the identity of the interests that spokesmen may represent in public debate over controversial issues and a requirement that the speaker have a sufficiently great interest in the subject to justify communication.

Section 8 permits a corporation to communicate to the public its views on certain referendum subjects—those materially affecting its business—but not others. It also singles out one kind of ballot question—individual taxation—as a subject about which corporations may never make their ideas public. The legislature has drawn the line between permissible and impermissible speech according to whether there is a sufficient nexus, as defined by the legislature, between the issue presented to the voters and the business interests of the speaker.

In the realm of protected speech, the legislature is constitutionally disqualified from dictating the subjects about which persons may speak and the speakers who may address a public issue. *Police Dept. of Chicago v. Mosley*, 408 U.S. 92 (1972). If a legislature may direct business corporations to "stick to business," it also may limit other corporations—religious, charitable, or civic—to their respective "business" when addressing the public. Such power in government to channel the expression of views is unacceptable under the First Amendment. Especially where, as here, the legislature's suppression of speech suggests an attempt to give one side of a debatable public question an advantage in expressing its views to the people, the First Amendment is plainly offended. Yet the State contends that its action is necessitated by governmental interests of the highest order. We next consider these asserted interests.

IV . . .

The Supreme Judicial Court did not subject § 8 to "the critical scrutiny demanded under accepted First Amendment and equal protection principles," *Buckley*, because of its view that the First Amendment does not apply to appellants' proposed speech. For this reason the court did not even discuss the State's interests in considering appellants' First Amendment argument. The court adverted to the conceivable interests served by § 8 only in rejecting appellants' equal protection claim. Appellee nevertheless advances two principal justifications for the prohibition of corporate speech. The first is the State's interest in sustaining the active role of the individual citizen in the electoral process and thereby preventing diminution of the citizen's confidence in government. The second is the interest in protecting the rights of shareholders whose views differ from those expressed by management on behalf of the corporation. However weighty these interests may be in the context of partisan candidate elections,[26] they either are not implicated in this case or are not served at all, or in other than a random manner, by the prohibition in § 8.

A

Preserving the integrity of the electoral process, preventing corruption, and "sustain[ing] the active, alert responsibility of the individual citizen in a democracy

26. In addition to prohibiting corporate contributions and expenditures for the purpose of influencing the vote on a ballot question submitted to the voters, § 8 also proscribes corporate contributions or expenditures "for the purpose of aiding, promoting or preventing the nomination or election of any person to public office, or aiding, promoting, or antagonizing the interests of any political party." In this respect, the statute is not unlike many other state and federal laws regulating corporate participation in partisan candidate elections. Appellants do not challenge the constitutionality of laws prohibiting or limiting corporate contributions to political candidates or committees, or other means of influencing candidate elections. About half of these laws, including the federal law, 2 U.S.C. § 441b [now 52 U.S.C. § 30118] (originally enacted as the Federal Corrupt Practices Act), by their terms do not apply to referendum votes. Several of the others proscribe or limit spending for "political" purposes, which may or may not cover referenda. The overriding concern behind the enactment of statutes such as the Federal Corrupt Practices Act was the problem of corruption of elected representatives through the creation of political debts. The importance of the governmental interest in preventing this occurrence has never been doubted. The case before us presents no comparable problem, and our consideration of a corporation's right to speak on issues of general public interest implies no comparable right in the quite different context of participation in a political campaign for election to public office. Congress might well be able to demonstrate the existence of a danger of real or apparent corruption in independent expenditures by corporations to influence candidate elections.

for the wise conduct of government" are interests of the highest importance. *Buckley*; *United States v. United Automobile Workers*, 352 U.S. 567 (1957). Preservation of the individual citizen's confidence in government is equally important. *Buckley*.

Appellee advances a number of arguments in support of his view that these interests are endangered by corporate participation in discussion of a referendum issue. They hinge upon the assumption that such participation would exert an undue influence on the outcome of a referendum vote, and—in the end—destroy the confidence of the people in the democratic process and the integrity of government. According to appellee, corporations are wealthy and powerful and their views may drown out other points of view. If appellee's arguments were supported by record or legislative findings that corporate advocacy threatened imminently to undermine democratic processes, thereby denigrating rather than serving First Amendment interests, these arguments would merit our consideration. *Red Lion Broadcasting Co. v. FCC*, 395 U.S. 367 (1969). But there has been no showing that the relative voice of corporations has been overwhelming or even significant in influencing referenda in Massachusetts,[28] or that there has been any threat to the confidence of the citizenry in government.

Nor are appellee's arguments inherently persuasive or supported by the precedents of this Court. Referenda are held on issues, not candidates for public office. The risk of corruption perceived in cases involving candidate elections simply is not present in a popular vote on a public issue. To be sure, corporate advertising may influence the outcome of the vote; this would be its purpose. But the fact that advocacy may persuade the electorate is hardly a reason to suppress it: The Constitution "protects expression which is eloquent no less than that which is unconvincing." *Kingsley Int'l Pictures Corp. v. Regents*, 360 U.S. 684 (1959). We noted only recently that "the concept that government may restrict the speech of some elements of our society in order to enhance the relative voice of others is wholly foreign to the First Amendment. . . ." *Buckley*. Moreover, the people in our democracy are entrusted

28. In his dissenting opinion, Mr. Justice WHITE relies on incomplete facts with respect to expenditures in the 1972 referendum election, in support of his perception as to the "domination of the electoral process by corporate wealth." The record shows only the extent of corporate and individual contributions to the two committees that were organized to support and oppose, respectively, the constitutional amendment. It does show that three of the appellants each contributed $3,000 to the "opposition" committee. The dissenting opinion makes no reference to the fact that amounts of money expended independently of organized committees need not be reported under Massachusetts law, and therefore remain unknown.

Even if viewed as material, any inference that corporate contributions "dominated" the electoral process on this issue is refuted by the 1976 election. There the voters again rejected the proposed constitutional amendment even in the absence of any corporate spending, which had been forbidden by the decision below.

[Although corporate spending was prohibited, opponents of the 1976 proposal outspent supporters by about $115,000 to $10,000. See John S. Shockley, *Money in Politics: Judicial Roadblocks to Campaign Finance Reform*, 10 Hastings Constitutional Law Quarterly 679, 703 n.117 (1983). Does this fact support or detract from Justice Powell's position?—Eds.]

with the responsibility for judging and evaluating the relative merits of conflicting arguments.[31] They may consider, in making their judgment, the source and credibility of the advocate.[32] But if there be any danger that the people cannot evaluate the information and arguments advanced by appellants, it is a danger contemplated by the Framers of the First Amendment. In sum, "[a] restriction so destructive of the right of public discussion [as § 8], without greater or more imminent danger to the public interest than existed in this case, is incompatible with the freedoms secured by the First Amendment." *Thomas v. Collins*, 323 U.S. 516 (1945).

B

Finally, appellee argues that § 8 protects corporate shareholders, an interest that is both legitimate and traditionally within the province of state law. *Cort v. Ash*, 422 U.S. 66 (1975). The statute is said to serve this interest by preventing the use of corporate resources in furtherance of views with which some shareholders may disagree. This purpose is belied, however, by the provisions of the statute, which are both underinclusive and overinclusive.

The underinclusiveness of the statute is self-evident. Corporate expenditures with respect to a referendum are prohibited, while corporate activity with respect to the passage or defeat of legislation is permitted, even though corporations may engage in lobbying more often than they take positions on ballot questions submitted to the voters. Nor does § 8 prohibit a corporation from expressing its views, by the expenditure of corporate funds, on any public issue until it becomes the subject of a referendum, though the displeasure of disapproving shareholders is unlikely to be any less.

The fact that a particular kind of ballot question has been singled out for special treatment undermines the likelihood of a genuine state interest in protecting shareholders. It suggests instead that the legislature may have been concerned with silencing corporations on a particular subject. Indeed, appellee has conceded that "the legislative and judicial history of the statute indicates . . . that the second crime

31. The State's paternalism evidenced by this statute is illustrated by the fact that Massachusetts does not prohibit lobbying by corporations, which are free to exert as much influence on the people's representatives as their resources and inclinations permit. Presumably the legislature thought its members competent to resist the pressures and blandishments of lobbying, but had markedly less confidence in the electorate. If the First Amendment protects the right of corporations to petition legislative and administrative bodies, see *California Motor Transp. Co. v. Trucking Unlimited*, 404 U.S. 508 (1972); *Eastern Railroad Presidents Conf. v. Noerr Motor Freight, Inc.*, 365 U.S. 127 (1961), there hardly can be less reason for allowing corporate views to be presented openly to the people when they are to take action in their sovereign capacity.

32. Corporate advertising, unlike some methods of participation in political campaigns, is likely to be highly visible. Identification of the source of advertising may be required as a means of disclosure, so that the people will be able to evaluate the arguments to which they are being subjected. See *Buckley*; *United States v. Harriss*, 347 U.S. 612, 625–626 (1954). In addition, we emphasized in *Buckley* the prophylactic effect of requiring that the source of communication be disclosed.

was 'tailor-made' to prohibit corporate campaign contributions to oppose a graduated income tax amendment."

Nor is the fact that § 8 is limited to banks and business corporations without relevance. Excluded from its provisions and criminal sanctions are entities or organized groups in which numbers of persons may hold an interest or membership, and which often have resources comparable to those of large corporations. Minorities in such groups or entities may have interests with respect to institutional speech quite comparable to those of minority shareholders in a corporation. Thus the exclusion of Massachusetts business trusts, real estate investment trusts, labor unions, and other associations undermines the plausibility of the State's purported concern for the persons who happen to be shareholders in the banks and corporations covered by § 8.

The overinclusiveness of the statute is demonstrated by the fact that § 8 would prohibit a corporation from supporting or opposing a referendum proposal even if its shareholders unanimously authorized the contribution or expenditure. Ultimately shareholders may decide, through the procedures of corporate democracy, whether their corporation should engage in debate on public issues.[34] Acting through

---

34. Appellee does not explain why the dissenting shareholder's wishes are entitled to such greater solicitude in this context than in many others where equally important and controversial corporate decisions are made by management or by a predetermined percentage of the shareholders. Mr. Justice WHITE's repeatedly expressed concern for corporate shareholders who may be "coerced" into supporting "causes with which they disagree" apparently is not shared by appellants' shareholders. Not a single shareholder has joined appellee in defending the Massachusetts statute or, so far as the record shows, has interposed any objection to the right asserted by the corporations to make the proscribed expenditures.

The dissent of Mr. Justice WHITE relies heavily on *Abood v. Detroit Board of Education*, 431 U.S. 209 (1977), and *International Assn. of Machinists v. Street*, 367 U.S. 740 (1961). These decisions involved the First Amendment rights of employees in closed or agency shops not to be compelled, as a condition of employment, to support with financial contributions the political activities of other union members with which the dissenters disagreed.

Street and *Abood* are irrelevant to the question presented in this case. In those cases employees were required, either by state law or by agreement between the employer and the union, to pay dues or a "service fee" to the exclusive bargaining representative. To the extent that these funds were used by the union in furtherance of political goals, unrelated to collective bargaining, they were held to be unconstitutional because they compelled the dissenting union member "'to furnish contributions of money for the propagation of opinions which he disbelieves. . . .'" *Abood.*

The critical distinction here is that no shareholder has been "compelled" to contribute anything. Apart from the fact, noted by the dissent, that compulsion by the State is wholly absent, the shareholder invests in a corporation of his own volition and is free to withdraw his investment at any time and for any reason. A more relevant analogy, therefore, is to the situation where an employee voluntarily joins a union, or an individual voluntarily joins an association, and later finds himself in disagreement with its stance on a political issue. The *Street* and *Abood* Courts did not address the question whether, in such a situation, the union or association must refund a portion of the dissenter's dues or, more drastically, refrain from expressing the majority's views. In addition, even apart from the substantive differences between compelled membership in a union and voluntary investment in a corporation or voluntary participation in any collective organization, it is by no means an automatic step from the remedy in *Abood*, which honored the interests of the minority

their power to elect the board of directors or to insist upon protective provisions in the corporation's charter, shareholders normally are presumed competent to protect their own interests. In addition to intracorporate remedies, minority shareholders generally have access to the judicial remedy of a derivative suit to challenge corporate disbursements alleged to have been made for improper corporate purposes or merely to further the personal interests of management.

Assuming, *arguendo*, that protection of shareholders is a "compelling" interest under the circumstances of this case, we find "no substantially relevant correlation between the governmental interest asserted and the State's effort" to prohibit appellants from speaking. *Shelton v. Tucker*, 364 U.S. 479 (1960).

V

Because that portion of § 8 challenged by appellants prohibits protected speech in a manner unjustified by a compelling state interest, it must be invalidated. The judgment of the Supreme Judicial Court is

Reversed.[a]

Mr. Justice WHITE, with whom Mr. Justice BRENNAN and Mr. Justice MARSHALL join, dissenting....

I

There is now little doubt that corporate communications come within the scope of the First Amendment. This, however, is merely the starting point of analysis, because an examination of the First Amendment values that corporate expression furthers and the threat to the functioning of a free society it is capable of posing reveals that it is not fungible with communications emanating from individuals and is subject to restrictions which individual expression is not. Indeed, what some have considered to be the principal function of the First Amendment, the use of communication as a means of self-expression, self-realization, and self-fulfillment, is not at all furthered by corporate speech. It is clear that the communications of profitmaking corporations are not "an integral part of the development of ideas, of mental exploration and of the affirmation of self."[4] They do not represent a manifestation of individual freedom or choice. Undoubtedly, as this Court has recognized, see *NAACP v. Button*, 371 U.S. 415 (1963), there are some corporations formed for the express purpose of advancing certain ideological causes shared by all their members, or, as in the case of the press, of disseminating information and ideas. Under such circumstances, association in a corporate form may be viewed as merely a means of achieving effective self-expression. But this is hardly the case generally with corporations operated for the purpose of making profits. Shareholders in such entities do not share a common set of political or social views, and they certainly

---

without infringing the majority's rights, to the position adopted by the dissent which would completely silence the majority because a hypothetical minority might object.

a. A concurring opinion by Chief Justice Burger is omitted. — Eds.

4. T. Emerson, Toward a General Theory of the First Amendment 5 (1966).

have not invested their money for the purpose of advancing political or social causes or in an enterprise engaged in the business of disseminating news and opinion. In fact, as discussed *infra*, the government has a strong interest in assuring that investment decisions are not predicated upon agreement or disagreement with the activities of corporations in the political arena.

Of course, it may be assumed that corporate investors are united by a desire to make money, for the value of their investment to increase. Since even communications which have no purpose other than that of enriching the communicator have some First Amendment protection, activities such as advertising and other communications integrally related to the operation of the corporation's business may be viewed as a means of furthering the desires of individual shareholders. This unanimity of purpose breaks down, however, when corporations make expenditures or undertake activities designed to influence the opinion or votes of the general public on political and social issues that have no material connection with or effect upon their business, property, or assets. Although it is arguable that corporations make such expenditures because their managers believe that it is in the corporations' economic interest to do so, there is no basis whatsoever for concluding that these views are expressive of the heterogeneous beliefs of their shareholders whose convictions on many political issues are undoubtedly shaped by considerations other than a desire to endorse any electoral or ideological cause which would tend to increase the value of a particular corporate investment. This is particularly true where, as in this case, whatever the belief of the corporate managers may be, they have not been able to demonstrate that the issue involved has any material connection with the corporate business. Thus when a profitmaking corporation contributes to a political candidate this does not further the self-expression or self-fulfillment of its shareholders in the way that expenditures from them as individuals would.

The self-expression of the communicator is not the only value encompassed by the First Amendment. One of its functions, often referred to as the right to hear or receive information, is to protect the interchange of ideas. Any communication of ideas, and consequently any expenditure of funds which makes the communication of ideas possible, it can be argued, furthers the purposes of the First Amendment. This proposition does not establish, however, that the right of the general public to receive communications financed by means of corporate expenditures is of the same dimension as that to hear other forms of expression. In the first place, as discussed *supra*, corporate expenditures designed to further political causes lack the connection with individual self-expression which is one of the principal justifications for the constitutional protection of speech provided by the First Amendment. Ideas which are not a product of individual choice are entitled to less First Amendment protection. Secondly, the restriction of corporate speech concerned with political matters impinges much less severely upon the availability of ideas to the general public than do restrictions upon individual speech. Even the complete curtailment of corporate communications concerning political or ideological questions not integral to day-to-day business functions would leave individuals, including corporate shareholders, employees, and customers, free to communicate their thoughts. Moreover, it is unlikely that any significant communication would be lost by such a prohibition. These individuals would remain perfectly free to communicate any ideas which could be conveyed by means of the corporate form. Indeed, such individuals could even form associations for the very purpose of promoting political or ideological causes. . . .

It bears emphasis here that the Massachusetts statute forbids the expenditure of corporate funds in connection with referenda but in no way forbids the board of directors of a corporation from formulating and making public what it represents as the views of the corporation even though the subject addressed has no material effect whatsoever on the business of the corporation. These views could be publicized at the individual expense of the officers, directors, stockholders, or anyone else interested in circulating the corporate view on matters irrelevant to its business.

The governmental interest in regulating corporate political communications, especially those relating to electoral matters, also raises considerations which differ significantly from those governing the regulation of individual speech. Corporations are artificial entities created by law for the purpose of furthering certain economic goals. In order to facilitate the achievement of such ends, special rules relating to such matters as limited liability, perpetual life, and the accumulation, distribution, and taxation of assets are normally applied to them. States have provided corporations with such attributes in order to increase their economic viability and thus strengthen the economy generally. It has long been recognized however, that the special status of corporations has placed them in a position to control vast amounts of economic power which may, if not regulated, dominate not only the economy but also the very heart of our democracy, the electoral process. Although *Buckley* provides support for the position that the desire to equalize the financial resources available to candidates does not justify the limitation upon the expression of support which a restriction upon individual contributions entails, the interest of Massachusetts and the many other States which have restricted corporate political activity is quite different. It is not one of equalizing the resources of opposing candidates or opposing positions, but rather of preventing institutions which have been permitted to amass wealth as a result of special advantages extended by the State for certain economic purposes from using that wealth to acquire an unfair advantage in the political process, especially where, as here, the issue involved has no material connection with the business of the corporation. The State need not permit its own creation to consume it. Massachusetts could permissibly conclude that not to impose limits upon the political activities of corporations would have placed it in a position of departing from neutrality and indirectly assisting the propagation of corporate views because of the advantages its laws give to the corporate acquisition of funds to finance such activities. Such expenditures may be viewed as seriously threatening the role of the First Amendment as a guarantor of a free marketplace of ideas. Ordinarily, the expenditure of funds to promote political causes may be assumed to bear some relation to the fervency with which they are held. Corporate political expression, however, is not only divorced from the convictions of individual corporate shareholders, but also, because of the ease with which corporations are permitted to accumulate capital, bears no relation to the conviction with which the ideas expressed are held by the communicator.

The Court's opinion appears to recognize at least the possibility that fear of corporate domination of the electoral process would justify restrictions upon corporate expenditures and contributions in connection with referenda but brushes this interest aside by asserting that "there has been no showing that the relative voice of corporations has been overwhelming or even significant in influencing referenda in Massachusetts," and by suggesting that the statute in issue represents an attempt to give an unfair advantage to those who hold views in opposition to positions which would otherwise be financed by corporations. It fails even to allude to the fact, however, that Massachusetts' most recent experience with unrestrained corporate expenditures in connection with ballot questions establishes precisely the contrary. In 1972, a proposed amendment to the Massachusetts Constitution which would have authorized the imposition of a graduated income tax on both individuals and corporations was put to the voters. The Committee for Jobs and Government Economy, an organized political committee, raised and expended approximately $120,000 to oppose the proposed amendment, the bulk of it raised through large corporate contributions. Three of the present appellant corporations each contributed $3,000 to this committee. In contrast, the Coalition for Tax Reform, Inc., the only political committee organized to support the 1972 amendment, was able to raise and expend only approximately $7,000. Perhaps these figures reflect the Court's view of the appropriate role which corporations should play in the Massachusetts electoral process, but it nowhere explains why it is entitled to substitute its judgment for that of Massachusetts and other States, as well as the United States, which have acted to correct or prevent similar domination of the electoral process by corporate wealth.

This Nation has for many years recognized the need for measures designed to prevent corporate domination of the political process. The Corrupt Practices Act, first enacted in 1907, has consistently barred corporate contributions in connection with federal elections. This Court has repeatedly recognized that one of the principal purposes of this prohibition is "to avoid the deleterious influences on federal elections resulting from the use of money by those who exercise control over large aggregations of capital." *United States v. Automobile Workers*, 352 U.S. 567 (1957). Although this Court has never adjudicated the constitutionality of the Act, there is no suggestion in its cases construing it . . . that this purpose is in any sense illegitimate or deserving of other than the utmost respect; indeed, the thrust of its opinions, until today, has been to the contrary.

II

There is an additional overriding interest related to the prevention of corporate domination which is substantially advanced by Massachusetts' restrictions upon corporate contributions: assuring that shareholders are not compelled to support and financially further beliefs with which they disagree where, as is the case here, the issue involved does not materially affect the business, property, or other affairs of the corporation. . . .

Mr. Justice REHNQUIST, dissenting.

This Court decided at an early date, with neither argument nor discussion, that a business corporation is a "person" entitled to the protection of the Equal Protection Clause of the Fourteenth Amendment. Likewise, it soon became accepted that the property of a corporation was protected under the Due Process Clause of that same Amendment. Nevertheless, we concluded soon thereafter that the liberty protected by that Amendment "is the liberty of natural, not artificial persons." *Northwestern Nat. Life Ins. Co. v. Riggs*, 203 U.S. 243 (1906). Before today, our only considered and explicit departures from that holding have been that a corporation engaged in the business of publishing or broadcasting enjoys the same liberty of the press as is enjoyed by natural persons, *Grosjean v. American Press Co.*, 297 U.S. 233 (1936), and that a nonprofit membership corporation organized for the purpose of "achieving . . . equality of treatment by all government, federal, state and local, for the members of the Negro community" enjoys certain liberties of political expression. *NAACP v. Button*, 371 U.S. 415 (1963).

The question presented today, whether business corporations have a constitutionally protected liberty to engage in political activities, has never been squarely addressed by any previous decision of this Court. However, the General Court of the Commonwealth of Massachusetts, the Congress of the United States, and the legislatures of 30 other States of this Republic have considered the matter, and have concluded that restrictions upon the political activity of business corporations are both politically desirable and constitutionally permissible. The judgment of such a broad consensus of governmental bodies expressed over a period of many decades is entitled to considerable deference from this Court. I think it quite probable that their judgment may properly be reconciled with our controlling precedents, but I am certain that under my views of the limited application of the First Amendment to the States, which I share with the two immediately preceding occupants of my seat on the Court, but not with my present colleagues, the judgment of the Supreme Judicial Court of Massachusetts should be affirmed.

Early in our history, Mr. Chief Justice Marshall described the status of a corporation in the eyes of federal law:

> A corporation is an artificial being, invisible, intangible, and existing only in contemplation of law. Being the mere creature of law, it possesses only those properties which the charter of creation confers upon it, either expressly, or as incidental to its very existence. These are such as are supposed best calculated to effect the object for which it was created.

Dartmouth College v. Woodward, 4 Wheat. 518, 636 (1819). The appellants herein either were created by the Commonwealth or were admitted into the Commonwealth only for the limited purposes described in their charters and regulated by state law. Since it cannot be disputed that the mere creation of a corporation does not invest it with all the liberties enjoyed by natural persons, our inquiry must seek to determine which constitutional protections are "incidental to its very existence." *Dartmouth College.*

There can be little doubt that when a State creates a corporation with the power to acquire and utilize property, it necessarily and implicitly guarantees that the corporation will not be deprived of that property absent due process of law. Likewise, when a State charters a corporation for the purpose of publishing a newspaper, it necessarily assumes that the corporation is entitled to the liberty of the press essential to the conduct of its business. *Grosjean* so held, and our subsequent cases have so assumed. Until recently, it was not thought that any persons, natural or artificial, had any protected right to engage in commercial speech. Although the Court has never explicitly recognized a corporation's right of commercial speech, such a right might be considered necessarily incidental to the business of a commercial corporation.

It cannot be so readily concluded that the right of political expression is equally necessary to carry out the functions of a corporation organized for commercial purposes. A State grants to a business corporation the blessings of potentially perpetual life and limited liability to enhance its efficiency as an economic entity. It might reasonably be concluded that those properties, so beneficial in the economic sphere, pose special dangers in the political sphere. Furthermore, it might be argued that liberties of political expression are not at all necessary to effectuate the purposes for which States permit commercial corporations to exist. So long as the Judicial Branches of the State and Federal Governments remain open to protect the corporation's interest in its property, it has no need, though it may have the desire, to petition the political branches for similar protection. Indeed, the States might reasonably fear that the corporation would use its economic power to obtain further benefits beyond those already bestowed.[6] I would think that any particular form of organization upon which the State confers special privileges or immunities different

6. The question of whether [restrictions such as § 8] are politically desirable is exclusively for decision by the political branches of the Federal Government and by the States, and may not be reviewed here. My Brother WHITE, in his dissenting opinion, puts the legislative determination in its most appealing light when he says:

"[T]he interest of Massachusetts and the many other States which have restricted corporate political activity . . . is not one of equalizing the resources of opposing candidates or opposing positions, but rather of preventing institutions which have been permitted to amass wealth as a result of special advantages extended by the State for certain economic purposes from using that wealth to acquire an unfair advantage in the political process . . ."

As I indicate in the text, I agree that this is a rational basis for sustaining the legislation here in question. But I cannot agree with my Brother WHITE's intimation that this is in fact the reason that the Massachusetts General Court enacted this legislation. If inquiry into legislative motives were to determine the outcome of cases such as this, I think a very persuasive argument could be made that the General Court, desiring to impose a personal income tax but more than once defeated in that desire by the combination of the Commonwealth's referendum provision and corporate expenditures in opposition to such a tax, simply decided to muzzle corporations on this sort of issue so that it could succeed in its desire.

from those of natural persons would be subject to like regulation, whether the organization is a labor union, a partnership, a trade association, or a corporation.

One need not adopt such a restrictive view of the political liberties of business corporations to affirm the judgment of the Supreme Judicial Court in this case. That court reasoned that this Court's decisions entitling the property of a corporation to constitutional protection should be construed as recognizing the liberty of a corporation to express itself on political matters concerning that property. Thus, the Court construed the statute in question not to forbid political expression by a corporation "when a general political issue materially affects a corporation's business, property or assets."

I can see no basis for concluding that the liberty of a corporation to engage in political activity with regard to matters having no material effect on its business is necessarily incidental to the purposes for which the Commonwealth permitted these corporations to be organized or admitted within its boundaries. Nor can I disagree with the Supreme Judicial Court's factual finding that no such effect has been shown by these appellants. Because the statute as construed provides at least as much protection as the Fourteenth Amendment requires, I believe it is constitutionally valid.

It is true, as the Court points out, that recent decisions of this Court have emphasized the interest of the public in receiving the information offered by the speaker seeking protection. The free flow of information is in no way diminished by the Commonwealth's decision to permit the operation of business corporations with limited rights of political expression. All natural persons, who owe their existence to a higher sovereign than the Commonwealth, remain as free as before to engage in political activity.

I would affirm the judgment of the Supreme Judicial Court.

Notes and Questions

1. Justice Powell wrote in *Bellotti*, "The Constitution 'protects expression which is eloquent no less than that which is unconvincing.'" Is eloquence in campaign speech equivalent to persuasiveness, as Justice Powell seems to assume? Consider the following anecdote, described by Arthur Samish, the most powerful lobbyist in California in the 1930s and 40s.

Samish placed an initiative proposal on the ballot to give a tax break to the bus and truck industry, which he represented. He tried to "educate the voting public on

---

If one believes, as my Brother WHITE apparently does, that a function of the First Amendment is to protect the interchange of ideas, he cannot readily subscribe to the idea that, if the desire to muzzle corporations played a part in the enactment of this legislation, the General Court was simply engaged in deciding which First Amendment values to promote....

But I think the Supreme Judicial Court was correct in concluding that, whatever may have been the motive of the General Court, the law thus challenged did not violate the United States Constitution.

the need for standard taxation for buses, pointing out that 1,700 small communities had no other public transportation besides buses." But railroad companies succeeded in defeating the initiative with a large advertising campaign.

The next election, Samish tried again. He hired "a well-known cartoonist named Johnny Argens to draw a picture of a big, fat, ugly pig." The pig was placed on billboards throughout California with the slogan:

> DRIVE THE HOG FROM THE ROAD! VOTE YES ON PROPOSITION NUMBER 2

Samish also distributed millions of handbills containing the pig and the same slogan. He points out that he always spelled out the word "Number." If he used the abbreviation "No. 2," "the voter might get confused and think he should vote 'No.'" Samish reports that his plan worked.

> Boy, did it work! Nobody likes a roadhog, and the voters flocked to the polls and passed the constitutional amendment by 700,000!
>
> All because the voters thought they were voting against roadhogs. That had nothing to do with it.

See Arthur H. Samish & Bob Thomas, The Secret Boss of California 37–38 (1971).

Was Samish's campaign literature in favor of "Proposition Number 2" eloquent? Was it persuasive? Was it the kind of speech that merits the full protection of the First Amendment?

2. Justice Powell's opinion contains the statement that if "appellee's arguments were supported by record or legislative findings that corporate advocacy threatened imminently to undermine democratic processes, thereby denigrating rather than serving First Amendment interests, these arguments would merit our consideration." Is it possible, then, that in a different case a ban on corporate financial resources being used in ballot measure campaigns would be upheld? What kind of record evidence or legislative findings, if any, would lead to such a result? Would Samish's anecdote in the previous note be relevant? Would evidence that corporations often achieved electoral success by such tactics be sufficient? See generally John S. Shockley, *Direct Democracy, Campaign Finance, and the Courts: Can Corruption, Undue Influence and Declining Voter Confidence be Found?*, 39 University of Miami Law Review 377 (1985). Shockley writes, at 389–90:

> The Court's distinction between domination and legitimate persuasion probably hinges on *perception*. In other words, only if voters perceive big money as dominating the process, thereby alienating citizens, reducing voter turnout, and undermining the democratic process, should campaign finance reform curb such influence. Requiring a public perception of domination adds a second stage to the process, complicating the matter considerably. If the public were to recognize the overwhelming impact of campaign funds on direct democracy, would money simultaneously become

> less influential, as in a self-negating prophecy? What if the public does not perceive money as being dominant, but it is? Or, less likely, what if the public perceives money as being dominant, but the public is wrong? On this question of perception, is it not relevant that so many states and municipalities—often through direct voter approval of the specific laws—have tried to limit money in ballot proposition campaigns? Is this an indication that the public already perceives and understands the power of money to dominate the electoral process? For what other purposes would these states enact such laws? Unfortunately, the Court has chosen not to answer these questions.

Consider the following more recent statistics:

> Public opinion polls conducted in California shed some light on the perception question. In 2004, 48% of respondents to a Field poll believed that statewide ballot proposition elections come out the way "a few organized special interests want" rather than "the way most people want." Only one-third believed that the initiative elections came out the way most people want (10% were mixed and 9% had no opinion). The "Special Interest" response was up five percentage points over the 1999 survey, and the "Most People Want" response was down nine percentage points. More negatively, a February 2001 survey by the Public Policy Institute found that 52% of Californians believe the initiative process was controlled "a lot" by special interests, and another 44% thought it was controlled "somewhat" by them. Some of this skepticism translates into support for campaign finance reform of ballot measure campaigns. In a 1997 Field poll study, 77% of voters favored limits on the amount of money that can be spent by supporters and opponents of statewide ballot measure campaigns. These statistics appear to show that a large number of voters (though not necessarily a majority) are concerned about the role of money in the initiative process.
>
> These statistics do not, however, tell the full story. By large majorities, Californians approve of statewide ballot measure elections. In 2004, 68% of Californians thought statewide ballot proposition elections were a "good thing" and another 17% had a "mixed" opinion while only 9% saw them as a bad thing. The "good thing" figure is down from a high of 83% in 1979, but is higher than the low of 62% in 1999. When asked in 2004 whether the voting public or elected representatives could be better trusted to make decisions in the public interest, respondents favored the voting public over the legislature 56% to 35%. In addition, 67% of respondents thought elected representatives were more easily influenced and manipulated by special interest groups, compared to 24% who thought the public was more easily influenced and manipulated.

Richard L. Hasen, *Rethinking the Unconstitutionality of Contribution and Expenditure Limits in Ballot Measure Campaigns*, 78 Southern California Law Review 885, 911–12 (2005).

3. *Bellotti* bars expenditure limits in ballot measure campaigns. In *Citizens Against Rent Control v. City of Berkeley*, 454 U.S. 290 (1981) (*CARC*), the Court struck down a $250 limit on contributions to committees formed to support or oppose municipal ballot measures. The Court relied heavily on *Bellotti* and on the First Amendment right of association. We return to a discussion of *CARC* in the next chapter.

4. Given *Buckley* (not to mention *Bellotti* and *CARC*), it is clear that a state may not limit total spending for or against ballot propositions. For a decision so holding, see *Citizens for Jobs and Energy v. Fair Political Practices Commission*, 547 P.2d 1386 (Cal. 1976).

5. Bellotti *as a Corporations Case.* Although we have considered *Bellotti* primarily for what it says about regulating the financing of ballot measure elections, it also has great significance for the law governing the regulation of campaign finance activities by corporations and other targeted entities. In *Bellotti*, Justice Powell avoided direct consideration whether corporations have First Amendment rights by stating that the significant issue was the right of the public to hear the speech that issues from corporations. The Supreme Court addressed the issue directly decades later in the 2010 *Citizens United* case, reprinted below.

6. Does the Court's opinion leave open the possibility of a statute that would require advance stockholder approval of a corporation's political contributions?

II. Limiting Spending by Corporations, Labor Unions, and Others in Candidate Elections

Bellotti involved a state law limiting expenditures by corporations in ballot measure campaigns. At the federal level (where there are no ballot measure elections), the earliest campaign finance restriction targeted contributions by corporations. Such contributions were prohibited, and during the World War II period the prohibition was extended to labor unions and clearly applied to prohibit corporate and union independent expenditures as well. For a detailed historical account, see Robert E. Mutch, Campaigns, Congress, and Courts (1988); see also Robert E. Mutch, *Before and After* Bellotti: *The Corporate Political Contribution Cases*, 5 Election Law Journal 293 (2006). In the 1970s, the Federal Corrupt Practices Act, which contained these prohibitions, was merged into the Federal Election Campaign Act. It was formerly codified at 2 U.S.C. § 441b and now appears at 52 U.S.C. § 30118.

Prior to the adoption of the FECA, the Corrupt Practices Act was rarely enforced. Most of the few cases that were prosecuted were brought against labor unions. Three of these cases reached the Supreme Court, and in each instance the union in question challenged the constitutionality of a ban on union contributions. In each case, the Court either interpreted the law so as not to apply to the alleged conduct or otherwise avoided deciding the constitutional issue. See *United States v. CIO*, 335 U.S. 106 (1948); *United States v. United Automobile Workers*, 352 U.S. 567 (1957);

Pipefitters Local Union No. 562 v. United States, 407 U.S. 385 (1972). In *UAW*, in particular, the Court seemed to stretch very hard to avoid adjudicating the constitutional question.[b]

When the ban on corporate and labor contributions was reenacted as part of the original FECA, adopted in 1971, it was qualified by express provisions authorizing corporations and unions to use their funds to pay administrative expenses of "separate segregated funds"—now almost universally referred to as PACs—which in turn could contribute to federal candidates out of voluntary contributions they received from individuals. Many unions and some corporations had been using PACs, but their legality had been questionable. In *Pipefitters, supra*, the Supreme Court finally ruled that under the prior law PACs were permissible, but by that time Congress, in the FECA, had adopted rules legalizing and governing PACs.

The Court in *Buckley* did not consider the constitutionality of the spending limits applied to corporations and labor unions in candidate elections, and footnote 26 of *Bellotti* the Court suggested that such limits could well be constitutional: "The overriding concern behind the enactment of statutes such as the Federal Corrupt Practices Act was the problem of corruption of elected representatives through the creation of political debts. The importance of the governmental interest in preventing this occurrence has never been doubted. The case before us presents no comparable problem, and our consideration of a corporation's right to speak on issues of general public interest implies no comparable right in the quite different context of participation in a political campaign for election to public office. Congress might well be able to demonstrate the existence of a danger of real or apparent corruption in independent expenditures by corporations to influence candidate elections."

The Court first confronted the question of corporate spending limits in candidate elections more directly in *Federal Election Commission v. Massachusetts Citizens for Life*, 479 U.S. 238 (1986) (*MCFL*). In that case, an incorporated anti-abortion group published a special edition of its newsletter

> prior to the September 1978 primary elections [for Congress]. While the May 1978 newsletter had been mailed to 2,109 people and the October 1978 newsletter to 3,119 people, more than 100,000 copies of the "Special Edition" were printed for distribution. The front page of the publication was headlined "EVERYTHING YOU NEED TO KNOW TO VOTE PRO-LIFE," and readers were admonished that "[n]o pro-life candidate can win in November without your vote in September." "VOTE PRO-LIFE" was printed in large bold-faced letters on the back page, and a coupon was provided to be clipped and taken to the polls to remind voters of the name of the "pro-life" candidates. Next to the exhortation to vote "pro-life" was a disclaimer:

b. *UAW*, written by Justice Frankfurter, is also noteworthy for its account of the history of federal campaign finance regulation.

> "This special election edition does not represent an endorsement of any particular candidate."
>
> To aid the reader in selecting candidates, the flyer listed the candidates for each state and federal office in every voting district in Massachusetts, and identified each one as either supporting or opposing what MCFL regarded as the correct position on three issues. A "y" indicated that a candidate supported the MCFL view on a particular issue and an "n" indicated that the candidate opposed it. An asterisk was placed next to the names of those incumbents who had made a "special contribution to the unborn in maintaining a 100% pro-life voting record in the state house by actively supporting MCFL legislation." While some 400 candidates were running for office in the primary, the "Special Edition" featured the photographs of only 13. These 13 had received a triple "y" rating, or were identified either as having a 100% favorable voting record or as having stated a position consistent with that of MCFL. No candidate whose photograph was featured had received even one "n" rating.

A complaint was filed alleging that *MCFL* violated section 441b (now 52 U.S.C. § 30118) by spending corporate treasury funds on the newsletter. The case eventually reached the Supreme Court.

The Court rejected MCFL's argument that it did not violate section 441b because its newsletter contained no express advocacy or because it should be entitled to an exemption from section 441b as a press entity:

> [Appellee] argues that the definition of an expenditure under § 441b necessarily incorporates the requirement that a communication "expressly advocate" the election of candidates, and that its "Special Edition" does not constitute express advocacy. The argument relies on the portion of *Buckley* that upheld the disclosure requirement for expenditures by individuals other than candidates and by groups other than political committees. There, in order to avoid problems of overbreadth, the Court held that the term "expenditure" encompassed "only funds used for communications that expressly advocate the election or defeat of a clearly identified candidate." . . .
>
> We agree with appellee that [the rationale for the *Buckley* ruling] requires a similar construction of the more intrusive provision that directly regulates independent spending. We therefore hold that an expenditure must constitute "express advocacy" in order to be subject to the prohibition of § 441b. We also hold, however, that the publication of the "Special Edition" constitutes "express advocacy."
>
> *Buckley* adopted the "express advocacy" requirement to distinguish discussion of issues and candidates from more pointed exhortations to vote for particular persons. We therefore concluded in that case that a finding of "express advocacy" depended upon the use of language such as "vote for,"

"elect," "support," etc. Just such an exhortation appears in the "Special Edition." The publication not only urges voters to vote for "pro-life" candidates, but also identifies and provides photographs of specific candidates fitting that description. The Edition cannot be regarded as a mere discussion of public issues that by their nature raise the names of certain politicians. Rather, it provides in effect an explicit directive: vote for these (named) candidates. The fact that this message is marginally less direct than "Vote for Smith" does not change its essential nature. The Edition goes beyond issue discussion to express electoral advocacy. The disclaimer of endorsement cannot negate this fact. The "Special Edition" thus falls squarely within § 441b, for it represents express advocacy of the election of particular candidates distributed to members of the general public.

Finally, MCFL argues that it is entitled to the press exemption under [52 U.S.C. § 30101(9)(B)(i)] reserved for "any news story, commentary, or editorial distributed through the facilities of any . . . newspaper, magazine, or other periodical publication, unless such facilities are owned or controlled by any political party, political committee, or candidate."

MCFL maintains that its regular newsletter is a "periodical publication" within this definition, and that the "Special Edition" should be regarded as just another issue in the continuing newsletter series. The legislative history on the press exemption is sparse; the House of Representatives' Report on this section states merely that the exemption was designed to

> make it plain that it is not the intent of Congress in the present legislation to limit or burden in any way the first amendment freedoms of the press or of association. [The exemption] assures the unfettered right of the newspapers, TV networks, and other media to cover and comment on political campaigns.

We need not decide whether the regular MCFL newsletter is exempt under this provision, because, even assuming that it is, the "Special Edition" cannot be considered comparable to any single issue of the newsletter. It was not published through the facilities of the regular newsletter, but by a staff which prepared no previous or subsequent newsletters. It was not distributed to the newsletter's regular audience, but to a group 20 times the size of that audience, most of whom were members of the public who had never received the newsletter. No characteristic of the Edition associated it in any way with the normal MCFL publication. The MCFL masthead did not appear on the flyer, and, despite an apparent belated attempt to make it appear otherwise, the Edition contained no volume and issue number identifying it as one in a continuing series of issues.

MCFL protests that determining the scope of the press exemption by reference to such factors inappropriately focuses on superficial considerations of form. However, it is precisely such factors that in combination permit the

> distinction of campaign flyers from regular publications. We regard such an inquiry as essential, since we cannot accept the notion that the distribution of such flyers by entities that happen to publish newsletters automatically entitles such organizations to the press exemption. A contrary position would open the door for those corporations and unions with in-house publications to engage in unlimited spending directly from their treasuries to distribute campaign material to the general public, thereby eviscerating § 441b's prohibition.[5]

The Court then considered whether it would be constitutional to limit independent spending by corporations, suggesting in dicta that the corporate limit ordinarily would be constitutional as applied to for-profit corporations, but holding that the rules could not be applied against an ideological corporation such as MCFL:

> When a statutory provision burdens First Amendment rights, it must be justified by a compelling state interest. The FEC first insists that justification for § 441b's expenditure restriction is provided by this Court's acknowledgment that "the special characteristics of the corporate structure require particularly careful regulation." *Federal Election Commission v. National Right to Work Committee*, 459 U.S. 197 (1982) ("*NRWC*") The Commission thus relies on the long history of regulation of corporate political activity as support for the application of § 441b to MCFL. Evaluation of the Commission's argument requires close examination of the underlying rationale for this longstanding regulation.
>
> We have described that rationale in recent opinions as the need to restrict "the influence of political war chests funneled through the corporate form," *NCPAC*; to "eliminate the effect of aggregated wealth on federal elections," *Pipefitters*; to curb the political influence of "those who exercise control over large aggregations of capital," *Automobile Workers*; and to regulate the "substantial aggregations of wealth amassed by the special advantages which go with the corporate form of organization," *NRWC*.
>
> This concern over the corrosive influence of concentrated corporate wealth reflects the conviction that it is important to protect the integrity of the marketplace of political ideas. It acknowledges the wisdom of Justice Holmes' observation that "the ultimate good desired is better reached by free trade in ideas — that the best test of truth is the power of the thought to get itself accepted in the competition of the market. . . ." *Abrams v. United States*, 250 U.S. 616, 630 (1919) (Holmes, J., joined by Brandeis, J., dissenting).

5. Nor do we find the "Special Edition" akin to the normal business activity of a press entity deemed by some lower courts to fall within the exemption, such as the distribution of a letter soliciting subscriptions, see *FEC v. Phillips Publishing Co.*, 517 F.Supp. 1308, 1313 (DC 1981), or the dissemination of publicity, see *Reader's Digest Assn. v. FEC*, 509 F.Supp. 1210 (SDNY 1981).

> Direct corporate spending on political activity raises the prospect that resources amassed in the economic marketplace may be used to provide an unfair advantage in the political marketplace. Political "free trade" does not necessarily require that all who participate in the political marketplace do so with exactly equal resources. See *NCPAC*; *Buckley*. Relative availability of funds is after all a rough barometer of public support. The resources in the treasury of a business corporation, however, are not an indication of popular support for the corporation's political ideas. They reflect instead the economically motivated decisions of investors and customers. The availability of these resources may make a corporation a formidable political presence, even though the power of the corporation may be no reflection of the power of its ideas.
>
> By requiring that corporate independent expenditures be financed through a political committee expressly established to engage in campaign spending, § 441b seeks to prevent this threat to the political marketplace. The resources available to *this* fund, as opposed to the corporate treasury, in fact reflect popular support for the political positions of the committee.[11] The expenditure restrictions of § 441b are thus meant to ensure that competition among actors in the political arena is truly competition among ideas.
>
> Regulation of corporate political activity thus has reflected concern not about use of the corporate form *per se*, but about the potential for unfair deployment of wealth for political purposes.[12] Groups such as MCFL, however, do not pose that danger of corruption. MCFL was formed to disseminate political ideas, not to amass capital. The resources it has available are not a function of its success in the economic marketplace, but its popularity in the political marketplace. While MCFL may derive some advantages from its corporate form, those are advantages that redound to its benefit as a political organization, not as a profit-making enterprise. In short, MCFL is not the type of "traditional corporatio[n] organized for economic gain," *NCPAC*, that has been the focus of regulation of corporate political activity.

The Court then summarized the features of MCFL relevant to its ability to gain an exemption from section 441b:

---

11. While business corporations may not represent the only organizations that pose this danger, they are by far the most prominent example of entities that enjoy legal advantages enhancing their ability to accumulate wealth. That Congress does not at present seek to regulate every possible type of firm fitting this description does not undermine its justification for regulating corporations. Rather, Congress' decision represents the "careful legislative adjustment of the federal electoral laws, in a 'cautious advance, step by step,'" to which we have said we owe considerable deference.

12. The regulation imposed as a result of this concern is of course distinguishable from the complete foreclosure of any opportunity for political speech that we invalidated in the state referendum context in *Bellotti*.

> In particular, MCFL has three features essential to our holding that it may not constitutionally be bound by § 441b's restriction on independent spending. *First*, it was formed for the express purpose of promoting political ideas, and cannot engage in business activities. If political fundraising events are expressly denominated as requests for contributions that will be used for political purposes, including direct expenditures, these events cannot be considered business activities. This ensures that political resources reflect political support. *Second*, it has no shareholders or other persons affiliated so as to have a claim on its assets or earnings. This ensures that persons connected with the organization will have no economic disincentive for disassociating with it if they disagree with its political activity. *Third*, MCFL was not established by a business corporation or a labor union, and it is its policy not to accept contributions from such entities. This prevents such corporations from serving as conduits for the type of direct spending that creates a threat to the political marketplace.

A few years after *MCFL*, the Supreme Court considered the constitutionality of campaign spending limits in candidate campaigns applied against corporations not entitled to the *MCFL* exemption. In *Austin v. Michigan Chamber of Commerce*, 494 U.S. 652 (1990), the Court upheld a Michigan law that barred the use of a corporation's general (treasury) funds spent on elections. As under federal law, Michigan law allowed the corporation to set up a separate PAC, soliciting funds from its executives and shareholders, to contribute and spend in candidate elections. The nonprofit Michigan Chamber of Commerce challenged the rule limiting its spending as a First Amendment violation. It also argued that it was treated worse than media corporations, raising an equal protection issue.

The Court first held that the chamber was not entitled to the *MCFL* exemption because it took money from for-profit business corporations, leaving the Court to address head-on whether or not direct corporate spending in candidate elections could be barred from the corporate treasury and limited to the corporate PAC. The Court, in a 6-3 opinion written by Justice Thurgood Marshall, answered in the affirmative:

> The State contends that the unique legal and economic characteristics of corporations necessitate some regulation of their political expenditures to avoid corruption or the appearance of corruption. See *NCPAC* ("[P]reventing corruption or the appearance of corruption are the only legitimate and compelling government interests thus far identified for restricting campaign finances"). State law grants corporations special advantages — such as limited liability, perpetual life, and favorable treatment of the accumulation and distribution of assets — that enhance their ability to attract capital and to deploy their resources in ways that maximize the return on their shareholders' investments. These state-created advantages not only allow corporations to play a dominant role in the Nation's economy, but also permit them to use "resources amassed in the economic marketplace" to

obtain "an unfair advantage in the political marketplace." *MCFL*. As the Court explained in *MCFL*, the political advantage of corporations is unfair because

> [t]he resources in the treasury of a business corporation . . . are not an indication of popular support for the corporation's political ideas. They reflect instead the economically motivated decisions of investors and customers. The availability of these resources may make a corporation a formidable political presence, even though the power of the corporation may be no reflection of the power of its ideas.

We therefore have recognized that "the compelling governmental interest in preventing corruption support[s] the restriction of the influence of political war chests funneled through the corporate form." *NCPAC*.

The Chamber argues that this concern about corporate domination of the political process is insufficient to justify a restriction on independent expenditures. Although this Court has distinguished these expenditures from direct contributions in the context of federal laws regulating individual donors, *Buckley*, it has also recognized that a legislature might demonstrate a danger of real or apparent corruption posed by such expenditures when made by corporations to influence candidate elections, *Bellotti*. Regardless of whether this danger of "financial *quid pro quo*" corruption, see *NCPAC*, may be sufficient to justify a restriction on independent expenditures, Michigan's regulation aims at a different type of corruption in the political arena: the corrosive and distorting effects of immense aggregations of wealth that are accumulated with the help of the corporate form and that have little or no correlation to the public's support for the corporation's political ideas. The Act does not attempt "to equalize the relative influence of speakers on elections," *post* (KENNEDY, J., dissenting); rather, it ensures that expenditures reflect actual public support for the political ideas espoused by corporations. We emphasize that the mere fact that corporations may accumulate large amounts of wealth is not the justification for § 54; rather, the unique state-conferred corporate structure that facilitates the amassing of large treasuries warrants the limit on independent expenditures. Corporate wealth can unfairly influence elections when it is deployed in the form of independent expenditures, just as it can when it assumes the guise of political contributions. We therefore hold that the State has articulated a sufficiently compelling rationale to support its restriction on independent expenditures by corporations.

The Court also rejected the Chamber's argument that the law was unconstitutional because it exempted labor unions and media corporations:

> The Chamber also attacks § 54(1) as underinclusive because it does not regulate the independent expenditures of unincorporated labor unions. Whereas unincorporated unions, and indeed individuals, may be able to

amass large treasuries, they do so without the significant state-conferred advantages of the corporate structure; corporations are "by far the most prominent example of entities that enjoy legal advantages enhancing their ability to accumulate wealth." *MCFL*. The desire to counterbalance those advantages unique to the corporate form is the State's compelling interest in this case; thus, excluding from the statute's coverage unincorporated entities that also have the capacity to accumulate wealth "does not undermine its justification for regulating corporations." *Ibid.*

Moreover, labor unions differ from corporations in that union members who disagree with a union's political activities need not give up full membership in the organization to avoid supporting its political activities. Although a union and an employer may require that all bargaining unit employees become union members, a union may not compel those employees to support financially "union activities beyond those germane to collective bargaining, contract administration, and grievance adjustment." *Communications Workers v. Beck*, 487 U.S. 735, 745 (1988). See also *Abood* (holding that compelling nonmember employees to contribute to union's political activities infringes employees' First Amendment rights). An employee who objects to a union's political activities thus can decline to contribute to those activities, while continuing to enjoy the benefits derived from the union's performance of its duties as the exclusive representative of the bargaining unit on labor-management issues. As a result, the funds available for a union's political activities more accurately reflect[] members' support for the organization's political views than does a corporation's general treasury. Michigan's decision to exclude unincorporated labor unions from the scope of § 54(1) is therefore justified by the crucial differences between unions and corporations. . . .

[W]e find that the Act's exemption of media corporations from the expenditure restriction does not render the statute unconstitutional. . . .

Although all corporations enjoy the same state-conferred benefits inherent in the corporate form, media corporations differ significantly from other corporations in that their resources are devoted to the collection of information and its dissemination to the public. We have consistently recognized the unique role that the press plays in "informing and educating the public, offering criticism, and providing a forum for discussion and debate." *Bellotti*. See also *Mills v. Alabama*, 384 U.S. 214, 219 (1966) ("[T]he press serves and was designed to serve as a powerful antidote to any abuses of power by governmental officials and as a constitutionally chosen means for keeping officials elected by the people responsible to all the people whom they were selected to serve"). . . . The media exception ensures that the Act does not hinder or prevent the institutional press from reporting on, and publishing editorials about, newsworthy events. A valid distinction thus exists between corporations that are part of the media industry and

> other corporations that are not involved in the regular business of imparting news to the public. Although the press' unique societal role may not entitle the press to greater protection under the Constitution, *Bellotti*, it does provide a compelling reason for the State to exempt media corporations from the scope of political expenditure limitations. We therefore hold that the Act does not violate the Equal Protection Clause.

Justices Scalia and Kennedy (joined by Justice O'Connor) wrote dissenting opinions, deriding the majority opinion as fostering censorship. Justice Scalia was particularly derisive of the majority's expansion of the definition of "corruption" to include a concern about the distorting influence of corporate spending. And he deeply criticized Michigan's exception for media corporations:

> The Court's opinion says that political speech of corporations can be regulated because "[s]tate law grants [them] special advantages" and because this "unique state-conferred corporate structure . . . facilitates the amassing of large treasuries." This analysis seeks to create one good argument by combining two bad ones. Those individuals who form that type of voluntary association known as a corporation are, to be sure, given special advantages—notably, the immunization of their personal fortunes from liability for the actions of the association—that the State is under no obligation to confer. But so are other associations and private individuals given all sorts of special advantages that the State need not confer, ranging from tax breaks to contract awards to public employment to outright cash subsidies. It is rudimentary that the State cannot exact as the price of those special advantages the forfeiture of First Amendment rights. See *Pickering v. Board of Education*, 391 U.S. 563 (1968); *Speiser v. Randall*, 357 U.S. 513 (1958). The categorical suspension of the right of any person, or of any association of persons, to speak out on political matters must be justified by a compelling state need. See *Buckley*. That is why the Court puts forward its second bad argument, the fact that corporations "amas[s] large treasuries." But that alone is also not sufficient justification for the suppression of political speech, unless one thinks it would be lawful to prohibit men and women whose net worth is above a certain figure from endorsing political candidates. Neither of these two flawed arguments is improved by combining them and saying, as the Court in effect does, that "since the State gives special advantages to these voluntary associations, and since they thereby amass vast wealth, they may be required to abandon their right of political speech."[1]

---

1. The Court's assertion that the Michigan law "does not impose an *absolute* ban on all forms of corporate political spending," (emphasis added) is true only in a respect that is irrelevant for purposes of First Amendment analysis. A corporation is absolutely prohibited from spending its own funds on this form of political speech, and would be guilty of misrepresentation if it asserted that a particular candidate was supported or opposed by the corporation. This is to say that the corporation *as a corporation* is prohibited from speaking. What the Michigan law permits the corporation to do is to serve as the founder and treasurer of a different association of individuals that can

The Court's extensive reliance upon the fact that the objects of this speech restriction, corporations, receive "special advantages" is in stark contrast to our opinion issued just six years ago in *FCC v. League of Women Voters of California*, 468 U.S. 364 (1984). In that decision, striking down a congressionally imposed ban upon editorializing by noncommercial broadcasting stations that receive federal funds, the *only* respect in which we considered the receipt of that "special advantage" relevant was in determining whether the speech limitation could be justified under Congress' spending power, as a means of assuring that the subsidy was devoted only to the purposes Congress intended, which did not include political editorializing. We held it could not be justified on that basis, since "a noncommercial educational station that receives only 1% of its overall income from [federal] grants is barred absolutely from all editorializing.... The station has no way of limiting the use of its federal funds to all noneditorializing activities, and, more importantly, it is barred from using even wholly private funds to finance its editorial activity." Of course the same is true here, even assuming that tax exemptions and other benefits accorded to incorporated associations constitute an exercise of the spending power. It is not just that portion of the corporation's assets attributable to the gratuitously conferred "special advantages" that is prohibited from being used for political endorsements, but *all* of the corporation's assets. I am at a loss to explain the vast difference between the treatment of the present case and *League of Women Voters*. Commercial corporations may not have a public *persona* as sympathetic as that of public broadcasters, but they are no less entitled to this Court's concern.

As for the second part of the Court's argumentation, the fact that corporations (or at least some of them) possess "massive wealth": Certain uses of "massive wealth" in the electoral process—whether or not the wealth is the result of "special advantages" conferred by the State—pose a substantial risk of corruption which constitutes a compelling need for the regulation of speech. Such a risk plainly exists when the wealth is given directly to the political candidate, to be used under his direction and control. We held in *Buckley*, however, that independent expenditures to express the political views of individuals and associations do not raise a sufficient threat of corruption to justify prohibition. Neither the Court's opinion nor either of the concurrences makes any effort to distinguish that case—except, perhaps, by misdescribing the case as involving "federal laws regulating individual donors," or as involving "individual expenditures," (STEVENS, J.,

endorse or oppose political candidates. The equivalent, where an individual rather than an association is concerned, would be to prohibit John D. Rockefeller from making political endorsements, but to permit him to form an association to which others (though not he himself) can contribute for the purpose of making political endorsements. Just as political speech by that association is not speech by John D. Rockefeller, so also speech by a corporate PAC that the Michigan law allows is not speech by the corporation itself.

concurring). Section 608(e)(1) of the Federal Election Campaign Act of 1971, which we found unconstitutional in *Buckley*, was directed, like the Michigan law before us here, to expenditures made for the purpose of advocating the election or defeat of a particular candidate. It limited to $1,000 (a *lesser* restriction than the absolute prohibition at issue here) such expenditures not merely by "individuals," but by "persons," specifically defined to include corporations. The plaintiffs in the case included corporations, and we specifically discussed § 608(e)(1) as a restriction addressed not just to individuals but to "individuals and groups," "persons and groups," "persons and organizations," "person[s] [and] association[s]." . . . In support of our determination that the restriction was "wholly at odds with the guarantees of the First Amendment" we cited *Miami Herald Publishing Co. v. Tornillo*, 418 U.S. 241 (1974), which involved limitations upon a corporation. Of course, if § 608(e)(1) had been unconstitutional only as applied to individuals and not as applied to corporations, we might nonetheless have invalidated it *in toto* for substantial overbreadth, see *Broadrick v. Oklahoma*, 413 U.S. 601, 611–613 (1973), but there is not a hint of that doctrine in our opinion. Our First Amendment law is much less certain than I had thought it to be if we are free to recharacterize each clear holding as a disguised "overbreadth" determination.

Buckley should not be overruled, because it is entirely correct. The contention that prohibiting overt advocacy for or against a political candidate satisfies a "compelling need" to avoid "corruption" is easily dismissed. As we said in *Buckley*, "[i]t would naively underestimate the ingenuity and resourcefulness of persons and groups desiring to buy influence to believe that they would have much difficulty devising expenditures that skirted the restriction on express advocacy of election or defeat but nevertheless benefited the candidate's campaign." Independent advocacy, moreover, unlike contributions, "may well provide little assistance to the candidate's campaign and indeed may prove counterproductive," thus reducing the danger that it will be exchanged "as a *quid pro quo* for improper commitments from the candidate." The latter point seems even more plainly true with respect to corporate advocates than it is with respect to individuals. I expect I could count on the fingers of one hand the candidates who would generally welcome, much less negotiate for, a formal endorsement by AT & T or General Motors. The advocacy of such entities that have "amassed great wealth" will be effective only to the extent that it brings to the people's attention *ideas* which—despite the invariably self-interested and probably uncongenial source—strike them as true.

The Court does not try to defend the proposition that independent advocacy poses a substantial risk of political "corruption," as English speakers understand that term. Rather, it asserts that that concept (which it defines as "'financial *quid pro quo*' corruption,") is really just a narrow subspecies of a hitherto unrecognized genus of political corruption. "Michigan's regulation," we are told, "aims at a different type of corruption in the political arena: the corrosive and distorting effects of immense aggregations of wealth that are accumulated with the help of the corporate form and that have little or no correlation to the public's support for the corporation's political ideas." Under this mode of analysis, virtually anything the Court deems politically undesirable can be turned into political corruption—by simply describing its effects as politically "corrosive," which is close enough to "corruptive" to qualify. It is sad to think that the First Amendment will ultimately be brought down not by brute force but by poetic metaphor.

The Court's opinion ultimately rests upon that proposition whose violation constitutes the "New Corruption": Expenditures must "reflect actual public support for the political ideas espoused." This illiberal free-speech principle of "one man, one minute" was proposed and soundly rejected in *Buckley*:

> It is argued, however, that the ancillary governmental interest in equalizing the relative ability of individuals and groups to influence the outcome of elections serves to justify the limitation on express advocacy of the election or defeat of candidates imposed by § 608(e)(1)'s expenditure ceiling. But the concept that government may restrict the speech of some elements of our society in order to enhance the relative voice of others is wholly foreign to the First Amendment, which was designed "to secure 'the widest possible dissemination of information from diverse and antagonistic sources,'" and "to assure unfettered interchange of ideas for the bringing about of political and social changes desired by the people."

But it can be said that I have not accurately quoted today's decision. It does not endorse the proposition that government may ensure that expenditures "reflect actual public support for the political ideas espoused," but only the more limited proposition that government may ensure that expenditures "reflect actual public support for the political ideas espoused by corporations." The limitation is of course entirely irrational. Why is it perfectly all right if advocacy by an individual billionaire is out of proportion with "actual public support" for his positions? There is no explanation, except the effort I described at the outset of this discussion to make one valid proposition out of two invalid ones: When the vessel labeled "corruption" begins to founder under weight too great to be logically sustained, the argumentation jumps to the good ship "special privilege"; and when that in turn begins to go down, it returns to "corruption." Thus hopping back and forth between the two, the argumentation may survive but makes no headway towards port, where its conclusion waits in vain. . . .

Finally, a few words are in order concerning the Court's approval of the Michigan law's exception for "media corporations." This is all right, we are told, because of "the unique role that the press plays in 'informing and educating the public, offering criticism, and providing a forum for discussion and debate.'" But if one believes in the Court's rationale of "compelling state need" to prevent amassed corporate wealth from skewing the political debate, surely that "unique role" of the press does not give Michigan justification for *excluding* media corporations from coverage, but provides especially strong reason to include them. Amassed corporate wealth that regularly sits astride the ordinary channels of information is much more likely to produce the New Corruption (too much of one point of view) than amassed corporate wealth that is generally busy making money elsewhere. Such media corporations not only have vastly greater power to perpetrate the evil of overinforming, they also have vastly greater opportunity. General Motors, after all, will risk a stockholder suit if it makes a political endorsement that is not plausibly tied to its ability to make money for its shareholders. But media corporations make money *by* making political commentary, including endorsements. For them, unlike any other corporations, the whole world of politics and ideology is fair game. Yet the Court tells us that it is reasonable to *exclude* media corporations, rather than target them specially.

Members of the institutional press, despite the Court's approval of their illogical exemption from the Michigan law, will find little reason for comfort in today's decision. The theory of New Corruption it espouses is a dagger at their throats. The Court today holds merely that media corporations *may* be excluded from the Michigan law, not that they *must* be. We have consistently rejected the proposition that the institutional press has any constitutional privilege beyond that of other speakers. See *Bellotti*. Thus, the Court's holding on this point must be put in the following unencouraging form: "Although the press' unique societal role may not entitle the press to greater protection under the Constitution, *Bellotti*, it does provide a compelling reason for the State to exempt media corporations from the scope of political expenditure limitations." One must hope, I suppose, that Michigan will continue to provide this generous and voluntary exemption.

Notes and Questions

1. *Austin*'s recognition that corporate spending could be limited to prevent "the corrosive and distorting effects of immense aggregations of wealth that are accumulated with the help of the corporate form and that have little or no correlation to the public's support for the corporation's political ideas" was presaged in the *MCFL* opinion. This is sometimes referred to as the "anti-distortion" rationale.

2. Is the *Austin/MCFL* anti-distortion rationale consistent with *Buckley*'s rejection of the equality rationale for limiting campaign spending?

3. When Justice Scalia asks why it is "perfectly all right if advocacy by an individual billionaire is out of proportion with 'actual public support' for his positions," might one response be that it is *not* all right, and that the inconsistency should be resolved by overruling *Buckley*'s strong protection of independent expenditures? But is there necessarily an inconsistency? Consider Marlene Arnold Nicholson, *Basic Principles or Theoretical Tangles: Analyzing the Constitutionality of Government Regulation of Campaign Finance*, 38 Case Western Reserve Law Review 589, 606 (1988):

> Corporate expression does not reflect the self-realization of actual people. [She adds, in a footnote, "It probably reflects only someone's determination of what will be most profitable for the corporation, which may or may not correspond with anyone's view of good political policy."] Perhaps we must be willing to tolerate the possibility of a coercive influence of concentrated wealth when it represents someone's self-fulfillment, but we need not do so when that element is missing.

Nicholson adds that although this would be a "principled conclusion," she would reject it because the self-realization interest should be considered together with other pertinent values. All would be accommodated, she suggests, "if very generous limitations were applied to independent expenditures, the use of candidate wealth and contributions in ballot measure elections."

4. Is *Austin* consistent with *Bellotti*? Why wouldn't *Austin*'s anti-distortion rationale also justify restrictions on corporate expenditures in ballot measure campaigns?

5. CEOs of two major corporations wish to use substantial corporate resources to elect candidates they prefer for federal office. One CEO is media mogul Rupert Murdoch; the other is the CEO of General Motors. Under *Austin* the government may bar the General Motors CEO from directly using corporate resources for contributions to or independent expenditures for federal candidates. 52 U.S.C. § 30118. But the FECA, like the Michigan statute at issue in *Austin*, contains an exception to the definition of expenditure for "any news story, commentary, or editorial distributed through the facilities of any broadcasting station, newspaper, magazine, or other periodical publication, unless such facilities are owned or controlled by any political party, political committee, or candidate." 52 U.S.C. § 30101(9)(B)(i). So Rupert Murdoch could publish editorial after editorial in his newspapers and magazines urging the election or defeat of candidates for federal office. *Austin* held that the different treatment of media corporations did not render the ban on non-media corporate independent expenditures in candidate campaigns unconstitutional. On what basis did Justice Marshall uphold the different treatment? Are you convinced that the press plays the role that Marshall describes? Does the answer depend upon how the "press" has evolved with the rise of the internet and social media? Reconsider this question after you read the next case.

III. The *Citizens United* Revolution

In the 1974 FECA amendments, Congress sought to impose limits on any spending "relative to a clearly identified candidate [in federal elections]" and to require "'[e]very person ... who makes contributions or expenditures' ... 'for the purpose of ... influencing' the nomination or election of candidates for federal office" to disclose the source of such contributions and expenditures. The Supreme Court in *Buckley* viewed both of these statutes as presenting problems of unconstitutional vagueness; people engaging in political speech might well not know if the statutes cover their conduct.

In order to save both statutes from unconstitutional vagueness, the Court construed them as reaching only "communications that in express terms advocate the election or defeat of a clearly identified candidate." The Court explained that such *express advocacy* required explicit words "of advocacy of election or defeat, such as 'vote for,' 'elect,' 'support,' 'cast your ballot for,' 'Smith for Congress,' 'vote against,' 'defeat,' [or] 'reject.'" So construed, the Court still struck down the spending limits as violating the First Amendment, but it upheld the disclosure requirements (as discussed in Chapter 16).

The upshot of this part of *Buckley* is that advertisements intended to or likely to influence the outcome of an election but lacking words of express advocacy were unregulated by FECA. Such advertisements became known as "issue advocacy," even though the prime issue at stake in many of these advertisements was the election or defeat of a candidate. Thus, an advertisement lacking express advocacy but criticizing Senator Smith in the weeks before the election was not subject to disclosure under FECA, and could be paid for with corporate or union funds, and is subject to no contribution limits. The conduct escapes FECA because the advertisement ends with something like, "Call Smith and tell her what you think of her Medicare plan" rather than "Defeat Smith."

Issue advocacy exploded on the federal election scene in the 1990s and grew quickly in the 2000s. In the face of this explosion after six years of failed attempts, and with impetus from an accounting scandal involving the Enron Corporation that became a hot political issue, Congress passed the most significant campaign finance changes since 1974. The campaign finance proposals had been known as the "McCain-Feingold" and "Shays-Meehan" bills before passage (named for their primary sponsors in the Senate and House, respectively), but campaign finance practitioners now refer to the law under its official title, the Bipartisan Campaign Reform Act of 2002, Pub. L. 107-155, 116 Stat. 81, or "BCRA." The law is quite complex.

We will examine one significant part of BCRA in the next chapter: Congress's ban on party "soft money." Here we focus on how Congress sought to regulate issue advocacy through a new "electioneering communications" test. Under BCRA, corporations and unions may not spend general treasury funds (but may spend PAC funds) on "electioneering communications." An electioneering communication "encompasses any broadcast, cable or satellite communication that refers to a candidate for federal office and that is aired within 30 days of a primary election or 60 days of a federal election in the jurisdiction in which that candidate is running for office." Thus, under section 203 of BCRA, a corporation or union could not use treasury funds to pay for a television advertisement broadcast shortly before the election criticizing Senator Smith by name for her lousy Medicare plan.

By a 5–4 vote, the Supreme Court upheld section 203 of BCRA. *McConnell v. FEC*, 540 U.S. 93 (2003). Eight of the nine Supreme Court Justices deciding *McConnell* rejected any constitutionally significant distinction between express advocacy and issue advocacy. Indeed, as the excerpts from *McConnell*'s disclosure discussion in Chapter 16 detail, eight Justices voted to uphold BCRA's main disclosure provisions, requiring that anyone who spends enough money on "electioneering communications" must disclose such spending as well as most contributions funding that spending. (Only Justice Thomas disagreed on these points.) Thus, eight Justices agreed that the presence of express words of advocacy did not limit the universe of election-related advertising that legislatures may constitutionally regulate.

That determination called *Austin* directly into question because, without a meaningful distinction between express advocacy and issue advocacy, the ban on independent spending by corporations and unions upheld in *Austin* was far more extensive than at the time *Austin* was decided. Furthermore, the only way to attack the electioneering provision was to attack the constitutionality of limits on *express* advocacy by corporations and unions. Thus, the focus shifted to the constitutionality of preventing corporations and unions from engaging in unlimited independent expenditures (whether containing words of express advocacy or not) mentioning candidates for federal office.

Recall that *Austin* was a 6–3 decision. Justices Kennedy, O'Connor, and Scalia dissented in *Austin*, and of the six-member majority, only Justice Stevens and Chief Justice Rehnquist remained on the Court. In *McConnell*, Chief Justice Rehnquist changed his vote, concurring with Justice Kennedy that *Austin* was wrongly decided and should be overruled. What saved *Austin*, and indeed led to its affirmation in *McConnell*, was the switch in position by Justice O'Connor, who joined with Justices Breyer, Ginsburg, Souter, and Stevens in the majority opinion on Title II. This was not the first time that Justice O'Connor had changed her vote on this question. Recall her vote in *MCFL*.

McConnell was also significant in extending the PAC requirement to labor unions. The *Austin* Court did not have before it a separate fund requirement for unions; indeed, the *Austin* Court held it was permissible to restrict corporations without extending the requirement to unions. Without any explicit discussion, the *McConnell* Court upheld the treatment of unions under the *Austin* rationale.

BCRA seemed to have a larger immediate effect on corporations than unions. Of corporations giving more than $100,000 in soft money in both 2000 and 2002, the amount of spending from corporate treasury funds fell in 2004 from $113.2 million (in soft money) in 2000 to $6.1 million (given to "527" organizations). Robert G.

Boatright et al., *Interest Group and Advocacy Organizations After BCRA*, in The Election After Reform: Money, Politics, and the Bipartisan Campaign Reform Act 112, 118 (Michael J. Malbin, ed., 2006). As for labor unions in the 2004 elections, "the flow of treasury funds to political parties was also halted, but most of the dollars appear to have been spent elsewhere, either directly or in the form of contributions to Democratic-leaning 527s." Thomas E. Mann, *Lessons for Reformers*, in Financing the 2004 Election 241, 249 (David B. Magleby et al., eds., 2006).

McConnell turned out to be a ringing endorsement of the deferential approach the Court had taken to campaign finance regulation beginning with *Shrink Missouri*, a contributions case we will consider in the next chapter. But *McConnell*'s endorsement of *Austin* was short-lived, and the replacement of Justice O'Connor with Justice Alito caused Supreme Court doctrine to reverse completely.

In *Wisconsin Right to Life v. Federal Election Commission* (*WRTL I*), 546 U.S. 410 (2006), decided as Justice O'Connor was leaving the Court, the Court held that *McConnell* did not preclude an "as applied" challenge to BCRA § 203 for a corporation or union whose ads were not the "'functional equivalent' of express advocacy." *WRTL I* involved a corporate-funded broadcast advertising that mentioned Senator Feingold's and Senator Kohl's position on judicial filibusters, and was to be broadcast in Wisconsin during the period of Senator Feingold's reelection campaign. After remand, in which the lower court found the ads were not entitled to an exemption because they were the functional equivalent of express advocacy, the case returned to the Supreme Court.

In *Federal Election Commission v. Wisconsin Right to Life*, (*WRTL II*), 551 U.S. 449 (2007), the Court held, on a 5–4 vote, that BCRA § 203 could not be constitutionally applied to such ads. Three Justices in the majority (Justices Kennedy, Scalia, and Thomas) held, consistent with their dissenting opinions in *McConnell*, that BCRA § 203 was unconstitutional as applied to *any* corporate advertising, stating that *McConnell* and *Austin* should be overruled. Chief Justice Roberts and Justice Alito, in a narrower controlling opinion, did not reach the question whether *McConnell* and *Austin* should be overruled. They wrote instead that the only corporate-funded advertisements that BCRA could bar constitutionally were those that were the "functional equivalent of express advocacy."

The controlling opinion held that in making the "functional equivalent" determination, the question the FEC or a court must consider is whether, without regard to context (such as the fact that the filibuster issue was one that conservatives were using to attack liberal Democrats) and without detailed discovery of the intentions of the advertisers, the advertisement was susceptible of no reasonable interpretation other than as an advertisement supporting or opposing a candidate for office. Unless the ad was susceptible to "no reasonable interpretation" other than as an advertisement supporting or opposing the candidate, it would be unconstitutional to apply BCRA § 203 to bar corporate funding for it. The controlling opinion then held that the ad at issue in *WRTL II* was susceptible to an interpretation as something other than an ad against Senator Feingold: it did not mention Senator Feingold's character or fitness for office, and had no other clear indicia of the functional equivalent of express advocacy. Accordingly, WRTL was entitled to an as-applied exemption and could pay for the ads with corporate funds. It created a loophole to BCRA § 203 that appeared quite extensive.

WRTL II's controlling "no reasonable interpretation" test too was short-lived, thanks to the following opinion, which overruled *Austin* and the relevant part of *McConnell* on corporate spending limits in candidate elections.

Citizens United v. Federal Election Commission

558 U.S. 310 (2010)

Justice KENNEDY delivered the opinion of the Court.

Federal law prohibits corporations and unions from using their general treasury funds to make independent expenditures for speech defined as an "electioneering communication" or for speech expressly advocating the election or defeat of a candidate. 2 U.S.C. § 441b [now codified at 52 U.S.C. § 30118]. Limits on electioneering communications were upheld in *McConnell v. Federal Election Comm'n* (2003). The holding of *McConnell* rested to a large extent on an earlier case, *Austin. Austin* had held that political speech may be banned based on the speaker's corporate identity.

In this case we are asked to reconsider *Austin* and, in effect, *McConnell.* It has been noted that "*Austin* was a significant departure from ancient First Amendment principles," (*WRTL*) (SCALIA, J., concurring in part and concurring in judgment). We agree with that conclusion and hold that *stare decisis* does not compel the continued acceptance of *Austin.* The Government may regulate corporate political speech through disclaimer and disclosure requirements, but it may not suppress that speech altogether. We turn to the case now before us.

I

A

Citizens United is a nonprofit corporation [with] an annual budget of about $12 million. Most of its funds are from donations by individuals; but, in addition, it accepts a small portion of its funds from for-profit corporations.

In January 2008, Citizens United released a film entitled *Hillary: The Movie.* We refer to the film as *Hillary.* It is a 90-minute documentary about then-Senator Hillary Clinton, who was a candidate in the Democratic Party's 2008 Presidential primary elections. *Hillary* mentions Senator Clinton by name and depicts interviews with political commentators and other persons, most of them quite critical of Senator Clinton. *Hillary* was released in theaters and on DVD, but Citizens United wanted to increase distribution by making it available through video-on-demand.

Video-on-demand allows digital cable subscribers to select programming from various menus, including movies, television shows, sports, news, and music.... In December 2007, a cable company offered, for a payment of $1.2 million, to make

Hillary available on a video-on-demand channel called "Elections '08." [T]he proposal was to make *Hillary* available to viewers free of charge.

To implement the proposal, Citizens United was prepared to pay for the video-on-demand; and to promote the film, it produced two 10-second ads and one 30-second ad for *Hillary*. Each ad includes a short (and, in our view, pejorative) statement about Senator Clinton, followed by the name of the movie and the movie's Website address. Citizens United desired to promote the video-on-demand offering by running advertisements on broadcast and cable television.

B

Before the Bipartisan Campaign Reform Act of 2002 (BCRA), federal law prohibited—and still does prohibit—corporations and unions from using general treasury funds to make direct contributions to candidates or independent expenditures that expressly advocate the election or defeat of a candidate, through any form of media, in connection with certain qualified federal elections. 2 U.S.C. § 441b (2000 ed.). BCRA § 203 amended § 441b to prohibit any "electioneering communication" as well. 2 U.S.C. § 441b(b)(2) (2006 ed.). An electioneering communication is defined as "any broadcast, cable, or satellite communication" that "refers to a clearly identified candidate for Federal office" and is made within 30 days of a primary or 60 days of a general election. § 434(f)(3)(A) [now 52 U.S.C. § 30104(f)(3)(A)]. The Federal Election Commission's (FEC) regulations further define an electioneering communication as a communication that is "publicly distributed." 11 CFR § 100.29(a)(2) (2009). "In the case of a candidate for nomination for President ... *publicly distributed* means" that the communication "[c]an be received by 50,000 or more persons in a State where a primary election ... is being held within 30 days." § 100.29(b)(3)(ii). Corporations and unions are barred from using their general treasury funds for express advocacy or electioneering communications. They may establish [a PAC,] however.... The moneys received by the segregated fund are limited to donations from stockholders and employees of the corporation or, in the case of unions, members of the union.

C

Citizens United wanted to make *Hillary* available through video-on-demand within 30 days of the 2008 primary elections. It feared, however, that both the film and the ads would be covered by § 441b's ban on corporate-funded independent expenditures, thus subjecting the corporation to civil and criminal penalties under § 437g [52 U.S.C. § 30109]. In December 2007, Citizens United sought declaratory and injunctive relief against the FEC. It argued that (1) § 441b is unconstitutional as applied to *Hillary;* and (2) BCRA's disclaimer and disclosure requirements, BCRA §§ 201 and 311, are unconstitutional as applied to *Hillary* and to the three ads for the movie....

II

Before considering whether *Austin* should be overruled, we first address whether Citizens United's claim that § 441b cannot be applied to *Hillary* may be resolved on other, narrower grounds.

A

Citizens United contends that § 441b does not cover *Hillary,* as a matter of statutory interpretation, because the film does not qualify as an "electioneering communication." § 441b(b)(2).... Under the definition of electioneering communication, the video-on-demand showing of *Hillary* on cable television would have been a "cable ... communication" that "refer[red] to a clearly identified candidate for Federal office" and that was made within 30 days of a primary election. 2 U.S.C. § 434(f)(3)(A)(i). Citizens United, however, argues that *Hillary* was not "publicly distributed," because a single video-on-demand transmission is sent only to a requesting cable converter box and each separate transmission, in most instances, will be seen by just one household—not 50,000 or more persons.

This argument ignores the regulation's instruction on how to determine whether a cable transmission "[c]an be received by 50,000 or more persons." § 100.29(b)(3)(ii). The regulation provides that the number of people who can receive a cable transmission is determined by the number of cable subscribers in the relevant area. §§ 100.29(b)(7)(i)(G), (ii). Here, Citizens United wanted to use a cable video-on-demand system that had 34.5 million subscribers nationwide. Thus, *Hillary* could have been received by 50,000 persons or more.

One *amici* brief asks us, alternatively, to construe the condition that the communication "[c]an be received by 50,000 or more persons," § 100.29(b)(3)(ii)(A), to require "a plausible likelihood that the communication will be viewed by 50,000 or more potential voters"—as opposed to requiring only that the communication is "technologically capable" of being seen by that many people. Whether the population and demographic statistics in a proposed viewing area consisted of 50,000 registered voters—but not "infants, pre-teens, or otherwise electorally ineligible recipients"—would be a required determination, subject to judicial challenge and review, in any case where the issue was in doubt.

In our view the statute cannot be saved by limiting the reach of 2 U.S.C. § 441b through this suggested interpretation. In addition to the costs and burdens of litigation, this result would require a calculation as to the number of people a particular communication is likely to reach, with an inaccurate estimate potentially subjecting the speaker to criminal sanctions. The First Amendment does not permit laws that force speakers to retain a campaign finance attorney, conduct demographic marketing research, or seek declaratory rulings before discussing the most salient political issues of our day. Prolix laws chill speech for the same reason that vague laws chill speech: People "of common intelligence must necessarily guess at [the law's] meaning and differ as to its application." *Connally v. General Constr. Co.,* 269 U.S. 385, 391 (1926). The Government may not render a ban on political speech constitutional by carving out a limited exemption through an amorphous regulatory interpretation. We must reject the approach suggested by the *amici*. Section 441b covers *Hillary*....

C

Citizens United further contends that § 441b should be invalidated as applied to movies shown through video-on-demand, arguing that this delivery system has a lower risk of distorting the political process than do television ads. On what we might call conventional television, advertising spots reach viewers who have chosen a channel or a program for reasons unrelated to the advertising. With video-on-demand, by contrast, the viewer selects a program after taking "a series of affirmative steps": subscribing to cable; navigating through various menus; and selecting the program.

While some means of communication may be less effective than others at influencing the public in different contexts, any effort by the Judiciary to decide which means of communications are to be preferred for the particular type of message and speaker would raise questions as to the courts' own lawful authority. Substantial questions would arise if courts were to begin saying what means of speech should be preferred or disfavored. And in all events, those differentiations might soon prove to be irrelevant or outdated by technologies that are in rapid flux.

Courts, too, are bound by the First Amendment. We must decline to draw, and then redraw, constitutional lines based on the particular media or technology used to disseminate political speech from a particular speaker. It must be noted, moreover, that this undertaking would require substantial litigation over an extended time, all to interpret a law that beyond doubt discloses serious First Amendment flaws. The interpretive process itself would create an inevitable, pervasive, and serious risk of chilling protected speech pending the drawing of fine distinctions that, in the end, would themselves be questionable. First Amendment standards, however, "must give the benefit of any doubt to protecting rather than stifling speech." *WRTL* (opinion of ROBERTS, C.J.) (citing *New York Times Co. v. Sullivan*).

D

Citizens United also asks us to carve out an exception to § 441b's expenditure ban for nonprofit corporate political speech funded overwhelmingly by individuals. As an alternative to reconsidering *Austin*, the Government also seems to prefer this approach. This line of analysis, however, would be unavailing.

In *MCFL*, the Court found unconstitutional § 441b's restrictions on corporate expenditures as applied to nonprofit corporations that were formed for the sole purpose of promoting political ideas, did not engage in business activities, and did not accept contributions from for-profit corporations or labor unions. BCRA's so-called Wellstone Amendment applied § 441b's expenditure ban to all nonprofit corporations. *McConnell* then interpreted the Wellstone Amendment to retain the *MCFL* exemption to § 441b's expenditure prohibition. Citizens United does not qualify for the *MCFL* exemption, however, since some funds used to make the movie were donations from for-profit corporations.

The Government suggests we could find BCRA's Wellstone Amendment unconstitutional, sever it from the statute, and hold that Citizens United's speech is exempt from § 441b's ban under BCRA's Snowe-Jeffords Amendment, § 441b(c)(2). The Snowe-Jeffords Amendment operates as a backup provision that only takes effect if the Wellstone Amendment is invalidated. The Snowe-Jeffords Amendment would exempt from § 441b's expenditure ban the political speech of certain nonprofit corporations if the speech were funded "exclusively" by individual donors and the funds were maintained in a segregated account. § 441b(c)(2). Citizens United would not qualify for the Snowe-Jeffords exemption, under its terms as written, because *Hillary* was funded in part with donations from for-profit corporations.

Consequently, to hold for Citizens United on this argument, the Court would be required to revise the text of *MCFL*, sever BCRA's Wellstone Amendment, § 441b(c)(6), and ignore the plain text of BCRA's Snowe-Jeffords Amendment, § 441b(c)(2). If the Court decided to create a *de minimis* exception to *MCFL* or the Snowe-Jeffords Amendment, the result would be to allow for-profit corporate general treasury funds to be spent for independent expenditures that support candidates. There is no principled basis for doing this without rewriting *Austin*'s holding that the Government can restrict corporate independent expenditures for political speech.

Though it is true that the Court should construe statutes as necessary to avoid constitutional questions, the series of steps suggested would be difficult to take in view of the language of the statute. In addition to those difficulties the Government's suggestion is troubling for still another reason.... We decline to adopt an interpretation that requires intricate case-by-case determinations to verify whether political speech is banned, especially if we are convinced that, in the end, this corporation has a constitutional right to speak on this subject.

E

As the foregoing analysis confirms, the Court cannot resolve this case on a narrower ground without chilling political speech, speech that is central to the meaning and purpose of the First Amendment. It is not judicial restraint to accept an unsound, narrow argument just so the Court can avoid another argument with broader implications.... Here, the lack of a valid basis for an alternative ruling requires full consideration of the continuing effect of the speech suppression upheld in *Austin*....

III . . .

The law before us is an outright ban, backed by criminal sanctions. Section 441b makes it a felony for all corporations — including nonprofit advocacy corporations — either to expressly advocate the election or defeat of candidates or to broadcast electioneering communications within 30 days of a primary election and 60 days of a general election. Thus, the following acts would all be felonies under § 441b: The Sierra Club runs an ad, within the crucial phase of 60 days before the general election, that exhorts the public to disapprove of a Congressman who favors logging in national forests; the National Rifle Association publishes a book urging the public to vote for the challenger because the incumbent U.S. Senator supports a handgun ban; and the American Civil Liberties Union creates a Web site telling the public to vote for a Presidential candidate in light of that candidate's defense of free speech. These prohibitions are classic examples of censorship.

Section 441b is a ban on corporate speech notwithstanding the fact that a PAC created by a corporation can still speak. A PAC is a separate association from the corporation. So the PAC exemption from § 441b's expenditure ban does not allow corporations to speak. Even if a PAC could somehow allow a corporation to speak — and it does not — the option to form PACs does not alleviate the First Amendment problems with § 441b. PACs are burdensome alternatives; they are expensive to administer and subject to extensive regulations. For example, every PAC must appoint a treasurer, forward donations to the treasurer promptly, keep detailed records of the identities of the persons making donations, preserve receipts for three years, and file an organization statement and report changes to this information within 10 days.

And that is just the beginning. PACs must file detailed monthly reports with the FEC, which are due at different times depending on the type of election that is about to occur. . . .

PACs have to comply with these regulations just to speak. This might explain why fewer than 2,000 of the millions of corporations in this country have PACs. PACs, furthermore, must exist before they can speak. Given the onerous restrictions, a corporation may not be able to establish a PAC in time to make its views known regarding candidates and issues in a current campaign.

Section 441b's prohibition on corporate independent expenditures is thus a ban on speech. As a "restriction on the amount of money a person or group can spend on political communication during a campaign," that statute "necessarily reduces the quantity of expression by restricting the number of issues discussed, the depth of their exploration, and the size of the audience reached." *Buckley*. Were the Court to uphold these restrictions, the Government could repress speech by silencing certain voices at any of the various points in the speech process. If § 441b applied to individuals, no one would believe that it is merely a time, place, or manner restriction on speech. Its purpose and effect are to silence entities whose voices the Government deems to be suspect. . . .

Laws that burden political speech are "subject to strict scrutiny," which requires the Government to prove that the restriction "furthers a compelling interest and is narrowly tailored to achieve that interest." *WRTL* (opinion of ROBERTS, C.J.). While it might be maintained that political speech simply cannot be banned or restricted as a categorical matter, see *Simon & Schuster*, 502 U.S., at 124 (KENNEDY, J., concurring in judgment), the quoted language from *WRTL* provides a sufficient framework for protecting the relevant First Amendment interests in this case. We shall employ it here.

Premised on mistrust of governmental power, the First Amendment stands against attempts to disfavor certain subjects or viewpoints. Prohibited, too, are restrictions distinguishing among different speakers, allowing speech by some but not others. See *Bellotti*. As instruments to censor, these categories are interrelated: Speech restrictions based on the identity of the speaker are all too often simply a means to control content.

Quite apart from the purpose or effect of regulating content, moreover, the Government may commit a constitutional wrong when by law it identifies certain preferred speakers. By taking the right to speak from some and giving it to others, the Government deprives the disadvantaged person or class of the right to use speech to strive to establish worth, standing, and respect for the speaker's voice. The Government may not by these means deprive the public of the right and privilege to determine for itself what speech and speakers are worthy of consideration. The First Amendment protects speech and speaker, and the ideas that flow from each. . . .

[I]t is inherent in the nature of the political process that voters must be free to obtain information from diverse sources in order to determine how to cast their votes. At least before *Austin*, the Court had not allowed the exclusion of a class of speakers from the general public dialogue.

We find no basis for the proposition that, in the context of political speech, the Government may impose restrictions on certain disfavored speakers. Both history and logic lead us to this conclusion.

A

1

The Court has recognized that First Amendment protection extends to corporations. [Justice Kennedy cites over twenty cases, including *Bellotti*.]

This protection has been extended by explicit holdings to the context of political speech. Under the rationale of these precedents, political speech does not lose First Amendment protection "simply because its source is a corporation." *Bellotti*. The Court has thus rejected the argument that political speech of corporations or other associations should be treated differently under the First Amendment simply because such associations are not "natural persons." *Id.*

At least since the latter part of the 19th century, the laws of some States and of the United States [have] imposed a ban on corporate direct contributions to candidates. See B. Smith, Unfree Speech: The Folly of Campaign Finance Reform 23 (2001). Yet not until 1947 did Congress first prohibit independent expenditures by corporations and labor unions in § 304 of the Labor Management Relations Act 1947. In passing this Act Congress overrode the veto of President Truman, who warned that the expenditure ban was a "dangerous intrusion on free speech."

For almost three decades thereafter, the Court did not reach the question whether restrictions on corporate and union expenditures are constitutional. [Justice Kennedy then discusses *United States v. CIO*, *United States v. Automobile Workers*, and *Pipefitters v. United States*, in each of which the issue was raised but not decided.]

2 . . .

The *Buckley* Court explained that the potential for *quid pro quo* corruption distinguished direct contributions to candidates from independent expenditures. The Court emphasized that "the independent expenditure ceiling . . . fails to serve any substantial governmental interest in stemming the reality or appearance of corruption in the electoral process," because "[t]he absence of prearrangement and coordination . . . alleviates the danger that expenditures will be given as a *quid pro quo* for improper commitments from the candidate." *Buckley* invalidated § 608(e)'s restrictions on independent expenditures, with only one Justice dissenting.

Buckley did not consider § 610's separate ban on corporate and union independent expenditures. . . . Had § 610 been challenged in the wake of *Buckley*, however, it could not have been squared with the reasoning and analysis of that precedent. The expenditure ban invalidated in *Buckley*, § 608(e), applied to corporations and unions, and some of the prevailing plaintiffs in *Buckley* were corporations. The *Buckley* Court did not invoke the First Amendment's overbreadth doctrine to suggest that § 608(e)'s expenditure ban would have been constitutional if it had applied only to corporations and not to individuals. *Buckley* cited with approval the *Automobile Workers* dissent, which argued that § 610 was unconstitutional.

Notwithstanding this precedent, Congress recodified § 610's corporate and union expenditure ban at 2 U.S.C. § 441b four months after *Buckley* was decided. Section 441b is the independent expenditure restriction challenged here.

Less than two years after *Buckley*, *Bellotti* reaffirmed the First Amendment principle that the Government cannot restrict political speech based on the speaker's corporate identity. . . .

It is important to note that the reasoning and holding of *Bellotti* did not rest on the existence of a viewpoint-discriminatory statute. It rested on the principle that the Government lacks the power to ban corporations from speaking.

Bellotti did not address the constitutionality of the State's ban on corporate independent expenditures to support candidates. In our view, however, that restriction would have been unconstitutional under *Bellotti*'s central principle: that the First Amendment does not allow political speech restrictions based on a speaker's corporate identity.

3

Thus the law stood until *Austin*. *Austin* "uph[eld] a direct restriction on the independent expenditure of funds for political speech for the first time in [this Court's] history" (KENNEDY, J., dissenting). There, the Michigan Chamber of Commerce sought to use general treasury funds to run a newspaper ad supporting a specific candidate. Michigan law, however, prohibited corporate independent expenditures that supported or opposed any candidate for state office. A violation of the law was punishable as a felony. The Court sustained the speech prohibition.

To bypass *Buckley* and *Bellotti,* the *Austin* Court identified a new governmental interest in limiting political speech: an antidistortion interest. *Austin* found a compelling governmental interest in preventing "the corrosive and distorting effects of immense aggregations of wealth that are accumulated with the help of the corporate form and that have little or no correlation to the public's support for the corporation's political ideas."

B

The Court is thus confronted with conflicting lines of precedent: a pre-*Austin* line that forbids restrictions on political speech based on the speaker's corporate identity and a post-*Austin* line that permits them. No case before *Austin* had held that Congress could prohibit independent expenditures for political speech based on the speaker's corporate identity....

In its defense of the corporate-speech restrictions in § 441b, the Government notes the antidistortion rationale on which *Austin* and its progeny rest in part, yet it all but abandons reliance upon it. It argues instead that two other compelling interests support *Austin*'s holding that corporate expenditure restrictions are constitutional: an anticorruption interest and a shareholder-protection interest. We consider the three points in turn.

1

As for *Austin*'s antidistortion rationale, the Government does little to defend it. And with good reason, for the rationale cannot support § 441b.

If the First Amendment has any force, it prohibits Congress from fining or jailing citizens, or associations of citizens, for simply engaging in political speech. If the antidistortion rationale were to be accepted, however, it would permit Government to ban political speech simply because the speaker is an association that has taken on the corporate form. The Government contends that *Austin* permits it to ban corporate expenditures for almost all forms of communication stemming from a corporation. If *Austin* were correct, the Government could prohibit a corporation from expressing political views in media beyond those presented here, such as by printing books. The Government responds "that the FEC has never applied this statute to a book," and if it did, "there would be quite [a] good as-applied challenge." This troubling assertion of brooding governmental power cannot be reconciled with the confidence and stability in civic discourse that the First Amendment must secure.

Political speech is "indispensable to decisionmaking in a democracy, and this is no less true because the speech comes from a corporation rather than an individual." *Bellotti.* This protection for speech is inconsistent with *Austin*'s antidistortion rationale. *Austin* sought to defend the antidistortion rationale as a means to prevent corporations from obtaining "'an unfair advantage in the political marketplace'" by using "'resources amassed in the economic marketplace.'" (quoting *MCFL*). But *Buckley* rejected the premise that the Government has an interest "in equalizing the relative ability of individuals and groups to influence the outcome of elections." *Buckley* was specific in stating that "the skyrocketing cost of political campaigns" could not sustain the governmental prohibition. The First Amendment's protections do not depend on the speaker's "financial ability to engage in public discussion."

The Court reaffirmed these conclusions when it invalidated the BCRA provision that increased the cap on contributions to one candidate if the opponent made certain expenditures from personal funds. See *Davis v. Federal Election Comm'n* ("Leveling electoral opportunities means making and implementing judgments about which strengths should be permitted to contribute to the outcome of an election. The Constitution, however, confers upon voters, not Congress, the power to choose the Members of the House of Representatives, Art. I, § 2, and it is a dangerous business for Congress to use the election laws to influence the voters' choices"). The rule that political speech cannot be limited based on a speaker's wealth is a necessary consequence of the premise that the First Amendment generally prohibits the suppression of political speech based on the speaker's identity.

Either as support for its antidistortion rationale or as a further argument, the *Austin* majority undertook to distinguish wealthy individuals from corporations on the ground that "[s]tate law grants corporations special advantages — such as limited liability, perpetual life, and favorable treatment of the accumulation and distribution of assets." This does not suffice, however, to allow laws prohibiting speech. "It is rudimentary that the State cannot exact as the price of those special advantages the forfeiture of First Amendment rights." (SCALIA, J., dissenting).

It is irrelevant for purposes of the First Amendment that corporate funds may "have little or no correlation to the public's support for the corporation's political ideas." (majority opinion). All speakers, including individuals and the media, use money amassed from the economic marketplace to fund their speech. The First Amendment protects the resulting speech, even if it was enabled by economic transactions with persons or entities who disagree with the speaker's ideas.

Austin's antidistortion rationale would produce the dangerous, and unacceptable, consequence that Congress could ban political speech of media corporations. Media corporations are now exempt from § 441b's ban on corporate expenditures. See [52 U.S.C. §§ 30101(9)(B)(i), 30104(f)(3)(B)(i)]. Yet media corporations accumulate wealth with the help of the corporate form, the largest media corporations have "immense aggregations of wealth," and the views expressed by media corporations often "have little or no correlation to the public's support" for those views. *Austin*. Thus, under the Government's reasoning, wealthy media corporations could have their voices diminished to put them on par with other media entities. There is no precedent for permitting this under the First Amendment.

The media exemption discloses further difficulties with the law now under consideration. There is no precedent supporting laws that attempt to distinguish between corporations which are deemed to be exempt as media corporations and those which are not. "We have consistently rejected the proposition that the institutional press has any constitutional privilege beyond that of other speakers." *Id.* (SCALIA, J., dissenting). With the advent of the Internet and the decline of print and broadcast media, moreover, the line between the media and others who wish to comment on political and social issues becomes far more blurred.

The law's exception for media corporations is, on its own terms, all but an admission of the invalidity of the antidistortion rationale. And the exemption results in a further, separate reason for finding this law invalid: Again by its own terms, the law exempts some corporations but covers others, even though both have the need or the motive to communicate their views. The exemption applies to media corporations owned or controlled by corporations that have diverse and substantial investments and participate in endeavors other than news. So even assuming the most doubtful proposition that a news organization has a right to speak when others do not, the exemption would allow a conglomerate that owns both a media business and an unrelated business to influence or control the media in order to advance its overall business interest. At the same time, some other corporation, with an identical business interest but no media outlet in its ownership structure, would be forbidden to speak or inform the public about the same issue. This differential treatment cannot be squared with the First Amendment.

There is simply no support for the view that the First Amendment, as originally understood, would permit the suppression of political speech by media corporations. The Framers may not have anticipated modern business and media corporations. Yet television networks and major newspapers owned by media corporations have become the most important means of mass communication in modern times. The First Amendment was certainly not understood to condone the suppression of political speech in society's most salient media. It was understood as a response to the repression of speech and the press that had existed in England and the heavy taxes on the press that were imposed in the colonies. The great debates between the Federalists and the Anti-Federalists over our founding document were published and expressed in the most important means of mass communication of that era—newspapers owned by individuals.... The Framers may have been unaware of certain types of speakers or forms of communication, but that does not mean that those speakers and media are entitled to less First Amendment protection than those types of speakers and media that provided the means of communicating political ideas when the Bill of Rights was adopted.

Austin interferes with the "open marketplace" of ideas protected by the First Amendment. It permits the Government to ban the political speech of millions of associations of citizens. See Statistics of Income 2 (5.8 million for-profit corporations filed 2006 tax returns). Most of these are small corporations without large amounts of wealth. This fact belies the Government's argument that the statute is justified on the ground that it prevents the "distorting effects of immense aggregations of wealth." It is not even aimed at amassed wealth.

The censorship we now confront is vast in its reach.... By suppressing the speech of manifold corporations, both for-profit and nonprofit, the Government prevents their voices and viewpoints from reaching the public and advising voters on which persons or entities are hostile to their interests. Factions will necessarily form in our

Republic, but the remedy of "destroying the liberty" of some factions is "worse than the disease." *Federalist No. 10.* Factions should be checked by permitting them all to speak and by entrusting the people to judge what is true and what is false.

The purpose and effect of this law is to prevent corporations, including small and nonprofit corporations, from presenting both facts and opinions to the public. This makes *Austin*'s antidistortion rationale all the more an aberration. "[T]he First Amendment protects the right of corporations to petition legislative and administrative bodies." *Bellotti.* Corporate executives and employees counsel Members of Congress and Presidential administrations on many issues, as a matter of routine and often in private.... When that phenomenon is coupled with § 441b, the result is that smaller or nonprofit corporations cannot raise a voice to object when other corporations, including those with vast wealth, are cooperating with the Government. That cooperation may sometimes be voluntary, or it may be at the demand of a Government official who uses his or her authority, influence, and power to threaten corporations to support the Government's policies. Those kinds of interactions are often unknown and unseen. The speech that § 441b forbids, though, is public, and all can judge its content and purpose. References to massive corporate treasuries should not mask the real operation of this law. Rhetoric ought not obscure reality.

Even if § 441b's expenditure ban were constitutional, wealthy corporations could still lobby elected officials, although smaller corporations may not have the resources to do so. And wealthy individuals and unincorporated associations can spend unlimited amounts on independent expenditures. Yet certain disfavored associations of citizens — those that have taken on the corporate form — are penalized for engaging in the same political speech.

When Government seeks to use its full power, including the criminal law, to command where a person may get his or her information or what distrusted source he or she may not hear, it uses censorship to control thought. This is unlawful. The First Amendment confirms the freedom to think for ourselves.

2

What we have said also shows the invalidity of other arguments made by the Government. For the most part relinquishing the antidistortion rationale, the Government falls back on the argument that corporate political speech can be banned in order to prevent corruption or its appearance. In *Buckley*, the Court found this interest "sufficiently important" to allow limits on contributions but did not extend that reasoning to expenditure limits. When *Buckley* examined an expenditure ban, it found "that the governmental interest in preventing corruption and the appearance of corruption [was] inadequate to justify [the ban] on independent expenditures."

With regard to large direct contributions, *Buckley* reasoned that they could be given "to secure a political *quid pro quo*," and that "the scope of such pernicious practices can never be reliably ascertained." The practices *Buckley* noted would be covered by bribery laws if a *quid pro quo* arrangement were proved. The Court, in consequence, has noted that restrictions on direct contributions are preventative, because few if any contributions to candidates will involve *quid pro quo* arrangements. *MCFL; National Right to Work Comm.* The *Buckley* Court, nevertheless, sustained limits on direct contributions in order to ensure against the reality or appearance of corruption. That case did not extend this rationale to independent expenditures, and the Court does not do so here.

"The absence of prearrangement and coordination of an expenditure with the candidate or his agent not only undermines the value of the expenditure to the candidate, but also alleviates the danger that expenditures will be given as a *quid pro quo* for improper commitments from the candidate." *Buckley.* Limits on independent expenditures, such as § 441b, have a chilling effect extending well beyond the Government's interest in preventing *quid pro quo* corruption. The anticorruption interest is not sufficient to displace the speech here in question. Indeed, 26 States do not restrict independent expenditures by for-profit corporations. The Government does not claim that these expenditures have corrupted the political process in those States.

A single footnote in *Bellotti* [n.26] purported to leave open the possibility that corporate independent expenditures could be shown to cause corruption. For the reasons explained above, we now conclude that independent expenditures, including those made by corporations, do not give rise to corruption or the appearance of corruption....

Seizing on this aside in *Bellotti*'s footnote, the Court in *NRWC* did say there is a "sufficient" governmental interest in "ensur[ing] that substantial aggregations of wealth amassed" by corporations would not "be used to incur political debts from legislators who are aided by the contributions." *NRWC*, however, has little relevance here. *NRWC* decided no more than that a restriction on a corporation's ability to solicit funds for its segregated PAC, which made direct contributions to candidates, did not violate the First Amendment. *NRWC* thus involved contribution limits which, unlike limits on independent expenditures, have been an accepted means to prevent *quid pro quo* corruption. Citizens United has not made direct contributions to candidates, and it has not suggested that the Court should reconsider whether contribution limits should be subjected to rigorous First Amendment scrutiny.

When *Buckley* identified a sufficiently important governmental interest in preventing corruption or the appearance of corruption, that interest was limited to *quid pro quo* corruption. The fact that speakers may have influence over or access to elected officials does not mean that these officials are corrupt:

> Favoritism and influence are not . . . avoidable in representative politics. It is in the nature of an elected representative to favor certain policies, and, by necessary corollary, to favor the voters and contributors who support those policies. It is well understood that a substantial and legitimate reason, if not the only reason, to cast a vote for, or to make a contribution to, one candidate over another is that the candidate will respond by producing

> those political outcomes the supporter favors. Democracy is premised on responsiveness. *McConnell,* (opinion of KENNEDY, J.).

Reliance on a "generic favoritism or influence theory . . . is at odds with standard First Amendment analyses because it is unbounded and susceptible to no limiting principle." *Id.*

The appearance of influence or access, furthermore, will not cause the electorate to lose faith in our democracy. By definition, an independent expenditure is political speech presented to the electorate that is not coordinated with a candidate. The fact that a corporation, or any other speaker, is willing to spend money to try to persuade voters presupposes that the people have the ultimate influence over elected officials. This is inconsistent with any suggestion that the electorate will refuse "'to take part in democratic governance'" because of additional political speech made by a corporation or any other speaker. *McConnell* (quoting *Shrink Missouri*).

Caperton [Chapter 10] is not to the contrary. *Caperton* held that a judge was required to recuse himself "when a person with a personal stake in a particular case had a significant and disproportionate influence in placing the judge on the case by raising funds or directing the judge's election campaign when the case was pending or imminent." The remedy of recusal was based on a litigant's due process right to a fair trial before an unbiased judge. *Caperton*'s holding was limited to the rule that the judge must be recused, not that the litigant's political speech could be banned.

The *McConnell* record was "over 100,000 pages" long, yet it "does not have any direct examples of votes being exchanged for . . . expenditures," (opinion of Kollar-Kotelly, J.). This confirms *Buckley*'s reasoning that independent expenditures do not lead to, or create the appearance of, *quid pro quo* corruption. In fact, there is only scant evidence that independent expenditures even ingratiate. Ingratiation and access, in any event, are not corruption. The BCRA record establishes that certain donations to political parties, called "soft money," were made to gain access to elected officials. This case, however, is about independent expenditures, not soft money. When Congress finds that a problem exists, we must give that finding due deference; but Congress may not choose an unconstitutional remedy. If elected officials succumb to improper influences from independent expenditures; if they surrender their best judgment; and if they put expediency before principle, then surely there is cause for concern. We must give weight to attempts by Congress to seek to dispel either the appearance or the reality of these influences. The remedies enacted by law, however, must comply with the First Amendment; and, it is our law and our tradition that more speech, not less, is the governing rule. An outright ban on corporate political speech during the critical preelection period is not a permissible remedy. Here Congress has created categorical bans on speech that are asymmetrical to preventing *quid pro quo* corruption.

3

The Government contends further that corporate independent expenditures can be limited because of its interest in protecting dissenting shareholders from being compelled to fund corporate political speech. This asserted interest, like *Austin*'s antidistortion rationale, would allow the Government to ban the political speech even of media corporations. Assume, for example, that a shareholder of a corporation that owns a newspaper disagrees with the political views the newspaper expresses. Under the Government's view, that potential disagreement could give the Government the authority to restrict the media corporation's political speech. The First Amendment does not allow that power. There is, furthermore, little evidence of abuse that cannot be corrected by shareholders "through the procedures of corporate democracy." *Bellotti.*

Those reasons are sufficient to reject this shareholder-protection interest; and, moreover, the statute is both underinclusive and overinclusive. As to the first, if Congress had been seeking to protect dissenting shareholders, it would not have banned corporate speech in only certain media within 30 or 60 days before an election. A dissenting shareholder's interests would be implicated by speech in any media at any time. As to the second, the statute is overinclusive because it covers all corporations, including nonprofit corporations and for-profit corporations with only single shareholders. As to other corporations, the remedy is not to restrict speech but to consider and explore other regulatory mechanisms. The regulatory mechanism here, based on speech, contravenes the First Amendment.

4

We need not reach the question whether the Government has a compelling interest in preventing foreign individuals or associations from influencing our Nation's political process. Cf. [52 U.S.C. § 30121] (contribution and expenditure ban applied to "foreign national[s]"). Section 441b is not limited to corporations or associations that were created in foreign countries or funded predominately by foreign shareholders. Section 441b therefore would be overbroad even if we assumed, *arguendo,* that the Government has a compelling interest in limiting foreign influence over our political process.

C

Our precedent is to be respected unless the most convincing of reasons demonstrates that adherence to it puts us on a course that is sure error. "Beyond workability, the relevant factors in deciding whether to adhere to the principle of *stare decisis* include the antiquity of the precedent, the reliance interests at stake, and of course whether the decision was well reasoned." We have also examined whether "experience has pointed up the precedent's shortcomings."

These considerations counsel in favor of rejecting *Austin,* which itself contravened this Court's earlier precedents in *Buckley* and *Bellotti.* . . .

For the reasons above, it must be concluded that *Austin* was not well reasoned. The Government defends *Austin,* relying almost entirely on "the quid pro quo interest, the corruption interest or the shareholder interest," and not *Austin*'s expressed antidistortion rationale. When neither party defends the reasoning of a precedent, the principle of adhering to that precedent through *stare decisis* is diminished. *Austin* abandoned First Amendment principles, furthermore, by relying on language in some of our precedents that traces back to the *Automobile Workers* Court's flawed historical account of campaign finance laws, see Hayward, 45 Harv. J. Legis. 421; R. Mutch, Campaigns, Congress, and Courts 33–35, 153–157 (1988).

Austin is undermined by experience since its announcement. Political speech is so ingrained in our culture that speakers find ways to circumvent campaign finance laws. Our Nation's speech dynamic is changing, and informative voices should not have to circumvent onerous restrictions to exercise their First Amendment rights. Speakers have become adept at presenting citizens with sound bites, talking points, and scripted messages that dominate the 24-hour news cycle. Corporations, like individuals, do not have monolithic views. On certain topics corporations may possess valuable expertise, leaving them the best equipped to point out errors or fallacies in speech of all sorts, including the speech of candidates and elected officials.

Rapid changes in technology—and the creative dynamic inherent in the concept of free expression—counsel against upholding a law that restricts political speech in certain media or by certain speakers. See Part II-C, *supra*. Today, 30-second television ads may be the most effective way to convey a political message. Soon, however, it may be that Internet sources, such as blogs and social networking Web sites, will provide citizens with significant information about political candidates and issues. Yet, § 441b would seem to ban a blog post expressly advocating the election or defeat of a candidate if that blog were created with corporate funds. The First Amendment does not permit Congress to make these categorical distinctions based on the corporate identity of the speaker and the content of the political speech.

No serious reliance interests are at stake.... Legislatures may have enacted bans on corporate expenditures believing that those bans were constitutional. This is not a compelling interest for *stare decisis*. If it were, legislative acts could prevent us from overruling our own precedents, thereby interfering with our duty "to say what the law is." *Marbury v. Madison*, 1 Cranch 137, 177 (1803).

Due consideration leads to this conclusion: *Austin* should be and now is overruled. We return to the principle established in *Buckley* and *Bellotti* that the Government may not suppress political speech on the basis of the speaker's corporate identity. No sufficient governmental interest justifies limits on the political speech of nonprofit or for-profit corporations.

D

Austin is overruled, so it provides no basis for allowing the Government to limit corporate independent expenditures. As the Government appears to concede, overruling *Austin* "effectively invalidate[s] not only BCRA Section 203, but also 2 U.S.C. 441b's prohibition on the use of corporate treasury funds for express advocacy." Section 441b's restrictions on corporate independent expenditures are therefore invalid and cannot be applied to *Hillary*.

Given our conclusion we are further required to overrule the part of *McConnell* that upheld BCRA § 203's extension of § 441b's restrictions on corporate independent expenditures. The *McConnell* Court relied on the antidistortion interest recognized in *Austin* to uphold a greater restriction on speech than the restriction upheld in *Austin* and we have found this interest unconvincing and insufficient. This part of *McConnell* is now overruled.

IV

[Both the spot ads advertising *Hillary* and the video-on-demand showing of the movie itself were subject to "disclaimer" requirements that the persons responsible be indentified on the face of the ads or the movies. In addition, the expenditures, if over $10,000, were subject to campaign disclosure requirements. Part IV of Justice Kennedy's opinion, joined by all members of the Court except Justice Thomas, upheld the disclaimer and disclosure requirements against challenge. See Chapter 16. Justice Thomas's opinion dissenting on this point is omitted here.]

V

When word concerning the plot of the movie *Mr. Smith Goes to Washington* reached the circles of Government, some officials sought, by persuasion, to discourage its distribution. Under *Austin,* though, officials could have done more than discourage its distribution — they could have banned the film. After all, it, like *Hillary,* was speech funded by a corporation that was critical of Members of Congress. *Mr. Smith Goes to Washington* may be fiction and caricature; but fiction and caricature can be a powerful force.

Modern day movies, television comedies, or skits on Youtube.com might portray public officials or public policies in unflattering ways. Yet if a covered transmission during the blackout period creates the background for candidate endorsement or opposition, a felony occurs solely because a corporation, other than an exempt media corporation, has made the "purchase, payment, distribution, loan, advance, deposit, or gift of money or anything of value" in order to engage in political speech. [52 U.S.C. § 30101(9)(A)(i)]. Speech would be suppressed in the realm where its necessity is most evident: in the public dialogue preceding a real election. Governments are often hostile to speech, but under our law and our tradition it seems stranger than fiction for our Government to make this political speech a crime. Yet this is the statute's purpose and design.

Some members of the public might consider *Hillary* to be insightful and instructive; some might find it to be neither high art nor a fair discussion on how to set the Nation's course; still others simply might suspend judgment on these points but decide to think more about issues and candidates. Those choices and assessments, however, are not for the Government to make. . . .

The judgment of the District Court is reversed with respect to the constitutionality of 2 U.S.C. § 441b's restrictions on corporate independent expenditures. The judgment is affirmed with respect to BCRA's disclaimer and disclosure requirements. The case is remanded for further proceedings consistent with this opinion.

It is so ordered.

[Justice Stevens, joined by Justices Breyer, Ginsburg, and Sotomayor, dissented except as to Part IV of the Court's opinion (on disclosure). Stevens's opinion is very long. Space here permits only brief excerpts of his opinion. For those with a serious interest in campaign finance, the whole opinion is worth reading. The same is true of concurring opinions by Chief Justice Roberts and Justice Scalia, responding to Stevens. Roberts addressed Stevens's arguments that the Court ought to have applied the doctrine of constitutional avoidance or decided the case on a narrower ground, and that *stare decisis* ought to have prevented the Court from overruling *Austin*. Justice Scalia addressed the original textual meaning of the First Amendment as applied to the question of independent spending by corporations.]

Justice STEVENS, with whom Justice GINSBURG, Justice BREYER, and Justice SOTOMAYOR join, concurring in part and dissenting in part.

The real issue in this case concerns how, not if, the appellant may finance its electioneering. Citizens United is a wealthy nonprofit corporation that runs a political action committee (PAC) with millions of dollars in assets. Under the Bipartisan Campaign Reform Act of 2002 (BCRA), it could have used those assets to televise and promote *Hillary: The Movie* wherever and whenever it wanted to. It also could have spent unrestricted sums to broadcast *Hillary* at any time other than the 30 days before the last primary election. Neither Citizens United's nor any other corporation's speech has been "banned." All that the parties dispute is whether Citizens United had a right to use the funds in its general treasury to pay for broadcasts during the 30-day period. The notion that the First Amendment dictates an affirmative answer to that question is, in my judgment, profoundly misguided. Even more misguided is the notion that the Court must rewrite the law relating to campaign expenditures by *for-profit* corporations and unions to decide this case.

The basic premise underlying the Court's ruling is its iteration, and constant reiteration, of the proposition that the First Amendment bars regulatory distinctions based on a speaker's identity, including its "identity" as a corporation. While that glittering generality has rhetorical appeal, it is not a correct statement of the law. Nor does it tell us when a corporation may engage in electioneering that some of its shareholders oppose. It does not even resolve the specific question whether Citizens United may be required to finance some of its messages with the money in its PAC. The conceit that corporations must be treated identically to natural persons in the political sphere is not only inaccurate but also inadequate to justify the Court's disposition of this case.

In the context of election to public office, the distinction between corporate and human speakers is significant. Although they make enormous contributions to our society, corporations are not actually members of it. They cannot vote or run for office. Because they may be managed and controlled by nonresidents, their interests may conflict in fundamental respects with the interests of eligible voters. The financial resources, legal structure, and instrumental orientation of corporations raise legitimate concerns about their role in the electoral process. Our lawmakers have a compelling constitutional basis, if not also a democratic duty, to take measures designed to guard against the potentially deleterious effects of corporate spending in local and national races.

The majority's approach to corporate electioneering marks a dramatic break from our past. Congress has placed special limitations on campaign spending by corporations ever since the passage of the Tillman Act in 1907. We have unanimously concluded that this "reflects a permissible assessment of the dangers posed by those entities to the electoral process," *FEC v. National Right to Work Comm.*, and have accepted the "legislative judgment that the special characteristics of the corporate structure require particularly careful regulation." The Court today rejects a century of history when it treats the distinction between corporate and individual campaign spending as an invidious novelty born of *Austin*. Relying largely on individual dissenting opinions, the majority blazes through our precedents, overruling or disavowing a body of case law including *Wisconsin Right to Life, McConnell, FEC v. Beaumont, Massachusetts Citizens for Life, Inc., NRWC,* and *California Medical Assn. v. FEC*. . . .

I.

The Court's ruling threatens to undermine the integrity of elected institutions across the Nation. The path it has taken to reach its outcome will, I fear, do damage to this institution. Before turning to the question whether to overrule *Austin* and part of *McConnell,* it is important to explain why the Court should not be deciding that question.

Scope of the Case

The first reason is that the question was not properly brought before us. In declaring § 203 of BCRA facially unconstitutional on the ground that corporations' electoral expenditures may not be regulated any more stringently than those of individuals, the majority decides this case on a basis relinquished below, not included in the questions presented to us by the litigants, and argued here only in response to the Court's invitation. This procedure is unusual and inadvisable for a court. Our colleagues' suggestion that "we are asked to reconsider *Austin* and, in effect, *McConnell,*" would be more accurate if rephrased to state that "we have asked ourselves" to reconsider those cases.

In the District Court, Citizens United initially raised a facial challenge to the constitutionality of § 203. In its motion for summary judgment, however, Citizens United expressly abandoned its facial challenge, and the parties stipulated to the dismissal of that claim. The District Court therefore resolved the case on alternative grounds, and in its jurisdictional statement to this Court, Citizens United properly advised us that it was raising only "an as-applied challenge to the constitutionality of . . . BCRA § 203." The jurisdictional statement never so much as cited *Austin*, the key case the majority today overrules. And not one of the questions presented suggested that Citizens United was surreptitiously raising the facial challenge to § 203 that it previously agreed to dismiss. In fact, not one of those questions raised an issue based on Citizens United's corporate status. . . .

This is not merely a technical defect in the Court's decision. The unnecessary resort to a facial inquiry "run[s] contrary to the fundamental principle of judicial restraint that courts should neither anticipate a question of constitutional law in advance of the necessity of deciding it nor formulate a rule of constitutional law broader than is required by the precise facts to which it is to be applied." *Washington State Grange.* Scanting that principle "threaten[s] to short circuit the democratic process by preventing laws embodying the will of the people from being implemented in a manner consistent with the Constitution." These concerns are heightened when judges overrule settled doctrine upon which the legislature has relied. The Court operates with a sledge hammer rather than a scalpel when it strikes down one of Congress' most significant efforts to regulate the role that corporations and unions play in electoral politics. It compounds the offense by implicitly striking down a great many state laws as well.

The problem goes still deeper, for the Court does all of this on the basis of pure speculation. Had Citizens United maintained a facial challenge, and thus argued that there are virtually no circumstances in which BCRA § 203 can be applied constitutionally, the parties could have developed, through the normal process of litigation, a record about the *actual* effects of § 203, its actual burdens and its actual benefits, on *all* manner of corporations and unions. "Claims of facial invalidity often rest on speculation," and consequently "raise the risk of premature interpretation of statutes on the basis of factually barebones records." In this case, the record is not simply incomplete or unsatisfactory; it is nonexistent. Congress crafted BCRA in response to a virtual mountain of research on the corruption that previous legislation had failed to avert. The Court now negates Congress' efforts without a shred of evidence on how § 203 or its state-law counterparts have been affecting any entity other than Citizens United . . .

Narrower Grounds

It is all the more distressing that our colleagues have manufactured a facial challenge, because the parties have advanced numerous ways to resolve the case that would facilitate electioneering by nonprofit advocacy corporations such as Citizens United, without toppling statutes and precedents. Which is to say, the majority has transgressed yet another "cardinal" principle of the judicial process: "[I]f it is not necessary to decide more, it is necessary not to decide more," *PDK Labs., Inc. v. Drug Enforcement Admin.*, 362 F.3d 786, 799 (C.A.D.C.2004) (Roberts, J., concurring in part and concurring in judgment). . . .

This brief tour of alternative grounds on which the case could have been decided is not meant to show that any of these grounds is ideal, though each is perfectly "valid."[16] It is meant to show that there were principled, narrower paths that a Court that was serious about judicial restraint could have taken. There was also the straightforward path: applying *Austin* and *McConnell* just as the District Court did in holding that the funding of Citizens United's film can be regulated under them. The only thing preventing the majority from affirming the District Court, or adopting a narrower ground that would retain *Austin* is its disdain for *Austin*.

II

The final principle of judicial process that the majority violates is the most transparent: *stare decisis*. . . .

[After discussing *stare decisis*, Justice Stevens turned to a lengthy discussion of the merits. He disagreed with the majority's repeated insistence that the PAC requirement "banned" political speech, calling the characterization "highly misleading and need[ing] to be corrected." The idea that corporate speech would be banned is "nonsense." Justice Stevens defended the media exemption, noting the "unique role played by the institutional press in sustaining public debate."

The dissent rejected the "identity-based" distinctions of the majority, noting that in the election context laws ban political activities of foreigners and government employees. It then turned to a very long discussion of the "original understandings" of the First Amendment, the pre-*Austin* campaign finance cases, and the post-*Austin* cases which "reaffirmed" its holding. The dissent also disagreed with the majority's reading of *Buckley* and *Bellotti*, stating that *Austin* did not conflict with *Buckley*'s rejection of the equalization rationale, and noting that *Bellotti* footnote 26 expressly left the anticorruption rationale open as to corporate spending limits in candidate elections. Finally, the dissent turned to discuss the anticorruption, antidistortion, and shareholder protection rationales.

On anticorruption, the dissent began by disagreeing with the narrow view of corruption embraced by the majority: "the difference between selling a vote and selling access is a matter of degree, not kind." Setting forth a broad view of "undue influence" that could justify campaign finance regulations, the dissent rejected the idea that *Buckley* compelled a conclusion that independent spending can never corrupt a candidate. It then concluded that corporations raised a special problem of *quid pro quo* corruption because corporations as a class "tend to be more attuned to the

---

16. THE CHIEF JUSTICE finds our discussion of these narrower solutions "quite perplexing" because we suggest that the Court should "latch on to one of them in order to avoid reaching the broader constitutional question," without doing the same ourselves. There is nothing perplexing about the matter, because we are not similarly situated to our colleagues in the majority. We do not share their view of the First Amendment. Our reading of the Constitution would not lead us to strike down any statutes or overturn any precedents in this case, and we therefore have no occasion to practice constitutional avoidance or to vindicate Citizens United's as-applied challenge. Each of the arguments made above is surely at least as strong as the statutory argument the Court accepted in last year's Voting Rights Act case, *Northwest Austin Municipal Utility District No. One v. Holder* [discussed *supra* Chapter 5, Part I].

complexities of the legislative process and more directly affected by tax and appropriation measures that received little public scrutiny; they also have vastly more money with which to try to buy access and votes." The dissent then saw the majority's rejection of these arguments as inconsistent with its opinion the term before in *Caperton*. It ended the section by brushing aside arguments that Congress passed the law as a means of incumbent self-protection.

The dissent then turned to *Austin* antidistortion. While acknowledging "that *Austin* can bear an egalitarian reading," the dissent rejected the argument that *Austin*'s antidistortion rationale was "just" an "equalization rationale in disguise." Instead, "understood properly" the argument "is simply a variant on the classic governmental interest in protecting against improper influences on officeholders that debilitate the democratic process." According to the dissent, corporations do not engage in self-expression the way human beings do. In any case, some corporations actually wanted limits on spending to prevent officeholders from "shak[ing] them down for supportive ads." Finally, large corporate spending could "marginalize" the opinions of "real people" by "drowning out non-corporate voices." This in turn "can generate the impression that corporations dominate our democracy" and give corporations "special advantages in the market for legislation."

Finally, considering shareholder protection, the dissent further stated that the law can "serve First Amendment values" by protecting the rights of shareholders from a "kind of coerced speech: electioneering communications that do not reflec[t] [their] support." The PAC mechanism prevents managers from advancing personal agendas, and limits the "rent seeking behavior of executives and respects views of dissenters."]

V

Today's decision is backwards in many senses. It elevates the majority's agenda over the litigants' submissions, facial attacks over as-applied claims, broad constitutional theories over narrow statutory grounds, individual dissenting opinions over precedential holdings, assertion over tradition, absolutism over empiricism, rhetoric over reality. Our colleagues have arrived at the conclusion that *Austin* must be overruled and that § 203 is facially unconstitutional only after mischaracterizing both the reach and rationale of those authorities, and after bypassing or ignoring rules of judicial restraint used to cabin the Court's lawmaking power. Their conclusion that the societal interest in avoiding corruption and the appearance of corruption does not provide an adequate justification for regulating corporate expenditures on candidate elections relies on an incorrect description of that interest, along with a failure to acknowledge the relevance of established facts and the considered judgments of state and federal legislatures over many decades.

In a democratic society, the longstanding consensus on the need to limit corporate campaign spending should outweigh the wooden application of judge-made rules. The majority's rejection of this principle "elevate[s] corporations to a level of deference which has not been seen at least since the days when substantive due process was regularly used to invalidate regulatory legislation thought to unfairly impinge upon established economic interests." *Bellotti* (White, J., dissenting). At bottom, the Court's opinion is thus a rejection of the common sense of the American people, who have recognized a need to prevent corporations from undermining self-government since the founding, and who have fought against the distinctive corrupting potential of corporate electioneering since the days of Theodore Roosevelt. It is a strange time to repudiate that common sense. While American democracy is imperfect, few outside the majority of this Court would have thought its flaws included a dearth of corporate money in politics.

I would affirm the judgment of the District Court.

Notes and Questions

1. May labor unions also spend unlimited general treasury funds in candidate elections?

2. Should the Court have decided the case on narrower grounds? Why not, for example, read the electioneering provisions so as not to apply to a full-length film offered on-demand?

3. The majority in *Citizens United* declined to opine on whether bans on spending on elections by foreign individuals, entities, or government would be constitutional. Yet two years later, the Supreme Court summarily affirmed a lower court opinion upholding the ban on foreign spending in elections. *Bluman v. FEC*, 565 U.S. 1104 (2012) (mem.) (affirming 800 F. Supp. 2d 281 (D.D.C. 2011) (three-judge court)). Recall that a summary affirmance is a decision on the merits that the lower court got the result right, although perhaps not for the same reasons as the Court would have given.

Here are the reasons the lower court gave for upholding the ban on foreign spending in elections:

> [T]he Supreme Court has drawn a fairly clear line: The government may exclude foreign citizens from activities "intimately related to the process of democratic self-government." As the Court has written, "a State's historical power to exclude aliens from participation in its democratic political institutions [is] part of the sovereign's obligation to preserve the basic conception of a political community." In other words, the government may reserve "participation in its democratic political institutions" for citizens of this country. When reviewing a statute barring foreign citizens from serving as probation officers, the Court explained that the "exclusion of aliens from basic governmental processes is not a deficiency in the democratic system but *a necessary consequence of the community's process of political self-definition.*" Upholding a statute barring aliens from teaching in public schools, the Court reasoned that the "distinction between citizens and aliens, though ordinarily irrelevant to private activity, is *fundamental to the definition and government of a State.* . . . It is because of this special

significance of citizenship that governmental entities, when exercising the functions of government, have wider latitude in limiting the participation of noncitizens." And in upholding a ban on aliens serving as police officers, the Court stated that, "although we extend to aliens the right to education and public welfare, along with the ability to earn a livelihood and engage in licensed professions, the right to govern is reserved to citizens."

We read these cases to set forth a straightforward principle: It is fundamental to the definition of our national political community that foreign citizens do not have a constitutional right to participate in, and thus may be excluded from, activities of democratic self-government. It follows, therefore, that the United States has a compelling interest for purposes of First Amendment analysis in limiting the participation of foreign citizens in activities of American democratic self-government, and in thereby preventing foreign influence over the U.S. political process.

Applying the Supreme Court's precedents, the question here is whether political contributions and express-advocacy expenditures — including donations to outside groups that in turn make contributions or express-advocacy expenditures — constitute part of the process of democratic self-government. In our view, the answer to that question is straightforward: Political contributions and express-advocacy expenditures are an integral aspect of the process by which Americans elect officials to federal, state, and local government offices. Political contributions and express-advocacy expenditures finance advertisements, get-out-the-vote drives, rallies, candidate speeches, and the myriad other activities by which candidates appeal to potential voters. We think it evident that those campaign activities are part of the overall process of democratic self-government. Moreover, it is undisputed that the government may bar foreign citizens from voting and serving as elected officers. It follows that the government may bar foreign citizens (at least those who are not lawful permanent residents of the United States) from participating in the campaign process that seeks to influence how voters will cast their ballots in the elections. Those limitations on the activities of foreign citizens are of a piece and are all "part of the sovereign's obligation to preserve the basic conception of a political community."

The three-judge court further quoted from Justice Stevens's dissent for four Justices in *Citizens United*: "To be sure, the other five Justices did not have occasion to expressly address this issue in *Citizens United,* but the majority's analysis in *Citizens United* certainly was not in conflict with Justice Stevens's conclusion on this particular question about foreign influence. Indeed, in our view, the majority opinion in *Citizens United* is entirely consistent with a ban on foreign contributions and expenditures. And we find the force of Justice Stevens's statement to be a telling and accurate indicator of where the Supreme Court's jurisprudence stands on the question of foreign contributions and expenditures."

Is the three-judge court's analysis "entirely consistent" with *Citizens United*? How, if at all, do these reasons for excluding foreign individuals differ from the anti-corruption and antidistortion arguments rejected by the Court in *Citizens United*? What other arguments might the Justices accept to support such a ban against foreign spending but not corporate spending? Does the Court's summary affirmance in *Bluman* mean that sometimes the identity of the speaker *does* matter? For an argument before *Citizens United* that the First Amendment prevents barring foreign spending, see Toni M. Massaro, *Foreign Nationals, Foreign Spending, and the First Amendment*, 34 Harvard Journal of Law and Public Policy 663 (2011).

4. The question of foreign spending in U.S. elections took on new urgency after extensive reports of foreign (especially Russian government) interference in the 2016 elections. As explained in Richard L. Hasen, *Cheap Speech and What It Has Done (to American Democracy)*, 16 First Amendment Law Review 200, 206–07 (2018):

> As part of a larger effort to influence the 2016 presidential election and U.S. politics, Russia undertook an extensive propaganda effort, which included publishing negative stories about [Democratic presidential candidate Hillary] Clinton and U.S. interests as well as inflaming passions and spreading false stories aimed at influencing the outcome of the election in Trump's favor. "For example, [Russian news website] Sputnik published an article that said the [John] Podesta email dump included certain incriminating comments about the Benghazi scandal, an allegation that turned out to be incorrect. Trump himself repeated this false story" at a campaign rally.
>
> Sources allied with the Russian government paid at least $100,000 to Facebook to spread election-related messages and false reports to specific populations (a process called "microtargeting"), including aiming certain false reports at journalists who might be expected to further spread the propaganda and misinformation. Russia and others also used automated "bots" to spread and amplify false news across social media platforms such as Facebook and Twitter.

But, according to Hasen, it was not clear how much of this activity violated the current federal ban on foreign spending in U.S. elections or, if federal law were amended to prohibit such activity, whether the Supreme Court would strike down some of the prohibitions as inconsistent with the First Amendment:

> After investigation, Facebook announced finding at least $100,000 in spending from sources connected to the Russian government on roughly 3,000 ads intended to influence the election. The ads reached at least 10 million people (44% before the 2016 election) and some focused on social controversies over immigration rights, gun rights, and racial justice.
>
> If Russia paid for these ads without coordinating with any campaign, then it almost certainly did not violate current federal campaign finance law as to most of the ads. Further, laws that would bar Russia from placing

these ads could well be found at least partially unconstitutional under the First Amendment as the Supreme Court currently construes it.

Federal law bars foreign nationals, including foreign governments, from making expenditures, independent expenditures, and electioneering communications in connection with a "Federal, State or local election." However, it is at best uncertain whether independent online ads that do not expressly advocate the election or defeat of candidates are covered by the foreign expenditure ban. For example, a Russian ad promoting a Black Lives Matter rally, but not mentioning or showing a candidate for office, likely would not be considered an election ad under current law, which does not cover pure issue advocacy even if intended to influence election outcomes.

These advertisements also would not be covered under proposed federal legislation, the "Honest Ads Act," which would extend rules barring foreign spending on television or radio "electioneering communications" to communications via digital outlets like Facebook. Electioneering communications must feature the name or likeness of a candidate for office to be covered.

Even if Congress passed a statute purporting to make illegal all of the activity Russians engaged in during the 2016 election, such a statute would likely run into First Amendment resistance. After the Supreme Court decided *Citizens United* ... the Court summarily affirmed a lower court decision in *Bluman v. Federal Election Commission*. *Bluman* upheld a federal law barring foreign nationals—in the case of Benjamin Bluman, a foreign national working in New York on a temporary work visa—from spending even fifty cents to print and distribute flyers expressly advocating the reelection of President Obama.

Bluman seems to indicate that, despite tensions with the holding in *Citizens United* that the identity of the speaker does not matter for First Amendment purposes, the government has a compelling interest in banning foreign spending in our elections....

But the *Bluman* court, in an opinion by conservative-libertarian D.C. Circuit judge Brett Kavanaugh, narrowly construed the foreign spending ban to cover only express advocacy and not issue advocacy. "This statute, as we interpret it, does not bar foreign nationals from issue advocacy—that is, speech that does not expressly advocate the election or defeat of a specific candidate." Indeed, three FEC Republican commissioners relied upon this dicta from *Bluman* in voting to hold that the foreign spending ban does not apply to ballot measure elections.

While this interpretation is not free from doubt—the statute is written broadly to cover all expenditures and not just independent expenditures—it seems like the kind of interpretation likely to be favored by the current Supreme Court.

> Indeed, it is not clear that the courts would accept a more clearly written foreign spending ban going beyond express advocacy and electioneering communications to cover foreign-funded ads meant to stir social unrest without using candidates' names or likenesses. These ads should be covered, not because they necessarily contain false speech, but because they constitute a foreign government's interference with American self-government.

Hasen, *supra*, at 217–19.

Do you agree? Should a statute barring foreign interference be able to ban more than express advocacy and electioneering communications by foreign individuals, governments, and entities? Just governments? What about foreign media corporations? If *The Guardian* newspaper from Great Britain editorializes in favor of a candidate for U.S. President, should it be allowed to post a link to that endorsement via a paid Facebook ad targeted at U.S. readers?

Judge Kavanaugh, the author of the unanimous *Bluman* opinion, is now Justice Kavanaugh, having been named to the Supreme Court by President Trump. Does his confirmation increase or decrease the chances of the Court construing the foreign spending ban to apply only to express advocacy?

Does the *WRTL II* "functional equivalent of express advocacy" apply to limits on foreign issue ads? This seems to be a huge unanswered question.

5. The much-anticipated report from Special Counsel Robert Mueller detailed Russian interference in the 2016 elections. Mueller's investigation "identified numerous links between the Russian government and the Trump Campaign. Although the investigation established that the Russian government perceived it would benefit from a Trump presidency and worked to secure that outcome, and that the [Trump] Campaign expected it would benefit electorally from information stolen and released through Russian efforts, the investigation did not establish that members of the Trump Campaign conspired or coordinated with the Russian government in its election interference activities." I Special Counsel Robert S. Mueller, III, Report on the Investigation into Russian Interference in the 2016 Presidential Election, 1-2 (Mar. 2019), https://perma.cc/9TEW-JD3Z.

Foreign interference in the 2020 U.S. elections continued, although the full scope remains under investigation. Julian E. Barnes, *Russia Continues Interfering in Election to Try to Help Trump, U.S. Intelligence Says*, N.Y. Times, Aug. 7, 2020 (updated Sept. 2, 2020); Natasha Bertrand & Daniel Lippman, *Ratcliffe Went Off Script with Iran Remarks, Officials Say*, Politico, Oct. 28, 2020; Julian E. Barnes, Nicole Perlroth & David E. Sanger, *Russia Poses Greater Election Threat Than Iran, Many U.S. Officials Say*, N.Y. Times, Oct. 22, 2020; Julian E. Barnes, *Russian Interference in 2020 Included Influencing Trump Associates, Report Says*, N.Y. Times, Mar. 16, 2021; Nat'l Intel. Council, *Foreign Threats to the US 2020 Federal Elections*, Mar. 10, 2021; *Joint Report of the Department of Justice and the Department of Homeland Security on Foreign Interference Targeting Election Infrastructure or Political Organization,*

Campaign, or Candidate Infrastructure Related to the 2020 US Federal Elections, Mar. 2021.

Relying upon the Supreme Court's summary affirmance in *Bluman*, the Ninth Circuit rejected a challenge to the federal foreign contribution ban's application to state and local elections, finding the law within Congress's powers and not a First Amendment violation. *United States v. Singh*, 924 F.3d 1030, 1043 (9th Cir. 2019), cert. denied, 140 S. Ct. 1265 (2020).

6. Which is more inconsistent: a Court which accepts a corporate spending ban but allows spending by media corporations on election-related activity, or a Court which rejects a corporate spending ban but allows a ban on spending by foreign individuals and entities? See Richard L. Hasen, Citizens United *and the Illusion of Coherence*, 109 Michigan Law Review 581 (2011). For another view, see Michael W. McConnell, *Reconsidering Citizens United as a Press Clause Case*, 123 Yale Law Journal 412 (2013). A rebuttal to Professor McConnell's argument appears in Chapter 6 of Richard L. Hasen, Plutocrats United: Campaign Money, the Supreme Court, and the Distortion of American Elections (2016).

7. *Citizens United* appears to apply to judicial elections. On what basis does the majority distinguish the *Caperton* case, considered in Chapter 10? Note that Justice Kennedy was the only Justice in the majority in both *Caperton* and *Citizens United*. Is his vote in these cases consistent? How could a contribution to a Super PAC merit recusal if such spending can neither corrupt nor create the appearance of corruption? Consider too the decision in *Williams-Yulee*, also discussed in Chapter 10, which recognized a compelling interest in preserving public confidence in the integrity of the judiciary. Would that interest justify limits on spending in judicial elections, by corporations or other groups?

8. *Citizens United* has had both a direct effect of freeing corporate (and labor union) money in candidate elections, and some indirect effects as well. One study found that "[i]n states where union membership is relatively high and corporations relatively weak, *Citizens United* did not have a discernible effect on the partisan balance of the state legislature. But in states with weak unions and strong corporations, the decision appeared to increase Republican seat share by as much as 12 points." Nour Abdul-Razzak, Carlo Prato & Stéphane Wolton, *How* Citizens United *Gave Republicans a Bonanza of Seats in U.S. State Legislatures*, Monkey Cage, Washington Post, Feb. 24, 2017. One of the most significant effects is the growth of independent groups (now commonly known as "Super PACs") spending money in federal elections. We consider the emergence of these groups, and their effects on the campaign finance system, in the following chapter.

9. Justice Kennedy suggests one way in which corporate spending might be limited: through shareholder democracy. In the wake of *Citizens United*, there have been attempts to get major institutional investors, such as pension funds, to push for shareholder approval of corporate political spending. Under what circumstances

will it be in the interest of corporate shareholders to limit corporate political spending? Under what circumstances could they overcome collective action problems to do so?

10. *Who gains from* Citizens United? Polling showed the *Citizens United* ruling unpopular among Democrats, Republicans, and independents. But among elites, Democrats have generally been broadly critical of the opinion, while Republicans have been generally supportive. Yet opinion does not always neatly break down upon party lines. Consider the views of Professor Joel Gora, one of the lawyers who represented the ACLU in the *Buckley* case.

> Of course, only time will tell what the real impact of the *Citizens United* decision will be, either doctrinally, practically or politically. But, whatever results, to me the case is a landmark of political freedom. It has already changed the campaign finance conversation away from limits and toward issues like disclosure, public subsidies, plus further deregulation of the limits on political funding. The decision will lead to increased political speech, a more informed electorate, and a more robust democracy. A win, win, win situation.
>
> The ultimate essence of the Court's ruling is that under the First Amendment there are no privileged speakers and no pariah speakers. The First Amendment protects all those individuals and groups that would exercise their right to speak and communicate by disabling government from abridging the freedom of speech. That is a true form of leveling the playing field, putting all people and groups on the same plane and footing where freedom of speech is concerned. Most of the press does not like the decision because they do not want the competition; most of the politicians do not like the decision because they do not want the criticism and the pushback. But the competition and the criticism will inevitably work to the benefit of the public and the political process, and ultimately, to the strength of our democracy.

Joel Gora, *The First Amendment . . . United*, 27 Georgia State University Law Review 935, 987 (2011). Do you agree that *Citizens United* strengthens democracy? Why or why not?

11. Given the great public controversy surrounding the *Citizens United* decision, some observers predicted (without any obvious basis for thinking so) that one or more Justices on the Supreme Court who were in the majority in the *Citizens United* case would be quickly willing to vote to reverse it. Critics focused upon a case in which the Montana Supreme Court held that Montana's history demonstrated corporate corruption of candidates through independent spending. It used these facts to distinguish *Citizens United* and uphold the state's corporate spending ban. *Western Tradition Partnership v. Attorney General*, 271 P.3d 1 (Mont. 2011). Hopes for a Supreme Court turnaround were quickly dashed by the following case, in an opinion the Court issued summarily from a cert. petition, without oral argument.

American Tradition Partnership v. Bullock

567 U.S. 516 (2012)

PER CURIAM.

A Montana state law provides that a "corporation may not make . . . an expenditure in connection with a candidate or a political committee that supports or opposes a candidate or a political party." Mont. Code Ann §13-25-227(1) (2011). The Montana Supreme Court rejected petitioners' claim that this statute violates the First Amendment. In *Citizens United*, this Court struck down a similar federal law, holding that "political speech does not lose First Amendment protection simply because its source is a corporation." The question presented in this case is whether the holding of *Citizens United* applies to the Montana state law. There can be no serious doubt that it does. See U.S. Const., Art. VI, cl. 2. Montana's arguments in support of the judgment below either were already rejected in *Citizens United*, or fail to meaningfully distinguish that case.

The petition for certiorari is granted. The judgment of the Supreme Court of Montana is reversed.

It is so ordered.

Justice BREYER, with whom Justice GINSBURG, Justice SOTOMAYOR, and Justice KAGAN join, dissenting.

In *Citizens United*, the Court concluded that "independent expenditures, including those made by corporations, do not give rise to corruption or the appearance of corruption." I disagree with the Court's holding for the reasons expressed in Justice Stevens' dissent in that case. As Justice Stevens explained, "technically independent expenditures can be corrupting in much the same way as direct contributions." Indeed, Justice Stevens recounted a "substantial body of evidence" suggesting that "[m]any corporate independent expenditures . . . had become essentially interchangeable with direct contributions in their capacity to generate *quid pro quo* arrangements."

Moreover, even if I were to accept *Citizens United*, this Court's legal conclusion should not bar the Montana Supreme Court's finding, made on the record before it, that independent expenditures by corporations did in fact lead to corruption or the appearance of corruption in Montana. Given the history and political landscape in Montana, that court concluded that the State had a compelling interest in limiting independent expenditures by corporations. Thus, Montana's experience, like considerable experience elsewhere since the Court's decision in *Citizens United*, casts grave doubt on the Court's supposition that independent expenditures do not corrupt or appear to do so.

Were the matter up to me, I would vote to grant the petition for certiorari in order to reconsider *Citizens United* or, at least, its application in this case. But given the Court's *per curiam* disposition, I do not see a significant possibility of reconsideration. Consequently, I vote instead to deny the petition.

Notes and Questions

1. Should state legislatures have greater authority to impose spending limits on their own elections than Congress has for federal elections? Is there a federalism argument that would support giving states more constitutional latitude? For an argument to that effect, grounded in the Republican Guarantee Clause, see Anthony Johnstone, *The Federalist Safeguards of Politics*, 39 Harvard Journal of Law & Policy 415 (2016). (The author was counsel for the State of Montana in *ATP v. Bullock*.)

2. If the Court were willing to reconsider evidence that independent spending could corrupt, what would it look like? Should the Court reconsider its rejection of the equality rationale for limiting campaign spending if there is insufficient evidence of corruption?

Chapter 14

Contribution Limits

In *Buckley v. Valeo*, the Supreme Court upheld several FECA provisions limiting campaign contributions to candidates for federal office. The Court held such limits only "marginally" restricted free speech rights and were justified by the government's interest in preventing corruption and the appearance of corruption.

Though *Buckley* answered some fundamental questions about the constitutionality of campaign contribution limits, it left open a number of others, including the following important questions:

- May a state or local government limit campaign contributions in ballot measure campaigns?
- Can campaign contribution limits be so low as to become unconstitutional?
- Under what circumstances may campaign contribution limits be applied against political party contributions?
- Is it constitutional to limit contributions to political groups that make *independent expenditures* favoring or opposing candidates, but do not make any contributions to candidates or coordinate spending with candidates?[a] "Super PACs" are among the groups now engaging in such activity.
- Is it permissible to *ban* direct contributions to candidates by corporations, or other persons or entities, such as lobbyists or government contractors?

On these last questions, we will consider not only *Buckley* but also the Supreme Court's 2010 opinion in *Citizens United v. FEC*, discussed in the last chapter.

We consider each of these questions in turn.

I. Campaign Contribution Limits in Ballot Measure Elections

Buckley concerned *federal* campaign finance law, which means it concerned exclusively *candidate* elections; there is no initiative process on the federal level. In *First National Bank of Boston v. Bellotti*, set forth in the last chapter, the Supreme Court held that the First Amendment bars any limit on spending by corporations in

---

a. As *Buckley* pointed out, federal law counts coordinated spending as a contribution rather than as an independent expenditure. See *FEC v. Wisconsin Right to Life*, 551 U.S. 449, 486 (2007) (Scalia, J., concurring in part and concurring in the judgment).

ballot measure campaigns. *Bellotti* is important for our purposes now because the *Bellotti* Court's premise was that "Referenda are held on issues, not candidates for public office. The risk of corruption perceived in cases involving candidate elections simply is not present in a popular vote on a public issue."

Building upon *Bellotti*, the Court in *Citizens against Rent Control v. City of Berkeley*, 454 U.S. 290 (1981) (*CARC*), struck down a $250 limit on contributions to committees formed to support or oppose municipal ballot measures. Writing for the majority, Chief Justice Burger relied heavily on the First Amendment right of association:

> We begin by recalling that the practice of persons sharing common views banding together to achieve a common end is deeply embedded in the American political process. The 18th-century Committees of Correspondence and the pamphleteers were early examples of this phenomena [*sic*] and the Federalist Papers were perhaps the most significant and lasting example. The tradition of volunteer committees for collective action has manifested itself in myriad community and public activities; in the political process it can focus on a candidate or on a ballot measure. Its value is that by collective effort individuals can make their views known, when, individually, their voices would be faint or lost.
>
> The Court has long viewed the First Amendment as protecting a marketplace for the clash of different views and conflicting ideas. That concept has been stated and restated almost since the Constitution was drafted. The voters of the city of Berkeley adopted the challenged ordinance which places restrictions on that marketplace.

The *CARC* Court then found the contribution limit unconstitutional under *Buckley*:

> [*Buckley* noted] that the freedom of association "is diluted if it does not include the right to pool money through contributions, for funds are often essential if 'advocacy' is to be truly or optimally 'effective.'" Under the Berkeley ordinance an affluent person can, acting alone, spend without limit to advocate individual views on a ballot measure. It is only when contributions are made in concert with one or more others in the exercise of the right of association that they are restricted by [the ordinance].
>
> *Buckley* identified a single narrow exception to the rule that limits on political activity were contrary to the First Amendment. The exception relates to the perception of undue influence of large contributors to a *candidate* . . .
>
> *Buckley* thus sustained limits on contributions to candidates and their committees.
>
> In *Bellotti*, we held that a state could not prohibit corporations any more than it could preclude individuals from making contributions or expenditures advocating views on ballot measures. The *Bellotti* Court relied on

Buckley to strike down state legislative limits on advocacy relating to ballot measures . . .

Notwithstanding *Buckley* and *Bellotti*, the city of Berkeley argues that [the ordinance] is necessary as a prophylactic measure to make known the identity of supporters and opponents of ballot measures. It is true that when individuals or corporations speak through committees, they often adopt seductive names that may tend to conceal the true identity of the source. Here, there is no risk that the Berkeley voters will be in doubt as to the identity of those whose money supports or opposes a given ballot measure since contributors must make their identities known under [another provision] of the ordinance, which requires publication of lists of contributors in advance of the voting.

Contributions by individuals to support concerted action by a committee advocating a position on a ballot measure is beyond question a very significant form of political expression. As we have noted, regulation of First Amendment rights is always subject to exacting judicial scrutiny. The public interest allegedly advanced by [the ordinance] — identifying the sources of support for and opposition to ballot measures — is insubstantial because voters may identify those sources under the [other] provisions. In addition, the record in this case does not support the California Supreme Court's conclusion that [the ordinance] is needed to preserve voters' confidence in the ballot measure process. Cf. *Bellotti*. It is clear, therefore, that [the ordinance] does not advance a legitimate governmental interest significant enough to justify its infringement of First Amendment rights.

Apart from the impermissible restraint on freedom of association, but virtually inseparable from it in this context, [the ordinance] imposes a significant restraint on the freedom of expression of groups and those individuals who wish to express their views through committees. As we have noted, an individual may make expenditures without limit under [the ordinance] on a ballot measure but may not contribute beyond the $250 limit when joining with others to advocate common views. The contribution limit thus automatically affects expenditures,[b] and limits on expenditures operate as a direct restraint on freedom of expression of a group or committee desiring to engage in political dialogue concerning a ballot measure.

Whatever may be the state interest or degree of that interest in regulating and limiting contributions to or expenditures of a candidate or a candidate's committees there is no significant state or public interest in curtailing

b. Is this statement consistent with the analysis in *Buckley* supporting the constitutionality of the FECA contribution limits? If not, which analysis is more sound, the *per curiam* opinion's in *Buckley* or Chief Justice Burger's here? — Eds.

> debate and discussion of a ballot measure. Placing limits on contributions which in turn limit expenditures plainly impairs freedom of expression. The integrity of the political system will be adequately protected if contributors are identified in a public filing revealing the amounts contributed; if it is thought wise, legislation can outlaw anonymous contributions.

Id. at 297–300. Justices Blackmun and O'Connor issued a brief opinion concurring in the judgment. On the question of the city's interest in preserving voter confidence in government, they wrote:

> We would not deny the legitimacy of that interest. . . . We did not find those interests threatened in *Bellotti*, however, in part because the State failed to show "by record or legislative findings that corporate advocacy threatened imminently to undermine democratic processes" or "the confidence of the citizenry in government." The city's evidentiary support in this case is equally sparse.

Id. at 302, 303. Justice Marshall agreed in his separate opinion concurring in the judgment that the city failed to present adequate evidence the ordinance was needed to preserve voter confidence. Justice White dissented, disagreeing with the majority and concurring justices' assessment of the city's interests.

> It is bad enough that the Court overstates the extent to which First Amendment interests are implicated. But the Court goes on to assert that the ordinance furthers no legitimate public interest and cannot survive "any degree of scrutiny." Apparently the Court assumes this to be so because the ordinance is not directed at *quid pro quos* between large contributors and candidates for office, "the single narrow exception" for regulation that it viewed *Buckley* as endorsing. The *Buckley* Court, however, found it "unnecessary to look beyond the Act's primary purpose," the prevention of corruption, to uphold the contribution limits, and thus did not consider other possible interests for upholding the restriction. Indeed, at least since *United States v. Automobile Workers*, 352 U.S. 567 (1957), the Court has recognized that "sustaining the active alert responsibility of the individual citizen in a democracy for the wise conduct of government" is a valid state interest. The *Bellotti* Court took care to note that this objective, along with "[p]reserving the integrity of the electoral process [and] the individual citizen's confidence in government" "are interests of the highest importance."
>
> In *Bellotti*, the Court found inadequate evidence in the record to support these interests, but it suggested that some regulation of corporate spending might be justified if "corporate advocacy threatened imminently to undermine democratic processes, thereby denigrating rather than serving First Amendment interests." The Court suggested that such a situation would arise if it could be shown that "the relative voice of corporations ha[d] been overwhelming [and] . . . significant in influencing referenda." It is quite possible that such a test is fairly met in this case. Large contributions, mainly

from corporate sources, have skyrocketed as the role of individuals has declined. Staggering disparities have developed between spending for and against various ballot measures. While it is not possible to prove that heavy spending "bought" a victory on any particular ballot proposition, there is increasing evidence that large contributors are at least able to block the adoption of measures through the initiative process. Recognition that enormous contributions from a few institutional sources can overshadow the efforts of individuals may have discouraged participation in ballot measure campaigns and undermined public confidence in the referendum process.

By restricting the size of contributions, the Berkeley ordinance requires major contributors to communicate directly with the voters. If the ordinance has an ultimate impact on speech, it will be to assure that a diversity of views will be presented to the voters. . . . Of course, entities remain free to make major direct expenditures. But because political communications must state the source of funds, voters will be able to identify the source of such messages and recognize that the communication reflects, for example, the opinion of a single powerful corporate interest rather than the views of a large number of individuals. As the existence of disclosure laws in many States suggests, information concerning who supports or opposes a ballot measure significantly affects voter evaluation of the proposal. The Court asserts, without elaboration, that existing disclosure requirements suffice to inform voters of the identity of contributors. Yet, the inadequacy of disclosure laws was a major reason for the adoption of the Berkeley ordinance. Section 101(d) of the ordinance constitutes a finding by the people of Berkeley that "the influence of large campaign contributors is increased because existing laws for disclosure of campaign receipts and expenditures have proved to be inadequate."

Admittedly, Berkeley cannot present conclusive evidence of a causal relationship between major undisclosed expenditures and the demise of the referendum as a tool of direct democracy. But the information available suffices to demonstrate that the voters had valid reasons for adopting contribution ceilings. It was on a similar foundation that the Court upheld contribution limits in *Buckley* and *California Medical Assn.* In my view, the ordinance survives scrutiny under the *Buckley* and *Bellotti* cases.

Notes and Questions

1. The Court in *Bellotti* and *CARC* proceeded on the assumption that there is a clear line separating candidate elections and ballot measure elections. That is not always true. In California, for example, governors and others have used ballot measure elections as a means to boost their own chances for reelection or to further other political goals. "There were at least thirty-seven committees controlled by candidates or elected officials and organized to affect the outcome of ballot measure elections from 1990 to 2004, and together they have raised at least

$84 million." See Richard L. Hasen, *Rethinking the Unconstitutionality of Contribution and Expenditure Limits in Ballot Measure Campaigns*, 78 Southern California Law Review 885, 898 (2005). On the strength of this evidence, may contributions to candidate-controlled ballot measure committees be limited consistent with the First Amendment?

2. The *CARC* Court rejected the California Supreme Court's view that a contribution limit could be justified as "needed to preserve voters' confidence in the ballot measure process," because it was not supported by the record. What evidence would be sufficient to sustain this argument? Consider the following evidence, which had not been published prior to the trial in *CARC* and therefore could not have been made part of the record.

Some scholars have asserted that even when one side greatly outspends its adversaries its chances for success do not increase materially. *E.g.*, Ronald J. Allen, *The National Initiative Proposal: A Preliminary Analysis*, 58 Nebraska Law Review 965, 1028–38 (1979). Others have found one-sided spending to have a dominant effect. *E.g.*, John S. Shockley, The Initiative Process in Colorado Politics: An Assessment (1980). Research relative to California ballot propositions held between 1968 and 1980 suggests that one-sided spending has generally been very effective, to the point of "dominance," when it has been on the negative side, but surprisingly ineffective when it has been on the affirmative side. See Lowenstein, *supra*. Lowenstein's study is deservedly criticized for its statistical crudeness by John R. Owens and Larry L. Wade, *Campaign Spending on California Ballot Propositions, 1924–1984: Trends and Voting Effects*, 39 Western Political Quarterly 675, 682–87 (1986). Owens and Wade considered vote percentages rather than passage or defeat of ballot propositions, and the effects of campaign spending that they found were relatively weak. Nevertheless, a study of California initiative campaigns for the period 1976–88 generally found the same effects on outcomes as had appeared in Lowenstein's study, i.e., dominance of big negative spending and ineffectiveness of big affirmative spending. See California Commission on Campaign Financing, Democracy By Initiative 290–91 (1992).

If another jurisdiction adopted a contribution limit, would introduction of that research be sufficient to sustain the limit? If you were persuaded that this conclusion (that one-sided spending usually prevails if it is on the negative side but not on the affirmative side) holds generally in ballot proposition campaigns, would it lead you to regard some control as desirable or as unnecessary? Would your answer be affected by whether you regard the institutions of direct democracy as desirable?

3. Elisabeth R. Gerber, The Populist Paradox: Interest Group Influence and the Promise of Direct Legislation (1999), argues that "it is a mistake to equate money with influence in the context of direct legislation." Gerber studied how both "economic" interest groups (such as trade associations) and "citizen" interest groups (such as the National Rifle Association or the Sierra Club) used the political process in states with initiatives. Gerber noted that economic groups are generally rich in capital and citizen groups are rich in labor, leading to different strategies:

> If citizen and economic interest groups have the comparative advantages described above, then I expect to observe the following patterns between group resources and strategies. Because citizen groups tend to have the personnel resources required to mobilize broad-based electoral support, they are better able to amass an electoral majority. When they have sufficient capital to participate at all, I therefore expect citizen groups to employ strategies aimed at proposing and passing new initiatives. Economic interest groups, by contrast, should anticipate a more difficult time using their resources to achieve victory at the ballot box and should instead pursue largely defensive or indirect strategies. Analyzing surveys of interest group activities and motivations, as well as campaign finance data from 161 initiative and referendum campaigns in eight states, I find strong empirical evidence in support of these theoretical conclusions. Citizen groups report using the direct legislation process to pass new laws and contribute to campaigns to support new initiative legislation. Economic groups report using the direct legislation process to pressure the legislature and direct a large share of their financial resources to opposition campaigns . . .
>
> I expect these patterns of interest group behavior to translate into patterns of policy outcomes. Specifically, I expect the laws that pass by initiative to reflect the interests of citizen groups that use the process to achieve direct modifying influence. I expect the laws that fail to reflect economic group interests. I also expect legislatures in initiative states to respond to interest group pressures by passing different laws than do legislatures in noninitiative states. Further analyses of the campaign finance data, plus comparisons of policies in the fifty states, provide strong empirical evidence that is consistent with these expectations.
>
> Together, these theoretical and empirical results show that citizen and economic interest groups use direct legislation for different purposes and to different ends. The largely conservative and indirect influence by economic interest groups is a form of influence much different from — although perhaps no less important than — the one portrayed by modern critics of direct legislation.[c]

Id. at 8–9. Assume Gerber's empirical evidence supports her case. Would that fact lead you to support different (or no) controls over initiative campaign finance?

4. Suppose that in a ballot proposition campaign side A can raise $1,000,000 in relatively small contributions, and side B can raise only $100,000 in such contributions. Suppose further that XYZ Corporation would like to contribute $900,000 to side B. Is it fair to permit the large contribution under these circumstances? Is it fair

---

c. On the specific question of blocking initiatives, Gerber found that economic groups have an easier time than citizen groups blocking initiatives they oppose. *Id.* at 119.

to prohibit it? From whose point of view are you applying a standard of fairness? Consider Lowenstein, *supra*, 29 UCLA Law Review at 515–17:

> There are two conceptions of fairness that may inform our evaluation. First, the campaign may be regarded as fair when both sides have a roughly equal opportunity to present their arguments to the voters. We shall call this the *equality* standard of fairness. Second, the campaign may be regarded as fair when the ability of either side to present its arguments more or less reflects the number of people who actively support that side and the strength of their feelings. We shall call this the *intensity* standard of fairness.
>
> The equality standard is based on the voter's interest in receiving a balanced presentation of the arguments. If the equality standard is met, the voter is least likely to be deceived and most likely to be apprised of considerations relevant to his assessment of the proposition. The intensity standard is based on the interest of activists on each side who wish to translate their own strong feelings into an advantage for their side. The intensity standard minimizes the likelihood that an apathetic majority will impose severe harm on an intense minority. In addition, it incorporates the idea that widespread political participation is desirable and therefore should be encouraged by assuring that participation will be effective.
>
> While both the equality and intensity standards have intuitive appeal, they can be incompatible. If large numbers of people feel strongly and are prepared to contribute money, speak out and otherwise assist one side of the issue while most of their opponents remain apathetic, under the intensity standard the result is regarded as fair although voters are exposed to a relatively one-sided debate. On the other hand, if measures are taken to assure a relatively even-handed debate, the intense feelings on one side will not significantly enhance that side's chances of success.

In the above problem, is permitting the contribution by the XYZ Corporation to Side B fair under the equality standard of fairness? Under the intensity standard? Suppose the XYZ Corporation instead wants to contribute $900,000 to side A. Is permitting this contribution fair under either or both standards of fairness?

Now consider a variation that is often more realistic in ballot measure campaigns. Side A has sufficiently widespread and intense support that it can raise $500,000 in small contributions, and it receives no large contributions. Side B receives virtually no small contributions, but four corporations contribute $5 million each. Because of the large size of the state and the high prices for advertising in media of all types, political experts agree that a $500,000 campaign will have almost no success in communicating its message to voters, whereas $20 million is just about what is needed to get a message heard often enough to make an impression. Furthermore, because of other, more newsworthy matters that will be on the ballot at the same time, newspapers and broadcasters are giving little attention to the proposition in question. The proposition is sufficiently complex and its likely consequences sufficiently debatable that the electorate would unquestionably benefit from debate and information. Under these circumstances, if the choice is between a one-sided campaign favoring side B and virtually no campaign at all, which is more in the public interest?

5. Would public financing of ballot measure campaigns be desirable? What would be the objective of public financing? Would money be provided in all ballot proposition campaigns? Bear in mind that many ballot propositions involve relatively obscure amendments to state constitutions that generate little interest. If money is not to be provided in all campaigns, how would it be decided which propositions would be eligible? Would funds go to both sides of the campaign or to one side only? If it were decided that a given side in a given campaign were entitled to funds, what would happen if more than one committee on that side applied for the funds? Would public financing be joined with a limit on the size of contributions or would it be an alternative to such limits? For discussion of these issues, see Elizabeth Garrett, *Money, Agenda Setting, and Direct Democracy*, 77 Texas Law Review 1845, 1876–79 (1999); Richard Briffault, *Ballot Propositions and Campaign Finance Reform,* 1 New York University Journal of Legislation & Public Policy 41 (1997); Lowenstein, *supra*, 29 UCLA Law Review at 578–83.

II. When Are Contribution Limits Too Low?

You may recall from *Buckley* that the Court rejected a challenge to the *amount* of the FECA's contribution limits as unconstitutionally low. The Court quoted approvingly from the lower court opinion that it lacked "a scalpel to probe, whether, say, a $2,000 ceiling might not serve as well as $1,000."[d] The Court continued that "[s]uch distinctions in degree become significant only when they can be said to amount to differences in kind." 424 U.S. 1, 30 (1976).

Over time, some lower courts upheld lower contribution limits, and others rejected them, relying on *Buckley*'s sparse analysis. In 2000, the Supreme Court in *Nixon v. Shrink Missouri Government PAC*, 528 U.S. 377 (2000), upheld a $1,075 individual contribution limit applied to statewide offices in Missouri. *Shrink Missouri* came during a period on the Court when it showed great deference to legislative judgments about the need for campaign finance regulation, and the opinion, written by Justice Souter, reflected this deference.

Although the Court said it was applying the same "exacting scrutiny" that *Buckley* applied to the review of contribution limits, it stressed deference owed to legislative judgments. It held that governments defending campaign finance laws need not provide proof of the danger of corruption when the claims are "neither novel nor implausible." It was enough for the state of Missouri to point to evidence such as an

d. As we will see in Part III of this chapter, the federal individual contribution limit was raised to $2,000 in 2003 and indexed to inflation.

affidavit of a state legislator that large contributions have the "real potential to buy votes."

The Court defined the meaning of "corruption" broadly to include the concern about politicians being "too compliant" with the wishes of contributors and for the public to believe that large contributors "call the tune." It held that the amounts of contributions could only be unconstitutional when a "contribution limitation was so radical in effect as to render political association ineffective, drive the sound of a candidate's voice below the level of notice, and render contributions pointless." The test seemed to make it all but impossible for a contribution limitation to be struck down as unconstitutionally low.[e]

The period of Supreme Court deference to campaign finance regulation did not last long. As we saw in the last chapter, soon after Justice Sandra Day O'Connor retired from the Court, its jurisprudence swung in a much more deregulatory direction. It began before *Citizens United* in *Randall v. Sorrell*, below, a case raising similar issues to those in *Shrink Missouri*, but with a very different result.

Randall v. Sorrell

548 U.S. 230 (2006)

Justice BREYER announced the judgment of the Court and delivered an opinion, in which THE CHIEF JUSTICE joins, and in which Justice ALITO joins except as to Parts II-B-1 and II-B-2.

We here consider the constitutionality of a Vermont campaign finance statute that limits both (1) the amounts that candidates for state office may spend on their campaigns (expenditure limitations) and (2) the amounts that individuals, organizations, and political parties may contribute to those campaigns (contribution limitations). Vt. Stat. Ann., Tit. 17, § 2801 *et seq.* (2002). We hold that both sets of limitations are inconsistent with the First Amendment. Well-established precedent makes clear that the expenditure limits violate the First Amendment. *Buckley.* The contribution limits are unconstitutional because in their specific details (involving low maximum levels and other restrictions) they fail to satisfy the First Amendment's requirement of careful tailoring. That is to say, they impose burdens upon First Amendment interests that (when viewed in light of the statute's legitimate objectives) are disproportionately severe.

---

e. *Shrink Missouri* is also notable for the concurring opinion of Justice Breyer, which sets forth his participatory democracy view that "constitutionally protected interests lie on both sides of the legal equation," and the dissenting opinion of Justice Thomas, which argues that all contribution limits should be subject to strict scrutiny and struck down as a violation of the First Amendment. Serious students of campaign finance would do well to read these dueling opinions on the permissibility of limiting money in politics consistent with the First Amendment.

I

A

Prior to 1997, Vermont's campaign finance law imposed no limit upon the amount a candidate for state office could spend. It did, however, impose limits upon the amounts that individuals, corporations, and political committees could contribute to the campaign of such a candidate. Individuals and corporations could contribute no more than $1,000 to any candidate for state office. Political committees, excluding political parties, could contribute no more than $3,000. The statute imposed no limit on the amount that political parties could contribute to candidates.

In 1997, Vermont enacted a more stringent campaign finance law, Pub. Act No. 64, codified at Vt. Stat. Ann., Tit. 17, § 2801 *et seq.* (2002) (hereinafter Act or Act 64), the statute at issue here. Act 64, which took effect immediately after the 1998 elections, imposes mandatory expenditure limits on the total amount a candidate for state office can spend during a "two-year general election cycle," *i.e.*, the primary plus the general election, in approximately the following amounts: governor, $300,000; lieutenant governor, $100,000; other statewide offices, $45,000; state senator, $4,000 (plus an additional $2,500 for each additional seat in the district); state representative (two-member district), $3,000; and state representative (single member district), $2,000. These limits are adjusted for inflation in odd-numbered years based on the Consumer Price Index. Incumbents seeking reelection to statewide office may spend no more than 85% of the above amounts, and incumbents seeking reelection to the State Senate or House may spend no more than 90% of the above amounts. The Act defines "[e]xpenditure" broadly to mean the

> payment, disbursement, distribution, advance, deposit, loan or gift of money or anything of value, paid or promised to be paid, for the purpose of influencing an election, advocating a position on a public question, or supporting or opposing one or more candidates.

With certain minor exceptions, expenditures over $50 made on a candidate's behalf by others count against the candidate's expenditure limit if those expenditures are "intentionally facilitated by, solicited by or approved by" the candidate's campaign. These provisions apply so as to count against a campaign's expenditure limit any spending by political parties or committees that is coordinated with the campaign and benefits the candidate. And any party expenditure that "primarily benefits six or fewer candidates who are associated with the political party" is "presumed" to be coordinated with the campaign and therefore to count against the campaign's expenditure limit.

Act 64 also imposes strict contribution limits. The amount any single individual can contribute to the campaign of a candidate for state office during a "two-year general election cycle" is limited as follows: governor, lieutenant governor, and other statewide offices, $400; state senator, $300; and state representative, $200. Unlike its expenditure limits, Act 64's contribution limits are not indexed for inflation.

A political committee is subject to these same limits. So is a political party, defined broadly to include "any subsidiary, branch or local unit" of a party, as well as any "national or regional affiliates" of a party (taken separately or together). Thus, for example, the statute treats the local, state, and national affiliates of the Democratic Party as if they were a single entity and limits their total contribution to a single candidate's campaign for governor (during the primary and the general election together) to $400.

The Act also imposes a limit of $2,000 upon the amount any individual can give to a political party during a 2-year general election cycle.

The Act defines "contribution" broadly in approximately the same way it defines "expenditure." Any expenditure made on a candidate's behalf counts as a contribution to the candidate if it is "intentionally facilitated by, solicited by or approved by" the candidate. And a party expenditure that "primarily benefits six or fewer candidates who are associated with the" party is "presumed" to count against the party's contribution limits.

There are a few exceptions. A candidate's own contributions to the campaign and those of the candidate's family fall outside the contribution limits. Volunteer services do not count as contributions. Nor does the cost of a meet-the-candidate function, provided that the total cost for the function amounts to $100 or less.

In addition to these expenditure and contribution limits, the Act sets forth disclosure and reporting requirements and creates a voluntary public financing system for gubernatorial elections. . . . None of these is at issue here. The Act also limits the amount of contributions a candidate, political committee, or political party can receive from out-of-state sources. The lower courts held these out-of-state contribution limits unconstitutional, and the parties do not challenge that holding.

B

The petitioners are individuals who have run for state office in Vermont, citizens who vote in Vermont elections and contribute to Vermont campaigns, and political parties and committees that participate in Vermont politics. Soon after Act 64 became law, they brought this lawsuit in Federal District Court against the respondents, state officials charged with enforcement of the Act. Several other private groups and individual citizens intervened in the District Court proceedings in support of the Act and are joined here as respondents as well.

The District Court agreed with the petitioners that the Act's expenditure limits violate the First Amendment. See *Buckley.* The court also held unconstitutional the Act's limits on the contributions of political parties to candidates. At the same time, the court found the Act's other contribution limits constitutional. *Landell v. Sorrell,* 118 F.Supp.2d 459, 470 (Vt.2000).

Both sides appealed. A divided panel of the Court of Appeals for the Second Circuit held that *all* of the Act's contribution limits are constitutional. It also held that the Act's expenditure limits may be constitutional. *Landell v. Sorrell,* 382 F.3d

91 (2004). It found those limits supported by two compelling interests, namely, an interest in preventing corruption or the appearance of corruption and an interest in limiting the amount of time state officials must spend raising campaign funds. The Circuit then remanded the case to the District Court with instructions to determine whether the Act's expenditure limits were narrowly tailored to those interests.

The petitioners and respondents all sought certiorari. They asked us to consider the constitutionality of Act 64's expenditure limits, its contribution limits, and a related definitional provision. We agreed to do so.

II

We turn first to the Act's expenditure limits. Do those limits violate the First Amendment's free speech guarantees? ...

B

1

The respondents recognize that, in respect to expenditure limits, *Buckley* appears to be a controlling — and unfavorable — precedent. They seek to overcome that precedent in two ways. First, they ask us in effect to overrule *Buckley.* Post-*Buckley* experience, they believe, has shown that contribution limits (and disclosure requirements) alone cannot effectively deter corruption or its appearance; hence experience has undermined an assumption underlying that case. Indeed, the respondents have devoted several pages of their briefs to attacking *Buckley's* holding on expenditure limits. See Brief for Respondent/Cross-Petitioner Vermont Public Interest Research Group et al. 6–39 (hereinafter VPIRG Brief) (arguing that "sound reasons exist to revisit the applicable standard of review" for expenditure limits); Brief for Respondent/Cross-Petitioner William H. Sorrell et al. 28–31 (hereinafter Sorrell Brief) (arguing that "the Court should revisit *Buckley* and consider alternative constitutional approaches to spending limits").

Second, in the alternative, they ask us to limit the scope of *Buckley* significantly by distinguishing *Buckley* from the present case. They advance as a ground for distinction a justification for expenditure limitations that, they say, *Buckley* did not consider, namely, that such limits help to protect candidates from spending too much time raising money rather than devoting that time to campaigning among ordinary voters. We find neither argument persuasive.

2

The Court has often recognized the "fundamental importance" of *stare decisis,* the basic legal principle that commands judicial respect for a court's earlier decisions and the rules of law they embody. See *Harris v. United States,* 536 U.S. 545, 556–557 (plurality opinion) (citing numerous cases). The Court has pointed out that *stare decisis* "'promotes the evenhanded, predictable, and consistent development of legal principles, fosters reliance on judicial decisions, and contributes to the actual and perceived integrity of the judicial process.'" *United States v. International Business Machines Corp.,* 517 U.S. 843, 856 (1996) (quoting *Payne v. Tennessee,* 501

U.S. 808, 827, (1991)). *Stare decisis* thereby avoids the instability and unfairness that accompany disruption of settled legal expectations. For this reason, the rule of law demands that adhering to our prior case law be the norm. Departure from precedent is exceptional, and requires "special justification." *Arizona v. Rumsey,* 467 U.S. 203, 212. This is especially true where, as here, the principle has become settled through iteration and reiteration over a long period of time.

We can find here no such special justification that would require us to overrule *Buckley.* Subsequent case law has not made *Buckley* a legal anomaly or otherwise undermined its basic legal principles. We cannot find in the respondents' claims any demonstration that circumstances have changed so radically as to undermine *Buckley's* critical factual assumptions. The respondents have not shown, for example, any dramatic increase in corruption or its appearance in Vermont; nor have they shown that expenditure limits are the only way to attack that problem. At the same time, *Buckley* has promoted considerable reliance. Congress and state legislatures have used *Buckley* when drafting campaign finance laws. And, as we have said, this Court has followed *Buckley,* upholding and applying its reasoning in later cases. Overruling *Buckley* now would dramatically undermine this reliance on our settled precedent.

For all these reasons, we find this a case that fits the *stare decisis* norm. And we do not perceive the strong justification that would be necessary to warrant overruling so well established a precedent. We consequently decline the respondents' invitation to reconsider *Buckley.*

3

The respondents also ask us to distinguish these cases from *Buckley.* But we can find no significant basis for that distinction. Act 64's expenditure limits are not substantially different from those at issue in *Buckley.* In both instances the limits consist of a dollar cap imposed upon a candidate's expenditures. Nor is Vermont's primary justification for imposing its expenditure limits significantly different from Congress' rationale for the *Buckley* limits: preventing corruption and its appearance.

The sole basis on which the respondents seek to distinguish *Buckley* concerns a further supporting justification. They argue that expenditure limits are necessary in order to reduce the amount of time candidates must spend raising money. Increased campaign costs, together with the fear of a better-funded opponent, mean that, without expenditure limits, a candidate must spend too much time raising money instead of meeting the voters and engaging in public debate. *Buckley,* the respondents add, did not fully consider this justification. Had it done so, they say, the Court would have upheld, not struck down, FECA's expenditure limits.

In our view, it is highly unlikely that fuller consideration of this time protection rationale would have changed *Buckley*'s result. The *Buckley* Court was aware of the connection between expenditure limits and a reduction in fundraising time. In a section of the opinion dealing with FECA's public financing provisions, it wrote that

Congress was trying to "free candidates from the rigors of fundraising." And, in any event, the connection between high campaign expenditures and increased fundraising demands seems perfectly obvious.

Under these circumstances, the respondents' argument amounts to no more than an invitation so to limit *Buckley*'s holding as effectively to overrule it. For the reasons set forth above, we decline that invitation as well. And, given *Buckley*'s continued authority, we must conclude that Act 64's expenditure limits violate the First Amendment.

III

We turn now to a more complex question, namely, the constitutionality of Act 64's contribution limits. The parties, while accepting *Buckley*'s approach, dispute whether, despite *Buckley's* general approval of statutes that limit campaign contributions, Act 64's contribution limits are so severe that in the circumstances its particular limits violate the First Amendment.

A

As with the Act's expenditure limits, we begin with *Buckley.* In that case, the Court upheld the $1,000 contribution limit before it. *Buckley* recognized that contribution limits, like expenditure limits, "implicate fundamental First Amendment interests," namely, the freedoms of "political expression" and "political association." But, unlike expenditure limits (which "necessarily reduc[e] the quantity of expression by restricting the number of issues discussed, the depth of their exploration, and the size of the audience reached," contribution limits "involv[e] little direct restraint on" the contributor's speech. They do restrict "one aspect of the contributor's freedom of political association," namely, the contributor's ability to support a favored candidate, but they nonetheless "permi[t] the symbolic expression of support evidenced by a contribution," and they do "not in any way infringe the contributor's freedom to discuss candidates and issues."

Consequently, the Court wrote, contribution limitations are permissible as long as the Government demonstrates that the limits are "closely drawn" to match a "sufficiently important interest." It found that the interest advanced in the case, "prevent[ing] corruption" and its "appearance," was "sufficiently important" to justify the statute's contribution limits.

The Court also found that the contribution limits before it were "closely drawn." It recognized that, in determining whether a particular contribution limit was "closely drawn," the amount, or level, of that limit could make a difference. Indeed, it wrote that "contribution restrictions could have a severe impact on political dialogue if the limitations prevented candidates and political committees from amassing the resources necessary for effective advocacy." But the Court added that such "distinctions in degree become significant only when they can be said to amount to differences in kind." Pointing out that it had "'no scalpel to probe, whether, say, a $2,000 ceiling might not serve as well as $1,000,'" *ibid.*, the Court found "no indication" that the $1,000 contribution limitations imposed by the Act would have "any dramatic adverse effect on the funding of campaigns." It therefore found the limitations constitutional.

Since *Buckley,* the Court has consistently upheld contribution limits in other statutes. *Shrink Missouri* ($1,075 limit on contributions to candidates for Missouri state auditor); *California Medical Assn.* [*v. FEC*], 453 U.S. 182 ($5,000 limit on contributions to multicandidate political committees). The Court has recognized, however, that contribution limits might *sometimes* work more harm to protected First Amendment interests than their anticorruption objectives could justify. And individual Members of the Court have expressed concern lest too low a limit magnify the "reputation-related or media-related advantages of incumbency and thereby insulat[e] legislators from effective electoral challenge." *Shrink Missouri* (BREYER, J., joined by GINSBURG, J., concurring). In the cases before us, the petitioners challenge Act 64's contribution limits on that basis.

B

Following *Buckley,* we must determine whether Act 64's contribution limits prevent candidates from "amassing the resources necessary for effective [campaign] advocacy," whether they magnify the advantages of incumbency to the point where they put challengers to a significant disadvantage; in a word, whether they are too low and too strict to survive First Amendment scrutiny. In answering these questions, we recognize, as *Buckley* stated, that we have "'no scalpel to probe'" each possible contribution level. We cannot determine with any degree of exactitude the precise restriction necessary to carry out the statute's legitimate objectives. In practice, the legislature is better equipped to make such empirical judgments, as legislators have "particular expertise" in matters related to the costs and nature of running for office. Thus ordinarily we have deferred to the legislature's determination of such matters.

Nonetheless, as *Buckley* acknowledged, we must recognize the existence of some lower bound. At some point the constitutional risks to the democratic electoral process become too great. After all, the interests underlying contribution limits, preventing corruption and the appearance of corruption, "directly implicate the integrity of our electoral process." *McConnell v. FEC* [discussed later in this Chapter — Eds]. Yet that rationale does not simply mean "the lower the limit, the better." That is because contribution limits that are too low can also harm the electoral process by preventing challengers from mounting effective campaigns against incumbent officeholders, thereby reducing democratic accountability. Were we to ignore that fact, a statute that seeks to regulate campaign contributions could itself prove an obstacle to the very electoral fairness it seeks to promote. Thus, we see no alternative to the exercise of independent judicial judgment as a statute reaches those outer limits. And, where there is strong indication in a particular case, *i.e.,* danger signs, that such risks exist (both present in kind and likely serious in degree), courts, including appellate courts, must review the record independently and carefully with an eye toward assessing the statute's "tailoring," that is, toward assessing the proportionality of the restrictions.

We find those danger signs present here. As compared with the contribution limits upheld by the Court in the past, and with those in force in other States, Act 64's limits are sufficiently low as to generate suspicion that they are not closely drawn. The Act sets its limits per election cycle, which includes both a primary and a general election. Thus, in a gubernatorial race with both primary and final election contests, the Act's contribution limit amounts to $200 per election per candidate (with significantly lower limits for contributions to candidates for State Senate and House of Representatives). These limits apply both to contributions from individuals and to contributions from political parties, whether made in cash or in expenditures coordinated (or presumed to be coordinated) with the candidate.

These limits are well below the limits this Court upheld in *Buckley.* Indeed, in terms of real dollars (*i.e.,* adjusting for inflation), the Act's $200 per election limit on individual contributions to a campaign for governor is slightly more than one-twentieth of the limit on contributions to campaigns for federal office before the Court in *Buckley.* Adjusted to reflect its value in 1976 (the year *Buckley* was decided), Vermont's contribution limit on campaigns for statewide office (including governor) amounts to $113.91 per 2-year election cycle, or roughly $57 per election, as compared to the $1,000 per election limit on individual contributions at issue in *Buckley.* (The adjusted value of Act 64's limit on contributions from political parties to candidates for statewide office, again $200 per candidate per election, is just over one one-hundredth of the comparable limit before the Court in *Buckley,* $5,000 per election.) Yet Vermont's gubernatorial district—the entire State—is no smaller than the House districts to which *Buckley's* limits applied. In 1976, the average congressional district contained a population of about 465,000. Dept. of Commerce, Bureau of Census, Statistical Abstract of the United States 459 (1976) (Statistical Abstract) (describing results of 1970 census). Indeed, Vermont's population is 621,000—about one-third *larger.* Statistical Abstract 21 (2006) (describing Vermont's population in 2004).

Moreover, considered as a whole, Vermont's contribution limits are the lowest in the Nation. Act 64 limits contributions to candidates for statewide office (including governor) to $200 per candidate per election. We have found no State that imposes a lower per election limit. Indeed, we have found only seven States that impose limits on contributions to candidates for statewide office at or below $500 per election, more than twice Act 64's limit. Cf. Ariz.Rev.Stat. Ann. § 16-905 (West Cum. Supp.2005) ($760 per election cycle, or $380 per election, adjusted for inflation); Colo. Const., Art. XXVIII, § 3 ($500 per election, adjusted for inflation); Fla. Stat. § 106.08(1)(a) (2003) ($500 per election); Me.Rev.Stat. Ann., Tit. 21-A, § 1015(1) (West Supp.2005) ($500 for governor, $250 for other statewide office, per election); Mass. Gen. Laws, ch. 55, § 7A (West Cum.Supp.2006) ($500 per year, or $250 per election); Mont.Code Ann. § 13-37-216(1)(a) (2005) ($500 for governor, $250 for other statewide office, per election); S.D. Codified Laws § 12-25-1.1 (2004) ($1,000 per year, or $500 per election). We are aware of no State that imposes a limit on contributions from political parties to candidates for statewide office lower than Act 64's $200 per candidate per election limit. Cf. Me.Rev.Stat. Ann., Tit. 21-A, § 1015(1) (next lowest: $500 for contribution from party to candidate for governor, $250 for contribution from party to candidate for other statewide office, both per election). Similarly, we have found only three States that have limits on contributions to candidates for state legislature below Act 64's $150 and $100 per election limits. Ariz.Rev.Stat. Ann. § 16–905 ($296 per election cycle, or $148 per election); Mont.Code Ann. § 13-37-216(1)(a) ($130 per election); S.D. Codified Laws § 12-25-1.1 ($250 per year, or $125 per election). And we are aware of no State that has a lower limit on contributions from political parties to state legislative candidates. Cf. Me.Rev.Stat. Ann., Tit. 21-A, § 1015(1) (next lowest: $250 per election).

Finally, Vermont's limit is well below the lowest limit this Court has previously upheld, the limit of $1,075 per election (adjusted for inflation every two years) for candidates for Missouri state auditor. *Shrink Missouri.* The comparable Vermont limit of roughly $200 per election, not adjusted for inflation, is less than one-sixth of Missouri's current inflation-adjusted limit ($1,275).

We recognize that Vermont's population is much smaller than Missouri's. Indeed, Vermont is about one-ninth of the size of Missouri. Statistical Abstract 21 (2006). Thus, *per citizen,* Vermont's limit is slightly more generous. As of 2006, the ratio of the contribution limit to the size of the constituency in Vermont is .00064, while Missouri's ratio is .00044, 31% lower.

But this does not necessarily mean that Vermont's limits are less objectionable than the limit upheld in *Shrink.* A campaign for state auditor is likely to be less costly than a campaign for governor; campaign costs do not automatically increase or decrease in precise proportion to the size of an electoral district. Moreover, Vermont's limits, unlike Missouri's limits, apply in the same amounts to contributions made by political parties. And, as we have said, Missouri's (current) $1,275 per election limit, unlike Vermont's $200 per election limit, is indexed for inflation.

The factors we have mentioned offset any neutralizing force of population differences. At the very least, they make it difficult to treat *Shrink's* (then) $1,075 limit as providing affirmative support for the lawfulness of Vermont's far lower levels. And even were that not so, Vermont's failure to index for inflation means that Vermont's levels would soon be far lower than Missouri's regardless of the method of comparison.

In sum, Act 64's contribution limits are substantially lower than both the limits we have previously upheld and comparable limits in other States. These are danger signs that Act 64's contribution limits may fall outside tolerable First Amendment limits. We consequently must examine the record independently and carefully to determine whether Act 64's contribution limits are "closely drawn" to match the State's interests.

C

Our examination of the record convinces us that, from a constitutional perspective, Act 64's contribution limits are too restrictive. We reach this conclusion based not merely on the low dollar amounts of the limits themselves, but also on the statute's effect on political parties and on volunteer activity in Vermont elections. *Taken together,* Act 64's substantial restrictions on the ability of candidates to raise the funds necessary to run a competitive election, on the ability of political parties to help their candidates get elected, and on the ability of individual citizens to volunteer their time to campaigns show that the Act is not closely drawn to meet its objectives. In particular, five factors together lead us to this decision.

First, the record suggests, though it does not conclusively prove, that Act 64's contribution limits will significantly restrict the amount of funding available for challengers to run competitive campaigns. For one thing, the petitioners' expert, Clark Bensen, conducted a race-by-race analysis of the 1998 legislative elections (the last to take place before Act 64 took effect) and concluded that Act 64's contribution limits would have reduced the funds available in 1998 to Republican challengers in competitive races in amounts ranging from 18% to 53% of their total campaign income. See 3 Tr. 52–57 (estimating loss of 47% of funds for candidate Tully, 50% for Harvey, 53% for Welch, 19% for Bahre, 29% for Delaney, 36% for LaRocque, 18% for Smith, and 31% for Brown).

For another thing, the petitioners' expert witnesses produced evidence and analysis showing that Vermont political parties (particularly the Republican Party) "target" their contributions to candidates in competitive races, that those contributions represent a significant amount of total candidate funding in such races, and that the contribution limits will cut the parties' contributions to competitive races dramatically. See also, *e.g.,* Gierzynski & Breaux, The Role of Parties in Legislative Campaign Financing, 15 Am. Rev. Politics 171 (1994); Thompson, Cassie, & Jewell, A Sacred Cow or Just a Lot of Bull? Party and PAC Money in State Legislative Elections, 47 Pol. Research Q. 223 (1994). Their statistics showed that the party contributions accounted for a significant percentage of the total campaign income in those races. And their studies showed that Act 64's contribution limits would cut the party contributions by between 85% (for the legislature on average) and 99% (for governor).

More specifically, Bensen pointed out that in 1998, the Republican Party made contributions to 19 Senate campaigns in amounts that averaged $2,001, which on average represented 16% of the recipient campaign's total income. 3 Tr. 84. Act 64 would reduce these contributions to $300 per campaign, an average reduction of about 85%. *Ibid.* The party contributed to 50 House campaigns in amounts averaging $787, which on average represented 28% of the recipient campaign's total income. Act 64 would reduce these contributions to $200 per campaign, an average reduction of 74.5%. And the party contributed $40,600 to its gubernatorial candidate, an amount that accounted for about 16% of the candidate's funding. *Id.,* at 86. The Act would have reduced that contribution by 99%, to $400.

Bensen added that 57% of all 1998 Senate campaigns and 30% of all House campaigns exceeded Act 64's expenditure limits, which were enacted along with the statute's contribution limits.... Moreover, 27% of all Senate campaigns and 10% of all House campaigns spent more than double those limits.

The respondents did not contest these figures. Rather, they presented evidence that focused, not upon *strongly contested* campaigns, but upon the funding amounts available for the *average* campaign. The respondents' expert, Anthony Gierzynski, concluded, for example, that Act 64 would have a "minimal effect on . . . candidates' ability to raise funds. But he rested this conclusion upon his finding that "only a small proportion of" *all* contributions to *all* campaigns for state office "made during the last three elections would have been affected by the new limits." The lower courts similarly relied almost exclusively on averages in assessing Act 64's effect.

The respondents' evidence leaves the petitioners' evidence unrebutted in certain key respects. That is because the critical question concerns not simply the *average* effect of contribution limits on fundraising but, more importantly, the ability of a candidate running against an incumbent officeholder to mount an effective *challenge.* And information about *average* races, rather than *competitive* races, is only distantly related to that question, because competitive races are likely to be far more expensive than the average race. See, *e.g.*, N. Ornstein, T. Mann, & M. Malbin, Vital Statistics on Congress 2001–2002, pp. 89–98 (2002) (data showing that spending in competitive elections, *i.e.*, where incumbent wins with less than 60% of vote or where incumbent loses, is far greater than in most elections, where incumbent wins with more than 60% of the vote). We concede that the record does contain some anecdotal evidence supporting the respondents' position, namely, testimony about a post-Act-64 competitive mayoral campaign in Burlington, which suggests that a challenger can "amas[s] the resources necessary for effective advocacy." *Buckley.* But the facts of that particular election are not described in sufficient detail to offer a convincing refutation of the implication arising from the petitioners' experts' studies.

Rather, the petitioners' studies, taken together with low *average* Vermont campaign expenditures and the typically higher costs that a challenger must bear to overcome the name-recognition advantage enjoyed by an incumbent, raise a reasonable inference that the contribution limits are so low that they may pose a significant obstacle to candidates in competitive elections. Cf. Ornstein, *supra* (In the 2000 U.S. House and Senate elections, successful challengers spent far more than the average candidate). Information about average races does not rebut that inference. Consequently, the inference amounts to one factor (among others) that here counts against the constitutional validity of the contribution limits.

Second, Act 64's insistence that political parties abide by *exactly* the same low contribution limits that apply to other contributors threatens harm to a particularly important political right, the right to associate in a political party. See, *e.g., California Democratic Party v. Jones* (describing constitutional importance of associating in political parties to elect candidates); *Timmons* (same); *Colorado I* [*infra* this chapter—Eds]; *Norman v. Reed,* 502 U.S. 279, 288, (1992) (same). Cf. *Buckley* (contribution limits constitute "only a marginal restriction" on First Amendment rights *because* contributor remains free to associate politically, *e.g.*, in a political party, and "assist personally" in the party's "efforts on behalf of candidates").

The Act applies its $200 to $400 limits—precisely the same limits it applies to an individual—to virtually all affiliates of a political party taken together as if they were a single contributor. That means, for example, that the Vermont Democratic Party, taken together with all its local affiliates, can make one contribution of at most $400 to the Democratic gubernatorial candidate, one contribution of at most $300 to a Democratic candidate for State Senate, and one contribution of at most $200 to a Democratic candidate for the State House of Representatives. The Act includes within these limits not only direct monetary contributions but also expenditures in kind: stamps, stationery, coffee, doughnuts, gasoline, campaign buttons, and so forth. See Indeed, it includes all party expenditures "intended to promote the election of a specific candidate or group of candidates" as long as the candidate's campaign "facilitate[s]," "solicit[s]," or "approve[s]" them. And a party expenditure that "primarily benefits six or fewer candidates who are associated with the" party is "presumed" to count against the party's contribution limits.

In addition to the negative effect on "amassing funds" that we have described, the Act would severely limit the ability of a party to assist its candidates' campaigns by engaging in coordinated spending on advertising, candidate events, voter lists, mass mailings, even yard signs. And, to an unusual degree, it would discourage those who wish to contribute small amounts of money to a party, amounts that easily comply with individual contribution limits. Suppose that many individuals do not know Vermont legislative candidates personally, but wish to contribute, say, $20 or $40, to the State Republican Party, with the intent that the party use the money to help elect whichever candidates the party believes would best advance its ideals and interests—the basic object of a political party. Or, to take a more extreme example, imagine that 6,000 Vermont citizens each want to give $1 to the State Democratic Party because, though unfamiliar with the details of the individual races, they would like to make a small financial contribution to the goal of electing a Democratic state legislature. And further imagine that the party believes control of the legislature will depend on the outcome of three (and only three) House races. The Act prohibits the party from giving $2,000 (of the $6,000) to each of its candidates in those pivotal races. Indeed, it permits the party to give no more than $200 to each candidate, thereby thwarting the aims of the 6,000 donors from making a meaningful contribution to state politics by giving a small amount of money to the party they support. Thus, the Act would severely inhibit collective political activity by preventing a political party from using contributions by small donors to provide meaningful assistance to any individual candidate.

We recognize that we have previously upheld limits on contributions from political parties to candidates, in particular the federal limits on coordinated party spending. *Colorado II* [*infra* this chapter—Eds.] And we also recognize that any such limit will negatively affect *to some extent* the fund-allocating party function just described. But the contribution limits at issue in *Colorado II* were far less problematic, for they were significantly higher than Act 64's limits. *See id.* (at least $67,560 in coordinated spending and $5,000 in direct cash contributions for U.S.

Senate candidates, at least $33,780 in coordinated spending and $5,000 in direct cash contributions for U.S. House candidates). And they were much higher than the federal limits on contributions from individuals to candidates, thereby reflecting an effort by Congress to balance (1) the need to allow individuals to participate in the political process by contributing to political parties that help elect candidates with (2) the need to prevent the use of political parties "to circumvent contribution limits that apply to individuals." *Id.* Act 64, by placing identical limits upon contributions to candidates, whether made by an individual or by a political party, gives to the former consideration *no weight at all.*

We consequently agree with the District Court that the Act's contribution limits "would reduce the voice of political parties" in Vermont to a "whisper." And we count the special party-related harms that Act 64 threatens as a further factor weighing against the constitutional validity of the contribution limits.

Third, the Act's treatment of volunteer services aggravates the problem. Like its federal statutory counterpart, the Act excludes from its definition of "contribution" all "services provided without compensation by individuals volunteering their time on behalf of a candidate." But the Act does not exclude the expenses those volunteers incur, such as travel expenses, in the course of campaign activities. The Act's broad definitions would seem to count those expenses against the volunteer's contribution limit, at least where the spending was facilitated or approved by campaign officials. And, unlike the Federal Government's treatment of comparable requirements, the State has not (insofar as we are aware) created an exception excluding such expenses.

The absence of some such exception may matter in the present context, where contribution limits are very low. That combination, low limits and no exceptions, means that a gubernatorial campaign volunteer who makes four or five round trips driving across the State performing volunteer activities coordinated with the campaign can find that he or she is near, or has surpassed, the contribution limit. So too will a volunteer who offers a campaign the use of her house along with coffee and doughnuts for a few dozen neighbors to meet the candidate, say, two or three times during a campaign. . . . Such supporters will have to keep careful track of all miles driven, postage supplied (500 stamps equals $200), pencils and pads used, and so forth. And any carelessness in this respect can prove costly, perhaps generating a headline, "Campaign laws violated," that works serious harm to the candidate.

These sorts of problems are unlikely to affect the constitutionality of a limit that is reasonably high. Cf. *Buckley* (Coordinated expenditure by a volunteer "provides material financial assistance to a candidate," and therefore "may properly be viewed as a contribution"). But Act 64's contribution limits are so low, and its definition of "contribution" so broad, that the Act may well impede a campaign's ability effectively to use volunteers, thereby making it more difficult for individuals to associate in this way. Cf. *Buckley* (Federal contribution limits "leave the contributor free to become a member of any political association and to assist personally in the association's efforts on behalf of candidates"). Again, the very low limits at issue help to transform differences in degree into difference in kind. And the likelihood of unjustified interference in the present context is sufficiently great that we must consider the lack of tailoring in the Act's definition of "contribution" as an added factor counting against the constitutional validity of the contribution limits before us.

Fourth, unlike the contribution limits we upheld in *Shrink,* Act 64's contribution limits are not adjusted for inflation. Its limits decline in real value each year. Indeed, in real dollars the Act's limits have already declined by about 20% ($200 in 2006 dollars has a real value of $160.66 in 1997 dollars). A failure to index limits means that limits which are already suspiciously low, see will almost inevitably become too low over time. It means that future legislation will be necessary to stop that almost inevitable decline, and it thereby imposes the burden of preventing the decline upon incumbent legislators who may not diligently police the need for changes in limit levels to ensure the adequate financing of electoral challenges.

Fifth, we have found nowhere in the record any special justification that might warrant a contribution limit so low or so restrictive as to bring about the serious associational and expressive problems that we have described. Rather, the basic justifications the State has advanced in support of such limits are those present in *Buckley.* The record contains no indication that, for example, corruption (or its appearance) in Vermont is significantly more serious a matter than elsewhere. Indeed, other things being equal, one might reasonably believe that a contribution of, say, $250 (or $450) to a candidate's campaign was less likely to prove a corruptive force than the far larger contributions at issue in the other campaign finance cases we have considered.

These five sets of considerations, taken together, lead us to conclude that Act 64's contribution limits are not narrowly tailored. Rather, the Act burdens First Amendment interests by threatening to inhibit effective advocacy by those who seek election, particularly challengers; its contribution limits mute the voice of political parties; they hamper participation in campaigns through volunteer activities; and they are not indexed for inflation. Vermont does not point to a legitimate statutory objective that might justify these special burdens. We understand that many, though not all, campaign finance regulations impose certain of these burdens to some degree. We also understand the legitimate need for constitutional leeway in respect to legislative line-drawing. But our discussion indicates why we conclude that Act 64 in this respect nonetheless goes too far. It disproportionately burdens numerous First Amendment interests, and consequently, in our view, violates the First Amendment.

We add that we do not believe it possible to sever some of the Act's contribution limit provisions from others that might remain fully operative. To sever provisions to avoid constitutional objection here would require us to write words into the statute (inflation indexing), or to leave gaping loopholes (no limits on party contributions), or to foresee which of many different possible ways the legislature might respond to the constitutional objections we have found. Given these difficulties, we believe the Vermont Legislature would have intended us to set aside the statute's contribution limits, leaving the legislature free to rewrite those provisions in light of the constitutional difficulties we have identified.

IV

We conclude that Act 64's expenditure limits violate the First Amendment as interpreted in *Buckley.* We also conclude that the specific details of Act 64's contribution limits require us to hold that those limits violate the First Amendment, for they burden First Amendment interests in a manner that is disproportionate to the public purposes they were enacted to advance. Given our holding, we need not, and do not, examine the constitutionality of the statute's presumption that certain party expenditures are coordinated with a candidate. Accordingly, the judgment of the Court of Appeals is reversed, and the cases are remanded for further proceedings.

It is so ordered.

Justice THOMAS, with whom Justice SCALIA joins, concurring in the judgment.

Although I agree with the plurality that [Act 64] is unconstitutional, I disagree with its rationale for striking down that statute. Invoking *stare decisis,* the plurality rejects the invitation to overrule *Buckley.* It then applies *Buckley* to invalidate the expenditure limitations and, less persuasively, the contribution limitations. I continue to believe that *Buckley* provides insufficient protection to political speech, the core of the First Amendment. The illegitimacy of *Buckley* is further underscored by the continuing inability of the Court (and the plurality here) to apply *Buckley* in a coherent and principled fashion. As a result, *stare decisis* should pose no bar to overruling *Buckley* and replacing it with a standard faithful to the First Amendment. Accordingly, I concur only in the judgment.

I

I adhere to my view that this Court erred in *Buckley* when it distinguished between contribution and expenditure limits, finding the former to be a less severe infringement on First Amendment rights. See *Shrink Missouri* (dissenting opinion); *(Colorado II)* (same); *(Colorado I)* (opinion concurring in judgment and dissenting in part). "[U]nlike the *Buckley* Court, I believe that contribution limits infringe as directly and as seriously upon freedom of political expression and association as do expenditure limits." *Id.* The *Buckley* Court distinguished contributions from expenditures based on the presence of an intermediary between a contributor and the speech eventually produced. But that reliance is misguided, given that "[e]ven in the case of a direct expenditure, there is usually some go-between that facilitates the dissemination of the spender's message." *Colorado I* (opinion of THOMAS, J.); *Shrink Missouri* (THOMAS, J., dissenting). Likewise, *Buckley*'s suggestion that contribution caps only marginally restrict speech, because "[a] contribution serves as a general expression of support for the candidate and his views, but does not communicate the underlying basis for the support," even if descriptively accurate, does not support restrictions on contributions. After all, statements of general support are as deserving of constitutional protection as those that communicate specific reasons for that support. Accordingly, I would overrule *Buckley* and subject both the contribution and expenditure restrictions of Act 64 to strict scrutiny, which they would fail. See *Colorado I* (opinion of THOMAS, J.) ("I am convinced that under traditional strict scrutiny, broad prophylactic caps on both spending and giving in the political process . . . are unconstitutional"). . . .

Justice STEVENS, dissenting.

Justice BREYER and Justice SOUTER debate whether the *per curiam* decision in *Buckley* forecloses any constitutional limitations on candidate expenditures. This is plainly an issue on which reasonable minds can disagree. The *Buckley* Court never explicitly addressed whether the pernicious effects of endless fundraising can serve as a compelling state interest that justifies expenditure limits), yet its silence, in light of the record before it, suggests that it implicitly treated this proposed interest insufficient,). Assuming this to be true, however, I am convinced that *Buckley*'s holding on expenditure limits is wrong, and that the time has come to overrule it. . . .

Justice SOUTER, with whom Justice GINSBURG joins, and with whom Justice STEVENS joins as to Parts II and III, dissenting.

In 1997, the Legislature of Vermont passed Act 64 after a series of public hearings persuaded legislators that rehabilitating the State's political process required campaign finance reform. A majority of the Court today decides that the expenditure and contribution limits enacted are irreconcilable with the Constitution's guarantee of free speech. I would adhere to the Court of Appeals's decision to remand for further enquiry bearing on the limitations on candidates' expenditures, and I think the contribution limits satisfy controlling precedent. I respectfully dissent.

I

Rejecting Act 64's expenditure limits as directly contravening of *Buckley*, is at least premature. . . .

II

Although I would defer judgment on the merits of the expenditure limitations, I believe the Court of Appeals correctly rejected the challenge to the contribution limits. Low though they are, one cannot say that "the contribution limitation[s are] so radical in effect as to render political association ineffective, drive the sound of a candidate's voice below the level of notice, and render contributions pointless." *Shrink Missouri*.

The limits set by Vermont are not remarkable departures either from those previously upheld by this Court or from those lately adopted by other States. The plurality concedes that on a per-citizen measurement Vermont's limit for statewide elections "is slightly more generous" than the one set by the Missouri statute approved by this Court in *Shrink*. Not only do those dollar amounts get more generous the smaller the district, they are consistent with limits set by the legislatures of many other States, all of them with populations larger than Vermont's, some significantly so. See, *e.g.*, *Montana Right to Life Assn. v. Eddleman*, 343 F.3d 1085, 1088 (C.A.9 2003) (approving $400 limit for candidates filed jointly for Governor and Lieutenant Governor, since increased to $500, see Mont.Code Ann. §13-37-216(1)(a)(i) (2005)); *Daggett v. Commission on Governmental Ethics and Election Practices,* 205 F.3d 445, 452 (C.A.1 2000) ($500 limit for gubernatorial candidates in Maine); *Minnesota Citizens Concerned for Life, Inc. v. Kelley,* 427 F.3d 1106, 1113 (C.A.8 2005) ($500 limit on contributions to legislative candidates in election years, $100 in other years); *Florida Right to Life, Inc. v. Mortham,* No. 6:98-770-CV.ORL–19A, 2000 WL 33733256, *3 (M.D.Fla., Mar.20, 2000) ($500 limit on contributions to any state candidate). The point is not that this Court is bound by judicial sanctions of those numbers; it is that the consistency in legislative judgment tells us that Vermont is not an eccentric party of one, and that this is a case for the judicial deference that our own precedents say we owe here. See *Shrink* (BREYER, J., concurring) ("Where a legislature has significantly greater institutional expertise, as, for example, in the field of election regulation, the Court in practice defers to empirical legislative judgments"); see also *ante* (plurality opinion) ("[O]rdinarily we have deferred to the legislature's determination of [matters related to the costs and nature of running for office]").

To place Vermont's contribution limits beyond the constitutional pale, therefore, is to forget not only the facts of *Shrink,* but also our self-admonition against second-guessing legislative judgments about the risk of corruption to which contribution limits have to be fitted. And deference here would surely not be overly complaisant. Vermont's legislators themselves testified at length about the money that gets their special attention, see Legislative Findings, App. 20 (finding that "[s]ome candidates and elected officials, particularly when time is limited, respond and give access to contributors who make large contributions in preference to those who make small or no contributions"); 382 F.3d, at 122 (testimony of Elizabeth Ready: "If I have only got an hour at night when I get home to return calls, I am much more likely to return [a donor's] call than I would [a non-donor's]. . . . [W]hen you only have a few minutes to talk, there are certain people that get access" (alterations in original)). The record revealed the amount of money the public sees as suspiciously large, see 118 F.Supp.2d, at 479–480 ("The limits set by the legislature . . . accurately reflect the level of contribution considered suspiciously large by the Vermont public. Testimony suggested that amounts greater than the contribution limits are considered large by the Vermont public"). And testimony identified the amounts high enough to pay for effective campaigning in a State where the cost of running tends to be on the low side, see *id.,* at 471 ("In the context of Vermont politics, $200, $300, and $400 donations are clearly large, as the legislature determined. Small donations are considered to be strong acts of political support in this state. William Meub testified that a contribution of $1 is meaningful because it represents a commitment by the contributor that is likely to become a vote for the candidate. Gubernatorial candidate Ruth Dwyer values the small contributions of $5 so much that she personally sends thank you notes to those donors"); *id.,* at 470–471 ("In Vermont, many politicians have run effective and winning campaigns with very little money, and some with no money at all. . . . Several candidates, campaign managers, and past and present government officials testified that they will be able to raise enough money to mount effective campaigns in the system of contribution limits established by Act 64"); *id.*, at 472 ("Spending in Vermont statewide elections is very low. . . . Vermont ranks 49th out of the 50 states in campaign spending. The majority of major party candidates for statewide office in the last three election cycles spent less than what the spending limits of Act 64 would allow. . . . In Vermont legislative races, low-cost methods such as door-to-door campaigning are standard and even expected by the voters").

Still, our cases do not say deference should be absolute. We can all imagine dollar limits that would be laughable, and per capita comparisons that would be meaningless because aggregated donations simply could not sustain effective campaigns. The plurality thinks that point has been reached in Vermont, and in particular that the low contribution limits threaten the ability of challengers to run effective races against incumbents. Thus, the plurality's limit of deference is substantially a function of suspicion that political incumbents in the legislature set low contribution limits because their public recognition and easy access to free publicity will effectively augment their own spending power beyond anything a challenger can muster. The suspicion is, in other words, that incumbents cannot be trusted to set fair limits, because facially neutral limits do not in fact give challengers an even break. But this received suspicion is itself a proper subject of suspicion. The petitioners offered, and the plurality invokes, no evidence that the risk of a pro-incumbent advantage has been realized; in fact, the record evidence runs the other way, as the plurality concedes. See *ante* ("[T]he record does contain some anecdotal evidence supporting the respondents' position, namely, testimony about a post-Act-64 competitive mayoral campaign in Burlington, which suggests that a challenger can 'amas[s] the resources necessary for effective advocacy,' *Buckley*"). I would not discount such evidence that these low limits are fair to challengers, for the experience of the Burlington race is confirmed by recent empirical studies addressing this issue of incumbent's advantage. See, *e.g.*, Eom & Gross, Contribution Limits and Disparity in Contributions Between Gubernatorial Candidates, 59 Pol. Research Q. 99 (2006) ("Analyses of both the number of contributors and the dollar amount of contributions [to gubernatorial candidates] suggest no support for an increased bias in favor of incumbents resulting from the presence of campaign contribution limits. If anything, contribution limits can work to reduce the bias that traditionally works in favor of incumbents. Also, contribution limits do not seem to increase disparities between gubernatorial candidates in general" (emphasis deleted)); Bardwell, Money and Challenger Emergence in Gubernatorial Primaries, 55 Pol. Research Q. 653 (2002) (finding that contribution limits favor neither incumbents nor challengers); Hogan, The Costs of Representation in State Legislatures: Explaining Variations in Campaign Spending, 81 Soc. Sci. Q. 941, 952 (2000) (finding that contribution limits reduce incumbent spending but have no effect on challenger or open-seat candidate spending). The Legislature of Vermont evidently tried to account for the realities of campaigning in Vermont, and I see no evidence of constitutional miscalculation sufficient to dispense with respect for its judgments.

III

Four issues of detail call for some attention, the first being the requirement that a volunteer's expenses count against the person's contribution limit. The plurality certainly makes out the case that accounting for these expenses will be a colossal nuisance, but there is no case here that the nuisance will noticeably limit volunteering, or that volunteers whose expenses reach the limit cannot continue with their efforts subject to charging their candidates for the excess. Granted, if the provisions for contribution limits were teetering on the edge of unconstitutionality, Act 64's treatment of volunteers' expenses might be the finger-flick that gives the fatal push, but it has no greater significance than that.

Second, the failure of the Vermont law to index its limits for inflation is even less important. This challenge is to the law as it is, not to a law that may have a different impact after future inflation if the state legislature fails to bring it up to economic date.

Third, subjecting political parties to the same contribution limits as individuals does not condemn the Vermont scheme. What we said in *Colorado II*, dealing with regulation of coordinated expenditures, goes here, too. The capacity and desire of parties to make large contributions to competitive candidates with uphill fights are shared by rich individuals, and the risk that large party contributions would be channels to evade individual limits cannot be eliminated. Nor are these reasons to support the party limits undercut by claims that the restrictions render parties impotent, for the parties are not precluded from uncoordinated spending to benefit their candidates. That said, I acknowledge the suggestions in the petitioners' briefs that such restrictions in synergy with other influences weakening party power would justify a wholesale reexamination of the situation of party organization today. But whether such a comprehensive reexamination belongs in courts or only in legislatures is not an issue presented by these cases. . . .

IV

Because I would not pass upon the constitutionality of Vermont's expenditure limits prior to further enquiry into their fit with the problem of fundraising demands on candidates, and because I do not see the contribution limits as depressed to the level of political inaudibility, I respectfully dissent.

[Concurring opinions of Justices Alito and Kennedy are omitted.]

Justice SOUTER delivered the opinion of the Court.

Notes and Questions

1. The plurality opinion notes that seven states "impose limits on contributions to candidates for statewide office at or below $500 per election." Are these statutes in danger of being struck down as unconstitutional? How should lower courts following *Randall* assess the constitutionality of these laws? In fact, arguments that state or local contribution limits are unconstitutionally low under the *Randall* plurality

standard generally had been unsuccessful for the first decade and a half after *Randall*. See, *e.g*, *Thalheimer v. City of San Diego*, 2012 WL 177414 (S.D. Cal. 2012) (upholding low contribution limits in San Diego, California); *Zimmerman v. City of Austin*, 881 F.3d 378, 387–88 (5th Cir.), cert. denied, 139 S. Ct. 639 (2018) (upholding Austin, Texas's individual campaign contribution limit of $300 indexed to inflation (and raised to $350 by the time of the lawsuit)). Why?

Perhaps part of the reason was uncertainty about whether the approach of the *Randall* plurality represented the view of the Court when only three Justices signed onto its reasoning. That uncertainty disappeared when the Supreme Court recently embraced Justice Breyer's plurality analysis in *Randall* as the position of the Court.

2. In *Thompson v. Hebdon*, 909 F.3d 1027 (9th Cir. 2018), the Ninth Circuit upheld a $500 individual contribution limit and a $5,000 political party contribution limit to candidates for state office in Alaska. The Supreme Court in a *per curiam* opinion reversed that portion of the Ninth Circuit opinion in *Hebdon* upholding the $500 individual limit. *Thompson v. Hebdon*, 140 S. Ct. 348 (2019). The Court held that the Ninth Circuit erred in failing to apply Justice Breyer's plurality opinion in *Randall.*

The Court did not revisit the question whether strict scrutiny should apply to the review of contribution limits, but *Hebdon* is not good news for supporters of the Alaska regulation. The Court suggested that under the *Randall* test, Alaska's limits were likely so low as to violate the First Amendment:

> In *Randall*, we identified several "danger signs" about Vermont's law that warranted closer review. Alaska's limit on campaign contributions shares some of those characteristics. First, Alaska's $500 individual-to-candidate contribution limit is "substantially lower than . . . the limits we have previously upheld." The lowest campaign contribution limit this Court has upheld remains the limit of $1,075 per two-year election cycle for candidates for Missouri state auditor in 1998 (citing *Shrink*). That limit translates to over $1,600 in today's dollars. Alaska permits contributions up to 18 months prior to the general election and thus allows a maximum contribution of $1,000 over a comparable two-year period. Accordingly, Alaska's limit is less than two-thirds of the contribution limit we upheld in *Shrink*.
>
> Second, Alaska's individual-to-candidate contribution limit is "substantially lower than . . . comparable limits in other States." *Randall.* Most state contribution limits apply on a per-election basis, with primary and general elections counting as separate elections. Because an individual can donate the maximum amount in both the primary and general election cycles, the per-election contribution limit is comparable to Alaska's annual limit and 18-month campaign period, which functionally allow contributions in both the election year and the year preceding it. Only five other States have any individual-to-candidate contribution limit of $500 or less per election: Colorado, Connecticut, Kansas, Maine, and Montana. Moreover, Alaska's $500 contribution limit applies uniformly to all offices, including Governor

and Lieutenant Governor. But Colorado, Connecticut, Kansas, Maine, and Montana all have limits above $500 for candidates for Governor and Lieutenant Governor, making Alaska's law the most restrictive in the country in this regard.

Third, Alaska's contribution limit is not adjusted for inflation. We observed in *Randall* that Vermont's "failure to index limits means that limits which are already suspiciously low" will "almost inevitably become too low over time." The failure to index "imposes the burden of preventing the decline upon incumbent legislators who may not diligently police the need for changes in limit levels to ensure the adequate financing of electoral challenges." So too here. In fact, Alaska's $500 contribution limit is the same as it was 23 years ago, in 1996.

In *Randall*, we noted that the State had failed to provide "any special justification that might warrant a contribution limit so low." The parties dispute whether there are pertinent special justifications here.

The Court sent the case back to the Ninth Circuit to consider Alaska's limits in light of *Randall*. On a 2-1 vote, the Ninth Circuit on remand held the $500 contribution limit unconstitutional. *Thompson v. Hebdon*, 7 F.4th 811 (9th Cir. 2021).

3. As is typical of Justice Breyer's opinions, *Randall* contains a multipart, multistage test for evaluating the constitutionality of Vermont's contribution limits. Do all these factors have to be considered in every case raising a claim that a contribution limit is unconstitutionally low? May other factors be considered? Justice Souter in dissent agreed that some contribution limit may be so laughably low as to be unconstitutional. How would he determine when that limit has been reached? Is Justice Breyer's "danger signs" test better than a "laughability" test?

4. Does *Randall* signal a shift towards the "political markets"/competition approach to election law of Professors Issacharoff and Pildes, described in Chapter 4? After all, in deciding whether or not a contribution limit is too low, courts have to ask if the amount makes it harder to run competitive campaigns. For an argument in the negative, see Hasen, *supra*. What role *should* a concern about incumbency protection play in evaluating the constitutionality of a campaign contribution limit?

5. Following *Randall*, the Supreme Court struck down another contribution limit law, a part of BCRA § 319 known as the "Millionaire's Amendment." *Davis v. Federal Elections Commission*, 554 U.S. 724 (2008). To simplify slightly, the Millionaire's Amendment allowed candidates running against self-financed opponents to accept contributions from individuals up to three times larger than the usual contribution limits. Justice Alito, writing for the Court, likened the increased contribution limits to expenditure limits, applied strict scrutiny, and struck them down.

The majority took issue with the equality-like rationale offered by the government for the provision of BCRA increasing candidate contribution limits when candidates face self-financed opponents:

The Government maintains that § 319(a)'s asymmetrical limits are justified because they "level electoral opportunities for candidates of different personal wealth." "Congress enacted Section 319," the Government writes, "to reduce *the natural advantage* that wealthy individuals possess in campaigns for federal office." (emphasis added). Our prior decisions, however, provide no support for the proposition that this is a legitimate government objective. See *Shrink Missouri* (THOMAS, J., dissenting) ("'[P]reventing corruption or the appearance of corruption are the only legitimate and compelling government interests thus far identified for restricting campaign finances'" (quoting *NCPAC*); *Randall* (THOMAS, J., concurring in judgment) (noting "the interests the Court has recognized as compelling, *i.e.*, the prevention of corruption or the appearance thereof"). On the contrary, in *Buckley* we held that "[t]he interest in equalizing the financial resources of candidates" did not provide a "justification for restricting" candidates' overall campaign expenditures, particularly where equalization "might serve . . . to handicap a candidate who lacked substantial name recognition or exposure of his views before the start of the campaign." We have similarly held that the interest "in equalizing the relative ability of individuals and groups to influence the outcome of elections" cannot support a cap on expenditures for "express advocacy of the election or defeat of candidates," as "the concept that government may restrict the speech of some elements of our society in order to enhance the relative voice of others is wholly foreign to the First Amendment." See also *McConnell* (noting, in assessing standing, that there is no legal right to have the same resources to influence the electoral process). Cf. *Austin* (KENNEDY, J., dissenting) (rejecting as "antithetical to the First Amendment" "the notion that the government has a legitimate interest in restricting the quantity of speech to equalize the relative influence of speakers on elections").

The argument that a candidate's speech may be restricted in order to "level electoral opportunities" has ominous implications because it would permit Congress to arrogate the voters' authority to evaluate the strengths of candidates competing for office. See *Bellotti* ("[T]he people in our democracy are entrusted with the responsibility for judging and evaluating the relative merits of conflicting arguments" and "may consider, in making their judgment, the source and credibility of the advocate"). Different candidates have different strengths. Some are wealthy; others have wealthy supporters who are willing to make large contributions. Some are celebrities; some have the benefit of a well-known family name. Leveling electoral opportunities means making and implementing judgments about which strengths should be permitted to contribute to the outcome of an election. The Constitution, however, confers upon voters, not Congress, the power to choose the Members of the House of Representatives, Art. I, § 2, and it is a dangerous business for Congress to use the election laws to influence the voters' choices.

> See *Bellotti* (The "[g]overnment is forbidden to assume the task of ultimate judgment, lest the people lose their ability to govern themselves").

Id. at 740–42.

Justice Stevens, speaking for four dissenters, wrote the following in response:

> [W]e have long recognized the strength of an independent governmental interest in reducing both the influence of wealth on the outcomes of elections, and the appearance that wealth alone dictates those results. In case after case, we have held that statutes designed to protect against the undue influence of aggregations of wealth on the political process—where such statutes are responsive to the identified evil—do not contravene the First Amendment. See, *e.g., Austin* (upholding statute designed to combat "the corrosive and distorting effects of immense aggregations of wealth that are accumulated with the help of the corporate form and that have little or no correlation to the public's support for the corporation's political ideas"); *MCFL* ("Th[e] concern over the corrosive influence of concentrated corporate wealth reflects the conviction that it is important to protect the integrity of the marketplace of political ideas.... Direct corporate spending on political activity raises the prospect that resources amassed in the economic marketplace may be used to provide an unfair advantage in the political marketplace"); cf. *Red Lion Broadcasting Co. v. FCC,* 395 U.S. 367, 390 (1969) (upholding constitutionality of several components of the FCC's "fair coverage" requirements, and explaining that "[i]t is the purpose of the First Amendment to preserve an uninhibited marketplace of ideas in which truth will ultimately prevail, rather than to countenance monopolization of that market").
>
> Although the focus of our cases has been on aggregations of corporate rather than individual wealth, there is no reason that their logic—specifically, their concerns about the corrosive and distorting effects of wealth on our political process—is not equally applicable in the context of individual wealth. For, as we explained in *McConnell,* "Congress' historical concern with the 'political potentialities of wealth' and their 'untoward consequences for the democratic process' ... has long reached beyond corporate money."
>
> Minimizing the effect of concentrated wealth on our political process, and the concomitant interest in addressing the dangers that attend the perception that political power can be purchased, are, therefore, sufficiently weighty objectives to justify significant congressional action. And, not only was Congress motivated by proper and weighty goals in crafting the Millionaire's Amendment, the details of the scheme it devised are genuinely responsive to the problems it identified. The statute's "Opposition Personal Funds Amount" formula permits a self-funding candidate to spend as much money as he wishes, while taking into account fundraising by the relevant campaigns; it thereby ensures that a candidate who happens to enjoy a significant fundraising advantage against a self-funding opponent does

> not reap a windfall as a result of the enhanced contribution limits. Rather, the self-funder's opponent may avail himself of the enhanced contribution limits only until parity is achieved, at which point he becomes again ineligible for contributions above the normal maximum.
>
> It seems uncontroversial that "there is no good reason to allow disparities in wealth to be translated into disparities in political power. A well-functioning democracy distinguishes between market processes of purchase and sale on the one hand and political processes of voting and reason-giving on the other." Sunstein, *Political Equality and Unintended Consequences*, 94 Colum. L.Rev. 1390 (1994). In light of that clear truth, Congress' carefully crafted attempt to reduce the distinct advantages enjoyed by wealthy candidates for congressional office does not offend the First Amendment.

Id. at 753–56.

In his *Citizens United* dissent, Justice Stevens wrote of *Davis*:

> Quite distinct from the interest in preventing improper influences on the electoral process, I have long believed that "a number of [other] purposes, both legitimate and substantial, may justify the imposition of reasonable limitations on the expenditures permitted during the course of any single campaign." *Davis* [Stevens, J., concurring in part and dissenting in part]. In my judgment, such limitations may be justified to the extent they are tailored to "improving the quality of the exposition of ideas" that voters receive, "free[ing] candidates and their staffs from the interminable burden of fundraising," and "protect[ing] equal access to the political arena," *Randall v. Sorrell* (Stevens, J., dissenting). I continue to adhere to these beliefs, but they have not been briefed by the parties or amici in this case, and their soundness is immaterial to its proper disposition.

III. Campaign Contributions and Political Parties

Even before *Shrink Missouri*, the Supreme Court considered the constitutionality of limits applied to political parties. One question is about money coming into parties, and whether it may be limited. The other is about money going out from the parties, that might be contributed or spent to support a party's candidates.

In *Colorado Republican Federal Campaign Committee v. Federal Election Commission*, 518 U.S. 604 (1996) (*Colorado I*), Democrats filed a complaint against spending by the Colorado Republican Party attacking Timothy Wirth, the likely Democratic Senate nominee in the 1986 Senate election. The FECA contained a special provision allowing political parties to make a certain amount of coordinated expenditures (set through a formula contained in the statute) supporting that party's Senate candidates. (Recall that coordinated spending is ordinarily treated like a contribution to a candidate, and subject to contribution limits.) The FECA did not allow for independent spending by parties, on the assumption that in the nature of things, the activities of parties and candidates are coordinated. The Colorado Republican Party had assigned its $103,000 in permissible coordinated expenditures to the National Republican Senatorial Committee, and when the Colorado Republican Party paid for a radio advertisement attacking Wirth, the Democrats claimed that the Republicans violated the FECA. The Colorado Republican Party claimed, first, that the spending was independent of any candidate—a plausible claim, because the anti-Wirth ads ran before the Republican candidate was known—and second, that it was unconstitutional to deny parties the right to engage in independent spending. The Republicans also contended that even if the expenditures in question were coordinated, parties had the constitutional right to unlimited coordinated spending.

The Supreme Court issued no majority opinion. Justice Breyer, joined by Justices O'Connor and Souter, declined to reach the question whether parties' *coordinated* expenditures could be limited. These Justices concluded that the FECA provision was unconstitutional insofar as it prohibited the party from making *independent* expenditures. Following *Buckley*, the three Justices held that the government could not demonstrate an adequate danger of corruption to justify limiting such expenditure:

> We are not aware of any special dangers of corruption associated with political parties that tip the constitutional balance in a different direction. When this Court considered, and held unconstitutional, limits that FECA had set on certain independent expenditures by PAC's, it reiterated *Buckley*'s observation that "the absence of prearrangement and coordination" does not eliminate, but it does help to "alleviate," any "danger" that a candidate will understand the expenditure as an effort to obtain a "*quid pro quo*." See *NCPAC*. The same is true of independent party expenditures.
>
> We recognize that FECA permits individuals to contribute more money ($20,000) to a party than to a candidate ($1,000) or to other political committees ($5,000). [52 U.S.C. § 30116(a)]. We also recognize that FECA permits unregulated "soft money" contributions to a party for certain activities, such as electing candidates for state office or for voter registration and "get out the vote" drives. But the opportunity for corruption posed by these greater opportunities for contributions is, at best, attenuated. Unregulated "soft money" contributions may not be used to influence a federal campaign, except when used in the limited, party-building activities specifically designated in the statute. [52 U.S.C. § 30101(8)]. Any contribution to a party that is earmarked for a particular campaign is considered a contribution to the candidate and is subject to the contribution limitations. [52 U.S.C. § 30116(a)(8)]. A party may not simply channel unlimited amounts of even undesignated contributions to a candidate, since such direct transfers are also considered contributions and are subject to the contribution limits on a "multicandidate political committee." [52 U.S.C. § 30116(a)(2)]. The greatest danger of corruption, therefore, appears to be from the ability of donors to give sums up to $20,000 to a party which may be used for

> independent party expenditures for the benefit of a particular candidate. We could understand how Congress, were it to conclude that the potential for evasion of the individual contribution limits was a serious matter, might decide to change the statute's limitations on contributions to political parties. Cf. *California Medical Assn.* (plurality opinion) (danger of evasion of limits on contribution to candidates justified prophylactic limitation on *contributions* to PAC's). But we do not believe that the risk of corruption present here could justify the "markedly greater burden on basic freedoms caused by" the statute's limitations on *expenditures*. *Buckley*. Contributors seeking to avoid the effect of the $1,000 contribution limit indirectly by donations to the national party could spend that same amount of money (or more) themselves more directly by making their own independent expenditures promoting the candidate.... If anything, an independent expenditure made possible by a $20,000 donation, but controlled and directed by a party rather than the donor, would seem less likely to corrupt than the same (or a much larger) independent expenditure made directly by that donor. In any case, the constitutionally significant fact, present equally in both instances, is the lack of coordination between the candidate and the source of the expenditure. See *Buckley*; *NCPAC*. This fact prevents us from assuming, absent convincing evidence to the contrary, that a limitation on political parties' independent expenditures is necessary to combat a substantial danger of corruption of the electoral system.

Justices Kennedy, Scalia and Chief Justice Rehnquist agreed that the provision was unconstitutional as applied to party independent expenditures, but they would have struck down the limit as applied to party *coordinated* expenditures as well: "We have a constitutional tradition of political parties and their candidates engaging in joint First Amendment activity; we also have a practical identity of interests between the two entities during an election. Party spending 'in cooperation, consultation, or concert with' a candidate therefore is indistinguishable in substance from expenditures by the candidate or his campaign committee. We held in *Buckley* that the First Amendment does not permit regulation of the latter, and it should not permit this regulation of the former." Justice Thomas issued a separate opinion in which he agreed with Justice Kennedy's analysis under *Buckley*, but also argued that the *Buckley* framework should be abandoned in favor of a strict scrutiny approach to all regulation. Justice Stevens, joined by Justice Ginsburg, dissented, identifying three reasons to limit even independent spending by political parties:

> First, such limits serve the interest in avoiding both the appearance and the reality of a corrupt political process. A party shares a unique relationship with the candidate it sponsors because their political fates are inextricably linked. That interdependency creates a special danger that the party—or the persons who control the party—will abuse the influence it has over the candidate by virtue of its power to spend. The provisions at issue are appropriately aimed at reducing that threat....

> Second, these restrictions supplement other spending limitations embodied in the Act, which are likewise designed to prevent corruption. Individuals and certain organizations are permitted to contribute up to $1,000 to a candidate. Since the same donors can give up to $5,000 to party committees, if there were no limits on party spending, their contributions could be spent to benefit the candidate and thereby circumvent the $1,000 cap. We have recognized the legitimate interest in blocking similar attempts to undermine the policies of the Act. See *CMA*; *Buckley*.
>
> Finally, I believe the Government has an important interest in leveling the electoral playing field by constraining the cost of federal campaigns.

On remand, the district court addressed the Colorado Republican Federal Campaign Committee's counterclaim that the ban on party spending coordinated with candidates was unconstitutional. Such coordinated spending is treated as a contribution under the FECA. See 52 U.S.C. § 30116(a)(7)(B)(i). The court struck down the party expenditure provision because the FEC "failed to offer relevant, admissible evidence which suggests that coordinated party expenditures must be limited to prevent corruption or the appearance thereof. . . ." *Federal Election Commission v. Colorado Republican Federal Campaign Committee*, 41 F. Supp. 2d 1197, 1213 (D. Colo. 1999). The Tenth Circuit affirmed. 213 F.3d 1221 (10th Cir. 2000).

In *Federal Election Commission v. Colorado Republican Federal Campaign Committee*, 533 U.S. 431 (2001) (*Colorado II*), the Supreme Court, by a 5–4 vote, reversed the Tenth Circuit. Following its opinion in *Shrink Missouri*, the Court treated the coordinated expenditure rules as a "functional[]" contribution limit. It then held that Congress could impose such a limit to prevent corruption and its appearance:

> When we look directly at a party's function in getting and spending money, it would ignore reality to think that the party role is adequately described by speaking generally of electing particular candidates. The money parties spend comes from contributors with their own personal interests. PACs, for example, are frequent party contributors who (according to one of the Party's own experts) "do not pursue the same objectives in electoral politics," that parties do (statement of Professor Anthony Corrado). PACs "are most concerned with advancing their narrow interest[s]" and therefore "provide support to candidates who share their views, regardless of party affiliation." *Ibid.* In fact, many PACs naturally express their narrow interests by contributing to both parties during the same electoral cycle, and sometimes even directly to two competing candidates in the same election. Parties are thus necessarily the instruments of some contributors whose object is not to support the party's message or to elect party candidates across the board, but rather to support a specific candidate for the sake of a position on one, narrow issue, or even to support any candidate who will be obliged to the contributors.

> Parties thus perform functions more complex than simply electing candidates; whether they like it or not, they act as agents for spending on behalf of those who seek to produce obligated officeholders. It is this party role, which functionally unites parties with other self-interested political actors, that the [challenged provision] targets. This party role, accordingly, provides good reason to view limits on coordinated spending by parties through the same lens applied to such spending by donors, like PACs, that can use parties as conduits for contributions meant to place candidates under obligation.

Justice Thomas, joined by Justices Scalia and Kennedy, dissented, calling for *Buckley* to be overruled. Then, joined by those Justices and Chief Justice Rehnquist, Justice Thomas argued that even under *Buckley* the law failed to pass constitutional muster. On the point raised by the majority about parties acting as agents for donors, Justice Thomas responded:

> The Court contends that parties are not organized simply to "elec[t] particular candidates" as evidenced by the fact that many political action committees donate money to both parties and sometimes even opposing candidates. According to the Court, "[p]arties are thus necessarily the instruments of some contributors whose object is not to support the party's message or to elect party candidates across the board." There are two flaws in the Court's analysis. First, no one argues that a party's role is merely to get particular candidates elected. Surely, among other reasons, parties also exist to develop and promote a platform. The point is simply that parties and candidates have shared interests, that it is natural for them to work together, and that breaking the connection between parties and their candidates inhibits the promotion of the party's message. Second, the mere fact that some donors contribute to both parties and their candidates does not necessarily imply that the donors control the parties or their candidates. It certainly does not mean that the parties are mere "instruments" or "agents" of the donors. Indeed, if a party receives money from donors on both sides of an issue, how can it be a tool of both donors? If the Green Party were to receive a donation from an industry that pollutes, would the Green Party necessarily become, through no choice of its own, an instrument of the polluters? The Court proffers no evidence that parties have become pawns of wealthy contributors. Parties might be the target of the speech of donors, but that does not suggest that parties are influenced (let alone improperly influenced) by the speech. Thus, the Court offers no explanation for why political parties should be treated the same as individuals and political committees.

Notes and Questions

1. Political parties and the candidates they nominate normally work closely together in campaigns. *Colorado I* and *Colorado II* taken together allow parties to spend independently without limit but permit controls on their spending that is

coordinated with candidates. The cases therefore create a strong incentive for parties to separate their activities from their candidates. Is any public purpose served?

2. Do political parties have a right to make direct campaign contributions to candidates? See *Thalheimer v. City of San Diego*, 2012 WL 177414 (S.D. Cal. 2012) (yes); *Thalheimer v. City of San Diego*, 645 F.3d 1109 (9th Cir. 2011) (maybe).

3. *"Soft Money."* As noted in the last chapter, Congress passed the most significant campaign finance changes since 1974 in the 2002 Bipartisan Campaign Reform Act. Aside from the new limits on corporate and labor union spending in federal elections, discussed in the last chapter, BCRA also made significant changes to the rules related to contribution limits. Putting aside much detail, the bill increased the individual campaign contribution limit to $2,000 per election (indexed, for the first time, to inflation), keeping the $5,000 contribution limit to PACs from individuals and from PACs to candidates the same. The law also barred various practices related to the raising of "soft money."

In *McConnell v. FEC*, 540 U.S. 93 (2003), the Court described the rise of soft money and the emergence of BCRA's new rules as follows:

> Under FECA, "contributions" must be made with funds that are subject to the Act's disclosure requirements and source and amount limitations. Such funds are known as "federal" or "hard" money. FECA defines the term "contribution," however, to include only the gift or advance of anything of value "made by any person for the purpose of influencing any election for *Federal* office." Donations made solely for the purpose of influencing state or local elections are therefore unaffected by FECA's requirements and prohibitions. As a result, prior to the enactment of BCRA, federal law permitted corporations and unions, as well as individuals who had already made the maximum permissible contributions to federal candidates, to contribute "nonfederal money"—also known as "soft money"—to political parties for activities intended to influence state or local elections.
>
> Shortly after *Buckley* was decided, questions arose concerning the treatment of contributions intended to influence both federal and state elections. Although a literal reading of FECA's definition of "contribution" would have required such activities to be funded with hard money, the FEC ruled that political parties could fund mixed-purpose activities—including get-out-the-vote drives and generic party advertising—in part with soft money. In 1995 the FEC concluded that the parties could also use soft money to defray the costs of "legislative advocacy media advertisements," even if the ads mentioned the name of a federal candidate, so long as they did not expressly advocate the candidate's election or defeat.
>
> As the permissible uses of soft money expanded, the amount of soft money raised and spent by the national political parties increased exponentially. Of the two major parties' total spending, soft money accounted for 5% ($21.6 million) in 1984, 11% ($45 million) in 1988, 16% ($80 million)

in 1992, 30% ($272 million) in 1996, and 42% ($98 million) in 2000. The national parties transferred large amounts of their soft money to the state parties, which were allowed to use a larger percentage of soft money to finance mixed-purpose activities under FEC rules. In the year 2000, for example, the national parties diverted $280 million — more than half of their soft money — to state parties.

Many contributions of soft money were dramatically larger than the contributions of hard money permitted by FECA. For example, in 1996 the top five corporate soft-money donors gave, in total, more than $9 million in nonfederal funds to the two national party committees. In the most recent election cycle the political parties raised almost $300 million — 60% of their total soft-money fundraising — from just 800 donors, each of which contributed a minimum of $120,000. Moreover, the largest corporate donors often made substantial contributions to both parties. Such practices corroborate evidence indicating that many corporate contributions were motivated by a desire for access to candidates and a fear of being placed at a disadvantage in the legislative process relative to other contributors, rather than by ideological support for the candidates and parties.

Not only were such soft-money contributions often designed to gain access to federal candidates, but they were in many cases solicited by the candidates themselves. Candidates often directed potential donors to party committees and tax-exempt organizations that could legally accept soft money. For example, a federal legislator running for reelection solicited soft money from a supporter by advising him that even though he had already "contributed the legal maximum" to the campaign committee, he could still make an additional contribution to a joint program supporting federal, state, and local candidates of his party. Such solicitations were not uncommon.

The solicitation, transfer, and use of soft money thus enabled parties and candidates to circumvent FECA's limitations on the source and amount of contributions in connection with federal elections. . . .

Title I is Congress' effort to plug the soft-money loophole. The cornerstone of Title I is new FECA § 323(a), which prohibits national party committees and their agents from soliciting, receiving, directing, or spending any soft money. In short, § 323(a) takes national parties out of the soft-money business.

The remaining provisions of new FECA § 323 largely reinforce the restrictions in § 323(a). New FECA § 323(b) prevents the wholesale shift of soft-money influence from national to state party committees by prohibiting state and local party committees from using such funds for activities that affect federal elections. These "Federal election activities," defined in new FECA § 301(20)(A), are almost identical to the mixed-purpose activities that have long been regulated under the FEC's pre-BCRA allocation

> egime. New FECA § 323(d) reinforces these soft-money restrictions by pro-ibiting political parties from soliciting and donating funds to tax-exempt rganizations that engage in electioneering activities. New FECA § 323(e) estricts federal candidates and officeholders from receiving, spending, or oliciting soft money in connection with federal elections and limits their ability to do so in connection with state and local elections. Finally, new FECA § 323(f) prevents circumvention of the restrictions on national, state, and local party committees by prohibiting state and local candidates from raising and spending soft money to fund advertisements and other public communications that promote or attack federal candidates.

This table from the FEC describes the inflation-adjusted federal contribution limits that were in effect, post-BCRA (and after the decision in *McCutcheon*, *infra* this Chapter), for the 2021–22 election season.

CONTRIBUTION LIMITS FOR 2021–2022

<table>
<tr><th rowspan="2">DONORS</th><th colspan="5">RECIPIENTS</th></tr>
<tr><th>Candidate Committee per election</th><th>PAC[1] (SSF and Nonconnected)</th><th>State/District/ Local Party Committee</th><th>National Party Committee</th><th>Additional National Party Committee Accounts[2]</th></tr>
<tr><td>Individual</td><td>$2,900* per election</td><td>$5,000 per year</td><td>$10,000 per year (combined)</td><td>$36,500* per year</td><td>$109,500* per account, per year</td></tr>
<tr><td>Candidate Committee</td><td>$2,000 per election</td><td>$5,000 per year</td><td>Unlimited Transfers</td><td>Unlimited Transfers</td><td></td></tr>
<tr><td>PAC Multicandidate</td><td>$5,000 per election</td><td>$5,000 per year</td><td>$5,000 per year (combined)</td><td>$15,000 per year</td><td>$45,000 per account, per year</td></tr>
<tr><td>PAC Nonmulticandidate</td><td>$2,900* per election</td><td>$5,000 per year</td><td>$10,000 per year (combined)</td><td>$36,500* per year</td><td>$109,500* per account, per year</td></tr>
<tr><td>State/District/Local Party Committee</td><td>$5,000 per election (combined)</td><td>$5,000 per year (combined)</td><td rowspan="2" colspan="2">Unlimited Transfers</td><td rowspan="2"></td></tr>
<tr><td>National Party Committee</td><td>$5,000 per election[3]</td><td>$5,000 per year</td></tr>
</table>

*- Indexed for inflation in odd-numbered years.

[1] "PAC" here refers to a committee that makes contributions to other federal political committees. Independent-expenditure-only political committees (sometimes called "super PACs") may accept unlimited contributions, including from corporations and labor organizations.

[2] The limits in this column apply to a national party committee's accounts for: (i) the presidential nominating convention; (ii) election recounts and contests and other legal proceedings; and (iii) national party headquarters buildings. A party's national committee, Senate campaign committee and House campaign committee are each considered separate national party committees with separate limits. Only a national party committee, not the parties' national congressional campaign committees, may have an account for the presidential nominating convention.

[3] Additionally, a national party committee and its Senatorial campaign committee may contribute up to $51,200 combined per campaign to each Senate candidate.

President Bush signed BCRA into law despite expressing reservations about the constitutionality of several of its provisions. Immediately upon the President signing the bill, it was challenged in federal court, first by the National Rifle Association and then by a varied collection of groups and individuals including Senator Mitch McConnell, a leading opponent of campaign finance regulation. The cases were consolidated under the name *McConnell v. FEC,* and heard, under expedited procedures set forth in the Act, by a three-judge district court in Washington D.C. with direct appeal to the Supreme Court. The three judges hearing the case were District Court judges Colleen Kollar-Kotelly and Richard Leon and D.C. Circuit Court judge Karen LeCraft Henderson.

The three judges on the panel issued four opinions in the case, *McConnell v. FEC*, 251 F. Supp. 2d 176 (D.D.C. 2003), totaling an astounding 1,638 typescript pages (a mere 774 pages in the printed volume). First came a *per curiam* opinion joined by Judges Kollar-Kotelly and Leon dealing with general issues and some of the law's disclosure provisions. But the *per curiam* opinion did not address the great majority of issues, including the most controversial ones. The bulk of the court's product appeared in individual opinions by each of the three judges. In broad terms, Judge Kollar-Kotelly upheld most of BCRA, while Judge Henderson regarded much of it as unconstitutional. Judge Leon took an in-between position, so that with few exceptions, his views were decisive.

The Supreme Court issued its decision in December 2003, upholding most of the BCRA, including the soft money and issue advocacy provisions (the latter of which were discussed in the last chapter). The opinions had the largest U.S. Reports page count (279, excluding the heading and syllabus) and second largest word count (89,694) in Supreme Court history.

The Court's majority opinion was divided into three parts, with Justices Stevens and O'Connor jointly writing the opinion for the Court as to the constitutionality of challenged provisions of BCRA's Title I and Title II, the act's soft money and issue advocacy provisions. Chief Justice Rehnquist and Justice Breyer each wrote opinions for the Court on other challenged provisions.

McConnell's greatest doctrinal significance came in its further relaxation of the definition of corruption to include "ingratiation" and "access." As we shall see in Part V, however, that significance has proven to be short-lived, as the Supreme Court rejected *McConnell*'s language in the contributions context in the *McCutcheon* case (after having rejected it in the spending context in *Citizens United*). The Court may soon consider whether to directly overrule *McConnell*'s soft money holding as well.

IV. The Growth of Super PACs and Other Outside Groups

Though we have focused thus far on the campaign finance activities of political parties, individuals, corporations, and labor unions, we turn our attention now to another important type of association: the political action committee (or "PAC").[f] The importance of PACs has waxed and waned over time. Since *Citizens United*, as we shall see, PACs (and other outside groups) have gained tremendous (some might say overwhelming) importance in federal campaign election financing. But we begin with some history to put things in context.

Before *Citizens United*, corporations and unions could not spend their general treasury funds on certain election-related activities. Instead, they were allowed to solicit contributions of up to $5,000 for their PACs.[g] The PACs themselves may make contributions of up to $5,000 per election to federal candidates, and spend unlimited sums supporting or opposing candidates for federal office. Corporate and union PACs are restricted on whom they may solicit. *See Federal Election Commission v. National Right to Work Committee*, 459 U.S. 197 (1982) (*NRWC*), upholding the constitutionality of the solicitation rules.[h]

---

f. "PAC," or "political action committee," is not a term that appears in the FECA. Most PACs are "multicandidate political committees," which the Act defines as "a political committee which has been registered . . . for a period of not less than 6 months, which has received contributions from more than 50 persons, and, except for any state political party organization, has made contributions to 5 or more candidates for Federal office." 52 U.S.C. § 30116(a)(4). A committee must qualify as a multicandidate political committee in order to be eligible for the $5,000 limit on contributions to federal candidates, as opposed to the $1,000 limit that is applicable to individuals and other entities. A "separate segregated fund" of a corporation or union will ordinarily qualify as a multicandidate political committee — or, in popular language, as a PAC.

g. The provisions in 52 U.S.C. § 30118(b)(4), specifying the individuals who may be solicited by corporate and labor PACs, were added to the FECA in 1976. In a controversial opinion the previous year, the Federal Election Commission had ruled by a 4–2 vote that corporations could solicit stockholders and employees. FEC Advisory Opinion 1975-23 (Sun Oil Co.) (1975). Many Democrats and union leaders had urged that corporations be limited to soliciting stockholders. Corporate leaders and many Republicans, recognizing that employees were much more likely than stockholders to contribute to corporate PACs, strenuously argued the contrary. The 1976 statutory amendments limited corporate PACs to soliciting "executive or administrative personnel." Although on the face of it this represented a compromise, as a practical matter it was a smashing victory for corporate PACs, whose expenditures increased rapidly and dramatically. In 1976, corporate PACs spent a total of $5.8 million. Corporate PAC spending exceeded $158 million in the 1999–2000 election period.

h. Labor union PACs commonly collect contributions by a "check-off" procedure, whereby members sign an authorization to have a small amount deducted from each paycheck. Suppose a union PAC uses a "reverse check-off," whereby the contribution is withheld from each member's paycheck unless the member submits a request that the contribution *not* be withheld? Is such a system constitutional? See *FEC v. National Education Association*, 457 F. Supp. 1102 (D.D.C. 1978). A Michigan statute requiring union members to reaffirm annually their desire to contribute to a union PAC was upheld in a 2–1 decision in *Michigan State AFL-CIO v. Miller*, 103 F.3d 1240 (6th Cir. 1997). Disagreeing with *Miller*, the Washington state Supreme Court, with three justices dissenting,

The restrictions on solicitation of contributions by PACs in 52 U.S.C. § 30118 apply to corporate and labor union PACs, which have the offsetting advantage of being able to use treasury funds of the sponsoring corporations and unions to pay their administrative expenses. This is no trivial advantage, as the administrative expenses often exceed the money received from contributors and donated to candidates.

The total number of federal political action committees grew rapidly in the first decade following the 1974 amendments to the FECA, and then leveled off. At the end of 1974, 608 PACs were registered with the FEC. According to the most recent FEC data, released in March 2021, the number was 8855. FEC, "Summary of PAC Activity, January 1, 2019 through December 31, 2020," https://perma.cc/5QBJ-CD5D.

In the past, PACs played some role, but not a dominating role, in federal election campaigns, primarily because of the $5,000 contribution limits to PACs. Thus, PACs cannot serve as a conduit for campaign contributions of large individuals. Nor could they take general treasury funds from corporations or labor unions (except to pay for administrative expenses). Still PACs contributed $412.8 million to House and Senate candidates in the 2007–08 election season, https://perma.cc/2C4B-A2RZ. During that same period, PACs spent about $36 million on independent expenditures in House and Senate races during the period, and $98 million on the presidential election.

With limits on PACs in place, and new restrictions in BCRA, some wealthy individuals, along with some corporations and labor unions, looked for ways to contribute sums larger than $5,000 to non-PAC organizations geared to influence federal elections. In the 2004 election, certain groups organized under section 527 of the Internal Revenue Code began accepting large donations to make electioneering communications in connection with the 2004 federal elections. The groups claimed they were not operating as "political committees" as defined in FECA, because they made no contributions to candidates and did not expressly advocate the election or defeat of candidates for office. Many saw them as "shadow parties" doing the work of political parties but not limited on the rules governing contributions to parties or PACs.

Although these groups were set up for both parties, in the 2004 election the largest and most important were Democratic groups supporting John Kerry against George Bush. The resulting controversy was pervasively ironic, as Republicans and many former opponents of BCRA claimed that it is illegal for individuals to make large donations to these groups for these purposes. Democrats and many who supported

---

struck down a state statute passed by initiative requiring public sector union members to "opt in" before the union could deduct from union member paychecks monies used for political purposes. *Washington State Public Disclosure Commission v. Washington Education Association*, 130 P.3d 352 (Wash. 2006) (en banc). The U.S. Supreme Court unanimously reversed, holding that a state does not violate the First Amendment when it requires public sector union members to opt in before spending nonmembers' fees for election-related purposes. *Davenport v. Washington Educ. Ass'n*, 551 U.S. 177 (2007). Whether the ruling applies to private sector employees remains to be seen.

of BCRA as a means of plugging loopholes called for a narrower construction to leave the section 527 organizations unregulated. As a matter of statutory interpretation, at least some of these organizations might have been considered political committees because their "major purpose" was to influence federal elections, even if they failed to engage in express advocacy. Individual donations to political committees were capped at $5,000 under the FECA.

Section 527 organizations played a major role in the 2004 election, with one estimate placing their spending at nearly $400 million in the 2004 federal elections. Steve Weissman & Ruth Hassan, *BCRA and the 527 Groups*, in The Election after Reform: Money, Politics, and the Bipartisan Campaign Reform Act (Michael J. Malbin, ed., 2007). George Soros topped the list of individual donors to 527s at $24 million, though labor unions gave about 4 times as much as Soros to pro-Democratic 527s. Some criticized the Federal Election Commission for not regulating 527s as political committees during the 2004 election season. Treating 527s as political committees would have a number of consequences, most importantly limiting contributions *to* such committees to $5,000 per person. Reform groups sued the FEC for failing to issue rules setting forth when 527s would be treated as political committees. The FEC responded by settling with some 527 groups that failed to register as political committees, fining others, and issuing an "Explanation and Justification" explaining what factors it would take into account in deciding on a 527's political committee status. A federal district court upheld the FEC's decision to judge 527s on a case-by-case basis. *Shays v. Federal Election Commission,* 511 F. Supp. 2d 19 (D.D.C. 2007). As the FEC began to regulate 527 organizations, albeit on a case-by-case basis, some election-related activity shifted to 501(c)(4) "social welfare" organizations and other" nonprofits. Among other things 501(c)(4) status made it easier for groups to hide the identity of their donors.

After *Citizens United*, opponents of campaign finance limits challenged limits on contributions to independent PACs in both the courts and at the FEC. They had remarkable success, and are transforming campaign financing in the U.S. Thanks in part to *Citizens United* and the next case, PAC spending in federal elections exceeded a staggering $4.2 billion in 2016. David B. Magleby, *Change and Continuity in the Financing of the 2016 U.S. Federal Election*, in Financing the 2016 Elections (David B. Magleby, ed., 2019), at 1, 27 tbl. 1. Many Super PACs and outside groups acted as "shadow" campaigns for presidential candidates. These groups could accept larger donations and support candidates, so long as they did not run afoul of the formal rules against "coordination" between campaigns and outside groups *Id.* at 30-33. For more on how Super PACs and other outside groups served as "de facto" campaign organizations for the presidential candidates in 2016, see Anthony Corrado, *The Regulatory Environment of the 2016 Election,* 55, 71-79, in Financing the 2016 Elections, *supra*.

SpeechNow.org v. Federal Election Commission

599 F.3d 686 (D.C. Cir. 2010) (en banc)

SENTELLE, Chief Judge:

David Keating is president of an unincorporated nonprofit association, SpeechNow.org (SpeechNow), that intends to engage in express advocacy supporting candidates for federal office who share his views on First Amendment rights of free speech and freedom to assemble. In January 2008, the Federal Election Committee (FEC) issued a draft advisory opinion concluding that under the Federal Election Campaign Act (FECA), SpeechNow would be required to organize as a "political committee" as defined by [52 U.S.C. § 30101(4)] and would be subject to all the requirements and restrictions concomitant with that designation. Keating and four other individuals availed themselves of [52 U.S.C. § 30110], under which an individual may seek declaratory judgment to construe the constitutionality of any provision of FECA. As required by that provision, the district court certified the constitutional questions directly to this court for en banc determination. Thereafter, the Supreme Court decided *Citizens United v. FEC*, which resolves this appeal. In accordance with that decision, we hold that the contribution limits of [52 U.S.C. § 30116(a)(1)(C) and (a)(3)] are unconstitutional as applied to individuals' contributions to SpeechNow. However, we also hold that the [PAC] reporting requirements and organizational requirements . . . can constitutionally be applied to SpeechNow. . . .

I. Background

SpeechNow is an unincorporated nonprofit association registered as a "political organization" under § 527 of the Internal Revenue Code Its purpose is to promote the First Amendment rights of free speech and freedom to assemble by expressly advocating for federal candidates whom it views as supporting those rights and against those whom it sees as insufficiently committed to those rights. It intends to acquire funds solely through donations by individuals. SpeechNow further intends to operate exclusively through "independent expenditures." FECA defines "independent expenditures" as expenditures "expressly advocating the election or defeat of a clearly identified candidate" that are "not made in concert or cooperation with or at the request or suggestion of such candidate, the candidate's authorized political committee, or their agents, or a political party committee or its agents." [52 U.S.C. § 30101(17)]. SpeechNow has five members, two of whom are plaintiffs in this case: David Keating, who is also SpeechNow's president and treasurer, and Edward Crane. Keating makes the operational decisions for SpeechNow, including in which election campaigns to run advertisements, which candidates to support or oppose, and all administrative decisions.

Though it has not yet begun operations, SpeechNow has made plans both for fundraising and for making independent expenditures. . . .

On November 19, 2007, SpeechNow filed with the FEC a request for an advisory opinion, asking whether it must register as a political committee and if donations to

SpeechNow qualify as "contributions" limited by [federal law]. At the time, the FEC did not have enough commissioners to issue an opinion, but it did issue a draft advisory opinion stating that SpeechNow would be a political committee and contributions to it would be subject to the political committee contribution limits. Believing that subjecting SpeechNow to all the restrictions imposed on political committees would be unconstitutional, SpeechNow and the five individual plaintiffs filed a complaint in the district court requesting declaratory relief against the FEC . . .

II. Analysis

A. Contribution Limits . . .

The First Amendment mandates that "Congress shall make no law . . . abridging the freedom of speech." In *Buckley*, the Supreme Court held that, although contribution limits do encroach upon First Amendment interests, they do not encroach upon First Amendment interests to as great a degree as expenditure limits. In *Buckley*, the Supreme Court first delineated the differing treatments afforded contribution and expenditure limits. In that case, the Court struck down limits on an individual's expenditures for political advocacy, but upheld limits on contributions to political candidates and campaigns. In making the distinction, the Court emphasized that in "contrast with a limitation upon expenditures for political expression, a limitation upon the amount that any one person or group may contribute to a candidate or political committee entails only a marginal restriction upon the contributor's ability to engage in free communication." However, contribution limits still do implicate fundamental First Amendment interests.

When the government attempts to regulate the financing of political campaigns and express advocacy through contribution limits, therefore, it must have a countervailing interest that outweighs the limit's burden on the exercise of First Amendment rights. Thus a "contribution limit involving significant interference with associational rights must be closely drawn to serve a sufficiently important interest." *Davis*. The Supreme Court has recognized only one interest sufficiently important to outweigh the First Amendment interests implicated by contributions for political speech: preventing corruption or the appearance of corruption. The Court has rejected each of the few other interests the government has, at one point or another, suggested as a justification for contribution or expenditure limits. Equalization of differing viewpoints is not a legitimate government objective. *Davis*. An informational interest in "identifying the sources of support for and opposition to" a political position or candidate is not enough to justify the First Amendment burden. *CARC*. And, though this rationale would not affect an unincorporated association such as SpeechNow, the Court has also refused to find a sufficiently compelling governmental interest in preventing "the corrosive and distorting effects of immense aggregations of wealth that are accumulated with the help of the corporate form." *Citizens United*.

Given this precedent, the only interest we may evaluate to determine whether the government can justify contribution limits as applied to SpeechNow is the government's anticorruption interest. Because of the Supreme Court's recent decision in

Citizens United, the analysis is straightforward. There, the Court held that the government has *no* anti-corruption interest in limiting independent expenditures.[3] . . .

The independence of independent expenditures was a central consideration in the Court's decision [in *Citizens United*]. By definition, independent expenditures are "not made in concert or cooperation with or at the request or suggestion of such candidate, the candidate's authorized political committee, or their agents, or a political party committee or its agents.". As the *Buckley* Court explained when it struck down a limit on independent expenditures, "[t]he absence of prearrangement and coordination of an expenditure with the candidate or his agent . . . alleviates the danger that expenditures will be given as a *quid pro quo* for improper commitments from the candidate." However, the *Buckley* Court left open the possibility that the future might bring data linking independent expenditures to corruption or the appearance of corruption. The Court merely concluded that independent expenditures "do [] not presently appear to pose dangers of real or apparent corruption comparable to those identified with large campaign contributions."

Over the next several decades, Congress and the Court gave little further guidance respecting *Buckley*'s reasoning that a lack of coordination diminishes the possibility of corruption. [The court summarized the history of *Austin and McConnell.*] The *Citizens United* Court reevaluated this line of cases and found them to be incompatible with *Buckley's* original reasoning. The Court overruled *Austin* and the part of *McConnell that* upheld BCRA's amendments to [52 U.S.C. § 30118]. More important for this case, the Court did so by expressly deciding the question left open by the footnoted caveat in *Bellotti.* The Court stated, "[W]e now conclude that independent expenditures, including those made by corporations, do not give rise to corruption or the appearance of corruption." *Citizens United.*

The Court came to this conclusion by looking to the definition of corruption and the appearance of corruption. For several decades after Buckley, the Court's analysis of the government's anti-corruption interest revolved largely around the "hallmark of corruption," "financial *quid pro quo*: dollars for political favors." *NCPAC.* However, in a series of cases culminating in *McConnell* Court expanded the definition to include "the appearance of undue influence" created by large donations given for the purpose of "buying access," The *McConnell* Court concluded that limiting the government's anticorruption interest to preventing *quid pro quo* was a "crabbed view of corruption, and particularly of the appearance of corruption" that "ignores precedent, common sense, and the realities of political fundraising." The *Citizens United* Court retracted this view of the government's interest, saying that "[t]he fact that speakers may have influence over or access to elected officials does not mean that these officials are corrupt." The Court returned to its older definition of corruption that focused on *quid pro quo,* saying that "[i]ngratiation and access . . . are not

---

3. Of course, the government still has an interest in preventing *quid pro quo* corruption. However, after *Citizens United*, independent expenditures do not implicate that interest.

corruption." Therefore, without any evidence that independent expenditures "lead to, or create the appearance of, *quid pro quo* corruption," and only "scant evidence" that they even ingratiate, the Court concluded that independent expenditures do not corrupt or create the appearance of corruption.

In its briefs in this case, the FEC relied heavily on *McConnell,* arguing that independent expenditures by groups like SpeechNow benefit candidates and that those candidates are accordingly grateful to the groups and to their donors. The FEC's argument was that large contributions to independent expenditure groups "lead to preferential access for donors and undue influence over officeholders." Whatever the merits of those arguments before *Citizens United,* they plainly have no merit after *Citizens United.*

In light of the Court's holding as a matter of law that independent expenditures do not corrupt or create the appearance of *quid pro quo* corruption, contributions to groups that make only independent expenditures also cannot corrupt or create the appearance of corruption. The Court has effectively held that there is no corrupting "quid" for which a candidate might in exchange offer a corrupt "quo."

Given this analysis from *Citizens United,* we must conclude that the government has no anti-corruption interest in limiting contributions to an independent expenditure group such as SpeechNow. This simplifies the task of weighing the First Amendment interests implicated by contributions to SpeechNow against the government's interest in limiting such contributions. As we have observed in other contexts, "something . . . outweighs nothing every time." *Nat'l Ass'n of Retired Fed. Employees v. Horner,* 879 F.2d 873, 879 (D.C. Cir. 1989). Thus, we do not need to quantify to what extent contributions to SpeechNow are an expression of core political speech. We do not need to answer whether giving money is speech per se, or if contributions are merely symbolic expressions of general support, or if it matters in this case that just one person, David Keating, decides what the group will say. All that matters is that the First Amendment cannot be encroached upon for naught.

At oral argument, the FEC insisted that *Citizens United* does not disrupt *Buckley*'s longstanding decision upholding contribution limits. This is literally true. But, as *Citizens United* emphasized, the limits upheld in *Buckley* were limits on contributions made *directly to candidates.* Limits on direct contributions to candidates, "unlike limits on independent expenditures, have been an accepted means to prevent *quid pro quo* corruption." *Citizens United.*

The FEC also argues that we must look to the discussion about the potential for independent expenditures to corrupt in *Colorado Republican.* This, too, is unavailing. In *Colorado Republican,* the Court considered the constitutionality of FECA provisions that exempted political party committees from the general political committee contribution limits, but imposed limitations on political party committees' independent expenditures. A majority of the Court agreed that the independent expenditure limitations were unconstitutional, but no more than three Justices joined any single opinion. It is true that the opinion of Justice Breyer did discuss the potential for corruption or the appearance of corruption potentially arising from independent expenditures, saying that "[t]he greatest danger of corruption ... appears to be from the ability of donors to give sums up to $20,000 to a party which may be used for independent party expenditures for the benefit of a particular candidate," thus evading the limits on direct contributions to candidates. (opinion of Breyer, J.). But *Colorado Republican* concerned expenditures by political parties, which are wholly distinct from "independent expenditures" as defined by [52 U.S.C. § 30101(17)]. Moreover, a discussion in a 1996 opinion joined by only three Justices cannot control our analysis when the more recent opinion of the Court in *Citizens United* clearly states as a matter of law that independent expenditures do not pose a danger of corruption or the appearance of corruption.

The FEC argues that the analysis of *Citizens United* does not apply because that case involved an expenditure limit while this case involves a contribution limit. Alluding to the divide between expenditure limits and contribution limits established by *Buckley,* the FEC insists that contribution limits are subject to a lower standard of review than expenditure limits, so that "what may be insufficient to justify an expenditure limit may be sufficient to justify a contribution limit." Plaintiffs, on the other hand, argue that *Citizens United* stands for the proposition that "burdensome laws trigger strict scrutiny." We do not find it necessary to decide whether the logic of *Citizens United* has any effect on the standard of review generally afforded contribution limits. The *Citizens United* Court avoided "reconsider[ing] whether contribution limits should be subjected to rigorous First Amendment scrutiny," and so do we. Instead, we return to what we have said before: because *Citizens United* holds that independent expenditures do not corrupt or give the appearance of corruption as a matter of law, then the government can have no anti-corruption interest in limiting contributions to independent expenditure-only organizations. No matter which standard of review governs contribution limits, the limits on contributions to SpeechNow cannot stand.

We therefore answer in the affirmative each of the first three questions certified to this Court. The contribution limits of [52 U.S.C. § 30116(a)(1)(C) and (a)(3)] violate the First Amendment by preventing plaintiffs from donating to SpeechNow in excess of the limits and by prohibiting SpeechNow from accepting donations in excess of the limits. We should be clear, however, that we only decide these questions as applied to contributions to SpeechNow, an independent expenditure-only group. Our holding does not affect, for example, [§ 30116(a)(3)'s] limits on direct contributions to candidates.

B. Organizational and Reporting Requirements ...

[The court upholds the organizational and reporting requirements for PACs.]

Conclusion

We conclude that the [limits on individual contributions to independent expenditure PACs] cannot be constitutionally applied against SpeechNow and the individual plaintiffs....

Notes and Questions

1. The decision of the en banc D.C. Circuit court was unanimous. The government did not file a cert. petition with the Supreme Court. Why not?

2. After *SpeechNow*, the Federal Election Commission issued two advisory opinions which determined that corporations and labor unions could also contribute (unlimited sums) to Super PACs. FEC Advisory Opinion 2010–09 (Club for Growth), https://perma.cc/AKE5-MYHK; FEC Advisory Opinion 2010–11 (Commonsense Ten), https://perma.cc/PED3-ZZVJ. Does this result follow unquestionably from *SpeechNow*?

3. Eliza Newlin Carney dubbed these independent expenditure committees "Super PACs," and the name has stuck. Eliza Newlin Carney, *FEC Rulings Open Door for 'Super' PACs,* National Journal, Aug. 2, 2010, https://bit.ly/3wpq5N0. These new organizations have played a major role in subsequent elections.

4. In *Carey v. Federal Election Commission*, 791 F. Supp. 2d 121 (D.D.C. 2011), a federal district court held that a PAC which makes direct donations to candidates also may accept unlimited donations, if it segregates the two funds. So every PAC, provided it does its paperwork right, can become a Super PAC.

5. These new rules put great pressure on the definition of "coordination." In the 2012 elections, Super PACs have included former campaign managers, been funded by relatives of candidates, share consultants, and engage in other activities (including fundraising for the Super PACs, so long as the candidates do not ask for more than $5,000) without running afoul of the FEC's rules on coordination. Mike McIntire & Michael Luo, *Fine Line Between 'Super PACs' and Campaigns*, N.Y. Times, Feb. 25, 2012. The coordination rules are under great pressure.

6. Super PACs are not the final frontier when it comes to outside groups. The amount of spending by 501(c)(4) groups and other groups that do not disclose their donors publicly has ballooned. Chapter 16 returns to the question of outside spending and disclosure.

V. The New Skepticism

McCutcheon v. Federal Election Commission

572 U.S. 185 (2014)

Chief Justice ROBERTS announced the judgment of the Court and delivered an opinion, in which Justice SCALIA, Justice KENNEDY, and Justice ALITO join.

There is no right more basic in our democracy than the right to participate in electing our political leaders. Citizens can exercise that right in a variety of ways: They can run for office themselves, vote, urge others to vote for a particular candidate, volunteer to work on a campaign, and contribute to a candidate's campaign. This case is about the last of those options.

The right to participate in democracy through political contributions is protected by the First Amendment, but that right is not absolute. Our cases have held that Congress may regulate campaign contributions to protect against corruption or the appearance of corruption. See, *e.g., Buckley.* At the same time, we have made clear that Congress may not regulate contributions simply to reduce the amount of money in politics, or to restrict the political participation of some in order to enhance the relative influence of others. See, *e.g.,* [*Arizona Free Enterprise Club's Freedom Club PAC v.*] *Bennett* [*infra*, Chapter 15—Eds.]

Many people might find those latter objectives attractive: They would be delighted to see fewer television commercials touting a candidate's accomplishments or disparaging an opponent's character. Money in politics may at times seem repugnant to some, but so too does much of what the First Amendment vigorously protects. If the First Amendment protects flag burning, funeral protests, and Nazi parades—despite the profound offense such spectacles cause—it surely protects political campaign speech despite popular opposition. Indeed, as we have emphasized, the First Amendment "has its fullest and most urgent application precisely to the conduct of campaigns for political office." *Monitor Patriot Co. v. Roy.*

In a series of cases over the past 40 years, we have spelled out how to draw the constitutional line between the permissible goal of avoiding corruption in the political process and the impermissible desire simply to limit political speech. We have said that government regulation may not target the general gratitude a candidate may feel toward those who support him or his allies, or the political access such support may afford. "Ingratiation and access ... are not corruption." *Citizens United.* They embody a central feature of democracy—that constituents support candidates who share their beliefs and interests, and candidates who are elected can be expected to be responsive to those concerns.

Any regulation must instead target what we have called "*quid pro quo*" corruption or its appearance. That Latin phrase captures the notion of a direct exchange of an official act for money. See *McCormick v. United States.* "The hallmark of corruption is the financial *quid pro quo* : dollars for political favors." *NCPAC.* Campaign finance restrictions that pursue other objectives, we have explained, impermissibly inject the Government "into the debate over who should govern." *Bennett.* And those who govern should be the *last* people to help decide who *should* govern.

The statute at issue in this case imposes two types of limits on campaign contributions. The first, called base limits, restricts how much money a donor may contribute to a particular candidate or committee. [52 U.S.C. § 30116(a)(1)]. The second, called aggregate limits, restricts how much money a donor may contribute in total to all candidates or committees. [52 U.S.C. § 30116(a)(3)].

This case does not involve any challenge to the base limits, which we have previously upheld as serving the permissible objective of combatting corruption. The Government contends that the aggregate limits also serve that objective, by preventing circumvention of the base limits. We conclude, however, that the aggregate limits do little, if anything, to address that concern, while seriously restricting participation in the democratic process. The aggregate limits are therefore invalid under the First Amendment.

I

A

For the 2013–2014 election cycle, the base limits in the Federal Election Campaign Act of 1971 (FECA), as amended by the Bipartisan Campaign Reform Act of 2002 (BCRA), permit an individual to contribute up to $2,600 per election to a candidate ($5,200 total for the primary and general elections); $32,400 per year to a national party committee; $10,000 per year to a state or local party committee; and $5,000 per year to a political action committee, or "PAC."[2] A national committee, state or local party committee, or multicandidate PAC may in turn contribute up to $5,000 per election to a candidate.

The base limits apply with equal force to contributions that are "in any way earmarked or otherwise directed through an intermediary or conduit" to a candidate. If, for example, a donor gives money to a party committee but directs the party committee to pass the contribution along to a particular candidate, then the transaction is treated as a contribution from the original donor to the specified candidate.

For the 2013–2014 election cycle, the aggregate limits in BCRA permit an individual to contribute a total of $48,600 to federal candidates and a total of $74,600 to other political committees. Of that $74,600, only $48,600 may be contributed to state or local party committees and PACs, as opposed to national party committees. All told, an individual may contribute up to $123,200 to candidate and noncandidate committees during each two-year election cycle.

The base limits thus restrict how much money a donor may contribute to any particular candidate or committee; the aggregate limits have the effect of restricting how many candidates or committees the donor may support, to the extent permitted by the base limits.

B

In the 2011–2012 election cycle, appellant Shaun McCutcheon contributed a total of $33,088 to 16 different federal candidates, in compliance with the base limits applicable to each. He alleges that he wished to contribute $1,776 to each of 12 additional candidates but was prevented from doing so by the aggregate limit on contributions to candidates. McCutcheon also contributed a total of $27,328 to several noncandidate political committees, in compliance with the base limits applicable to each. He alleges that he wished to contribute to various other political committees, including

2. A PAC is a business, labor, or interest group that raises or spends money in connection with a federal election, in some cases by contributing to candidates. A so-called "Super PAC" is a PAC that makes only independent expenditures and cannot contribute to candidates. The base and aggregate limits govern contributions to traditional PACs, but not to independent expenditure PACs. See *SpeechNow.Org*.

$25,000 to each of the three Republican national party committees, but was prevented from doing so by the aggregate limit on contributions to political committees. McCutcheon further alleges that he plans to make similar contributions in the future. In the 2013–2014 election cycle, he again wishes to contribute at least $60,000 to various candidates and $75,000 to non-candidate political committees.

Appellant Republican National Committee is a national political party committee charged with the general management of the Republican Party. The RNC wishes to receive the contributions that McCutcheon and similarly situated individuals would like to make—contributions otherwise permissible under the base limits for national party committees but foreclosed by the aggregate limit on contributions to political committees.

In June 2012, McCutcheon and the RNC filed a complaint before a three-judge panel of the U.S. District Court for the District of Columbia. McCutcheon and the RNC asserted that the aggregate limits on contributions to candidates and to non-candidate political committees were unconstitutional under the First Amendment. They moved for a preliminary injunction against enforcement of the challenged provisions, and the Government moved to dismiss the case.

The three-judge District Court denied appellants' motion for a preliminary injunction and granted the Government's motion to dismiss. Assuming that the base limits appropriately served the Government's anticorruption interest, the District Court concluded that the aggregate limits survived First Amendment scrutiny because they prevented evasion of the base limits.

In particular, the District Court imagined a hypothetical scenario that might occur in a world without aggregate limits. A single donor might contribute the maximum amount under the base limits to nearly 50 separate committees, each of which might then transfer the money to the same single committee. That committee, in turn, might use all the transferred money for coordinated expenditures on behalf of a particular candidate, allowing the single donor to circumvent the base limit on the amount he may contribute to that candidate. The District Court acknowledged that "it may seem unlikely that so many separate entities would willingly serve as conduits" for the single donor's interests, but it concluded that such a scenario "is not hard to imagine." It thus rejected a constitutional challenge to the aggregate limits, characterizing the base limits and the aggregate limits "as a coherent system rather than merely a collection of individual limits stacking prophylaxis upon prophylaxis."

McCutcheon and the RNC appealed directly to this Court, as authorized by law. In such a case, "we ha[ve] no discretion to refuse adjudication of the case on its merits," *Hicks v. Miranda,* 422 U.S. 332, 344 (1975), and accordingly we noted probable jurisdiction.

II

A

Buckley v. Valeo presented this Court with its first opportunity to evaluate the constitutionality of the original contribution and expenditure limits set forth in

FECA. FECA imposed a $1,000 per election base limit on contributions from an individual to a federal candidate. It also imposed a $25,000 per year aggregate limit on all contributions from an individual to candidates or political committees. On the expenditures side, FECA imposed limits on both independent expenditures and candidates' overall campaign expenditures.

Buckley recognized that "contribution and expenditure limitations operate in an area of the most fundamental First Amendment activities." But it distinguished expenditure limits from contribution limits based on the degree to which each encroaches upon protected First Amendment interests. Expenditure limits, the Court explained, "necessarily reduce[ ] the quantity of expression by restricting the number of issues discussed, the depth of their exploration, and the size of the audience reached." The Court thus subjected expenditure limits to "the exacting scrutiny applicable to limitations on core First Amendment rights of political expression." Under exacting scrutiny, the Government may regulate protected speech only if such regulation promotes a compelling interest and is the least restrictive means to further the articulated interest. See *Sable Communications of Cal., Inc. v. FCC,* 492 U.S. 115, 126 (1989).

By contrast, the Court concluded that contribution limits impose a lesser restraint on political speech because they "permit . . . the symbolic expression of support evidenced by a contribution but do[ ] not in any way infringe the contributor's freedom to discuss candidates and issues." *Buckley.* As a result, the Court focused on the effect of the contribution limits on the freedom of political association and applied a lesser but still "rigorous standard of review." Under that standard, "[e]ven a '"significant interference" with protected rights of political association' may be sustained if the State demonstrates a sufficiently important interest and employs means closely drawn to avoid unnecessary abridgement of associational freedoms."

The primary purpose of FECA was to limit *quid pro quo* corruption and its appearance; that purpose satisfied the requirement of a "sufficiently important" governmental interest. As for the "closely drawn" component, *Buckley* concluded that the $1,000 base limit "focuses precisely on the problem of large campaign contributions . . . while leaving persons free to engage in independent political expression, to associate actively through volunteering their services, and to assist to a limited but nonetheless substantial extent in supporting candidates and committees with financial resources." The Court therefore upheld the $1,000 base limit under the "closely drawn" test.

The Court next separately considered an overbreadth challenge to the base limit. The challengers argued that the base limit was fatally overbroad because most large donors do not seek improper influence over legislators' actions. Although the Court accepted that premise, it nevertheless rejected the overbreadth challenge for two reasons: First, it was too "difficult to isolate suspect contributions" based on a contributor's subjective intent. Second, "Congress was justified in concluding that the interest in safeguarding against the appearance of impropriety requires that the opportunity for abuse inherent in the process of raising large monetary contributions be eliminated."

Finally, in one paragraph of its 139-page opinion, the Court turned to the $25,000 aggregate limit under FECA. As a preliminary matter, it noted that the constitutionality of the aggregate limit "ha[d] not been separately addressed at length by the parties." Then, in three sentences, the Court disposed of any constitutional objections to the aggregate limit that the challengers might have had:

> The overall $25,000 ceiling does impose an ultimate restriction upon the number of candidates and committees with which an individual may associate himself by means of financial support. But this quite modest restraint upon protected political activity serves to prevent evasion of the $1,000 contribution limitation by a person who might otherwise contribute massive amounts of money to a particular candidate through the use of unearmarked contributions to political committees likely to contribute to that candidate, or huge contributions to the candidate's political party. The limited, additional restriction on associational freedom imposed by the overall ceiling is thus no more than a corollary of the basic individual contribution limitation that we have found to be constitutionally valid.

B

1

The parties and *amici curiae* spend significant energy debating whether the line that *Buckley* drew between contributions and expenditures should remain the law. Notwithstanding the robust debate, we see no need in this case to revisit *Buckley*'s distinction between contributions and expenditures and the corollary distinction in the applicable standards of review. *Buckley* held that the Government's interest in preventing *quid pro quo* corruption or its appearance was "sufficiently important;" we have elsewhere stated that the same interest may properly be labeled "compelling," see *NCPAC*, so that the interest would satisfy even strict scrutiny. Moreover, regardless whether we apply strict scrutiny or *Buckley*'s "closely drawn" test, we must assess the fit between the stated governmental objective and the means selected to achieve that objective. See, e.g. *NCPAC; Randall* (opinion of BREYER, J.). Or to put it another way, if a law that restricts political speech does not "avoid unnecessary abridgement" of First Amendment rights, *Buckley*, it cannot survive "rigorous" review.

Because we find a substantial mismatch between the Government's stated objective and the means selected to achieve it, the aggregate limits fail even under the "closely drawn" test. We therefore need not parse the differences between the two standards in this case.

2

Buckley treated the constitutionality of the $25,000 aggregate limit as contingent upon that limit's ability to prevent circumvention of the $1,000 base limit, describing the aggregate limit as "no more than a corollary" of the base limit. The Court determined that circumvention could occur when an individual legally contributes "massive amounts of money to a particular candidate through the use of unearmarked contributions" to entities that are themselves likely to contribute to the candidate. For that reason, the Court upheld the $25,000 aggregate limit.

Although *Buckley* provides some guidance, we think that its ultimate conclusion about the constitutionality of the aggregate limit in place under FECA does not control here. *Buckley* spent a total of three sentences analyzing that limit; in fact, the opinion pointed out that the constitutionality of the aggregate limit "ha[d] not been separately addressed at length by the parties." We are now asked to address appellants' direct challenge to the aggregate limits in place under BCRA. BCRA is a different statutory regime, and the aggregate limits it imposes operate against a distinct legal backdrop.

Most notably, statutory safeguards against circumvention have been considerably strengthened since *Buckley* was decided, through both statutory additions and the introduction of a comprehensive regulatory scheme. With more targeted anticircumvention measures in place today, the indiscriminate aggregate limits under BCRA appear particularly heavy-handed.

The 1976 FECA Amendments, for example, added another layer of base contribution limits. The 1974 version of FECA had already capped contributions *from* political committees to candidates, but the 1976 version added limits on contributions *to* political committees. This change was enacted at least "in part to prevent circumvention of the very limitations on contributions that this Court upheld in *Buckley*." *California Medical Assn. v. FEC*, 453 U.S. 182, 197–198 (1981) (plurality opinion); see also *id.*, at 203 (Blackmun, J., concurring in part and concurring in judgment). Because a donor's contributions to a political committee are now limited, a donor cannot flood the committee with "huge" amounts of money so that each contribution the committee makes is perceived as a contribution from him. *Buckley.* Rather, the donor may contribute only $5,000 to the committee, which hardly raises the specter of abuse that concerned the Court in *Buckley.* Limits on contributions to political committees consequently create an additional hurdle for a donor who seeks both to channel a large amount of money to a particular candidate and to ensure that he gets the credit for doing so.

The 1976 Amendments also added an antiproliferation rule prohibiting donors from creating or controlling multiple affiliated political committees. The Government acknowledges that this antiproliferation rule "forecloses what would otherwise be a particularly easy and effective means of circumventing the limits on contributions to any particular political committee." In effect, the rule eliminates a donor's ability to create and use his own political committees to direct funds in excess of the individual base limits. It thus blocks a straightforward method of achieving the circumvention that was the underlying concern in *Buckley.*

The intricate regulatory scheme that the Federal Election Commission has enacted since *Buckley* further limits the opportunities for circumvention of the base limits via "unearmarked contributions to political committees likely to contribute" to a particular candidate. Although the earmarking provision was in place when *Buckley* was decided, the FEC has since added regulations that define earmarking broadly. For example, the regulations construe earmarking to include any designation, "whether direct or indirect, express or implied, oral or written." The regulations specify that an individual who has contributed to a particular candidate may not also contribute to a single-candidate committee for that candidate. Nor may an individual who has contributed to a candidate also contribute to a political committee that has supported or anticipates supporting the same candidate, if the individual knows that "a substantial portion [of his contribution] will be contributed to, or expended on behalf of," that candidate.

In addition to accounting for statutory and regulatory changes in the campaign finance arena, appellants' challenge raises distinct legal arguments that *Buckley* did not consider. For example, presumably because of its cursory treatment of the $25,000 aggregate limit, *Buckley* did not separately address an overbreadth challenge with respect to that provision. The Court rejected such a challenge to the *base* limits because of the difficulty of isolating suspect contributions. The propriety of large contributions to individual candidates turned on the subjective intent of donors, and the Court concluded that there was no way to tell which donors sought improper influence over legislators' actions. The aggregate limit, on the other hand, was upheld as an anticircumvention measure, without considering whether it was possible to discern which donations might be used to circumvent the base limits. The Court never addressed overbreadth in the specific context of aggregate limits, where such an argument has far more force.

Given the foregoing, this case cannot be resolved merely by pointing to three sentences in *Buckley* that were written without the benefit of full briefing or argument on the issue. We are confronted with a different statute and different legal arguments, at a different point in the development of campaign finance regulation. Appellants' substantial First Amendment challenge to the system of aggregate limits currently in place thus merits our plenary consideration.[4]

III

The First Amendment "is designed and intended to remove governmental restraints from the arena of public discussion, putting the decision as to what views shall be voiced largely into the hands of each of us, . . . in the belief that no other approach would comport with the premise of individual dignity and choice upon

4. The dissent contends that we should remand for development of an evidentiary record before answering the question with which we were presented. But the parties have treated the question as a purely legal one, and the Government has insisted that the aggregate limits can be upheld under the existing record alone. We take the case as it comes to us.

which our political system rests." *Cohen v. California,* 403 U.S. 15, 24 (1971). As relevant here, the First Amendment safeguards an individual's right to participate in the public debate through political expression and political association. See *Buckley.* When an individual contributes money to a candidate, he exercises both of those rights: The contribution "serves as a general expression of support for the candidate and his views" and "serves to affiliate a person with a candidate." *Id.*

Those First Amendment rights are important regardless whether the individual is, on the one hand, a "lone pamphleteer[] or street corner orator[] in the Tom Paine mold," or is, on the other, someone who spends "substantial amounts of money in order to communicate [his] political ideas through sophisticated" means. *NCPAC.* Either way, he is participating in an electoral debate that we have recognized is "integral to the operation of the system of government established by our Constitution." *Buckley.*

Buckley acknowledged that aggregate limits at least diminish an individual's right of political association. As the Court explained, the "overall $25,000 ceiling does impose an ultimate restriction upon the number of candidates and committees with which an individual may associate himself by means of financial support." But the Court characterized that restriction as a "quite modest restraint upon protected political activity." We cannot agree with that characterization. An aggregate limit on *how many* candidates and committees an individual may support through contributions is not a "modest restraint" at all. The Government may no more restrict how many candidates or causes a donor may support than it may tell a newspaper how many candidates it may endorse.

To put it in the simplest terms, the aggregate limits prohibit an individual from fully contributing to the primary and general election campaigns of ten or more candidates, even if all contributions fall within the base limits Congress views as adequate to protect against corruption. The individual may give up to $5,200 each to nine candidates, but the aggregate limits constitute an outright ban on further contributions to any other candidate (beyond the additional $1,800 that may be spent before reaching the $48,600 aggregate limit). At that point, the limits deny the individual all ability to exercise his expressive and associational rights by contributing to someone who will advocate for his policy preferences. A donor must limit the number of candidates he supports, and may have to choose which of several policy concerns he will advance — clear First Amendment harms that the dissent never acknowledges.

It is no answer to say that the individual can simply contribute less money to more people. To require one person to contribute at lower levels than others because he wants to support more candidates or causes is to impose a special burden on broader participation in the democratic process. And as we have recently admonished, the Government may not penalize an individual for "robustly exercis[ing]" his First Amendment rights. *Davis.*

The First Amendment burden is especially great for individuals who do not have ready access to alternative avenues for supporting their preferred politicians and policies. In the context of base contribution limits, *Buckley* observed that a supporter could vindicate his associational interests by personally volunteering his time and energy on behalf of a candidate. Such personal volunteering is not a realistic alternative for those who wish to support a wide variety of candidates or causes. Other effective methods of supporting preferred candidates or causes without contributing money are reserved for a select few, such as entertainers capable of raising hundreds of thousands of dollars in a single evening.[5]

The dissent faults this focus on "the individual's right to engage in political speech," saying that it fails to take into account "the public's interest" in "collective speech." This "collective" interest is said to promote "a government where laws reflect the very thoughts, views, ideas, and sentiments, the expression of which the First Amendment protects."

But there are compelling reasons not to define the boundaries of the First Amendment by reference to such a generalized conception of the public good. First, the dissent's "collective speech" reflected in laws is of course the will of the majority, and plainly can include laws that restrict free speech. The whole point of the First Amendment is to afford individuals protection against such infringements. The First Amendment does not protect the government, even when the government purports to act through legislation reflecting "collective speech."

Second, the degree to which speech is protected cannot turn on a legislative or judicial determination that particular speech is useful to the democratic process. The First Amendment does not contemplate such "ad hoc balancing of relative social costs and benefits."

Third, our established First Amendment analysis already takes account of any "collective" interest that may justify restrictions on individual speech. Under that accepted analysis, such restrictions are measured against the asserted public interest (usually framed as an important or compelling governmental interest). As explained below, we do not doubt the compelling nature of the "collective" interest in preventing corruption in the electoral process. But we permit Congress to pursue that interest only so long as it does not unnecessarily infringe an individual's right to freedom of speech; we do not truncate this tailoring test at the outset.

IV

A

With the significant First Amendment costs for individual citizens in mind, we turn to the governmental interests asserted in this case. This Court has identified only one legitimate governmental interest for restricting campaign finances: preventing corruption or the appearance of corruption. See *Davis*; *NCPAC*. We have

5. See, *e.g.*, Felsenthal, Obama Attends Fundraiser Hosted by Jay-Z, Beyonce, Reuters, Sept. 18, 2012; Coleman, Kid Rock Supports Paul Ryan at Campaign Fundraiser, Rolling Stone, Aug. 25, 2012; Mason, Robert Duvall to Host Romney Fundraiser, L.A. Times, July 25, 2012; Piazza, Hillary Lands 2.5M with Rocket Man, N.Y. Daily News, Apr. 10, 2008, p. 2.

consistently rejected attempts to suppress campaign speech based on other legislative objectives. No matter how desirable it may seem, it is not an acceptable governmental objective to "level the playing field," or to "level electoral opportunities," or to "equaliz[e] the financial resources of candidates." *Bennett*; *Davis*; *Buckley*. The First Amendment prohibits such legislative attempts to "fine-tun[e]" the electoral process, no matter how well intentioned. *Bennett.*

As we framed the relevant principle in *Buckley*, "the concept that government may restrict the speech of some elements of our society in order to enhance the relative voice of others is wholly foreign to the First Amendment." The dissent's suggestion that *Buckley* supports the opposite proposition simply ignores what *Buckley* actually said on the matter. See also *CARC* ("*Buckley* . . . made clear that contributors cannot be protected from the possibility that others will make larger contributions").

Moreover, while preventing corruption or its appearance is a legitimate objective, Congress may target only a specific type of corruption — "*quid pro quo* " corruption. As *Buckley* explained, Congress may permissibly seek to rein in "large contributions [that] are given to secure a political *quid pro quo* from current and potential office holders." In addition to "actual *quid pro quo* arrangements," Congress may permissibly limit "the appearance of corruption stemming from public awareness of the opportunities for abuse inherent in a regime of large individual financial contributions" to particular candidates. *Id.*; see also *Citizens United* ("When *Buckley* identified a sufficiently important governmental interest in preventing corruption or the appearance of corruption, that interest was limited to *quid pro quo* corruption").

Spending large sums of money in connection with elections, but not in connection with an effort to control the exercise of an officeholder's official duties, does not give rise to such *quid pro quo* corruption. Nor does the possibility that an individual who spends large sums may garner "influence over or access to" elected officials or political parties. *Id*; see *McConnell* (KENNEDY, J., concurring in judgment in part and dissenting in part). And because the Government's interest in preventing the appearance of corruption is equally confined to the appearance of *quid pro quo* corruption, the Government may not seek to limit the appearance of mere influence or access. See *Citizens United.*

The dissent advocates a broader conception of corruption, and would apply the label to any individual contributions above limits deemed necessary to protect "collective speech." Thus, under the dissent's view, it is perfectly fine to contribute $5,200 to nine candidates but somehow corrupt to give the same amount to a tenth.

It is fair to say, as Justice Stevens has, "that we have not always spoken about corruption in a clear or consistent voice." *Id.* (opinion concurring in part and dissenting in part). The definition of corruption that we apply today, however, has firm roots in *Buckley* itself. The Court in that case upheld base contribution limits because they targeted "the danger of actual *quid pro quo* arrangements" and "the impact of the appearance of corruption stemming from public awareness" of such a system of unchecked direct contributions. *Buckley* simultaneously rejected limits on spending that was less likely to "be given as a *quid pro quo* for improper commitments from the candidate." In any event, this case is not the first in which the debate over the proper breadth of the Government's anticorruption interest has been engaged.

The line between *quid pro quo* corruption and general influence may seem vague at times, but the distinction must be respected in order to safeguard basic First Amendment rights. In addition, "[i]n drawing that line, the First Amendment requires us to err on the side of protecting political speech rather than suppressing it." *WRTL* (2007) (opinion of ROBERTS, C.J.).

The dissent laments that our opinion leaves only remnants of FECA and BCRA that are inadequate to combat corruption. Such rhetoric ignores the fact that we leave the base limits undisturbed.[6] Those base limits remain the primary means of regulating campaign contributions — the obvious explanation for why the aggregate limits received a scant few sentences of attention in *Buckley*.[7]

B

"When the Government restricts speech, the Government bears the burden of proving the constitutionality of its actions." *United States v. Playboy Entertainment Group, Inc.*, 529 U.S. at 816. Here, the Government seeks to carry that burden by arguing that the aggregate limits further the permissible objective of preventing *quid pro quo* corruption.

The difficulty is that once the aggregate limits kick in, they ban all contributions of *any* amount. But Congress's selection of a $5,200 base limit indicates its belief that contributions of that amount or less do not create a cognizable risk of corruption. If there is no corruption concern in giving nine candidates up to $5,200 each, it is difficult to understand how a tenth candidate can be regarded as corruptible if given $1,801, and all others corruptible if given a dime. And if there is no risk that additional candidates will be corrupted by donations of up to $5,200, then the Government must defend the aggregate limits by demonstrating that they prevent circumvention of the base limits.

The problem is that they do not serve that function in any meaningful way. In light of the various statutes and regulations currently in effect, *Buckley*'s fear that an individual might "contribute massive amounts of money to a particular candidate

6. The fact that this opinion does not address the base limits also belies the dissent's concern that we have silently overruled the Court's holding in *McConnell*. At issue in *McConnell* was BCRA's extension of the base limits to so-called "soft money" — previously unregulated contributions to national party committees. Our holding about the constitutionality of the aggregate limits clearly does not overrule *McConnell*'s holding about "soft money."

7. It would be especially odd to regard aggregate limits as essential to enforce base limits when state campaign finance schemes typically include base limits but not aggregate limits. Just eight of the 38 States that have imposed base limits on contributions from individuals to candidates have also imposed aggregate limits (excluding restrictions on a specific subset of donors). The Government presents no evidence concerning the circumvention of base limits from the 30 States with base limits but no aggregate limits.

through the use of unearmarked contributions" to entities likely to support the candidate is far too speculative. And—importantly—we "have never accepted mere conjecture as adequate to carry a First Amendment burden." *Shrink Missouri.*

As an initial matter, there is not the same risk of *quid pro quo* corruption or its appearance when money flows through independent actors to a candidate, as when a donor contributes to a candidate directly. When an individual contributes to a candidate, a party committee, or a PAC, the individual must by law cede control over the funds. The Government admits that if the funds are subsequently re-routed to a particular candidate, such action occurs at the initial recipient's discretion—not the donor's. As a consequence, the chain of attribution grows longer, and any credit must be shared among the various actors along the way. For those reasons, the risk of *quid pro quo* corruption is generally applicable only to "the narrow category of money gifts that are directed, in some manner, to a candidate or officeholder." *McConnell* (opinion of KENNEDY, J.).

Buckley nonetheless focused on the possibility that "unearmarked contributions" could eventually find their way to a candidate's coffers. Even accepting the validity of *Buckley*'s circumvention theory, it is hard to see how a candidate today could receive a "massive amount[ ] of money" that could be traced back to a particular contributor uninhibited by the aggregate limits. *Ibid.* The Government offers a series of scenarios in support of that possibility. But each is sufficiently implausible that the Government has not carried its burden of demonstrating that the aggregate limits further its anticircumvention interest. [Chief Justice Roberts's opinion considers in detail, then rejects, a number of these scenarios.]

These scenarios, along with others that have been suggested, are either illegal under current campaign finance laws or divorced from reality. The three examples posed by the dissent are no exception. The dissent does not explain how the large sums it postulates can be legally rerouted to a particular candidate, why most state committees would participate in a plan to redirect their donations to a candidate in another State, or how a donor or group of donors can avoid regulations prohibiting contributions to a committee "with the knowledge that a substantial portion" of the contribution will support a candidate to whom the donor has already contributed.

The dissent argues that such knowledge may be difficult to prove, pointing to eight FEC cases that did not proceed because of insufficient evidence of a donor's incriminating knowledge. It might be that such guilty knowledge could not be shown because the donors were not guilty—a possibility that the dissent does not entertain. In any event, the donors described in those eight cases were typically alleged to have exceeded the base limits by $5,000 or less. The FEC's failure to find the requisite knowledge in those cases hardly means that the agency will be equally powerless to prevent a scheme in which a donor routes *millions of dollars* in excess of the base limits to a particular candidate.... And if an FEC official cannot establish knowledge of circumvention (or establish affiliation) when the same ten donors contribute $10,000 each to 200 newly created PACs, and each PAC writes a $10,000 check to the same ten candidates... then that official has not a heart but a head of stone.

The dissent concludes by citing three briefs for the proposition that, even with the aggregate limits in place, individuals "have transferred large sums of money to specific candidates" in excess of the base limits. But the cited sources do not provide any real-world examples of circumvention of the base limits along the lines of the various hypotheticals. The dearth of FEC prosecutions, according to the dissent, proves only that people are getting away with it. And the violations that surely must be out there elude detection "because in the real world, the methods of achieving circumvention are more subtle and more complex" than the hypothetical examples. This sort of speculation, however, cannot justify the substantial intrusion on First Amendment rights at issue in this case.

Buckley upheld aggregate limits only on the ground that they prevented channeling money to candidates beyond the base limits. The absence of such a prospect today belies the Government's asserted objective of preventing corruption or its appearance. The improbability of circumvention indicates that the aggregate limits instead further the impermissible objective of simply limiting the amount of money in political campaigns.

C

Quite apart from the foregoing, the aggregate limits violate the First Amendment because they are not "closely drawn to avoid unnecessary abridgment of associational freedoms." *Buckley,* 424 U.S. at 25. In the First Amendment context, fit matters. Even when the Court is not applying strict scrutiny, we still require "a fit that is not necessarily perfect, but reasonable; that represents not necessarily the single best disposition but one whose scope is 'in proportion to the interest served,' . . . that employs not necessarily least restrictive means but . . . a means narrowly tailored to achieve the desired objective." *Board of Trustees of State Univ. of N.Y. v. Fox,* 492 U.S. 469, 480 (1989) (quoting *In re R.M.J.,* 455 U.S. 191, 203 (1982)). Here, because the statute is poorly tailored to the Government's interest in preventing circumvention of the base limits, it impermissibly restricts participation in the political process.

1

The Government argues that the aggregate limits are justified because they prevent an individual from giving to too many initial recipients who might subsequently recontribute a donation. After all, only recontributed funds can conceivably give rise to circumvention of the base limits. Yet all indications are that many types of recipients have scant interest in regifting donations they receive.

Some figures might be useful to put the risk of circumvention in perspective. We recognize that no data can be marshaled to capture perfectly the counterfactual world in which aggregate limits do not exist. But, as we have noted elsewhere, we can nonetheless ask "whether experience under the present law confirms a serious threat of abuse." *FEC v. Colorado Republican Federal Campaign Comm.,* 533 U.S. 431, 457 (2001). It does not. Experience suggests that the vast majority of contributions made in excess of the aggregate limits are likely to be retained and spent by their recipients rather than rerouted to candidates. . . .

Based on what we can discern from experience, the indiscriminate ban on all contributions above the aggregate limits is disproportionate to the Government's interest in preventing circumvention. The Government has not given us any reason to believe that parties or candidates would dramatically shift their priorities if the aggregate limits were lifted. Absent such a showing, we cannot conclude that the sweeping aggregate limits are appropriately tailored to guard against any contributions that might implicate the Government's anticircumvention interest.

A final point: It is worth keeping in mind that the *base limits* themselves are a prophylactic measure. As we have explained, "restrictions on direct contributions are preventative, because few if any contributions to candidates will involve *quid pro quo* arrangements." *Citizens United.* The aggregate limits are then layered on top, ostensibly to prevent circumvention of the base limits. This "prophylaxis-upon-prophylaxis approach" requires that we be particularly diligent in scrutinizing the law's fit. *WRTL* (opinion of ROBERTS, C.J.); see *McConnell,* (opinion of THOMAS, J.).

Importantly, there are multiple alternatives available to Congress that would serve the Government's anticircumvention interest, while avoiding "unnecessary abridgment" of First Amendment rights. *Buckley.*

The most obvious might involve targeted restrictions on transfers among candidates and political committees. There are currently no such limits on transfers among party committees and from candidates to party committees. . . .

Other alternatives might focus on earmarking. . . .

We do not mean to opine on the validity of any particular proposal. The point is that there are numerous alternative approaches available to Congress to prevent circumvention of the base limits.

D

Finally, disclosure of contributions minimizes the potential for abuse of the campaign finance system. Disclosure requirements are in part "justified based on a governmental interest in 'provid[ing] the electorate with information' about the sources of election-related spending." *Citizens United* (quoting *Buckley*). They may also "deter actual corruption and avoid the appearance of corruption by exposing large contributions and expenditures to the light of publicity." *Id.* Disclosure requirements burden speech, but—unlike the aggregate limits—they do not impose a ceiling on speech. For that reason, disclosure often represents a less restrictive alternative to flat bans on certain types or quantities of speech.

With modern technology, disclosure now offers a particularly effective means of arming the voting public with information. In 1976, the Court observed that Congress could regard disclosure as "only a partial measure." *Buckley.* That perception was understandable in a world in which information about campaign contributions was filed at FEC offices and was therefore virtually inaccessible to the average member of the public. Today, given the Internet, disclosure offers much more robust protections against corruption. See *Citizens United.* Reports and databases are available on the FEC's Web site almost immediately after they are filed, supplemented by private entities such as OpenSecrets.org and FollowTheMoney.org. Because massive quantities of information can be accessed at the click of a mouse, disclosure is effective to a degree not possible at the time *Buckley,* or even *McConnell,* was decided.

The existing aggregate limits may in fact encourage the movement of money away from entities subject to disclosure. Because individuals' direct contributions are limited, would-be donors may turn to other avenues for political speech. See *Citizens United.* Individuals can, for example, contribute unlimited amounts to 501(c) organizations, which are not required to publicly disclose their donors. Such organizations spent some $300 million on independent expenditures in the 2012 election cycle.

V

At oral argument, the Government shifted its focus from *Buckley*'s anticircumvention rationale to an argument that the aggregate limits deter corruption regardless of their ability to prevent circumvention of the base limits. The Government argued that there is an opportunity for corruption whenever a large check is given to a legislator, even if the check consists of contributions within the base limits to be appropriately divided among numerous candidates and committees. The aggregate limits, the argument goes, ensure that the check amount does not become too large. That new rationale for the aggregate limits—embraced by the dissent—does not wash. It dangerously broadens the circumscribed definition of *quid pro quo* corruption articulated in our prior cases, and targets as corruption the general, broad-based support of a political party.

In analyzing the base limits, *Buckley* made clear that the risk of corruption arises when an individual makes large contributions to the candidate or officeholder himself. *Buckley*'s analysis of the aggregate limit under FECA was similarly confined. The Court noted that the aggregate limit guarded against an individual's funneling—through circumvention—"massive amounts of money to *a particular candidate.*" *Id.* (emphasis added). We have reiterated that understanding several times.

Of course a candidate would be pleased with a donor who contributed not only to the candidate himself, but also to other candidates from the same party, to party committees, and to PACs supporting the party. But there is a clear, administrable line between money beyond the base limits funneled in an identifiable way to a candidate—for which the candidate feels obligated—and money within the base limits given widely to a candidate's party—for which the candidate, like all other members of the party, feels grateful.

When donors furnish widely distributed support within all applicable base limits, all members of the party or supporters of the cause may benefit, and the leaders of the party or cause may feel particular gratitude. That gratitude stems from the basic nature of the party system, in which party members join together to further common political beliefs, and citizens can choose to support a party because they share some, most, or all of those beliefs. See *Tashjian.* To recast such shared interest, standing alone, as an opportunity for *quid pro quo* corruption would dramatically expand government regulation of the political process. Cf. *California Democratic Party v. Jones* (recognizing the Government's "role to play in structuring and monitoring the election process," but rejecting "the proposition that party affairs are public affairs, free of First Amendment protections").

The Government suggests that it is the *solicitation* of large contributions that poses the danger of corruption, but the aggregate limits are not limited to any direct solicitation by an officeholder or candidate. Cf. *McConnell* (opinion of KENNEDY, J.) (rejecting a ban on "soft money" contributions to national parties, but approving a ban on the solicitation of such contributions as "a direct and necessary regulation of federal candidates' and officeholders' receipt of *quids*"). We have no occasion to consider a law that would specifically ban candidates from soliciting donations—within the base limits—that would go to many other candidates, and would add up to a large sum. For our purposes here, it is enough that the aggregate limits at issue are not directed specifically to candidate behavior.

* * *

For the past 40 years, our campaign finance jurisprudence has focused on the need to preserve authority for the Government to combat corruption, without at the same time compromising the political responsiveness at the heart of the democratic process, or allowing the Government to favor some participants in that process over others. As Edmund Burke explained in his famous speech to the electors of Bristol, a representative owes constituents the exercise of his "mature judgment," but judgment informed by "the strictest union, the closest correspondence, and the most unreserved communication with his constituents." The Speeches of the Right Hon. Edmund Burke 129–130 (J. Burke ed. 1867). Constituents have the right to support candidates who share their views and concerns. Representatives are not to follow constituent orders, but can be expected to be cognizant of and responsive to those concerns. Such responsiveness is key to the very concept of self-governance through elected officials.

The Government has a strong interest, no less critical to our democratic system, in combatting corruption and its appearance. We have, however, held that this interest must be limited to a specific kind of corruption—*quid pro quo* corruption—in order to ensure that the Government's efforts do not have the effect of restricting the First Amendment right of citizens to choose who shall govern them. For the reasons set forth, we conclude that the aggregate limits on contributions do not further the only governmental interest this Court accepted as legitimate in *Buckley*. They instead intrude without justification on a citizen's ability to exercise "the most fundamental First Amendment activities." *Buckley*.

The judgment of the District Court is reversed, and the case is remanded for further proceedings.

It is so ordered.

Justice THOMAS, concurring in the judgment.

I adhere to the view that this Court's decision in *Buckley v. Valeo* denigrates core First Amendment speech and should be overruled. . . .

Although today's decision represents a faithful application of our precedents, the plurality's discussion of *Buckley* omits any reference to these discarded rationales. Instead, the plurality alludes only to *Buckley*'s last remaining reason for devaluing political contributions relative to expenditures. The relevant sentence from *Buckley* reads as follows:

> A limitation on the amount of money a person may give to a candidate or campaign organization thus involves little direct restraint on his political communication, for it permits the symbolic expression of support evidenced by a contribution but does not in any way infringe the contributor's freedom to discuss candidates and issues.

That proposition, read in full, cannot be squared with a key premise of today's decision.

Among the Government's justifications for the aggregate limits set forth in the Bipartisan Campaign Reform Act of 2002 (BCRA) is that "an individual can engage in the 'symbolic act of contributing' to as many entities as he wishes." That is, the Government contends that aggregate limits are constitutional as long as an individual can still contribute some token amount (a dime, for example) to each of his preferred candidates. The plurality, quite correctly, rejects that argument, noting that "[i]t is no answer to say that the individual can simply contribute less money to more people." That is so because "[t]o require one person to contribute at lower levels than others because he wants to support more candidates or causes is to impose a special burden on broader participation in the democratic process."

What the plurality does not recognize is that the same logic also defeats the reasoning from *Buckley* on which the plurality purports to rely. Under the plurality's analysis, limiting the amount of money a person may give to a candidate *does* impose a direct restraint on his political communication; if it did not, the aggregate limits at issue here would not create "a special burden on broader participation in the democratic process." I am wholly in agreement with the plurality's conclusion on this point: "[T]he Government may not penalize an individual for 'robustly exercis[ing]' his First Amendment rights." I regret only that the plurality does not acknowledge that today's decision, although purporting not to overrule *Buckley,* continues to chip away at its footings.

In sum, what remains of *Buckley* is a rule without a rationale. Contributions and expenditures are simply "two sides of the same First Amendment coin," and our efforts to distinguish the two have produced mere "word games" rather than any cognizable principle of constitutional law. *Buckley,* (Burger, C.J., concurring in part and dissenting in part). For that reason, I would overrule *Buckley* and subject the aggregate limits in BCRA to strict scrutiny, which they would surely fail.

This case represents yet another missed opportunity to right the course of our campaign finance jurisprudence by restoring a standard that is faithful to the First Amendment. Until we undertake that reexamination, we remain in a "halfway house" of our own design. *Shrink Missouri* (KENNEDY, J., dissenting). For these reasons, I concur only in the judgment.

Justice BREYER, with whom Justice GINSBURG, Justice SOTOMAYOR, and Justice KAGAN join, dissenting.

Nearly 40 years ago in *Buckley* v. *Valeo* this Court considered the constitutionality of laws that imposed limits upon the overall amount a single person can contribute to all federal candidates, political parties, and committees taken together. The Court held that those limits did not violate the Constitution. Accord, *McConnell* (citing with approval *Buckley*'s aggregate limits holding).

The *Buckley* Court focused upon the same problem that concerns the Court today, and it wrote:

> The overall $25,000 ceiling does impose an ultimate restriction upon the number of candidates and committees with which an individual may associate himself by means of financial support. But this quite modest restraint upon protected political activity serves to prevent evasion of the $1,000 contribution limitation by a person who might otherwise contribute massive amounts of money to a particular candidate through the use of unearmarked contributions to political committees likely to contribute to that candidate, or huge contributions to the candidate's political party. The limited, additional restriction on associational freedom imposed by the overall ceiling is thus no more than a corollary of the basic individual contribution limitation that we have found to be constitutionally valid.

Today a majority of the Court overrules this holding. It is wrong to do so. Its conclusion rests upon its own, not a record-based, view of the facts. Its legal analysis is faulty: It misconstrues the nature of the competing constitutional interests at stake. It understates the importance of protecting the political integrity of our governmental institutions. It creates a loophole that will allow a single individual to contribute millions of dollars to a political party or to a candidate's campaign. Taken together with *Citizens United*, today's decision eviscerates our Nation's campaign finance laws, leaving a remnant incapable of dealing with the grave problems of democratic legitimacy that those laws were intended to resolve.

I

The plurality concludes that the aggregate contribution limits "unnecessar[ily] abridg[e]" First Amendment rights. It notes that some individuals will wish to "spen[d] 'substantial amounts of money in order to communicate [their] political ideas through sophisticated' means." Aggregate contribution ceilings limit an individual's ability to engage in such "broader participation in the democratic process," while insufficiently advancing any legitimate governmental objective. Hence, the plurality finds, they violate the Constitution.

The plurality's conclusion rests upon three separate but related claims. Each is fatally flawed. First, the plurality says that given the base limits on contributions to candidates and political committees, aggregate limits do not further any independent governmental objective worthy of protection. And that is because, given the base limits, "[s]pending large sums of money in connection with elections" does not "give rise to . . . corruption." In making this argument, the plurality relies heavily upon a narrow definition of "corruption" that excludes efforts to obtain "'influence over or access to' elected officials or political parties." *Ibid.* (quoting *Citizens United*).

Second, the plurality assesses the instrumental objective of the aggregate limits, namely, safeguarding the base limits. It finds that they "do not serve that function in any meaningful way." That is because, even without the aggregate limits, the possibilities for circumventing the base limits are "implausible" and "divorced from reality."

Third, the plurality says the aggregate limits are not a "reasonable" policy tool. Rather, they are "poorly tailored to the Government's interest in preventing circumvention of the base limits." The plurality imagines several alternative regulations that it says might just as effectively thwart circumvention. Accordingly, it finds, the aggregate caps are out of "proportion to the [anticorruption] interest served."

II

The plurality's first claim—that large aggregate contributions do not "give rise" to "corruption"—is plausible only because the plurality defines "corruption" too narrowly. The plurality describes the constitutionally permissible objective of campaign finance regulation as follows: "Congress may target only a specific type of corruption—'*quid pro quo*' corruption." It then defines *quid pro quo* corruption to mean no more than "a direct exchange of an official act for money"—an act akin to bribery. It adds specifically that corruption does *not* include efforts to "garner 'influence over or access to' elected officials or political parties." (quoting *Citizens United*). Moreover, the Government's efforts to prevent the "appearance of corruption" are "equally confined to the appearance of *quid pro quo* corruption," as narrowly defined. In the plurality's view, a federal statute could not prevent an individual from writing a million dollar check to a political party (by donating to its various committees), because the rationale for any limit would "dangerously broade[n] the circumscribed definition of *quid pro quo* corruption articulated in our prior cases."

This critically important definition of "corruption" is inconsistent with the Court's prior case law (with the possible exception of *Citizens United,* as I will explain below). It is virtually impossible to reconcile with this Court's decision in *McConnell,* upholding the Bipartisan Campaign Reform Act of 2002 (BCRA). And it misunderstands the constitutional importance of the interests at stake. In fact, constitutional interests—indeed, First Amendment interests—lie on both sides of the legal equation.

A

In reality, as the history of campaign finance reform shows and as our earlier cases on the subject have recognized, the anticorruption interest that drives Congress to regulate campaign contributions is a far broader, more important interest than the plurality acknowledges. It is an interest in maintaining the integrity of our public governmental institutions. And it is an interest rooted in the Constitution and in the First Amendment itself.

Consider at least one reason why the First Amendment protects political speech. Speech does not exist in a vacuum. Rather, political communication seeks to secure government action. A politically oriented "marketplace of ideas" seeks to form a public opinion that can and will influence elected representatives.

This is not a new idea. Eighty-seven years ago, Justice Brandeis wrote that the First Amendment's protection of speech was "essential to effective democracy." *Whitney v. California,* 274 U.S. 357, 377 (1927) (concurring opinion). Chief Justice Hughes reiterated the same idea shortly thereafter: "A fundamental principle of our constitutional system" is the "maintenance of the opportunity for free political discussion *to the end* that government may be responsive to the will of the people." *Stromberg v. California,* 283 U.S. 359, 369 (1931) (emphasis added). In *Citizens United,* the Court stated that "[s]peech is an essential mechanism of democracy, for it is *the means* to hold officials accountable to the people." (Emphasis added).

The Framers had good reason to emphasize this same connection between political speech and governmental action. An influential 18th-century continental philosopher had argued that in a representative democracy, the people lose control of their representatives between elections, during which interim periods they were "in chains." J. Rousseau, An Inquiry Into the Nature of the Social Contract 265–266 (transl. 1791).

The Framers responded to this criticism both by requiring frequent elections to federal office, and by enacting a First Amendment that would facilitate a "chain of communication between the people, and those, to whom they have committed the exercise of the powers of government." J. Wilson, Commentaries on the Constitution of the United States of America 30–31 (1792). This "chain" would establish the necessary "communion of interests and sympathy of sentiments" between the people and their representatives, so that public opinion could be channeled into effective governmental action. The Federalist No. 57, p. 386 (J. Cooke ed. 1961) (J. Madison); accord, T. Benton, 1 Abridgement of the Debates of Congress, from 1789 to 1856, p. 141 (1857) (explaining that the First Amendment will strengthen American democracy by giving "the people" a right to "publicly address their representatives," "privately advise them," or "declare their sentiments by petition to the whole body" (quoting James Madison)). Accordingly, the First Amendment advances not only the individual's right to engage in political speech, but also the public's interest in preserving a democratic order in which collective speech *matters.*

What has this to do with corruption? It has everything to do with corruption. Corruption breaks the constitutionally necessary "chain of communication" between the people and their representatives. It derails the essential speech-to-government-action tie. Where enough money calls the tune, the general public will not be heard. Insofar as corruption cuts the link between political thought and political action, a free marketplace of political ideas loses its point. That is one reason why the Court has stressed the constitutional importance of Congress' concern that a few large donations not drown out the voices of the many. See, *e.g., Buckley.*

That is also why the Court has used the phrase "subversion of the political process" to describe circumstances in which "[e]lected officials are influenced to act contrary to their obligations of office by the prospect of financial gain to themselves or infusions of money into their campaigns." *NCPAC.* See also *NRWC* (the Government's interests in preventing corruption "directly implicate the integrity of our electoral process" (internal quotation marks and citation omitted)). See generally R. Post, Citizens Divided: Campaign Finance Reform and the Constitution 7–16, 80–94 (forthcoming 2014) (arguing that the efficacy of American democracy depends on "electoral integrity" and the responsiveness of public officials to public opinion).

The "appearance of corruption" can make matters worse. It can lead the public to believe that its efforts to communicate with its representatives or to help sway public opinion have little purpose. And a cynical public can lose interest in political participation altogether. *Shrink Missouri* ("[T]he cynical assumption that large donors call the tune could jeopardize the willingness of voters to take part in democratic governance"). Democracy, the Court has often said, cannot work unless "the people have faith in those who govern." *United States v. Mississippi Valley Generating Co.,* 364 U.S. 520, 562 (1961).

The upshot is that the interests the Court has long described as preventing "corruption" or the "appearance of corruption" are more than ordinary factors to be weighed against the constitutional right to political speech. Rather, they are interests rooted in the First Amendment itself. They are rooted in the constitutional effort to create a democracy responsive to the people—a government where laws reflect the very thoughts, views, ideas, and sentiments, the expression of which the First Amendment protects. Given that end, we can and should understand campaign finance laws as resting upon a broader and more significant constitutional rationale than the plurality's limited definition of "corruption" suggests. We should see these laws as seeking in significant part to strengthen, rather than weaken, the First Amendment. To say this is not to deny the potential for conflict between (1) the need to permit contributions that pay for the diffusion of ideas, and (2) the need to limit payments in order to help maintain the integrity of the electoral process. But that conflict takes place within, not outside, the First Amendment's boundaries.

B

Since the kinds of corruption that can destroy the link between public opinion and governmental action extend well beyond those the plurality describes, the plurality's notion of corruption is flatly inconsistent with the basic constitutional rationale I have just described. Thus, it should surprise no one that this Court's case law (*Citizens United* excepted) insists upon a considerably broader definition.

In *Buckley,* for instance, the Court said explicitly that aggregate limits were constitutional because they helped "prevent evasion . . . [through] huge contributions to the candidate's political party," (the contrary to what the plurality today seems to believe). Moreover, *Buckley* upheld the base limits in significant part because they helped thwart "the appearance of corruption stemming from public awareness of the opportunities for abuse *inherent in a regime of large individual financial contributions.*" (Emphasis added). And it said that Congress could reasonably conclude that criminal laws forbidding "the giving and taking of bribes" did *not* adequately "deal with the reality or appearance of corruption." Bribery laws, the Court recognized, address "only the most blatant and specific attempts of those with money to influence governmental action." The concern with corruption extends further.

Other cases put the matter yet more strongly. In *Beaumont,* for example, the Court found constitutional a ban on direct contributions by corporations because of the need to prevent corruption, properly "understood not only as *quid pro quo* agreements, but also as undue influence on an officeholder's judgment." *FEC v. Beaumont,* 539 U.S. 146, 155–156 (2003). In *FEC v. Colorado Republican Federal Campaign Comm.,* 533 U.S. 431, 441, 457-460 (2001) (*Colorado II*), the Court upheld limits imposed upon coordinated expenditures among parties and candidates because it found they thwarted corruption and its appearance, again understood as including "undue influence" by wealthy donors. In *Shrink Missouri,* the Court upheld limitations imposed by the Missouri Legislature upon contributions to state political candidates, not only because of the need to prevent bribery, but also because of "the broader threat from politicians too compliant with the wishes of large contributors."

C

Most important, in *McConnell,* this Court considered the constitutionality of the Bipartisan Campaign Reform Act of 2002, an Act that set new limits on "soft money" contributions to political parties. "Soft money" referred to funds that, prior to BCRA, were freely donated to parties for activities other than directly helping elect a federal candidate—activities such as voter registration, "get out the vote" drives, and advertising that did not expressly advocate a federal candidate's election or defeat. BCRA imposed a new ban on soft money contributions to national party committees, and greatly curtailed them in respect to state and local parties.

The Court in *McConnell* upheld these new contribution restrictions under the First Amendment for the very reason the plurality today discounts or ignores. Namely, the Court found they thwarted a significant risk of corruption—understood not as *quid pro quo* bribery, but as privileged access to and pernicious influence upon elected representatives.

In reaching its conclusion in *McConnell,* the Court relied upon a vast record compiled in the District Court. That record consisted of over 100,000 pages of material and included testimony from more than 200 witnesses. What it showed, in detail, was the web of relationships and understandings among parties, candidates, and large donors that underlies privileged access and influence. The District Judges in *McConnell* made clear that the record did "*not* contain any evidence of bribery or vote buying in exchange for donations of nonfederal money." (Emphasis added). Indeed, no one had identified a "single discrete instance of *quid pro quo* corruption" due to soft money. But what the record did demonstrate was that enormous soft money contributions, ranging between $1 million and $5 million among the largest donors, enabled wealthy contributors to gain disproportionate "access to federal lawmakers" and the ability to "influenc[e] legislation." There was an indisputable link between generous political donations and opportunity after opportunity to make one's case directly to a Member of Congress.

Testimony by elected officials supported this conclusion.... This Court upheld BCRA's limitations on soft money contributions by relying on just the kind of evidence I have described.... Insofar as today's decision sets forth a significantly narrower definition of "corruption," and hence of the public's interest in political integrity, it is flatly inconsistent with *McConnell.*

D

One case, however, contains language that offers the plurality support. That case is *Citizens United.* There, as the plurality points out, the Court said that "[w]hen *Buckley* identified a sufficiently important governmental interest in preventing corruption or the appearance of corruption, that interest was limited to *quid pro quo* corruption." Further, the Court said that *quid pro quo* corruption does not include "influence over or access to elected officials," because "generic favoritism or influence theory . . . is at odds with standard First Amendment analyses." (quoting *McConnell* (KENNEDY, J., concurring in judgment in part and dissenting in part)).

How should we treat these statements from *Citizens United* now? They are not essential to the Court's holding in the case—at least insofar as it can be read to require federal law to treat corporations and trade unions like individuals when they independently pay for, *e.g.,* television advertising during the last 60 days of a federal election. Taken literally, the statements cited simply refer to and characterize still-earlier Court cases. They do not require the more absolute reading that the plurality here gives them.

More than that. Read as the plurality reads them today, the statements from *Citizens United* about the proper contours of the corruption rationale conflict not just with language in the *McConnell* opinion, but with *McConnell*'s very holding. Did the Court in *Citizens United* intend to overrule *McConnell* ? I doubt it, for if it did, the Court or certainly the dissent would have said something about it. The total silence of all opinions in *Citizens United* with respect to this matter argues strongly in favor of treating the language quoted above as dictum, as an overstatement, or as limited to the context in which it appears. *Citizens United* itself contains language that supports the last mentioned reading, for it says that "[*Buckley*] did not extend this rationale [about the reality or appearance of corruption] to *independent* expenditures, and the Court does not do so here." (Emphasis added). And it adds that, while "[t]he BCRA record establishes that certain donations to political parties, called 'soft money,' were made to gain access to elected officials," "*[t]his case, however, is about independent expenditures, not soft money.*" (Emphasis added.)

The plurality's use of *Citizens United*'s narrow definition of corruption here, however, is a different matter. That use does not come accompanied with a limiting context (independent expenditures by corporations and unions) or limiting language. It applies to the whole of campaign finance regulation. And, as I have pointed out, it is flatly inconsistent with the broader definition of corruption upon which *McConnell*'s holding depends.

So: Does the Court intend today to overrule *McConnell*? Or does it intend to leave *McConnell* and BCRA in place? The plurality says the latter. But how does the plurality explain its rejection of the broader definition of corruption, upon which *McConnell*'s holding depends?

III

The plurality invalidates the aggregate contribution limits for a second reason. It believes they are no longer needed to prevent contributors from circumventing federal limits on direct contributions to individuals, political parties, and political action committees. Other "campaign finance laws," combined with "experience" and "common sense," foreclose the various circumvention scenarios that the Government hypothesizes. Accordingly, the plurality concludes, the aggregate limits provide no added benefit.

The plurality is wrong. Here, as in *Buckley*, in the absence of limits on aggregate political contributions, donors can and likely will find ways to channel millions of dollars to parties and to individual candidates, producing precisely the kind of "corruption" or "appearance of corruption" that previously led the Court to hold aggregate limits constitutional. Those opportunities for circumvention will also produce the type of corruption that concerns the plurality today. The methods for using today's opinion to evade the law's individual contribution limits are complex, but they are well known, or will become well known, to party fundraisers. I shall describe three. [Justice Breyer then offers three scenarios for this "evasion."]

B

The plurality believes that the three scenarios I have just depicted either pose no threat, or cannot or will not take place.... The plurality's view depends in large part upon its claim that since this Court decided *Buckley* in 1976, changes in either statutory law or in applicable regulations have come to make it difficult, if not impossible, for these circumvention scenarios to arise. Hence, it concludes, there is no longer a need for aggregate contribution limits. But a closer examination of the five legal changes to which the plurality points makes clear that those changes cannot effectively stop the abuses that I have depicted....

IV

The plurality concludes that even if circumvention were a threat, the aggregate limits are "poorly tailored" to address it. The First Amendment requires "a fit that is . . . reasonable," and there is no such "fit" here because there are several alternative ways Congress could prevent evasion of the base limits. For instance, the plurality posits, Congress (or the FEC) could "tighten . . . transfer rules"; it could require "contributions above the current aggregate limits to be deposited into segregated, nontransferable accounts and spent only by their recipients"; it could define "how many candidates a PAC must support in order to ensure that 'a substantial portion' of a donor's contribution is not rerouted to a certain candidate"; or it could prohibit "donors who have contributed the current maximum sums from further contributing to political committees that have indicated they will support candidates to whom the donor has already contributed."

The plurality, however, does not show, or try to show, that these hypothetical alternatives could effectively replace aggregate contribution limits. . . . In sum, the explanation of why aggregate limits are needed is complicated, as is the explanation of why other methods will not work. But the conclusion is simple: There is no "substantial mismatch" between Congress' legitimate objective and the "means selected to achieve it." The Court, as in *Buckley*, should hold that aggregate contribution limits are constitutional.

V

The District Court in this case, holding that *Buckley* foreclosed McCutcheon's constitutional challenge to the aggregate limits, granted the Government's motion to dismiss the complaint prior to a full evidentiary hearing. If the plurality now believes the District Court was wrong, then why does it not return the case for the further evidentiary development which has not yet taken place?

In the past, when evaluating the constitutionality of campaign finance restrictions, we have typically relied upon an evidentiary record amassed below to determine whether the law served a compelling governmental objective. And, typically, that record contained testimony from Members of Congress (or state legislators) explaining why Congress (or the legislature) acted as it did. See, *e.g., McConnell*; *Colorado II*; *Shrink Missouri*. If we are to overturn an act of Congress here, we should do so on the basis of a similar record.

For one thing, an evidentiary record can help us determine whether or the extent to which we should defer to Congress' own judgments, particularly those reflecting a balance of the countervailing First Amendment interests I have described. Determining whether anticorruption objectives justify a particular set of contribution limits requires answering empirically based questions, and applying significant discretion and judgment. To what extent will unrestricted giving lead to corruption or its appearance? What forms will any such corruption take? To what extent will a lack of regulation undermine public confidence in the democratic system? To what extent can regulation restore it?

These kinds of questions, while not easily answered, are questions that Congress is far better suited to resolve than are judges. Thus, while court review of contribution limits has been and should be "rigorous," *Buckley*, we have also recognized that "deference to legislative choice is warranted." *Beaumont*. And that deference has taken account of facts and circumstances set forth in an evidentiary record.

For another thing, a comparison of the plurality's opinion with this dissent reveals important differences of opinion on fact-related matters. We disagree, for example, on the possibilities for circumvention of the base limits in the absence of aggregate limits. We disagree about how effectively the plurality's "alternatives" could prevent evasion. An evidentiary proceeding would permit the parties to explore these matters, and it would permit the courts to reach a more accurate judgment. The plurality rationalizes its haste to forgo an evidentiary record by noting that "the parties have treated the question as a purely legal one." But without a doubt, the legal question—whether the aggregate limits are closely drawn to further a compelling governmental interest—turns on factual questions about whether corruption, in the absence of such limits, is a realistic threat to our democracy. The plurality itself spends pages citing figures about campaign spending to defend its "legal" conclusion. The problem with such reasoning is that this Court's expertise does not lie in marshaling facts in the primary instance. That is why in the past, when answering similar questions about the constitutionality of restrictions on campaign contributions, we have relied on an extensive evidentiary record produced below to inform our decision.

Without further development of the record, however, I fail to see how the plurality can now find grounds for overturning *Buckley*. The justification for aggregate contribution restrictions is strongly rooted in the need to assure political integrity and ultimately in the First Amendment itself. Part II, *supra*. The threat to that integrity posed by the risk of special access and influence remains real. Part III, *supra*. Even taking the plurality on its own terms and considering solely the threat of *quid pro quo* corruption (*i.e.*, money-for-votes exchanges), the aggregate limits are a necessary tool to stop circumvention. *Ibid*. And there is no basis for finding a lack of "fit" between the threat and the means used to combat it, namely the aggregate limits.

The plurality reaches the opposite conclusion. The result, as I said at the outset, is a decision that substitutes judges' understandings of how the political process works for the understanding of Congress; that fails to recognize the difference between influence resting upon public opinion and influence bought by money alone; that overturns key precedent; that creates huge loopholes in the law; and that undermines, perhaps devastates, what remains of campaign finance reform.

With respect, I dissent.

Notes and Questions

1. Compare how Chief Justice Roberts began his opinion here with how he began his opinion in the *Shelby County* case (Chapter 5). Why extol the right to vote and

participate in a campaign finance case but not a voting rights case? Are voting and donating similar enough to justify the Chief's opening?

2. Justice Breyer claimed that the Court did not need to import the definition of corruption used in *Citizens United* into the context of contribution limitation challenges. How could the Court with a straight face have one definition of corruption for contribution limitations and one for spending limitations?

3. Although the *McCutcheon* majority said it was merely hypothetical that joint fundraising committees would raise large donations from wealthy donors, six- and seven-figure donations have become fairly common. For the latest data, see https://opensecrets.org/jfc.

4. How has the law related to review of contribution limits changed since *Shrink Missouri* in terms of (1) *Buckley*'s standard of review; (2) the definition of corruption; (3) the definition of the appearance of corruption; and (4) the evidence necessary to support the constitutionality of a contribution limitation? Given these changes, how vulnerable to constitutional challenge are federal individual (base) $2,700 contribution limits following *McCutcheon*?

The Supreme Court declined the opportunity to explore the fourth question. In *Lair v. Motl*, 873 F.3d 1170 (9th Cir. 2017), cert. denied *sub nom. Lair v. Mangan*, 139 S. Ct. 916 (2019), a divided Ninth Circuit panel upheld Montana's campaign contribution limits against constitutional challenge. The court had upheld the limits in an earlier case, *Montana Right to Life Ass'n v. Eddleman*, 343 F.3d 1085 (9th Cir. 2003), and after the Supreme Court decided *Randall*, plaintiffs renewed their challenge in the *Lair* case. Among the arguments plaintiffs raised was that there was insufficient evidence of quid pro quo corruption or its appearance in Montana to justify the law. The *Lair* majority disagreed, relying on the test it set out in *Eddleman*:

> Montana's evidence shows the threat of actual or perceived quid pro quo corruption in Montana politics is not illusory. State Representative Hal Harper testified groups "funnel[] more money into campaigns when certain special interests know an issue is coming up, because it gets results." State Senator Mike Anderson sent a "destroy after reading" letter to his party colleagues, urging them to vote for a bill so a PAC would continue to funnel contributions to the party:
>
>> Dear Fellow Republicans. Please destroy this after reading. Why? Because the Life Underwriters Association in Montana is one of the larger Political Action Committees in the state, and I don't want the Demo's to know about it! In the last election they gave $8,000 to state candidates. . . . Of this $8,000 — Republicans got $7,000 — you probably got something from them. This bill is important to the underwriters and I have been able to keep the contributions coming our way. In 1983, the PAC will be $15,000. Let's keep it in our camp.

> State Senator Bruce Tutvedt stated in a declaration that during the 2009 legislative session the National Right to Work group promised to contribute at least $100,000 to elect Republican majorities in the next election if he and his colleagues introduced and voted for a right-to-work bill in the 2011 legislative session. Finally, a state court found two 2010 state legislature candidates violated state election laws by accepting large contributions from a corporation that "bragged . . . that those candidates that it supported 'rode into office in 100% support of [the corporation's] . . . agenda.'"

Lair, 873 F.3d at 1179.

Judge Bea dissented, arguing that the majority's standard was inconsistent with Supreme Court precedent, including *McCutcheon*, and suggesting that all campaign contribution limits are unconstitutional. "Absent a showing of the existence or appearance of quid pro quo corruption based on objective evidence, the presence of a subjective sense that there is a risk of such corruption or its appearance does not justify a limit on campaign contributions." *Id.* at 1191 (Bea, J., dissenting).

The Ninth Circuit denied en banc rehearing, with five judges dissenting. 889 F.3d 571 (9th Cir. 2018) (en banc). Judge Ikuta, writing for the dissenters, argued that the Ninth Circuit's *Eddleman* test had been "swept away" by the Supreme Court's decisions in *Citizens United* and *McCutcheon. Id.* at 572 (Ikuta, J., dissenting from denial of rehearing en banc). "In light of the Supreme Court's clarification, a state can justify imposing regulations limiting individuals' political speech (via limiting political contributions) only by producing evidence that it has a real problem in combating actual or apparent quid pro quo corruption." Judge Ikuta wrote that a "risk" of corruption is not enough.

5. How would you describe the standard of review of contribution limitations after *McCutcheon*? How does it differ from strict scrutiny? Reconsider this question in light of *Americans for Prosperity Foundation v. Bonta*, in Chapter 16.

6. *Soft Money Again.* Twice before *McCutcheon*, opponents of soft money limitations tried to challenge those party limits but faced rejection at the Supreme Court. *Republican Nat'l Committee v. FEC*, 698 F. Supp. 2d 150 (D.D.C. 2010) (three-judge court), affirmed, 561 U.S. 1040 (2010). Justices Kennedy, Scalia and Thomas indicated they would have heard this case. *Cao v. FEC*, 619 F.3d 410 (5th Cir. 2010) (en banc), cert. denied 562 U.S. 1286 (2011). The Republican National Committee filed a new suit, relying on *Citizens United* and *McCutcheon*, to allow the party to raise unlimited sums much like a Super PAC does. Matea Gold, *RNC Files Lawsuit Seeking to Raise Unlimited Sums*, Washington Post, May 23, 2014. However, a year later the RNC, without explanation, voluntarily dismissed the lawsuit. Then in 2015, the Republican Party of Louisiana filed yet another lawsuit against the soft money rules. A three-judge court rejected the new challenge in *Republican Party of Louisiana v. FEC*, 219 F. Supp. 3d 86 (D.D.C. 2016). Granting summary judgment for the FEC, it held that *McConnell* had already resolved the issues in the case. The Supreme Court summarily affirmed. 137 S. Ct. 2178 (2017). Justices Gorsuch and Thomas voted to hear the case. A sign of things to come from Justice Gorsuch?

Does *McCutcheon* support an argument against the soft money ban? Consider Richard L. Hasen, *Die Another Day: The Supreme Court Takes a Big Step Closer to Gutting the Last Bits of Campaign Finance Reform*, Slate, Apr. 2, 2014, https://perma.cc/AC27-W5L5:

> Third and most dramatically, the court [in *McCutcheon*] seems to open the door for a future challenge to what remains of the McCain-Feingold law: the ban on large, "soft money" contributions collected by political parties. These contributions were banned because it had become clear that political parties were becoming conduits for access between elected officials and big donors. Today Roberts rejects ingratiation and access as a problem, and says that this funnel of significant money to parties could serve the purpose of strengthening political parties and thus be a good thing. He writes: "When donors furnish widely distributed support within all applicable base limits, all members of the party or supporters of the cause may benefit, and the leaders of the party or cause may feel particular gratitude. That gratitude stems from the basic nature of the party system, in which party members join together to further common political beliefs, and citizens can choose to support a party because they share some, most, or all of those beliefs.... To recast such shared interest, standing alone, as an opportunity for *quid pro quo* corruption would dramatically expand government regulation of the political process."

Is there any plausible defense of BCRA's soft money restrictions after *McCutcheon*? For one possible argument, see Michael Kang, *Party-Based Corruption and McCutcheon v. FEC*, 108 Northwestern University Law Review Online 240 (2014). Kang suggests that parties may serve as a vehicle for *quid pro quo* arrangements between contributors and groups of candidates.

7. *Corporate Contribution Bans*. Before *Citizens United*, federal law banned not only independent corporate and labor union spending in candidate elections. It also banned *contributions* from these entities to federal candidates. These limits remain in effect. In *FEC v. Beaumont*, 539 U.S. 146 (2003), a case decided while Justice O'Connor was still on the Court, the Court held that the ban could be applied even to *MCFL* corporations (that is, those corporations who, before *Citizens United*, were ideological corporations entitled to a Court-created exemption from the corporate spending ban). The Court in *Beaumont* held the corporate ban justified, for among other reasons, by the state's interest in preventing circumvention of valid individual contribution limits. If individuals could set up an unlimited number of corporations to make contributions, there would be no effective contribution limit for individuals.

The *Beaumont* Court also made the following statement about corporate speech:

> Within the realm of contributions generally, corporate contributions are furthest from the core of political expression, since corporations' First Amendment speech and association interests are derived largely from those

> of their members, see, *e.g., NAACP v. Alabama*, and of the public in receiving information, see, *e.g., Bellotti.* A ban on direct corporate contributions leaves individual members of corporations free to make their own contributions and deprives the public of little or no material information.

Does this reasoning survive *Citizens United* and *McCutcheon*? If not, is the anti-circumvention interest enough to save the corporate contribution ban? So far, the Court has repeatedly declined to reconsider the question. *United States v. Danielczyk*, 683 F.3d 611 (4th Cir. 2012), cert. denied, 568 U.S. 1193 (2013); *Iowa Right to Life v. Tooker*, 717 F.3d 576 (8th Cir. 2013), cert. denied, 572 U.S. 1046 (2014); *1A Auto, Inc. v. Dir. of Office of Campaign & Political Fin.*, 105 N.E.3d 1175 (Mass. 2018), cert. denied, 139 S. Ct. 2613 (2019). The Court denied cert. in *Tooker* right after deciding *McCutcheon*. Why does a Court that has embraced deregulation keep passing on this issue?

8. *Other Contribution Limitations.* Corporations and unions are not the only entities targeted for special regulation. For example, federal law prohibits contributions in *any* election—federal, state or local—by national banks and corporations specially chartered by acts of Congress (52 U.S.C. § 30118); in any election or for *any political purpose* by federal contractors (52 U.S.C. § 30119); and in any *candidate* election by foreign nationals (52 U.S.C. § 30121). Federal law does not prohibit permanent resident aliens from contributing to campaigns. See 52 U.S.C. § 30121(b)(2) (defining a "foreign national" as, "an individual who is not a citizen of the United States and who is not lawfully admitted for permanent residence . . .").[i] The Federal Election Commission deadlocked over whether the ban on foreign money in U.S. elections applies to state and local ballot measure elections. Michelle Conlins & Lucas Iberico Lozada, *FEC Decision May Allow More Foreign Money in U.S. Votes, Critics Say*, Reuters, Apr. 24, 2015. State and local prohibitions may still bar foreign money, however.

The United States Court of Appeals for the D.C. Circuit sitting en banc pursuant to a special jurisdictional provision of the FECA unanimously rejected a challenge to the constitutionality of the federal contractor ban in *Wagner v. FEC*, 793 F.3d 1, 26 (D.C. Cir. 2015) (en banc). Judge Merrick Garland, who President Obama unsuccessfully nominated to fill the vacant Supreme Court seat previously occupied by Justice Scalia, wrote the opinion for the court (before being nominated, and before the Senate declined to take up his nomination). "We conclude that the ban on contractor contributions is closely drawn to the government's interests in preventing corruption and its appearance, and in protecting against interference with merit-based administration. It strikes at the dangers Congress most feared while preserving contractors' freedom to engage in many other forms of political expression. We do not discount the possibility that Congress could have narrowed its aim even further, targeting only certain specific kinds of government contracting or doing so only during specific periods. But as the Court has made clear, 'most problems arise in

---

i. American subsidiaries of foreign corporations also appear to be outside of section 30121's prohibition. See Note, *"Foreign" Campaign Contributions and the First Amendment*, 110 Harvard Law Review 1886 (1997).

greater and lesser gradations, and the First Amendment does not confine a State to addressing evils in their most acute form.' *Williams-Yulee*." The Ninth Circuit similarly upheld Hawaii's ban on campaign contributions by state contractors. *Yamada v. Snipes*, 786 F.3d 1182 (9th Cir.), cert. denied, 577 U.S. 1007 (2015). It held that the ban survived closely drawn scrutiny and was justified on anticorruption grounds.

Lobbyists are individuals who are employed to influence governmental decisions in the executive and, especially, the legislative branch. Not surprisingly, lobbyists often desire to or are pressured to make campaign contributions. Some states have attempted to place special restrictions on contributions by lobbyists. In one sense, such restrictions are more precisely targeted than restrictions on corporations, unions, or PACs, because, by definition, lobbyists are employed to influence public officials. But lobbyists are individuals, not organizations, and as individuals they enjoy the same constitutional rights as anyone else. Are restrictions directed at lobbyists' contributions constitutional? See *North Carolina Right to Life, Inc. v. Bartlett*, 168 F.3d 705 (4th Cir. 1999), cert. denied 528 U.S. 1153 (2000), where the court, applying strict scrutiny, upheld a North Carolina law prohibiting a lobbyist, a lobbyist's agent, or a political committee that employs a lobbyist from contributing to a member of or candidate for the North Carolina General Assembly or Council of State (an advisory body) while the General Assembly is in session. The law also prohibited candidates or incumbents from soliciting lobbyists or political committees that employ them during the session. Note that this provision applies to both lobbyists and to political committees that employ lobbyists. As to political committees, is the prohibition constitutional under *NCPAC*?

Would the North Carolina prohibition on contributions by lobbyists be constitutional if it applied at all times, not only during legislative sessions? See *Fair Political Practices Commission v. Superior Court*, 25 Cal. 3d 33 (Cal. 1979), cert. denied 444 U.S. 1049 (1980); *Institute of Governmental Advocates v. Fair Political Practices Commission*, 164 F. Supp. 2d 1183 (E.D. Cal. 2001). Does *Citizens United* change the equation? See *Green Party of Connecticut v. Garfield*, 616 F.3d 189 (2d Cir. 2010); see also Richard L. Hasen, *Lobbying, Rent Seeking and the Constitution*, 64 Stanford Law Review 191 (2012) (stating that some courts may reject the anticorruption argument for a lobbyist contribution ban and considering whether the government's interest in promoting national economic welfare may support such a ban).

Some targeted prohibitions of contributions have been upheld by state courts, including a ban on contributions by officers and "key employees" of casinos in *Petition of Soto*, 565 A.2d 1088 (N.J. Super. 1989), cert. denied 496 U.S. 937 (1990), and by liquor licensees in *Schiller Park Colonial Inn v. Berz*, 349 N.E.2d 61 (Ill. 1976). The Louisiana Supreme Court reached a result contrary to *Soto* in *Penn v. State*, 751 So. 2d 823 (La. 1999), cert. denied 529 U.S. 1109 (2000). The court there struck down a state statute prohibiting some in the video poker gaming industry from making campaign contributions to state and local candidates and their committees. The court pointed to the fact that the ban applied only to some persons in the gaming industry and also maintained that the ban was unnecessary, given generally applicable campaign contribution limits. But the main problem for the majority appeared to be that "[t]his absolute ban on political contributions by a particular segment of society goes far beyond what *Buckley* endorsed. The First Amendment simply does not allow the State to target groups and exclude them from the political process" (Johnson, J., concurring). Citing Louisiana's rich history of corruption associated with the gaming industry, two dissenting justices would have upheld the provision as narrowly tailored to prevent corruption and the appearance of corruption. In *Casino Association of Louisiana v. State*, 820 So.2d 494 (La. 2002), cert. denied *sub nom. Casino Association of Louisiana v. Louisiana*, 537 U.S. 1226 (2003), the Louisiana Supreme Court upheld a law barring campaign contributions by casinos. The court both distinguished and questioned the reasoning of its earlier *Penn* decision. In *Deon v. Barasch*, 960 F.3d 152 (3d Cir. 2020), the Third Circuit held that Pennsylvania statute that prohibited individuals with interests in businesses that had gaming licenses from making any contributions, no matter how small, to any politician, political candidate, public official, or political organization violated the First Amendment.

In addition to bans on particular individuals or entities, courts have considered challenges to the *timing* of contributions. The Ninth Circuit upheld a ban on collecting contributions more than a year before an election, *Thalheimer v. City of San Diego*, 645 F.3d 1109 (9th Cir. 2011), but rejected a ban on large contributions in the 21 days before an election. *Family PAC v. McKenna*, 685 F.3d 800 (9th Cir. 2012). Why the difference? The Fifth Circuit held unconstitutional an Austin, Texas law barring city candidates from soliciting or accepting campaign contributions within 180 days of an election. *Zimmerman v. City of Austin*, 881 F.3d 378, 393 (5th Cir.), cert. denied, 139 S. Ct. 639 (2018). The court distinguished *Thalheimer* and an earlier Fourth Circuit case upholding temporal limits by noting that they predated *McCutcheon* and "upheld temporal limits on campaign contributions without any specific evidence that the timing of a contribution creates a risk of actual corruption or its appearance that is distinct from that created by the size of a contribution." Such evidence is now required after *McCutcheon*, the *Zimmerman* court ruled. Compare to *Platt v. Bd. of Comm'rs on Grievs. & Discipline*, 894 F.3d 235 (6th Cir. 2018), upholding temporal campaign finance limits in judicial elections. The Eighth Circuit upheld a preliminary injunction against an Arkansas law that prohibited public officials from raising funds more than two years before election. *Jones v. Jegley*, 947 F.3d 1100 (8th Cir. 2020). "Arkansas has not shown that contributions made more than two years before an election present a greater risk of actual or apparent quid pro quo corruption than those made later."

Oregon voters amended their constitution to penalize state and local candidates who accepted more than ten percent of their funds from out-of-district contributors. The Ninth Circuit struck down the ban as unconstitutional. *VanNatta v. Keisling*, 151 F.3d 1215 (9th Cir. 1998), cert. denied *sub nom. Miller v. VanNatta*, 525 U.S. 1104 (1999). It held that the ban was not narrowly tailored to prevent corruption because the measure "bans all out-of-district donations, regardless of size or any other factor that would tend to indicate corruption." In *State v. Alaska Civil Liberties Union*, 978 P.2d 597, 616 (Alaska 1999), the Alaska Supreme Court distinguished *VanNatta* in upholding Alaska's ban on campaign contributions by non-residents. "Oregon's out-of-district restrictions applied to both nonresidents and residents of Oregon. But Alaska's challenged provisions apply only to nonresidents of Alaska, and do not limit speech of those most likely to be directly affected by the outcome of a campaign for state office—Alaska residents regardless of what district they live in." Does one need to be affected by an issue to have a First Amendment right to speak on it? The Alaska court further rejected the relevance of what it termed the "largeness" of the outside contributions. The restrictions "are aimed not at very large individual contributions, by which a single contributor can influence a candidate, but at cumulatively vast out-of-state contributions." Does this reasoning mean that people lose their constitutional right to make a campaign contribution because others who are similarly situated also try to exercise those rights?

In *Thompson v. Hebdon*, 7 F.4th 811 (9th Cir. 2021) (discussed on another question as detailed earlier in this chapter), the Ninth Circuit held unconstitutional a provision of Alaska law limiting candidates from accepting more than $3,000 per year from out-of-state residents. The dissenting judge would have accepted as compelling Alaska's stated interest in "self-governance" to justify the limitation on accepting contributions from out-of-state residents, citing *Bluman v. FEC*'s acceptance of a foreign contribution ban. Along similar lines, a federal district court blocked a South Dakota ballot measure which banned out-of-state contributions to South Dakota ballot measure committees, rejecting the self-government interest. *SD Voice v. Noem*, 380 F. Supp. 3d 939 (D.S.D. 2019). Is there a good analogy between the ban on foreign money in elections (upheld by the Court in *Bluman*) and out-of-state money? See Anthony Johnstone, *Outside Influence*, 13 Election Law Journal 117 (2014).

Most of the rulings summarized in this note upholding various contribution limits predate *Citizens United* and *McCutcheon*. Which ones survive the Supreme Court's New Skepticism?

Chapter 15

Public Financing

For many reformers, public financing is the *sine qua non* of campaign finance reform. The logic supporting public financing is simple. Many Americans willingly contribute modest amounts to campaigns for such reasons as ideology, party, or the candidate's leadership abilities, without expecting the contribution to exert any particular pressure on the recipient. But experience shows that contributions of this type do not consistently meet the need of candidates and parties for funds in amounts sufficient to bring their messages home to voters and to allow for vigorous electoral competition. Sometimes this gap is not filled, as is often the case for challengers in House and state legislative races. In other cases—especially for incumbents in the same races—the gap is filled by contributors who hope to apply pressure or, perhaps, are pressured into making contributions. Public financing, according to supporters, is the only way to reduce or eliminate this gap so that informative, competitive campaigns can be run, while reducing campaign financing as a source of undue pressure and influence.

Some reformers also support public financing on grounds it promotes political equality. Consider Richard Briffault's argument:

> It is not possible to truly equalize influence over elections. Indeed, given the value of robust and uninhibited political participation and the extensive regulation it would take to assure total equality, assuring absolutely equal influence over elections is not even desirable. Nevertheless, dramatically unequal campaign spending that reflects underlying inequalities of wealth is in sharp tension with the one person, one vote principle enshrined in our civil culture and our constitutional law. Public funding is necessary to bring our campaign finance system more in line with our central value of political equality. In privately funded systems, donors and independent spenders can have a bigger impact on the election than those who neither contribute nor spend, and big donors and spenders can have a bigger impact than smaller financial participants. Contribution and expenditure caps could ameliorate this, but at the cost of cutting into the ability of candidates to campaign effectively and possibly reinforcing the advantages of incumbents. Public funding can break the tie between private wealth and electoral influence while simultaneously supplementing campaign resources. Money from the public fisc comes from everyone and, thus, from no one in particular. No one gains influence over the election through public funding. The more the funds for election campaigns come from the public treasury, the

> more evenly is financial influence over election outcomes spread across the populace.

Richard Briffault, *Public Funding and Democratic Elections*, 148 University of Pennsylvania Law Review 563, 577–78 (1999).

Other reformers support public financing not for its own merits, but because they believe it is important to have some form or other of spending limits. Under *Buckley v. Valeo*, such limitations generally cannot be imposed except as a voluntary condition of accepting a public benefit that is offered in exchange. Ordinarily that benefit is public funding, though we shall see in Part II of this chapter that there have been some efforts to fashion incentives for the acceptance of spending limits other than public funding. Whether these will pass constitutional muster is not yet clear, but as will be briefly noted, their prospects were dampened by a recent Supreme Court decision.

The opposition to public financing is as vigorous as the support. In part it reflects a general opposition to new or expanded government programs. Opponents of public financing argue that in a time of fiscal pressure in which many vital programs are competing for funds, a new appropriation for political campaigns is objectionable. Furthermore, they contend taxes should not be used for the propagation of political views that the taxpayers may disagree with or even find offensive. In addition, some people oppose public funding because they believe such programs would be accompanied by contribution and/or spending limits, which are themselves objectionable. See, *e.g.*, Bradley A. Smith, *Some Problems with Taxpayer-Funded Political Campaigns*, 148 University of Pennsylvania Law Review 591, 628 (1999) (contending that "[g]overnment subsidies of political campaigns, if not tied to bans on private contributions and spending limits, may indeed have certain benefits for political life[,]" but that "[g]overnment financing plans which include limits on contributions and spending, whether deemed 'voluntary' or not, are doomed to failure").

Perhaps the most telling argument against public financing is that it would endanger the autonomy of the political process from the state. Even laws that merely regulate the flow of money in campaigns are often enacted and implemented with political advantage—partisan or personal—in mind. To make candidates and parties dependent on public funds and the strings that are or might be attached to them would greatly magnify the danger of abuse, according to opponents of public funding. See Roy A. Schotland, *Demythologizing Public Funding*, 21 Georgetown Journal of Law & Ethics 1254 (2008) (part of a dialogue between Schotland and Bert Brandenburg of Justice at Stake).

Whatever may be the force of this last argument, there can be little doubt that partisanship and calculation of advantage have been central to the politics of public financing. In general and with a number of exceptions, Democrats have supported public financing and Republicans have opposed it. Part of the reason, of course, is that some of the ideological arguments against public financing are likely to appeal more to Republicans than to Democrats. In addition, both Republicans and Democrats may believe that in the long run, Republicans—with their affinity to the corporate sector—have a natural advantage over Democrats in a privately financed campaign system. Probably a third reason, less frequently mentioned, is that most of the public financing schemes that have been proposed and debated in the last couple of decades have been fashioned by Democrats and therefore have been more attuned to the needs of Democrats than Republicans. Recent survey work by Professors Primo and Milyo on the popularity of various campaign finance reform proposals finds less than a quarter of survey recipients supporting public financing (at least as to how it was presented in their survey), making it less popular than other reforms. Republicans like public financing less than Democrats, and over one-third of liberal Democrats "do favor public financing, which could explain why it is often proposed by Democratic politicians . . . seeking to appeal to their base." David M. Primo & Jeffrey D. Milyo, Campaign Finance and American Democracy 160 (2020).

The debate on public financing is complicated not merely because of the competing pro and con arguments and the political cross-currents that surround it, but because "public financing" is not a single concept. Following are only a handful of the options that must be considered in fashioning any public financing plan:

- Who will be eligible for public financing? All major party candidates? If so, will public financing be available in primaries? If so, on what terms? Or will eligibility be determined by other standards? The most common method proposed is that candidates be required to raise a threshold amount in private contributions. If this method is used, what will be the terms and conditions?
- How much should the candidates receive? Will all eligible candidates for the same office receive the same amount? Or will public funds match, on a dollar-for-dollar or other basis, private contributions the candidates receive?
- Will funds be paid directly from the public treasury? More commonly, a special "fund" is created. Individuals, when they pay their federal or state income taxes, are permitted to "check off" one or a few dollars of their taxes to go into the fund. This device is intended to deflect criticism that taxpayers' funds are used to support propagation of views to which they object. But many regard this device as deceptive, because the taxpayer who checks the box on a tax return pays no additional tax for doing so. To say that the taxes of individuals who decline to check the box are not being used is thus a dubious proposition.
- Should public funding take the form of cash grants that can be used for any campaign purpose, or should it consist of "in-kind" benefits, such as reduced postage rates or free or discounted radio and television advertising?
- What additional rules and regulations should control campaign financing to complement public funding?
- If public financing is adopted, would it be better to use political parties to distribute funds?

Supporters of public financing are by no means agreed on the answers to these and many other questions. Take the last one, for example. As we have seen, some people support public financing solely or primarily because they must do so in order to advocate spending limits. But there are other supporters of public financing who oppose spending limits. This single disagreement may be sufficient to create deep division within any coalition for public financing, and it is only one of a large number of disagreements.

Part I of this chapter surveys public financing as it presently exists on both the state and local level and through the presidential public financing system. Part II of this chapter considers in depth an issue the Supreme Court dealt with only cryptically in *Buckley*: what constraints, such as expenditure limits, may be placed upon candidates running for public office who agree to accept public financing of their campaigns? In Part III, we review various novel methods that scholars have proposed for doling out public funds for campaigns.

I. Existing Public Financing Systems

A. In the States

Kenneth Mayer, Timothy Werner, and Amanda Williams, *Do Public Funding Programs Enhance Electoral Competition?*

in The Marketplace of Democracy 245–67 (Michael P. McDonald and John Samples, eds., 2006)

Advocates of public funding offer four main arguments about the consequences of taxpayer-financed elections. First, public funding can help potential candidates overcome the barriers that might deter them from running. In a vicious cycle, potential candidates who lack the ability to raise campaign funds are not taken seriously, and candidates who are not taken seriously cannot raise campaign funds. The cost of a campaign, even at the state legislative level, prevents potentially qualified candidates from even entering. A system of public grants can give candidates the seed money necessary to launch broader fundraising efforts, or even provide them all the resources they need to run credible campaigns. By reducing the campaign funding barrier, public funding systems might encourage candidates to emerge. Grants can be especially crucial for challengers, who face particularly daunting prospects in taking on an incumbent.

A corollary advantage to public financing is that it can encourage the emergence of candidates who lack substantial personal resources. Because campaigning is so expensive, candidates (especially challengers) routinely put thousands of dollars of their own money—sometimes millions—into their campaigns. Candidates without deep pockets have more difficulty persuading potential contributors (and political parties) to take them seriously. Public funding lowers this barrier, and therefore might increase the ideological and demographic diversity of candidates, as well as the range of policy positions that are put before the electorate.

Second, public grants can make elections more competitive. By reducing the fund-raising advantages that, in particular, incumbents have over challengers, public funding systems can "level the playing field" and reduce the number of landslide victories.

Third, public funding can reduce the influence of private contributions on both candidates and officeholders. By replacing individual, corporate, labor, or political action committee contributions with public funds not tied to any particular interest, public funding can, in theory, refocus attention away from parochial concerns to those of the broader public.

A fourth argument put forth by advocates is that public financing can control campaign costs. Since candidates who accept public grants must, as a general rule, agree to abide by spending limits, higher participation in public funding programs can prevent further escalation in the spiral of campaign spending.

Does public financing achieve any of these goals? The short answer is that nobody knows because there has been no comprehensive evaluation of public finance systems to identify what conditions and program elements lead to successful outcomes. The conventional wisdom is based on either a limited amount of data or anecdotal impression. Consequently, the elements of clean elections programs—funding amounts, eligibility rules, spending limits, and other regulations—are based more on guesswork than on solid evidence. The clean elections movement is in part motivated by axioms about the political process: that the need to raise funds deters many candidates from emerging; that candidates need protection against independent expenditures and issue ads; and that incumbents are as a rule unbeatable. While these are reasonable conclusions, they have not been subjected to rigorous analysis and testing. "The justifications normally offered for public funding," wrote Michael Malbin and Thomas Gais, "all rest on long strings of difficult assumptions."[2]

The question was also uninteresting, since only a handful of states had public funding programs. That changed, though, when Arizona and Maine adopted full public funding (dubbed "clean elections" by proponents) beginning with the 2000 cycle. For the first time, public grants would pay the full cost of a state legislative campaign. Hawaii changed its public funding law in 1995, raising grant size from what had been a trivial amount ($50 for State House candidates) to several thousand dollars, depending on the number of registered voters in each district. New York City changed its public funding program for city council candidates to a four-to-one matching formula, in which each $1 raised in qualifying contributions is matched by a public grant of $4 (in December 2004, the city council raised the maximum matching rate to six-to-one). We summarize provisions of the state legislative programs in Table 15.1 on the following page.

2. [Michael J. Malbin & Thomas L. Gais, The Day After Reform: Sobering Campaign Finance Lessons from the American States 70 (1998).]

Table 15.1 Characteristics of Public Funding Programs in Five States

	State and date effective				
Characteristic	*Arizona 2000*	*Maine 2000*	*Wisconsin 1978*	*Minnesota 1976*	*Hawaii 1996*
Qualification	Raise $1,050 in qualifying contributions ($5 each)	Raise $250 (House) or $750 (Senate) in qualifying contributions ($5 each)	Win primary with at least 6 percent of total vote for office Raise threshold amount in $100 contributions ($1,725 for Assembly, $3,450 for Senate)	Raise $1,500 (House) or $3,000 (Senate) in qualifying contributions ($100 each)	Raise $1,500 (House) or $2,500 (Senate)
Maximum grant	Up to spending limit Bonus provisions against privately funded candidates and independent expenditures	Up to spending limit Bonus provisions against privately funded candidates and independent expenditures	$15,525 for Senate (2002) $7,763 for Assembly (2002) Grants for general election only	Up to 50 percent of spending limit Small contribution refund program reimburses individuals up to $50 for contribution to participating candidate	Amount of grant restricted to 15 percent of spending limit
Spending limit (2004)	$28,300 for primary/general in House and Senate elections	$4,406 for primary/general in House $23,278 for primary/general in Senate	$17,250 for Assembly $34,500 for Senate Limits unchanged since 1986	$34,100 for House (2004) $64,866 for Senate (2002) Separate spending limits for election and non-election years	$1.40 x number of registered voters in district 2004 ranges (approx.): House: $14,000–19,000 Senate: $23,000–45,000
Special conditions	Unopposed candidates not eligible for public funds beyond qualifying contributions	Nonparticipating candidates face additional reporting requirements	Spending limits apply only if all candidates accept public funds	Spending limits increase by 10 percent for first-time candidates and by 20 percent for candidates running in competitive primary Spending limits waived when nonparticipating opponent exceeds threshold expenditures	

Source: Compiled by authors.

This combination of major change and continuity presents an unusually favorable opportunity to see if public funding has made any difference or achieved the goals that it was intended to achieve. We are particularly interested in how public funding affects legislative elections. With legislatures, because multiple elections occur at precisely the same time, we have a much larger set of races to analyze (than, for example, after a single gubernatorial or attorney general election). We also believe a plausible case can be made that public funding is more likely to affect legislative elections, since statewide races are more likely to attract well-known and experienced candidates who may be less influenced by the existence of a public funding program. For legislative candidates, especially first-time challengers, public funding is more likely to make a difference in their decision to run.

There has been some research on the consequences of these reforms, but these initial evaluations are incomplete. Some reports, especially those produced by advocacy groups that strongly support public funding, overstate the effect of the new law and ignore other factors, such as term limits or redistricting, that have without question shaped outcomes.[4] Others, including the General Accounting Office's evaluation of the Maine and Arizona programs, understate the reforms' impact.[5] We will navigate between these two edges and make an effort to specify the conditional nature of our conclusions, which can be summarized as follows:

— Public funding programs increase the pool of candidates willing and able to run for state legislative office. This effect is most pronounced for challengers, who were far more likely than incumbents to accept public funding.

— Public funding increases the likelihood that an incumbent will have a competitive race.

— Public funding has reduced the incumbency reelection rates in Arizona and Maine, although the effects are marginal. We can say with certainty, though, that public funding has *not* made incumbents safer. Fears that public funding would amount to an incumbency protection act are unfounded.

— Public funding programs have a threshold effect: if grants sizes and spending limits do not have a realistic connection to what candidates actually need, programs will have no effect.

In the end, we conclude that public funding programs — particularly the full "clean elections" systems in Arizona and Maine — increase the competitiveness of state legislative elections. . . .

---

4. [Clean Elections Institute. http://www.azclean.org/; Breslow, Gorat, and Saba. 2002. Revitalizing Democracy: Clean Election Reform Shows the Way Forward. January 2002. http://www.neaction.org/revitalizingdemocracy.pdf.]

5. [General Accounting Office. 2003. *Campaign Finance Reform: Early Experiences of Two States That Offer Full Public Funding for Political Candidates.* GAO-03-453, May 2003.] http://www.gao.gov/htext/d03453.html.

Does It Work? The GAO Report and Beyond

Past work on public funding has come to a mixed result: some studies find evidence that grant programs increase election competitiveness, while others find no effect. As we noted earlier, the significant recent changes in Arizona and Maine make another round of investigation worthwhile. Until recently, any analysis of public funding was confined to a comparison of Wisconsin and Minnesota, since Hawaii's program offered only trivial grants to candidates until 1996. . . . In one of the few studies to even attempt to measure the impact, across states, of public funding on competitiveness, Malbin and Gais concluded that "there is no evidence to support the claim that programs combining public funding with spending limits have leveled the playing field, countered the effects of incumbency, and made elections more competitive."[19] However, this study, of necessity, was again limited to a focus on Wisconsin and Minnesota; other research has concluded that public funding can indeed make a difference.[20] More recent work has begun to challenge the efficacy of New York City's public funding program, noting that it has not done much to make municipal elections more competitive.[21] Through the 2000 election cycle, public funding did not have a good track record in creating competitive electoral environments, and a comprehensive study of state-level programs concluded that "full-blown public funding programs with spending limits do not *seem* to do much for competition.[22]

Section 310 of the Bipartisan Campaign Reform Act (BCRA) — more commonly known as McCain-Feingold — directed the General Accounting Office to study the Maine and Arizona public funding systems in the 2000 and 2002 election cycles. The GAO's cautious May 2003 report offered some support for the clean elections programs, but concluded that "it is too soon to determine the extent to which the goals of Maine's and Arizona's public financing programs are being met." The report found that more candidates in both states were running and winning with public funding, and that funding differences between incumbents and challengers had narrowed. But it also found no evidence that elections had become more competitive, or that interest group influence had diminished.

The GAO report received scant press attention, with no major mentions in the national media, perhaps in part because of its tentative nature (a LexisNexis search did not result in a single mention in any national newspaper). The reform group Public Campaign, which supports public funding, criticized the report as "too cautious in [its] analysis" and argued that the GAO's own evidence could have supported

---

19. Malbin and Gais (1998, p. 137).

20. [Mayer, Kenneth R. 1998. *Public Financing and Electoral Competition in Minnesota and Wisconsin.* Citizens' Research Foundation, University of Southern California (April).]

21. [Kraus, Jeffrey. 2006. "Campaign Finance Reform Reconsidered: New York City's Public Finance Program after Fifteen Years." *The Forum 3 (4).* http://www.bepress.com/forum/vol3/iss4/art6/.]

22. Malbin and Gais (1998, p. 158).

stronger conclusions. The publisher of the trade newsletter *Political Finance* argued that the authorizing language resulted in a report that intentionally overstated the impact of the clean elections law, attributing to public funding outcomes that actually resulted from term limits.

A review of the GAO's methods reveals that the office did significantly underestimate most measures of electoral competitiveness, in large part because the authors performed many of their calculations using unorthodox measures. . . .

We now turn to our own analysis of electoral competition, which offers a somewhat clearer picture of the impact of the Maine and Arizona reforms.

Data on Electoral Competition

To measure the extent to which public funding has affected electoral competition, we calculated the following indicators, from 1990–2004, for elections to the lower house in the state legislatures in Arizona, Hawaii, Maine, Minnesota, and Wisconsin:

—the percentage of incumbents who faced a major-party opponent (contestedness)

—the percentage of incumbents who were in a competitive race, defined as one in which the winner received less than 60 percent of the two-party vote (competitiveness)

—the percentage of incumbents who ran for and were reelected to office (reelection rate)

For the first and third indicators, we controlled for the presence of paired incumbents in the 2002 elections. We did not count a race as contested if the two (or more) major-party candidates were paired through redistricting, and we removed losing paired incumbents from our calculations of incumbent reelection rates. For comparison, we also calculated these figures for states that do not offer public funding.

Assessing the effect of the clean elections law in Arizona is more difficult since its implementation coincided with two other significant changes to state election law. In 1992, Arizona enacted term limits for state legislators, limiting them to four consecutive terms. The 2000 elections were the first in which members were "termed out," and fifteen legislators (nine representatives and six senators) were ineligible for reelection in 2002. Second, in 2000 voters opted to conduct the decennial reapportionment process using an Independent Redistricting Commission (IRC), rather than allow state legislators to draw district lines. Advocates of the independent commission approach hoped that the new approach would produce districts less tied to incumbent interests (indeed, the law prohibited the commission from identifying or taking into account incumbents' residency when drawing the new districts). The near simultaneous effects of these three major reforms—public funding, term limits, and a new approach to redistricting—produced significant turnover in both chambers, and it is not immediately apparent how the effects should be allocated.

Figure 15.1 Incumbents Facing Major-Party Challengers in General State House/Assembly Elections, Excluding Incumbent Pairings, 1990–2004[a]

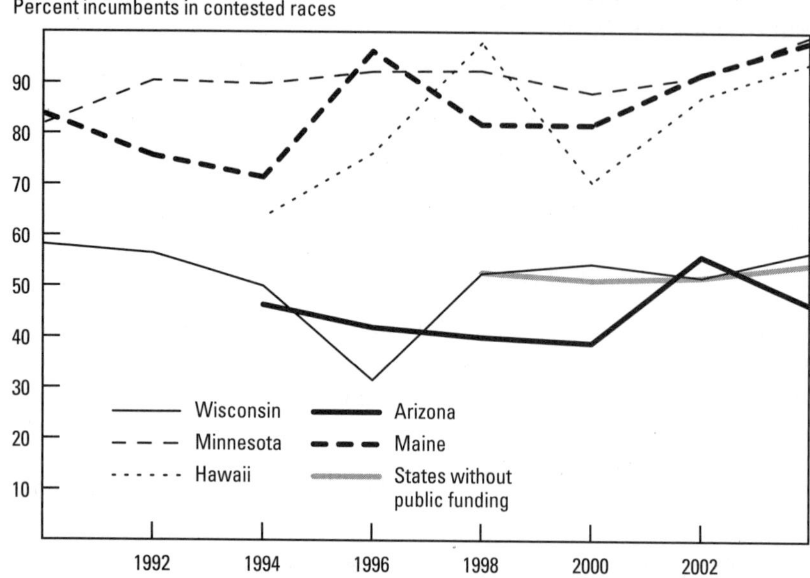

a. Incumbent pairings refer to incumbents running against each other.

In addition, the 2004 election cycle was unusually tumultuous because of legal disputes surrounding the new legislative districts that the IRC created for the 2002 elections. In January 2004, a state court rejected the redistricting plan in a lawsuit challenging the constitutionality of the proposed districts. Holding that the commission did not comply with the constitutional language requiring it to create competitive districts, a State Superior Court judge ordered the IRC to draw up a new plan for the 2004 elections. The commission complied, and in April 2004 submitted a map to the U.S. Department of Justice for preclearance under section 5 of the "Voting Rights Act." But the filing deadline for state office passed before the DOJ had approved the new plan, so state officials were forced to use a version of the 2002 plan for the upcoming 2004 elections. The uncertainty over the district maps meant that some prospective candidates had no idea which district they lived in, and some of these may have chosen to stay out of the ring until 2006.

A final problem is that Arizona's House elects its members from multimember districts, which do not translate into head-to-head campaigns. We address some of these methodological difficulties, and describe our application of an existing method of measuring competitiveness in multicandidate systems, in the appendix.

In Figure 15.1, we report contestedness from 1990 to 2004. The key to this and subsequent figures is the change in the period 2000–04 in Maine and Arizona, when the full public funding system was in place. Several patterns emerge from this graph. Arizona experienced a significant jump in the number of contested races in 2002 and 2004, increasing from under 40 percent in 2000 to over 50 percent in 2002 and 2004. This increase was not only large; it also reversed the previous trend of uniformly fewer contested elections between 1994 and 2000. While we cannot attribute this shift entirely to public funding (which was also in place in 2000), it is likely to have played a key role. Of the twenty-five major-party challengers who took on an incumbent in the general election in 2002, twelve were publicly funded. Given that these races present poor electoral odds for the challenger — incumbents are difficult to beat except in unusual circumstances — it is a defensible inference that some of these candidates would have stayed away without the existence of public funding.

The patterns for Maine and Hawaii are murkier, though in the expected direction. Both saw the percentage of contested incumbents increase in 2002, and again in 2004. Maine's contested rate in 2004 (98 percent) was higher than it was at any point since 1990.

Wisconsin and Minnesota show a continuation of patterns that existed throughout the 1990s. Minnesota's public funding program, which combines direct grants with refunds of small individual contributions, is generally regarded as effective in both encouraging candidate participation and in fostering a competitive environment. Wisconsin, which provides grants that have not changed since 1986, is at the other end of the spectrum, with low candidate participation rates and a program generally considered close to irrelevant. In Minnesota, uncontested House elections are rare, with contested rates almost always higher than 90 percent. In Wisconsin, uncontested incumbents are almost the norm, with just over half of incumbents facing a major-party opponent.

For comparison, we also show the contested rate for states that do not have public funding programs, using data from the Institute on Money in State Politics (IMSP). In these states, incumbents face major-party challenges about 50 percent of the time; that figure changed little from 1998 through 2004.

In Figure 15.2 we report on the competitiveness of an election when an incumbent is running. We defined a competitive race as one in which the incumbent received less than 60 percent of the two-party vote. This is not a universally accepted threshold — many political professionals would consider a 60–40 race something of a blowout — but we regard it as an acceptable minimum baseline of competitiveness, especially given the advantages that incumbents have in these low-visibility races.

Figure 15.2 shows that the percentage of competitive races went up in Hawaii, Maine, and Minnesota between 1998 and 2004. In Maine, 64 percent of incumbents were in competitive races in 2004, nearly double the 1998 rate (35 percent), and higher than the rate in Minnesota. The increase in Hawaii was much more modest, with only a slight improvement over the 2002 and 2000 rates.

Figure 15.2 Incumbents in Competitive Races Assembly/House Elections, 1990–2004[a]

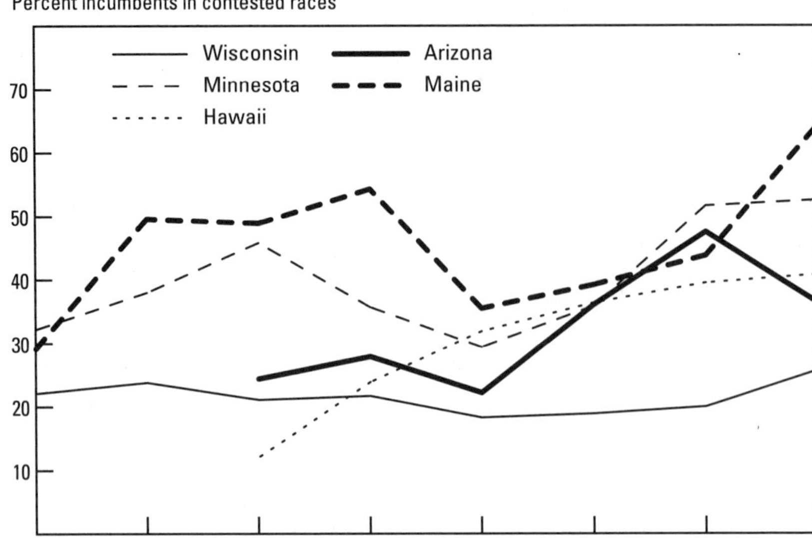

a. A competitive race is defined here as one in which the winner received less than 60 percent of the two-party vote. Reprinted with permission. © 2006, the Brookings Institution.

The 2004 Arizona House elections proved something of a disappointment to campaign finance reformers: the percentage of incumbents in competitive races in 2004 was the same as it was in 2000 (about 36 percent), declining from a post-1990 record of 47 percent in 2002. At the same time, in Arizona this measure of competition remained higher than it had been during the pre-public-funding era (1998 and earlier).

In 2004, Minnesota continued its pattern of close races, with over half of its House incumbents facing competitive challengers. Wisconsin trails the pack, with only one incumbent in four having faced a competitive race in 2004.

Figure 15.3 shows the incumbent reelection rate—that is, the percentage of incumbents who run and are reelected to another term. This represents what many would consider to be the payoff measure. Opponents of public funding often argue that it is nothing but an incumbent protection act: since incumbents have formidable advantages in name recognition, experience, and ability to mobilize supporters, the spending limits that always accompany public grants could, in this view, simply institutionalize the inability of challengers to overcome the incumbency advantage. But this has not happened. In Arizona, the incumbent reelection rate dropped from a Congresslike 98 percent in 1998 to 75 percent in 2002 (even after controlling for incumbency pairings), and remained low in 2004, at 83 percent. In comparison with 1998, incumbent reelection rates in 2004 were also lower in Maine, Hawaii, and Minnesota. The changes in these states, though, appear to be within normal limits and are not radically different from levels that existed throughout the 1990s.

Figure 15.3 Incumbent Reelection Rates in the State Assembly/House, Excluding Incumbent Pairings

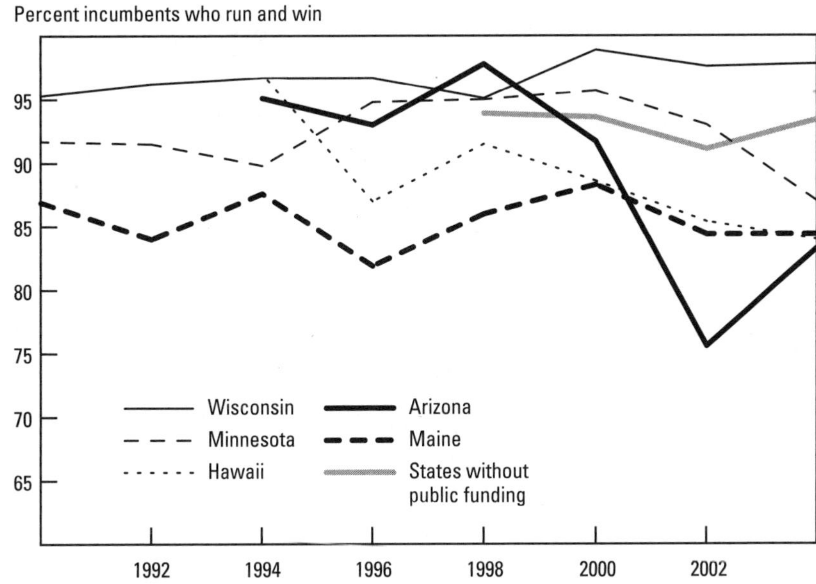

Wisconsin, making a three-for-three sweep, again holds the record for the least competitive elections. Ninety-eight percent of unpaired incumbents won reelection in 2004 (eighty-eight out of ninety won).

We also include a measure of incumbency reelection for the states that do not have public funding, again using IMSP data. These data are not fully comparable to the lines for publicly funded states, both because they do not control for pairings and because they consider as incumbents lower House members running for Senate seats. This is one reason why the incumbency reelection rate dipped in 2002, after redistricting had occurred in most states. However, we calculated reelection rates using several different methods, and all were within a percentage point of the others. In the states without public funding, the incumbency reelection rate has remained stable, at about 93 percent.

What accounts for these results? Obviously, they cannot be attributed entirely to changes in campaign finance law, but all of the trends are in the expected direction. The dramatic changes in Arizona cannot be attributed to term limits, since we are focusing on incumbents who are running for reelection; nor can the Maine results be the result of redistricting, since the state did not begin the process until 2003. And the stark lack of electoral competition in Wisconsin clearly sets it apart from the other states in this group—even from Hawaii, which has been dominated by the Democratic Party for decades.

One difference among these states is the varying amounts of money available to candidates through the public funding programs. We can distinguish between the full public funding systems (Arizona and Maine), those that provide multiple sources of public grants (Minnesota), and those that provide relatively small grants (Hawaii and Wisconsin). . . .

These data suggest a clear explanation for why public funding has apparently made so little difference in Wisconsin, as public grants make up only a tiny and shrinking share of overall campaign spending. During the 1980s, public funds made up as much as one-third of candidate spending. But in 1986, grant levels and spending limits were fixed and have not changed since then. When a candidate has to raise $80,000 or more to run a competitive Assembly campaign, and $250,000 or more for the Senate, the maximum grants—$15,525 for a Senate candidate, $7,763 for the Assembly—are hardly worth the bother.

The data also confirm that public funding could not possibly have had any effect in Hawaii, since grants continue to make up only a trivial fraction of overall campaign spending. This is a limiting case which shows that campaign finance is not the only factor that affects election competition.

Hawaii's experience with public funding—minimal grants, but a trend toward increased electoral competitiveness—highlights some of the limits of public funding as a comprehensive reform strategy. Although the evidence from Maine and Arizona, in particular, point to a significant improvement in electoral competition, even dramatic changes in campaign finance practices do not by themselves uproot electoral systems or produce fundamental rearrangements of political influence (at least none that we can detect so far). More to the point, when the political context does change, it may be the result of broader political forces, or even idiosyncratic events.

Although Hawaii was considered a Republican state in its early years of statehood, the Democratic Party ascended in the early 1960s to dominate state politics, with a coalition of labor unions and minority groups organized into a powerful majority by skilled politicians like Daniel Inouye and John Burns.

But the Democratic hold on state elections began to waver in the mid-1990s in response to because of a combination of stagnant economic growth, ethics scandals, and efforts to organize in response to a 1993 state Supreme Court decision opening the door to same-sex marriages. Republicans held only seven of fifty-one State House seats in 1995, but won nineteen of fifty-one in the 2000 elections (Democrats now have a 41–10 majority). And although the state GOP has failed to cut into the Democratic legislative lock, in 2002 Hawaii elected its first Republican governor since 1962, and was considered competitive—for a time, at least—during the 2004 presidential election.

Conclusion: Does Public Funding Make Elections More Competitive?

We are left with something of a mixed picture. There is compelling evidence that Arizona and Maine have become much more competitive states in the wake of the

1998 clean elections programs. The fact that indicators of competitiveness in Arizona remained stable through the 2002 and 2004 cycles is evidence that the electoral dynamic has indeed changed. We have revised our view of the impact of Maine's program: based on the 2002 elections, we concluded that it was too early to tell whether public funding had changed the electoral landscape. With the 2004 results in hand, we can say that public funding appears to have significantly increased the competitiveness of State House elections, based on the percentage of incumbents who face major-party opponents and run in reasonably close races. Minnesota's program continues to show a high degree of efficacy.

Not everyone agrees with our conclusions. Elsewhere in this volume [see Note 1 below — Eds.], Primo, Milyo, and Groseclose argue that "the jury is still very much out on clean elections laws," observing that the changes we noted here may be fleeting. In particular, they note that the decline in incumbency reelection rates may be the result of a culling effect, in which the best and most experienced incumbents are the first to be forced out by term limits. The incumbents who are left are, by definition, the ones with less experience. It is possible, then, that the incumbents we are observing in 2002 and 2004 — that is, post-reform — are less experienced and of lower quality than those who stayed in office before term limits. If this is true, these incumbents would have wound up in closer races (because they are less experienced and skilled, or because term limits reduced the incumbency advantage in some other way) even without clean elections.

It is of course possible that the effects we have observed will ebb. Everyone who studies elections will concede that the environment is complex, with many interactions, simultaneous relationships, and causal chains that are hard to pin down. Even so, we are confident in our results, because while we cannot claim to have controlled for every possible alternative explanation, we have eliminated the most obvious ones. Moreover, a growing literature suggests that term limits may *decrease* electoral competition by giving potential challengers a reason to bide their time until a seat opens up. In any case, we expect that a few more election cycles will clear up disagreement over the public funding effect.[37]

Hawaii and Wisconsin are states with ineffective programs; the key characteristic in both states is that public funds make up only a fraction of what candidates raise and spend. Although there is some evidence from Hawaii that elections have become slightly more competitive, this has more to do with long-term changes in the political composition of the electorate than with campaign finance law (and in

37. Early data from 2006, while not definitive, are consistent with our argument. In Maine, 321 candidates have filed for the 151 House seats, with 81 percent stating an intention to accept public funding. One hundred forty-six of the 151 seats are contested. In the Senate, all thirty-five seats are contested by the major parties, with 71 percent of candidates accepting public funding. These figures will change, since Maine ballot laws are flexible. But they suggest that the competitive effects observed have not yet dissipated. See Maine Commission on Governmental Ethics and Election Practices (www.state.me.us/ethics/candidate-list.htm).

any event, Hawaii Republicans have yet to seriously challenge the Democratic Party's hold on the legislature, even as they have achieved some statewide successes).

One significant inference that we draw is that there is no merit in the argument that public funding programs amount to an incumbent protection act. The fear that spending limits would put challengers in an impossible strategic situation and make incumbents even more unbeatable has simply not been realized.

There are limits to what these data can tell us, in any event. We do not yet have evidence that public funding has altered roll-call voting patterns or legislative coalitions, as might be expected if interest group influence or party influence has declined as legislators utilize their newfound independence. But the evidence points strongly to the conclusion that, under the right set of circumstances, public grants can significantly increase the level of election competition.

Notes and Questions

1. *Competition.* How much do "clean election"-style public financing systems stimulate political competition?

> To my eye, the changes [in competitiveness described in the Mayer, Werner, and Williams article] are noteworthy enough to make good political science but hardly enough to qualitatively improve the electoral system, even if one indulges the assumption that a more competitive system would be a major improvement.
>
> For example, the reelection rate for incumbents in Maine declined by about five percent from the high 80s from 2000 to 2004. But the 2004 figure was still not quite as low as in 1996, before "clean elections" went into effect, and the rate in all the years from 2000 to 2004 was within the normal range defined in the previous decade. Arizona saw a much sharper decline of about 20 percentage points in the incumbency reelection rate between 1998 and 2002, but the rate bounced up about ten percentage points in 2004.

Daniel H. Lowenstein, *Competition and Competitiveness in American Elections*, 6 Election Law Journal 278, 292 (2007) (reviewing The Marketplace of Democracy).

Another study found that "[b]efore the institution of clean elections in Maine and Arizona, only 14% of challengers won in general elections; after the program was in place, 22% of challengers did." Dorie E. Apollonio & Raymond J. LaRaja, "Incumbent Spending under Clean Election Laws," paper presented to Western Political Science Association (2005). Should this count as a qualitative difference in levels of competition? If so, does it make you more likely to favor this system of public financing? Using different methodology and focusing on competitiveness of gubernatorial elections, Primo, Milyo and Groseclose conclude that "[p]ublic funding has only a modest and statistically insignificant effect on winning margins." David M. Primo, Jeffrey Milyo, & Tim Groseclose, *State Campaign Finance Reform,*

Competitiveness, and Party Advantage in Gubernatorial Elections, 268, 278, in The Marketplace of Democracy, *supra*. Perhaps public financing is more helpful to legislative challengers than gubernatorial candidates.

Another study finding that these types of public financing systems increase political competition. Neil Malhotra, *The Impact of Public Financing on Political Competition: Evidence from Arizona and Maine*, 8 State Politics and Policy Quarterly 263 (2008). For a debate on the methodology behind the GAO report, see Michael G. Miller, *After the GAO Report: What Do We Know About Public Election Funding?*, 10 Election Law Journal 273 (2011) and William O. Jenkins, Jeff Tessin, and Anna Maria Ortiz, *GAO Response to "After the GAO Report: What do We Know About Public Election Funding?*," 10 Election Law Journal 291 (2011).

2. *Who Participates?* "The conventional wisdom holds that public funding programs should be especially advantageous for candidates who are not part of existing recruitment efforts or lack access to key political elites. According to this line of thought, women and challengers — two categories of candidates traditionally shut out from established political networks — will benefit from this alternative source of campaign funds." Timothy Werner & Kenneth R. Mayer, *Public Election Funding, Competition, and Candidate Gender*, 40 PS: Political Science & Politics 661, 661 (2007). Looking at the results in Maine and Arizona, the authors conclude that "female candidates are substantially more likely than male candidates to accept public funding in races for the state house . . . At the same time, this effect disappears in state senate races." *Id.* at 666. The authors suggest that this difference between state houses might be due to the fact that state senate candidates are less likely to be entry-level candidates, and therefore that public financing helps non-traditional candidates most at the entry level.

3. *Strategic Responses to the Matching Funds Aspect of "Clean Elections" Programs.* As initially enacted, candidates who accepted full public financing in Maine and Arizona were entitled to additional funding beyond the initial allocation when their opponents engage in large amounts of spending or when someone runs a major independent expenditure campaign against the candidate. This feature apparently led to some strategic timing of campaign spending. Michael Miller, examining the new Arizona public financing program, found that "traditionally-funded candidates try to maximize the competitive effect of the money that they do spend by releasing funds at the last moment, giving the Clean Elections candidate little time to react." Michael Miller, *Gaming Arizona: Public Money and Shifting Candidate Strategies*, 41 PS: Political Science & Politics 527 (2008). Whether such gaming presented a serious challenge to these public financing systems became a moot point when the United States Supreme Court struck down this aspect of the Arizona program in the next principal case below. More generally, it is not clear if the effects identified by Mayer, Werner, and Williams can survive the elimination of additional matching funds.

4. *Ideological Extremism?* Do programs such as Maine's and Arizona's produce candidates who are more or less ideologically extreme than privately-funded candidates? There are plausible arguments in each direction but the evidence shows that the programs likely do not increase or decrease ideological polarization:

> It is not wholly implausible to suggest a link between candidate extremism and campaign finance regulations and/or campaign contributions. For instance, as frequent contributors tend to be more ideologically extreme (see, for example, Bonica 2014), it seems possible that donors may exert a polarizing influence on legislative candidates, who might seek to repay their supporters after the election. Alternatively, assuming that political money exists in a marketplace in which candidates with a high likelihood of winning attract the most donations, the difficulty in fundraising that very extreme candidates are likely to face may serve a gate-keeping function, keeping ideologically extreme candidates out of contention. That is, candidates with highly extreme policy views may simply have a difficult time finding enough donors willing to support their agenda. It therefore remains a largely open question whether privately donated money affects the tone of legislative politics. Put another way: If campaign contributions could be removed from the equation, would legislators be more or less ideologically extreme? . . .
>
> Our study finds that there was essentially no important difference in the legislative voting behavior of "clean" funded legislators and traditionally funded ones in either Arizona or Maine during the 2000s, after Clean Elections was implemented. This finding is consistent with others suggesting only minimal impacts of campaign fundraising on the behavior of elected officials (Levitt 1994) but calls into question some concerns about the effects on polarization of money generally and public funding in particular. Our findings suggest that concerns about the influence of money on political tone may be overstated: spending and polarization may be increasing simultaneously, but one is not necessarily leading to the other.

Seth E. Masket & Michael G. Miller, *Does Public Election Funding Create More Extreme Legislators? Evidence from Arizona and Maine*, 15 State Politics & Policy Quarterly 24, 25 (2015). Andrew Hall, *How the Public Funding of Elections Increases Candidate Polarization* (draft dated Aug. 13, 2014), https://perma.cc/BSW6-VHUX, finds greater concern about polarization. Sundeep Iyer, Elizabeth Genn, Brenda Glavin, and Michael J. Malbin in a 2012 report, *Donor Diversity of Matching Funds,* https://perma.cc/HPF6-JX89, found that New York City's multiple matching system increased the diversity of donors, potentially blunting political polarization. Professor Richard Pildes cautions that if small donors tend to be more ideologically extreme, then multiple match programs could fuel polarization. Richard H. Pildes, *Small-Donor-Based Campaign-Finance Reform and Political Polarization*, 129 Yale Law Journal Forum 149 (2019). For an argument that campaign finance law has not caught up with the consequences of deep party polarization, see Michael S. Kang, *Hyperpartisan Campaign Finance*, 70 Emory Law Journal 1171 (2021).

In light of the concern over polarization, would it be better to distribute public financing through political parties? See Richard H. Pildes, *Romanticizing Democracy, Political Fragmentation, and the Decline of American Government*, 124 Yale Law Journal 804, 824-825 (2014); Daniel Hays Lowenstein, *On Campaign Finance Reform: The Root of All Evil Is Deeply Rooted*, 18 Hofstra Law Review 301, 365–66 (1989). For evidence on the potential moderating effects of political party contributions, see Raymond J. LaRaja and Brian F. Schaffner, Campaign Finance and Political Polarization: When Purists Prevail (2015).

5. *Vouchers*. The city of Seattle has instituted a program for city elections in which each voter receives four $25 vouchers to distribute to candidates of their choice in each election. The program has been in place for a few election cycles, and an early study found that the program both broadened the pool of donors and increased the number of candidates running for office. Alan Griffth & Thomas Noonen, *Does Public Campaign Funding Crowd Out Private Donation Activity? Evidence from Seattle's Democracy Voucher Program* (draft dated April 20, 2021), https://osf.io/preprints/socarxiv/9wtzs/. Another study of the program found that voucher users were more likely to be white, older, and wealthier than non-users, but they were more representative of the voters in the city than those who made private contributions. Jennifer A. Heerwig & Brian J. McCabe, *Building a More Diverse Donor Coalition: An Analysis of the Seattle Democracy Voucher Program in the 2019 Cycle* (2020), https://georgetown.app.box.com/s/r2skgxfnc230ukkb3dfqgm4576phzabd. What does this say about the risk of polarization from voucher-based public financing?

Why vouchers? Consider Richard L. Hasen, *Clipping Coupons for Democracy: An Egalitarian/Public Choice Defense of Campaign Finance Vouchers*, 84 California Law Review 1 (1996):

> Generally, campaign finance reform plans either seek to "level-up," by increasing the ability of those shut out of the political system to participate, or to "level-down," by decreasing the ability of those with disproportionate political capital to exercise greater influence over the political system. A voluntary public financing system, which allows candidates either to accept public funds or solicit private contributions, is a classic level-up program; it amplifies the voice of the poor but does not limit the influence of the rich. A law limiting the amount an individual or PAC can contribute to a candidate is a classic level-down program.
>
> Past proposals to use publicly funded vouchers have been of the level-up variety only. For example, in 1967, Senator Lee Metcalf proposed a plan under which taxpayers would receive campaign vouchers from the government, but politicians could accept private money as well.

Recently, however, Bruce Ackerman and I independently have proposed publicly financed voucher systems which both level-up and level-down.[1] These voucher plans level-up in the sense that all voters, even those voters who have never made campaign contributions before, are given vouchers to contribute to candidates for federal office. Vouchers facilitate the representation of groups which lack a voice in the current system. But these vouchers also level-down by prohibiting all other sources of campaign money; the rich can no longer exercise greater influence through private contributions and independent expenditures.

Here are the key elements of my voucher plan. The government provides every voter with a voucher for each bi-annual federal election. . . . Voters may donate their voucher dollars either directly to candidates, to licensed interest groups, or to political parties. The groups may serve whatever goals they please, whether ideological or economic. Thus, the NRA, NOW, and other ideological groups will compete for voucher dollars with the Beef Industry Council, the AFL-CIO, and other economic groups.

All campaign contributions and independent expenditures in support of or in opposition to a candidate must be made with voucher dollars. Candidates and elected officials cannot receive any other direct donations, honoraria, soft money benefits, in-kind contributions, or other donations. . . .

Independent expenditure campaigns must be financed only through collected vouchers; with limited exceptions, no private funds may be used. Individuals like Ross Perot, Herbert Kohl, and Michael Huffington could not bankroll their own campaigns. Corporations (other than licensed interest groups) could not donate money to candidates or make independent expenditures for or against a candidate. However, political activity not directly endorsing or opposing a candidate would not be subject to any limits.

Only licensed interest groups could collect voucher dollars from others to run independent expenditure campaigns supporting candidates, and

1. I proposed a voucher plan originally in my unpublished dissertation. Bruce Ackerman then independently proposed a voucher plan in a short article in the journal *American Prospect. See* Bruce Ackerman, *Crediting the Voters: A New Beginning for Campaign Finance*, 13 American Prospect 71 (1993). He has not had occasion to provide a scholarly treatment of his plan. Edward Foley discussed Ackerman's voucher plan in an article arguing for "equal-dollars-per-voter" as a matter of constitutional principle. Edward B. Foley, *Equal-Dollars-Per-Voter: A Constitutional Principle of Campaign Finance*, 94 Columbia Law Review 1204, 1208–13 (1994) [a portion of which is reprinted in Chapter 12—Eds.]. Smurzynski hinted at a voucher plan in his discussion of campaign finance reforms. Kenneth C. Smurzynski, Note, *Modeling Campaign Contributions: The Market for Access and Its Implications for Regulation*, 80 Georgetown Law Journal 1891, 1911 (1992) (suggesting that public financing could be done through the "intermediary" of interest groups). This Article is the first published scholarly look at the efficacy and fairness of a post-voucher political system. [We discuss Ackerman's recent ideas with Ian Ayres to combine vouchers with mandatory donor anonymity in the next chapter.—Eds.]

> only those groups and the voters themselves could contribute vouchers to candidates. Any voter could register for a license to create an interest group, and the license would be free. An independent federal agency would process license requests. The agency could not turn down a group's licensing request for ideological reasons.[a]

It seems likely that a voucher plan *supplementing* private financing of campaigns would be as constitutional as other public financing plans which do not key support to the spending of opponents. What advantages and disadvantages do you see from use of vouchers to dole out public financing of campaigns?

Consider Daniel H. Lowenstein, *Voting with Votes*, 116 Harvard Law Review 1971, 1989–90 (2003) (book review):

> The advantage of vouchers is not . . . that they bring about a marketlike solution, but rather that they provide an alternative to the formulaic distribution of public funds among congressional candidates. Unfortunately, the alternative that vouchers provide is far from perfect. Citizens situated in the collective action problem that vouchers would create are not likely to have the desire or the ability to figure out which races are the most competitive, in which their vouchers could be put to the best use. Even if they could overcome this problem, collectively they would face a difficult coordination problem in achieving a distribution of voucher funds reasonably well-calibrated along a spectrum of the most to the least competitive races. The only way these problems could be solved, or at least mitigated, would be if citizens were to contribute a large percentage of their congressional vouchers to parties or political organizations.
>
> If vouchers were the only public financing alternative to formulaic distribution, I would embrace them warmly. But they are not. Political parties are better situated than individual citizens to distribute campaign funds for maximum competitive effect. I have proposed a public financing scheme built around grants to the Democratic and Republican campaign committees in the House and Senate, to be distributed to candidates as the committees see fit. To be sure, there are drawbacks to parties' distributing public funds, but this is not the place for an extended argument for the superiority of my plan over [a recent voucher proposal by Bruce] Ackerman and [Ian] Ayres. Much will depend on whether one accepts my criticism of the voting-with-dollars concept.
>
> In that respect, this is an appropriate place to revisit briefly the citizenship effect that Ackerman and Ayres claim will result from vouchers. They

---

a. Hasen modifies his voucher proposal in Plutocrats United: Campaign Money, the Supreme Court, and the Distortion of American Elections (2016). In that plan, each individual could contribute and/or spend a total of $25,000 per candidate per federal election (and up to $500,000 in each two-year federal election cycle). Does that make the plan more or less desirable? Constitutional?

> contend that the ability to make voucher contributions will stimulate citizens to take a new interest in federal campaigns and to perceive that they have a new stake in the political system. The existence of vouchers would likely stimulate some discussion and participation. But Ackerman and Ayres give no reason for us to believe that the stimulation will be greater than (or even as great as) the level provided by elections generally, or by other forms of participation, such as signing petitions. Indeed, it may be instructive to consider the means by which signatures are obtained in the states that allow statutes and constitutional amendments to be placed on the ballot by initiative petitions. In many such states, notably California, companies have arisen whose business it is to qualify initiatives for the ballot. The circulators paid by these companies to obtain signatures can perform their function virtually without regard to the content of the petitions. A significant percentage of people will sign petitions simply because they are asked. Whether similar techniques would work for obtaining voucher contributions under Ackerman and Ayres' system is hard to say. It may be that the logistics of getting a citizen to swipe a credit card or ATM card through a machine are sufficiently different from the efforts required to obtain a signature that individuals would be somewhat more attentive to what they were doing. However that may be, it seems inevitable that under the Ackerman and Ayres plan, solicitors would obtain voucher contributions through mass marketing techniques comparable to those used for signature collection, mass fundraising, and electioneering. This circumstance is not necessarily bad, but it means that vouchers are not likely to produce much of a citizenship effect. Moreover, the voucher system is likely to frustrate many reformers—though not necessarily Ackerman and Ayres—who believe deep down that election campaigns ought to be run like college seminars.

Regardless of the merits, the city of Seattle, Washington has become the first to use "democracy vouchers" as a supplement to the campaign finance system. The Washington Supreme Court rejected a First Amendment challenge to Seattle's voucher program, and the Supreme Court declined to intervene. *Elster v. City of Seattle*, 444 P.3d 590 (Wash. 2019), cert. denied, 140 S. Ct. 2564 (2020).

B. In Presidential Elections

Public financing is available to presidential candidates in both primaries and general elections, but the system works differently before and after the parties have chosen their nominees. In presidential primaries, partial public financing is provided on a matching basis. In the general election, the campaigns are entirely funded from public funds. At least that was the original conception. Beginning in the 2012 election season, not a single credible major party candidate accepted public funding. As Anthony Corrado explains, "the presidential public funding program, which gave $239 million to candidates at its peak in 2000, has deteriorated into no more than a last resort for candidates with no viable alternative. In 2016, all the major-party presidential candidates rejected the public funding option, with one exception. Democrat Martin O'Malley, who gained little support in his bid for the nomination, qualified for $1.09 million of primary matching funds, which was largely used to pay off campaign debts. Jill Stein, the Green Party presidential nominee, also accepted primary matching funds, receiving $456,000 before her formal nomination." Anthony Corrado, *The Regulatory Environment of the 2016 Election,* 55, 56-57, in Financing the 2016 Elections (David B. Magleby, ed., 2019).

The material below, aside from being of historical interest, is valuable in exploring what a revived presidential public financing system would look like. In primaries, candidates become eligible for public funding by raising $5,000 or more in contributions of $250 or less in at least twenty states. Candidates who accept public financing are subject to campaign spending limits. The nationwide spending limit for presidential primaries is adjusted for changes in the cost of living, starting from $10 million in base year 1974. In addition to this basic limit, candidates may spend an additional twenty percent in fundraising costs. For the 2016 election, the nationwide spending limit including the allowance for fundraising was estimated to be about $57.7 million. Campaign Finance Institute, *Pre-Nomination and General Election Spending Limits Mandated as a Condition for Candidates Who Accept Voluntary Public Financing Candidates*, 1976-2016, tbl. 1, https://perma.cc/L2RG-P9LN.

In addition to the nationwide limit, there is a spending limit for each state. The state-by-state limit serves no apparent purpose. It was initially explained as assuring "that relatively unknown candidates would have an opportunity to compete effectively against better-known or better-financed candidates in individual states."[b] If that was a plausible expectation in 1974, the information regarding incumbency and campaign spending in Chapter 12 of this book suggests that, if anything, lesser-known candidates may have a greater need than their better-known opponents to spend large amounts. As it is, the state-by-state limit interferes for no clear reason with the strategies of candidates who wish to spend disproportionate amounts in states with crucial caucuses or primaries. In practice, this means Iowa and New Hampshire, which are usually the only states in which the state-by-state limits are a factor. In the past, some have evaded the limits. For example, staffers in the New Hampshire campaign would be lodged across the border in neighboring states, with the costs attributed to those states. Many candidates simply violated the limits, with no consequence beyond having to repay modest amounts of public financing after audits conducted long after the election year was over.[c] Prior to the 1992 election, the Federal Election Commission adopted revised accounting rules that make it possible for virtually any campaign to avoid the state-by-state spending limits legally.

---

b. See Anthony Corrado, Paying for Presidents: Public Financing in National Elections 6 (1993).

c. See Anthony Corrado, Creative Campaigning: PACs and the Presidential Selection Process 37–40 (1992).

Candidates who agree to the spending limits and who receive contributions sufficient to satisfy the threshold amounts described above get public funds for their campaigns equal in amount to the contributions they receive from individuals in amounts up to $250. The maximum amount a candidate can receive in public funds is half the nationwide spending limit. However, some of the money candidates raise, such as amounts over $250 and contributions from PACs, is not eligible for matching. On average, public funding amounts to about a third of major candidates' money in presidential primaries.

After the primaries, the major parties receive flat grants to pay the costs of their national nominating conventions. The parties are not permitted to raise private funds to add to the public funds they receive.

In the general election, the major party candidates receive a flat grant, which is equal to the spending limit. In other words, presidential candidates who accept public funding cannot spend any private funds in the general election campaign. The amounts of the grant are adjusted for changes in the cost of living, based on $20 million for the base year, 1974. In 2008, the amount for each major party candidate was eligible to receive was $84.1 million. (Republican John McCain took the money; Democrat Barack Obama did not.) Each national party also received $16.8 million for nominating conventions.

Candidate acceptance of public funding was nearly universal in the early years of the program. In 1980, Republican John Connolly became the first eligible major party candidate to decline public funding in the primaries. Later, Steve Forbes declined public funding in the 1996 Republican primaries and both Forbes and now-President George W. Bush declined the money in the Republican primaries leading up to the 2000 election. Unlike Connolly and Forbes, who drew on their own private funds, Bush relied primarily on fundraising. By June 2000, he had raised an impressive $94.5 million under the FECA rules limiting contributions to federal candidates to $1,000 from individuals and $5,000 from PACs, over $91 million in individual contributions. Nonetheless, Bush agreed to accept public financing for the general election as the Republican Party nominee. Until 2008, no major party candidate declined public funding in the general election. (Primaries and the general are treated as separate elections, but all the presidential primaries are treated as one for purposes of the contribution limits.)

Both President Bush and Democratic candidate John Kerry decided to decline public financing in the primaries leading to the 2004 election. Bush raised $269.6 million and Senator Kerry raised $234.6 million. Additionally, a number of independent but Democratic-leaning "527 organizations" (discussed in Chapter 14) raised and spent tens of millions of dollars during the primary period. Both Bush and Kerry opted for public funding in the general election. Should presidential candidates be able to opt into public financing for the primary season but not the general election? In the 2008 election, many of the leading major party primary candidates declined to take public financing in the primary season. Although Democratic nominee Barack Obama had pledged to accept public funds in the general election if the Republican nominee did likewise, he broke precedent and declined public financing when he concluded he could raise more money on his own, within the contribution limits. Since Obama's decision in 2008, no major party candidate has taken public funding in the general election, and no serious contender for a major party presidential nomination has taken public financing in the primary season. Aside from weak major party candidates and minor party candidates, the presidential public financing system is essentially dead though still on the books.

The public money for presidential public financing has been paid out of the Presidential Election Campaign Fund. Money is deposited into the Fund at the behest of taxpayers, who are permitted to "check off" an amount to go into the fund out of their taxes each year. Until 1993, each individual taxpayer could designate one dollar to go into the fund. Two dollars could be designated on a joint tax return. However, the Fund was barely adequate to cover the claims of candidates in 1992, and projections made it clear that the Fund would be inadequate in 1996. Accordingly, Congress in 1993 raised the check-off amount to $3 for individual returns and $6 for joint returns.

The main reason the amount in the Fund became inadequate was that the check-off was fixed at one dollar, whereas the amounts candidates could collect were raised with the cost of living. Thus, in 1976, the total amount paid out of the Fund to candidates and parties was $72.3 million. In 2004, that amount was $207.5 million. A lesser reason was that taxpayer use of the check-off appears to have declined. One reason may be that only people who have tax liability are eligible for the check-off, and the percentage of individuals who file tax returns but have no tax liability increased after the 1986 Tax Reform Act. Another reason was probably heightened disenchantment with government and politics. A major point of contention is whether the decline reflected disapproval of the public financing system itself and whether, indeed, most taxpayers understand the system, whether or not they use the check-off. Unfortunately, poor record-keeping by the Internal Revenue Service makes it impossible to be sure of the extent of the decline, and even less is understood of its causes.[d]

Public funding worked well until the early 2000s to accomplish many of the objectives of campaign finance regulation. As Anthony Corrado wrote:

> [T]he matching funds program has proven to be an extremely popular form of campaign finance and an important source of revenue. It has been widely accepted by candidates and has encouraged them to solicit small contributions instead of large gifts and PAC donations. The program has been

d. For a careful analysis of these issues, see Corrado, Paying for Presidents, at 16–36. For prospective consideration of the need to keep the Fund solvent, see Joseph Michael Pace, *Public Funding of Presidential Campaigns and Elections: Is There a Viable Future?*, 24 Presidential Studies Quarterly 139 (1994).

> especially helpful to lesser-known aspirants who lack broad bases of financial support and to candidates who lack ready access to substantial numbers of large donors. By providing such candidates with the funds needed to introduce themselves to voters, public funding has increased the choices available to the electorate and enhanced the competitiveness of nomination contests.... At the same time, it has served to diminish the role of special interest money in presidential campaigns. Because PAC contributions are not eligible for matching funds, candidates can raise more money by soliciting small contributions than PAC contributions.... The law thus gives candidates a strong incentive to choose small private gifts over PAC money. This incentive, as well as the practice of many PACs to forego making contributions in processes that select major party candidates, has led to a system in which PAC contributions play an insignificant role. On average, only two to four percent of the total monies raised by presidential aspirants comes from PACs, as compared to congressional campaigns, which often rely on PACs for 30 to 40 percent of their total revenue.[e]

So what explained the change in 2008?

> By 2008, it was clear that the public financing system, with its relatively paltry spending limits, was a luxury no serious candidate could afford, at least in the primary season. Indeed, in 2008, the only candidates opting for public financing were the weak ones who could not raise funds well on their own. John Edwards agreed to take public financing as his personal fundraising collapsed, and John McCain agreed to take it when he too was written off as having no chance at securing the Republican nomination. Once McCain became the front-runner, he backed out of his commitment to take public financing in the primary election season.
>
> During the primary season, (up to each party's national convention), eventual Democratic Party nominee Barack Obama raised $414.2 million through private contributions, and eventual Republican party nominee John McCain raised $216.3 million, without taking any public financing. In one month alone, July 2008, Obama raised $50 million and spent $55 million, spending more in one month than he would have been able to spend *for the entire primary campaign season* had he opted for public financing and its accompanying $52 million spending cap.

Richard L. Hasen, *The Changing Nature of Campaign Financing for Presidential Primary Candidates,* in Nominating the President: Evolution and Revolution in 2008 and Beyond 27, 29 (Jack Citrin & David Karol, eds., 2009). Obama's unprecedented fundraising relied upon "micro-donations" (donations under $200), collected primarily via the Internet, and the extensive use of campaign finance

---

e. Corrado, *supra*, at 38, 44–45.

"bundlers." Obama raised $117.7 million from donors giving less than $200 in the aggregate. *Id.* at 33. He reported over 2 million individual donors during both election periods. *Id.* at 45 n.13. Does fundraising from small donations and small donors achieve the same goals as the primary campaign finance system, as the Obama campaign claimed during the election? Senator McCain's fundraising relied much more heavily on bundling than on Internet-based small donations. McCain raised 31 percent of his primary funds (over $62 million) in small donations, while Obama raised 53 percent of his primary funds in this way. *Id.* at 32.

In the general election, Senator McCain, the Republican party nominee, opted into the public financing system, entitling him to $84.1 million in public funds (plus an additional $46 million in funds for legal and accounting expenses). Senator Obama opted out, and continued to raise unprecedented sums privately, much through internet micro-donations and bundling. Much of the disparity between the candidates, however, was made up by the Republican National Committee fundraising, some of that as part of a joint fundraising program with the McCain campaign. In the general election, during September Senator Obama raised $150 million and the DNC raised another $42 million. Senator McCain in the same period received his $84.1 million in public financing, while the RNC raised a little over $67 million." Richard L. Hasen, *Senator Obama's $150-Million September and $600-Million Campaign: Signs that Our Campaign Finance Laws are Broken or Working?*, Findlaw, Oct. 28, 2008, https://perma.cc/UL2Y-H5V5.

What, if anything, can or should be done to fix the now-defunct presidential public financing system?

II. Constitutional Questions with Public Financing

In footnote 65 of *Buckley v. Valeo*, the Supreme Court wrote:

> For the reasons discussed in Part III, *infra*, Congress may engage in public financing of election campaigns and may condition acceptance of public funds on an agreement by the candidate to abide by specified expenditure limitations. Just as a candidate may voluntarily limit the size of the contributions he chooses to accept, he may decide to forgo private fundraising and accept public funding.

In Part III of its opinion the Court does give reasons for the permissibility of public financing, but contrary to the statement in footnote 65, there is no explanation in Part III or elsewhere in *Buckley* why Congress may "condition acceptance of public funds on an agreement by the candidate to abide by . . . expenditure limitations."

Critics of public financing conditioned on the acceptance of spending limits point out that the simultaneous enactment of contribution limits may put considerable pressure on candidates to accept the public financing/spending limits package. The argument is made cogently by Brice M. Clagett and John R. Bolton, Buckley v. Valeo, *Its Aftermath, and Its Prospects: The Constitutionality of Government Restraints on Campaign Financing*, 29 Vanderbilt Law Review 1327, 1336–37 (1976):

> [T]he candidate is presented with a particularly invidious form of the twentieth century "Catch 22" which threatens to reduce the private sector to adjuncts and servants of the state: government imposes restrictions upon, and by taxation or otherwise dries up funds formerly available to, a private activity; government then offers public funds to subsidize the activity it itself has crippled; the courts then hold that by virtue of the regulation and the subsidies the formerly private activity has become "state action" and thus subject to even greater governmental control. When this process involves a virtually coerced surrender of first amendment rights in an area going to the heart of the political process, it is difficult to see how the Court's unexplained result can be sustained if the issue is brought before it and fully analyzed.

Judge Leventhal, one of the members of the Court of Appeals panel in *Buckley*, was friendlier to FECA and therefore found footnote 65 not anomalous but evidence that despite its rhetoric, the Court regarded spending limits as "substantially and significantly less restrictive than content prohibitions." Harold Leventhal, *Courts and Political Thickets*, 77 Columbia Law Review 345, 361 (1977). Professor Daniel Polsby took a similar but less approving view:

> [T]he Court made a mistake in allowing expenditure ceilings to ride in on the coattails of public financing. There is no good reason for the Court to allow this restraint, especially when it takes the strong position on expenditure ceilings that it does. The Court's failure even to allude to this issue has the flavor of a tacit agreement among the Justices that expenditures of private money in elections is a bad thing for which there exists no obviously constitutional remedy. Hence, expenditure limits are to be cursed with the tongue but blessed with the hand, an understandable political compromise, not dismissible out-of-hand as bad policy, but unconvincing as law and contrary to the fundamental logic of the bulk of the decision.

Daniel D. Polsby, Buckley v. Valeo*: The Special Nature of Political Speech*, 1976 Supreme Court Review 1, 30–31. If, as Polsby is willing to concede, spending limits tied to public financing may be good policy, then why is a ruling that the policy is constitutionally permissible "unconvincing as law"? There are some campaign finance reformers who are less than enthusiastic about spending limits but who strongly favor public financing of campaigns and either favor or are willing to tolerate spending limits so long as they are accompanied by public financing. Is it possible that some or all of the *Buckley* majority were of this mind and that they hoped or expected that the result of the *Buckley* decision would be to induce Congress to extend public financing to congressional elections? If so, would such considerations be proper influences on a Supreme Court decision? Whether or not they existed or were proper, any such hopes or expectations on the part of the Justices have failed to come to fruition. Continuous efforts to extend public financing to congressional campaigns have consistently failed over a period of 30 years.

Whatever the merits of Clagett and Bolton's criticism of footnote 65, their prediction that the footnote would fail to withstand further scrutiny has turned out to be incorrect. The issue was presented more concretely in *Republican National Committee v. Federal Election Commission*, 487 F. Supp. 280 (S.D.N.Y.) summarily aff'd 445 U.S. 955 (1980). That case was a challenge to 26 U.S.C. § 9003(b), which requires major party presidential candidates to certify, as a condition of receiving public funding, that they will not "incur qualified campaign expenses in excess of the aggregate payments to which they will be entitled," and that no private contributions will be accepted unless necessary to make up the difference in the event that the amount available in the government's "Presidential Election Campaign Fund" should fall short of the amount candidates are entitled to receive.

Plaintiffs in *RNC* contended that as a practical matter, candidates had no choice but to accept the public funding and that in any event, the conditioning of public funding on the waiver of First Amendment rights constituted an unconstitutional condition. The district court regarded the contention that candidates had no choice but to accept public funding as unproved. Relying on *Buckley*'s footnote 65 and on other decisions applying the "unconstitutional conditions" doctrine, the district court held that "the fact that a statute requires an individual to choose between two methods of exercising the same constitutional right does not render the law invalid, provided the statute does not diminish a protected right or, where there is such a diminution, the burden is justified by a compelling state interest." The district court did not think the conditions attached to presidential public funding infringed on First Amendment rights, and in any event, it found a compelling state interest in assuring that candidates who receive public funding should be "relieved of the burdens of soliciting private contributions and of avoiding unhealthy obligations to private contributors." The Supreme Court's summary affirmance (i.e., without issuing its own opinion) is an authoritative reaffirmation that expenditure limits may be imposed as a condition on public funding, but it is no indication whether the Supreme Court relied on any or all of the reasons given by the district court.

The question whether particular public financing laws are voluntary or coercive continues to be litigated as jurisdictions pass new laws conditioning the receipt of public financing on a candidate agreeing to give up certain fundraising techniques the law otherwise would allow. See, *e.g., Daggett v. Commission on Governmental Ethics and Election Practices*, 205 F.3d 445 (1st Cir. 2000). But the ability of states to design public financing systems which are both constitutional and attractive enough to get serious candidates to participate was put to the test by the next case.

Arizona Free Enterprise Club's Freedom Club PAC v. Bennett

564 U.S. 721 (2011)

CHIEF JUSTICE ROBERTS delivered the opinion of the Court.

Under Arizona law, candidates for state office who accept public financing can receive additional money from the State in direct response to the campaign activities of privately financed candidates and independent expenditure groups. Once a set spending limit is exceeded, a publicly financed candidate receives roughly one dollar for every dollar spent by an opposing privately financed candidate. The publicly financed candidate also receives roughly one dollar for every dollar spent by independent expenditure groups to support the privately financed candidate, or to oppose the publicly financed candidate. We hold that Arizona's matching funds scheme substantially burdens protected political speech without serving a compelling state interest and therefore violates the First Amendment.

I

A

The Arizona Citizens Clean Elections Act, passed by initiative in 1998, created a voluntary public financing system to fund the primary and general election campaigns of candidates for state office. All eligible candidates for Governor, secretary of state, attorney general, treasurer, superintendent of public instruction, the corporation commission, mine inspector, and the state legislature (both the House and Senate) may opt to receive public funding. Eligibility is contingent on the collection of a specified number of five-dollar contributions from Arizona voters, and the acceptance of certain campaign restrictions and obligations. Publicly funded candidates must agree, among other things, to limit their expenditure of personal funds to $500; participate in at least one public debate; adhere to an overall expenditure cap; and return all unspent public moneys to the State.

In exchange for accepting these conditions, participating candidates are granted public funds to conduct their campaigns. In many cases, this initial allotment may be the whole of the State's financial backing of a publicly funded candidate. But when certain conditions are met, publicly funded candidates are granted additional "equalizing" or matching funds.

Matching funds are available in both primary and general elections. In a primary, matching funds are triggered when a privately financed candidate's expenditures, combined with the expenditures of independent groups made in support of the privately financed candidate or in opposition to a publicly financed candidate, exceed the primary election allotment of state funds to the publicly financed candidate. During the general election, matching funds are triggered when the amount of money a privately financed candidate receives in contributions, combined with the expenditures of independent groups made in support of the privately financed candidate or in opposition to a publicly financed candidate, exceed the general election allotment of state funds to the publicly financed candidate. A privately financed candidate's expenditures of his personal funds are counted as contributions for purposes of calculating matching funds during a general election.

Once matching funds are triggered, each additional dollar that a privately financed candidate spends during the primary results in one dollar in additional state funding to his publicly financed opponent (less a 6% reduction meant to account for fundraising expenses). During a general election, every dollar that a candidate receives in contributions—which includes any money of his own that a candidate spends on his campaign—results in roughly one dollar in additional state funding to his publicly financed opponent. In an election where a privately funded candidate faces multiple publicly financed candidates, one dollar raised or spent by the privately financed candidate results in an almost one dollar increase in public funding to each of the publicly financed candidates.

Once the public financing cap is exceeded, additional expenditures by independent groups can result in dollar-for-dollar matching funds as well. Spending by independent groups on behalf of a privately funded candidate, or in opposition to a publicly funded candidate, results in matching funds. Independent expenditures made in support of a publicly financed candidate can result in matching funds for other publicly financed candidates in a race. The matching funds provision is not activated, however, when independent expenditures are made in opposition to a privately financed candidate. Matching funds top out at two times the initial authorized grant of public funding to the publicly financed candidate.

Under Arizona law, a privately financed candidate may raise and spend unlimited funds, subject to state-imposed contribution limits and disclosure requirements. Contributions to candidates for statewide office are limited to $840 per contributor per election cycle and contributions to legislative candidates are limited to $410 per contributor per election cycle.

An example may help clarify how the Arizona matching funds provision operates. Arizona is divided into 30 districts for purposes of electing members to the State's House of Representatives. Each district elects two representatives to the House biannually. In the last general election, the number of candidates competing for the two available seats in each district ranged from two to seven. Arizona's Fourth District had three candidates for its two available House seats. Two of those candidates opted to accept public funding; one candidate chose to operate his campaign with private funds.

In that election, if the total funds contributed to the privately funded candidate, added to that candidate's expenditure of personal funds and the expenditures of supportive independent groups, exceeded $21,479—the allocation of public funds for the general election in a contested State House race—the matching funds provision would be triggered. At that point, a number of different political activities could result in the distribution of matching funds. For example:

- If the privately funded candidate spent $1,000 of his own money to conduct a direct mailing, each of his publicly funded opponents would receive $940 ($1,000 less the 6% offset).
- If the privately funded candidate held a fundraiser that generated $1,000 in contributions, each of his publicly funded opponents would receive $940.
- If an independent expenditure group spent $1,000 on a brochure expressing its support for the privately financed candidate, each of the publicly financed candidates would receive $940 directly.
- If an independent expenditure group spent $1,000 on a brochure opposing one of the publicly financed candidates, but saying nothing about the privately financed candidate, the publicly financed candidates would receive $940 directly.
- If an independent expenditure group spent $1,000 on a brochure supporting one of the publicly financed candidates, the other publicly financed candidate would receive $940 directly, but the privately financed candidate would receive nothing.
- If an independent expenditure group spent $1,000 on a brochure opposing the privately financed candidate, no matching funds would be issued.

A publicly financed candidate would continue to receive additional state money in response to fundraising and spending by the privately financed candidate and independent expenditure groups until that publicly financed candidate received a total of $64,437 in state funds (three times the initial allocation for a State House race).[3]

B

Petitioners in this case, plaintiffs below, are five past and future candidates for Arizona state office—four members of the House of Representatives and the Arizona state treasurer—and two independent groups that spend money to support and oppose Arizona candidates. They filed suit challenging the constitutionality of the matching funds provision. The candidates and independent expenditure groups argued that the matching funds provision unconstitutionally penalized their speech and burdened their ability to fully exercise their First Amendment rights.

[The District Court held the measure unconstitutional. The Ninth Circuit reversed. The Supreme Court issued a stay of the Ninth Circuit while it considered this case.]

---

3. Maine and North Carolina have both passed matching funds statutes that resemble Arizona's law. Minnesota, Connecticut, and Florida have also adopted matching funds provisions, but courts have enjoined the enforcement of those schemes after concluding that their operation violates the First Amendment. See *Day v. Holahan,* 34 F.3d 1356, 1362 (C.A.8 1994); *Green Party of Conn. v. Garfield,* 616 F.3d 213, 242 (C.A.2 2010); *Scott v. Roberts,* 612 F.3d 1279, 1297–1298 (C.A.11 2010).

II

"Discussion of public issues and debate on the qualifications of candidates are integral to the operation" of our system of government. *Buckley.* As a result, the First Amendment "'has its fullest and most urgent application' to speech uttered during a campaign for political office." *Eu.* "Laws that burden political speech are" accordingly "subject to strict scrutiny, which requires the Government to prove that the restriction furthers a compelling interest and is narrowly tailored to achieve that interest." *Citizens United; see MCFL.*

Applying these principles, we have invalidated government-imposed restrictions on campaign expenditures, *Buckley,* restraints on independent expenditures applied to express advocacy groups, *MCFL,* limits on uncoordinated political party expenditures, (*Colorado I*), and regulations barring unions, nonprofit and other associations, and corporations from making independent expenditures for electioneering communication, *Citizens United.*

At the same time, we have subjected strictures on campaign-related speech that we have found less onerous to a lower level of scrutiny and upheld those restrictions. For example, after finding that the restriction at issue was "closely drawn" to serve a "sufficiently important interest," see, *e.g., McConnell*; *Shrink Missouri,* we have upheld government-imposed limits on contributions to candidates, *Buckley,* caps on coordinated party expenditures, (*Colorado II*), and requirements that political funding sources disclose their identities, *Citizens United.*

Although the speech of the candidates and independent expenditure groups that brought this suit is not directly capped by Arizona's matching funds provision, those parties contend that their political speech is substantially burdened by the state law in the same way that speech was burdened by the law we recently found invalid in *Davis* . . .

A

1

The logic of *Davis* largely controls our approach to this case. Much like the burden placed on speech in *Davis,* the matching funds provision "imposes an unprecedented penalty on any candidate who robustly exercises [his] First Amendment right[s]." Under that provision, "the vigorous exercise of the right to use personal funds to finance campaign speech" leads to "advantages for opponents in the competitive context of electoral politics."

Once a privately financed candidate has raised or spent more than the State's initial grant to a publicly financed candidate, each personal dollar spent by the privately financed candidate results in an award of almost one additional dollar to his opponent. That plainly forces the privately financed candidate to "shoulder a special and potentially significant burden" when choosing to exercise his First Amendment right to spend funds on behalf of his candidacy. If the law at issue in *Davis* imposed a burden on candidate speech, the Arizona law unquestionably does so as well.

The penalty imposed by Arizona's matching funds provision is different in some respects from the penalty imposed by the law we struck down in *Davis*. But those differences make the Arizona law *more* constitutionally problematic, not less. First, the penalty in *Davis* consisted of raising the contribution limits for one of the candidates. The candidate who benefited from the increased limits still had to go out and raise the funds. He may or may not have been able to do so. The other candidate, therefore, faced merely the possibility that his opponent would be able to raise additional funds, through contribution limits that remained subject to a cap. And still the Court held that this was an "unprecedented penalty," a "special and potentially significant burden" that had to be justified by a compelling state interest—a rigorous First Amendment hurdle. Here the benefit to the publicly financed candidate is the direct and automatic release of public money. That is a far heavier burden than in *Davis*.

Second, depending on the specifics of the election at issue, the matching funds provision can create a multiplier effect. In the Arizona Fourth District House election previously discussed, if the spending cap were exceeded, each dollar spent by the privately funded candidate would result in an additional dollar of campaign funding to each of that candidate's publicly financed opponents. In such a situation, the matching funds provision forces privately funded candidates to fight a political hydra of sorts. Each dollar they spend generates two adversarial dollars in response. Again, a markedly more significant burden than in *Davis*.

Third, unlike the law at issue in *Davis*, all of this is to some extent out of the privately financed candidate's hands. Even if that candidate opted to spend less than the initial public financing cap, any spending by independent expenditure groups to promote the privately financed candidate's election—regardless whether such support was welcome or helpful—could trigger matching funds. What is more, that state money would go directly to the publicly funded candidate to use as he saw fit. That disparity in control—giving money directly to a publicly financed candidate, in response to independent expenditures that cannot be coordinated with the privately funded candidate—is a substantial advantage for the publicly funded candidate. That candidate can allocate the money according to his own campaign strategy, which the privately financed candidate could not do with the independent group expenditures that triggered the matching funds. Cf. *Citizens United* ("'The absence of prearrangement and coordination of an expenditure with the candidate or his agent . . . undermines the value of the expenditure to the candidate'" (quoting *Buckley*).

The burdens that this regime places on independent expenditure groups are akin to those imposed on the privately financed candidates themselves. Just as with the candidate the independent group supports, the more money spent on that candidate's behalf or in opposition to a publicly funded candidate, the more money the publicly funded candidate receives from the State. And just as with the privately financed candidate, the effect of a dollar spent on election speech is a guaranteed financial payout to the publicly funded candidate the group opposes. Moreover, spending one dollar can result in the flow of dollars to multiple candidates the group disapproves of, dollars directly controlled by the publicly funded candidate or candidates.

In some ways, the burden the Arizona law imposes on independent expenditure groups is worse than the burden it imposes on privately financed candidates, and thus substantially worse than the burden we found constitutionally impermissible in *Davis*. If a candidate contemplating an electoral run in Arizona surveys the campaign landscape and decides that the burdens imposed by the matching funds regime make a privately funded campaign unattractive, he at least has the option of taking public financing. Independent expenditure groups, of course, do not.

Once the spending cap is reached, an independent expenditure group that wants to support a particular candidate—because of that candidate's stand on an issue of concern to the group—can only avoid triggering matching funds in one of two ways. The group can either opt to change its message from one addressing the merits of the candidates to one addressing the merits of an issue, or refrain from speaking altogether. Presenting independent expenditure groups with such a choice makes the matching funds provision particularly burdensome to those groups. And forcing that choice—trigger matching funds, change your message, or do not speak—certainly contravenes "the fundamental rule of protection under the First Amendment, that a speaker has the autonomy to choose the content of his own message." *Hurley v. Irish-American Gay, Lesbian and Bisexual Group of Boston, Inc.*, 515 U.S. 557, 573 (1995); cf. *Citizens United* ("the First Amendment stands against attempts to disfavor certain subjects or viewpoints"); *WRTL II* (opinion of ROBERTS, C.J.) (the argument that speakers can avoid the burdens of a law "by changing what they say" does not mean the law complies with the First Amendment).[6]

2

Arizona, the Clean Elections Institute, and the United States offer several arguments attempting to explain away the existence or significance of any burden imposed by matching funds. None is persuasive.

Arizona contends that the matching funds provision is distinguishable from the law we invalidated in *Davis*. The State correctly points out that our decision in *Davis* focused on the asymmetrical contribution limits imposed by the Millionaire's Amendment. But that is not because—as the State asserts—the reach of that opinion is limited to asymmetrical contribution limits. It is because that was the particular burden on candidate speech we faced in *Davis*. And whatever the significance of the distinction in general, there can be no doubt that the burden on speech is significantly greater in this case than in *Davis*: That means that the law here—like the one in *Davis*—must be justified by a compelling state interest.

6. The dissent sees "*chutzpah*" in candidates exercising their right not to participate in the public financing scheme, while objecting that the system violates their First Amendment rights. See *post* (opinion of KAGAN, J.). The charge is unjustified, but, in any event, it certainly cannot be leveled against the independent expenditure groups. The dissent barely mentions such groups in its analysis, and fails to address not only the distinctive burdens imposed on these groups—as set forth above—but also the way in which privately financed candidates are particularly burdened when matching funds are triggered by independent group speech.

The State argues that the matching funds provision actually results in more speech by "increas[ing] debate about issues of public concern" in Arizona elections and "promot[ing] the free and open debate that the First Amendment was intended to foster." In the State's view, this promotion of First Amendment ideals offsets any burden the law might impose on some speakers.

Not so. Any increase in speech resulting from the Arizona law is of one kind and one kind only—that of publicly financed candidates. The burden imposed on privately financed candidates and independent expenditure groups reduces their speech; "restriction[s] on the amount of money a person or group can spend on political communication during a campaign necessarily reduces the quantity of expression." *Buckley.* Thus, even if the matching funds provision did result in more speech by publicly financed candidates and more speech in general, it would do so at the expense of impermissibly burdening (and thus reducing) the speech of privately financed candidates and independent expenditure groups. This sort of "beggar thy neighbor" approach to free speech—"restrict[ing] the speech of some elements of our society in order to enhance the relative voice of others"—is "wholly foreign to the First Amendment."[7]

We have rejected government efforts to increase the speech of some at the expense of others outside the campaign finance context. In *Miami Herald Publishing Co. v. Tornillo,* 418 U.S. 241, 244, 258 (1974), we held unconstitutional a Florida law that required any newspaper assailing a political candidate's character to allow that candidate to print a reply. We have explained that while the statute in that case "purported to advance free discussion, . . . its effect was to deter newspapers from speaking out in the first instance" because it "penalized the newspaper's own expression." *Pacific Gas & Elec. Co. v. Public Util. Comm'n of Cal.,* 475 U.S. 1, 10 (1986) (plurality opinion). Such a penalty, we concluded, could not survive First Amendment scrutiny. The Arizona law imposes a similar penalty: The State grants funds to publicly financed candidates as a direct result of the speech of privately financed candidates and independent expenditure groups. The argument that this sort of burden promotes free and robust discussion is no more persuasive here than it was in *Tornillo.*

Arizona asserts that no "candidate or independent expenditure group is 'obliged personally to express a message he disagrees with'" or "'required by the government to subsidize a message he disagrees with.'" True enough. But that does not mean that the matching funds provision does not burden speech. The direct result of the speech of privately financed candidates and independent expenditure groups is a

7. The dissent also repeatedly argues that the Arizona matching funds regime results in "*more* political speech," (emphasis in original); but—given the logic of the dissent's position—that is only as a step to *less* speech. If the matching funds provision achieves its professed goal and causes candidates to switch to public financing, there will be less speech: no spending above the initial state-set amount by formerly privately financed candidates, and no associated matching funds for anyone. Not only that, the level of speech will depend on the State's judgment of the desirable amount, an amount tethered to available (and often scarce) state resources.

state-provided monetary subsidy to a political rival. That cash subsidy, conferred in response to political speech, penalizes speech to a greater extent and more directly than the Millionaire's Amendment in *Davis*. The fact that this may result in more speech by the other candidates is no more adequate a justification here than it was in *Davis*.

In disagreeing with our conclusion, the dissent relies on cases in which we have upheld government subsidies against First Amendment challenge, and asserts that "[w]e have never, not once, understood a viewpoint-neutral subsidy given to one speaker to constitute a First Amendment burden on another." But none of those cases—not one—involved a subsidy given in direct response to the political speech of another, to allow the recipient to counter that speech. And nothing in the analysis we employed in those cases suggests that the challenged subsidies would have survived First Amendment scrutiny if they were triggered by someone else's political speech.

The State also argues, and the Court of Appeals concluded, that any burden on privately financed candidates and independent expenditure groups is more analogous to the burden placed on speakers by the disclosure and disclaimer requirements we recently upheld in *Citizens United* than to direct restrictions on candidate and independent expenditures. This analogy is not even close. A political candidate's disclosure of his funding resources does not result in a cash windfall to his opponent, or affect their respective disclosure obligations.

The State and the Clean Elections Institute assert that the candidates and independent expenditure groups have failed to "cite specific instances in which they decided not to raise or spend funds," and have "failed to present any reliable evidence that Arizona's triggered matching funds deter their speech." The record in this case, which we must review in its entirety, does not support those assertions. See *Bose Corp. v. Consumers Union of United States, Inc.*, 466 U.S. 485, 499 (1984).

That record contains examples of specific candidates curtailing fundraising efforts, and actively discouraging supportive independent expenditures, to avoid triggering matching funds. The record also includes examples of independent expenditure groups deciding not to speak in opposition to a candidate, or in support of a candidate, to avoid triggering matching funds. In addition, Dr. David Primo, an expert involved in the case, "found that privately financed candidates facing the prospect of triggering matching funds changed the timing of their fundraising activities, the timing of their expenditures, and, thus, their overall campaign strategy."

The State contends that if the matching funds provision truly burdened the speech of privately financed candidates and independent expenditure groups, spending on behalf of privately financed candidates would cluster just below the triggering level, but no such phenomenon has been observed. That should come as no surprise. The hypothesis presupposes a privately funded candidate who would spend his own money just up to the matching funds threshold, when he could have simply taken matching funds in the first place.

Furthermore, the Arizona law takes into account all manner of uncoordinated political activity in awarding matching funds. If a privately funded candidate wanted to hover just below the triggering level, he would have to make guesses about how much he will receive in the form of contributions and supportive independent expenditures. He might well guess wrong.

In addition, some candidates may be willing to bear the burden of spending above the cap. That a candidate is willing to do so does not make the law any less burdensome. See *Davis* (that candidates may choose to make "personal expenditures to support their campaigns" despite the burdens imposed by the Millionaire's Amendment does not change the fact that "they must shoulder a special and potentially significant burden if they make that choice"). If the State made privately funded candidates pay a $500 fine to run as such, the fact that candidates might choose to pay it does not make the fine any less burdensome.

While there is evidence to support the contention of the candidates and independent expenditure groups that the matching funds provision burdens their speech, "it is never easy to prove a negative"—here, that candidates and groups did not speak or limited their speech because of the Arizona law. *Elkins v. United States,* 364 U.S. 206, 218 (1960). In any event, the burden imposed by the matching funds provision is evident and inherent in the choice that confronts privately financed candidates and independent expenditure groups. Cf. *Davis.* Indeed even candidates who sign up for public funding recognize the burden matching funds impose on private speech, stating that they participate in the program because "matching funds ... discourage[ ] opponents, special interest groups, and lobbyists from campaigning against" them. GAO, Campaign Finance Reform: Experiences of Two States that Offered Full Public Funding for Political Candidates 27 (GAO-10-390, 2010). As in *Davis,* we do not need empirical evidence to determine that the law at issue is burdensome. See *Davis* (requiring no evidence of a burden whatsoever).

It is clear not only to us but to every other court to have considered the question after *Davis* that a candidate or independent group might not spend money if the direct result of that spending is additional funding to political adversaries [discussing lower court cases]. The dissent's disagreement is little more than disagreement with *Davis.*

The State correctly asserts that the candidates and independent expenditure groups "do not ... claim that a single lump sum payment to publicly funded candidates," equivalent to the maximum amount of state financing that a candidate can obtain through matching funds, would impermissibly burden their speech. The State reasons that if providing all the money up front would not burden speech, providing it piecemeal does not do so either. And the State further argues that such incremental administration is necessary to ensure that public funding is not under- or over-distributed.

These arguments miss the point. It is not the amount of funding that the State provides to publicly financed candidates that is constitutionally problematic in this case. It is the manner in which that funding is provided—in direct response to the political speech of privately financed candidates and independent expenditure groups. And the fact that the State's matching mechanism may be more efficient than other alternatives—that it may help the State in "finding the sweet-spot" or "fine-tuning" its financing system to avoid a drain on public resources (KAGAN, J., dissenting)—is of no moment; "the First Amendment does not permit the State to sacrifice speech for efficiency." *Riley v. National Federation of Blind of N. C., Inc.*, 487 U.S. 781, 795 (1988).

The United States as *amicus* contends that "[p]roviding additional funds to petitioners' opponents does not make petitioners' own speech any less effective" and thus does not substantially burden speech. Of course it does. One does not have to subscribe to the view that electoral debate is zero sum to see the flaws in the United States' perspective. All else being equal, an advertisement supporting the election of a candidate that goes without a response is often more effective than an advertisement that is directly controverted. And even if the publicly funded candidate decides to use his new money to address a different issue altogether, the end goal of that spending is to claim electoral victory over the opponent that triggered the additional state funding. See *Davis*.

B

Because the Arizona matching funds provision imposes a substantial burden on the speech of privately financed candidates and independent expenditure groups, "that provision cannot stand unless it is 'justified by a compelling state interest,'" *id.*

There is a debate between the parties in this case as to what state interest is served by the matching funds provision. The privately financed candidates and independent expenditure groups contend that the provision works to "level [ ] electoral opportunities" by equalizing candidate "resources and influence." The State and the Clean Elections Institute counter that the provision "furthers Arizona's interest in preventing corruption and the appearance of corruption."

1

There is ample support for the argument that the matching funds provision seeks to "level the playing field" in terms of candidate resources. The clearest evidence is of course the very operation of the provision: It ensures that campaign funding is equal, up to three times the initial public funding allotment. The text of the Citizens Clean Elections Act itself confirms this purpose. The statutory provision setting up the matching funds regime is titled "Equal funding of candidates." The Act refers to the funds doled out after the Act's matching mechanism is triggered as "equalizing funds." And the regulations implementing the matching funds provision refer to those funds as "equalizing funds" as well.

Other features of the Arizona law reinforce this understanding of the matching funds provision. If the Citizens Clean Election Commission cannot provide publicly financed candidates with the moneys that the matching funds provision envisions because of a shortage of funds, the statute allows a publicly financed candidate to "accept private contributions to bring the total monies received by the candidate" up to the matching funds amount. Limiting contributions, of course, is the primary means we have upheld to combat corruption. *Buckley.* Indeed the State argues that one of the principal ways that the matching funds provision combats corruption is by eliminating the possibility of any *quid pro quo* between private interests and publicly funded candidates by eliminating contributions to those candidates altogether. But when confronted with a choice between fighting corruption and equalizing speech, the drafters of the matching funds provision chose the latter. That significantly undermines any notion that the "Equal funding of candidates" provision is meant to serve some interest other than an interest in equalizing funds.[10]

We have repeatedly rejected the argument that the government has a compelling state interest in "leveling the playing field" that can justify undue burdens on political speech. See, *e.g., Citizens United.* In *Davis,* we stated that discriminatory contribution limits meant to "level electoral opportunities for candidates of different personal wealth" did not serve "a legitimate government objective," let alone a compelling one. And in *Buckley,* we held that limits on overall campaign expenditures could not be justified by a purported government "interest in equalizing the financial resources of candidates." After all, equalizing campaign resources "might serve not to equalize the opportunities of all candidates, but to handicap a candidate who lacked substantial name recognition or exposure of his views before the start of the campaign."

"Leveling electoral opportunities means making and implementing judgments about which strengths should be permitted to contribute to the outcome of an election," *Davis*—a dangerous enterprise and one that cannot justify burdening protected speech. The dissent essentially dismisses this concern, but it needs to be taken seriously; we have, as noted, held that it is not legitimate for the government to attempt to equalize electoral opportunities in this manner. And such basic intrusion by the government into the debate over who should govern goes to the heart of First Amendment values.

"Leveling the playing field" can sound like a good thing. But in a democracy, campaigning for office is not a game. It is a critically important form of speech. The First Amendment embodies our choice as a Nation that, when it comes to such speech, the guiding principle is freedom—the "unfettered interchange of ideas"—not whatever the State may view as fair. *Buckley.*

10. Prior to oral argument in this case, the Citizens Clean Elections Commission's Web site stated that "'The Citizens Clean Elections Act was passed by the people of Arizona in 1998 to level the playing field when it comes to running for office.'" The Web site now says that "The Citizens Clean Elections Act was passed by the people of Arizona in 1998 to restore citizen participation and confidence in our political system."

2

As already noted, the State and the Clean Elections Institute disavow any interest in "leveling the playing field." They instead assert that the "Equal funding of candidates" provision, serves the State's compelling interest in combating corruption and the appearance of corruption. See, *e.g., Davis; WRTL II* (opinion of ROBERTS, C. J.). But even if the ultimate objective of the matching funds provision is to combat corruption — and not "level the playing field" — the burdens that the matching funds provision imposes on protected political speech are not justified.

Burdening a candidate's expenditure of his own funds on his own campaign does not further the State's anticorruption interest. Indeed, we have said that "reliance on personal funds *reduces* the threat of corruption" and that "discouraging [the] use of personal funds[] disserves the anticorruption interest." *Davis.* That is because "the use of personal funds reduces the candidate's dependence on outside contributions and thereby counteracts the coercive pressures and attendant risks of abuse" of money in politics. *Buckley.* The matching funds provision counts a candidate's expenditures of his own money on his own campaign as contributions, and to that extent cannot be supported by any anticorruption interest.

We have also held that "independent expenditures . . . do not give rise to corruption or the appearance of corruption." *Citizens United.* "By definition, an independent expenditure is political speech presented to the electorate that is not coordinated with a candidate." The candidate-funding circuit is broken. The separation between candidates and independent expenditure groups negates the possibility that independent expenditures will result in the sort of *quid pro quo* corruption with which our case law is concerned. See *id.* Including independent expenditures in the matching funds provision cannot be supported by any anticorruption interest.

We have observed in the past that "[t]he interest in alleviating the corrupting influence of large contributions is served by . . . contribution limitations." Arizona already has some of the most austere contribution limits in the United States. See *Randall* (plurality opinion). Contributions to statewide candidates are limited to $840 per contributor per election cycle and contributions to legislative candidates are limited to $410 per contributor per election cycle. Arizona also has stringent fundraising disclosure requirements. In the face of such ascetic contribution limits, strict disclosure requirements, and the general availability of public funding, it is hard to imagine what marginal corruption deterrence could be generated by the matching funds provision.

Perhaps recognizing that the burdens the matching funds provision places on speech cannot be justified in and of themselves, either as a means of leveling the playing field or directly fighting corruption, the State and the Clean Elections Institute offer another argument: They contend that the provision indirectly serves the anticorruption interest, by ensuring that enough candidates participate in the State's public funding system, which in turn helps combat corruption.[11] We have said that a voluntary system of "public financing as a means of eliminating the improper influence of large private contributions furthers a significant governmental interest." *Buckley.* But the fact that burdening constitutionally protected speech might indirectly serve the State's anticorruption interest, by encouraging candidates to take public financing, does not establish the constitutionality of the matching funds provision.

We have explained that the matching funds provision substantially burdens the speech of privately financed candidates and independent groups. It does so to an even greater extent than the law we invalidated in *Davis.* We have explained that those burdens cannot be justified by a desire to "level the playing field." We have also explained that much of the speech burdened by the matching funds provision does not, under our precedents, pose a danger of corruption. In light of the foregoing analysis, the fact that the State may feel that the matching funds provision is necessary to allow it to "find[] the sweet-spot" and "fine-tun[e]" its public funding system (KAGAN, J., dissenting), to achieve its desired level of participation without an undue drain on public resources, is not a sufficient justification for the burden.

The flaw in the State's argument is apparent in what its reasoning would allow. By the State's logic it could grant a publicly funded candidate five dollars in matching funds for every dollar his privately financed opponent spent, or force candidates who wish to run on private funds to pay a $10,000 fine in order to encourage participation in the public funding regime. Such measures might well promote participation in public financing, but would clearly suppress or unacceptably alter political speech. How the State chooses to encourage participation in its public funding system matters, and we have never held that a State may burden political speech — to the extent the matching funds provision does — to ensure adequate participation in a public funding system. Here the State's chosen method is unduly burdensome and not sufficiently justified to survive First Amendment scrutiny.

III

We do not today call into question the wisdom of public financing as a means of funding political candidacy. That is not our business. But determining whether laws governing campaign finance violate the First Amendment is very much our business. In carrying out that responsibility over the past 35 years, we have upheld some restrictions on speech and struck down others. See, *e.g., Buckley* (upholding contribution limits and striking down expenditure limits); *Colorado I* (opinion of BREYER, J.) (invalidating ban on independent expenditures for electioneering communication);

11. The State claims that the Citizens Clean Elections Act was passed in response to rampant corruption in Arizona politics — elected officials "literally taking duffle bags full of cash in exchange for sponsoring legislation." That may be. But, as the candidates and independent expenditure groups point out, the corruption that plagued Arizona politics is largely unaddressed by the matching funds regime. Public financing does nothing to prevent politicians from accepting bribes in exchange for their votes.

Colorado II (upholding caps on coordinated party expenditures); *Davis* (invalidating asymmetrical contribution limits triggered by candidate spending).

We have said that governments "may engage in public financing of election campaigns" and that doing so can further "significant governmental interest[s]," such as the state interest in preventing corruption. *Buckley.* But the goal of creating a viable public financing scheme can only be pursued in a manner consistent with the First Amendment. The dissent criticizes the Court for standing in the way of what the people of Arizona want. But the whole point of the First Amendment is to protect speakers against unjustified government restrictions on speech, even when those restrictions reflect the will of the majority. When it comes to protected speech, the speaker is sovereign.

Arizona's program gives money to a candidate in direct response to the campaign speech of an opposing candidate or an independent group. It does this when the opposing candidate has chosen not to accept public financing, and has engaged in political speech above a level set by the State. The professed purpose of the state law is to cause a sufficient number of candidates to sign up for public financing, which subjects them to the various restrictions on speech that go along with that program. This goes too far; Arizona's matching funds provision substantially burdens the speech of privately financed candidates and independent expenditure groups without serving a compelling state interest.

"[T]here is practically universal agreement that a major purpose of" the First Amendment "was to protect the free discussion of governmental affairs," "includ[ing] discussions of candidates." *Buckley.* That agreement "reflects our 'profound national commitment to the principle that debate on public issues should be uninhibited, robust, and wide-open.'" *Ibid.* True when we said it and true today. Laws like Arizona's matching funds provision that inhibit robust and wide-open political debate without sufficient justification cannot stand.

The judgment of the Court of Appeals for the Ninth Circuit is reversed.

It is so ordered.

Justice KAGAN, with whom Justice GINSBURG, Justice BREYER, and Justice SOTOMAYOR join, dissenting.

Imagine two States, each plagued by a corrupt political system. In both States, candidates for public office accept large campaign contributions in exchange for the promise that, after assuming office, they will rank the donors' interests ahead of all others. As a result of these bargains, politicians ignore the public interest, sound public policy languishes, and the citizens lose confidence in their government.

Recognizing the cancerous effect of this corruption, voters of the first State, acting through referendum, enact several campaign finance measures previously approved by this Court. They cap campaign contributions; require disclosure of substantial donations; and create an optional public financing program that gives candidates a fixed public subsidy if they refrain from private fundraising. But these measures do not work. Individuals who "bundle" campaign contributions become indispensable to candidates in need of money. Simple disclosure fails to prevent shady dealing. And candidates choose not to participate in the public financing system because the sums provided do not make them competitive with their privately financed opponents. So the State remains afflicted with corruption.

Voters of the second State, having witnessed this failure, take an ever-so-slightly different tack to cleaning up their political system. They too enact contribution limits and disclosure requirements. But they believe that the greatest hope of eliminating corruption lies in creating an effective public financing program, which will break candidates' dependence on large donors and bundlers. These voters realize, based on the first State's experience, that such a program will not work unless candidates agree to participate in it. And candidates will participate only if they know that they will receive sufficient funding to run competitive races. So the voters enact a program that carefully adjusts the money given to would-be officeholders, through the use of a matching funds mechanism, in order to provide this assurance. The program does not discriminate against any candidate or point of view, and it does not restrict any person's ability to speak. In fact, by providing resources to many candidates, the program creates more speech and thereby broadens public debate. And just as the voters had hoped, the program accomplishes its mission of restoring integrity to the political system. The second State rids itself of corruption.

A person familiar with our country's core values — our devotion to democratic self-governance, as well as to "uninhibited, robust, and wide-open" debate, *New York Times Co. v. Sullivan,* 376 U.S. 254, 270 (1964) — might expect this Court to celebrate, or at least not to interfere with, the second State's success. But today, the majority holds that the second State's system — the system that produces honest government, working on behalf of all the people — clashes with our Constitution. The First Amendment, the majority insists, requires us all to rely on the measures employed in the first State, even when they have failed to break the stranglehold of special interests on elected officials.

I disagree. The First Amendment's core purpose is to foster a healthy, vibrant political system full of robust discussion and debate. Nothing in Arizona's anti-corruption statute, the Arizona Citizens Clean Elections Act, violates this constitutional protection. To the contrary, the Act promotes the values underlying both the First Amendment and our entire Constitution by enhancing the "opportunity for free political discussion to the end that government may be responsive to the will of the people." I therefore respectfully dissent.

I

A

Campaign finance reform over the last century has focused on one key question: how to prevent massive pools of private money from corrupting our political system. If an officeholder owes his election to wealthy contributors, he may act for their benefit alone, rather than on behalf of all the people. As we recognized in *Buckley*, our seminal campaign finance case, large private contributions may result in "political *quid pro quo[s]*," which undermine the integrity of our democracy. And even if these contributions are not converted into corrupt bargains, they still may weaken confidence in our political system because the public perceives "the opportunities for abuse[s]." To prevent both corruption and the appearance of corruption — and so to protect our democratic system of governance — citizens have implemented reforms designed to curb the power of special interests.

Among these measures, public financing of elections has emerged as a potentially potent mechanism to preserve elected officials' independence. President Theodore Roosevelt proposed the reform as early as 1907 in his State of the Union address. "The need for collecting large campaign funds would vanish," he said, if the government "provided an appropriation for the proper and legitimate expenses" of running a campaign, on the condition that a "party receiving campaign funds from the Treasury" would forgo private fundraising. The idea was — and remains — straightforward. Candidates who rely on public, rather than private, moneys are "beholden [to] no person and, if elected, should feel no post-election obligation toward any contributor." *Republican Nat. Comm. v. FEC*, 487 F. Supp. 280, 284 (S.D.N.Y.), aff'd 445 U.S. 955, (1980). By supplanting private cash in elections, public financing eliminates the source of political corruption.

For this reason, public financing systems today dot the national landscape. Almost one-third of the States have adopted some form of public financing, and so too has the Federal Government for presidential elections. See R. Garrett, Congressional Research Service Report for Congress, Public Financing of Congressional Campaigns: Overview and Analysis 2, 32 (2009). The federal program — which offers presidential candidates a fixed public subsidy if they abstain from private fundraising — originated in the campaign finance law that Congress enacted in 1974 on the heels of the Watergate scandal. Congress explained at the time that the "potentia[l] for abuse" inherent in privately funded elections was "all too clear." In Congress's view, public financing represented the "only way . . . [to] eliminate reliance on large private contributions" and its attendant danger of corruption, while still ensuring that a wide range of candidates had access to the ballot.

We declared the presidential public financing system constitutional in *Buckley v. Valeo*. Congress, we stated, had created the program "for the 'general welfare' — to reduce the deleterious influence of large contributions on our political process," as well as to "facilitate communication by candidates with the electorate, and to free candidates from the rigors of fundraising." We reiterated "that public financing as a means of eliminating the improper influence of large private contributions furthers a significant governmental interest." And finally, in rejecting a challenge based on the First Amendment, we held that the program did not "restrict[ ] or censor speech, but rather . . . use[d] public money to facilitate and enlarge public discussion and participation in the electoral process." We declared this result "vital to a self-governing people," and so concluded that the program "further[ed], not abridge[d], pertinent First Amendment values." We thus gave state and municipal governments the green light to adopt public financing systems along the presidential model.

But this model, which distributes a lump-sum grant at the beginning of an election cycle, has a significant weakness: It lacks a mechanism for setting the subsidy at a level that will give candidates sufficient incentive to participate, while also conserving public resources. Public financing can achieve its goals only if a meaningful number of candidates receive the state subsidy, rather than raise private funds. But a public funding program must be voluntary to pass constitutional muster, because of its restrictions on contributions and expenditures. See *Buckley*. And candidates will choose to sign up only if the subsidy provided enables them to run competitive races. If the grant is pegged too low, it puts the participating candidate at a disadvantage: Because he has agreed to spend no more than the amount of the subsidy, he will lack the means to respond if his privately funded opponent spends over that threshold. So when lump-sum grants do not keep up with campaign expenditures, more and more candidates will choose not to participate. But if the subsidy is set too high, it may impose an unsustainable burden on the public fisc. At the least, hefty grants will waste public resources in the many state races where lack of competition makes such funding unnecessary.

The difficulty, then, is in finding the Goldilocks solution — not too large, not too small, but just right. And this in a world of countless variables — where the amount of money needed to run a viable campaign against a privately funded candidate depends on, among other things, the district, the office, and the election cycle. A state may set lump-sum grants district-by-district, based on spending in past elections; but even that approach leaves out many factors — including the resources of the privately funded candidate — that alter the competitiveness of a seat from one election to the next. In short, the dynamic nature of our electoral system makes *ex ante* predictions about campaign expenditures almost impossible. And that creates a chronic problem for lump-sum public financing programs, because inaccurate estimates produce subsidies that either dissuade candidates from participating or waste taxpayer money. And so States have made adjustments to the lump-sum scheme that we approved in *Buckley*, in attempts to more effectively reduce corruption.

B

The people of Arizona had every reason to try to develop effective anti-corruption measures. Before turning to public financing, Arizonans voted by referendum to establish campaign contribution limits. But that effort to abate corruption, standing alone, proved unsuccessful. Five years after the enactment of these limits, the State suffered "the worst public corruption scandal in its history." In that scandal, known as "AzScam," nearly 10% of the State's legislators were caught accepting campaign contributions or bribes in exchange for supporting a piece of legislation. Following that incident, the voters of Arizona decided that further reform was necessary. Acting once again by referendum, they adopted the public funding system at issue here.

The hallmark of Arizona's program is its inventive approach to the challenge that bedevils all public financing schemes: fixing the amount of the subsidy. For each electoral contest, the system calibrates the size of the grant automatically to provide sufficient—but no more than sufficient—funds to induce voluntary participation. In effect, the program's designers found the Goldilocks solution, which produces the "just right" grant to ensure that a participant in the system has the funds needed to run a competitive race.

As the Court explains, Arizona's matching funds arrangement responds to the shortcoming of the lump-sum model by adjusting the public subsidy in each race to reflect the expenditures of a privately financed candidate and the independent groups that support him.... The question here is whether this modest adjustment to the public financing program that we approved in *Buckley* makes the Arizona law unconstitutional. The majority contends that the matching funds provision "substantially burdens protected political speech" and does not "serv[e] a compelling state interest." But the Court is wrong on both counts.

II

Arizona's statute does not impose a "restriction," or "substantia[l] burde[n]" on expression. The law has quite the opposite effect: It subsidizes and so produces *more* political speech. We recognized in *Buckley* that, for this reason, public financing of elections "facilitate[s] and enlarge[s] public discussion," in support of First Amendment values. And what we said then is just as true today. Except in a world gone topsy-turvy, additional campaign speech and electoral competition is not a First Amendment injury.

A

At every turn, the majority tries to convey the impression that Arizona's matching fund statute is of a piece with laws prohibiting electoral speech. The majority invokes the language of "limits," "bar[s]," and "restraints." It equates the law to a "restrictio[n] on the amount of money a person or group can spend on political communication during a campaign. It insists that the statute "restrict[s] the speech of some elements of our society" to enhance the speech of others. And it concludes by reminding us that the point of the First Amendment is to protect "against unjustified government restrictions on speech."

There is just one problem. Arizona's matching funds provision does not restrict, but instead subsidizes, speech. The law "impose[s] no ceiling on [speech] and do[es] not prevent anyone from speaking." *Citizens United*; see *Buckley* (holding that a public financing law does not "abridge, restrict, or censor" expression). The statute does not tell candidates or their supporters how much money they can spend to convey their message, when they can spend it, or what they can spend it on. Rather, the Arizona law, like the public financing statute in *Buckley,* provides funding for political speech, thus "facilitat[ing] communication by candidates with the electorate." *Id.*, at 91. By enabling participating candidates to respond to their opponents' expression, the statute expands public debate, in adherence to "our tradition that more speech, not less, is the governing rule." *Citizens United.*[2]

And under the First Amendment, that makes all the difference. In case after case, year upon year, we have distinguished between speech restrictions and speech subsidies. "'There is a basic difference,'" we have held, "'between direct state interference with [First Amendment] protected activity and state encouragement'" of other expression.... Government subsidies of speech, designed "to stimulate... expression[,] ... [are] consistent with the First Amendment," so long as they do not discriminate on the basis of viewpoint. That is because subsidies, by definition and contra the majority, do not restrict any speech.

No one can claim that Arizona's law discriminates against particular ideas, and so violates the First Amendment's sole limitation on speech subsidies. The State throws open the doors of its public financing program to all candidates who meet minimal eligibility requirements and agree not to raise private funds. Republicans and Democrats, conservatives and liberals may participate; so too, the law applies equally to independent expenditure groups across the political spectrum. Arizona disburses funds based not on a candidate's (or supporter's) ideas, but on the candidate's decision to sign up for public funding. So under our precedent, Arizona's subsidy statute should easily survive First Amendment scrutiny.[3]

This suit, in fact, may merit less attention than any challenge to a speech subsidy ever seen in this Court. In the usual First Amendment subsidy case, a person complains that the government declined to finance his speech, while bankrolling someone else's; we must then decide whether the government differentiated between these speakers on a prohibited basis—because it preferred one speaker's ideas to another's. But the candidates bringing this challenge do not make that claim—because they were never denied a subsidy. Arizona, remember, offers to support any person running for state office. Petitioners here *refused* that assistance. So they are making a novel argument: that Arizona violated *their* First Amendment rights by

2. And the law appears to do that job well. Between 1998 (when the statute was enacted) and 2006, overall candidate expenditures increased between 29% and 67%; overall independent expenditures rose by a whopping 253%; and average candidate expenditures grew by 12% to 40%.

3. The majority claims that none of our subsidy cases involved the funding of "respons[ive]" expression. But the majority does not explain why this distinction, created to fit the facts of this case, should matter so long as the government is not discriminating on the basis of viewpoint. Indeed, the difference the majority highlights should cut in the opposite direction, because facilitating responsive speech fosters "uninhibited, robust, and wide-open" public debate. *New York Times v. Sullivan.* In any event, the majority is wrong to say that we have never approved funding to "allow the recipient to counter" someone else's political speech. That is *exactly* what we approved in *Buckley.* The majority notes that the public financing scheme in *Buckley* lacked the trigger mechanism used in the Arizona law. But again, that is just to describe a difference, not to say why it matters. As I will show, the trigger is constitutionally irrelevant—as we made clear in the very case (*Davis*) on which the majority principally relies.

disbursing funds to *other* speakers even though they could have received (but chose to spurn) the same financial assistance. Some people might call that *chutzpah*.

Indeed, what petitioners demand is essentially a right to quash others' speech through the prohibition of a (universally available) subsidy program. Petitioners are able to convey their ideas without public financing—and they would prefer the field to themselves, so that they can speak free from response. To attain that goal, they ask this Court to prevent Arizona from funding electoral speech—even though that assistance is offered to every state candidate, on the same (entirely unobjectionable) basis. And this Court gladly obliges.

If an ordinary citizen, without the hindrance of a law degree, thought this result an upending of First Amendment values, he would be correct. That Amendment protects no person's, nor any candidate's, "right to be free from vigorous debate." *Pacific Gas & Elec. Co. v. Public Util. Comm'n of Cal.*, 475 U.S. 1, 14, (1986) (plurality opinion). Indeed, the Amendment exists so that this debate can occur—robust, forceful, and contested. It is the theory of the Free Speech Clause that "falsehood and fallacies" are exposed through "discussion," "education," and "more speech." *Whitney v. California*, 274 U.S. 357, 377 (1927) (Brandeis, J., concurring). Or once again from *Citizens United:* "[M]ore speech, not less, is the governing rule." And this is no place more true than in elections, where voters' ability to choose the best representatives depends on debate—on charge and countercharge, call and response. So to invalidate a statute that restricts no one's speech and discriminates against no idea—that only provides more voices, wider discussion, and greater competition in elections—is to undermine, rather than to enforce, the First Amendment.[4]

We said all this in *Buckley*, when we upheld the presidential public financing system—a ruling this Court has never since questioned. The principal challenge to that system came from minor-party candidates not eligible for benefits—surely more compelling plaintiffs than petitioners, who could have received funding but refused it. Yet we rejected that attack in part because we understood the federal program as supporting, rather than interfering with, expression. *Buckley* rejected any idea, along the lines the majority proposes, that a subsidy of electoral speech was in truth a restraint. And more: *Buckley* recognized that public financing of elections *fosters* First Amendment principles....

---

4. The majority argues that more speech will quickly become "less speech," as candidates switch to public funding. But that claim misunderstands how a voluntary public financing system works. Candidates with significant financial resources will likely decline public funds, so that they can spend in excess of the system's expenditure caps. Other candidates accept public financing because they believe it will enhance their communication with voters. So the system continually pushes toward more speech. That is exactly what has happened in Arizona, and the majority offers no counter-examples.

B

The majority has one, and only one, way of separating this case from *Buckley* and our other, many precedents involving speech subsidies. According to the Court, the special problem here lies in Arizona's matching funds mechanism, which the majority claims imposes a "substantia[l] burde[n]" on a privately funded candidate's speech. Sometimes, the majority suggests that this "burden" lies in the way the mechanism "diminish[es] the effectiveness" of the privately funded candidate's expression by enabling his opponent to respond. At other times, the majority indicates that the "burden" resides in the deterrent effect of the mechanism: The privately funded candidate "might not spend money" because doing so will trigger matching funds. Either way, the majority is wrong to see a substantial burden on expression.[5]

Most important, and as just suggested, the very notion that additional speech constitutes a "burden" is odd and unsettling. Here is a simple fact: Arizona imposes nothing remotely resembling a coercive penalty on privately funded candidates. The State does not jail them, fine them, or subject them to any kind of lesser disability. (So the majority's analogies to a fine on speech are inapposite.) The only "burden" in this case comes from the grant of a subsidy to another person, and the opportunity that subsidy allows for responsive speech. But that means the majority cannot get out from under our subsidy precedents. Once again: We have never, not once, understood a viewpoint-neutral subsidy given to one speaker to constitute a First Amendment burden on another. (And that is so even when the subsidy is not open to all, as it is here.) Yet in this case, the majority says that the prospect of more speech — responsive speech, competitive speech, the kind of speech that drives public debate — counts as a constitutional injury. That concept, for all the reasons previously given, is "wholly foreign to the First Amendment." *Buckley.*

But put to one side this most fundamental objection to the majority's argument; even then, has the majority shown that the burden resulting from the Arizona statute is "substantial"? See *Clingman* (holding that stringent judicial review is "appropriate only if the burden is severe"). I will not quarrel with the majority's assertion that responsive speech by one candidate may make another candidate's speech less effective, that, after all, is the whole idea of the First Amendment, and a *benefit* of having more responsive speech. See *Abrams v. United States,* 250 U.S. 616, 630 (1919) (Holmes., J., dissenting) ("[T]he best test of truth is the power of the thought to get itself accepted in the competition of the market"). And I will assume that the operation of this statute may on occasion deter a privately funded candidate from

---

5. The majority's error on this score extends both to candidates and to independent expenditure groups. Contrary to the majority's suggestion, nearly all of my arguments showing that the Clean Elections Act does not impose a substantial burden apply to both sets of speakers (and apply regardless of whether independent or candidate expenditures trigger the matching funds). That is also true of every one of my arguments demonstrating the State's compelling interest in this legislation. But perhaps the best response to the majority's view that the Act inhibits independent expenditure groups lies in an empirical fact already noted: Expenditures by these groups have risen by 253% since Arizona's law was enacted. See n. 2, *supra.*

spending money, and conveying ideas by that means.[6] My guess is that this does not happen often: Most political candidates, I suspect, have enough faith in the power of their ideas to prefer speech on both sides of an issue to speech on neither. But I will take on faith that the matching funds provision may lead one or another privately funded candidate to stop spending at one or another moment in an election. Still, does that effect count as a severe burden on expression? By the measure of our prior decisions—which have upheld campaign reforms with an equal or greater impact on speech—the answer is no.

Number one: *Any* system of public financing, including the lump-sum model upheld in *Buckley*, imposes a similar burden on privately funded candidates. Suppose Arizona were to do what all parties agree it could under *Buckley*—provide a single upfront payment (say, $150,000) to a participating candidate, rather than an initial payment (of $50,000) plus 94% of whatever his privately funded opponent spent, up to a ceiling (the same $150,000). That system would "diminis[h] the effectiveness" of a privately funded candidate's speech at least as much, and in the same way: It would give his opponent, who presumably would not be able to raise that sum on his own, more money to spend. And so too, a lump-sum system may deter speech. A person relying on private resources might well choose not to enter a race at all, because he knows he will face an adequately funded opponent. And even if he decides to run, he likely will choose to speak in different ways—for example, by eschewing dubious, easy-to-answer charges—because his opponent has the ability to respond. Indeed, privately funded candidates may well find the lump-sum system *more* burdensome than Arizona's (assuming the lump is big enough). Pretend you are financing your campaign through private donations. Would you prefer that your opponent receive a guaranteed, upfront payment of $150,000, or that he receive only $50,000, with the *possibility*—a possibility that you mostly get to control—of collecting another $100,000 somewhere down the road? Me too. That's the first reason the burden on speech cannot command a different result in this case than in *Buckley*.

Number two: Our decisions about disclosure and disclaimer requirements show the Court is wrong. Starting in *Buckley* and continuing through last Term, the Court has repeatedly declined to view these requirements as a substantial First Amendment burden, even though they discourage some campaign speech. "It is undoubtedly true," we stated in *Buckley*, that public disclosure obligations "will deter some individuals" from engaging in expressive activity. Yet we had no difficulty upholding

6. I will note, however, that the record evidence of this effect is spotty at best. The majority finds anecdotal evidence supporting its argument on just 6 pages of a 4500-page summary judgment record. That is consistent with the assessment of the District Court Judge who presided over the proceedings in this case: He stated that petitioners had presented only "vague" and "scattered" evidence of the law's deterrent impact. The appellate court discerned even less evidence of any deterrent effect. I understand the majority to essentially concede this point and to say it does not matter. So I will not belabor the issue by detailing the substantial testimony (much more than 6 pages worth) that the matching funds provision has not put a dent in privately funded candidates' spending.

these requirements there. And much more recently, in *Citizens United* and *Doe v. Reed*, we followed that precedent. "'Disclosure requirements may burden the ability to speak," we reasoned, but they "do not prevent anyone from speaking.'" So too here. Like a disclosure rule, the matching funds provision may occasionally deter, but "impose[s] no ceiling" on electoral expression.

The majority breezily dismisses this comparison, labeling the analogy "not even close" because disclosure requirements result in no payment of money to a speaker's opponent. That is indeed the factual distinction: A matching fund provision, we can all agree, is not a disclosure rule. But the majority does not tell us why this difference matters. Nor could it. The majority strikes down the matching funds provision because of its ostensible *effect*—most notably, that it may deter a person from spending money in an election. But this Court has acknowledged time and again that disclosure obligations have the selfsame effect. If that consequence does not trigger the most stringent judicial review in the one case, it should not do so in the other.

Number three: Any burden that the Arizona law imposes does not exceed the burden associated with contribution limits, which we have also repeatedly upheld. Contribution limits, we have stated, "impose *direct quantity restrictions* on political communication and association," *Buckley* (emphasis added), thus "'significant[ly] interfer[ing]'" with First Amendment interests, *Shrink Missouri*. Rather than potentially deterring or "'diminish[ing] the effectiveness'" of expressive activity, these limits stop it cold. Yet we have never subjected these restrictions to the most stringent review. See *Buckley*. I doubt I have to reiterate that the Arizona statute imposes no restraints on any expressive activity. So the majority once again has no reason here to reach a different result.

In this way, our campaign finance cases join our speech subsidy cases in supporting the constitutionality of Arizona's law. Both sets of precedents are in accord that a statute funding electoral speech in the way Arizona's does imposes no First Amendment injury.

C

The majority thinks it has one case on its side—*Davis*— and it pegs everything on that decision. But *Davis* relies on principles that fit securely within our First Amendment law and tradition—most unlike today's opinion....

Under the First Amendment, the similarity between *Davis* and this case matters far less than the differences. Here is the similarity: In both cases, one candidate's campaign expenditure triggered... something. Now here are the differences: In *Davis*, the candidate's expenditure triggered a discriminatory speech restriction, which Congress could not otherwise have imposed consistent with the First Amendment; by contrast, in this case, the candidate's expenditure triggers a nondiscriminatory speech subsidy, which all parties agree Arizona could have provided in the first instance. In First Amendment law, that difference makes a difference—indeed, it makes *all* the difference. As I have indicated before, two great fault lines run through our First Amendment doctrine: one, between speech restrictions and speech subsidies, and the other, between discriminatory and neutral government action. The Millionaire's Amendment fell on the disfavored side of both divides: To reiterate, it imposed a discriminatory speech restriction. The Arizona Clean Elections Act lands on the opposite side of both: It grants a non-discriminatory speech subsidy. So to say that *Davis* "largely controls" this case is to decline to take our First Amendment doctrine seriously....

III

For all these reasons, the Court errs in holding that the government action in this case substantially burdens speech and so requires the State to offer a compelling interest. But in any event, Arizona has come forward with just such an interest, explaining that the Clean Elections Act attacks corruption and the appearance of corruption in the State's political system. The majority's denigration of this interest — the suggestion that it either is not real or does not matter — wrongly prevents Arizona from protecting the strength and integrity of its democracy.

A

Our campaign finance precedents leave no doubt: Preventing corruption or the appearance of corruption is a compelling government interest. See, *e.g., Davis; NCPAC.* And so too, these precedents are clear: Public financing of elections serves this interest. As *Buckley* recognized, and as I earlier described, public financing "reduce[s] the deleterious influence of large contributions on our political process." When private contributions fuel the political system, candidates may make corrupt bargains to gain the money needed to win election. See *NCPAC.* And voters, seeing the dependence of candidates on large contributors (or on bundlers of smaller contributions), may lose faith that their representatives will serve the public's interest. See *Shrink Missouri.* (the "assumption that large donors call the tune [may] jeopardize the willingness of voters to take part in democratic governance"). Public financing addresses these dangers by minimizing the importance of private donors in elections. Even the majority appears to agree with this premise.

This compelling interest appears on the very face of Arizona's public financing statute....[11]

---

11. The majority briefly suggests that the State's "austere contribution limits" lessen the need for public financing, but provides no support for that dubious claim. As Arizona and other jurisdictions have discovered, contribution limits may not eliminate the risk of corrupt dealing between candidates and donors, especially given the widespread practice of bundling small contributions into large packages. For much this reason, *Buckley* upheld *both* limits on contributions to federal candidates *and* public financing of presidential campaigns. Arizona, like Congress, was "surely entitled to conclude" that contribution limits were only a "partial measure," and that a functional public financing system was also necessary to eliminate political corruption. In stating otherwise, the Court substitutes its judgment for that of Arizona's voters, contrary to our practice of declining to "second-guess a ... determination as to the need for prophylactic measures where corruption is the evil feared." *NRWC.*

And that interest justifies the matching funds provision at issue because it is a critical facet of Arizona's public financing program. The provision is no more than a disbursement mechanism; but it is also the thing that makes the whole Clean Elections Act work. As described earlier, public financing has an Achilles heel—the difficulty of setting the subsidy at the right amount. Too small, and the grant will not attract candidates to the program; and with no participating candidates, the program can hardly decrease corruption. Too large, and the system becomes unsustainable, or at the least an unnecessary drain on public resources. But finding the sweet-spot is near impossible because of variation, across districts and over time, in the political system. Enter the matching funds provision, which takes an ordinary lump-sum amount, divides it into thirds, and disburses the last two of these (to the extent necessary) via a self-calibrating mechanism. That provision is just a fine-tuning of the lump-sum program approved in *Buckley*—a fine-tuning, it bears repeating, that prevents no one from speaking and discriminates against no message. But that fine-tuning can make the difference between a wholly ineffectual program and one that removes corruption from the political system.[12] If public financing furthers a compelling interest—and according to this Court, it does—then so too does the disbursement formula that Arizona uses to make public financing effective. The one conclusion follows directly from the other.

Except in this Court, where the inescapable logic of the State's position is . . . virtually ignored. The Court, to be sure, repeatedly asserts that the State's interest in preventing corruption does not "sufficiently justif[y]" the mechanism it has chosen to disburse public moneys. Only one thing is missing from the Court's response: any reasoning to support this conclusion. Nowhere does the majority dispute the State's view that the success of its public financing system depends on the matching funds mechanism; and nowhere does the majority contest that, if this mechanism indeed spells the difference between success and failure, the State's interest in preventing corruption justifies its use. And so the majority dismisses, but does not actually answer the State's contention—even though that contention is the linchpin of the entire case. Assuming (against reason and precedent) that the matching funds provision substantially burdens speech, the question becomes whether the State has offered a sufficient justification for imposing that burden. Arizona has made a forceful argument on this score, based on the need to establish an effective public financing system. The majority does not even engage that reasoning.

12. For this reason, the majority is quite wrong to say that the State's interest in combating corruption does not support the matching fund provisions application to a candidate's expenditure of his own money or to an independent expenditure. The point is not that these expenditures themselves corrupt the political process. Rather, Arizona includes these, as well as all other, expenditures in the program to ensure that participating candidates receive the funds necessary to run competitive races—and so to attract those candidates in the first instance. That is in direct service of the State's anti-corruption interest.

B

The majority instead devotes most of its energy to trying to show that "level[ing] the playing field," not fighting corruption, was the State's real goal. But the majority's distaste for "leveling" provides no excuse for striking down Arizona's law.

1

For starters, the Court has no basis to question the sincerity of the State's interest in rooting out political corruption. As I have just explained, that is the interest the State has asserted in this Court; it is the interest predominantly expressed in the "findings and declarations" section of the statute; and it is the interest universally understood (stretching back to Teddy Roosevelt's time) to support public financing of elections. As against all this, the majority claims to have found three smoking guns that reveal the State's true (and nefarious) intention to level the playing field. But the only smoke here is the majority's, and it is the kind that goes with mirrors.

The majority first observes that the matching funds provision is titled "'Equal funding of candidates'" and that it refers to matching grants as "'equalizing funds.'" Well, yes. The statute provides for matching funds (above and below certain thresholds); a synonym for "match" is "equal"; and so the statute uses that term. In sum, the statute describes what the statute does. But the relevant question here (according to the majority's own analysis) is *why* the statute does that thing—otherwise said, what interest the statute serves. The State explains that its goal is to prevent corruption, and nothing in the Act's descriptive terms suggests any other objective.

Next, the majority notes that the Act allows participating candidates to accept private contributions if (but only if) the State cannot provide the funds it has promised (for example, because of a budget crisis). That provision, the majority argues, shows that when push comes to shove, the State cares more about "leveling" than about fighting corruption. But this is a plain misreading of the law. All the statute does is assure participating candidates that they will not be left in the lurch if public funds suddenly become unavailable. That guarantee helps persuade candidates to enter the program by removing the risk of a state default. And so the provision directly advances the Act's goal of combating corruption.

Finally, the Court remarks in a footnote that the Clean Elections Commission's website once stated that the "'Act was passed by the people of Arizona . . . to level the playing field.'" I can understand why the majority does not place much emphasis on this point. Some members of the majority have ridiculed the practice of relying on subsequent statements by legislators to demonstrate an earlier Congress's intent in enacting a statute. See, *e.g., Sullivan v. Finkelstein,* 496 U.S. 617, 631–632 (1990) (SCALIA, J., concurring in part); *United States v. Hayes,* 555 U.S. 415, 434–435 (2009) (ROBERTS, C. J., dissenting). Yet here the majority makes a much stranger claim: that a statement appearing on a government website in 2011 (written by who-knows-whom?) reveals what hundreds of thousands of Arizona's voters sought to do in 1998 when they enacted the Clean Elections Act by referendum. Just to state that proposition is to know it is wrong.

So the majority has no evidence — zero, none — that the objective of the Act is anything other than the interest that the State asserts, the Act proclaims, and the history of public financing supports: fighting corruption.

2

But suppose the majority had come up with some evidence showing that Arizona had sought to "equalize electoral opportunities." Would that discovery matter? Our precedent says no, so long as Arizona had a compelling interest in eliminating political corruption (which it clearly did). In these circumstances, any interest of the State in "leveling" should be irrelevant. That interest could not support Arizona's law (assuming the law burdened speech), but neither would the interest invalidate the legislation.

To see the point, consider how the matter might arise. Assume a State has two reasons to pass a statute affecting speech. It wants to reduce corruption. But in addition, it wishes to "level the playing field." Under our First Amendment law, the interest in preventing corruption is compelling and may justify restraints on speech. But the interest in "leveling the playing field," according to well-established precedent, cannot support such legislation. So would this statute (assuming it met all other constitutional standards) violate the First Amendment?

The answer must be no. This Court, after all, has never said that a law restricting speech (or any other constitutional right) demands two compelling interests. One is enough. And this statute has one: preventing corruption. So it does not matter that equalizing campaign speech is an insufficient interest. The statute could violate the First Amendment only if "equalizing" qualified as a forbidden motive — a motive that itself could annul an otherwise constitutional law. But we have never held that to be so. And that should not be surprising: It is a "fundamental principle of constitutional adjudication," from which we have deviated only in exceptional cases, "that this Court will not strike down an otherwise constitutional statute on the basis of an alleged illicit legislative motive." *United States v. O'Brien*, 391 U.S. 367, 383 (1968); see *id.*, at 384 (declining to invalidate a statute when "Congress had the undoubted power to enact" it without the suspect motive); accord, *Turner Broadcasting System, Inc. v. FCC*, 512 U.S. 622, 652 (1994); *Renton v. Playtime Theatres, Inc.*, 475 U.S. 41, 47–48 (1986). When a law is otherwise constitutional — when it either does not restrict speech or rests on an interest sufficient to justify any such restriction — that is the end of the story.

That proposition disposes of this case, even if Arizona had an adjunct interest here in equalizing electoral opportunities. No special rule of automatic invalidation applies to statutes having some connection to equality; like any other laws, they pass muster when supported by an important enough government interest. Here, Arizona has demonstrated in detail how the matching funds provision is necessary to serve a compelling interest in combating corruption. So the hunt for evidence of "leveling" is a waste of time; Arizona's law survives constitutional scrutiny no matter what that search would uncover.

IV

This case arose because Arizonans wanted their government to work on behalf of all the State's people. On the heels of a political scandal involving the near-routine purchase of legislators' votes, Arizonans passed a law designed to sever political candidates' dependence on large contributors. They wished, as many of their fellow Americans wish, to stop corrupt dealing—to ensure that their representatives serve the public, and not just the wealthy donors who helped put them in office. The legislation that Arizona's voters enacted was the product of deep thought and care. It put into effect a public financing system that attracted large numbers of candidates at a sustainable cost to the State's taxpayers. The system discriminated against no ideas and prevented no speech. Indeed, by increasing electoral competition and enabling a wide range of candidates to express their views, the system "further[ed] . . . First Amendment values." *Buckley.* Less corruption, more speech. Robust campaigns leading to the election of representatives not beholden to the few, but accountable to the many. The people of Arizona might have expected a decent respect for those objectives.

Today, they do not get it. The Court invalidates Arizonans' efforts to ensure that in their State, "'[t]he people . . . possess the absolute sovereignty.'" *Buckley* (quoting James Madison in 4 Elliot's Debates on the Federal Constitution 569–570 (1876)). No precedent compels the Court to take this step; to the contrary, today's decision is in tension with broad swaths of our First Amendment doctrine. No fundamental principle of our Constitution backs the Court's ruling; to the contrary, it is the law struck down today that fostered both the vigorous competition of ideas and its ultimate object—a government responsive to the will of the people. Arizonans deserve better. Like citizens across this country, Arizonans deserve a government that represents and serves them all. And no less, Arizonans deserve the chance to reform their electoral system so as to attain that most American of goals.

Truly, democracy is not a game. I respectfully dissent.

Notes and Questions

1. *Level of Scrutiny.* The Court applies strict scrutiny to the trigger provision of Arizona's law. It was an odd application, given when the burden here was that more money would be provided to pay for someone else's speech. Does strict scrutiny now apply to all public financing laws? If not, when does strict scrutiny apply to a public financing law? Some opponents of campaign finance laws read portions of *Citizens United* as calling into question whether strict scrutiny should now apply to review of campaign contribution limits. Does the *Arizona Free Enterprise* majority's recognition of the lower standard of review applicable to campaign contribution limit laws have the force of precedent as lower courts review challenges to campaign contribution limit laws?

2. After the Court's decision removing the matching funds provision, private funding of campaigns did not go up relative to other states, suggesting the matching funds were not chilling speech. Conor M. Dowling, Ryan D. Enos, Anthony Fowler & Costas Panagopoulos, *Does Public Financing Chill Political Speech?* 11 Election

Law Journal 302 (2012). The authors also found that non-participating candidates did not act strategically when the law was in place to avoid triggering the provisions. What does this tell us about the Supreme Court's ability to predict the empirical consequences of election laws?

3. *Matching Funds for Small Contributions.* Under New York City's public financing law, candidates who agree to take public financing and stick with a spending limit get an 8-to-1 match on contributions from city residents, for contributions up to $175 of $250 (depending on the office). For an analysis of the early years of the program, see Michael J. Malbin, Peter W. Briscoe & Brendan Glavin, *Small Donors, Big Democracy: New York City's Matching Funds as a Model for the Nation and States*, 11 Election Law Journal 3 (2012).

Is such a system constitutional under *Arizona Free Enterprise*? The New York City Campaign Finance Board Web site says this about "how democracy benefits" from its program: "The Program maximizes the voices of ordinary voters, amplifying small contributions and helping ensure politicians are accountable to the people they serve, not to big-money special interest contributors." https://perma.cc/39CV-257T (last visited June 2021, "How Democracy Benefits" tab). Is that statement constitutionally relevant? If so, how does it cut? If you were helping to secure the constitutionality of a multiple-match-for-small-contributions public financing plan, what interests would you put forward on your website in defending the law against a First Amendment challenge? For an argument that matching funds present the only hope for viable public financing schemes (short of a reversal of constitutional precedent by the Supreme Court), see James Sample, *The Last Rites of Public Campaign Financing?*, 92 Nebraska Law Review 349 (2013).

4. *Justice Kagan's Dissent.* This was Justice Kagan's first vote (and opinion) in a campaign finance case. Before she was confirmed by the Senate, there were some questions about how she would vote in these cases, given some of her academic writings on the First Amendment. If Justice Kagan had been on the Court during *Citizens United*, and not the Solicitor General defending federal law on behalf of the United States, how would she have voted? On the merits, isn't she right that if Arizona had a valid anticorruption interest in its law, it is irrelevant whether it *also* had an equality interest?

5. *A Constitutional and Effective Campaign Finance System?* After *Arizona Free Enterprise*, how would you design a campaign finance system that would satisfy the Supreme Court and induce participation from those candidates who fear large independent expenditure campaigns against them?

6. *A Partisan Dimension to the Case?* All five Justices appointed by Republican Presidents voted to strike down this law, and more generally express broad skepticism for the constitutionality and wisdom of campaign finance laws. All four Justices appointed by Democratic Presidents voted to uphold this law, and more generally express support for the constitutionality and wisdom of campaign finance laws. Coincidence? Ideology? Party?

7. *Debates.* Some jurisdictions condition receipt of public funding upon candidates' agreement to debate their opponents. New Jersey's election commission proposed that publicly funded gubernatorial candidates participate in three debates. Is such a condition constitutional under *Arizona Free Enterprise*?

8. After *Arizona Free Enterprise*, a federal district court rejected a challenge to aspects of Vermont's voluntary public financing law. Plaintiffs argued, among other things, that the law interfered with the right of political parties to campaign with their preferred candidates. *Corren v. Sorrell,* 167 F. Supp. 3d. 647 (D. Vt. 2016). While rejecting that argument, the court left the door open to reconsidering the constitutional question if the law as implemented chilled protected political activity: "Briefly stated, the Court finds no constitutional infirmity with the Vermont statute so long as it is construed as allowing supporters to associate and communicate with publicly-funded candidates consistent with the intent of the Vermont Legislature. If the state courts construe the law in a way that significantly restricts those communications, Plaintiffs may re-file their objections so that this Court can revisit the constitutionality of the entire public financing scheme." The Second Circuit unanimously affirmed. *Corren v. Condos*, 898 F.3d 209 (2d Cir. 2018).

Chapter 16

Disclosure

I. The Government Interests in Disclosure Versus the Right to Anonymity

We turn now to campaign finance disclosure. Those who favor broad campaign finance regulation champion disclosure as well. Many opponents of contribution and expenditure limits also favor disclosure, seeing it as a more narrowly tailored solution to the problem of money in politics. Larry J. Sabato & Glenn R. Simpson, Dirty Little Secrets 330–36 (1996); Kathleen M. Sullivan, *Political Money and Freedom of Speech*, 30 U.C. Davis Law Review 663, 668–69 (1997); *Nixon v. Shrink Missouri Government PAC*, 528 U.S. 377, 430 (2000) (Thomas J., dissenting) ("States are free to enact laws that directly punish those engaged in corruption and require the disclosure of large contributions, but they are not free to enact generalized laws that suppress a tremendous amount of protected speech along with the targeted corruption."). At least this was the view until recently. With many limits gone after the *Citizens United* revolution, some who proposed disclosure as a more narrowly tailored solution to concerns about corruption have come to regard disclosure itself as threatening protected First Amendment rights.

As we shall see, the Supreme Court in *Buckley v. Valeo* recognized three government interests in disclosure:

(1) *Disclosure deters corruption* (the "anti-corruption" interest). Disclosure allows interested parties to look for connections between campaign contributors or spenders and the candidates who benefit from those contributions or spending.

(2) *Disclosure provides information helpful to voters* (the "information" interest). Chapter 2 demonstrated that voters often are rationally ignorant regarding details about the candidates or issues on the ballot. Disclosure provides information helpful to voters. For example, a voter knowing that the insurance industry or the Sierra Club backs a particular ballot measure may use that information as a proxy for whether the measure is in the voter's interest.

(3) *Disclosure aids in the enforcement of other campaign finance laws* (the "enforcement" interest). For example, without disclosure, contributors could evade contribution laws more easily.

Disclosure, however, has drawbacks that implicate the First Amendment. Consider the case of the Ohio Socialist Workers Party. The FBI harassed leaders and members of the party. For example, the FBI visited potential landlords of SWP members and suggested that the landlords not rent to them. Party leaders also were victims of violence. See *Brown v. Socialist Workers '74 Campaign Committee*, 459 U.S. 87 (1982). Those individuals who otherwise might contribute to the SWP could be deterred by disclosure of their identities. Should the state be allowed to compel SWP contributors to disclose their identities? More broadly, is there a constitutional right to engage in anonymous political speech? Recall that many famous political documents at the time of the American Revolution were penned anonymously. Should that history be relevant? See Justice Scalia's dissenting opinion in the *McIntyre* case below.

The Supreme Court first addressed this conflict between the state's three interests in disclosure of campaign finance information and First Amendment claims of a right to anonymity in a portion of *Buckley v. Valeo* reprinted below. *Buckley* upheld the disclosure provisions of the FECA. The Court has revisited the disclosure issue in subsequent cases, most importantly in the *McIntyre* case reprinted immediately after the *Buckley* excerpt. *McIntyre* struck down an Ohio law preventing a lone pamphleteer from distributing anonymously a pamphlet advocating the defeat of a local ballot proposition. As you read the two cases together, consider which factor or factors led the Court to different results in the two cases. In Part II of this Chapter, we will consider whether the Court's long support for the constitutionality of campaign finance disclosure laws is under threat.

Buckley v. Valeo

424 U.S. 1, 60–84 (1976)

PER CURIAM . . .

II. Reporting and Disclosure Requirements

Unlike the limitations on contributions and expenditures imposed by 18 U.S.C. § 608,[a] the disclosure requirements of the Act, 2 U.S.C. § 431 *et seq.* [now codified at 52 U.S.C. § 30101 *et seq.*] are not challenged by appellants as *per se* unconstitutional restrictions on the exercise of First Amendment freedoms of speech and association. Indeed, appellants argue that "narrowly drawn disclosure requirements are the proper solution to virtually all of the evils Congress sought to remedy." The particular requirements embodied in the Act are attacked as overbroad—both in their application to minor-party and independent candidates and in their extension to contributions as small as $11 or $101. Appellants also challenge the provision for disclosure by those who make independent contributions and expenditures, § 434(e) [now 52 U.S.C. § 30104(e)]. The Court of Appeals found no constitutional infirmities

a. Chapter 12 reprints the portion of *Buckley* reviewing the constitutionality of contribution and expenditure limits.—Eds.

in the provisions challenged here. We affirm the determination on overbreadth and hold that § 434(e), if narrowly construed, also is within constitutional bounds.

[The Court described earlier federal disclosure requirements, dating back to 1910. These had contained various loopholes and were "widely circumvented."]

The Act presently under review replaced all prior disclosure laws. Its primary disclosure provisions impose reporting obligations on "political committees" and candidates. "Political committee" is defined ... as a group of persons that receives "contributions" or makes "expenditures" of over $1,000 in a calendar year. "Contributions" and "expenditures" are defined in lengthy parallel provisions similar to those in Title 18, discussed above. Both definitions focus on the use of money or other objects of value "for the purpose of . . . influencing" the nomination or election of any person to federal office.

Each political committee is required to register with the Commission and to keep detailed records of both contributions and expenditures. These records must include the name and address of everyone making a contribution in excess of $10, along with the date and amount of the contribution. If a person's contributions aggregate more than $100, his occupation and principal place of business are also to be included. These files are subject to periodic audits and field investigations by the Commission.

Each committee and each candidate also is required to file quarterly reports. The reports are to contain detailed financial information, including the full name, mailing address, occupation, and principal place of business of each person who has contributed over $100 in a calendar year, as well as the amount and date of the contributions. They are to be made available by the Commission "for public inspection and copying." Every candidate for federal office is required to designate a "principal campaign committee," which is to receive reports of contributions and expenditures made on the candidate's behalf from other political committees and to compile and file these reports, together with its own statements, with the Commission.

Every individual or group, other than a political committee or candidate, who makes "contributions" or "expenditures" of over $100 in a calendar year "other than by contribution to a political committee or candidate" is required to file a statement with the Commission. Any violation of these record-keeping and reporting provisions is punishable by a fine of not more than $1,000 or a prison term of not more than a year, or both.

A. General Principles

Unlike the overall limitations on contributions and expenditures, the disclosure requirements impose no ceiling on campaign-related activities. But we have repeatedly found that compelled disclosure, in itself, can seriously infringe on privacy of association and belief guaranteed by the First Amendment. *E.g., Gibson v. Florida Legislative Comm.*, 372 U.S. 539 (1963); *NAACP v. Button*, 371 U.S. 415 (1963); *Shelton v. Tucker*, 364 U.S. 479 (1960); *Bates v. Little Rock*, 361 U.S. 516 (1960); *NAACP v. Alabama*, 357 U.S. 449 (1958).

We long have recognized that significant encroachments on First Amendment rights of the sort that compelled disclosure imposes cannot be justified by a mere showing of some legitimate governmental interest. Since *NAACP v. Alabama* we have required that the subordinating interests of the State must survive exacting scrutiny. We also have insisted that there be a "relevant correlation" or "substantial relation" between the governmental interest and the information required to be disclosed. This type of scrutiny is necessary even if any deterrent effect on the exercise of First Amendment rights arises, not through direct government action, but indirectly as an unintended but inevitable result of the government's conduct in requiring disclosure.

Appellees argue that the disclosure requirements of the Act differ significantly from those at issue in *NAACP v. Alabama* and its progeny because the Act only requires disclosure of the names of contributors and does not compel political organizations to submit the names of their members.

[T]he invasion of privacy of belief may be as great when the information sought concerns the giving and spending of money as when it concerns the joining of organizations, for "[f]inancial transactions can reveal much about a person's activities, associations, and beliefs." *California Bankers Assn v. Shultz*, 416 U.S. 21, 78–79 (1974) (POWELL, J., concurring). Our past decisions have not drawn fine lines between contributors and members but have treated them interchangeably. In *Bates*, for example, we applied the principles of *NAACP v. Alabama* and reversed convictions for failure to comply with a city ordinance that required the disclosure of "dues, assessments, and contributions paid, by whom and when paid."

The strict test established by *NAACP v. Alabama* is necessary because compelled disclosure has the potential for substantially infringing the exercise of First Amendment rights. But we have acknowledged that there are governmental interests sufficiently important to outweigh the possibility of infringement, particularly when the "free functioning of our national institutions" is involved. *Communist Party v. Subversive Activities Control Bd.*, 367 U.S. 1, 97 (1961).

The governmental interests sought to be vindicated by the disclosure requirements are of this magnitude. They fall into three categories. First, disclosure provides the electorate with information "as to where political campaign money comes from and how it is spent by the candidate" in order to aid the voters in evaluating those who seek federal office. It allows voters to place each candidate in the political spectrum more precisely than is often possible solely on the basis of party labels and campaign speeches. The sources of a candidate's financial support also alert the voter to the interests to which a candidate is most likely to be responsive and thus facilitate predictions of future performance in office.

Second, disclosure requirements deter actual corruption and avoid the appearance of corruption by exposing large contributions and expenditures to the light of publicity. This exposure may discourage those who would use money for improper purposes either before or after the election. A public armed with information about a candidate's most generous supporters is better able to detect any post-election special favors that may be given in return. And, as we recognized in *Burroughs v. United States*, 290 U.S. 534 (1934), Congress could reasonably conclude that full disclosure during an election campaign tends "to prevent the corrupt use of money to affect elections." In enacting these requirements it may have been mindful of Mr. Justice Brandeis' advice:

> Publicity is justly commended as a remedy for social and industrial diseases. Sunlight is said to be the best of disinfectants; electric light the most efficient policeman.[80]

Third, and not least significant, recordkeeping, reporting, and disclosure requirements are an essential means of gathering the data necessary to detect violations of the contribution limitations described above.

The disclosure requirements, as a general matter, directly serve substantial governmental interests. In determining whether these interests are sufficient to justify the requirements we must look to the extent of the burden that they place on individual rights.

It is undoubtedly true that public disclosure of contributions to candidates and political parties will deter some individuals who otherwise might contribute. In some instances, disclosure may even expose contributors to harassment or retaliation. These are not insignificant burdens on individual rights, and they must be weighed carefully against the interests which Congress has sought to promote by this legislation. In this process, we note and agree with appellants' concession that disclosure requirements — certainly in most applications — appear to be the least restrictive means of curbing the evils of campaign ignorance and corruption that Congress found to exist.[82] Appellants argue, however, that the balance tips against disclosure when it is required of contributors to certain parties and candidates. We turn now to this contention.

B. Application to Minor Parties and Independents

Appellants contend that the Act's requirements are overbroad insofar as they apply to contributions to minor parties and independent candidates because the governmental interest in this information is minimal and the danger of significant infringement on First Amendment rights is greatly increased.

1. Requisite Factual Showing

In *NAACP v. Alabama* the organization had "made an uncontroverted showing that on past occasions revelation of the identity of its rank-and-file members [had]

---

80. L. Brandeis, Other People's Money 62 (National Home Library Foundation ed. 1933).

82. Post-election disclosure by successful candidates is suggested as a less restrictive way of preventing corrupt pressures on officeholders. Delayed disclosure of this sort would not serve the equally important informational function played by pre-election reporting. Moreover, the public interest in sources of campaign funds is likely to be at its peak during the campaign period; that is the time when improper influences are most likely to be brought to light.

exposed these members to economic reprisal, loss of employment, threat of physical coercion, and other manifestations of public hostility," and the State was unable to show that the disclosure it sought had a "substantial bearing" on the issues it sought to clarify. Under those circumstances, the Court held that "whatever interest the State may have in [disclosure] has not been shown to be sufficient to overcome petitioner's constitutional objections."

The Court of Appeals rejected appellants' suggestion that this case fits into the *NAACP v. Alabama* mold. It concluded that substantial governmental interests in "informing the electorate and preventing the corruption of the political process" were furthered by requiring disclosure of minor parties and independent candidates, and therefore found no "tenable rationale for assuming that the public interest in minority party disclosure of contributions above a reasonable cutoff point is uniformly outweighed by potential contributors' associational rights." The court left open the question of the application of the disclosure requirements to candidates (and parties) who could demonstrate injury of the sort at stake in *NAACP v. Alabama.* No record of harassment on a similar scale was found in this case. We agree with the Court of Appeals' conclusion that *NAACP v. Alabama* is inapposite where, as here, any serious infringement on First Amendment rights brought about by the compelled disclosure of contributors is highly speculative.

It is true that the governmental interest in disclosure is diminished when the contribution in question is made to a minor party with little chance of winning an election. As minor parties usually represent definite and publicized viewpoints, there may be less need to inform the voters of the interests that specific candidates represent. Major parties encompass candidates of greater diversity. In many situations the label "Republican" or "Democrat" tells a voter little. The candidate who bears it may be supported by funds from the far right, the far left, or any place in between on the political spectrum. It is less likely that a candidate of, say, the Socialist Labor Party will represent interests that cannot be discerned from the party's ideological position.

The Government's interest in deterring the "buying" of elections and the undue influence of large contributors on officeholders also may be reduced where contributions to a minor party or an independent candidate are concerned, for it is less likely that the candidate will be victorious. But a minor party sometimes can play a significant role in an election. Even when a minor-party candidate has little or no chance of winning, he may be encouraged by major-party interests in order to divert votes from other major-party contenders.

We are not unmindful that the damage done by disclosure to the associational interests of the minor parties and their members and to supporters of independents could be significant. These movements are less likely to have a sound financial base and thus are more vulnerable to falloffs in contributions. In some instances fears of reprisal may deter contributions to the point where the movement cannot survive. The public interest also suffers if that result comes to pass, for there is a consequent reduction in the free circulation of ideas both within and without the political arena.

There could well be a case, similar to those before the Court in *NAACP v. Alabama* and *Bates*, where the threat to the exercise of First Amendment rights is so serious and the state interest furthered by disclosure so insubstantial that the Act's requirements cannot be constitutionally applied. But no appellant in this case has tendered record evidence of the sort proffered in *NAACP v. Alabama*. Instead, appellants primarily rely on "the clearly articulated fears of individuals, well experienced in the political process." At best they offer the testimony of several minor-party officials that one or two persons refused to make contributions because of the possibility of disclosure. On this record, the substantial public interest in disclosure identified by the legislative history of this Act outweighs the harm generally alleged.

2. Blanket Exemption

Appellants agree that "the record here does not reflect the kind of focused and insistent harassment of contributors and members that existed in the NAACP cases." They argue, however, that a blanket exemption for minor parties is necessary lest irreparable injury be done before the required evidence can be gathered. . . .

We recognize that unduly strict requirements of proof could impose a heavy burden, but it does not follow that a blanket exemption for minor parties is necessary. Minor parties must be allowed sufficient flexibility in the proof of injury to assure a fair consideration of their claim. The evidence offered need show only a reasonable probability that the compelled disclosure of a party's contributors' names will subject them to threats, harassment, or reprisals from either Government officials or private parties. The proof may include, for example, specific evidence of past or present harassment of members due to their associational ties, or of harassment directed against the organization itself. A pattern of threats or specific manifestations of public hostility may be sufficient. New parties that have no history upon which to draw may be able to offer evidence of reprisals and threats directed against individuals or organizations holding similar views.

Where it exists the type of chill and harassment identified in *NAACP v. Alabama* can be shown. We cannot assume that courts will be insensitive to similar showings when made in future cases. We therefore conclude that a blanket exemption is not required.

C. Section 434(e)

Section 434(e) requires "[e]very person (other than a political committee or candidate) who makes contributions or expenditures" aggregating over $100 in a calendar year "other than by contribution to a political committee or candidate" to file a statement with the Commission. Unlike the other disclosure provisions, this section does not seek the contribution list of any association. Instead, it requires direct disclosure of what an individual or group contributes or spends.

In considering this provision we must apply the same strict standard of scrutiny. . . .

Appellants attack § 434(e) as a direct intrusion on privacy of belief, in violation of *Talley v. California*, 362 U.S. 60 (1960), and as imposing "very real, practical burdens . . . certain to deter individuals from making expenditures for their independent political speech" analogous to those held to be impermissible in *Thomas v. Collins*, 323 U.S. 516 (1945).

1. The Role of § 434(e)

. . . Section 434(e) is part of Congress' effort to achieve "total disclosure" by reaching "every kind of political activity"[92] in order to insure that the voters are fully informed and to achieve through publicity the maximum deterrence to corruption and undue influence possible. The provision is responsive to the legitimate fear that efforts would be made, as they had been in the past, to avoid the disclosure requirements by routing financial support of candidates through avenues not explicitly covered by the general provisions of the Act.

2. Vagueness Problems

In its effort to be all-inclusive, however, the provision raises serious problems of vagueness, particularly treacherous where, as here, the violation of its terms carries criminal penalties and fear of incurring these sanctions may deter those who seek to exercise protected First Amendment rights.

Section 434(e) applies to "(e)very person . . . who makes contributions or expenditures." "Contributions" and "expenditures" are defined in parallel provisions in terms of the use of money or other valuable assets "for the purpose of . . . influencing" the nomination or election of candidates for federal office. It is the ambiguity of this phrase that poses constitutional problems.

Due process requires that a criminal statute provide adequate notice to a person of ordinary intelligence that his contemplated conduct is illegal, for "no man shall be held criminally responsible for conduct which he could not reasonably understand to be proscribed." *United States v. Harriss*, 347 U.S. 612 (1954). Where First Amendment rights are involved, an even "greater degree of specificity" is required.

There is no legislative history to guide us in determining the scope of the critical phrase "for the purpose of . . . influencing." It appears to have been adopted without comment from earlier disclosure Acts. . . . Where the constitutional requirement of definiteness is at stake, we have the further obligation to construe the statute, if

92. S. Rep. No. 92-229, p. 57 (1971).

that can be done consistent with the legislature's purpose, to avoid the shoals of vagueness.

In enacting the legislation under review Congress addressed broadly the problem of political campaign financing. It wished to promote full disclosure of campaign-oriented spending to insure both the reality and the appearance of the purity and openness of the federal election process. Our task is to construe "for the purpose of... influencing," incorporated in § 434(e) through the definitions of "contributions" and "expenditures," in a manner that precisely furthers this goal.

In Part I we discussed what constituted a "contribution" for purposes of the contribution limitations set forth in 18 U.S.C. § 608(b). We construed that term to include not only contributions made directly or indirectly to a candidate, political party, or campaign committee, and contributions made to other organizations or individuals but earmarked for political purposes, but also all expenditures placed in cooperation with or with the consent of a candidate, his agents, or an authorized committee of the candidate. The definition of "contribution" in § 431(e) for disclosure purposes parallels the definition in Title 18 almost word for word, and we construe the former provision as we have the latter. So defined, "contributions" have a sufficiently close relationship to the goals of the Act, for they are connected with a candidate or his campaign.

When we attempt to define "expenditure" in a similarly narrow way we encounter line-drawing problems of the sort we faced in 18 U.S.C. § 608(e)(1). Although the phrase, "for the purpose of... influencing" an election or nomination, differs from the language used in § 608(e)(1), it shares the same potential for encompassing both issue discussion and advocacy of a political result. The general requirement that "political committees" and candidates disclose their expenditures could raise similar vagueness problems, for "political committee" is defined only in terms of amount of annual "contributions" and "expenditures," and could be interpreted to reach groups engaged purely in issue discussion. The lower courts have construed the words "political committee" more narrowly. To fulfill the purposes of the Act they need only encompass organizations that are under the control of a candidate or the major purpose of which is the nomination or election of a candidate. Expenditures of candidates and of "political committees" so construed can be assumed to fall within the core area sought to be addressed by Congress. They are, by definition, campaign related.

But when the maker of the expenditure is not within these categories — when it is an individual other than a candidate or a group other than a "political committee" — the relation of the information sought to the purposes of the Act may be too remote. To insure that the reach of § 434(e) is not impermissibly broad, we construe "expenditure" for purposes of that section in the same way we construed the terms of § 608(e) to reach only funds used for communications that expressly advocate[108]

108. See n. 52, *supra*.

the election or defeat of a clearly identified candidate. This reading is directed precisely to that spending that is unambiguously related to the campaign of a particular federal candidate.

In summary, § 434(e), as construed, imposes independent reporting requirements on individuals and groups that are not candidates or political committees only in the following circumstances: (1) when they make contributions earmarked for political purposes or authorized or requested by a candidate or his agent, to some person other than a candidate or political committee, and (2) when they make expenditures for communications that expressly advocate the election or defeat of a clearly identified candidate.

[I]t is not fatal that § 434(e) encompasses purely independent expenditures uncoordinated with a particular candidate or his agent. The corruption potential of these expenditures may be significantly different, but the informational interest can be as strong as it is in coordinated spending, for disclosure helps voters to define more of the candidates' constituencies.

Section 434(e), as we have construed it, does not contain the infirmities of the provisions before the Court in *Talley v. California* and *Thomas v. Collins*. The ordinance found wanting in *Talley* forbade all distribution of handbills that did not contain the name of the printer, author, or manufacturer, and the name of the distributor. The city urged that the ordinance was aimed at identifying those responsible for fraud, false advertising, and libel, but the Court found that it was "in no manner so limited." Here, as we have seen, the disclosure requirement is narrowly limited to those situations where the information sought has a substantial connection with the governmental interests sought to be advanced. *Thomas* held unconstitutional a prior restraint in the form of a registration requirement for labor organizers. The Court found the State's interest insufficient to justify the restrictive effect of the statute. The burden imposed by § 434(e) is no prior restraint, but a reasonable and minimally restrictive method of furthering First Amendment values by opening the basic processes of our federal election system to public view.[109]

D. Thresholds

Appellants' third contention, based on alleged overbreadth, is that the monetary thresholds in the record keeping and reporting provisions lack a substantial nexus with the claimed governmental interests, for the amounts involved are too low even to attract the attention of the candidate, much less have a corrupting influence.

The provisions contain two thresholds. Records are to be kept by political committees of the names and addresses of those who make contributions in excess of $10, and these records are subject to Commission audit. If a person's contributions

---

109. Of course, independent contributions and expenditures made in support of the campaigns of candidates of parties that have been found to be exempt from the general disclosure requirements because of the possibility of consequent chill and harassment would be exempt from the requirements of § 434(e).

to a committee or candidate aggregate more than $100, his name and address, as well as his occupation and principal place of business, are to be included in reports filed by committees and candidates with the Commission, and made available for public inspection. . . .

The $10 and $100 thresholds are indeed low. Contributors of relatively small amounts are likely to be especially sensitive to recording or disclosure of their political preferences. These strict requirements may well discourage participation by some citizens in the political process, a result that Congress hardly could have intended. Indeed, there is little in the legislative history to indicate that Congress focused carefully on the appropriate level at which to require recording and disclosure. Rather, it seems merely to have adopted the thresholds existing in similar disclosure laws since 1910. But we cannot require Congress to establish that it has chosen the highest reasonable threshold. The line is necessarily a judgmental decision, best left in the context of this complex legislation to congressional discretion. We cannot say, on this bare record, that the limits designated are wholly without rationality.

We are mindful that disclosure serves informational functions, as well as the prevention of corruption and the enforcement of the contribution limitations. Congress is not required to set a threshold that is tailored only to the latter goals. In addition, the enforcement goal can never be well served if the threshold is so high that disclosure becomes equivalent to admitting violation of the contribution limitations.

The $10 recordkeeping threshold, in a somewhat similar fashion, facilitates the enforcement of the disclosure provisions by making it relatively difficult to aggregate secret contributions in amounts that surpass the $100 limit. We agree with the Court of Appeals that there is no warrant for assuming that public disclosure of contributions between $10 and $100 is authorized by the Act. Accordingly, we do not reach the question whether information concerning gifts of this size can be made available to the public without trespassing impermissibly on First Amendment rights.

In summary, we find no constitutional infirmities in the recordkeeping reporting, and disclosure provisions of the Act.

McIntyre v. Ohio Elections Commission

514 U.S. 334 (1995)

Justice STEVENS delivered the opinion of the Court.

The question presented is whether an Ohio statute that prohibits the distribution of anonymous campaign literature is a "law . . . abridging the freedom of speech" within the meaning of the First Amendment.

I

On April 27, 1988, Margaret McIntyre distributed leaflets to persons attending a public meeting at the Blendon Middle School in Westerville, Ohio. At this meeting, the superintendent of schools planned to discuss an imminent referendum on a proposed school tax levy. The leaflets expressed Mrs. McIntyre's opposition to the levy.[2] There is no suggestion that the text of her message was false, misleading, or libelous. She had composed and printed it on her home computer and had paid a professional printer to make additional copies. Some of the handbills identified her as the author; others merely purported to express the views of "CONCERNED PARENTS AND TAX PAYERS." Except for the help provided by her son and a friend, who placed some of the leaflets on car windshields in the school parking lot, Mrs. McIntyre acted independently.

While Mrs. McIntyre distributed her handbills, an official of the school district, who supported the tax proposal, advised her that the unsigned leaflets did not conform to the Ohio election laws. Undeterred, Mrs. McIntyre appeared at another meeting on the next evening and handed out more of the handbills.

The proposed school levy was defeated at the next two elections, but it finally passed on its third try in November 1988. Five months later, the same school official filed a complaint with the Ohio Elections Commission charging that Mrs. McIntyre's distribution of unsigned leaflets violated § 3599.09(A) of the Ohio Code.[3] The commission agreed and imposed a fine of $100. . . .

---

2. The following is one of Mrs. McIntyre's leaflets, in its original typeface:

VOTE NO

ISSUE 19 SCHOOL TAX LEVY

Last election Westerville Schools, asked us to vote yes for new buildings and expansions programs. We gave them what they asked. We knew there was crowded conditions and new growth in the district.

Now we find out there is a 4 million dollar deficit—WHY?

We are told the 3 middle schools must be split because of over-crowding, and yet we are told 3 schools are being closed—WHY?

A magnet school is not a full operating school, but a specials school.

Residents were asked to work on a 20 member commission to help formulate the new boundaries. For 4 weeks they worked long and hard and came up with a very workable plan. Their plan was totally disregarded—WHY?

WASTE of tax payers dollars must be stopped. Our children's education and welfare must come first. WASTE CAN NO LONGER BE TOLERATED.

PLEASE VOTE NO

ISSUE 19

THANK YOU.

CONCERNED PARENTS

3. Ohio Rev.Code Ann. § 3599.09(A) (1988) provides:

"No person shall write, print, post, or distribute, or cause to be written, printed, posted, or distributed, a notice, placard, dodger, advertisement, sample ballot, or any other form of general publication which is designed to promote the nomination or election or defeat of a candidate, or to promote the adoption or defeat of any issue, or to influence the voters in any election, or make an expenditure for the purpose of financing political communications through newspapers, magazines, outdoor advertising facilities, direct mailings, or other similar types of general public political advertising, or through flyers, handbills, or other nonperiodical printed matter, unless there appears on such form of publication in a conspicuous place or is contained within said statement the name and residence or business address of the chairman, treasurer, or secretary of the organization issuing the

Mrs. McIntyre passed away during the pendency of this litigation. Even though the amount in controversy is only $100, petitioner, as the executor of her estate, has pursued her claim in this Court. Our grant of certiorari reflects our agreement with his appraisal of the importance of the question presented.

II

Ohio maintains that the statute under review is a reasonable regulation of the electoral process. The State does not suggest that all anonymous publications are pernicious or that a statute totally excluding them from the marketplace of ideas would be valid. This is a wise (albeit implicit) concession, for the anonymity of an author is not ordinarily a sufficient reason to exclude her work product from the protections of the First Amendment.

"Anonymous pamphlets, leaflets, brochures and even books have played an important role in the progress of mankind." *Talley v. California*, 362 U.S. 60 (1960). Great works of literature have frequently been produced by authors writing under assumed names. Despite readers' curiosity and the public's interest in identifying the creator of a work of art, an author generally is free to decide whether or not to disclose his or her true identity. The decision in favor of anonymity may be motivated by fear of economic or official retaliation, by concern about social ostracism, or merely by a desire to preserve as much of one's privacy as possible. Whatever the motivation may be, at least in the field of literary endeavor, the interest in having anonymous works enter the marketplace of ideas unquestionably outweighs any public interest in requiring disclosure as a condition of entry.[5] Accordingly, an

---

> same, or the person who issues, makes, or is responsible therefor. The disclaimer 'paid political advertisement' is not sufficient to meet the requirements of this division. When such publication is issued by the regularly constituted central or executive committee of a political party, organized as provided in Chapter 3517. of the Revised Code, it shall be sufficiently identified if it bears the name of the committee and its chairman or treasurer. No person, firm, or corporation shall print or reproduce any notice, placard, dodger, advertisement, sample ballot, or any other form of publication in violation of this section. This section does not apply to the transmittal of personal correspondence that is not reproduced by machine for general distribution.
>
> "The secretary of state may, by rule, exempt, from the requirements of this division, printed matter and certain other kinds of printed communications such as campaign buttons, balloons, pencils, or like items, the size or nature of which makes it unreasonable to add an identification or disclaimer. The disclaimer or identification, when paid for by a campaign committee, shall be identified by the words 'paid for by' followed by the name and address of the campaign committee and the appropriate officer of the committee, identified by name and title."

Section 3599.09(B) contains a comparable prohibition against unidentified communications uttered over the broadcasting facilities of any radio or television station. No question concerning that provision is raised in this case. Our opinion, therefore, discusses only written communications and, particularly, leaflets of the kind Mrs. McIntyre distributed....

5. Though such a requirement might provide assistance to critics in evaluating the quality and significance of the writing, it is not indispensable. To draw an analogy from a nonliterary context, the now-pervasive practice of grading law school examination papers "blindly" (*i.e.*, under a system in which the professor does not know whose paper she is grading) indicates that such evaluations

author's decision to remain anonymous, like other decisions concerning omissions or additions to the content of a publication, is an aspect of the freedom of speech protected by the First Amendment.

The freedom to publish anonymously extends beyond the literary realm. In *Talley*, the Court held that the First Amendment protects the distribution of unsigned handbills urging readers to boycott certain Los Angeles merchants who were allegedly engaging in discriminatory employment practices. Writing for the Court, Justice Black noted that "[p]ersecuted groups and sects from time to time throughout history have been able to criticize oppressive practices and laws either anonymously or not at all." Justice Black recalled England's abusive press licensing laws and seditious libel prosecutions, and he reminded us that even the arguments favoring the ratification of the Constitution advanced in the Federalist Papers were published under fictitious names. On occasion, quite apart from any threat of persecution, an advocate may believe her ideas will be more persuasive if her readers are unaware of her identity. Anonymity thereby provides a way for a writer who may be personally unpopular to ensure that readers will not prejudge her message simply because they do not like its proponent. Thus, even in the field of political rhetoric, where "the identity of the speaker is an important component of many attempts to persuade," *City of Ladue v. Gilleo*, 512 U.S. 43, 56 (1994) (footnote omitted), the most effective advocates have sometimes opted for anonymity. The specific holding in *Talley* related to advocacy of an economic boycott, but the Court's reasoning embraced a respected tradition of anonymity in the advocacy of political causes. This tradition is perhaps best exemplified by the secret ballot, the hard-won right to vote one's conscience without fear of retaliation.

III

California had defended the Los Angeles ordinance at issue in *Talley* as a law "aimed at providing a way to identify those responsible for fraud, false advertising and libel." We rejected that argument because nothing in the text or legislative history of the ordinance limited its application to those evils. We then made clear that we did "not pass on the validity of an ordinance limited to prevent these or any other supposed evils." The Ohio statute likewise contains no language limiting its application to fraudulent, false, or libelous statements; to the extent, therefore, that Ohio seeks to justify § 3599.09(A) as a means to prevent the dissemination of untruths, its defense must fail for the same reason given in *Talley*. As the facts of this case demonstrate, the ordinance plainly applies even when there is no hint of falsity or libel.

Ohio's statute does, however, contain a different limitation: It applies only to unsigned documents designed to influence voters in an election. In contrast, the Los Angeles ordinance prohibited all anonymous handbilling "in any place under any

---

are possible — indeed, perhaps more reliable — when any bias associated with the author's identity is prescinded. [How persuasive is the analogy between grading exams on an anonymous basis (or anonymous literature) and voting on the basis of anonymous campaign literature? — Eds.]

circumstances." For that reason, Ohio correctly argues that *Talley* does not necessarily control the disposition of this case. We must, therefore, decide whether and to what extent the First Amendment's protection of anonymity encompasses documents intended to influence the electoral process.

Ohio places its principal reliance on cases such as *Anderson v. Celebrezze*, 460 U.S. 780 (1983); *Storer v. Brown*, 415 U.S. 724 (1974); and *Burdick v. Takushi*, 504 U.S. 428 (1992), in which we reviewed election code provisions governing the voting process itself. See *Anderson* (filing deadlines); *Storer* (ballot access); *Burdick* (write-in voting); see also *Tashjian v. Republican Party of Conn.* 479 U.S. 208 (1986) (eligibility of independent voters to vote in party primaries). In those cases we refused to adopt "any 'litmus-paper test' that will separate valid from invalid restrictions." *Anderson*, quoting *Storer.* Instead, we pursued an analytical process comparable to that used by courts "in ordinary litigation": We considered the relative interests of the State and the injured voters, and we evaluated the extent to which the State's interests necessitated the contested restrictions. Applying similar reasoning in this case, the Ohio Supreme Court upheld § 3599.09(A) as a "*reasonable*" and "*nondiscriminatory*" burden on the rights of voters.

The "ordinary litigation" test does not apply here. Unlike the statutory provisions challenged in *Storer* and *Anderson*, § 3599.09(A) of the Ohio Code does not control the mechanics of the electoral process. It is a regulation of pure speech. Moreover, even though this provision applies evenhandedly to advocates of differing viewpoints,[8] it is a direct regulation of the content of speech. Every written document covered by the statute must contain "the name and residence or business address of the chairman, treasurer, or secretary of the organization issuing the same, or the person who issues, makes, or is responsible therefor." § 3599.09(A). Furthermore, the category of covered documents is defined by their content — only those publications containing speech designed to influence the voters in an election need bear the required markings. Consequently, we are not faced with an ordinary election restriction; this case "involves a limitation on political expression subject to exacting scrutiny." *Meyer v. Grant.*

Indeed, as we have explained on many prior occasions, the category of speech regulated by the Ohio statute occupies the core of the protection afforded by the First Amendment....

Of course, core political speech need not center on a candidate for office. The principles enunciated in *Buckley* extend equally to issue-based elections such as the school tax referendum that Mrs. McIntyre sought to influence through her handbills. See *Bellotti*. Indeed, the speech in which Mrs. McIntyre engaged — handing out leaflets in the advocacy of a politically controversial viewpoint — is the essence of First Amendment expression. That this advocacy occurred in the heat of a controversial

---

8. Arguably, the disclosure requirement places a more significant burden on advocates of unpopular causes than on defenders of the status quo. For purposes of our analysis, however, we assume the statute evenhandedly burdens all speakers who have a legitimate interest in remaining anonymous.

referendum vote only strengthens the protection afforded to Mrs. McIntyre's expression: Urgent, important, and effective speech can be no less protected than impotent speech, lest the right to speak be relegated to those instances when it is least needed. No form of speech is entitled to greater constitutional protection than Mrs. McIntyre's.

When a law burdens core political speech, we apply "exacting scrutiny," and we uphold the restriction only if it is narrowly tailored to serve an overriding state interest. Our precedents thus make abundantly clear that the Ohio Supreme Court applied a significantly more lenient standard than is appropriate in a case of this kind.

IV

Nevertheless, the State argues that, even under the strictest standard of review, the disclosure requirement in § 3599.09(A) is justified by two important and legitimate state interests. Ohio judges its interest in preventing fraudulent and libelous statements and its interest in providing the electorate with relevant information to be sufficiently compelling to justify the anonymous speech ban. These two interests necessarily overlap to some extent, but it is useful to discuss them separately.

Insofar as the interest in informing the electorate means nothing more than the provision of additional information that may either buttress or undermine the argument in a document, we think the identity of the speaker is no different from other components of the document's content that the author is free to include or exclude.[11] We have already held that the State may not compel a newspaper that prints editorials critical of a particular candidate to provide space for a reply by the candidate. *Miami Herald Publishing Co. v. Tornillo*, 418 U.S. 241 (1974). The simple interest in providing voters with additional relevant information does not justify a state requirement that a writer make statements or disclosures she would otherwise omit. Moreover, in the case of a handbill written by a private citizen who is not known to the recipient, the name and address of the author add little, if anything, to the reader's ability to evaluate the document's message. Thus, Ohio's informational interest is plainly insufficient to support the constitutionality of its disclosure requirement.

The state interest in preventing fraud and libel stands on a different footing. We agree with Ohio's submission that this interest carries special weight during election campaigns when false statements, if credited, may have serious adverse consequences for the public at large. Ohio does not, however, rely solely on § 3599.09(A) to protect that interest. Its Election Code includes detailed and specific prohibitions against making or disseminating false statements during political campaigns. Ohio

---

11. "Of course, the identity of the source is helpful in evaluating ideas. But 'the best test of truth is the power of the thought to get itself accepted in the competition of the market' (*Abrams v. United States*, [250 U.S. 616, 630 (1919) (Holmes, J., dissenting)]). Don't underestimate the common man. People are intelligent enough to evaluate the source of an anonymous writing. They can see it is anonymous. They know it is anonymous. They can evaluate its anonymity along with its message, as long as they are permitted, as they must be, to read that message. And then, once they have done so, it is for them to decide what is 'responsible', what is valuable, and what is truth." *New York v. Duryea*, 351 N.Y.S.2d 978, 996 (1974) (striking down similar New York statute as overbroad).

Rev. Code Ann. §§3599.09.1(B), 3599.09.2(B) (1988). These regulations apply both to candidate elections and to issue-driven ballot measures. Thus, Ohio's prohibition of anonymous leaflets plainly is not its principal weapon against fraud. Rather, it serves as an aid to enforcement of the specific prohibitions and as a deterrent to the making of false statements by unscrupulous prevaricators. Although these ancillary benefits are assuredly legitimate, we are not persuaded that they justify §3599.09(A)'s extremely broad prohibition.

As this case demonstrates, the prohibition encompasses documents that are not even arguably false or misleading. It applies not only to the activities of candidates and their organized supporters, but also to individuals acting independently and using only their own modest resources. It applies not only to elections of public officers, but also to ballot issues that present neither a substantial risk of libel nor any potential appearance of corrupt advantage. It applies not only to leaflets distributed on the eve of an election, when the opportunity for reply is limited, but also to those distributed months in advance. It applies no matter what the character or strength of the author's interest in anonymity. Moreover, as this case also demonstrates, the absence of the author's name on a document does not necessarily protect either that person or a distributor of a forbidden document from being held responsible for compliance with the Election Code. Nor has the State explained why it can more easily enforce the direct bans on disseminating false documents against anonymous authors and distributors than against wrongdoers who might use false names and addresses in an attempt to avoid detection. We recognize that a State's enforcement interest might justify a more limited identification requirement, but Ohio has shown scant cause for inhibiting the leafletting at issue here.

V

Finally, Ohio vigorously argues that our opinions in *Bellotti* and *Buckley v. Valeo* amply support the constitutionality of its disclosure requirement. Neither case is controlling: The former concerned the scope of First Amendment protection afforded to corporations; The relevant portion of the latter concerned mandatory disclosure of campaign-related expenditures. Neither case involved a prohibition of anonymous campaign literature.

In *Bellotti* . . . we noted that the "inherent worth of the speech in terms of its capacity for informing the public does not depend upon the identity of its source, whether corporation, association, union, or individual." We also made it perfectly clear that we were not deciding whether the First Amendment's protection of corporate speech is coextensive with the protection it affords to individuals. Accordingly, although we commented in dicta on the prophylactic effect of requiring identification of the source of corporate advertising,[18] that footnote did not necessarily apply to independent communications by an individual like Mrs. McIntyre.

18. "Corporate advertising, unlike some methods of participation in political campaigns, is likely to be highly visible. Identification of the source of advertising may be required as a means

Our reference in [*Bellotti*] to the "prophylactic effect" of disclosure requirements cited a portion of our earlier opinion in *Buckley*, in which we stressed the importance of providing "the electorate with information 'as to where political campaign money comes from and how it is spent by the candidate.'" We observed that the "sources of a candidate's financial support also alert the voter to the interests to which a candidate is most likely to be responsive and thus facilitate predictions of future performance in office." Those comments concerned contributions to the candidate or expenditures authorized by the candidate or his responsible agent. They had no reference to the kind of independent activity pursued by Mrs. McIntyre. Required disclosures about the level of financial support a candidate has received from various sources are supported by an interest in avoiding the appearance of corruption that has no application to this case.

True, in another portion of the *Buckley* opinion we expressed approval of a requirement that even "independent expenditures" in excess of a threshold level be reported to the Federal Election Commission. But that requirement entailed nothing more than an identification to the Commission of the amount and use of money expended in support of a candidate. Though such mandatory reporting undeniably impedes protected First Amendment activity, the intrusion is a far cry from compelled self-identification on all election-related writings. A written election-related document—particularly a leaflet—is often a personally crafted statement of a political viewpoint. Mrs. McIntyre's handbills surely fit that description. As such, identification of the author against her will is particularly intrusive; it reveals unmistakably the content of her thoughts on a controversial issue. Disclosure of an expenditure and its use, without more, reveals far less information. It may be information that a person prefers to keep secret, and undoubtedly it often gives away something about the spender's political views. Nonetheless, even though money may "talk," its speech is less specific, less personal, and less provocative than a handbill—and as a result, when money supports an unpopular viewpoint it is less likely to precipitate retaliation.

Not only is the Ohio statute's infringement on speech more intrusive than the *Buckley* disclosure requirement, but it rests on different and less powerful state interests. The Federal Election Campaign Act of 1971, at issue in *Buckley*, regulates only candidate elections, not referenda or other issue-based ballot measures; and we construed "independent expenditures" to mean only those expenditures that "expressly advocate the election or defeat of a clearly identified candidate." In candidate elections, the Government can identify a compelling state interest in avoiding the corruption that might result from campaign expenditures. Disclosure of expenditures lessens the risk that individuals will spend money to support a candidate as a *quid pro quo* for special treatment after the candidate is in office. Curriers of

---

of disclosure, so that the people will be able to evaluate the arguments to which they are being subjected. See *Buckley*; *United States v. Harriss*, 347 U.S. 612, 625–626 (1954). In addition, we emphasized in *Buckley* the prophylactic effect of requiring that the source of communication be disclosed." *Bellotti*.

favor will be deterred by the knowledge that all expenditures will be scrutinized by the Federal Election Commission and by the public for just this sort of abuse.[20] Moreover, the federal Act contains numerous legitimate disclosure requirements for campaign organizations; the similar requirements for independent expenditures serve to ensure that a campaign organization will not seek to evade disclosure by routing its expenditures through individual supporters. See *Buckley*. In short, although *Buckley* may permit a more narrowly drawn statute, it surely is not authority for upholding Ohio's open-ended provision.

VI

Under our Constitution, anonymous pamphleteering is not a pernicious, fraudulent practice, but an honorable tradition of advocacy and of dissent. Anonymity is a shield from the tyranny of the majority. See generally J. Mill, On Liberty and Considerations on Representative Government 1, 3–4 (R. McCallum ed. 1947). It thus exemplifies the purpose behind the Bill of Rights, and of the First Amendment in particular: to protect unpopular individuals from retaliation—and their ideas from suppression—at the hand of an intolerant society. The right to remain anonymous may be abused when it shields fraudulent conduct. But political speech by its nature will sometimes have unpalatable consequences, and, in general, our society accords greater weight to the value of free speech than to the dangers of its misuse. Ohio has not shown that its interest in preventing the misuse of anonymous election-related speech justifies a prohibition of all uses of that speech. The State may, and does, punish fraud directly. But it cannot seek to punish fraud indirectly by indiscriminately outlawing a category of speech, based on its content, with no necessary relationship to the danger sought to be prevented. One would be hard pressed to think of a better example of the pitfalls of Ohio's blunderbuss approach than the facts of the case before us.

The judgment of the Ohio Supreme Court is reversed.

It is so ordered.

Justice GINSBURG, concurring.

The dissent is stirring in its appreciation of democratic values. But I do not see the Court's opinion as unguided by "bedrock principle," tradition, or our case law. Margaret McIntyre's case, it seems to me, bears a marked resemblance to Margaret Gilleo's case[1] and Mary Grace's.[2] All three decisions, I believe, are sound, and hardly sensational, applications of our First Amendment jurisprudence.

---

20. This interest also serves to distinguish *United States v. Harriss* in which we upheld limited disclosure requirements for lobbyists. The activities of lobbyists who have direct access to elected representatives, if undisclosed, may well present the appearance of corruption.

1. See *City of Ladue v. Gilleo*, in which we held that the city of Ladue could not prohibit homeowner Gilleo's display of a small sign, on her lawn or in a window, opposing war in the Persian Gulf.

2. Grace was the "lone picketer" who stood on the sidewalk in front of this Court with a sign containing the text of the First Amendment, prompting us to exclude public sidewalks from the

In for a calf is not always in for a cow. The Court's decision finds unnecessary, overintrusive, and inconsistent with American ideals the State's imposition of a fine on an individual leafleteer who, within her local community, spoke her mind, but sometimes not her name. We do not thereby hold that the State may not in other, larger circumstances require the speaker to disclose its interest by disclosing its identity. Appropriately leaving open matters not presented by McIntyre's handbills, the Court recognizes that a State's interest in protecting an election process "might justify a more limited identification requirement." But the Court has convincingly explained why Ohio lacks "cause for inhibiting the leafletting at issue here."

Justice THOMAS, concurring in the judgment.

I agree with the majority's conclusion that Ohio's election law, § 3599.09(A), is inconsistent with the First Amendment. I would apply, however, a different methodology to this case. Instead of asking whether "an honorable tradition" of anonymous speech has existed throughout American history, or what the "value" of anonymous speech might be, we should determine whether the phrase "freedom of speech, or of the press," as originally understood, protected anonymous political leafletting. I believe that it did. [The remainder of Justice Thomas's opinion examining the historical evidence regarding the Framers' understanding of the First Amendment is omitted.]

Justice SCALIA, with whom THE CHIEF JUSTICE joins, dissenting.

At a time when both political branches of Government and both political parties reflect a popular desire to leave more decisionmaking authority to the States, today's decision moves in the opposite direction, adding to the legacy of inflexible central mandates (irrevocable even by Congress) imposed by this Court's constitutional jurisprudence. In an opinion which reads as though it is addressing some peculiar law like the Los Angeles municipal ordinance at issue in *Talley*, the Court invalidates a species of protection for the election process that exists, in a variety of forms, in every State except California, and that has a pedigree dating back to the end of the 19th century. Preferring the views of the English utilitarian philosopher John Stuart Mill to the considered judgment of the American people's elected representatives from coast to coast, the Court discovers a hitherto unknown right-to-be-unknown while engaging in electoral politics. I dissent from this imposition of free-speech imperatives that are demonstrably not those of the American people today, and that there is inadequate reason to believe were those of the society that begat the First Amendment or the Fourteenth.

I

The question posed by the present case is not the easiest sort to answer for those who adhere to the Court's (and the society's) traditional view that the Constitution bears its original meaning and is unchanging. Under that view, "[o]n every question

---

statutory ban on display of a "flag, banner, or device" on Court grounds. *United States v. Grace*, 461 U.S. 171, 183 (1983).

of construction, [we should] carry ourselves back to the time when the Constitution was adopted; recollect the spirit manifested in the debates; and instead of trying [to find] what meaning may be squeezed out of the text, or invented against it, conform to the probable one in which it was passed." T. Jefferson, Letter to William Johnson (June 12, 1823), in 15 Writings of Thomas Jefferson 439, 449 (A. Lipscomb ed. 1904). That technique is simple of application when government conduct that is claimed to violate the Bill of Rights or the Fourteenth Amendment is shown, upon investigation, to have been engaged in without objection at the very time the Bill of Rights or the Fourteenth Amendment was adopted. There is no doubt, for example, that laws against libel and obscenity do not violate "the freedom of speech" to which the First Amendment refers; they existed and were universally approved in 1791. Application of the principle of an unchanging Constitution is also simple enough at the other extreme, where the government conduct at issue was *not* engaged in at the time of adoption, and there is ample evidence that the *reason* it was not engaged in is that it was thought to violate the right embodied in the constitutional guarantee. Racks and thumbscrews, well-known instruments for inflicting pain, were not in use because they were regarded as cruel punishments.

The present case lies between those two extremes. Anonymous electioneering was not prohibited by law in 1791 or in 1868. In fact, it was widely practiced at the earlier date, an understandable legacy of the revolutionary era in which political dissent could produce governmental reprisal. I need not dwell upon the evidence of that, since it is described at length in today's concurrence. See *ante* (THOMAS, J., concurring in judgment). The practice of anonymous electioneering may have been less general in 1868, when the Fourteenth Amendment was adopted, but at least as late as 1837 it was respectable enough to be engaged in by Abraham Lincoln. See 1 A. Beveridge, Abraham Lincoln 1809–1858, pp. 215–216 (1928); 1 Uncollected Works of Abraham Lincoln 155–161 (R. Wilson ed. 1947).

But to prove that anonymous electioneering was used frequently is not to establish that it is a constitutional right. Quite obviously, not every restriction upon expression that did not exist in 1791 or in 1868 is *ipso facto* unconstitutional, or else modern election laws such as those involved in *Burson v. Freeman*, 504 U.S. 191 (1992), and *Buckley v. Valeo*, would be prohibited, as would (to mention only a few other categories) modern antinoise regulation of the sort involved in *Kovacs v. Cooper*, 336 U.S. 77 (1949), and *Ward v. Rock Against Racism*, 491 U.S. 781 (1989), and modern parade-permitting regulation of the sort involved in *Cox v. New Hampshire*, 312 U.S. 569 (1941).

Evidence that anonymous electioneering was regarded as a constitutional right is sparse, and as far as I am aware evidence that it was *generally* regarded as such is nonexistent.

[T]he sum total of the historical evidence marshaled by the concurrence for the principle of *constitutional entitlement* to anonymous electioneering is partisan claims in the debate on ratification (which was *almost* like an election) that a viewpoint-based restriction on anonymity by newspaper editors violates freedom of speech. This absence of historical testimony concerning the point before us is hardly remarkable. The issue of a governmental prohibition upon anonymous electioneering in particular (as opposed to a government prohibition upon anonymous publication in general) simply never arose. Indeed, there probably never arose even the abstract question whether electoral openness and regularity was worth such a governmental restriction upon the normal right to anonymous speech. The idea of close government regulation of the electoral process is a more modern phenomenon, arriving in this country in the late 1800's.

What we have, then, is the most difficult case for determining the meaning of the Constitution. No accepted existence of governmental restrictions of the sort at issue here demonstrates their constitutionality, but neither can their nonexistence clearly be attributed to constitutional objections. In such a case, constitutional adjudication necessarily involves not just history but judgment: judgment as to whether the government action under challenge is consonant with the concept of the protected freedom (in this case, the freedom of speech and of the press) that existed when the constitutional protection was accorded. In the present case, *absent other indication*, I would be inclined to agree with the concurrence that a society which used anonymous political debate so regularly would not regard as constitutional even moderate restrictions made to improve the election process. (I would, however, want further evidence of common practice in 1868, since I doubt that the Fourteenth Amendment time-warped the post-Civil War States back to the Revolution.)

But there *is* other indication, of the most weighty sort: the widespread and longstanding traditions of our people. Principles of liberty fundamental enough to have been embodied within constitutional guarantees are not readily erased from the Nation's consciousness. A governmental practice that has become general throughout the United States, and particularly one that has the validation of long, accepted usage, bears a strong presumption of constitutionality. And that is what we have before us here. Ohio Rev. Code Ann. § 3599.09(A) (1988) was enacted by the General Assembly of the State of Ohio almost 80 years ago. Even at the time of its adoption, there was nothing unique or extraordinary about it. The earliest statute of this sort was adopted by Massachusetts in 1890, little more than 20 years after the Fourteenth Amendment was ratified. No less than 24 States had similar laws by the end of World War I, and today every State of the Union except California has one, as does the District of Columbia, and as does the Federal Government where advertising relating to candidates for federal office is concerned, see [52 U.S.C. § 30120(a)]. Such a universal and long-established American legislative practice must be given precedence, I think, over historical and academic speculation regarding a restriction that assuredly does not go to the heart of free speech.

It can be said that we ignored a tradition as old, and almost as widespread, in *Texas v. Johnson*, 491 U.S. 397 (1989), where we held unconstitutional a state law prohibiting desecration of the United States flag. See also *United States v. Eichman*, 496 U.S. 310 (1990). But those cases merely stand for the proposition that postadoption tradition cannot alter the core meaning of a constitutional guarantee. As we said in

Johnson, "[i]f there is a bedrock principle underlying the First Amendment, it is that the government may not prohibit the expression of an idea simply because society finds the idea itself offensive or disagreeable." Prohibition of expression of contempt for the flag, whether by contemptuous words, see *Street v. New York*, 394 U.S. 576 (1969), or by burning the flag, came, we said, within that "bedrock principle." The law at issue here, by contrast, forbids the expression of no idea, but merely requires identification of the speaker when the idea is uttered in the electoral context. It is at the periphery of the First Amendment, like the law at issue in *Burson*, where we took guidance from tradition in upholding against constitutional attack restrictions upon electioneering in the vicinity of polling places.

II

The foregoing analysis suffices to decide this case for me. Where the meaning of a constitutional text (such as "the freedom of speech") is unclear, the widespread and long-accepted practices of the American people are the best indication of what fundamental beliefs it was intended to enshrine. Even if I were to close my eyes to practice, however, and were to be guided exclusively by deductive analysis from our case law, I would reach the same result.

Three basic questions must be answered to decide this case. Two of them are readily answered by our precedents; the third is readily answered by common sense and by a decent regard for the practical judgment of those more familiar with elections than we are. The first question is whether protection of the election process justifies limitations upon speech that cannot constitutionally be imposed generally. (If not, *Talley v. California*, which invalidated a flat ban on *all* anonymous leafletting, controls the decision here.) Our cases plainly answer that question in the affirmative—indeed, they suggest that no justification for regulation is more compelling than protection of the electoral process....

The second question relevant to our decision is whether a "right to anonymity" is such a prominent value in our constitutional system that even protection of the electoral process cannot be purchased at its expense. The answer, again, is clear: no. Several of our cases have held that *in peculiar circumstances* the compelled disclosure of a person's identity would unconstitutionally deter the exercise of First Amendment associational rights. See, *e.g.*, *Brown v. Socialist Workers '74 Campaign Comm. (Ohio)*, 459 U.S. 87 (1982); *Bates v. Little Rock*, 361 U.S. 516 (1960); *NAACP v. Alabama*. But those cases did not acknowledge any general right to anonymity, or even any right on the part of *all* citizens to ignore the particular laws under challenge. Rather, they recognized a right to an *exemption* from otherwise valid disclosure requirements on the part of someone who could show a "reasonable probability" that the compelled disclosure would result in "threats, harassment, or reprisals from either Government officials or private parties." This last quotation is from *Buckley v. Valeo*, which prescribed the safety valve of a similar exemption in upholding the disclosure requirements of the Federal Election Campaign Act. That is the answer our case law provides to the Court's fear about the "tyranny of the majority," and to its concern that "'[p]ersecuted groups and sects from time to time throughout history have been able to criticize oppressive practices and laws either anonymously or not at all." Anonymity can still be enjoyed by those who require it, without utterly destroying useful disclosure laws. The record in this case contains not even a hint that Mrs. McIntyre feared "threats, harassment, or reprisals"; indeed, she placed her name on some of her fliers and meant to place it on all of them.

The existence of a generalized right of anonymity in speech was rejected by this Court in *Lewis Publishing Co. v. Morgan*, 229 U.S. 288 (1913), which held that newspapers desiring the privilege of second-class postage could be required to provide to the Postmaster General, and to publish, a statement of the names and addresses of their editors, publishers, business managers, and owners. We rejected the argument that the First Amendment forbade the requirement of such disclosure. The provision that gave rise to that case still exists, see 39 U.S.C. § 3685, and is still enforced by the Postal Service. It is one of several federal laws seemingly invalidated by today's opinion.

The Court's unprecedented protection for anonymous speech does not even have the virtue of establishing a clear (albeit erroneous) rule of law. For after having announced that this statute, because it "burdens core political speech," requires "exacting scrutiny" and must be "narrowly tailored to serve an overriding state interest," (ordinarily the kiss of death), the opinion goes on to proclaim soothingly (and unhelpfully) that "a State's enforcement interest might justify a more limited identification requirement." See also *ante* (GINSBURG, J., concurring) ("We do not . . . hold that the State may not in other, larger circumstances require the speaker to disclose its interest by disclosing its identity"). Perhaps, then, not *all* the state statutes I have alluded to are invalid, but just *some* of them; or indeed maybe *all* of them remain valid in "larger circumstances"! It may take decades to work out the shape of this newly expanded right-to-speak-incognito, even in the elections field. And in other areas, of course, a whole new boutique of wonderful First Amendment litigation opens its doors. Must a parade permit, for example, be issued to a group that refuses to provide its identity, or that agrees to do so only under assurance that the identity will not be made public? Must a municipally owned theater that is leased for private productions book anonymously sponsored presentations? Must a government periodical that has a "letters to the editor" column disavow the policy that most newspapers have against the publication of anonymous letters? Must a public university that makes its facilities available for a speech by Louis Farrakhan or David Duke refuse to disclose the on-campus or off-campus group that has sponsored or paid for the speech? Must a municipal "public-access" cable channel permit anonymous (and masked) performers? The silliness that follows upon a generalized right to anonymous speech has no end.

The third and last question relevant to our decision is whether the prohibition of anonymous campaigning is effective in protecting and enhancing democratic elections. In answering this question no, the Justices of the majority set their own views — on a practical matter that bears closely upon the real-life experience of elected politicians and *not* upon that of unelected judges — up against the views of 49 (and perhaps all 50) state legislatures and the Federal Congress. We might also add to the list on the other side the legislatures of foreign democracies: Australia, Canada, and England, for example, all have prohibitions upon anonymous campaigning. How is it, one must wonder, that all of these elected legislators, from around the country and around the world, could not see what six Justices of this Court see so clearly that they are willing to require the entire Nation to act upon it: that requiring identification of the source of campaign literature does not improve the quality of the campaign?

The Court says that the State has not explained "why it can more easily enforce the direct bans on disseminating false documents against anonymous authors and distributors than against wrongdoers who might use false names and addresses in an attempt to avoid detection." I am not sure what this complicated comparison means. I am sure, however, that (1) a person who is required to put his name to a document is much less likely to lie than one who can lie anonymously, and (2) the distributor of a leaflet which is unlawful because it is anonymous runs much more risk of immediate detection and punishment than the distributor of a leaflet which is unlawful because it is false. Thus, people will be more likely to observe a signing requirement than a naked "no falsity" requirement; and, having observed that requirement, will then be significantly less likely to lie in what they have signed.

But the usefulness of a signing requirement lies not only in promoting observance of the law against campaign falsehoods (though that alone is enough to sustain it). It lies also in promoting a civil and dignified level of campaign debate — which the State has no power to command, but ample power to encourage by such undemanding measures as a signature requirement. Observers of the past few national elections have expressed concern about the increase of character assassination — "mudslinging" is the colloquial term — engaged in by political candidates and their supporters to the detriment of the democratic process. Not all of this, in fact not much of it, consists of actionable untruth; most is innuendo, or demeaning characterization, or mere disclosure of items of personal life that have no bearing upon suitability for office. Imagine how much all of this would increase if it could be done anonymously. The principal impediment against it is the reluctance of most individuals and organizations to be publicly associated with uncharitable and uncivil expression. Consider, moreover, the increased potential for "dirty tricks." It is not unheard-of for campaign operatives to circulate material over the name of their opponents or their opponents' supporters (a violation of election laws) in order to attract or alienate certain interest groups. See, *e.g.*, B. Felknor, Political Mischief: Smear, Sabotage, and Reform in U.S. Elections 111–112 (1992) (fake United Mine Workers' newspaper assembled by the National Republican Congressional Committee); *New York v. Duryea*, 351 N.Y.S.2d 978 (Sup. 1974) (letters purporting to be from the "Action Committee for the Liberal Party" sent by Republicans). How much easier — and sanction free! — it would be to circulate anonymous material (for example, a *really* tasteless, though not actionably false, attack upon one's own candidate) with the hope and expectation that it will be attributed to, and held against, the other side.

The Court contends that demanding the disclosure of the pamphleteer's identity is no different from requiring the disclosure of any other information that may reduce the persuasiveness of the pamphlet's message. It cites *Miami Herald Publishing Co. v. Tornillo*, which held it unconstitutional to require a newspaper that had published an editorial critical of a particular candidate to furnish space for that candidate to reply. But it is not *usual* for a speaker to put forward the best arguments against himself, and it is a great imposition upon free speech to make him do so. Whereas it is quite usual—it is expected—for a speaker to *identify* himself, and requiring that is (at least when there are no special circumstances present) virtually no imposition at all.

We have approved much more onerous disclosure requirements in the name of fair elections. In *Buckley*, we upheld provisions of the Federal Election Campaign Act that required private individuals to report to the Federal Election Commission independent expenditures made for communications advocating the election or defeat of a candidate for federal office. Our primary rationale for upholding this provision was that it served an "informational interest" by "increas[ing] the fund of information concerning those who support the candidates." The provision before us here serves the same informational interest, as well as more important interests, which I have discussed above. The Court's attempt to distinguish *Buckley* would be unconvincing, even if it were accurate in its statement that the disclosure requirement there at issue "reveals far less information" than requiring disclosure of the identity of the author of a specific campaign statement. That happens not to be accurate, since the provision there at issue required not merely "[d]isclosure of an expenditure and its use, without more." It required, among other things:

> the identification of *each person to whom expenditures have been made . . .* within the calendar year in an aggregate amount or value in excess of $100, the amount, date, *and purpose of each such expenditure* and the name and address of, and office sought by, *each candidate on whose behalf* such expenditure was made. (emphasis added).

Surely in many if not most cases, this information will readily permit identification of the particular message that the would-be-anonymous campaigner sponsored. Besides which the burden of complying with this provision, which includes the filing of quarterly reports, is infinitely more onerous than Ohio's simple requirement for signature of campaign literature. If *Buckley* remains the law, this is an easy case.

* * *

I do not know where the Court derives its perception that "anonymous pamphleteering is not a pernicious, fraudulent practice, but an honorable tradition of advocacy and of dissent." I can imagine no reason why an anonymous leaflet is any more honorable, as a general matter, than an anonymous phone call or an anonymous letter. It facilitates wrong by eliminating accountability, which is ordinarily the very purpose of the anonymity. There are of course exceptions, and where anonymity is needed to avoid "threats, harassment, or reprisals" the First Amendment will require an exemption from the Ohio law. Cf. *NAACP v. Alabama*. But to strike down the Ohio law in its general application — and similar laws of 49 other States and the Federal Government — on the ground that all anonymous communication is in our society traditionally sacrosanct, seems to me a distortion of the past that will lead to a coarsening of the future.

I respectfully dissent.

Notes and Questions

1. The Court in *Buckley* recognized an exception to the FECA's disclosure requirements when a minor party shows "a reasonable probability that the compelled disclosure of a party's contributors' names will subject them to threats, harassment, or reprisals from either Government officials or private parties." Under the facts related to the Ohio Socialist Workers Party discussed in the introduction to this chapter, the Court held in *Brown v. Socialist Workers '74 Campaign Comm.*, 459 U.S. 87 (1982), that the party was entitled to such an exemption. Three Justices agreed that the evidence showed the SWP deserved an exemption as to campaign *contributors*, but disagreed that the evidence showed that those who received *expenditures* from the SWP were reasonably likely to be subject to threats, harassment, or reprisals. We return to this issue in the next case.

2. *Buckley* recognized three interests served by disclosure, as outlined in the introduction to this chapter: the anti-corruption interest, the information interest, and the enforcement interest. In *McIntyre*, the Court held that the anti-corruption interest could not be invoked to support the Ohio disclosure law. Citing *Buckley*, the Court wrote that "[d]isclosure of expenditures [in candidate elections] lessens the risk that individuals will spend money to support a candidate as a *quid pro quo* for special treatment after the candidate is in office." Ohio could not rely upon the anti-enforcement interest in *McIntyre* as the federal government did in *Buckley* because disclosure was unnecessary to support any other Ohio campaign finance regulation. That left only the information interest, which the Court held was inadequate in McIntyre's case.

Following *McIntyre*, is the information interest standing alone ever adequate grounds for disclosure in a campaign finance case? If not, it would be unconstitutional to require disclosure of contributions and expenditures in any ballot measure campaign, where the anti-corruption interest (at least in the sense of *quid pro quo* corruption) is irrelevant because there is no candidate to corrupt, and the enforcement interest is inapplicable because existing precedent (such as *Bellotti* and *CARC*) prevents contribution and expenditure limits in ballot campaigns. For a case upholding the ability of the state to require disclosure of express advocacy in ballot measure elections, see *California Pro-Life Council, Inc. v. Getman*, 328 F.3d 1088 (9th Cir. 2003).

3. Despite the serious questions raised about the limits of campaign disclosure in *McIntyre*, in more recent years the Supreme Court has repeatedly upheld campaign

finance disclosure laws against First Amendment challenge. Recall that the *Buckley* Court found part of the disclosure law to be vague, and it interpreted the law to apply only to what has come to be known as "express advocacy," advertising such as "Vote for Senator X." The result of this interpretation was that contributions and spending for many "issue advocacy" ads went unreported. Congress fixed the vagueness problem in BCRA. Among other things, BCRA requires disclosure of contributions and spending on so-called "electioneering communications," which are radio and television advertisements featuring a federal candidate and broadcasting to a wide audience close to the election. The Supreme Court upheld the disclosure provisions in *McConnell v. FEC*, 540 U.S. 93, 106 (2003), and held that the provisions could be applied to a broad array of ads—even those that are not the functional equivalent of express advocacy—in the *Citizens United* case. In both cases, the vote was 8–1. In both cases Justice Thomas cited *McIntyre* in dissent, but the majority did not cite it.

4. *Buckley* and *McIntyre* are different in one other important way. *Buckley* required disclosure in documents filed with a government agency after the expenditure or contribution, while *McIntyre* required disclosure on the face of the document itself. Indeed, the Court in *McIntyre* distinguished *Buckley* and *Bellotti* on grounds that "[n]either case involved a prohibition of anonymous campaign literature." Should the time and place of disclosure matter?

Another U.S. Supreme Court case sent mixed signals on the question whether the time and place of disclosure matter. In *Buckley v. American Constitutional Law Foundation*, 525 U.S. 182 (1999), the Justices unanimously agreed that it was unconstitutional for Colorado to require paid initiative petition circulators to wear an identification badge displaying their names.

> [T]he restraint on speech in this case is more severe than was the restraint in *McIntyre*. Petition circulation is the less fleeting encounter, for the circulator must endeavor to persuade electors to sign the petition.... The injury to speech is heightened for the petition circulator because the badge requirement compels personal name identification at the precise moment when the circulator's interest in anonymity is the greatest.

Id. at 199. This holding suggests that the time and place of disclosure do matter. However, the *ACLF* Court in a footnote distinguished the case (and *Meyer v. Grant*, 486 U.S. 414 (1988), which struck down a Colorado law prohibiting the payment of petition circulators) from campaign finance disclosure cases: "[T]oday's decision ... like *Meyer*, separates petition circulators from the proponents and financial backers of ballot initiatives."

By a 6–3 vote, the *ACLF* Court also struck down a requirement that initiative proponents file disclosure reports listing paid circulators and their income from circulation. Thus, the time and place of disclosure apparently were not dispositive to the six Justices in the *ACLF* majority. That holding, however, appeared to turn at least in part on the fact that initiative circulators already disclosed their names and addresses on affidavits accompanying initiative petitions filed for public inspection—thus, the additional challenged disclosure requirement was unnecessary.

5. Does government-required disclosure of information on the face of documents (or through spoken words on radio or superimposed words on television broadcasts) violate First Amendment prohibitions against compelled speech? For a skeptical look at BCRA's "Stand by your ad" required disclosures, see Nicholas Stephanopoulos, *Stand by Your First Amendment Values—Not Your Ad: The Court's Wrong Turn in* McConnell v. FEC, 23 Yale Law & Policy Review 369 (2005).

California passed a series of provisions requiring publishers of "slate mailers" advocating the election or defeat of several candidates or ballot measures to include certain information on the face of the mailers. For example, slate mailers making a recommendation contrary to the "official endorsement" of a party "which the mailer appears by representation or indicia to represent" had to include a statement that the recommendation was "NOT THE POSITION" of the party in question. This requirement was void under the general principle that "a statute compelling speech, like a statute forbidding speech, falls within the purview of the First Amendment." See *Levine v. Fair Political Practices Commission*, 222 F. Supp. 2d 1182 (E.D.Cal. 2002). An earlier decision struck down a requirement that three dollar signs accompany the publication of an endorsement of a candidate or proposition when someone paid the publisher to cover some of the cost of the mailing. The court relied upon *McIntyre's* statement that the state's information interest did "not justify a requirement that a writer make statements or disclosures she would otherwise omit." *California Prolife Council Political Action Committee v. Scully*, No. Civ. S-96-1965 LKK/DAD (E.D. Cal. Mar. 1, 2001). If the government cannot require disclosure on the face of slate mailers, can it require that a radio or television communication governed by federal campaign law include "in a clearly spoken manner, the following audio statement: '_____ is responsible for the content of this advertising.' (with the blank to be filled in with the name of the political committee or other person paying for the communication and the name of any connected organization of the payor.)"? See BCRA, § 311, upheld by the Supreme Court in *McConnell v. Federal Election Commission*, and imposing a similar requirement.

6. With all of this talk about disclosure, might there be a virtue in *mandatory* donor anonymity? The secrecy of the voting booth is sometimes defended as a way of preventing the corruption of voters; might a secret "donation booth" prevent the corruption of candidates and elected officials? See Bruce Ackerman & Ian Ayres, Voting with Dollars: A New Paradigm for Campaign Finance (2002), arguing for a combination of mandatory anonymity of donations and campaign finance vouchers. The book has received an extraordinary amount of scholarly commentary, including two symposia and a number of other reviews. Volume 91, Issue 3 (May 2003) of the California Law Review features commentaries on the book by Richard Briffault, John Ferejohn, Pamela S. Karlan, and David Strauss (with a rejoinder by Ackerman and Ayres). Volume 37, Number 4 (May 2003) of the University of Richmond Law Review features commentaries on the book by Kathryn Abrams, Bruce E. Cain,

Daniel A. Farber, Elizabeth Garrett, Richard L. Hasen, Kenneth R. Mayer, and Fred Wertheimer & Alexandra T.V. Edsall (with a response by Ackerman and Ayres). See also Lillian R. BeVier, Book Review, *What Ails Us?*, 112 Yale Law Journal 1135 (2003); Guy-Uriel E. Charles, Book Review, *Mixing Metaphors: Voting, Dollars and Campaign Finance Reform*, 2 Election Law Journal 271 (2003); and Daniel H. Lowenstein, Book Review, *Voting with Votes*, 116 Harvard Law Review 1971 (2003).

II. The New Skepticism About Disclosure

As we saw in earlier chapters on spending limits and contribution limits, the Supreme Court has moved in a decisively deregulatory direction. Until recently, skepticism of regulation did not extend to laws that required disclosure of campaign finance information, even among most of the conservatives on the Court aside from Justice Thomas. Justices such as Antonin Scalia and Anthony Kennedy, both in the majority in *Citizens United* on the spending limits question, also saw disclosure as a much more narrowly tailored solution than limits to deal with the potential for corruption. The Court consistently upheld disclosure rules, including in *McConnell* and *Citizens United.*

But the addition of new conservative Justices on the Court, as well as the ease with which disclosed campaign finance information now flows on the Internet and on social media, seems to be changing the constitutional calculus. See William McGeveran, *Mrs. McIntyre's Checkbook: Privacy Costs of Political Contribution Disclosure*, 6 University of Pennsylvania Journal of Constitutional Law 1 (2003). We may be moving into a period of New Skepticism about disclosure as well.

The first signs of a potential shift came into sharp relief in *Doe v. Reed*, 561 U.S. 186 (2010). *Reed* concerned not a campaign finance disclosure law but one that required disclosure of the names of Washington state voters who sign petitions to place measures on the ballot. The dispute concerned the disclosure of the names of signers of a referendum petition that would have given voters the opportunity to reverse a Washington law giving certain rights to same-sex couples.

In a majority opinion written by Chief Justice Roberts, the Court upheld the law against a facial challenge and remanded for consideration of an as-applied challenge. In other words, the Court held that the disclosure law constitutionally could be applied to most petition signers, but that the signers of the same-sex rights referendum might be entitled to an exemption if they could prove a threat of harassment. The Court remanded the case to consider this as-applied challenge.

In addressing the facial challenge, the Court described the applicable standard of review of mandatory disclosure laws:

> We have a series of precedents considering First Amendment challenges to disclosure requirements in the electoral context. These precedents have

> reviewed such challenges under what has been termed "exacting scrutiny." See, *e.g.*, *Buckley v. Valeo*; *Citizens United*; *Davis v. FEC*; *ACLF.*
>
> That standard "requires a 'substantial relation' between the disclosure requirement and a 'sufficiently important' governmental interest." *Citizens United.* To withstand this scrutiny, "the strength of the governmental interest must reflect the seriousness of the actual burden on First Amendment rights."

Washington State sought to justify its disclosure law based on two interests: "(1) preserving the integrity of the electoral process by combating fraud, detecting invalid signatures, and fostering government transparency and accountability; and (2) providing information to the electorate about who supports the petition." The Court held that the first interest was sufficient to defeat the constitutional argument against it: "Because we determine that the State's interest in preserving the integrity of the electoral process suffices to defeat the argument that the PRA is unconstitutional with respect to referendum petitions in general, we need not, and do not, address the State's 'informational' interest." It remanded the case to the lower court to consider whether the risk of harassment for signers of the particular referendum justified as as-applied exception.

Although the decision was 8-1, with only Justice Thomas dissenting, many Justices wrote concurring opinions. Justices Scalia and Sotomayor wrote strong defenses of the interests in disclosure, while Justice Alito stressed the potential for disclosure to chill protected First Amendment activity, especially in the Internet era. On the risks of disclosure chilling participation, Justice Scalia concluded his concurring opinion with this often-quoted passage:

> Plaintiffs raise concerns that the disclosure of petition signatures may lead to threats and intimidation. Of course nothing prevents the people of Washington from keeping petition signatures secret to avoid that—just as nothing prevented the States from moving to the secret ballot. But there is no constitutional basis for this Court to impose that course upon the States—or to insist (as today's opinion does) that it can only be avoided by the demonstration of a "sufficiently important governmental interest." And it may even be a bad idea to keep petition signatures secret. There are laws against threats and intimidation; and harsh criticism, short of unlawful action, is a price our people have traditionally been willing to pay for self-governance. Requiring people to stand up in public for their political acts fosters civic courage, without which democracy is doomed. For my part, I do not look forward to a society which, thanks to the Supreme Court, campaigns anonymously (*McIntyre*) and even exercises the direct democracy of initiative and referendum hidden from public scrutiny and protected from the accountability of criticism. This does not resemble the Home of the Brave.

A decade after *Reed*, the Supreme Court returned to the question of disclosure. With a different conservative majority on the Court, the tone and standard of the Court's analysis took a dramatic turn.

Americans for Prosperity Foundation v. Bonta

141 S. Ct. 2373 (2021)

Chief Justice ROBERTS delivered the opinion of the Court, except as to Part II-B-1.

To solicit contributions in California, charitable organizations must disclose to the state Attorney General's Office the identities of their major donors. The State contends that having this information on hand makes it easier to police misconduct by charities. We must decide whether California's disclosure requirement violates the First Amendment right to free association.

I

The California Attorney General's Office is responsible for statewide law enforcement, including the supervision and regulation of charitable fundraising. Under state law, the Attorney General is authorized to "establish and maintain a register" of charitable organizations and to obtain "whatever information, copies of instruments, reports, and records are needed for the establishment and maintenance of the register." In order to operate and raise funds in California, charities generally must register with the Attorney General and renew their registrations annually. Over 100,000 charities are currently registered in the State, and roughly 60,000 renew their registrations each year.

California law empowers the Attorney General to make rules and regulations regarding the registration and renewal process. Pursuant to this regulatory authority, the Attorney General requires charities renewing their registrations to file copies of their Internal Revenue Service Form 990, along with any attachments and schedules. Form 990 contains information regarding tax-exempt organizations' mission, leadership, and finances. Schedule B to Form 990 — the document that gives rise to the present dispute — requires organizations to disclose the names and addresses of donors who have contributed more than $5,000 in a particular tax year (or, in some cases, who have given more than 2 percent of an organization's total contributions).

The petitioners are tax-exempt charities that solicit contributions in California and are subject to the Attorney General's registration and renewal requirements. Americans for Prosperity Foundation is a public charity that is "devoted to education and training about the principles of a free and open society, including free markets, civil liberties, immigration reform, and constitutionally limited government." Thomas More Law Center is a public interest law firm whose "mission is to protect religious freedom, free speech, family values, and the sanctity of human life." Since 2001, each petitioner has renewed its registration and has filed a copy of its Form 990 with the Attorney General, as required by [California law]. Out of concern for their donors' anonymity, however, the petitioners have declined to file their Schedule Bs (or have filed only redacted versions) with the State.

For many years, the petitioners' reluctance to turn over donor information presented no problem because the Attorney General was not particularly zealous about collecting Schedule Bs. That changed in 2010, when the California Department of Justice "ramped up its efforts to enforce charities' Schedule B obligations, sending thousands of deficiency letters to charities that had not complied with the Schedule B requirement." The Law Center and the Foundation received deficiency letters in 2012 and 2013, respectively. When they continued to resist disclosing their contributors' identities, the Attorney General threatened to suspend their registrations and fine their directors and officers.

The petitioners each responded by filing suit in the Central District of California. In their complaints, they alleged that the Attorney General had violated their First Amendment rights and the rights of their donors. The petitioners alleged that disclosure of their Schedule Bs would make their donors less likely to contribute and would subject them to the risk of reprisals. Both organizations challenged the disclosure requirement on its face and as applied to them.

In each case, the District Court granted preliminary injunctive relief prohibiting the Attorney General from collecting their Schedule B information. The Ninth Circuit vacated and remanded. The court held that it was bound by Circuit precedent to reject the petitioners' facial challenge. And reviewing the petitioners' as-applied claims under an "exacting scrutiny" standard, the panel narrowed the injunction, allowing the Attorney General to collect the petitioners' Schedule Bs so long as he did not publicly disclose them.

On remand, the District Court held bench trials in both cases, after which it entered judgment for the petitioners and permanently enjoined the Attorney General from collecting their Schedule Bs. Applying exacting scrutiny, the District Court held that disclosure of Schedule Bs was not narrowly tailored to the State's interest in investigating charitable misconduct. The court credited testimony from California officials that Schedule Bs were rarely used to audit or investigate charities. And it found that even where Schedule B information was used, that information could be obtained from other sources.

The court also determined that the disclosure regime burdened the associational rights of donors. In both cases, the court found that the petitioners had suffered from threats and harassment in the past, and that donors were likely to face similar retaliation in the future if their affiliations became publicly known. For example, the CEO of the Foundation testified that a technology contractor working at the Foundation's headquarters had posted online that he was "inside the belly of the beast" and "could easily walk into [the CEO's] office and slit his throat." And the Law Center introduced evidence that it had received "threats, harassing calls, intimidating and obscene emails, and even pornographic letters."

The District Court also found that California was unable to ensure the confidentiality of donors' information. During the course of litigation, the Foundation identified nearly 2,000 confidential Schedule Bs that had been inadvertently posted to the Attorney General's website, including dozens that were found the day before trial. One of the Foundation's expert witnesses also discovered that he was able to access hundreds of thousands of confidential documents on the website simply by changing a digit in the URL. The court found after trial that "the amount of careless mistakes made by the Attorney General's Registry is shocking." And although California subsequently codified a policy prohibiting disclosure — an effort the District Court described as "commendable" — the court determined that "[d]onors and potential donors would be reasonably justified in a fear of disclosure given such a context" of past breaches.

The Ninth Circuit again vacated the District Court's injunctions, and this time reversed the judgments and remanded for entry of judgment in favor of the Attorney General. The court held that the District Court had erred by imposing a narrow tailoring requirement. And it reasoned that the disclosure regime satisfied exacting scrutiny because the up-front collection of charities' Schedule Bs promoted investigative efficiency and effectiveness. The panel also found that the disclosure of Schedule Bs would not meaningfully burden donors' associational rights, in part because the Attorney General had taken remedial security measures to fix the confidentiality breaches identified at trial.

The Ninth Circuit denied rehearing en banc. Judge Ikuta dissented, joined by four other judges. In her view, the panel had impermissibly overridden the District Court's factual findings and evaluated the disclosure requirement under too lenient a degree of scrutiny.

We granted certiorari.

II

A

The First Amendment prohibits government from "abridging the freedom of speech, or of the press; or the right of the people peaceably to assemble, and to petition the Government for a redress of grievances." This Court has "long understood as implicit in the right to engage in activities protected by the First Amendment a corresponding right to associate with others." *Roberts v. United States Jaycees*, 468 U.S. 609, 622 (1984). Protected association furthers "a wide variety of political, social, economic, educational, religious, and cultural ends," and "is especially important in preserving political and cultural diversity and in shielding dissident expression from suppression by the majority." *Ibid.* Government infringement of this freedom "can take a number of forms." *Ibid.* We have held, for example, that the freedom of association may be violated where a group is required to take in members it does not want, see *id.*, at 623, where individuals are punished for their political affiliation, see *Elrod v. Burns* [Chapter 8 — Eds.] (plurality opinion), or where members of an organization are denied benefits based on the organization's message, see *Healy v. James*, 408 U.S. 169, 181–182 (1972).

We have also noted that "[i]t is hardly a novel perception that compelled disclosure of affiliation with groups engaged in advocacy may constitute as effective a restraint on freedom of association as [other] forms of governmental action." *NAACP v. Alabama ex rel. Patterson*, 357 U.S. 449, 462 (1958). *NAACP v. Alabama* involved this chilling effect in its starkest form. The NAACP opened an Alabama office that supported racial integration in higher education and public transportation. In response, NAACP members were threatened with economic reprisals and violence. As part of an effort to oust the organization from the State, the Alabama Attorney General sought the group's membership lists. We held that the First Amendment prohibited such compelled disclosure. We explained that "[e]ffective advocacy of both public and private points of view, particularly controversial ones, is undeniably enhanced by group association," and we noted "the vital relationship between freedom to associate and privacy in one's associations." Because NAACP members faced a risk of reprisals if their affiliation with the organization became known — and because Alabama had demonstrated no offsetting interest "sufficient to justify the deterrent effect" of disclosure — we concluded that the State's demand violated the First Amendment.

B

1

NAACP v. Alabama did not phrase in precise terms the standard of review that applies to First Amendment challenges to compelled disclosure. We have since settled on a standard referred to as "exacting scrutiny." *Buckley* (*per curiam*). Under that standard, there must be "a substantial relation between the disclosure requirement and a sufficiently important governmental interest." *Doe v. Reed*. "To withstand this scrutiny, the strength of the governmental interest must reflect the seriousness of the actual burden on First Amendment rights." *Ibid.* Such scrutiny, we have held, is appropriate given the "deterrent effect on the exercise of First Amendment rights" that arises as an "inevitable result of the government's conduct in requiring disclosure."

The Law Center (but not the Foundation) argues that we should apply strict scrutiny, not exacting scrutiny. Under strict scrutiny, the government must adopt "the least restrictive means of achieving a compelling state interest," *McCullen v. Coakley*, 573 U.S. 464, 478 (2014), rather than a means substantially related to a sufficiently important interest. The Law Center contends that only strict scrutiny adequately protects the associational rights of charities. And although the Law Center acknowledges that we have applied exacting scrutiny in prior disclosure cases, it argues that those cases arose in the electoral context, where the government's important interests justify less searching review. *Buckley*.

It is true that we first enunciated the exacting scrutiny standard in a campaign finance case. See *Buckley*. And we have since invoked it in other election-related settings. See, *e.g.*, *Citizens United; Davis v. Federal Election Comm'n*. But exacting scrutiny is not unique to electoral disclosure regimes. To the contrary, *Buckley* derived the test from *NAACP v. Alabama* itself, as well as other nonelection cases. See *Buckley* (citing *Gibson v. Florida Legislative Investigation Comm.*, 372 U.S. 539

(1963); *NAACP v. Button*, 371 U.S. 415 (1963); *Shelton v. Tucker*, 364 U.S. 479 (1960); *Bates v. Little Rock*, 361 U.S. 516 (1960)). As we explained in *NAACP v. Alabama*, "it is immaterial" to the level of scrutiny "whether the beliefs sought to be advanced by association pertain to political, economic, religious or cultural matters." Regardless of the type of association, compelled disclosure requirements are reviewed under exacting scrutiny.

2

The Law Center (now joined by the Foundation) argues in the alternative that even if exacting scrutiny applies, such review incorporates a least restrictive means test similar to the one imposed by strict scrutiny. The United States and the Attorney General respond that exacting scrutiny demands no additional tailoring beyond the "substantial relation" requirement noted above. We think that the answer lies between those two positions. While exacting scrutiny does not require that disclosure regimes be the least restrictive means of achieving their ends, it does require that they be narrowly tailored to the government's asserted interest.

The need for narrow tailoring was set forth early in our compelled disclosure cases. In *Shelton v. Tucker*, we considered an Arkansas statute that required teachers to disclose every organization to which they belonged or contributed. We acknowledged the importance of "the right of a State to investigate the competence and fitness of those whom it hires to teach in its schools." On that basis, we distinguished prior decisions in which we had found "no substantially relevant correlation between the governmental interest asserted and the State's effort to compel disclosure." But we nevertheless held that the Arkansas statute was invalid because even a "legitimate and substantial" governmental interest "cannot be pursued by means that broadly stifle fundamental personal liberties when the end can be more narrowly achieved."

Shelton stands for the proposition that a substantial relation to an important interest is not enough to save a disclosure regime that is insufficiently tailored. This requirement makes sense. Narrow tailoring is crucial where First Amendment activity is chilled — even if indirectly — "[b]ecause First Amendment freedoms need breathing space to survive." *Button*.

Our more recent decisions confirm the need for tailoring. In *McCutcheon v. Federal Election Commission*, for example, a plurality of the Court explained:

> "In the First Amendment context, fit matters. Even when the Court is not applying strict scrutiny, we still require a fit that is not necessarily perfect, but reasonable; that represents not necessarily the single best disposition but one whose scope is in proportion to the interest served, that employs not necessarily the least restrictive means but a means narrowly tailored to achieve the desired objective."

McCutcheon is instructive here. A substantial relation is necessary but not sufficient to ensure that the government adequately considers the potential for First Amendment harms before requiring that organizations reveal sensitive information about their members and supporters. Where exacting scrutiny applies, the challenged requirement must be narrowly tailored to the interest it promotes, even if it is not the least restrictive means of achieving that end.

The dissent reads our cases differently. It focuses on the words "broadly stifle" in the quotation from *Shelton* above, and it interprets those words to mean that narrow tailoring is required only for disclosure regimes that "impose a severe burden on associational rights." Because, in the dissent's view, the petitioners have not shown such a burden here, narrow tailoring is not required.

We respectfully disagree. The "government may regulate in the [First Amendment] area only with narrow specificity," *Button*, and compelled disclosure regimes are no exception. When it comes to "a person's beliefs and associations," "[b]road and sweeping state inquiries into these protected areas . . . discourage citizens from exercising rights protected by the Constitution." *Baird v. State Bar of Ariz.*, 401 U.S. 1, 6 (1971) (plurality opinion). Contrary to the dissent, we understand this Court's discussion of rules that are "broad" and "broadly stifle" First Amendment freedoms to refer to the scope of challenged restrictions—their breadth—rather than the severity of any demonstrated burden. That much seems clear to us from *Shelton*'s statement (in the sentence following the one quoted by the dissent) that "[t]he breadth of legislative abridgment must be viewed in the light of less drastic means for achieving the same basic purpose." It also seems clear from the immediately preceding paragraph, which stressed that "[t]he scope of the inquiry required by [the law] is completely unlimited. . . . It requires [the teacher] to list, without number, every conceivable kind of associational tie—social, professional, political, avocational, or religious. Many such relationships could have no possible bearing upon the teacher's occupational competence or fitness." In other words, the law was not narrowly tailored to the State's objective.

Nor does our decision in *Reed* suggest that narrow tailoring is required only for laws that impose severe burdens. The dissent casts *Reed* as a case involving only "'modest burdens,'" and therefore "a correspondingly modest level of tailoring." But it was only after we concluded that various narrower alternatives proposed by the plaintiffs were inadequate, that we held that the strength of the government's interest in disclosure reflected the burden imposed. The point is that a reasonable assessment of the burdens imposed by disclosure should begin with an understanding of the extent to which the burdens are unnecessary, and that requires narrow tailoring.

III

The Foundation and the Law Center both argued below that the obligation to disclose Schedule Bs to the Attorney General was unconstitutional on its face and as applied to them. The petitioners renew their facial challenge in this Court, and they argue in the alternative that they are entitled to as-applied relief. For the reasons below, we conclude that California's blanket demand for Schedule Bs is facially unconstitutional.

A

As explained, exacting scrutiny requires that there be "a substantial relation between the disclosure requirement and a sufficiently important governmental interest," *Reed*, and that the disclosure requirement be narrowly tailored to the interest it promotes, see *Shelton*. The Ninth Circuit found that there was a substantial relation between the Attorney General's demand for Schedule Bs and a sufficiently strong governmental interest. Of particular relevance, the court found that California had such an interest in preventing charitable fraud and self-dealing, and that "the up-front collection of Schedule B information improves the efficiency and efficacy of the Attorney General's important regulatory efforts." The court did not apply a narrow tailoring requirement, however, because it did not read our cases to mandate any such inquiry. That was error. And properly applied, the narrow tailoring requirement is not satisfied by the disclosure regime.

We do not doubt that California has an important interest in preventing wrongdoing by charitable organizations. It goes without saying that there is a "substantial governmental interest[] in protecting the public from fraud." *Schaumburg v. Citizens for Better Environment*, 444 U.S. 620, 636 (1980). The Attorney General receives complaints each month that identify a range of misconduct, from "misuse, misappropriation, and diversion of charitable assets," to "false and misleading charitable solicitations," to other "improper activities by charities soliciting charitable donations." Such offenses cause serious social harms. And the Attorney General is the primary law enforcement officer charged with combating them under California law.

There is a dramatic mismatch, however, between the interest that the Attorney General seeks to promote and the disclosure regime that he has implemented in service of that end. Recall that 60,000 charities renew their registrations each year, and nearly all are required to file a Schedule B. Each Schedule B, in turn, contains information about a charity's top donors — a small handful of individuals in some cases, but hundreds in others. This information includes donors' names and the total contributions they have made to the charity, as well as their addresses.

Given the amount and sensitivity of this information harvested by the State, one would expect Schedule B collection to form an integral part of California's fraud detection efforts. It does not. To the contrary, the record amply supports the District Court's finding that there was not "a single, concrete instance in which pre-investigation collection of a Schedule B did anything to advance the Attorney General's investigative, regulatory or enforcement efforts."

The dissent devotes much of its analysis to relitigating factual disputes that the District Court resolved against the Attorney General, notwithstanding the applicable clear error standard of review. For example, the dissent echoes the State's argument that, in some cases, it relies on up-front Schedule B collection to prevent and police fraud. But the record before the District Court tells a different story. And even if the State relied on up-front collection in some cases, its showing falls far short of satisfying the means-end fit that exacting scrutiny requires. California is not free to enforce *any* disclosure regime that furthers its interests. It must instead demonstrate its need for universal production in light of any less intrusive alternatives. Cf. *Shelton*.

The Attorney General and the dissent contend that alternative means of obtaining Schedule B information—such as a subpoena or audit letter—are inefficient and ineffective compared to up-front collection. It became clear at trial, however, that the Office had not even considered alternatives to the current disclosure requirement. The Attorney General and the dissent also argue that a targeted request for Schedule B information could tip a charity off, causing it to "hide or tamper with evidence." But again, the States' witnesses failed to substantiate that concern. Nor do the actions of investigators suggest a risk of tipping off charities under suspicion, as the standard practice is to send audit letters asking for a wide range of information early in the investigative process. Furthermore, even if tipoff were a concern in some cases, the State's indiscriminate collection of Schedule Bs in all cases would not be justified.

The upshot is that California casts a dragnet for sensitive donor information from tens of thousands of charities each year, even though that information will become relevant in only a small number of cases involving filed complaints. California does not rely on Schedule Bs to initiate investigations, and in all events, there are multiple alternative mechanisms through which the Attorney General can obtain Schedule B information after initiating an investigation. The need for up-front collection is particularly dubious given that California—one of only three States to impose such a requirement—did not rigorously enforce the disclosure obligation until 2010. Certainly, this is not a regime "whose scope is in proportion to the interest served." *McCutcheon*.

In reality, then, California's interest is less in investigating fraud and more in ease of administration. This interest, however, cannot justify the disclosure requirement. The Attorney General may well prefer to have every charity's information close at hand, just in case. But "the prime objective of the First Amendment is not efficiency." Mere administrative convenience does not remotely "reflect the seriousness of the actual burden" that the demand for Schedule Bs imposes on donors' association rights. *Reed*.

B

The foregoing discussion also makes clear why a facial challenge is appropriate in these cases. Normally, a plaintiff bringing a facial challenge must "establish that no set of circumstances exists under which the [law] would be valid," *United States v. Salerno*, 481 U.S. 739, 745, 7 (1987), or show that the law lacks "a plainly legitimate sweep," *Washington State Grange v. Washington State Republican Party* [discussed in Chapter 8—Eds.]. In the First Amendment context, however, we have recognized "a second type of facial challenge, whereby a law may be invalidated as overbroad if a substantial number of its applications are unconstitutional, judged in relation to the statute's plainly legitimate sweep." *United States v. Stevens*, 559 U.S. 460, 473 (2010). We have no trouble concluding here that the Attorney General's disclosure requirement is overbroad. The lack of tailoring to the State's investigative goals is categorical—present in every case—as is the weakness of the State's interest in administrative convenience. Every demand that might chill association therefore fails exacting scrutiny.

The Attorney General tries to downplay the burden on donors, arguing that "there is no basis on which to conclude that California's requirement results in any broad-based chill." He emphasizes that "California's Schedule B requirement is confidential," and he suggests that certain donors—like those who give to noncontroversial charities—are unlikely to be deterred from contributing. He also contends that disclosure to his office imposes no added burdens on donors because tax-exempt charities already provide their Schedule Bs to the IRS.

We are unpersuaded. Our cases have said that disclosure requirements can chill association "[e]ven if there [is] no disclosure to the general public." *Shelton*. In *Shelton*, for example, we noted the "constant and heavy" pressure teachers would experience simply by disclosing their associational ties to their schools. Exacting scrutiny is triggered by "state action which *may* have the effect of curtailing the freedom to associate," and by the "*possible* deterrent effect" of disclosure. *NAACP v. Alabama* (emphasis added); see *Talley v. California*, 362 U.S. 60, 65 (1960) ("identification and fear of reprisal *might* deter perfectly peaceful discussions of public matters of importance" (emphasis added)). While assurances of confidentiality may reduce the burden of disclosure to the State, they do not eliminate it.*

It is irrelevant, moreover, that some donors might not mind—or might even prefer—the disclosure of their identities to the State. The disclosure requirement "creates an unnecessary risk of chilling" in violation of the First Amendment, indiscriminately sweeping up the information of *every* major donor with reason to remain anonymous. The petitioners here, for example, introduced evidence that they and their supporters have been subjected to bomb threats, protests, stalking, and physical violence. Such risks are heightened in the 21st century and seem to grow with each passing year, as "anyone with access to a computer [can] compile a wealth of information about" anyone else, including such sensitive details as a person's home address or the school attended by his children. *Reed* (ALITO, J., concurring).

---

* Here the State's assurances of confidentiality are not worth much. The dissent acknowledges that the Foundation and Law Center "have unquestionably provided evidence that their donors face a reasonable probability of threats, harassment, and reprisals if their affiliations are made public," but it concludes that the petitioners have no cause for concern because the Attorney General "has implemented security measures to ensure that Schedule B information remains confidential." The District Court—whose findings, again, we review only for clear error—disagreed. After two full bench trials, the court found that the Attorney General's promise of confidentiality "rings hollow," and that "[d]onors and potential donors would be reasonably justified in a fear of disclosure."

The gravity of the privacy concerns in this context is further underscored by the filings of hundreds of organizations as *amici curiae* in support of the petitioners. Far from representing uniquely sensitive causes, these organizations span the ideological spectrum, and indeed the full range of human endeavors: from the American Civil Liberties Union to the Proposition 8 Legal Defense Fund; from the Council on American-Islamic Relations to the Zionist Organization of America; from Feeding America — Eastern Wisconsin to PBS Reno. The deterrent effect feared by these organizations is real and pervasive, even if their concerns are not shared by every single charity operating or raising funds in California.

The dissent argues that — regardless of the defects in California's disclosure regime — a facial challenge cannot succeed unless a plaintiff shows that donors to a substantial number of organizations will be subjected to harassment and reprisals. As we have explained, plaintiffs may be required to bear this evidentiary burden where the challenged regime is narrowly tailored to an important government interest. Such a demanding showing is not required, however, where — as here — the disclosure law fails to satisfy these criteria.

Finally, California's demand for Schedule Bs cannot be saved by the fact that donor information is already disclosed to the IRS as a condition of federal tax-exempt status. For one thing, each governmental demand for disclosure brings with it an additional risk of chill. For another, revenue collection efforts and conferral of tax-exempt status may raise issues not presented by California's disclosure requirement, which can prevent charities from operating in the State altogether.

We are left to conclude that the Attorney General's disclosure requirement imposes a widespread burden on donors' associational rights. And this burden cannot be justified on the ground that the regime is narrowly tailored to investigating charitable wrongdoing, or that the State's interest in administrative convenience is sufficiently important. We therefore hold that the up-front collection of Schedule Bs is facially unconstitutional, because it fails exacting scrutiny in "a substantial number of its applications . . . judged in relation to [its] plainly legitimate sweep." *Stevens.*

The dissent concludes by saying that it would be "sympathetic" if we "had simply granted as-applied relief to petitioners based on [our] reading of the facts." But the pertinent facts in these cases are the same across the board: Schedule Bs are not used to initiate investigations. That is true in every case. California has not considered alternatives to indiscriminate up-front disclosure. That is true in every case. And the State's interest in amassing sensitive information for its own convenience is weak. That is true in every case. When it comes to the freedom of association, the protections of the First Amendment are triggered not only by actual restrictions on an individual's ability to join with others to further shared goals. The risk of a chilling effect on association is enough, "[b]ecause First Amendment freedoms need breathing space to survive." *Button.*

* * *

The District Court correctly entered judgment in favor of the petitioners and permanently enjoined the Attorney General from collecting their Schedule Bs. The Ninth Circuit erred by vacating those injunctions and directing entry of judgment for the Attorney General. The judgment of the Ninth Circuit is reversed, and the cases are remanded for further proceedings consistent with this opinion.

It is so ordered.

Justice THOMAS, concurring in Parts I, II-A, II-B-2, and III-A, and concurring in the judgment.

The Court correctly holds that California's disclosure requirement violates the First Amendment. It also correctly concludes that the District Court properly enjoined California's attorney general from collecting the forms at issue, which contain sensitive donor information. But, while I agree with much of the Court's opinion, I would approach three issues differently.

First, the bulk of "our precedents . . . require application of strict scrutiny to laws that compel disclosure of protected First Amendment association." *Reed* (THOMAS, J., dissenting). California's law fits that description. Although the Court rightly holds that even the less demanding "exacting scrutiny" standard requires narrow tailoring for laws that compel disclosure, invoking exacting scrutiny is at odds with our repeated recognition "that privacy of association is protected under the First Amendment." The text and history of the Assembly Clause suggest that the right to assemble includes the right to associate anonymously. See 4 Annals of Cong. 900–902, 941–942 (1795) (defending the Democratic-Republican societies, many of which met in secret, as exercising individuals' "leave to assemble"); see also *NAACP v. Alabama* (discussing the history of anonymous publications). And the right to associate anonymously often operates as a vehicle to protect other First Amendment rights, such as the freedom of the press. *McIntyre* (1995) (THOMAS, J., concurring) ("Founding-era Americans" understood the freedom of the press to include the right of printers and publishers not to be compelled to disclose the authors of anonymous works). Laws directly burdening the right to associate anonymously, including compelled disclosure laws, should be subject to the same scrutiny as laws directly burdening other First Amendment rights. *Reed.*

Second, the Court holds the law "overbroad" and, thus, invalid in all circumstances. But I continue to have "doubts about [the] origins and application" of our "overbreadth doctrine." *United States v. Sineneng-Smith*, 140 S.Ct. 1575, 1583 (2020) (THOMAS, J., concurring). . . .

Third, and relatedly, this Court also lacks the power "to 'pronounce that the statute is unconstitutional in *all* applications,'" even if the Court suspects that the law will likely be unconstitutional in every future application as opposed to just a substantial number of its applications. *Borden v. United States*, 141 S.Ct., at — — (THOMAS, J., concurring). . . .

With those points of difference clarified, I join Parts I, II-A, II-B-2, and III-A of the majority's opinion and concur in the judgment.

Justice ALITO, with whom Justice GORSUCH joins, concurring in Parts I, II-A, II-B-2, and III, and concurring in the judgment.

I am pleased to join most of THE CHIEF JUSTICE's opinion. In particular, I agree that the exacting scrutiny standard drawn from our election-law jurisprudence has real teeth. It requires both narrow tailoring and consideration of alternative means of obtaining the sought-after information. For the reasons THE CHIEF JUSTICE explains, California's blunderbuss approach to charitable disclosures fails exacting scrutiny and is facially unconstitutional. The question is not even close. And for the same reasons, California's approach necessarily fails strict scrutiny.

THE CHIEF JUSTICE would hold that the particular exacting scrutiny standard in our election-law jurisprudence applies categorically "to First Amendment challenges to compelled disclosure." Justice THOMAS, by contrast, would hold that strict scrutiny applies in all such cases. I am not prepared at this time to hold that a single standard applies to all disclosure requirements. And I do not read our cases to have broadly resolved the question in favor of exacting scrutiny. . . .

Because the choice between exacting and strict scrutiny has no effect on the decision in these cases, I see no need to decide which standard should be applied here or whether the same level of scrutiny should apply in all cases in which the compelled disclosure of associations is challenged under the First Amendment.

Justice SOTOMAYOR, with whom Justice BREYER and Justice KAGAN join, dissenting.

Although this Court is protective of First Amendment rights, it typically requires that plaintiffs demonstrate an actual First Amendment burden before demanding that a law be narrowly tailored to the government's interests, never mind striking the law down in its entirety. Not so today. Today, the Court holds that reporting and disclosure requirements must be narrowly tailored even if a plaintiff demonstrates no burden at all. The same scrutiny the Court applied when NAACP members in the Jim Crow South did not want to disclose their membership for fear of reprisals and violence now applies equally in the case of donors only too happy to publicize their names across the websites and walls of the organizations they support.

California oversees nearly a quarter of this Nation's charitable assets. As part of that oversight, it investigates and prosecutes charitable fraud, relying in part on a registry where it collects and keeps charitable organizations' tax forms. The majority holds that a California regulation requiring charitable organizations to disclose tax forms containing the names and contributions of their top donors unconstitutionally burdens the right to associate even if the forms are not publicly disclosed.

In so holding, the Court discards its decades-long requirement that, to establish a cognizable burden on their associational rights, plaintiffs must plead and prove that disclosure will likely expose them to objective harms, such as threats, harassment, or reprisals. It also departs from the traditional, nuanced approach to First Amendment challenges, whereby the degree of means-end tailoring required is commensurate to the actual burdens on associational rights. Finally, it recklessly holds a state regulation facially invalid despite petitioners' failure to show that a substantial proportion of those affected would prefer anonymity, much less that they are objectively burdened by the loss of it.

Today's analysis marks reporting and disclosure requirements with a bull's-eye. Regulated entities who wish to avoid their obligations can do so by vaguely waving toward First Amendment "privacy concerns." It does not matter if not a single individual risks experiencing a single reprisal from disclosure, or if the vast majority of those affected would happily comply. That is all irrelevant to the Court's determination that California's Schedule B requirement is facially unconstitutional. Neither precedent nor common sense supports such a result. I respectfully dissent.

I

Charitable organizations that wish to solicit tax-deductible contributions from California residents must maintain membership in a registry managed by the California attorney general. As a condition of membership, the attorney general requires charities to submit a complete copy of Internal Revenue Service (IRS) Form 990, including Schedule B, on which 501(c)(3) organizations report the names and contributions of their major donors. California regulations expressly require that Schedule Bs remain confidential, and the attorney general's office has implemented enhanced protocols to ensure confidentiality.[1] California relies on Schedule Bs to investigate fraud and other malfeasance.

After the attorney general's office stepped up its efforts to enforce California's Schedule B reporting requirement, petitioners Americans for Prosperity Foundation (Foundation) and Thomas More Law Center (Law Center) sought an injunction against the requirement. They alleged that the requirement "unconstitutionally burden[ed] their First Amendment right to free association by deterring individuals from financially supporting them." They pointed to evidence that their supporters experienced threats, reprisals, and harassment when their identities and associations became publicly known in other contexts. Importantly, however, the Foundation and Law Center failed to show that such consequences would result from the confidential submission of their top donors' identities to California's attorney general's office in light of the security mechanisms the office has now implemented.

1. Schedule Bs are kept in a confidential database used only by the Charitable Trusts Section and inaccessible to others in California's attorney general's office. Employees who fail to safeguard confidential information are subject to discipline. In light of previous security breaches disclosed in this litigation, the attorney general's office instituted a series of measures to ensure that Schedule B information remains confidential. The office has adopted a system of text searching forms before they are uploaded onto the Internet to ensure that none contain Schedule B information. The office now also runs automated scans of publicly accessible government databases to identify and remove any documents containing Schedule B information that may be inadvertently uploaded.

II

Because the freedom to associate needs "breathing space to survive," *Button*, this Court has recognized that associational rights must be "protected not only against heavy-handed frontal attack, but also from being stifled by more subtle governmental interference," *Bates v. Little Rock*, 361 U.S. 516, 523 (1960). Publicizing individuals' association with particular groups might expose members to harassment, threats, and reprisals by opponents of those organizations. Individuals may choose to disassociate themselves from a group altogether rather than face such backlash.

Acknowledging that risk, this Court has observed that "privacy in group association may in many circumstances be indispensable to preservation of freedom of association, particularly where a group espouses dissident beliefs." *NAACP v. Alabama* (1958). That observation places special emphasis on the risks actually resulting from disclosure. Privacy "may" be indispensable to the preservation of freedom of association, but it need not be. It depends on whether publicity will lead to reprisal. For example, privacy can be particularly important to "dissident" groups because the risk of retaliation against their supporters may be greater. For groups that promote mainstream goals and ideas, on the other hand, privacy may not be all that important. Not only might their supporters feel agnostic about disclosing their association, they might actively seek to do so.

Given the indeterminacy of how disclosure requirements will impact associational rights, this Court requires plaintiffs to demonstrate that a requirement is likely to expose their supporters to concrete repercussions in order to establish an actual burden. It then applies a level of means-end tailoring proportional to that burden. The Court abandons that approach here, instead holding that narrow tailoring applies to disclosure requirements across the board, even if there is no evidence that they burden anyone at all.

A

Before today, to demonstrate that a reporting or disclosure requirement would chill association, litigants had to show "a reasonable probability that the compelled disclosure of . . . contributors' names will subject them to threats, harassment, or reprisals from either Government officials or private parties. *Buckley.* Proof could include "specific evidence of past or present harassment of members due to their associational ties, or of harassment directed against the organization itself," *ibid.*, as well as evidence that "fear of community hostility and economic reprisals that would follow public disclosure . . . had discouraged new members from joining" an organization or caused "former members to withdraw," *Bates.* Although the Court has never imposed an "unduly strict requiremen[t] of proof," *Buckley*, it has consistently required at least some record evidence demonstrating a risk of such objective harms.

Indeed, the Court has expressly held that parties do not have standing to bring claims where they assert nothing more than that government action will cause a "subjective 'chill.'" *Laird v. Tatum*, 408 U.S. 1, 13–14 (1972). It does not matter if an individual perceives a government regulation "as inappropriate," or believes "it is inherently dangerous for the [government] to be concerned with" a particular activity, or has "generalized yet speculative apprehensiveness that the [government] may at some future date misuse the information in some way that would cause direct harm" to her. *Id.* She must still allege a risk of objective harm. See *id.*

Consistent with this approach, the Court has carefully scrutinized record evidence to determine whether a disclosure requirement actually risks exposing supporters to backlash. . . .

Hence, in *Doe v. Reed*, the Court rejected a facial challenge to the public disclosure of referenda signatories on the ground that the "typical referendum" concerned revenue, budget, and tax policies unlikely to incite threats or harassment. Any judge who has witnessed local fights over raising taxes, funding schools, building sewer systems, or rerouting roads can surely envisage signatories with reason to keep their support for such measures private. But in *Reed*, such subjective reasons did not suffice to establish a cognizable burden on associational rights.

Today, the Court abandons the requirement that plaintiffs demonstrate that they are chilled, much less that they are reasonably chilled. Instead, it presumes (contrary to the evidence, precedent, and common sense) that all disclosure requirements impose associational burdens. For example, the Court explains that there is a risk of chill in this suit because the government requires disclosure of the identity of any donor "with reason to remain anonymous." The Court does not qualify that statement, nor does it require record evidence of such reasons. If the Court did, it would not be able to strike California's Schedule B requirement down in all its applications, because the only evidence in the record of donors with any reason to remain anonymous is that of petitioners'.

At best, then, a subjective preference for privacy, which previously did not confer standing, now subjects disclosure requirements to close scrutiny. Of course, all disclosure requires some loss of anonymity, and courts can always imagine that someone might, for some reason, prefer to keep their donations undisclosed. If such speculation is enough (and apparently it is), then all disclosure requirements *ipso facto* impose cognizable First Amendment burdens.

Indeed, the Court makes obvious its presumption that all disclosure requirements are burdensome by beginning its analysis of "burden" with an evaluation of means-end fit instead. "[A] reasonable assessment of the burdens imposed by disclosure," the Court explains, "should begin with an understanding of the extent to which the burdens are unnecessary, and that requires narrow tailoring."

I disagree. A reasonable assessment of the burdens imposed by disclosure should begin by determining whether those burdens even exist. If a disclosure requirement imposes no burdens at all, then of course there are no "unnecessary" burdens. Likewise, if a disclosure requirement imposes no burden for the Court to remedy, there is no need for it to be closely scrutinized. By forgoing the requirement that plaintiffs adduce evidence of tangible burdens, such as increased vulnerability to harassment or reprisals, the Court gives itself license to substitute its own policy preferences for those of politically accountable actors.

B

All this would be less troubling if the Court still required means-end tailoring commensurate to the actual burden imposed. It does not. Instead, it adopts a new rule that every reporting or disclosure requirement be narrowly tailored.

1

Disclosure requirements burden associational rights only indirectly and only in certain contexts. For that reason, this Court has never necessarily demanded such requirements to be narrowly tailored. Rather, it has reserved such automatic tailoring for state action that "directly and immediately affects associational rights." *Boy Scouts of America v. Dale*, 530 U.S. 640, 659 (2000); see also *Buckley* (requiring a "closely drawn" fit for political contribution limits, which directly "limit one important means of associating with a candidate or committee"). When it comes to reporting and disclosure requirements, the Court has instead employed a more flexible approach, which it has named "exacting scrutiny."

Exacting scrutiny requires two things: first, there must be "'a "substantial relation" between the disclosure requirement and a "sufficiently important" government interest,'" and second, "'the strength of the governmental interest must reflect the seriousness of the actual burden on First Amendment rights.'" *Reed*. Exacting scrutiny thus incorporates a degree of flexibility into the means-end analysis. The more serious the burden on First Amendment rights, the more compelling the government's interest must be, and the tighter must be the fit between that interest and the government's means of pursuing it. By contrast, a less substantial interest and looser fit will suffice where the burden on First Amendment rights is weaker (or nonexistent). In other words, to decide how closely tailored a disclosure requirement must be, courts must ask an antecedent question: How much does the disclosure requirement actually burden the freedom to associate?

This approach reflects the longstanding principle that the requisite level of scrutiny should be commensurate to the burden a government action actually imposes on First Amendment rights. See, *e.g., Burdick v. Takushi* [discussed in Chapter 9—Eds.] ("[T]he rigorousness of our inquiry . . . depends upon the extent to which a challenged regulation burdens" First Amendment rights); *Board of Trustees of State Univ. of N.Y. v. Fox*, 492 U.S. 469, 477 (1989) ("[C]ommercial speech enjoys a limited measure of protection, commensurate with its subordinate position in the scale of First Amendment values, and is [thus] subject to modes of regulation that might be impermissible in the realm of noncommercial expression" (internal quotation marks and alterations omitted)); see also *Fulton v. Philadelphia*, 141 S.Ct. — — (2021) (BARRETT, J., concurring) (noting the "nuanced" approach the Court generally takes in the "resolution of conflicts between generally applicable laws and . . . First Amendment rights").

Compare, for instance, the Court's approaches in *Shelton v. Tucker* and *Doe v. Reed.* At issue in *Shelton* was an Arkansas statute passed in 1958 that compelled all public school teachers, as a condition of employment, to submit annually a list of every organization to which they belonged or regularly contributed.. The Court held that the disclosure requirement "comprehensive[ly] interfere[d] with associational freedom," because record evidence demonstrated a significant risk that the information would be publicly disclosed, and such disclosure could lead to public pressure on school boards "to discharge teachers who belong to unpopular or minority organizations." Arkansas's statute did not require that the information remain confidential; each school board was "free to deal with the information as it wishe[d]." Indeed, "a witness who was a member of the Capital Citizens['] Council" (an organization dedicated to resisting school integration) "testified that his group intended to gain access" to the teachers' affidavits "with a view to eliminating from the school system persons who supported organizations unpopular with the group." Moreover, a starkly asymmetric power dynamic existed between teachers, who were "hired on a year-to-year basis," and the hiring authorities to whom their membership lists were submitted. The Arkansas Legislature had made no secret of its desire for teachers' disclosures to be used for hiring and firing decisions. One year after enacting the disclosure requirement at issue in *Shelton*, the legislature enacted another provision that made it outright unlawful for state governmental bodies to employ members of the NAACP. It is thus unsurprising that the Court found that Arkansas teachers would feel a "constant and heavy" pressure "to avoid any ties which might displease those who control [their] professional destin[ies]." Because Arkansas's purpose (ensuring teachers' fitness) was "pursued by means that broadly stifle fundamental personal liberties," the Court demanded that Arkansas "more narrowly achiev[e]" its interest.

Now consider this Court's approach in *Reed. Reed* involved a facial challenge to a Washington law permitting the public disclosure of referendum petitions that included signatories' names and addresses. The Court found that Washington had a number of other mechanisms in place to pursue its stated interest in preventing fraudulent referendum signatures. For instance, the secretary of state was charged with verifying and canvassing the names on referendum petitions, advocates and opponents of a measure could observe the canvassing process, and citizens could challenge the secretary's actions in court. Publicly disclosing referendum signatories was thus a mere backstop, giving citizens the opportunity to catch the secretary's mistakes. Had Washington been required to achieve its interests narrowly, as in *Shelton*, it is unlikely the disclosure requirement would have survived.[4]

---

4. For instance, the Court did not ask whether the public disclosure of signatories' names and addresses was "in proportion to the" government's interest in policing fraud. Nor did it feel any need to respond to the dissent's description of ways in which Washington's interest could be met without public disclosure. It was enough that public disclosure could "help" advance electoral integrity. The Court is clearly wrong to suggest it applied narrow tailoring in *Reed.*

In crucial contrast to *Shelton*, however, the *Reed* Court found "scant evidence" that disclosure exposed signatories of typical referendums to "threats, harassment, or reprisals from either Government officials or private parties." Given the "modest burdens" imposed by the requirement, the Court required a correspondingly modest level of tailoring. Under that standard, the disclosure requirement passed muster, and the Court refused to facially strike it down.

The public disclosure regimes in both *Shelton* and *Reed* served important government goals. Yet the Court's assessment of each differed considerably because the First Amendment burdens differed. This flexible approach is necessary because not all reporting and disclosure regimes burden associational rights in the same way.

2

The Court now departs from this nuanced approach in favor of a "one size fits all" test. Regardless of whether there is any risk of public disclosure, and no matter if the burdens on associational rights are slight, heavy, or nonexistent, disclosure regimes must always be narrowly tailored.

The Court searches in vain to find a foothold for this new approach in precedent. The Court first seizes on *Shelton*'s statement that a governmental interest "'cannot be pursued by means that broadly stifle fundamental personal liberties when the end can be more narrowly achieved.'" The Court could not have cherry-picked a less helpful quote. By its own terms, *Shelton* held that an end must be "more narrowly achieved" only if the means "broadly stifle" First Amendment liberties, that is, only if the means impose a severe burden on associational rights.[5] . . .

The Court next looks to *McCutcheon*, which addressed political contribution limits, not disclosure regimes. It is no surprise that the Court subjected the former to narrow tailoring, as *Buckley* had already held that contribution limits directly "impinge on protected associational freedoms." *Buckley*; see also *McCutcheon* (explaining that aggregate limits on contributions "diminish an individual's right of political association" by "limit[ing] the number of candidates he supports" or the amount of money he gives). *Buckley* itself distinguished the First Amendment burdens of disclosure requirements and contribution limits. *Buckley* (noting that, unlike contribution limits, "disclosure requirements impose no ceiling on campaign-related activities" and concluding only that compelled disclosure "can" infringe associational rights). Apparently, those distinctions no longer matter.

Neither *Shelton* nor *McCutcheon*, then, supports the idea that all disclosure requirements must be narrowly tailored. *McCutcheon* arose in the context of a direct limit on associational freedoms, while the law in *Shelton* "broadly stifle[d]" associational rights. Ignoring these distinctions, the Court decides that it will

5. The Court claims that "broadly stifle" refers "to the scope of challenged restrictions" rather than "the severity of any demonstrated burden." That reading ignores the verb "stifle" and its object, "fundamental personal liberties." The Court wishes the sentence said that a government interest "cannot be pursued by [broad] means." It does not.

indiscriminately require narrow tailoring for every single disclosure regime. The Court thus trades precision for blunt force, creating a significant risk that it will topple disclosure regimes that should be constitutional, and that, as in *Reed*, promote important governmental interests.

III

A

Under a First Amendment analysis that is faithful to this Court's precedents, California's Schedule B requirement is constitutional. Begin with the burden it imposes on associational rights. Petitioners have unquestionably provided evidence that their donors face a reasonable probability of threats, harassment, and reprisals if their affiliations are made public. California's Schedule B regulation, however, is a nonpublic reporting requirement, and California has implemented security measures to ensure that Schedule B information remains confidential.

Nor have petitioners shown that their donors, or any organization's donors, will face threats, harassment, or reprisals if their names remain in the hands of a few California state officials. The Court notes that, under *Shelton*, disclosure requirements can chill association even absent public disclosure. In *Shelton*, however, there was a serious concern that hiring authorities would punish teachers for their organizational affiliations. By contrast, the Court in no way suggests that California officials will use Schedule B information to retaliate against any organization's donors. If California's reporting requirement imposes any burden at all, it is at most a very slight one.

B

1

Given the modesty of the First Amendment burden, California may justify its Schedule B requirement with a correspondingly modest showing that the means achieve its ends. See *Reed*. California easily meets this standard.

California collects Schedule Bs to facilitate supervision of charities that operate in the State. As the Court acknowledges, this is undoubtedly a significant governmental interest. In the United States, responsibility for overseeing charities has historically been vested in States' attorneys general, who are tasked with prosecuting charitable fraud, self-dealing, and misappropriation of charitable funds. Effective policing is critical to maintaining public confidence in, and continued giving to, charitable organizations. California's interest in exercising such oversight is especially compelling given the size of its charitable sector. Nearly a quarter of the country's charitable assets are held by charities registered in California.

The Schedule B reporting requirement is properly tailored to further California's efforts to police charitable fraud. See *Reed* (noting that disclosure "helps" combat fraud, even if it is not the least restrictive method of doing so). The IRS Schedule B form requires organizations to disclose the names and addresses of their major donors, the total amount of their contributions, and whether the donation was cash or in-kind. If the gift is in-kind, Schedule B requires a description of the property and its fair market value.

Schedule B and other parts of Form 990 help attorneys in the Charitable Trusts Section of the California Department of Justice (Section) uncover whether an officer or director of a charity is engaged in self-dealing, or whether a charity has diverted donors' charitable contributions for improper use. It helps them determine whether a donor is using the charity as a pass-through entity, including as a source of improper loans that the donor repays as a contribution. It helps them identify red flags, such as discrepancies in reporting contributions across different schedules. And it helps them determine whether a charity has inflated the value of a donor's in-kind contribution in order, for instance, to overstate how efficiently the charity expends resources....

In sum, the evidence shows that California's confidential reporting requirement imposes trivial burdens on petitioners' associational rights and plays a meaningful role in Section attorneys' ability to identify and prosecute charities engaged in malfeasance. That is more than enough to satisfy the First Amendment here.

2

Much of the Court's tailoring analysis is categorically inappropriate under the correct standard of review. In any event, the Court greatly understates the importance to California of collecting information on charitable organizations' top donors.

The Court claims that the collection of Schedule Bs does not form an "integral" part of California's fraud detection efforts and has never done "'anything'" to advance investigative efforts. The record reveals otherwise....

The Court next insists that California can rely on alternative mechanisms, such as audit letters or subpoenas, to obtain Schedule B information. But the Section receives as many as 100 charity-related complaints a month. It is not feasible for the Section, which has limited staff and resources, to conduct that many audits. The subpoena process is also time consuming: Letters must go through multiple layers of review and waiting for a response causes further delays during which a charity can continue its malfeasance.

Implicitly acknowledging that audits and subpoenas are more cumbersome and time consuming, the Court trivializes the State's interest in what it calls "ease of administration." Yet in various contexts, the Court has recognized that an interest in "efficiency" is critical to the effective operation of public agencies....

IV

In a final coup de grâce, the Court concludes that California's reporting requirement is unconstitutional not just as applied to petitioners, but on its very face. "In the First Amendment context," such broad relief requires proof that the requirement is unconstitutional in "'a substantial number of... applications..., judged in relation to the statute's plainly legitimate sweep.'" *Stevens*. "Facial challenges are disfavored for several reasons," prime among them because they "often rest on speculation." *Washington State Grange*. Speculation is all the Court has. The Court points to not a single piece of record evidence showing that California's reporting requirement will chill "a substantial number" of top donors from giving to their charities of choice.[11] Yet it strikes the requirement down in every application.

The average donor is probably at most agnostic about having their information confidentially reported to California's attorney general. A significant number of the charities registered in California engage in uncontroversial pursuits. They include hospitals and clinics; educational institutions; orchestras, operas, choirs, and theatrical groups; museums and art exhibition spaces; food banks and other organizations providing services to the needy, the elderly, and the disabled; animal shelters; and organizations that help maintain parks and gardens. It is somewhat hard to fathom that donors to the Anderson Elementary School PTA, the Loomis-Eureka Lakeside Little League, or the Santa Barbara County Horticultural Society ("[c]elebrating plants since 1880") are less likely to give because their donations are confidentially reported to California's Charitable Trusts Section.

In fact, research shows that the vast majority of donors prefer to publicize their charitable contributions. See Drennan, Where Generosity and Pride Abide: Charitable Naming Rights, 80 U. Cin. L. Rev. 45, 50 (2011) ("Research reveals that anonymous largesse from the wealthy has become rare"); Posner, Altruism, Status, and Trust in the Law of Gifts and Gratuitous Promises, 1997 Wis. L. Rev. 567, 574, n. 17 ("[C]haritable gifts are rarely made anonymously"). One study found that anonymous gifting accounted for less than 1% of all donations to Yale Law School, Harvard Law School, and Carnegie Mellon University. Glazer & Konrad, A Signaling Explanation for Charity, 86 Am. Econ. Rev. 1019, 1021 (1996). Symptomatic of this trend is the explosion in charitable naming rights since the mid-1990s. Drennan, 80 U. Cin. L. Rev., at 50, 55. As one author has recounted, "every nook and cranny of [public] buildings" is now "tagged by some wealthy, generous and obviously not publicity-shy donor." Isherwood, The Graffiti of the Philanthropic Class, N.Y. Times, Dec. 2, 2007.

Of course, it is always possible that an organization is inherently controversial or for an apparently innocuous organization to explode into controversy. The answer, however, is to ensure that confidentiality measures are sound or, in the case of public disclosures, to require a procedure for governments to address requests for

11. The Court highlights the "filings of hundreds of organizations as *amici curiae* in support of" petitioners in this suit. Those briefs, of course, are not record evidence. Moreover, even if those organizations had each provided evidence that California's reporting requirement would subject their top donors to harassment and reprisals (they did not), this still would not demonstrate that a substantial proportion of the reporting requirement's applications are unconstitutional when "'judged in relation to [its] plainly legitimate sweep.'" *Stevens*. Some 60,000 charities renew their registrations with California each year, and nearly all must file a Schedule B. The *amici* are just a small fraction of the disclosure requirement's reach.

exemptions in a timely manner. It is not to hamper all government law enforcement efforts by forbidding confidential disclosures en masse.

Indeed, this Court has already rejected such an indiscriminate approach in the specific context of disclosure requirements. Just over a decade ago, in *Reed*, petitioners demonstrated that their own supporters would face reprisal if their opposition to expanding domestic partnership laws became public. That evidence did not support a facial challenge to Washington's public disclosure law, however, because the "typical referendum petitio[n] concern[ed] tax policy, revenue, budget, or other state law issues," and "there [was] no reason to assume that any burdens imposed by disclosure of typical referendum petitions would be remotely like the burdens plaintiffs fear in this case." *Reed*; see also *id.* (ALITO, J., concurring) ("Many referendum petitions concern relatively uncontroversial matters, and plaintiffs have provided no reason to think that disclosure of signatory information in those contexts would significantly chill the willingness of voters to sign. Plaintiffs' facial challenge therefore must fail").

So too here. Many charitable organizations "concern relatively uncontroversial matters" and petitioners "have provided no reason to think that" confidential disclosure of donor information "would significantly chill the willingness of " most donors to give. Nor does the Court provide such a reason. It merely highlights threats that public disclosure would pose to these two petitioners' supporters. Those threats provide "scant evidence" of anything beyond "the specific harm" that petitioners' donors might experience were their Schedule B information publicly disclosed. Petitioners' "facial challenge therefore must fail." *Reed* (ALITO, J., concurring).

How, then, can their facial challenge succeed? Only because the Court has decided, in a radical departure from precedent, that there no longer need be any evidence that a disclosure requirement is likely to cause an objective burden on First Amendment rights before it can be struck down.

* * *

Today's decision discards decades of First Amendment jurisprudence recognizing that reporting and disclosure requirements do not directly burden associational rights. There is no other explanation for the Court's conclusion that, first, plaintiffs do not need to show they are actually burdened by a disclosure requirement; second, every disclosure requirement demands narrow tailoring; and third, a facial challenge can succeed in the absence of any evidence a state law burdens the associational rights of a substantial proportion of affected individuals.

That disclosure requirements directly burden associational rights has been the view of Justice THOMAS, but it has never been the view of this Court. Just 11 years ago, eight Members of the Court, including two Members of the current majority, recognized that disclosure requirements do not directly interfere with First Amendment rights. In an opinion barely mentioned in today's decision, the Court in *Reed* did the opposite of what the Court does today. First, it demanded objective evidence that disclosure risked exposing supporters to threats and reprisals; second, it required only a loose means-end fit in light of the "modest" burden it found; and third, it rejected a facial challenge given petitioners' failure to establish that signatories to the "typical" referendum had any reason to fear disclosure. In so doing, the Court ensured that it would not "short circuit the democratic process by preventing laws embodying the will of the people from being implemented in a manner consistent with the Constitution." *Washington State Grange.*

The Court 11 years later apparently has a different view of its role. It now calls upon the federal courts to serve "as virtually continuing monitors of the wisdom and soundness of [governmental] action." *Laird.* There is no question that petitioners have shown that their donors reasonably fear reprisals if their identities are publicly exposed. The Court and I, however, disagree about the likelihood of that happening and the role Schedule Bs play in the investigation of charitable malfeasance. If the Court had simply granted as-applied relief to petitioners based on its reading of the facts, I would be sympathetic, although my own views diverge. But the Court's decision is not nearly so narrow or modest. Instead, the Court jettisons completely the longstanding requirement that plaintiffs demonstrate an actual First Amendment burden before the Court will subject government action to close scrutiny. It then invalidates a regulation in its entirety, even though it can point to no record evidence demonstrating that the regulation is likely to chill a substantial proportion of donors. These moves are wholly inconsistent with the Court's precedents and our Court's long-held view that disclosure requirements only indirectly burden First Amendment rights. With respect, I dissent.

Notes and Questions

1. *Petition Signing, Charity Disclosures, and Campaign Finance.* Neither *Reed* nor *AFPF* is about campaign finance disclosure, but the Supreme Court has now made abundantly clear that the same "exacting scrutiny" standard that applies in those cases also applies to campaign finance disclosure challenges.

2. *Exacting Scrutiny.* What *is* the exacting scrutiny standard? It appears to have changed in two significant ways from *Reed* to *AFPF.* First, the Court has adopted a "narrow tailoring" requirement: "While exacting scrutiny does not require that disclosure regimes be the least restrictive means of achieving their ends, it does require that they be narrowly tailored to the government's asserted interest." And this narrow tailoring requirement applies even if the law imposes only a modest burden on a plaintiff's First Amendment rights. Second, plaintiffs need not demonstrate "chill," and it may be presumed in a facial challenge. Plaintiffs in *AFPF* proved that they faced a danger of harassment, which would justify success in an as-applied challenge. The Court nonetheless allowed the facial challenge, striking down the law for everyone, even those not chilled by disclosure. How can this be squared with the approach in *Reed*? See Lloyd Mayer, *Justices Open the Door Wider for Donor Info Challenges*, Law 360 (July 2, 2021).

3. *Standards for Judging Contribution Limits.* The Court in *AFPF* cites *McCutcheon* in setting out the need for narrow tailoring and the dissent seems to accept the idea of narrow tailoring in the campaign finance context. Does *AFPF* make it harder

for jurisdictions to defend the constitutionality of their contribution limits? For an argument in the affirmative, see Richard L. Hasen, *The Supreme Court is Putting Democracy at Risk*, N.Y. Times, July 1, 2021.

4. *Chill and the Result of As-Applied Challenges.* On remand in *Reed* on the as-applied challenge, the district court found very little evidence of harassment, with nothing more serious than ballot petition signature gatherers being "mooned" by passers-by. A federal district court considering similar evidence in the context of contributors to California's Proposition 8, barring gay marriage, similarly found evidence of harassment lacking. *Doe v. Reed*, 823 F. Supp. 2d 1195 (W.D. Wash. 2011); *ProtectMarriage.com v. Bowen*, 830 F. Supp. 2d 914 (E.D. Cal. 2011). For an argument that opponents of disclosure have been overstating the threat of harassment, see Richard L. Hasen, *Chill Out: A Qualified Defense of Campaign Finance Disclosure in the Internet Era*, 27 Journal of Law and Politics 557 (2012). Is such evidence no longer relevant in cases challenging disclosure laws? Does the rise of social media and the ability to harass people online change the constitutional calculus? Or does it just create an appearance that harassment is more common? Note that the dissenters in *AFPF* were "sympathetic" to an as-applied challenge based on evidence that the plaintiffs faced a real danger of harassment. Why did they not concur in the judgment favoring the plaintiffs?

5. *The "Information Interest."* The majority opinion in *Reed* did not need to address the question whether the information interest could justify Washington State's law, given the anti-fraud rationale. However, in the *Citizens United* case the Court recognized the information interest as a sufficient basis for broad disclosure in the campaign finance context:

> The Court has explained that disclosure is a less restrictive alternative to more comprehensive regulations of speech. In *Buckley* the Court upheld a disclosure requirement for independent expenditures even though it invalidated a provision that imposed a ceiling on those expenditures. In *McConnell* three Justices who would have found § 441b [52 U.S.C. § 30118] to be unconstitutional nonetheless voted to uphold BCRA's disclosure and disclaimer requirements. And the Court has upheld registration and disclosure requirements on lobbyists, even though Congress has no power to ban lobbying itself. *United States v. Harriss*, 347 U.S. 612, 625 (1954) (Congress "has merely provided for a modicum of information from those who for hire attempt to influence legislation or who collect or spend funds for that purpose"). For these reasons, we reject Citizens United's contention that the disclosure requirements must be limited to speech that is the functional equivalent of express advocacy.
>
> Citizens United also disputes that an informational interest justifies the application of [BCRA's disclosure requirements] to its ads, which only attempt to persuade viewers to see the film. Even if it disclosed the funding sources for the ads, Citizens United says, the information would not help viewers make informed choices in the political marketplace. This is

> similar to the argument rejected above with respect to disclaimers. Even if the ads only pertain to a commercial transaction, the public has an interest in knowing who is speaking about a candidate shortly before an election. Because the informational interest alone is sufficient to justify application of [the disclosure law] to these ads, it is not necessary to consider the Government's other asserted interests.

Can the information interest help campaign finance laws survive the new exacting scrutiny standard under *AFPF*? Is that stronger or weaker than arguments for disclosure based upon (the Court's new narrow definition of) corruption.

6. *Campaign Finance Disclosure Challenges in the Lower Courts.* Following *Citizens United* and *Reed*, many lower courts have rejected general constitutional challenges to campaign finance disclosure laws. *E.g.*, *National Association for Gun Rights v. Mangan*, 933 F.3d 1102 (9th Cir. 2019), cert. denied, 140 S. Ct. 2825 (2020); *Doe v. Federal Election Commission*, 920 F.3d 866 (D.C. Cir. 2019), cert. denied, 140 S. Ct. 2506 (2020); *Chula Vista Citizens for Jobs and Fair Competition v. Norris*, 782 F.3d 520 (9th Cir. 2015) (en banc); *Independence Institute v. FEC*, 216 F. Supp. 3d. 176 (D.D.C. 2016); *Ctr. for Individual Freedom, Inc. v. Tennant*, 706 F.3d 270 (4th Cir. 2013); *Ctr. for Individual Freedom v. Madigan*, 697 F.3d 464 (7th Cir. 2012); *The Real Truth About Abortion, Inc. v. FEC*, 681 F.3d 544, 546 (4th Cir. 2012), cert. denied, 568 U.S. 1114 (2013); *Free Speech v. FEC*, 720 F.3d 788 (10th Cir. 2013); *ProtectMarriage .Com—Yes on 8 v. Bowen*, 752 F.3d 827 (9th Cir. 2014); *National Organization for Marriage v. McKee*, 723 F. Supp. 2d 245 (D. Maine 2010). See Ciara Torres-Spelliscy, *Has the Tide Turned in Favor of Disclosure? Revealing Money in Politics After* Citizens United *and* Doe v. Reed, 27 Georgia State University Law Review 1057 (2011).

Some courts have, however, struck down more burdensome reporting requirements. See, *e.g.*, *Minnesota Citizens Concerned for Life, Inc. v. Swanson*, 692 F.3d 864 (8th Cir. 2012). In *Washington Post v. McManus*, 944 F.3d 506 (4th Cir. 2019), the Fourth Circuit held unconstitutional a Maryland law requiring online publishers to self-publish information about paid political advertisements posted on their websites and to make records about those ads available for state inspection, which news outlets alleged were unconstitutional. Nothing prevented the state from requiring those running their ads to make the required disclosures.

And some lower courts have turned much more hostile to disclosure generally. In a long-running dispute over the Federal Election Commission's disclosure rules for McCain-Feingold's "electioneering communications," a panel of D.C. Circuit judges upheld the FEC's rules despite reformers' contention that the rules were impermissibly lax given the language of the McCain-Feingold law. In the course of siding with the FEC, the appeals court criticized the Supreme Court's disclosure doctrine as not sufficiently protective of the right to engage in anonymous political speech:

> Both an individual's right to speak anonymously and the public's interest in contribution disclosures are now firmly entrenched in the Supreme

Court's First Amendment jurisprudence. And yet they are also fiercely antagonistic. The deleterious effects of disclosure on speech have been ably catalogued. "Disclaimer and disclosure requirements enable private citizens and elected officials to implement political strategies *specifically calculated* to curtail campaign-related activity and prevent the lawful, peaceful exercise of First Amendment rights." *Citizens United* (Thomas, J., dissenting) (highlighting how mandatory disclosure of contributors to California's controversial "Yes on Proposition 8" campaign led to their being singled out for ruthless retaliation and intimidation). "[T]he advent of the Internet enables prompt disclosure of expenditures, which provides political opponents with the information needed to intimidate and retaliate against their foes." *Id.* "Disclosure also makes it easier to see who has not done his bit for the incumbents, so that arms may be twisted and pockets tapped." *Majors v. Abell,* 361 F.3d 349, 356 (7th Cir.2004) (Easterbrook, J., dubitante).

In addition to these general burdens, the specific disclosure requirement Van Hollen advocates here would present its own unique harms. For instance, an American Cancer Society donor who supports cancer research but not ACS's political communications must decide whether a cancer cure or her associational rights are more important to her. This is categorically distinct from deciding whether a political issue, such as tax reform, is as important as one's associational right. Cancer research isn't a political issue, but disclosure rules of this sort would undeniably transform it into one. These disclosure rules also burden privacy rights in another crucial way: modest individuals who'd prefer the amount of their charitable donations remain private lose that privilege the minute their nonprofit of choice decides to run an issue ad. The Supreme Court routinely invalidates laws that chill speech far less than a disclosure rule that might scare away charitable donors. *See Watchtower Bible and Tract Soc'y of New York, Inc. v. Stratton,* 536 U.S. 150 (2002) (striking a law requiring religious canvassers to obtain a permit before advocating door-to-door on private property).

The ones who would truly bear the burden of Van Hollen's preferred rule would not be the wealthy corporations or the extraordinarily rich private donors that likely motivated Congress to compel disclosure in the first place. Such individuals would have "little difficulty complying" with these laws, as they can readily hire "legal counsel who specialize in election matters," who "not only will assure compliance but also will exploit the inevitable loopholes." *Majors* (Easterbrook, J., dubitante). Instead, such requirements "have their real bite when flushing small groups, political clubs, or solitary speakers into the limelight, or reducing them to silence." *Id.*

Van Hollen v. FEC, 811 F.3d 486, 500-01 (D.C. Cir. 2016). Why did the appeals court include this dicta? Who has the better of the argument on the benefits and risks of mandated disclosure?

The group Citizens United was partially able to obtain an as-applied exemption from Colorado's disclosure laws on grounds that it was entitled to a media exemption:

> Citizens United brought the present action against the Colorado Secretary of State (the Secretary) in the United States District Court for the District of Colorado to challenge under the First Amendment the disclosure provisions both on their face and as applied to Citizens United because it is treated differently from various media that are exempted from the provisions (the exempted media). It sought a preliminary injunction against enforcing the provisions that do not apply to exempted media. The district court denied relief, and Citizens United appeals.
>
> Although we agree with much of what the district court said, we must reverse. We do not address the facial challenge to the disclosure provisions, because we afford Citizens United the relief it requested through its as-applied challenge. We hold that on the record before us Citizens United would likely prevail on the merits and therefore is entitled to a preliminary injunction. In light of (1) the Colorado disclosure exemptions for printed periodicals, cable and over-the-air broadcasters, and Internet periodicals and blogs, (2) the rationale presented for these exemptions, and (3) Citizen United's history of producing and distributing two dozen documentary films over the course of a decade, the Secretary has not shown a substantial relation between a sufficiently important governmental interest and the disclosure requirements that follow from treating *Rocky Mountain Heist* as an "electioneering communication" or treating the costs of producing and distributing the film as an "expenditure" under Colorado's campaign laws. Citizens United has also sought to have its advertising for *Rocky Mountain Heist* exempted from the disclosure provisions. But it has not demonstrated that the Secretary would exempt advertising placed by the exempted media if the advertisements mentioned a candidate or advocated for the election or defeat of a candidate. Having failed to show that in this respect it would be treated differently from the exempted media, Citizens United is not entitled to relief regarding advertising. To explain our holding, we begin by describing the pertinent disclosure provisions of Colorado law....

Citizens United v. Gessler, 773 F.3d 200, 202-03 (10th Cir. 2014).

In the meantime, scholars continue to explore the tradeoffs accompanying compelled disclosure of campaign finance information. See Michael D. Gilbert, *Campaign Finance Disclosure and the Information Tradeoff*, 98 Iowa Law Review 1847 (2013).

7. *FEC Enforcement.* For years, the FEC has deadlocked along party lines in important cases, including those involving disclosure requirements. See Michael M. Franz, *Federal Election Commission Divided: Measuring Conflict in Commission Votes Since 1990*, Election L.J., https://doi.org/10.1089/elj.2019.0560 (2020). When the

FEC deadlocks or otherwise fails to act in an enforcement matter, campaign finance watchdogs may seek judicial review. 52 U.S.C. § 30109(a)(8)(A), (C). In *Citizens for Responsibility & Ethics in Washington v. Federal Election Commission*, 993 F.3d 880 (D.C. Cir. 2021) ("CREW"), the court held that when a non-enforcement decision is based upon an exercise of "prosecutorial discretion," that decision is judicially unreviewable, even if it is just part of the rationale for non-enforcement. The dissenting judge saw the issue differently:

> The question in this case is whether a federal agency can immunize its conclusive legal determinations and evidentiary analyses from judicial review simply by tacking a cursory reference to prosecutorial discretion onto the end of a lengthy and substantive merits decision. In holding that such an incantation precludes all scrutiny, the majority opinion creates an easy and automatic "get out of judicial review free" card for the Federal Election Commission. That should not be the law of this circuit.

Id. at 895 (Millet, J. dissenting).

Soon after this ruling, Republican commissioners cited "prosecutorial discretion" in declining to investigate former President Donald Trump for payments made to adult film actress Stormy Daniels allegedly to keep her silence about an affair with Trump to benefit his campaign. Democratic commissioner Ellen Weintraub used the decision as an opportunity to urge the entire D.C. Circuit to rehear the *CREW* case en banc. Ellen L. Weintraub, Opinion: *Close This FEC Loophole That Killed the Case Over Trump's Payment to Stormy Daniels*, Washington Post, May 9, 2021.

8. *Lobbying Disclosure.* To what extent do the government interests supporting campaign finance disclosure also justify disclosure of lobbying activities? Because lobbying is protected by the First Amendment, mandatory disclosure is the primary means by which such activities are regulated. See Chapter 12, Part III. Congress first adopted comprehensive lobbying disclosure in 1946. The current scheme of federal lobbying disclosure derives from the Lobbying Disclosure Act of 1995, as amended in by the Honest Leadership and Open Government Act of 2007. These statutes require that those engaged in specified lobbying contacts make periodic reports regarding their lobbying activities, including disclosure of their clients and the income received from them. Should compelled disclosure of lobbying activities be subject to the same level of scrutiny as campaign finance disclosure?

In *National Association of Manufacturers v. Taylor*, 582 F.3d 1 (D.C. Cir. 2009), the D.C. Circuit rejected a First Amendment challenge to some of the disclosure requirements imposed by federal law. In an opinion by Judge Merrick Garland, the court assumed without deciding that strict scrutiny was the proper standard, and upheld the challenged provisions under that standard. Relying on the text of the federal lobbying statute, the court concluded that Congress's goal was to increase "public awareness of paid lobbyists to influence the public decisionmaking process." *Id.* at 13 (citing 2 U.S.C. § 1601(1)). The court found this interest compelling based largely on *Buckley v. Valeo*, reasoning that "[t]ransparency in government, no less than transparency in choosing our government, remains a vital national interest in a democracy." *Id.* at 14. The court proceeded to find the challenged lobbying disclosure requirements narrowly tailored to this informational interest. Should lobbying disclosure requirements be subjected to strict scrutiny or the slightly more relaxed standard of exacting scrutiny? Are the interests served by lobbying disclosure as strong as those served by campaign finance disclosure?

9. *Political Impediments to Fuller Disclosure.* In *Citizens United*, Justice Kennedy remarked that "A campaign finance system that pairs corporate independent expenditures with effective disclosure has not existed before today . . . With the advent of the Internet, prompt disclosure of expenditures can provide shareholders and citizens with the information needed to hold corporations and elected officials accountable for their positions and supporters."

The world Justice Kennedy imagined has not materialized. Thanks in part because of inaction from the FEC and Internal Revenue Service, spending by groups that do not disclose, or fully disclose, their donors continues to rise, amounting to over $1 billion in the first decade since *Citizens United.* Opensecrets.org, *Dark Money Basics* (last accessed July 7, 2021), https://perma.cc/PK9S-FN2T. The means of avoiding disclosure include using the 501(c)(4) status, as well as having limited liability companies (LLCs) contribute money to Super PACs. Many disclosure rules also do not cover spending on campaign ads avoiding express advocacy appearing on the Internet.

Congress for years has debated beefing up disclosure rules, but political stalemate in Washington has blocked new legislation, with most Democrats supporting new legislation and most Republicans opposing it. Until recently, constitutional constraints on disclosure legislation were minimal. Now, *AFPF* changes the calculus, adding legal constraints to political impediments for fuller disclosure.

The Court also finds meaning in the fact that *Shelton* criticized Arkansas' challenged disclosure regime for not being narrowly tailored. But the *Shelton* Court had already explained why the failure to narrowly tailor was problematic: because the statute significantly burdened Arkansas teachers' associational rights. In no way did the Court suggest that narrow tailoring was necessary in the absence of a significant burden on associational rights.

Appendix

I. Election Law Research

Sara Sampson[a]

Researching in the area of election law can be much more complicated than expected. One reason is that the search terms used to find cases and statutes on election law are frequently found in other legal areas in which elections occur. For example, even a well-written electronic database search to find cases concerning the proper procedure for counting ballots may return cases about corporate, church, or union elections as well as state, federal, and municipal government elections. Sometimes there is no way to avoid having to examine each case to determine its germaneness to your topic.

When writing a scholarly paper or doing in-depth research, it is important to find as many relevant sources as possible, while minimizing the number of irrelevant sources. Many of the resources described below allow searching by subject, as opposed to by particular words. Terms & connectors (also called "key word") searching merely finds a specific combination of words in a particular document. Terminology can vary across jurisdictions and over time. Overlooking a few key words or their synonyms may cause results that miss important articles, cases, or statutory provisions.

One way to avoid these problems is to search by subject. Westlaw, Lexis Advance, and Bloomberg Law all use their own systems of headnotes and topics to classify cases by subject. These topic systems or outlines can be browsed to find all the cases dealing with that particular subject. The different topic systems vary in their level of detail, but all will allow you the option to further filter and sort the cases under a particular topic.

When looking for federal or state law and regulations, be sure to use an index. While the United States Code was reorganized to move all of the federal election laws into Title 52, not every jurisdiction's law is as organized. When looking for state

---

a. Sara Sampson is the Assistant Dean for Information Services and Director of the Law Library at The Ohio State University Moritz College of Law. This chapter is dedicated to the memory of Paul Gatz, who served as a Reference Librarian and Adjunct Professor at The Ohio State University Moritz College of Law and contributed to the previous edition of this appendix. Paul taught many future lawyers how to effectively analyze and research complex legal topics. He will continue to do so through this appendix.

statutes and federal regulations, it is important to use the index to find all relevant material, especially in an unfamiliar jurisdiction. Relevant laws or regulations may be scattered throughout the code, even though an election law title or chapter exists. Furthermore, the code may use antiquated or local terminology.

Always consult the jurisdiction's election official's web page as there may be directives, regulations and even letters to local election officials that affect the law at issue. For example, Ohio's Secretary of State's web page has links to directives that interpret Ohio election law provisions. These directives won't always be found in a typical Westlaw or Lexis search.

You may also need to look outside of legal publications. Political science, sociology, history, economics, psychology and other disciplines may provide the support you need. For example, if you are advocating a change to the presidential elections from a weekday to the weekend to increase voter turnout, you may turn to sociology to determine how to predict group behavior, psychology to look at how to motivate individuals to vote, or world history to compare turnout and voting schedules in other jurisdictions.

When searching for law review articles, it is important to use an online index in addition to conducting key word searching in full text databases, such as Westlaw, Lexis, HeinOnline, or Google Scholar. The index allows for subject searching and, therefore, ensures that all articles on a particular topic are found. Westlaw and Lexis provide the full-text of many articles, but both online services begin coverage for virtually all law journals in the early 1980s. HeinOnline, a subscription database, begins coverage for most journals with the first volume.

The next few pages list election law resources by topic. Journals, blogs and websites of advocacy and interest groups are especially helpful places to find a topic on which to write. Note that your library may not have access to all the resources described below. If you are not sure whether you have access or have trouble using a particular source or research technique (such as subject searching), consult your law librarian.

II. Election Law Resources

A. General Resources

Books & Journals

There is no currently updated general treatise on election law. A legal encyclopedia, such as *American Jurisprudence*, provides a general overview of most election law related topics as well as citations to important primary sources. To locate books on election law, searching your library's online catalog using the Library of Congress Subject Headings will provide precise search results. Possible subject headings are: Election law — United States, Voting research — United States, and Elections — United States. To browse your library's collection, be sure to visit the collection near

JK1800-2300 (which may include materials on the right to vote, voter behavior, election and campaign reform, money and politics, corruption, and political parties) and KF 4900 (which deals with all aspects of election law). If you have access to a large university library, be sure to explore their collection as well. To find materials your library does not have, you can search many library catalogs simultaneously via WorldCat (www.worldcat.org) and request materials via inter-library loan (ILL).

America Votes! Challenges to Modern Election Law & Voting is published by the American Bar Association. This text provides an overview of current election law and voting rights issues, including redistricting, voter qualification and participation, the voting process, and audit recounts. Previous editions, published under the title *America Votes! A Guide to Modern Election Law & Voting* can provide historical information.

Congressional Quarterly's Guide to U.S. Elections provides extensive information about America's electoral system and political parties as well as statistics and summaries of presidential, congressional, and gubernatorial elections. Use the list of tables and figures at the beginning of each volume to quickly find compilations of statistics.

Election Law in a Nutshell 2d, written by Professor Tokaji, serves as a brief introduction to the U.S. law of elections and politics, covering voting rights, districting and gerrymandering, election administration, and campaign finance, among other topics.

Election Law Journal: Rules, Politics and Policy started publication in 2002. Each issue has articles and book reviews. Some issues include case summaries and reprints of important election law documents that may be difficult to find. The journal covers United States and foreign election law topics. This journal is not available on Westlaw or Lexis.

International Election Principles: Democracy & the Rule of Law (American Bar Association 2009) focuses on three main topics: electoral and democratic principles, election administration and resolution of election-related disputes. It covers both international law and the law of select foreign countries.

Legislation, Statutory Interpretation, and Election Law: Examples and Explanations 2d, written by Professor Hasen, contains sections on voting rights and representation and campaign finance law. As a study aid from the Examples & Explanations series, it includes clear descriptions of the law along with illustrative hypotheticals to aid students in preparing for class.

Online Resources

CQ Voting and Elections Collection is the online version of many of CQ Press' popular publications. It has a wealth of statistical data and information on presidential, congressional, and gubernatorial elections, campaigns and elections political parties, & voters and demographics. It also includes a summary of legislation proposed and enacted by each federal congress and special reports on federal investigations and actions on related topics. A subscription is required to access this database.

Brennan Center for Justice (www.brennancenter.org) litigates cases and writes reports on various election law topics. The reports and case documents are available on its website.

Campaign Legal Center (www.campaignlegal.org) focuses on campaign finance and elections, political communication, and government ethics. It brings together information from the many government agencies responsible for campaign finance regulation.

Electionline.org (https://electionline.org) is a non-partisan aggregator of election news and information from across the United States.

Election Law Blog (https://electionlawblog.org) is a great way to stay up to date with election law news and developments.

Election Law at Ohio State (https://u.osu.edu/electionlaw/) focuses on election administration, tracking pending election law litigation, and expert commentary.

Institute for Free Speech (https://www.ifs.org) seeks to educate the public on the actual effects of money in politics, and the results of a more free and competitive electoral process. Its website contains a blog and various studies.

B. Regulation of Campaign Finance & Campaign Speech

Books & Journals

To find materials on campaign finance topics in your library, do a subject search in the catalog for Campaign funds — Law and legislation — United States or browse near call numbers JK 1990 and KF 4920. Finding materials on free speech and campaign regulation is a bit more difficult because there is not a specific category for this topic in your library. Instead, you can do a key word search in the library catalog or combine these subjects: Campaign funds — Law and legislation — United States and Freedom of speech — United States.

American Law Reports (ALR) also has many annotations on campaign finance topics. ALR annotations give a general overview of a topic along with a survey of the laws in many, if not all, United States jurisdictions. For example, *Validity, Construction, and Application of Campaign Finance Laws — Supreme Court Cases,* 19 A.L.R. Fed. 2d 1 (2007) provides a summary of the Supreme Court's jurisprudence in this area. Although originally published in 2007, they are updated with new cases. These annotations will also provide references to relevant topic and key numbers, law review articles, and ALR annotations on closely related topics. ALR annotations are available on Lexis and Westlaw.

Corporate Political Activities: Complying with Campaign Finance, Lobbying & Ethics Laws (PLI, currently published annually) is a compilation of handouts from a continuing education program on corporate political activities. While the content may vary each year, it usually provides an overview of current law and controversies. In recent years, it has included several 50 state surveys on campaign finance and lobbying laws. It is available on the PLI Plus database.

Lobbying, PACs, and Campaign Finance: 50 State Handbook (Thomson West, published annually) surveys state legal requirements affecting lobbying (including government ethics rules) and campaign finance. Some editions are available on Westlaw.

Online Resources

The FEC's website (www.fec.gov) contains the laws and regulations relating to federal campaigns, agency actions, and a disclosure database. On the Finance Disclosure Portal (https://www.fec.gov/data/) campaign finance data for presidential and congressional candidates is available to search, download, and view in various graphic formats.

National Institute on Money in State Politics (https://followthemoney.org) offers access to campaign contribution data from all 50 states. The Institute also provides reports based on that data to track trends in state-level campaign contributions.

OpenSecrets.org (https://www.opensecrets.org) is run by the Center for Responsive Politics, the "nation's premier research group tracking money in U.S. politics." This website collects and disseminates data on federal campaign contributions, including information on industries, contributors, and donor demographics. The site also includes data on personal finances of candidates, party fundraising, lobbyists, and PACs.

Political MoneyLine (https://politicalmoneyline.com) provides data and detailed financial profiles of candidates, political action committees, party committees, 527 organizations, and registered lobbyists. It also provides daily news updates on campaign finance, government ethics, and lobbying.

C. Election Administration

Because this topic concerns both federal and state law, be sure to search both federal and state case law using subject searching tools such as Westlaw's topic and key numbers as well as federal and state statutes.

Books & Journals

To find books on this topic, do a key word search in the library catalog for the particular issue. Be sure to browse both the JK 1800-2300 area of your library as well as near KF 4900.

American Law Reports (ALR) also has many annotations on election administration topics. These annotations provide a general overview of a topic along with a survey of the laws in many, if not all, United States jurisdictions. For example, *Elections:*

Validity of State or Local Legislative Ban on Write-in Votes, 69 A.L.R.4th 948 (1989) provides a nationwide summary of such bans and cases challenging their legality. While the annotation was published in 1989, it is kept current online and new cases are added regularly. These annotations will also provide references to relevant topic and key numbers, law review articles, and closely related ALR annotations. ALR annotations are available in print and on Lexis and Westlaw.

Election Administration Reports is a biweekly newsletter focused on issues affecting election officials, covering new legislation, major court decisions, and changes in voting technology and election administration practices.

Principles of Election Law: Election Administration (American Law Institute). The *Principles* series are recommendations for best practices in particular areas of law written by leading academics and practitioners. The Election Law project concerns two main topics: non-precinct voting (voting by any means other than at a polling place on election day) and resolving disputed elections. Available in Lexis, Westlaw and HeinOnline

Online Resources

The Election Assistance Commission (www.eac.gov) was created by the Help America Vote Act of 2002 and is charged with running the federal voting system certification program and issuing guidance to states about HAVA (including best practices guidance to state election officials). The EAC collects reports and statistics on all election administration issues such as turnout, alternative voting methods, voting systems, voting machines, and registration. The EAC periodically publishes a summary of state election laws, called the Statutory Overview.

Electionline.org (https://electionline.org) is a non-partisan aggregator of election news and information from across the United States. In-depth reports on election administration are available in the "Training & Resources" area of the website.

Election Law at Ohio State (https://u.osu.edu/electionlaw/) focuses on election administration, tracking pending election law litigation, and expert commentary.

The National Conference of State Legislatures maintains several databases of pending and existing election legislation, available at https://www.ncsl.org/research/elections-and-campaigns.aspx. NCSL's resources include summaries of state laws on numerous election administration topics, such as voter ID, provisional ballots, and online voter registration. https://www.ncsl.org/research/elections-and-campaigns/election-laws-and-procedures-overview.aspx.

D. Voting Rights Act & Redistricting

The Voting Rights Act is available at 52 U.S.C. §§ 10101 et seq. Peruse the annotations of the code and use subject searching in case law databases to find relevant cases. The regulations implementing the Act are found in 28 C.F.R. §§ 51.1 et seq. and §§ 55.1 et seq.

Books & Journals

There have been many books and articles published on this topic. *The Voting Rights Act of 1965: A Selected Annotated Bibliography,* 98 Law Lib. J. 663 (2006) lists major books, articles, and online resources about the history and initial implementation of the Act, voting rights litigation, and the impact of the Act and its reauthorization. To find books about the Act, use the following subject headings in your library's catalog: Voting Rights Act of 1965 (United States), African Americans—Suffrage, and Minorities—Suffrage—United States, or browse near KF 4905. To find books and reports specifically about reapportionment, search your library's catalog with these subject headings: Apportionment (Election law)—United States, Election districts—United States, and Gerrymandering—United States, or browse the library stacks near JK 1920 and KF 4890.

Redistricting Litigation: An Overview of the Legal, Statistical, and Case Management Issues (Federal Judicial Center 2002) covers the basics of redistricting, including a chapter on race-polarized voting. It is available on Westlaw.

Online Resources

United States Department of Justice, Civil Rights Division, Voting Section (https://www.justice.gov/crt/voting-section) is tasked with enforcing the Voting Rights Act. The website includes links to the text of the law, litigation brought by the section, and an introduction to federal voting rights legislation.

All About Redistricting (https://redistricting.lls.edu) provides an overview of the redistricting process in each state including interactive maps that summarize the progress of ongoing redistricting in each state. It also tracks redistricting litigation.

E. Ballot Propositions

Books & Journals

These direct democracy tools are available at the state level, so be sure to search both federal and state case law and statutes. To find books about ballot propositions use the following subject headings in your library's catalog: Referendum or Initiative, Right of, and browse near JF 494 and KF 4800.

The Initiative and Referendum Almanac (Carolina Academic Press 2d 2018) provides a general overview of the topic and a step-by-step guide to using them. This text is not updated, so verify the text by reviewing state codes and case law. Some of this information is available online at the Initiative & Referendum Institute (www.iandrinstitute.org).

The Routledge Handbook to Referendums and Direct Democracy (Routledge 2020) discusses the history, impact, and policy surrounding referendums and other direct democracy tools throughout the world.

F. Violations of Election Law & Political Corruption

Books & Journals

American Jurisprudence 2d has an overview of this area in *Elections* §§ 444-465. It includes bribery, illegal voting, intimidation of voters and offenses by election officials and campaign related offenses. In addition to a summary of the law and references to primary authority, *American Jurisprudence* identifies relevant topic and key numbers that can be used to find cases on the topic in a particular jurisdiction.

To find books related to this topic, search your library's catalog for the following subjects: Bribery and Political Corruption. For other topics, a key word search will be necessary.

G. Political Parties

Books & Journals

To find books, reports and other information about political parties, use the Political Parties—United States subject headings in your library's catalog and browse near JK 2260.

National Party Conventions (CQ Press, updated every four years) includes information on the conventions, including a narrative summary and a table of key votes, back to 1831.

Online Resources

Party websites often provide the party's platform and rules that govern the selection of party candidates. The Republican National Committee's website is available at https://www.gop.com and the Democratic National Committee's online presence is at www.democrats.org.

H. Election Statistics

There are many compilations of election statistics. To find books in your library, browse near call numbers JK 518-524 for presidential elections, JK 1010-1041 for congressional elections, and JK 1965-67 for general election related statistics.

Books & Journals

America Votes (CQ Press, published annually) provides voting statistics by state for presidential, gubernatorial, and Congressional elections. Breaks some vote counts down by county, city or town.

The Almanac of State Legislative Elections: Voting Patterns and Demographics (CQ Press) uses detailed demographic data to analyze voting behavior of all 6,744 state legislative districts.

Almanac of American Politics has election results for state and national races.

America at the Polls (CQ Press) is a comprehensive analysis of presidential elections back to 1916.

Exit Polls: Surveying the American Electorate (Sage/CQ Press) provides an overview of the evolution of exit polls and their results in federal elections over time. An in-depth analysis of federal elections from 1972 to 2010 is also included.

Vital Statistics on American Politics (CQ Press) includes statistics on all types of political issues, including elections; specifically campaign finance, districting, minority elected officials, public opinion, results of national elections, term limits, turnout, voting equipment, and voting rights. Some statistical compilations and tables go back to 1789.

Online Resources

ANES (American National Election Studies) (www.electionstudies.org) produces statistics, data sets, and reports on voting, public opinion, and political participation in the United States. It also maintains a list of similar programs in other countries.

The United States Census Bureau provides data on voting and registration, with some measures available back to 1964 (https://www.census.gov/topics/public-sector/voting.html). The Census Bureau site also includes Redistricting Census data.

The United States Election Assistance Commission, under the Help America Vote Act, collects and shares information on election administration from across the country. The reports and data from its Election Administration and Voting Survey are available on its Research and Data page, https://www.eac.gov/research-and-data.

ProQuest Statistical Insight provides statistical data, including election information, from government and private sources. This is a subscription database.

I. Politics and Current Election News

CQ Roll Call (https://www.rollcall.com) specializes in congressional news, but also follows congressional and presidential elections. The site also includes Race Ratings for Senate, House, and Governor races.

Election Law Blog (https://electionlawblog.org/) is Professor Rick Hasen's blog and covers election law news and analysis as well as current scholarship in the field. Professors Stephanopoulos and Tokaji are contributors as well.

Nate Silver's data-based journalism blog Five Thirty Eight (https://fivethirtyeight.com) covers a number of topics, including elections, and provides election forecasts and other interactive features.

The Hill (https://thehill.com) covers politics and campaigns, with a particular focus on Congress.

Political Wire (https://politicalwire.com) is a blog by Taegan Goddard that follows and comments on national political news.

Politico (https://www.politico.com) focuses on politics and government at the federal level and includes coverage of elections as well.

Sabato's Crystal Ball (https://www.centerforpolitics.org/crystalball) is maintained by the University of Virginia's Center for Politics and features blogposts alongside its highly-regarded ratings system for predicting presidential, congressional, and gubernatorial elections.

III. Interdisciplinary Research

Looking beyond legal topics can help support your arguments. Finding policy reasons that the law should be different or that one interpretation of a law or regulation is better can make an argument more persuasive. The resources described below can supply these policy arguments as well as support factual assertions with statistics, historical facts, and news accounts of events.

CRS Reports are written for members of Congress by the Congressional Research Service (a division of the Library of Congress). The reports can analyze the policy, economic, and legal issues surrounding potential legislation, current issues, or any other topic requested by a member of Congress. The reports occasionally provide a statistical analysis of a current or proposed government program. CRS Reports are available at https://crsreports.congress.gov/. Your library may also subscribe to ProQuest Congressional, which is one of the more comprehensive sources for CRS reports and offers more sophisticated searching of the reports.

EconLit indexes worldwide economic scholarship. Because this is an index, full-text searching is not possible. Only the title, author, abstract, and subjects can be searched, so simple and broad searches will work well. This database can also lead to statistical reports. Your school may subscribe to EconLit with Full Text, which includes the full text of many economic journals.

Google Scholar uses the Google search functionality to search scholarly databases that are not included in Google. Unlike Google, the results are not always part of the free web, and unless your library has a subscription to the database, you may have to purchase access to particular results. To make sure that you get the full benefit of your library's resources, set your Google Scholar settings to include your school.

PAIS indexes scholarship and other publications in public policy, social policy, and the social sciences. Because this is an index, full-text searching is not possible. Only the title, author, abstract, and descriptors can be searched, so simple and broad searches will work well. This database can also lead to statistical reports.

PsycINFO is the leading index to worldwide psychology scholarship. Its interdisciplinary content includes psychology's relationship to areas such as law, medicine, sociology, education, and business. A law library is unlikely to have a subscription to this database. If your law school is affiliated with a University, you are likely to have access to the database through the University library.

Polling the Nations (from InfoBase) is a database of over 750,000 poll questions conducted by many groups around the world. There are polls relating to elections and voting and it is possible to search for polls by election year and location.

Sociological Abstracts indexes international scholarship on sociology and other social and behavior sciences. Because this is an index, full-text searching is not possible. Only the title, author, abstract, and descriptors can be searched, so simple and broad searches will work well. This database can also lead to statistical reports. A law library is unlikely to have a subscription to this database. If your law school is affiliated with a University, you are likely to have access to the database through the University library.

Web of Science: Social Sciences Citation Index is a citator (like Shepard's or KeyCite) for social science literature. If you have a relevant journal article or book, you can use it to find other sources from a variety of disciplines that cite the journal article or book and, presumably, are on the same topic. This database is sometimes included with the Web of Science Core Collection and is a subscription database.

Table of Cases

Page numbers in **bold** identify principal items. Page numbers in *italics* identify extended discussion or quotation. Only the first pages of items are indicated. Subsequent histories of cases are omitted in this table.

Table of Authorities

Page numbers in **bold** identify principal items. Page numbers in *italics* identify extended discussion or quotation. Only the first pages of these items are indicated.

Vanderbilt Law Review 1327 (1976) *884*, 888
Clark, Sherman J., The Character of Direct Democracy, 13 Journal of Contemporary Legal Issues 341 (2004) 522
Codrington, Wilfred U. III, Purcell in Pandemic, 96 New York University Law Review (forthcoming 2021) 502
Coffee, John C., Modern Mail Fraud: The Restoration of the Public/Private Distinction, 35 American Criminal Law Review 427 (1998) 834
Cohen, Aloni et al., Census TopDown: The Impacts of Differential Privacy on Redistricting (Apr. 14, 2021) 113
Colby, Thomas B., In Defense of the Equal Sovereignty Principle, 65 Duke Law Journal 1087 (2016) 261
Coleman, Kevin J., Congressional Research Service, Presidential Nominating Process: Current Issues (2011) 603
Cooter, Robert D. & Michael D. Gilbert, A Theory of Direct Democracy and the Single Subject Rule, 110 Columbia Law Review 687 (2010) 562
Corrado, Anthony, Creative Campaigning: PACs and the Presidential Selection Process (1992) 1097
Corrado, Anthony, Paying for Presidents: Public Financing in National Elections (1993) 1097
Corrado, Anthony, The Regulatory Environment of the 2016 Election, in Financing the 2016 Election (David B. Magleby ed., 2019) 1034, 1097
Cover, Benjamin Plener, Quantifying Partisan Gerrymandering: An Evaluation of the Efficiency Gap Proposal, 70 Stanford Law Review 1131 (2018) 153
Cox, Adam B. & Richard T. Holden, Reconsidering Racial and Partisan Gerrymandering, 78 University of Chicago Law Review 553 (2011) 363
Cox, Adam B. & Thomas J. Miles, Documenting Discrimination?, 108 Columbia Law Review Sidebar 31 (2008) 262
Cox, Adam B. & Thomas J. Miles, Judging the Voting Rights Act, 108 Columbia Law Review 1 (2008) 298
Cox, Adam B. & Thomas J. Miles, Judicial Ideology and the Transformation of Voting Rights Jurisprudence, 75 University of Chicago Law Review 1493 (2008) 298
Cox, Gary W. & Jonathan N. Katz, Elbridge Gerry's Salamander: The Electoral Consequences of the Reapportionment Revolution (2002) 102
Cronin, Thomas E., Direct Democracy (1989) *515*
Crum, Travis, The Voting Rights Act's Secret Weapon: Pocket Trigger Litigation and Dynamic Preclearance, 119 Yale Law Journal 1992 (2010) 264
Cunningham, Dayna L., Who Are to Be the Electors? A Reflection on the History of Voter Registration in the United States, 9 Yale Law & Policy Review 370 (1991) 483
Dahl, Robert A., A Preface to Democratic Theory 1 (1956) 3, 99
Daniels, Gilda R., A Vote Delayed is a Vote Denied: A Preemptive Approach to Eliminating Election Administration That Disenfranchises Unwanted Voters, 47 University of Louisville Law Review 57 (2008) 469
Daniels, Gilda R., Unfinished Business: Protecting Voting Rights in the Twenty-First Century, 81 George

Madison, James, The Federalist Papers, No. 10 (Clinton Rossiter, ed., 1961) 4

Magarian, Gregory P., Regulating Political Parties Under a "Public Rights" First Amendment, 44 William & Mary Law Review 1939 (2003) 630

Magleby, David B., Change and Continuity in the Financing of the 2016 U.S. Federal Election, in Financing the 2016 Election (David B. Magleby, ed., 2019) 854, 1034

Magleby, David B., Direct Legislation (1984) *521*, 523

Magleby, David B., Direct Legislation in the States, in Referendums around the World (David Butler & Austin Ranney, eds., 1994) *564*

Magleby, David B., ed., Financing the 2000 Election (2002) 853, 854

Magleby, David B., ed., Financing the 2012 Election (2014) 853

Magleby, David B., ed., Financing the 2016 Election (2019) 853, 854, 1034, 1097

Magleby, David B., Anthony Corrado, & Kelly D. Patterson, eds., Financing the 2004 Election (2006) 959

Magleby, David B. & Anthony Corrado, eds., Financing the 2008 Election (2011) 853

Malbin, Michael J., ed., The Election After Reform: Money, Politics, and the Bipartisan Campaign Reform Act (2006) 853, 959, 1034

Malbin, Michael J. & Thomas L. Gais, The Day After Reform: Sobering Campaign Finance Lessons from the American States (1998) 1079

Malbin, Michael J. et al., Small Donors, Big Democracy: New York City's Matching Funds as a Model for the Public Financing of Congressional Campaigns, 11 Election Law Journal 3 (2012) 1132

Malhotra, Neil, The Impact of Public Financing on Political Competition: Evidence from Arizona and Maine, 8 State Politics and Policy Quarterly 263 (2008) 1091

Manheim, Lisa Marshall & Elizabeth G. Porter, The Elephant in the Room: Intentional Vote Suppression, 2019 Supreme Court Review 213 (2019) 477

Mann, Thomas E. & E.J. Dionne, Jr., The Futility of Nostalgia and the Romanticism of the New Political Realists: Why Praising the 19th-Century Political Machine Won't Solve the 21st Century's Problems (2015) 587

Mann, Thomas E., Lessons for Reformers, in Financing the 2004 Election (David B. Magleby et al., eds., 2006) 959

Mansker, Nicole & Neal Devins, Do Judicial Elections Facilitate Popular Constitutionalism; Can They?, 111 Columbia Law Review Sidebar 27 (2011) 742

Manza, Jeff & Christopher Uggen, Punishment and Democracy: Disenfranchisement of Nonincarcerated Felons in the United States, 2 Perspectives on Politics 491 (2004) 72

Martinez, Michael D. & David Hill, Did Motor Voter Work?, 27 American Politics Quarterly 296 (1999) 473

Masket, Seth E. & Michael G. Miller, Does Public Election Funding Create More Extreme Legislators? Evidence from Arizona and Maine, 15 State Politics & Policy Quarterly 24 (2015) 1092

Masket, Seth E., No Middle Ground: How Informal Party Organizations

Amendment an Obstacle to Political Equality?, 82 Columbia Law Review 611 (1982) *880*

Wright, J. Skelly, Politics and the Constitution: Is Money Speech? 85 Yale Law Journal 1001 (1976) 22, *885*

Zaller, John R., The Nature and Origin of Mass Public Opinion 267 (1992) 718

Ziegler, Reuven, Legal Outlier Again? U.S. Felon Suffrage: Comparative and International Human Rights Perspectives, 29 Boston University International Law Journal 197 (2011) 70

Zimmerman, Joseph F., The Initiative: Citizen Law-Making (1999) 516

Index

Page numbers in **bold** identify principal discussion. Page numbers in *italics* identify extended discussion or quotation. Only the first pages of items are indicated.